Design of
Machine
Elements I
(DME I)

W0235509

Other CBS Book by the Same Author

- Design of Machine Elements II (DME II)

Design of
Machine
Elements I
(DME I)

K Raghavendra MTech
Assistant Professor
Department of Mechanical Engineering
Ballari Institute of Technology and Management (BITM)
Ballari, Karnataka

CBS Publishers & Distributors Pvt Ltd

New Delhi • Bengaluru • Chennai • Kochi • Kolkata • Mumbai
Bhopal • Bhubaneswar • Hyderabad • Jharkhand • Nagpur • Patna • Pune • Uttarakhand • Dhaka (Bangladesh)

Disclaimer

Science and technology are constantly changing fields. New research and experience broaden the scope of information and knowledge. The author has tried his best in giving information available to him while preparing the material for this book. Although, all efforts have been made to ensure optimum accuracy of the material, yet it is quite possible some errors might have been left uncorrected. The publisher, the printer and the author will not be held responsible for any inadvertent errors, omissions or inaccuracies.

Design of
**Machine
Elements I**
(DME I)

ISBN: 978-93-86478-11-5

Copyright © Author and Publisher

First Edition: 2017
Reprint: 2019

All rights reserved. No part of this book may be reproduced or transmitted in any form or by any means, electronic or mechanical, including photocopying, recording, or any information storage and retrieval system without the prior permission in written from the author and the publisher.

Published by Satish Kumar Jain and produced by Varun Jain for

CBS Publishers & Distributors Pvt Ltd

4819/XI Prahlad Street, 24 Ansari Road, Daryaganj, New Delhi 110 002, India.
Ph: 23289259, 23266861, 23266867   Fax: 011-23243014   Website: www.cbspd.com
e-mail: delhi@cbspd.com; cbspubs@airtelmail.in

Corporate Office: 204 FIE, Industrial Area, Patparganj, Delhi 110 092
Ph: 4934 4934   Fax: 4934 4935   e-mail: publishing@cbspd.com; publicity@cbspd.com

Branches

- **Bengaluru:** Seema House, 2975, 17th Cross, K.R. Road, Banasankari 2nd Stage, Bengaluru 560 070, Karnataka
  Ph: +91-80-26771678/79   Fax: +91-80-26771680   e-mail: bangalore@cbspd.com
- **Chennai:** 7, Subbaraya Street, Shenoy Nagar, Chennai 600 030, Tamil Nadu
  Ph: +91-44-26680620, 26681266   Fax: +91-44-42032115   e-mail: chennai@cbspd.com
- **Kochi:** 42/1325, 1326, Power House Road, Opposite KSEB Power House, Ernakulam 682 018, Kochi, Kerala
  Ph: +91-484-4059061-65   Fax: +91-484-4059065   e-mail: kochi@cbspd.com
- **Kolkata:** 6/B, Ground Floor, Rameswar Shaw Road, Kolkata-700 014, West Bengal
  Ph: +91-33-22891126, 22891127, 22891128   e-mail: kolkata@cbspd.com
- **Mumbai:** 83-C, Dr E Moses Road, Worli, Mumbai-400018, Maharashtra
  Ph: +91-22-24902340/41   Fax: +91-22-24902342   e-mail: mumbai@cbspd.com

Representatives

• **Bhopal**	0-8319310552	• **Bhubaneswar**	0-9911037372	• **Hyderabad**	0-9885175004	• **Jharkhand**	0-9811541605
• **Nagpur**	0-9021734563	• **Patna**	0-9334159340	• **Pune**	0-9623451994	• **Uttarakhand**	0-9716462459
• **Dhaka (Bangladesh)**	01912-003485						

Printed at : Swastik Packagings, Patparganj Industrial Area, Delhi, India

*In loving memory
of
my father
Late Sri K Sivaramulu*

Preface

It gives me a great satisfaction in presenting this book titled *Design of Machine Elements I (DME I)*, written according to the syllabus prescribed by VTU, Belagavi, for Vth semester students of Mechanical Engineering.

The manuscript is based on the lectures delivered by the author with reference to the fourth edition of *Design Data Handbook for Mechanical Engineers*, by Prof K Mahadevan and Prof K Balaveera Reddy. The concepts are presented in simple and lucid language to explain the subject within the scope of the topics given in the syllabus.

I owe my gratitude to my mother Smt B Susheela, whose blessings inspired me in bringing out this book. I am thankful to my wife Smt V Radhika, son Chi K Naga Ganesh and daughter Chi K Shanvi for their continuous support and encouragement in preparing this book.

I would like to express my sincere thanks to Dr Kori Nagaraj, Professor and Head, Department of Mechanical Engineering, RYME College, Ballari; Dr Yadavalli Basavaraj, Professor and Head, Department of Mechanical Engineering, BITM, Ballari, for their support and cooperation while preparing the manuscript.

In spite of care being taken, errors might have crept in without knowledge. The author would be grateful to the readers if they could bring to attention, the errors if any, noticed by them.

Last but not the least, I would like to thank the entire team of CBS Publishers & Distributors, New Delhi, who has taken immense pain in publishing this book.

K Raghavendra

Contents

Preface   *vii*
Syllabus   *xiii*

PART A

1. INTRODUCTION   3–33

1.1 Overview 3
    1.1.1 Classification of Machine Design 3
    1.1.2 Types of Design Based on Methods 3
1.2 Basic Procedure in Machine Design 4
1.3 Engineering Materials and their Mechanical Properties 5
    1.3.1 Selection of Materials for Engineering Purposes 5
1.4 Mechanical Properties of Metals 5
1.5 Factors Influencing Machine Design/Design Considerations 6
1.6 Codes and Standards 7
1.7 Indian Standards for Designation of Materials (BIS System) 7
1.8 Stress Analysis (Fundamentals from Strength of Materials) 10
1.9 Stress-Strain Diagram 12
1.10 Material Subjected to Combined Direct and Shear Stress 14
1.11 Biaxial/Two Dimensional Stress 16
1.12 Triaxial Stress/Three Dimensional Stress 17
1.13 Stress Tensor/Components of Stress 17
1.14 Biaxial Deformation/Strain 18
1.15 Triaxial Deformation/Strain 18

    VTU Question Papers 28

2. DESIGN FOR STATIC AND IMPACT STRENGTH   34–162

Design For Static Strength

2.1 Static Load 34
2.2 Factor of Safety 34
    2.2.1 Selection of Factor of Safety 35
2.3 Combined Stresses 35
    2.3.1 Direct Stress 35
    2.3.2 Bending Stress 36
    2.3.3 Torsional Stress 36
2.4 Eccentric Loading (Superposition) 58
2.5 Theories of Failure: Static Loading 70
    2.5.1 Maximum Normal Stress Theory (MNST) or Principal Stress Theory or
        Rankine's Theory 70
    2.5.2 Maximum Normal Strain Theory or Principal Strain Theory or
        Saint Venant Theory 71

2.5.3 Maximum Shear Stress Theory (MSST) or Guest's or Tresca's Theory or Shear Difference Theory *71*

2.5.4 Maximum Shear Energy Theory or Distortion Theory or von Mises Theory (DET) *72*

2.5.5 Maximum Strain Energy Theory (MSET) or Haigh's Theory *73*

2.6 Difference Between Ductile and Brittle Fracture *73*

2.7 Failure of Ductile and Brittle Materials *74*

2.8 Stress Concentration *90*

2.8.1 Characteristics of Stress Concentration Factor *91*

2.9 Stress Concentration in Contrast to Ductile and Brittle Materials under Static Loading *92*

2.10 Determination of Stress Concentration Factor *92*

2.11 Methods of Reducing Stress Concentration *93*

Design For Impact Strength

2.12 Impact Loading: Introduction *121*

2.13 Methods of Selecting Members to Withstand Impact Load *121*

2.14 Properties of Material to Resist Impact Load *121*

2.15 Strain Energy Due to Impact Load (Impact Stresses Due to Axial Load) *121*

2.16 Impact Stresses Due to Bending *128*

2.17 Impact and Torsion *130*

2.18 Effect of Inertia *130*

VTU Question Papers *142*

3. DESIGN FOR FATIGUE STRENGTH   163–246

3.1 Introduction to Fatigue *163*

3.2 Characteristics of Fatigue *164*

3.3 Factors to be Considered to Avoid Fatigue Failure *164*

3.4 Phenomenon of Fatigue Failure/Nature of Fatigue *164*

3.5 High Cycle and Low Cycle Fatigue *165*

3.5.1 Low Cycle Fatigue (LCF) *166*

3.5.2 High Cycle Fatigue (HCF) *166*

3.6 Definitions/ Nomenclature *166*

3.7 S-N Curve: General S-N Behaviour or Wohler Curves *169*

3.8 Endurance Limits Modifying Factors/Strength Reduction Factors/Factors Influencing S-N Behavior *170*

3.9 Factor of Safety for Fatigue Loading *174*

3.10 Fatigue Strength under Fluctuating Stresses: Fatigue Failure Theories *174*

3.10.1 Soderberg Criteria or Yield Criteria *174*

3.10.2 Goodman Criteria or Fracture Criteria *176*

3.11 Relation Between Endurance Limit and Ultimate Tensile Strength *177*

3.12 Relation Between Direct Stress Endurance Limit and Ultimate Tensile Strength *177*

3.13 Relation Between Cyclic Torsion Endurance Limit and Ultimate Tensile Strength *178*

3.14 Stresses due to Combined Loading *201*

3.15 Cumulative Fatigue Damage *230*

VTU Question Papers *235*

4. THREADED FASTENERS   247–317

4.1 Introduction *247*

4.2 Important Definitions *247*

4.3 Forms of Screw Threads *248*

4.4 Designation of Screw Threads *248*

4.5 Materials Used for Bolts *249*

4.6 Working Stress in Bolts—Initial Tension Unknown *249*

4.7 Stresses in Screwed Fastening Due to Static Loading *250*

    4.7.1 Initial Stress due to Screwing up of Forces *250*

    4.7.2 Stresses due to External Forces *252*

    4.7.3 Stresses due to the above Combination (Sections 4.7.1 and 4.7.2) *252*

4.8 Effect of Fatigue or Dynamic Loading *266*

4.9 Effect of Impact Loading *280*

4.10 Eccentric Loading or Bolted Joints in Shear *282*

    4.10.1 Eccentric Load Acting Parallel to the Axis of the Bolt *282*

    4.10.2 Eccentric Load Acting Perpendicular to the Axis of the Bolt *285*

    4.10.3 Load Acting in a Plane Containing the Bolts *302*

VTU Question Papers *307*

PART B

5. DESIGN OF SHAFTS

321–401

5.1 Introduction *321*

5.2 Types of Shafts *321*

5.3 Some Definitions *321*

5.4 Materials Used for Shafts *321*

5.5 Maximum Permissible Working or Design Stress *322*

5.6 Design of Shaft *322*

5.7 Shaft Design Based on Strength *322*

    5.7.1 Shafts Subjected to Torque (*T*) only *322*

    5.7.2 Shafts Subjected to Bending Moment (BM) Only *323*

    5.7.3 Shafts Subjected to Combined T and BM *323*

5.8 Shaft Design Based on Rigidity *324*

    5.8.1 Torsional Rigidity (Shaft as Torsion Bars) *324*

    5.8.2 Lateral Rigidity (Shafts as Beams) *325*

5.9 ASME Code for Shaft Design *325*

5.10 Shafts Subjected to Combined Axial Load, Together with Torsional and Bending Moments (F, T and BM) *327*

5.11 Shaft Subjected to Fluctuating Loads *328*

5.12 Power Equation *329*

5.13 Evaluation of Transmission Forces *329*

VTU Question Papers *391*

6. COTTER AND KNUCKLE JOINTS, KEYS AND COUPLINGS

402–486

6.1 Cotter Joint *402*

6.2 Types of Cotter Joint *402*

6.3 Socket and Spigot Cotter Joint *402*

6.4 Knuckle Joint *413*

6.5 Keys *417*

6.6 Types of Keys *418*

6.7 Design of Sunk Key *420*

6.8 Effect of Keyways for Sunk Key *421*

6.9 Design of a Taper Key *432*

6.10 Splines *435*

6.11 Couplings *439*

6.12 Flange Coupling *439*

6.13 Flexible Coupling: Bush-pin Type *463*

6.14 Oldham's Coupling *477*

VTU Question Papers *478*

7. RIVETED AND WELDED JOINTS

487–645

Riveted Joints

7.1 Introduction *487*
7.2 Types of Fastening *487*
7.3 Types of Riveted Joints *488*
7.4 Important Terms Used in Riveted Joints *490*
7.5 Types of Rivet Heads *490*
7.6 Materials for Rivets *491*
7.7 Failures of Riveted Joints *491*
7.8 Strength of a Riveted Joint *493*
7.9 Efficiency of a Riveted Joint *493*
7.10 Design of Boiler Joints *496*
7.11 Design Procedure for Longitudinal Butt Joint *496*
7.12 Design Procedure for Circumferential Lap Joint *498*
7.13 Structural Joints or Ties [Diamond or Lozenge Joint] *532*
7.14 Eccentric Loaded Riveted Joints *544*
    7.14.1 Load Acting in a Plane Containing the Rivets—Compound Group *545*
    7.14.2 Load Acting Perpendicular to the Axis of the Rivet *564*

Welded Joints

7.15 Introduction *569*
7.16 Types of Welded Joints *570*
7.17 Details of Fillet Weld *571*
7.18 Strength of Butt Weld *572*
7.19 Strength of Fillet Weld *573*
    7.19.1 Transverse or Normal Fillet Welds *573*
    7.19.2 Parallel or Longitudinal Fillet Welds *574*
    7.19.3 Combined Parallel and Transverse Fillet Welds *575*
7.20 Stress Concentration Factors *576*
7.21 Unsymmetrical Welds Subjected to Axial Loads *586*
7.22 Special Cases of Fillet Weld *594*
    7.22.1 Tee Joint: Parallel Fillet Weld Subjected to Bending Moment *594*
    7.22.2 Tee Joint: Parallel Fillet Weld Subjected to Eccentric Load *595*
    7.22.3 Tee Joint: Transverse Fillet Weld Subjected to Bending Moment *596*
    7.22.4 Tee Joint: Transverse Fillet Weld Subjected to Eccentric Load *597*
    7.22.5 Annular or Circular Fillet Weld Subjected to Torsion *598*
    7.22.6 Annular or Circular Fillet Weld Subjected to Bending Moment *599*
7.23 Eccentric Load on Welded Connections *603*
    7.23.1 Welded Connection Subjected to Moment in a Plane Normal to the Plane of Weld *604*
    7.23.2 Welded Connection Subjected to Moment in a Plane of the Weld *614*
    VTU Question Papers *628*

8. POWER SCREWS

646–708

8.1 Introduction *646*
8.2 Types of Screw Thread *646*
8.3 Terminology of Power Screws *647*
8.4 Mechanics of Power Screw: Force and Torque Analysis *648*
8.5 Efficiency of Square Threaded Screw *652*
8.6 Self locking and Overhauling in Power Screws *652*
8.7 Efficiency of Self Locking Screw *653*
8.8 V-threads or Angular Threads *653*
8.9 Stresses in Power Screws *672*
8.10 Design of Screw Jack *680*

    VTU Question Papers *701*

Index

709–710

Syllabus

DESIGN OF MACHINE ELEMENTS I (DME I)

Sub Code: 10ME52   **5th Semester**

PART A

UNIT-1: INTRODUCTION

Definitions: Normal, shear, biaxial and tri-axial stresses, Stress tensor, Principal stresses. Engineering Materials and their mechanical properties, Stress–Strain diagrams, Stress Analysis, Design considerations: Codes and Standards.   **05 Hours**

UNIT-2: DESIGN FOR STATIC AND IMPACT STRENGTH

Static Strength: Static loads and factor of safety, Theories of failure: Maximum normal stress theory, Maximum shear stress theory, Maximum strain theory, Strain energy theory, Distortion energy theory. Failure of brittle and ductile materials, Stress concentration, Determination of Stress concentration factor.

Impact Strength: Introduction, Impact stresses due to axial, bending and torsional loads, effect of inertia.   **07 Hours**

UNIT-3: DESIGN FOR FATIGUE STRENGTH

Introduction, S-N Diagram, Low cycle fatigue, High cycle fatigue, Endurance limit, Modifying factors: size effect, surface effect, Stress concentration effects, Fluctuating stresses, Goodman and Soderberg relationship, stresses due to combined loading, cumulative fatigue damage.   **08 Hours**

UNIT-4: THREADED FASTENERS

Stresses in threaded fasteners, Effect of initial tension, Design of threaded fasteners under static, dynamic and impact loads, Design of eccentrically loaded bolted joints.
06 Hours

PART B

UNIT-5: DESIGN OF SHAFTS

Torsion of shafts, design for strength and rigidity with steady loading, ASME codes for power transmission shafting, shafts under fluctuating loads and combined loads.
07 Hours

UNIT-6: COTTER AND KNUCKLE JOINTS, KEYS AND COUPLINGS

Design of Cotter and Knuckle joints, Keys: Types of keys, Design of keys, Couplings: Rigid and flexible couplings, Flange coupling, Bush and Pin type coupling and Oldham's coupling. **07 Hours**

UNIT-7: RIVETED AND WELDED JOINTS

Types, rivet materials, failures of riveted joints, Joint Efficiency, Boiler Joints, Lozenge Joints, Riveted Brackets. Welded Joints—Types, Strength of butt and fillet welds, eccentrically loaded welded joints. **07 Hours**

UNIT-8: POWER SCREWS

Mechanics of power screw, Stresses in power screws, efficiency and self-locking, Design of Power Screw, Design of Screw Jack (Complete Design). **05 Hours**

DATA HANDBOOK

Design Data Handbook for Mechanical Engineers, 4th ed., by Prof K Mahadevan and Prof K Balaveera Reddy.

Part A

1. Introduction

2. Design for Static and Impact Strength

3. Design for Fatigue Strength

4. Threaded Fasteners

1

Introduction

1.1 OVERVIEW

A *machine* is a device consisting of interrelated components that modifies force or motion. *Machine design* is the art of planning new or improved machine(s) to accomplish specific purpose. The aim of design process is to shape and size the elements so that the resulting system can be expected to perform the intended function without failure.

Machine design may also be defined as the use of scientific principles, technical information and imagination in the design of mechanical structure, machine or a system to perform prescribed functions with maximum economy and efficiency. Design is an iterative process with many interactive phases so as to produce better machines and improving the existing ones. A new or better machine is one which is more economical in the overall cost of production and operation.

1.1.1 Classification of Machine Design

The machine design may be classified as follows.
- *Adaptive design*: Here the designer makes minor alterations to the existing design and as such does not require special skills.
- *Development design*: Here the designer starts from the existing design but the final product may vary markedly from that of original design.
- *New design*: This type of design is entirely new but based on existing scientific principles. No scientific invention is involved but requires creative thinking to solve a problem.

1.1.2 Types of Design Based on Methods

- **Rational design:** This is based on determining the stresses and strains of components and thereby deciding their dimensions.
- **Empirical design:** This is based on empirical formulae which in turn are based on past experience and experiments.
  For example, when we tighten a nut on a bolt the force exerted or the stresses induced cannot be determined exactly but experience shows that the tightening force may be given by $P = 2840d$, where d is the bolt diameter in mm and P is the applied force in newton. There is no mathematical backing of this equation but it is based on observations and experience.
- **Industrial design:** These are based on industrial considerations and norms, viz. market survey, external look, production facilities, low cost, use of existing standard products.

- **Optimum design:** It refers to design of a component under a set of specified constraints.
- **System design:** It refers to design of orderly combination of parts in a complex mechanical system into a whole.
  Example: Automobiles.
- **Element design:** It refers to design of any element/component of the mechanical system.
  Example: Piston, crankshaft, connecting rod, etc.
- **Computer aided design:** It refers to the use of computer systems to assist in the creation, modification, analysis and optimization of a design.

1.2 BASIC PROCEDURE IN MACHINE DESIGN

The basic procedure of machine design consists of a step by step approach from given specifications of functional requirement of a product to the complete description in the form of blueprints of the final product. It is to be noted that the process is neither exhaustive nor rigid and will probably be modified to suit individual problems. It can be outlined by flow diagrams with feedback loops as shown in **Fig. 1.1**.

Identification of Need

- Design process begins with recognition of the need, real or imagined, and a decision to do something about it.
  Example: The need for present equipment requires improving durability, efficiency, weight and cost.

Definition of the Problem

- It includes all the specifications for the object that is to be designed.
- Specifications include all forms of input and output quantities must be spelled out. It also includes the definitions of the members to be manufactured, cost, the expected life, the range, the operating temperature, and reliability.
- Once the specifications have been prepared, relevant design information is collected to make a feasibility study.
- As a result of this study, changes are made in the specifications and requirements.

Synthesis

- After defining the problem, now finding a solution and putting together is the most challenging and interesting part of design.
- This is sometimes called the iteration and invention phase (where the largest possible number of creative solutions is originated).
- The designer combines separate parts to form a complex whole of various new and old ideas and concepts to produce an overall new idea or concept.

Analysis and Optimization

- Analysis refers to finding out whether the system satisfies the requirements.
- Optimization refers to the best performance given by the system for which it is designed.

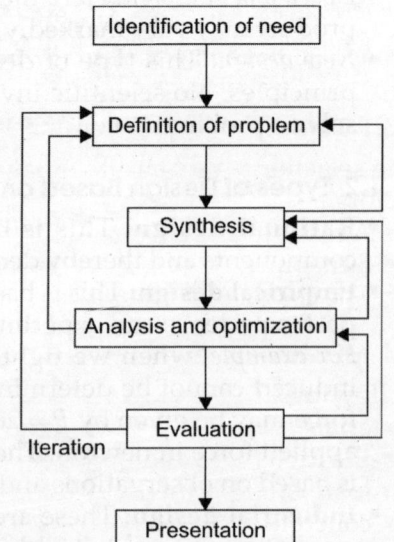

Fig. 1.1: Basic procedure in machine design

- If the design fails, the synthesis procedure must begin again till optimum performance is achieved.
- After synthesizing the system, the designer must specify the dimensions, select the components and materials, and consider the manufacturing cost, reliability, serviceability, and safety.

Evaluation

- This step is the final proof of a successful design and usually involves the testing of a prototype in the laboratory.
- Here we discover whether the design really satisfies the needs and other desirable features.

Presentation

- It refers to communicating the design to others.
- It is a selling job. The engineer, when presenting a new solution, attempts to prove that this solution is a better one.

1.3 ENGINEERING MATERIALS AND THEIR MECHANICAL PROPERTIES

Engineering materials are classified as follows.
1. Metals and alloys
   Metals are further classified as:
   a. Ferrous metals
   b. Nonferrous metals
2. Nonmetals.

Metal is defined as a substance which is solid at room temperature, has good mechanical properties (high strength, toughness, ductility, etc.) along with good thermal and electrical conductivity.

- Metals which contain iron as the main constituent are referred to as *ferrous metals*.
  Example: Cast iron, wrought iron, steel.
- Metals which do not contain iron as their main constituent are referred to as *non-ferrous metals*.
  Example: Aluminium, copper, brass, tin, etc.
- An alloy is a combination of two or more metals of which one is the base metal.

1.3.1 Selection of Materials for Engineering Purposes

The selection of proper material(s) for a given application is based on the following factors.
- Availability of the materials
- Suitability of the materials for the working conditions in service
- The cost of the materials.

1.4 MECHANICAL PROPERTIES OF METALS

Following are some of the most important mechanical properties of engineering materials.
- **Elasticity** is the ability of a material to regain its original shape and size, when the load causing the deformation is removed. *Example:* Steel, copper, aluminium, concrete, etc.
- **Plasticity** is the property of a material which does not regain its original shape and size, when the load causing the deformation is removed.
- **Strength** is the ability of a material to withstand the action of external forces.

- **Toughness** is the property of a material which absorbs energy elastically before failure, i.e. to withstand elastic and plastic deformation.
- **Stiffness/rigidity** is the ability of a material to resist elastic deformation.
- **Hardness** is the property of a material which resists indentation and/or penetration, or it is the property of a material to resist plastic deformation.
- **Resilience** is the property of a material to absorb energy elastically.
- **Ductility** is the property of a material of drawing it into wires.
  Example: Mild steel (MS)
- **Brittleness** is the property of the material by the virtue of which it breaks easily into pieces. *Example:* Cast iron
- **Malleability** is the property of the material by the virtue of which it can be rolled into sheets. *Example:* MS, aluminium, etc.
- **Creep** refers to the slow and progressive deformation of a material with time at constant stress.
- **Fatigue** refers to the behavior of a material when subjected to fluctuating or repeated loads.
- **Fracture** refers to the separation of a material into two/more parts under stress.
  - *Ductile fracture*: This occurs after extensive plastic deformation and is characterized by slow crack propagation.
  - *Brittle fracture*: This occurs by rapid propagation of a crack after a little or no plastic deformation.

1.5 FACTORS INFLUENCING MACHINE DESIGN/DESIGN CONSIDERATIONS

These refer to the characteristics which influence the design of element of the entire system. Following are some of the characteristics to be considered.

- **Strength:** This is the most important consideration while designing a new machine and its components. The machine should be sufficiently strong so that there is no damage or permanent deformation during its service life.
  The most commonly used proverb in designing a component is *"sacrifice everything but not strength"*.
- **Stiffness or rigidity:** Under the effects of applied load, the machine should be rigid enough so that elastic deformation of the component is within the specified limits.
- **Availability of material:** Materials selected should be available easily at the lowest possible costs.
- **Cost:** Cost is the major factor to be considered while designing the machine and its components. The shape and material of the machine selected should be such that it can be produced with minimum labor and processing methods. The best design is the one which helps to get the finished product at the lowest possible cost.
- **Wear resistance:** Wear is defined as the damage to a surface that generally involves progressive loss of material and is due to relative motion between that surface and a contacting substance or substances. Wear resistance of the machine elements can be increased by increasing strength and hardness of the working surfaces. The wear of friction parts can be reduced by proper lubrication.
- **Reliability:** It is defined as the ability of the machine and/or component to perform its intended function without failure under stated conditions for a stated period of time. The reliability of the machine is very important for its proper functioning.
- **Light weight and minimum dimensions:** The machine elements should be strong, rigid and wear resistant with minimum weight and least dimensions. This can be achieved by:

– Employing light weight rolled sections.
– Employing latest methods of surface hardening.
– Using high strength grades of cast iron and light alloys.
– Introducing nonmetallic materials to replace ferrous and nonferrous materials.
– Improving the design of machine elements.

- **Safety:** For the safety of the operator from the machine, the hazard producing elements from the machine should be eliminated and the design should confirm to the safety codes.
- **Use of standard parts:** As far as possible, standard parts should be used in the design of the machine. This will help reduce the cost of the machine and ensure easy replacement of the damaged parts, etc.

1.6 CODES AND STANDARDS

A *standard* is a set of specifications given for materials, parts or processes so as to achieve uniformity, efficiency, and quality. The purpose of a standard is to limit the number of items in the specifications, thereby providing a reasonable inventory of tooling, sizes, shapes and varieties.

A *code* is a set of specifications for the analysis, design, manufacture, and construction of items. The purpose is to achieve a specified degree of safety, efficiency, and quality.

The most commonly used standards include:

- Standards for materials, their chemical composition, mechanical properties and heat treatment.
- Shapes and dimensions of commonly used elements, viz. bolts, rivets, nuts, chains belts, bearings, etc.
- Standards for fits, tolerances and surface finish of components.
- Standards for pressure vessels, boilers, overhead cranes, wire ropes, etc.
- Standards for engineering drawings of components.

Following are some of the standard organizations. The name of the organization provides a clue to the nature of the standard or code.

- American Bearing Manufacturers Association (ABMA)
- American Gear Manufacturers Association (AGMA)
- American National Standards Institute (ANSI)
- American Society of Mechanical Engineers (ASME)
- American Society of Testing and Materials (ASTM)
- International Standards Organization (ISO)
- National Association of Power Engineers (NAPE)
- National Institute for Standards and Technology (NIST)
- Society of Automotive Engineers (SAE), etc.

1.7 INDIAN STANDARDS FOR DESIGNATION OF MATERIALS (BIS SYSTEM)
... APPENDIX I/ Pg 453, DHB

1.7.1 Steels Designated on the Basis of Mechanical Properties (Letter Symbols)

The designation consists of the following in order.

i. Symbol 'Fe' or 'FeE' depending on whether the steel has been specified on the basis of minimum tensile strength or yield strength.

ii. Figure indicating the minimum tensile strength or yield stress in N/mm^2.
Example: Fe 360 means a steel having minimum tensile strength of $360 \, N/mm^2$ and FeE 270 means steel having yield strength of $270 \, N/mm^2$. ... **Tb I.7/ Pg 462, DHB**

1.7.2 Steels Designated on the Basis of Chemical Composition

A. Unalloyed Steels

1. **Carbon steels:** The designation consists of the following in order.
   i. Figure indicating 100 times the average percentage of carbon content
   ii. Letter 'C'
   iii. Figure indicating 10 times the average percentage of manganese content. The figure after multiplying shall be rounded off to the nearest integer.

   Example: 25C means a carbon steel containing 0.20 to 0.30 per cent (0.25 per cent on average) carbon and 0.30 to 0.60 per cent (0.45 per cent rounded off to 0.5 per cent on an average) manganese. ... **Tb I.8/ Pg 463, DHB**

2. **Unalloyed free cutting steels:** The designation consists of the following in order.
   i. Figure indicating 100 times the average percentage of carbon
   ii. Symbol 'C' for tool steel
   iii. Figure indicating 10 times the average percentage of manganese
   iv. Symbol 'S' followed by the figure indicating the 100 times the average content of sulphur.

   Example: 35C10S14K indicates free cutting steel with 0.35% (average) carbon, 1% manganese and 0.14% sulphur. ... **App. I/ Pg 455, DHB**

3. **Unalloyed tool steels:** The designation consists of the following in order.
   i. Figure indicating 100 times the average percentage of carbon
   ii. Letter 'T'
   iii. Figure indicating 10 times the average percentage of manganese.

   Example: 75T5 indicates unalloyed tool steel with average 0.75% carbon and 0.5% manganese. ... **App. I/ Pg 455, DHB**

B. Alloy Steels

Alloy steel may be defined as a steel to which elements other than carbon are added in sufficient amount to produce an improvement in properties. The commonly added elements are nickel, chromium, manganese, silicon, molybdenum, cobalt, vanadium and tungsten.

1. **Low and medium alloy steels:** The term low and medium alloy steels is used for alloy steels containing less than 10% of alloying elements. The designation consists of the following in order.
   i. Figure indicating 100 times the average percentage carbon.
   ii. Chemical symbol for alloying elements each followed by the figure for its average percentage content multiplied by a factor as given below.

Element	Multiplying factor
Cr, Co, Ni, Mn, Si and W	4
Al, Be, V, Pb, Cu, Nb, Ti, Ta, Zr and Mo	10
P, S and N	100

... **App. I/ Pg 456, DHB**

Note:
- The figure after multiplying shall be rounded off to the nearest integer.
- Symbol 'Mn' for manganese shall be included in case manganese content is equal to or greater than 1%.

- The chemical symbols and their figures shall be listed in the designation in the order of decreasing content.

  Example: 40Cr4Mo2 means alloy steel having 0.4% average carbon, 1% chromium and 0.20% molybdenum. ... **App. I/ Pg 456, DHB**

2. **High alloy steels:** The term high alloy steels is used for alloy steels containing more than 10% of alloying elements. The designation consists of the following in order.

   i. Letter 'X'
   ii. Figure indicating 100 times the percentage of carbon content
   iii. Chemical symbol for alloying elements each followed by a figure for its average percentage content rounded off to the nearest integer
   iv. Chemical symbol to indicate specially added element to allow the desired properties.

   Example: X15Cr25Ni12 means high alloy steel with 0.15% carbon, 25% chromium and 12% nickel. ... **App. I/ Pg 456, DHB**

3. **Alloy tool steels**

   i. *Low and medium alloy tool steel*: The designation consists of the following in order.
      a. Letter 'T'
      b. Figure indicating 100 times the percentage of carbon content
      c. Chemical symbol for alloying elements each followed by the figure for its average percentage content rounded off to the nearest integer
      d. Chemical symbol to indicate specially added element to attain the desired properties.

   Example: X75W18Cr4V1 means low alloy tool steel having 0.75% average carbon, 18% tungsten, 4% chromium and 1% vanadium.
   ... **App. I/ Pg 456, DHB**

   ii. *High alloy tool steel*: The designation consists of the following in order.
      a. Letter 'XT'
      b. Figure indicating 100 times the percentage of carbon content
      c. Chemical symbol for alloying elements each followed by the figure for its average percentage content rounded off to the nearest integer
      d. Chemical symbol to indicate specially added element to attain the desired properties.

   Example: XT98W6Mo5Cr4V1 means a high alloy tool steel having 0.98% average carbon, 6% tungsten, 5% molybdenum, 4% chromium and 1% vanadium. ... **App. I/ Pg 456, DHB**

4. **Free cutting alloy steels:** The designation is same as indicate in alloy tool steels except that depending upon the percentage or S, Se, Te and Zr present, the designation shall also consist of the chemical symbol of the element present followed by the figure indicating 100 times its content.

   Example: X15Cr25Ni15S40 means alloy free cutting steel having 0.15% carbon, 25% chromium, 15% nickel and 0.40% vanadium. ... **App. I/ Pg 457, DHB**

1.7.3 Designation of Ferrous Castings   ... **App. I/ Pg 456, DHB**

1. **On the basis of mechanical properties:** The designation used is *300.
   * refers to any of the symbols listed below
      FG = grey iron castings
      SG = spheroidal or nodular graphite iron
      CS = steel castings etc.
      300 = minimum tensile strength in N/mm^2.

2. **On the basis of chemical composition:** The designation used is *33Ni4Cr2.
* refers to any of the symbols listed in **App. I/Pg 457, DHB.**

     33 = total carbon 3.3%

     Ni4 = 4% nickel (average)

     Cr2 = 2% chromium.

1.7.4 Designation of Pig Iron

The designation used is PG 12 Mn3P15.   **... App. I/ Pg 457, DHB**

  PG = designation for pig iron

   12 = indicates silicon as four times its average percentage rounded to the nearest integer without its symbol (Si)

Mn3 = indicates manganese as four times its average percentage rounded to the nearest integer

P15 = indicates phosphorous as 100 times the average percentage.

1.8 STRESS ANALYSIS (FUNDAMENTALS FROM STRENGTH OF MATERIALS)

1.8.1 Load (*F*)

Load may be defined as the combined effect of external forces acting on a body.
- The loads may be classified as:
  - a. Dead/steady load
  - b. Live/variable/fluctuating load
  - c. Inertia load
  - d. Centrifugal load.
- Apart from these, loads may also be classified as:
  - a. Tensile load
  - b. Compressive load
  - c. Torsional/twisting load
  - d. Bending load
  - e. Shear load.
- Further, loads can also be either as:
  - a. Point/concentrated load
  - b. Distributed load.

In general, loads can be of following types.
- *Transverse loading*: It refers to the forces applied perpendicular to the longitudinal axis of a member. Transverse loading causes the member to bend and deflect from its original position, with internal tensile and compressive strains accompanying change in curvature. Transverse loading also induces shear forces that cause shear deformation of the material and increase the transverse deflection of the member.
- *Axial loading*: Here the applied forces are collinear with the longitudinal axes of the member. The forces cause the member to either stretch or shorten.
- *Torsional loading*: Twisting action caused by a pair of externally applied equal and oppositely directed couples acting on parallel planes or by a single external couple applied to a member that has one end fixed against rotation.

1.8.2 Stress

When a body is subjected to a load within the elastic limits, it develops an equal and opposite resisting force within the body. This resisting force per unit area is called stress.

$$\sigma = \pm F/A \text{ (MPa or N/mm}^2) \quad \dots \text{(Eq. 1.1)} \textbf{ 1.1(a)/ Pg 2, DHB}$$

where F = force [(+)tensile, (–) compressive] (N)

A = cross-sectional area (mm^2)

It is a property at a specific point within a body, which is a function of load, geometry, temperature, and manufacturing processing.

The stresses are of the following types.

- *Tensile stress*: It is the stress state caused by an applied load that tends to elongate the material in the axis of the applied load, in other words, the stress caused by pulling the material. Due to this the length of the member increases, while its cross-section decreases, as shown in **Fig. 1.2(a)**.

  The strength of structures of equal cross-sectional area loaded in tension is independent of shape of the cross-section. Materials loaded in tension are susceptible to stress concentrations such as material defects or abrupt changes in geometry. However, materials exhibiting ductile behavior (most metals, for example) can tolerate some defects while brittle materials (such as ceramics) can fail well below their ultimate material strength.

- *Compressive stress*: It is the stress state caused by an applied load that acts to reduce the length of the material (compression member) in the axis of the applied load. In other words, the stress state caused by squeezing/pushing the material. Due to this the length of the member decreases, while its cross-section increases, as shown in **Fig. 1.2(b)**.

  Compressive strength for materials is generally higher than their tensile strength. However, structures loaded in compression are subject to additional failure modes dependent on geometry, such as Euler buckling.

  In general the tensile and compressive stresses are referred to as normal stresses.

- *Shear stress* (τ): It is the stress state caused by a pair of opposing forces acting along parallel lines of action through the material, in other words, the stress caused by faces of the material sliding relative to one another.

  An example is cutting paper with scissors or stresses due to torsional loading, or a rivet subjected to tensile loading, as shown in **Fig. 1.2(c)**.

$$\tau = F_s/A_s \text{ (MPa or N/mm}^2) \quad \dots \text{(Eq. 1.2)} \textbf{ 1.1(c)/ Pg 2, DHB}$$

where F_s = shear force (N); A_s = shear area (mm^2)

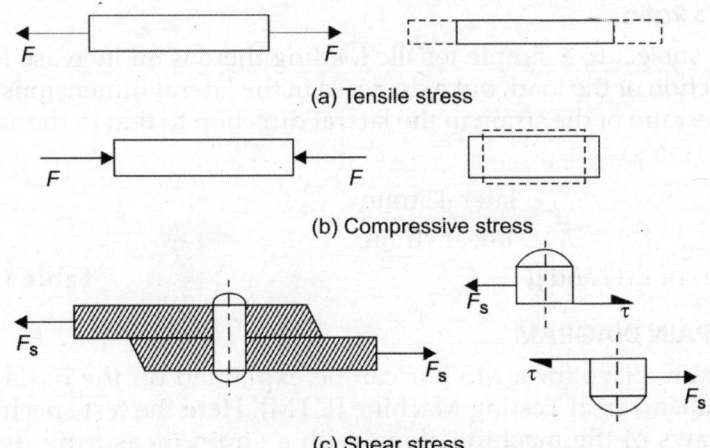

(a) Tensile stress

(b) Compressive stress

(c) Shear stress

Fig. 1.2: Types of stresses

1.8.3 Strain (ε)

The deformation of a body per unit length is called strain. The deformation can be elongation/contraction.

$$\varepsilon = \delta/L \qquad \qquad \text{...(Eq. 1.3)}$$

where δ = deformation (mm), L = length (mm)

The strains are of the following types.
- *Tensile strain*: When a body is subjected to tensile stress, the strain produced in the body is referred to as tensile strain. Due to this the length of the member increases, while its cross-section decreases, as shown in **Fig. 1.2(a)**.
- *Compressive strain*: When a body is subjected to compressive stress, the strain produced in the body is referred to as compressive strain. Due to this the length of the member decreases, while its cross-section increases, as shown in **Fig. 1.2(b)**.
- *Shear strain* (γ): When a body is subjected to shear stress, the strain produced in the body is referred to as shear strain.

$$\gamma = \delta/L \qquad \qquad \text{...(Eq. 1.4)}$$

1.8.4 Hooke's Law

It states that, "when a body is loaded within the elastic limits, stress is directly proportional to strain", i.e. $\sigma \propto \varepsilon$

i.e.
$$\sigma = E \cdot \varepsilon$$
$$E = \sigma/\varepsilon$$

or
$$\varepsilon = \sigma/E = F/AE \qquad \qquad \text{...(Eq. 1.5) 1.2(a)/ Pg 2, DHB}$$

∴
$$\delta = FL/AE = \sigma L/E \quad \text{...using (Eqs 1.1 and 1.3)}$$
$$\text{...(Eq. 1.6) 1.2(b)/ Pg 3, DHB}$$

where E is a proportionality constant, known as ***modulus of elasticity or Young's modulus***.

1.8.5 Shear Modulus/Modulus of Rigidity (G)

It is defined as the ratio of shear stress to shear strain

i.e.
$$G = \tau/\gamma \qquad \qquad \text{...(Eq. 1.7) 1.2(c)/ Pg 3, DHB}$$

∴
$$\delta = F_s L/A_s G = \tau L/G \quad \text{...using (Eqs 1.2 and 1.4)} \quad \text{...(Eq. 1.8)}$$

where G = shear modulus or modulus of rigidity.

1.8.6 Poisson's Ratio

When a bar is subject to a simple tensile loading there is an increase in length of the bar in the direction of the load, but a decrease in the lateral dimensions perpendicular to the load. The ratio of the strain in the lateral direction to that in the axial direction is defined as Poisson's ratio.

$$\mu = \frac{\text{lateral strain}}{\text{linear strain}} \qquad \qquad \text{...(Eq. 1.9)}$$

Note: Values of E, G and μ **... Table 1.1/ Pg 11, DHB**

1.9 STRESS–STRAIN DIAGRAM

The stress–strain curve for a MS bar can be explained on the basis of tensile test performed in a Universal Testing Machine (UTM). Here the test specimen is gripped between the jaws of the machine along with a strain measuring device and load measuring device.

Referring to **Fig. 1.3**, the relation between stress and strain is initially linear (OP), where P defines the limit of proportionality. On further straining, the relation is no longer linear but is still elastic, i.e. the material regains its original shape and size upon the removal of applied load. The maximum load that can be applied without causing the material to undergo permanent deformation defines the elastic limit (PE). Point A marks the end of elastic state and initiation of plastic state, known as upper yield point (Y_U).

Upon further straining, there is a sudden drop in stress and then extension occurs at approximately constant stress, known as lower yield point (Y_L). After Y_L, stress increases with further increase in strain. This effect of the material being able to withstand greater stress despite uniform reduction in cross-sectional area is called strain or work hardening.

At S (design or working stress) the rate of work hardening is unable to keep pace with the rate of reduction in c/s area. Hence 'necking' (local strain hardening) takes place leading to fracture at B (ultimate or fracture or breaking stress).

- *Limit of proportionality* refers to the limit until which stress is directly proportional to strain.

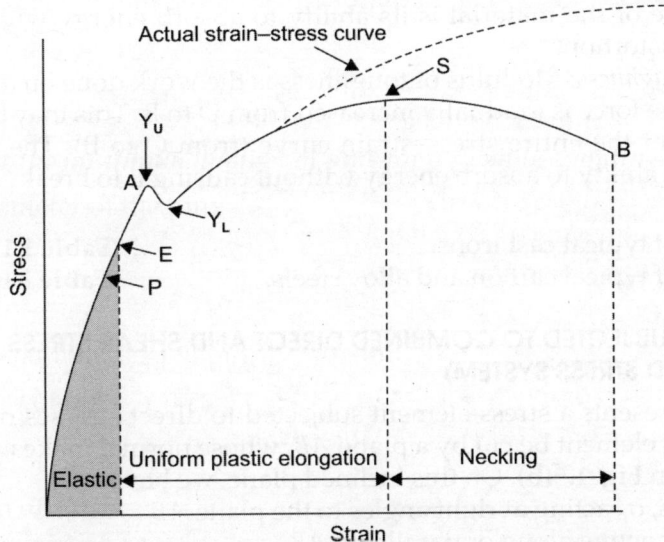

Fig. 1.3: Stress–strain curve for ductile material (MS)

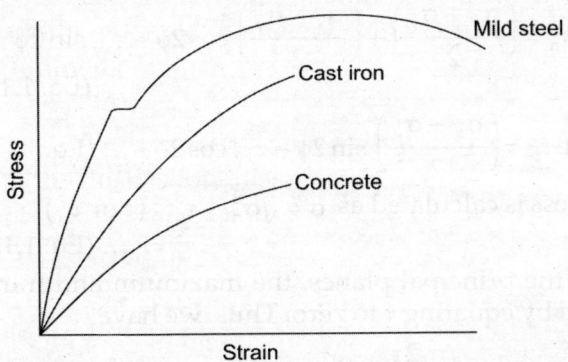

Fig. 1.4: Stress–strain diagram for various materials

- *Elastic limit*: The elastic limit is the limit beyond which the material will no longer regain its original shape when the load is removed, or it is the maximum stress that may be developed such that there is no permanent or residual deformation when the load is entirely removed.
- *Yield point*: Yield point is the point at which the material will have an appreciable elongation or yielding without any increase in load.
- *Upper yield point* (Y_U): It is the stress at which the extension increases without further increase in load.
- *Lower yield point* (Y_L): Here stress remains constant while the strain increases for some time.
- *Ultimate strength* (S): The maximum ordinate in the stress–strain diagram is the ultimate strength or tensile strength.
- *Rupture strength* (B): Rupture strength is the strength of the material at rupture. This is also known as the breaking strength.
- *Modulus of resilience*: Modulus of resilience is the work done on a unit volume of material as the force is gradually increased from O to P. This may be calculated as the area under the stress–strain curve from the origin O up to the elastic limit E (the shaded area in Fig. 1.3).
  The resilience of the material is its ability to absorb energy without creating a permanent distortion.
- *Modulus of toughness*: Modulus of toughness is the work done on a unit volume of material as the force is gradually increased from O to B. This may be calculated as the area under the entire stress–strain curve (from O to B). The toughness of a material is its ability to absorb energy without causing it to break.

Note:
- Properties of typical cast irons.   ... **Table I.17/ Pg 472, DHB**
- Properties of typical carbon and alloy steels.   ... **Table i.18/ Pg 473, DHB**

1.10 MATERIAL SUBJECTED TO COMBINED DIRECT AND SHEAR STRESS (GENERAL 2D STRESS SYSTEM)

Figure 1.5(a) represents a stress element subjected to direct stresses σ_x, σ_y and shear stress τ_{xy}. Let this element be cut by a plane *AB*, whose normal makes an angle ϕ with Y-axis as shown in **Fig. 1.5(b)**. On this inclined plane, we have:
- Normal stress, σ_n acting at right angles to the plane *AB*
- Shear stress, τ acting along or parallel to *AB*

The magnitudes of these stresses are

- Normal stress, $\sigma_n = \left(\dfrac{\sigma_x + \sigma_y}{2}\right) + \left(\dfrac{\sigma_x - \sigma_y}{2}\right)\cos 2\phi + \tau_{xy}\sin 2\phi$

$$\text{... (Eq. 1.10) } \textbf{1.8(a)/ Pg 5, DHB}$$

- Shear stress, τ or $\tau_n = \left(\dfrac{\sigma_x - \sigma_y}{2}\right)\sin 2\phi - \tau_{xy}\cos 2\phi$ ... (Eq. 1.11) **1.8(b)/ Pg 5, DHB**

- The resultant stress is calculated as $\sigma = \sqrt{\sigma_n^2 + \tau^2}$ (τ or τ_n)

$$\text{... (Eq. 1.12) } \textbf{1.7(g)/ Pg 4, DHB}$$

In order to find the principal planes, the maximum and minimum values of σ_n must be obtained by equating τ to zero. Thus, we have

$$\tan 2\phi_1 = \left(\frac{2\tau_{xy}}{\sigma_x - \sigma_y}\right) \qquad \text{... (Eq. 1.13) } \textbf{1.8(e)/ Pg 5, DHB}$$

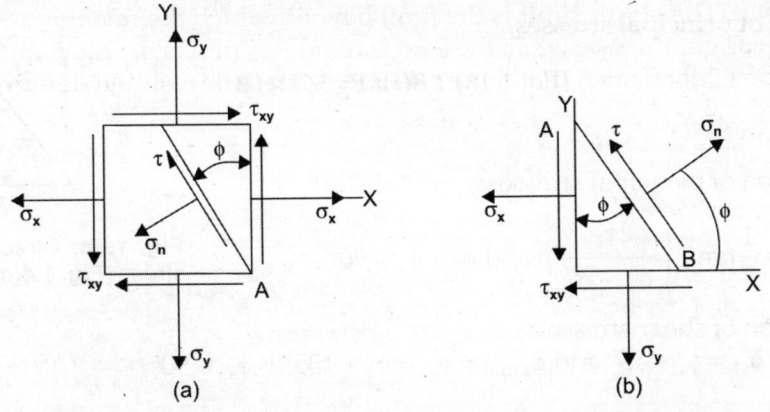

Fig. 1.5: The general condition of two dimensional stress [**Fig. 1.4(a) Plane stress system/Pg 5, DHB**]

Equation 1.13 can be represented as shown in **Fig. 1.6(a).** From this equation we have two values of $2\phi_1$ which differ by 180° [i.e. ϕ_1 and ϕ_2 differ by 90°].

- The values of $2\phi_1$ obtained from (Eq. 1.13) are 180° apart. Equation (1.13) is satisfied at two possible values of ϕ_1. Substituting this value of $2\phi_1$ in (Eq. 1.10) we get two principal stresses, represented by σ_1 and σ_2, which is given as:

Maximum principal stress,

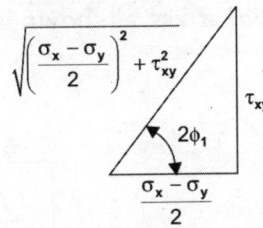

Fig. 1.6a: Direction of principal stress [**Fig. 1.4(b)/Pg 5, DHB**]

$$\sigma_1 = \left(\frac{\sigma_x + \sigma_y}{2}\right) + \sqrt{\left(\frac{\sigma_x - \sigma_y}{2}\right)^2 + \tau_{xy}^2} \qquad \text{... (Eq. 1.14) 1.8(c)/ Pg 5, DHB}$$

Minimum principal stress,

$$\sigma_2 = \left(\frac{\sigma_x + \sigma_y}{2}\right) - \sqrt{\left(\frac{\sigma_x - \sigma_y}{2}\right)^2 + \tau_{xy}^2} \qquad \text{... (Eq. 1.15) 1.8(d)/ Pg 5, DHB}$$

- Further there are two values of $2\phi_1$ at which the shear stress are maximum. For maximum value of τ, differentiating (Eq. 1.11) with respect to ϕ and equating to zero, we have

$$\tan 2\phi_s = -\left(\frac{\sigma_x - \sigma_y}{2\tau_{xy}}\right) \qquad \text{... (Eq. 1.16) 1.8(g)/ Pg 5, DHB}$$

Equation 1.16 can be represented as shown in **Fig. 1.6(b).** From this equation we have two values of $2\phi_s$ which differ by 180° [i.e. ϕ_{s1} and ϕ_{s2} differ by 90°].

- The values of $2\phi_s$ obtained from (Eq. 1.16) are 180° apart and the maximum shear stress occurs on planes that are 90° apart. The maximum shear stress is found as:

$$\tau_{max} = \pm\sqrt{\left(\frac{\sigma_x - \sigma_y}{2}\right)^2 + \tau_{xy}^2} \qquad \text{... (Eq. 1.17) 1.8(f)/ Pg 5, DHB}$$

In terms of principal stresses,

$$\tau_{max} = \frac{\sigma_1 - \sigma_2}{2} \quad \dots \text{(Eq. 1.18)} \ \textbf{1.8(f)/ Pg 5, DHB}$$

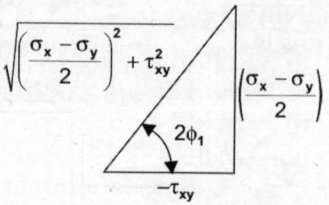

Note:

- Direction of principal stresses:

$$\phi_1 = \frac{1}{2}\tan^{-1}\left(\frac{2\tau_{xy}}{\sigma_x - \sigma_y}\right) \text{ and } \phi_2 = \phi_1 + 90°$$

Fig. 1.6b: Direction of shear stress **[Fig. 1.4(c)/Pg 5, DHB]**

- Direction of shear stresses:

$$\phi_{s\,max} = \phi_{s1} = \phi_1 + 45° \text{ and } \phi_{s\,min} = \phi_{s2} = \phi_1 + 135° = \phi_{s1} + 90°$$

1.11 BIAXIAL/ TWO DIMENSIONAL STRESS

When a component is subjected to different forces such that the stresses produced act only on two planes perpendicular to each other then the state of stress is referred to as *biaxial stress*, as shown in **Fig. 1.7.**

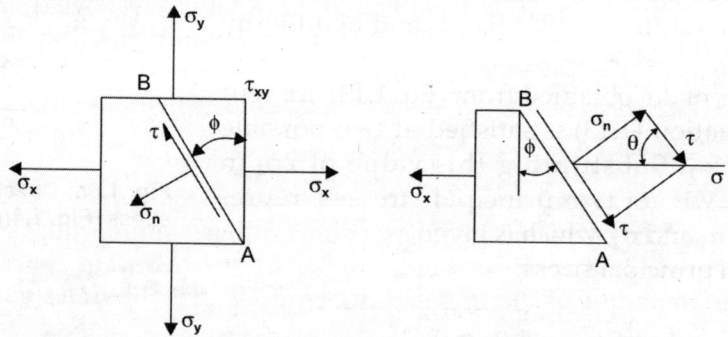

Fig. 1.7: Biaxial stress system **[Fig. 1.3(b)/Pg 4, DHB]**

Figure 1.7 represents a stress element subjected to direct stresses σ_x and σ_y. Let this element be cut by a plane *AB*, whose normal makes an angle ϕ with Y-axis as shown. On this inclined plane, we have:

- Normal stress, σ_n acting at right angles to the plane *AB*
- Shear stress, τ acting along or parallel to '*AB*'

The magnitudes of these stresses are

- Normal stress, $\quad \sigma_n = \left(\dfrac{\sigma_x + \sigma_y}{2}\right) + \left(\dfrac{\sigma_x - \sigma_y}{2}\right)\cos 2\phi$

$$\dots \text{(Eq. 1.19)} \ \textbf{1.7(a)/ Pg 4, DHB}$$

- Shear stress, $\quad \tau \text{ or } \tau_n = \left(\dfrac{\sigma_x - \sigma_y}{2}\right)\sin^2 \phi \qquad \dots \text{(Eq. 1.20)} \ \textbf{1.7(b)/ Pg 4, DHB}$

- The resultant stress is calculated as $\sigma = \sqrt{\sigma_n^2 + \tau^2} \quad \dots \text{(Eq. 1.21)} \ \textbf{1.7(g)/ Pg 4, DHB}$

- Direction of resultant stress or angle of obliquity, $\tan\theta = \left(\dfrac{\sigma_n}{\tau}\right)$

$$\dots \text{(Eq. 1.22)} \ \textbf{1.7(h)/ Pg 4, DHB}$$

Note:
- Referring to **Fig. 1.3(b)/Pg 4, DHB**, equations for biaxial stress system are available under **Eq. 1.7(a) to 1.7(h)/Pg 4, DHB.**
- Referring to **Fig. 1.3(a)/Pg 4, DHB**, equations for uniaxial stress system are available under **Eq. 1.6(a) to 1.6(f)/Pg 4, DHB.**

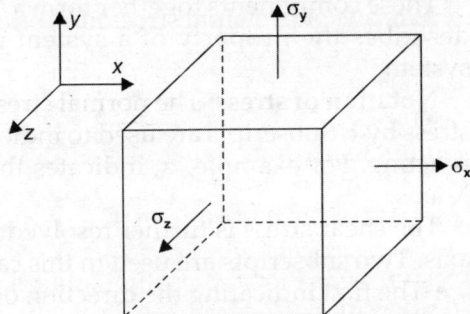

Fig. 1.8: Triaxial stress system **[Fig. 1.7(a)/Pg 7, DHB]**

1.12 TRIAXIAL STRESS/THREE DIMENSIONAL STRESS

A state of **triaxial stress** exists in an element if it is subjected to normal stresses σ_x, σ_y and σ_z in three mutually perpendicular directions and there are no shear stresses on the faces of the element as shown in Fig. 1.8. Since there are no shear stresses on the x, y and z faces, the stresses σ_x, σ_y and σ_z are the principal stresses (σ_1, σ_2 and σ_3) in the material, i.e. the principal normal stresses are σ_1, σ_2 and σ_3 where $\sigma_1 \geq \sigma_2 \geq \sigma_3$, then τ_{max} is largest of

$$\frac{\sigma_1 - \sigma_2}{2}, \frac{\sigma_2 - \sigma_3}{2}, \frac{\sigma_1 - \sigma_3}{2} \qquad \text{... (Eq. 1.23)}$$

1.13 STRESS TENSOR/COMPONENTS OF STRESS

Consider a rectangular parallelepiped (cubical element) as shown in **Fig. 1.9.** The state of stress at any point of a continuous body is determined entirely by the components of stress in three mutually perpendicular planes which pass through the chosen point. These planes are usually taken perpendicular to the orthogonal coordinate system.

To define the stresses acting on six faces of the cubical element, we need three normal stresses: σ_x, σ_y and σ_z and six shear stresses:

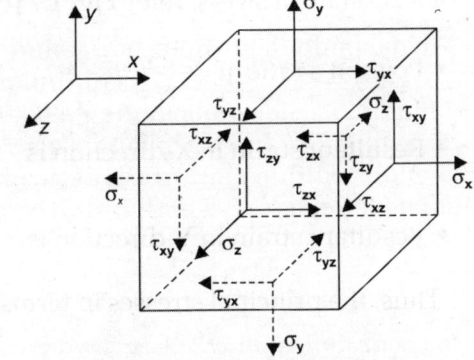

Fig. 1.9: Components of stress

τ_{xy}, τ_{yx}, τ_{yz}, τ_{zy}, τ_{zx} and τ_{xz}. Thus the state of stress at a point using three mutually perpendicular (orthogonal) planes can be described by the nine distinct values of stress represented in the matrix form shown below.

$$\tau_{ij} = \begin{bmatrix} \tau_{xx} & \tau_{xy} & \tau_{xz} \\ \tau_{yx} & \tau_{yy} & \tau_{yz} \\ \tau_{zx} & \tau_{zy} & \tau_{zz} \end{bmatrix} = \begin{bmatrix} \sigma_x & \tau_{xy} & \tau_{xz} \\ \tau_{yx} & \sigma_y & \tau_{yz} \\ \tau_{zx} & \tau_{zy} & \sigma_z \end{bmatrix} \qquad \text{... (Eq. 1.24)}$$

To ensure the static equilibrium, the following equations must hold.

$$\tau_{xy} = \tau_{yx}, \tau_{yz} = \tau_{zy}, \text{ and } \tau_{zx} = \tau_{xz} \qquad \text{... (Eq. 1.25)}$$

$\therefore$ Equation (1.24) yields $\tau_{ij} = \begin{bmatrix} \sigma_x & \tau_{xy} & \tau_{xz} \\ \tau_{yx} & \sigma_y & \tau_{yz} \\ \tau_{zx} & \tau_{zy} & \sigma_z \end{bmatrix}$ ... (Eq. 1.26)

These components together form a *'stress tensor' or 'stress matrix'*. A tensor matrix describes the property of a system which is invariant with respect to coordinate system.

Notation of stress: The normal stress is represented by σ_n and the tangential (shear) stress by τ. Subscripts are used to indicate the direction of the plane on which the stress is acting. For example, σ_x indicates that the stress is acting on a plane normal to the X-axis.

The shear stress is further resolved into two components parallel to the coordinate axis. Two subscripts are used in this case:
- The first indicating the direction of normal to the plane (face) and
- The second indicates the direction of component of stress as shown below:

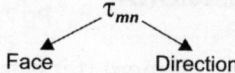

This shows that the first is the plane in which the stress acts and the second is the direction in which the stress acts.

For example, τ_{yz} is the shear stress in the plane perpendicular to Y-axis in the Z-direction. Each component represents a magnitude for that particular plane and direction.

1.14 BIAXIAL DEFORMATION/STRAIN

For a 2D state of stress, refer **Fig. 1.7 [Fig. 1.3(b)/ Pg 4, DHB]**

- Poisson's ratio $\mu = \dfrac{-\varepsilon_y}{\varepsilon_x} = \dfrac{-\varepsilon_z}{\varepsilon_x}$ ... (Eq. 1.27) **1.11(a)/ Pg 7, DHB**

- Resultant strain in X-direction is $\varepsilon_x = \dfrac{\sigma_x}{E} - \mu\dfrac{\sigma_y}{E}$ ... (Eq. 1.28) **1.11(b)/ Pg 7, DHB**

- Resultant strain in Y-direction is $\varepsilon_y = \dfrac{\sigma_y}{E} - \mu\dfrac{\sigma_x}{E}$ ... (Eq. 1.29) **1.11(c)/ Pg 7, DHB**

Thus, the principal stresses in terms of principal strains are calculated as below.

- Normal stress in X-direction, $\sigma_x = \dfrac{(\varepsilon_x + \mu\varepsilon_y)E}{1-\mu^2}$ ... (Eq. 1.30) **1.11(d)/ Pg 7, DHB**

- Normal stress in Y-direction, $\sigma_y = \dfrac{(\varepsilon_y + \mu\varepsilon_x)E}{1-\mu^2}$ ... (Eq. 1.31) **1.11(e)/ Pg 7, DHB**

1.15 TRIAXIAL DEFORMATION/STRAIN

On similar lines, for a 3D state of stress, **Fig. 1.9 [Fig. 1.7(b)/ Pg 7, DHB]**
- Resultant strain in X-direction is

$$\varepsilon_x = \frac{1}{E}[\sigma_x - \mu(\sigma_y + \sigma_z)] \quad \text{... (Eq. 1.32) } \textbf{1.12(a)/ Pg 7, DHB}$$

- Resultant strain in Y-direction is

$$\varepsilon_y = \frac{1}{E}[\sigma_y - \mu(\sigma_z + \sigma_x)] \quad \text{... (Eq. 1.33) } \textbf{1.12(b)/ Pg 7, DHB}$$

- Resultant strain in Z-direction is

$$\varepsilon_z = \frac{1}{E}[\sigma_z - \mu(\sigma_x + \sigma_y)] \qquad \text{... (Eq. 1.34) } \mathbf{1.12(c)/ \ Pg \ 7, \ DHB}$$

1. **Identify the following engineering materials giving specifications:**
   i. **FG350** ii. **FeE300** iii. **C35Mn75** iv. **X20Cr18Ni2**

VTU – June 12 – 04 Marks

Solution:
   i. FG350: Grey cast iron with ultimate strength of 350 N/mm^2.
      ... Tb I.4/ Pg 461, DHB
   ii. FeE300: Plain carbon steel having yield strength of 360 N/mm^2.
      ... Tb I.7/ Pg 462, DHB
   iii. C35Mn75: Free cutting steel with 0.35% (average) carbon, 0.75% manganese.
      ... Tb I.8/ Pg 463, DHB
   iv. X20Cr18Ni2: High alloy steel with 0.20% carbon, 18% chromium and 2% nickel.
      ... Pg 456, DHB

2. **The principal stresses at a point in a strained material are σ_x and σ_y. Show that the resultant stress σ_r on the plane carrying the maximum shear stress is**

$$\sigma_r = \sqrt{\frac{\sigma_x^2 + \sigma_y^2}{2}}$$

Solution:
We know that the resultant stress,

$$\sigma_r = \sqrt{\sigma_n^2 + \tau^2} \qquad \text{... Eq. (i) } \mathbf{1.7(g)/ \ Pg \ 4, \ DHB}$$

But normal stress, $\sigma_n = \left(\dfrac{\sigma_x + \sigma_y}{2}\right) + \left(\dfrac{\sigma_x - \sigma_y}{2}\right)\cos 2\phi + \tau_{xy}\sin 2\phi$

$$\text{... } \mathbf{1.8(a)/ \ Pg \ 5, \ DHB}$$

i.e. $\sigma_n = \left(\dfrac{\sigma_x + \sigma_y}{2}\right) + \left(\dfrac{\sigma_x - \sigma_y}{2}\right)\cos 2\phi \ (\text{since } \tau_{xy} = 0)$

$$\text{... Eq. (ii) } \mathbf{1.7(a)/ \ Pg \ 4, \ DHB}$$

and shear stress, $\tau = \left(\dfrac{\sigma_x - \sigma_y}{2}\right)\sin 2\phi - \tau_{xy}\cos 2\phi \qquad \text{... } \mathbf{1.8(b)/ \ Pg \ 5, \ DHB}$

i.e. $\tau \text{ or } \tau_n = \left(\dfrac{\sigma_x - \sigma_y}{2}\right)\sin 2\phi$

$$\text{... Eq. (iii) } \mathbf{1.7(b)/ \ Pg \ 4, \ DHB}$$

For maximum shear stress, $\phi = 45°$

$\therefore$ Eq. (i) yields

$$\sigma_r = \sqrt{\left[\left(\frac{\sigma_x + \sigma_y}{2}\right) + \left(\frac{\sigma_x - \sigma_y}{2}\right)\cos(2\times 45)°\right]^2 + \left[\left(\frac{\sigma_x - \sigma_y}{2}\right)\sin(2\times 45)°\right]}$$

$$= \sqrt{\left(\frac{\sigma_x + \sigma_y}{2}\right) + \left(\frac{\sigma_x - \sigma_y}{2}\right)^2}$$

i.e.
$$\sigma_r^2 = \frac{1}{4}(\sigma_x^2 + \sigma_y^2 + 2\sigma_x\sigma_y) + \frac{1}{4}(\sigma_x^2 + \sigma_y^2 - 2\sigma_x\sigma_y)$$

$$= \frac{1}{4}(2\sigma_x^2 + 2\sigma_y^2)$$

$$= \frac{1}{2}(\sigma_x^2 + \sigma_y^2)$$

$$\therefore \qquad \sigma_r = \sqrt{\frac{\sigma_x^2 + \sigma_y^2}{2}}$$

3. **At a point in a 2D stress system, the normal stresses on two mutually perpendicular planes are σ_x and σ_y (both alike) and the shear stress is τ_{xy}. If $\tau_{xy}^2 = \sigma_x \cdot \sigma_y$, show that one of the principal stresses is zero.**

Solution:

We know that
$$\sigma_{1,2} = \left(\frac{\sigma_x + \sigma_y}{2}\right) \pm \sqrt{\left(\frac{\sigma_x - \sigma_y}{2}\right)^2 + \tau_{xy}^2} \quad ... \ 1.8(c)\&(d)/ \ Pg \ 5, \ DHB$$

$$= \left(\frac{\sigma_x + \sigma_y}{2}\right) \pm \sqrt{\frac{\sigma_x^2 + \sigma_y^2 - 2\sigma_x\sigma_y}{4} + \sigma_x\sigma_y}$$

$$= \left(\frac{\sigma_x + \sigma_y}{2}\right) \pm \sqrt{\frac{\sigma_x^2 + \sigma_y^2 - 2\sigma_x\sigma_y + 4\sigma_x\sigma_y}{4}}$$

$$= \left(\frac{\sigma_x + \sigma_y}{2}\right) \pm \sqrt{\frac{\sigma_x^2 + \sigma_y^2 + 2\sigma_x\sigma_y}{4}}$$

$$= \left(\frac{\sigma_x + \sigma_y}{2}\right) \pm \sqrt{\left(\frac{\sigma_x + \sigma_y}{2}\right)^2}$$

$$\sigma_{1,2} = \left(\frac{\sigma_x + \sigma_y}{2}\right) \pm \left(\frac{\sigma_x + \sigma_y}{2}\right)$$

$$\therefore \qquad \sigma_1 = (\sigma_x + \sigma_y) \text{ and } \sigma_2 = 0$$

4. **A rectangular bar of section 50 mm × 25 mm is subjected to a tensile load of 25 kN. Determine the values of normal and shear stresses on a plane 30° with the vertical. Also calculate the magnitude and direction of the maximum shear stress.**

VTU – Dec.08/ Jan.2009 – 08 Marks

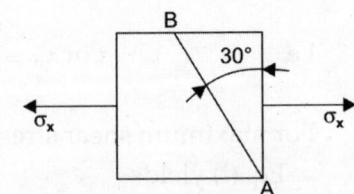

Fig. 1.10: Problem 4

Solution: $A = 50 \times 25 = 1250 \text{ mm}^2$, $F = 25$ kN, $\sigma_n = ?$, $\tau = ?$, $\phi = 30°$.

• We know that $\sigma_n = \sigma_x \cos^2\phi$ ... 1.6(a)/ Pg 4, DHB

But $\sigma_x = \dfrac{F}{A} = \dfrac{25000}{1250} = 20$ MPa   ... 1.1(a)/ Pg 2, DHB

$$\sigma_n = 20 \times \cos^2(30) = 15 \text{ MPa}$$

- Also $\qquad \tau = \dfrac{\sigma_x}{2} \sin 2\phi = \dfrac{20}{2} \sin(2 \times 30) = 8.66 \text{ MPa}$

... **1.6(b)/ Pg 4, DHB**

- Maximum shear stress

$$\tau_{max} = \dfrac{\sigma_x}{2} = \dfrac{20}{2} = 10 \text{ MPa} \qquad \qquad \text{... } \textbf{1.6(e)/ Pg 4, DHB}$$

- Direction of maximum shear stress
  $$\phi_s = 45°$$

5. For the system shown in Fig. 1.11, determine the normal and tangential stress intensities. Also find the direction of resultant stress.

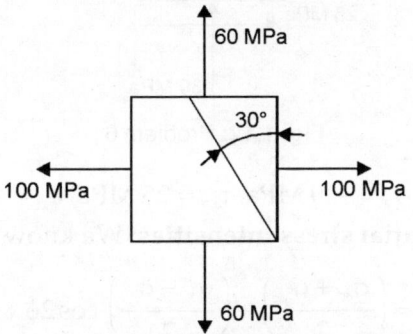

Fig. 1.11: Problem 5

Solution: $\sigma_x = 100 \text{ MPa}$, $\sigma_y = 60 \text{ MPa}$, $\phi = 30°$, $\sigma_n = ?$, $\tau = ?$, $\theta = ?$

- Normal stress $\quad \sigma_n = \left(\dfrac{\sigma_x + \sigma_y}{2}\right) + \left(\dfrac{\sigma_x - \sigma_y}{2}\right) \cos 2\phi \qquad \text{... } \textbf{1.7(a)/ Pg 4, DHB}$

$$= \left(\dfrac{100 + 60}{2}\right) + \left(\dfrac{100 - 60}{2}\right) \cos(2 \times 30)$$

$$\sigma_n = 90 \text{ MPa}$$

- Shear stress $\quad \tau = \left(\dfrac{\sigma_x - \sigma_y}{2}\right) \sin 2\phi \qquad \qquad \text{... } \textbf{1.7(b)/ Pg 4, DHB}$

$$= \left(\dfrac{100 - 60}{2}\right) \sin(2 \times 30)$$

$$\tau = 17.32 \text{ MPa}$$

- Direction of resultant stress of angle of obliquity,

$$\tan \theta = \left(\dfrac{\sigma_n}{\tau}\right) = \left(\dfrac{90}{17.32}\right) \qquad \qquad \text{... } \textbf{1.7(h)/ Pg 4, DHB}$$

$$\theta = 79.11°$$

6. A point in a structural member is subjected to plane state of stress as shown in Fig. 1.12. Determine the following:
  i. Normal and tangential stress intensities at an angle of $\theta = 45°$

ii. **Principal stresses σ_1 and σ_2 and their directions**

iii. **Maximum shear stress and its plane.**

VTU – June 2012 – 10 Marks; Dec.09/ Jan.2010 – 10 Marks;
(Similar) June/ July 2011 – 14 Marks; (similar) June/ July 2015 – 10 Marks

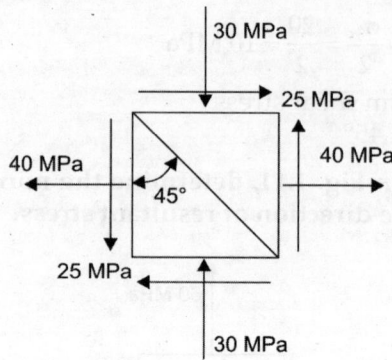

Fig. 1.12: Problem 6

Solution: $\sigma_x = 40$ MPa, $\sigma_y = -30$ MPa, $\tau_{xy} = 25$ MPa, $\phi_n = 45°$.

i. **Normal and tangential stress intensities:** We know that normal stress

$$\sigma_n = \left(\frac{\sigma_x + \sigma_y}{2}\right) + \left(\frac{\sigma_x - \sigma_y}{2}\right)\cos 2\phi + \tau_{xy}\sin 2\phi$$

$$\text{... 1.8(a)/ Pg 5, DHB}$$

$$= \left(\frac{40 - 30}{2}\right) + \left[\left(\frac{40 + 30}{2}\right)\cos(2 \times 45)\right] + 25\sin(2 \times 45)$$

$$\sigma_n = 30 \text{ MPa}$$

Also tangential stress,

$$\tau = \left(\frac{\sigma_x - \sigma_y}{2}\right)\sin 2\phi - \tau_{xy}\cos 2\phi \qquad \text{... 1.8(b)/ Pg 5, DHB}$$

$$= \left[\left(\frac{40 + 30}{2}\right)\sin(2 \times 45)\right] - 25\cos(2 \times 45)$$

$$\tau = 35 \text{ MPa}$$

ii. **Principal stresses and their directions:**

We know that $\sigma_{1,2} = \left(\frac{\sigma_x + \sigma_y}{2}\right) \pm \sqrt{\left(\frac{\sigma_x - \sigma_y}{2}\right)^2 + \tau_{xy}^2}$ ... 1.8(c)&(d)/ Pg 5, DHB

$$= \left(\frac{40 - 30}{2}\right) \pm \sqrt{\left(\frac{40 + 30}{2}\right)^2 + 25^2}$$

$$\therefore \qquad \sigma_{1,2} = 48.01, -38.01 \text{ MPa}$$

i.e. $\qquad \sigma_1 = 48.01$ MPa

and $\qquad \sigma_2 = -38.01$ MPa

Directions: We know that

$$\tan 2\phi_1 = \left(\frac{2\tau_{xy}}{\sigma_x - \sigma_y}\right) \qquad \dots \textbf{1.8(e)/ Pg 5, DHB}$$

$$\tan 2\phi_1 = \left(\frac{2 \times 25}{40 - (-30)}\right) = 0.714$$

$$2\phi_1 = 35.54°$$

$$\therefore \qquad \phi_1 = 17.77°$$

$$\phi_2 = \phi_1 + 90° = 17.77° + 90° = 107.77°$$

iii. **Maximum shear stress:** We know that

$$\tau_{max} = \pm \sqrt{\left(\frac{\sigma_x - \sigma_y}{2}\right)^2 + \tau_{xy}^2} \qquad \dots \textbf{1.8(f)/ Pg 5, DHB}$$

$$= \pm \sqrt{\left(\frac{40 + 30}{2}\right)^2 + 25^2}$$

$$\tau_{max} = \pm 43.01 \text{ MPa}$$

Directions: We know that

$$\tan 2\phi_s = -\left(\frac{\sigma_x - \sigma_y}{2\tau_{xy}}\right) \qquad \dots \textbf{1.8(g)/ Pg 5, DHB}$$

$$\tan 2\phi_s = -\left(\frac{40 - (-30)}{2 \times 25}\right) = -1.4$$

$$2\phi_s = -54.46°$$

$$\therefore \qquad \phi_{s1} = -27.23°$$

$$\text{and} \qquad \phi_{s2} = \phi_1 + 90° = -27.23° + 90° = 62.77°$$

or Direction of maximum shear stress,

$$\phi_{s1} = \phi_1 + 45° = 17.77 + 45° = 62.77°$$

Direction of minimum shear stress

$$\phi_{s2} = \phi_1 + 135° = 17.77 + 135° = 152.77° \quad [\text{or } \phi_{s1} + 90°]$$

7. **A machine component is subjected to stresses as shown in Fig. 1.13. Determine:**

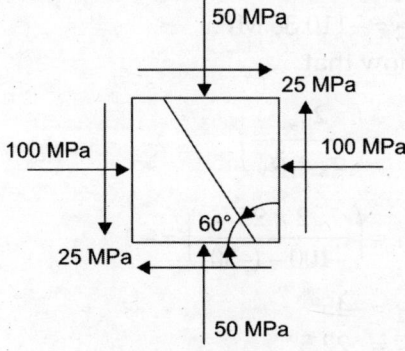

Fig. 1.13: Problem 7

    a. Normal, shear and resultant stresses
    b. Principal stresses and their directions

Solution: $\sigma_x = -100$ MPa, $\sigma_y = -50$ MPa, $\tau_{xy} = 25$ MPa, $\phi' = 60°$ (with horizontal), $\phi' = 90° - 30°$ (with vertical).

    a. Normal, shear and resultant stresses: We know that normal stress

$$\sigma_n = \left(\frac{\sigma_x + \sigma_y}{2}\right) + \left(\frac{\sigma_x - \sigma_y}{2}\right)\cos 2\phi + \tau_{xy}\sin 2\phi$$

$$\text{... 1.8(a)/ Pg 5, DHB}$$

$$= \left(\frac{-100 - 50}{2}\right) + \left[\left(\frac{-100 + 50}{2}\right)\cos(2 \times 30)\right] + 25\sin(2 \times 30)$$

$$\sigma_n = -65.85 \text{ MPa}$$

Also shear stress,

$$\tau = \left(\frac{\sigma_x - \sigma_y}{2}\right)\sin 2\phi - \tau_{xy}\cos 2\phi \qquad \text{... 1.8(b)/ Pg 5, DHB}$$

$$= \left[\left(\frac{-100 + 50}{2}\right)\sin(2 \times 30)\right] - 25\cos(2 \times 30)$$

$$\tau = -34.15 \text{ MPa}$$

and resultant stress,

$$\sigma_r = \sqrt{\sigma_n^2 + \tau^2} \qquad \text{... 1.7(g)/ Pg 4, DHB}$$

$$= \sqrt{(-65.85)^2 + (-34.15)^2}$$

$$\sigma_r = 74.18 \text{ MPa}$$

    b. Principal stresses and their directions: We know that

$$\sigma_{1,2} = \left(\frac{\sigma_x + \sigma_y}{2}\right) \pm \sqrt{\left(\frac{\sigma_x - \sigma_y}{2}\right)^2 + \tau_{xy}^2} \quad \text{... 1.8(c)\&(d)/ Pg 5, DHB}$$

$$= \frac{-100 - 50}{2} \pm \sqrt{\left(\frac{-100 + 50}{2}\right)^2 + 25^2}$$

$\therefore$ $\sigma_{1,2} = -39.64, -110.36$ MPa

i.e. $\sigma_1 = -39.64$ MPa

and $\sigma_2 = -110.36$ MPa

Directions: We know that

$$\tan 2\phi_1 = \left(\frac{2\tau_{xy}}{\sigma_x - \sigma_y}\right) \qquad \text{... 1.8(e)/ Pg 5, DHB}$$

$$\tan 2\phi_1 = \left(\frac{2 \times 25}{-100 - (-50)}\right) = -1$$

$$2\phi_1 = -45°$$

$\therefore$ $\phi_1 = -22.5°$

and $\phi_2 = \phi_1 + 90° = -22.5° + 90° = 67.5°$

8. **A point in a structural member is subjected to plane stress as shown in Fig. 1.14. Determine (a) the principal stresses and (b) their directions.**

VTU – Dec.13/ Jan.2014 – 08 Marks

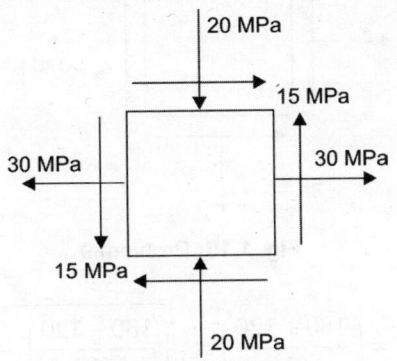

Fig. 1.14: Problem 8

Solution: $\sigma_x = 30$ MPa, $\sigma_y = -20$ MPa, $\tau_{xy} = 15$ MPa.

a. **Principal stresses:** We know that

$$\sigma_{1,2} = \left(\frac{\sigma_x + \sigma_y}{2}\right) \pm \sqrt{\left(\frac{\sigma_x - \sigma_y}{2}\right)^2 + \tau_{xy}^2}$$

... 1.8(c)&(d)/ Pg 5, DHB

$$= \left(\frac{30 - 20}{2}\right) \pm \sqrt{\left(\frac{30 + 20}{2}\right)^2 + 15^2}$$

∴ $\sigma_{1,2} = 34.15$ MPa, -24.15 MPa

i.e. $\sigma_1 = 34.15$ MPa

and $\sigma_2 = -24.15$ MPa

b. **Principal stresses directions:** We know that

$$\tan 2\phi_1 = \left(\frac{2\tau_{xy}}{\sigma_x - \sigma_y}\right)$$

... 1.8(e)/ Pg 5, DHB

$$\tan 2\phi_1 = \left(\frac{2 \times 15}{30 - (20)}\right) = 0.6$$

∴ $2\phi_1 = 30.96°$

i.e. $\phi_1 = 15.48°$

and $\phi_2 = \phi_1 + 90° = 15.48° + 90° = 105.48°$

9. **For the stress element shown in Fig. 1.15, find (a) the principal stresses and (b) directions.**

VTU – June/ July 2014 – 06 Marks

Solution: $\sigma_x = 180$ MPa, $\sigma_y = 120$ MPa, $\tau_{xy} = 80$ MPa.

a. **Principal stresses:** We know that

$$\sigma_{1,2} = \left(\frac{\sigma_x + \sigma_y}{2}\right) \pm \sqrt{\left(\frac{\sigma_x - \sigma_y}{2}\right)^2 + \tau_{xy}^2}$$

... 1.8(c)&(d)/ Pg 5, DHB

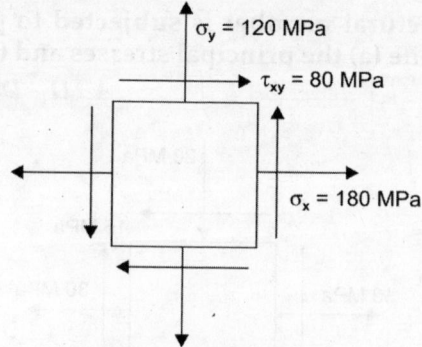

Fig. 1.15: Problem 9

$$= \left(\frac{180 + 120}{2}\right) \pm \sqrt{\left(\frac{180 - 120}{2}\right)^2 + 80^2}$$

∴ $\sigma_{1,2} = 235.44$ MPa, 64.56 MPa

i.e. $\sigma_1 = 235.44$ MPa

and $\sigma_2 = 64.56$ MPa

b. **Principal stresses directions:** We know that

$$\tan 2\phi_1 = \left(\frac{2\tau_{xy}}{\sigma_x - \sigma_y}\right)$$ ... 1.8(e)/ Pg 5, DHB

$$\tan 2\phi_1 = \left(\frac{2 \times 80}{180 - 120}\right) = 2.67$$

∴ $2\phi_1 = 69.44°$

i.e. $\phi_1 = 34.72°$

and $\phi_2 = \phi_1 + 90° = 34.72° + 90° = 124.72°$

10. **For the system in Fig. 1.16, find:**
    a. **Principal stresses and their directions**
    b. **Maximum shear stress and their planes.**

Solution: $\sigma_x = 70$ MPa, $\sigma_y = -35$ MPa, $\tau_{xy} = -17.5$ MPa.

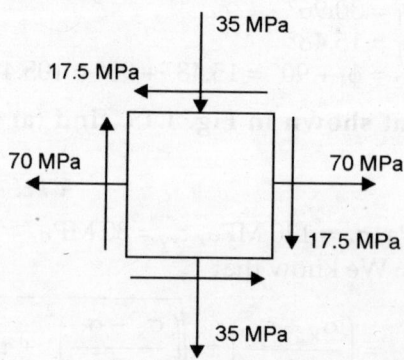

Fig. 1.16: Problem 10

a. **Principal stresses:** We know that

$$\sigma_{1,2} = \left(\frac{\sigma_x + \sigma_y}{2}\right) \pm \sqrt{\left(\frac{\sigma_x - \sigma_y}{2}\right)^2 + \tau_{xy}^2} \quad \dots \textbf{1.8(c)\&(d)/ Pg 5, DHB}$$

$$= \left(\frac{70 - 35}{2}\right) \pm \sqrt{\left(\frac{70 + 35}{2}\right)^2 + (-17.5)^2}$$

$\therefore \qquad\qquad \sigma_{1,2} = 72.84, -37.84 \text{ MPa}$

i.e. $\qquad\qquad \sigma_1 = 72.84 \text{ MPa}$

and $\qquad\qquad \sigma_2 = -37.84 \text{ MPa}$

Principal stresses directions: We know that

$$\tan 2\phi_1 = \left(\frac{2\tau_{xy}}{\sigma_x - \sigma_y}\right) \qquad\qquad \dots \textbf{1.8(e)/ Pg 5, DHB}$$

$$\tan 2\phi_1 = \left(\frac{2 \times (-17.5)}{70 - (-35)}\right) = -0.334$$

$\qquad 2\phi_1 = -18.43°$

$\therefore \qquad \phi_1 = -9.22°$

$\qquad \phi_2 = \phi_1 + 90° = -9.22° + 90° = 80.78°$

b. **Maximum shear stress:** We know that

$$\tau_{max} = \pm \sqrt{\left(\frac{\sigma_x - \sigma_y}{2}\right)^2 + \tau_{xy}^2} \qquad\qquad \dots \textbf{1.8(f)/ Pg 5, DHB}$$

$$= \pm \sqrt{\left(\frac{70 + 35}{2}\right)^2 + (-17.5)^2}$$

$\qquad \tau_{max} = \pm 55.34 \text{ MPa}$

or $\qquad \tau_{max} = \left(\frac{\sigma_1 - \sigma_2}{2}\right) = \frac{72.84 - (-37.84)}{2} = 55.34 \text{ MPa}$

Shear stress directions: We know that

$$\tan 2\phi_s = -\left(\frac{\sigma_x - \sigma_y}{2\tau_{xy}}\right) \qquad\qquad \dots \textbf{1.8(g)/ Pg 5, DHB}$$

$$\tan 2\phi_s = -\left(\frac{70 - (-35)}{2 \times (-17.5)}\right) = 3$$

$\qquad 2\phi_s = 71.57°$

$\therefore \qquad \phi_s = \phi_{s1} = 35.78°$

and $\qquad \phi_{s2} = \phi_{s1} + 90° = 35.78° + 90° = 125.78°$

or direction of maximum shear stress,

$\qquad \phi_{s1} = \phi_1 + 45° = -9.22° + 45° = 35.78°$

direction of minimum shear stress

$\qquad \phi_{s2} = \phi_1 + 135° = -9.22° + 135° = 125.78° \quad [\text{or } \phi_{s1} + 90°]$

11. **The state of stress at a point in a structural member is shown in Fig. 1.17. The tensile principal stress is known to be 84 N/mm². Determine:**
   a. **The shear stress τ_{xy}.**
   b. **The maximum shear stress at the point and orientation of its plane**

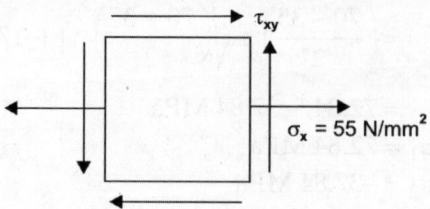

Fig. 1.17: Problem 11

Solution: $\sigma_x = 55\,\text{N/mm}^2$, $\sigma_1 = 84\,\text{N/mm}^2$ (i) $\tau_{max} = ?$, $2\phi_s = ?$ (ii) $\tau_{xy} = ?$

i. **Shear stress τ_{xy}:** We know that

$$\sigma_1 = \left(\frac{\sigma_x + \sigma_y}{2}\right) \pm \sqrt{\left(\frac{\sigma_x - \sigma_y}{2}\right)^2 + \tau_{xy}^2} \qquad \text{... 1.8(c)/ Pg 5, DHB}$$

$$84 = \left(\frac{55 + 0}{2}\right) + \sqrt{\left(\frac{55 + 0}{2}\right)^2 + \tau_{xy}^2}$$

$\therefore$ $\qquad\qquad \tau_{xy} = 49.36\,\text{MPa}$

ii. **Maximum shear stress at the point and orientation of its plane:** We know that

$$\tau_{max} = \pm\sqrt{\left(\frac{\sigma_x - \sigma_y}{2}\right)^2 + \tau_{xy}^2} \qquad \text{... 1.8(f)/ Pg 5, DHB}$$

$$= \pm\sqrt{\left(\frac{55 + 0}{2}\right)^2 + (49.36)^2}$$

$\tau_{max} = \pm 56.50\,\text{MPa}$

Shear stress directions: We know that

$$\tan 2\phi_s = -\left(\frac{\sigma_x - \sigma_y}{2\tau_{xy}}\right) \qquad \text{... 1.8(g)/ Pg 5, DHB}$$

$$\tan 2\phi_s = -\left(\frac{55 - 0}{2 \times 49.36}\right) = -0.56$$

$$2\phi_s = -29.13°$$

$\therefore$ $\qquad\qquad \phi_{s1} = -14.56°$

and $\qquad\qquad \phi_{s2} = \phi_{s1} + 90° = -14.56° + 90° = 75.44°$

VTU QUESTION PAPERS

Mar. 2001 (ME5T2)

1. Briefly discuss factors influencing the selection of suitable material for machine element. **(05 Marks)**

July/Aug. 2004 (AU46)

2. a. Draw the stress–strain diagram and name the salient points for the following materials:
   i. C60 steel **(03 Marks)**
   ii. Cast iron FG200 **(02 Marks)**
   b. On a rectangular stress element show the triaxial stress components and the corresponding stress tensor. **(05 Marks)**

Jan/Feb. 2005 (AU46)

3. a. List the three factors which govern the selection of a material for a machine component. **(03 Marks)**
   b. Define standardization. State the standards used in machine design. **(03 Marks)**

July/ Aug. 2005 (AU46)

4. Discuss factors to be considered for selection of an appropriate material for a machine element in the design process. **(08 Marks)**

Jan/Feb. 2006 (AU46)

5. a. Draw stress–strain diagram for a ductile material subjected to tension. Explain the significance of salient points. **(06 Marks)**
   b. Explain principal planes and principal stresses. **(04 Marks)**

July 2006 (AU46)

6. Draw the stress–strain diagrams for the ductile material and a brittle material and show the salient points on them. **(06 Marks)**

Dec. 07/Jan. 2008 (AU46)

7. Explain the factors which govern the selection of material for a given machine component. **(05 Marks)**

Dec. 08/Jan. 2009 (06ME-AU52)

8. a. Sketch and explain biaxial and triaxial stresses, stress tensor, and principal stresses. **(08 Marks)**
   b. A rectangular bar of section 50 mm × 25 mm is subjected to a tensile load of 25 kN. Determine the values of normal and shear stresses on a plane 30° with the vertical. Also calculate the magnitude and direction of the maximum shear stress. **(08 Marks)**
   c. Briefly explain the design codes and standards. **(04 Marks)**

June/July 2009 (AU46)

9. Define standardization. State the standards used in machine design. **(03 Marks)**

June/July 2009 (06ME52)

10. Write brief note on general procedure used in design. **(05 Marks)**

Dec. 2009/ Jan. 2010 (AU46)

11. Draw stress–strain diagram for ductile material subjected to tension. Explain the significance of salient points. **(04 Marks)**

Dec. 2009/Jan. 2010 (06ME52)

12. A point in a structural member subjected to plane stress is shown in **Fig. U1.1**. Determine the following.

   i. Normal and tangential stress intensities on a plane inclined at 45°.

   ii. Principal stresses and their directions.

   iii. Maximum shear stress and the direction of plane on which they occur.

   (10 Marks)

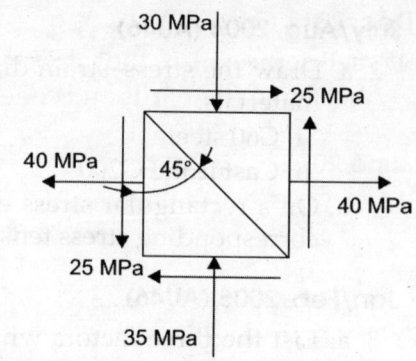

Fig. U1.1

May/June 2010 (06ME52)

13. a. Sketch and explain biaxial and triaxial stresses, shear tensor and principal stresses. **(06 Marks)**

   b. The state of stress at a point in a structural member is as shown in **Fig. U1.2**. The tensile principal stress is known to be 84 N/mm². Determine:

   i. The maximum shear stress at the point and orientation of its plane.

   ii. The shearing stress τ_{xy}.

   (10 Marks)

   c. Briefly discuss the factors influencing the selection of suitable material for machine element. **(04 Marks)**

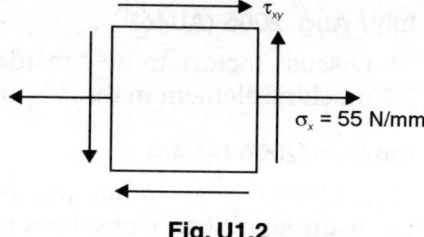

Fig. U1.2

Dec. 2010 (AU46)

14. a. Classify the standards with examples and list the purposes of standardization. **(05 Marks)**

   b. Discuss the factors which govern the selection of a material in the design of machine elements. **(05 Marks)**

Dec. 2010 (06ME52)

15. Sketch and explain biaxial, triaxial and principal stresses. **(08 Marks)**

June/ July 2011 (06ME52)

16. a. Draw the stress–strain diagram for mild steel subjected to tension. Explain the significance of salient points. **(06 Marks)**

   b. A point in a structural member subjected to plane stress is shown in **Fig. U1.3**. Determine the following.

   i. Normal and tangential stress intensities on plane MN inclined at 45°.

   ii. Principal stresses and their direction.

   iii. Maximum shear stress and the direction of the planes on which it occurs.

   (14 Marks)

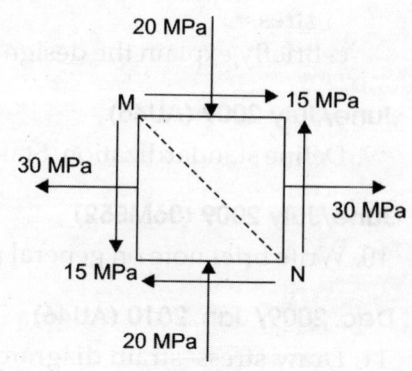

Fig. U1.3

Dec. 2011 (06ME52)

17. a. Briefly explain the important mechanical properties of metals. **(06 Marks)**
   b. Define standards and codes. **(04 Marks)**

June 2012 (06ME52-06AU52)

18. a. Identify the following engineering materials
   giving specifications.
      i. FG350
      ii. FeE300
      iii. C35Mn75
      iv. X20Cr18Ni2 **(04 Marks)**
   b. A point in a structural member is subjected to
   plane state of stress as shown in **Fig. U1.4**.
   Determine the following.
      i. Normal and tangential stress intensities at
      an angle of $\theta = 45°$.
      ii. Principle stresses σ_1 and σ_2 and their directions.
      iii. Maximum shear stress and its plane. **(10 Marks)**

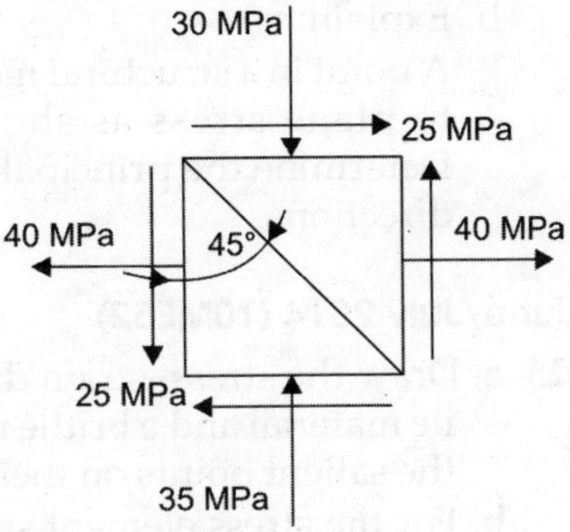

Fig. U1.4

Dec. 2012 (10ME52)

19. a. What is mechanical engineering design? Explain. **(03 Marks)**
   b. Explain the importance of standards in design. Give examples. **(03 Marks)**

Dec. 2012 (06ME52)

20. a. Draw the stress–strain curve for mild steel and cast iron. Name the salient points. **(06 Marks)**
   b. What are the important mechanical properties of metals? Explain each of them
   briefly. **(10 Marks)**
   c. What is standardization? What are the advantages of standardization? **(04 Marks)**

June/July 2013 (06ME52)

21. a. Briefly explain the following.
      i. Design considerations **(04 Marks)**
      ii. Design codes and standards **(02 Marks)**
      iii. Stress tensor **(02 Marks)**

June/July 2013 (10ME52)

22. a. What are the requirements of machine elements? Explain briefly. **(05 Marks)**
   b. What are the factors to be considered for selection of material for a machine
   component? **(05 Marks)**

Dec. 2013/Jan. 2014 (06ME52)

23. a. Write a brief note on general procedure used in design. **(05 Marks)**
   b. Discuss factors influencing the selection of a suitable material for a machine
   element. **(10 Marks)**
   c. Explain the codes and standards used in machine design. **(05 Marks)**

Dec. 2013/Jan. 2014 (10ME52)

24. a. Explain:
    i. Mechanical engineering design
    ii. Standards in design. **(04 Marks)**
    b. Explain:
    A point in a structural member is subjected to plane stress as shown in **Fig. U1.5**. Determine the principal stresses and their directions. **(08 Marks)**

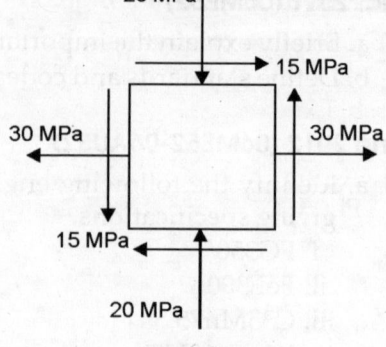

Fig. U1.5

June/July 2014 (10ME52)

25. a. Draw the stress–strain diagram for a ductile material and a brittle material and show the salient points on them. **(05 Marks)**
    b. For the stress element shown in **Fig. U1.6**, find the principal stresses and directions. **(06 Marks)**

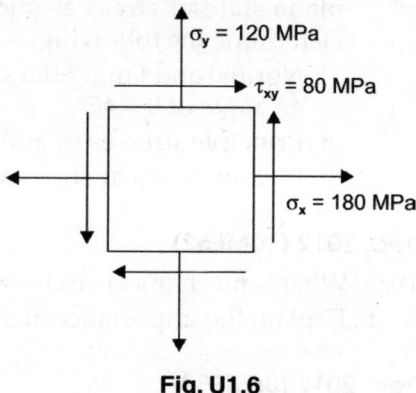

Fig. U1.6

Dec. 2014/ Jan. 2015 (06ME52)

26. a. Explain the material code for any two engineering materials. **(02 Marks)**
    b. Explain in brief, any six important factors governing the selection of materials for a machine member. **(06 Marks)**

Dec. 2014/ Jan 2015 (10ME52)

27. Briefly discuss three dimensional stress field and stress tensor. **(10 Marks)**

June/July 2015 (06ME52)

28. a. Draw stress–strain diagram for mild steel. Name the salient points. **(05 Marks)**
    b. Explain with a neat sketch, biaxial and triaxial stresses. **(05 Marks)**
    c. A point in a structural member subjected to plane stress is shown in **Fig. U1.7**. Determine the following.
       i. Normal and tangential stress intensities on plane MN inclined at 45°.
       ii. Principal stresses and their directions.
       iii. Maximum shear stress and the directions on the planes on which it occurs. **(10 Marks)**

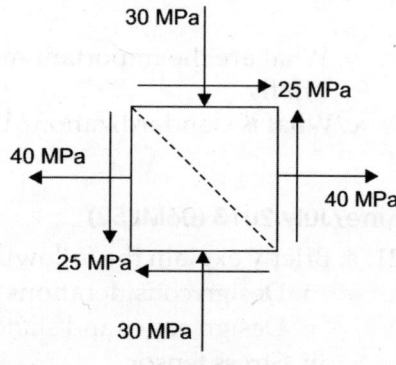

Fig. U1.7

June/July 2015 (10ME52)

29. a. What is mechanical engineering design? State the steps involved in mechanical engineering design. **(04 Marks)**
    b. Explain biaxial and triaxial stresses with neat sketches. **(04 Marks)**

Dec. 2015/ Jan. 2016 (10ME52)

30. a. Explain briefly the selection of factor of safety in engineering design.

(03 Marks)

b. Explain briefly the selection of materials in the process of machine design.

(03 Marks)

31. A point in a structural member is subjected to plane state of stress as shown in **Fig. U1.8**. Determine the following:

i. Normal and tangential stresses on a plane inclined at 45°.
ii. Principal stresses directions
iii. Maximum shear stress.

(07 Marks)

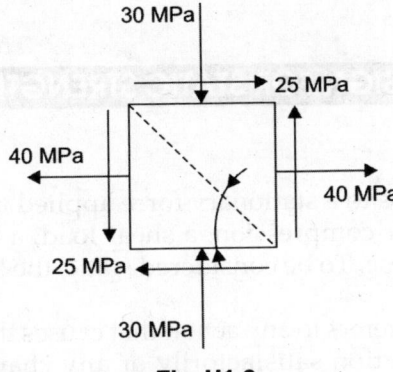

Fig. U1.8

2

Design for Static and Impact Strength

DESIGN FOR STATIC STRENGTH

2.1 STATIC LOAD

The term static loading refers to a stationary force applied to a member. A static load can produce axial tension or compression, a shear load, a bending load, a torsional load, or a combination of these. To be considered static, the load cannot change in any manner with respect to time.

Modes of failure: Failure refers to any action that causes the member of the machine or structure to cease to function satisfactorily or any change in the size, shape, or material properties of a structure, machine, or component that renders it incapable of performing its intended function is regarded as a mechanical failure of the device.

A mechanical component may fail as a result of any one of following three modes of failure.

- Failure by elastic deflection
- Failure by general yielding
- Failure by fracture.

2.2 FACTOR OF SAFETY

The term factor of safety is applied to a factor used to evaluate the safeness of a member. It is used separately for uncertainties that may occur in the strength of a part and uncertainties that might occur with loads acting on the part.

It is defined as the ratio of ultimate stress or load to the working stress or load.

i.e. $\qquad$ Factor of safety $= \dfrac{\text{ultimate stress}}{\text{working stress}}$ i.e. $n = \dfrac{\sigma_u}{\sigma_d}$ $\qquad$ ... (Eq. 2.1)

Working stress is based on yield point stress for ductile materials and ultimate strength for brittle materials.

- For ductile materials, $\quad n = \dfrac{\text{yield stress}}{\text{working stress}} = \dfrac{\sigma_y}{\sigma_d}$ $\qquad$ ... (Eq. 2.2)

- For brittle materials, $\quad n = \dfrac{\text{ultimate stress}}{\text{working stress}} = \dfrac{\sigma_u}{\sigma_d}$ $\qquad$ ... (Eq. 2.3)

Appendix III/ Pg 477, DHB

σ_d = working stress or design stress or allowable stress or applied stress

34

The appropriate factor of safety for static loading in case of:
- Ductile materials is the yield strength
- Brittle materials is the ultimate strength
- Cyclic/variable loading is the endurance limit.

Ultimate stress is defined as the maximum stress that the material is subjected to during a test.

Working or design or allowable or applied stress (σ_d) is defined as the maximum safe stress that the material can carry under a given loading. The allowable stress should be limited to a value not exceeding the proportional limit of the material so that Hooke's law is not invalidated.

Note:
- **Recommended values of factor of safety.**   **... Appendix III/ Pg 477, DHB**
- A higher value of factor of safety increases the dimensions, volume of the material and the cost of the component.

2.2.1 Selection of Factor of Safety

The selection of the factor of safety to be used for various applications is one of the most important engineering tasks. On the one hand, if a factor of safety is chosen too small, the possibility of failure becomes unacceptably large; on the other hand, if a factor of safety is chosen unnecessarily large, the result is an uneconomical or nonfunctional design. Hence, the choice of factor of safety that is appropriate for a given design application requires engineering judgment based on many considerations.

In general the following points are to be considered while selecting the factor of safety.
- Nature of material: Homogeneous or isotropic
- Nature of loading: Dead, live, gradual, sudden, alternating, constant, etc.
- Type of stress
- Exact mode of failure
- Localized stress or stress concentrations
- Environmental factors: Corrosion, wear, humidity, etc.
- Reliability of the component
- Previous case histories: Possible results of failure
- Workmanship: Errors in manufacturing/fabrication
- Cost of component
- Human safety and economy.

2.3 COMBINED STRESSES

In practical applications, machine members are subjected to combined stresses due to simultaneous action of direct stress (either tensile or compressive) combined with shear stresses and/or bending stress.

Examples of direct stress (applied externally) and shear stress (due to torsion) and C-frames, propeller shafts, etc.

Example of torsion and bending is crankshafts.

2.3.1 Direct Stress

- A direct stress may be tensile or compressive. **[Fig. 1.1(a)/ Pg 2, DHB]**

$$\sigma = \pm\, F/A \qquad\qquad \text{... (Eq. 2.4)}\ \textbf{1.1(a)/ Pg 2, DHB}$$

where F = force [(+) tensile, (–) compressive] (N), A = cross-sectional area (mm^2)

- Also direct shear stress [**Fig. 1.1(c)/ Pg 2, DHB**]

$$\tau = F_s/A_s \qquad \qquad \text{... (Eq. 2.5) 1.1(c)/ Pg 2, DHB}$$

where F_s = shear force (N) and A_s = shear area (mm²)

2.3.2 Bending Stress

The bending stress is given as [**Fig. 1.1(b)/ Pg 2, DHB**]

$$\frac{M}{I} = \frac{E}{R} = \frac{\sigma}{c} \qquad \qquad \text{... (Eq. 2.6) 1.3(a)/ Pg 3, DHB}$$

where

M = bending moment (N·mm)

I = moment of inertia about neutral axis (mm⁴)

E = Young's modulus (MPa)

R = radius of curvature of the beam (mm)

c = distance from neutral axis to extreme fibre (mm)

σ = bending stress (MPa)

$$\sigma = \sigma_b = \frac{M}{Z} = \frac{32M}{\pi d^3} = \frac{32FL}{\pi d^3} \qquad \qquad \text{... (Eq. 2.7) 1.1(b)/ Pg 3, DHB}$$

d = diameter of the rod or shaft

Note:

- *Properties of various cross-sections* ... **Table 1.3(a) & (b)/ Pg 12, DHB**
- *Standard expressions for shear, moment and deflection for various beams* ...**Table 1.4/ Pg 15, DHB**

2.3.3 Torsional Stress

The torsional equation is given as [**Fig. 1.1(d)/ Pg 2, DHB**]

$$\frac{T}{J} = \frac{G\theta}{L} = \frac{\tau}{r} \qquad \qquad \text{... (Eq. 2.8) 1.3(b)/ Pg 3, DHB}$$

where

T = maximum twisting torque (N·mm)

r = radius of the shaft (mm)

J = polar moment of inertia (mm⁴)

τ = shear stress (MPa)

G = modulus of rigidity (MPa)

θ = angle of twist (rad)

L = length of the shaft (mm)

$Z = I/c$ = section modulus (mm³)

$$T = \frac{(9.55 \times 10^6)P}{n} \qquad \qquad \text{... (Eq. 2.9) 3.3(a)/ Pg 50, DHB}$$

P = power (kW)

n = speed (rpm)

$$d = \text{diameter of shaft (mm)} = \sqrt[3]{\frac{16T}{\pi\tau}} \qquad \qquad \text{... (Eq. 2.10) 3.1/ Pg 50, DHB}$$

Note:

- *Values of moment of inertia* ... **Table 1.3(a)/ Pg 12, DHB**
- *Standard values of shaft diameter* ...**Table 3.5(a)/ Pg 57, DHB**

- For a solid shaft, $J = \dfrac{\pi d^4}{32}$ ... (Eq. 2.11)

- For a hollow shaft, $J = \dfrac{\pi}{32}(d_o^4 - d_i^4) = \dfrac{\pi}{32}d_o^4(1 - K^4),$ ... (Eq. 2.12)
  where

  $K = \dfrac{d_i}{d_o}$

  d = diameter of solid shaft
  d_o, d_i = outside and inside diameters of hollow shaft respectively.

- **Figure 1.2(a) to 1.2(d)/ Pg 3, DHB** represents different cases of combined loading. Axial load = F or F_1; Bending load = W or F_2; Torque or twisting moment = T
- The resultant stress due to combined axial and bending loads, $\sigma_{max} = \sigma_D \pm \sigma_b$
  ... (Eq. 2.13) **1.4/ Pg 3, DHB**

1. **A cast iron beam 30 mm × 30 mm in cross-section is 1.2 m long and supported at ends fails when a central load of 750 N is applied. What udl will break a cantilever of same material 40 mm wide × 80 mm deep and 2 m long?**

   Solution:
   Case (a): Simply supported beam: $b = h = 30$ mm, $L = 1.2$ m, W or $F = 750$ N
   Case (b): Cantilever beam: $b = 40$ mm, $h = 80$ mm, $L = 2$ m, $w = ?$

   Case (a): Simply supported beam:

   We know that $\dfrac{M}{I} = \dfrac{\sigma}{c}$ ... **1.3(a)/ Pg 3, DHB**

   $$\sigma = \sigma_b = \dfrac{Mc}{I}$$ ... Eq. (i) **1.1(b)/ Pg 2, DHB**

   For a SS beam with central load,

   $$M = \dfrac{WL}{4} \quad (W \text{ or } F)$$ ... **Tb 1.4, (Fig. 4)/ Pg 15, DHB**

   $$= \dfrac{750 \times 1200}{4}$$

   $$M = 225 \times 10^3 \text{ N·mm}$$

   For a rectangular cross-section, moment of inertia,

   $$I = \dfrac{bh^3}{12}$$ ... **Tb 1.3(a), (Fig. a)/ Pg 12, DHB**

   $$= \dfrac{30 \times 30^3}{12} = 67.5 \times 10^3 \text{ N·mm}$$

   Distance from neutral axis to extreme fiber, $c = h/2 = 30/2 = 15$ mm

   $\therefore$ Eq. (i) yields... $\sigma_b = \dfrac{(225 \times 10^3) \times 15}{67.5 \times 10^3} = 50$ MPa

   Case (b): Cantilever beam:
   For a cantilever with udl,

   $$M = \dfrac{WL}{2} = \dfrac{wL^2}{2} \quad (\because W = w \cdot L) \quad \text{... } \textbf{Tb 1.4, (Fig. 3)/ Pg 15, DHB}$$

$$= \frac{w \times 2000^2}{2}$$

$$M = (2w \times 10^6) \text{ N·mm}$$

For a rectangular cross-section, moment of inertia,

$$I = \frac{bh^3}{12} = \frac{40 \times 80^3}{12} \qquad \text{... Tb 1.3(a), (Fig. a)/ Pg 12, DHB}$$

$$= 1.71 \times 10^6 \text{ N·mm}$$

Distance from neutral axis to extreme fiber, $c = h/2 = 80/2 = 40$ mm

$$\therefore \text{ Eq. (i) yields...} \qquad 50 = \frac{(2w \times 10^6) \times 40}{1.71 \times 10^6}$$

$$w = 1.07 \text{ N/mm} = 107 \text{ kN/m}$$

2. **A steel blade 1 mm thick is bent into an arc of circle 500 mm radius. Determine the flexural stresses induced and the bending moment required to bend the blade, which is 15 mm wide. Take $E = 210$ GPa.**

VTU – Mar 2001 – 05 Marks

Solution: $h = 1$ mm, $R = 500$ mm, $\sigma_b = ?$, $M = ?$, $E = 210$ GPa $= 210 \times 10^3$ N/mm^2, $b = 15$ mm

We know that $\qquad \dfrac{M}{I} = \dfrac{E}{R} = \dfrac{\sigma}{c} \qquad$ ... 1.3(a)/ Pg 3, DHB

Bending stress, $\qquad \sigma = \sigma_b = \dfrac{Ec}{R}$

But $\qquad c = \dfrac{h}{2} = \dfrac{1}{2} = 0.5$ mm

$\therefore \qquad \sigma = \sigma_b = \dfrac{(210 \times 10^3) \times 0.5}{500} = 210 \text{ N/mm}^2$

Bending moment, $\quad M = \dfrac{EI}{R} = \dfrac{E}{R}\left(\dfrac{bh^3}{12}\right) = \left(\dfrac{210 \times 10^3}{500}\right) \times \left(\dfrac{15 \times 1^3}{12}\right) = 525 \text{ N·mm}$

3. **A solid shaft is subjected to a torque of 15 kN·m. Find the necessary diameter of the shaft if the allowable shear stress is 60 MPa and angle of twist is 1° for every 20 diameter length of the shaft. Take $G = 80$ GPa.**

Solution: $T = 15 \times 10^6$ N·mm, $d = ?$, $\tau = 60$ MPa, $\theta = 1° = 0.0174$ rad, $L = 20d$, $G = 80$ GPa $= 80 \times 10^3$ MPa.

We know that $\qquad \dfrac{T}{J} = \dfrac{G\theta}{L} = \dfrac{\tau}{r} \qquad$ ... 1.3(b)/ Pg 3, DHB

Based on strength:

We know that $\qquad \dfrac{T}{J} = \dfrac{\tau}{r}$

Substituting $\qquad J = \dfrac{\pi d^4}{32}$ and $r = d/2$, we get

... Tb 1.3(b), (Fig. a)/ Pg 14, DHB

$$\tau = \frac{16T}{\pi d^3} \qquad \text{... 1.1(d)/ Pg 2, DHB or 3.1/ Pg 50, DHB}$$

$$d^3 = \frac{16 \times (15 \times 10^6)}{\pi \times 60}$$

$$d = 108.39 \text{ mm} \qquad \text{... Eq. (i)}$$

Based on rigidity:

We know that $\qquad \dfrac{T}{J} = \dfrac{G\theta}{L} \Rightarrow J = \dfrac{TL}{G\theta}$

Substituting $\qquad J = \dfrac{\pi d^4}{32}$ and $L = 20d$, we get

$$\frac{\pi d^4}{32} = \frac{T(20d)}{G\theta}$$

$$\frac{\pi d^4}{32} = \frac{(15 \times 10^6) \times 20d}{(80 \times 10^3) \times 0.0174}$$

$$d = 129.96 \text{ mm} \qquad \text{... Eq. (ii)}$$

Based on Eqs. (i) and (ii), select maximum value of diameter for design
i.e. $\qquad\qquad d = 129.96$ mm.

Thus, the standard values of shaft diameter, $d = 140$ mm ... **Tb 3.5(a)/ Pg 57, DHB**

4. **A cantilever circular rod has a diameter of 50 mm and 300 mm length. Find out the values of principal stress and maximum shear stress under the following conditions.**
   i. **Applying an axial load of 20 kN**
   ii. **Applying 4 kN load at an end, acting downwards creating bending stress.**
   iii. **Applying a torque of 1.5 kN·m**

   VTU – June/ July 2013 – 12 Marks

Solution: $L = 300$ mm, $d = 50$ mm. Stresses at critical point (principal stresses at A and B) = ?

Case (i): $F = F_1 = 20$ kN $= 20 \times 10^3$ N ($\rightarrow$) (Fig. 2.1a)

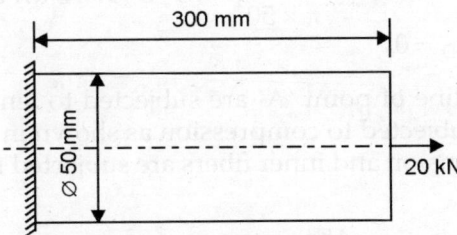

300 mm

Ø 50 mm

20 kN

Fig. 2.1a: Problem 4

- We know that the axial stress,

$$\sigma_D = \frac{F_1}{A} = \frac{20 \times 10^3}{\pi \times (50^2)/4} = 10.19 \text{ MPa} \qquad \text{... 1.1(a)/ Pg 2, DHB}$$

Here all points in the member are subjected to the same stress.

Principal stresses:

Here $\qquad \sigma_x = \sigma_D = 10.19$ MPa; $\sigma_y = 0$; $\tau_{xy} = 0$

Maximum principal stress,

$$\sigma_1 = \left(\frac{\sigma_x + \sigma_y}{2}\right) + \sqrt{\left(\frac{\sigma_x - \sigma_y}{2}\right)^2 + \tau_{xy}^2}$$

... Eq. (i) **1.8(c) / Pg 5, DHB**

$$= \left(\frac{10.19 + 0}{2}\right) + \sqrt{\left(\frac{10.19 - 0}{2}\right) + 0^2}$$

∴ $\sigma_1 = 10.19$ MPa

Minimum principal stress,

$$\sigma_2 = \left(\frac{\sigma_x + \sigma_y}{2}\right) - \sqrt{\left(\frac{\sigma_x - \sigma_y}{2}\right)^2 + \tau_{xy}^2}$$

... Eq. (ii) **1.8(d) / Pg 5, DHB**

$$= \left(\frac{10.19 + 0}{2}\right) - \sqrt{\left(\frac{10.19 - 0}{2}\right) + 0^2}$$

∴ $\sigma_2 = 0$ MPa

Maximum shear stress,

$$\tau_{max} = \pm \sqrt{\left(\frac{\sigma_x - \sigma_y}{2}\right)^2 + \tau_{xy}^2}$$ ... Eq. (iii) **1.8(f) / Pg 5, DHB**

$$\pm \sqrt{\left(\frac{10.19 - 0}{2}\right) + 0^2}$$

$$\tau_{max} = \pm 5.09 \text{ MPa}$$

Case ii: $W = F_2 = 4$ kN $= 4000$ N($\downarrow$) (Fig. 2.1b)

- Bending stress, $\sigma_b = \dfrac{M}{Z} = \dfrac{32 F_2 L}{\pi d^3}$ $[F_2 \text{ or } W]$

$$= \frac{32 \times [(4 \times 10^3) \times 300]}{\pi \times 50^3} = 97.78 \text{ MPa}$$ ... **1.1(b)/ Pg 2, DHB**

- In this case, $\sigma_D = 0$

The fibers along the line of point 'A' are subjected to tension and that along the line of point 'B' are subjected to compression as shown in **Fig. 2.1(b)-(i)**, i.e. outer fibers are subject to tension and inner fibers are subjected to compression.

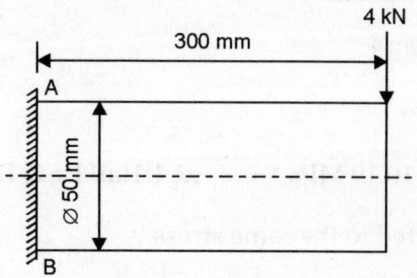

Fig. 2.1b: Problem 4

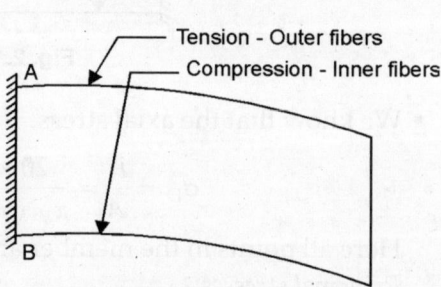

Fig. 2.1b(i): Problem 4

- Resultant stress at 'A', $\sigma_A = \sigma_D + \sigma_b = 0 + 97.78 = 97.78$ MPa (Outer fibers)
- Resultant stress at 'B', $\sigma_B = \sigma_D - \sigma_b = 0 - 97.78 = -97.78$ MPa (Inner fibers)

Principal stresses:

Principal stresses at A: Here $\sigma_x = \sigma_A = 97.79$ MPa; $\sigma_y = 0$; $\tau_{xy} = 0$

∴ Eq. (i) yields maximum principal stress,

$$\sigma_{1A} = \left(\frac{97.78 + 0}{2}\right) + \sqrt{\left(\frac{97.78 - 0}{2}\right)^2 + 0^2} = 97.78 \text{ MPa}$$

∴ Eq. (ii) yields minimum principal stress,

$$\sigma_{2A} = \left(\frac{97.78 + 0}{2}\right) - \sqrt{\left(\frac{97.78 - 0}{2}\right)^2 + 0^2} = 0 \text{ MPa}$$

∴ Eq. (iii) yields maximum shear stress,

$$\tau_{maxA} = \sqrt{\left(\frac{97.78 - 0}{2}\right)^2 + 0^2} = 48.89 \text{ MPa}$$

Principal stresses at B: Here $\sigma_x = \sigma_B = -97.79$ MPa; $\sigma_y = 0$; $\tau_{xy} = 0$

∴ Eq. (i) yields maximum principal stress,

$$\sigma_{1B} = \left(\frac{-97.78 + 0}{2}\right) + \sqrt{\left(\frac{-97.78 - 0}{2}\right)^2 + 0^2} = 0 \text{ MPa}$$

∴ Eq. (ii) yields minimum principal stress,

$$\sigma_{2B} = \left(\frac{-97.78 + 0}{2}\right) - \sqrt{\left(\frac{-97.78 - 0}{2}\right)^2 + 0^2} = -97.78 \text{ MPa}$$

∴ Eq. (iii) yields maximum shear stress,

$$\tau_{maxB} = \sqrt{\left(\frac{-97.78 - 0}{2}\right)^2 + 0^2} = 48.89 \text{ MPa}$$

Case iii: T = 1.5 kN·m = 1.5 × 10⁶ N·mm. Fig. 2.1(c)

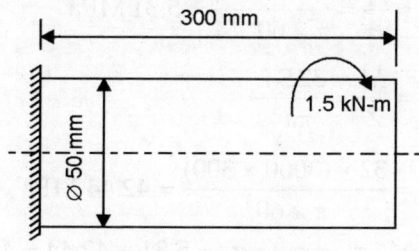

Fig. 2.1c: Problem 4

- Shear stress, $\tau = \dfrac{16T}{\pi d^3} = \dfrac{16 \times (1.5 \times 10^6)}{\pi \times 50^3} = 61.12 \text{ MPa}$

… 3.1/ Pg 50, DHB or 1.1(d)/ Pg 2, DHB

- In this case, $\sigma_D = 0$ and $\sigma_b = 0$

Here critical points occur along the outer surface of the member.

Principal stresses: Here $\sigma_x = \sigma_D = 0$ MPa; $\sigma_y = 0$; $\tau = \tau_{xy} = 61.12$ MPa

$\therefore$ Eq. (i) yields maximum principal stress,

$$\sigma_1 = \left(\frac{0+0}{2}\right) + \sqrt{\left(\frac{0-0}{2}\right)^2 + 61.12^2} = 61.12 \text{ MPa}$$

$\therefore$ Eq. (ii) yields minimum principal stress,

$$\sigma_2 = \left(\frac{0+0}{2}\right) - \sqrt{\left(\frac{0-0}{2}\right)^2 + 61.12^2} = -61.12 \text{ MPa}$$

$\therefore$ Eq. (iii) yields maximum shear stress,

$$\sigma_3 = \sqrt{\left(\frac{0-0}{2}\right)^2 + 61.12^2} = 61.12 \text{ MPa}$$

5. **A shaft is subjected to a bending load of 3 kN and an axial load of 15 kN as shown in Fig. 2.2. Determine the stresses at critical point.**

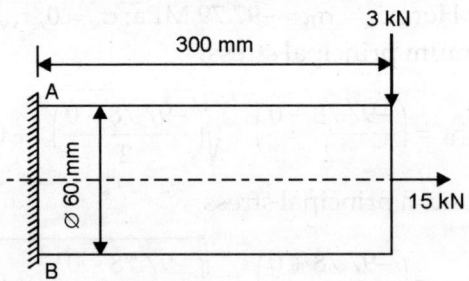

Fig. 2.2: Problem 5

Solution: $L = 300$ mm, $F = F_1 = 15$ kN $= 15 \times 10^3$ N, $W = F_2 = 3$ kN $= 3000$ N, $s = 60$ mm. Stresses at critical point (principal stresses at A and B) = ?

Resultant stress:

• We know that axial stress,

$$\sigma_D = \frac{F_1}{A} = \frac{15 \times 10^3}{\pi \times 60^2/4} = 5.31 \text{ MPa} \qquad \text{... 1.1(a)/ Pg 2, DHB}$$

• Bending stress, $\sigma_b = \dfrac{M}{Z} = \dfrac{32 F_2 L}{\pi d^3}$

$$= \frac{32 \times (3000 \times 300)}{\pi \times 60^3} = 42.44 \text{ MPa} \qquad \text{... 1.1(b)/ Pg 2, DHB}$$

Resultant stress at 'A', $\sigma_A = \sigma_D - \sigma_b = 5.31 + 42.44 = 47.55$ MPa

Resultant stress at 'B', $\sigma_B = \sigma_D - \sigma_b = 5.31 - 42.44 = -37.13$ MPa

Principal stresses at A: Here $\sigma_x = \sigma_A = 47.55$ MPa; $\sigma_y = 0$; $\tau_{xy} = 0$ MPa

Maximum principal stress,

$$\sigma_{1A} = \left(\frac{\sigma_x + \sigma_y}{2}\right) + \sqrt{\left(\frac{\sigma_x - \sigma_y}{2}\right)^2 + \tau_{xy}^2}$$

... Eq. (i) **1.8(c) / Pg 5, DHB**

$$= \left(\frac{47.45 + 0}{2}\right) + \sqrt{\left(\frac{47.45 - 0}{2}\right) + 0^2}$$

$$\therefore \qquad \sigma_{1A} = 47.75 \text{ MPa}$$

Minimum principal stress,

$$\sigma_{2A} = \left(\frac{\sigma_x + \sigma_y}{2}\right) - \sqrt{\left(\frac{\sigma_x - \sigma_y}{2}\right)^2 + \tau_{xy}^2}$$

... Eq. (ii) **1.8(d) / Pg 5, DHB**

$$= \left(\frac{47.75 + 0}{2}\right) - \sqrt{\left(\frac{47.75 - 0}{2}\right) + 0^2}$$

$$\therefore \qquad \sigma_2 = 0 \text{ MPa}$$

Maximum shear stress,

$$\tau_{maxA} = \sqrt{\left(\frac{\sigma_x - \sigma_y}{2}\right)^2 + \tau_{xy}^2} \qquad \text{... Eq. (iii) } \mathbf{1.8(f) / Pg 5, DHB}$$

$$= \sqrt{\left(\frac{47.75 - 0}{2}\right) + 0^2}$$

$$\tau_{maxA} = 23.88 \text{ MPa}$$

$$\text{or} \qquad \tau_{maxA} = \left(\frac{\sigma_{1A} - \sigma_{2A}}{2}\right) = \frac{47.75 - 0}{2} = 23.88 \text{ MPa}$$

Principal stresses at B: Here $\sigma_x = \sigma_B = -37.15$ MPa; $\sigma_y = 0$; $\tau = \tau_{xy} = 0$ MPa
$\therefore$ Eq. (i) yields maximum principal stress,

$$\sigma_{1B} = \left(\frac{-37.13 + 0}{2}\right) + \sqrt{\left(\frac{-37.13 - 0}{2}\right)^2 + 0^2} = 0 \text{ MPa}$$

$\therefore$ Eq. (ii) yields minimum principal stress,

$$\sigma_{2B} = \left(\frac{-37.13 + 0}{2}\right) - \sqrt{\left(\frac{-37.13 - 0}{2}\right)^2 + 0^2} = -37.13 \text{ MPa}$$

$\therefore$ Eq. (iii) yields maximum shear stress,

$$\sigma_3 = \sqrt{\left(\frac{-37.13 - 0}{2}\right)^2 + 0^2} = 18.57 \text{ MPa}$$

6. **A circular shaft 50 mm diameter fixed at one end is subjected to an axial load of 20 kN and a torque of 1.5 kN·m. If the length of the shaft is 300 mm, determine the nature and magnitude of stresses at the critical point.**

VTU – Dec. 06/ Jan. 07 – 10 Marks; (Similar) Jan/Feb. 2005 – 04 Marks

Solution: $L = 300$ mm, $F = F_1 = 20$ kN $= 20 \times 10^3$ N, $T = 1.5$ kN·m $= 1.5 \times 10^6$ N·mm, $d = 50$ mm. Stresses at critical point (principal stresses at A and B) = ?

Figure 2.3 represents the problem as per the given conditions.

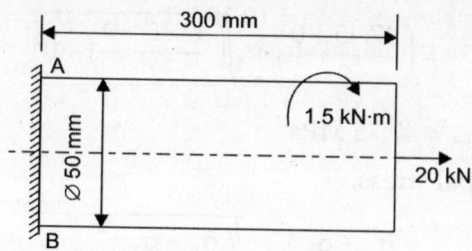

Fig. 2.3: Problem 6

Resultant stress:

- We know that axial stress,

$$\sigma_D = \frac{F_1}{A} = \frac{20 \times 10^3}{\pi \times 50^2/4} = 10.18 \text{ MPa} \qquad \text{... 1.1(a)/ Pg 2, DHB}$$

- Shear stress, $\quad \tau = \frac{16T}{\pi d^3} = \frac{16 \times (1.5 \times 10^6)}{\pi \times 50^3} = 61.12 \text{ MPa} \quad \text{... 1.1(d)/ Pg 2, DHB}$

Resultant stress at 'A', $\sigma_A = \sigma_D + \sigma_b = 10.18 + 0 = 10.18 \text{ MPa}$

Resultant stress at 'B', $\sigma_B = \sigma_D - \sigma_b = 10.18 - 0 = 10.18 \text{ MPa}$

Principal stresses at A: Here $\sigma_x = \sigma_A = 10.18 \text{ MPa}$; $\sigma_y = 0$; $\tau_{xy} = 61.12 \text{ MPa}$

Maximum principal stress,

$$\sigma_{1A} = \left(\frac{\sigma_x + \sigma_y}{2}\right) + \sqrt{\left(\frac{\sigma_x - \sigma_y}{2}\right)^2 + \tau_{xy}^2}$$

$$\text{... Eq. (i) 1.8(c) / Pg 5, DHB}$$

$$= \left(\frac{10.18 + 0}{2}\right) + \sqrt{\left(\frac{10.18 - 0}{2}\right)^2 + 61.12^2}$$

$$\therefore \qquad \sigma_{1A} = 66.42 \text{ MPa}$$

Minimum principal stress,

$$\sigma_{2A} = \left(\frac{\sigma_x + \sigma_y}{2}\right) - \sqrt{\left(\frac{\sigma_x - \sigma_y}{2}\right)^2 + \tau_{xy}^2}$$

$$\text{... Eq. (ii) 1.8(d) / Pg 5, DHB}$$

$$= \left(\frac{10.18 + 0}{2}\right) - \sqrt{\left(\frac{10.18 - 0}{2}\right)^2 + 61.12^2}$$

$$\therefore \qquad \sigma_{2A} = -56.24 \text{ MPa}$$

Maximum shear stress,

$$\tau_{maxA} = \sqrt{\left(\frac{\sigma_x - \sigma_y}{2}\right)^2 + \tau_{xy}^2} \qquad \text{... Eq. (iii) 1.8(f) / Pg 5, DHB}$$

$$= \sqrt{\left(\frac{10.18 - 0}{2}\right)^2 + 61.12^2}$$

$$\tau_{maxA} = 61.33 \text{ MPa}$$

Principal stresses at B: Here $\sigma_x = \sigma_B = 10.18$ MPa; $\sigma_y = 0$; $\tau = \tau_{xy} = 61.12$ MPa

$\therefore$ Eq. (i) yields maximum principal stress,

$$\sigma_{1B} = \left(\frac{10.18 + 0}{2}\right) + \sqrt{\left(\frac{10.18 - 0}{2}\right)^2 + 61.12^2} = 66.42 \text{ MPa}$$

$\therefore$ Eq. (ii) yields minimum principal stress,

$$\sigma_{2B} = \left(\frac{10.18 + 0}{2}\right) - \sqrt{\left(\frac{10.18 - 0}{2}\right)^2 + 61.12^2} = -56.24 \text{ MPa}$$

$\therefore$ Eq. (iii) yields maximum shear stress,

$$\tau_{maxB} = \sqrt{\left(\frac{10.18 - 0}{2}\right)^2 + 61.12^2} = 61.33 \text{ MPa}$$

Since critical points occur at outer surface of the member, $\sigma_{1A} = \sigma_{1B}$; $\sigma_{2A} = \sigma_{2B}$; $\tau_{maxA} = \tau_{maxB}$.

7. **Calculate the principal stresses at all critical points of the shaft shown in Fig. 2.4.**

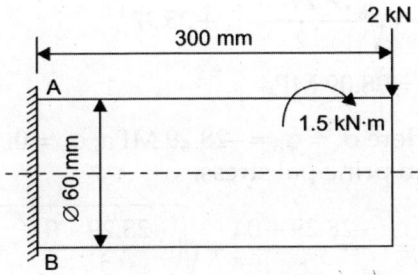

Fig. 2.4: Problem 7

Solution: $L = 300$ mm, $W = F_2 = 2$ kN $= 2000$ N, $T = 1.5$ kN·m $= 1.5 \times 10^6$ N·mm, $d = 60$ mm. Stresses at critical point (principal stresses at A and B) = ?

Resultant stress:

• We know that axial stress,

$$\sigma_D = \frac{M}{Z} = \frac{32 F_2 L}{\pi d^3} = \frac{32 \times 2000 \times 300}{\pi \times 60^3} = 28.29 \text{ MPa}$$

$$\text{... 1.1(b)/ Pg 2, DHB}$$

• Shear stress, $\quad \tau = \frac{16T}{\pi d^3} = \frac{16 \times (1.5 \times 10^6)}{\pi \times 60^3} = 35.57 \text{ MPa} \quad \text{... 1.1(d)/ Pg 2, DHB}$

Resultant stress at 'A', $\sigma_A = \sigma_D + \sigma_b = 0 + 28.29 = 28.29$ MPa

Resultant stress at 'B', $\sigma_B = \sigma_D - \sigma_b = 0 - 28.29 = -28.29$ MPa

Principal stresses at A: Here $\sigma_x = \sigma_A = 28.29$ MPa; $\sigma_y = 0$; $\tau_{xy} = 35.37$ MPa

Maximum principal stress,

$$\sigma_{1A} = \left(\frac{\sigma_x + \sigma_y}{2}\right) + \sqrt{\left(\frac{\sigma_x - \sigma_y}{2}\right)^2 + \tau_{xy}^2}$$

$$\text{... Eq. (i) 1.8(c) / Pg 5, DHB}$$

$$= \left(\frac{28.29+0}{2}\right) + \sqrt{\left(\frac{28.29-0}{2}\right)^2 + 35.37^2}$$

$$\therefore \qquad \sigma_{1A} = 52.24 \text{ MPa}$$

Minimum principal stress,

$$\sigma_{2A} = \left(\frac{\sigma_x + \sigma_y}{2}\right) - \sqrt{\left(\frac{\sigma_x - \sigma_y}{2}\right)^2 + \tau_{xy}^2}$$

$$\text{... Eq. (ii) } \textbf{1.8(d) / Pg 5, DHB}$$

$$= \left(\frac{28.29+0}{2}\right) - \sqrt{\left(\frac{28.29-0}{2}\right)^2 + 35.37^2}$$

$$\therefore \qquad \sigma_{2A} = -23.95 \text{ MPa}$$

Maximum shear stress,

$$\tau_{maxA} = \sqrt{\left(\frac{\sigma_x - \sigma_y}{2}\right)^2 + \tau_{xy}^2} \qquad \text{... Eq. (iii) } \textbf{1.8(f) / Pg 5, DHB}$$

$$= \sqrt{\left(\frac{28.29-0}{2}\right)^2 + 35.37^2}$$

$$\tau_{maxA} = 38.09 \text{ MPa}$$

Principal stresses at B: Here $\sigma_x = \sigma_B = -28.29$ MPa; $\sigma_y = 0$; $\tau = \tau_{xy} = 35.37$ MPa
∴ Eq. (i) yields maximum principal stress,

$$\sigma_{1B} = \left(\frac{-28.29+0}{2}\right) + \sqrt{\left(\frac{-28.29-0}{2}\right)^2 + 35.37^2} = 23.95 \text{ MPa}$$

∴ Eq. (ii) yields minimum principal stress,

$$\sigma_{2B} = \left(\frac{-28.29+0}{2}\right) - \sqrt{\left(\frac{-28.29-0}{2}\right)^2 + 35.37^2} = -52.24 \text{ MPa}$$

∴ Eq. (iii) yields maximum shear stress,

$$\tau_{maxB} = \sqrt{\left(\frac{-28.29-0}{2}\right)^2 + 35.37^2} = 38.09 \text{ MPa}$$

8. **A cantilever beam of circular cross-section is loaded as shown in Fig. 2.5. Determine the maximum and minimum normal stresses and maximum shear stress at points A and B.**

VTU – Dec. 2011 – 10 Marks; June/ July – 2015 – 12 Marks

Solution: $L = 250$ mm, $W = F_2 = 3$ kN $= 3000$ N, $F = F_1 = 15$ kN $= 1.5 \times 10^3$ N, $d = 50$ mm, $T = 1$ kN·m $= 1 \times 10^6$ N·mm. Stresses at critical point (principal stresses at A and B) = ?

Resultant stress:

• Axial stress, $\qquad \sigma_D = \dfrac{F_1}{A} = \dfrac{15 \times 10^3}{\pi \times 50^2/4} = 7.64 \text{ MPa} \qquad \text{... 1.1(a)/ Pg 2, DHB}$

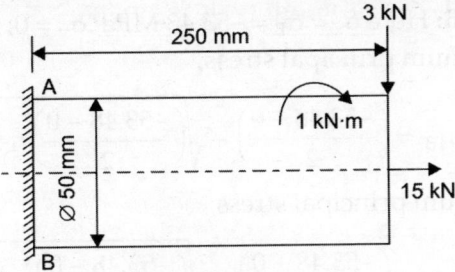

Fig. 2.5: Problem 8

- Bending stress, $\sigma_b = \dfrac{M}{Z} = \dfrac{32F_2 L}{\pi d^3} = \dfrac{32 \times 3000 \times 250}{\pi \times 50^3} = 61.12 \text{ MPa}$

$$\qquad \qquad \qquad \qquad \qquad \qquad \qquad \qquad \textbf{... 1.1(b)/ Pg 2, DHB}$$

- Shear stress, $\tau = \dfrac{16T}{\pi d^3} = \dfrac{16 \times (1 \times 10^6)}{\pi \times 50^3} = 40.74 \text{ MPa} \qquad \textbf{... 1.1(d)/ Pg 2, DHB}$

Resultant stress at 'A', $\sigma_A = \sigma_D + \sigma_b = 7.64 + 61.12 = 68.76 \text{ MPa}$

Resultant stress at 'B', $\sigma_B = \sigma_D - \sigma_b = 7.64 - 61.12 = -53.48 \text{ MPa}$

Principal stresses at A: Here $\sigma_x = \sigma_A = 68.76 \text{ MPa}$; $\sigma_y = 0$; $\tau = \tau_{xy} = 40.74 \text{ MPa}$

Maximum principal stress,

$$\sigma_{1A} = \left(\frac{\sigma_x + \sigma_y}{2}\right) + \sqrt{\left(\frac{\sigma_x - \sigma_y}{2}\right)^2 + \tau_{xy}^2}$$

$$\qquad \qquad \qquad \qquad \qquad \qquad \textbf{... Eq. (i) 1.8(c) / Pg 5, DHB}$$

$$= \left(\frac{68.76 + 0}{2}\right) + \sqrt{\left(\frac{68.76 - 0}{2}\right)^2 + 40.74^2}$$

$$\therefore \qquad \sigma_{1A} = 87.69 \text{ MPa}$$

Minimum principal stress,

$$\sigma_{2A} = \left(\frac{\sigma_x + \sigma_y}{2}\right) - \sqrt{\left(\frac{\sigma_x - \sigma_y}{2}\right)^2 + \tau_{xy}^2}$$

$$\qquad \qquad \qquad \qquad \qquad \qquad \textbf{... Eq. (ii) 1.8(d) / Pg 5, DHB}$$

$$= \left(\frac{68.76 + 0}{2}\right) - \sqrt{\left(\frac{68.76 - 0}{2}\right)^2 + 40.74^2}$$

$$\therefore \qquad \sigma_{2A} = -18.93 \text{ MPa}$$

Maximum shear stress,

$$\tau_{maxA} = \sqrt{\left(\frac{\sigma_x - \sigma_y}{2}\right)^2 + \tau_{xy}^2} \qquad \qquad \textbf{... Eq. (iii) 1.8(f) / Pg 5, DHB}$$

$$= \sqrt{\left(\frac{68.76 - 0}{2}\right)^2 + 40.74^2}$$

$$\tau_{maxA} = 53.31 \text{ MPa}$$

Principal stresses at B: Here $\sigma_x' = \sigma_B = -53.48$ MPa; $\sigma_y = 0$; $\tau = \tau_{xy} = 40.74$ MPa

∴ Eq. (i) yields maximum principal stress,

$$\sigma_{1B} = \left(\frac{-53.48 + 0}{2}\right) + \sqrt{\left(\frac{-53.48 - 0}{2}\right)^2 + 40.74^2} = 22 \text{ MPa}$$

∴ Eq. (ii) yields minimum principal stress,

$$\sigma_{2B} = \left(\frac{-53.48 + 0}{2}\right) - \sqrt{\left(\frac{-53.48 - 0}{2}\right)^2 + 40.74^2} = -75.47 \text{ MPa}$$

∴ Eq. (iii) yields maximum shear stress,

$$\tau_{maxB} = \sqrt{\left(\frac{-53.48 - 0}{2}\right)^2 + 40.74^2} = 48.73 \text{ MPa}$$

9. **A hollow shaft of 40 mm external diameter and 25 mm inner diameter is subjected to a twisting moment of 118 N·m, an axial thrust of 9806 N and a bending moment of 79 N·m. Calculate the maximum compressive and shear stresses.**

VTU – June/ July 2013 – 10 Marks

Solution: $d_o = 40$ mm, $d_i = 25$ mm, $M = 79$ N·m $= 79 \times 10^3$ N·mm, $F = F_1 = 9806$ N, $T = 118$ N·m $= 118 \times 10^3$ N·mm. Stresses at critical point (principal stresses at A and B) = ?

Figure 2.6 represents the problem as per the given conditions.

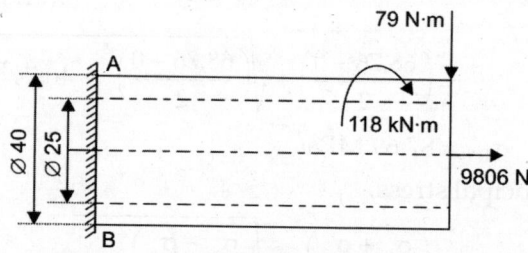

Fig. 2.6: Problem 9

Resultant stress:

• Axial stress, $\sigma_D = \dfrac{F_1}{A} = \dfrac{9806}{\pi \times (40^2 - 25^2)/4} = 12.81$ MPa

... 1.1(a)/ Pg 2, DHB

• Bending stress, $\sigma_b = \dfrac{M}{Z} = \dfrac{M}{\pi(d_o^4 - d_i^4)/32d_o}$ ... Tb 1.3(a), (Fig. h)/ Pg 13, DHB

$$= \dfrac{79 \times 10^3}{\pi \times (40^4 - 25^4)/(32 \times 40)}$$

$\sigma_b = 14.84$ MPa

• Shear stress, $\tau = \dfrac{16T}{\pi d_o^3} = \left(\dfrac{1}{1 - K^4}\right)$ ... 1.1(d)/ Pg 2, DHB

$$= \left[\frac{16 \times (118 \times 10^3)}{\pi \times 40^3} \right] \left(\frac{1}{1 - 0.625^4} \right) \quad K = \frac{d_i}{d_o} = \frac{25}{40} = 0.625$$

where $\qquad K = \dfrac{d_i}{d_o} = \dfrac{25}{40} = 0.625$ $\qquad$ ... **1.1(d)/ Pg 2, DHB**

$$\tau = 11.08 \text{ MPa}$$

Resultant stress at 'A', $\sigma_A = \sigma_D + \sigma_b = 12.81 + 14.84 = 27.65$ MPa

Resultant stress at 'B', $\sigma_B = \sigma_D - \sigma_b = 12.81 - 14.84 = -2.03$ MPa

Principal stresses at A: Here $\sigma_x = \sigma_A = 27.65$ MPa; $\sigma_y = 0$; $\tau = \tau_{xy} = 11.08$ MPa

Maximum principal stress,

$$\sigma_{1A} = \left(\frac{\sigma_x + \sigma_y}{2} \right) + \sqrt{\left(\frac{\sigma_x - \sigma_y}{2} \right)^2 + \tau_{xy}^2}$$

$$\dots \text{ Eq. (i) } \textbf{1.8(c) / Pg 5, DHB}$$

$$= \left(\frac{27.65 + 0}{2} \right) + \sqrt{\left(\frac{27.65 - 0}{2} \right)^2 + 11.08^2}$$

$\therefore \qquad \sigma_{1A} = 31.54$ MPa

Minimum principal stress,

$$\sigma_{2A} = \left(\frac{\sigma_x + \sigma_y}{2} \right) - \sqrt{\left(\frac{\sigma_x - \sigma_y}{2} \right)^2 + \tau_{xy}^2}$$

$$\dots \text{ Eq. (ii) } \textbf{1.8(d) / Pg 5, DHB}$$

$$= \left(\frac{27.65 + 0}{2} \right) - \sqrt{\left(\frac{27.65 - 0}{2} \right)^2 + 11.08^2}$$

$\therefore \qquad \sigma_{2A} = -3.89$ MPa

Maximum shear stress,

$$\tau_{maxA} = \sqrt{\left(\frac{\sigma_x - \sigma_y}{2} \right)^2 + \tau_{xy}^2} \qquad \dots \text{ Eq. (iii) } \textbf{1.8(f) / Pg 5, DHB}$$

$$= \sqrt{\left(\frac{27.65 - 0}{2} \right)^2 + 11.08^2}$$

$$\tau_{maxA} = 17.71 \text{ MPa}$$

Principal stresses at B: Here $\sigma_x = \sigma_B = -2.03$ MPa; $\sigma_y = 0$; $\tau = \tau_{xy} = 11.08$ MPa

$\therefore$ Eq. (i) yields maximum principal stress,

$$\sigma_{1B} = \left(\frac{-2.03 + 0}{2} \right) + \sqrt{\left(\frac{-2.03 - 0}{2} \right)^2 + 11.08^2} = 10.11 \text{ MPa}$$

$\therefore$ Eq. (ii) yields minimum principal stress,

$$\sigma_{2B} = \left(\frac{-2.03 + 0}{2} \right) - \sqrt{\left(\frac{-2.03 - 0}{2} \right)^2 + 11.08^2} = -12.14 \text{ MPa}$$

$\therefore$ Eq. (iii) yields maximum shear stress,

$$\tau_{maxB} = \sqrt{\left(\frac{-2.03 - 0}{2}\right)^2 + 11.08^2} = 11.13 \text{ MPa}$$

10. **Determine the maximum normal stress and maximum shear stress at section A–A for the crank shown in Fig. 2.7, when a load of 10 kN is assumed to be concentrated at the center of the crank pin.**

VTU – June/ July 2008 – 08 Marks

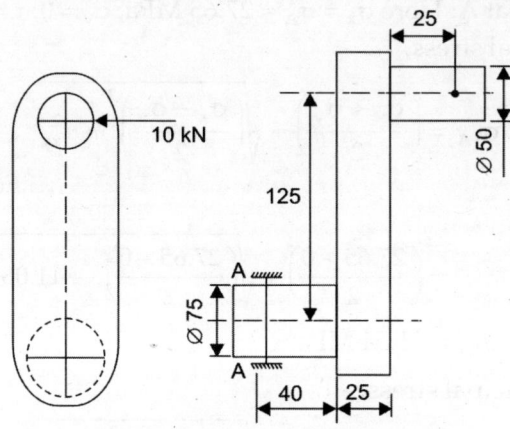

Fig. 2.7: Problem 10

Solution: $L_1 = (40 + 25 + 25) = 90$ mm, $L_2 = 125$ mm, $W = F_2 = 10$ kN $= 10000$ N, $d = 75$ mm, $\sigma_1 = ?$, $\tau_{max} = ?$

Resultant stress:

- Bending stress, $\sigma_b = \dfrac{M}{Z} = \dfrac{32 F_2 L_1}{\pi d^3}$ ... **1.1(b)/ Pg 2, DHB**

$$= \frac{32 \times (10 \times 10)^3 \times 90}{\pi \times 75^3} = 21.73 \text{ MPa}$$

- Shear stress, $\tau = \dfrac{16T}{\pi d^3} = \dfrac{16(F_2 L_2)}{\pi d^3}$ ... **1.1(d)/ Pg 2, DHB**

$$= \frac{16 \times (10 \times 10^3 \times 125)}{\pi \times 75^3} = 15.10 \text{ MPa} \quad ... \textbf{1.1(d)/ Pg 2, DHB}$$

Resultant stress: Here 'A', $\sigma_x = \sigma_A + \sigma_b = 0 + 21.73 = 21.73$ MPa

Principal stresses : Here $\sigma_x = \sigma_A = 21.73$ MPa; $\sigma_y = 0$; $\tau = \tau_{xy} = 15.10$ MPa
Maximum principal stress,

$$\sigma_1 = \left(\frac{\sigma_x + \sigma_y}{2}\right) + \sqrt{\left(\frac{\sigma_x - \sigma_y}{2}\right)^2 + \tau_{xy}^2} \qquad \textbf{1.8(c) / Pg 5, DHB}$$

$$= \left(\frac{21.73 + 0}{2}\right) + \sqrt{\left(\frac{21.73 - 0}{2}\right)^2 + 15.10^2}$$

$\therefore \qquad \sigma_1 = 29.47$ MPa

Maximum shear stress,

$$\tau_{max} = \sqrt{\left(\frac{\sigma_x - \sigma_y}{2}\right)^2 + \tau_{xy}^2} \qquad \text{... 1.8(f) / Pg 5, DHB}$$

$$= \sqrt{\left(\frac{21.73 - 0}{2}\right)^2 + 15.10^2}$$

$$\tau_{max} = 18.60 \text{ MPa}$$

11. **For the crank shown in Fig. 2.8, determine the diameter at section A-A using maximum shear stress. Take τ_y = 150 MPa and factor of safety as 1.5, W = 2 kN.**

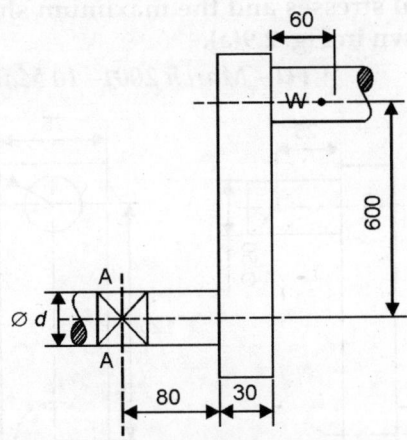

Fig. 2.8: Problem 11

Solution: L_1 = (80 + 60 + 30) = 170 mm, L_2 = 600 mm, $W = F_2$ = 2 kN = 2000 N, τ_y = 150 MPa, $n = 2$, $d = ?$

We know that $\qquad \tau_{max} = \dfrac{\tau_y}{n} = \dfrac{150}{1.5} = 100 \text{ MPa}$

Resultant stress:

• Bending stress, $\quad \sigma_b = \dfrac{M}{Z} = \dfrac{32 F_2 L_1}{\pi d^3}$

$$= \frac{32 \times 2000 \times 170}{\pi \times d^3} = \frac{3.46 \times 10^6}{d^3} \qquad \text{... 1.1(b)/ Pg 2, DHB}$$

• Shear stress, $\quad \tau = \dfrac{16T}{\pi d^3} = \dfrac{16(WL_2)}{\pi d^3} \qquad \text{... 1.1(d)/ Pg 2, DHB}$

$$= \frac{16 \times (2 \times 10^3 \times 600)}{\pi \times d^3} = \frac{6.11 \times 10^6}{d^3}$$

Resultant stress at 'A',

$$\sigma_A = \sigma_D + \sigma_b = 0 + \frac{3.46 \times 10^6}{d^3} = \frac{3.46 \times 10^6}{d^3}$$

We know that maximum shear stress, $\tau_{max} = \sqrt{\left(\dfrac{\sigma_x - \sigma_y}{2}\right)^2 + \tau_{xy}^2}$

Here $\sigma_x = \sigma_A = \dfrac{3.46 \times 10^6}{d^3}$ MPa; $\sigma_y = 0$; $\tau_{xy} = \dfrac{6.11 \times 10^6}{d^3}$ MPa

$\therefore \quad 100 = \sqrt{\left(\dfrac{3.46 \times 10^6}{2d^3}\right)^2 + \left(\dfrac{6.11 \times 10^6}{d^3}\right)^2}$

$100^2 = \dfrac{4.03 \times 10^{13}}{d^6}$

$\therefore \quad d = 39.89 \text{ mm} \approx 40 \text{ mm}$

12. **Determine the principal stresses and the maximum shear stress at A-A for the crankshaft bearing shown in Fig. 2.9(a).**

VTU – March 2001– 10 Marks; Dec. 2011 – 10 Marks

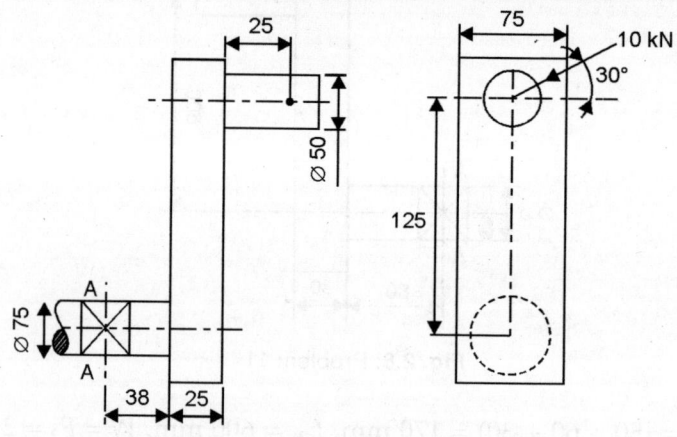

Fig. 2.9a: Problem 12

Solution: $L_1 = (38 + 25 + 25) = 88$ mm, $L_2 = 125$ mm, $d = 75$ mm, $W = F_2 = 10$ kN $= 10000$ N, $\theta = 30°$, principal stresses = ?, maximum shear stress = ?

Force components: Referring to **Fig. 2.9b**, we have:
Horizontal component
$W_H = F_{2H} = F_2 \cos\theta = 10\cos 30 = 8.66$ kN
Vertical component
$W_v = F_{2V} = F_2 \cos\theta = 10\sin 30 = 5$ kN

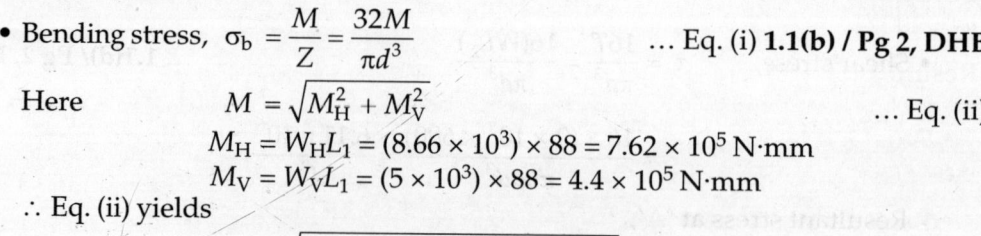

Fig. 2.9b: Problem 12

Resultant stress:

• Bending stress, $\sigma_b = \dfrac{M}{Z} = \dfrac{32M}{\pi d^3}$ ... Eq. (i) **1.1(b) / Pg 2, DHB**

Here $M = \sqrt{M_H^2 + M_V^2}$ ... Eq. (ii)

$M_H = W_H L_1 = (8.66 \times 10^3) \times 88 = 7.62 \times 10^5$ N·mm
$M_V = W_V L_1 = (5 \times 10^3) \times 88 = 4.4 \times 10^5$ N·mm

$\therefore$ Eq. (ii) yields

$M = \sqrt{(7.62 \times 10^5)^2 + (4.4 \times 10^5)^2}$

$\therefore \quad = 8.80 \times 10^5$ N·mm

$\therefore$ Eq. (i) yields $\quad \sigma_b = \dfrac{32 \times 8.80 \times 10^5}{\pi \times 75^3} = 21.25$ MPa

- Shear stress, $\quad \tau = \dfrac{16T}{\pi d^3} = \dfrac{16(W_H L_2)}{\pi d^3} = \dfrac{16 \times (8.66 \times 10^3 \times 125)}{\pi \times 75^3} = 13.07$ MPa

$$\ldots \textbf{1.1(d) / Pg 2, DHB}$$

Resultant stress at 'A', $\sigma_A = \sigma_D + \sigma_b = 0 + 21.25 = 21.25$ MPa

Principal stresses: Here $\sigma_x = \sigma_A = 21.25$ MPa; $\sigma_y = 0$; $\tau = \tau_{xy} = 13.07$ MPa

Maximum principal stress,

$$\sigma_1 = \dfrac{\sigma_x + \sigma_y}{2} + \sqrt{\left(\dfrac{\sigma_x - \sigma_y}{2}\right)^2 + \tau_{xy}^2} \qquad \ldots \textbf{1.8(c) / Pg 5, DHB}$$

$$= \dfrac{21.25 + 0}{2} + \sqrt{\left(\dfrac{21.25 - 0}{2}\right)^2 + 13.07^2}$$

$\therefore \qquad \sigma_1 = 27.46$ MPa

Minimum principal stress,

$$\sigma_2 = \dfrac{\sigma_x + \sigma_y}{2} - \sqrt{\left(\dfrac{\sigma_x - \sigma_y}{2}\right)^2 + \tau_{xy}^2} \qquad \ldots \textbf{1.8(c) / Pg 5, DHB}$$

$$= \dfrac{21.25 + 0}{2} + \sqrt{\left(\dfrac{21.25 - 0}{2}\right)^2 + 13.07^2}$$

$\therefore \qquad \sigma_2 = -6.22$ MPa

Maximum shear stress,

$$\tau_{max} = \sqrt{\left(\dfrac{\sigma_x - \sigma_y}{2}\right)^2 + \tau_{xy}^2} \qquad \ldots \text{Eq. (iii) } \textbf{1.8(f) / Pg 5, DHB}$$

$$= \sqrt{\left(\dfrac{21.25 - 0}{2}\right)^2 + 13.07^2}$$

$\tau_{maxA} = 16.84$ MPa

13. **Find the maximum numerical normal stress and the maximum shear stress at section X–X for the member shown in Fig. 2.10.**

Solution: $F = 2000$ N, $W = 4000$ N, $d = 60$ mm, $x = 200$ mm, $y_1 = 150$ mm, $y_2 = 300$ mm, maximum, normal and shear stress = ?

Resultant stress:

- Axial stress, $\quad \sigma_D = \dfrac{W}{A} = \dfrac{4000}{\pi \times 60^2 / 4} = 1.415$ MPa $\qquad \ldots \textbf{1.1(b) / Pg 2, DHB}$

- Bending stress, $\quad \sigma_b = \dfrac{M}{Z} = \dfrac{32M}{\pi d^3} \qquad \ldots \text{Eq. (i) } \textbf{1.1(b) / Pg 2, DHB}$

Here $\qquad M = \sqrt{M_H^2 + M_V^2} \qquad \ldots \text{Eq. (ii)}$

Bending moment due to horizontal load,
$$M_H = F \cdot y_2 = 2000 \times 300$$
$$= 6 \times 10^5 \text{ N·mm}$$

Bending moment due to vertical load,
$$M_V = W \cdot x = 4000 \times 200$$
$$= 8 \times 10^5 \text{ N·mm}$$

∴ Eq. (ii) yields
$$M = \sqrt{(6 \times 10^5)^2 + (8 \times 10^5)^2}$$
∴ $$M = 1.0 \times 10^6 \text{ N·mm}$$

∴ Eq. (i) yields
$$\sigma_b = \frac{32 \times 1.0 \times 10^6}{\pi \times 60^3}$$
$$= 47.16 \text{ MPa}$$

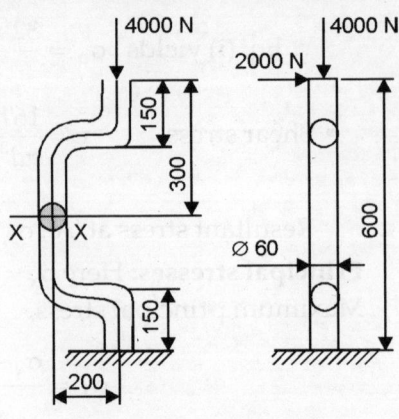

Fig. 2.10: Problem 13

- Shear stress, $\tau = \dfrac{16T}{\pi d^3} = \dfrac{16(Fx)}{\pi d^3} = \dfrac{16 \times (2000 \times 200)}{\pi \times 60^3} = 9.43 \text{ MPa}$

... **1.1(d) / Pg 2, DHB**

Resultant stress $\sigma_A = \sigma_D + \sigma_b = 1.414 + 47.16 = 48.57 \text{ MPa}$

Maximum numerical normal stress: Since the member is subjected to bending, the maximum normal numerical stress refers to minimum principal stress σ_2.

Here $\sigma_x = \sigma_A = -48.57 \text{ MPa (compression)}$; $\sigma_y = 0$; $\tau = \tau_{xy} = 18.86 \text{ MPa}$

i.e. minimum principal stress,

$$\sigma_2 = \frac{\sigma_x + \sigma_y}{2} - \sqrt{\left(\frac{\sigma_x - \sigma_y}{2}\right)^2 + \tau_{xy}^2} \qquad \text{... } \mathbf{1.8(d) / Pg\ 5, DHB}$$

$$= \frac{-48.57 + 0}{2} - \sqrt{\left(\frac{-48.57 - 0}{2}\right)^2 + 9.43^2}$$

∴ $$\sigma_2 = -50.34 \text{ MPa}$$

Maximum shear stress,

$$\tau_{max} = \sqrt{\left(\frac{\sigma_x - \sigma_y}{2}\right)^2 + \tau_{xy}^2} \qquad \text{... Eq. (iii) } \mathbf{1.8(f) / Pg\ 5, DHB}$$

$$= \sqrt{\left(\frac{-48.57 - 0}{2}\right)^2 + 9.43^2}$$

$$\tau_{maxA} = 26.05 \text{ MPa}$$

14. **A steel member is loaded as shown in Fig. 2.11. Determine the magnitude of:**
    i. **The maximum normal stress**
    ii. **The minimum normal stress**
    iii. **The maximum shear stress.**

VTU – July 2006 – 12 Marks

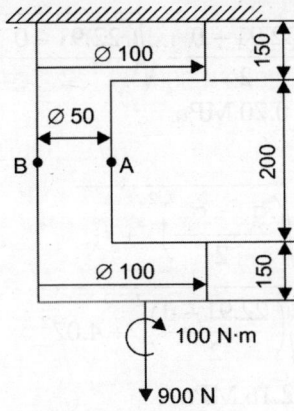

Fig. 2.11: Problem 14

Solution: $T = 100 \, \text{N·m} = 100 \times 10^3 \, \text{N·mm}$, $d = 50 \, \text{mm}$, $F = 9000 \, \text{N}$, stresses at critical point (principal stresses at A and B) = ?

Resultant stress: We know that

- Axial stress, $\quad \sigma_D = \dfrac{F}{A} = \dfrac{9000}{\pi \times 50^2/4} = 4.58 \, \text{MPa}$ ... **1.1(a) / Pg 2, DHB**

- Bending stress, $\quad \sigma_b = \dfrac{M}{Z} = \dfrac{Mc}{I}$ ... **1.1(b) / Pg 2, DHB**

  But $\qquad c = d/2 \, \text{m} = 50/2 = 25 \, \text{mm};$

  $\qquad M = 9000 \times (50/2) = 225 \times 10^3 \, \text{N·mm}$

  $\qquad = \left[\dfrac{225 \times 10^3}{\pi \times 50^4/64} \right] \times 25$

  $\qquad \sigma_b = 18.33 \, \text{MPa}$

- Shear stress, $\quad \tau = \dfrac{16T}{\pi d^3} = \dfrac{16 \times (100 \times 10^3)}{\pi \times 50^3} = 4.07 \, \text{MPa}$ ... **1.1(d) / Pg 2, DHB**

Resultant stress at 'A', $\sigma_A = \sigma_D + \sigma_b = 4.58 + 18.33 = 22.91 \, \text{MPa}$

Resultant stress at 'B', $\sigma_B = \sigma_D - \sigma_b = 4.58 - 18.33 = -13.75 \, \text{MPa}$

Principal stresses at A: Here $\sigma_x = \sigma_A = 22.91 \, \text{MPa}$; $\sigma_y = 0$; $\tau = \tau_{xy} = 4.07 \, \text{MPa}$

Maximum principal stress,

$$\sigma_1 = \frac{\sigma_x + \sigma_y}{2} + \sqrt{\left(\frac{\sigma_x - \sigma_y}{2} \right)^2 + \tau_{xy}^2}$$

... Eq. (i) **1.8(c) / Pg 5, DHB**

$$= \frac{22.91 + 0}{2} + \sqrt{\left(\frac{22.91 - 0}{2} \right)^2 + 4.07^2}$$

$\therefore \qquad \sigma_1 = 23.61 \, \text{MPa}$

Minimum principal stress,

$$\sigma_1 = \frac{\sigma_x + \sigma_y}{2} - \sqrt{\left(\frac{\sigma_x - \sigma_y}{2} \right)^2 + \tau_{xy}^2}$$

... Eq. (ii) **1.8(d) / Pg 5, DHB**

$$= \frac{22.91 + 0}{2} - \sqrt{\left(\frac{22.91 - 0}{2}\right)^2 + 4.07^2}$$

$$\therefore \quad \sigma_1 = -0.70 \text{ MPa}$$

Maximum shear stress,

$$\tau_{max} = \sqrt{\left(\frac{\sigma_x - \sigma_y}{2}\right)^2 + \tau_{xy}^2} \qquad \dots \text{Eq. (ii) } \mathbf{1.8(f) / Pg 5, DHB}$$

$$= \sqrt{\left(\frac{22.91 - 0}{2}\right)^2 + 4.07^2}$$

$$\therefore \quad \tau_{max} = 12.16 \text{ MPa}$$

Principal stresses at B: Here $\sigma_x = \sigma_B = -13.75$ MPa; $\sigma_y = 0$; $\tau = \tau_{xy} = 4.07$ MPa
$\therefore$ Eq. (i) yields maximum principal stress,

$$\sigma_1 = \frac{-13.75 + 0}{2} + \sqrt{\left(\frac{-13.75 - 0}{2}\right)^2 + 4.07^2} = 1.11 \text{ MPa}$$

$\therefore$ Eq. (ii) yields minimum principal stress,

$$\sigma_2 = \frac{-13.75 + 0}{2} - \sqrt{\left(\frac{-13.75 - 0}{2}\right)^2 + 4.07^2} = -14.86 \text{ MPa}$$

$\therefore$ Eq. (iii) yields maximum shear stress,

$$\tau_{max} = \sqrt{\left(\frac{-13.75 - 0}{2}\right)^2 + 4.07^2} = 7.99 \text{ MPa}$$

Thus   i. The maximum normal stress = 23.61 MPa
    ii. The minimum normal stress = −14.86 MPa
    iii. The maximum shear stress = 12.16 MPa

15. **A machine member 50 mm diameter and 200 mm long can be treated as a cantilever for stress analysis. The loading of the member is shown in Fig. 2.12. Determine the maximum and minimum normal stress and maximum shear stress at critical stress point "A" and point "B".**

VTU – Dec. 2014 - Jan 2015 – 12 Marks

Solution: $L = (200 - 20) = 180$ mm, $d = 50$ mm, $F = F_1 = 10$ kN $= 10 \times 10^3$ N, $W = F_2 = 3.5$ kN $= 3500$ N, $T = 3$ kN·m $= 3 \times 10^6$ N·mm. Stresses at critical point (principal stresses at A and B) = ?

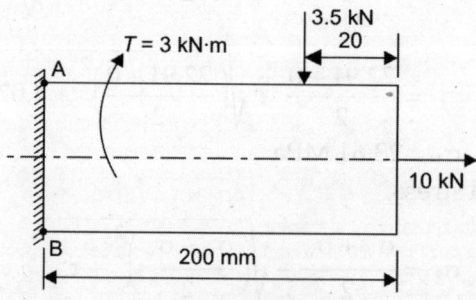

Fig. 2.12: Problem 15

Resultant stress:

- Axial stress, $\sigma_D = \dfrac{F_1}{A} = \dfrac{10 \times 10^3}{\pi \times 50^2/4} = 5.10$ MPa   ... **1.1(a) / Pg 2, DHB**

- Bending stress, $\sigma_b = \dfrac{M}{Z} = \dfrac{32 F_2 L}{\pi d^3} = \dfrac{32 \times 3500 \times 180}{\pi \times 50^3} = 51.33$ MPa

  ... **1.1(b) / Pg 2, DHB**

- Shear stress, $\tau = \dfrac{16T}{\pi d^3} = \dfrac{16 \times (3 \times 10^6)}{\pi \times 50^3} = 122.23$ MPa   ... **1.1(d) / Pg 2, DHB**

Resultant stress at 'A', $\sigma_A = \sigma_D + \sigma_b = 5.10 + 51.33 = 56.43$ MPa

Resultant stress at 'B', $\sigma_B = \sigma_D - \sigma_b = 5.10 - 51.33 = -46.23$ MPa

Principal stresses at A: Here $\sigma_x = \sigma_A = 56.43$ MPa; $\sigma_y = 0$; $\tau = \tau_{xy} = 122.23$ MPa
Maximum principal stress,

$$\sigma_{1A} = \frac{\sigma_x + \sigma_y}{2} + \sqrt{\left(\frac{\sigma_x - \sigma_y}{2}\right)^2 + \tau_{xy}^2}$$

... Eq. (i) **1.8(c) / Pg 5, DHB**

$$= \left(\frac{56.43 + 0}{2}\right) + \sqrt{\left(\frac{56.43 - 0}{2}\right)^2 + 122.23^2}$$

$\therefore$ $\sigma_{1A} = 153.65$ MPa

Minimum principal stress,

$$\sigma_{2A} = \frac{\sigma_x + \sigma_y}{2} - \sqrt{\left(\frac{\sigma_x - \sigma_y}{2}\right)^2 + \tau_{xy}^2}$$

... Eq. (ii) **1.8(d) / Pg 5, DHB**

$$= \left(\frac{56.43 + 0}{2}\right) - \sqrt{\left(\frac{56.43 - 0}{2}\right)^2 + 122.23^2}$$

$\therefore$ $\sigma_{2A} = -97.23$ MPa

Maximum shear stress,

$$\tau_{\max A} = \sqrt{\left(\frac{\sigma_x - \sigma_y}{2}\right)^2 + \tau_{xy}^2}$$ ... Eq. (ii) **1.8(f) / Pg 5, DHB**

$$= \sqrt{\left(\frac{56.43 - 0}{2}\right)^2 + 122.23^2}$$

$\therefore$ $\tau_{\max A} = 125.44$ MPa

Principal stresses at B: Here $\sigma_x = \sigma_B = -46.23$ MPa; $\sigma_y = 0$; $\tau = \tau_{xy} = 122.23$ MPa
$\therefore$ Eq. (i) yields maximum principal stress,

$$\sigma_{1B} = \left(\frac{-46.23 + 0}{2}\right) + \sqrt{\left(\frac{-46.23 - 0}{2}\right)^2 + 122.23^2} = 101.28 \text{ MPa}$$

∴ Eq. (ii) yields minimum principal stress,

$$\sigma_{2B} = \left(\frac{-46.23 + 0}{2}\right) - \sqrt{\left(\frac{-46.23 - 0}{2}\right)^2 + 122.23^2} = -147.51 \text{ MPa}$$

∴ Eq. (iii) yields maximum shear stress,

$$\tau_{\text{max}B} = \sqrt{\left(\frac{-46.23 - 0}{2}\right)^2 + 122.23^2} = 124.40 \text{ MPa}$$

2.4 ECCENTRIC LOADING (SUPERPOSITION)

An external load, whose line of action is parallel but does not coincide with the centroidal axis of the machine component, is known as an ***eccentric load.*** The distance between the centroidal axis of the machine component and the eccentric load is called *eccentricity(e)*.

Consider an axial bar as shown in **Fig. 2.13(a)** subjected to eccentric load F at an eccentricity of e. In order to bring the load point to the centroidal axis we make use of principle of superposition, thereby forming a couple ($F \cdot e$) as shown in **Fig. 2.13 (b)** thus forming an equivalent load.

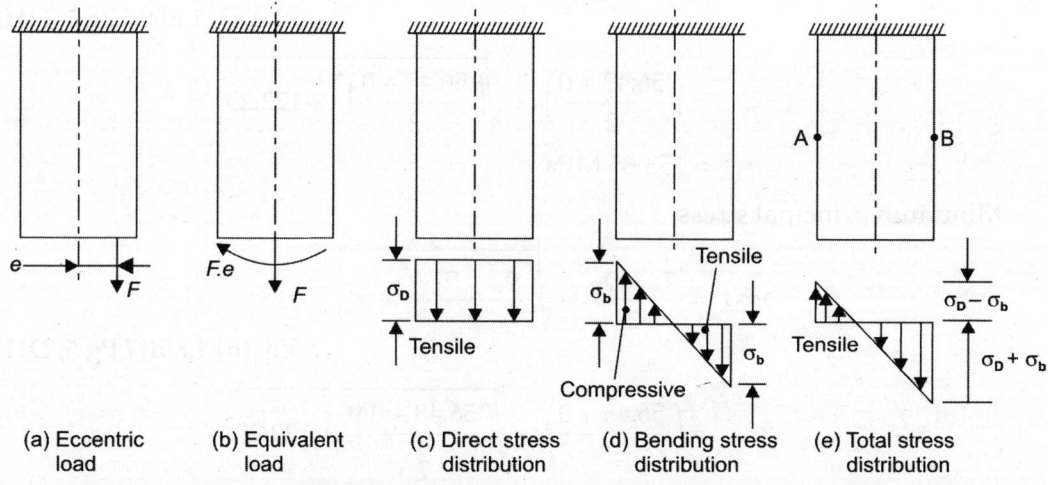

| (a) Eccentric load | (b) Equivalent load | (c) Direct stress distribution | (d) Bending stress distribution | (e) Total stress distribution |

Fig. 2.13: Eccentric load (superposition)

Referring to **Fig. 2.13(c)**, magnitude of direct stress,

$$\sigma_D = \frac{F}{A} \qquad \qquad \text{... 1.1(a)/ Pg 2, DHB}$$

Referring to **Fig. 2.13(d)**, bending stress,

$$\sigma_b = \frac{M}{Z} = \frac{F \cdot e}{Z} \qquad \qquad \text{... 1.1(b)/ Pg 2, DHB}$$

where $M = F \cdot e$.

This moment will be compressive on one side and tensile on the other side as shown in **Fig. 2.13(d)**.

Thus, the resultant stress at the cross-section are obtained by using the principle of superposition and is given as

$$\sigma = \sigma_D \pm \sigma_b = \frac{F}{A} \pm \frac{M}{Z} = \frac{F}{A} \pm \frac{F \cdot e}{Z}$$
$$\text{... (Eq. 2.14a) } \textbf{1.10/ Pg 7, DHB}$$

Equation (2.14a) gives the maximum normal stress due to direct stress (tensile/compressive) combined with bending.

The magnitude of bending stress at the right side edge (B) is tensile and that at the left edge (A) is compressive,

i.e. Combined stress at edge B $= \dfrac{F}{A} + \dfrac{F \cdot e}{Z}$ … (Eq. 2.14b)

Combined stress at edge A $= \dfrac{F}{A} - \dfrac{F \cdot e}{Z}$ … (Eq. 2.14c)

16. **A steel column is subjected to eccentric load as shown in Fig. 2.14. Find the maximum and minimum intensities of stress in the section.**

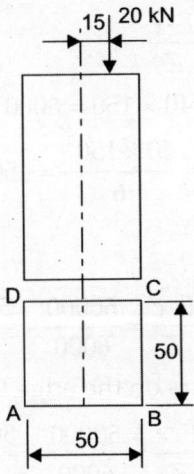

Fig. 2.14: Problem 16

Solution: $F = 20$ kN $= 20000$ N, $e = 15$ mm, $b = h = 50$ mm, $\sigma = ?$

For eccentric load, $\sigma = \dfrac{F}{A} \pm \dfrac{F \cdot e}{Z}$ … **1.10/ Pg 7, DHB**

Here area $A = b \cdot h = 50 \times 50 = 2500$ mm^2

$$Z = \frac{bh^2}{6} = \frac{50 \times 50^2}{6} = 20833.33 \text{ mm}^2$$
$$\text{... Tb. 1.3, (Fig. a)/ Pg 12, DHB}$$

Maximum stress intensity occurs on the edge AD

i.e. $\qquad \sigma = \dfrac{F}{A} + \dfrac{F \cdot e}{Z} = \dfrac{20000}{2500} + \dfrac{20000 \times 15}{20833.33} = 22.40$ MPa (tensile)

Minimum stress intensity occurs on the edge BC

i.e. $\qquad \sigma = \dfrac{F}{A} - \dfrac{F \cdot e}{Z} = \dfrac{20000}{2500} + \dfrac{20000 \times 15}{20833.33}$

$\qquad\qquad = -6.40$ MPa (compressive)

17. **For the link shown in Fig. 2.15, find the stresses induced if the load acts at an eccentricity of one-third the depth of the link.**

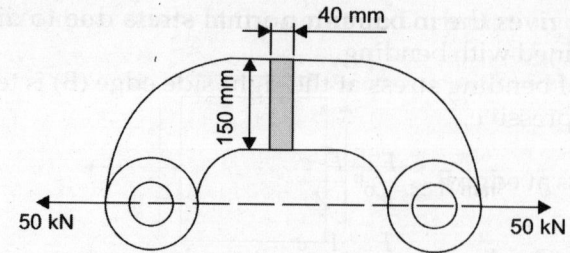

Fig. 2.15: Problem 17

Solution: $F = 50$ kN $= 50000$ N, $b = 40$ mm, $h = 150$ mm, $e = h/3$ mm $= 150/3 = 50$ mm, $\sigma = ?$

For eccentric load, $\sigma = \dfrac{F}{A} \pm \dfrac{F \cdot e}{Z}$ ... 1.10/ Pg 7, DHB

Here area $A = b \cdot h = 40 \times 150 = 6000$ mm^2

$$Z = \frac{bh^2}{6} = \frac{40 \times 150^2}{6} = 150000 \text{ mm}^2$$

... Tb. 1.3, (Fig. a)/ Pg 12, DHB

Maximum stress intensity,

i.e. $\sigma = \dfrac{F}{A} + \dfrac{F \cdot e}{Z} = \dfrac{50000}{6000} + \dfrac{50000 \times 50}{150000} = 25$ MPa (tensile)

Minimum stress intensity occurs on the edge BC

i.e. $\sigma = \dfrac{F}{A} - \dfrac{F \cdot e}{Z} = \dfrac{50000}{6000} - \dfrac{50000 \times 50}{150000}$

$= -8.34$ MPa (compressive)

18. **A 50 mm diameter steel rod supports a 9 kN load and in addition is subjected to torsional moment of 100 N·m as shown in Fig. 2.16. Determine the maximum tensile and the maximum shear stress.**

VTU – Dec. 13/ Jan. 2014 – 08 Marks; June/ July 14 – 09 Marks; Dec.14/ Jan.15 – 10 Marks

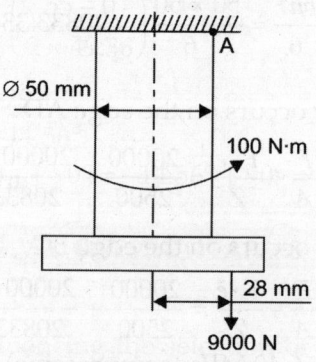

Fig. 2.16: Problem 18

Solution: $d = 50$ mm, $F = 9$ kN $= 9000$ N, $T = 100$ N·m, maximum tensile and shear stress at A = ?

Resultant stress:

For eccentric load, $\quad \sigma = \dfrac{F}{A} \pm \dfrac{F \cdot e}{Z}$ $\qquad\qquad$ ... 1.10/ Pg 7, DHB

Here area $\qquad A = \pi \times 50^2 / 4 = 1963.50$ mm^2

$$Z = \frac{\pi d^3}{32} = \frac{\pi \times 50^3}{32} = 12271.85 \text{ mm}^3$$

$\qquad\qquad\qquad\qquad\qquad\qquad\qquad\qquad$ ... Tb. 1.3, (Fig. g)/ Pg 12, DHB

i.e. maximum stress intensity at 'A',

$$\sigma = \frac{F}{A} + \frac{F \cdot e}{Z} = \frac{9000}{1963.50} + \frac{9000 \times 28}{12271.85} = 25.12 \text{ MPa}$$

Shear stress $\qquad \tau = \dfrac{16T}{\pi d^3} = \dfrac{16 \times (1 \times 10^5)}{\pi \times 50^3} = 4.07$ MPa $\qquad$ ... 1.1(d)/ Pg 2, DHB

OR

- We know that axial stress,

$$\sigma = \frac{F}{A} = \frac{9000}{\pi \times 50^2 / 4} = 4.58 \text{ MPa} \qquad \text{... 1.1(a)/ Pg 2, DHB}$$

- Bending stress, $\sigma_b = \dfrac{M}{Z} = \dfrac{F \cdot e}{Z} = \dfrac{(9000 \times 28)}{\pi \times 50^3 / 32}$

$$= 20.54 \text{ MPa} \quad [M = F \cdot e \text{ and } e = 28 \text{ mm}]$$

$\qquad\qquad\qquad\qquad\qquad\qquad\qquad\qquad$ ... 1.1(b)/ Pg 2, DHB

Resultant stress at 'A', $\sigma_x = \sigma_A = 25.12$ MPa; $\sigma_y = 0$; $\tau = \tau_{xy} = 4.07$ MPa

Principal stresses at A: Here $\sigma_x = \sigma_A = 25.12$ MPa; $\sigma_y = 0$; $\tau = \tau_{xy} = 4.07$ MPa

Maximum principal stress,

$$\sigma_1 = \frac{\sigma_x + \sigma_y}{2} + \sqrt{\left(\frac{\sigma_x - \sigma_y}{2}\right)^2 + \tau_{xy}^2}$$

$\qquad\qquad\qquad\qquad\qquad\qquad\qquad\qquad$ ... Eq. (i) 1.8(c) / Pg 5, DHB

$$= \frac{25.12 + 0}{2} + \sqrt{\left(\frac{25.12 - 0}{2}\right)^2 + 4.07^2}$$

$\therefore \qquad\qquad \sigma_1 = 25.76$ MPa

Maximum shear stress,

$$\tau_{max} = \sqrt{\left(\frac{\sigma_x - \sigma_y}{2}\right)^2 + \tau_{xy}^2} \qquad \text{... Eq. (ii) 1.8(f) / Pg 5, DHB}$$

$$= \sqrt{\left(\frac{25.12 - 0}{2}\right)^2 + 4.07^2}$$

$\therefore \qquad\qquad \tau_{max} = 13.20$ MPa

19. **Find the dimensions of the link shown in Fig. 2.17. Take 30 kN, 120 MPa.**

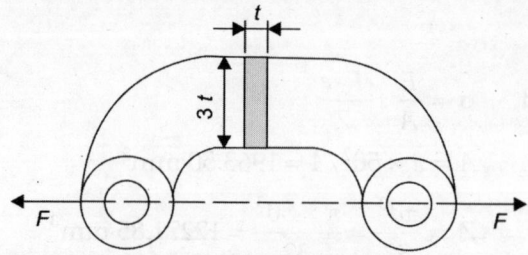

Fig. 2.17: Problem 19

Solution: $F = 30$ kN $= 30000$ N, $\sigma = 120$ MPa, $b = t$, $h = 3t$, $t = ?$
We know that maximum stress intensity,

$$\sigma = \frac{F}{A} \pm \frac{F \cdot e}{Z} \qquad \text{... 1.10/ Pg 7, DHB}$$

Here area
$$A = b \cdot h = t \times 3t = 3t^2$$

$$e = \frac{h}{2} = \frac{3t}{2} = 1.5t$$

$$Z = \frac{bh^2}{6} \qquad \text{... Tb. 1.3(a), (Fig. a)/ Pg 12, DHB}$$

$$Z = \frac{t \times (3t)^2}{6} = 1.5t^3 \text{ mm}^3$$

$\therefore$ Eq. (i) yields...
$$120 = \frac{3000}{3t^2} = \frac{30000 \times (1.5t)}{1.5t^3}$$

$$= \frac{10000}{t^2} + \frac{30000}{t^2}$$

$\therefore$
$$t = 18.26 \text{ mm} \approx 20 \text{ mm}$$

20. **Figure 2.18 shows a symmetrical link as dotted lines which transmit 50 kN. Determine the dimensions b and h_1 assuming a permissible tensile stress of 60 MPa and that $h_1 = 2b$. If the original link is replaced by an unsymmetrical link as shown by full lines, having the same thickness as the original link, determine the depth b of the new link.**

Solution: $F = 50$ kN $= 50000$ N, $\sigma = 60$ MPa
Case 1: If $h_1 = 2b$, $b = ?$, $h_1 = ?$
Case 2: $h = ?$, if b is same as obtained from case 1

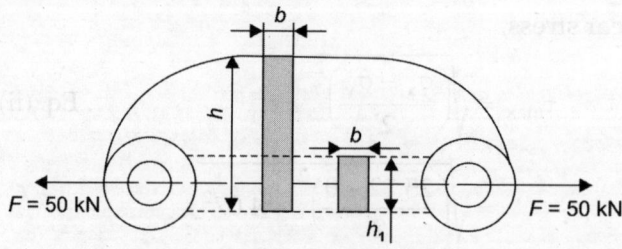

Fig. 2.18: Problem 20

Case 1: Symmetrical link

We know that $\sigma = \dfrac{F}{A}$ ... **1.1(a)/ Pg 2, DHB**

$$A = b \cdot h_1 = (2b) \cdot b = 2b^2$$

$$60 = \frac{50000}{2b^2}$$

$\therefore$ $b = 20.41 \text{ mm} \; \square \; 21 \text{ mm}$

and $h_1 = 2b = 2 \times 21 = 42 \text{ mm}$

Case 2: Unsymmetrical link

We know that maximum stress intensity

$$\sigma = \frac{F}{A} + \frac{F \cdot e}{Z} \qquad \text{... Eq. (i) } \textbf{1.10/ Pg 7, DHB}$$

$$A = b \cdot h = 21 \times h = 21h \text{ mm}^2$$

$$e = \frac{h}{2}$$

$$Z = \frac{bh^2}{6} = \frac{21h^2}{6} = 3.5h^2 \qquad \text{... } \textbf{Tb. 1.3(a), (Fig. a)/ Pg 12, DHB}$$

$\therefore$ Eq. (i) yields... $60 = \dfrac{50000}{21h} + \dfrac{50000 \times (h/2)}{3.5h^2}$

$$= \frac{2380.95}{h} + \frac{7142.86}{h}$$

$\therefore$ $h = 158.73 \text{ mm} \approx 160 \text{ mm}$

21. **Determine the required thickness 'b' of the steel bracket at a section A–A, when loaded as shown in Fig. 2.19 in order to limit the maximum tensile stress to 70 MPa.**

VTU – June 2012 – 06 Marks

Solution: $F = 50 \text{ kN} = 50000 \text{ N}$, $\sigma = 60 \text{ MPa}$.

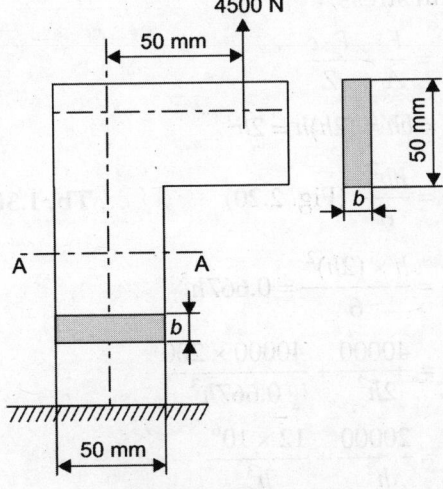

Fig. 2.19: Problem 21

We know that maximum stress intensity

$$\sigma = \frac{F}{A} + \frac{F \cdot e}{Z} \qquad \text{...Eq. (i) } \mathbf{1.1(a)/ Pg\ 2,\ DHB}$$

Here $\qquad A = b \cdot h = 50b$

$$Z = \frac{bh^2}{6} \qquad \text{... Tb. 1.3(a), (Fig. a)/ Pg 12, DHB}$$

$$Z = \frac{b \times (50)^2}{6} = 416.67b$$

$\therefore$ Eq. (i) yields... $\qquad 70 = \dfrac{4500}{50b} + \dfrac{4500 \times 50}{416.67b}$

$$70 = \frac{90}{b} + \frac{540}{b} = \frac{630}{b} \Rightarrow b = 9 \text{ mm}$$

22. The load acting on a C-clamp as shown in Fig. 2.20 is 40 kN. Assuming that, $b = 2h$, determine the dimensions of the clamp if the allowable stress is 100 MPa.

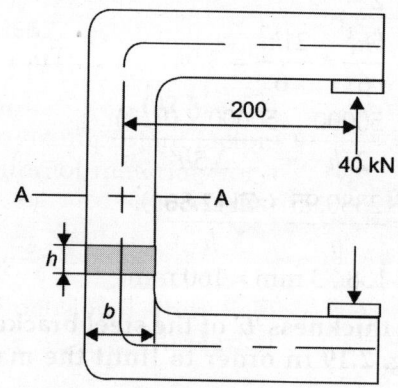

200

40 kN

A — A

h

b

Fig. 2.20: Problem 22

Solution: $F = 40$ kN $= 40000$ N, $e = 200$ mm, $b = 2h$, $\sigma = 100$ MPa, $b = ?$, $h = ?$
We know that maximum stress,

$$\sigma = \frac{F}{A} + \frac{F \cdot e}{Z} \qquad \text{...Eq. (i) } \mathbf{1.10/ Pg\ 7,\ DHB}$$

Here $\qquad A = bh = (2h)h = 2h^2$

$$Z = \frac{hb^2}{6} \quad \text{(Fig. 2.20)} \qquad \text{... Tb. 1.3(a), (Fig. a)/ Pg 12, DHB}$$

$$Z = \frac{h \times (2h)^2}{6} = 0.667h^3$$

$\therefore$ Eq. (i) yields... $\qquad 100 = \dfrac{40000}{2h^2} + \dfrac{40000 \times 200}{0.667h^3}$

$$= \frac{20000}{h^2} + \frac{12 \times 10^6}{h^3}$$

$$h^3 = 200h + (12 \times 10^4)$$
$$h = 50.68 \text{ mm} \approx 52 \text{ mm}$$
and
$$b = 2 \times 52 = 104 \text{ mm}$$

23. **Determine the stress at extreme fibers for the cross-section X-X of the C-clamp loaded as shown in Fig. 2.21, where $P = 100$ kN.**

VTU – July 2006 – 14 Marks

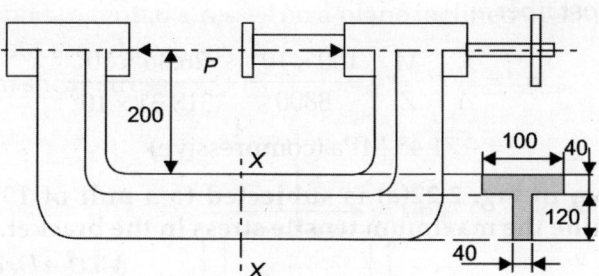

Fig. 2.21: Problem 23

Solution: $P = 100$ kN $= 100 \times 10^3$ N, $\sigma_t = ?$, $\sigma_c = ?$

We know that $\qquad \sigma = \dfrac{F}{A} \pm \dfrac{M}{Z}$ $\qquad$ ... Eq. (i) **1.10/ Pg 7, DHB**

Comparing the given cross-section with **Tb 1.3(a), Fig. d/Pg 12, DHB**, we have
$B = 100$ mm, $d = 40$ mm, $a = 40$ mm, $H = 160$ mm

- Area, $A = (Bd) + (H - d)a = (100 \times 40) + (160 - 40) \times 40 = 8800$ mm^2

- $c_1 = \dfrac{aH^2 + bd^2}{2(aH + bd)}$ $\qquad$ ... **Tb 1.3(a), Fig. d / Pg 12, DHB**

  $b = B - a = 100 - 40 = 60$ mm

  $c_1 = \dfrac{40 \times 160^2 + 60 \times 40^2}{2 \times (40 \times 160 + 60 \times 40)} = 63.64$ mm

- $c_2 = H - c_1 = 160 - 63.64 = 96.36$ mm

- $I = \dfrac{Bc_1^2 - bh^3 + ac_2^3}{3}$

  $h = c_1 - d = 63.64 - 40 = 23.64$ mm

  $= \dfrac{(100 \times 63.64^3) - (60 \times 23.64^3) + (40 \times 96.36^3)}{3}$

  $I = 20.26 \times 10^6$ mm^4

- $Z = \dfrac{I}{c_1} = \dfrac{20.26 \times 10^6}{63.64} = 318.31 \times 10^3$ mm^3

From **Fig. 2.21**, Moment
$$M = F \times \text{distance wrt } C_g \quad (C_g = \text{centre of gravity})$$
$$= F \times (200 + c_1)$$
$$= (100 \times 10^3) \times (200 + 63.64)$$
$$M = 26.36 \times 10^6 \text{ N·mm}$$

∴ Eq. (i) yields...

Stress in outermost fiber,

$$\sigma_t = \frac{F}{A} + \frac{M}{Z} = \frac{100 \times 10^3}{8800} + \frac{26.36 \times 10^6}{318.31 \times 10^3}$$

$$= 94.17 \text{ MPa (tensile)}$$

Stress in innermost fiber,

$$\sigma_c = \frac{F}{A} - \frac{M}{Z} = \frac{100 \times 10^3}{8800} - \frac{26.36 \times 10^6}{318.31 \times 10^3}$$

$$= -71.45 \text{ MPa (compressive)}$$

24. A bracket shown in Fig. 2.22(a) is subjected to a pull of 15 kN at 60° to the vertical. Determine the maximum tensile stress in the bracket.

VTU – Dec. 2010 – 12 Marks

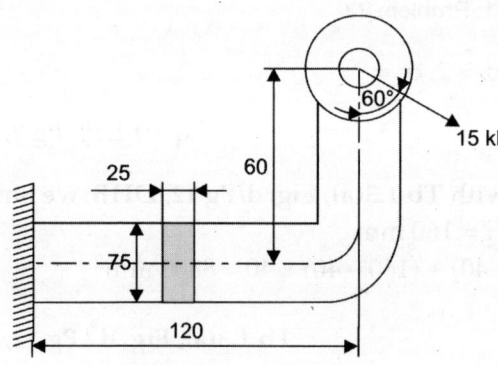

Fig. 2.22a: Problem 24

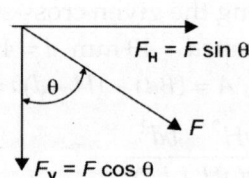

Fig. 2.22b: Problem 24

Solution: $P = 15$ kN $= 15 \times 10^3$ N, $\theta = 60°$ (with vertical), $b = 25$ mm, $h = 75$ mm, $\sigma_t = ?$, $x = 120$ mm, $y = 60$ mm

We know that maximum stress,

$$\sigma = \frac{F}{A} + \frac{F \cdot e}{Z} = \sigma_D + \sigma_b \qquad \text{... Eq. (i) 1.10/ Pg 7, DHB}$$

Here

$$A = bh = 75 \times 25 = 1875 \text{ mm}^2$$

$$Z = \frac{bh^2}{6} \qquad \text{... Tb. 1.3(a), (Fig. a)/ Pg 12, DHB}$$

$$Z = \frac{25 \times 75^2}{6} = 23437.5 \text{ mm}^2$$

Force components:

Referring to **Fig. 2.22(b)**, we have

Horizontal component, $F_H = F \sin \theta = 15 \sin 60 = 13$ kN

Vertical component, $F_V = F \cos \theta = 15 \cos 60 = 7.5$ kN

Resultant stress:

- Axial stress, $\sigma_D = \dfrac{F_H}{A} = \dfrac{13 \times 10^3}{1875} = 6.93$ MPa   ... **1.1(a)/ Pg 2, DHB**

- Bending stress, $\sigma_b = \dfrac{M}{Z}$ ... Eq. (ii) **1.1(b)/ Pg 2, DHB**

Here $M = M_H + M_y$

$M_H = F_H y = (13 \times 10^3) \times 60 = 7.80 \times 10^5$ N·mm

$M_V = F_V x = (7.5 \times 10^3) \times 120 = 9.0 \times 10^5$ N·mm

∴ Eq. (iii) yields...

$M = (7.80 \times 10^5) + (9 \times 10^5)$

∴ $M = 16.80 \times 10^5$ N·mm

∴ Eq. (ii) yields...

$\sigma_b = \dfrac{16.80 \times 10^5}{23437.5} = 71.68$ MPa

∴ Eq. (i) yields...

$\sigma = 6.93 + 71.68 = 78.61$ MPa

- Shear stress, $\tau = \dfrac{F_V}{A} = \dfrac{7.5 \times 10^3}{1875} = 4$ MPa   ... **1.1(d)/ Pg 2, DHB**

Principal stresses: Here $\sigma_x = \sigma = 78.61$ MPa; $\sigma_y = 0$; $\tau = \tau_{xy} = 4$ MPa

Maximum principal stress,

$$\sigma_1 = \frac{\sigma_x + \sigma_y}{2} + \sqrt{\left(\frac{\sigma_x - \sigma_y}{2}\right)^2 + \tau_{xy}^2}$$

... Eq. (i) **1.8(c) / Pg 5, DHB**

$$= \frac{78.61 + 0}{2} + \sqrt{\left(\frac{78.61 - 0}{2}\right)^2 + 4^2}$$

∴ $\sigma_1 = 78.81$ MPa

25. **Determine the dimensions of the bracket as shown in Fig. 2.23. The bracket is of rectangular cross-section whose depth is twice its width. The permissible stress is limited to 90 MPa.**

Solution: $F = 8$ kN $= 8000$ N, $h = 2b$, $\sigma = 90$ MPa, $\theta = 30°$, $x = 120$ mm, $y = 80$ mm, $b = ?, h = ?$

We know that maximum stress,

$$\sigma = \frac{F}{A} + \frac{F \cdot e}{Z} = \sigma_D + \sigma_b$$ ... Eq. (i) **1.10/ Pg 7, DHB**

Here $A = bh = b(2b) = 2b^2$

$Z = \dfrac{bh^2}{6}$ ... **Tb. 1.3(a), (Fig. a)/ Pg 12, DHB**

$Z = \dfrac{b \times (2b)^2}{6} = 0.667b^3$

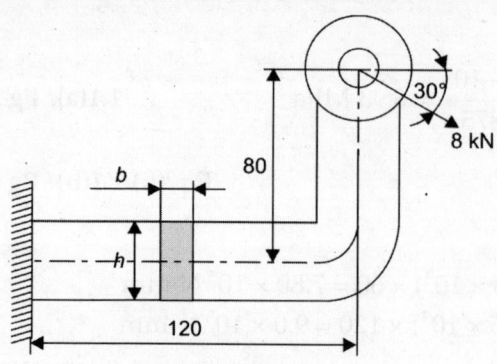

Fig. 2.23a: Problem 25

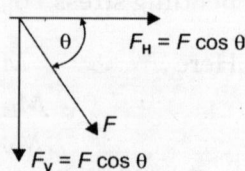

Fig. 2.23b: Problem 25

Force components: Referring to **Fig. 2.22(b)**, we have

Horizontal component, $F_H = F \cos \theta = 8 \times \cos 30 = 6.93$ kN

Vertical component, $F_V = F \sin \theta = 8 \times \sin 30 = 4$ kN

Resultant stress:

- Axial stress, $\quad \sigma_D = \dfrac{F_H}{A} = \dfrac{6.93 \times 10^3}{2b^2} = \dfrac{3465}{b^2}$ $\qquad$ ... **1.1(a)/ Pg 2, DHB**

- Bending stress, $\sigma_b = \dfrac{M}{Z}$ $\qquad$ ... Eq. *(ii)* **1.1(b)/ Pg 2, DHB**

Here $\qquad M = M_H + M_y$

$\qquad\qquad M_H = F_H y = (6.93 \times 10^3) \times 80 = 5.54 \times 10^5$ N·mm

$\qquad\qquad M_V = F_V x = (4 \times 10^3) \times 120 = 4.80 \times 10^5$ N·mm

∴ Eq. (iii) yields...

$\qquad\qquad M = (5.54 \times 10^5) + (4.80 \times 10^5)$

∴ $\qquad\qquad M = 10.30 \times 10^5$ N·mm

∴ Eq. (ii) yields...

$\qquad\qquad \sigma_b = \dfrac{10.34 \times 10^5}{0.667 b^3} = \dfrac{15.5 \times 10^6}{b^3}$

∴ Eq. (i) yields...

$\qquad\qquad 90 = \dfrac{3465}{b^2} + \dfrac{15.51 \times 10^6}{b^3}$

$\qquad\qquad b^3 = 38.5b + (17.23 \times 10^3)$

$\qquad\qquad b = 26.34$ mm ≈ 28 mm $\quad$ and $h = 2 \times 28 = 56$ mm

26. **A wall bracket of rectangular cross-section whose depth is twice its width carries a load of 60 kN as shown in Fig. 2.24(a). Find the required width and depth of cross-section taking allowable stress as 90 MPa.**

VTU – June/ July 2014 – 10 Marks

Solution: $P = 60$ kN $= 60 \times 10^3$ N, $\theta = 60°$, $h = 2b$, $\sigma_t = 90$ MPa, $x = 420$ mm, $y = 300$ mm, $b = ?, h = ?$

We know that maximum stress,

$$\sigma = \frac{F}{A} + \frac{F \cdot e}{Z} = \sigma_D + \sigma_b \qquad \text{... Eq. (i) } \textbf{1.10/ Pg 7, DHB}$$

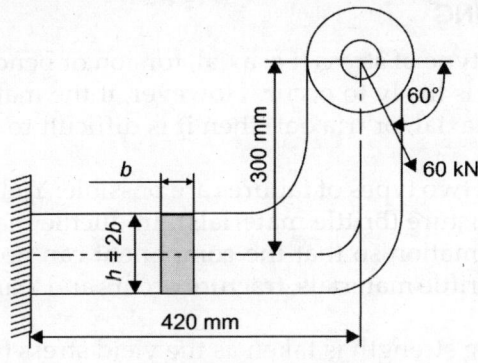

Fig. 2.24a: Problem 26

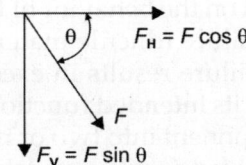

Fig. 2.24b: Problem 26

Here $A = bh = b(2b) = 2b^2$

$$Z = \frac{bh^2}{6}$$ **... Tb. 1.3(a), (Fig. a)/ Pg 12, DHB**

$$Z = \frac{b \times (2b)^2}{6} = 0.667b^3$$

Force components: Referring to **Fig. 2.24(b)**, we have

Horizontal component, $F_H = F \cos \theta = 60 \times \cos 60 = 30$ kN

Vertical component, $F_V = F \sin \theta = 60 \times \sin 60 = 52$ kN

Resultant stress:

• Axial stress, $\sigma_D = \dfrac{F_H}{A} = \dfrac{30 \times 10^3}{2b^2} = \dfrac{15000}{b^2}$ **... 1.1(a)/ Pg 2, DHB**

• Bending stress, $\sigma_b = \dfrac{M}{Z}$ **... Eq. (ii) 1.1(b)/ Pg 2, DHB**

Here $M = M_H + M_V$

$M_H = F_H y = (30 \times 10^3) \times 300 = 9 \times 10^6$ N·mm

$M_V = F_V x = (52 \times 10^3) \times 420 = 21.84 \times 10^6$ N·mm

∴ Eq. (iii) yields...

$M = (9 \times 10^6) + (21.84 \times 10^6)$

∴ $M = 30.84 \times 10^6$ N·mm

∴ Eq. (ii) yields...

$$\sigma_b = \frac{30.84 \times 10^6}{0.667b^3} = \frac{46.24 \times 10^6}{b^3}$$

∴ Eq. (i) yields...

$$90 = \frac{15000}{b^2} + \frac{46.24 \times 10^6}{b^3}$$

$b^3 = 166.67b + (513.78 \times 10^3)$

$b = 80.78$ mm ≈ 82 mm

and $h = 2 \times 82 = 164$ mm

2.5 THEORIES OF FAILURE: STATIC LOADING

When a material is subjected to a single type of stress (i.e. axial, torsion or bending), it is very easy to predict when the failure is likely to occur. However, if the material is subjected to a complex stress system (biaxial, or triaxial) then it is difficult to predict the failure of the material.

Based on the behavior of the material, two types of failures are possible: Yielding or elastic failure (ductile materials) and fracture (brittle materials). In ductile materials, elastic failure results in excessive deformation so that the component can no longer perform its intended function; while in brittle materials, fracture occurs and tears apart the component into two or more pieces.

Hence for *ductile materials*, the limiting strength is taken as the yield stress (tension or compression), while for *brittle materials*, the limiting strength is taken as the ultimate stress (tension or compression).

In order to predict the failure of material under combined stresses, the following theories of failure have been postulated.

a. Maximum normal stress theory (MNST) or principal stress theory or Rankine's theory
b. Maximum shear stress theory (MSST) or Guest's or Tresca's theory or shear difference theory
c. Maximum normal strain theory or principal strain theory or Saint Venant theory
d. Maximum strain energy theory or Haigh's theory
e. Maximum shear energy theory or distortion theory or von Mises theory (DET)

It is to be noted that, in static loading and ductile behavior, stress concentrations are harmless as they only create small localized yielding which do not lead to any objectionable dimensional changes.

2.5.1 Maximum Normal Stress Theory (MNST) or Principal Stress Theory or Rankine's Theory

According to this theory, "the failure of a machine component subjected to combined action of normal and shear stresses occurs whenever the maximum principal stress (σ_1) of the component becomes equal to the elastic strength $(\sigma_e$ or $\sigma_y)$ of the material in simple tension test".

Elastic strength = Maximum principal stress

$$\sigma_e = \sigma_1 \qquad \qquad \text{... (Eq. 2.15)}$$

$$\sigma_e = \left(\frac{\sigma_x + \sigma_y}{2}\right) + \sqrt{\left(\frac{\sigma_x - \sigma_y}{2}\right)^2 + \tau_{xy}^2}$$

... (Eq. 2.16a) **2.8(a)/ Pg 21, DHB**

or

$$\sigma_e = \left(\frac{\sigma_x + \sigma_y}{2}\right) + \frac{1}{2}\sqrt{(\sigma_x - \sigma_y)^2 + 4\tau_{xy}^2} \qquad \text{... (Eq. 2.16b)}$$

If factor of safety is considered,

$$n = \frac{\sigma_e}{\sigma_1} \qquad \qquad \text{... (Eq. 2.17)}$$

where

σ_1 = maximum principal stress (MPa)
σ_e or σ_y = yield strength of the material (MPa)

For design,
$$\frac{\sigma_e}{n} = \left(\frac{\sigma_x + \sigma_y}{2}\right) + \sqrt{\left(\frac{\sigma_x - \sigma_y}{2}\right)^2 + \tau_{xy}^2} \qquad \text{... (Eq. 2.18)}$$

The principal stresses are found as follows.

- Maximum principal stress,

$$\sigma_1 = \left(\frac{\sigma_x + \sigma_y}{2}\right) + \sqrt{\left(\frac{\sigma_x - \sigma_y}{2}\right)^2 + \tau_{xy}^2}$$

... (Eq. 2.19a) **1.8 (c)/ Pg 5, DHB**

- Minimum principal stress,

$$\sigma_2 = \left(\frac{\sigma_x + \sigma_y}{2}\right) - \sqrt{\left(\frac{\sigma_x - \sigma_y}{2}\right)^2 + \tau_{xy}^2}$$

... (Eq. 2.19b) **1.8(d)/ Pg 5, DHB**

Applicable only for brittle materials. This theory disregards the effects of other principal stresses and the effects of shear stress on other planes and hence it is not used for ductile materials.

2.5.2 Maximum Normal Strain Theory or Principal Strain Theory or Saint Venant Theory

According to this theory, "the failure of a machine component subjected to combined action of normal and shear stresses occurs whenever the maximum principal strain of the component becomes equal to the maximum strain of the material in simple tension test"

i.e.
$$\sigma_e = (1 - \mu)\left(\frac{\sigma_x + \sigma_y}{2}\right) + (1 + \mu)\sqrt{\left(\frac{\sigma_x - \sigma_y}{2}\right)^2 + \tau_{xy}^2}$$

or $\qquad \sigma = (\sigma_1 - \mu\sigma_2) \qquad$ ... (Eq. 2.20) **2.8(b)/ Pg 22, DHB**

If factor of safety is considered, then

$$n = \frac{\sigma_e}{(\sigma_1 - \mu\sigma_2)} \qquad \text{... (Eq. 2.21)}$$

For design,
$$\frac{\sigma_e}{n} = (1 - \mu)\left(\frac{\sigma_x + \sigma_y}{2}\right) + (1 + \mu)\sqrt{\left(\frac{\sigma_x - \sigma_y}{2}\right)^2 + \tau_{xy}^2}$$

... (Eq. 2.22a)

or $\qquad \dfrac{\sigma_e}{n} = (\sigma_1 - \mu\sigma_2) \qquad\qquad$ ... (Eq. 2.22b)

where μ = Poisson's ratio

This theory is not used in general.

2.5.3 Maximum Shear Stress Theory (MSST) or Guest's or Tresca's Theory or Shear Difference Theory

According to this theory, "the failure of a machine component subjected to combined action of normal and shear stresses occurs whenever the shear stress of the component becomes equal to the shear stress experienced by the material in simple tension test".

i.e. $\qquad \tau_{max} = \tau_e \qquad\qquad$ ... (Eq. 2.23)

Since the shear stress at yield point in a simple tension test is equal to one-half the yield stress in tension, we have

$$\tau_e = \frac{\sigma_e}{2} \qquad \text{... (Eq. 2.24)}$$

$$\therefore \quad \sqrt{\left(\frac{\sigma_x - \sigma_y}{2}\right)^2 + \tau_{xy}^2} = \frac{\sigma_e}{2} \qquad \text{... (Eq. 2.25a) \textbf{2.8(c)/ Pg 22, DHB}}$$

$$\frac{1}{2}\sqrt{(\sigma_x - \sigma_y)^2 + 4\tau_{xy}^2} = \frac{\sigma_e}{2}$$

$$\sqrt{(\sigma_x - \sigma_y)^2 + 4\tau_{xy}^2} = \sigma_e \qquad \text{... (Eq. 2.25b) \textbf{2.8(c)/ Pg 22, DHB}}$$

or $$\sigma_1 - \sigma_2 = \sigma_e \qquad \text{... (Eq. 2.25c) \textbf{2.8(c)/ Pg 22, DHB}}$$

If factor of safety is considered, then

$$n = \frac{\sigma_e}{\sigma_1 - \sigma_2} \qquad \text{... (Eq. 2.26)}$$

For design, $$\frac{\sigma_e}{n} = \sqrt{(\sigma_x - \sigma_y)^2 + 4\tau_{xy}^2} \qquad \text{... (Eq. 2.27a)}$$

or $$\sigma_1 - \sigma_2 = \frac{\sigma_e}{n} \qquad \text{... (Eq. 2.27b)}$$

For a 3D case: If the principal normal stresses are σ_1, σ_2 and σ_3, where $\sigma_1 \geq \sigma_2 \geq \sigma_3$, then τ_{max} is the largest of:

$$\tau_{1-2} = \frac{\sigma_1 - \sigma_2}{2}; \quad \tau_{2-3} = \frac{\sigma_2 - \sigma_3}{2}; \quad \tau_{3-1} = \frac{\sigma_1 - \sigma_3}{2}$$

(Eq. 2.27b) yields...

$$\sigma_1 - \sigma_3 = \frac{\sigma_e}{n} \qquad \text{... (Eq. 2.28)}$$

Applicable to ductile materials. The results are on the safer side.

2.5.4 Maximum Shear Energy Theory or Distortion Theory or von Mises Theory (DET)

According to this theory, "the failure of a machine component subjected to combined action of normal and shear stresses occurs whenever the shear strain energy (distortion energy) per unit volume of the component becomes equal to the shear strain energy (distortion energy) per unit volume of the material in simple tension test"

i.e. $$\sigma_e = \sqrt{\sigma_x^2 + \sigma_y^2 - \sigma_x\sigma_y + 3\tau_{xy}^2} \quad \text{... (Eq. 2.29a) \textbf{2.8(d)/ Pg 22, DHB}}$$

or $$\sigma_e = \sqrt{\sigma_1^2 + \sigma_2^2 - \sigma_1\sigma_2} \qquad \text{... (Eq. 2.29b) \textbf{2.8(d)/ Pg 22, DHB}}$$

If factor of safety is considered, then

$$n = \frac{\sigma_e}{\sqrt{\sigma_1^2 + \sigma_2^2 - \sigma_1\sigma_2}} \qquad \text{... (Eq. 2.30)}$$

For design, $$\frac{\sigma_e}{n} = \sqrt{\sigma_x^2 + \sigma_y^2 - \sigma_x\sigma_y + 3\tau_{xy}^2} \qquad \text{... (Eq. 2.31a)}$$

or $$\frac{\sigma_e}{n} = \sqrt{\sigma_1^2 + \sigma_2^2 - \sigma_1\sigma_2} \qquad \text{... (Eq. 2.31b)}$$

For a 3D case: If the principal normal stresses are σ_1, σ_2 and σ_3, where $\sigma_1 \geq \sigma_2 \geq \sigma_3$, then τ_{max} is the largest of:

$$\frac{\sigma_e}{n} = \sqrt{\sigma_1^2 + \sigma_2^2 + \sigma_3^2 - (\sigma_1\sigma_2 + \sigma_2\sigma_3 + \sigma_1\sigma_3)} \qquad \text{... (Eq. 2.32a)}$$

or

$$\frac{\sigma_e}{n} = \sqrt{\frac{(\sigma_1 - \sigma_2)^2 + (\sigma_2 - \sigma_3)^2 + (\sigma_3 - \sigma_1)^2}{2}} \qquad \text{... (Eq. 2.32b)}$$

In terms of applied stresses, we have

$$\frac{\sigma_e}{n} = \sqrt{\frac{(\sigma_x - \sigma_y)^2 + (\sigma_y - \sigma_z)^2 + (\sigma_z - \sigma_x)^2 + 6(\tau_{xy}^2 + \tau_{yz}^2 + \tau_{zx}^2)}{2}} \qquad \text{... (Eq. 2.33)}$$

Applicable to ductile materials. This theory gives satisfactory results.

2.5.5 Maximum Strain Energy Theory (MSET) or Haigh's Theory

According to this theory, "the failure of a machine component subjected to combined action of normal and shear stresses occurs whenever the strain energy per unit volume of the component becomes equal to the strain energy per unit volume of the material in simple tension test".

i.e.

$$\sigma_e = \sqrt{\sigma_1^2 + \sigma_2^2 - 2\mu\sigma_1\sigma_2} \qquad \text{... (Eq. 2.34) \textbf{2.8(e)/ Pg 22, DHB}}$$

If factor of safety is considered, then

$$n = \frac{\sigma_e}{\sqrt{\sigma_1^2 + \sigma_2^2 - 2\mu\sigma_1\sigma_2}} \qquad \text{... (Eq. 2.35)}$$

For design,

$$\frac{\sigma_e}{n} = \sqrt{\sigma_1^2 + \sigma_2^2 - 2\mu\sigma_1\sigma_2} \qquad \text{... (Eq. 2.36)}$$

Applicable to ductile materials. This theory yields good approximation.

2.6 DIFFERENCE BETWEEN DUCTILE AND BRITTLE FRACTURE

Sl. No.	Ductile fracture	Brittle fracture
1	All fractures involve crack formation followed by crack propagation	
2	Mode of fracture highly dependent on crack propagation mechanism	
3	Ductile crack propagation – stable	Brittle crack propagation – unstable
4	$\sigma_f \geq \sigma_y$ σ_f = fracture stress, σ_y = yield stress	$\sigma_f < \sigma_y$
5	Material fails by yielding	Material fails by fracture
6	Fracture occurs due to failure of atoms	Due to breaking of bonds
7	Yielding and necking occurs	Does not occur
8	Fracture is fibrous in nature	Crystalline
9	Fracture surfaces cannot be joined	Can be joined
10	Surfaces are dull/rough	Reflective
11	Energy required for fracture is high	Low
12	Toughness is more	Less
13	Ductile fracture is always preferred as it gives warning signs	Brittle fracture is not always preferred—no warning signs

2.7 FAILURE OF DUCTILE AND BRITTLE MATERIALS

For ductile materials the *distortion theory* gives accurate results. However, *maximum shear stress theory* is also preferred as it gives results on safer side.

For brittle materials which fail by fracture, the *maximum normal or principal stress theory* and *distortion theory* are preferred. In majority of the cases, maximum normal stress theory is preferred.

27. **A bolt is designed to take up direct tensile load of 30 kN and a shear load of 16 kN with a factor of safety of 4. The yield strength of the material used is 400 MPa. Calculate the size of the bolt based on various theories of failure. Take μ = 0.3.**

Solution: $F = 30$ kN $= 30 \times 10^3$ N, $F_s = 16$ kN $= 16 \times 10^3$ N, factor of safety $n = 4$, yield of elastic stress, $\sigma_e = 400$ MPa, $d = ?$

- Axial stress, $\qquad \sigma_D = \dfrac{F}{A} = \dfrac{30 \times 10^3}{\pi d^2 / 4} = \dfrac{38.20 \times 10^3}{d^2}$ MPa $\qquad$ ... **1.1(a)/ Pg 2, DHB**

- Shear stress, $\qquad \tau = \dfrac{F_s}{A_s} \; (A_s = A)$ $\qquad\qquad\qquad\qquad$ ... **1.1(c)/ Pg 2, DHB**

$$\tau = \frac{16 \times 10^3}{\pi d^2 / 4} = \frac{20.37 \times 10^3}{d^2} \text{ MPa}$$

State of stress: Here

$$\sigma_x = \sigma_D = \frac{38.20 \times 10^3}{d^2} \text{ MPa}; \; \sigma_y = 0; \; \tau = \tau_{xy} = \frac{20.37 \times 10^3}{d^2} \text{ MPa}$$

a. **Maximum normal stress theory:**

For design $\qquad \dfrac{\sigma_e}{n} = \dfrac{\sigma_x + \sigma_y}{2} + \sqrt{\left(\dfrac{\sigma_x - \sigma_y}{2}\right)^2 + \tau_{xy}^2}$ $\qquad$ ... **2.8(a) / Pg 21, DHB**

$$\frac{400}{4} = \left(\frac{38.20 \times 10^3 + 0}{2d^2}\right) + \sqrt{\left(\frac{38.20 \times 10^3 - 0}{2d^2}\right)^2 + \left(\frac{20.37 \times 10^3}{d^2}\right)}$$

$$100 = \left(\frac{19.10 \times 10^3}{d^2}\right) + \left(\frac{27.92 \times 10^3}{d^2}\right)$$

$$100 = \left(\frac{47 \times 10^3}{d^2}\right)$$

$$\therefore \qquad d = 21.68 \text{ MPa}$$

b. **Maximum shear stress theory:**

For design $\qquad \dfrac{\sigma_e}{n} = \sqrt{(\sigma_x - \sigma_y)^2 + 4\tau_{xy}^2}$ $\qquad$ ... **2.8(c) / Pg 22, DHB**

$$\frac{400}{4} = \sqrt{\left(\frac{38.20 \times 10^3 - 0}{d^2}\right)^2 + \left[4 \times \left(\frac{20.37 \times 10^3}{d^2}\right)^2\right]}$$

$$100 = \left(\frac{55.84 \times 10^3}{d^2}\right)$$

$$\therefore \qquad d = 23.63 \text{ MPa}$$

c. **Maximum strain theory:**

For design $\qquad \dfrac{\sigma_e}{n} = (1 - \mu)\left(\dfrac{\sigma_x + \sigma_y}{2}\right) + \left[(1 + \mu)\sqrt{\left(\dfrac{\sigma_x - \sigma_y}{2}\right)^2 + \tau_{xy}^2}\right]$

... **2.8(b) / Pg 22, DHB**

$$\frac{400}{4} = \left[(1 - 0.3) \times \left(\frac{38.20 \times 10^3 + 0}{2d^2}\right)\right]$$

$$+ \left[(1 + 0.3) \times \sqrt{\left(\frac{38.20 \times 10^3 - 0}{2d^2}\right)^2 + \left(\frac{20.37 \times 10^3 - 0}{2d^2}\right)^2}\right]$$

$$100 = \left(\frac{13.37 \times 10^3}{d^2}\right) + \left(\frac{36.30 \times 10^3}{d^2}\right)$$

$$100 = \left(\frac{49.67 \times 10^3}{d^2}\right)$$

$$\therefore \qquad d = 22.28 \text{ MPa}$$

d. **Distortion energy theory or von Mises theory:**

For design

$$\frac{\sigma_e}{n} = \sqrt{\sigma_x^2 + \sigma_y^2 - \sigma_x \sigma_y + 3\tau_{xy}^2} \qquad\qquad \text{... 2.8(d) / Pg 22, DHB}$$

$$\frac{400}{4} = \sqrt{\left(\frac{38.20 \times 10^3}{d^2}\right)^2 + 0 - \left[\left(\frac{38.20 \times 10^3}{d^2}\right)^2 \times 0\right] + \left[\left(3 \times \frac{20.37 \times 10^3}{d^2}\right)^2\right]}$$

$$100 = \left(\frac{52 \times 10^3}{d^2}\right)$$

$$\therefore \quad d = 22.80 \text{ MPa}$$

e. **Strain energy theory:**

For design

$$\frac{\sigma_e}{n} = \sqrt{\sigma_1^2 + \sigma_2^2 - 2\mu\sigma_1\sigma_2} \qquad\qquad \text{... 2.8(e) / Pg 22, DHB}$$

$$\sigma_{1,2} = \left(\frac{\sigma_x + \sigma_y}{2}\right) \pm \sqrt{\left(\frac{\sigma_x - \sigma_y}{2}\right)^2 + \tau_{xy}^2}$$

$$= \left(\frac{19.10 \times 10^3}{d^2}\right) \pm \left(\frac{27.92 \times 10^3}{d^2}\right) \qquad\qquad \text{... 1.8(c) \& (d) / Pg 5, DHB}$$

$$\therefore \quad \sigma_1 = \frac{47 \times 10^3}{d^2}, \sigma_2 = \left(\frac{-8820}{d^2}\right)$$

$$\therefore \quad \frac{400}{4} = \sqrt{\left(\frac{47 \times 10^3}{d^2}\right)^2 + \left(\frac{-8820}{d^2}\right)^2 - \left[2 \times 0.3 \times \left(\frac{47 \times 10^3}{d^2}\right) \times \left(\frac{-8820}{d^2}\right)\right]}$$

$$100 = \left(\frac{50.35 \times 10^3}{d^2}\right)$$

$$\therefore \quad d = 22.44 \text{ MPa}$$

Theories of failure	Diameter d 'mm'	Bolt size ...Tb. 9.8/Pg - 142 - Col (5) & (3)
Maximum normal stress theory	21.68	M24
Maximum shear stress theory	23.63	M27
Maximum strain theory	22.29	M24
Distortion theory	22.80	M27
Strain energy theory	22.45	M24

Based on above theories, the maximum diameter is $d = 23.63$ mm $= M27$ mm.

28. **A bolt is subjected to a direct tensile load of 30 kN and a transverse shear force of 15 kN. The material of the bolt has a normal stress of 350 MPa at yield and Poisson's ratio of 0.25. Compute the root diameter of the bolt according to:**
    a. Maximum shear stress theory of failure
    b. von Mises criterion for failure.
    Hence suggest suitable size of the bolt. Take value of 3 for factor of safety.
    VTU – June/ July 2013 – 07 Marks; Dec.14/ Jan.15 – 09 Marks

Solution: $F = 30$ kN $= 30 \times 10^3$ N, $F_s = 15$ kN $= 15 \times 10^3$ N, yield stress $\sigma_e = 350$ MPa, $\mu = 0.25$, factor of safety, $n = 3$, $d = ?$

- Axial stress, $\sigma_D = \dfrac{F}{A} = \dfrac{30 \times 10^3}{\pi d^2/4} = \dfrac{38.20 \times 10^3}{d^2}$ MPa $\quad$ ... **1.1(a)/ Pg 2, DHB**

- Shear stress, $\tau = \dfrac{F_s}{A_s} \quad (A_s = A)$ $\quad$ ... **1.1(c)/ Pg 2, DHB**

$$\tau = \frac{15 \times 10^3}{\pi d^2/4} = \frac{19.09 \times 10^3}{d^2} \text{ MPa}$$

State of stress: Here

$$\sigma_x = \sigma_D = \frac{38.20 \times 10^3}{d^2} \text{ MPa}; \sigma_y = 0, \tau = \tau_{xy} = \frac{19.09 \times 10^3}{d^2} \text{ MPa}$$

a. **Maximum shear stress theory:**

For design $\quad \dfrac{\sigma_e}{n} = \sqrt{(\sigma_x - \sigma_y)^2 + 4\tau_{xy}^2}$ $\quad$ ... **2.8(c)/ Pg 22, DHB**

$$\frac{350}{3} = \sqrt{\left(\frac{38.20 \times 10^3 - 0}{d^2}\right)^2 \left[4 \times \left(\frac{19.09 \times 10^3}{d^2}\right)^2\right]}$$

$$116.67 = \left(\frac{54 \times 10^3}{d^2}\right)$$

$$d = 21.52 \text{ mm}$$

b. **Distortion energy theory or von Mises theory:**
For design

$$\frac{\sigma_e}{n} = \sqrt{\sigma_x^2 + \sigma_y^2 - \sigma_x\sigma_y + 3\tau_{xy}^2} \qquad \text{... 2.8(d)/ Pg 22, DHB}$$

$$\frac{350}{3} = \sqrt{\left(\frac{38.20 \times 10^3}{d^2}\right)^2 + 0 - \left[\left(\frac{38.20 \times 10^3}{d^2}\right) \times 0\right] + \left[3 \times \left(\frac{19.09 \times 10^3}{d^2}\right)^2\right]}$$

$$116.67 = \left(\frac{50.53 \times 10^3}{d^2}\right)$$

$$d = 21.52 \text{ mm}$$

Theories of failure	Diameter d 'mm'	Bolt size ..... Tb. 9.8/ Pg 142 - Col (5) & (3)
Maximum shear stress theory	21.52	M24
Distortion theory	20.81	M24

29. **A bolt in an assembly is subjected to a pull of 1000 N along its axis and a shear force of 500 N, what will be the maximum stress induced in the bolt. If the bolt is made of SAE 1045 annealed steel, is the bolt safe given that the diameter of the bolt is 12 mm.**

VTU – June/ July 2009 – 07 Marks

Solution: $F = 1000$ N, $F_s = 500$ N, $\sigma_e = ?$, Material: SAE 1045, $d = 12$ mm.

- Axial stress, $\quad \sigma_D = \dfrac{1000}{\pi \times 12^2/4} = 8.84$ MPa $\qquad$ ... 1.1(a)/ Pg 2, DHB

- Shear stress, $\quad \tau = \dfrac{F_s}{A_s} \quad (A_s = A)$ $\qquad$ ... 1.1(c)/ Pg 2, DHB

$$\tau = \frac{500}{\pi \times 12^2/4} = 4.42 \text{ MPa}$$

State of stress: Here $\sigma_x = \sigma_x = \sigma_D = 8.84$ MPa; $\sigma_y = 0$; $\tau = \tau_{xy} = 4.42$ MPa

For ductile materials the distortion theory gives accurate results. However, maximum shear stress theory is also preferred as it gives results on safer side.

a. **Maximum shear stress theory:**

For design $\quad \sigma_e = \sqrt{(\sigma_x - \sigma_y)^2 + 4\tau_{xy}^2}$ $\qquad$ ... 2.8(c)/ Pg 22, DHB

$$= \sqrt{(8.84 - 0)^2 + [4 \times 4.42^2]}$$

$$\sigma_e = 12.50 \text{ MPa}$$

b. **Distortion energy theory or von Mises theory:**
For design

$$\sigma_e = \sqrt{\sigma_x^2 + \sigma_y^2 - \sigma_x\sigma_y + 3\tau_{xy}^2} \qquad \text{... 2.8(d)/ Pg 22, DHB}$$

$$= \sqrt{8.84^2 + 0^2 - (8.84 \times 0) + [3 \times 4.42^2]}$$

$$\sigma_e = 11.31 \text{ MPa}$$

30. **A mild steel shaft is subjected to 3500 N·m of bending moment at it critical point and transmits a torque of 2500 N·m. The shaft is made of steel having yield strength of 231 MPa. Estimate the size of the shaft based on various theories of failure and specify the final size. Take FOS = 2 and μ = 0.3.**

VTU – Dec. 2013/ Jan. 2014 – 14 Marks

Solution: $M = 3500$ N·m $= 3.5 \times 10^6$ N·mm, $T = 2500$ N·m $= 2.5 \times 10^6$ N·mm, yield stress, $\sigma_e = 231$ MPa, $d = ?$, $n = 2$, $\sigma = 0.3$.

- Bending stress, $\sigma_D = \dfrac{M}{Z} = \dfrac{32M}{\pi d^3} = \dfrac{3.5 \times 10^6}{\pi d^3/32} = \dfrac{35.65 \times 10^6}{d^3}$ ... **1.1(b)/ Pg 2, DHB**

- Shear stress, $\tau = \dfrac{16T}{\pi d^3} = \left(\dfrac{16 \times (2.5 \times 10^6)}{\pi d^3}\right) = \dfrac{12.73 \times 10^6}{d^3}$

  ... **1.1(d)/ Pg 2, DHB**

State of stress: Here

$$\sigma_x = \sigma_D = \frac{35.65 \times 10^6}{d^3} \text{ MPa}; \sigma_y = 0, \tau = \tau_{xy} = \frac{12.73 \times 10^6}{d^2} \text{ MPa}$$

a. **Maximum normal stress theory:**

For design $\quad \dfrac{\sigma_e}{n} = \left(\dfrac{\sigma_x + \sigma_y}{2}\right) + \sqrt{\left(\dfrac{\sigma_x - \sigma_y}{2}\right)^2 + \tau_{xy}^2}$ ... **2.8(a)/ Pg 21, DHB**

$$\frac{231}{2} = \left(\frac{35.65 \times 10^6 + 0}{2d^3}\right) + \sqrt{\left(\frac{35.65 \times 10^6 - 0}{2d^2}\right)^2 + \left(\frac{12.73 \times 10^6}{d^3}\right)^2}$$

$$115.5 = \left(\frac{17.83 \times 10^6}{d^3}\right) + \left(\frac{21.90 \times 10^6}{d^3}\right) \qquad \text{... Eq. (a)}$$

$$115.5 = \left(\frac{39.73 \times 10^6}{d^3}\right)$$

$$d = 70.06 \text{ mm}$$

∴ Standard shaft diameter = 71 mm $\qquad$ ... **Tb. 3.5(a)/ Pg 57, DHB**

b. **Maximum shear stress theory:**

For design $\quad \dfrac{\sigma_e}{n} = \sqrt{(\sigma_x - \sigma_y)^2 + 4\tau_{xy}^2}$ $\qquad$ ... **2.8(c)/ Pg 22, DHB**

$$\frac{231}{2} = \sqrt{\left(\frac{35.65 \times 10^6 - 0}{d^3}\right)^2 + \left[4 \times \left(\frac{12.73 \times 10^6}{d^3}\right)^2\right]}$$

$$115.5 = \left(\frac{43.80 \times 10^6}{d^3}\right)$$

$$d = 72.38 \text{ mm}$$

∴ Standard shaft diameter = 80 mm $\qquad$ ... **Tb. 3.5(a)/ Pg 57, DHB**

c. **Maximum strain theory:**

For design

$$\frac{\sigma_e}{n} = (1-\mu)\left(\frac{\sigma_x + \sigma_y}{2}\right) + \left[(1+\mu)\sqrt{\left(\frac{\sigma_x - \sigma_y}{2}\right)^2 + \tau_{xy}^2}\right]$$

... **2.8(b)/ Pg 22, DHB**

$$\frac{231}{2} = \left[(1-0.3) \times \left(\frac{35.65 \times 10^6 + 0}{2d^3}\right)\right]$$

$$+ \left[(1-0.3) \times \sqrt{\left(\frac{35.65 \times 10^6 - 0}{2d^3}\right)^2 + \left(\frac{12.73 \times 10^6}{d^3}\right)^2}\right]$$

$$115.5 = \left(\frac{12.48 \times 10^6}{d^3}\right) + \left(\frac{28.47 \times 10^6}{d^3}\right)$$

$$115.5 = \left(\frac{40.95 \times 10^6}{d^3}\right)$$

$$\therefore \qquad d = 21.52 \text{ mm}$$

$\therefore$ Standard shaft diameter = 71 mm   ... **Tb. 3.5(a)/ Pg 57, DHB**

d. **Distortion energy theory or von Mises theory:**

For design

$$\frac{\sigma_e}{n} = \sqrt{(\sigma_x^2 + \sigma_y^2 - \sigma_x\sigma_y + 3\tau_{xy}^2)}$$

... **2.8(d)/ Pg 22, DHB**

$$\frac{231}{2} = \sqrt{\left(\frac{35.65 \times 10^6}{d^3}\right)^2 + 0 - \left[\left(\frac{35.65 \times 10^6}{d^3}\right) \times 0\right] + \left[3 \times \left(\frac{12.73 \times 10^6}{d^3}\right)^2\right]}$$

$$115.5 = \left(\frac{41.92 \times 10^6}{d^3}\right)$$

$$\therefore \qquad d = 71.33 \text{ mm}$$

$\therefore$ Standard shaft diameter = 80 mm   ... **Tb. 3.5(a)/ Pg 57, DHB**

e. **Strain energy theory:**

For design

$$\frac{\sigma_e}{n} = \sqrt{(\sigma_1^2 + \sigma_2^2 - 2\mu\sigma_1\sigma_2})$$

... **2.8(e)/ Pg 22, DHB**

$$\sigma_{1,2} = \left(\frac{\sigma_x + \sigma_y}{2}\right) \pm \sqrt{\left(\frac{\sigma_x + \sigma_y}{2}\right)^2 + \tau_{xy}^2}$$

... **1.8(c)&(d)/ Pg 5, DHB**

$$= \left(\frac{17.83 \times 10^6}{d^3}\right) \pm \left(\frac{21.90 \times 10^6}{d^3}\right)$$

$$\sigma_1 = \left(\frac{39.73 \times 10^6}{d^3}\right), \sigma_2 = \left(\frac{-4.07 \times 10^6}{d^3}\right)$$

$$\frac{231}{2} = \sqrt{\left(\frac{39.73 \times 10^6}{d^3}\right)^2 + \left(\frac{-4.07 \times 10^6}{d^3}\right)^2 - \left[2 \times 0.3 \times \left(\frac{39.73 \times 10^6}{d^3}\right) \times \left(\frac{-4.07 \times 10^6}{d^3}\right)\right]}$$

$$115.5 = \left(\frac{41.13 \times 10^6}{d^3}\right)$$

$\therefore \quad d = 71.33 \text{ mm}$

$\therefore$ Standard shaft diameter = 80 mm   ... **Tb. 3.5(a)/ Pg 57, DHB**

Based on above theories, the maximum shaft diameter is $d = 72.38$ mm

$\therefore$ Standard shaft diameter, $d = 80$ mm

31. **A cylindrical shaft made of steel is subjected to a static load, consisting of bending moment of 10 kN·m and a torsional moment of 30 kN·m. Determine the diameter of the shaft according to:**
    i. Maximum shear stress theory
    ii. Strain energy theory
    Take yield strength = 700 MPa, Young's modulus = 210 GPa, Poisson's ratio = 0.25, factor of safety = 2.

VTU – Dec. 2010 – 14 Marks; (Similar) Dec. 2009/ Jan 2010 – 10 Marks; (similar) Dec. 07/ Jan. 2008 – 15 Marks; (similar) June/ July 2014 – 10 Marks.

Solution: $M = 10$ kN·m $= 10 \times 10^6$ N·mm, $T = 30$ kN·m $= 30 \times 10^6$ N·mm, yield stress, $\sigma_e = 700$ MPa, $d = ?$, $n = 2$, $\mu = 0.25$.

- Bending stress, $\sigma_b = \dfrac{M}{Z} = \dfrac{32M}{\pi d^3} = \dfrac{10 \times 10^6}{\pi d^3/32} = \dfrac{101.86 \times 10^6}{d^3}$ ... **1.1(b)/ Pg 2, DHB**

- Shear stress, $\quad \tau = \dfrac{16T}{\pi d^3} = \dfrac{16 \times (30 \times 10^6)}{\pi d^3} = \dfrac{152.78 \times 10^6}{d^3}$ ... **1.1(d)/ Pg 2, DHB**

State of stress: Here

$$\sigma_x = \sigma_b = \frac{101.86 \times 10^6}{d^3} \text{ MPa}; \; \sigma_y = 0, \; \tau = \tau_{xy} = \frac{152.78 \times 10^6}{d^3} \text{ MPa}$$

i. **Maximum shear stress theory:**

For design $\quad \dfrac{\sigma_e}{n} = \sqrt{(\sigma_x - \sigma_y)^2 + 4\tau_{xy}^2}$ ... **2.8(c)/ Pg 22, DHB**

$$\frac{700}{2} = \sqrt{\left(\frac{101.86 \times 10^6 - 0}{d^3}\right)^2 + \left[4 \times \left(\frac{152.78 \times 10^6}{d^3}\right)^2\right]}$$

$$350 = \left(\frac{322.1 \times 10^6}{d^3}\right)$$

$\therefore \qquad d = 97.26$ mm

$\therefore$ Standard shaft diameter = 100 mm   ... **Tb. 3.5(a)/ Pg 57, DHB**

ii. **Strain energy theory:**

For design

$$\frac{\sigma_e}{n} = \sqrt{(\sigma_1^2 - \sigma_2^2 - 2\mu\sigma_1\sigma_2)} \qquad \ldots \textbf{2.8(e)/Pg 22, DHB}$$

$$\sigma_{1,2} = \left(\frac{\sigma_x + \sigma_y}{2}\right) \pm \sqrt{\left(\frac{\sigma_x - \sigma_y}{2}\right)^2 + \tau_{xy}^2} \qquad \ldots \textbf{1.8(c) \& (d)/Pg 5, DHB}$$

$$= \left(\frac{101.86 \times 10^6 + 0}{2d^3}\right) \pm \sqrt{\left(\frac{101.86 \times 10^6 - 0}{2d^3}\right)^2 + \left(\frac{152.78 \times 10^6}{d^3}\right)^2}$$

$$= \left(\frac{50.93 \times 10^6}{d^3}\right) \pm \left(\frac{161.05 \times 10^6}{d^3}\right)$$

$$\sigma_1 = \left(\frac{211.98 \times 10^6}{d^3}\right), \sigma_2 = \left(\frac{-110.12 \times 10^6}{d^3}\right)$$

$$\therefore \frac{700}{2} = \sqrt{\left(\frac{211.98 \times 10^6}{d^3}\right)^2 + \left(\frac{-110.12 \times 10^6}{d^3}\right)^2 - \left[2 \times 0.25 \times \left(\frac{211.98 \times 10^6}{d^3}\right)\left(\frac{-110.12 \times 10^6}{d^3}\right)\right]}$$

$$350 = \left(\frac{262.17 \times 10^6}{d^3}\right)$$

$\therefore \quad d = 90.82$ mm

$\therefore$ Standard shaft diameter = 100 mm $\qquad \ldots$ **Tb. 3.5(a)/ Pg 57, DHB**

32. **A MS shaft of 50 mm diameter is subjected to a bending moment of 2 kN·m and a torque 'T'. If the yield point of steel in simple tension is 200 MPa, find the value of this torque according: a. MSST, b. DET.**

Solution: $d = 50$ mm, $M = 2 \times 10^6$ N·mm, $\sigma_e = 200$ MPa, torque, $T = ?$, a. MSST, b. DET.

- Bending stress, $\sigma_b = \dfrac{M}{Z} = \dfrac{32M}{\pi d^3} = \dfrac{32(2 \times 10^6)}{\pi \times 50^3} = 163$ MPa $\ldots$ **1.1(b)/ Pg 2, DHB**

- Shear stress, $\tau = \dfrac{16T}{\pi d^3} = \dfrac{16 \times T}{\pi \times 50^3} = (40.74 \times 10^{-6})T$ MPa

$\qquad \ldots$ **1.1(d)/ Pg 2, DHB**

State of stress: Here $\sigma_x = \sigma_b = 163$ MPa; $\sigma_y = 0$; $\tau = \tau_{xy} = (40.74 \times 10^{-6})$ T MPa

a. **According to MSST:**

For design $\qquad \dfrac{\sigma_e}{n} = \sqrt{(\sigma_x - \sigma_y)^2 + 4\tau_{xy}^2} \qquad \ldots$ **2.8(c)/ Pg 22, DHB**

$$\sigma_e = \sqrt{(\sigma_x - \sigma_y)^2 + 4\tau_{xy}^2} \quad \text{(Assume } n = 1, \text{ if not given)}$$

$$200 = \sqrt{(163^2 + [4 \times (40.74 \times 10^{-6}T)^2]}$$

$$= \sqrt{26569 + (6.64 \times 10^{-9})T^2}$$

$$\therefore \qquad 200^2 = 26569 + (6.64 \times 10^{-9})T^2$$

$$T = 1.42 \times 10^6 \text{ N·mm} = 1.42 \text{ kN·m}$$

b. According to DET:

For design $\quad \dfrac{\sigma_e}{n} = \sqrt{\sigma_x^2 + \sigma_y^2 - \sigma_x\sigma_y + 3\tau_{xy}^2}$ $\qquad$ **... 2.8(d)/ Pg 22, DHB**

$\sigma_e = \sqrt{\sigma_x^2 + \sigma_y^2 - \sigma_x\sigma_y + 3\tau_{xy}^2}$ (Assume $n = 1$, if not given)

$200 = \sqrt{(163^2 + 0 - 0 + [3 \times (40.74 \times 10^{-6}T)^2]}$

$= \sqrt{26569 + (4.98 \times 10^{-9})T^2}$

$\therefore \qquad 200^2 = 26569 + (4.98 \times 10^{-9})T^2$

$T = 1.64 \times 10^6$ N·mm $= 1.64$ kN·m

33. **A mild steel shaft 60 mm diameter is subjected to a bending moment of 25 × 10⁵ N·mm and torque M_t. If the yield point of steel in tension is 230 N/mm², find the maximum value of this torque without causing yielding of the shaft according to:**
    a. **Maximum principal stress theory of failure**
    b. **Maximum shear stress theory of failure**
    c. **Maximum distortion energy theory of failure.**

    Adopt a factor of safety of 1.5

VTU – Mar. 2001 – 14 Marks; Dec. 2014/ Jan. 2015 – 10 Marks

Solution: $d = 60$ mm, $M = 25 \times 10^5$ N·mm, $\sigma_e = 230$ MPa, $n = 1.5$, torque $M_t = ?$, a. MNST, b. MSST, c. DET.

Bending stress $\qquad \sigma_b = \dfrac{32M}{\pi d^3} = \dfrac{32(25 \times 10^5)}{\pi \times 60^3} = 117.90$ MPa $\quad$ **... 1.1(b)/ Pg 2, DHB**

Shear stress, $\qquad \tau = \dfrac{16T}{\pi d^3} = \dfrac{16T}{\pi \times 60^3} = (2.36 \times 10^{-5})T$ $\quad$ **... 1.1(d)/ Pg 2, DHB**

State of stress $\quad \sigma_x = \sigma_b = 117.90$ MPa, $\sigma_y = 0$ and $\tau_{xy} = (2.36 \times 10^{-5})T$

a. According to MNST:

For design $\quad \dfrac{\sigma_e}{n} = \left(\dfrac{\sigma_x + \sigma_y}{2}\right) + \sqrt{\left(\dfrac{\sigma_x + \sigma_y}{2}\right)^2 + \tau_{xy}^2}$ $\qquad$ **... 2.8(a)/ Pg 21, DHB**

$\dfrac{230}{1.5} = \left(\dfrac{117.90 + 0}{2}\right) + \sqrt{\left(\dfrac{117.90 + 0}{2}\right)^2 + (2.36 \times 10^{-5}T)^2}$

$153.33 = 58.95 + \sqrt{58.95^2 + (2.36 \times 10^{-5}T)^2}$

$94.38 = \sqrt{3475.10 + (5.57 \times 10^{-10})T^2}$

$\therefore \qquad 94.38^2 = 3475.10 + (5.57 \times 10^{-10})T^2$

$T = M_t = 3.12 \times 10^6$ N·mm $= 3.12$ kN·m

b. According to MSST:

For design $\quad \dfrac{\sigma_e}{n} = \sqrt{(\sigma_x + \sigma_y)^2 + 4\tau_{xy}^2}$ $\qquad$ **... 2.8(c)/ Pg 22, DHB**

$$\frac{230}{1.5} = \sqrt{117.90^2 + [4 \times (2.36 \times 10^{-5}T)^2]}$$

$$153.33 = \sqrt{13900.41 + (2.23 \times 10^{-9})T^2}$$

$$\therefore \qquad 153.33^2 = 13900.41 + (2.23 \times 10^{-11})T^2$$

$$T = 2.08 \times 10^6 \text{ N·mm} = 2.08 \text{ kN·m}$$

c. **According to DET:**

For design $\qquad \dfrac{\sigma_e}{n} = \sqrt{\sigma_x^2 + \sigma_y^2 - \sigma_x\sigma_y + 3\tau_{xy}^2}$ $\qquad$ ... **2.8(d)/ Pg 22, DHB**

$$\sigma_e = \sqrt{\sigma_x^2 + \sigma_y^2 - \sigma_x\sigma_y + 3\tau_{xy}^2}$$

$$\frac{230}{1.5} = \sqrt{117.90^2 + 0 - 0 + \left[3 \times (2.36 \times 10^{-5}T)^2\right]}$$

$$153.33 = \sqrt{13900.41 + (1.67 \times 10^{-9})T^2}$$

$$\therefore \qquad 153.33^2 = 13900.41 + (1.67 \times 10^{-9})T^2$$

$$T = 1.64 \times 10^6 \text{ N·mm} = 1.64 \text{ kN·m}$$

34. **A round rod of diameter 30 mm is to sustain an axial compressive load of 20 kN and twisting moment of 1.5 kN·m. The rod is made of carbon steel C40 ($\sigma_{yt} = 328.6$ MPa). Determine the factor of safety as per the following theories of failure:**
   i. **Maximum principal strain theory**
   ii. **Maximum elastic strain energy theory**
   iii. **Maximum shear stress theory of failure.**

VTU – May/ June 2010 – 08 Marks; July 2006 – 08 Marks; (Similar) July/Aug. 2005 – 08 Marks; (Similar) June 2012 – 10 Marks

Solution: $d = 30$ mm, $F = -20$ kN $= -20 \times 10^3$ N, $T = 1.5$ kN·m, $\sigma_y = \sigma_e = 328.6$ MPa, $n = ?$

- Axial stress, $\qquad \sigma_D = \dfrac{F}{A} = \dfrac{-20 \times 10^3}{\pi \times 30^2/4} = -28.29$ MPa $\qquad$ ... **1.1(a)/ Pg 2, DHB**

- Shear stress, $\qquad \tau = \dfrac{16T}{\pi d^3} = \dfrac{16 \times (1.5 \times 10^6)}{\pi \times 30^3} = 282.94$ MPa

$\qquad\qquad\qquad\qquad\qquad\qquad\qquad\qquad\qquad$ ... **1.1(d)/ Pg 2, DHB**

State of stress: Here $\sigma_x = \sigma_D = -28.29$ MPa; $\sigma_y = 0$; $\tau = \tau_{xy} = 282.94$ MPa

i. **Maximum principal strain theory:**

For design $\quad \dfrac{\sigma_e}{n} = (1 - \mu)\left(\dfrac{\sigma_x + \sigma_y}{2}\right) + \left[(1 + \mu)\sqrt{\left(\dfrac{\sigma_x - \sigma_y}{2}\right)^2 + \tau_{xy}^2}\right]$

$\qquad\qquad\qquad\qquad\qquad\qquad\qquad\qquad\qquad$ ... **2.8(b) / Pg 21, DHB**

$$\frac{328.6}{n} = (1 - 0.25) \times \left(\frac{-28.29 + 0}{2}\right)$$

$$+ \left[(1 + 0.25) \times \sqrt{\left(\frac{-28.29 - 0}{2d^2}\right)^2 + 282.94^2}\right] \quad \text{(Assume } \mu = 0.25\text{)}$$

$$\frac{328.6}{n} = 343.50$$

$$\therefore \qquad n = 0.956$$

ii. Maximum shear stress theory:

For design $\qquad \dfrac{\sigma_e}{n} = \sqrt{(\sigma_1^2 - \sigma_2^2 - 2\mu\sigma_1\sigma_2)}$ $\qquad$ ... **2.8(e) / Pg 22, DHB**

$$\sigma_{1,2} = \left(\frac{\sigma_x + \sigma_y}{2}\right) \pm \sqrt{\left(\frac{\sigma_x + \sigma_y}{2}\right)^2 + \tau_{xy}^2} \quad ... \textbf{1.8(c) \& (d)/ Pg 5, DHB}$$

$$= \left(\frac{-28.29 + 0}{2}\right) \pm \sqrt{\left(\frac{-28.29 - 0}{2}\right)^2 + 282.94^2}$$

$$= -14.15 \pm 283.30$$

$$\therefore \qquad \sigma_1 = 269.15 \text{ MPa}, \sigma_2 = -297.44 \text{ MPa}$$

$$\therefore \qquad \frac{328.6}{n} = \sqrt{(269.15)^2 + (-297.44)^2 - [2 \times 0.25 \times (269.15) \times (-297.44)]}$$

$$\frac{328.6}{n} = 448.26$$

$$n = 0.733$$

iii. Maximum strain theory:

For design $\qquad \dfrac{\sigma_e}{n} = \sqrt{(\sigma_x - \sigma_y)^2 + 4\tau_{xy}^2}$ $\qquad$ ... **2.8(c) / Pg 22, DHB**

$$\frac{328.6}{n} = \sqrt{(-28.29 - 0)^2 + 4(282.94)^2}$$

$$\frac{328.6}{n} = 566.60$$

$$\therefore \qquad n = 0.580 \text{ MPa}$$

35. **A rotating shaft of diameter 16 mm shown in Fig. 2.25 is subjected to axial tensile load of 5000 N, a steady torque of 50 N·m and a maximum bending moment of 75 N·m. Assume $\sigma_y = 350$ MPa and $\sigma = 0.3$. Calculate the factor of safety based on**
   a. **Maximum normal stress theory**
   b. **Maximum shear stress theory.**

   VTU – Dec. 2009/ Jan 2010 – 10 Marks: (Similar) July 2007 – 08 Marks

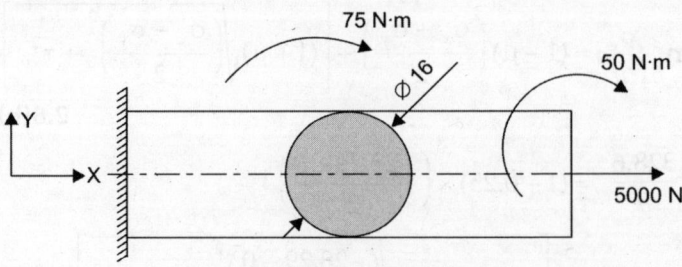

Fig. 2.25: Problem 35

Solution: $d = 16$ mm, $F = 5000$ N, $T = 50$ N·m $= 50 \times 10^3$ N·mm, $M = 75$ N·m $= 75 \times 10^3$ N·mm, $n = ?$

- Axial stress, $\sigma_D = \dfrac{F}{A} = \dfrac{5000}{\pi \times 16^2/4} = 24.86$ MPa   ... 1.1(a)/ Pg 2, DHB

- Bending stress, $\sigma_b = \dfrac{M}{Z} = \dfrac{32M}{\pi d^3} = \dfrac{75 \times 10^3}{\pi \times 16^3/32} = 186.51$ MPa

   ... 1.1(b)/ Pg 2, DHB

- Shear stress, $\tau = \dfrac{16T}{\pi d^3} = \dfrac{16 \times (50 \times 10^6)}{\pi \times 16^3} = 62.17$ MPa

   ... 1.1(d)/ Pg 2, DHB

Resultant stress: $\sigma_x = \sigma_D + \sigma_b = 24.86 + 186.51 = 211.37$ MPa

State of stress: Here $\sigma_x = 211.37$ MPa; $\sigma_y = 0$; $\tau = \tau_{xy} = 62.17$ MPa

a. **Maximum normal stress theory:**

For design $\dfrac{\sigma_e}{n} = \left(\dfrac{\sigma_x + \sigma_y}{2}\right) + \sqrt{\left(\dfrac{\sigma_x - \sigma_y}{2}\right)^2 + \tau_{xy}^2}$ ... 2.8(a) / Pg 21, DHB

$\dfrac{350}{n} = \left(\dfrac{211.37 + 0}{2}\right) + \sqrt{\left(\dfrac{211.37 - 0}{2}\right)^2 + 62.17^2}$

$\dfrac{350}{n} = 228.30$

$\therefore \qquad n = 1.53$

b. **Maximum shear stress theory:**

For design $\dfrac{\sigma_e}{n} = \sqrt{(\sigma_x - \sigma_y)^2 + 4\tau_{xy}^2}$ ... 2.8(c) / Pg 22, DHB

$\therefore \qquad \dfrac{350}{n} = \sqrt{(211.37 - 0)^2 + (4 \times 62.17^2)}$

$\dfrac{350}{n} = 245.22$

$n = 1.43$

36. **The state of plane stress occurs at critical point of a steel member for which the tensile yield strength is 250 MPa, as shown in Fig. 2.26. Determine the factor of safety (FoS) using: a. MSST b. DET.**

Solution: $\sigma_{yt} = \sigma_e = 250$ MPa, $n = ?$, $\sigma_x = 80$ MPa, $\sigma_y = -40$ MPa (comp.), $\tau_{xy} = 25$ MPa.

a. **Maximum normal stress theory:**

For design $\dfrac{\sigma_e}{n} = \sqrt{(\sigma_x - \sigma_y)^2 + 4\tau_{xy}^2}$ ... 2.8(c) / Pg 21, DHB

$\dfrac{250}{n} = \sqrt{[80 - (-40)]^2 + [4 \times 25^2]}$

$\dfrac{250}{n} = 130$

$\therefore \qquad n = 1.923$

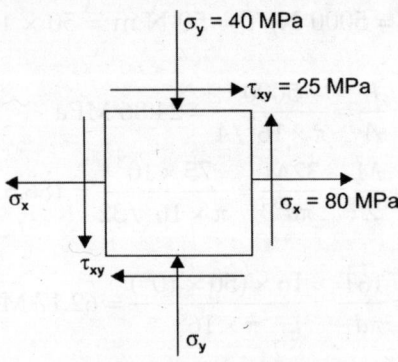

Fig. 2.26: Problem 36

b. **DET:**

For design $\qquad \dfrac{\sigma_e}{n} = \sqrt{\sigma_x^2 + \sigma_y^2 - \sigma_x\sigma_y + 3\tau_{xy}^2}$ $\qquad$ ... **2.8(d) / Pg 22, DHB**

$\therefore \qquad \dfrac{250}{n} = \sqrt{80^2 + (-40)^2 - [80 \times (-40)] + [3 \times 25^2]}$

$\dfrac{250}{n} = 114.35$

$n = 2.186$

37. **The stresses induced at a critical point in a machine component made of 45C8 with yield strength (σ_{yt}) of 380 MPa are as follows: σ_x = 100 MPa, σ_y = 40 MPa, τ_{xy} = 80 MPa. Calculate factor of safety by:**

i. **The maximum normal stress theory**

ii. **The maximum shear stress theory**

iii. **The distortion energy theory.**

VTU – Dec. 2012 – 10 Marks; (similar) June/ July 2008 – 06 Marks; (Similar) Dec. 2013/ Jan 2014 – 08 Marks

Solution: $\sigma_{yt} = \sigma_e$ = 380 MPa, σ_x = 100 MPa, σ_y = 40 MPa, τ_{xy} = 80 MPa, n = ?

i. **Maximum normal stress theory:**

For design $\qquad \dfrac{\sigma_e}{n} = \left(\dfrac{\sigma_x + \sigma_y}{2}\right) + \sqrt{\left(\dfrac{\sigma_x - \sigma_y}{2}\right)^2 + \tau_{xy}^2}$ $\qquad$ ... **2.8(a) / Pg 21, DHB**

$\dfrac{380}{n} = \left(\dfrac{100 + 40}{2}\right) + \sqrt{\left(\dfrac{100 - 40}{2}\right)^2 + 80^2}$

$\dfrac{380}{n} = 155.44$

$\therefore \qquad n = 2.44$

ii. **Maximum shear stress theory:**

For design $\quad \dfrac{\sigma_e}{n} = \sqrt{(\sigma_x - \sigma_y)^2 + 4\tau_{xy}^2} \qquad$ ... **2.8(c) / Pg 22, DHB**

$\therefore \qquad \dfrac{380}{n} = \sqrt{(100-40)^2 + (4 \times 80^2)}$

$\dfrac{380}{n} = 170.88$

$n = 2.22$

iii. **DET:**

For design $\quad \dfrac{\sigma_e}{n} = \sqrt{\sigma_x^2 + \sigma_y^2 - \sigma_x\sigma_y + 3\tau_{xy}^2} \qquad$ ... **2.8(d) / Pg 22, DHB**

$\therefore \qquad \dfrac{380}{n} = \sqrt{100^2 + 40^2 - (100 \times 40) + (3 \times 80^2)}$

$\dfrac{380}{n} = 163.71$

$n = 2.32$

38. **A machine member is statically loaded and has a yield strength of 350 MPa. For each of the stress state indicated below, find the factor of safety according to:**
    a. **Maximum normal stress theory**
    b. **Maximum shear stress theory**
    c. **Maximum distortion energy theory.**
       i. $\sigma_1 = 70$ MPa, $\sigma_2 = 70$ MPa
       ii. $\sigma_1 = 70$ MPa, $\sigma_2 = 35$ MPa
       iii. $\sigma_1 = 70$ MPa, $\sigma_2 = -70$ MPa
       iv. $\sigma_1 = 70$ MPa, $\sigma_2 = 0$ MPa

VTU – Dec. 2011 – 12 Marks

Solution: $\sigma_e = 350$ MPa, $n = ?$

Case i: $\sigma_1 = 70$ MPa, $\sigma_2 = 70$ MPa
 a. **Maximum normal stress theory:**

For design $\quad \dfrac{\sigma_e}{n} = \left(\dfrac{\sigma_x + \sigma_y}{2}\right) + \dfrac{1}{2}\sqrt{(\sigma_x - \sigma_y)^2 + 4\tau^2} = \sigma_1$

... **2.8(a) / Pg 21, DHB**

i.e. $\qquad \dfrac{\sigma_e}{n} = \sigma_1$

$\dfrac{350}{n} = 70$

$\therefore \qquad n = 5.0$

 b. **Maximum shear stress theory:**

For design $\quad \dfrac{\sigma_e}{n} = \sigma_1 - \sigma_2 \qquad$ ... **2.8(c) / Pg 22, DHB**

$$\therefore \qquad \frac{350}{n} = (70 - 70)$$

$$\frac{350}{n} = 0$$

$$n = \infty \text{ (infinity)}$$

c. Distortion energy theory:

For design $\qquad \dfrac{\sigma_e}{n} = \sqrt{\sigma_1^2 + \sigma_2^2 - \sigma_1 \sigma_2}$ $\qquad$ ... 2.8(d) / Pg 22, DHB

$$\therefore \qquad \frac{350}{n} = \sqrt{70^2 + 70^2 - (70 \times 70)}$$

$$\frac{350}{n} = 70$$

$$n = 5.0$$

On similar lines, we have

Case		Factor of safety (N)	
Stresses: $\sigma_1 > \sigma_2$	MNST	MSST	DET
$\sigma_1 = 70$ MPa, $\sigma_2 = 35$ MPa	5.00	10.00	5.77
$\sigma_1 = 70$ MPa, $\sigma_2 = -70$ MPa	5.00	2.50	2.89
$\sigma_1 = 0$ MPa, $\sigma_2 = -70$ MPa (rearranged)	infinity	5.00	5.00

39. **A hot rolled steel has a yield strength of $\sigma_{yt} = \sigma_{yc} = 690$ MPa. Estimate the factor of safety for the following principal stresses using:**
    a. MSST
    b. DET
        i. 480, 480, 0
        ii. 210, 480, 0
        iii. 0, 480, –210
        iv. 0, –210, –480
        v. 210, 210, 210

Solution: $\sigma_{yt} = \sigma_{yc} = \sigma_e = 690$ MPa, $n = ?$

Case i: $\sigma_1 = 480, \sigma_2 = 480, \sigma_3 = 0$ (*arrangement* $\sigma_1 > \sigma_2 > \sigma_3$)

a. According to maximum shear stress theory:

For design $\qquad \dfrac{\sigma_e}{n} = \sigma_1 - \sigma_3$ $\qquad$ ... 2.8(c) / Pg 22, DHB

$$\therefore \qquad \frac{690}{n} = (480 - 0)$$

$$n = 1.438$$

b. According to distortion energy theory:

For design $\qquad \dfrac{\sigma_e}{n} = \sqrt{\sigma_1^2 + \sigma_2^2 + \sigma_3^2 - (\sigma_1\sigma_2 + \sigma_2\sigma_3 + \sigma_1\sigma_3)}$ $\qquad$ ...using (Eq. 2.32a)

$$\therefore \qquad \frac{690}{n} = \sqrt{480^2 + 480^2 + 0 - [(480 \times 480) + 0 + 0]}$$

$$n = 1.438$$

On similar lines, we have

Case		
		Factor of safety (N)
Arrangement ($\sigma_1 > \sigma_2 > \sigma_3$)	MSST	DET
480, 210, 0	1.438	1.656
480, 0, –210	1.0	1.126
0, –210, –480	1.438	1.656
210, 210, 210	infinity	infinity

40. **A material has a yield strength of 600 MPa. Compute the factor of safety for each of the failure theories for ductile material. Use following stress states.**
    i. $\sigma_1 = 420$ MPa $\sigma_2 = 410$ MPa $\sigma_3 = 0$ MPa
    ii. $\sigma_1 = 420$ MPa $\sigma_2 = 180$ MPa $\sigma_3 = 0$ MPa
    iii. $\sigma_1 = 420$ MPa $\sigma_2 = 0$ MPa $\sigma_3 = -180$ MPa
    iv. $\sigma_1 = 0$ MPa $\sigma_2 = -180$ MPa $\sigma_3 = -420$ MPa

    VTU – Jan/ Feb. 2005 – 12 Marks; (Similar) Dec. 06/ Jan. 2007 – 10 Marks

Solution: $\sigma_y = \sigma_e = = 600$ MPa, $n = ?$
For ductile materials the *distortion theory* gives accurate results. However, *maximum shear stress theory* is also preferred as it gives results on safer side.
Case i: $\sigma_1 = 420$, $\sigma_2 = 410$, $\sigma_3 = 0$ MPa (*arrangement* $\sigma_1 > \sigma_2 > \sigma_3$)
   a. **According to maximum shear stress theory:**

For design $\dfrac{\sigma_e}{n} = \sigma_1 - \sigma_3$ ... 2.8(c) / Pg 22, DHB

$$\therefore \qquad \frac{600}{n} = (420 - 0)$$

$$n = 1.429$$

   b. **According to distortion energy theory:**

For design $\dfrac{\sigma_e}{n} = \sqrt{\sigma_1^2 + \sigma_2^2 + \sigma_3^2 - (\sigma_1\sigma_2 + \sigma_2\sigma_3 + \sigma_1\sigma_3)}$ ...using (Eq. 2.32a)

$$\therefore \qquad \frac{600}{n} = \sqrt{420^2 + 410^2 + 0 - (420 \times 410) + 0 + 0}$$

$$n = 1.445$$

On similar lines, we have

Case		
		Factor of safety (N)
Arrangement ($\sigma_1 > \sigma_2 > \sigma_3$)	MSST	DET
420, 180, 0	1.429	1.644
480, 0, –180	1	1.125
0, –180, –420	1.429	1.644

41. **A material is tested under a state of stress $\sigma_1 = 3\sigma_2 = -2\sigma_3$. Yielding is observed at $\sigma_2 = 140$ MPa.**
    a. **What is the yield stress in simple tension?**
    b. **If the material is tested under the condition $\sigma_1 = -\sigma_3$, and $\sigma_2 = 0$, under what value of σ_3 will yielding occur?**

Solution: $\sigma_1 = 3\sigma_2 = -2\sigma_3$, $\sigma_2 = 140$ MPa.

a. **To find σ_e:** According to DET, failure/yielding occurs when

$$(\sigma_1 - \sigma_2)^2 + (\sigma_2 - \sigma_3)^2 + (\sigma_3 - \sigma_1)^2 \geq 2\sigma_e^2 \qquad \text{...Eq. (i)}$$

From data, $\quad \sigma_1 = 3\sigma_2 = -2\sigma_3$ and $\sigma_2 = 140$ MPa

i.e. $\quad\quad\quad \sigma_1 = 3 \times 140 = 420$ MPa

and $\quad\quad\quad \sigma_3 = -210$ MPa

Eq. (i) yields... $(420 - 140)^2 + (140 + 210)^2 + (-210 - 420)^2 \geq 2\sigma_e^2$

$$\sigma_e = 546.72 \text{ MPa}$$

b. **To find σ_3, if $\sigma_1 = -\sigma_3$ and $\sigma_2 = 0$**

Eq. (i) yields... $(-\sigma_1 - 0)^2 + (0 - \sigma_3)^2 + (\sigma_3 + \sigma_3)^2 \geq 2\sigma_e^2$

$$6\sigma_3^2 = 2 \times 546.72^2$$

$$\sigma_3 = 315.65 \text{ MPa}$$

2.8 STRESS CONCENTRATION

The formulas dealt till now for computing simple stresses due to direct tensile and compressive forces, bending moments, and torsional moments are applicable to members having uniform cross-section. But in actual practice it is difficult to design a machine without permitting some changes in the cross-sections of the members.

For example:
- Rotating shafts are stepped to different diameters to accommodate gears, bearings, pulleys, etc.
- The shafts should have keyways machined into them for securing the gears and pulleys.
- A bolt has a head at one end and screw threads at the other end, both of which are abrupt changes in cross-section.
- Other factors include openings, cavities, cracks, grooves, incisions, corners, protrusions, sharp edges, or engraving, as well as various surface irregularities, such as notches, scratches, markings, and irregularities of welded seams.

Failure of machines and structures always initiate at sites of local stress concentration caused by geometrical or microstructural discontinuities. Thus, any discontinuity in a machine part alters the stress distribution in the neighbourhood of the discontinuity and the elementary stress equations no longer holds good in the neighbourhood of the discontinuity. Such discontinuities are called **stress raisers or notches**, and the regions in which they occur are called areas of **stress concentration**. These stress concentrations or stress raisers often lead to local stresses many times higher than the stresses obtained by elementary equations.

Stress concentration is defined as the localization of high stresses due to abrupt changes in the cross-section of the component or the condition where high localized stresses are produced due to abrupt change in geometry is called stress concentration.

In order to consider the effect of stress concentration and determine the localized stresses, a factor called stress concentration factor K_t is used. It is given as

$$K_t = \frac{\text{maximum stress}}{\text{nominal stress}} = \frac{\sigma_{max}}{\sigma} \qquad \text{... Eq. (2.37)}$$

where
  K_t = theoretical elastic stress concentration factor for normal stress (tension or bending)
  σ_{max} = maximum stress at the notch
   σ = Nominal stress

- For direct stress, $\sigma_{max} = \sigma K_t = \left(\dfrac{F}{A}\right) K_t$

$$\text{... (Eq. 2.38) } \textbf{2.1(a)/ Pg 20, DHB [Fig. 2.1(a)/ Pg 20, DHB]}$$

- For bending, $\sigma_{max} = \sigma_b K_t = \left(\dfrac{M}{Z}\right) K_t$

$$\text{... (Eq. 2.39) } \textbf{2.1(b)/ Pg 20, DHB [Fig. 2.1(b)/ Pg 20, DHB]}$$

- For torsion, $\tau_{max} = \tau K_s = \left(\dfrac{Tr}{J}\right) K_s = \left(\dfrac{T}{z_p}\right) K_s$

$$\text{... (Eq. 2.40) } \textbf{2.1(c)/ Pg 20, DHB [Fig. 2.1(c)/ Pg 20, DHB]}$$

  K_s = theoretical elastic stress concentration factor for shear stress.

2.8.1 Characteristics of Stress Concentration Factor
- K_t is a function of the geometry or shape of the part, but not its size or material.
- K_t is a function of the type of loading applied to the part (axial, bending or torsional).
- K_t is a function of the specific geometric stress raiser in the part (e.g. fillet radius, notch, or hole).
- K_t is always defined with respect to a particular nominal stress.
- K_t typically assumes a linear elastic, homogeneous, isotropic material.

Stress concentration charts
- **Fig. 2.2/Pg 21, DHB** *gives form stress factor due to hole in narrow plate.*
- **Fig. 2.9/Pg 30, DHB** *gives stress concentration factor for a plate with a hole in tension.*
- **Fig. 2.10/Pg 30, DHB** *gives form factor ratio due to notches of various shapes.*
- **Fig. 2.11/Pg 36, DHB** *gives stress concentration for an elliptical hole in a plate.*
- **Fig. 2.12/Pg 36, DHB** *gives stress concentration factor for a plate with a hole in tension.*
- **Fig. 2.13/Pg 37, DHB** *gives stress concentration factor for a flat bar with a transverse hole in bending.*
- **Fig. 2.14/Pg 37, DHB** *gives stress concentration factor for a notched flat bar in tension.*
- **Fig. 2.15/Pg 38, DHB** *gives stress concentration factor for a notched flat bar in bending.*

- Fig. 2.16/Pg 38, DHB *gives stress concentration factor for a stepped flat bar in tension.*
- Fig. 2.17/Pg 39, DHB *gives stress concentration factor for a stepped flat bar in bending.*
- Fig. 2.18/Pg 39, DHB *gives stress concentration factor for a grooved shaft in tension.*
- Fig. 2.20/Pg 40, DHB *gives stress concentration factor for a grooved shaft in bending.*
- Fig. 2.22/Pg 41, DHB *gives stress concentration factor (K_s) for a grooved shaft in torsion.*
- Fig. 2.23/Pg 42, DHB *gives stress concentration factor for a stepped shaft in tension.*
- Fig. 2.25/Pg 43, DHB *gives stress concentration factor for a stepped shaft in bending.*
- Fig. 2.27/Pg 44, DHB *gives stress concentration factor (K_s) for a stepped shaft in torsion.*
- Fig. 2.28/ Pg 44, DHB *gives stress concentration factor for a shaft with transverse hole.*

2.9 STRESS CONCENTRATION IN CONTRAST TO DUCTILE AND BRITTLE MATERIALS UNDER STATIC LOADING

Under static loading, the effect of stress concentration is well defined in a brittle material than that in a ductile material.

- In ductile materials, stress concentrations are relatively unimportant since yielding which occurs at the concentration, e.g. tip of a notch, will merely redistribute the stresses and not necessarily lead to failure. Thus a ductile material loaded statically will not develop full theoretical stress concentration factor. Hence, it is common to ignore the effects of geometric stress concentration in ductile materials under static loading. However, appreciable stress concentration effects will occur under fatigue conditions of alternating stresses.
- Brittle materials will not yield locally, since they do not have a plastic range. Thus, stress concentrations have a greater effect on their behavior even under static loads. Once the stress at the stress raiser (notch, hole) exceeds the fracture strength, a crack begins to form. This reduces the material available to resist the load and also increases the stress concentration in the narrow crack, thereby leading to failure of the material.

It is to be noted that, in static loading and ductile behavior, stress concentrations are harmless as they only create small localized yielding which do not lead to any objectionable dimensional changes.

2.10 DETERMINATION OF STRESS CONCENTRATION FACTOR

Stress concentration factor may also be obtained using any one of the following *experimental* techniques.

- Finite element method
- Strain gauge method
- Photo elasticity method
- Brittle coating technique
- Grid method

Finite element method is the most powerful method made in the field of CAD. Here the member is first divided into a large number of finite elements (triangles and rectangles) of different sizes. Starting from the known loading and boundary configurations as well as constraints, a computer analysis is made and iterated until all conditions are satisfied.

This method requires the knowledge of matrices and linear elasticity and familiarity with computer language.

Photo elasticity method is the most dependable and widely used method of determining stresses at a point. A transparent material having double refraction properties, when stressed, is cut into the same shape as the part whose stresses are desired. The model is placed in a loading frame, and a beam of polarized light is directed through it onto a photographic plate or screen. When the model is loaded, fringes of colored light originate at the points of maximum stress and when the load is increased, move from the edges of image towards the center. A certain stress is associated with each fringe so that one can determine the stresses at the edges merely by counting the fringes as they originate.

Brittle coating method employs a plaster (lacquer). A uniform layer of stress coat is sprayed on to the part under carefully controlled temperature and humidity conditions. After the lacquer has dried up, load is applied to the part causing tiny cracks to form at all areas of high tensile stress. The directions of cracks are always perpendicular to the direction of tensile stresses, because the lacquer is brittle and fails in tension. The first crack formed on the part is the region of highest tensile stress. As load is increased further, other cracks form indicating the areas of lower stress. Each specimen is loaded until fracture occurs and the respective loads are compared to obtain the stress concentration factor.

Grid method consists of drawing a grid of lines on the part. In order to form a grid, two sets of equally spaced lines at right angles to each other may be used or a series of concentric circles intersected by radial lines is employed. The part is placed under a known load and the change in line spacing is used to map the strain. After the strains are mapped, the stresses are calculated using biaxial stress–strain relations.

2.11 METHODS OF REDUCING STRESS CONCENTRATION

A number of methods are available to reduce stress concentration in machine parts. Some of them are as follows.

- Provide a fillet radius at shoulders so that the cross-section may change gradually [Fig. 2.27].

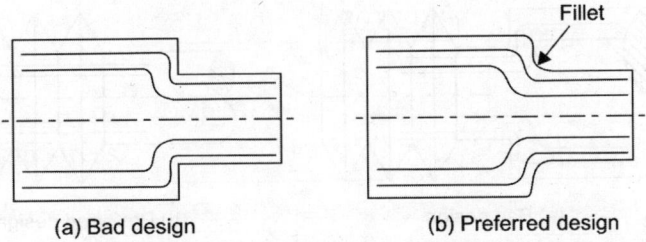

(a) Bad design (b) Preferred design

Fig. 2.27: Use of filters at shoulders

- Using multiple holes in place of a single hole [Fig. 2.28].
- If a notch is unavoidable it is better to provide a number of small notches rather than a long one. This reduces the stress concentration to a large extent. [Fig. 2.29].

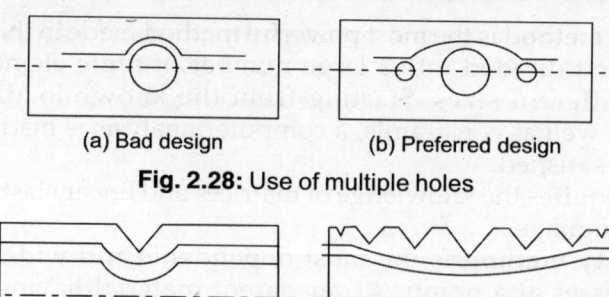

(a) Bad design   (b) Preferred design

Fig. 2.28: Use of multiple holes

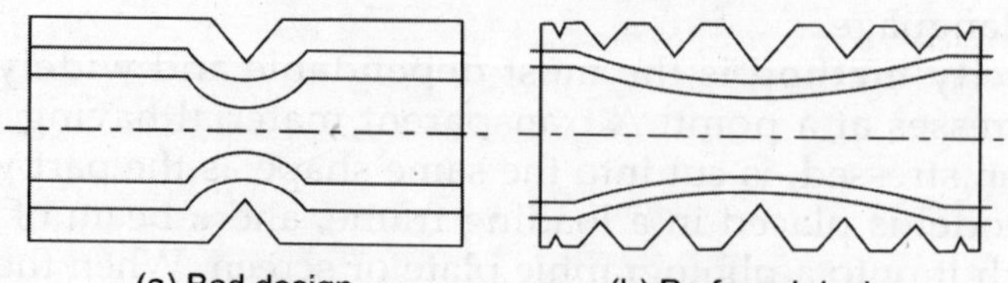

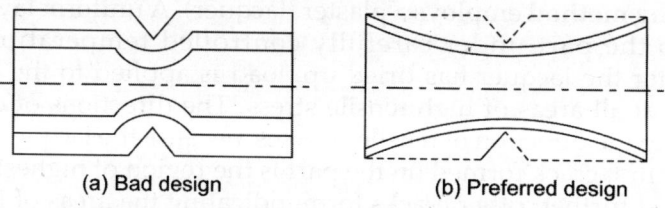

(a) Bad design   (b) Preferred design

Fig. 2.29: Use of multiple notches

- Removal of unwanted material [**Fig. 2.30**].

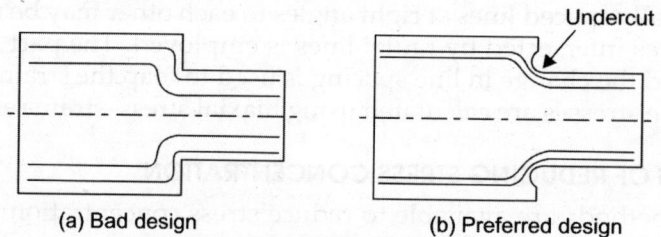

(a) Bad design   (b) Preferred design

Fig. 2.30: Removal of unwanted material

- Use of undercuts [**Fig.2.31**].

Undercut

(a) Bad design   (b) Preferred design

Fig. 2.31: Use of undercuts

- Reduced shank diameter for threaded members [**Fig. 2.32**].

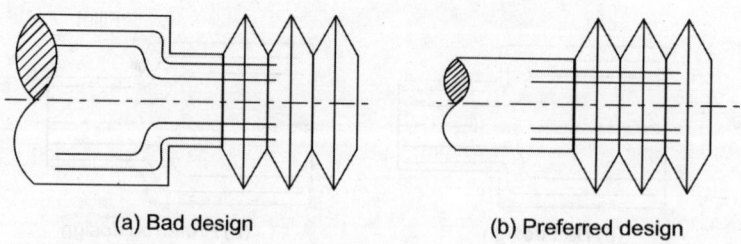

(a) Bad design   (b) Preferred design

Fig. 2.32: Reduced shank diameter for threaded members

Problems on stresses

42. Find the maximum stress induced in the following cases, if concentration factor is taken into account.

a. Rectangular plate 60 mm × 10 mm with a hole of 12 mm and subjected to tensile load of 12 kN.

b. A shaft of diameter 50 mm, stepped down to diameter 25 mm having fillet radius of 5 mm and subjected to a tensile load of 12 kN.

VTU – Jan/ Feb. 2006 –08 Marks, (Similar) June/July 2013 – 07 Marks

Solution: σ_{max} = ?

Case a: Rectangular plate with a hole in tension: Comparing **Fig. 2.33a** with **Fig. 2.12/Pg 36, DHB**, we have $F = 12$ kN, $B = 60$ mm, $t = 10$ mm, $a = 12$ mm

For axial load, $\qquad \sigma_{max} = \left(\dfrac{F}{A}\right) K_t$ $\qquad\qquad$ ... Eq. (i) **2.1(a)/Pg 20, DHB**

Area, $\qquad\qquad A = (B - a)t = (60 - 12) \times 10 = 480$ mm^2

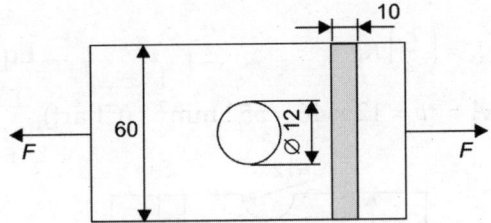

Fig. 2.33a: Problem 42

Now $\qquad\qquad \dfrac{a}{B} = \dfrac{12}{60} = 0.2$

At $\qquad\qquad \dfrac{a}{B} = 0.2$, we have $K_t = 2.55$

$\therefore$ Eq. (i) yields... $\quad \sigma_{max} = \left(\dfrac{12 \times 10^3}{480}\right) \times 2.55 = 63.75$ MPa

Case b: Stepped shaft with fillet in axial loading: Comparing **Fig. 2.33(b)** with **Fig. 2.23/ Pg 42, DHB**, we have $F = 12$ kN, $D = 50$ mm, $d = 25$ mm, $r = 5$ mm

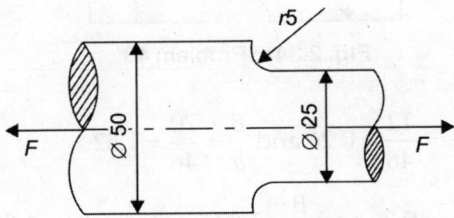

Fig. 2.33b: Problem 42

Here $\qquad\qquad A = \dfrac{\pi d^2}{4} = \dfrac{\pi \times 25^2}{4} = 490.87$ mm^2 (Chart)

Now $\qquad\qquad \dfrac{r}{d} = \dfrac{5}{25} = 0.2$ and $\dfrac{D}{d} = \dfrac{50}{25} = 2$

At $\qquad\qquad \dfrac{r}{d} = 0.2$, and $\dfrac{D}{d} = 2$, we have $K_t = 1.65$

∴ Eq. (i) yields... $\sigma_{max} = \left(\dfrac{12 \times 10^3}{490.87}\right) \times 1.65 = 40.33$ MPa

43. **A rectangular plate with semi-circular groove of radius 12 mm, as shown in Fig. 2.34 is subjected to:**
    a. **Tensile force of 10 kN**
    b. **BM of 15 N·m.**
    Determine the maximum stress induced in each case.

VTU – Dec. 06/ Jan. 2007 – 10 Marks

Solution: $\sigma_{max} = ?$, $F = 10$ kN, $M = 15$ N·m

Case a: Rectangular plate with a semi-circular groove in tension: Comparing **Fig. 2.34(a)** with **Fig. 2.14/ Pg 37, DHB**, we have $B = 70$ mm, $r = 12$ mm, $b = B - 2r = 46$ mm, $t = 12$ mm, $F = 10$ kN

For axial load, $\sigma_{max} = \left(\dfrac{F}{A}\right) K_t$ ... Eq. (i) **2.1(a)/Pg 20, DHB**

Area, $A = tb = 12 \times 46 = 552$ mm^2 (Chart)

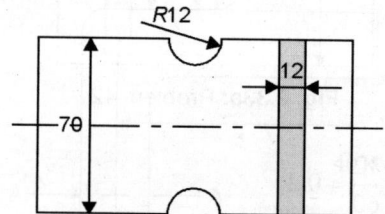

Fig. 2.34: Problem 43

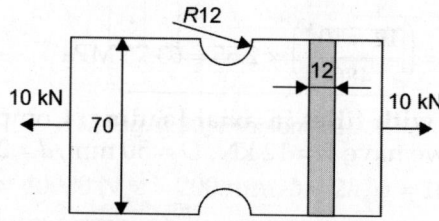

Fig. 2.34a: Problem 43

Now $\dfrac{r}{b} = \dfrac{12}{46} = 0.26$ and $\dfrac{B}{b} = \dfrac{70}{46} = 1.52$

At $\dfrac{r}{b} = 0.26$ and $\dfrac{B}{b} = 1.52$, we have $K_t = 1.53$

∴ Eq. (i) yields... $\sigma_{max} = \left(\dfrac{10 \times 10^3}{552}\right) \times 1.86 = 33.70$ MPa

Case b: Rectangular plate with a semi-circular groove subjected to bending moment: Comparing **Fig. 2.34(b)** with **Fig. 2.15/ Pg 38, DHB**, we have $B = 70$ mm, $r = 12$ mm, $b = B - 2r = 46$ mm, $t = 12$ mm, $M = 15$ N·m

For bending load, $\sigma_{max} = \left(\dfrac{Mc}{I}\right) K_t$ ... Eq. (ii) **2.1(b)/Pg 20, DHB**

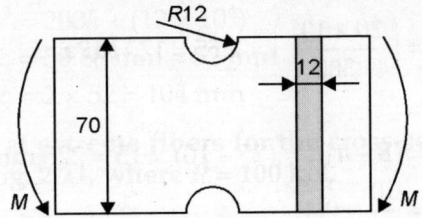

Fig. 2.34b: Problem 43

But
$$\frac{I}{c} = \frac{tb^2}{6} = \frac{12 \times 46^2}{6} = 4232 \text{ mm}^3 \quad \text{(Chart)}$$

Now
$$\frac{r}{b} = \frac{12}{46} = 0.26 \quad \text{and} \quad \frac{B}{b} = \frac{70}{36} = 1.52$$

At
$$\frac{r}{b} = 0.26, \text{ and } \frac{D}{b} = 1.52, \text{ we have } K_t = 1.53$$

$\therefore$ Eq. (ii) yields... $\sigma_{max} = \left(\dfrac{15 \times 10^3}{4232}\right) \times 1.53 = 5.42 \text{ MPa}$

44. **A rectangular plate 15 mm thick made of a brittle material is shown in Fig. 2.35. Calculate the stresses at each of three holes.**

VTU – Jan/ Feb. 2005 – 08 Marks

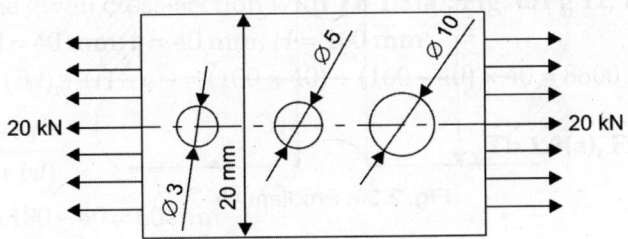

Fig. 2.35: Problem 44

Solution: $\sigma_{max} = ?$, $t = 15$ mm. Comparing **Fig. 2.35** with **Fig. 2.12/ Pg 36, DHB**, we have $F = 20$ kN, $B = 25$ mm, $t = 15$ mm, $a_1 = 3$ mm, $a_2 = 5$ mm, $a_3 = 10$ mm.

For axial load, $\sigma_{max} = \left(\dfrac{F}{A}\right) K_t$ ... Eq. (i) **2.1(a)/Pg 20, DHB**

Case 1: $a_1 = 3$ mm

Here $A = (B - a_1)t = (25 - 3) \times 15 = 330 \text{ mm}^2$ (Chart)

Now $\dfrac{a_1}{B} = \dfrac{3}{25} = 0.12$

At $\dfrac{a_1}{B} = 0.12$, we have $K_t = 2.7$

$\therefore$ Eq. (i) yields... $\sigma_{max} = \left(\dfrac{20 \times 10^3}{330}\right) \times 2.7 = 163.44 \text{ MPa}$

Case 2: $a_2 = 5$ mm

Here $A = (B - a_2)t = (25 - 5) \times 15 = 300 \text{ mm}^2$ (Chart)

Now $\dfrac{a_2}{B} = \dfrac{5}{25} = 0.2$; At $\dfrac{a_2}{B} = 0.2$, we have $K_t = 2.55$

∴ Eq. (i) yields... $\sigma_{max} = \left(\dfrac{20 \times 10^3}{300}\right) \times 2.55 = 170$ MPa

Case 3: $a_3 = 10$ mm

Here $\qquad A = (B - a_3)t = (25 - 10) \times 15 = 225$ mm² (Chart)

Now $\qquad \dfrac{a_3}{B} = \dfrac{10}{25} = 0.4$

At $\qquad \dfrac{a_3}{B} = 0.4$, we have $K_t = 2.25$

∴ Eq. (i) yields... $\sigma_{max} = \left(\dfrac{12 \times 10^3}{225}\right) \times 2.25 = 200$ MPa

45. **Determine the maximum stress induced in the semi-grooved shaft as shown in Fig. 2.36 if it is subjected to:**
    a. **An axial load of 40 kN**
    b. **A bending moment of 400 N·m**
    c. **A twisting moment of 500 N·m**
    Take stress concentration into account.

    VTU – Dec. 2009/ Jan 2010 – 10 Marks

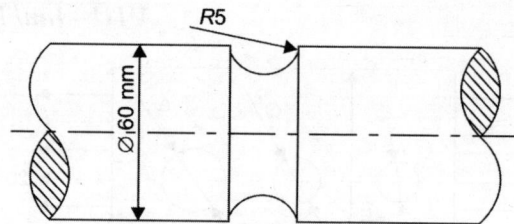

Fig. 2.36: Problem 45

Solution:
Case a: An axial load of 40 kN. Comparing **Fig. 2.36(a)** with **Fig. 2.18/ Pg 39, DHB**, we have $F = 40$ kN, $D = 60$ mm, $r = 5$ mm, $d = D - 2r = 50$ mm.

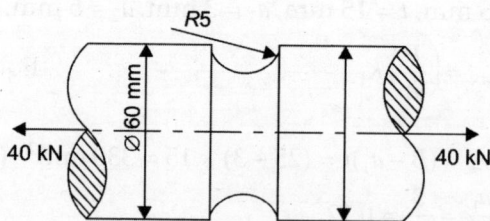

Fig. 2.36a: Problem 45

For axial load, $\qquad \sigma_{max} = \left(\dfrac{F}{A}\right)K_t$ $\qquad\qquad$ ... Eq. (i) **2.1(a)/Pg 20, DHB**

Here $\qquad A = \dfrac{\pi d^2}{4} = \dfrac{\pi \times 50^2}{4} = 1963.50$ mm²

Now $\qquad \dfrac{r}{d} = \dfrac{5}{50} = 0.1$ and $\dfrac{D}{d} = \dfrac{60}{50} = 1.2$

At $\qquad \dfrac{r}{d} = 0.1$, and $\dfrac{D}{d} = 1.2$, we have $K_t = 2.18$

$\therefore$ Eq. (i) yields... $\sigma_{max} = \left(\dfrac{40 \times 10^3}{1963.50}\right) \times 2.18 = 55.41$ MPa

Case b: A bending moment of 400 N·m. Comparing Fig. 2.36(b) with Fig. 2.20/ Pg 40, DHB, we have $M = 400$ N·m, $D = 60$ mm, $r = 5$ mm, $d = D - 2r = 50$ mm

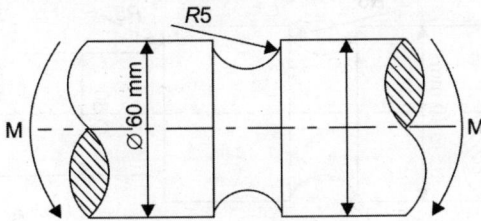

Fig. 2.36b: Problem 45

For bending load, $\sigma_{max} = \left(\dfrac{Mc}{I}\right) K_t$ $\qquad$ ... Eq. (ii) **2.1(b)/Pg 20, DHB**

But $\qquad \dfrac{I}{c} = \dfrac{\pi d^3}{32} = \dfrac{\pi \times 50^3}{32} = 12271.85$ mm^3 (Chart)

Now $\qquad \dfrac{r}{d} = \dfrac{5}{50} = 0.1$ and $\dfrac{D}{d} = \dfrac{60}{50} = 1.2$

At $\qquad \dfrac{r}{d} = \dfrac{5}{50} = 0.1$ and $\dfrac{D}{d} = \dfrac{60}{50} = 1.2$, we have $K_t = 1.88$

$\therefore$ Eq. (ii) yields... $\sigma_{max} = \left(\dfrac{400 \times 10^3}{12271.85}\right) \times 1.88 = 61.28$ MPa

Case c: A twisting moment of 500 N·m. Comparing Fig. 2.36(c) with Fig. 2.22/ Pg 41, DHB, we have $T = 500$ N·m, $D = 60$ mm, $r = 5$ mm, $d = D - 2r = 50$ mm

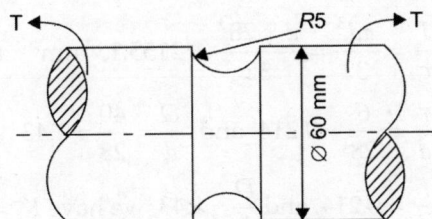

Fig. 2.36c: Problem 45

For torsion, $\qquad \tau_{max} = \left(\dfrac{T}{Z_p}\right) K_s$ $\qquad$ ... Eq. (iii) **2.1(c)/Pg 20, DHB**

but $\qquad Z_p = \dfrac{\pi d^3}{16} = \dfrac{\pi \times 50^3}{16} = 24543.70$ mm^2 (Chart)

Now $\qquad \dfrac{r}{d} = \dfrac{5}{50} = 0.1$ and $\dfrac{D}{d} = \dfrac{60}{50} = 1.2$

At $\qquad \dfrac{r}{d} = 0.1$, and $\dfrac{D}{d} = 1.2$, we have $K_s = 1.52$

$\therefore$ Eq. (iii) yields... $\sigma_{max} = \left(\dfrac{500 \times 10^3}{24543.70}\right) \times 1.52 = 30.97$ MPa

46. A shaft as shown in Fig. 2.37 is subjected to BM of 550 N·m, determine the maximum stress.

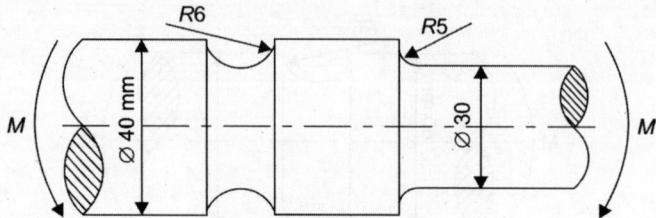

Fig. 2.37: Problem 46

Solution: $M = 550$ N·m, $\sigma_{max} = ?$ Here the stresses are critical at two sections: Shoulder and fillet.

Case a: Shoulder section: [Fig. 2.37(a)]: Comparing **Fig. 2.37(a)** with **Fig. 2.20/Pg 40, DHB**, we have $M = 550$ N·m, $D = 40$ mm, $r = 6$ mm, $d = D - 2r = 28$ mm.

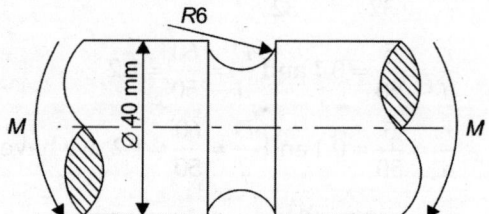

Fig. 2.37a: Problem 46

For bending load, $\sigma_{max} = \left(\dfrac{Mc}{I}\right) K_t$ $\qquad$ ... Eq. (i) **2.1(b)/Pg 20, DHB**

But $\qquad \dfrac{I}{c} = \dfrac{\pi d^3}{32} = \dfrac{\pi \times 28^3}{32} = 2155.13$ mm³ (Chart)

Now $\qquad \dfrac{r}{d} = \dfrac{6}{28} = 0.214$ and $\dfrac{D}{d} = \dfrac{40}{28} = 1.43$

At $\qquad \dfrac{r}{d} = 0.214$, and $\dfrac{D}{b} = 1.43$, we have $K_t = 1.55$

$\therefore$ Eq. (i) yields... $\sigma_{max} = \left(\dfrac{15 \times 10^3}{4232}\right) \times 1.53 = 5.42$ MPa

Case b: Fillet section [Fig. 2.37(b)]: Comparing **Fig. 2.37(b)** with **Fig. 2.25/ Pg 43, DHB**, we have $D = 40$ mm, $r = 5$ mm, $d = 30$ mm

Here $\qquad \dfrac{I}{c} = \dfrac{\pi d^3}{32} = \dfrac{\pi \times 30^3}{32} = 2650.72$ mm³ (Chart)

Now $\qquad \dfrac{r}{d} = \dfrac{5}{30} = 0.167$ and $\dfrac{D}{d} = \dfrac{40}{30} = 1.34$

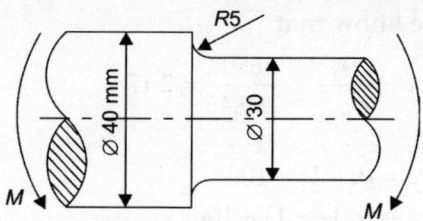

Fig. 2.37b: Problem 46

At $\dfrac{r}{d} = 0.167$, and $\dfrac{D}{b} = 1.34$, we have $K_t = 1.47$

$\therefore$ Eq. (i) yields... $\sigma_{max} = \left(\dfrac{550 \times 10^3}{2650.72}\right) \times 1.47 = 305$ MPa

Therefore taking higher value, we have $\sigma_{max} = 395.56$ MPa, i.e. maximum stress occurs in shoulder.

47. **A shaft as shown in Fig. 2.38 is subjected to a bending moment of 1.5 kN·m. Determine the maximum stress induced in the shaft.**
    Also find the factor of safety if the yield stress of the material is 650 MPa. What is the margin of safety?

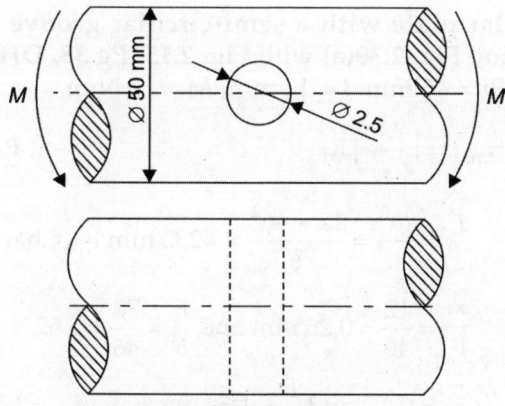

Fig. 2.38: Problem 47

Solution: $M = 1.5$ kN·m, $\sigma_{max} = ?$, $n = ?$, margin of safety = ?

Comparing **Fig. 2.38** with **Fig. 2.28/Pg 44, DHB**, we have $D = 50$ mm, $a = 2.5$ mm

For bending load, $\sigma_{max} = \left(\dfrac{Mc}{I}\right) K_t$ ... Eq. (i) **2.1(b)/Pg 20, DHB**

But $\dfrac{I}{c} = \dfrac{\pi D^3}{32} = \dfrac{\pi \times 50^3}{32} = 12271.85$ mm^3 (Chart)

At $\dfrac{a}{D} = 0.05$, we have $K_t = 2.45$

$\therefore$ Eq. (i) yields... $\sigma_{max} = \left(\dfrac{15 \times 10^6}{12271.85}\right) \times 2.45 = 299.46$ MPa

b. **Factor of safety:** We know that

$$n = \frac{\sigma_y}{\sigma_{max}} = \frac{650}{299.46} = 2.17$$

c. **Margin of safety:**

Margin of safety $= (n - 1) \times 100$

$= (2.17 - 1) \times 100$

∴ Margin of safety $= 117\%$

48. **Find the maximum stress induced in the following cases shown in Figs 2.39(a) and (b) taking stress concentration into account.**

Dec. 2014 - Jan 2015 – 08 Marks

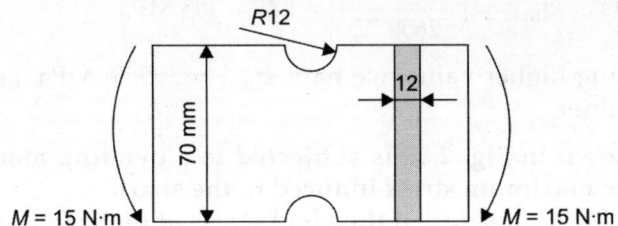

Fig. 2.39a: Problem 48

Case a: Rectangular plate with a semi-circular groove subjected to bending moment: Comparing **Fig. 2.39(a)** with **Fig. 2.15/ Pg 38, DHB**, we have $B = 70$ mm, $r = 12$ mm, $b = B = 2r = 46$ mm, $t = 12$ mm, $M = 15$ N·m

For bending load, $\sigma_{max} = \left(\dfrac{Mc}{I}\right) K_t$ … Eq. (i) **2.1(b)/Pg 20, DHB**

But $\dfrac{I}{c} = \dfrac{tb^2}{6} = \dfrac{12 \times 46^2}{6} = 4232 \text{ mm}^3$ (Chart)

Now $\dfrac{r}{b} = \dfrac{12}{46} = 0.26$ mm and $\dfrac{B}{b} = \dfrac{70}{46} = 1.52$

At $\dfrac{r}{b} = 0.26$, and $\dfrac{B}{b} = 1.52$, we have $K_t = 1.53$

∴ Eq. (i) yields... $\sigma_{max} = \left(\dfrac{15 \times 10^3}{4232}\right) \times 1.53 = 5.42$ MPa

Case b: Stepped shaft subjected to torque: Comparing **Fig. 2.39(b)** with **Fig. 2.27/ Pg 44, DHB**, we have $T = 400$ N·m, $D = 60$ mm, $r = 5$ mm, $d = 30$ mm

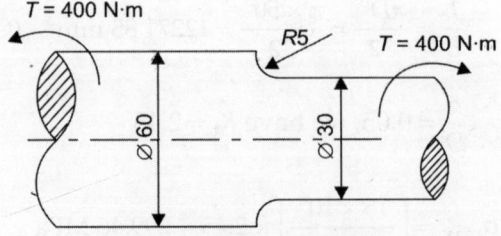

Fig. 2.39b: Problem 48

For torsion, $\tau_{max} = \left(\dfrac{T}{Z_p}\right) K_s$ ... Eq. (ii) **2.1(c)/Pg 20, DHB**

but $Z_p = \dfrac{\pi d^3}{16} = \dfrac{\pi \times 30^3}{16} = 5301.44 \text{ mm}^2$ (Chart)

Now $\dfrac{r}{d} = \dfrac{5}{30} = 0.17$ and $\dfrac{D}{d} = \dfrac{60}{30} = 2$

At $\dfrac{r}{d} = 0.17$, and $\dfrac{D}{d} = 2$, we have $K_s = 1.28$

$\therefore$ Eq. (ii) yields... $\tau_{max} = \left(\dfrac{400 \times 10^3}{5301.44}\right) \times 1.28 = 96.56 \text{ MPa}$

PROBLEMS ON LOAD

49. **Determine the maximum tensile load that a flat 25 mm × 3 mm can carry if it has a central hole of 10 mm diameter and $\sigma_{max} = 120$ MPa.**

VTU – Dec. 08/ Jan. 2009 – 12 Marks

Solution: $F = ?$, $\sigma_{max} = 120 \text{ MPa}$

Figure 2.40 represents the given condition of the problem.

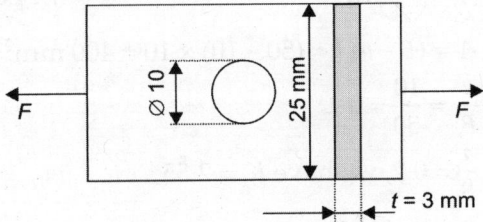

Fig. 2.40: Problem 49

Comparing **Fig. 2.40** with **Fig. 2.12/ Pg 36, DHB**, we have $F = ?$, $B = 25$ mm, $t = 3$ mm, $a = 10$ mm

For axial load, $\sigma_{max} = \left(\dfrac{F}{A}\right) K_t$ ... Eq. (i) **2.1(a)/Pg 20, DHB**

$A = (B - a)\, t = (25 - 10) \times 3 = 45 \text{ mm}^2$

Now $\dfrac{a}{B} = \dfrac{10}{25} = 0.4$

At $\dfrac{a}{B} = 0.4$, we have $K_t = 2.25$

$\therefore$ Eq. (i) yields... $120 = \left(\dfrac{F}{45}\right) \times 2.25$

$F = 2400 \text{ N}$

50. **Determine the safe load that can be carried by a bar of rectangular cross-section shown in Fig. 2.41 limiting the maximum stress to 130 MPa and taking stress concentration into account.**

VTU – Dec. 2013/ Jan 2014 – 06 Marks, July 2006 – 10 Marks.

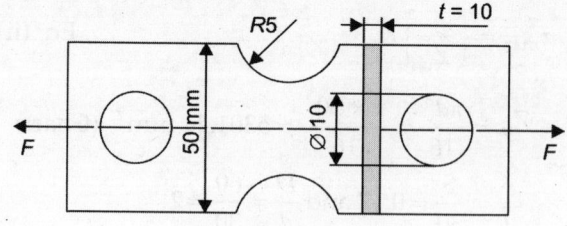

Fig. 2.41: Problem 50

Solution: $F = ?$, $\sigma_{max} = 130$ MPa

Case 1: Plate with hole: Comparing **Fig. 2.41(a)** with **Fig. 2.12/ Pg 36, DHB**, we have $F = ?$, $B = 50$ mm, $t = 10$ mm, $a = 10$ mm

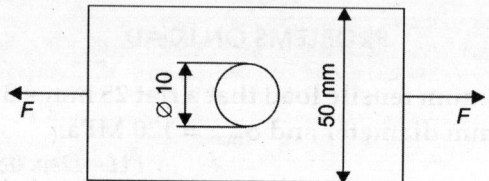

Fig. 2.41a: Problem 50

For axial load, $\qquad \sigma_{max} = \left(\dfrac{F}{A}\right) K_t \qquad\qquad$ … Eq. (i) **2.1(a)/Pg 20, DHB**

$$A = (B - a)\, t = (50 - 10) \times 10 = 400 \text{ mm}^2$$

Now $\qquad\qquad \dfrac{a}{B} = \dfrac{10}{50} = 0.2$

At $\qquad\qquad \dfrac{a}{B} = 0.2$, we have $K_t = 2.55$

$\therefore$ Eq. (i) yields... $\quad 130 = \left(\dfrac{F}{400}\right) \times 2.55$

$$F = 20392 \text{ N}$$

Case 2: Plate with notch: Comparing **Fig. 2.41(b)** with **Fig. 2.14/ Pg 37, DHB**, we have $B = 50$ mm, $r = 5$ mm, $b = D - 2r = 40$ mm, $t = 10$ mm.

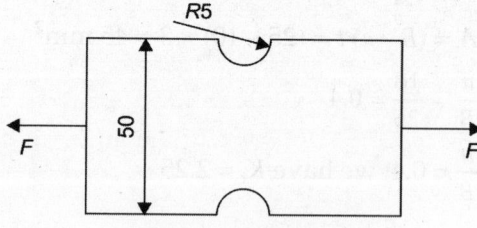

Fig. 2.41b: Problem 50

Here area, $\qquad A = tb = 10 \times 40 = 400 \text{ mm}^2$

Now $\qquad \dfrac{r}{b} = \dfrac{5}{50} = 0.125$ and $\dfrac{B}{b} = \dfrac{50}{40} = 1.25$

At $\qquad \dfrac{r}{b} = 0.125$, and $\dfrac{B}{b} = 1.25$, we have $K_t = 2.25$

$\therefore$ Eq. (i) yields... $130 = \left(\dfrac{F}{400}\right) \times 2.25$

$F = 23111.11$ N

Thus, the safe load carried by the bar is $F = 20392.16$ N (Lower value).

51. **A shaft shown in Fig. 2.42 is subjected to a load W. Determine the load such that the maximum stress is limited to 250 MPa.**

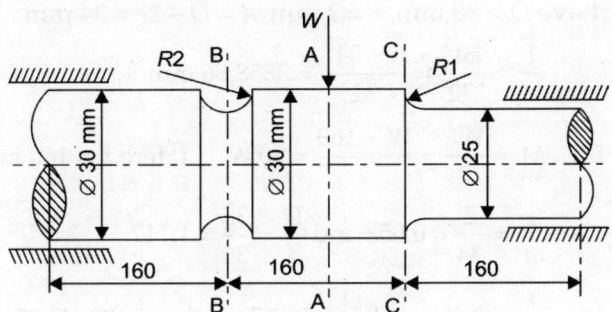

Fig. 2.42: Problem 51

Solution: $W = ?$, $\sigma_{max} = 250$ MPa.

The given shaft acts like a simply supported beam subjected to point load at mid-span, as shown in **Fig. 2.42(a)**, thereby causing a bending moment as shown in **Fig. 2.42(b)**.

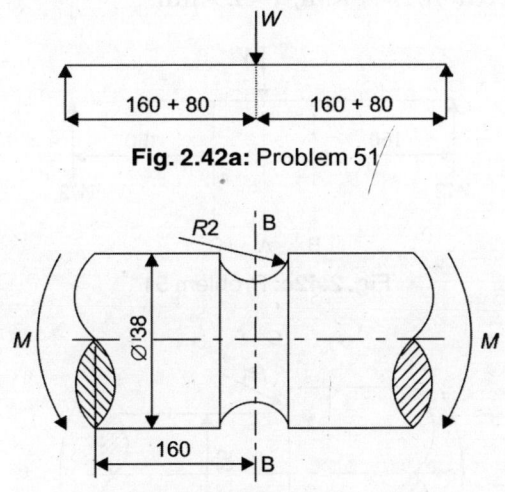

Fig. 2.42a: Problem 51

Fig. 2.42b: Problem 51

Case 1: Bending moment at section A – A: For a SS beam with central load,

$$M = \frac{WL}{4} = \frac{W \times (160 \times 3)}{4} = 120\,W$$

... **Tb 1.4, (Fig. 4)/ Pg 15, DHB**

For bending load, $\sigma_{max} = \left(\dfrac{Mc}{I}\right) K_t$

... Eq. (i) **2.1(b)/Pg 20, DHB**

But
$$\frac{I}{c} = \frac{\pi d^3}{32} = \frac{\pi \times 38^3}{32} = 5387.05 \text{ mm}^3 \quad \text{(Chart)}$$

$\therefore$ Eq. (i) yields... $\sigma_{max} = \left(\dfrac{120\,W}{5387.05}\right) \times 1$ [since diameter is uniform at A – A, $K = 1$]

$$\sigma_{max} = 0.022\,W \qquad \qquad \text{... Eq. (ii)}$$

Case 2: Section B – B, shaft with groove: Comparing **Fig. 2.42(b)** with **Fig. 2.20/ Pg 40, DHB**, we have $D = 38$ mm, $r = 2$ mm, $d = D - 2r = 34$ mm

Here
$$\frac{I}{c} = \frac{\pi d^3}{32} = \frac{\pi \times 34^3}{32} = 3858.66 \text{ mm}^3$$

and
$$M = \frac{WL}{2} = \frac{W \times 160}{2} = 80\,W \quad \text{(Here } L = 160 \text{ mm at B–B)}$$

Now
$$\frac{r}{d} = \frac{2}{34} = 0.058 \text{ and } \frac{D}{d} = \frac{38}{34} = 1.117$$

At
$$\frac{r}{d} = 0.058 \text{ and } \frac{D}{d} = 1.117, \text{ we have, } K_t = 2.25$$

$\therefore$ Eq. (i) yields... $\sigma_{max} = \left(\dfrac{80W}{3858.66}\right) \times 2.25$

$$\sigma_{max} = 0.047\,W \qquad \qquad \text{... Eq. (iii)}$$

Case 3: Section C – C, stepped shaft: Comparing **Fig. 2.42(d)** with **Fig. 2.25/ Pg 43, DHB**, we have $D = 38$ mm, $r = 1$ mm, $d = 25$ mm.

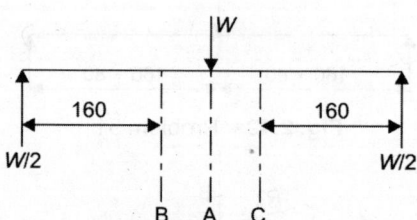

Fig. 2.42c: Problem 51

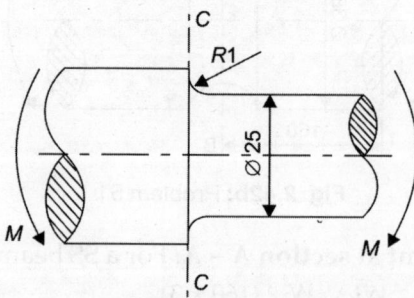

Fig. 2.42d: Problem 51

Here
$$\frac{I}{c} = \frac{\pi d^3}{32} = \frac{\pi \times 25^3}{32} = 1534 \text{ mm}^3$$

and $\qquad M = \dfrac{WL}{2} = \dfrac{W \times 160}{2} = 80\,W$

$\qquad\qquad\qquad$ [here $L = 160$ mm from RHS to section C–C]

Now $\qquad \dfrac{r}{d} = \dfrac{1}{25} = 0.04$ and $\dfrac{D}{d} = \dfrac{38}{25} = 1.52$

At $\qquad \dfrac{r}{d} = 0.04$, and $\dfrac{D}{d} = 1.52$, we have $K_t = 2.21$

$\therefore$ Eq. (i) yields... $\sigma_{max} = \left(\dfrac{80W}{1534}\right) \times 2.21$

$\qquad\qquad \sigma_{max} = 0.1153\,W$ $\qquad\qquad\qquad\qquad$ ... Eq. (iv)

Therefore, σ_{max} is the largest of Eqs. (ii), (iii) and (iv), i.e. Eq. (iii) yields...

$\qquad\qquad \sigma_{max} = 0.1153\,W$

$\qquad\qquad 250 = 0.1153\,W$

$\therefore \qquad\qquad W = 2169.12$ N

PROBLEMS ON THICKNESS

52. **A flat plate subjected to a tensile force of 5 kN is shown in Fig. 2.43. The plate material is grey cast iron having $\sigma_u = 200$ MPa. Determine the thickness of the plate. Factor of safety is 2.5.**

VTU – May/ June 2010 – 08 Marks; June/ July 14 – 07 Marks

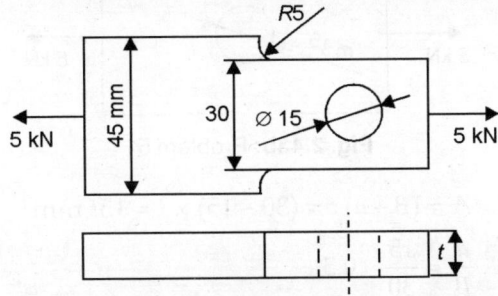

Fig. 2.43: Problem 52

Solution: $F = 5$ kN, $\sigma_u = 200$ MPa, $n = 2.5$, $t = ?$

We know that, $\qquad n = \dfrac{\sigma_u}{\sigma_{max}}$

$\qquad\qquad \sigma_{max} = \dfrac{200}{2.5}$

$\qquad\qquad\qquad = 80$ MPa

$\quad$ **Case 1: Fillet section: Figure 2.43(a):** Comparing **Fig. 2.43(a)** with **Fig. 2.16/ Pg 38, DHB**, we have $B = 45$ mm, $b = 30$ mm, $r = 5$ mm

For axial load, $\qquad \sigma_{max} = \left(\dfrac{F}{A}\right) K_t$ $\qquad\qquad$ ... Eq. (i) **2.1(a)/Pg 20, DHB**

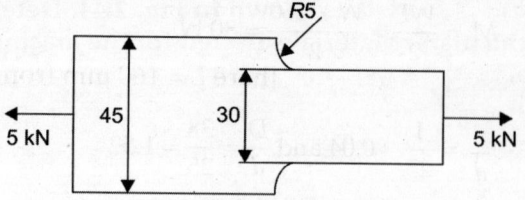

Fig. 2.43a: Problem 51

Area, $A = tb = t \times 30 = 30t \text{ mm}^2$

Now $\dfrac{r}{b} = \dfrac{5}{30} = 0.167$ and $\dfrac{B}{b} = \dfrac{45}{30} = 1.5$

At $\dfrac{r}{b} = 0.167$ and $\dfrac{B}{b} = 1.5$, we have $K_t = 1.8$

∴ Eq. (i) yields... $\sigma_{max} = \left(\dfrac{5000}{30t}\right) \times 1.8$

$$\sigma_{max} = \dfrac{300}{t}$$ ... Eq. (iv)

Case 2: Hole section: Fig 2.43(b): Comparing Fig. 2.43(b) with Fig. 2.12/ Pg 36, DHB, we have $F = 5000 \text{ N}$, $B = 30 \text{ mm}$, $a = 15 \text{ mm}$

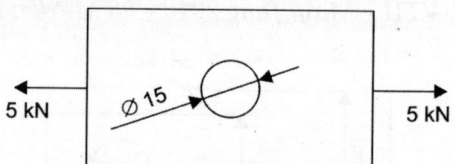

Fig. 2.43b: Problem 51

Here $A = (B - a)\, t = (30 - 15) \times t = 15t \text{ mm}^2$

Now $\dfrac{a}{B} = \dfrac{15}{30} = 0.5$

At $\dfrac{a}{B} = 0.5$, we have $K_t = 2.18$

∴ Eq. (i) yields... $\sigma_{max} = \left(\dfrac{5000}{15t}\right) \times 2.18$

$$\sigma_{max} = \dfrac{726.67}{t}$$ ... Eq. (ii)

Taking larger value of σ_{max} from Eqs. (ii) and (iii), we have

$$\sigma_{max} = \dfrac{726.67}{t}$$

$$80 = \dfrac{726.67}{t}$$

∴ $t = 9.08 \text{ mm} \approx 10 \text{ mm}$

53. **A machine element is loaded as shown in Fig. 2.44. Determine a safe value for the thickness of the plate. Material selected for the machine element has design stress of 200 MPa.**

VTU – Dec. 2009/ Jan 2010 – 10 Marks;(Similar) Dec. 2010 – 05 Marks

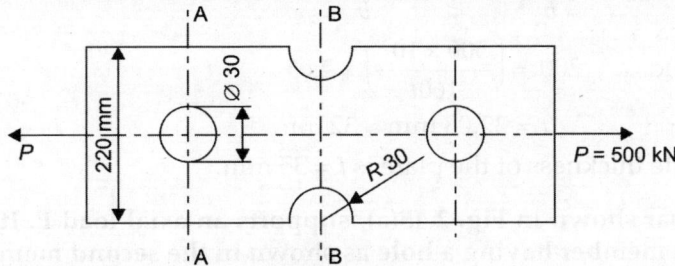

Fig. 2.44: Problem 53

Solution: $P = 500$ kN, $t = ?$ $\sigma_{max} = 200$ MPa

Case 1: Plate with hole: Comparing **Fig. 2.44(a)** with **Fig. 2.12/ Pg 36, DHB**, we have $P = F = 500$ kN, $B = 220$ mm, $a = 30$ mm, $t = ?$

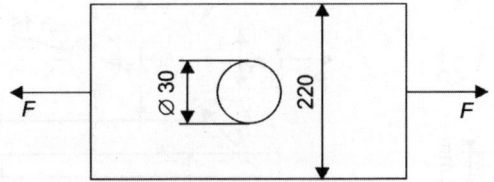

Fig. 2.44a: Problem 53

For axial load, $\qquad \sigma_{max} = \left(\dfrac{F}{A}\right) K_t$ $\qquad\qquad$ ... Eq. (i) **2.1(a)/Pg 20, DHB**

$$A = (B - a)\, t = (220 - 30) \times t = 190t$$

Now $\qquad \dfrac{a}{B} = \dfrac{30}{220} = 0.14$

At $\qquad \dfrac{a}{B} = 0.14$, we have $K_t = 2.65$

$\therefore$ Eq. (i) yields... $\quad 200 = \left(\dfrac{500 \times 10^3}{190}\right) \times 2.65$

$$t = 34.86 \text{ mm} \approx 35 \text{ mm}$$

Case 2: Plate with notch: Comparing **Fig. 2.44(b)** with **Fig. 2.14/ Pg 37, DHB**, we have $B = 220$ mm, $r = 30$ mm, $b = B - 2r = 160$ mm, $t = ?$

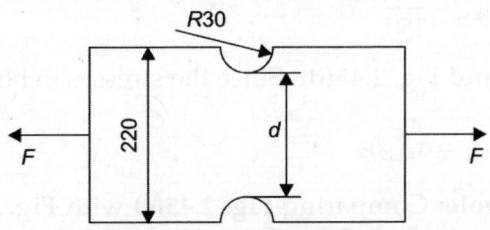

Fig. 2.44b: Problem 53

Here area, $A = tb = t \times 160 = 160t$

Now $\dfrac{r}{b} = \dfrac{30}{160} = 0.19$ and $\dfrac{D}{d} = \dfrac{220}{160} = 1.38$

At $\dfrac{r}{b} = 0.19$, and $\dfrac{B}{b} = 1.38$, we have $K_t = 2.05$

$\therefore$ Eq. (i) yields... $200 = \left(\dfrac{500 \times 10^3}{160t}\right) \times 2.05$

$$t = 32.03 \text{ mm} \approx 32 \text{ mm}$$

Thus, the safe thickness of the plate is $t = 35$ mm.

54. **A tension bar shown in Fig. 2.45(a), supports an axial load P. It is necessary to replace this member having a hole as shown in the second member. Determine the thickness 'h' and fillet radius 'r' at the member by one having a 15 mm hole as shown Fig. 2.45(b), so that, the maximum stress will not exceed that of the first member.**

VTU – Dec. 2011 – 08 Marks

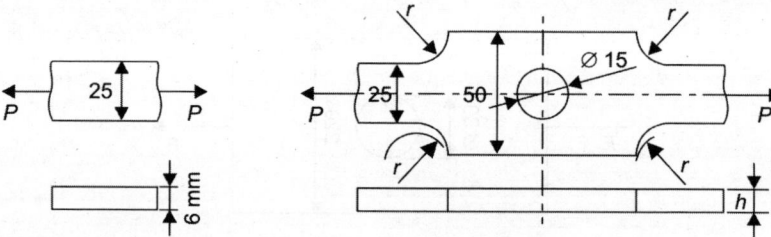

Fig. 2.45a: Problem 54   **Fig. 2.45b:** Problem 54

Solution: $h = ?$, $t = ?$

Plate 1: Fig. 2.45(a)

For axial load, $\sigma_{max} = \left(\dfrac{F}{A}\right) K_t$ ... Eq. (i) **2.1(a)/Pg 20, DHB**

Since the plate is uniform,

$$K_t = 1$$

Here $F = P$

$$\sigma_{max} = \left(\dfrac{P}{25 \times 6}\right) \times 1$$

$\therefore$ $\sigma_{max} = \dfrac{P}{150}$ ... Eq. (ii)

Plate 2: Fig. 2.45(b) and Fig. 2.45(d): Since the stresses in both the plates are same (data),

$$\sigma_{max})_1 = \sigma_{max})_2$$ ... Eq. (iiii)

Case 1: Plate with hole: Comparing **Fig. 2.45(c)** with **Fig. 2.12/ Pg 36, DHB**, we have $P = F$, $B = 50$ mm, $t = ?$, $a = 15$ mm

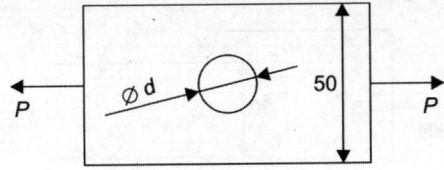

Fig. 2.45c: Problem 54

Eq. (i) yields $\quad \sigma_{max})_1 = \left(\dfrac{F}{A}\right) K_t$ $\hspace{4cm}$ ... Eq. (iv)

Here $\quad A = (B - a)t = (50 - 15) \times t = 35t$

Now $\quad \dfrac{a}{B} = \dfrac{15}{50} = 0.3$

At $\quad \dfrac{a}{B} = 0.3$, we have $K_t = 2.37$

$\therefore$ Eq. (i) yields... $\quad \dfrac{P}{150} = \left(\dfrac{P}{35t}\right) \times 2.37$ $\hspace{3cm}$ ... using Eq. (iii)

$\therefore$ $\hspace{3.5cm} t = 10.16$ mm

Case 2: Plate with fillet: Comparing **Fig. 2.45(d)** with **Fig. 2.16/ Pg 38, DHB**, we have $B = 50$ mm, $b = 25$ mm, $r = ?$

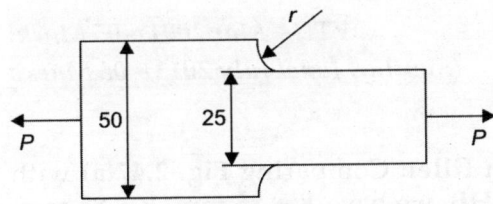

Fig. 2.45d: Problem 54

Eq. (i) yields... $\quad \sigma_{max})_2 = \left(\dfrac{F}{A}\right) K_t$ $\hspace{4cm}$ ... Eq. (v)

Here $\quad A = tb = 10.16 \times 25 = 254$ mm^2 $\;$ (Here $h = t$)

$\therefore$ Eq. (v) yields $\quad \dfrac{P}{150} = \left(\dfrac{P}{254}\right) \times K_t$ $\hspace{3cm}$ ... using Eq. (iii)

$\therefore$ $\hspace{3.5cm} K_t = 1.69$ mm

Now at $\quad K_t = 1.69 \;$ and $\; \dfrac{B}{b} = \dfrac{50}{25} = 2, \dfrac{r}{b} = 0.26$

$\therefore$ $\hspace{3.5cm} r = 0.26 \times 25 = 6.5$ mm

PROBLEMS ON DIAMETER

55. **A plate 10 mm thick is subjected to a tensile load of 25 kN as shown in Fig. 2.46. If the maximum stress in the plate is 150 MPa, determine the radius of the fillet.**

Solution: $\sigma_{max} = 150$ MPa.

Comparing **Fig. 2.46** with **Fig. 2.16/ Pg 38, DHB**, we have $F = 25$ kN, $t = 10$ mm, $B = 45$ mm, $b = 30$ mm, $r = ?$

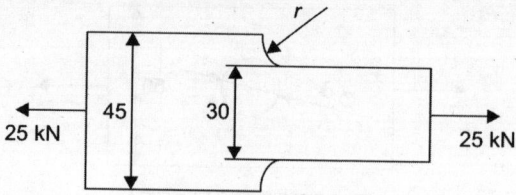

Fig. 2.46: Problem 55

For axial load, $\sigma_{max} = \left(\dfrac{F}{A}\right) K_t$ ... Eq. (i) **2.1(a)/Pg 20, DHB**

$$A = tb = 10 \times 30 = 300 \text{ mm}^2$$

∴ Eq. (i) yields... $150 = \left(\dfrac{25000}{300}\right) \times K_t$

∴ $K_t = 1.8$

At $K_t = 1.8$ and $\dfrac{B}{b} = \dfrac{45}{30} = 1.5$, we have $\dfrac{r}{b} = 0.17$

∴ $r = 0.17 \times 30 = 5.1 \text{ mm}$

56. **Find the diameter of the hole in Fig. 2.47, if the stress concentration factor at the hole is to be same as at the fillet.**

VTU – Mar 2001 – 05 Mark;
(Similar) June/ July 2013 – 06 Marks

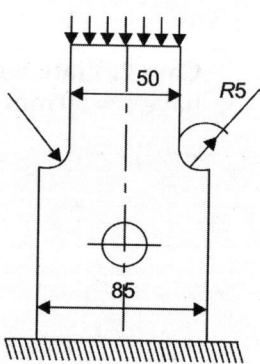

Solution: $d = ?$

Case 1: Plate with fillet: Comparing **Fig. 2.47(a)** with **Fig. 2.16/ Pg 38, DHB**, we have $B = 85$ mm, $b = 85$ mm, $b = 50$ mm, $r = 5$ mm

Fig. 2.47: Problem 56

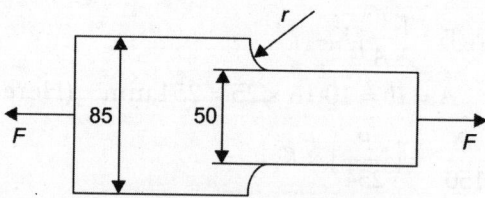

Fig. 2.47a: Problem 56

Now $\dfrac{r}{b} = \dfrac{5}{50} = 0.1$ and $\dfrac{B}{b} = \dfrac{85}{50} = 1.7$

At $\dfrac{r}{b} = 0.1$ and $\dfrac{B}{b} = 1.7$, we have $K_t = 2.18$

Case 2: Hole section: Comparing **Fig. 2.47(b)** with **Fig. 2.12/ Pg 36, DHB**, we have $B = 50$ mm, $a = d = ?$

Since K_c is same for fillet and hole, we have $K_t = 2.18$

At $K_t = 2.18$, we have $\dfrac{a}{B} = 0.5$

∴ $a = 0.5 \times 85 = 5 \text{ mm}$

∴ $a = 42.5 \text{ mm} = d$

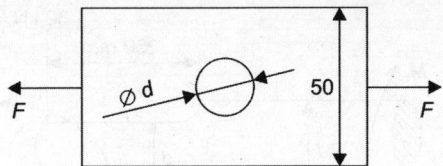

Fig. 2.47b: Problem 56

57. **A round stepped shaft is made of brittle material cast iron FG 260 and subjected to a bending moment of 15 N·m as shown in Fig. 2.48. The stress concentration factor at the fillet is 1.5. Determine the following:**

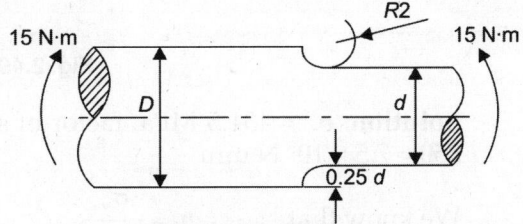

Fig. 2.48: Problem 57

   a. **Step diameter**
   b. **magnitude of stress at fillet**
   c. **factor of safety.**

VTU – June 2012 – 10 Marks

Solution: $M = 1.5$ N·m, $K_t = 1.5$

For cast iron FG 260, ultimate tensile strength, $\sigma_u = 260$ MPa

… **Tb. I.4/ Pg 461, DHB**

From Fig. 2.48, $D = d + (2 \times 0.25d) = 1.5d$

   a. **Step diameter:** Comparing **Fig. 2.48** with **Fig. 2.25/ Pg 43, DHB**, we have
   $D = 1.5d, d = d, r = 2$ mm.

At $\qquad \dfrac{D}{d} = \dfrac{1.5d}{d} = 1.5$ and $K_t = 1.5$, we have $\dfrac{r}{d} = 0.16$

∴ $\qquad \dfrac{2}{d} = 0.16$

$\qquad d = 12.5$ mm

   b. **Magnitude of stress at fillet:**
   For bending load,

$$\sigma_{max} = \left(\dfrac{Mc}{I}\right) K_t \qquad \text{… 2.1(b)/Pg 20, DHB}$$

But $\qquad \dfrac{I}{c} = \dfrac{\pi d^3}{32} = \dfrac{\pi \times 12.5^3}{32} = 191.75 \text{ mm}^3$ (Chart)

$$\sigma_{max} = \left(\dfrac{15 \times 10^3}{191.75}\right) \times 1.5 = 117.34 \text{ MPa}$$

   c. **Factor of safety:** We know that

$$n = \dfrac{\sigma_u}{\sigma_{max}} = \dfrac{260}{117.34} = 2.216$$

58. **A stepped shaft of circular cross-section shown in Fig. 2.49 is made of 20MN2 steel ($\sigma_y = 431.5$ MPa). Determine the value of 'd' and the fillet radius 'r' so that the maximum stress will be limited to a ratio corresponding to a factor of safety of 2.5 and taking stress concentration factor into account.**

VTU – Dec. 07/Jan. 2008 – 10 Marks

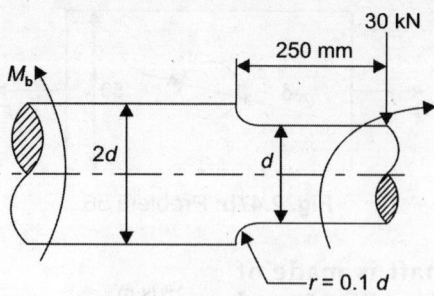

Fig. 2.49: Problem 58

Solution: $\sigma_y = 431.5$ MPa, factor of safety, $n = 2.5$, $d = ?$, $r = ?$, $M_b = (30 \times 10^3) \times 250 = 7.5 \times 10^6$ N·mm

We know that $\qquad n = \dfrac{\sigma_y}{\sigma_{max}}$

$$2.5 = \frac{431.5}{\sigma_{max}}$$

$$\sigma_{max} = 172.6 \text{ MPa}$$

Comparing **Fig. 2.49** with **Fig. 2.25/ Pg 43, DHB**, we have $D = 1.2d$, $d = d$, $r = 0.1d$

Now $\qquad \dfrac{r}{d} = \dfrac{0.1d}{d} = 0.1$ and $\dfrac{D}{d} = \dfrac{1.2d}{d} = 1.2$

At $\qquad \dfrac{r}{d} = 0.1$, and $\dfrac{D}{d} = 1.2$, we have $K_t = 1.63$

For bending load, $\sigma_{max} = \left(\dfrac{Mc}{I}\right) K_t$ $\qquad\qquad$ ... **2.1(b)/Pg 20, DHB**

But $\qquad \dfrac{I}{c} = \dfrac{\pi d^3}{32}$ (Chart)

$\therefore \qquad 172.6 = \left(\dfrac{7.5 \times 10^6}{\pi d^3/32}\right) \times 1.63$

$$d = 89.68 \text{ mm} \approx 90 \text{ mm}$$

59. **A round bar of diameter 1.2*d* has a semi-circular groove of radius 0.1*d*. Determine the safe value of *d* to sustain a bending moment of 2 kN·m. Select a suitable material and choose appropriate value for factor of safety.**

VTU – July/ Aug. 2005 – 05 Marks

Solution: Based on the given data the problem is represented as shown in **Fig. 2.50**
Material selection: Assuming that the material for the bar is C40 steel, we have:

$\qquad\qquad \sigma_y = 324$ MPa $\qquad\qquad\qquad$ ... **Tb. I.8/ Pg 464, DHB**
Assume $\qquad n = 2$

We know that $\qquad n = \dfrac{\sigma_u}{\sigma_{max}}$

$$2 = \frac{324}{\sigma_{max}}$$

$$\sigma_{max} = 162 \text{ MPa}$$

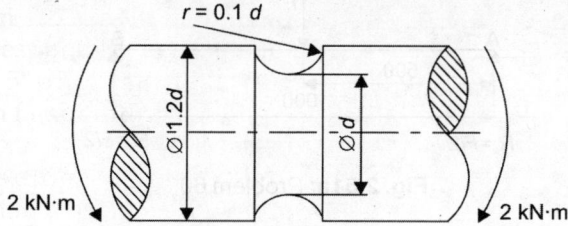

Fig. 2.50: Problem 59

Comparing **Fig. 2.50** with **Fig. 2.20/ Pg 40, DHB**, we have $D = 1.2d, d = d, r = 0.1d$

Now $\qquad \dfrac{r}{d} = \dfrac{0.1d}{d} = 0.1$ and $\dfrac{D}{d} = \dfrac{1.2d}{d} = 1.2$

At $\qquad \dfrac{r}{d} = 0.1$, and $\dfrac{D}{d} = 1.2$, we have $K_t = 1.88$

For bending load, $\sigma_{max} = \left(\dfrac{Mc}{I}\right) K_t$ $\qquad$ ... **2.1(b)/Pg 20, DHB**

But $\qquad \dfrac{I}{c} = \dfrac{\pi d^3}{32}$ (Chart)

$\therefore \qquad 162 = \left(\dfrac{2 \times 10^6}{\pi d^3 / 32}\right) \times 1.88$

$$d = 61.82 \text{ mm} \approx 62 \text{ mm}$$

60. **A stepped shaft is subjected to a transverse load of 10 kN as shown in Fig. 2.51. The shaft is made of steel with ultimate tensile strength of 300 MPa. Determine the diameter of the shaft based on factor of safety of 2.**

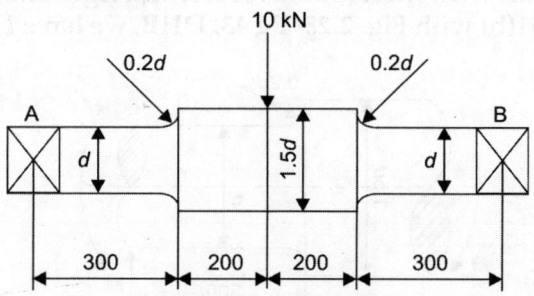

Fig. 2.51: Problem 60

Solution: $F = 10$ kN, $\sigma_u = 300$ MPa, factor of safety, $n = 2$, $d = ?$

We know that $\qquad n = \dfrac{\sigma_u}{\sigma_{max}}$

$$2 = \dfrac{300}{\sigma_{max}}$$

$$\sigma_{max} = 150 \text{ MPa}$$

The given shaft acts like a simply supported beam subjected to point load at mid-span, thereby causing a bending moment as shown in **Fig. 2.51(a)**.

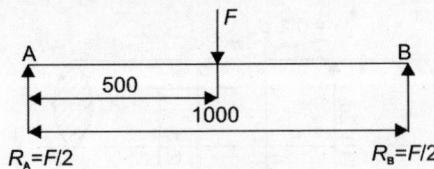

Fig. 2.51a: Problem 60

Case 1: Bending moment at mid span [Fig. 2.51(a)]: For a simply supported beam with point load at center span [**Fig. 2.51(a)**],

$$M = \frac{FL}{4} \qquad \text{... Tb. 1.4, (Fig. 4)/ Pg 15, DHB}$$

i.e. $\qquad M = R_A L/2$

$$= \frac{(10 \times 10^3) \times 1000}{4}$$

$\therefore \qquad M = 2.5 \times 10^6 \text{ N·mm}$

For bending load, $\sigma_{max} = \left(\dfrac{Mc}{I}\right) K_t \qquad$ ... Eq. (i) **2.1(b)/Pg 20, DHB**

But $\qquad \dfrac{I}{c} = \dfrac{\pi d^3}{32} = \dfrac{\pi(1.5d)^3}{32} = 0.3313 d^3$ (Chart)

$\therefore$ Eq. (i) yields... $\quad 150 = \left(\dfrac{2.5 \times 10^6}{0.3313 d^3}\right) \times 1$

$\qquad\qquad\qquad$ [since diameter is uniform at mid span, $K_t = 1$]

$\qquad d = 36.91 \text{ mm} \qquad\qquad$ ... Eq. (ii)

Case 2: Stepped shaft with fillet [Same for left and right shoulder] [Fig. 2.51(b)]: Comparing **Fig. 2.51(b)** with **Fig. 2.25/ Pg 43, DHB**, we have $D = 1.5d$, $r = 0.2d$.

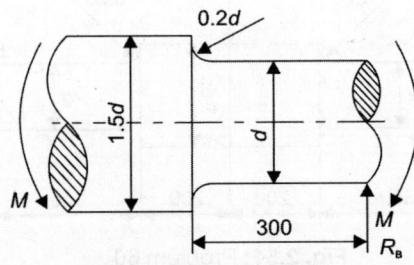

Fig. 2.51b: Problem 60

Here $\qquad \dfrac{I}{c} = \dfrac{\pi d^3}{32} = \dfrac{\pi d^3}{32} = 0.098 d^3$

and $\qquad M = R_B \times 300 = \dfrac{F}{2} \times 300 \qquad$ ... **Tb. 1.4(Fig. 4)/Pg 15, DHB**

$$= \frac{(10 \times 10^3) \times 300}{2}$$

$\therefore \qquad M = 1.5 \times 10^6 \text{ N·mm}$

Now $\qquad \dfrac{r}{d} = \dfrac{0.2d}{d} = 0.2$ and $\dfrac{D}{d} = \dfrac{1.5d}{d} = 1.5$

At $\qquad \dfrac{r}{d} = 0.2$, and $\dfrac{D}{d} = 1.5$, we have $K_t = 1.42$

$\therefore$ Eq. (i) yields... $\quad 150 = \left(\dfrac{1.5 \times 10^6}{0.098d^3}\right) \times 1.42$

$\qquad\qquad\qquad d = 61.82 \text{ mm} \approx 62 \text{ mm}$ $\qquad\qquad$ ... Eq. (iii)

From Eqs. (ii) and (iii), taking larger value of diameter for design, we have $d = 52$ mm.

Therefore, standard shaft size, $d = 56$ mm. $\qquad$ ... Tb 3.5(a)/ Pg 57, DHB

61. **A stepped shaft is subjected to a transverse load of 8 kN as shown in Fig. 2.52. The shaft is made of steel with ultimate tensile strength of 400 MPa. Determine the diameter of the shaft based on factor of safety of 2.**

VTU – July 2007 – 12 Marks

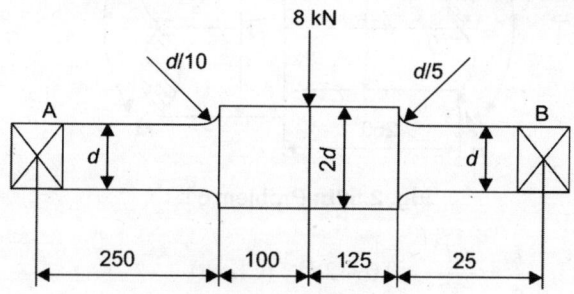

Fig. 2.52: Problem 61

Solution: $F = 8$ kN, $\sigma_u = 400$ MPa, factor of safety, $n = 2$, $d = ?$

We know that $\qquad n = \dfrac{\sigma_u}{\sigma_{max}}$

$\qquad\qquad\qquad 2 = \dfrac{400}{\sigma_{max}}$

$\qquad\qquad\qquad \sigma_{max} = 200$ MPa

The given shaft acts like a simply supported beam subjected to point load, thereby causing a bending moment as shown in **Fig. 2.52(a)**.

Method 1: For a simply supported beam with intermediate load **[Fig. 2.52(a)]**,

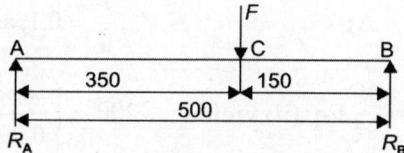

Fig. 2.52a: Problem 61

$\qquad\qquad M = \dfrac{Fab}{L}$ $\qquad$ ... Tb. 1.4, (Fig. 5)/ Pg 16, DHB

$\qquad\qquad\quad = \dfrac{(8 \times 10^3) \times 350 \times 150}{500}$

$\therefore \qquad M = 840 \times 10^3 \text{ N·mm}$

For bending load, $\sigma_{max} = \left(\dfrac{Mc}{I}\right) K_t$ ... Eq. (i) **2.1(b)/Pg 20, DHB**

But $\dfrac{I}{c} = \dfrac{\pi d^3}{32} = \dfrac{\pi (2d)^3}{32} = 0.7854 d^3$ (Chart)

∴ Eq. (i) yields... $200 = \left(\dfrac{840 \times 10^3}{0.7854 d^3}\right) \times 1$

[since diameter is uniform at mid span, $K_t = 1$]

$d = 17.48$ mm   ... Eq. (ii)

Case 2: Stepped shaft having left fillet [Fig. 2.52(b)]: Comparing **Fig. 2.52(b)** with **Fig. 2.25/ Pg 43, DHB**, we have $D = 2d$, $r = d/10$.

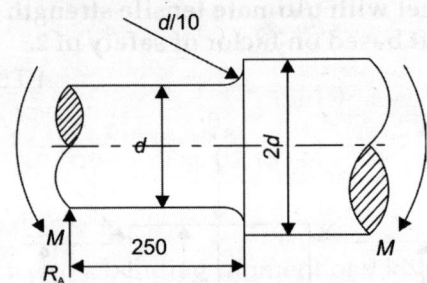

Fig. 2.52b: Problem 61

But $\dfrac{I}{c} = \dfrac{\pi d^3}{32} = 0.0982 d^3$ (Chart)

Also $M = R_A \times 250 = \dfrac{Fb}{L} \times 250$ ... **Tb. 1.4(Fig. 5)/Pg 16, DHB**

$= \dfrac{(8 \times 10^3) \times 150}{500} \times 250$

∴ $M = 6 \times 10^5$ N·mm

Now $\dfrac{r}{d} = \dfrac{d/10}{d} = 0.1$ and $\dfrac{D}{d} = \dfrac{2d}{d} = 2$

At $\dfrac{r}{d} = 0.1$, and $\dfrac{D}{d} = 2$, we have $K_t = 1.74$

∴ Eq. (ii) yields... $200 = \left(\dfrac{6 \times 10^5}{0.0982 d^3}\right) \times 1.74$

$d = 37.60$ mm   ... Eq. (iii)

Case 3: Stepped shaft having left fillet [Fig. 2.52(c)]: Comparing **Fig. 2.52(c)** with **Fig. 2.25/ Pg 43, DHB**, we have $D = 2d$, $r = d/5$

But $\dfrac{I}{c} = \dfrac{\pi d^3}{32} = 0.0982 d^3$ (Chart)

Also $M = R_B \times 25 = \dfrac{Fa}{L} \times 25$ ... **Tb. 1.4(Fig. 5)/Pg 16, DHB**

$$= \frac{(8 \times 10^3) \times 350}{500} \times 25$$

$\therefore \qquad M = 1.4 \times 10^5 \, \text{N·mm}$

Now $\quad \dfrac{r}{d} = \dfrac{d/5}{d} = 0.2$ and $\dfrac{D}{d} = \dfrac{2d}{d} = 2$

At $\quad \dfrac{r}{d} = 0.2$, and $\dfrac{D}{d} = 2$, we have $K_t = 1.44$

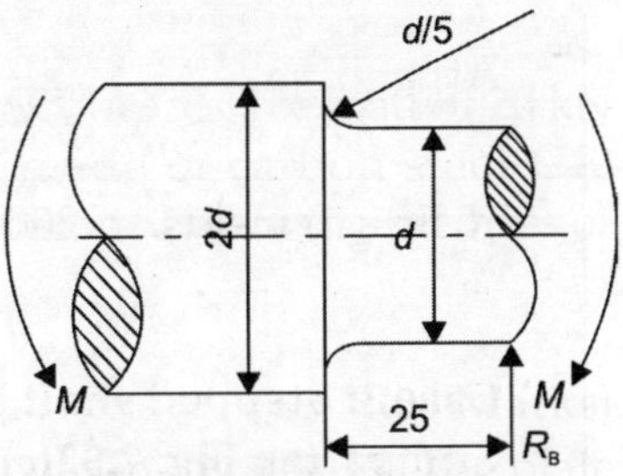

$\therefore$ Eq. (ii) yields... $\quad 200 = \left(\dfrac{1.4 \times 10^5}{0.0982d^3}\right) \times 1.44$

$$d = 21.73 \, \text{mm} \qquad \qquad \text{... Eq. (iv)}$$

Fig. 2.52c: Problem 61

From Eqs. (ii), (iii) and (iv), taking larger value of diameter for design, we have $d = 37.60$ mm.

Therefore, standard shaft size, $d = 40$ mm $\qquad$ **... Tb 3.5(a)/ Pg 57, DHB**

Method 1: From fundamentals:
Case 1: Bending moment at eccentric distance [Fig. 2.52(a)]
From **Fig. 2.52(a)**, $R_A + R_B = W$ $\qquad\qquad$ ... Eq. (i)
Taking moments about 'A', we have
$\qquad\qquad R_B \times 500 = W \times 350$

$$R_B = \frac{W \times 350}{600} = \frac{8000 \times 350}{500}$$

$\therefore \qquad\qquad R_B = 5600 \, \text{N}$
$\therefore$ Eq. (i) yields... $\quad R_A = W - R_B = 8000 - 5600$
$\qquad\qquad\qquad = 2400 \, \text{N}$

For bending load, $\sigma_{max} = \left(\dfrac{Mc}{I}\right) K_t$ $\qquad$ ... Eq. (ii) **2.1(b)/Pg 20, DHB**

But $\qquad \dfrac{I}{c} = \dfrac{\pi d^3}{32} = \dfrac{\pi(2d)^3}{32} = 0.7854d^3$ (Chart)

$\qquad M = M_C = R_A \times 350 = 2400 \times 3500 = 840 \times 10^3 \, \text{N·mm}$

$\therefore$ Eq. (ii) yields... $\quad 200 = \left(\dfrac{840 \times 10^3}{0.7854d^3}\right) \times 1$

$\qquad\qquad\qquad$ [since diameter is uniform at mid span, $K_t = 1$]
$\qquad\qquad d = 17.48 \, \text{mm}$

Case 2: Stepped shaft having left fillet [Fig. 2.52(b)]: Comparing **Fig. 2.52(b)** with **Fig. 2.25/ Pg 43, DHB**, we have $D = 2d, r = d/10$

But $\qquad \dfrac{I}{c} = \dfrac{\pi d^3}{32} = 0.0982d^3$ (Chart)

Also $\qquad M = R_A \times 250$
$\qquad\qquad = 2400 \times 25$
$\therefore \qquad M = 6 \times 10^5 \, \text{N·mm}$

Now $\qquad \dfrac{r}{d} = \dfrac{d/10}{d} = 0.1$ and $\dfrac{D}{d} = \dfrac{2d}{d} = 2$

At $\dfrac{r}{d} = 0.1$, and $\dfrac{D}{d} = 2$, we have $K_t = 1.74$

$\therefore$ Eq. (ii) yields... $200 = \left(\dfrac{6 \times 10^5}{0.0982d^3}\right) \times 1.74$

$$d = 37.60 \text{ mm} \qquad \text{... Eq. (iii)}$$

Case 3: Stepped shaft having left fillet [Fig. 2.52(c)]

Comparing **Fig. 2.52(c)**, with **Fig. 2.25/Pg 43, DHB**, we have

$$D = 2d, r = d/5$$

Here $M = R_B \times 25$

$$= 5600 \times 25$$

$\therefore$ $M = 1.4 \times 10^5 \text{ N·mm}$

Now $\dfrac{r}{d} = \dfrac{d/5}{d} = 0.2$ and $\dfrac{D}{d} = \dfrac{2d}{d} = 2$

At $\dfrac{r}{d} = 0.2$, and $\dfrac{D}{d} = 2$, we have $K_t = 1.44$

$\therefore$ Eq. (ii) yields... $200 = \left(\dfrac{1.4 \times 10^5}{0.0982d^3}\right) \times 1.44$

$$d = 21.73 \text{ mm} \qquad \text{... Eq. (iv)}$$

Taking larger diameter for design, we have $d = 37.60$ mm

Therefore, standard size, $d = 40$ mm **... Tb 3.5(a)/Pg 57, DHB**

62. **An infinite plate with a elliptical cut out having major axis 50 mm and minor axis 25 mm is subjected to a tensile load F. Determine the stress concentration factor when:**
    a. **The load is perpendicular to major axis**
    b. **The load is parallel to the major axis.**

VTU – Dec. 08/ Jan. 2009 – 08 Marks

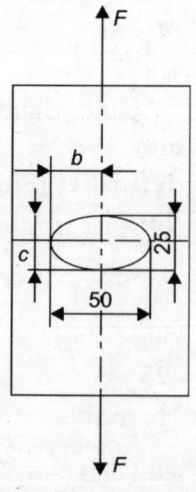

Fig. 2.53: Problem 62

Solution: Major axis, $2b = 50$ mm $\Rightarrow b = 25$ mm, minor axis, $2c = 25$ mm $\Rightarrow c + 12.5$ mm, $K_t = ?$

Case a) Load perpendicular to major axis: For an elliptical hole,

$$K_t = 1 + \frac{2b}{c} = 1 + \left(\frac{2 \times 25}{12.5} \right) = 5 \qquad \text{... Tb 2.1/ Pg 30, DHB}$$

Case b) Load parallel to major axis: For an elliptical hole,

$$K_t = 1 + \frac{2c}{b} = 1 + \left(\frac{2 \times 12.5}{25} \right) = 2 \qquad \text{... Tb 2.1/ Pg 30, DHB}$$

DESIGN FOR IMPACT STRENGTH

2.12 IMPACT LOADING: INTRODUCTION

A load is said to be an impact load, if it is applied with some initial velocity. In general, impact load is an external force applied to a structure or a part if the time of application is less than one-third its lowest natural period of vibration. It can occur in the following ways.

- A direct impact by another member or an external body moving with considerable velocity, e.g. punch press, two cars colliding.
- Sudden application of forces without a blow being involved
  - Sudden creation of force on a member, e.g. power stroke in IC engines.
  - Sudden moving of force on to a member, e.g. heavily loaded train or truck moving rapidly over the floor of the bridge.
- The inertia of the member resisting high acceleration and retardation, e.g. reciprocating levers.

2.13 METHODS OF SELECTING MEMBERS TO WITHSTAND IMPACT LOAD

The following two methods are employed for selection of member subjected to impact loads.

- Maximum force exerted by moving body on resisting member is estimated by applying an *impact factor*. Later this force is considered as static and the design formulas are used.
- Energy to be absorbed by resisting member is to be estimated and from this value, stresses or deformations by formula for impact load on members are determined.

2.14 PROPERTIES OF MATERIAL TO RESIST IMPACT LOAD

The two most important properties of a material that indicate its resistance to impact load are:

- *Modulus of resilience*: It is defined as the capacity of a material to absorb energy within its elastic range without undergoing permanent deformation.
- *Ultimate energy resilience*: This property indicates the material toughness or its ability to resist fracture under impact loading. Both properties are obtained from stress–strain diagram.

2.15 STRAIN ENERGY DUE TO IMPACT LOAD (IMPACT STRESSES DUE TO AXIAL LOAD)

Consider a bar shown in **Fig. 2.54** with a rigid collar firmly attached at the end. The load W is free to slide vertically and is suspended by some means at a distance *h* above the collar.

Let

W = load applied with impact

h = height through which the load falls

A = cross-sectional area of the bar

L = length of the bar

σ = static stress

δ = deformation of bar due to static action

σ′ = impact stress

δ′ = deformation due to impact action

E = Young's modulus of the bar material

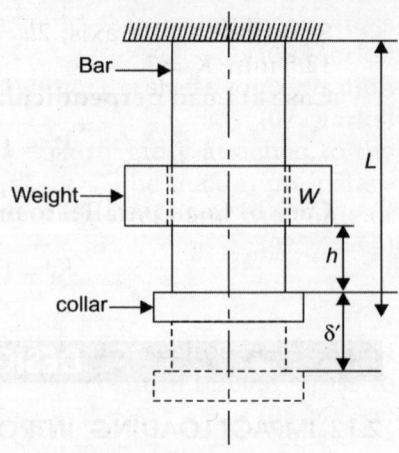

When the load is dropped it will produce a maximum instantaneous extension δ′ of the bar, and thus

Fig. 2.54: Impact stress due to axial load [(Fig. 2.8(a)/Pg 28, DHB]

$$\text{Work done} = \text{Force} \times \text{distance moved}$$
$$= W \times (h + \delta') \qquad \text{... (Eq. 2.41) } \textbf{2.25(c)/ Pg 27, DHB}$$

Also strain energy or resilience,

$$U = \frac{1}{2}W\delta' \qquad \text{... (Eq. 2.42) } \textbf{2.27(a)/ Pg 28, DHB}$$

Equating (Eq. 2.41) and (Eq. 2.42), we have

$$\frac{1}{2}W\delta' = W \times (h + \delta')$$

Since $\sigma' = W/A$, and $\delta' = \dfrac{\sigma'L}{E}$, we have ... (Eq. 2.43)

$$\frac{1}{2}(\sigma'A)\left(\frac{\sigma'L}{E}\right) = W\left[h + \frac{\sigma'L}{E}\right]$$

$$\left(\frac{\sigma'^2}{2}\right)\left(\frac{AL}{E}\right) = Wh + \frac{W\sigma'L}{E}$$

$$\left(\frac{\sigma'^2}{2}\right)\left(\frac{AL}{E}\right) - \left(\frac{WL}{E}\right)\sigma' - Wh = 0 \qquad \text{... (Eq. 2.44)}$$

Multiplying with $\left(\dfrac{E}{AL}\right)$ on both sides of (Eq. 2.44), we have

$$\left(\frac{\sigma'^2}{2}\right) - \left(\frac{W}{A}\right)\sigma' - Wh\cdot\left(\frac{E}{AL}\right) = 0 \qquad \text{... (Eq. 2.45)}$$

Equation (2.45) is a quadratic equation, the roots of which are found as

$$\sigma = \frac{-\left(\dfrac{-W}{A}\right) \pm \sqrt{\left(\dfrac{-W}{A}\right) - \left[4 \times \left(\dfrac{1}{2}\right) \times \left(\dfrac{-WEh}{AL}\right)\right]}}{2 \times \left(\dfrac{1}{2}\right)}$$

$$= \left(\frac{W}{A}\right) \pm \sqrt{\left(\frac{W}{A}\right)^2 + \left[\frac{2WEh}{AL}\right]}$$

$$= \left(\frac{W}{A}\right) \pm \left(\frac{W}{A}\right)\sqrt{1 + \left(\frac{2Eh}{AL}\right)\left(\frac{A}{W}\right)}$$

$$\sigma' = \left(\frac{W}{A}\right)\left[1 + \sqrt{1 + \left(\frac{2AEh}{WL}\right)}\right] \quad \text{(neglecting negative sign)}$$

... (Eq. 2.46a) **2.26(a)/ Pg 27, DHB**

or
$$\sigma' = \sigma\left[1 + \sqrt{1 + \left(\frac{2AEh}{WL}\right)}\right] = \sigma\left[1 + \sqrt{1 + \left(\frac{2h}{\delta}\right)}\right]$$

... (Eq. 2.46b) **2.26(a)/ Pg 27, DHB**

The term $\quad \dfrac{\sigma'}{\sigma} = \left[1 + \sqrt{1 + \left(\dfrac{2h}{\delta}\right)}\right]$ is called the **impact/ shock factor** for

stress. ... (Eq. 2.46c)

Equation (2.46b) indicates that an impact load produces much larger effects than when the same load is applied statically.

But static deflection, $\quad \delta = \dfrac{WL}{AE}$ ... (Eq. 2.47) **1.2(b)/ Pg 3, DHB**

Multiplying with $\left(\dfrac{L}{E}\right)$ on both sides of (Eq. 2.46a), we have

$$\sigma'\left(\frac{L}{E}\right) = \left(\frac{W}{A}\right)\left(\frac{L}{E}\right)\left[1 \pm \sqrt{1 + \left(\frac{2AEh}{WL}\right)}\right]$$

$$\delta' = \delta\left[1 + \sqrt{1 + \left(\frac{2h}{\delta}\right)}\right] \quad \text{... using (Eq. 2.43)}$$

... (Eq. 2.48a) **2.26(b)/ Pg 27, DHB**

The term $\dfrac{\delta'}{\delta} = \left[1 + \sqrt{1 + \left(\dfrac{2h}{8}\right)}\right]$ is called the **impact/shock factor** for elongation.

... (Eq. 2.48b)

Impact factor is defined as the ratio of the dynamic response of a structure to the static response. This factor represents the amount by which the static elongation is amplified due to the dynamic effects of the impact.

Note:

- Impact stress due to sudden load, $\sigma' = 2\sigma$, $\sigma_b' = 2\sigma_b$ and $\tau' = 2\tau$

  ... **2.26(g)/ Pg 28, DHB**

- Deformation under the action of sudden load, $\delta' = 2\delta$, $y' = 2y$ and $\theta' = 2\theta$

  ... **2.26(h)/ Pg 28, DHB**

- Kinetic energy, $E_k = \dfrac{Wv^2}{2g} = \dfrac{1}{2}mv^2$ ... **2.25(a)/ Pg 27, DHB**

- Impact energy of a body falling from a height h (potential energy) is

  $$E_k = Wh = (mg)h \quad \text{... } \textbf{2.25(b)/ Pg 27, DHB}$$

- Strain energy or resilience,

$$U = WD = \frac{\sigma^2 V}{2E}, \text{ where volume } V = AL \quad ...2.27(b)/ \text{ Pg 29, DHB}$$

- Equations for modulus of resilience for various loadings are available in

  ...Table 2.9/ Pg 34, DHB

63. **A bar of 16 mm diameter gets stretched by 4 mm under a steady load of 10 kN. What stress would be produced in the bar by a weight of 1000 N, which falls through 100 mm before commencing the stretch of rod which is initially unstressed? Take $E = 200$ GPa.**

Solution: $d = 16$ mm $\Rightarrow$ area $A = \pi d^2/4 = 201.06$ mm^2, static deformation $\delta = 4$ mm, static load $F = 10000$ N, impact stress $\sigma' = ?$, if impact load $W = 1000$ N, $h = 100$ mm, $E = 200$ GPa $= 2 \times 10^5$ MPa.

To find σ':

We know that $\qquad \sigma' = \left(\dfrac{W}{A}\right)\left[1 + \sqrt{1 + \left(\dfrac{2AEh}{WL}\right)}\right] \qquad$ ... 2.26(a)/Pg 27, DHB

But static deformation

$$\delta = \frac{FL}{AE} \qquad\qquad\qquad ... 1.2(b)/ \text{ Pg 3, DHB}$$

$$4 = \frac{10000 \times L}{201.06 \times (2 \times 10^5)}$$

$$L = 16084.95 \text{ mm}$$

$\therefore$ Eq. (i) yields... $\quad \sigma' = \left(\dfrac{1000}{201.06}\right)\left[1 + \sqrt{1 + \dfrac{2 \times 201.06 \times (2 \times 10^5) \times 100}{1000 \times 16084.95}}\right]$

$$\sigma' = 116.30 \text{ MPa}$$

64. **Two brasses of an automobile connecting rod have worn, so as to apply play which gives shock loading equivalent to a weight of 5886 N falling through a height of 0.2 mm. The connecting rod is 250 mm long and has a cross-sectional area of 3×10^{-4} m^2. Determine the stress induced in the connecting rod. Compare the maximum stress induced with that of a static load of 5886 N. Take $E = 80$ GPa.**

VTU – June/ July 2013 – 06 Marks

Solution: a. Impact load $W = 5886$ N, $L = 250$ mm, $A = 3 \times 10^{-4}$ m$^2 = 300$ mm^2, $h = 0.2$ mm, impact stress $\sigma' = ?$ b. Static stress $\sigma = ?$, static load $F = 5886$ N

a. **To find σ':**

We know that $\qquad \sigma' = \left(\dfrac{W}{A}\right)\left[1 + \sqrt{1 + \left(\dfrac{2AEh}{WL}\right)}\right] \qquad$ ... 2.26(a)/Pg 27, DHB

$$= \left(\frac{5886}{300}\right)\left[1 + \sqrt{1 + \frac{2 \times 300 \times (80 \times 10^3) \times 0.2}{5886 \times 250}}\right]$$

$$\sigma' = 73.44 \text{ MPa}$$

b. **To find σ:**

We know that $\qquad \sigma = \dfrac{F}{A} = \dfrac{5886}{300} = 19.62$ MPa $\qquad$ ... 1.2(b)/ Pg 3, DHB

65. **An unknown weight falls through 10 mm on a collar rigidly attached to the lower end of a bar 3 m long and 600 mm² in section. If the maximum instantaneous extension is 2 mm, what are the corresponding stress and the value of unknown weight? Take $E = 200$ GPa.**

> *VTU – June/July 2015–10 Marks; Dec. 2011–07 Marks; June/ July 2011–12 Marks; (Similar) Dec. 13/Jan. 14 – 06 Marks; (Similar) Dec. 2012 – 10 Marks; (Similar) June/July 08 – 08 Marks; (Similar) Jan./ Feb. 06 – 10 Marks.*

Solution: $h = 10$ mm, $L = 3000$ mm, $A = 600$ mm², $\delta' = 2$ mm, impact stress $\sigma' = ?$, $W = ?$, $E = 2 \times 10^5$ MPa

To find σ':

Instantaneous deflection,

$$\delta' = \frac{\sigma' L}{E}$$

$$2 = \frac{\sigma' \times 3000}{2 \times 10^5}$$

∴ $\qquad \sigma' = 133.34$ MPa

To find W:

We know that $\qquad \sigma' = \left(\dfrac{W}{A}\right)\left[1 + \sqrt{1 + \left(\dfrac{2AEh}{WL}\right)}\right] \qquad$ ... 2.26(a)/ Pg 27, DHB

$$133.34 = \left(\frac{W}{600}\right)\left[1 + \sqrt{1 + \frac{2 \times 600 \times (2 \times 10^5) \times 10}{W \times 3000}}\right]$$

$$\frac{80 \times 10^3}{W} = 1 + \sqrt{1 + \left(\frac{8 \times 10^5}{W}\right)}$$

$$\frac{80 \times 10^3}{W} - 1 = \sqrt{1 + \left(\frac{8 \times 10^5}{W}\right)}$$

Squaring both sides, we have

$$\left(\frac{80 \times 10^3}{W} - 1\right)^2 = 1 + \left(\frac{8 \times 10^5}{W}\right)$$

$$\frac{6400 \times 10^6}{W^2} + 1 - \frac{160 \times 10^3}{W} = 1 + \left(\frac{8 \times 10^5}{W}\right)$$

$$\frac{6400 \times 10^6}{W^2} = \left(\frac{960 \times 10^3}{W}\right)$$

∴ $\qquad W = 6.67$ kN

66. **A rectangular bar 200 mm long is subjected to an impact load of 2 kN that falls from a height of 20 mm. Determine the dimensions of the bar if the allowable stress is 125 MPa. Assume the thickness as twice the width. Take $E = 200$ GPa.**

Solution: $L = 200$ mm, impact load $W = 2000$ N, $h = 20$ mm, dimensions $b, t = ?$, if $t = 2b$, $\sigma' = 125$ MPa, $E = 2 \times 10^5$ MPa

We know that
$$\sigma' = \left(\frac{W}{A}\right)\left[1 + \sqrt{1 + \left(\frac{2AEh}{WL}\right)}\right] \qquad \text{... 2.26(a)/ Pg 27, DHB}$$

$$125 = \left(\frac{2000}{A}\right)\left[1 + \sqrt{1 + \frac{2A \times (2 \times 10^5) \times 20}{2000 \times 200}}\right]$$

$$0.0625A = [1 + \sqrt{1 + 20A}]$$

$$0.0625A - 1 = \sqrt{1 + 20A}$$

Squaring both sides, we have

$$(0.0625A - 1)^2 = 1 + 20A$$

$$(3.91 \times 10^{-3})A^2 + 1 - 0.125A = 1 + 20A$$

$$(3.91 \times 10^{-3})A^2 = 20.125A$$

$$A = 5147.05 \text{ mm}^2$$

But
$$A = bt = b(2b) \qquad \text{...(data)}$$

$$5147.05 = 2b^2$$

$$b = 50.73 \text{ mm} \approx 52 \text{ mm}$$

and
$$t = 2 \times 52 = 104 \text{ mm}$$

67. **A steel rod 1.5 m long resists an impact load of 2 kN dropped through a distance of 50 mm along its axis. Limiting the maximum stress in the rod to 150 MPa, determine:**
    a. **The diameter of the rod required.**
    b. **Impact factor. Use $E = 200$ GPa**

VTU – June/ July 2009 – 10 Marks; Dec. 2012 – 12 Marks

Solution: $L = 1500$ mm, impact load $W = 2000$ N, $h = 50$ mm, $\sigma' = 150$ MPa, $E = 2 \times 10^5$ MPa, $d = ?$, impact factor $= ?$

a. To find d:

We know that
$$\sigma' = \left(\frac{W}{L}\right)\left[1 + \sqrt{1 + \left(\frac{2AEh}{WL}\right)}\right] \qquad \text{... 2.26(a)/Pg 27, DHB}$$

$$150 = \left(\frac{2000}{A}\right)\left[1 + \sqrt{1 + \frac{2A \times (2 \times 10^5) \times 50}{2000 \times 1500}}\right]$$

$$0.075A = [1 + \sqrt{1 + 6.67A}]$$

$$0.075A - 1 = \sqrt{1 + 6.67A}$$

Squaring both sides, we have

$$(0.075A - 1)^2 = 1 + 6.67A$$

$$(5.625 \times 10^{-3})A^2 + 1 - 0.15A = 1 + 6.67A$$

$$(5.625 \times 10^{-3}) A^2 = 6.82A$$
$$A = 1212.44 \text{ mm}^2$$

But
$$A = \pi d^2 / 4$$
$$1212.44 = \pi d^2 / 4$$
$$d = 39.29 \text{ mm} \approx 40 \text{ mm}$$

b. Impact factor:

We know that Impact factor $= \left[1 + \sqrt{1 + \left(\dfrac{2h}{\delta} \right)} \right]$ ... Eq. (i)

but $\qquad \delta = \dfrac{WL}{AE} = \dfrac{2000 \times 1500}{(\pi \times 40^2 / 4) \times 2 \times 10^5} = 0.0119 \text{ mm}$

∴ Eq. (i) yields...

$$\text{impact factor} = \left[1 + \sqrt{1 + \left(\dfrac{2 \times 50}{0.0119} \right)} \right] = 92.53$$

68. **A steel rod 1.5 m long has to resist longitudinally an impact of 2.5 kN falling under gravity at a velocity of 0.9925 m/s. The maximum computed stress is to be limited to 150 MPa. Determine the diameter of the rod.**

VTU – June/ July 2013 – 10 Marks

Solution: $L = 1500$ mm, impact load $W = 2500$ N, $v = 0.9925$ m/s, $\sigma' = 150$ MPa, $d = ?$

We know that $\qquad \sigma' = \left(\dfrac{W}{A} \right) \left[1 + \sqrt{1 + \left(\dfrac{2AEh}{WL} \right)} \right]$ ... Eq. (i) **2.26(a)/Pg 27, DHB**

But kinetic energy, $E_k = \dfrac{Wv^2}{2g}$ ... Eq. (ii) **2.25(a)/Pg 27, DHB**

Also impact energy of a body falling from a height h is $E_k = Wh$

... Eq. (iii) **2.25(b)/Pg 27, DHB**

Equations (ii) and (iii), we have

$$\frac{Wv^2}{2g} = Wh$$

i.e. $\qquad \dfrac{v^2}{2g} = h$

$$h = \frac{0.9925^2}{2 \times 9.81} = 0.0502 \text{ m} = 50.2 \text{ mm} \approx 51 \text{ mm}$$

∴ Eq. (i) yields... $\quad 150 = \left(\dfrac{2500}{A} \right) \left[1 + \sqrt{\dfrac{2A \times (2 \times 10^5) \times 51}{2500 \times 1500}} \right]$ (assume $E = 2 \times 10^5$ MPa)

$$0.06A = [1 + \sqrt{1 + 5.44A}]$$

$$0.06A - 1 = \sqrt{1 + 5.44A}$$

Squaring both sides, we have
$$(0.06A - 1)^2 = 1 + 5.44A$$
$$(3.6 \times 10^{-3}) A^2 + 1 - 0.12A = 1 + 5.44A$$
$$(3.6 \times 10^{-3}) A^2 = 5.56A$$
$$A = 1544.44 \text{ mm}^2$$
But
$$A = \pi d^2 / 4$$
$$1544.44 = \pi d^2 / 4$$
$$d = 44.34 \text{ mm} \approx 45 \text{ mm}$$

2.16 IMPACT STRESSES DUE TO BENDING

Figure 2.55 represents two different beams subjected to bending load. Consider a simply supported beam as shown in **Fig. 2.55(a)**.

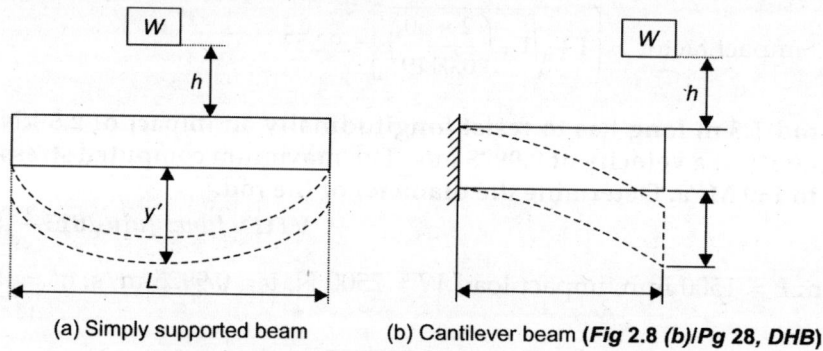

(a) Simply supported beam   (b) Cantilever beam (*Fig 2.8 (b)/Pg 28, DHB*)

Fig. 2.55: Impact stress due to bending load

Let
W = weight of falling body
h = height through which the load falls
L = Length of the bar
A = cross-sectional area of the bar
y = static deflection of the beam due to weight W
y' = deflection of the beam due to impact
σ_b = bending stress due to static weight
σ_b' = impact stress
M = bending moment of the beam

$$\text{Work done} = \text{Force} \times \text{distance moved}$$
$$= W \times (h + y') \qquad \text{... (Eq. 2.49)} \textbf{ 2.25(c)/ Pg 27, DHB}$$

Also strain energy, $U = \dfrac{1}{2} W_E y' \qquad \text{... (Eq. 2.50)} \textbf{ 2.27(a)/ Pg 28, DHB}$

$$W_E = \text{Equivalent static load}$$

Equating (Eq. 2.49) and (Eq. 2.50), we have
$$\frac{1}{2} W_E y' = W \times (h + y') \qquad \qquad \text{... (Eq. 2.51)}$$
$$W_E = \frac{2W(h + y')}{y'}$$

For a static beam deflection,

$$y = \frac{WL^3}{48EI} \qquad \text{… (Eq. 2.52) **Tb. 1.4/ Pg 15, DHB**}$$

On similar lines for W_E,

$$y' = \frac{W_E L^3}{48EI} \qquad \text{… (Eq. 2.53)}$$

Substituting (Eq. 2.51) in (Eq. 2.53), we have

$$y' = \frac{2W(h + y')}{y'} \left(\frac{L^3}{48EI} \right)$$

$$y' = \frac{2(h + y')}{y'} \times y \qquad \text{… using (Eq. 2.52)}$$

i.e. $\qquad y'^2 - 2yy' - 2hy = 0 \qquad \text{… (Eq. 2.54)}$

Equation (2.54) is a quadratic equation, the roots of which are found as

$$y' = \frac{-(-2y) \pm \sqrt{(-2y)^2 - [4 \times (1) \times (-2hy)]}}{2 \times (1)} = \frac{2y \pm \sqrt{4y^2 + 8hy}}{2}$$

$$= \frac{2y + \sqrt{4y^2 + 8hy}}{2} \quad \text{(neglecting negative sign)}$$

$$= \frac{2y + 2y\sqrt{1 + \left(\frac{2h}{y}\right)}}{2} = \frac{2y + \left[1 + \sqrt{1 + \left(\frac{2h}{y}\right)}\right]}{2}$$

$$y' = y\left[1 + \sqrt{1 + \left(\frac{2h}{y}\right)}\right] \qquad \text{… (Eq. 2.55) **2.26(d)/ Pg 28, DHB**}$$

Multiplying with $\left(\frac{8Ec}{L^2}\right)$ on both sides of (Eq. 2.55), we have

$$y'\left(\frac{8Ec}{L^2}\right) = y\left(\frac{8Ec}{L^2}\right)\left[1 + \sqrt{1 + \left(\frac{2h}{y}\right)}\right]$$

i.e. $\qquad \sigma'_b = \sigma_b \left[1 + \sqrt{1 + \left(\frac{2h}{y}\right)}\right] \qquad \text{… (Eq. 2.56a) **2.26(c)/ Pg 27, DHB**}$

The term $\dfrac{\sigma'_b}{\sigma_b} = \left[1 + \sqrt{1 + \left(\frac{2h}{y}\right)}\right]$ is called the ***impact/shock factor*** for stress

$$\text{… (Eq. 2.56b)}$$

Note:

We know that $\qquad \dfrac{M}{I} = \dfrac{\sigma_b}{c} = \dfrac{E}{R} \qquad \text{… (Eq. 2.45) **1.3(a)/ Pg 3, DHB**}$

$$R = \frac{EI}{M} \qquad \text{… (Eq. 2.57)}$$

But the deflection at the centre of a SS beam,

$$y = \frac{L^2}{8R}$$

$$= \frac{ML^2}{8EI} \qquad \text{... (Eq. 2.58) using (Eq. 2.46)}$$

$$= \frac{L^2}{8E}\left(\frac{\sigma_b}{c}\right) \qquad \text{... using (Eq. 2.45)}$$

$$\sigma_b = \left(\frac{8Ec}{L^2}\right)y \qquad \text{... (Eq. 2.59)}$$

2.17 IMPACT AND TORSION

In this case

- Impact shear stress,

$$\tau' = \tau\left[1 + \sqrt{1 + \left(\frac{2h}{r\theta}\right)}\right] \qquad \text{... (Eq. 2.60) 2.26(e)/ Pg 28, DHB}$$

- Angular deflection due to impact loading

$$\theta' = \theta\left[1 + \sqrt{1 + \left(\frac{2h}{r\theta}\right)}\right] \qquad \text{... (Eq. 2.61) 2.26(f)/ Pg 28, DHB}$$

2.18 EFFECT OF INERTIA

When a body of weight W strikes another body that has a weight of W', then according to the laws of collsion of inelastic bodies the impact energy Wh is reduced to nWh. The value of n can be found as

$$n = \frac{1 + am}{(1 + bm)^2} \qquad \text{... (Eq. 2.62) 2.26(i)/ Pg 28, DHB}$$

where $m = W'/W$

Values of a and b ... **Table 2.8/ Pg 34, DHB**

69. **A beam of rectangular cross-section has a width of 30 mm and 40 mm depth. The beam is simply supported for the length of 0.9 m. If it is struck by a mass of 10 kg falling through a height of 80 mm, find the instantaneous stress developed. Take E = 210 GPa.**

Solution: $b = 30$ mm, $d = 40$ mm, $L = 900$ mm, $m = 10$ kg $\Rightarrow W = mg = 10 \times 9.81 = 98.1$ N, $h = 80$ mm, $\sigma'_b = ?$, $E = 210$ GPa $= 210 \times 10^3$ MPa.

Maximum instantaneous stress: We know that

$$\sigma'_b = \sigma_b\left[1 + \sqrt{1 + \left(\frac{2h}{y}\right)}\right] \qquad \text{... Eq. (i) 2.26(c)/ Pg 27, DHB}$$

But bending stress,

$$\sigma_b = \frac{M}{Z} \qquad \text{... Eq. (ii) 1.1(b)/ Pg 2, DHB}$$

- $$I = \frac{bd^3}{12} = \frac{30 \times 40^3}{12} = 160000 \text{ mm}^4$$

    ... **Tb 1.3(a), (Fig. a)/ Pg 12, DHB**

- $$Z = \frac{bd^2}{6} = \frac{30 \times 40^2}{6} = 8000 \text{ mm}^3$$

    ... **Tb 1.3(a), (Fig. a)/ Pg 12, DHB**

- For a simply supported beam (SS beam) with point load at mid span

$$M = \frac{WL}{4} = \frac{98.10 \times 900}{4} = 22.07 \times 10^3 \text{ N} \cdot \text{mm}$$

    ... **Tb 1.4, (Fig. 4)/ Pg 15, DHB**

Deflection, $$y = \frac{WL^3}{48EI} \quad [F \text{ or } W]$$ ... **Tb 1.4, (Fig. 4)/ Pg 15, DHB**

$$\therefore \qquad y = \frac{98.1 \times 900^3}{48 \times 210 \times 10^3 \times 160000} = 0.0433 \text{ mm}$$

$$\therefore \text{ Eq. (ii) yields...} \quad \sigma_b = \frac{22.07 \times 10^3}{8000} = 2.76 \text{ MPa}$$

$$\therefore \text{ Eq. (i) yields...} \quad \sigma_b' = 2.76 \left[1 + \sqrt{1 + \left(\frac{2 \times 80}{0.0443} \right)} \right] = 168.57 \text{ MPa}$$

Note: While using deflection equations from DHB, neglect sign for solving the problems.

70. **A rectangular beam of 100 mm width and 200 mm depth is freely supported over a span of 2 m. A load of 10 kN is dropped on the middle of the beam from a height of 10 mm. Find the maximum instantaneous deflection and stress induced in the beam. Take $E = 2 \times 10^5$ MPa.**

VTU – June/ July 2015 – 10 Marks; (Similar) Dec. 12 – 05 Marks

Solution: $b = 100$ mm, $d = 200$ mm, $L = 2000$ mm, $W = 10 \times 10^3$ N, $h = 10$ mm, $\sigma_b' = ?$, $y' = ?$, $E = 2 \times 10^5$ MPa.

Maximum instantaneous stress: We know that

$$\sigma_b' = \sigma_b \left[1 + \sqrt{1 + \left(\frac{2h}{y} \right)} \right] \qquad \text{... Eq. (i) 2.26(c)/ Pg 27, DHB}$$

But bending stress,

$$\sigma_b = \frac{M}{Z} \qquad \text{... Eq. (ii) 1.1(b)/ Pg 2, DHB}$$

- $$I = \frac{bd^3}{12} = \frac{100 \times 200^3}{12} = 66.67 \times 10^6 \text{ mm}^4$$

    ... **Tb 1.3(a), (Fig. a)/ Pg 12, DHB**

- $$Z = \frac{bd^2}{6} = \frac{100 \times 200^2}{6} = 666.7 \times 10^3 \text{ mm}^3$$

    ... **Tb 1.3(a), (Fig. a)/ Pg 12, DHB**

- For a simply supported beam (SS beam) with point load at mid span

$$M = \frac{WL}{4} = \frac{(10 \times 10^3) \times 2000}{4} = 5 \times 10^6 \ \text{N·mm}$$

... **Tb 1.4, (Fig. 4)/ Pg 15, DHB**

Deflection, $\qquad y = \dfrac{WL^3}{48EI}$ ... **Tb 1.4, (Fig. 4)/ Pg 15, DHB**

$\therefore \qquad\qquad y = \dfrac{(10 \times 10^3) \times 2000^3}{48 \times (2 \times 10^5) \times 66.67 \times 10^6} = 0.1250 \ \text{mm}$

$\therefore$ Eq. (ii) yields... $\quad \sigma_b = \dfrac{5 \times 10^6}{666.67 \times 10^3} = 7.50 \ \text{MPa}$

$\therefore$ Eq. (i) yields... $\quad \sigma_b' = 7.50 \left[1 + \sqrt{1 + \left(\dfrac{2 \times 10}{0.1250}\right)} \right] = 102.66 \ \text{MPa}$

Maximum instantaneous deflection: We know that

$$y' = y \left[1 + \sqrt{1 + \left(\frac{2h}{y}\right)} \right]$$

   ... **2.26(d)/ Pg 28, DHB**

$$= 0.1250 \left[1 + \sqrt{1 + \left(\frac{2 \times 10}{0.1250}\right)} \right] = 1.71 \ \text{mm}$$

71. **A 5 kg block is dropped from a height of 200 mm onto a beam as shown in Fig. 2.56. The material has an allowable stress of 50 MPa. Determine the dimensions of the rectangular cross-section whose depth is 1.5 times the width. Take $E = 70$ GPa.**

VTU – Dec. 07/ Jan. 2008 – 10 Marks

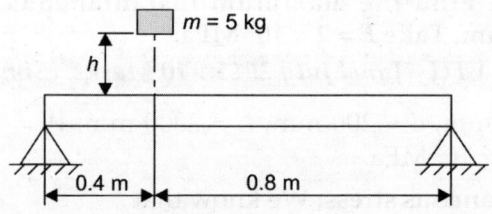

Fig. 2.56: Problem 71

Solution: $m = 5$ kg $\Rightarrow W = mg = 5 \times 9.81 = 49.05$ N, $h = 200$ mm, $\sigma_b' = 50$ MPa, $b = ?$, $d = ?$, $d = 1.5b$, $E = 70 \times 10^3$ MPa.

To find b and d: We know that

$$\sigma_b' = \sigma_b \left[1 + \sqrt{1 + \left(\frac{2h}{y}\right)} \right]$$

   ... Eq. (i) **2.26(c)/ Pg 27, DHB**

But bending stress,

$$\sigma_b = \frac{M}{Z}$$

   ... Eq. (ii) **1.1(b)/ Pg 2, DHB**

$$I = \frac{bd^3}{12} = \frac{b \times (1.5b)^3}{12} = 0.2813b^4$$

   ... **Tb 1.3(a), (Fig. a)/ Pg 12, DHB**

- $$Z = \frac{bd^2}{6} = \frac{b \times (1.5b)^2}{6} = 0.375b^3$$

  ... Tb 1.3(a), (Fig. a)/ Pg 12, DHB

- For a simply supported beam (SS beam) with point load at intermediate span

  $$M = \frac{Wab}{L} = \frac{49.05 \times 400 \times 800}{1200} = 13080 \text{ N·mm}$$

  ... Tb 1.4, (Fig. 5)/ Pg 15, DHB

Deflection, $\qquad y = \frac{Fbx}{6EIL}[2L(L-x) - b^2 - (L-x)^2]$

... Tb 1.4, (Fig. 5)/ Pg 15, DHB

From **Fig. 2.56**, $x = a; (L-x) = b; (L-b) = a; L = 1200$ mm

$\therefore \qquad y = \frac{Fba}{6EIL}[2Lb - b^2 - b^2]$

$$= \frac{Fba}{6EIL}[2Lb - 2b^2] = \frac{Fba}{6EIL}[2b(L-b)]$$

$$= \frac{Fa^2b^2}{3EIL} \qquad\qquad \text{... [}I \text{ missing in DHB]}$$

$$= \frac{49.05 \times 400^2 \times 800^2}{3 \times (70 \times 10^3) \times (0.2813b^4) \times 1200} = \frac{70.85 \times 10^3}{b^4}$$

$\therefore$ Eq. (ii) yields... $\qquad \sigma_b = \frac{13080}{0.375b^3} = \frac{34880}{b^3}$

$\therefore$ Eq. (i) yields... $\qquad 50 = \frac{34880}{b^3}\left[1 + \sqrt{1 + \left(\frac{2 \times 200}{70.85 \times 10^3 / b^4}\right)}\right]$

$$(1.433 \times 10^{-3})b^3 = \left[1 + \sqrt{1 + (5.65 \times 10^{-3})b^4}\right]$$

$$(1.433 \times 10^{-3})b^3 - 1 = \sqrt{1 + (5.65 \times 10^{-3})b^4}$$

Squaring both sides, we have

$$[(1.433 \times 10^{-3})b^3 - 1]^2 = 1 + (5.65 \times 10^{-3})b^4$$

$$(2.05 \times 10^{-6})b^6 + 1 - (2.866 \times 10^{-3})b^3 = 1 + (5.65 \times 10^{-3})b^4$$

$$(2.05 \times 10^{-6})b^6 - (5.65 \times 10^{-3})b^4 - (2.866 \times 10^{-3})b^3 = 0$$

Dividing throughout by b^3, we have

$$(2.05 \times 10^{-6})b^3 - (5.65 \times 10^{-3})b - 2.866 \times 10^{-3} = 0 \qquad\qquad \text{... Eq. (ii)}$$

which upon solving yields $\qquad\qquad b = 52.75$ mm

$\therefore \qquad\qquad\qquad\qquad b \approx 55$ mm

and $\qquad\qquad\qquad\qquad d = 1.5 \times 55 = 82.5$ mm

72. **A weight of 600 N drops through a height of 20 mm and impacts the center of 300 mm long simply supported circular cross-section beam. Find the diameter of the beam and the maximum deflection, if the allowable stress is limited to 90 MPa. Neglect the inertia effect and take $E = 200$ GPa.**

VTU – Dec. 2009/ Jan 2010 – 10 Marks; June - July 2014 – 07 Marks

Solution: $W = 600$ N, $h = 20$ mm, $L = 300$ mm, diameter $D = ?$, $y' = ?$, $\sigma'_b = 90$ MPa, $E = 200 \times 10^3$ MPa.

To find diameter D: We know that

$$\sigma'_b = \sigma_b \left[1 + \sqrt{1 + \left(\frac{2h}{y}\right)} \right] \qquad \text{... Eq. (i) } \textbf{2.26(c)/ Pg 27, DHB}$$

But bending stress,

$$\sigma_b = \frac{M}{Z} \qquad \text{... Eq. (ii) } \textbf{1.1(b)/ Pg 2, DHB}$$

- $$I = \frac{\pi D^4}{64} = 0.0491 D^4 \qquad \text{... Tb 1.3(a), (Fig. g)/ Pg 13, DHB}$$

- $$Z = \frac{\pi D^3}{32} = 0.0982 D^3 \qquad \text{... Tb 1.3(a), (Fig. g)/ Pg 13, DHB}$$

- For a simply supported beam (SS beam) with point load at mid span

$$M = \frac{WL}{4} = \frac{600 \times 300}{4} = 45000 \text{ N} \cdot \text{mm}$$
$$\text{... Tb 1.4, (Fig. 4)/ Pg 15, DHB}$$

Deflection, $\qquad y = \dfrac{WL^3}{48EI} \qquad \text{... Tb 1.4, (Fig. 4)/ Pg 15, DHB}$

$$\therefore \qquad y = \frac{600 \times 300^3}{48 \times (200 \times 10^3) \times 0.0491 D^4} = \frac{34.37 \times 10^3}{D^4} \qquad \text{... Eq. (iii)}$$

$\therefore$ Eq. (ii) yields... $\qquad \sigma_b = \dfrac{45000}{0.0982 D^3} = \dfrac{458.25 \times 10^3}{D^3}$

$\therefore$ Eq. (i) yields... $\qquad 90 = \dfrac{458.25 \times 10^3}{D^3} \left[1 + \sqrt{1 + \left(\dfrac{2 \times 20}{34.37 \times 10^3 / D^4}\right)} \right]$

$$(1.964 \times 10^{-4}) D^3 = \left[1 + \sqrt{1 + (1.164 \times 10^{-3}) D^4} \right]$$

$$(1.964 \times 10^{-4}) D^3 - 1 = \sqrt{1 + (1.164 \times 10^{-3}) D^4}$$

Squaring both sides, we have

$$[(1.964 \times 10^{-4}) D^3 - 1]^2 = 1 + (1.164 \times 10^{-3}) D^4$$

$$(3.857 \times 10^{-8}) D^6 + 1 - (3.928 \times 10^{-4}) D^3 = 1 + (1.164 \times 10^{-3}) D^4$$

$$(3.857 \times 10^{-8}) D^6 - (1.164 \times 10^{-3}) D^4 - (3.928 \times 10^{-4}) D^3 = 0$$

Dividing throughout by D^3, we have

$$(3.857 \times 10^{-8}) D^3 - (1.164 \times 10^{-3}) D - 3.928 \times 10^{-4} = 0 \qquad \text{... Eq. (ii)}$$

which upon solving yields $\qquad\qquad\qquad\qquad D = 173.88$ mm

$\therefore \qquad\qquad\qquad\qquad\qquad\qquad\qquad\qquad D \approx 175$ mm

Maximum instantaneous deflection: We know that

$$y' = y\left[1 + \sqrt{1 + \left(\frac{2h}{y}\right)}\right] \qquad \textbf{2.26(d)/ Pg 28, DHB}$$

$\therefore$ Eq. (iii) yields... $\quad y = \dfrac{34.37 \times 10^3}{175^4} = 3.66 \times 10^{-5}$ mm

$$y' = 3.66 \times 10^{-5}\left[1 + \sqrt{1 + \left(\frac{2 \times 20}{3.66 \times 10^{-5}}\right)}\right] = 0.0383 \text{ mm}$$

73. **A steel cantilever beam of rectangular cross-section is loaded 400 mm from the supports. The width of the beam is 16 mm and the depth is 20 mm. Determine the maximum bending stress in the beam, when a weight of 100 N is dropped on the beam through a height of 5 mm. Take $E = 210$ GPa.**

VTU – Dec. 2010 – 06 Marks

Solution: $L = 400$ mm, $b = 16$ mm, $d = 20$ mm, $\sigma'_b = ?$, $W = 100$ N, $h = 5$ mm, $E = 200 \times 10^3$ MPa.

Maximum instantaneous stress: We know that

$$\sigma'_b = \sigma_b\left[1 + \sqrt{1 + \left(\frac{2h}{y}\right)}\right] \qquad \text{... Eq. (i) } \textbf{2.26(c)/ Pg 27, DHB}$$

But bending stress,

$$\sigma_b = \frac{M}{Z} \qquad \text{... Eq. (ii) } \textbf{1.1(b)/ Pg 2, DHB}$$

- $$I = \frac{bd^3}{12} = \frac{16 \times 20^3}{12} = 10.67 \times 10^3 \text{ mm}^4 \qquad \text{...}$$
  Tb 1.3(a), (Fig. a)/ Pg 12, DHB

- $$Z = \frac{bd^3}{12} = \frac{16 \times 20^2}{6} = 1066.67 \text{ mm}^3$$
  ... Tb 1.3(a), (Fig. a)/ Pg 12, DHB

- For a cantilever beam with end load,
  $$M = WL = 100 \times 400 = 40000 \text{ N·m}$$
  ... Tb 1.4, (Fig. 1)/ Pg 15, DHB

  Deflection, $\quad y = \dfrac{WL^3}{3EI} \qquad$ **... Tb 1.4, (Fig. 1)/ Pg 15, DHB**

$\therefore \quad y = \dfrac{100 \times 400^3}{3 \times (210 \times 10^3) \times 10.67 \times 10^3} = 0.952$ mm

$\therefore$ Eq. (ii) yields... $\quad \sigma_b = \dfrac{40000}{1066.67} = 37.50$ MPa

$\therefore$ Eq. (i) yields... $\quad \sigma'_b = 3750\left[1 + \sqrt{1 + \left(\frac{2 \times 5}{0.952}\right)}\right] = 164.70$ MPa

74. **A cantilever beam 12 mm deep, 8 mm wide and 300 mm long is loaded as follows, at the free end. Determine the maximum bending stress in each case.**
    i. A load of 50 N applied gradually.
    ii. A load of 50 N dropped through a distance of 5 mm.

VTU – Dec. 2010 – 10 Marks

Solution: $b = 8$ mm, $d = 12$ mm, $L = 300$ mm, $\sigma'_b = ?$

Case i: Gradually applied load $F = W = 50$ kN: We know that

$$\sigma'_b = \sigma_b \left[1 + \sqrt{1 + \left(\frac{2h}{y} \right)} \right] \qquad \text{... Eq. (i) } \textbf{2.26(c)/ Pg 27, DHB}$$

In case of gradually applied load, $h = 0$, thus we have

$$\sigma'_b = \sigma_b = \frac{M}{Z} \qquad \text{... Eq. (ii) } \textbf{1.1(b)/ Pg 2, DHB}$$

- $$I = \frac{bd^3}{12} = \frac{8 \times 12^3}{12} = 1152 \text{ mm}^4 \qquad \text{...}$$

Tb 1.3(a), (Fig. a)/ Pg 12, DHB

- $$Z = \frac{bd^2}{6} = \frac{8 \times 12^2}{6} = 192 \text{ mm}^3$$

... Tb 1.3(a), (Fig. a)/ Pg 12, DHB

- For a cantilever beam with end load,
  $$M = WL = 50 \times 300 = 15000 \text{ N·m}$$

... Tb 1.4, (Fig. 1)/ Pg 15, DHB

Deflection, $\qquad y = \frac{WL^3}{3EI}$ **... Tb 1.4, (Fig. 1)/ Pg 15, DHB**

$$\therefore \qquad y = \frac{50 \times 300^3}{3 \times (210 \times 10^3) \times 1152} = 1.86 \text{ mm}$$

$\therefore$ Eq. (ii) yields... $\qquad \sigma_b = \frac{15000}{192} = 78.125$ MPa

Case ii: Impact load $F = W = 50$ kN:

$\therefore$ Eq. (i) yields... $\qquad \sigma'_b = 78.125 \left[1 + \sqrt{1 + \left(\frac{2 \times 5}{1.86} \right)} \right] = 275.40$ MPa

75. **A machine element in the form of a cantilever beam is made of rod of circular cross-section with a span of 800 mm. The material of the rod is carbon steel C30. Determine the safe value for a transverse load that falls on to the free end of the beam from a height of 25 mm, if the diameter of the rod is 40 mm. Use a value of 2.5 for factor of safety.**

VTU – July/ Aug. 2005 – 07 Marks

Solution: $L = 800$ mm, material: carbon steel C30, $W = ?$, $h = 25$ mm, diameter, $D = 40$ mm, $n = 2.5$.

We know that factor of safety,

$$n = \frac{\sigma_y}{\sigma'_b}$$

Material	Yield strength, $(\sigma_y) = 294$ MPa	... Tb I.8/ Pg 463, DHB
C30	Young's modulus for steel (E) $= 202$ GPa	... Tb 1.18/ Pg 11, DHB

$$\sigma'_b = \frac{294}{2.5} = 117.6 \text{ MPa}$$

Also
$$\sigma'_b = \sigma_b \left[1 + \sqrt{1 + \left(\frac{2h}{y} \right)} \right]$$

But bending stress,

$$\sigma_b = \frac{M}{Z} \qquad \text{... Eq. (ii) } \textbf{1.1(b)/ Pg 2, DHB}$$

- $$I = \frac{\pi D^4}{64} = \frac{\pi \times 40^4}{64} = 125.66 \times 10^3 \text{ mm}^4$$

  ... Tb 1.3(a), (Fig. g)/ Pg 13, DHB

- $$Z = \frac{\pi D^3}{32} = \frac{\pi \times 40^3}{32} = 6283.19 \text{ mm}^3$$

  ... Tb 1.3(a), (Fig. g)/ Pg 13, DHB

- For a cantilever beam with end load,
$$M = WL = (800 \, W) \text{ N·mm}$$

  ... Tb 1.4, (Fig. 1)/ Pg 15, DHB

Deflection,
$$y = \frac{WL^3}{3EI} \qquad \text{... Tb 1.4, (Fig. 1)/ Pg 15, DHB}$$

$$\therefore \qquad y = \frac{W \times 800^3}{3 \times (202 \times 10^3) \times 125.66 \times 10^3} = 6.72 \times 10^{-3} \, W$$

$\therefore$ Eq. (ii) yields...
$$\sigma_b = \frac{800 \, W}{6283.19} = 0.127 \, W \text{ MPa}$$

$\therefore$ Eq. (i) yields...
$$117.6 = 0.127 \, W \left[1 + \sqrt{1 + \left(\frac{2 \times 25}{6.72 \times 10^{-3} \, W} \right)} \right]$$

$$\left(\frac{925.98}{W} \right) - 1 = \sqrt{1 + \left(\frac{7440.48}{W} \right)}$$

Squaring both sides, we have

$$\left[\left(\frac{925.98}{W} \right) - 1 \right]^2 = 1 + \left(\frac{7440.48}{W} \right)$$

$$\frac{857.44 \times 10^3}{W^2} + 1 - \frac{1851.96}{W} = 1 + \left(\frac{7440.48}{W} \right)$$

$$\frac{857.44 \times 10^3}{W^2} = \left(\frac{9292.44}{W} \right)$$

$\therefore \qquad W = 92.27 \text{ N}$

76. A machine element in the form of a cantilever beam has a rectangular cross-section of 40 mm width and 120 mm depth. The span of the beam is 600 mm. A transverse load of 5 kN falls from a height of '*h*' at the free end of the beam. Determine the safe value of '*h*' limiting the normal stress induced in the machine element, due to impact, to 120 MPa. The modulus of elasticity of the material of the beam is 210 GPa.

VTU – July 2006 – 07 Marks

Solution: $b = 40$ mm, $d = 120$ mm, $L = 600$ mm, $F = W = 5$ kN, $h = ?$, $\sigma_b' = 120$ MPa, $E = 210$ MPa.

To find *h*: We know that

$$\sigma_b = \frac{M}{Z} \qquad \text{... Eq. (ii) } \textbf{1.1(b)/ Pg 2, DHB}$$

• $$I = \frac{bd^3}{12} = \frac{40 \times 120^3}{12} = 5.76 \times 10^6 \text{ mm}^4$$

... **Tb 1.3(a), (Fig. a)/ Pg 12, DHB**

• $$Z = \frac{bd^2}{6} = \frac{40 \times 120^2}{6} = 96000 \text{ mm}^3$$

... **Tb 1.3(a), (Fig. a)/ Pg 12, DHB**

• For a cantilever beam with end load,
$$M = WL = 5000 \times 600 = 3 \times 10^6 \text{ N·mm}$$

... **Tb 1.4, (Fig. 1)/ Pg 15, DHB**

Deflection, $$y = \frac{WL^3}{3EI} \qquad \text{... \textbf{Tb 1.4, (Fig. 1)/ Pg 15, DHB}}$$

$$\therefore \quad y = \frac{5000 \times 600^3}{3 \times (210 \times 10^3) \times 5.76 \times 10^6} = 0.298 \text{ mm} \qquad \text{... Eq. (iii)}$$

$\therefore$ Eq. (ii) yields... $$\sigma_b = \frac{3 \times 10^6}{96000} = 31.25 \text{ MPa}$$

$\therefore$ Eq. (i) yields... $$120 = 31.25 \left[1 + \sqrt{1 + \left(\frac{2h}{0.298} \right)} \right]$$

$$3.84 - 1 = \sqrt{1 + 6.71h}$$
$$2.94 = \sqrt{1 + 6.71h}$$

Squaring both sides, we have
$$8.066 = 1 + 6.71h$$
$$7.066 = 6.71h$$
$$\therefore \qquad h = 1.053 \text{ mm}$$

PROBLEMS ON ENERGY AND RESILIENCE

77. A mass of 500 kg is being lowered by means of a steel wire rope having cross-sectional area of 250 mm². The velocity of weight is 0.5 m/sec. When the length of the extended rope is 20 m, the sheave gets stuck up. Determine the stresses induced in the rope due to sudden stoppage of the sheave. Neglect friction. Take $E = 190$ GPa

VTU – July 2007 – 08 Marks; Dec. 2014/ Jan 2015 – 10 Marks

Solution: $m = 5$ kg, $A = 250$ mm^2, $v = 0.5$ m/s, $L = 20$ m, $\sigma = ?$, $E = 190$ GPa = 190×10^3 MPa.

We know that strain energy

$$U = \frac{\sigma^2 V}{2E} \qquad \text{... 2.27(b)/ Pg 29, DHB}$$

Volume $\qquad V = AL = 250 \times (20 \times 10^3) = 5 \times 10^6$ mm^3

$$U = \frac{\sigma^2 \times (5 \times 10^6)}{2 \times (190 \times 10^3)} = 13.157\sigma^2 \text{ N·mm} = 0.01357\sigma^2 \text{ N·m}$$

$$\text{... Eq. (i)}$$

Also kinetic energy,

$$E_k = \frac{Wv^2}{2g} = \frac{mv^2}{2} \qquad \text{... 2.25(a)/ Pg 27, DHB}$$

$$= \frac{500 \times 0.5^2}{2} = 62.5 \text{ N·m} \qquad \text{... Eq. (ii)}$$

Equating Eqs. (i) and (ii), we have

$$0.01357\sigma^2 = 62.5$$

$$\therefore \qquad \sigma = 68.92 \text{ MPa}$$

78. **A wagon weighing 35 kN is attached to a wire rope and moving down an incline at 3.6 km/hr, when the rope jams and the wagon is suddenly brought to rest. If the length of the rope is 60 m at the time of sudden stoppage, calculate the maximum instantaneous stress and the maximum instantaneous elongation produced. Take the diameter of rope = 30 mm and $E = 200$ GPa.**

Solution: $W = 35$ kN, $v = 3.6$ km/hr = 1 m/s, $L = 60$ m, $\sigma = ?$, $\delta = ?$, diameter of rope $d = 30$ mm, $E = 200$ GPa.

Maximum instantaneous stress: We know that strain energy

$$U = \frac{\sigma^2 V}{2E} \qquad \text{... 2.27(b)/ Pg 29, DHB}$$

Volume $\qquad V = AL = (\pi \times 30^2/4) \times (60 \times 10^3) = 42.41 \times 10^6$ mm^3

$$U = \frac{\sigma^2 \times (42.41 \times 10^6)}{2 \times (200 \times 10^3)} = 106.03\sigma^2 \text{ N·mm} = 0.10603\,\sigma^2 \text{ N·m}$$

$$\text{... Eq. (i)}$$

Also kinetic energy,

$$E_k = \frac{Wv^2}{2g} = \frac{35000 \times 1^2}{2 \times 9.81} = 1783.89 \text{ N·m}$$

$$\text{... Eq. (ii) **2.25(a)/ Pg 27, DHB**}$$

Equating Eqs. (i) and (ii), we have

$$0.10603\,\sigma^2 = 1783.89$$

$$\therefore \qquad \sigma = 129.71 \text{ MPa}$$

Maximum instantaneous deflection: We know that

$$\delta = \frac{\sigma L}{E} = \frac{129.71 \times 60000}{200 \times 10^3} = 38.91 \text{ mm}$$

79. **A weight of 5 kN is being lowered with a velocity of 2 m/s with the help of a wire rope and a sheave. When the sheave stops suddenly after the weight has reached a distance of 15 m, find the maximum stress in the rope. The area resisting the stress is 707 mm² and modulus of elasticity is 190 GPa. Neglect the inertia effect.**

VTU – Dec. 06/ Jan. 2007 – 10 Marks

Solution: $W = 5$ kN, $v = 2$ m/s $= L = 15$ m, $\sigma = ?$, $A = 707$ mm², $E = 190$ GPa.

Maximum instantaneous stress: We know that strain energy

$$U = \frac{\sigma^2 V}{2E} \qquad \text{... 2.27(b)/ Pg 29, DHB}$$

$$U = \frac{\sigma^2 \times (707 \times 15 \times 10^3)}{2 \times (190 \times 10^3)} = 27.91\sigma^2 \text{ N·mm} = 0.02791\sigma^2 \text{ N·m}$$

$$\text{... Eq. (i)}$$

Also kinetic energy,

$$E_k = \frac{Wv^2}{2g} = \frac{5000 \times 2^2}{2 \times 9.81} = 1019.37 \text{ N·m}$$

Equating Eqs. (i) and (ii), we have

$$0.02791\sigma^2 = 1019.37 \qquad \text{... Eq. (ii) 2.25(a)/ Pg 27, DHB}$$

$$\therefore \qquad \sigma = 191.11 \text{ MPa}$$

80. **An elevator car carrying a load of 10 kN is descending by means of a steel rope at a speed of 1 m/sec. The cross-section area of the rope is 400 mm². The rope is suddenly brought to rest by braking after 30 seconds of descent. Calculate the stress induced in the rope due to sudden stoppage if Young's modulus for the rope is 80000 MPa.**

VTU – July/ Aug. 2004 – 10 Marks

Solution: $W = 10$ kN, $v = 1$ m/s $= A = 400$ mm², $t = 30$ sec, $\sigma = ?$, $E = 80000$ GPa.

We know that strain energy

$$U = \frac{\sigma^2 V}{2E} \qquad \text{... Eq. (i) 2.27(b)/ Pg 29, DHB}$$

But volume $\qquad V = AL \qquad \text{... Eq. (ii)}$

Also $\qquad v^2 = u^2 + 2as$

Here $\qquad a = \dfrac{v}{t} = \dfrac{1}{30} = 0.0334$ m/s² and $u = 0$ m/s

$$1^2 = 0 + (2 \times 0.0334 \times s)$$

$$s = 15 \text{ m}$$

$$\therefore \qquad s = L = 15000 \text{ mm}$$

$\therefore$ Eq. (i) yields... $\quad U = \dfrac{\sigma^2 \times (400 \times 15000)}{2 \times 80000} = 37.5\sigma^2 \text{ N·m} = 0.0375\sigma^2 \text{ N·m}$

$$\text{... Eq. (iii)}$$

Also kinetic energy,

$$E_k = \frac{Wv^2}{2g} = \frac{10000 \times 1^2}{2 \times 9.81} = 509.58 \text{ N·m}$$

$$\text{... Eq. (iv) 2.25(a)/ Pg 27, DHB}$$

Equating Eqs. (iii) and (iv), we have

$$0.0375\sigma^2 = 509.68$$

$$\therefore \qquad \sigma = 116.58 \text{ MPa}$$

81. **A steel wire 5 mm diameter is firmly held in clamp from which it hangs vertically. An anvil, the weight of which may be neglected is secured to the wire 2 m below the clamp. The wire is to be tested allowing a weight bored to the slide over the wire to drop freely from 1.5 m above the anvil. Calculate the weight required to stress the wire to 700 MPa, assuming the wire to be elastic up to this stress. Take $E = 210$ GPa.**

Solution: Diameter of wire $d = 5$ mm, $L = 2$ m, $h = 1.5$ m, $W = ?$, $\sigma = 700$ MPa, $E = 210$ GPa.

We know that $\qquad U = W \times (h + y') \qquad\qquad$ ... Eq. (i) **2.25(c)/ Pg 27, DHB**

Also $\qquad\qquad U = \dfrac{\sigma^2 V}{2E} \qquad\qquad$ ... Eq. (ii) **2.27(b)/ Pg 29, DHB**

Equating Eqs. (i) and (ii), we have

$$W \times (h + y') = \frac{\sigma^2 V}{2E} \qquad\qquad \text{... Eq. (iii)}$$

But $\qquad\qquad y' = \dfrac{\sigma L}{E} = \dfrac{700 \times 2000}{(210 \times 10^3)} = 6.67 \text{ mm}$

$\therefore$ Eq. (iii) yields...

$$W \times (1500 + 6.67) = \frac{700^2 \times [(\pi \times 5^2/4) \times 2000]}{2 \times (210 \times 10^3)}$$

$$\therefore \qquad\qquad W = 30.41 \text{ N}$$

82. **A vertical steel rod of 20 mm diameter checks the fall on its end of weight 2 kN, which drops through a distance of 10 mm before it strikes the rod. Find the shortest length of the rod which will bear the impact, if the stress is not to exceed 150 MPa. Take $E = 200$ GPa.**

Solution: Diameter of rod $d = 20$ mm, $W = 2$ kN, $h = 10$ mm, $L = ?$, $\sigma = 150$ MPa, $E = 200$ GPa.

We know that $\qquad U = W \times (h + y') \qquad\qquad$ Eq. (i) **2.25(c)/ Pg 27, DHB**

Also $\qquad\qquad U = \dfrac{\sigma^2 V}{2E} \qquad\qquad$ ... Eq. (ii) **2.27(b)/ Pg 29, DHB**

Equating Eqs. (i) and (ii), we have

$$W \times (h + y') = \frac{\sigma^2 V}{2E} \qquad\qquad \text{... Eq. (iii)}$$

But $\qquad\qquad y' = \dfrac{\sigma L}{E} = \dfrac{150 L}{200 \times 10^3} = 7.5 \times 10^{-4} L \text{ mm}$

$\therefore$ Eq. (iii) yields...

$$2000 \times (10 + 7.5 \times 10^{-4} L) = \frac{150^2 \times [(\pi \times 20^2/4) \times L]}{2 \times (200 \times 10^3)}$$

$$\therefore \qquad (10 + 7.5 \times 10^{-4}L) = 8.836 \times 10^{-3}L$$
$$10 = 8.086 \times 10^{-3}L$$
$$\therefore \qquad L = 1236.71 \text{ mm} = 1.236 \text{ m}$$

PROBLEMS ON TORSION

83. **Determine the maximum torsional impact that can withstand, without permanent deformation by a 100 mm cylindrical shaft 5 m long and made of SAE 1045 annealed steel ($\tau_y = 180$ MPa and $G = 82$ GPa). Factor of safety = 3.**

VTU – May/ June 2010 – 04 Marks

Solution: $\tau' =$?, diameter, $d = 100$ mm, $L = 5000$ mm, $\tau_y = 180$ MPa, $G = 82$ GPa, $n = 3$.

For a round solid bar, resilience in torsion

Also
$$U_s = \frac{\tau_e^2 V}{4G} \qquad \qquad \text{... Eq. (i) Tb. 2.9/ Pg 34, DHB}$$

But
$$\tau_e = \frac{\tau_y}{n} = \frac{180}{3} = 60 \text{ MPa}$$

Volume
$$V = A \cdot L = (\pi \times 100^2/4) \times 5000 = 3.93 \times 10^7 \text{ N·mm}$$

$\therefore$ Eq. (i) yields...
$$U_s = \frac{60^2 \times 3.93 \times 10^7}{4 \times 82 \times 10^3} = 4.31 \times 10^5 \text{ N·m} = 431 \text{ N·m}$$

VTU QUESTION PAPERS

Mar. 2001 (ME5T2)

1. a. A steel blade 1 mm thick is bent into an arc of circle 500 mm radius. Determine the flexural stresses induced and the bending moment required to bend the blade, which is 15 mm wide. Take $E = 210$ GPa. **(05 Marks)**

   b. Determine the maximum normal and maximum shear stress at section A – A for the crank shown in **Fig. U2.1**, when a load of 10 kN, assumed concentrated, is applied at the center of the crank pin. Neglect the effect of transverse shear. **(10 Marks)**

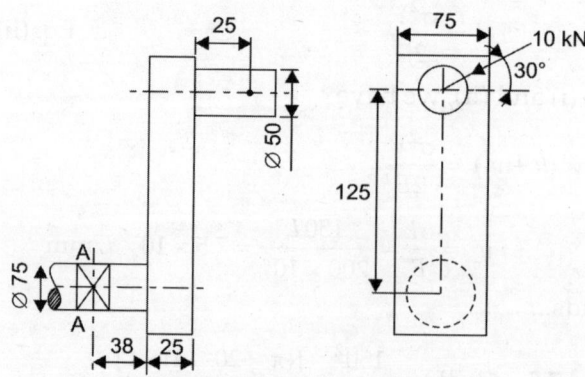

Fig. U2.1

2. a. List the factors to be considered in arriving at an appropriate value of factor of safety in the design process of a machine component. **(05 Marks)**

   b. Find the diameter of the hole in **Fig. U2.2**, if the stress concentration factor at the hole is to be same as at the fillet. **(05 Marks)**

3. A mild steel shaft 60 mm diameter is subjected to a bending moment of 25×10^5 N·mm and torque M_t. If the yield point of steel in tension is 230 N/mm^2, find the maximum value of this torque without causing yielding of the shaft according to:

   i. Maximum principal stress theory of failure
   ii. Maximum shear stress theory of failure
   iii. Maximum distortion energy theory of failure.
   Adopt a factor of safety of 1.5. **(14 Marks)**

Fig. U2.2

July/Aug. 2004 (AU46)

4. An elevator car carrying a load of 10 kN is descending by means of a steel rope at a speed of 1 m/sec. The cross-section area of the rope is 400 mm^2. The rope is suddenly brought to rest by braking after 30 seconds of descent, calculate the stress induced in the rope due to sudden stoppage if Young's modulus for the rope is 80000 MPa. **(10 Marks)**

5. State the following theories of failure. When are they used?

   i. Maximum normal stress theory
   ii. Maximum shear stress theory. **(05 Marks)**

Jan/Feb. 2005 (AU46)

6. A vertical bar of uniform cross-section has a flange at the lower end. A weight W is released from the top of the box and falls freely along the bar until it strikes the flange. Determine the maximum stress induced in the bar. State the assumptions used while determining the same. **(10 Marks)**

7. a. A material has yield strength of 600 MPa. Compute the factor of safety for each of the failure theories for ductile material. Use following stress states:

   i. $\sigma_1 = 420$ MPa $\sigma_2 = 410$ MPa $\sigma_3 = 0$ MPa
   ii. $\sigma_1 = 420$ MPa $\sigma_2 = 180$ MPa $\sigma_3 = 0$ MPa
   iii. $\sigma_1 = 420$ MPa $\sigma_2 = 0$ MPa $\sigma_3 = -180$ MPa
   iv. $\sigma_1 = 0$ MPa $\sigma_2 = -180$ MPa $\sigma_3 = -420$ MPa   **(12 Marks)**

   b. A rectangular plate 15 mm thick made of a brittle material is shown in **Fig. U2.3**. Calculate the stresses at each of three holes. **(08 Marks)**

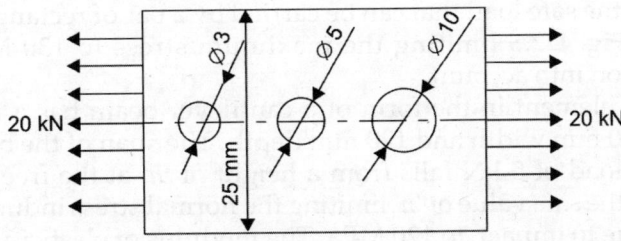

Fig. U2.3

July/Aug. 2005 (AU46)

8. a. Derive an expression for impact/shock factor. **(05 Marks)**

   b. A machine element in the form of a cantilever beam is made of rod of circular cross-section with a span of 800 mm. The material of the rod is carbon steel C30. Determine a safe value for a transverse load that falls on to the free end of the beam from a height of 25 mm, if the diameter of the rod is 40 mm. Use a value of 2.5 for factor of safety. **(07 Marks)**

9. a. A round bar of diameter $1.2d$ has a semi-circular groove of radius $0.1d$. Determine the safe value of d to sustain a bending moment of 2 kN·m. Select a suitable material and choose appropriate value for factor of safety. **(05 Marks)**

   b. Explain the following theories of failure.
      i. Maximum normal stress theory
      ii. Maximum shear stress theory
      iii. Distortion energy theory. **(06 Marks)**

   c. A round bar of diameter 50 mm is to sustain an axial tensile load of 25 kN together with a twisting moment of 1.5 kN·m. The material for the rod is carbon steel C40. Determine the factor of safety as per the following theory of failure: Maximum normal stress theory. **(8 Marks)**

Jan/Feb. 2006 (AU46)

10. An unknown weight falls through 15 mm on a collar rigidly attached to the lower end of a vertical bar 3 meter long and 500 sq mm section. If the maximum instantaneous extension is 2 mm, what is the corresponding stress and the value of unknown weight? Take $E = 200$ kN/mm^2. **(10 Marks)**

11. a. Explain the following theories of failure:
       i. Maximum normal stress theory
       ii. Maximum shear stress theory
       iii. Distortion energy theory **(09 Marks)**

    b. Discuss the statement, "In static loading, stress concentration in ductile materials is not as serious as in brittle materials". **(03 Marks)**

    c. Find the maximum stress induced in the following cases taking stress concentration into account:
       i. A rectangular plate of 60 mm × 90 mm with a hole of 12 mm in the center loaded in axial tension of 12 kN. Thickness of plate is 10 mm.
       ii. A circular shaft of 50 mm diameter stepped down to 25 mm diameter having a fillet radius of 5 mm subjected to an axial tensile load of 12 kN. **(08 Marks)**

July 2006 (AU46)

12. Determine the stress at extreme fibers for the cross-section X-X of the C-clamp loaded as shown in **Fig. U2.4**, where $P = 100$ kN. **(14 Marks)**

13. a. Determine the safe load that can be carried by a bar of rectangular cross-section shown in **Fig. U2.5** limiting the maximum stress to 130 MPa taking stress concentration into account. **(10 Marks)**

    b. A machine element in the form of a cantilever beam has a rectangular cross-section of 40 mm width and 120 mm depth. The span of the beam is 600 mm. A transverse load of 5 kN falls from a height of 'h' at the free end of the beam. Determine the safe value of 'h' limiting the normal stress induced in the machine element, due to impact, to 120 MPa. The modulus of elasticity of the material of the beam is 210 MPa. **(07 Marks)**

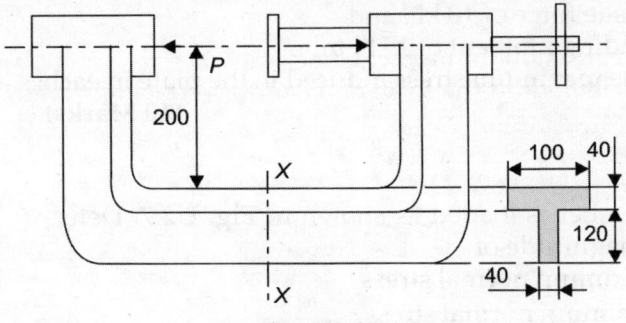

Fig. U2.4

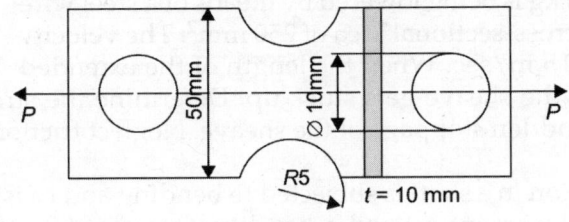

Fig. U2.5

Dec. 06/Jan. 2007 (AU46)

14. a. A circular shaft 50 mm diameter fixed at one end is subjected to an axial load of 20 kN and a torque of 1.5 kN·m. If the length of the shaft is 300 mm, determine the nature and magnitude of stresses at the critical point. **(10 Marks)**

b. A weight of 5 kN is being lowered with a velocity of 2 m/s with the help of a wire rope and a sheave. When the sheave stops suddenly after the weight has reached a distance of 15 m, find the maximum stress in the rope. The area resisting the stress is 707 mm^2 and modulus of elasticity is 190 GPa. Neglect the inertia effect. **(10 Marks)**

15. a. A hot rolled bar has an yield strength of 390 MPa. Compute the factor of safety for the following theories of failure:

   i. Maximum normal stress theory

   ii. Maximum shear stress theory

   iii. Distortion energy theory, for the following states of stress.

   - $\sigma_1 = 225$ MPa $\sigma_2 = 225$ MPa $\sigma_3 = 0$ MPa
   - $\sigma_1 = 225$ MPa $\sigma_2 = 120$ MPa $\sigma_3 = 0$ MPa
   - $\sigma_1 = 225$ MPa $\sigma_2 = 0$ MPa $\sigma_3 = -120$ MPa   **(10 Marks)**

b. A rectangular plate with semi-circular groove of radius 12 mm as shown in **Fig. U2.6** is subjected to:

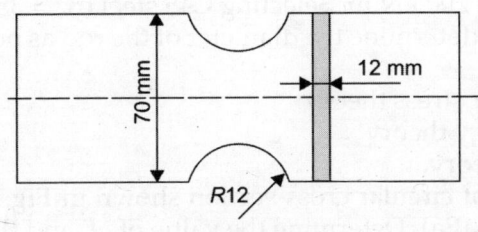

Fig. U2.6

i. A tensile force of 10 kN and

ii. A bending moment of 15 N·m.

Determine the maximum stress induced in the plate in each case.   **(10 Marks)**

July 2007 (AU46)

16. a. A steel member is loaded as shown in **Fig. U2.7**. Determine the magnitude of

    i. The maximum normal stress

    ii. The minimum normal stress

    iii. The maximum shear stress.   **(12 Marks)**

    b. A mass of 500 kg is being lowered by means of a steel wire rope having cross-sectional area of 250 mm². The velocity of weight is 0.5 m/sec. When the length of the extended rope is 20 m, the sheave gets stuck up. Determine the stresses induced in the rope due to sudden stoppage of the sheave. Neglect friction. Take $E = 190$ GPa   **(08 Marks)**

Figure, top right:

Ø 100, 150, Ø 50, 200, Ø 100, 150, 100 N·m, 9000 N

Fig. U2.7

17. a. A critical section in a shaft is subjected to bending and twisting simultaneously. The bending moment caused a bending stress of 50 MPa and the twisting moment causes a shear stress of 31.5 MPa. Determine the factor of safety according to:

    i. Maximum normal stress theory

    ii. Maximum shear stress theory if a tensile test gives a proportionality limit of 284 MPa and a yield stress of 324 MPa.   **(08 Marks)**

    b. A stepped shaft is subjected to a transverse load of 8 kN as shown in **Fig. U2.8**. The shaft is made of steel with ultimate tensile strength of 400 MPa. Determine the diameter of the shaft based on factor of safety of 2.   **(12 Marks)**

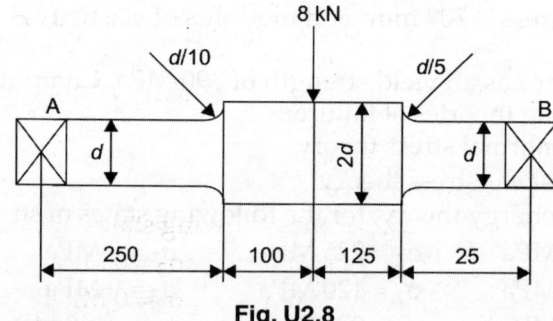

Fig. U2.8

Dec. 07/Jan. 2008 (AU46)

18. A rod of circular cross-section is to sustain a torsional moment of 300 kN·m and bending moment of 200 kN·m. Selecting C45 steel ($\sigma_y = 353$ MPa) and assuming a factor of safety of 3, determine the diameter of the rod as per the following theories of failure:

    i. Maximum shear stress theory

    ii. Distortion energy theory

    iii. Total energy theory.   **(15 Marks)**

19. a. A stepped shaft of circular cross-section shown in **Fig. U2.9** is made of 20Mn2 steel ($\sigma_y = 431.5$ MPa). Determine the value of 'd' and the fillet radius 'r' so that

the maximum stress will be limited to a ratio corresponding to a factor of safety of 2.5 and taking stress concentration factor into account.
(10 Marks)

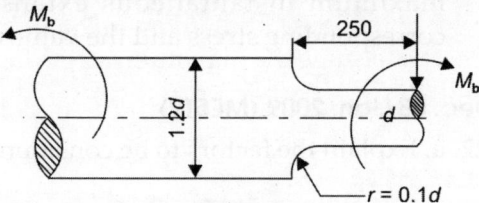

Fig. U2.9

b. A 5 kg block is dropped from a height of 200 mm on to a beam as shown in **Fig. U2.10**. The material has as allowable stress of 50 MPa. Determine the dimensions of the rectangular cross-section whose depth is 1.5 times the width. Take $E = 70$ GPa.
(10 Marks)

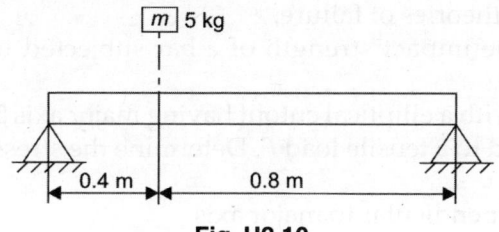

Fig. U2.10

June/July 2008 (AU46)

20. a. Explain the following:
    i. Maximum shear stress theory
    ii. Distortion energy theory
    (06 Marks)

   b. The state of stresses at a point in a body is given below:
   $\sigma_x = 81$ MPa, $\sigma_y = 21$ MPa and $\tau_{xy} = 84$ MPa. The yield stress of the material is 280 MPa. Find the factor of safety by:
   i. Maximum shear stress
   ii. Distortion energy theory
   (06 Marks)

   c. Determine the maximum normal stress and maximum shear stress at section A – A for the crank shown in **Fig. U2.11** when a load of 10 kN is assumed to be concentrated at the center of the crank pin.
   (08 Marks)

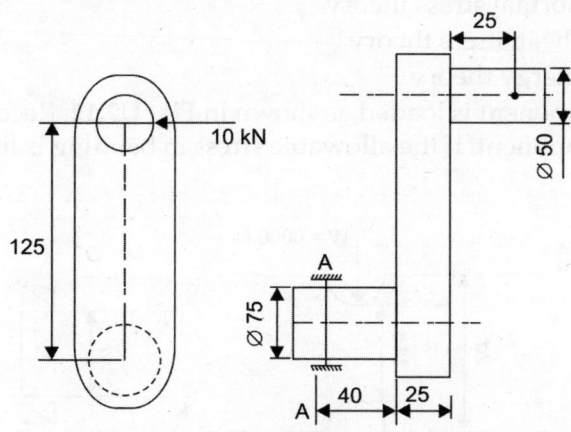

Fig. U2.11

21. An unknown weight falls through 15 mm on to a collar rigidly attached to the lower end of a bar 3 meter long and 625 mm² in cross-sectional area. If the

maximum instantaneous extension of the shaft is 1.25 mm, what is the corresponding stress and the value of unknown weight? **(08 Marks)**

Dec. 08/Jan. 2009 (ME5T2)

22. a. Explain the factors to be considered in the selection of factor of safety.
    (08 Marks)
    b. Determine the maximum tensile load that a flat 25 mm × 3 mm can carry if it has a central hole of 10 mm dia. and σ_{max} = 120 MPa. **(12 Marks)**

Dec. 08/Jan. 2009 (06ME-AU52)

23. a. State and explain theories of failure. **(06 Marks)**
    b. Briefly explain the impact strength of a bar subjected to axial, bending and torsional loading. **(06 Marks)**
    c. An infinite plate with a elliptical cutout having major axis 50 mm and minor axis 25 mm is subjected to a tensile load F. Determine the stress concentration factor when
       i. The load is perpendicular to major axis.
       ii. The load is parallel to the major axis. **(08 Marks)**

June/July 2009 (AU46)

24. a. Briefly explain the following terms:
       i. Stress concentration factor
       ii. Endurance limit
       iii. Fatigue stress concentration factor
       iv. Notch sensitivity. **(08 Marks)**
    b. Determine the cross-section dimensions for the cantilever of length 200 mm, when it is subjected to impact by a weight of 1000 N falling though 1 mm height at the free end. Take depth of section as 4 times the width and allowable stress of 80 N/mm². **(09 Marks)**

25. a. Explain the following theories of failure:
       i. Maximum normal stress theory
       ii. Maximum shear stress theory
       iii. Distortion energy theory. **(06 Marks)**
    b. A machine component is loaded as shown in **Fig. U2.12**. Recommend a suitable size for the component, if the allowable stress in bending is limited to 100 MPa. **(05 Marks)**

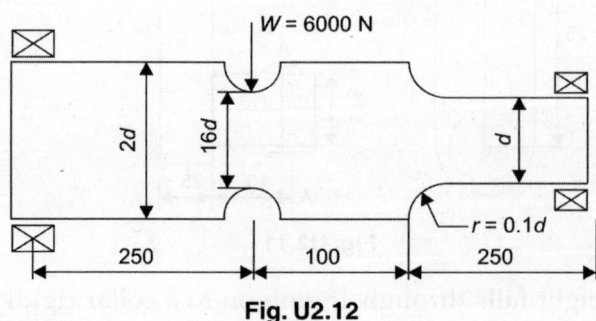

Fig. U2.12

June/July 2009 (06ME52)

26. a. Explain the following theories of failure:
    i. Maximum normal stress theory
    ii. Distortion energy theory. **(05 Marks)**
   b. A steel rod 1.5 m long resists an impact load of 2 kN dropped through a distance of 50 mm along its axis. Limiting the maximum stress in the rod to 150 MPa, determine:
    i. The diameter of the rod required.
    ii. Impact factor. Use $E = 200$ GPa **(10 Marks)**

27. a. Explain the following:
    i. Notch sensitivity
    ii. Stress concentration factor **(05 Marks)**
   b. A bolt in an assembly is subjected to a pull of 1000 N along its axis and a shear force of 500 N, what will be the maximum stress induced in the bolt. If the bolt is made of SAE 1045 annealed steel, is the bolt safe given that the diameter of the bolt is 12 mm. **(07 Marks)**
   c. A 50 mm diameter steel rod supports a 9000 N load in addition is subjected to torsional moment of 100 N·m. Determine the maximum normal and the maximum shear stresses. **(08 Marks)**

Dec. 2009/ Jan. 2010 (AU46)

28. a. Define impact load and derive an expression for impact stress. **(06 Marks)**
   b. Find the diameter 'd' and the dimensions 'b' and 't' of the machine member shown in **Fig. U2.13**. The permissible normal stress in the member is 80 N/mm^2 and the permissible shear stress is 55 N/mm^2. Assume $b/t = 5$. **(10 Marks)**

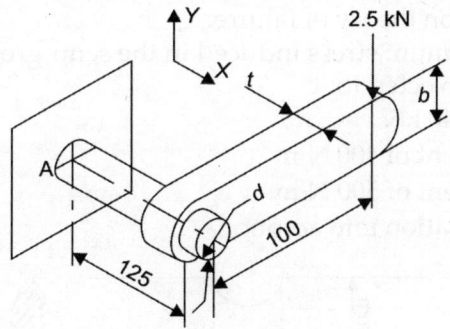

Fig. U2.13

29. a. A rotating shaft of diameter 16 mm shown in **Fig. U2.14** is subjected to axial tensile load of 5000 N, a steady torque of 50 N·m and a maximum bending moment of 75 N·m. Calculate the factor of safety based on
    i. Maximum normal stress theory
    ii. Maximum shear stress theory. Assume 400 MPa. **(10 Marks)**
   b. A machine element is loaded as shown in **Fig. U2.15**. Determine a safe value for the thickness of the plate. Material selected for the machine element has design stress of 200 MPa. **(10 Marks)**

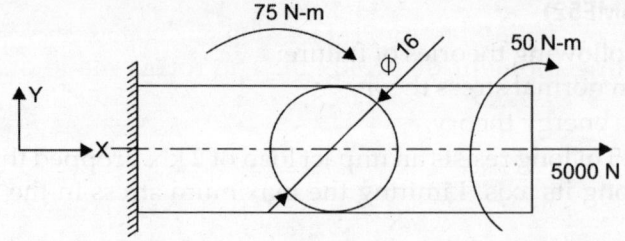

Fig. U2.14

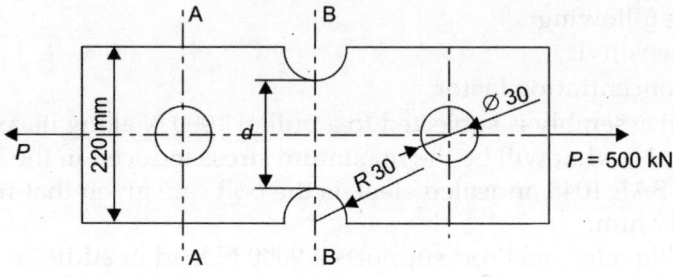

Fig. U2.15

Dec. 2009/Jan. 2010 (06ME52)

30. A steel shaft is subjected to a bending moment of 9 kN·m and a twisting moment of 12 kN·m. The yield strength of steel is 360 MPa in tension and compression and the Poisson's ratio is 0.3. If a factor of safety of 2 with respect to failure is specified, determine the permissible diameter of the shaft according to:
    i. Maximum shear stress theory of failure
    ii. Maximum normal stress theory of failure
    iii. Maximum distortion theory of failure. **(10 Marks)**

31. a. Determine the maximum stress induced in the semi-grooved shaft as shown in **Fig. U2.16**, if it is subjected to:
    i. An axial load of 40 kN
    ii. A bending moment of 400 N·m
    iii. A twisting moment of 500 N·m.
    Take stress concentration into account **(10 Marks)**

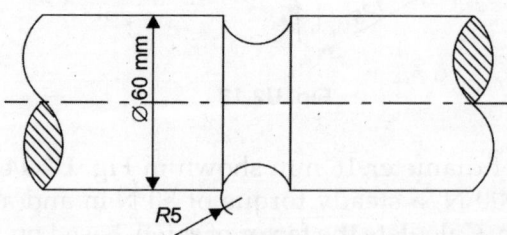

Fig. U2.16

b. A weight of 600 N drops through a height of 20 mm and impacts the center of 300 mm long simply supported circular cross-section beam. Find the diameter of the beam and the maximum deflection, if the allowable stress is limited to 90 MPa. Neglect the inertia effect and take $E = 200$ GPa. **(10 Marks)**

May/June 2010 (06ME52)

32. a. A round rod of diameter 30 mm is to sustain an axial compressive load of 20 kN and a twisting moment of 1.5 kN·m. The rod is made of carbon steel C40 (σ_{yt} = 328.6 MPa). Determine the factor of safety as per the following theories of failure:

   i. Maximum principal strain theory

   ii. Maximum elastic strain energy theory **(08 Marks)**

   b. A flat plate subjected to a tensile force of 5 kN is shown in **Fig. U2.17**. The plate material is grey cast iron having σ_u MPa. Determine the thickness of the plate. Factor of safety is 2.5. **(08 Marks)**

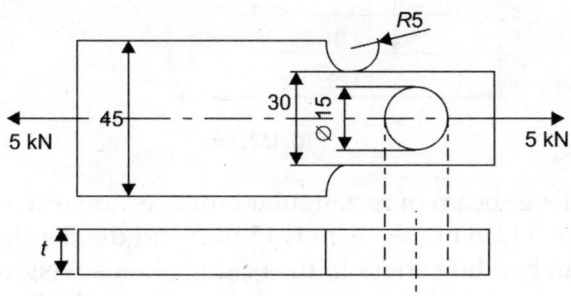

Fig. U2.17

   c. Determine the maximum torsional impact that can withstand, without permanent deformation by a 100 mm cylindrical shaft 5 m long and made of SAE 1045 annealed steel (τ_y = 180 MPa and G = 82 GPa). Factor of safety = 3. **(04 Marks)**

Dec. 2010 (AU46)

33. What is stress concentration factor? Explain any two methods of determining the stress concentration factor. **(10 Marks)**

34. a. Explain the significance of the theories of failure. Using Distortion energy theory of failure, derive an expression for the factor of safety. **(10 Marks)**

   b. A rectangular cross-section plate is loaded as shown in **Fig. U2.18**. If the allowable tensile stress of the material is 150 MPa, calculate the minimum thickness of the plate required for an axial load of 60 kN. **(05 Marks)**

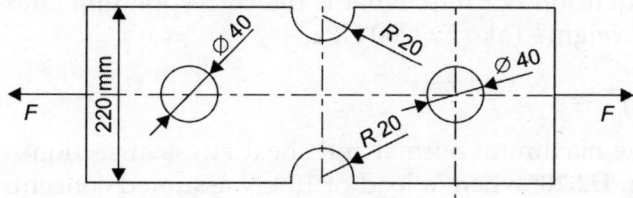

Fig. U2.18

35. A cantilever beam 12 mm deep, 8 mm wide and 300 mm long is loaded as follows, at the free end. Determine the maximum bending stress in each case.

   i. A load of 50 N applied gradually.

   ii. A load of 50 N dropped through a distance of 5 mm. **(10 Marks)**

Dec. 2010 (06ME52)

36. A bracket shown in **Fig. U2.19** is subjected to a pull of 15 kN at 60° to the vertical. Determine the maximum tensile stress in the bracket. **(12 Marks)**

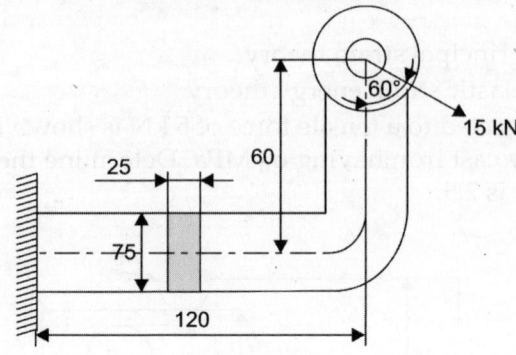

Fig. U2.19

37. a. A steel cantilever beam of rectangular cross-section is loaded 400 mm from the supports. The width of the beam is 15 mm and the depth is 20 mm. Determine the maximum bending stress in the beam, when a weight of 100 N is dropped on the beam through a height of 5 mm. Take $E = 210$ GPa. **(06 Marks)**

b. A cylindrical shaft made of steel is subjected to a static load, consisting of bending moment of 10 kN·m and a torsional moment of 30 kN·m. Determine the diameter of the shaft according to:
   i. Maximum shear stress theory
   ii. Shear energy theory

Take yield strength = 700 MPa, Young's modulus = 210 GPa, Poisson's ratio = 0.25. Factor of safety = 2. **(14 Marks)**

June/July 2011 (06ME52)

38. a. Explain the following theories of failure:
   i. Maximum normal stress theory
   ii. Maximum distortion energy theory. **(08 Marks)**

b. An unknown weight falls through 10 mm on a collar rigidly attached to the lower end of a bar 3 m long and 600 mm² in section. If the maximum instantaneous extension is 2 mm, what is the corresponding stress and the value of unknown weight? Take $E = 200$ GPa. **(12 Marks)**

Dec. 2011 (AU46)

39. Determine the maximum normal and shear stress at section A – A for the crank shown in **Fig. U2.20,** when a load of 10 kN assumed concentrated, is applied at the center of the crank pin. **(10 Marks)**

40. a. A tension bar shown in **Fig. U2.21(a)** supports an axial load P. It is necessary to replace this member having a hole as shown in the second member. Determine the thickness 'h' and fillet radius '' at the member by one having a 15 mm hole as shown **Fig. U2.21 (b)**, so that, the maximum stress will not exceed that of the first member. **(08 Marks)**

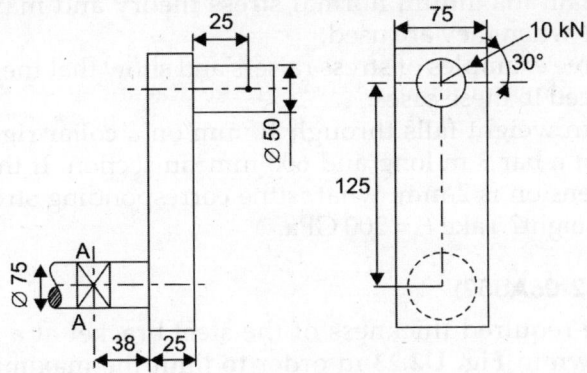

Fig. U2.20

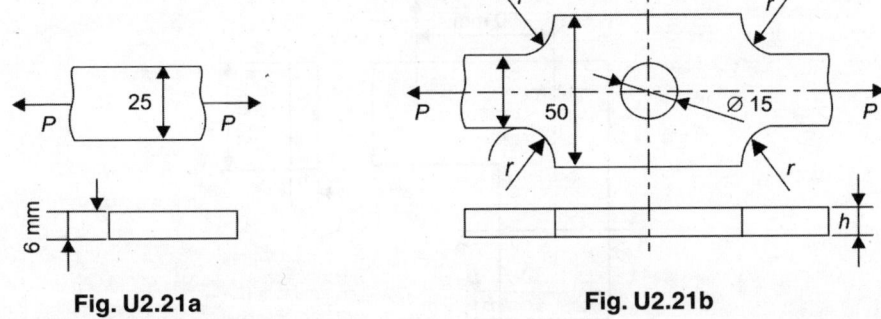

Fig. U2.21a   **Fig. U2.21b**

   b. A machine member is statically loaded and has a yield strength of 350 MPa. For each of the stress state indicated below. Find the factor of safety according to

     i. Maximum normal stress theory

     ii. Maximum shear stress theory

     iii. Maximum distortion energy theory.

       i. $\sigma_1 = 70$ MPa, $\sigma_2 = 70$ MPa

       ii. $\sigma_1 = 70$ MPa, $\sigma_2 = 35$ MPa

       iii. $\sigma_1 = 70$ MPa, $\sigma_2 = 70$ MPa

       iv. $\sigma_1 = -70$ MPa, $\sigma_1 = 0$ MPa   **(12 Marks)**

Dec. 2011 (06ME52)

41. A cantilever beam of circular cross-section is loaded as shown in **Fig. U2.22**. Determine the maximum and minimum normal stresses and maximum shear stress at points A and B.   **(10 Marks)**

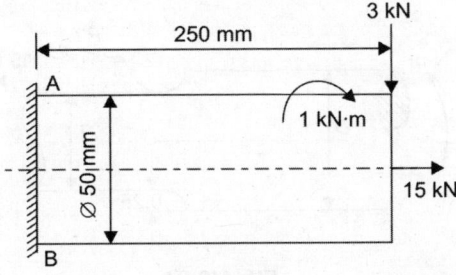

Fig. U2.22

42. a. Briefly explain maximum normal stress theory and maximum shear stress theory. State when they are used. **(06 Marks)**
    b. Give any three examples of stress raisers and show that the stress concentration can be reduced in these cases. **(07 Marks)**
    c. An unknown weight falls through 10 mm on a collar rigidly attached to the lower end of a bar 3 m long and 600 mm² in section. If the maximum instantaneous extension is 2 mm, what is the corresponding stress and the value of unknown weight? Take $E = 200$ GPa. **(07 Marks)**

June 2012 (06ME52-06AU52)

43. Determine the required thickness of the steel bracket at a section A–A, when loaded as shown in **Fig. U2.23** in order to limit the maximum tensile stress to 70 MPa. **(06 Marks)**

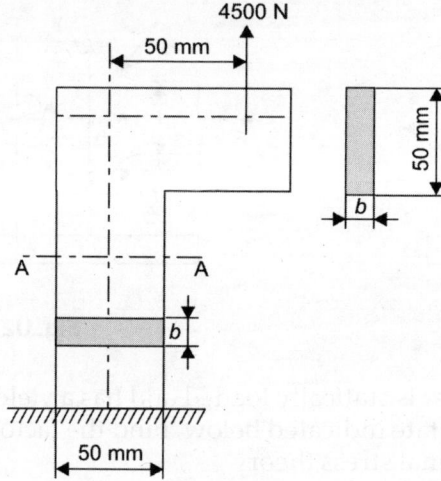

Fig. U2.23

44. a. Explain the following theories of failure and state when they are used:
    i. Maximum principal stress theory
    ii. Maximum shear stress theory. **(05 Marks)**
    b. A round stepped shaft is made of brittle material cast iron FG 260 and subjected to a bending moment of 15 N·m as shown in **Fig. U2.24**. The stress concentration factor at the fillet is 1.5. Determine the following:
    i. Step diameter
    ii. Magnitude of stress at fillet
    iii. Factor of safety. **(10 Marks)**

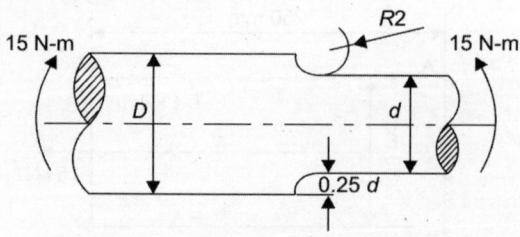

Fig. U2.24

c. Derive an impact stress in an axial bar of cross-section and length due to impact of a load falling from a height on the bar, as shown in **Fig. U2.25**. **(05 Marks)**

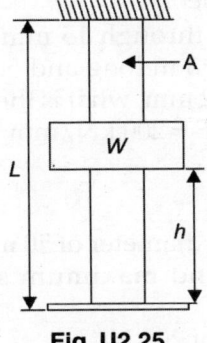

Fig. U2.25

Dec. 2012 (10ME52)

45. Determine the extreme fiber stresses at the critical section of a machine member loaded as shown in **Fig. U2.26**. Also show the distribution of stresses at this section.
(14 Marks)

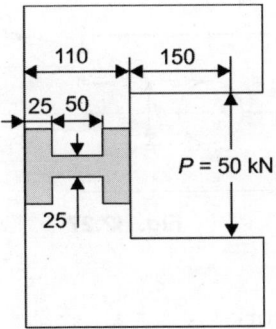

Fig. U2.26

46. a. State and explain the following theories of failure:
    i. Maximum principal stress theory
    ii. Maximum shear stress theory. **(05 Marks)**
   b. A round rod of diameter 60 mm is subjected to an axial tensile load of 10 kN and a twisting moment of 3 kN·m. The rod is made of steel C30. Factor of safety is 3. Determine whether the design is safe according to:
    i. Maximum principal stress theory of failure
    ii. Maximum shear stress theory of failure. **(10 Marks)**
   c. A machine member can be considered as a simply supported beam of 1 m length, cross-section of the beam is 60 mm². Determine the instantaneous maximum deflection and bending stress if a mass of 15 kg falls from a height of 250 mm at the midpoint of the beam made of steel. **(05 Marks)**

Dec. 2012 (06ME52)

47. a. The stresses induced at a critical point in a machine component made of 45C8 with yield strength (σ_{yt}) of 380 MPa are as follows: σ_x = 100 MPa, σ_y = 40 MPa and τ_{xy} = 80 MPa. Calculate factor of safety by:

i. The maximum normal stress theory

ii. The maximum shear stress theory

iii. The distortion energy theory.   **(10 Marks)**

b. An unknown weight falls through 15 mm on a collar rigidly attached to the lower end of a vertical bar 3 m long and 500 mm² in section. If the maximum instantaneous extension is 2 mm, what is the corresponding stress and the value of unknown weight? Take $E = 200$ kN/mm².   **(10 Marks)**

June/July 2013 (06ME52)

48. A cantilever circular rod has a diameter of 50 mm and 300 mm length. Find out the values of principal stress and maximum shear stress under the following conditions:

    i. Applying an axial load of 20 kN

    ii. Applying 4 kN load at an end, acting downwards creating bending stress.

    iii. Applying a torque of 1.5 kN·m   **(12 Marks)**

49. a. What diameter of maximum hole that can be derived in a flat plate shown in **Fig. U2.27**, if the stress concentration at the step is same as that of a hole.

                                                       (06 Marks)

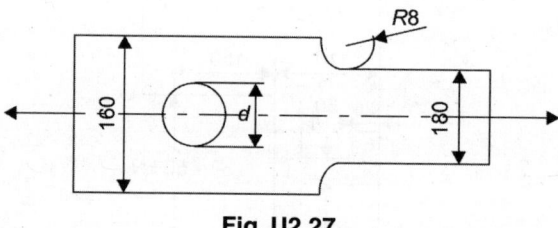

Fig. U2.27

b. Explain:

    i. Distortion energy theory

    ii. Maximum shear stress theory   **(04 Marks)**

c. A steel rod 1.5 m long has to resist longitudinally an impact of 2.5 kN falling under gravity at a velocity of 0.9925 m/s. The maximum computed stress is to be limited to 150 MPa. Determine the diameter of the round bar.   **(10 Marks)**

June/July 2013 (10ME52)

50. A hollow shaft of 40 mm diameter and 25 mm inner diameter is subjected to a twisting moment of 118 N·m, an axial thrust of 9806 N and a bending moment of 79 N·m. Calculate the maximum compressive and shear stresses.   **(10 Marks)**

51. a. The brasses of an automobile connecting rod have worn, so as to apply play which gives shock loading equivalent to a weight of 5886 N falling through a height of 0.2 mm. The connecting rod is 250 mm and has a cross-sectional area of 3×10^{-4} m². Determine the stress induced in the connecting rod. Compare the maximum stress induced with that of a static load of 5886 N.   **(06 Marks)**

b. A bolt is subjected to a direct tensile load of 30 kN and a transverse shear force of 15 kN. Material of the bolt has a normal stress of 350 MPa at yield and Poisson's ratio of 0.25. Compute the root diameter of the bolt according to:

    i. Maximum shear stress theory of failure

    ii. von Mises criterion for failure.

Hence suggest suitable size of the bolt. Take a value of 3 for factor of safety.

(07 Marks)

c. Determine the maximum stress induced in the following cases taking stress concentration into account:
  i. A rectangular plate 50 mm wide, 8 mm thick with a central hole of 10 mm loaded in axial tension of 14.7 kN.
  ii. A stepped shaft stepped down from 45 mm to 30 mm with a filet radius of 6 mm is subjected to a twisting moment of 90 N·m. **(07 Marks)**

Dec. 2013/Jan. 2014 (06ME52)

52. a. What is stress concentration? What are the factors affecting the stress concentration? Explain. **(05 Marks)**
  b. A mild steel shaft is subjected to 3500 N·m of bending moment at its critical point and transmits a torque of 2500 N·m. The shaft is made of steel having yield strength of 231 N/mm². Estimate the size based on various theories of failure with factor of safety of 2 and specify the final size. **(10 Marks)**

Dec. 2013/Jan. 2014 (10ME52)

53. A 50 mm diameter steel rod supports a 9 kN load and in addition is subjected to torsional moment of 100 N·m as shown in **Fig. U2.28**. Determine the maximum tensile and the maximum shear stress. **(08 Marks)**

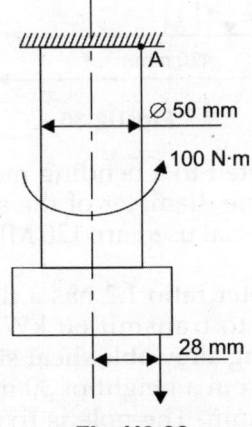

Fig. U2.28

54. a. In a plate of C45 steel (σ_y = 353 MPa) subjected to a system of loads, following stresses are induced at critical point: σ_x = 150 N/mm², σ_y = 100 N/mm² and τ_{xy} = 50 N/mm². Find the factor of safety according to:
  i. Maximum normal stress theory
  ii. Maximum shear stress theory
  iii. Distortion energy theory. **(08 Marks)**
  b. Determine the safe load that can be carried by a bar of rectangular cross-section shown in **Fig. U2.29** limiting the maximum stress to 130 MPa taking stress concentration into account. **(06 Marks)**
  c. An unknown weight falls through 20 mm on to a collar rigidly attached to the lower end of a vertical bar 2 meter long and 500 sq mm section. If the maximum instantaneous extension is 2 mm, what is the corresponding stress and the value of unknown weight? Take E = 200 GPa. **(06 Marks)**

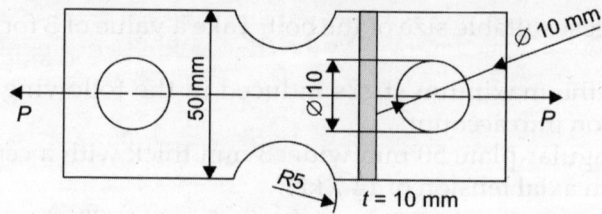

Fig. U2.29

June/July 2014 (06ME52)

55. a. A wall bracket of rectangular cross-section whose depth is twice its width carries a load of 60 kN as shown in **Fig. U2.30**. Find the required width and depth of cross-section taking allowable stress as 90 MPa. **(10 Marks)**

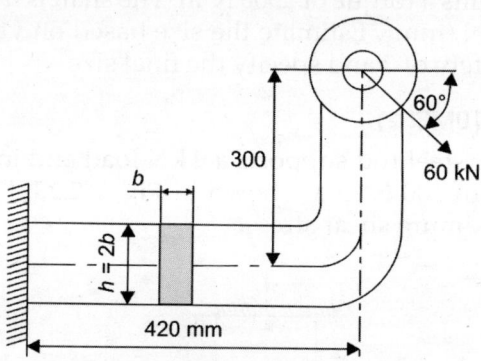

Fig. U2.30

b. A machine shaft is subjected to a bending moment of 3 kN·m and a torque of 1.5 kN·m. Find the suitable diameter of the shaft if the allowable normal and shear stresses for the material used are 120 MPa and 75 MPa respectively.
(10 Marks)

56. a. A stepped shaft of diameter ratio 1.2 has a fillet radius of 1/10 of the smaller diameter. It is required to transmit 60 kW at 1200 rpm. Find the suitable diameter of the shaft taking allowable shear stress as 60 MPa. **(10 Marks)**

b. A weight of 20 kN falls from a height of 30 mm on a vertical pole of 6 m long having a diameter of 30 mm. The pole is fixed at the lower end. Modulus of elasticity may be taken as 206 GPa. Determine the maximum instantaneous stress produced and the maximum instantaneous deflection. **(10 Marks)**

June/July 2014 (10ME52)

57. Determine the maximum normal stress and shear stress for the element shown in **Fig. U2.31**.
(09 Marks)

58. a. Explain the following theories of failure:
    i. Maximum shear stress theory
    ii. Distortion energy theory **(05 Marks)**

b. A flat plate subjected to a tensile load of 5 kN is shown in **Fig. U2.32**. The plate material is grey cast

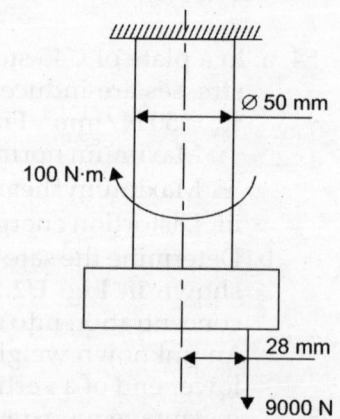

Fig. U2.31

iron having σ_u = 200 MPa. Determine the thickness of the plate. Take factor of safety as 2.5. **(07 Marks)**

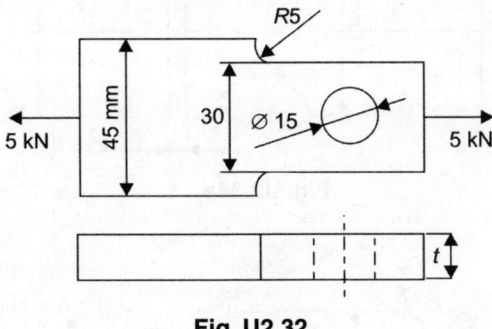

Fig. U2.32

c. A weight 600 N drops through a height of 20 mm and impacts the centre of 300 mm long simply supported circular cross-section beam. Find the diameter of the beam and the maximum deflection, if the allowable stress is limited to 90 MPa. Neglect the inertia effect and take E = 200 GPa. **(07 Marks)**

Dec. 2014/Jan. 2015 (06ME52)

59. A machine member 50 mm diameter and 200 mm long can be treated as a cantilever for stress analysis. The loading of the member is shown in **Fig. U2.33**. Determine the maximum and minimum normal stress and maximum shear stress at critically stresses point "A" and point "B". **(12 Marks)**

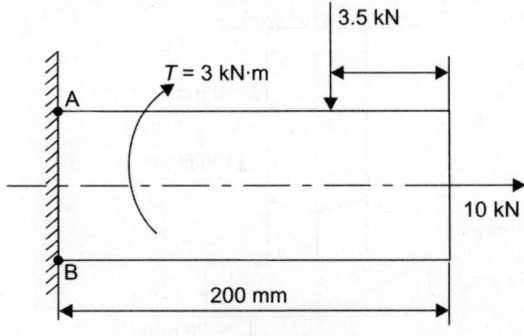

Fig. U2.33

60. a. A bolt is subjected to a direct axial tensile load of 20 kN and a shear load of 15 kN. Material of the bolt is ductile and has a yield strength of 360 N/mm^2 and Poisson's ratio of 0.25. Compute the root diameter of the bolt according to:
   i. Maximum shear stress theory
   ii. Maximum normal stress theory
   iii. Maximum strain energy theory.
   Factor of safety = 3 **(09 Marks)**
   b. Discuss the statement "In static loading, stress concentration in ductile material is not so serious as in brittle material". **(03 Marks)**
   c. Find the maximum stress induced in the following cases shown in **Fig. U2.34(a)** and **Fig. U2.34(b)** taking stress concentration into account. **(08 Marks)**

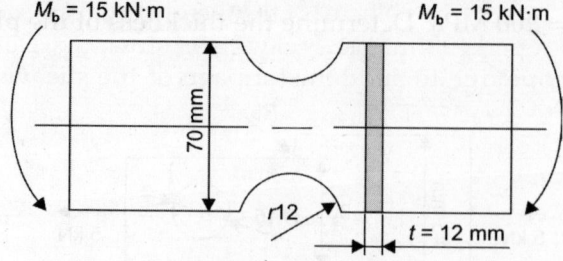

Fig. U2.34a

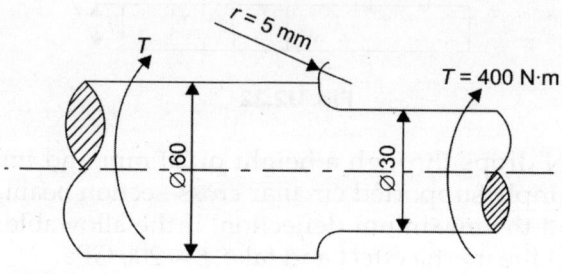

Fig. U2.34b

Dec. 2014/ Jan. 2015 (10ME52)

61. A 50 mm steel rod supports a 9 kN load and in addition to this a torsional moment of 100 N·m is applied on it as shown in **Fig. U2.35**. Determine the maximum tensile and maximum shear stresses. **(10 Marks)**

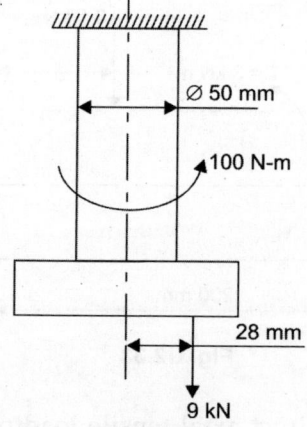

Fig. U2.35

62. a. A mild steel shaft of 60 mm diameter is subjected to bending moment of 25×10^5 N·mm and torque M_c. If the yield stress in tension is 300 N/mm^2, find the maximum value of torque without causing yielding of the shaft according to:
   i. Maximum shear stress theory of failure
   ii. Maximum distortion theory of failure.
   Adopt a factor of safety of 1.5. **(10 Marks)**
   b. A mass of 500 kg is being lowered by means of steel wire rope having cross-

sectional area 250 mm². The velocity of the weight is 0.5 m/sec. When the length of the extended rope is 20 m, the sheave gets stuck up. Determine the stress induced in the rope due to sudden stoppage of the sheave. Neglect friction. Take $E = 190$ GPa. **(10 Marks)**

June/ July 2015 (06ME52)

63. a. Explain the following theories of failure:
   i. Maximum normal stress theory
   ii. Maximum shear stress theory **(10 Marks)**

   b. An unknown weight falls through 10 mm on a collar rigidly attached to the lower end of a vertical bar 3 m long and 600 mm² in section. If the maximum instantaneous extension is known to be 2 mm, what is the corresponding stress and the value of unknown weight? Take $E = 200$ kN/mm². **(10 Marks)**

June/July 2015 (10ME52)

64. A shaft as shown in **Fig. U2.36** is subjected to bending load of 3 kN, torque of 1×10^6 N·mm and an axial load of 15 kN. Calculate the stresses at A and B. **(12 Marks)**

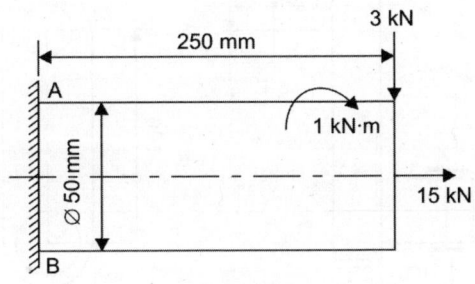

Fig. U2.36

65. a. State and explain the theories of failure applicable to
   i. Ductile materials
   ii. Brittle materials. **(06 Marks)**

   b. What is stress concentration? Explain the factors affecting the stress concentration. **(04 Marks)**

   c. A rectangular beam of 100 mm width and 200 mm depth is freely supported over a span of 2 m. A load of 10 kN is dropped on the middle of the beam from a height of 10 mm. Find the maximum instantaneous deflection and stress induced in the beam. Take $E = 2 \times 10^5$ MPa. **(10 Marks)**

Dec. 2015/Jan. 2016 (10ME52)

66. A wall bracket with a rectangular cross-section is shown in **Fig. U2.37**. The force P acting on the bracket at 60° to the vertical is 5 kN. The material of the bracket is gray cast iron (ordinary) and factor of safety is 2. Determine the cross-section of the bracket for maximum normal stress. All dimensions shown are in mm. **(07 Marks)**

67. a. Explain the theories of elastic failure. Mention five types of theories of elastic failures. **(05 Marks)**

   b. An overhung crank with pin and shaft is as shown in **Fig. U2.38**. A tangential load of 15 kN acts on the crank pin. Determine the diameter at section 'XX' using

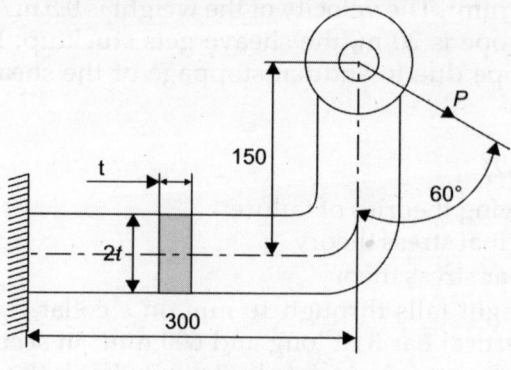

Fig. U2.37

maximum shear stress theory. The crank is made of C60 carbon steel. Take factor of safety as 2. All dimensions are in mm. **(05 Marks)**

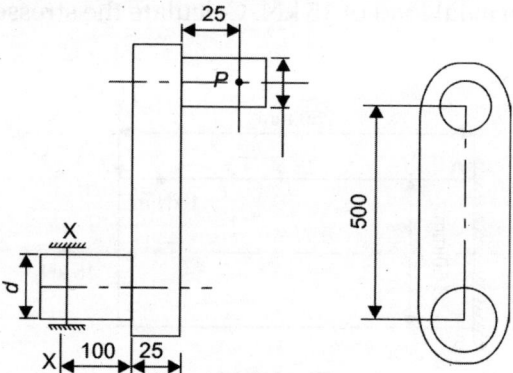

Fig. U2.38

c. A flat plate subjected to tensile force of 5 kN is shown in **Fig. U2.39**. The plate material is gray cast iron (good) and the factor of safety is 2.5. Determine the thickness of the plate. All dimensions are in mm. **(07 Marks)**

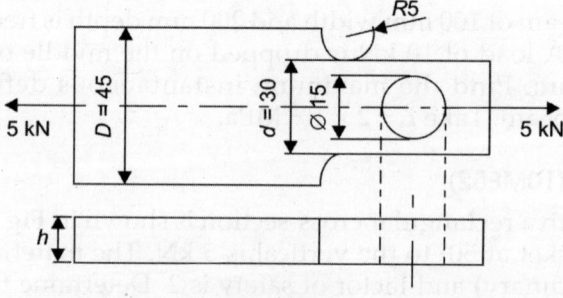

Fig. U2.39

d. Design a rod of solid circular cross-section of length 200 mm (placed vertical) to sustain an axial compressive load of 1000 N, that falls on it from a height of 10 mm. The material selected has a design stress of 80 N/mm² and $E = 2.1 \times 10^5$ N/mm². **(03 Marks)**

Design for Fatigue Strength

3.1 INTRODUCTION TO FATIGUE

Fatigue and fracture, like other forms of material degradation such as corrosion and wear, are common engineering concerns that often limit the life of engineering materials. The majority of engineering failures are caused by fatigue.

The fatigue of the material is affected by the size of component, relative magnitude of static and fluctuating loads and the number of load reversals. On the other hand, the shape of the structure will significantly affect the fatigue life, *square holes or sharp corners* will lead to elevated local stresses where fatigue cracks can initiate.

A good example of fatigue failure is breaking a thin steel rod or wire with your hands after bending it back and forth several times in the same place.

Fatigue failures occur in every field of engineering. Following are some of the examples.
- Automobiles in mechanical engineering
- Bridges in civil engineering
- Aircrafts in aeronautical engineering
- Ship hull in marine engineering
- Pressure vessels in chemical engineering
- Tractors (tie rod) involving agricultural engineering
- Nuclear piping involving nuclear engineering.

Definition

- When a material is subjected to repeated stresses (repeated loads/ alternating loads), it fails at a stress far below the yield point stress. Such type of failure is referred to as fatigue.
- According to ASTM, fatigue is defined as *"the process of progressive localized permanent structural change occurring in a material subjected to conditions that produce fluctuating stresses and strains at some point or points and that may culminate in cracks or complete fracture after a sufficient number of fluctuations"*.

The term localized indicates that the fatigue process opiates at local areas (notches, fillets, etc.) than throughout the entire structure/component. These local areas can have high stresses and strains due to external load transfer, abrupt change in geometry, temperature variations, residual stresses and material imperfections.

The term fluctuating indicates that the stresses and strains are cyclic in nature.

How is it different from static failure?

- Fatigue failure occurs at stresses well below the yield strength of a material.

- Fatigue failure is always brittle and catastrophic in nature with no visible warning prior to failure.
- Fatigue accounts for about 90% of all failures in metals.

3.2 CHARACTERISTICS OF FATIGUE

- In metals and alloys, the process starts with dislocation movements, eventually forming persistent slip bands (PSBs) that nucleate short cracks.
- Fatigue is a stochastic process, often showing considerable scatter even in controlled environments.
- The greater the applied stress range, the shorter the life.
- Fatigue life scatter tends to increase for longer fatigue lives.
- Damage is cumulative. Materials do not recover when rested.
- Fatigue life is influenced by a variety of factors, such as temperature, surface finish, microstructure, presence of oxidizing or inert chemicals, residual stresses, contact (fretting), etc.
- Some materials (e.g. some steel and titanium alloys) exhibit a theoretical fatigue limit below which continued loading does not lead to structural failure.
- High cycle fatigue strength (about 10^3 to 10^8 cycles) can be described by stress-based parameters.
- Low cycle fatigue (typically less than 10^3 cycles) is associated with widespread plasticity in metals; thus, a strain-based parameter should be used for fatigue life prediction in metals and alloys.

3.3 FACTORS TO BE CONSIDERED TO AVOID FATIGUE FAILURE

- Variation in size of component should be as gradual as possible.
- Holes, notches and other stress raisers should be avoided.
- Proper stress de-concentrators such as fillets and notches should be provided wherever necessary.
- Parts should be protected from corrosion.
- To provide smooth finish on the outer surface of the component, thereby increasing its fatigue life.
- Materials with high fatigue strength should be selected.
- Residual compressive stresses over the parts surface increases its fatigue strength.

3.4 PHENOMENON OF FATIGUE FAILURE/NATURE OF FATIGUE

Figure 3.1 shows typical propagation of a fatigue crack. There are three stages involved in fatigue failure: 1. Crack initiation, 2. Crack propagation, and 3. Fracture.

1. **Crack initiation:** A fatigue failure begins with a small crack. The initial crack may be very minute and cannot be detected. The crack usually develops at areas of localized stress concentrations such as fillets, notches, key ways, and bolt holes. Even scratches and/or tool marks are potential zones for crack initiation. As a result of the local stress concentrations at these locations, the induced stress goes above the yield strength (in normal ductile materials) and cyclic plastic straining results due to cyclic variations in the stresses. During plastic straining slip occurs and results in gliding of planes one over the other. During the cyclic stressing, slip saturation results which make further plastic deformation difficult. As a result, intrusion and extrusion occurs creating a notch like discontinuity in the material.

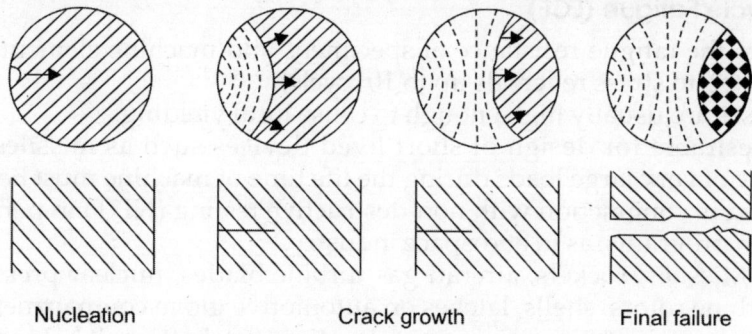

Nucleation   Crack growth   Final failure

Fig. 3.1: Typical propagation of a fatigue crack

2. **Crack propagation:** This further increases the stress levels by propagating the cracks across the grains or along the grain boundaries, slowly increasing the crack size. As the size of the crack increases the cross-sectional area resisting the applied stress decreases and reaches a threshold level at which it is insufficient to resist the applied stress.

3. **Final fracture:** Beyond the threshold region, the area decreases and becomes insufficient to resist the induced stresses any further and a sudden fracture results in the component.

3.5 HIGH CYCLE AND LOW CYCLE FATIGUE

Based on investigations, the fatigue process embraces two domains of cyclic stresses or strains that are significantly different in character and in each of which failure is probably produced by different physical mechanisms.

- One domain of cyclic loading is the *low-cycle fatigue (LCF)/strain controlled fatigue*, for which significant plastic strain occurs during each cycle. This domain is associated with high loads and short lives, or low numbers of cycles to produce failure.

  Example: Missiles, rockets, aircraft gas turbine blades, nuclear pressure vessels, steam turbine rotors, shells, latches on automotive glove compartments, studs on truck wheels, and setscrews fixing gear locations on shafts, bolt hole and fillet areas of compressor and turbine discs, etc.

- The other domain of cyclic loading is the *high-cycle fatigue (HCF)/stress controlled fatigue*, for which strain cycles are largely confined to elastic range. This domain is associated with lower loads and longer lives, or high numbers of cycles to produce failure.

  Example: Airfoil subjected to repeated bending, car door hinges, aircraft body panels, etc.

There is no sharp dividing line between the two. However, if:

- The loads or deformations are of such magnitude that less than about 1,000 cycles ($<10^3$) are required to produce failure, the phenomenon is usually termed *low cycle fatigue*.

- The loads or deformations are of such magnitude that more than about 1,000 cycles ($\geq 10^3$) are required to produce failure, the phenomenon is usually termed *high-cycle fatigue*.

3.5.1 Low Cycle Fatigue (LCF)

- It refers to the fatigue resistance of specimens and machine elements when they are subjected to stress reversals up to 10^3 cycles.
- The stresses are usually high enough to cause local yielding.
- This is desirable for design of short lived devices such as missiles, where the possibility of very large loads during the life time of machine must be considered.
- Often used in conjunction with non-destructive testing (NDT) in periodic service inspection programs, as in aerospace industry.
  Example: Missiles, rockets, aircraft gas turbine blades, nuclear pressure vessels, steam turbine rotors, shells, latches on automotive glove compartments, studs on truck wheels, and setscrews fixing gear locations on shafts, bolt hole and fillet areas of compressor and turbine discs, etc.

Advantages of LCF	Disadvantages of LCF
More conservative than HCF	Analysis depends on testing, strain data must be available
Widely used in industry	Analysis is more complicated than with HCF methods

3.5.2 High Cycle Fatigue (HCF)

- It refers to fatigue resistance of machine elements when they are subjected to stress reversals beyond 10^3 cycles.
- Stresses are usually low.
- Desired for design of long life machine elements where loads are low.
- Loads are predictable and consistent in amplitude.
  Example: Airfoil subjected to repeated bending, car door hinges, aircraft body panels, etc.

Advantages of HCF	Disadvantages of HCF
Empirical parameters for a lot of materials has been determined: Marin factors, fatigue strengths	Cannot be used for low cycle applications
Easy to use for design applications.	If loads are fluctuating in a pseudo-random way, HCF methods can yield non-conservative results

3.6 DEFINITIONS/ NOMENCLATURE (Fig. 2.5/ Pg 24, DHB)

- **Endurance limit/Fatigue limit** (σ_{en}) is defined as maximum value of the completely reversed bending stress which a polished standard specimen can withstand without failure, for infinite number of cycles (usually 10^7 cycles).
- **Endurance strength:** It is defined as the safe maximum stress which can be applied to the machine part working under actual conditions.

The term endurance limit is used for reversed bending only while for other types of loading, the term endurance strength is used when referring the fatigue strength of the material.

- **Varying stresses:**
  - *Fluctuating stress* is the stress which varies from a maximum value to a minimum value of the same nature (tensile/compressive).
  - *Repeated/released stress* is the stress which varies from zero to a maximum value (tensile/compressive).
    Here $\qquad \sigma_{min} = 0, R = 0, A = 1$ $\qquad$ ... (Eq. 3.1)
  - *Completely reversed/cyclic stress* is the stress which varies from one value in

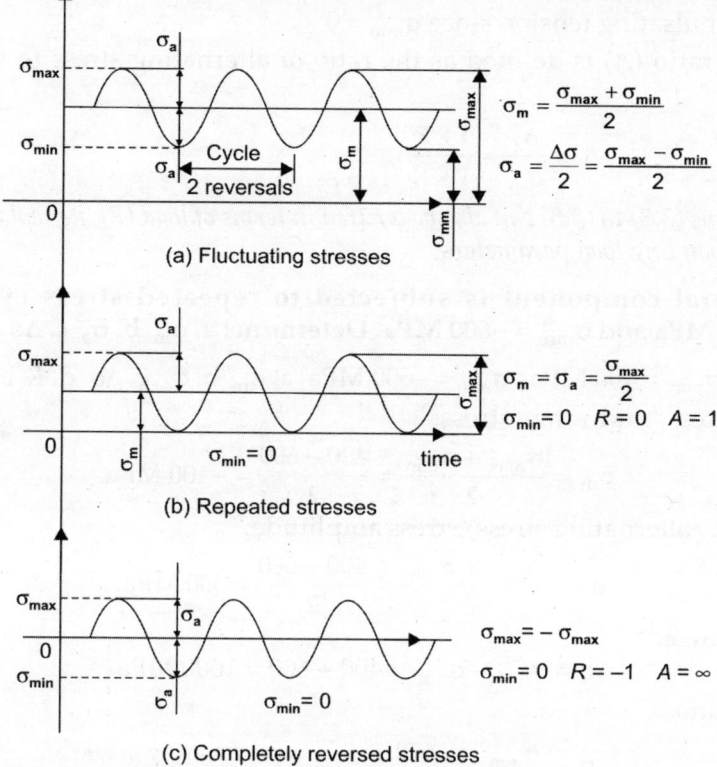

$$\sigma_m = \frac{\sigma_{max} + \sigma_{min}}{2}$$

$$\sigma_a = \frac{\Delta\sigma}{2} = \frac{\sigma_{max} - \sigma_{min}}{2}$$

(a) Fluctuating stresses

$$\sigma_m = \sigma_a = \frac{\sigma_{max}}{2}$$

$$\sigma_{min} = 0 \quad R = 0 \quad A = 1$$

(b) Repeated stresses

$$\sigma_{max} = -\sigma_{max}$$

$$\sigma_{min} = 0 \quad R = -1 \quad A = \infty$$

(c) Completely reversed stresses

Fig. 3.2: Nomenclature of constant amplitude cyclic loading

compression to the same value in tension, i.e. the maximum and minimum stresses are equal in magnitude but opposite in direction.

Here $\quad \sigma_{max} = -\sigma_{min}; \sigma_m = 0, R = -1, A = \infty$ ... (Eq. 3.2)

- **Maximum stress** (σ_{max}) is the largest algebraic stress in a stress cycle.
- **Minimum stress** (σ_{min}) is the smallest algebraic stress in a given cycle.
- **Stress cycle** is the smallest portion of the $\sigma - t$ curve which is repeated periodically. *In constant amplitude loading 1 cycle = 2 stress reversals*
- **Range of stress** ($\Delta\sigma$) is the difference between the maximum and minimum stresses.

$$\Delta\sigma = \sigma_{max} - \sigma_{min} \qquad \text{... (Eq. 3.3)}$$

- **Mean/average/mid-range stress** (σ_m) is the average of the maximum and minimum stresses in a cycle.

$$\sigma_m = \frac{\sigma_{max} + \sigma_{min}}{2} \qquad \text{... (Eq. 3.4) **2.16(a)/ Pg 23, DHB**}$$

- **Variable/ alternating stress/stress amplitude** (σ_a) is defined as half the value of stress range.

$$\sigma_a = \frac{\Delta\sigma}{2} = \frac{\sigma_{max} - \sigma_{min}}{2} \qquad \text{... (Eq. 3.5) **2.16(b)/ Pg 23, DHB**}$$

- **Stress ratio** (R) is defined as the ratio of minimum stress to the maximum stress.

$$R = \frac{\sigma_{min}}{\sigma_{max}} \qquad \text{... (Eq. 3.6)}$$

$R = -1$, is the fully reversed condition since $\sigma_{min} = -\sigma_{max}$

$R = 0$, is the pulsating tension since $\sigma_{min} = 0$

- **Amplitude ratio** (A) is defined as the ratio of alternating stress to that of mean stress.

$$A = \frac{\sigma_a}{\sigma_m} = \frac{1 - R}{1 + R} \qquad \qquad \dots \text{(Eq. 3.7)}$$

Note: Equations (3.3) to (3.5) can also be written in terms of load (F), i.e replace σ with F to obtain the corresponding load parameters.

1. **A structural component is subjected to repeated stress cycles where $\sigma_{max} = 400$ MPa and $\sigma_{min} = -600$ MPa. Determine: a. σ_m b. σ_a c. $\Delta\sigma$ d. R e. A**

   Solution: $\sigma_{max} = 400$ MPa, $\sigma_{min} = -600$ MPa. a. σ_m b. σ_a c. $\Delta\sigma$ d. R e. A.

   a. Mean stress/mid-range stress:

   $$\sigma_m = \frac{\sigma_{max} + \sigma_{min}}{2} = \frac{400 - 600}{2} = -100 \text{ MPa}$$

   b. Variable/alternating stress/stress amplitude:

   $$\sigma_a = \frac{\sigma_{max} + \sigma_{min}}{2} = \frac{400 + 600}{2} = 500 \text{ MPa}$$

   c. Stress range:

   $$\Delta\sigma = \sigma_{max} - \sigma_{min} = 400 + 600 = 1000 \text{ MPa}$$

   d. Stress ratio:

   $$R = \frac{\sigma_{min}}{\sigma_{max}} = \frac{-600}{400} = -1.5$$

   e. Amplitude ratio:

   $$A = \frac{\sigma_a}{\sigma_m} = \frac{500}{-100} = -5$$

2. **A tuning fork vibrates with a frequency of 440 Hz. The maximum bending stress in the tuning fork is 4 MPa at the end positions. Calculate the mean stress, range of stress, the stress amplitude, the stress ratio, and the amplitude ratio.**

   Solution: $\sigma_{max} = 4$ MPa, $\sigma_{min} = -4$ MPa. a. σ_m b. σ_a c. $\Delta\sigma$ d. R e. A.

   a. Mean stress/mid-range stress:

   $$\sigma_m = \frac{\sigma_{max} + \sigma_{min}}{2} = \frac{4 - 4}{2} = 0 \text{ MPa}$$

   b. Variable/alternating stress/stress amplitude:

   $$\sigma_a = \frac{\sigma_{max} - \sigma_{min}}{2} = \frac{4 + 4}{2} = 4 \text{ MPa}$$

   c. Stress range:

   $$\Delta\sigma = \sigma_{max} - \sigma_{min} = 4 + 4 = 8 \text{ MPa}$$

   d. Stress ratio:

   $$R = \frac{\sigma_{min}}{\sigma_{max}} = \frac{-4}{4} = -1$$

   e. Amplitude ratio

   $$A = \frac{\sigma_a}{\sigma_m} = \frac{4}{0} = \infty$$

3.7 *S–N* CURVE: GENERAL *S–N* BEHAVIOUR OR WOHLER CURVES

The basis of stress life method is the *S–N* diagram or the Wohler diagram, which is a plot of fatigue alternating stress (σ_a) versus the number of cycles of failure (*N* or N_f), plotted on semi-log paper. The most common procedure for generating *S–N* data is the RR Moore test which utilizes a high-speed rotating-beam machine using four point loading to apply a constant moment. The rotating hour-glass shaped specimen shown in **Fig. 3.3** is very carefully machined and polished, with a final polishing in an axial direction to avoid circumferential scratches.

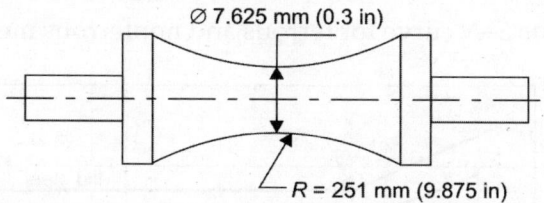

Fig. 3.3: Test specimen for R R Moore rotating-beam machine

This machine subjects the specimen to pure bending by means of weights and the number of revolutions (stress reversals) of the beam required for failure is recorded. As the specimen rotates, the bending stress at the upper fibers varies from maximum compressive to maximum tensile while the bending stress at the lower fibers varies from maximum tensile to maximum compressive. In other words, the specimen is subjected to a completely reversed stress cycle ($\sigma_m = 0$). The highest level of stress occurs at the center where the diameter of the specimen is 7.625 mm (0.3 in). The large radius of curvature prevents a stress concentration.

The first test is made at a stress which is less than the ultimate strength of the material. The second test is made at a stress that is less than the value used for the first test specimen. This process is continued, and the results are plotted on semi-log or log-log paper as an *S–N* diagram as shown in **Fig. 3.4**.

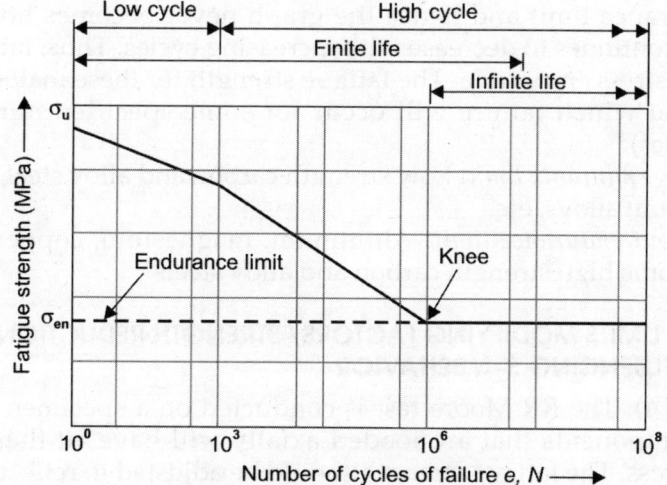

Fig. 3.4: A typical *S–N* diagram

For steel, a **"knee"** occurs between 10^6 and 10^7 cycles and beyond this knee, failure will not occur, irrespective of the increase in the number of cycles. The strength corresponding to the knee is called the *endurance limit/the fatigue limit* (σ_{en}). For many steels the endurance limit ranges between 35% and 60% of the material's ultimate strength.

Two points of interest can be observed from **Fig. 3.4**.

- Fatigue failure from $N = 1$ to $N = 1000$ cycles is generally classified as low cycle fatigue (LCF) and that more than 1000 cycles is referred to as high cycle fatigue (HCF).
- Another distinguishing feature is the finite-life region and an infinite-life region. The boundary between these regions cannot be clearly defined except for a specific material. For steels it lies somewhere between 10^6 and 10^7 cycles.

Figure 3.5 represents S–N curve for ferrous and nonferrous metals.

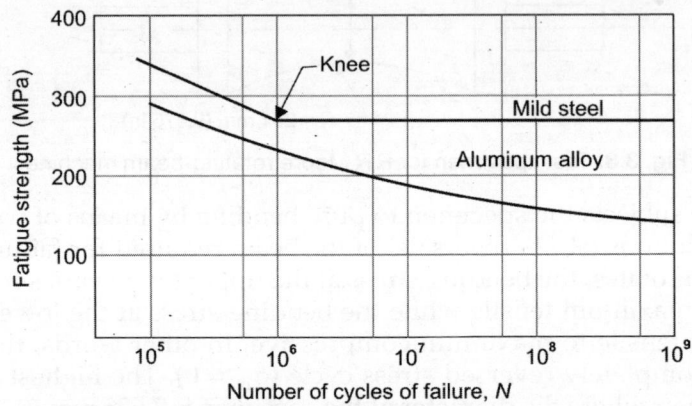

Fig. 3.5: S–N curves for ferrous and nonferrous metals

In the case of ferrous metals and alloys, the graph becomes horizontal after the material has been stressed for a certain number of cycles, indicating that an endurance limit (σ_{en}) is reached below which failure will not occur.

Most nonferrous alloys, e.g. aluminum, copper, and magnesium, do not have a significant endurance limit and hence the graph never becomes horizontal. Their fatigue strength continues to decrease with increasing cycles. Thus, fatigue will occur regardless of the stress amplitude. The fatigue strength for these materials is taken as the stress level at which failure will occur for some specified number of cycles (*Example*: 10^7 cycles).

Materials having endurance limit: Low strength carbon and alloy steel, some stainless steels, iron, titanium alloys, etc.

Materials without endurance limit: Aluminum, magnesium, copper, nickel, some stainless steels, some high strength carbon and alloy steels.

3.8 ENDURANCE LIMITS MODIFYING FACTORS/ STRENGTH REDUCTION FACTORS/ FACTORS INFLUENCING S–N BEHAVIOR

1. **Load factor (A):** The RR Moore test is conducted on a specimen that is in pure bending. Components that are loaded axially will have all their fibers under maximum stress. The fatigue strength should be adjusted to reflect this condition. The correction factor (A) for load is incorporated to take care of different loads, viz. reversed bending, reversed axial load and reversed torsional load.

   $A = 1.0$, for reversed bending
   $\quad = 0.7$ to 1.0 for reversed axial loading
   $\quad = 0.5$ to 0.6 for reversed torsional loading $\qquad$ ... (Eq. 3.8) **2.21(e)/ Pg 25, DHB**

2. **Size effects (B):** The fatigue failure of a material is based on the probability that a larger part is more likely to fail at lower stress due to the presence of flaw in larger stressed volume. This is due to the fact that a longer specimen will have more defects than a smaller one.

The size factor is given as

$$1/B = \frac{250}{300 - 4h + (\sigma_{e3}/\sigma_e)\,(4h - 50)}$$

… (Eq. 3.9) **2.9(b)/ Pg 22, DHB**

The value of the ratio (σ_{e3}/σ_e) for various materials is given in

… **Tb 2.5/Pg 33, DHB**.

In general

$\quad\quad\quad B = 1$, for $d < 8$ mm

$\quad\quad\quad\quad = 0.85$, for $8 < d < 50$ mm

$\quad\quad\quad\quad = 0.7$, for $d > 50$ mm

… (Eq. 3.10)

3. **Surface effects (C):** The rotating beam specimen has a highly polished surface finish with final polishing in the axial direction to smooth any circumferential scratches. Most machine elements do not usually have such high-quality finish. The surface modification factor depends on process used to generate the surface and on the ultimate strength.

- The values of C based on ultimate stress for cold and hot rolled surfaces are given in … **Tb 2.2/Pg 32, DHB**.
- The value of C based on ultimate tensile strength can be obtained from Fig. 3.5(a). … **(Fig. 2.33/ Pg 46, DHB)**

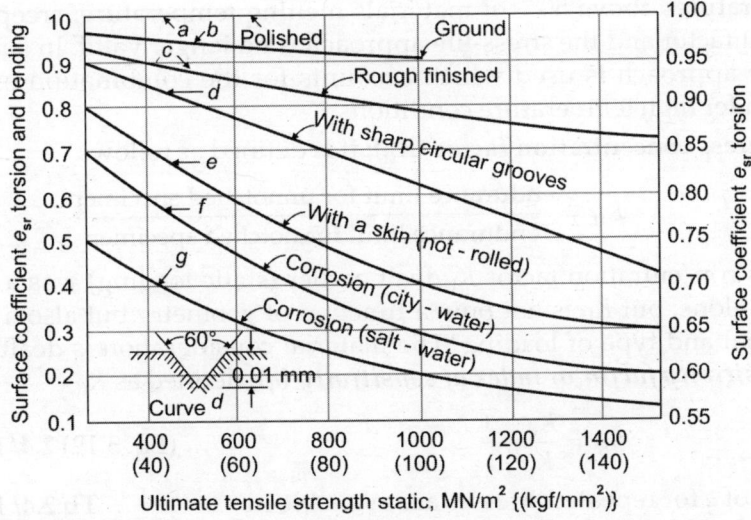

Fig. 3.5a: Reciprocals of stress concentration factors caused by surface conditions
(Fig. 2.33/Pg 46, DHB)

4. **Reliability factor:** The reliability factor depends on the survival rate of the component at a particular stress. **Table 3.1** gives reliability factors for some standard specified levels, based on the fatigue limits having a standard deviation of 8%.

Table 3.1: Reliability factors							
Reliability %	50	90	95	99	99.9	99.99	99.999	99.9999
R_f or C_{reliab}	1	0.897	0.868	0.814	0.753	0.702	0.659	0.620

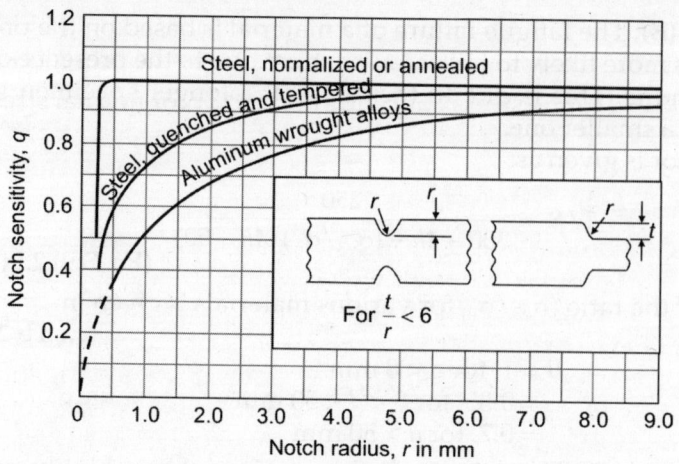

Fig. 3.6: Average notch sensitivity for different materials **[Fig. 2.51/Pg 46, DHB]**

5. **Temperature effects:** Fatigue tests are commonly done at room temperature. The fracture toughness decreases at low temperatures and increases at moderately high temperatures (up to 350°C). On the other hand, at high temperatures the endurance limit (knee) in the S–N diagram disappears, making the fatigue strength continue to decline with the number of cycles. Further the yield strength declines continuously with temperatures above room ambient and, in some cases, this can cause yielding before fatigue failure.

At temperatures above 50% of materials melting temperature, creep becomes a significant factor and the stress-life approach is no longer valid. In such cases the strain life approach is used which accounts for the combination of creep and fatigue under high temperature conditions.

6. **Fatigue stress concentration factor (K_{tf}):** It is defined as follows

$$K_{tf} = \frac{\text{endurance limit for unnotched specimen}}{\text{endurance limit for notched specimen}} \quad \text{... (Eq. 3.11)}$$

The stress concentration factor K_t dealt earlier (static loading) was a function of geometry alone; but K_{tf} is not only a function of geometry but also a function of the material and type of loading. The material consideration is dealt by using a **notch sensitivity factor or index of sensitivity (q)**, defined as K_{tf}

$$q = \frac{K_{tf} - 1}{K_t - 1} \quad \text{... (Eq. 3.12)} \textbf{ 2.4/ Pg 21, DHB}$$

– Value of q for repeated stresses are available in ... **Tb 2.4/ Pg 32, DHB**
– The value of q based on notched radius can be obtained from Fig. 3.6.
   ... **Fig. 2.31/ Pg 46, DHB**

The reason for subtracting 1 from both numerator and denominator is to provide a scale for q that ranges from 0 to 1.

– If $q = 0$, then $K_{tf} = 1$ and material has no sensitivity to notches (notch blunting effect), and
– If $q = 1$, then $K_{tf} = K_t$ and material has full sensitivity to notches.

In analysis or design work, find K_t first, from the geometry of the part; then specify the material, find q, and solve for K_{tf} from the following equations.

– For normal stress, $K_{tf} = 1 + q(K_t - 1)$ ... (Eq. 3.13) **2.5/ Pg 21, DHB**
– For shear stress, $K_{sf} = 1 + q(K_s - 1)$ ... (Eq. 3.14) **2.7/ Pg 21, DHB**

where K_{tf} = fatigue stress concentration factor for normal stress
        K_{sf} = fatigue stress concentration factor for shear stress
        K_t = theoretical stress concentration factor for normal stress
        K_s = theoretical stress concentration factor for shear stress

Note: It was observed that, in static loading and ductile behavior, stress concentrations were harmless as they resulted in small localized yielding which does not lead to any objectionable dimensional changes. But in dynamic/cyclic/fatigue loading the ductile materials would behave as if they are brittle leading to failure. Thus, regardless of ductility/brittleness of material, the stress concentration factor has to be applied when dynamic loads (fatigue/impact) are present. Hence for dynamic loading, the theoretical stress concentration factor (K_t) is modified based on the notch sensitivity (q) of the material to obtain fatigue stress concentration factor (K_{tf}).

3. **For the part shown in Fig. 3.7, calculate the maximum induced stress when**
   a. **The part is made of steel and subjected to static load.**
   b. **The part is made of cast iron and subjected to static load.**
   c. **The part is made of steel with notch sensitivity 0.9 and the load is cyclic.**
   d. **The part is made of cast iron and the load is cyclic.**

The plate is 20 mm thick.

VTU – July/Aug. 2004 – 15 Marks

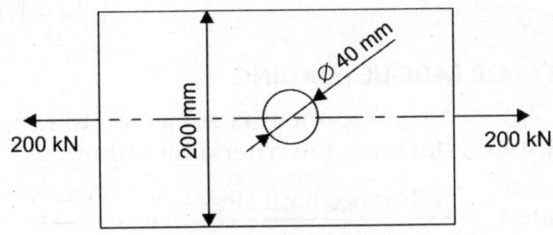

Fig. 3.7: Problem 3

Solution: $F = 200$ kN $= 200 \times 10^3$ N, $\sigma_{max} = ?$

Case a: Part is made of steel and subjected to static load: Referring to **Fig. 2.12/ Pg 36, DHB**, we have $B = 200$ mm, $t = 20$ mm, $a = 40$ mm.

We know that, $\sigma_{max} = \dfrac{F}{A}, \; K_t = \dfrac{F}{(B-a)t} K_t$ ... Eq. (i) **2.1(a)/ Pg 20, DHB**

On the other hand, if we use the fatigue stress concentration factor, then

$$K_{tf} = 1 + q(K_t - 1)$$ ... **2.5/ Pg 21, DHB**

$\therefore$ Eq. (i) yields... $\sigma_{max} = \dfrac{F}{(B-a)t} K_{tf} = \dfrac{F}{(B-a)t}[1 + q(K_t - 1)]$ ... Eq. (ii)

Now $\dfrac{a}{B} = \dfrac{40}{200} = 0.2$

at $\dfrac{a}{B} = 0.2$, we have $K_t = 2.55$

$\therefore$ Eq. (i) yields... $\sigma_{max} = \dfrac{200 \times 10^3}{(200 - 40)20} \times 2.55 = 159.38 \text{ MPa}$

$\therefore$ Eq. (ii) yields... $\sigma_{max} = \dfrac{200 \times 10^3}{(200 - 40)20} [1 + 0(2.55 - 1)] = 62.5 \text{ MPa}$

$[\because q = 0 \text{ (negligible), for ductile materials}]$

Case b: Part is made of cast iron and subjected to static load:

$\therefore$ Eq. (i) yields... $\sigma_{max} = \dfrac{200 \times 10^3}{(200 - 40)20} \times 2.55 = 159.38 \text{ MPa}$

$\therefore$ Eq. (ii) yields... $\sigma_{max} = \dfrac{200 \times 10^3}{(200 - 40)20} [1 + 1(2.55 - 1)] = 159.38 \text{ MPa}$

$[\because q = 1, \text{ for brittle materials}]$

Case c: Part is made of steel with notch sensitivity 0.9 and the load is cyclic:

$\therefore$ Eq. (ii) yields... $\sigma_{max} = \dfrac{200 \times 10^3}{(200 - 40)20} [1 + 0.9(2.55 - 1)] = 149.69 \text{ MPa}$

Case d: Part is made of cast iron and the load is cyclic:

$\therefore$ Eq. (ii) yields... $\sigma_{max} = \dfrac{200 \times 10^3}{(200 - 40)20} [1 + 1(2.55 - 1)] = 159.38 \text{ MPa}$

$[\because q = 1, \text{ for brittle materials}]$

3.9 FACTOR OF SAFETY FOR FATIGUE LOADING

As discussed in Unit 2, when a component is subjected to fatigue/cyclic/variable loading the endurance limit is taken as the criteria for failure.

i.e. $\qquad$ Factor of safety $= \dfrac{\text{endurance limit stress}}{\text{working stress}}$ i.e. $n = \dfrac{\sigma_{en}}{\sigma_d}$ $\qquad$ ... Eq. (3.15)

3.10 FATIGUE STRENGTH UNDER FLUCTUATING STRESSES: FATIGUE FAILURE THEORIES

The commonly used fatigue failure theories are:
- Soderberg criteria or yield criteria
- Goodman criteria or fracture criteria and
- Gerber's criteria.

3.10.1 Soderberg Criteria or Yield Criteria

This method is used for ductile materials when the design is based on yield stress. This method is used to find the limiting stress condition when the endurance limit (σ_{en}) and the yield strength (σ_{yp}) of the member are known, as shown in **Fig. 3.8**. Here X-axis represents the mean stress and the Y-axis represents the alternating stress. Point A represents the yield point stress and point B represents the endurance limit. The line joining points A and B is called the *Soderberg failure stress line.*

If a factor of safety is applied to endurance limit and yield strength, a safe stress line CD may be drawn parallel to the line AB. Then σ_{en}/n and σ_{yp}/n is the limiting condition. Any stress coming within the triangle DOC is considered to be safe.

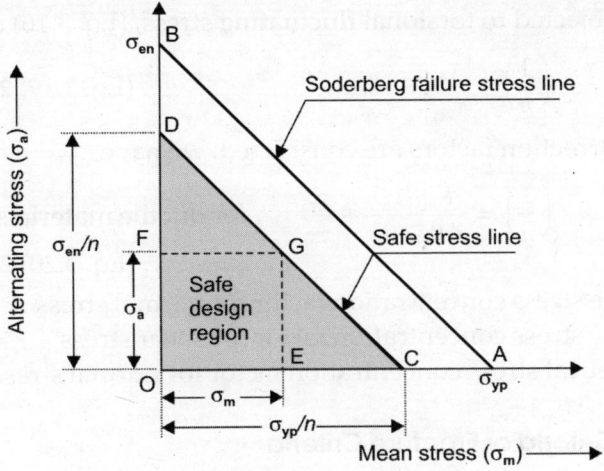

Fig. 3.8: Soderberg method or yield criteria

Consider a stress point G on the line CD. From similar triangles DOC and GEC, we have

$$\frac{EG}{OD} = \frac{EC}{OC}$$

$$= \frac{OC - OE}{OC} = 1 - \frac{OE}{OC}$$

$$\frac{\sigma_a}{\sigma_{en}/n} = 1 - \frac{\sigma_m}{\sigma_{yp}/n}$$

$$\sigma_a = \left(\frac{\sigma_{en}}{n}\right)\left[1 - \frac{\sigma_m}{\sigma_{yp}/n}\right]$$

$$\sigma_a = \sigma_{en}\left[\frac{1}{n} - \frac{\sigma_m}{\sigma_{yp}}\right]$$

$$\left(\frac{1}{n}\right) = \frac{\sigma_a}{\sigma_{en}} + \frac{\sigma_m}{\sigma_{yp}} \qquad \text{... (Eq. 3.16)} \textbf{ 2.19(c)/ Pg 24, DHB}$$

Equation (3.16) is used for ductile material subjected to static loading, wherein the stress concentration is neglected.

In case of fatigue loading, the effect of stress concentration has to be considered. If the correction factors, i.e. effect of load (*A*), size (*B*) and surface (*C*) are taken into account, then (Eq. 3.16) is modified as

$$\left(\frac{1}{n}\right) = \frac{K_{tf} \cdot \sigma_a}{ABC\,\sigma_{en}} + \frac{\sigma_m}{\sigma_{yp}} \quad \text{... for ductile materials}$$

$$\text{... (Eq. 3.17)} \textbf{ 2.21(c)/ Pg 25, DHB}$$

$$\left(\frac{1}{n}\right) = \frac{K_{tf} \cdot \sigma_a}{ABC\,\sigma_{en}} + \frac{K_t\sigma_m}{\sigma_{yp}} \quad \text{... for brittle materials}$$

$$\text{... (Eq. 3.18)} \textbf{ 2.21(d)/ Pg 25, DHB}$$

For materials subjected to torsional fluctuating stress, (Eq. 3.16) can be written as

$$\left(\frac{1}{n}\right) = \frac{\tau_a}{\tau_{en}} + \frac{\tau_m}{\tau_{yp}} \qquad \dots \text{(Eq. 3.19)} \textbf{ 2.19(e)/ Pg 25, DHB}$$

If the effect of correction factors are considered, we have

$$\left(\frac{1}{n}\right) = \frac{K_{sf} \cdot \tau_a}{ABC\,\sigma_{en}} + \frac{\tau_m}{\tau_{yp}} \dots \text{ for ductile materials subjected to shear}$$

$$\dots \text{(Eq. 3.20)} \textbf{ 2.21(e)/ Pg 25, DHB}$$

where K_{tf} = fatigue stress concentration factor for normal stress
   K_{sf} = fatigue stress concentration factor for shear stress
   K_t = theoretical stress concentration factor for normal stress.

3.10.2 Goodman Criteria or Fracture Criteria

This method is used for both ductile as well as brittle materials when the design is based on ultimate stress. This method is used to find the limiting stress condition when the endurance limit (σ_{en}) and the ultimate strength (σ_u) of the member are known, as shown in **Fig. 3.9**. Here X-axis represents the mean stress and the Y-axis represents the alternating stress. Point A represents the ultimate stress and point B represents the endurance limit. The line joining points A and B is called the *Goodman failure stress line*.

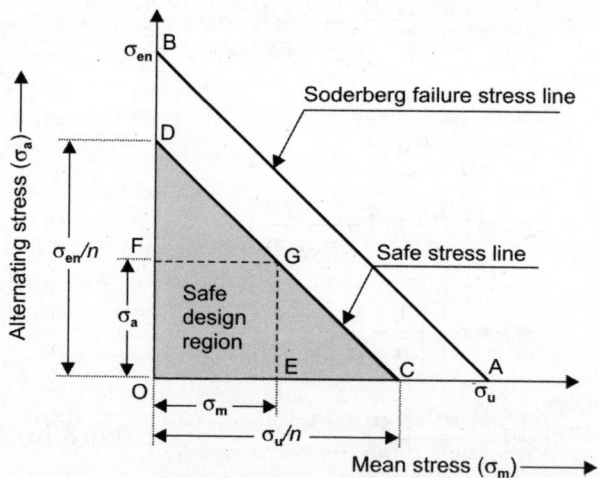

Fig. 3.9: Goodman method of fracture criteria

If a factor of safety is applied to endurance limit and ultimate strength, a safe stress line CD may be drawn parallel to the line AB. Then σ_{en}/n and σ_u/n is the limiting condition. Any stress coming within the triangle DOC is considered to be safe.

Consider a stress point G on the line CD. From similar triangles DOC and GEC, we have

$$\frac{EG}{OD} = \frac{EC}{OC}$$

$$= \frac{OC - OE}{OC} = 1 - \frac{OE}{OC}$$

$$\frac{\sigma_a}{\sigma_{en}/n} = 1 - \frac{\sigma_m}{\sigma_u/n}$$

$$\sigma_a = \left(\frac{\sigma_{en}}{n}\right)\left[1 - \frac{\sigma_m}{\sigma_u/n}\right]$$

$$\sigma_a = \sigma_{en}\left[\frac{1}{n} - \frac{\sigma_m}{\sigma_u}\right]$$

$$\left(\frac{1}{n}\right) = \frac{\sigma_a}{\sigma_{en}} + \frac{\sigma_m}{\sigma_u} \qquad \text{... (Eq. 3.21) } \mathbf{2.19(b)/ Pg\ 24,\ DHB}$$

In case of fatigue loading, the effect of stress concentration has to be considered. If the correction factors, i.e. effect of load (*A*), size (*B*) and surface (*C*) are taken into account, then (Eq. 3.21) is modified as

$$\left(\frac{1}{n}\right) = \frac{K_{tf}\cdot\sigma_a}{ABC\,\sigma_{en}} + \frac{\sigma_m}{\sigma_u} \quad \text{... for ductile materials}$$
$$\text{... (Eq. 3.22) } \mathbf{2.21(a)/ Pg\ 25,\ DHB}$$

$$\left(\frac{1}{n}\right) = \frac{K_{tf}\cdot\sigma_a}{ABC\,\sigma_{en}} + \frac{K_t\sigma_m}{\sigma_u} \quad \text{... for brittle materials}$$
$$\text{... (Eq. 3.23) } \mathbf{2.21(b)/ Pg\ 25,\ DHB}$$

For materials subjected to torsional fluctuating stress, (Eq. 3.21) can be written as

$$\left(\frac{1}{n}\right) = \frac{\tau_a}{\tau_{en}} + \frac{\tau_m}{\tau_u} \qquad \text{... (Eq. 3.24) } \mathbf{2.19(d)/ Pg\ 25,\ DHB}$$

3.11 RELATION BETWEEN ENDURANCE LIMIT AND ULTIMATE TENSILE STRENGTH

The relation between endurance limit and ultimate tensile stress of the material for different materials are given below.

For steel $\qquad\qquad\qquad\qquad \sigma_{en} = \left(\frac{1}{2} \text{ to } \frac{5}{8}\right)\sigma_u \qquad$ **... 2.13(a)/ Pg 23, DHB**

For cast iron $\qquad\qquad\qquad \sigma_{en} = 0.4\,\sigma_u \qquad\qquad$ **... 2.13(b)/ Pg 23, DHB**

For nonferrous metals and alloys $\quad \sigma_{en} = \left(\frac{1}{4} \text{ to } \frac{1}{3}\right)\sigma_u \qquad$ **... 2.13(c)/ Pg 23, DHB**

3.12 RELATION BETWEEN DIRECT STRESS ENDURANCE LIMIT AND ULTIMATE TENSILE STRENGTH

The relation between direct stress endurance limit and ultimate tensile stress of the material for different materials are given below.

For steel $\qquad\qquad\qquad\quad \sigma_{en-a} = (0.7 \text{ to } 1)\,\sigma_{en} = (0.35 \text{ to } 5/8)\,\sigma_u$
$$\text{... } \mathbf{2.14(a)/ Pg\ 23,\ DHB}$$

For cast iron $\qquad\qquad\quad \sigma_{en-a} = (0.7 \text{ to } 1)\,\sigma_{en} = (0.28 \text{ to } 0.4)\,\sigma_u$
$$\text{... } \mathbf{2.14(b)/ Pg\ 23,\ DHB}$$

For nonferrous metals and alloys $\quad \sigma_{en-a} = (0.7 \text{ to } 1)\,\sigma_{en} = (0.175 \text{ to } 1/3)\,\sigma_u$
$$\text{... } \mathbf{2.14(c)/ Pg\ 23,\ DHB}$$

3.13 RELATION BETWEEN CYCLIC TORSION ENDURANCE LIMIT AND ULTIMATE TENSILE STRENGTH

The relation between endurance limit and ultimate tensile stress of the material for different materials are given below:

For steel $\quad\quad\quad\quad\quad\quad\quad\quad\quad$ $\tau_{en} = (0.5 \text{ to } 0.6)\, \sigma_{en} = (0.25 \text{ to } 0.3)\, \sigma_u$

$\quad\quad\quad\quad\quad\quad\quad\quad\quad\quad\quad\quad\quad\quad\quad\quad\quad\quad$ **... 2.15(a)/ Pg 23, DHB**

For cast iron $\quad\quad\quad\quad\quad\quad\quad\quad$ $\tau_{en} = 0.8\, \sigma_u$ $\quad\quad\quad$ **... 2.15(b)/ Pg 23, DHB**

For nonferrous metals and alloys $\quad$ $\tau_{en} = 0.2\, \sigma_u$ $\quad\quad\quad$ **... 2.15(c)/ Pg 23, DHB**

PROBLEMS BASED ON CROSS-SECTION

4. **A steel rod (σ_{ut} = 1089.5 MPa, σ_{yt} = 689.4 MPa, σ_{-1} = 427.6 MPa) is subjected to a tensile load, which varies from 120 kN to 40 kN. Design the safe diameter of the rod using 'Soderberg diagram'. Adopt factor of safety as 2, stress concentration factor as unity and correction factors for load, size and surface as 0.75, 0.85 and 0.91 respectively.**

VTU – Dec. 07/ Jan. 2008 – 10 Marks

Solution: σ_{out} = 1089.5 MPa, $\sigma_{yt} = \sigma_{yp}$ = 689.4 MPa, $\sigma_{-1} = \sigma_{en}$ = 427.6 MPa, F_{max} = 120 kN = 120 × 10³ N. F_{min} = 40 kN = 40 × 10³ N, d = ? Using Soderberg criteria, n = 2, K_t = 1, load factor A = 0.75, size factor B = 0.85, surface factor C = 0.91.

According to Soderberg, for ductile material (steel),

$$\left(\frac{1}{n}\right) = \frac{K_{tf} \cdot \sigma_a}{ABC\,\sigma_{en}} + \frac{\sigma_m}{\sigma_{yp}} \quad \text{... Eq. (i) 2.21(c)/ Pg 25, DHB}$$

- Mean or average

$$\sigma_m = \frac{\sigma_{max} + \sigma_{min}}{2} = \frac{F_m}{A} \quad\quad \text{... 2.16(a)/ Pg 23, DHB}$$

But $\quad\quad$ $F_m = \dfrac{F_{max} + F_{min}}{2}$ and $F_a = \dfrac{F_{max} - F_{min}}{2}$ $\quad$ **... 2.17(a)/ Pg 24, DHB**

$$\sigma_m = \frac{F_{max} + F_{min}}{2A} = \frac{120 \times 10^3 + 40 \times 10^3}{2(\pi d^2/4)} = \frac{101.86 \times 10^3}{d^2}$$

- Variable or alternating stress,

$$\sigma_a = \frac{\sigma_{max} - \sigma_{min}}{2} = \frac{F_m}{A} \quad\quad \text{... 2.16(b)/ Pg 23, DHB}$$

$$\sigma_a = \frac{F_{max} - F_{min}}{2A} = \frac{120 \times 10^3 - 40 \times 10^3}{2(\pi d^2/4)} = \frac{50.91 \times 10^3}{d^2}$$

- Also $\quad\quad$ $K_{tf} = 1 + q(K_t - 1)$ $\quad\quad\quad\quad\quad\quad$ **... 2.5/ Pg 21, DHB**

Since the cross-section is uniform, K_t = 1 and q = 0

$$K_{tf} = 1 + 0(1 - 1) = 1$$

- *Correction factors*: From data A = 0.75, B = 0.85, C = 0.91

$\therefore$ Eq. (i) yields... $\left(\dfrac{1}{2}\right) = \dfrac{1}{(0.75 \times 0.85 \times 0.91) \times 427.6}\left(\dfrac{50.91 \times 10^3}{d^2}\right) + \dfrac{101.86 \times 10^3}{689.4 \times d^2}$

$$0.5 = \frac{352.98}{d^2}$$

$$d = 26.57 \text{ mm} \approx 30 \text{ mm}$$

5. **Determine the diameter of a circular rod made of ductile material with fatigue strength of σ_e = 265 MPa and tensile yield strength of 350 MPa. The member is subjected to a varying axial load from F_{min} = −300 × 10³ N to F_{max} = 700 × 10³ N and has a fatigue stress concentration factor = 1.8. Use factor of safety as 2.0.**

VTU – June/ July 2015 – 10 Marks

Solution: d = ?, σ_{en} = 265 MPa, σ_{yp} = 350 MPa, F_{max} = 700 × 10³ N, F_{min} = −300 × 10³ N, K_{tf} = 1.8, n = 2.

Since yield strength is given, Soderberg equation forms the criteria for failure

We know that $\quad \left(\dfrac{1}{n}\right) = \dfrac{K_{tf} \cdot \sigma_a}{ABC\,\sigma_{en}} + \dfrac{\sigma_m}{\sigma_{yp}} \qquad$ ... Eq. (i) **2.21(c)/ Pg 25, DHB**

- Mean or average stress,

$$\sigma_m = \frac{\sigma_{max} + \sigma_{min}}{2} = \frac{F_m}{A} \qquad \text{... 2.16(a)/ Pg 23, DHB}$$

But $\quad F_m = \dfrac{F_{max} + F_{min}}{2}$ and $F_a = \dfrac{F_{max} - F_{min}}{2} \quad$ ... **2.17(a)/ Pg 24, DHB**

$$\sigma_m = \frac{F_{max} + F_{min}}{2A} = \frac{700 \times 10^3 - 300 \times 10^3}{2(\pi d^2 / 4)} = \frac{2.55 \times 10^5}{d^2}$$

- Variable or alternating stress,

$$\sigma_a = \frac{\sigma_{max} - \sigma_{min}}{2} = \frac{F_a}{A} \qquad \text{... 2.16(b)/ Pg 23, DHB}$$

$$\sigma_a = \frac{F_{max} - F_{min}}{2A} = \frac{700 \times 10^3 + 300 \times 10^3}{2(\pi d^2 / 4)} = \frac{6.37 \times 10^5}{d^2}$$

K_{tf} = 1.8 (data)

- *Correction factors*:

  Load factor A = 0.85 (average value), for reversed axial load $\quad$ ... **Pg 25, DHB**

  Size correction factor B = 0.85, assumed, since size is unknown

  Surface correction factor C = 1, assumed since σ_u is unknown

∴ Eq. (i) yields... $\quad \left(\dfrac{1}{2}\right) = \dfrac{1.8}{(0.85 \times 0.85 \times 1) \times 265}\left(\dfrac{6.37 \times 10^5}{d^2}\right) + \dfrac{2.55 \times 10^5}{350 \times d^2}$

$$0.5 = \frac{6712.63}{d^2}$$

$$d = 115.87 \text{ mm} \approx 120 \text{ mm}$$

6. **The maximum pressure in the cylinder of a double acting type is 0.9 MPa. The bore of the cylinder is 500 mm in diameter. What should be the diameter of the piston rod if there are no stress raisers and column action? Take the factor of safety as 1.75 based on Soderberg's criteria, ultimate tensile strength of the material of the piston rod is 1750 MPa. Choose a modifying factor of 0.85 for the type of loading, 0.85 for the size and 0.78 for the surface effects.**

VTU – June/ July 2008 – 08 Marks

Solution: $p = 0.9$ MPa, $D = 500$ mm, $d = ?$. Using Soderberg criteria, $K_{tf} = 1$ (no stress raisers), $n = 1.75$, $\sigma_u = 1750$ MPa, load factor $A = 0.85$, size factor $B = 0.85$, surface factor $C = 0.78$.

According to Soderberg,

$$\left(\frac{1}{n}\right) = \frac{K_{tf} \cdot \sigma_a}{ABC\,\sigma_{en}} + \frac{\sigma_m}{\sigma_{yp}} \qquad \text{... Eq. (i)}\ \textbf{2.21(c)/ Pg 25, DHB}$$

- But $\qquad p = \dfrac{F}{A} = \dfrac{F}{\pi D^2/4}$

$$F = 0.9 \times (\pi \times 500^2/4) = 176.71 \times 10^3\ \text{N}$$

$\therefore \qquad F_{max} = 176.71 \times 10^3$ N, $F_{min} = -176.71 \times 10^3$ N

- Mean stress $\qquad \sigma_m = \dfrac{\sigma_{max} + \sigma_{min}}{2} = \dfrac{F_m}{A}$ $\qquad$ **... 2.16(a)/ Pg 23, DHB**

- But $\qquad F_m = \dfrac{F_{max} + F_{min}}{2}$ and $F_a = \dfrac{F_{max} - F_{min}}{2}$ $\qquad$ **... 2.17(a)/ Pg 24, DHB**

$$\sigma_m = \frac{F_{max} + F_{min}}{2A} = \frac{176.71 \times 10^3 - 176.71 \times 10^3}{2(\pi d^2/4)} = 0\ \text{MPa}$$

- Variable stress, $\quad \sigma_a = \dfrac{\sigma_{max} - \sigma_{min}}{2} = \dfrac{F_a}{A}$ $\qquad$ **... 2.16(b)/ Pg 23, DHB**

$$\sigma_a = \frac{F_{max} - F_{min}}{2A} = \frac{176.71 \times 10^3 + 176.71 \times 10^3}{2(\pi d^2/4)} = \frac{225 \times 10^3}{d^2}$$

- Also $\qquad K_{tf} = 1 + q(K_t - 1)$ $\qquad$ **... 2.5/ Pg 21, DHB**

   Since there are no stress raisers, $K_t = 1$ and $q = 0$
   $$K_{tf} = 1 + 0(1 - 1) = 1$$

- For steel, $\qquad \sigma_{en} = 0.5\sigma_u = 0.5 \times 1750 = 875$ MPa $\qquad$ **... 2.13(a)/ Pg 23, DHB**

- *Correction factors:* From data $A = 0.85$, $B = 0.85$, $C = 0.78$

$\therefore$ Eq. (i) yields...

$$\left(\frac{1}{1.75}\right) = \frac{1.8}{(0.85 \times 0.85 \times 0.78) \times 875} = \left(\frac{225 \times 10^3}{d^2}\right)$$

$$\left(\frac{1}{1.75}\right) = \frac{456.29}{d^2}$$

$$d = 28.26\ \text{mm} \approx 30\ \text{mm}$$

7. **A cold drawn steel bar is to withstand a tensile preload of 36.3 kN, a fluctuating tensile load varying from 0 to 72.6 kN. The bar has geometric stress concentration factor of 2.02 corresponding to a fillet whose radius is 4.75 mm. Determine the size of the bar for an infinite life and a factor of safety of 2. The material properties are $\sigma_{yp} = 588$ N/mm^2, $\sigma_{ut} = 700$ N/mm^2.**

VTU – Jan/ Feb. 2005 – 08 Marks

Solution: Preload $F = 36.3$ kN $= 36.3 \times 10^3$ N, $F_{max} = 72.6 \times 10^3$ N, $F_{min} = 0$ kN, $K_t = 2.02$, fillet radius $r = 4.75$ mm, bar size $d = ?$, $n = 2$, $\sigma_{yp} = 588$ N/mm^2, $\sigma_u = 700$ N/mm^2.

According to Soderberg,

$$\left(\frac{1}{n}\right) = \frac{K_{tf} \cdot \sigma_a}{ABC\,\sigma_{en}} + \frac{\sigma_m}{\sigma_{yp}} \qquad \text{... Eq. (i) } \textbf{2.21(c)/ Pg 25, DHB}$$

- Static stress, $\quad \sigma_D = \dfrac{F}{A} = \dfrac{36.3 \times 10^3}{(\pi d^2/4)} = \dfrac{46.22 \times 10^3}{d^2}$

- Mean stress $\quad \sigma_m = \dfrac{\sigma_{max} + \sigma_{min}}{2} = \dfrac{F_m}{A} \qquad \text{... } \textbf{2.16(a)/ Pg 23, DHB}$

- But $\quad F_m = \dfrac{F_{max} + F_{min}}{2}$ and $F_a = \dfrac{F_{max} - F_{min}}{2} \qquad \text{... } \textbf{2.17(a)/ Pg 24, DHB}$

$$\sigma_m = \frac{F_{max} + F_{min}}{2A} = \frac{72.6 \times 10^3 + 0}{2(\pi d^2/4)} = \frac{46.22 \times 10^3}{d^2}$$

Thus, the total mean stress

$$= \frac{46.22 \times 10^3}{d^2} + \frac{46.22 \times 10^3}{d^2} = \frac{92.44 \times 10^3}{d^2}$$

- Variable stress, $\quad \sigma_a = \dfrac{\sigma_{max} - \sigma_{min}}{2} = \dfrac{F_a}{A} \qquad \text{... } \textbf{2.16(b)/ Pg 23, DHB}$

$$\sigma_a = \frac{F_{max} - F_{min}}{2A} = \frac{72.6 \times 10^3 + 0}{2(\pi d^2/4)} = \frac{46.22 \times 10^3}{d^2}$$

- Also $\quad K_{tf} = 1 + q(K_t - 1) \qquad \text{... } \textbf{2.5/ Pg 21, DHB}$

  Based on notch radius of $r = 4.75$ mm and $q = 0.96 \quad \text{... } \textbf{Fig. 2.31/ Pg 46, DHB}$

  $K_{tf} = 1 + 0.96(2.02 - 1) = 1.98$

- *Correction factors*:

  Load factor $A = 0.85$ (average value), for reversed axial load $\quad \text{... } \textbf{Pg 25, DHB}$

  Size correction factor $B = 1$, assumed, since size is unknown

  Surface correction factor $C = 0.73$, based on $\sigma_u = 700$ MPa.

  $$\text{... } \textbf{Fig. 2.33 (curve-d)/Pg 46, DHB}$$

- *Endurance strength*:

  $$\sigma_{en} = 0.5\sigma_u = 0.5 \times 700 = 350 \text{ MPa}$$

$\therefore$ Eq. (i) yields... $\left(\dfrac{1}{2}\right) = \dfrac{1.98}{(0.85 \times 1 \times 0.73) \times 350}\left(\dfrac{46.22 \times 10^3}{d^2}\right) + \dfrac{92.44 \times 10^3}{588 \times d^2}$

$$0.5 = \frac{578.60}{d^2}$$

$$d = 34.01 \text{ mm} \approx 34 \text{ mm}$$

8. **A component machined from a plate made of steel 45C8 ($\sigma_{ut} = 630$ MPa) is shown in Fig. 3.10. It is subjected to a completely reversed axial force of 50 kN. The expected reliability is 90% and the factor of safety is 2. Determine the plate thickness 't' for infinite life, if the notch sensitivity factor is 0.8.**

VTU – Dec. 08/ Jan. 2009 – 12 Marks

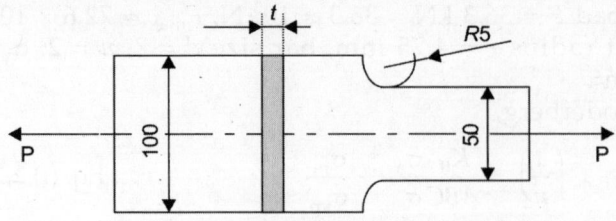

Fig. 3.10: Problem 8

Solution: $\sigma_{ut} = \sigma_u = 630$ MPa, $F_{max} = 50$ kN $= 50 \times 10^3$ N, $F_{min} = -50 \times 10^3$ N, reliability = 90%, $n = 2$, $t = ?$, $q = 0.8$.

Since yield stress is not given, design is based on Goodman criterion for ductile materials.

According to Goodman,

$$\left(\frac{1}{n}\right) = \frac{K_{tf} \cdot \sigma_a}{ABC\,\sigma_{en}} + \frac{\sigma_m}{\sigma_u} \qquad \text{... 2.21(a)/ Pg 25, DHB}$$

Since reliability is given, the above equation is modified as

$$\left(\frac{1}{n}\right) = \frac{K_{tf} \cdot \sigma_a}{ABC\,R_f\sigma_{en}} + \frac{\sigma_m}{\sigma_u} \qquad \text{... Eq. (i)}$$

- Mean stress $\sigma_m = \dfrac{\sigma_{max} + \sigma_{min}}{2} = \dfrac{F_m}{A}$ **... 2.16(a)/ Pg 23, DHB**

  But $F_m = \dfrac{F_{max} + F_{min}}{2}$ and $F_a = \dfrac{F_{max} - F_{min}}{2}$ **... 2.17(a)/ Pg 24, DHB**

  Referring the given problem to **Fig. 2.16/Pg 38, DHB**, we have

  $$A = bt = 50t$$

  $$\sigma_m = \frac{F_{max} + F_{min}}{2A} = \frac{50 \times 10^3 - 50 \times 10^3}{2(50t)} = 0$$

- Variable stress, $\sigma_a = \dfrac{\sigma_{max} - \sigma_{min}}{2} = \dfrac{F_a}{A}$ **... 2.16(b)/ Pg 23, DHB**

  $$\sigma_a = \frac{F_{max} - F_{min}}{2A} = \frac{50 \times 10^3 + 50 \times 10^3}{2(50t)} = \frac{1000}{t}$$

- Also $K_{tf} = 1 + q(K_t - 1)$ **... Eq. (ii) 2.5/ Pg 21, DHB**

  Referring the given problem to **Fig. 2.16/Pg 38, DHB,** we have

  $$B = 100 \text{ mm}, b = 50 \text{ mm}, r = 5 \text{ mm}, t = ?$$

  Now $\dfrac{r}{b} = \dfrac{5}{50} = 0.1$; and $\dfrac{B}{b} = \dfrac{100}{50} = 2$

  At $\dfrac{r}{b} = 0.1$; and $\dfrac{B}{b} = 2$, $K_t = 2.27$

  $\therefore$ Eq. (ii) yields...

  $$K_{tf} = 1 + 0.8(2.27 - 1) = 2.02$$

- *Correction factors:*

  Load factor $A = 0.85$ (average value), for reversed axial load   **... Pg 25, DHB**

  Size correction factor $B = 0.85$, assumed, since size is unknown

Surface correction factor $C = 0.85$, based on $\sigma_u = 630$ MPa.

... Fig. 2.33 (curve c)/Pg 46, DHB

For a reliability of 90%, $R_f = 0.897$ **... Tb 3.1/Pg 171**

- Endurance strength,

$$\sigma_{en} = 0.5\sigma_u = 0.5 \times 630 = 315 \text{ MPa} \qquad \text{... 2.13(a)/Pg 23, DHB}$$

$\therefore$ Eq. (i) yields...

$$\left(\frac{1}{2}\right) = \frac{2.02}{(0.85 \times 0.85 \times 0.85 \times 0.897) \times 315}\left(\frac{1000}{t}\right) + 0$$

$$0.5 = \frac{11.64}{t}$$

$$d = 23.28 \text{ mm} \approx 30 \text{ mm}$$

9. **Figure 3.11 shows a plate subjected to a fluctuating load which varies from 50 kN (tensile) to 100 kN (tensile). The strengths of the material are $\sigma_u = 480$ MPa, $\sigma_{en} = 240$ MPa, The correction factors $K_{sr} = 0.67$, $K_{sz} = 0.85$ and $K_l = 0.7$ corresponds to surface, size and type of load. Find the maximum value of D using a factor of safety of 2.**

VTU – Jan/ Feb. 2006 – 10 Marks

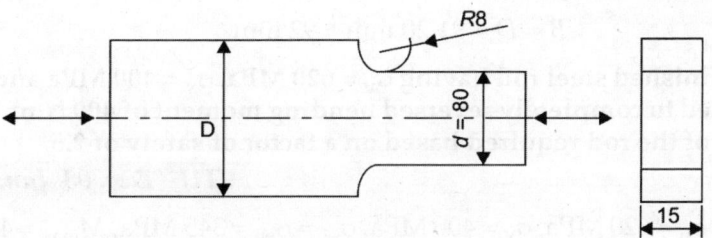

Fig. 3.11: Problem 9

Solution: $F_{max} = 100 \text{ kN} = 100 \times 10^3$ N, $F_{min} = 50 \text{ kN} = 50 \times 10^3$ N, $\sigma_u = 480$ MPa, $\sigma_{en} = 240$ MPa, load factor $A = 0.7$, size factor $B = 0.85$, surface factor $C = 0.67$, $D = ?$, $n = 2$.

According to Goodman,

$$\left(\frac{1}{n}\right) = \frac{K_{tf} \cdot \sigma_a}{ABC\,\sigma_{en}} + \frac{\sigma_m}{\sigma_u} \qquad \text{... Eq. (i) 2.21(a)/ Pg 25, DHB}$$

- Mean stress

$$\sigma_m = \frac{\sigma_{max} + \sigma_{min}}{2} = \frac{F_m}{A} \qquad \text{... 2.16(a)/ Pg 23, DHB}$$

But

$$F_m = \frac{F_{max} + F_{min}}{2} \text{ and } F_a = \frac{F_{max} - F_{min}}{2} \qquad \text{... 2.17(a)/ Pg 24, DHB}$$

Referring the given problem to **Fig. 2.16/Pg 38, DHB**, we have

$$A = bt = 80 \times 15 = 1200 \text{ mm}^2$$

$$\sigma_m = \frac{F_{max} + F_{min}}{2A} = \frac{100 \times 10^3 + 50 \times 10^3}{2 \times 1200} = 62.5 \text{ MPa}$$

- Variable stress,

$$\sigma_a = \frac{\sigma_{max} - \sigma_{min}}{2} = \frac{F_a}{A} \qquad \text{... 2.16(b)/ Pg 23, DHB}$$

$$\sigma_a = \frac{F_{max} - F_{min}}{2A} = \frac{100 \times 10^3 - 50 \times 10^3}{2 \times 1200} = 20.83 \text{ MPa}$$

- *Correction factors*: From data $A = 0.7$, $B = 0.85$, $C = 0.67$

∴ Eq. (i) yields... $\left(\dfrac{1}{2}\right) = \dfrac{K_{tf} \times 20.83}{(0.7 \times 0.85 \times 0.67) \times 240} + \left(\dfrac{62.5}{480}\right)$

$$K_{tf} = 1.70$$

But $\qquad K_{tf} = 1 + q(K_t - 1)$ ... Eq. (ii) **2.5/ Pg 21, DHB**

Referring the given problem to **Fig. 2.16/Pg 38, DHB**, we have

$$B = D = ?, b = 80 \text{ mm}, r = 8 \text{ mm}$$

Since B is unknown, using **Fig. 2.31/Pg 46, DHB**, we have the value of q based on r as $q = 1$

∴ Eq. (ii) yields... $1.70 = 1 + 1(K_t - 1)$

$$K_t = 1.70$$

Now at $\qquad \dfrac{r}{b} = \dfrac{8}{80} = 0.1$; and $K_t = 1.70$, we have $\dfrac{B}{b} = 1.14$

∴ $\qquad \dfrac{B}{80} = 1.14$

$$B = D = 91.20 \text{ mm} \approx 92 \text{ mm}$$

10. **A rough finished steel rod having $\sigma_u = 620$ MPa, $\sigma_y = 400$ MPa and $\sigma_{-1} = 345$ MPa is subjected to completely reversed bending moment of 400 N·m. Determine the diameter of the rod required based on a factor of safety of 2.5.**

VTU – Dec. 08/ Jan. 2009 12 Marks

Solution: $\sigma_u = 620$ MPa, $\sigma_y = 400$ MPa, $\sigma_{-1} = \sigma_{en} = 345$ MPa, $M_{max} = 400 \times 10^3$ N·mm, $M_{min} = -400 \times 10^3$ N·mm, $d = ?$, $n = 2.5$.

According to Soderberg,

$$\left(\dfrac{1}{n}\right) = \dfrac{K_{tf} \cdot \sigma_a}{ABC\,\sigma_{en}} + \dfrac{\sigma_m}{\sigma_{yp}} \qquad \text{... Eq. (i) } \textbf{2.21(c)/ Pg 25, DHB}$$

- Mean stress $\qquad \sigma_m = \dfrac{\sigma_{max} + \sigma_{min}}{2} = \dfrac{M_m}{Z}$ ... **2.16(a)/ Pg 23, DHB**

But $\qquad M_m = \dfrac{M_{max} + M_{min}}{2Z}$ and $M_a = \dfrac{M_{max} - M_{min}}{2}$

$$\sigma_m = \dfrac{M_{max} + M_{min}}{2Z} = \dfrac{400 \times 10^3 - 400 \times 10^3}{2(\pi d^3/32)} = 0$$

- Variable stress, $\sigma_a = \dfrac{\sigma_{max} - \sigma_{min}}{2} = \dfrac{M_a}{A}$ ... **2.16(b)/ Pg 23, DHB**

$$\sigma_a = \dfrac{M_{max} - M_{min}}{2Z} = \dfrac{400 \times 10^3 + 400 \times 10^3}{2(\pi d^3/32)} = \dfrac{4.07 \times 10^6}{d^3}$$

- Also $\qquad K_{tf} = 1 + q(K_t - 1)$ ... **2.5/ Pg 21, DHB**

Since the cross-section is uniform, $K_t = 1$ and $q = 0$

∴ $\qquad K_{tf} = 1$

- *Correction factors*:

Load factor $A = 1$, for reversed axial load ... **Pg 25, DHB**

Size correction factor $B = 0.85$, assumed since size is unknown

Surface correction factor $C = 0.86$, based on $\sigma_u = 620$ MPa.

... **Tb. 2.2/Pg 32, DHB**

$$\therefore \text{ Eq. (i) yields...} \left(\frac{1}{2.5}\right) = \frac{1}{(1 \times 0.85 \times 0.86) \times 345} \left(\frac{4.07 \times 10^6}{d^3}\right) + 0$$

$$0.4 = \left(\frac{16.02 \times 10^3}{d^3}\right)$$

$$d = 34.29 \text{ mm} \approx 35 \text{ mm}$$

11. **A circular bar of 500 mm length is supported freely at its two ends. It is acted upon by a central concentrated cyclic load having a minimum value of 20 kN and a maximum value of 50 kN. Determine the diameter of the bar by taking a factor of safety of 2, size effect of 0.85, and surface finish factor of 0.9. The material properties of the bar are given by ultimate strength of 650 MPa, yield strength of 500 MPa and endurance strength of 350 MPa.**

VTU – June/ July 2011 – 12 Marks

Solution: $L = 500$ mm, $F_{max} = 50$ kN $= 50 \times 10^3$ N, $F_{min} = 20$ kN $= 20 \times 10^3$ N, $d = ?$, $n = 2$, $B = 0.85$, $C = 0.9$, $\sigma_u = 650$ MPa, $\sigma_{yp} = 500$ MPa, $\sigma_{en} = 350$ MPa.

According to Soderberg,

$$\left(\frac{1}{n}\right) = \frac{K_{tf} \cdot \sigma_a}{ABC\,\sigma_{en}} + \frac{\sigma_m}{\sigma_{yp}} \qquad \text{... Eq. (i) } \textbf{2.21(c)/ Pg 25, DHB}$$

For a simply supported beam with point load at mid-span

$$M = \frac{FL}{4} \qquad \text{... \textbf{Tb. 1.4 (Fig. 4)/ Pg 15, DHB}}$$

- **Maximum BM,**

$$M_{max} = \frac{F_{max}L}{4} = \frac{(50 \times 10^3) \times 400}{4} = 6.25 \times 10^6 \text{ N·mm}$$

- **Minimum BM,**

$$M_{min} = \frac{F_{min}L}{4} = \frac{(20 \times 10^3) \times 500}{4} = 2.5 \times 10^6 \text{ N·mm}$$

- **Mean stress** $\sigma_m = \dfrac{\sigma_{max} + \sigma_{min}}{2} = \dfrac{M_m}{Z}$ ... **2.16(a)/ Pg 23, DHB**

But $\quad M_m = \dfrac{M_{max} + M_{min}}{2}$ and $M_a = \dfrac{M_{max} - M_{min}}{2}$

$$\sigma_m = \frac{M_{max} + M_{min}}{2Z} = \frac{6.25 \times 10^6 + 2.5 \times 10^6}{2(\pi d^3/32)} = \frac{44.56 \times 10^6}{d^3}$$

- **Variable stress,** $\sigma_a = \dfrac{\sigma_{max} - \sigma_{min}}{2} = \dfrac{M_a}{Z}$ ... **2.16(b)/ Pg 23, DHB**

$$\sigma_a = \frac{M_{max} - M_{min}}{2Z} = \frac{6.25 \times 10^3 - 2.5 \times 10^3}{2(\pi d^3/32)} = \frac{19.10 \times 10^6}{d^3}$$

- **Also** $\qquad K_{\mathrm{tf}} = 1 + q(K_t - 1)$ $\qquad\qquad$ ... **2.5/ Pg 21, DHB**

  Since the cross-section is uniform, $K_t = 1$ and $q = 0$

  $$K_{\mathrm{tf}} = 1$$

- *Correction factors*:

  Load factor $A = 1$, for reversed bending load $\qquad\qquad$ ... **Pg 25, DHB**

  $\qquad B = 0.85, C = 0.9$ (Data)

$\therefore$ Eq. (i) yields... $\quad \left(\dfrac{1}{2}\right) = \dfrac{1}{(1 \times 0.85 \times 0.9) \times 350}\left(\dfrac{19.10 \times 10^6}{d^3}\right) + \dfrac{44.56 \times 10^6}{500 \times d^3}$

$$0.5 = \left(\dfrac{160.45 \times 10^3}{d^3}\right)$$

$$d = 68.46 \text{ mm} \approx 70 \text{ mm}$$

12. **A hot rolled steel rod is subjected to a torsional load that varies from −100 N·m to 300 N·m. Determine the required diameter of the rod using a factor of safety of 2. The material has an ultimate tensile strength of 550 MPa and yield strength of 410 MPa.**

Solution: $T_{\max} = 300 \text{ N·m} = 300 \times 10^3 \text{ N·mm}$, $T_{\min} = -100 \text{ N·m} = -100 \times 10^3 \text{ N·mm}$, $d = ?$, $n = 2$, $\sigma_u = 550 \text{ MPa}$, $\sigma_{yp} = 410 \text{ MPa}$.

According to Soderberg,

$$\left(\frac{1}{n}\right) = \frac{K_{\mathrm{sf}} \cdot \tau_a}{ABC\,\sigma_{\mathrm{en}}} + \frac{\tau_m}{\tau_{\mathrm{yp}}} \qquad \text{... Eq. (i) } \mathbf{2.21(e)/ Pg\ 25,\ DHB}$$

- **Mean stress** $\qquad \tau_m = \dfrac{\tau_{\max} + \tau_{\min}}{2} = \dfrac{T_m}{Z_p}$ $\qquad\qquad$ ... **2.16(a)/ Pg 23, DHB**

  But $\qquad\qquad T_m = \dfrac{T_{\max} + T_{\min}}{2}$ and $T_a = \dfrac{T_{\max} - T_{\min}}{2}$

  $$\tau_m = \frac{T_{\max} + T_{\min}}{2Z_p} = \frac{300 \times 10^3 - 100 \times 10^3}{2(\pi d^3/16)} = \frac{5.09 \times 10^5}{d^3}$$

- **Variable stress,** $\quad \tau_a = \dfrac{\tau_{\max} - \tau_{\min}}{2} = \dfrac{T_a}{Z_p}$ $\qquad\qquad$ ... **2.16(b)/ Pg 23, DHB**

  $$\tau_a = \frac{T_{\max} - T_{\min}}{2Z_p} = \frac{300 \times 10^3 + 100 \times 10^3}{2(\pi d^3/16)} = \frac{1.02 \times 10^6}{d^3}$$

- **Also** $\qquad K_{\mathrm{sf}} = 1 + q(K_s - 1)$ $\qquad\qquad$ ... **2.7/ Pg 21, DHB**

  Since the cross-section is uniform, $K_t = 1$ and $q = 0$

  $$K_{\mathrm{sf}} = 1$$

- *Correction factors*:

  Load factor $A = 0.5$, for reversed axial load $\qquad\qquad$ ... **Pg 25, DHB**

  Size correction factor $B = 0.85$, assumed since size is unknown

  Surface correction factor $C = 0.62$, based on $\sigma_u = 550 \text{ MPa}$.

  $\qquad\qquad\qquad\qquad\qquad\qquad\qquad\qquad\qquad\qquad$ ... **Tb. 2.2/Pg 32, DHB**

- Endurance strength,

$$\sigma_{en} = 0.5\sigma_u \qquad \dots \textbf{2.13(a)/ Pg 23, DHB}$$

$$\sigma_{en} = 0.5 \times 550 = 275 \text{ MPa}$$

and $\qquad \tau_{yp} = 0.5\sigma_{yp} = 0.5 \times 410 = 205 \text{ MPa}$

$\therefore$ Eq. (i) yields... $\left(\dfrac{1}{2}\right) = \dfrac{1}{(0.5 \times 0.85 \times 0.62) \times 275}\left(\dfrac{1.02 \times 10^6}{d^3}\right) + \dfrac{5.09 \times 10^5}{205 \times d^3}$

$$0.5 = \left(\dfrac{16.56 \times 10^3}{d^3}\right)$$

$$d = 32.11 \text{ mm} \approx 35 \text{ mm}$$

13. **A steel shaft is subjected to a torque that varies over a range of $\pm 40\%$. Determine the diameter of the shaft if it transmits 15 kW at 250 rpm. The material has an ultimate tensile strength of 600 MPa and yield strength of 400 MPa. Assume a factor of safety of 3.**

Solution: $T = \pm 40\%$, $d = ?$, $P = 15$ kW, $n' = 250$ rpm, $\sigma_u = 600$ MPa, $\sigma_{yp} = 400$ MPa, $n = 3$.

According to Soderberg,

$$\left(\dfrac{1}{n}\right) = \dfrac{K_{sf} \cdot \tau_a}{ABC\,\sigma_{en}} + \dfrac{\tau_m}{\tau_{yp}} \qquad \dots \text{Eq. (i) } \textbf{2.21(e)/ Pg 25, DHB}$$

- Torque $\qquad T = \dfrac{9.55 \times 10^6 (P)}{n'} \qquad \dots \textbf{3.3(a)/ Pg 50, DHB}$

$$T = \dfrac{9.55 \times 10^6 \times (15)}{250} = 573 \times 10^3 \text{ N} \cdot \text{mm}$$

Therefore $\quad T_{max} = +40\%T = 1.4T = 1.4 \times (573 \times 10^3) = 802.2 \times 10^3 \text{ N·mm}$

and $\qquad T_{min} = -40\%T = 0.6T = 0.6 \times (573 \times 10^3) = 343.8 \times 10^3 \text{ N·mm}$

- Mean stress $\quad \tau_m = \dfrac{\tau_{max} + \tau_{min}}{2} = \dfrac{T_m}{Z_p} \qquad \dots \textbf{2.16(a)/ Pg 23, DHB}$

But $\qquad T_m = \dfrac{T_{max} + T_{min}}{2}$ and $T_a = \dfrac{T_{max} - T_{min}}{2}$

$$\tau_m = \dfrac{T_{max} + T_{min}}{2Z_p} = \dfrac{802.2 \times 10^3 + 343.8 \times 10^3}{2(\pi d^3/16)} = \dfrac{2.92 \times 10^6}{d^3}$$

- Variable stress, $\tau_a = \dfrac{\tau_{max} - \tau_{min}}{2} = \dfrac{T_a}{Z_p} \qquad \dots \textbf{2.16(b)/ Pg 23, DHB}$

$$\tau_a = \dfrac{T_{max} - T_{min}}{2Z_p} = \dfrac{802.2 \times 10^3 - 343.8 \times 10^3}{2(\pi d^3/16)} = \dfrac{1.17 \times 10^6}{d^3}$$

- Also $\qquad K_{sf} = 1 + q(K_s - 1) \qquad \dots \textbf{2.7/ Pg 21, DHB}$

Since the cross-section is uniform, $K_t = 1$ and $q = 0$

$$K_{sf} = 1$$

- *Correction factors*:

  $A = 0.5$, for reversed axial load   ... **Pg 25, DHB**

  $B = 0.85$, assumed since size is unknown

  $C = 0.93$, based on $\sigma_u = 600$ MPa   ... **Fig. 2.33 (curve b)/Pg 46, DHB**

- Endurance strength,

$$\sigma_{en} = 0.5\sigma_u \qquad \text{... 2.13(a)/Pg 23, DHB}$$

$$\sigma_{en} = 0.5 \times 600 = 300 \text{ MPa}$$

and $\tau_{yp} = 0.5\sigma_{yp} = 0.5 \times 400 = 200$ MPa

$\therefore$ Eq. (i) yields...
$$\left(\frac{1}{3}\right) = \frac{1}{(0.5 \times 0.85 \times 0.93) \times 300}\left(\frac{1.17 \times 10^6}{d^3}\right) + \frac{2.92 \times 10^6}{200 \times d^3}$$

$$0.334 = \left(\frac{24.50 \times 10^3}{d^3}\right)$$

$$d = 41.88 \text{ mm} \approx 35 \text{ mm}$$

Thus, the standard diameter of the shaft is $d = 45$ mm.   ... **Tb. 3.5(a)/Pg 57, DHB**

14. **Determine the wall thickness of a pressure vessel of diameter 900 mm subjected to an internal pressure that fluctuates between 10 MPa and 6 MPa. The material used for the vessel has a yield stress of 450 MPa and endurance stress of 300 MPa. Take FoS = 2, A = 1, B = 0.7, C = 0.6.**

Solution: $t = ?$, $d_i = 900$ mm, $p_{max} = 10$ MPa, $p_{min} = 6$ MPa, $\sigma_{yp} = 450$ MPa, $n = 2$, $\sigma_{en} = 300$ MPa, $A = 1$, $B = 0.7$, $C = 0.6$.

According to Soderberg,

$$\left(\frac{1}{n}\right) = \frac{K_{tf}\sigma_a}{ABC\,\sigma_{en}} + \frac{\sigma_m}{\sigma_{yp}} \qquad \text{... Eq. (i) 2.21(c)/ Pg 25, DHB}$$

For a pressure vessel subjected to internal pressure,

$$\sigma_m = \frac{pd_i}{4t} \qquad \text{... 7.1(d)/ Pg 100, DHB}$$

- Mean stress $\sigma_m = \dfrac{p_m d_i}{4t}$ ... **2.16(a)/ Pg 23, DHB**

But $p_m = \dfrac{p_{max} + p_{min}}{2}$ and $p_a = \dfrac{p_{max} - p_{min}}{2}$

$$\sigma_m = \frac{(p_{max} + p_{min})d_i}{2(4t)} = \frac{(10 + 6) \times 900}{8t} = \frac{1800}{t}$$

- Variable stress, $\sigma_a = \dfrac{p_a d_i}{4t} = \dfrac{(p_{max} - p_{min})d_i}{2(4t)} = \dfrac{(10 - 6) \times 900}{8t} = \dfrac{450}{t}$

- Also $K_{tf} = 1 + q(K_t - 1)$ ... **2.5/ Pg 21, DHB**

  Since the cross-section is uniform, $K_t = 1$ and $q = 0$

  $\therefore$ $K_{tf} = 1$

- *Correction factors*: From data, $A = 1$, $B = 0.7$, $C = 0.6$

$\therefore$ Eq. (i) yields... $\quad \left(\dfrac{1}{2}\right) = \dfrac{1}{(1 \times 0.7 \times 0.6) \times 300}\left(\dfrac{450}{t}\right) + \dfrac{1800}{450t}$

$$0.5 = \left(\dfrac{7.57}{t}\right)$$

$$d = 15.14 \text{ mm} \approx 16 \text{ mm}$$

PROBLEMS BASED ON LOAD

15. **Determine the completely reversed axial load $\pm$ F for the member shown in Fig. 3.12 made of AISI 1040 cold drawn steel (σ_{ut} = 520 MPa). The thickness of the member is 25 mm. Assume q = 0.8 and B = 0.85.**

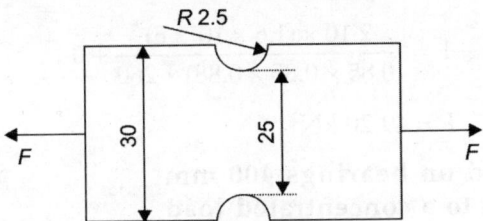

Fig. 3.12: Problem 15

Solution: $F_{max} = +F$, $F_{min} = -F$, $\sigma_u = 520$ MPa, $q = 0.8$, $B = 0.85$.
According to Goodman,

$$\left(\dfrac{1}{n}\right) = \dfrac{K_{tf} \cdot \sigma_a}{ABC\,\sigma_{en}} + \dfrac{\sigma_m}{\sigma_u} \qquad \text{... Eq. (i) 2.21(a)/ Pg 25, DHB}$$

- Mean or average stress

$$\sigma_m = \dfrac{\sigma_{max} + \sigma_{min}}{2} = \dfrac{F_m}{A} \qquad \text{... 2.16(a)/ Pg 23, DHB}$$

But $\quad F_m = \dfrac{F_{max} + F_{min}}{2}$ and $F_a = \dfrac{F_{max} - F_{min}}{2} \qquad \text{... 2.17(a)/ Pg 24, DHB}$

$$\sigma_m = \dfrac{F_{max} + F_{min}}{2} = \dfrac{F - F}{2(bt)} = 0$$

- Variable or alternating stress,

$$\sigma_a = \dfrac{\sigma_{max} - \sigma_{min}}{2} = \dfrac{F_a}{A} \qquad \text{... 2.16(b)/ Pg 23, DHB}$$

$$\sigma_a = \dfrac{F_{max} - F_{min}}{2A} = \dfrac{F + F}{2(bt)} = \dfrac{2F}{2(25 \times 25)} = 1.6 \times 10^{-3}\, F$$

- Also $\quad K_{tf} = 1 + q(K_t - 1) \qquad \text{... Eq. (ii) 2.5/ Pg 21, DHB}$

Referring the given problem to **Fig. 2.14/Pg 37, DHB**, we have

$$B = 30 \text{ mm}, b = 25 \text{ mm}, r = 25 \text{ mm}$$

Now $\quad \dfrac{r}{b} = \dfrac{2.5}{25} = 0.1$; and $\dfrac{B}{b} = \dfrac{30}{25} = 1.2$

At $\qquad$ $\dfrac{r}{b} = 0.1$ and $\dfrac{B}{b} = 1.2$, $K_t = 2.37$ and $q = 0.8$ (data)

$\therefore$ Eq. (ii) yields...

$$K_{tf} = 1 + 0.8(2.37 - 1) = 2.10$$

- *Correction factors:*

  Load factor $A = 0.85$ (average value) for reversed axial load $\quad$ ... **Pg 25, DHB**

  $\qquad$ $B = 0.85$ (Data)

  For $\sigma_u = 520$ MPa and rough finished specimen, $C = 0.88$
  $$\text{... \textbf{Fig. 2.33 (curve c)/Pg 46, DHB}}$$

- **Endurance strength,**

  $$\sigma_{en} = 0.5\sigma_u \qquad \text{... \textbf{2.13(a)/Pg 23, DHB}}$$

  $$\sigma_{en} = 0.5 \times 520 = 260 \text{ MPa}$$

$\therefore$ Eq. (i) yields... $\qquad$ $1 = \dfrac{2.10 \times (1.6 \times 10^{-3}\ F)}{(0.85 \times 0.85 \times 0.88) \times 260} + 0$

$$F = 49.20 \text{ kN}$$

16. **A shaft supported on bearings 400 mm apart is subjected to a concentrated load varying from W to $3W$ at its midpoint. The shaft is of 50 mm diameter. Estimate the value of W with a factor of safety of 1.5. The material has an ultimate strength of 700 MPa, endurance limit of 350 MPa and yield strength of 525 MPa. Take size factor as 0.85 and surface finish factor of 0.848.**

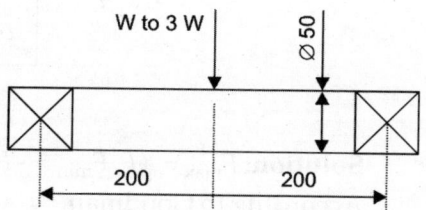

Fig. 3.13: Problem 16

VTU – Dec. 2013/ Jan. 2014 – 14 Marks

Solution: $L = 400$ mm, $F_{max} = 3W$, $F_{min} = W$, $d = 50$ mm, $W = ?$, $\sigma_u = 700$ MPa, $n = 1.5$, $\sigma_{en} = 350$ MPa, $\sigma_{yp} = 525$ MPa, $B = 0.85$, $C = 0.848$.

Case 1: Soderberg method: According to Soderberg,

$$\left(\dfrac{1}{n}\right) = \dfrac{K_{tf} \cdot \sigma_a}{ABC\, \sigma_{en}} + \dfrac{\sigma_m}{\sigma_{yp}} \qquad \text{... Eq. (i) \textbf{2.21(c)/ Pg 25, DHB}}$$

For a simply supported beam with point load at mid-span,

$$M = \dfrac{FL}{4} \qquad \text{... \textbf{Tb. 1.4 (Fig. 4)/ Pg 15, DHB}}$$

- **Maximum BM,**

  $$M_{max} = \dfrac{F_{max}L}{4} = \dfrac{(3W) \times 400}{4} = 300\,W$$

- **Minimum BM,**

  $$M_{min} = \dfrac{F_{min}L}{4} = \dfrac{(W) \times 400}{4} = 100\,W$$

- Mean stress $\qquad \sigma_m = \dfrac{\sigma_{max} + \sigma_{min}}{2} = \dfrac{M_m}{Z}$ $\qquad$ **... 2.16(a)/ Pg 23, DHB**

But $\qquad M_m = \dfrac{M_{max} + M_{min}}{2}$ and $M_a = \dfrac{M_{max} - M_{min}}{2}$

$$\sigma_m = \frac{M_{max} + M_{min}}{2Z} = \frac{300W + 100W}{2(\pi \times 50^3/32)} = 0.0163W$$

- Variable stress, $\sigma_a = \dfrac{\sigma_{max} - \sigma_{min}}{2} = \dfrac{M_a}{Z}$ $\qquad$ **... 2.16(b)/ Pg 23, DHB**

$$\sigma_a = \frac{M_{max} - M_{min}}{2Z} = \frac{300W - 100W}{2(\pi \times 50^3/32)} = 0.00815\,W$$

Also $\qquad K_{tf} = 1 + q(K_t - 1)$ $\qquad$ **... 2.5/ Pg 21, DHB**

Since the cross-section is uniform, $K_t = 1$ and $q = 0$

$$K_{tf} = 1$$

- *Correction factors*:
  Load factor $A = 1$, for reversed bending load $\qquad$ **... Pg 25, DHB**
  $\qquad B = 0.85, C = 0.848$ (Data)

$\therefore$ Eq. (i) yields... $\left(\dfrac{1}{1.5}\right) = \dfrac{0.00815\,W}{(1 \times 0.85 \times 0.848) \times 350} + \dfrac{0.0163\,W}{525}$

$$0.667 = 6.335 \times 10^{-5}\,W$$

$$W = 10528.55 \text{ N} = 10.528 \text{ kN}$$

and $\qquad 3W = 31.584 \text{ kN}$

Case 2: Goodman criteria: According to Goodman,

$$\left(\frac{1}{n}\right) = \frac{K_{tf} \cdot \sigma_a}{ABC\,\sigma_{en}} + \frac{\sigma_m}{\sigma_u} \qquad \text{... 2.21(a)/ Pg 25, DHB}$$

$$\left(\frac{1}{1.5}\right) = \frac{0.00815\,W}{(1 \times 0.85 \times 0.848) \times 350} + \frac{0.0163\,W}{700}$$

$$0.667 = 5.560 \times 10^{-5}\,W$$

$$W = 11992.33 \text{ N} = 11.99 \text{ kN}$$

and $\qquad 3W = 35.97 \text{ kN}$

17. **A cantilever beam made of cold drawn carbon steel of circular cross-section as shown in Fig. 3.14 is subjected to a load which varies from $-F$ and $3F$. Determine the maximum load that this member can withstand for an indefinite life using a factor of safety of 2. The theoretical stress concentration factor is 1.42 and the notch sensitivity is 0.9. Assume the following values.**
    Ultimate stress = 550 MPa $\qquad$ **Yield stress = 470 MPa**
    Endurance limit = 275 MPa $\qquad$ **Size factor = 0.85**
    Surface finish factor = 0.89

VTU – Jan/ Feb. 2006 – 15 Marks; (Similar) July 2007 – 15 Marks;
(Similar) June 2012 – 10 Marks

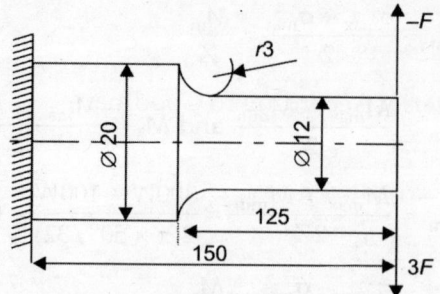

Fig. 3.14: Problem 17 (all dimensions in mm)

Solution: $F_{max} = 3F$, $F_{min} = -F$, $L = 125$ mm (step section), $d = 12$ mm, $F = ?$, $n = 2$, $K_t = 1.42$, $q = 0.9$, $\sigma_u = 550$ MPa, $\sigma_{yp} = 470$ MPa, $\sigma_{en} = 275$ MPa, $B = 0.85$, $C = 0.89$.

Case 1: Soderberg method: According to Soderberg,

$$\left(\frac{1}{n}\right) = \frac{K_{tf} \cdot \sigma_a}{ABC\,\sigma_{en}} + \frac{\sigma_m}{\sigma_{yp}} \qquad \text{... Eq. (i) 2.21(c)/ Pg 25, DHB}$$

For a cantilever beam with point load at end,

$$M = FL \qquad \text{... Tb. 1.4 (Fig. 1)/ Pg 15, DHB}$$

- Maximum BM,
$$M_{min} = F_{max}L = (3F) \times 125 = 375F$$

- Minimum BM,
$$M_{max} = F_{min}L = (-F) \times 125 = -125F$$

- Mean stress $\quad \sigma_m = \dfrac{\sigma_{max} + \sigma_{min}}{2} = \dfrac{M_m}{Z} \qquad$ ... **2.16(a)/ Pg 23, DHB**

  But $\qquad M_m = \dfrac{M_{max} + M_{min}}{2}$ and $M_a = \dfrac{M_{max} - M_{min}}{2}$

$$\sigma_m = \frac{M_{max} + M_{min}}{2Z} = \frac{375\,F - 125\,F}{2(\pi \times 12^3/32)} = 0.7368\,F$$

- Variable stress, $\quad \sigma_a = \dfrac{\sigma_{max} - \sigma_{min}}{2} = \dfrac{M_a}{Z} \qquad$ ... **2.16(b)/ Pg 23, DHB**

$$\sigma_a = \frac{M_{max} - M_{min}}{2Z} = \frac{375\,F + 125\,F}{2(\pi \times 12^3/32)} = 1.4737\,F$$

- Also $\qquad K_{tf} = 1 + q(K_t - 1) \qquad$ ... **2.5/ Pg 21, DHB**
$$= 1 + 0.9 \times (1.42 - 1)$$
$$\therefore \qquad K_{tf} = 1.378$$

- *Correction factors*:
  Load factor $A = 1$, for reversed bending load $\qquad$ **Pg 25, DHB**
$$B = 0.85,\, C = 0.89 \text{ (Data)}$$

$\therefore$ Eq. (i) yields... $\left(\dfrac{1}{2}\right) = \dfrac{1.378 \times 1.4737\,F}{(1 \times 0.85 \times 0.89) \times 275} + \dfrac{0.7368\,F}{470}$

$$0.5 = 8.651 \times 10^{-3}\,F$$

$$F = 44.130 \text{ N}$$

and $$3F = 122.40 \text{ N}$$

Case 2: Goodman criteria: According to Goodman,

$$\left(\frac{1}{n}\right) = \frac{K_{tf} \cdot \sigma_a}{ABC\sigma_{en}} + \frac{\sigma_m}{\sigma_u} \qquad \ldots \textbf{2.21(a)/ Pg 25, DHB}$$

$$\left(\frac{1}{2}\right) = \frac{1.378 \times 1.4737 \, F}{(1 \times 0.85 \times 0.89) \times 275} + \frac{0.7368 \, F}{550}$$

$$0.5 = 11.10 \times 10^{-3} \, F$$

$$F = 45.04 \text{ N}$$

and $$3F = 135.12 \text{ kN}$$

18. **A SAE 1025 water quenched steel rod (σ_u = 620.8 MPa, σ_y = 400.1 MPa, σ_{-1} = 345.2 MPa) of circular cross-section, shown in Fig. 3.15 is subjected to a load varying from P to 3P. Determine the value of P. The stress concentration factor may be taken as 1.4. Analyze the member at the change of cross-section. Use factor of safety = 3. Assume the surface to be rough finished.**

VTU – Dec. 06/ Jan. 2007 – 10 Marks; June/ July 2014 – 15 Marks

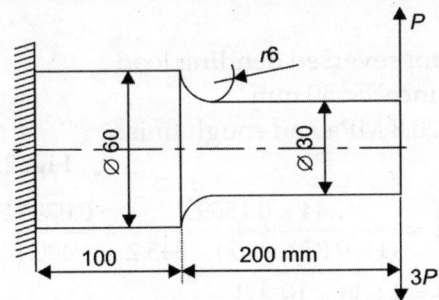

Fig. 3.15: Problem 18

Solution: σ_u = 620 MPa, σ_y = 400.1 MPa, σ_{en} = 345.2 MPa, F_{max} = 3P, F_{min} = –P, L = 200 mm (step section), d = 30 mm, P = ?, K_t = 1.4, n = 3.

Case 1: Soderberg method: According to Soderberg,

$$\left(\frac{1}{n}\right) = \frac{K_{tf} \cdot \sigma_a}{ABC\sigma_{en}} + \frac{\sigma_m}{\sigma_{yp}} \qquad \ldots \text{Eq. (i) } \textbf{2.21(c)/ Pg 25, DHB}$$

For a cantilever beam with point load at end,

$$M = FL \qquad \ldots \textbf{Tb. 1.4 (Fig. 1)/ Pg 15, DHB}$$

• Maximum BM,
$$M_{min} = F_{max}L = (3P) \times 200 = 600P$$

• Minimum BM,
$$M_{max} = F_{min}L = (-P) \times 200 = -200P$$

• Mean stress $$\sigma_m = \frac{\sigma_{max} + \sigma_{min}}{2} = \frac{M_m}{Z} \qquad \ldots \textbf{2.16(a)/ Pg 23, DHB}$$

But
$$M_m = \frac{M_{max} + M_{min}}{2} \text{ and } M_a = \frac{M_{max} - M_{min}}{2}$$

$$\sigma_m = \frac{M_{max} + M_{min}}{2Z} = \frac{600\,P - 200\,P}{2(\pi \times 30^3/32)} = 0.0755\,P$$

- Variable stress, $\sigma_a = \dfrac{\sigma_{max} - \sigma_{min}}{2} = \dfrac{M_a}{Z}$ ... **2.16(b)/ Pg 23, DHB**

$$\sigma_a = \frac{M_{max} - M_{min}}{2Z} = \frac{600\,P + 200\,P}{2(\pi \times 30^3/32)} = 0.1509\,P$$

- Also $K_{tf} = 1 + q(K_t - 1)$ ... Eq. (ii) **2.5/ Pg 21, DHB**

Referring the given problem to **Fig. 2.25/Pg 43, DHB**, we have

$$D = 60 \text{ mm}, d = 30 \text{ mm}, r = 6 \text{ mm}$$

Now $\dfrac{r}{d} = \dfrac{6}{30} = 0.2;$ and $\dfrac{D}{d} = \dfrac{60}{30} = 2$

At $\dfrac{r}{d} = 0.2;$ and $\dfrac{D}{d} = 2, K_t = 1.44$

Based on notch radius of $r = 6$ mm, we have $q = 1$ ... **Fig. 2.31/ Pg 46, DHB**
∴ Eq. (ii) yields...

$$K_{tf} = 1 + 1 \,(1.44 - 1) = 1.44$$

- *Correction factors*:
Load factor $A = 1$, for reversed bending load   ... **Pg 25, DHB**
Assume $B = 0.85$, since $d < 50$ mm
$C = 0.87$, for $\sigma_u = 620.8$ MPa and rough finish
         ... **Fig. 2.33 (curve c)/Pg 46, DHB**

∴ Eq. (i) yields... $\left(\dfrac{1}{3}\right) = \dfrac{1.44 \times 0.1509\,P}{(1 \times 0.85 \times 0.87) \times 345.2} + \dfrac{0.0755\,P}{400.1}$

$$0.334 = 1.038 \times 10^{-3}\,P$$
$$P = 320.92 \text{ N}$$
and $3P = 962.76 \text{ N}$

Case 2: Goodman criteria: According to Goodman,

$$\left(\frac{1}{n}\right) = \frac{K_{tf} \cdot \sigma_a}{ABC\,\sigma_{en}} + \frac{\sigma_m}{\sigma_u}$$ ... **2.21(a)/ Pg 25, DHB**

$$\left(\frac{1}{3}\right) = \frac{1.44 \times 0.1509\,P}{(1 \times 0.85 \times 0.87) \times 345.2} + \frac{0.0755\,P}{620.8}$$

$$0.334 = 9.728 \times 10^{-4}\,P$$
$$P = 342.64 \text{ N}$$
and $3P = 1027.92 \text{ N}$

PROBLEM BASED ON LIFE (N_f)

According to Goodman,

$$\left(\frac{1}{n}\right) = \frac{K_{tf} \cdot \sigma_a}{ABC\,\sigma_{en}} + \frac{\sigma_m}{\sigma_u}$$ ... **2.21(a)/ Pg 25, DHB**

If reliability factor and the number of cycles are given, the above equation is modified as

$$\left(\frac{1}{n}\right) = \frac{K_{tf} \cdot \sigma_a}{\sigma_{Nf}} + \frac{\sigma_m}{\sigma_u} \qquad \text{... Eq. (a)}$$

But

$$\sigma_{Nf} = P(N_f)^Q \qquad \text{... Eq. (b)}$$

where

$$P = \left[\frac{(f \cdot \sigma_u)^2}{\sigma'_{en}}\right], Q = -\frac{1}{3}\left[\log\left(\frac{f \cdot \sigma_u}{\sigma'_{en}}\right)\right] \text{ and } \sigma'_{en} = ABCR_f\sigma_{en}$$

$$\text{... Eq. (c)}$$

$f = 0.75$ for axial load; and 0.9 for bending load

The same may be modified for Soderberg relation.

19. **A cantilever beam made of 35C8 steel (σ_u = 540 MPa) is subjected to a completely reversed load of 1000 N as shown in Fig. 3.16. The notch sensitivity factor q at the fillet can be taken as 0.85 and expected reliability is 90%. Determine the diameter of the beam for a life cycle of 10000 cycles.**

VTU – June 2012 – 10 Marks

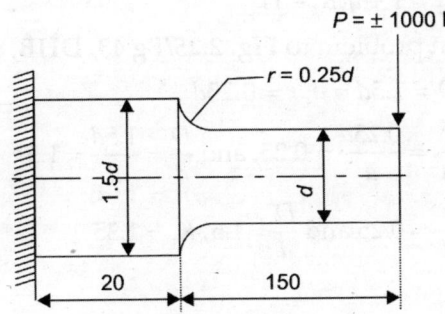

Fig. 3.16: Problem 19

Solution: σ_u = 540 MPa, P_{max} = 1000 N, P_{min} = −1000 N, q = 0.85, reliability R = 90%, d = ?, N_f = 10000 cycles.

According to Goodman,

$$\left(\frac{1}{n}\right) = \frac{K_{tf} \cdot \sigma_a}{ABC\sigma_{en}} + \frac{\sigma_m}{\sigma_u} \qquad \text{... Eq. (i) 2.21(c)/ Pg 25, DHB}$$

Since reliability and number of cycles are given, the above equation is modified as

$$\left(\frac{1}{n}\right) = \frac{K_{tf} \cdot \sigma_a}{\sigma_{Nf}} + \frac{\sigma_m}{\sigma_u} \qquad \text{... Eq. (i)}$$

But

$$\sigma_{Nf} = P(N_f)^Q \qquad \text{... Eq. (ii)}$$

where

$$P = \left[\frac{(f \cdot \sigma_u)^2}{\sigma'_{en}}\right], Q = -\frac{1}{3}\log\left[\frac{(f \cdot \sigma_u)}{\sigma'_{en}}\right] \text{ and } \sigma'_{en} = ABCR_f\sigma_{en}$$

$$\text{... Eq. (iii)}$$

$f = 0.75$ for axial load and 0.9 for bending load

For a cantilever beam point at end of the span

$$M = PL \qquad \text{... Tb. 1.4 (Fig. 1)/Pg 15, DHB}$$

- Maximum BM,
$$M_{max} = F_{max}L = 1000 \times 150 = 150 \times 10^3 \, \text{N·mm}$$

- Minimum BM,
$$M_{min} = F_{min}L = -1000 \times 150 = -150 \times 10^3 \, \text{N·mm}$$

- Mean stress $\quad \sigma_m = \dfrac{\sigma_{max} + \sigma_{min}}{2} = \dfrac{M_m}{Z} \qquad$ ... **2.16(a)/ Pg 23, DHB**

But $\qquad M_m = \dfrac{M_{max} + M_{min}}{2}$ and $M_a = \dfrac{M_{max} - M_{min}}{2}$

$$\sigma_m = \frac{M_{max} + M_{min}}{2Z} = \frac{150 \times 10^3 - 150 \times 10^3}{2(\pi \times d^3/32)} = 0$$

- Variable stress, $\quad \sigma_a = \dfrac{\sigma_{max} - \sigma_{min}}{2} = \dfrac{M_a}{Z} \qquad$ ... **2.16(b)/ Pg 23, DHB**

$$\sigma_a = \frac{M_{max} - M_{min}}{2Z} = \frac{150 \times 10^3 + 150 \times 10^3}{2(\pi d^3/32)} = \frac{1.53 \times 10^6}{d^3}$$

- Also $\qquad K_{tf} = 1 + q(K_t - 1) \qquad$ ... Eq. (iv) **2.5/ Pg 21, DHB**

Referring the given problem to **Fig. 2.25/Pg 43, DHB**, we have
$$D = 1.5d = d, r = 0.25d$$

Now $\qquad \dfrac{r}{d} = \dfrac{0.25d}{d} = 0.25;$ and $\dfrac{D}{d} = \dfrac{1.5d}{d} = 1.5$

At $\qquad \dfrac{r}{d} = 0.25$ and $\dfrac{D}{d} = 1.5, K_t = 1.35$

∴ Eq. (iv) yields...
$$K_{tf} = 1 + 0.85(1.35 - 1) = 1.29$$

- *Correction factors*:
  Load factor $A = 1$, for reversed bending load $\qquad$ ... **Pg 25, DHB**
  Assume $B = 0.85$, assumed since diameter is unknown.
  For $\sigma_u = 540$ MPa and rough finished specimen $C = 0.87$
  $\qquad$ ... **Fig. 2.33 (curve c)/Pg 46, DHB**
  For a reliability of 90%,
  $$R_f = 0.897 \qquad \text{... } \textbf{Tb 3.1/Pg 171}$$

- Endurance strength,
  $$\sigma_{en} = 0.5\sigma_u \qquad \text{... } \textbf{2.13(a)/Pg 23, DHB}$$
  $$\sigma_{en} = 0.5 \times 540 = 270 \, \text{MPa}$$

∴ Eq. (iii) yields... $\quad \sigma'_{en} = 1 \times 0.85 \times 0.87 \times 0.897 \times 270 = 179.10$ MPa

$$P = \left[\frac{(0.9\sigma_u)^2}{\sigma'_{en}} \right] = \left[\frac{(0.9 \times 540)^2}{179.10} \right] = 1318.80$$

$$Q = -\frac{1}{3}\left[\log\left(\frac{0.9\sigma_u}{\sigma'_{en}} \right) \right] = -\frac{1}{3}\left[\log\left(\frac{0.9 \times 540}{179.10} \right) \right] = -0.1445$$

$\therefore$ Eq. (ii) yields... $\sigma_{Nf} = 1318.80 \times (10000)^{-0.1445} = 348.48$ MPa

$\therefore$ Eq. (i) yields... $\qquad 1 = \dfrac{1.29}{348.48}\left(\dfrac{1.53 \times 10^6}{d^3}\right) + 0 \qquad$ Here $n = 1$, if not given

$$d = 17.83 \text{ mm} \approx 18 \text{ mm}$$

20. **A round steel part with the ultimate strength $\sigma_u = 760$ MPa and the yield strength $\sigma_{yp} = 530$ MPa has average machined surfaces. The diameter of the part is less than 25 mm. The part is subjected to an axial load fluctuating between 4450 N and 26700 N. A safety factor of 2 is applied to the loads. Determine the required diameter for infinite life (10^6 cycles of life) and for 10^3 cycles of life. No yielding is permitted.**

Solution: $\sigma_u = 760$ MPa, $\sigma_{yp} = 530$ MPa, surface—machined, $F_{max} = 26700$ N, $F_{min} = 4450$ N, $n = 2, d = ?$.

(a) For infinite life: ($N_f = 10^6$ cycles of life)

According to Goodman,

$$\left(\frac{1}{n}\right) = \frac{K_{tf} \cdot \sigma_a}{ABC\,\sigma_{en}} + \frac{\sigma_m}{\sigma_u} \qquad \text{... Eq. (i) 2.21(a)/ Pg 25, DHB}$$

- Mean or average stress

$$\sigma_m = \frac{\sigma_{max} + \sigma_{min}}{2} = \frac{F_m}{A} \qquad \text{... 2.16(a)/ Pg 23, DHB}$$

But $\qquad F_m = \dfrac{F_{max} + F_{min}}{2}$ and $F_a = \dfrac{F_{max} - F_{min}}{2}$

$$\text{... 2.17(a)/ Pg 24, DHB}$$

$$\sigma_m = \frac{F_{max} + F_{min}}{2A} = \frac{26700 + 4450}{2(\pi d^2/4)} = \frac{19.83 \times 10^3}{d^2}$$

- Variable or alternating stress,

$$\sigma_a = \frac{\sigma_{max} - \sigma_{min}}{2} = \frac{F_a}{A} \qquad \text{... 2.16(b)/ Pg 23, DHB}$$

$$\sigma_a = \frac{F_{max} - F_{min}}{2A} = \frac{26700 - 4450}{2(\pi d^2/4)} = \frac{14.16 \times 10^6}{d^2}$$

- Also $\qquad K_{tf} = 1 + q(K_t - 1) \qquad \text{... 2.5/ Pg 21, DHB}$

Since the cross-section is uniform, $K_t = 1$ and $q = 0$

$$K_{tf} = 1$$

- *Correction factors:*
  Load factor $A = 0.7$, for reversed bending load $\qquad\qquad$ **... Pg 25, DHB**
  Size correction factor $B = 0.85$, assumed since diameter is unknown
  Surface correction factor, $C = 0.84$, for machined surface based on $\sigma_u = 760$ MPa
  $$\text{... Tb. 2.2/Pg 32, DHB}$$

- Endurance strength,

$$\sigma_{en} = 0.5\sigma_u \qquad \text{... 2.13(a)/Pg 23, DHB}$$

$$\sigma_{en} = 0.5 \times 760 = 380 \text{ MPa}$$

∴ Eq. (i) yields... $\left(\dfrac{1}{2}\right) = \dfrac{1}{(0.7 \times 0.85 \times 0.84) \times 380}\left(\dfrac{14.16 \times 10^3}{d^2}\right) + \dfrac{19.83 \times 10^3}{760 \times d^2}$

$$0.5 = \frac{100.44}{d^2}$$

$$d = 14.17 \text{ mm} \approx 15 \text{ mm} \le 25 \text{ mm}$$

Hence the design is satisfactory.

(b) For finite life: ($N_f = 10^3$ cycles of life)
Method 1: Since the number of cycles is given, Eq. (i) is modified as

$$\left(\frac{1}{n}\right) = \frac{K_{tf} \cdot \sigma_a}{\sigma_{Nf}} + \frac{\sigma_m}{\sigma_u} \qquad \text{... Eq. (ii)}$$

But $\qquad \sigma_{Nf} = P(N_f)^Q \qquad \text{... Eq. (iii)}$

where $\qquad P = \left(\dfrac{(f \cdot \sigma_u)^2}{\sigma'_{en}}\right), Q = -\dfrac{1}{3}\left[\log\left(\dfrac{f \cdot \sigma_u}{\sigma'_{en}}\right)\right]$ and $\sigma'_{en} = ABC \sigma_{en}$

$$\text{... Eq. (iv)}$$

$$f = 0.75 \text{ for axial load and } 0.9 \text{ for bending load}$$

∴ Eq. (iv) yields... $\sigma'_{en} = 0.7 \times 0.85 \times 0.84 \times 380 = 189.92 \text{ MPa}$

$$P = \left[\frac{(0.75 \sigma_u)^2}{\sigma'_{en}}\right] = \left[\frac{(0.75 \times 760)^2}{189.92}\right] = 1710.72$$

$$Q = -\frac{1}{3}\left[\log\left(\frac{0.75 \sigma_u}{\sigma'_{en}}\right)\right] = -\frac{1}{3}\left[\log\left(\frac{0.75 \times 760}{189.92}\right)\right] = -0.1591$$

∴ Eq. (iii) yields...
But $\qquad \sigma_{Nf} = 1710.72 \times (1000)^{-0.1591} = 570 \text{ MPa}$

∴ Eq. (ii) yields... $\left(\dfrac{1}{2}\right) = \dfrac{1}{570}\left(\dfrac{14.16 \times 10^3}{d^2}\right) + \dfrac{19.83 \times 10^3}{760 \times d^2}$

$$0.5 = \frac{50.93}{d^2}$$

$$d = 10.09 \text{ mm} \approx 12 \text{ mm} \le 25 \text{ mm}$$

Hence the design is satisfactory.

Method 2:
Here $\qquad P = \sigma_u = 760 \text{ MPa @ } 10^6 \text{ cycles}$
and $\qquad \sigma_{Nf} = \sigma'_{en} = 189.92 \text{ MPa}$
∴ Eq. (iv) yields...
$$189.92 = 760 \times (10^6)^Q$$

$$\left(\frac{189.02}{760}\right) = (10^6)^Q$$

Taking log on both sides

$$\log\left(\frac{189.02}{760}\right) = Q \log(10^6)$$

$$Q = \frac{\log(189.92/760)}{\log(10^6)} = -0.1003$$

∴ Eq. (iii) yields...

$$\sigma_{Nf})_{@10^3} = 760 \times (10^3)^{-0.1003}$$

$$\sigma_{Nf})_{@10^3} = 379.92 \text{ MPa}$$

∴ Eq. (ii) yields... $\left(\dfrac{1}{2}\right) = \dfrac{1}{379.92}\left(\dfrac{14.16 \times 10^3}{d^2}\right) + \dfrac{19.83 \times 10^3}{760 \times d^2}$

$$0.5 = \frac{63.36}{d^2}$$

$$d = 11.25 \text{ mm} \approx 12 \text{ mm} \leq 25 \text{ mm}$$

Hence the design is satisfactory.

21. **A solid round bar, 25 mm in diameter, has a groove 2.5 mm deep with a 2.5 mm radius machined into it. The bar has an ultimate strength of $\sigma_u = 440$ MPa and is subjected to a pure reversing torque of 200 N·m. Estimate the number of cycles of failure, assuming $B = 0.85$, $q = 0.85$, factor of safety as 2 and $f = 0.9$.**

Solution: $D = 25$ mm, $r = 2.5$ mm, $d = D - 2r = 20$ mm, $\sigma_u = 440$ MPa, $T = \pm 200$ N·m, $T_{max} = 200 \times 10^3$ N·mm, $T_{min} = -200 \times 10^3$ N·mm, $B = 0.85$, $q = 0.85$, $n = 2$, $f = 0.9$ (multiplying factor for σ_u), $N_f = ?$

As per the given data, the part/specimen is as shown in **Fig. 3.17**.

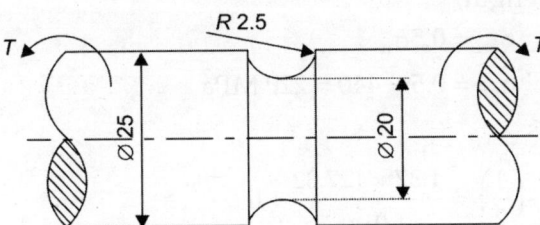

Fig. 3.17: Problem 21

According to Soderberg,

$$\left(\frac{1}{n}\right) = \frac{K_{sf} \cdot \tau_a}{ABC\,\sigma_{en}} + \frac{\tau_m}{\tau_{yp}} \qquad \text{... Eq. (i) } \textbf{2.21(e)/ Pg 25, DHB}$$

Since number of cycles is given, the above equation is modified as

$$\left(\frac{1}{n}\right) = \frac{K_{sf} \cdot \tau_a}{\sigma_{Nf}} + \frac{\tau_m}{\tau_{yp}} \qquad \text{... Eq. (i)}$$

• Mean stress $\tau_m = \dfrac{\tau_{max} + \tau_{min}}{2} = \dfrac{T_m}{Z_p}$ ... **2.16(a)/ Pg 23, DHB**

But $T_m = \dfrac{T_{max} + T_{min}}{2}$ and $T_a = \dfrac{T_{max} - T_{min}}{2}$

$$\tau_m = \frac{T_{max} + T_{min}}{2Z_p} = \frac{200 \times 10^3 - 200 \times 10^3}{2(\pi \times 20^3/16)} = 0$$

- Variable stress,

$$\tau_a = \frac{\tau_{max} - \tau_{min}}{2} = \frac{T_a}{Z_p} \qquad \dots \textbf{2.16(b)/ Pg 23, DHB}$$

$$\tau_a = \frac{T_{max} - T_{min}}{2Z_p} = \frac{200 \times 10^3 + 200 \times 10^3}{2(\pi \times 20^3/16)} = 127.32 \text{ MPa}$$

- Also $\qquad K_{sf} = 1 + q(K_s - 1) \qquad \dots$ Eq. (ii) **2.7/ Pg 21, DHB**

Referring the given problem to **Fig. 2.22/Pg 41, DHB**, we have

$$D = 25 \text{ mm}, d = 20 \text{ mm}, r = 2.5 \text{ mm}$$

Now $\qquad \dfrac{r}{d} = \dfrac{2.5}{20} = 0.13$; and $\dfrac{D}{d} = \dfrac{25}{20} = 1.25$

At $\qquad \dfrac{r}{d} = 0.13$ and $\dfrac{D}{d} = 1.25$, $K_s = 1.44$

$$q = 0.85 \text{ (data)}$$

∴ Eq. (ii) yields...

$$K_{sf} = 1 + 0.85(1.44 - 1) = 1.37$$

- *Correction factors*:

Load factor $A = 0.5$, for reversed bending load $\qquad$ **... Pg 25, DHB**

Size correction factor, $B = 0.85$ (data)

Surface factor $C = 0.84$, for circular grooves (curve d) based on $\sigma_u = 440$ MPa
$$\textbf{... Fig. 2.33/Pg 46, DHB}$$

- Endurance strength,

$$\sigma_{en} = 0.5\sigma_u \qquad \dots \textbf{2.13(a)/Pg 23, DHB}$$

$$\sigma_{en} = 0.5 \times 440 = 220 \text{ MPa}$$

∴ Eq. (i) yields...

$$\left(\frac{1}{2}\right) = \frac{1.37 \times 127.32}{\sigma_{Nf}} + 0$$

$$\sigma_{Nf} = 348.86 \text{ MPa}$$

We know that $\qquad \sigma_{Nf} = P(N_f)^Q$

where $\qquad P = \left(\dfrac{(f \cdot \sigma_u)^2}{\sigma'_{en}}\right)$, $Q = -\dfrac{1}{3}\left[\log\left(\dfrac{f \cdot \sigma_u}{\sigma'_{en}}\right)\right]$ and $\sigma'_{en} = ABC\sigma_{en}$

$$\dots \text{ Eq. (iv)}$$

$$f = 0.9 \text{ (data)}$$

$$\sigma'_{en} = 0.5 \times 0.85 \times 0.84 \times 220 = 78.54 \text{ MPa}$$

$$P = \left[\frac{(0.9 \times 440)^2}{78.54}\right] = 1996.64$$

$$Q = -\frac{1}{3}\left[\log\left(\frac{0.9 \times 440}{78.54}\right)\right] = -0.2342$$

∴ Eq. (iii) yields...

$$N_f = 1718.10 \text{ cycles.}$$

3.14 STRESSES DUE TO COMBINED LOADING

Combined stresses refer to a condition wherein the component or machine part is subjected to a combination of variable axial, variable bending and variable torsional loads. Examples include crankshafts, propeller shafts and airplane wings. The following may be the cases.

- Variable axial and variable bending load
- Variable axial and variable torsional load
- Variable bending load and variable torsional load.

Thus, whenever a component is subjected to a variable/fluctuating normal stress (axial and/or bending) and a variable shear stress, the equivalent stresses are found based on Soderberg criteria using the following relations:

- Equivalent normal stress,

$$\sigma_{eq-n} = \sigma_m + \left(\frac{\sigma_{yp}}{\sigma_{en}}\right)\frac{K_{tf} \cdot \sigma_a}{ABC} \qquad \text{... (Eq. 3.25)} \textbf{ 2.22(a)/Pg 26, DHB}$$

- Equivalent shear stress,

$$\tau_{eq} = \tau_m + \left(\frac{\tau_{yp}}{\sigma_{en}}\right)\frac{K_{sf} \cdot \tau_a}{ABC} \qquad \text{... (Eq. 3.26)} \textbf{ 2.22(b)/Pg 26, DHB}$$

For ductile materials,

- Equivalent maximum shear stress

$$\tau_{eq})_{max} = \sqrt{\left(\frac{\sigma_{eq-n}}{2}\right)^2 + (\tau_{eq})^2} \qquad \text{... (Eq. 3.27)}$$

If factor of safety is considered, then we have

$$\tau_{eq})_{max} = \sqrt{\left(\frac{\sigma_{eq-n}}{2}\right)^2 + (\tau_{eq})^2} = \frac{\tau_{yp}}{n}$$

$$\text{... (Eq. 3.27a)} \textbf{ 2.23(a)/Pg 26, DHB}$$

For brittle materials,

- Equivalent maximum shear stress

$$\sigma_{eq-n})_{max} = \left(\frac{\sigma_{eq-n}}{2}\right) + \sqrt{\left(\frac{\sigma_{eq-n}}{2}\right)^2 + (\tau_{eq})^2} \qquad \text{... (Eq. 3.28a)}$$

If factor of safety is considered, then we have

$$\sigma_{eq-n})_{max} = \left(\frac{\sigma_{eq-n}}{2}\right) + \sqrt{\left(\frac{\sigma_{eq-n}}{2}\right)^2 + (\tau_{eq})^2} = \frac{\sigma_{yp}}{n}$$

$$\text{... (Eq. 3.28b)} \textbf{ 2.23(b)/Pg 26, DHB}$$

PROBLEMS ON AXIAL AND BENDING LOADS

22. **A cantilever beam of circular cross-section is subjected to an alternating stress at a point on the outer fiber in the plane of support that varies from 21 MPa (compression) to 28 MPa (tension). At the same time there is an alternating stress due to axial loading that varies from 14 MPa (compression) to 28 MPa (tension). The material has an ultimate strength of 412 MPa, yield strength of 309 MPa. Assume that actual stress concentration factor = 1, size correction factor = 0.85 and surface correction factor = 0.9. Determine:**

a. the equivalent normal stress due to axial loading.
b. the equivalent normal stress due to bending and
c. the total equivalent normal stress due to axial loading and bending.

VTU – Jan/ Feb. 2005 – 12 Marks

Solution: Let suffix '1' refer to axial stress and suffix '2' refer to bending stress.
Bending stress: $\sigma_{max})_2 = 28$ MPa, $\sigma_{min})_2 = -21$ MPa; axial stress: $\sigma_{max})_1 = 28$ MPa,
$\sigma_{max})_1 = -14$ MPa, $\sigma_u = 412$ MPa, $\sigma_{yp} = 309$ MPa, $K_t = 1$, $B = 0.85$, $C = 0.9$.
a. $\sigma_{eq-n})_1 = ?$, b. $\sigma_{eq-n})_2 = ?$, c. $\sigma_{eq-n})_T = ?$

a. Equivalent normal stress due to axial loading: We know that equivalent normal
stress,

$$\sigma_{eq-n} = \sigma_m + \left(\frac{\sigma_{yp}}{\sigma_{en}}\right)\frac{K_{tf} \cdot \sigma_a}{ABC} \qquad \text{... Eq. (i) 2.22(a)/ Pg 26, DHB}$$

- Mean or average stress

$$\sigma_m)_1 = \frac{\sigma_{max})_1 + \sigma_{min})_1}{2} = \frac{28 - 14}{2} = 7 \text{ MPa} \quad \text{... 2.16(a)/ Pg 23, DHB}$$

- Variable or alternating stress,

$$\sigma_a)_1 = \frac{\sigma_{max})_1 - \sigma_{min})_1}{2} = \frac{28 + 14}{2} = 21 \text{ MPa}$$

$$\text{... 2.16(b)/ Pg 23, DHB}$$

- Also $\qquad K_{tf} = 1 + q(K_{t1} - 1) \qquad \text{...2.5/ Pg 21, DHB}$

$\qquad\qquad K_{t1} = 1$ (data) and $q = 0$ since the cross-section is uniform

$\qquad\qquad K_{tf1} = 1$

- *Correction factors*:
  Load factor $A = 0.7$, for reversed axial load $\qquad\qquad\qquad$ ... Pg 25, DHB
  $\qquad\qquad\quad = 1$ for reversed bending load

$$\left.\begin{array}{l} B = 0.85 \\ C = 0.9 \end{array}\right\} \text{data for both cases}$$

- Endurance strength, $\sigma_{en} = 0.5\sigma_u \qquad\qquad\qquad$ ... 2.13(a)/Pg 23, DHB
  $\qquad\qquad \sigma_{en} = 0.5 \times 412 = 206$ MPa

$\therefore$ Eq. (i) yields...

$$\sigma_{eq-n})_1 = 7 + \left(\frac{309}{206}\right)\frac{1 \times 21}{0.7 \times 0.85 \times 0.9} = 65.82 \text{ MPa}$$

b. Equivalent normal stress due to bending loading:

- Mean or average stress

$$\sigma_m)_2 = \frac{\sigma_{max})_2 + \sigma_{min})_2}{2} = \frac{28 - 21}{2} = -3.5 \text{ MPa}$$

$$\text{... 2.16(a)/ Pg 23, DHB}$$

- Variable or alternating stress,

$$\sigma_a)_2 = \frac{\sigma_{max})_2 - \sigma_{min})_2}{2} = \frac{28 + 21}{2} = 24.5 \text{ MPa}$$

$$\text{... 2.16(b)/ Pg 23, DHB}$$

- Also $\qquad K_{tf2} = 1 + q(K_{t2} - 1)$ $\qquad$ ...2.5/ Pg 21, DHB

$\qquad K_{t2} = 1$ (data) and $q = 0$ since the cross-section is uniform

$\qquad K_{tf2} = 1$

$\therefore$ Eq. (i) yields...

$$\sigma_{eq-n})_2 = -3.5 + \left(\frac{309}{206}\right)\frac{1 \times 24.5}{1 \times 0.85 \times 0.9} = 51.54 \text{ MPa}$$

c. Total equivalent normal stress due to axial loading and bending:
Total equivalent normal stress

$$\sigma_{eq-n})_T = \sigma_{eq-n})_1 + \sigma_{eq-n})_2$$

$$= 65.82 + 51.54 = 117.36 \text{ MPa}$$

23. **A cold drawn steel rod of circular section is subjected to a variable bending moment of 565 N·m to 1130 N·m as the axial load varies from 4500 N to 13500 N. The maximum bending moment occurs at the same instant that the axial load is maximum. Determine the required diameter of the rod for a factor of safety of 2. Neglect stress concentration and column effect. Take $\sigma_u = 550$ MPa, $\sigma_y = 470$ MPa, endurance limit as 50% of the ultimate strength and size, load and surface correction coefficients as 0.85, 1 and 0.85 respectively.**

VTU – Dec. 2009/ Jan. 2010 – 14 Marks

Solution: Let suffix '1' refer to axial load and suffix '2' refer to bending load.
Bending moment: $M_{max})_2 = 1130$ N·m $= 1130 \times 10^3$ N·mm, $M_{min})_2 = 565$ N·m $= 565 \times 10^3$ N·mm; Axial load: $F_{max})_1 = 13500$ N, $F_{min})_1 = 4500$ N.

$d = ?$, $n = 2$, $K_{tf} = 1$, $\sigma_u = 550$ MPa, $\sigma_{yp} = 470$ MPa, $A = 1$, $B = 0.85$, $C = 0.85$, $\sigma_{en} = 0.5$, $\sigma_u = 275$ MPa.

We know that equivalent normal stress,

$$\sigma_{eq-n} = \sigma_m + \left(\frac{\sigma_{yp}}{\sigma_{en}}\right)\frac{K_{tf} \cdot \sigma_a}{ABC} \qquad \text{... Eq. (i) 2.22(a)/ Pg 26, DHB}$$

If factor of safety is considered,

$$\sigma_{eq-n} = \frac{\sigma_{yp}}{n} = \sigma_m + \left(\frac{\sigma_{yp}}{\sigma_{en}}\right)\frac{K_{tf} \cdot \sigma_a}{ABC}$$

Since the normal stress include both axial and/or bending stresses, we have

$$\sigma_{eq-n})_T = \sigma_{eq-n})_{axial} + \sigma_{eq-n})_{bend} = \sigma_{eq-n})_1 + \sigma_{eq-n})_2 = \frac{\sigma_{yp}}{n} \qquad \text{... Eq. (ii)}$$

Axial load:
- Mean or average stress

$$\sigma_m)_1 = \frac{\sigma_{max})_1 + \sigma_{min})_1}{2} \qquad \text{... 2.16(a)/ Pg 23, DHB}$$

$$\sigma_m)_1 = \frac{F_{max})_1 + F_{min})_1}{2A} = \frac{13500 + 4500}{2(\pi d^2/4)} = \frac{11.46 \times 10^3}{d^2}$$

- Variable or alternating stress,

$$\sigma_a)_1 = \frac{\sigma_{max})_1 - \sigma_{min})_1}{2} \qquad \dots \textbf{2.16(b)/ Pg 23, DHB}$$

$$\sigma_a)_1 = \frac{F_{max})_1 - F_{min})_1}{2A} = \frac{13500 - 4500}{2(\pi d^2/4)} = \frac{5.73 \times 10^3}{d^2}$$

Also

$$K_{tf1} = 1 + q(K_{t1} - 1) \qquad \dots \textbf{2.5/ Pg 21, DHB}$$

$K_{tf1} = 1$ since stress concentration and column effect are neglected (data)

- *Correction factors*:

Load factor $A = 0.85$, (average) for reversed axial load $\qquad \dots \textbf{Pg 25, DHB}$
$\quad = 1$ for reversed bending load

$\left. \begin{array}{l} B = 0.85 \\ C = 0.85 \end{array} \right\}$ data for both cases

∴ Eq. (i) yields...

$$\sigma_{eq-n})_1 = \frac{11.46 \times 10^3}{d^2} + \left(\frac{470}{275}\right) \frac{1 \times 5.73 \times 10^3}{(0.85 \times 0.85 \times 0.85)d^2} = \frac{27.41 \times 10^3}{d^2}$$

Bending loading:

- Mean or average stress

$$\sigma_m)_2 = \frac{\sigma_{max})_2 + \sigma_{min})_2}{2} \qquad \dots \textbf{2.16(a)/ Pg 23, DHB}$$

$$\sigma_m)_2 = \frac{M_{max})_2 + M_{min})_2}{2Z} = \frac{1130 \times 10^3 + 565 \times 10^3}{2(\pi d^3/32)} = \frac{8.63 \times 10^6}{d^3}$$

- Variable or alternating stress,

$$\sigma_a)_2 = \frac{\sigma_{max})_2 - \sigma_{min})_2}{2} \qquad \dots \textbf{2.16(b)/ Pg 23, DHB}$$

$$\sigma_a)_2 = \frac{M_{max})_2 - M_{min})_2}{2Z} = \frac{1130 \times 10^3 - 565 \times 10^3}{2(\pi d^3/32)} = \frac{2.88 \times 10^6}{d^3}$$

- Also

$$K_{tf2} = 1 + q(K_{t2} - 1) \qquad \dots \textbf{2.5/ Pg 21, DHB}$$

$K_{tf2} = 1$ since stress concentration and column effect are neglected (data)

∴ Eq. (i) yields...

$$\sigma_{eq-n})_2 = \frac{8.63 \times 10^3}{d^3} + \left(\frac{470}{275}\right) \frac{1 \times 2.88 \times 10^6}{(1 \times 0.85 \times 0.85)d^3} = \frac{15.44 \times 10^6}{d^3}$$

∴ Eq. (ii) yields...

$$\sigma_{eq-n})_T = \frac{27.41 \times 10^3}{d^2} + \frac{15.44 \times 10^6}{d^3} = \frac{470}{2}$$

$$\frac{27.41 \times 10^3}{d^2} + \frac{15.44 \times 10^6}{d^3} - 235 = 0$$

i.e.

$$27.41 \times 10^3 d + 15.44 \times 10^6 - 235d^3 = 0$$

$$235d^3 - 27.41 \times 10^3 d - 15.44 \times 10^6 = 0$$

∴

$$d = 41.30 \text{ mm} \approx 45 \text{ mm}$$

24. **A steel cantilever of 200 mm long is subjected to combined loading as shown in Fig. 3.18. The cantilever is of circular cross-section. Determine its diameter taking a factor of safety of 2. Take σ_y = 330 MPa, σ_{en} = 300 MPa, stress concentration factor static axial and bending load as 1.64 and 1.44 respectively. Choose proper values for modifying factors "A", "B" and "C" from data handbook. Notch sensitivity index is 0.9.**

VTU – Dec. 2014/ Jan. 2015 – 15 Marks; June/ July 2015 – 10 Marks

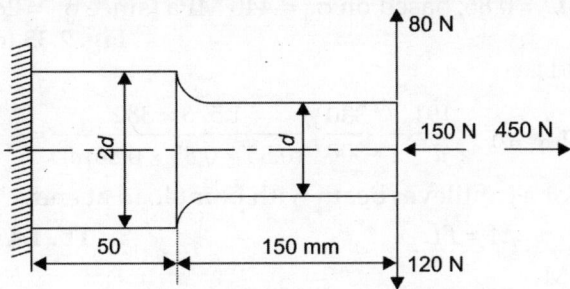

Fig. 3.18: Problem 24

Solution: Let suffix '1' refer to axial load and suffix '2' refer to bending load.

Axial load: $F_{max})_1$ = 450 N, $F_{min})_1$ = –150 N; Bending load: $F_{max})_2$ = 120 N, $F_{min})_2$ = –80 N, L = 150 mm, d = ?, n = 2, σ_{yp} = 330 MPa, σ_{en} = 300 MPa, K_{t1} = 1.64 for axial, K_{t2} = 1.44 for bending, q = 0.9.

We know that equivalent normal stress,

$$\sigma_{eq-n} = \sigma_m + \left(\frac{\sigma_{yp}}{\sigma_{en}}\right)\frac{K_{tf}\cdot\sigma_a}{ABC} \qquad \text{... Eq. (i) } \textbf{2.22(a)/ Pg 26, DHB}$$

If factor of safety is considered,

$$\sigma_{eq-n} = \frac{\sigma_{yp}}{n} = \sigma_m + \left(\frac{\sigma_{yp}}{\sigma_{en}}\right)\frac{K_{tf}\cdot\sigma_a}{ABC}$$

Since the normal stress includes both axial and/or bending stresses, we have

$$\sigma_{eq-n})_T = \sigma_{eq-n})_{axial} + \sigma_{eq-n})_{bend} = \sigma_{eq-n})_1 + \sigma_{eq-n})_2 = \frac{\sigma_{yp}}{n}$$
$$\text{... Eq. (ii)}$$

Axial load:

• Mean or average stress

$$\sigma_m)_1 = \frac{\sigma_{max})_1 + \sigma_{min})_1}{2} \qquad \text{... 2.16(a)/ Pg 23, DHB}$$

$$\sigma_m)_1 = \frac{F_{max})_1 + F_{min})_1}{2A} = \frac{450 - 150}{2(\pi d^2/4)} = \frac{191}{d^2}$$

• Variable or alternating stress,

$$\sigma_a)_1 = \frac{\sigma_{max})_1 - \sigma_{min})_1}{2} \qquad \text{... 2.16(b)/ Pg 23, DHB}$$

$$\sigma_a)_1 = \frac{F_{max})_1 - F_{min})_1}{2A} = \frac{450 + 150}{2(\pi d^2/4)} = \frac{382}{d^2}$$

- Also
$$K_{tf1} = 1 + q(K_{t1} - 1)$$
$$= 1 + 0.9(1.64 - 1)$$
$$K_{tf1} = 1.576$$

...**2.5/ Pg 21, DHB**
($q = 0.9$, data)

- *Correction factors*:
Load factor $A = 0.85$, (average) for reversed axial load   ... **Pg 25, DHB**
$= 1$ for reversed bending load
$B = 0.85$, assumed since diameter is unknown
$C = 0.86$, based on $\sigma_u = 440$ MPa [since $\sigma_u = 2\sigma_{en} = 600$ MPa]
... **Fig. 2.33 (curve c)/Pg 46, DHB**

$\therefore$ Eq. (i) yields...

$$\sigma_{eq-n})_1 = \frac{191}{d^2} + \left(\frac{330}{300}\right) \frac{1.576 \times 382}{(0.85 \times 0.85 \times 0.86)\, d^2} = \frac{1256.71}{d^2}$$

Bending load: For a cantilever beam with point load at end,
$$M = FL \qquad\qquad ... \textbf{Tb. 1.4 (Fig. 1)/ Pg 15, DHB}$$

- Maximum BM
$$M_{max} = F_{max})_2 L = 120 \times 150 = 18000 \text{ N·mm}$$

- Minimum BM
$$M_{min} = F_{min})_2 L = (-80) \times 150 = -12000 \text{ N·mm}$$

- Mean or average stress
$$\sigma_m)_2 = \frac{\sigma_{max})_2 + \sigma_{min})_2}{2} \qquad\qquad ... \textbf{2.16(a)/ Pg 23, DHB}$$

$$\sigma_m)_2 = \frac{M_{max})_2 + M_{min})_2}{2Z} = \frac{18000 - 12000}{2(\pi d^3/32)} = \frac{30.56 \times 10^3}{d^3}$$

- Variable or alternating stress,
$$\sigma_a)_2 = \frac{\sigma_{max})_2 - \sigma_{min})_2}{2} \qquad\qquad ... \textbf{2.16(b)/ Pg 23, DHB}$$

$$\sigma_a)_2 = \frac{M_{max})_2 - M_{min})_2}{2Z} = \frac{18000 + 12000}{2(\pi d^3/32)} = \frac{152.79 \times 10^6}{d^3}$$

- Also
$$K_{tf2} = 1 + q(K_{t2} - 1)$$
$$= 1 + 0.9(1.44 - 1)$$
$$K_{tf2} = 1.396$$

...**2.5/ Pg 21, DHB**
($q = 0.9$, data)

$\therefore$ Eq. (i) yields...

$$\sigma_{eq-n})_2 = \frac{30.56 \times 10^3}{d^3} + \left(\frac{330}{300}\right) \frac{1.396 \times 152.79 \times 10^3}{(1 \times 0.85 \times 0.86)\, d^3} = \frac{3.51 \times 10^5}{d^3}$$

$\therefore$ Eq. (ii) yields...

$$\sigma_{eq-n})_T = \frac{1256.71}{d^2} + \frac{3.51 \times 10^5}{d^3} = \frac{330}{2}$$

i.e.
$$\frac{1256.71}{d^2} + \frac{3.51 \times 10^5}{d^3} - 165 = 0$$

$$1256.71d + 3.51 \times 10^5 - 165d^3 = 0$$
$$165d^3 - 1256.71 - 3.51 \times 10^5 = 0$$

$\therefore$ $\qquad\qquad\qquad\qquad\qquad d = 13.17 \text{ mm} \approx 15 \text{ mm}$

25. **A ground steel cantilever member as shown in Fig. 3.19 is subjected to a transverse load at its free end that varies from 100 N up to 200 N down as an axial load varies from 500 N in compression to 1000 N in tension. Determine the required diameter of the section using a factor of safety of 2. The strength properties of the material are: Ultimate strength = 550 MPa, yield strength = 480 MPa, and endurance limit = 270 MPa.**

VTU – Dec. 2009/ Jan. 2010 – 20 Marks; Dec. 2011 – 15 Marks

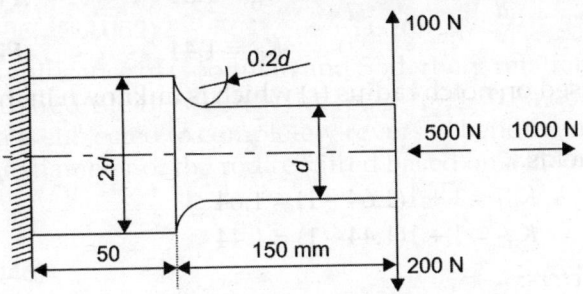

Fig. 3.19: Problem 25

Solution: Let suffix '1' refer to axial load and suffix '2' refer to bending load.

Axial load: $F_{max})_1 = 1000$ N, $F_{min})_1 = -500$ N; Bending load: $F_{max})_2 = 200$ N, $F_{min})_2 = -100$ N, $L = 150$ mm, $d = ?$, $n = 2$, $\sigma_u = 550$ MPa, $\sigma_{yp} = 480$ MPa, $\sigma_{en} = 270$ MPa, Surface finish – ground.

We know that equivalent normal stress,

$$\sigma_{eq-n} = \sigma_m + \left(\frac{\sigma_{yp}}{\sigma_{en}}\right)\frac{K_{tf}\cdot\sigma_a}{ABC} \qquad \text{... Eq. (i) } \mathbf{2.22(a)/ \ Pg \ 26, \ DHB}$$

If factor of safety is considered,

$$\sigma_{eq-n} = \frac{\sigma_{yp}}{n} = \sigma_m + \left(\frac{\sigma_{yp}}{\sigma_{en}}\right)\frac{K_{tf}\cdot\sigma_a}{ABC}$$

Since the normal stress includes both axial and/or bending stresses, we have

$$\sigma_{eq-n})_T = \sigma_{eq-n})_{axial} + \sigma_{eq-n})_{bend} = \sigma_{eq-n})_1 + \sigma_{eq-n})_2 = \frac{\sigma_{yp}}{n} \qquad \text{... Eq. (ii)}$$

Axial load:

• Mean or average stress

$$\sigma_m)_1 = \frac{\sigma_{max})_1 + \sigma_{min})_1}{2} \qquad \text{... } \mathbf{2.16(a)/ \ Pg \ 23, \ DHB}$$

$$\sigma_m)_1 = \frac{F_{max})_1 + F_{min})_1}{2A} = \frac{1000 - 500}{2(\pi d^2/4)} = \frac{318.31}{d^2}$$

• Variable or alternating stress,

$$\sigma_a)_1 = \frac{\sigma_{max})_1 - \sigma_{min})_1}{2} \qquad \text{... } \mathbf{2.16(b)/ \ Pg \ 23, \ DHB}$$

$$\sigma_a)_1 = \frac{F_{max})_1 - F_{min})_1}{2A} = \frac{1000 + 500}{2(\pi d^2/4)} = \frac{954.93}{d^2}$$

- Also $\qquad K_{tf1} = 1 + q(K_{t1} - 1) \qquad$ ... Eq. (iii) **2.5/ Pg 21, DHB**

Referring the given problem to **Fig. 2.23 and 2.25/Pg 42 and 43, DHB,** we have
$$D = 2d, d = d, r = 0.2d$$

Now $\qquad \dfrac{r}{d} = \dfrac{0.2d}{d} = 0.2;$ and $\dfrac{D}{d} = \dfrac{2d}{d} = 2$

At $\qquad \dfrac{r}{d} = 0.2$ and $\dfrac{D}{d} = 2, K_{t1} = 1.64 \qquad$ ...**Fig. 2.23/ Pg 42, DHB**

$$K_{t2} = 1.44 \qquad$$ ...**Fig. 2.25/ Pg 43, DHB**

Since q is based on notch radius (r) which is unknown in this problem, assume $q = 1$

$\therefore$ Eq. (iii) yields...
$$K_{tf1} = 1 + 1(1.64 - 1) = 1.64$$
and $\qquad K_{tf2} = 1 + 1(1.44 - 1) = 1.44$

- *Correction factors*:

Load factor $\quad A = 0.85$, (average) for reversed axial load $\qquad$ ... **Pg 25, DHB**
$\qquad\qquad\quad = 1$ for reversed bending load
$\qquad\qquad B = 0.85$, assumed since diameter is unknown
$\qquad\qquad C = 0.93$, based on $\sigma_u = 550$ MPa, for ground surface
$\qquad\qquad\qquad\qquad\qquad$ ... **Fig. 2.33 (curve b)/Pg 46, DHB**

$\therefore$ Eq. (i) yields...
$$\sigma_{eq-n})_1 = \frac{318.31}{d^2} + \left(\frac{480}{270}\right)\frac{1.64 \times 945.93}{(0.85 \times 0.85 \times 0.93)d^2} = \frac{4461.85}{d^2}$$

Bending load: For a cantilever beam with point load at end,
$$M = FL \qquad$$ ... **Tb. 1.4 (Fig. 1)/ Pg 15, DHB**

- Maximum BM
$$M_{max} = F_{max})_2 L = 200 \times 150 = 30000 \text{ N·mm}$$

- Minimum BM
$$M_{min} = F_{min})_2 = (-100) \times 150 = -15000 \text{ N·mm}$$

- Mean or average stress
$$\sigma_m)_2 = \frac{\sigma_{max})_2 + \sigma_{min})_2}{2} \qquad$$ ... **2.16(a)/ Pg 23, DHB**

$$\sigma_m)_2 = \frac{M_{max})_2 + M_{min})_2}{2Z} = \frac{30000 - 15000}{2(\pi d^3/32)} = \frac{76.40 \times 10^3}{d^3}$$

- Variable or alternating stress,
$$\sigma_a)_2 = \frac{\sigma_{max})_2 - \sigma_{min})_2}{2} \qquad$$ ... **2.16(b)/ Pg 23, DHB**

$$\sigma_a)_2 = \frac{M_{max})_2 - M_{min})_2}{2Z} = \frac{30000 + 15000}{2(\pi d^3/32)} = \frac{229.18 \times 10^3}{d^3}$$

- Also $\qquad K_{tf2} = 1.44$

∴ Eq. (i) yields...

$$\sigma_{eq-n})_2 = \frac{76.40 \times 10^3}{d^3} + \left(\frac{480}{270}\right) \frac{1.44 \times 229.18 \times 10^3}{(1 \times 0.85 \times 0.93)d^3} = \frac{818.59 \times 10^3}{d^3}$$

∴ Eq. (ii) yields...

$$\sigma_{eq-n})_T = \frac{4461.85}{d^2} + \frac{818.59 \times 10^3}{d^3} = \frac{480}{2}$$

i.e.

$$\frac{4461.85}{d^2} + \frac{818.59 \times 10^3}{d^3} - 240 = 0$$

$$4461.85d + 818.59 \times 10^3 - 240d^3 = 0$$

$$240d^3 - 4461.85d - 818.59 \times 10^3 = 0$$

∴ $d = 15.46\,\text{mm} \approx 16\,\text{mm}$

26. **A machine component shown in Fig. 3.20 is loaded as indicated in the figure. Determine the cross-section dimensions 'd' for the component, its fatigue stress concentration factor in bending and axial loading are 1.8 and 1.6 respectively. The allowable stress for the component is 100 N/mm², the material properties are σ_y = 250 N/mm², σ_u = 400 N/mm².**

VTU – June/ July 2009 – 15 Marks

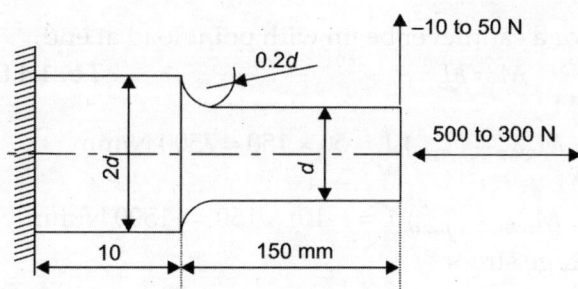

Fig. 3.20: Problem 26

Solution: Let suffix '1' refer to axial load and suffix '2' refer to bending load.

Axial load: $F_{max})_1 = 500$ N, $F_{min})_1 = -300$ N; Bending load: $F_{max})_2 = 50$ N, $F_{min})_2 = -10$ N, $L = 150$ mm, $d = ?$, $K_{tf1} = 1.6$, $K_{tf2} = 1.8$, $\sigma_{eq-n})_T = 100$ MPa, $\sigma_{yp} = 250$ MPa, $\sigma_u = 400$ MPa.

We know that equivalent normal stress,

$$\sigma_{eq-n} = \sigma_m + \left(\frac{\sigma_{yp}}{\sigma_{en}}\right) \frac{K_{tf} \cdot \sigma_a}{ABC} \qquad \text{... Eq. (i) } \mathbf{2.22(a)/\,Pg\ 26,\ DHB}$$

Since the normal stress includes both axial and/or bending stresses, we have

$$\sigma_{eq-n})_T = \sigma_{eq-n})_{axial} + \sigma_{eq-n})_{bend} = \sigma_{eq-n})_1 + \sigma_{eq-n})_2 \qquad \text{... Eq. (ii)}$$

Axial load:

• Mean or average stress

$$\sigma_m)_1 = \frac{\sigma_{max})_1 + \sigma_{min})_1}{2} \qquad \text{... } \mathbf{2.16(a)/\,Pg\ 23,\ DHB}$$

$$\sigma_m)_1 = \frac{F_{max})_1 + F_{min})_1}{2A} = \frac{500 - 300}{2(\pi d^2/4)} = \frac{127.32}{d^2}$$

- Variable or alternating stress,

$$\sigma_a)_1 = \frac{\sigma_{max})_1 - \sigma_{min})_1}{2} \qquad \text{... 2.16(b)/ Pg 23, DHB}$$

$$\sigma_a)_1 = \frac{F_{max})_1 - F_{min})_1}{2A} = \frac{500 + 300}{2(\pi d^2/4)} = \frac{509.30}{d^2}$$

- Also $\qquad K_{tf1} = 1.6 \text{ (data)}$
- *Correction factors*:

    Load factor $A = 0.85$, (average) for reversed axial load $\qquad$ **... Pg 25, DHB**

    $\qquad\qquad = 1$ for reversed bending load

    $\qquad\qquad B = 0.85$, assumed since diameter is unknown

    $\qquad\qquad C = 0.9$, based on $\sigma_u = 400$ MPa ... **Fig. 2.33 (curve b)/Pg. 46, DHB**

- Endurance strength,

    $\qquad\qquad \sigma_{en} = 0.5\sigma_u \qquad\qquad$ **... 2.13 (a)/Pg. 23, DHB**

    $\qquad\qquad \sigma_{en} = 0.5 \times 400 = 200$ MPa

    $\therefore$ Eq. (i) yields...

$$\sigma_{eq-n})_1 = \frac{127.32}{d^2} + \left(\frac{250}{200}\right)\frac{1.6 \times 509.30}{(0.85 \times 0.85 \times 0.9)d^2} = \frac{1693.80}{d^2}$$

Bending load: For a cantilever beam with point load at end,

$$M = FL \qquad\qquad \text{... Tb. 1.4 (Fig. 1)/ Pg 15, DHB}$$

- Maximum BM

    $\qquad M_{max} = F_{max})_2 L = 50 \times 150 = 7500 \text{ N·mm}$

- Minimum BM

    $\qquad M_{min} = F_{min})_2 L = (-10) \times 150 = -1500 \text{ N·mm}$

- Mean or average stress

$$\sigma_m)_2 = \frac{\sigma_{max})_2 + \sigma_{min})_2}{2} \qquad \text{... 2.16(a)/ Pg 23, DHB}$$

$$\sigma_m)_2 = \frac{M_{max})_2 + M_{min})_2}{2Z} = \frac{7500 - 1500}{2(\pi d^3/32)} = \frac{30.56 \times 10^3}{d^3}$$

- Variable or alternating stress,

$$\sigma_a)_2 = \frac{\sigma_{max})_2 - \sigma_{min})_2}{2} \qquad \text{... 2.16(b)/ Pg 23, DHB}$$

$$\sigma_a)_2 = \frac{M_{max})_2 - M_{min})_2}{2Z} = \frac{7500 + 1500}{2(\pi d^3/32)} = \frac{45.84 \times 10^3}{d^3}$$

- Also $\qquad K_{tf2} = 1.8 \text{ (Data)}$

    $\therefore$ Eq. (i) yields...

$$\sigma_{eq-n})_2 = \frac{30.56 \times 10^3}{d^3} + \left(\frac{250}{200}\right)\frac{1.8 \times 45.84 \times 10^3}{(1 \times 0.85 \times 0.9)d^3} = \frac{165.37 \times 10^3}{d^3}$$

$\therefore$ Eq. (ii) yields...

$$100 = \frac{1693.80}{d^2} + \frac{165.37 \times 10^3}{d^3}$$

i.e.
$$\frac{1693.80}{d^2} + \frac{165.37 \times 10^3}{d^3} - 100 = 0$$

$$1693.80d + 165.37 \times 10^3 - 100d^3 = 0$$

$$100d^3 - 1693.80d - 165.37 \times 10^3 = 0$$

∴ $d = 12.30 \text{ mm} \approx 15 \text{ mm}$

PROBLEMS ON BENDING AND TORSIONAL LOADS

27. **A hot rolled steel shaft is subjected to a torsional load that varies from 330 N·m (clockwise) to 110 N·m (counterclockwise) as the applied bending moment at the critical section varies from +440 N·m to –220 N·m. The shaft is of uniform cross-section and no key way is present at the critical section. Determine the required shaft diameter. The material has an ultimate tensile strength of 550 MPa and yield strength of 410 MPa. Take the endurance limit as half of the ultimate strength, factor of safety = 2, size factor = 0.85 and a surface finish factor = 0.62.**

VTU – May/June 2010 – 14 Marks; Dec. 08/Jan. 2009 – 20 Marks;
June/July 2009 – 15 Marks; Dec. 2010 – 15 Marks; Dec. 2013/Jan. 2014 – 15 Marks;
June/July 2014 – 15 Marks; (Similar) June/July 2013 – 15 Marks

Solution: Torsional moment: $T_{max} = 330 \times 10^3$ N·mm, $T_{min} = -110 \times 10^3$ N; Bending moment: $M_{max} = 440 \times 10^3$ N·mm, $M_{min} = -220 \times 10^3$ N·mm, $d = ?$, $K_t = K_s = 1$, $d = ?$, $\sigma_u = 550$ MPa, $\sigma_{yp} = 410$ MPa, $\sigma_{en} = 0.5\sigma_u = 275$ MPa, $n = 2$, $B = 0.85$, $C = 0.62$.

We know that equivalent maximum shear stress,

$$\tau_{eq})_{max} = \frac{\tau_{yp}}{\sigma_n} = \sqrt{\left(\frac{\sigma_{eq-n}}{2}\right)^2 + (\tau_{eq})^2} \quad \dots \text{ Eq. (i) } \textbf{2.23(a)/ Pg 26, DHB}$$

Bending load:

Equivalent normal stress

$$\sigma_{eq-n} = \sigma_m + \left(\frac{\sigma_{yp}}{\sigma_{en}}\right)\frac{K_{tf} \cdot \sigma_a}{ABC} \quad \dots \text{ Eq. (ii) } \textbf{2.22(a)/ Pg 26, DHB}$$

• Mean stress $\sigma_m = \dfrac{\sigma_{max} + \sigma_{min}}{2} = \dfrac{M_m}{Z}$ **2.16(a)/ Pg 23, DHB**

But $M_m = \dfrac{M_{max} + M_{min}}{2}$ and $M_a = \dfrac{M_{max} - M_{min}}{2}$

$$\sigma_m = \frac{M_{max} + M_{min}}{2Z} = \frac{440 \times 10^3 - 220 \times 10^3}{2(\pi d^3/32)} = \frac{1.12 \times 10^6}{d^3}$$

• Variable or alternating stress,

$$\sigma_a = \frac{\sigma_{max} - \sigma_{min}}{2} = \frac{M_a}{Z} \quad \dots \textbf{2.16(b)/ Pg 23, DHB}$$

$$\sigma_a = \frac{M_{max} - M_{min}}{2Z} = \frac{440 \times 10^3 + 220 \times 10^3}{2(\pi d^3/32)} = \frac{3.36 \times 10^6}{d^3}$$

• Also $K_{tf} = 1 + q(K_t - 1)$ $\dots$**2.5/ Pg 21, DHB**

since the cross-section is uniform, $K_{t1} = 1$ and $q = 0$

∴ $K_{tf} = 1$

- *Correction factors*:
  Load factor $A = 1$, for reversed bending load   **... Pg 25, DHB**
            $= 0.55$ for reversed torsional load
       $B = 0.85, C = 0.62$ (data)
- Endurance strength,
  $$\sigma_{en} = 0.5\sigma_u \qquad \text{... 2.13(a)/Pg. 23, DHB}$$
  $$\sigma_{en} = 0.5 \times 540 = 270 \text{ MPa}$$

$\therefore$ Eq. (ii) yields...

$$\sigma_{eq-n} = \frac{1.12 \times 10^6}{d^3} + \left(\frac{410}{275}\right)\frac{1 \times 3.36 \times 10^6}{(1 \times 0.85 \times 0.62)d^3} = \frac{10.62 \times 10^6}{d^3}$$

Torsional load: Equivalent shear stress,

$$\tau_{eq} = \tau_m + \left(\frac{\tau_{yp}}{\sigma_{en}}\right)\frac{K_{sf} \cdot \tau_a}{ABC} \qquad \text{...Eq. (iii) 2.22(b)/Pg. 26, DHB}$$

- Mean stress $\tau_m = \dfrac{\tau_{max} + \tau_{min}}{2} = \dfrac{T_m}{Z_p}$ **... 2.16(a)/ Pg 23, DHB**

  But $T_m = \dfrac{T_{max} + T_{min}}{2}$ and $T_a = \dfrac{T_{max} - T_{min}}{2}$

  $$\tau_m = \frac{T_{max} + T_{min}}{2Z_p} = \frac{330 \times 10^3 - 110 \times 10^3}{2(\pi d^3/16)} = \frac{560.23 \times 10^3}{d^3}$$

- Variable stress,

  $$\tau_a = \frac{\tau_{max} - \tau_{min}}{2} = \frac{T_a}{Z_p} \qquad \text{... 2.16(b)/ Pg 23, DHB}$$

  $$\tau_a = \frac{T_{max} - T_{min}}{2Z} = \frac{330 \times 10^3 + 110 \times 10^3}{2(\pi d^3/16)} = \frac{1.12 \times 10^6}{d^3}$$

- Also $K_{sf} = 1 + q(K_s - 1)$ **...2.5/ Pg 21, DHB**
       Since the cross-section is uniform, $K_s = 1$ and $q = 0$

  $\therefore$ $K_{sf} = 1$

- Yield strength in shear,
  $$\tau_{yp} = 0.5\sigma_{yp} \qquad (\because \tau = 0.5\sigma)$$
  $$\tau_{yp} = 0.5 \times 410 = 205 \text{ MPa}$$

$\therefore$ Eq. (iii) yields...

$$\tau_{eq} = \frac{560.23 \times 10^3}{d^3} + \left(\frac{205}{275}\right)\frac{1 \times 1.12 \times 10^6}{(0.55 \times 0.85 \times 0.62)d^3} = \frac{3.44 \times 10^6}{d^3}$$

$\therefore$ Eq. (i) yields...

$$\frac{205}{2} = \sqrt{\left(\frac{10.62 \times 10^6/d^3}{2}\right)^2 + \left(\frac{3.44 \times 10^6}{d^3}\right)^2}$$

$$10506.25 = \frac{4 \times 10^{13}}{d^6}$$

$\therefore$ $d = 39.52 \text{ mm} \approx 40 \text{ mm}$

28. **A pulley is keyed to a shaft midway between two antifriction bearings. The bending moment at the pulley varies from –170 N·m to 510 N·m as the torsional moment in the shaft varies from 55 N·m to 165 N·m. The frequency of the variation of the loads is same as the shaft speed. The shaft is made of cold drawn steel having an ultimate strength of 538 MPa and yield strength of 400 MPa. Determine the required diameter for an indefinite life. The stress concentration factor for the keyway in bending and torsion may be taken as 1.6 and 1.3 respectively. Use design factor of 1.5.**

VTU – July 2007 – 12 Marks; (Similar) June/July 2008 – 12 Marks; (Similar) June 2012 – 16 Marks; (Similar) June/ July 2013 – 15 Marks

Solution: Bending moment: $M_{max} = 510 \times 10^3$ N·mm, $M_{min} = -170 \times 10^3$ N·mm; Torsional moment: $T_{max} = 165 \times 10^3$ N·mm, $T_{min} = 55 \times 10^3$ N·mm; $\sigma_u = 538$ MPa, $\sigma_{yp} = 400$ MPa, $d = ?$, $K_{tf} = 1.6$, $K_{sf} = 1.3$, $n = 1.5$.

We know that equivalent maximum shear stress,

$$\tau_{eq})_{max} = \frac{\tau_{yp}}{\sigma_n} = \sqrt{\left(\frac{\sigma_{eq-n}}{2}\right)^2 + (\tau_{eq})^2} \quad \text{... Eq. (i) } \mathbf{2.23(a)/ \ Pg \ 26, \ DHB}$$

Bending load:

Equivalent normal stress

$$\sigma_{eq-n} = \sigma_m + \left(\frac{\sigma_{yp}}{\sigma_{en}}\right)\frac{K_{tf} \cdot \sigma_a}{ABC} \quad \text{... Eq. (ii) } \mathbf{2.22(a)/ \ Pg \ 26, \ DHB}$$

- **Mean stress** $\quad \sigma_m = \dfrac{\sigma_{max} + \sigma_{min}}{2} = \dfrac{M_m}{Z} \qquad \mathbf{2.16(a)/ \ Pg \ 23, \ DHB}$

  But $\qquad M_m = \dfrac{M_{max} + M_{min}}{2}$ and $M_a = \dfrac{M_{max} - M_{min}}{2}$

  $$\sigma_m = \frac{M_{max} + M_{min}}{2Z} = \frac{510 \times 10^3 - 170 \times 10^3}{2(\pi d^3/32)} = \frac{1.73 \times 10^6}{d^3}$$

- **Variable or alternating stress,**

  $$\sigma_a = \frac{\sigma_{max} - \sigma_{min}}{2} = \frac{M_a}{Z} \qquad \text{... } \mathbf{2.16(b)/ \ Pg \ 23, \ DHB}$$

  $$\sigma_a = \frac{M_{max} - M_{min}}{2Z} = \frac{510 \times 10^3 + 170 \times 10^3}{2(\pi d^3/32)} = \frac{3.46 \times 10^6}{d^3}$$

- **Also** $\qquad K_{tf} = 1.6$ (data)
- *Correction factors:*

  Load factor $A = 1$, for reversed bending load $\qquad$ ... **Pg 25, DHB**

  $\qquad\qquad\qquad = 0.55$ for reversed torsional load

  $B = 0.85$, assumed since diameter is unknown

  $\qquad C = 0.88$, based on $\sigma_u = 538$ MPa... **Fig. 2.33(curve c)/Pg. 46, DHB**
- **Endurance strength,**

  $$\sigma_{en} = 0.5\sigma_u \qquad\qquad \text{... } \mathbf{2.13(b)/Pg. \ 23, \ DHB}$$

  $$\sigma_{en} = 0.5 \times 538 = 269 \text{ MPa}$$

∴ Eq. (ii) yields...

$$\sigma_{eq-n} = \frac{1.73 \times 10^6}{d^3} + \left(\frac{400}{269}\right)\frac{1.6 \times 3.46 \times 10^6}{(1 \times 0.85 \times 0.88)d^3} = \frac{12.71 \times 10^6}{d^3}$$

Torsional load: Equivalent shear stress,

$$\tau_{eq} = \tau_m + \left(\frac{\tau_{yp}}{\sigma_{en}}\right)\frac{K_{sf} \cdot \tau_a}{ABC} \qquad \text{...Eq. (iii) } \textbf{2.22(b)/Pg. 26, DHB}$$

- **Mean stress** $\quad \tau_m = \dfrac{\tau_{max} + \tau_{min}}{2} = \dfrac{T_m}{Z_p} \qquad \text{... } \textbf{2.16(a)/ Pg 23, DHB}$

  But $\quad T_m = \dfrac{T_{max} + T_{min}}{2}$ and $T_a = \dfrac{T_{max} - T_{min}}{2}$

  $$\tau_m = \frac{T_{max} + T_{min}}{2Z_p} = \frac{165 \times 10^3 + 55 \times 10^3}{2(\pi d^3/16)} = \frac{560.23 \times 10^3}{d^3}$$

- **Variable stress,**

  $$\tau_a = \frac{\tau_{max} - \tau_{min}}{2} = \frac{T_a}{Z_p} \qquad \text{... } \textbf{2.16(b)/ Pg 23, DHB}$$

  $$\tau_a = \frac{T_{max} - T_{min}}{2Z} = \frac{165 \times 10^3 - 55 \times 10^3}{2(\pi d^3/16)} = \frac{280.12 \times 10^6}{d^3}$$

- **Also** $\quad K_{sf} = 1.3$ (data)

- **Yield strength in shear,**

  $$\tau_{yp} = 0.5\sigma_{yp} \qquad\qquad (\because \tau = 0.5\sigma)$$
  $$\tau_{yp} = 0.5 \times 400 = 200 \text{ MPa}$$

∴ Eq. (iii) yields...

$$\tau_{eq} = \frac{560.23 \times 10^3}{d^3} + \left(\frac{200}{269}\right)\frac{1.3 \times 280.12 \times 10^3}{(0.55 \times 0.85 \times 0.88)d^3} = \frac{1.21 \times 10^6}{d^3}$$

∴ Eq. (i) yields...

$$\frac{200}{1.5} = \sqrt{\left(\frac{12.71 \times 10^6/d^3}{2}\right)^2 + \left(\frac{1.21 \times 10^6}{d^3}\right)^2}$$

$$17.78 \times 10^3 = \frac{4.18 \times 10^{13}}{d^6}$$

∴ $\qquad\qquad d = 36.47 \text{ mm} \approx 40 \text{ mm}$

29. **A transmission shaft carries a pulley midway between two bearings. The bending moment at the pulley varies from 200 N·m to 600 N·m, as the torsional moment of the shaft varies from 70 N·m to 200 N·m. The frequencies of variation of bending and torsional moments are equal to the shaft speed. The shaft is made of steel Fe 400 (σ_u = 540 MPa, σ_{yt} = 400 MPa). The corrected endurance strength of the shaft is 200 MPa. Determine the diameter of the shaft using a factor of safety of 2.**

Solution: Bending moment: $M_{max} = 600 \times 10^3$ N·mm, $M_{min} = 200 \times 10^3$ N·mm; Torsional moment: $T_{max} = 200 \times 10^3$ N·mm, $T_{min} = 70 \times 10^3$ N·mm; $\sigma_u = 540$ MPa, $\sigma_{yp} = 400$ MPa, $d = ?$, $n = 2$, corrected endurance strength ABC $\sigma_{en} = 200$ MPa. We know that equivalent maximum shear stress,

$$\tau_{eq})_{max} = \frac{\tau_{yp}}{\sigma_n} = \sqrt{\left(\frac{\sigma_{eq-n}}{2}\right)^2 + (\tau_{eq})^2} \quad \text{... Eq. (i) } \mathbf{2.23(a)/ Pg\ 26,\ DHB}$$

Bending load:

Equivalent normal stress

$$\sigma_{eq-n} = \sigma_m + \left(\frac{\sigma_{yp}}{\sigma_{en}}\right)\frac{K_{tf}\cdot\sigma_a}{ABC} \quad \text{... Eq. (ii) } \mathbf{2.22(a)/ Pg\ 26,\ DHB}$$

- Mean stress $\quad \sigma_m = \dfrac{\sigma_{max} + \sigma_{min}}{2} = \dfrac{M_m}{Z} \qquad\qquad \mathbf{2.16(a)/ Pg\ 23,\ DHB}$

  But $\quad M_m = \dfrac{M_{max} + M_{min}}{2}$ and $M_a = \dfrac{M_{max} - M_{min}}{2}$

  $$\sigma_m = \frac{M_{max} + M_{min}}{2Z} = \frac{600 \times 10^3 + 200 \times 10^3}{2(\pi d^3/32)} = \frac{4.07 \times 10^6}{d^3}$$

- Variable or alternating stress,

  $$\sigma_a = \frac{\sigma_{max} - \sigma_{min}}{2} = \frac{M_a}{Z} \qquad \text{... } \mathbf{2.16(b)/ Pg\ 23,\ DHB}$$

  $$\sigma_a = \frac{M_{max} - M_{min}}{2Z} = \frac{600 \times 10^3 - 200 \times 10^3}{2(\pi d^3/32)} = \frac{2.04 \times 10^6}{d^3}$$

- Also $\quad K_{tf} = 1 + q(K_t - 1) \qquad\qquad \text{...} \mathbf{2.5/ Pg\ 21,\ DHB}$

  since the cross-section is uniform, $K_{t1} = 1$ and $q = 0$

  $\therefore \quad K_{tf} = 1$

- *Correction factors*: Corrected endurance strength $ABC\sigma_{en} = 200$ MPa

  $\therefore$ Eq. (ii) yields...

  $$\sigma_{eq-n} = \frac{4.07 \times 10^6}{d^3} + \frac{400 \times 1 \times 2.04 \times 10^6}{200\,d^3} = \frac{8.15 \times 10^6}{d^3}$$

Torsional load: Equivalent shear stress,

$$\tau_{eq} = \tau_m + \left(\frac{\tau_{yp}}{\sigma_{en}}\right)\frac{K_{sf}\cdot\tau_a}{ABC} \quad \text{...Eq. (iii) } \mathbf{2.22(b)/Pg.\ 26,\ DHB}$$

- Mean stress $\quad \tau_m = \dfrac{\tau_{max} + \tau_{min}}{2} = \dfrac{T_m}{Z_p} \qquad\qquad \text{... } \mathbf{2.16(a)/ Pg\ 23,\ DHB}$

  But $\quad T_m = \dfrac{T_{max} + T_{min}}{2}$ and $T_a = \dfrac{T_{max} - T_{min}}{2}$

  $$\tau_m = \frac{T_{max} + T_{min}}{2Z_p} = \frac{200 \times 10^3 + 70 \times 10^3}{2(\pi d^3/16)} = \frac{6.88 \times 10^5}{d^3}$$

- Variable stress,

$$\tau_a = \frac{\tau_{max} - \tau_{min}}{2} = \frac{T_a}{Z_p} \qquad \text{... 2.16(b)/ Pg 23, DHB}$$

$$\tau_a = \frac{T_{max} - T_{min}}{2Z} = \frac{200 \times 10^3 - 70 \times 10^3}{2(\pi d^3/16)} = \frac{3.31 \times 10^5}{d^3}$$

- Also $\qquad K_{sf} = 1 + q(K_s - 1) \qquad$ ...2.5/ Pg 21, DHB

  Since the cross-section is uniform, $K_s = 1$ and $q = 0$
  $\therefore \qquad K_{sf} = 1$

- Yield strength in shear,
  $$\tau_{yp} = 0.5\sigma_{yp} \qquad (\because \tau = 0.5\sigma)$$
  $$\tau_{yp} = 0.5 \times 400 = 200 \text{ MPa}$$

$\therefore$ Eq. (iii) yields...

$$\tau_{eq} = \frac{6.88 \times 10^5}{d^3} + \frac{200 \times 1 \times 3.31 \times 10^5}{200\,d^3} = \frac{10.20 \times 10^5}{d^3}$$

$\therefore$ Eq. (i) yields...

$$\frac{200}{2} = \sqrt{\left(\frac{8.15 \times 10^6/d^3}{2}\right)^2 + \left(\frac{10.20 \times 10^5}{d^3}\right)^2}$$

$$10000 = \frac{1.78 \times 10^{13}}{d^6}$$

$\therefore \qquad d = 34.77 \text{ mm} \approx 40 \text{ mm}$

30. **A round bar is subjected to the following variable loads: Torque varying from 2 kN·m to 5 kN·m, bending moment varying from 10 kN·m to 12 kN·m. Calculate the size of the bar if it is made of C40 steel. Adopt a factor of safety of 2.5 on yield stress for shear.**

VTU – July/ Aug. 2004 – 15 Marks

Solution: Bending moment: $M_{max} = 12 \times 10^6$ N·mm, $M_{min} = 10 \times 10^6$ N·mm; Torsional moment: $T_{max} = 5 \times 10^6$ N·mm, $T_{min} = 2 \times 10^6$ N·mm; $d = ?$, $n = 2.5$, Material: C40.

For C40 steel, $\sigma_u = (570 \text{ to } 667) = 600$ MPa, $\sigma_{yp} = 324$ MPa $\quad$ **... Tb 1.8/ Pg 464, DHB**

> **Hint:** As per **Appendix 1.8/Pg 464, DHB**, for C40 steel, $\sigma_u = (570 \text{ to } 667)$ MPa, $\sigma_{yp} = 324$ MPa. If σ_u is taken as 600 MPa, then $\sigma_{en} = 0.5\sigma_u = 330$ MPa, which is close to σ_{yp} and thus there would be no effect of σ_{yp} and σ_{en} in the problem. Hence students are requested to take a value close to the lower value in the given range, say $\sigma_u = 590$ MPa or 600 MPa.

We know that equivalent maximum shear stress,

$$(\tau_{eq})_{max} = \frac{\tau_{yp}}{\sigma_n} = \sqrt{\left(\frac{\sigma_{eq-n}}{2}\right)^2 + (\tau_{eq})^2} \qquad \text{... Eq. (i) 2.23(a)/ Pg 26, DHB}$$

Bending load:

Equivalent normal stress

$$\sigma_{eq-n} = \sigma_m + \left(\frac{\sigma_{yp}}{\sigma_{en}}\right) \frac{K_{tf} \cdot \sigma_a}{ABC} \qquad \text{... Eq. (ii) } \textbf{2.22(a)/ Pg 26, DHB}$$

- Mean stress $\qquad \sigma_m = \dfrac{\sigma_{max} + \sigma_{min}}{2} = \dfrac{M_m}{Z}$ **2.16(a)/ Pg 23, DHB**

  But $\qquad M_m = \dfrac{M_{max} + M_{min}}{2}$ and $M_a = \dfrac{M_{max} - M_{min}}{2}$

  $$\sigma_m = \frac{M_{max} + M_{min}}{2Z} = \frac{12 \times 10^6 + 10 \times 10^6}{2(\pi d^3/32)} = \frac{112.05 \times 10^6}{d^3}$$

- Variable or alternating stress,

  $$\sigma_a = \frac{\sigma_{max} - \sigma_{min}}{2} = \frac{M_a}{Z} \qquad \text{... } \textbf{2.16(b)/ Pg 23, DHB}$$

  $$\sigma_a = \frac{M_{max} - M_{min}}{2Z} = \frac{12 \times 10^6 - 10 \times 10^6}{2(\pi d^3/32)} = \frac{10.18 \times 10^6}{d^3}$$

- Also $\qquad K_{tf} = 1 + q(K_t - 1) \qquad \text{...} \textbf{2.5/ Pg 21, DHB}$

  since the cross-section is uniform, $K_t = 1$ and $q = 0$

  $\therefore \qquad K_{tf} = 1$

- *Correction factors*:

  Load factor $\;A = 1$, for reversed bending load $\qquad\qquad$ **... Pg 25, DHB**

  $\qquad\qquad = 0.55$ for reversed torsional load

  $\qquad B = 0.85$, assumed since diameter is unknown

  $\qquad C = 0.87$, based on $\sigma_u = 600$ MPa ... **Fig. 2.33 (curve c)/Pg 46, DHB**

- Endurance strength,

  $\qquad \sigma_{en} = 0.5\sigma_u \qquad\qquad\qquad\qquad\qquad$ **... 2.13(a)/Pg. 23, DHB**

  $\qquad \sigma_{en} = 0.5 \times 600 = 300$ MPa

  $\therefore$ Eq. (ii) yields...

  $$\sigma_{eq-n} = \frac{112.05 \times 10^6}{d^3} + \left(\frac{324}{300}\right) \frac{1 \times 10.18 \times 10^6}{(1 \times 0.85 \times 0.87)d^3} = \frac{126.9 \times 10^6}{d^3}$$

Torsional load: Equivalent shear stress,

$$\tau_{eq} = \tau_m + \left(\frac{\tau_{yp}}{\sigma_{en}}\right) \frac{K_{sf} \cdot \tau_a}{ABC} \qquad \text{...Eq. (iii) } \textbf{2.22(b)/Pg. 26, DHB}$$

- Mean stress $\qquad \tau_m = \dfrac{\tau_{max} + \tau_{min}}{2} = \dfrac{T_m}{Z_p} \qquad$ **... 2.16(a)/ Pg 23, DHB**

  But $\qquad T_m = \dfrac{T_{max} + T_{min}}{2}$ and $T_a = \dfrac{T_{max} - T_{min}}{2}$

  $$\tau_m = \frac{T_{max} + T_{min}}{2Z_p} = \frac{5 \times 10^6 + 2 \times 10^6}{2(\pi d^3/16)} = \frac{17.83 \times 10^6}{d^3}$$

- Variable stress,

$$\tau_a = \frac{\tau_{max} - \tau_{min}}{2} = \frac{T_a}{Z_p} \qquad \text{... 2.16(b)/ Pg 23, DHB}$$

$$\tau_a = \frac{T_{max} - T_{min}}{2Z} = \frac{5 \times 10^6 - 2 \times 10^6}{2(\pi d^3/16)} = \frac{7.64 \times 10^6}{d^3}$$

- Also $\qquad K_{sf} = 1 + q(K_s - 1) \qquad \qquad \text{...2.5/ Pg 21, DHB}$

  Since the cross-section is uniform, $K_s = 1$ and $q = 0$

  $\therefore \qquad K_{sf} = 1$

- Yield strength in shear,

$$\tau_{yp} = 0.5\sigma_{yp} \qquad \qquad (\because \tau = 0.5\sigma)$$

$$\tau_{yp} = 0.5 \times 324 = 162 \text{ MPa}$$

$\therefore$ Eq. (iii) yields...

$$\tau_{eq} = \frac{17.83 \times 10^6}{d^3} + \left(\frac{162}{300}\right)\frac{1 \times 7.64 \times 10^6}{(0.55 \times 0.85 \times 0.87)d^3} = \frac{27.97 \times 10^6}{d^3}$$

$\therefore$ Eq. (i) yields...

$$\frac{162}{2.5} = \sqrt{\left(\frac{126.9 \times 10^6/d^3}{2}\right)^2 + \left(\frac{25.97 \times 10^6}{d^3}\right)^2}$$

$$4.20 \times 10^3 = \frac{4.81 \times 10^{15}}{d^6}$$

$$d = 102.28 \text{ mm} \approx 105 \text{ mm}$$

31. **Determine the diameters of a hollow rod to sustain a twisting moment that fluctuates between 2.5 kN·m and 1.5 kN·m together with a bending moment that fluctuates between +2 kN·m and –2 kN·m. Assume the inner diameter to be 0.6 times the outer diameter. Select a suitable material and assume an appropriate value for factor of safety.**

VTU – July/ Aug. 2004 – 14 Marks

Solution: Torsional moment: $T_{max} = 2.5 \times 10^6$ N·mm, $T_{min} = 1.5 \times 10^6$ N·mm; Bending moment: $M_{max} = 2 \times 10^6$ N·mm, $M_{min} = -2 \times 10^6$ N·mm; $d_i = 0.6d_o$. Assume C40 steel and FoS = 2.

For C40 steel, $\sigma_u = (570 \text{ to } 667) = 600$ MPa, $\sigma_{yp} = 324$ MPa **... Tb 1.8/ Pg 464, DHB**

We know that equivalent maximum shear stress,

$$\tau_{eq})_{max} = \frac{\tau_{yp}}{\sigma_n} = \sqrt{\left(\frac{\sigma_{eq-n}}{2}\right)^2 + (\tau_{eq})^2} \qquad \text{... Eq. (i) 2.23(a)/ Pg 26, DHB}$$

Bending load:

- Equivalent normal stress

$$\sigma_{eq-n} = \sigma_m + \left(\frac{\sigma_{yp}}{\sigma_{en}}\right)\frac{K_{tf} \cdot \sigma_a}{ABC} \qquad \text{... Eq. (ii) 2.22(a)/ Pg 26, DHB}$$

- Mean stress $\qquad \sigma_m = \frac{\sigma_{max} + \sigma_{min}}{2} = \frac{M_m}{Z} \qquad \text{... 2.16(a)/ Pg 23, DHB}$

But $\qquad M_m = \dfrac{M_{max} + M_{min}}{2}$ and $M_a = \dfrac{M_{max} - M_{min}}{2}$

$$\sigma_m = \frac{M_{max} + M_{min}}{2Z} = \frac{2 \times 10^6 - 2 \times 10^6}{2[\pi(d_o^4 - d_i^4)/32d_o]} = 0$$

- Variable or alternating stress,

$$\sigma_a = \frac{\sigma_{max} - \sigma_{min}}{2} = \frac{M_a}{Z} \qquad \text{... } \textbf{2.16(b)/ Pg 23, DHB}$$

$$\sigma_a = \frac{M_{max} - M_{min}}{2Z} = \frac{2 \times 10^6 + 2 \times 10^6}{2[\pi(d_o^4 - d_i^4)/32d_o]}$$

$$= \frac{4 \times 10^6}{2[\pi(d_o^4 - (0.6d_o)^4)/32d_o]} = \frac{23.41 \times 10^6}{d_o^3}$$

- Also $\qquad K_{tf} = 1 + q(K_t - 1)$ $\qquad\qquad$ **...2.5/ Pg 21, DHB**

Since the cross-section is uniform, $K_t = 1$ and $q = 0$

$\therefore \qquad\qquad K_{tf} = 1$

- *Correction factors*:

Load factor $\;A = 1$, for reversed bending load $\qquad$ **... Pg 25, DHB**

$\qquad\qquad\quad = 0.55$ for reversed torsional load

$\qquad\qquad B = 0.85$, assumed since diameter is unknown

$\qquad\qquad C = 0.87$, based on $\sigma_u = 600$ MPa ... **Fig. 2.33 (curve c)/Pg 46, DHB**

- Endurance strength,

$$\sigma_{en} = 0.5\sigma_u \qquad\qquad\qquad \text{... } \textbf{2.13(a)/Pg. 23, DHB}$$

$$\sigma_{en} = 0.5 \times 600 = 300 \text{ MPa}$$

$\therefore$ Eq. (ii) yields...

$$\sigma_{eq-n} = 0 + \left(\frac{324}{300}\right) \frac{1 \times 23.41 \times 10^6}{(1 \times 0.85 \times 0.87)d_o^3} = \frac{34.18 \times 10^6}{d_o^3}$$

Torsional load: Equivalent shear stress,

$$\tau_{eq} = \tau_m + \left(\frac{\tau_{yp}}{\sigma_{en}}\right) \frac{K_{sf} \cdot \tau_a}{ABC} \qquad \text{...Eq. (iii) } \textbf{2.22(b)/Pg. 26, DHB}$$

- Mean stress $\qquad \tau_m = \dfrac{\tau_{max} + \tau_{min}}{2} = \dfrac{T_m}{Z_p}$ $\qquad$ **... 2.16(a)/ Pg 23, DHB**

But $\qquad T_m = \dfrac{T_{max} + T_{min}}{2}$ and $T_a = \dfrac{T_{max} - T_{min}}{2}$

$$\tau_m = \frac{T_{max} + T_{min}}{2Z_p} = \frac{2.5 \times 10^6 + 1.5 \times 10^6}{2[\pi(d_o^4 - d_i^4)/16d_o]}$$

$$= \frac{4 \times 10^6}{2[\pi(d_o^4 - (0.6d_o)^4)/16d_o]} = \frac{11.70 \times 10^6}{d_o^3}$$

- Variable stress,

$$\tau_a = \frac{\tau_{max} - \tau_{min}}{2} = \frac{T_a}{Z_P} \qquad\qquad \text{... 2.16(b)/ Pg 23, DHB}$$

$$\tau_a = \frac{T_{max} + T_{min}}{2Z_P} = \frac{2.5 \times 10^6 - 1.5 \times 10^6}{2(\pi(d_o^4 - d_i^4)/16d_o)}$$

$$= \frac{1 \times 10^6}{2(\pi(d_o^4 - 0.6d_o)^4/16d_o)} = \frac{2.92 \times 10^6}{d_o^3}$$

- Also $\qquad\qquad K_{sf} = 1 + q(K_s - 1) \qquad\qquad$ ...2.5/ Pg 21, DHB

  Since the cross-section is uniform, $K_s = 1$ and $q = 0$

  $\therefore \qquad\qquad K_{sf} = 1$

- Yield strength in shear,

$$\tau_{yP} = 0.5\sigma_{yP} \qquad\qquad (\because \tau = 0.5\sigma)$$

$$\tau_{yP} = 0.5 \times 324 = 162\ \text{MPa}$$

$\therefore$ Eq. (iii) yields...

$$\tau_{eq} = \frac{11.70 \times 10^6}{d_0^3} + \left(\frac{162}{300}\right)\frac{1 \times 2.92 \times 10^6}{(0.55 \times 0.85 \times 0.87)d_o^3} = \frac{15.58 \times 10^6}{d_o^3}$$

$\therefore$ Eq. (i) yields...

$$\frac{162}{2} = \sqrt{\left(\frac{34.18 \times 10^6/d_o^3}{2}\right)^2 + \left(\frac{15.58 \times 10^6}{d_o^3}\right)^2}$$

$$6561 = \frac{5.35 \times 10^{14}}{d_o^6}$$

$$d_o = 65.84\ \text{mm} \approx 70\ \text{mm and } d_i = 0.6 \times 70 = 42\ \text{mm}$$

32. **A round bar of diameter 1.2*d* has a semicircular groove of diameter 2*d*. This rod is to sustain a twisting moment that fluctuates between 2.5 kN·m and 1.5 kN·m together with a bending moment that fluctuates between 1 kN·m and –1 kN·m. Selecting carbon steel C30 as material for the road and choosing 2.5 as a value for factor of safety, determine the safe value of *d*.**

VTU – July/ Aug. 2004 – 14 Marks

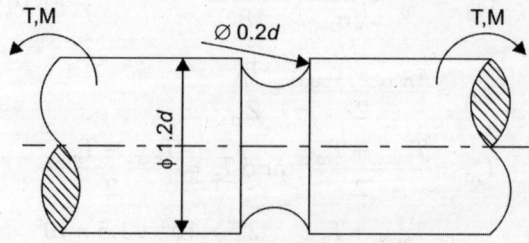

Fig. 3.21: Problem 32

Solution: Twisting moment: $T_{max} = 2.5 \times 10^6$ N·mm, $T_{min} = 1.5 \times 10^3$ N·mm; Bending moment: $M_{max} = 1 \times 10^6$ N·mm, $M_{min} = -1 \times 10^6$ N·mm; $d = ?$, $n = 2.5$. Material: C30.

As per the given data, the part/specimen is shown in **Fig. 3.21.**

For C30 steel, $\sigma_u = (490 \text{ to } 558) = 540$ MPa, $\sigma_{yp} = 294$ MPa.   ... **Tb 1.8/ Pg 463, DHB**

We know that equivalent maximum shear stress,

$$\tau_{eq})_{max} = \frac{\tau_{yp}}{\sigma_n} = \sqrt{\left(\frac{\sigma_{eq-n}}{2}\right)^2 + (\tau_{eq})^2} \quad \text{... Eq. (i) } \textbf{2.23(a)/ Pg 26, DHB}$$

Bending load:

Equivalent normal stress

$$\sigma_{eq-n} = \sigma_m + \left(\frac{\sigma_{yp}}{\sigma_{en}}\right)\frac{K_{tf} \cdot \sigma_a}{ABC} \quad \text{... Eq. (ii) } \textbf{2.22(a)/ Pg 26, DHB}$$

- Mean stress $\sigma_m = \dfrac{\sigma_{max} + \sigma_{min}}{2} = \dfrac{M_m}{Z}$ **2.16(a)/ Pg 23, DHB**

But $M_m = \dfrac{M_{max} + M_{min}}{2}$ and $M_a = \dfrac{M_{max} - M_{min}}{2}$

$$\sigma_m = \frac{M_{max} + M_{min}}{2Z} = \frac{1 \times 10^6 - 1 \times 10^6}{2(\pi d^3/32)} = 0$$

- Variable or alternating stress,

$$\sigma_a = \frac{\sigma_{max} - \sigma_{min}}{2} = \frac{M_a}{Z} \quad \text{... } \textbf{2.16(b)/ Pg 23, DHB}$$

$$\sigma_a = \frac{M_{max} - M_{min}}{2Z} = \frac{1 \times 10^6 + 1 \times 10^6}{2(\pi d^3/32)} = \frac{10.18 \times 10^6}{d^3}$$

- Also $K_{tf} = 1 + q(K_t - 1)$ **...2.5/ Pg 21, DHB**

Referring the given problem to **Fig. 2.20 and 2.22/Pg 40 and 41, DHB**, we have

$$D = 1.2d, r = 0.1d, d = d$$

Now $\dfrac{r}{d} = \dfrac{0.1d}{d} = 0.1$; and $\dfrac{D}{d} = \dfrac{1.2d}{d} = 1.2$

At $\dfrac{r}{d} = 0.1$ and $\dfrac{D}{d} = 1.2$, $K_t = 1.88$ **...Fig. 2.20/ Pg 40, DHB**

$$K_s = 1.52 \quad \textbf{...Fig. 2.21/ Pg 41, DHB}$$

Since q is based on notch radius (r) which is unknown in this problem, assume $q = 1$

∴ Eq. (iii) yields...

$$K_{tf} = 1 + 1(1.88 - 1) = 1.88$$

- *Correction factors*:

Load factor $A = 1$, for reversed bending load

$= 0.55$, for reversed torsional load   **... Pg 25, DHB**

$B = 0.85$, assumed since diameter is unknown

$C = 0.87$, based on $\sigma_u = 540$ MPa... **Fig. 2.33 (curve c)/Pg 46, DHB**

- Endurance strength,

$$\sigma_{en} = 0.5\sigma_u \quad \text{... } \textbf{2.13(a)/Pg. 23, DHB}$$

$$\sigma_{en} = 0.5 \times 540 = 270 \text{ MPa}$$

∴ Eq. (ii) yields...

$$\sigma_{eq-n} = 0 + \left(\frac{294}{270}\right) \frac{1.88 \times 10.18 \times 10^6}{(1 \times 0.85 \times 0.86)d^3} = \frac{28.51 \times 10^6}{d^3}$$

Torsional load: Equivalent shear stress,

$$\tau_{eq} = \tau_m + \left(\frac{\tau_{yp}}{\sigma_{en}}\right) \frac{K_{sf} \cdot \tau_a}{ABC} \qquad \text{...Eq. (iv) \textbf{2.22(b)/Pg. 26, DHB}}$$

- Mean stress $\quad \tau_m = \dfrac{\tau_{max} + \tau_{min}}{2} = \dfrac{T_m}{Z_p} \qquad \text{... \textbf{2.16(a)/ Pg 23, DHB}}$

  But $\qquad T_m = \dfrac{T_{max} + T_{min}}{2}$ and $T_a = \dfrac{T_{max} - T_{min}}{2}$

  $$\tau_m = \frac{T_{max} + T_{min}}{2Z_p} = \frac{2.5 \times 10^6 + 1.5 \times 10^6}{2(\pi d^3/16)} = \frac{10.18 \times 10^6}{d^3}$$

- Variable stress,

  $$\tau_a = \frac{\tau_{max} - \tau_{min}}{2} = \frac{T_a}{Z_p} \qquad \text{... \textbf{2.16(b)/ Pg 23, DHB}}$$

  $$\tau_a = \frac{T_{max} - T_{min}}{2Z_p} = \frac{2.5 \times 10^6 - 1.5 \times 10^6}{2(\pi d^3/16)} = \frac{2.55 \times 10^6}{d^3}$$

- Also $\qquad K_{sf} = 1 + q(K_s - 1) \qquad\qquad \text{...\textbf{2.7/ Pg 21, DHB}}$

  ∴ $\qquad\qquad K_{sf} = 1 + 1(1.52 - 1) = 1.52$

- Yield strength in shear,

  $$\tau_{yp} = 0.5\sigma_{yp} \qquad\qquad (\because \tau = 0.5\sigma)$$

  $$\tau_{yp} = 0.5 \times 294 = 147 \text{ MPa}$$

∴ Eq. (iv) yields...

$$\tau_{eq} = \frac{10.18 \times 10^6}{d^3} + \left(\frac{147}{270}\right) \frac{1.52 \times 2.55 \times 10^6}{(0.55 \times 0.85 \times 0.86)d^3} = \frac{15.43 \times 10^6}{d^3}$$

∴ Eq. (i) yields...

$$\frac{147}{2.5} = \sqrt{\left(\frac{28.51 \times 10^6/d^3}{2}\right)^2 + \left(\frac{15.43 \times 10^6}{d^3}\right)^2}$$

$$3457.44 = \frac{4.41 \times 10^{14}}{d^6}$$

∴ $\qquad\qquad d_o = 70.96 \text{ mm} \approx 75 \text{ mm}$

PROBLEM ON TORSIONAL AND AXIAL LOADS

33. **A hot rolled steel shaft is subjected to a torsional load that varies from 330 N·m (clockwise) to 110 N·m (counterclockwise) and at the same time it is subjected to an axial load that varies from +1000 N to −500 N. The shaft is of uniform cross-section and no key way is present at the critical section. Determine the required shaft diameter. The material has an ultimate tensile strength of 550 MPa and yield strength of 410 MPa. Take the endurance limit as half of the ultimate strength, factor of safety = 2, size factor = 0.85 and a surface finish factor = 0.62.**

Solution: Torsional moment: $T_{max} = 330 \times 10^3$ N·mm, $T_{min} = -110 \times 10^3$ N·mm; Axial load: $F_{max} = 1000$ N, $F_{min} = -500$ N; $K_t = K_s = 1$, $d = ?$, $\sigma_u = 550$ MPa, $\sigma_{yp} = 410$ MPa, $\sigma_{en} = 0.5\sigma_u = 275$ MPa, $n = 2$, $B = 0.85$, $C = 0.62$.

We know that equivalent maximum shear stress,

$$\tau_{eq})_{max} = \frac{\tau_{yp}}{\sigma_n} = \sqrt{\left(\frac{\sigma_{eq-n}}{2}\right)^2 + (\tau_{eq})^2} \quad \dots \text{Eq. (i) } \mathbf{2.23(a)/ Pg\ 26, DHB}$$

Axial load:

Equivalent normal stress

$$\sigma_{eq-n} = \sigma_m + \left(\frac{\sigma_{yp}}{\sigma_{en}}\right)\frac{K_{tf}\cdot\sigma_a}{ABC} \quad \dots \text{Eq. (ii) } \mathbf{2.22(a)/ Pg\ 26, DHB}$$

- Mean stress $\quad \sigma_m = \dfrac{\sigma_{max} + \sigma_{min}}{2} = \dfrac{F_m}{A} \quad \dots \mathbf{2.16(a)/ Pg\ 23, DHB}$

But $\quad F_m = \dfrac{F_{max} + F_{min}}{2}$ and $F_a = \dfrac{F_{max} - F_{min}}{2} \quad \dots \mathbf{2.17(a)/ Pg\ 24, DHB}$

$$\sigma_m = \frac{F_{max} + F_{min}}{2A} = \frac{1000 - 500}{2(\pi d^2/4)} = \frac{318.31}{d^2}$$

- Variable or alternating stress,

$$\sigma_a = \frac{\sigma_{max} - \sigma_{min}}{2} = \frac{F_a}{A} \quad \dots \mathbf{2.16(b)/ Pg\ 23, DHB}$$

$$\sigma_a = \frac{F_{max} - F_{min}}{2A} = \frac{1000 + 500}{2(\pi d^2/4)} = \frac{955}{d^2}$$

- Also $\quad K_{tf} = 1 + q(K_t - 1) \quad \dots \mathbf{2.5/ Pg\ 21, DHB}$

Since the cross-section is uniform, $K_t = 1$ and $q = 0$

$\therefore \quad K_{tf} = 1$

- *Correction factors*:
Load factor $A = 0.85$ (average) for reversed axial load
$\quad\quad = 0.55$ for reversed torsional load $\quad \dots \mathbf{Pg\ 25, DHB}$
$B = 0.85$, $C = 0.62$ (data)

$\therefore$ Eq. (ii) yields...

$$\sigma_{eq-n} = \frac{318.31}{d^2} + \left(\frac{410}{275}\right)\frac{1 \times 955}{(0.85 \times 0.85 \times 0.62)d^2} = \frac{3496.83}{d^2}$$

Torsional load: Equivalent shear stress,

$$\tau_{eq} = \tau_m + \left(\frac{\tau_{yp}}{\sigma_{en}}\right)\frac{K_{sf}\cdot\tau_a}{ABC} \quad \dots\text{Eq. (iii) } \mathbf{2.22(b)/Pg.\ 26, DHB}$$

- Mean stress $\quad \tau_m = \dfrac{\tau_{max} + \tau_{min}}{2} = \dfrac{T_m}{Z_p} \quad \dots \mathbf{2.16(a)/ Pg\ 23, DHB}$

But $T_m = \dfrac{T_{max} + T_{min}}{2}$ and $T_a = \dfrac{T_{max} - T_{min}}{2}$

$$\tau_m = \frac{T_{max} + T_{min}}{2Z_p} = \frac{330 \times 10^3 - 110 \times 10^3}{2(\pi d^3/16)} = \frac{0.56 \times 10^6}{d^3}$$

- Variable stress,

$$\tau_a = \frac{\tau_{max} - \tau_{min}}{2} = \frac{T_a}{Z_p} \qquad \text{... 2.16(b)/ Pg 23, DHB}$$

$$\tau_a = \frac{T_{max} - T_{min}}{2Z_p} = \frac{330 \times 10^6 + 110 \times 10^6}{2(\pi d^3/16)} = \frac{1.12 \times 10^6}{d^3}$$

- Also $\qquad K_{sf} = 1 + q(K_s - 1) \qquad$ ...2.7/ Pg 21, DHB

Since the cross-section is uniform, $K_s = 1$ and $q = 0$

$\therefore \qquad K_{sf} = 1$

- Yield strength in shear,

$$\tau_{yp} = 0.5\sigma_{yp} \qquad (\because \tau = 0.5\sigma)$$

$$\tau_{yp} = 0.5 \times 410 = 205 \text{ MPa}$$

$\therefore$ Eq. (iii) yields...

$$\tau_{eq} = \frac{0.56 \times 10^6}{d^3} + \left(\frac{205}{275}\right) \frac{1 \times 1.12 \times 10^6}{(0.55 \times 0.85 \times 0.62)d^3} = \frac{3.44 \times 10^6}{d^3}$$

$\therefore$ Eq. (i) yields...

$$\frac{205}{2} = \sqrt{\left(\frac{3496.83/d^2}{2}\right)^2 + \left(\frac{3.44 \times 10^6}{d^3}\right)^2}$$

$$10.51 \times 10^3 = \frac{3.06 \times 10^6}{d^4} + \frac{1.18 \times 10^{13}}{d^6}$$

i.e. $10.51 \times 10^3 d^6 - 3.06 \times 10^6 d^2 - 1.18 \times 10^{13} = 0$

$$d = 32.24 \text{ mm} \approx 35 \text{ mm}$$

34. **A steel member of circular cross-section is subjected to a torsional stress that varies from 0 to 35 MPa and at the same time it is subjected to an axial stress that varies from −14 MPa to +28 MPa. Neglecting stress concentration and column effect and assuming that the maximum stresses in torsion and axial load occur at the same time, determine:**
    i. **The maximum equivalent shear stress**
    ii. **The design factor of safety based on yield in shear.**

    The material has an endurance limit $\sigma_{-1} = 206$ MPa, and a yield strength of $\sigma_y = 480$ MPa. The diameter of the member is less than 12 mm. Take load concentration factor = 1. Surface finish factor = 1.

    VTU – Mar. 2001 – 10 Marks; Dec. 2011 – 15 Marks

Solution: $\tau_{max} = 35$ MPa, $\tau_{min} = 0$ MPa, $\sigma_{max} = 28$ MPa, $\sigma_{min} = -14$ MPa, $K_t = K_s = 1$, $d = 12$ mm, $\sigma_{yp} = 480$ MPa, $\sigma_{en} = 206$ MPa, $A = 1$, $C = 1$, $(\tau_{eq})_{max} = ?$, $n = ?$

i. To find $\tau_{eq})_{max}$: We know that equivalent maximum shear stress,

$$\tau_{eq})_{max} = \frac{\tau_{yp}}{\sigma_n} = \sqrt{\left(\frac{\sigma_{eq-n}}{2}\right)^2 + (\tau_{eq})^2} \quad \text{... Eq. (i) 2.23(a)/ Pg 26, DHB}$$

Axial load:

Equivalent normal stress

$$\sigma_{eq-n} = \sigma_m + \left(\frac{\sigma_{yp}}{\sigma_{en}}\right)\frac{K_{tf}\cdot\sigma_a}{ABC} \quad \text{... Eq. (ii) 2.22(a)/ Pg 26, DHB}$$

- Mean or average stress

$$\sigma_m = \frac{\sigma_{max} + \sigma_{min}}{2} = \frac{28 - 14}{2} = 7\text{ MPa} \quad \text{... 2.16(a)/ Pg 23, DHB}$$

- Variable or alternating stress,

$$\sigma_a = \frac{\sigma_{max} - \sigma_{min}}{2} = \frac{28 + 14}{2} = 21\text{ MPa} \quad \text{... 2.16(b)/ Pg 23, DHB}$$

- Also $\qquad K_{tf} = 1 + q(K_t - 1)$ $\qquad$ ...2.5/ Pg 21, DHB

  Since the cross-section is uniform, $K_t = 1$ and $q = 0$

  $\therefore \qquad\qquad K_{tf} = 1$

- *Correction factors:*

  Load factor $A = 1$, for reversed axial load

  $\qquad\qquad = 1$, for reversed torsional load $\qquad$ **... Pg 25, DHB**

  $\qquad B = 0.85$, assumed since $d < 12$ mm

  $\qquad C = 1$ (data)

  $\therefore$ Eq. (ii) yields...

$$\sigma_{eq-n} = 7 + \left(\frac{480}{206}\right)\frac{1 \times 21}{(1 \times 0.85 \times 1)} = 64.57\text{ MPa}$$

Torsional load: Equivalent shear stress,

$$\tau_{eq} = \tau_m + \left(\frac{\tau_{yp}}{\sigma_{en}}\right)\frac{K_{sf}\cdot\tau_a}{ABC} \quad \text{...Eq. (iii) 2.22(b)/Pg. 26, DHB}$$

- Mean stress $\qquad \tau_m = \dfrac{\tau_{max} + \tau_{min}}{2} = \dfrac{35 + 0}{2} = 17.5\text{ MPa} \quad$ **... 2.16(a)/ Pg 23, DHB**

- Variable stress, $\tau_a = \dfrac{\tau_{max} - \tau_{min}}{2} = \dfrac{35 - 0}{2} = 17.5\text{ MPa} \quad$ **... 2.16(b)/ Pg 23, DHB**

- Also $\qquad K_{sf} = 1 + q(K_s - 1)$ $\qquad$ ...2.7/ Pg 21, DHB

  Since the cross-section is uniform, $K_s = 1$ and $q = 0$

  $\therefore \qquad\qquad K_{sf} = 1$

- Yield strength in shear,

  $$\tau_{yp} = 0.5\sigma_{yp} \qquad\qquad (\because \tau = 0.5\sigma)$$
  $$\tau_{yp} = 0.5 \times 480 = 240\text{ MPa}$$

$\therefore$ Eq. (iii) yields...

$$\tau_{eq} = 17.5 + \left(\frac{240}{206}\right)\frac{1 \times 17.5}{(1 \times 0.85 \times 1)} = 41.49\text{ MPa}$$

∴ Eq. (i) yields...

$$\tau_{eq})_{max} = \sqrt{\left(\frac{64.57}{2}\right)^2 + (41.49)^2} = 52.56 \text{ MPa}$$

ii. To find _n_: We know that

$$\tau_{eq})_{max} = \frac{\tau_{yp}}{n}$$

$$52.56 = \frac{240}{n}$$

∴ $n = 4.57$

35. **A cast iron shaft with an ultimate tensile strength of 180 MPa is subjected to a torsional load which is completely reversal. The load is to be applied at indefinite number of cycles. The shaft is 50 mm diameter and is joined with 75 mm diameter shaft with a fillet radius of 12.5 mm. Using factor of safety of 2, what is the maximum torque that can be applied to the shaft? Take surface factor = 0.75, size factor = 0.85 and load factor = 1.**

VTU – June/ July 2013 – 12 Marks

Solution: $\sigma_u = 180$ MPa, $d = 50$ mm, $T_{max} = T$, $T_{min} = -T$, $n = 2$, $T = ?$, $C = 0.75$, $B = 0.85$, $A = 1$.

For brittle materials, the equivalent normal stress is

$$\sigma_{eq-n})_{max} = \frac{\sigma_{yp}}{n} = \left(\frac{\sigma_{eq-n}}{2}\right) + \sqrt{\left(\frac{\sigma_{eq-n}}{2}\right)^2 + (\tau_{eq})^2}$$

... **2.23(b)/ Pg 26, DHB**

Here $\sigma_{eq-n} = 0$, since there are no normal (axial/bending) components in the problem. Thus, the above equation reduces to the form,

$$\frac{\sigma_{yp}}{n} = \tau_{eq}$$

But equivalent shear stress,

$$\tau_{eq} = \tau_m + \left(\frac{\tau_{yp}}{\sigma_{en}}\right)\frac{K_{sf} \cdot \tau_a}{ABC} \qquad \text{... Eq. (ii) } \textbf{2.22(b)/ Pg 26, DHB}$$

- **Mean stress** $\tau_m = \dfrac{\tau_{max} + \tau_{min}}{2} = \dfrac{T_m}{Z_p}$ **2.16(a)/ Pg 23, DHB**

  But $T_m = \dfrac{T_{max} + T_{min}}{2}$ and $T_a = \dfrac{T_{max} + T_{min}}{2}$

  $$\tau_m = \frac{T_{max} + T_{min}}{2} = \frac{T - T}{2(\pi d^3/16)} = 0$$

- **Variable stress,** $\tau_a = \dfrac{\tau_{max} - \tau_{min}}{2} = \dfrac{T_a}{Z_p}$ ... **2.16(b)/ Pg 23, DHB**

  $$\tau_a = \frac{T_{max} - T_{min}}{2Z_p} = \frac{T + T}{2(\pi \times 50^3/16)} = 4.074 \times 10^{-5}\, T$$

- **Also** $K_{sf} = 1 + q(K_s - 1)$ ...Eq. (iii) **2.7/ Pg 21, DHB**

Referring the given problem to **Fig. 2.27/Pg 44, DHB**, we have

$$D = 75 \text{ mm}, d = 50 \text{ mm}, r = 12.5 \text{ mm}$$

Now $\qquad \dfrac{r}{d} = \dfrac{12.5}{50} = 0.25;$ and $\dfrac{D}{d} = \dfrac{75}{50} = 1.5$

At $\qquad \dfrac{r}{d} = 0.25$ and $\dfrac{D}{d} = 1.5, K_s = 1.25$

But the brittle materials, $q = 0$.

∴ Eq. (iii) yields...

$$K_{sf} = 1 + 0(1.25 - 1) = 1$$

- *Correction factors*:

$$A = 1, B = 0.85, C = 0.75 \text{ (data)}$$

- Endurance strength,

$$\sigma_{en} = 0.4\sigma_u, \text{ for cast iron} \qquad\qquad \text{... 2.13(b)/Pg. 23, DHB}$$

$$\sigma_{en} = 0.4 \times 180 = 72 \text{ MPa}$$

- Assuming yield strength in shear,

$$\tau_{yp} = 0.5\sigma_u \qquad\qquad (\because \tau = 0.5\sigma)$$

$$\tau_{yp} = 0.5 \times 180 = 90 \text{ MPa}$$

For cast iron, the yield strength in shear is usually taken equal to the yield strength in tension

i.e. $\qquad \tau_{yp} = \sigma_{yp} = 90 \text{ MPa}$

∴ Eq. (ii) yields...

$$\tau_{eq} = 0 + \left(\dfrac{90}{72}\right) \dfrac{1 \times 4.074 \times 10^{-5} T}{(1 \times 0.85 \times 0.75)} = 7.99 \times 10^{-5} T$$

∴ Eq. (i) yields...

$$\dfrac{90}{2} = 7.99 \times 10^{-5} T$$

∴ $\qquad\qquad T = 563.33 \times 10^3 \text{ N·mm} = 563.33 \text{ N·m}$

PROBLEM ON AXIAL, BENDING AND TORSIONAL LOADS

36. **A hot rolled steel shaft is subjected to a torsional load that varies from 330 N·m (clockwise) to 110 N·m (counterclockwise), a variable bending moment of 563 N·m to 1130 N·m and at the same time it is subjected to an axial load that varies from +1000 N to –500 N. The shaft is of uniform cross-section and no key way is present at the critical section. Determine the required shaft diameter. The material has an ultimate tensile strength of 550 MPa and yield strength of 470 MPa. Take the endurance limit as half of the ultimate strength, factor of safety = 2, size factor = 0.85 and a surface finish factor = 0.62.**

Solution: Let suffix '1' refer to axial load and suffix '2' refer to bending load.

Axial load: $F_{max})_1 = 1000 \text{ N}, F_{min})_1 = -500 \text{ N}$; Bending moment: $M_{max})_2 = 1130 \times 10^3$ N·mm, $M_{min})_2 = 565 \times 10^3$ N·mm; Torsional moment: $T_{max} = 300 \times 10^3$ N·mm, $F_{min} = -110 \times 10^3$ N·mm; $d = ?, K_{t1} = K_{t2} = K_s = 1, \sigma_u = 550$ MPa, $\sigma_{yp} = 470$ MPa, $n = 2$, $\sigma_{en} = 0.5\sigma_u = 275$ MPa, $B = 0.85, C = 0.62$.

We know that equivalent maximum shear stress,

$$\tau_{eq})_{max} = \frac{\tau_{yp}}{n} = \sqrt{\left(\frac{\sigma_{eq-n}}{2}\right)^2 + (\tau_{eq})^2} \quad \text{... Eq. (i) } \textbf{2.23(a)/ Pg 26, DHB}$$

Since the normal stress includes both axial and/or bending stresses, we have

$$\sigma_{eq-n})_T = \sigma_{eq-n})_{axial} + \sigma_{eq-n})_{bend} = \sigma_{eq-n})_1 + \sigma_{eq-n})_2 \quad \text{... Eq. (ii)}$$

Axial load: Equivalent normal stress

$$\sigma_{eq-n} = \sigma_m + \left(\frac{\sigma_{yp}}{\sigma_{en}}\right)\frac{K_{tf} \cdot \sigma_a}{ABC} \quad \text{...Eq. (iii) } \textbf{2.16(a)/ Pg 23, DHB}$$

- Mean or average stress

$$\sigma_m)_1 = \frac{\sigma_{max})_1 + \sigma_{min})_1}{2} \quad \text{... } \textbf{2.16(a)/ Pg 23, DHB}$$

$$\sigma_m)_1 = \frac{F_{max})_1 + F_{min})_1}{2A} = \frac{1000 - 500}{2(\pi d^2/4)} = \frac{318.31}{d^2}$$

- Variable or alternating stress,

$$\sigma_a)_1 = \frac{\sigma_{max})_1 - \sigma_{min})_1}{2} \quad \text{... } \textbf{2.16(b)/ Pg 23, DHB}$$

$$\sigma_a)_1 = \frac{F_{max})_1 - F_{min})_1}{2A} = \frac{1000 + 500}{2(\pi d^2/4)} = \frac{955}{d^2}$$

- Also $\qquad K_{tf1} = 1 + q(K_{t1} - 1) \qquad \text{...2.5/ Pg 21, DHB}$

  Since the cross-section is uniform, $K_{t1} = 1$ and $q = 0$

  $\therefore \qquad K_{tf1} = 1$

- *Correction factors*:

  Load factor $A = 0.85$ (average) for reversed axial load $\qquad$ **... Pg 25, DHB**

  $\qquad\qquad = 1$ for reversed bending load

  $\qquad\qquad = 0.55$ for torsional load

  $B = 0.85,$

  $C = 0.62$ (data)

$\therefore$ Eq. (i) yields...

$$\sigma_{eq-n})_1 = \frac{318.31}{d^2} + \left(\frac{470}{275}\right)\frac{1 \times 955}{(0.85 \times 0.85 \times 0.62)d^2} = \frac{3961.98}{d^2}$$

Bending loading:

- Mean or average stress

$$\sigma_m)_2 = \frac{\sigma_{max})_2 + \sigma_{min})_2}{2} \quad \text{... } \textbf{2.16(a)/ Pg 23, DHB}$$

$$\sigma_m)_2 = \frac{M_{max})_2 + M_{min})_2}{2Z} = \frac{1130 \times 10^3 + 565 \times 10^3}{2(\pi d^3/32)} = \frac{8.63 \times 10^6}{d^3}$$

- Variable or alternating stress,

$$\sigma_a)_2 = \frac{\sigma_{max})_2 - \sigma_{min})_2}{2} \quad \text{... } \textbf{2.16(b)/ Pg 23, DHB}$$

$$\sigma_a)_2 = \frac{M_{max})_2 - M_{min})_2}{2Z} = \frac{1130 \times 10^3 - 565 \times 10^3}{2(\pi d^3/32)} = \frac{2.88 \times 10^6}{d^3}$$

- Also $\qquad K_{tf2} = 1 + q(K_{t2} - 1)$ $\qquad\qquad$ ...2.5/ Pg 21, DHB

Since the cross-section is uniform $K_{t2} = 1$ and $q = 0$

$\therefore$ Eq. (iii) yields...

$$\sigma_{eq-n})_2 = \frac{8.63 \times 10^6}{d^3} + \left(\frac{470}{275}\right)\frac{1 \times 2.88 \times 10^6}{(1 \times 0.85 \times 0.62)d^3} = \frac{17.97 \times 10^6}{d^3}$$

$\therefore$ Eq. (ii) yields...

$$\sigma_{eq-n})_T = \frac{3961.98 \times 10^3}{d^2} + \frac{17.97 \times 10^6}{d^3} \qquad \text{... Eq. (iv)}$$

Torsional load: Equivalent shear stress,

$$\tau_{eq} = \tau_m + \left(\frac{\tau_{yp}}{\sigma_{en}}\right)\frac{K_{sf} \cdot \tau_a}{ABC} \qquad \text{...Eq. (v) 2.22(b)/Pg. 26, DHB}$$

- Mean stress $\qquad \tau_m = \dfrac{\tau_{max} + \tau_{min}}{2} = \dfrac{T_m}{Z_p}$ $\qquad$ ... 2.16(a)/ Pg 23, DHB

  But $\qquad T_m = \dfrac{T_{max} + T_{min}}{2}$ and $T_a = \dfrac{T_{max} - T_{min}}{2}$

  $$\tau_m = \frac{T_{max} + T_{min}}{2Z_p} = \frac{330 \times 10^3 - 110 \times 10^3}{2(\pi d^3/16)} = \frac{0.56 \times 10^6}{d^3}$$

- Variable stress,

  $$\tau_a = \frac{\tau_{max} - \tau_{min}}{2} = \frac{T_a}{Z_p} \qquad\qquad \text{... 2.16(b)/ Pg 23, DHB}$$

  $$\tau_a = \frac{T_{max} - T_{min}}{2Z_p} = \frac{330 \times 10^6 + 110 \times 10^6}{2(\pi d^3/16)} = \frac{1.12 \times 10^6}{d^3}$$

- Also $\qquad K_{sf} = 1 + q(K_s - 1)$ $\qquad\qquad$ ...2.7/ Pg 21, DHB

Since the cross-section is uniform, $K_s = 1$ and $q = 0$

$\therefore \qquad\qquad K_{sf} = 1$

- Yield strength in shear,

  $$\tau_{yp} = 0.5\sigma_{yp} \qquad\qquad (\because \tau = 0.5\sigma)$$

  $$\tau_{yp} = 0.5 \times 470 = 235 \text{ MPa}$$

$\therefore$ Eq. (v) yields...

$$\tau_{eq} = \frac{0.56 \times 10^6}{d^3} + \left(\frac{235}{275}\right)\frac{1 \times 1.12 \times 10^6}{(0.55 \times 0.85 \times 0.62)d^3} = \frac{3.86 \times 10^6}{d^3}$$

$\therefore$ Eq. (i) yields...

$$\left(\frac{235}{2}\right)^2 = \left[\frac{1}{2}\left(\frac{3961.98}{d^2} + \frac{17.97 \times 10^6}{d^3}\right)\right]^2 + \left(\frac{3.86 \times 10^6}{d^3}\right)^2$$

$$13.80 \times 10^3 = \frac{3.92 \times 10^6}{d^4} + \frac{8.07 \times 10^{13}}{d^6} + \frac{7.12 \times 10^{10}}{d^5} + \frac{1.49 \times 10^{13}}{d^6}$$

$$= \frac{3.92 \times 10^6}{d^4} + \frac{7.12 \times 10^{10}}{d^5} + \frac{9.56 \times 10^{13}}{d^6}$$

i.e. $13.80 \times 10^3 \, d^6 - 3.92 \times 10^6 \, d^2 - 7.12 \times 10^{10} \, d - 9.56 \times 10^{13} = 0$

$\therefore$ $d = 43.89 \text{ mm} \approx 45 \text{ mm}$

3.15 CUMULATIVE FATIGUE DAMAGE

The term "cumulative damage" refers to the fatigue effects of loading events other than constant amplitude cycles. Earlier fatigue tests on test specimens, components and structures were carried out using constant amplitude fatigue loading. However, many structures and components are subjected to *variable amplitude fatigue loading* or *variable amplitude loading*, with variations following either a regular or a random pattern. A variable amplitude load history is sometimes called a load spectrum. The term "spectrum" refers to a series of fatigue loading events other than uniformly repeated cycles.

Examples: Automotive suspension and aircraft structural components.

According to this theory, damage caused by 1 cycle is defined as

$$D = \frac{1}{N_f} \qquad \qquad \text{... (Eq. 3.29)}$$

where N_f = number of repetitions of same cycle that equals medial life to failure.

D = damage fraction

The damage produced by n such cycles is

$$nD = \frac{n}{N_f} \qquad \qquad \text{... (Eq. 3.30)}$$

Figures 3.22(a) and (b) represent two blocks of constant amplitude cycles and the corresponding *S–N* curve with fatigue life at stress amplitudes σ_{a1} and σ_{a2}, denoted by N_{f1} and N_{f2} respectively.

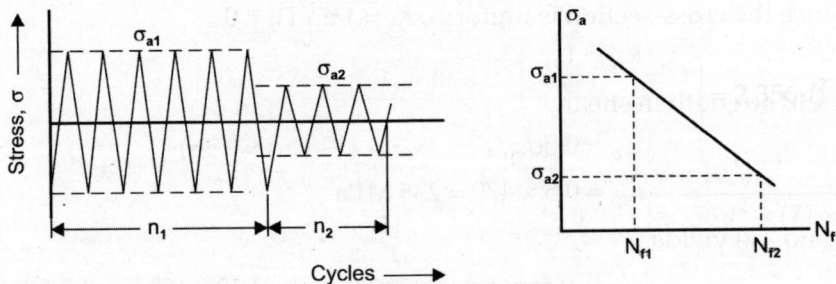

Fig. 3.22: a. Constant amplitude stress block, b. *S–N* curve

The damaging effect of n_1 cycles at σ_{a1} stress amplitude is

$$n_1 D_1 = \frac{n_1}{N_{f1}}$$

and damaging effect of cycles at σ_{a2} stress amplitude is

$$n_2 D_2 = \frac{n_2}{N_{f2}}$$

On similar lines, the cycle ratio of n_i cycles at σ_{ai} stress amplitude is

$$n_i D_i = \frac{n_i}{N_{fi}}$$

Failure is predicted when the sum of all ratios becomes 1 or 100%

i.e.
$$D = \sum\left(\frac{n_i}{N_{fi}}\right) = 1 \,(\text{or } 100\%)$$

or
$$\frac{n_1}{N_{f1}} + \frac{n_2}{N_{f2}} + \ldots = 1 \qquad \ldots \text{(Eq. 3.31)}$$

Equation 3.31 expresses the linear damage rule, proposed by Palmgren and later again by Miner. Thus, for any given arbitrary load sequence, failure is associated with the sum of cumulative fractional damage from successive load cycles attaining unity.

Limitations

- A major limitation of the Palmgren–Miner rule is that it does not consider sequence effects, i.e. the order of the loading makes no difference in this rule. Sequence effects are definitely observed in many cases.
- A second limitation is that the damage accumulation is independent of stress level.

37. **Tests show the median life of a certain model bearings operating at high frequency to be 2×10^8 cycles under 1 kN load and 3×10^7 cycles under 2 kN load. How many cycles can we expect the bearing to last if the load is 1 kN 90% of the time and 2 kN 10% of the time?**

    Solution: Number of cycles at 1 kN, $n_1 = 0.9n$, number of cycles at 2 kN, $n_2 = 0.1n$, $N_{f1} = 2 \times 10^8$ cycles, $N_{f2} = 3 \times 10^7$ cycles, $n = ?$
    We know that total damage,

    $$\frac{n_1}{N_{f1}} + \frac{n_2}{N_{f2}} = 1$$

    $$\frac{0.9n}{2 \times 10^8} + \frac{0.1n}{3 \times 10^7} = 1$$

    $$7.834 \times 10^{-9} n = 1$$

    $$n = 1.27 \times 10^8 \text{ cycles}$$

38. **A pressure vessel is made of aluminum alloy and operates in two states at 20 cycles per minute. It operates in the first state 60% of the time at a stress change of 10 MPa; the cycles to failure in this state are 1×10^6 cycles. In state 2 (40% of the time), a stress change of 16.5 MPa is exerted on the vessel, and the cycles to failure in state 2 is 2.15×10^5 to find the expected life in hours.**

    Solution: $n = 20$ cycles/min, $p_1 = 10.5$ MPa. Number of cycles at 10.5 MPa, $n_1 = 0.6n = 0.6 \times 20 = 12$ cycles/min, $N_{f1} = 1 \times 10^6$ cycles, $p_2 = 16.5$ MPa, number of cycles at 16.5 MPa, $n_2 = 0.4n = 0.4 \times 20 = 8$ cycles/min, $N_{f2} = 2.15 \times 10^5$ cycles.

We know damage caused by 1 cycle is defined as

$$D = \frac{1}{N_f} \qquad \qquad \qquad \text{...Eq. (i)}$$

But total damage $D = \dfrac{n_1}{N_{f1}} + \dfrac{n_2}{N_{f2}}$

$$= \frac{12}{1 \times 10^6} + \frac{8}{2.15 \times 10^5}$$

$$D = 4.921 \times 10^{-5} \text{ cycles/min} = 2.953 \times 10^{-3} \text{ cycles/hour}$$

∴ Eq. (i) yields... $N_f = \dfrac{1}{2.953 \times 10^{-3}} = 338.68 \text{ hours} \approx 340 \text{ hours}$

39. **A particular type of ball bearing operating at 3000 rpm has a rated life of 50000 hours, 6500 hours and 1000 hours respectively, when subjected to constant amplitude loads of 1 kN, 2 kN and 4 kN. During each hour of operation, the load is 4 kN for 5 min, 2 kN for 15 min and 1 kN for 40 min.**
    a. How many hours of operation do you expect the bearing to last?
    b. What percentage of damage is caused by each of the load levels?

Solution: Speed $N = 3000$ rpm, number of hours at 1 kN, $n_1 = (40/60)n = 0.667\, n$, $N_{f1} = 50000$ hours, number of hours at 2 kN, $n_2 = (15/60)n = 0.25\, n$, $N_{f2} = 6500$ hours, number of hours at 1 kN, $n_3 = (5/60)n = 0.0834n$, $N_{f3} = 1000$ hours.
a. $n = ?$ b. Percentage D in each load case.

a. To find n:

We know that total damage

$$\frac{n_1}{N_{f1}} + \frac{n_2}{N_{f2}} + \frac{n_3}{N_{f3}} = 1$$

$$\frac{0.6667\, n}{50000} + \frac{0.25\, n}{6500} + \frac{0.0834\, n}{1000} = 1$$

$$1.3520 \times 10^{-4}\, n = 1$$

$$n = 7396.70 \text{ hours} \; \therefore \; 7400 \text{ hours}$$

b. To find percentage damage:

We know damage caused by 1 cycle as

$$D = \frac{1}{N_f}$$

Hence for 1 kN, $D_1 = \dfrac{n_1}{N_{f1}} = \dfrac{0.6667 \times 7400}{50000} = 0.0987 = 98.7\%$

Hence for 2 kN, $D_2 = \dfrac{n_2}{N_{f2}} = \dfrac{0.25 \times 7400}{6500} = 0.2846 = 28.46\%$

Hence for 4 kN, $D_3 = \dfrac{n_3}{N_{f3}} = \dfrac{0.0834 \times 7400}{1000} = 0.6172 = 61.72\%$

Check:

$$D = \Sigma D_i = 1$$

i.e. $D_1 + D_2 + D_3 = 0.0987 + 0.2846 + 0.6172 = 1.000 = 100\%$

40. **A part with a machined surface is subjected to a reversed bending stress of 600 MPa for 10% of time, a reversed bending stress of 500 MPa for 40% of time and a reversed bending stress of 400 MPa for 50% of time. Find the expected life of the cycle if the material has the following fatigue life under various stresses: 600 MPa for 10000 cycles; 500 MPa for 45000 cycles; 400 MPa for 260000 cycles.**

Solution: Number of cycles at 600 MPa, $n_1 = 0.1\,n$, $N_{f1} = 10000$ cycles, number of cycles at 500 MPa, $n_2 = 0.4\,n$, $N_{f2} = 45000$ cycles, number of cycles at 400 MPa, $n_3 = 0.5\,n$, $N_{f3} = 260000$ cycles, $n = ?$

We know that total damage

$$\frac{n_1}{N_{f1}} + \frac{n_2}{N_{f2}} + \frac{n_3}{N_{f3}} = 1$$

$$\frac{0.1n}{10000} + \frac{0.4n}{45000} + \frac{0.5n}{260000} = 1$$

$$2.081 \times 10^{-5}\, n = 1$$

$$n = 48050 \text{ cycles}$$

41. **The work cycle of a mechanical component subjected to completely reversed bending stresses consist of the following three elements: i) $\pm$ 350 MPa for 85% of time; ii) 400 MPa for 12% of time; iii) 500 MPa for 3% of time. The material for the component is 50C4 (σ_u = 660 MPa) and the corrected endurance strength of the component is 280 MPa. Determine the life of the component.**

VTU – Dec. 2012 – 14 Marks

Solution: Number of cycles at $\sigma_1 = 350$ MPa, $n_1 = 0.85\,n$, number of cycles at $\sigma_2 = 400$ MPa, $n_2 = 0.12\,n$, number of cycles at $\sigma_3 = 500$ MPa, $n_3 = 0.03\,n$, $\sigma_u = 660$ MPa, corrected endurance strength, $\sigma'_{en} = 280$ MPa, $n = ?$

We know that total damage

$$\frac{n_1}{N_{f1}} + \frac{n_2}{N_{f2}} + \frac{n_3}{N_{f3}} = 1 \qquad \qquad \text{... Eq. (i)}$$

But $\qquad \qquad \sigma_{Nf} = P(N_f)^Q$

where $\qquad P = \left[\frac{(f \cdot \sigma_u)^2}{\sigma'_{en}} \right], Q = -\frac{1}{3}\left[\log\left(\frac{f \cdot \sigma_u}{\sigma'_{en}} \right) \right]$ and $\sigma'_{en} = ABC\,\sigma_{en}$

$$f = 0.9, \text{ for reversed bending stress}$$

Here $\qquad \sigma'_{en} = 280$ MPa (data)

$$P = \left[\frac{(0.9 \times 660)^2}{280} \right] = 1260.13$$

$$Q = -\frac{1}{3}\left[\log\left(\frac{(0.9 \times 660)}{280} \right) \right] = -0.1089$$

For $\sigma_{Nf} = \sigma_1 = 350$ MPa, Eq. (ii) yields...

$$350 = 1260.13\,(N_{f1})^{-0.1089} \Rightarrow N_{f1} = 128466.74 \text{ cycles}$$

For $\sigma_{Nf} = \sigma_2 = 400$ MPa, Eq. (ii) yields...

$$400 = 1260.13\,(N_{f1})^{-0.1089} \Rightarrow N_{f2} = 37693.45 \text{ cycles}$$

For $\sigma_{Nf} = \sigma_3 = 500$ MPa, Eq. (ii) yields...

$$500 = 1260.13\,(N_{f1})^{-0.1089} \Rightarrow N_{f3} = 4857 \text{ cycles}$$

∴ Eq. (i) yields...

$$\frac{0.85n}{128466.74} + \frac{0.12n}{37693.45} + \frac{0.03n}{4857} = 1$$

$$1.5976 \times 10^{-5}\,n = 1$$

$$n = 62591 \text{ cycles.}$$

Note: If the entire value (all decimals) of constants P and Q are taken into account, then

Eq. (ii) yields... $N_{f1} = 128797.03$ cycles,
$N_{f2} = 37780.21$ cycles

and $N_{f3} = 4866$ cycles, respectively

and Eq. (i) yields... $n = 62731.22$ cycles

42. **A machine member made of SAE 1095 steel (oil quenched) is subjected to a reversed stress cycles. If the effective endurance strength of the component is 600 MPa, compute the cycles of life for the machine member.**
    i. 70% of time with 650 MPa
    ii. 15% of time with 700 MPa
    iii. 10% of time with 750 MPa
    iv. 5% of time with 800 MPa

VTU – Dec. 2010 – 12 Marks

Solution: Material: SAE 1095 steel (oil quenched), number of cycles at $\sigma_1 = 650$ MPa, $n_1 = 0.70\,n$, number of cycles at $\sigma_2 = 700$ MPa, $n_2 = 0.15\,n$, number of cycles at $\sigma_3 = 750$ MPa, $n_3 = 0.1\,n$, number of cycles at $\sigma_4 = 800$ MPa, $n_4 = 0.05\,n$, $\sigma_u = 660$ MPa, corrected endurance strength, $\sigma'_{en} = 600$ MPa, $n = ?$

For SAE 1095 steel (oil quenched) at $\sigma_{en} = 600$ MPa, $\sigma_u = 1300$ MPa.

... Tb 1.17/ Pg 473, DHB

We know that total damage,

$$\frac{n_1}{N_{f1}} + \frac{n_2}{N_{f2}} + \frac{n_3}{N_{f3}} + \frac{n_4}{N_{f4}} = 1 \qquad\qquad \text{... Eq. (i)}$$

But $\sigma_{Nf} = P(N_f)^Q$

where $P = \left[\dfrac{(f \cdot \sigma_u)^2}{\sigma'_{en}}\right], Q = -\dfrac{1}{3}\left[\log\left(\dfrac{f \cdot \sigma_u}{\sigma'_{en}}\right)\right]$ and $\sigma'_{en} = ABC\,\sigma_{en}$

$f = 0.9$, for reversed bending stress

Here $\sigma'_{en} = 600$ MPa (data)

$$P = \left[\frac{(0.9 \times 1300)^2}{600}\right] = 2281.5$$

$$Q = -\frac{1}{3}\left[\log\left(\frac{(0.9 \times 1300)}{600}\right)\right] = -0.09668$$

For $\sigma_{Nf} = \sigma_1 = 650$ MPa, Eq. (ii) yields...

$$650 = 2281.5\,(N_{f1})^{-0.9668} \Rightarrow N_{f1} = 436.85 \times 10^3 \text{ cycles}$$

For $\sigma_{Nf} = \sigma_2 = 700$ MPa, Eq. (ii) yields...
$$700 = 2281.5 \,(N_{f2})^{-0.9668} \Rightarrow N_{f2} = 202.96 \times 10^3 \text{ cycles}$$

For $\sigma_{Nf} = \sigma_3 = 750$ MPa, Eq. (ii) yields...
$$750 = 2281.5 \,(N_{f3})^{-0.9668} \Rightarrow N_{f3} = 99.43 \times 10^3 \text{ cycles}$$

For $\sigma_{Nf} = \sigma_3 = 800$ MPa, Eq. (ii) yields...
$$800 = 2281.5 \,(N_{f4})^{-0.9668} \Rightarrow N_{f3} = 51 \times 10^3 \text{ cycles}$$

$\therefore$ Eq. (i) yields...
$$\frac{0.70\,n}{436.85 \times 10^3} + \frac{0.15\,n}{202.96 \times 10^3} + \frac{0.10\,n}{99.43 \times 10^3} + \frac{0.05\,n}{51 \times 10^3} = 1$$
$$4.328 \times 10^{-6}\,n = 1$$
$$n = 231 \times 10^3 \text{ cycles}$$

VTU QUESTION PAPERS

Mar. 2001 (ME5T2)

1. a. A steel member of circular cross-section is subjected to a torsional stress that varies from 0 to 35 MPa and at the same time it is subjected to an axial stress that varies from −14 MPa to +28 MPa. Neglecting stress concentration and column effect and assuming that the maximum stresses in torsion and axial load occur at the same time, determine:
     i. The maximum equivalent shear stress
     ii. The design factor of safety based on yield in shear.
   The material has an endurance limit $\sigma_{-1} = 206$ MPa, and a yield strength of $\sigma_y = 480$ MPa. The diameter of the member is less than 12 mm. Take load concentration factor = 1. Surface finish factor = 1. **(10 Marks)**
2. Explain the significance of Goodman's line and Soderberg's line in the design of members subjected to reversal of stresses. **(06 Marks)**

July/Aug. 2004 (AU46)

3. For the part shown in **Fig. U3.1,** calculate the maximum induced stress when

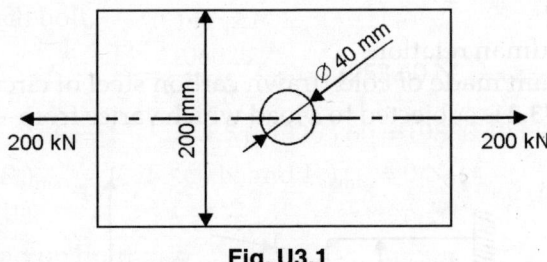

Fig. U3.1

   i. The part is made of steel and subjected to static load.
   ii. The part is made of cast iron and subjected to static load.
   iii. The part is made of steel with notch sensitivity 0.9 and the load is cyclic.
   iv. The part is made of cast iron and the load is cyclic. The plate is 20 mm thick
   (15 Marks)
4. a. Derive the Soderberg equation. **(05 Marks)**
   b. A round bar is subjected to the following variable loads:

Torque varying from 2kN·m to 5 kN·m

Bending moment varying from 10 kN·m to 12 kN·m.

Calculate the size of the bar if it is made of C40 steel. Adopt a factor of safety of 2.5 on yield stress for shear.   **(15 Marks)**

Jan/Feb. 2005 (AU46)

5. a. A cantilever beam of circular cross-section is subjected to an alternating stress at a point on the outer fiber in the plane of support that varies from 21 MPa (compression) to 28 MPa (tension). At the same time there is an alternating stress due to axial loading that varies from 14 MPa (compression) to 28 MPa (tension). The material has an ultimate strength of 412 MPa, yield strength of 309 MPa. Assume that actual stress concentration factor = 1, size correction factor = 0.85 and surface correction factor = 0.9. Determine:

   i. The equivalent normal stress due to axial loading.

   ii. The equivalent normal stress due to bending and

   iii. The total equivalent normal stress due to axial loading and bending.

        (12 Marks)

   b. A cold drawn steel bar is to withstand a tensile preload of 36.3 kN, a fluctuating tensile load varying from 0 to 72.6 kN. The bar has geometric stress concentration factor of 2.02 corresponding to a fillet whose radius is 4.75 mm. Determine the size of the bar for an infinite life and a factor of safety of 2. The material properties are $\sigma_{yp} = 588$ N/mm^2, $\sigma_{ut} = 700$ N/mm^2.   **(08 Marks)**

July/Aug. 2005 (AU46)

6. a. Derive Soderberg's equation for designing a machine element, with change in cross-section to sustain loads that fluctuate between two limits.   **(06 Marks)**

   b. Determine the diameters of a hollow rod to sustain a twisting moment that fluctuates between 2.5 kN·m and 1.5 kN·m together with a bending moment that fluctuates between +2 kN·m and –2 kN·m. Assume the inner diameter to be 0.6 times the outer diameter. Select a suitable material and assume an appropriate value for factor of safety.   **(14 Marks)**

Jan/Feb. 2006 (AU46)

7. a. Derive the Goodman relation.   **(05 Marks)**

   b. A cantilever beam made of cold drawn carbon steel of circular cross-section as shown in **Fig. U3.2** is subjected to a load which varies from –F and 3F. Determine

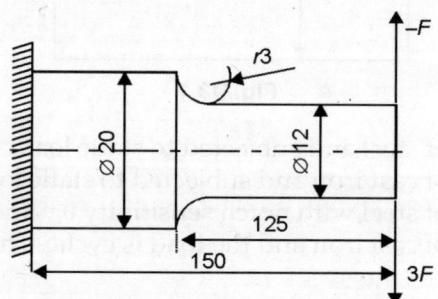

Fig. U3.2: All dimensions in mm

the maximum load that this member can withstand for an indefinite life using a factor of safety of 2. The theoretical stress concentration factor is 1.42 and the notch sensitivity is 0.9. Assume the following values:
Ultimate stress = 550 MPa
Yield stress = 470 MPa
Endurance limit = 275 MPa
Size factor = 0.85
Surface finish factor = 0.89 **(15 Marks)**

July 2006 (AU46)

8. A round bar of diameter 1.2d has a semicircular groove of diameter 0.2d. This rod is to sustain a twisting moment that fluctuates between 2.5 kN·m and 1.5 kN·m together with a bending moment that fluctuates between 2 kN·m and −1 kN·m. Selecting carbon steel C30 as material for the rod and choosing 2.5 as a value for factor of safety, determine the safe value of d. **(12 Marks)**

Dec. 06/Jan. 2007 (AU46)

9. a. Derive the Soderberg equation. **(06 Marks)**
   b. A SAE 1025 water quenched steel rod (σ_u = 620.8 MPa, σ_y = 400.1 MPa, σ_{-1} = 345.2 MPa) of circular cross-section, shown in **Fig. U3.3** is subjected to a load varying from P to 3P. Determine the value of P. The stress concentration factor may be taken as 1.4. Analyze the member at the change of cross-section. Use factor of safety as 3. Assume the surface to be rough finished. **(10 Marks)**

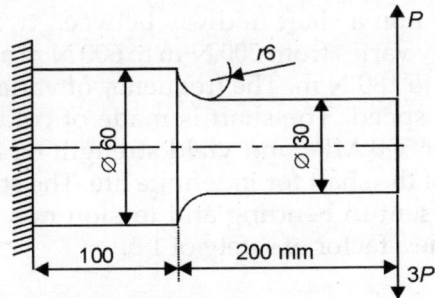

Fig. U3.3: All dimensions in mm

   c. How is cumulative fatigue failure predicted? **(04 Marks)**

July 2007 (AU46)

10. a. Derive Soderberg equation. **(05 Marks)**
    b. A cantilever shaft is subjected to a load of F newton (up) to 3F newton (down). The shaft is stepped down from 20 mm diameter to 13 mm diameter and is provided with a fillet of radius of 3 mm. the length of the shaft is 150 mm. The fillet section is at a distance of 25 mm from the fixed end. Determine the maximum load that the member can withstand for infinite life. Assume a factor of safety of 2. The material is cold drawn C26 steel for which σ_u = 550 N/mm^2, σ_y = 470 N/mm^2. Notch sensitivity for a 3 mm radius for this material is 0.9. **(15 Marks)**

11. A pulley is keyed to a shaft midway between two antifriction bearings. The bending moment at the pulley varies from 170 N·m to 510 N·m as the torsional

moment in the shaft varies from 55 N·m to 165 N·m. The frequency of the variation of the loads is same as that of the shaft speed. The shaft is made of cold drawn steel having an ultimate strength of 538 MPa and a yield strength of 400 MPa. Determine the required diameter for an indefinite life. The stress concentration factor for the keyway in bending and torsion may be taken as 1.6 and 1.3 respectively. Use design factor of 1.5. **(12 Marks)**

Dec. 07/Jan. 2008 (AU46)

12. a. Define endurance limit. List the factors affecting endurance limit. Explain any one factor. **(06 Marks)**
    b. Derive Goodman's relation. **(05 Marks)**
    c. A steel rod (σ_{ut} = 1089.5 MPa, σ_{yt} = 689.4 MPa, σ_{-1} = –427.6 MPa) is subjected to a tensile load, which varies from 120 kN to 40 kN. Design the safe diameter of the rod using 'Soderberg diagram'. Adopt factor of safety as 2, stress concentration factor as unity and correction factors for load, size and surface as 0.75, 0.85, and 0.91 respectively. **(10 Marks)**

June/July 2008 (AU46)

13. a. The maximum pressure in the cylinder of a double acting type is 0.9 MPa. The bore of the cylinder is 500 mm in diameter. What should be the diameter of the piston rod if there are no stress raisers and column action? Take the factor of safety as 1.75 based on Soderberg's criterion, ultimate tensile strength of the material of the piston rod is 1750 MPa. Choose a modifying factor of 0.85 for the type of loading, 0.85 for the size and 0.78 for the surface effects. **(08 Marks)**
    b. A pulley is mounted on a shaft midway between two bearings. The bending moment at the pulley varies from 200 N·m to 600 N·m and the torsional moment varies from 60 N·m to 180 N·m. The frequency of variation of loads is the same as that of the shaft speed. The shaft is made of cold drawn steel having an ultimate strength of 550 MPa and yield strength of 400 MPa. Determine the required diameter of the shaft for indefinite life. The stress concentration factor for the keyway present in bending and torsion may be taken as 1.5 and 1.2 respectively. Assume a factor of safety of 1.5. **(12 Marks)**

Dec. 08/Jan. 2009 (ME5T2)

14. a. Derive the Soderberg's relation $\dfrac{1}{N} = \dfrac{\sigma_m}{\sigma_y} + \dfrac{K_{tf}\sigma_a}{ABC\sigma_{en}}$. **(08 Marks)**
    b. A component machined from a plate made of steel 45C8 (σ_{ut} = 630 MPa) is shown in **Fig. U3.4**. It is subjected to a completely reversed axial force of 50 kN. The expected reliability is 90% and the factor of safety is 2. Determine the plate thickness 't' for infinite life, if the notch sensitivity factor is 0.8. **(12 Marks)**

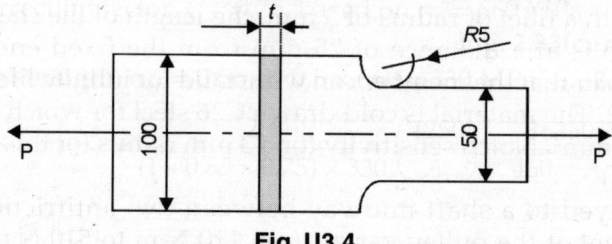

Fig. U3.4

15. A hot rolled steel shaft is subjected to a torsional load that varies from 330 N·m CW to 110 N·m CCW as an applied bending moment at a critical section varies from 440 N·m to –220 N·m. The shaft is of uniform cross-section and no keyway is present at the critical section. Determine the required shaft diameter. The material has an ultimate strength of 550 MPa and yield strength of 410 MPa. Base design on a factor of safety of 1.5. Take endurance limit as half the ultimate strength.

(20 Marks)

Dec. 08/Jan. 2009 (06ME-AU52)

16. a. Explain the significance of Goodman and Soderberg relations. **(08 Marks)**
    b. A rough finished steel rod having σ_u = 620 MPa, σ_y = 400 MPa and σ_{-1} = 345 MPa is subjected to completely reversed bending moment of 400 N·m. Determine the diameter of the rod required based on a factor of safety of 2.5.

(12 Marks)

June/July 2009 (AU46)

17. a. Explain endurance limit and endurance strength with the help of S–N diagram.
    (05 Marks)

    b. A machine component shown in **Fig. U3.5** is loaded as indicated on the diagram. Determine the cross-section dimensions 'd' for the component, if fatigue stress concentration factor in bending and axial loading are 1.8 and 1.6 respectively. The allowable stress for the component is 100 N/mm², the material properties are σ_y = 250 N/mm², σ_u = 400 N/mm². **(15 Marks)**

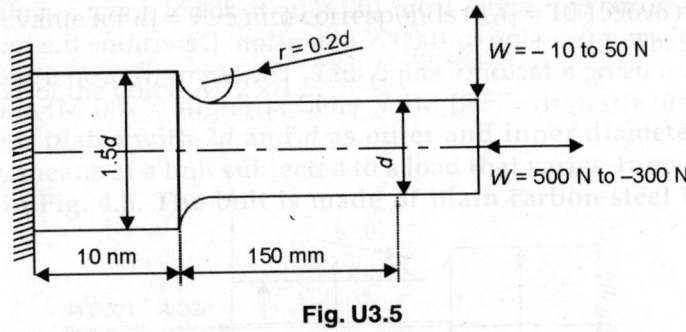

Fig. U3.5

June /July 2009 (06ME52)

18. a. Explain endurance limit and endurance strength with the help of S–N diagram.
    (05 Marks)

    b. A hot rolled steel rod is subjected to a torsional load that varies from +330 N·m clockwise to 110 N·m counter clockwise and an applied bending moment varies from +440 N·m to –220 N·m. The rod is of uniform cross-section. Determine the required rod diameter. The material has an ultimate tensile strength of 550 MPa and yield strength of 410 MPa. Design based on a factor of safety of 1.5. Take the endurance limit as half of the ultimate strength. **(15 Marks)**

19. A machine component is subjected to bending load which is completely cyclic as shown in **Fig. U3.6**. Determine the suitable value of load W. If the maximum stress induced is not to exceed 100 N/mm². Take σ_y = 250 N/mm² and σ_{end} = 200 N/mm². **(10 Marks)**

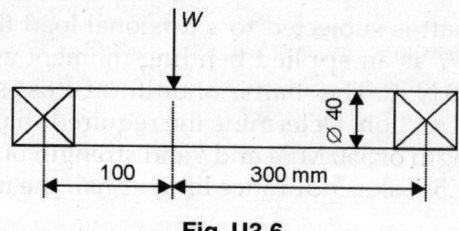

Fig. U3.6

Dec. 2009/ Jan. 2010 (AU46)

20. a. Derive Soderberg's equation $\dfrac{1}{N} = \dfrac{\sigma_m}{\sigma_y} + \dfrac{K_{tf}\sigma_a}{ABC\sigma_{en}}$, where A is the surface finish factor, B is the size factor and C is the load factor. **(06 Marks)**

b. A cold drawn steel rod of circular section is subjected to a variable bending moment of 565 N·m to 1130 N·m as the axial load varies from 4500 N to 13500 N. The maximum bending moment occurs at the same instant that the axial load is maximum. Determine the required diameter of the rod for a factor of safety of 2. Neglect stress concentration and column effect. Take $\sigma_u = 550$ MPa, $\sigma_y = 470$ MPa, endurance limit as 50% of the ultimate strength and size, load and surface correction coefficients as 0.85, 1 and 0.85 respectively. **(14 Marks)**

DEC. 2009/JAN. 2010 (06ME52)

21. A ground steel cantilever member as shown in **Fig. U3.7** is subjected to a transverse load at its free end that varies from 100 N up to 200 N down as an axial load varies from 500 N in compression to 1000 N in tension. Determine the required diameter of the section using a factor of safety of 2. The strength properties of the material are: Ultimate strength = 550 MPa, yield strength = 480 MPa, and endurance limit = 270 MPa. **(20 Marks)**

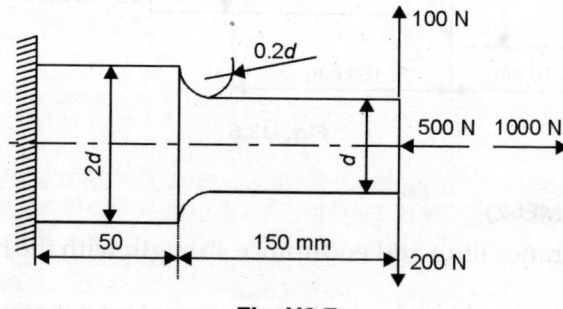

Fig. U3.7

May/June 2010 (06ME52)

22. a. Derive the Soderberg equation.

$$\frac{1}{N} = \frac{\sigma_m}{\sigma_y} + K_{ft}\frac{\sigma_a}{A \cdot B \cdot C\sigma_{en}}$$

where A = surface finish factor, B = size factor and C = load factor. **(06 Marks)**

b. A hot rolled steel shaft is subjected to a torsional load that varies from 330 N·m (clockwise) to 110 N·m (counterclockwise) as the applied bending moment at the critical section varies from +440 N·m to –220 N·m. The shaft is of uniform cross-section and no key way is present at the critical section. Determine the required shaft diameter. The material has an ultimate tensile strength of 550 MPa and yield strength of 410 MPa. Take the endurance limit as half of the ultimate strength, factor of safety = 2, size factor = 0.85 and a surface finish factor = 0.62. **(14 Marks)**

Dec. 2010 (AU46)

23. a. Sketch the Soderberg and Goodman diagrams and explain their uses in the design of machine components against fluctuating loads. **(08 Marks)**

    b. A machine member made of SAE 1095 steel (oil quenched) is subjected to a reversed stress cycles. If the effective endurance strength of the component is 600 MPa, compute the cycles of life for the machine member.

       i. 70% of time with 650 MPa

       ii. 15% of time with 700 MPa

       iii. 10% of time with 750 MPa

       iv. 5% of time with 800 MPa **(12 Marks)**

Dec. 2010 (06ME52)

24. a. Derive the Soderberg equation for members subjected to variable stresses. **(05 Marks)**

    b. A hot rolled steel rod is subjected to a torsional load that varies from +330 N·m clockwise to 110 N·m counter clockwise and an applied bending moment varies from +440 N-m to –220 N·m. The rod is of uniform cross-section. Determine the required rod diameter. The material has an ultimate tensile strength of 550 MPa and yield strength of 410 MPa. Design based on a factor of safety of 1.5. Take the endurance limit as half of the ultimate strength. **(15 Marks)**

June/July 2011 (06ME52)

25. a. Derive Goodman's equation. **(04 Marks)**

    b. Explain cumulative fatigue damage. **(04 Marks)**

    c. A circular bar of 500 mm length is supported freely at its two ends. It is acted upon by a central concentrated cyclic load having a minimum value of 20 kN and a maximum value of 50 kN. Determine the diameter of the bar by taking a factor of safety of 2, size effect of 0.85, and surface finish factor of 0.9. The material properties of the bar are given by ultimate strength of 650 MPa, yield strength of 500 MPa and endurance strength of 350 MPa. **(12 Marks)**

Dec. 2011 (AU46)

26. a. Derive the Soderberg relation. **(05 Marks)**

    b. A steel member of circular section is subjected to a torsional shear stress that varies from 0 to 35 MPa. At the same time, it is subjected to an axial stress that varies from –14 MPa to +28 MPa. Neglecting stress concentration and column effect and assuming that the maximum stress in bending and axial load occur at the same time, determine:

       i. The maximum equivalent shear stress

       ii. The design factor of safety based upon yield in shear.

The material has an endurance limit of $\sigma_{-1} = 206$ MPa and yield strength of $\sigma_y = 480$ MPa. The size factor $k_{sz} = 1$ and the surface has a mirror polish, i.e. $k_{sr} = 1$. **(15 Marks)**

Dec. 2011 (06ME52)

27. A cold drawn cantilever member shown in **Fig. U3.8** is subjected to a transverse load at its end that varies from 50 N to 150 N and an axial load varies from 100 N (compression) to 500 N (tension). Determine the required diameter at the change of section for infinite life using a factor of safety of 2. The material has an ultimate strength of 550 MPa and yield strength of 470 MPa. Take a notch sensitivity factor for the fillet as 0.9. **(15 Marks)**

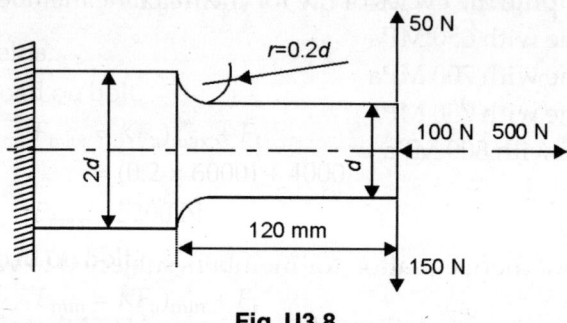

Fig. U3.8

June 2012 (06ME52-06AU52)

28. a. A cantilever beam made of 35C8 steel ($\sigma_{ut} = 540$ MPa) is subjected to a completely reversed load of 1000 N as shown in **Fig. U3.9**. The notch sensitivity factor q at the fillet can be taken as 0.85 and expected reliability is 90%. Determine the diameter of the beam for a life cycle of 10000 cycles. **(10 Marks)**

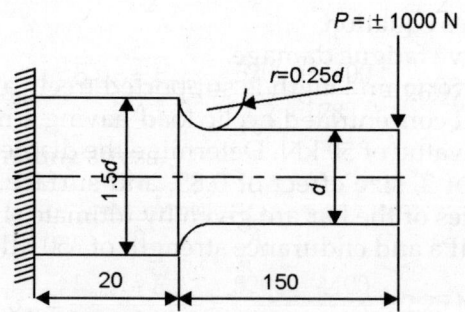

Fig. U3.9: All dimensions in mm

b. A cantilever beam made of cold drawn C30 steel ($\sigma_{ut} = 550$ MPa and $\sigma_{yt} = 470$ MPa) subjected to a load which varies from $-F$ and $3F$, as shown in **Fig. U3.10**. Determine the maximum load that this member can withstand for an indefinite life using a factor of safety of 2. The stress concentration factor effect has to be considered with notch sensitivity of 0.9. Analyze at the fillet section only. **(10 Marks)**

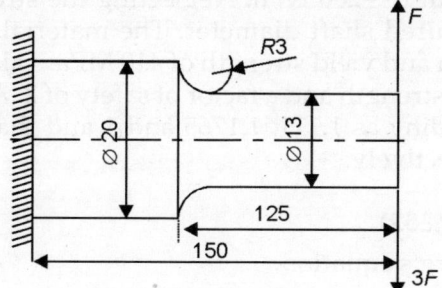

Fig. U3.10: All dimensions in mm

June 2012 (06ME52-06AU52)

29. a. Explain briefly the following:
    i. High cycle and low cycle fatigue
    ii. Stress concentration and its effects. **(04 Marks)**
  b. A pulley is keyed to a shaft midway between two bearings. The shaft is made of steel (σ_y = 3890 MPa). Bending moment at the pulley varies from –300 N·m to +500 N·m and the torque varies from –100 N·m to +200 N·m. The fatigue stress concentration factors for the key way in bending and torsion are 1.6 and 1.3 respectively. The factor of safety is 1.5. Determine the diameter of the shaft.
  (16 Marks)

Dec. 2012 (06ME52)

30. a. Define endurance limit. State and explain the factors for modifying it.
  (06 Marks)
  b. The work cycle of a mechanical component subjected to completely reversed bending stresses consist of the following three elements:
    i. ± 350 MPa for 85% of time
    ii. ± 400 MPa for 12% of time
    iii. ± 500 MPa for 3% of time.
    The material for the component is 50 C4 (σ_u = 660 N/mm^2) and the corrected endurance strength of the component is 280 MPa. Determine the life of the component. **(14 Marks)**

June/July 2013 (06ME52)

31. a. Derive the Soderberg relationship for designing machine components subjected to variable loads. **(08 Marks)**
  b. A cast iron shaft with an ultimate tensile strength of 180 MPa is subjected to a torsional load which is completely reversal. The load is to be applied at indefinite number of cycles. The shaft is 50 mm diameter and is joined with 75 mm diameter shaft with a fillet radius of 12.5 mm. Using factor of safety of 2, what is the maximum torque that can be applied to the shaft? Take surface factor = 0.75, size factor = 0.85 and load factor = 1. **(12 Marks)**

June/July 2013 (10ME52)

32. a. Derive Soderberg's equation for designing of a machine element, with change in cross-section to sustain loads that fluctuate between two limits. **(05 Marks)**
  b. A hot rolled steel rod is subjected to a torsional moment that varies from 300 N·m clockwise to 100 N·m counterclockwise and the bending moment

varies from 400 N·m to –200 N·m. Neglecting the stress concentration effect, determine the required shaft diameter. The material has an ultimate tensile strength of 550 MPa and yield strength of 410 MPa. Take the endurance limit as half of the ultimate strength and a factor of safety of 2. Assume surface, size and load factor for bending as 1.111, 1.1765 and 1 and that for torsion as 1.05263, 1.1765 and 1.7 respectively. **(15 Marks)**

Dec. 2013/Jan. 2014 (06ME52)

33. a. Derive the Soderberg's equation.

$$K_{ft}\frac{\sigma_a}{ABC\sigma_{en}} + \frac{\sigma_m}{\sigma_y} = \frac{1}{N}$$

where K_{ft} is the effect of stress concentration
      A is the load factor
      B is the size factor
      C is the surface finish factor   **(06 Marks)**

   b. A shaft supported on bearings 400 mm apart is subjected to a concentrated load varying from W to $3W$ at its midpoint. The shaft is of 50 mm diameter. Estimate the value of W with a factor of safety of 1.5. The material has an ultimate strength of 700 N/mm², endurance limit of 350 N/mm² and yield strength of 525 N/mm². Take size factor as 0.85 and surface finish factor of 0.848. **(14 Marks)**

Dec. 2013/Jan. 2014 (10ME52)

34. a. Derive the Soderberg equation. **(05 Marks)**
   b. A hot rolled steel rod is subjected to a torsional load that varies from +330 N·m clockwise to 110 N-m counterclockwise and an applied bending moment varies from +440 N·m to –220 N·m. The rod is of uniform cross-section. Determine the required rod diameter. The material has an ultimate tensile strength of 550 MPa and yield strength of 410 MPa. Design based on a factor of safety of 1.5. Take the endurance limit as half of the ultimate strength. **(15 Marks)**

June/July 2014 (06ME52)

35. a. Derive the Soderberg equation for fluctuating loads. **(05 Marks)**
   b. A SAE water quenched steel rod (σ_u = 600 MPa, σ_y = 390 MPa, and σ_{-1} = 320 MPa) of circular section shown in **Fig. U3.11** is subjected to a load varying from P upward to $3P$ downward. Determine the value of P taking a factor of safety of 3. Analyze at the change of cross-section. The size and surface factors may be taken as 0.85 and 0.9 respectively. **(15 Marks)**

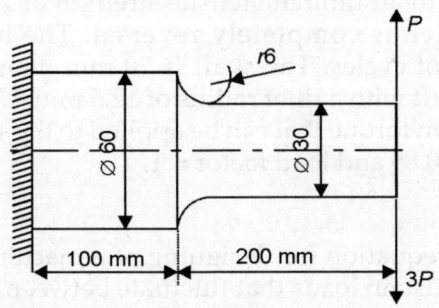

Fig. U3.11

Dec. 2014/Jan. 2015 (06ME52)

36. a. Derive the Soderberg's equation. **(05 Marks)**

b. A steel cantilever of 200 mm long is subjected to combined loading as shown in **Fig. U3.12**. The cantilever is of circular cross-section. Determine its diameter taking a factor of safety of 2. Take σ_y = 330 MPa, σ_{en} = 300 MPa, stress concentration factor static axial and bending load as 1.64 and 1.44 respectively. Choose proper values for modifying factors "A", "B" and "C" from data handbook. Notch sensitivity index is 0.9. **(15 Marks)**

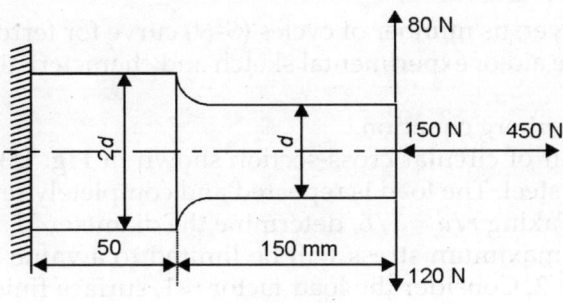

Fig. U3.12

Dec. 2014/Jan. 2015 (10ME52)

37. A transmission shaft carries a pulley midway between two bearings. The bending moment at the pulley varies from 200 N·m to 600 N·m, as the torsional moment of the shaft varies from 70 N·m to 200 N·m. The frequencies of variation of bending and torsional moments are equal to the shaft speed. The shaft is made of steel Fe 400 (σ_u = 540 MPa, σ_{ut} = 400 MPa). The corrected endurance strength of the shaft is 200 MPa. Determine the diameter of the shaft using a factor of safety of 2.

(20 Marks)

June/July 2015 (06ME52)

38. a. Derive the Soderberg equation. **(05 Marks)**

b. Explain cumulative fatigue damage. **(05 Marks)**

c. Determine the diameter of a circular rod made of ductile material with fatigue strength of σ_e = 265 MPa and a tensile yield strength of 350 MPa. The member is subjected to a varying axial load from W_{min} = −300 × 10³ N to W_{max} = 700 × 10³ N and has a stress concentration factor = 1.8. Use factor of safety as 2.0. **(10 Marks)**

June/July 2015 (10ME52)

39. a. Explain with neat sketches, the different types of varying stresses. **(05 Marks)**

b. Write a note on S–N diagram. **(05 Marks)**

c. A steel cantilever is 200 mm long. It is subjected to an axial load which varies from 150 N (compression) to 450 N (tension) and a transverse load at its free end which varies from 80 N (up) to 120 N (down). The cantilever beam is of circular cross-section having a diameter of 2d for the first 50 mm and diameter d for the remaining length. Determine its diameter assuming the following:

Factor of safety   = 2
Yield stress   = 330 MPa
Endurance limit   = 300 MPa

Stress concentration factor = 1.44 for bending.
= 1.64 for axial loading.
Correction factors = 0.7 for reverse axial loading.
= 1 for bending.
Size factor = 0.8
Surface correction factor = 0.9
Notch sensitivity = 0.9 **(10 Marks)**

Dec. 2015/Jan. 2016 (10ME52)

40. a. Explain stress versus number of cycles (*S-N*) curve for ferrous and non-ferrous metals with the aid of experimental sketch and characteristic curves.
(06 Marks)
   b. Derive the Soderberg equation. **(06 Marks)**
   c. A stepped shaft of circular cross-section shown in **Fig. U3.13** is made of SAE 1045 annealed steel. The load is repeated and completely reversed with a value of 100,000 N. Taking $r/d = 1/8$, determine the diameter 'd' and the fillet radius 'r' so that the maximum stress will be limited to a value corresponding to a factor of safety 2. Consider the load factor = 1, surface finish factor = 0.85 and size factor = 0.9. **(08 Marks)**

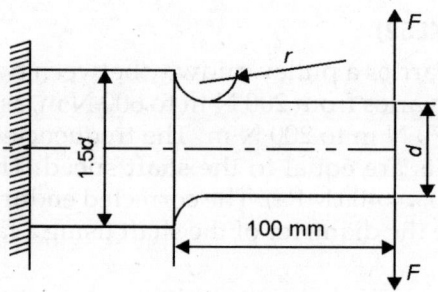

Fig. U3.13

4

Threaded Fasteners

4.1 INTRODUCTION

A fastener is a device to connect or join two or more members. The threaded fasteners are used to fasten the various parts of an assembly together. Fasteners may be classified into groups and subgroups according to their functions as follows.

1. Detachable fasteners:
   a. Threaded fasteners: Bolt and nut, screws and studs, etc.
   b. Cotter joint
   c. Knuckle joint
2. Permanent or nondetachable fasteners:
   a. Riveted joints
   b. Welded joints

A screw thread is formed by cutting a continuous helical groove on a cylindrical surface. The helical grooves may be cut either **right hand** or **left hand**. Unless otherwise specified, all threads are assumed to be right hand.

- A screw made by cutting a single helical groove on the cylinder is known as **single threaded** or single-start screw.
- If a second thread is cut in the space between the grooves of the first, a **double threaded** or double-start screw is formed and so on.

4.2 IMPORTANT DEFINITIONS

- *Pitch*: It is defined as the distance between two consecutive threads, denoted by 'p'.
- *Lead*: It is defined as the distance which a screw thread advances axially in one rotation of the nut, denoted by 'l'.

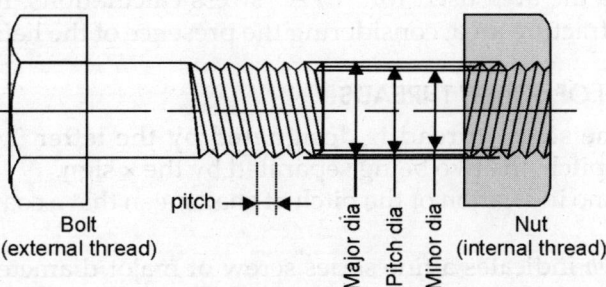

Fig. 4.1: Thread terminology

247

In general   Lead = number of starts × pitch

i.e. $l = n \cdot p$ ... (Eq. 4.1) **9.10(b)/Pg 133, DHB**

where $n = 1$, for single start threads

         $n = 2$, for double start threads

         $n = 3$, for triple start threads and so on.

- *Nominal or major or outer diameter (d)*: It is the largest diameter of a screw thread.
- *Root or core or minor or inner diameter (d_1)*: It is the smallest diameter of an external or internal screw thread.
- *Mean or pitch diameter (d_2)*: It is defined as the theoretical diameter between the major and minor diameters.

$$d_2 = [d - (p/2)] = [(d + d_1)/2] \qquad ... (Eq. 4.2)$$

Note: From *Tb. 9.8/Pg 140, DHB*

	External thread	Internal thread
Major or nominal or outside diameter [Column 3]	d	D
Mean or pitch diameter [Column 4]	d_2	D_2
Root or core or minor diameter	d_1 [Column 5]	D_1 [Column 6]

4.3 FORMS OF SCREW THREADS

The basic forms of screw threads include:

   a. British Standard Whitworth (BSW) thread

   b. British Association (BA) thread

   c. American National Standard(ANS) thread

   d. Unified Standard thread

   e. Square thread

   f. Acme thread

   g. Knuckle thread

   h. Buttress thread

   i. Metric thread

V-threads are mainly used for fastening purpose, i.e. to secure one member to another. V-threads are generally used for securing because they do not shake loose due to the wedging action provided by the thread. The included angle is 60 degrees. This form is prevalent in the Unified Screw Thread (UN, UNC, UNF, UNRC, UNRF) form as well as the ISO/Metric thread.

The standard proportions of ISO metric thread is shown in **Fig. 4.2**. The stress area tabulated in **Tb. 9.8/ Pg 140, DHB,** is based on the average of the pitch and root diameters. This is the area used for "P/A" stress calculations. It approximates the smallest possible fracture area, considering the presence of the helical thread.

4.4 DESIGNATION OF SCREW THREADS

- The size of the screw thread is designated by the letter '*M*' followed by the diameter and pitch, the two being separated by the × sign.

When there is no indication of the pitch, it shall mean that a coarse pitch is implied.

Example:

   ☛ M12 × 2–9*h* indicates a fine series screw of major diameter 12 mm and pitch 2 mm.

   ☛ M8–8*d* indicates a coarse series screw of major diameter 8 mm and pitch 1 mm.

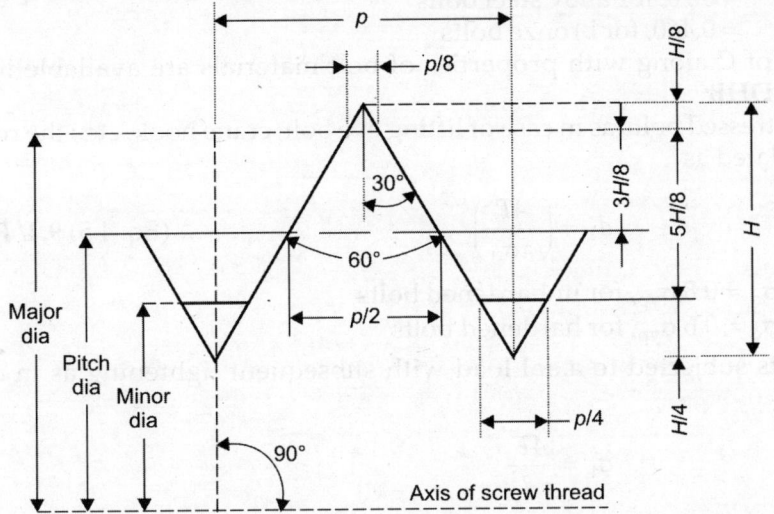

Fig. 4.2: Basic profile of ISO metric screw thread **[Fig. 9.8/Pg 145, DHB]**

- To specify the tolerances, the following tolerance grades are used:
  - ☞ '7' for fine grade
  - ☞ '8' for normal (medium) grade
  - ☞ '9' for coarse grade
- The tolerance position is specified as follows:
  - ☞ 'H' for unit thread
  - ☞ 'd' for bolt thread with allowance and
  - ☞ 'h' for bolt thread without allowance.

  Example:
  - ☞ M12 × 2–9h indicates a bolt thread of 12 mm size having a fine pitch of 2 mm of normal grade and with allowance on the thread.
  - ☞ M8–8d indicates a bolt thread of 8 mm size having coarse pitch of 1 mm of normal grade and with allowance on the thread.

4.5 MATERIALS USED FOR BOLTS

Most fasteners are made from steel because of its high strength, high stiffness, good ductility, and good machinability. Commonly used materials are plain carbon steels and free cutting steels. Alloy steels with nickel, chromium and molybdenum are used for fatigue loading and in corrosive environment. Nonferrous metals such as brass, bronze, aluminium, etc. are also used.

4.6 WORKING STRESS IN BOLTS—INITIAL TENSION UNKNOWN

- According to Seaton and Routhwaite, the working stress for bolts made of steel containing 0.08 to 0.25 carbon and with diameters above 20 mm,

$$\sigma_d = C(A_r)^{0.418} \qquad \text{... (Eq. 4.3) } \textbf{9.3(a)/ Pg 128, DHB}$$

- The total load capacity of the bolt is calculated as

$$F_a = \sigma_d A_r = C(A_r)^{1.418} \qquad \text{... (Eq. 4.4) } \textbf{9.3(b)/ Pg 129, DHB}$$

where A_r = stress area of the bolt

C = coefficient

= 2.29, for low carbon steels

= 0.70, for alloy steel bolts

= 0.460, for bronze bolts

Values of C along with properties of bolt materials are available in **Table 9.2/ Pg 136, DHB**

- For unstressed bolts as in case of lifting eye bolt, crane hook, etc., the root diameter is calculated as

$$d_1 = \left(\frac{4F}{\pi\sigma_d} \right)^{1/2} \qquad \text{... (Eq. 4.5) 9.4/ Pg 129, DHB}$$

where $\sigma_d = 0.8\,\sigma_{yp}$, for unhardened bolts

$\sigma_d = 0.6\,\sigma_{yp}$, for hardened bolts

- For bolts subjected to axial load with subsequent tightening as in case of turn buckle,

$$\sigma_t = \frac{4F}{\pi d_1^2} \qquad \text{... (Eq. 4.6)}$$

It is found that the resultant stress will be 20% to 30% greater than the axial tensile load. Assuming an average of 25% greater than the tensile load, the root diameter (as in turn buckle) is calculated as

$$d_1 = \left[\frac{1.25F}{(\pi/4)\sigma_d} \right]^{1/2} \qquad \text{... (Eq. 4.7) 9.5/ Pg 129, DHB}$$

where $\sigma_d = (0.25 \text{ to } 0.40)\sigma_{yp}$, for $d = 16$ to 30 mm

$\sigma_d = (0.40 \text{ to } 0.60)\sigma_{yp}$, for $d = 30$ to 60 mm

- The relation between the torque applied to the nut and the axial tension load in the bolt is

$$T = 0.2\,F_a d \qquad \text{... (Eq. 4.8) 9.1(d)/ Pg 127, DHB}$$

4.7 STRESSES IN SCREWED FASTENING DUE TO STATIC LOADING

Under static loading, the following stresses are considered.

A. Initial stresses due to screwing up of forces

B. Stressed due to external forces

C. Stresses due to the above combination.

4.7.1 Initial Stresses Due to Screwing up of Forces

The following stresses are induced in a bolt, screw or stud when it is screwed up tightly.

a. Tensile stresses due to stretching of the bolt

b. Torsional shear stress due to frictional resistance at the threads

c. Shear stress across threads

d. Compressive or crushing stress on the threads

e. Bending stress if the surfaces under the bolt head or nut are not perfectly parallel to the bolt axis.

a. **Tensile stresses due to stretching of the bolt:**

- Bolts are designed on the basis of direct tensile stress with a large factor of safety as

$$\sigma_t = \frac{F_i}{A_s} \qquad \text{... (Eq. 4.9)}$$

where stress area,

$$A_s = \frac{\pi}{4}\left[\frac{(d_1 + d_2)^2}{2}\right] \qquad \dots \text{(Eq. 4.9a)}$$

- According to experiments conducted at Cornell university, the initial tension or preload in the bolt is calculated as

$$F_i = 2805d \qquad \dots \text{Eq. (4.10) } \textbf{9.1(c)/ Pg 127, DHB}$$

where d = nominal or major diameter of the bolt
d_1 = root or core or minor diameter of the bolt
d_2 = mean or pitch diameter of the bolt

This equation is used for making fluid tight or leak proof as in pressure vessels and cylinder covers. Bolts less than M18 are not permitted for fluid tight joints.

- If a fluid tight joint is not required, then half of the above estimated load may be used,
i.e. $\qquad F_i = 1402.5d \qquad \dots \text{Eq. (4.11)}$

b. **Torsional shear stress:** The torsional shear stress induced due to tightening is computed as

$$\tau = \frac{16T}{\pi d_1^3} \qquad \dots \text{(Eq. 4.12) } \textbf{3.1/ Pg 51, DHB}$$

c. **Shear stress across threads:** The screw thread is considered to be loaded as a cantilevered beam. The load is assumed to be uniformly distributed over the mean radius of the screw. Hence, both the threads on the screw and the threads on the nut experience a transverse shear stress at their roots.
Shear stress in the screw,

$$\tau_{screw} = \frac{W}{A_s)_{screw}} = \frac{W}{n\pi d_1 t} \qquad \dots \text{(Eq. 4.13)}$$

Shear stress in the nut,

$$\tau_{nut} = \frac{W}{A_s)_{nut}} = \frac{W}{n\pi D_1 t} \qquad \dots \text{(Eq. 4.14)}$$

where n = number of threads in contact
d_1 = root or core or minor diameter of the bolt
D_1 = root or core or minor diameter of the nut
t = thickness or width of thread ($= p/2$)
p = pitch

d. **Compressive or crushing stress:** The crushing stress is calculated as

$$\sigma_c = \frac{4F}{n\pi(d^2 - d_1^2)} \qquad \dots \text{(Eq. 4.15) } \textbf{9.13(a)/Pg 135, DHB}$$

e. **Bending stress:** If the surfaces under the bolt head or nut are not perfectly parallel to the bolt axis, then the bolt will be subjected to bending moment and the bending stress induced in the shank of the bolt is calculated as

$$\sigma_b = \frac{xE}{2l} \qquad \dots \text{(Eq. 4.16)}$$

where x = difference in height between the extreme corners of the nut or head
E = Young's modulus of bolt material
l = length of the shank

4.7.2 Stresses Due to External Forces

The following stresses are induced in a bolt due to external force.
a. Tensile stress
b. Shear stress
c. Combined tensile and shear stresses

a. **Tensile stress:** Bolts, studs and screws are subjected to tensile stresses by the external forces acting on them, but occasionally are subjected to shear loads also, the common example being the bolts of a flange coupling. When the bolt is subjected to tensile load, the weakest section will be at the root of the thread

i.e. $$F = \sigma_t \frac{\pi d_1^2}{4} \qquad \ldots \text{(Eq. 4.17)}$$

If the load is taken up by n bolts, then the

$$F = \sigma_t \left(\frac{\pi d_1^2}{4} \right) n$$

In the absence of standard tables, the following relations may be employed to calculate the nominal diameter (d) from the core diameter (d_1)

$$d_1 = 0.84\,d, \text{ for coarse threads}$$
$$d_1 = 0.88\,d, \text{ for fine threads}$$

b. **Shear stress:** When the bolts are used to prevent the relative movement of two or more parts, then the shear stress is induced in the bolts. The shear stresses should be avoided as far as possible. When a number of bolts are used to share the shearing load, the finished bolts should be fitted to the reamed holes.

$$F_s = \tau \left(\frac{\pi d^2}{4} \right) n. \qquad \ldots \text{(Eq. 4.18)}$$

c. **Combined tensile and shear stresses:** When the bolt is subjected to combined action of both tensile and shear loads, then the design must be checked for the maximum principal stress and maximum shear stress using the following relations:

Maximum principal stress,

$$\sigma_1 = \left(\frac{\sigma}{2} \right) + \sqrt{\left(\frac{\sigma}{2} \right)^2 + \tau^2} \qquad \ldots \text{(Eq. 4.19)} \ \textbf{1.5(a)/ Pg 3, DHB}$$

Maximum shear stress,

$$\tau_{max} = \sqrt{\left(\frac{\sigma}{2} \right)^2 + \tau^2} \qquad \ldots \text{(Eq. 4.20)} \ \textbf{1.5(b)/ Pg 3, DHB}$$

For safe design, the calculated stresses should be less than the allowable stresses.

4.7.3 Stresses due to the above Combination (Sections 4.7.1 and 4.7.2)

When a bolt is subjected to both initial tightening and external loads, i.e. when a preloaded bolt is in tension or compression the resultant load on the bolt will depend upon:
• The initial tension due to tightening of the bolt
• The external load
• The relative elastic yielding of the bolt and the connected members.

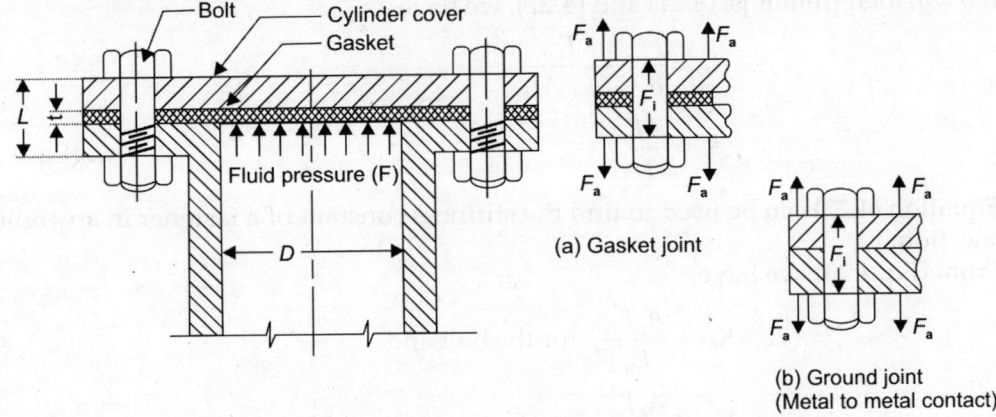

Bolt — Cylinder cover
Gasket

Fluid pressure (F)

D

(a) Gasket joint

F_a F_a F_i F_a F_a

F_a F_a F_i F_a F_a

(b) Ground joint
(Metal to metal contact)

Fig. 4.3: Bolted assembly subjected to external force

Figure 4.3 represents two cases of bolted connections. **Figure 4.3(a)** represents a connection between two parts separated by a gasket while **Fig. 4.3(b)** represents bolted connected without gasket.

In **Fig. 4.3(a)**, the connected members are very yielding as compared with the bolt. Hence, the resultant load on the bolt is approximately equal to the sum of the initial tension and the external load. On the other hand, if the bolt is very yielding as compared with the connected members, as shown in **Fig. 4.3(b)**, then the resultant load will be either the initial tension or the external load, whichever is greater.

When a load F is applied to the assembly, both the bolt and the connected parts have tensile stresses because the load is shared partly by the bolt and partly by the connected part (gasket). Hence, F_i and F_a are the tensile loads on the bolt due to initial tightening and external load respectively, as shown in **Figs 4.3(a) and (b)**.

Let F_i = initial load on the bolt

     F_a = external load applied upon the joint

     F = resultant or final load acting on the joint

     F_b = part of the load F_a taken by bolt

     F_g = part of the load F_a taken by connected members (gasket)

     K_b = stiffness of the bolt

     K_g = stiffness of connected members (gasket)

     L = length of the bolt

     t = thickness of gasket

In analyzing an elastic member such as a bolt, we introduce a term called spring rate or stiffness in order to examine the loads and deflections carried by each member. Spring rate or stiffness or spring constant is defined as the ratio between the force applied to the member and the deflection produced by that force,

i.e. spring rate $$K = \frac{F}{y}$$ ... (Eq. 4.21)

Also the deformation of a uniform bar in pure tension or compression is given as

$$\delta = \frac{FL}{AE}$$ ... (Eq. 4.22) **1.2(b)/Pg 3, DHB**

If $\delta = y$, then from Eqs. (4.21) and (4.22), we have,

$$K = \frac{F}{\delta} = \frac{F}{FL/AE}$$

$$\therefore \quad K = \frac{AE}{L} \qquad \qquad \qquad \text{... (Eq. 4.23)}$$

Equation (4.23) can be used to find the stiffness constant of a fastener in any bolted connection.

From (Eq. 4.23), we have,

$$K_b = \frac{A_b E_b}{L_b}, \text{ for the bolt and}$$

$$K_g = \frac{A_g E_g}{L_g}, \text{ for the connected member (gasket), respectively}$$

The deformation of the bolt is $\delta_b = \dfrac{F_b}{K_b}$ and that of the connected member is $\delta_g = \dfrac{F_g}{K_g}$.

Since the deformation is equal we have $\delta_b = \delta_g$

$$\frac{F_b}{K_b} = \frac{F_g}{K_g} \qquad \qquad \qquad \text{... (Eq. 4.24)}$$

Therefore, the total applied load F_a due to steam pressure is given by

$$F_a = F_b + F_g \qquad \qquad \qquad \text{... (Eq. 4.25)}$$

$$= F_b + \left(\frac{K_g}{K_b}\right) F_b$$

$$= F_b \left[1 + \left(\frac{K_g}{K_b}\right)\right]$$

$$F_a = F_b \left(\frac{K_b + K_g}{K_b}\right)$$

$$\therefore \quad F_b = F_a \left(\frac{K_b}{K_b + K_g}\right) = F_a K \qquad \qquad \text{... (Eq. 4.26)}$$

Thus the resultant load on bolt is

$$F = F_i + F_b$$
$$F = F_i + K F_a \qquad \qquad \text{... (Eq. 4.27) **9.2(a)/Pg 128, DHB**}$$

where

$$K = \left(\frac{K_b}{K_b + K_g}\right) = \frac{A_b E_b}{L_b} \Bigg/ \left(\frac{A_b E_b}{L_b} + \frac{A_g E_g}{L_g}\right)$$

$$= \frac{A_b E_b}{L} \Bigg/ \left(\frac{A_b E_b}{L} + \frac{A_g E_g}{t}\right)$$

$$= 0 \text{ to } 1, \text{ depending upon the nature of gasket.}$$

... Table 9.1/ Pg 136, DHB

A_b = Cross-sectional area of the bolt
A_g = Loaded area of the gasket
E_b = Modulus of elasticity for bolt material
E_g = Modulus of elasticity for gasket material
L_b = Length of the bolt from nut to head
$L_g = t$ = Thickness of the gasket

On similar lines, $F_g = F_a \left(\dfrac{K_g}{K_b + K_g} \right)$ ... (Eq. 4.28)

Since the connected part receives an equal and opposite force of compression F_i, the resultant load on the connected member is

$$F_g)_{min} = KF_a - F_i = F_a \left(\frac{K_g}{K_b + K_g} \right) - F_i \qquad \text{... (Eq. 4.29)}$$

A negative answer from this equation indicates that no force acts on the connected parts (i.e. no separation occurs).

Note:
- **Table 9.1/ Pg 136, DHB,** *gives value of K to be used* in **Eq. 9.2(a)/ Pg 128, DHB**
- **Table 9.2/ Pg 136, DHB,** *gives properties of some bolt material.*
- **Table 9.4/ Pg 137, DHB,** *gives working stress and load for Indian metric coarse thread.*
- **Table 9.8/ Pg 140, DHB,** *gives basic dimensions of ISO metric screw thread.*
- **Fig. 9.9/ Pg 145, DHB,** *indicates basic profile of ISO metric screw thread.*

1. **Determine the safe tensile load for the following bolts assuming a safe tensile stress of 42 MPa.**
   a. *M16*
   b. *M20*
   c. *M30*

Solution: F = ?, σ_t = 42 MPa.
Assuming that the bolts are not initially stressed, we have

$$\sigma_t = \frac{F}{A_1} \qquad \text{... Eq. (i)}$$

where A_1 = tensile stress area
From **Tb. 9.8/Pg 141, DHB,**
For *M16* bolt $A_1 = 157$ mm^2
     M20 bolt $A_1 = 245$ mm^2
     M30 bolt $A_1 = 561$ mm^2

Thus Eq. (i) yields...
For *M16* bolt $F = 42 \times 157 = 6594$ N
     M20 bolt $F = 42 \times 245 = 10290$ N
     M30 bolt $F = 42 \times 561 = 23562$ N

2. **Two machine parts are fastened together tightly by means of a *M25* bolt. If the load tending to separate these parts is neglected, find the stress set up in the bolt due to initial tightening.**

Solution: $M25 \Rightarrow d = 25$ mm, σ_t = ?

We know that $\sigma_t = \dfrac{F}{A_1}$ ... Eq. *(i)*

For initial tightening $F = F_i = 2805\,d$ ... 9.1(c)/ Pg 127, DHB
$$= 2805 \times 25$$
∴ $\qquad\qquad\qquad F = F_i = 70125$ N
For *M25* bolt, $\qquad d_1 = 21.319392$ mm ... Tb. 9.8/ Pg 142, DHB

Thus Eq. (i) yields... $\sigma_t = \dfrac{70125}{[\pi \times (21.319392)^2 / 4]} = 196.44$ MPa

3. **Two shafts are connected by means of a flange coupling to transmit torque of 60 N·m using 4 bolts at a PCD of 90 mm. The flanges and the coupling are made of same material. Determine the size of the bolts if the allowable shear stress for the bolt material is 35 MPa.**

Solution: $T = 60 \times 10^3$ N·mm, $i = 4$, $D_2 = 90$ mm, $d = ?$, $\tau = 35$ MPa.
Torque capacity based on shear of bolts,

$$T = \frac{\tau \pi i d_1^2 D_2}{8} \qquad\qquad \text{... 13.2(c)/ Pg 252, DHB}$$

$$60 \times 10^3 = \frac{35\pi \times 4 \times d_1^2 \times 90}{8}$$

∴ $\qquad\qquad\qquad d_1 = 3.48$ mm

The nearest value for $d_1 = 3.48$ mm corresponds to $d_1 = 3.598487$ mm for *M4.5*.
... Tb. 9.8/ Pg 140, DHB

Thus the size of the bolt is *M4.5* × 0.75.

4. **A bolt subjected to initial loading of 5 kN and final tensile load of 9 kN. Determine the size of the bolt, if the allowable stress is 80 MPa and K = 0.05.**

VTU – Dec. 08/Jan. 2009 – 08 Marks; June/July 2014 – 08 Marks

Solution: $F_i = 5000$ N, $F_a = 9000$ N, $d = ?$, $\sigma_t = 80$ MPa, $K = 0.05$.

We know that $\qquad \sigma_t = \dfrac{F}{A_1}$ ... Eq. *(i)*

For final load on the bolt, $\quad F = KF_a = F_i$ ... 9.2(a)/ Pg 128, DHB
$$= (0.05 \times 9000) + 5000$$
∴ $\qquad\qquad\qquad F = 5450$ N

Since $\qquad\qquad F_a > F$, take $F = 9000$ N

Eq. (i) yields... $\qquad 80 = \dfrac{9000}{A_1}$

$$A_1 = 112.5 \text{ mm}^2$$

i.e. $\qquad\qquad \dfrac{\pi d_1^2}{4} = 112.5 \text{ mm}^2$

∴ $\qquad\qquad\qquad d_1 = 11.97$ mm

The nearest value of $d_1 = 11.97$ mm corresponds to $d_1 = 12.159696$ mm for *M14*.
... 9.8/ Pg 141, DHB

Thus the size of the bolt is *M14* × 1.5.

5. **A bolt carries a tensile load of 8 kN and tightening load is 3 kN. It is made of steel having allowable tensile stress of 120 MPa. Find its size. A soft copper gasket is used.**

VTU – Dec. 2011 – 06 Marks

Solution: $F_a = 8000$ N, $F_i = 3000$ N, $d = ?$, $\sigma_t = 120$ MPa, soft copper gasket

We know that $\qquad \sigma_t = \dfrac{F}{A_1}$ $\qquad\qquad$ ... Eq. (i)

But final load on the bolt, $F = KF_a + F_i$ $\qquad$ ... **9.2(a)/ Pg 128, DHB**

For soft copper gasket, $\quad K = 0.5$ $\qquad\qquad$ ... **Tb. 9.1/ Pg 136, DHB**

$$F = (0.5 \times 8000) + 3000$$
$$F = 7000 \text{ N}$$

Since $\qquad\qquad F_a > F$, take $F = 8000$ N

Eq. (i) yields... $\qquad\qquad 120 = \dfrac{8000}{A_1}$

$$A_1 = 66.67 \text{ mm}^2$$

i.e. $\qquad\qquad \dfrac{\pi d_1^2}{4} = 66.67 \text{ mm}^2$

$\therefore \qquad\qquad d_1 = 9.21$ mm

The nearest value of $d_1 = 9.21$ mm corresponds to $d_1 = 9.852979$ mm for $M12$.

... **9.8/ Pg 141, DHB**

Thus the size of the bolt is $M12 \times 1.75$.

6. **A steam engine cylinder of 300 mm diameter is supplied with steam at 1.5 MPa. The cylinder cover is fastened by means of 8 bolts of size $M20$. The joint is made leak proof by means of suitable gaskets. Find the stress produced in the bolts.**

Solution: $D = 300$ mm, $p = 1.5$ MPa, $i = 8$, $d = 20$ mm, $\sigma_t = ?$

We know that $\qquad\qquad \sigma_t = \dfrac{F}{A_1}$ $\qquad\qquad$ ... Eq. (i)

But final load on the bolt, $F = KF_a + F_i$ $\quad$ ... Eq. (ii) **9.2(a)/ Pg 128, DHB**

Also $\qquad\qquad F_i = 2805\, d = 2805 \times 20 = 56100$ N $\quad$ ... **9.1(c)/ Pg 127, DHB**

Total external load,

$$F_a' = p\left(\frac{\pi D^2}{4}\right) = 1.5 \times \left(\frac{\pi \times 300^2}{4}\right) = 106028.75 \text{ N}$$

Load on each bolt,

$$F_a = \frac{F_a'}{i} = \frac{106028.75}{8} = 13253.60 \text{ N}$$

Assuming soft copper gasket, we have $K = 0.5$ $\qquad$ ... **Tb. 9.1/ Pg 136, DHB**

$\therefore$ Eq. (ii) yields... $\qquad\qquad F = (0.5 \times 13253.60) + 56100$

$$= 62726.50 \text{ N}$$

For $M20$ bolt,　　　　　　$A_1 = 245$ mm^2　　　　　　**... Tb. 9.8/ Pg 141, DHB**

Eq. (i) yields...　　　　　$\sigma_t = \dfrac{62726.50}{245} = 256.03$ MPa

7. **The cylinder head of a steam engine is held by 14 bolts. The effective diameter of the cylinder is 350 mm and the steam pressure is 0.85 MPa. Assuming that the bolts are not initially stressed, find the size of the bolt if permissible tensile stress is 20 MPa. Take $K = 0.5$.**

Solution: $i = 14$, $D = 350$ mm, $p = 0.85$ MPa, $d = ?$, $\sigma_t = 20$ MPa, $K = 0.5$.

We know that　　　　　$\sigma_t = \dfrac{F}{A_1}$　　　　　　　　　　**... Eq. (i)**

But final load on the bolt, $F = KF_a + F_i$　　　　**... Eq. (ii) 9.2(a)/ Pg 128, DHB**

Since the bolts are initially stressed, $F_i = 0$ N

Total external load,

$$F_a' = p\left(\frac{\pi D^2}{4}\right) = 0.85 \times \left(\frac{\pi \times 350^2}{4}\right) = 81779.58 \text{ N}$$

Load on each bolt,

$$F_a = \frac{F_a'}{i} = \frac{81779.58}{14} = 5841.40 \text{ N}$$

∴ Eq. (ii) yields...　　$F = 0 + 5841.40 = 5841.40$ N

Eq. (i) yields...　　　$20 = \dfrac{5841.40}{A_1}$

　　　　　　　　　　$A_1 = 292.06$ mm^2

i.e.　　　　　　　　$\dfrac{\pi d_1^2}{4} = 292.06$ mm^2

∴　　　　　　　　　$d_1 = 19.28$ mm

The nearest value for $d_1 = 19.28$ mm corresponds to $d_1 = 19.546261$ mm for $M22$.

　　　　　　　　　　　　　　　　　　... 9.8/ Pg 141, DHB

Thus the size of the bolt is $M22 \times 2$.

8. **The cylinder head of a steam engine is subjected to a steam pressure of 0.7 MPa. It is held in position by means of 12 bolts. A soft copper gasket is used to make the joint leak proof. The effective diameter of the cylinder is 300 mm. Find the size of the bolt so that the stresses in the bolt is not to exceed 100 MPa.**

VTU – July 2007 – 10 Marks; June/July 2011 – 10 Marks

Solution: $p = 0.7$ MPa, $i = 12$, copper gasket, $D = 300$ mm, $d = ?$, $\sigma_t = 100$ MPa.

We know that　　　$\sigma_t = \dfrac{F}{A_1}$

$$F = \sigma_t\left(\frac{\pi d_1^2}{4}\right) = 100 \times \left(\frac{\pi d_1^2}{4}\right)$$

$$= 78.54 d_1^2 = 78.54 \times (0.84 d)^2$$

(Assuming $d_1 = 0.84\, d$, for coarse threads)

$$F = 55.42\, d^2 \qquad\qquad \text{... Eq. (i)}$$

But final load on the bolt, $F = KF_a + F_i$ ... Eq. (ii) **9.2(a)/ Pg 128, DHB**

Also $F_i = 2805d$ ... **9.1(c)/ Pg 127, DHB**

Total external load,

$$F_a' = p\left(\frac{\pi D^2}{4}\right) = 0.7 \times \left(\frac{\pi \times 300^2}{4}\right) = 49480.08 \text{ N}$$

Load on each bolt,

$$F_a = \frac{F_a'}{i} = \frac{49480.08}{12} = 4123.34 \text{ N}$$

For soft copper gasket, we have $K = 0.5$ ... **9.1/ Pg 136, DHB**

$\therefore$ Eq. (ii) yields... $F = (0.5 \times 4123.34) + 2805\,d$

$$F = 2061.67 + 2805d \qquad \text{... Eq. (iii)}$$

Equating Eqs (i) and (iii), we have

$$55.42d^2 = 2061.67 + 2805d$$

$$55.42d^2 - 2805d - 2061.67 = 0$$

$$\therefore \qquad\qquad d = 51.34 \text{ mm}$$

The nearest value of $d = 51.34$ mm corresponds to $M52$.

9. **A cover plate is bolted on to the flanged end of a pressure vessel through 6 bolts. The inner diameter of the pressure vessel is 200 mm and is subjected to an internal pressure of 10 MPa. Selecting carbon steel C40 as the material for the bolts, determine the size of the bolts also considering the initial tension for the following cases:**
   a. Metal to metal joint
   b. A gasket joint.

VTU – July/ Aug. 2005 – 10 Marks; Dec. 2012 – 10 Marks; June/ July 2014 – 10 Marks

Solution: $i = 6$, $D = 200$ mm, $p = 10$ MPa, Material: C40, $d = ?$

For C40, steel $\sigma_{yt} = 324$ MPa   ... **Tb. I.8/ Pg 464, DHB**

Assume factor of safety, $n = 2$

$$\sigma_t = \frac{\sigma_{yt}}{n} = \frac{324}{2} = 162 \text{ MPa} \qquad \text{... App. III/Pg 477, DHB}$$

We know that $\sigma_t = \dfrac{F}{A_1}$

$$F = \sigma_t\left(\frac{\pi d_1^2}{4}\right) = 162 \times \left(\frac{\pi d_1^2}{4}\right)$$

$$= 127.23\,d_1^2 = 127.23 \times (0.84\,d)^2$$

(Assuming $d_1 = 0.84\,d$, for coarse threads)

$$F = 89.78\,d^2 \qquad\qquad \text{... Eq. (i)}$$

But final load on the bolt, $F = KF_a + F_i$ ... Eq. (ii) **9.2(a)/ Pg 128, DHB**

Also $F_i = 2805$ N

Total external load,

$$F_a' = p\left(\frac{\pi D^2}{4}\right) = 10 \times \left(\frac{\pi \times 200^2}{4}\right) = 314159.27 \text{ N}$$

Load on each bolt,

$$F_a = \frac{F_a'}{i} = \frac{314159.27}{6} = 52359.88 \text{ N}$$

∴ Eq. (ii) yields... $F = 52359.88\, K + 2805\, d$ ... Eq. (iii)

a. Metal to metal joint:

For metal to metal joint $K = 0$, ... **Tb. 9.1/Pg 136, DHB**

∴ Eq. (iii) yields... $F = 0 + 2805\, d$

$F = 2805\, d$ ... Eq. (iv)

Equating Eqs. (i) and (iv), we have

$89.78\, d^2 = 2805\, d$

∴ $d = 31.24$ mm

The nearest value for $d = 31.24$ mm corresponds to $M33$. ... **Tb. 9.8/Pg 140, DHB**

b. A gasket joint:

Here $K = 0.5$ assuming soft copper gasket ... **Tb. 9.1/Pg 136, DHB**

∴ Eq. (iii) yields... $F = (0.5 \times 52359.88) + 2805\, d$ ... Eq. (v)

$F = 26179.14 + 2805\, d$

Equating Eqs. (i) and (v), we have

$89.78\, d^2 = 26179.14 + 2805\, d$

$89.78\, d^2 - 2805\, d - 26179.4 = 0$

∴ $d = 38.77$ mm

The nearest value for $d = 38.77$ mm corresponds to $M39$. ... **Tb. 9.8/Pg 142, DHB**

10. **A bolted assembly consists of two components. The bolts are tightened with a preload of 1500 N. The external force acting on the assembly is 3000 N. The bolt with coarse thread is made of plain carbon steel having σ_{yt} = 400 MPa and FoS = 2. The combined thickness of the parts held together is 3 times the stiffness of the bolt. Specify the bolt size.**

Solution: $F_i = 1500$ N, $F_a = 3000$ N, $\sigma_{yt} = 400$ MPa and FoS, $n = 2$, $K_g = 3K_b$, $d = ?$

$$\sigma_t = \frac{\sigma_{yt}}{n} = \frac{400}{2} = 200 \text{ MPa}$$ ... **App. III/Pg 477, DHB**

We know that $\sigma_t = \dfrac{F}{A_1}$

$$F = \sigma_t\left(\frac{\pi d_1^2}{4}\right) = 200 \times \left(\frac{\pi d_1^2}{4}\right)$$

$$= 157.07\, d_1^2 = 157.07 \times (0.84\, d)^2$$

(Assuming $d_1 = 0.84\, d$, for coarse threads)

$$F = 110.84\, d^2$$ ... Eq. (i)

Also final load on the bolt, $F = KF_a + F_i$ ... **9.2(a)/ Pg 128, DHB**

But
$$K = \left(\frac{K_b}{K_b + K_g}\right) = \left(\frac{K_b}{K_b + 2.5K_g}\right) = \left(\frac{K_b}{4K_b}\right)$$

∴
$$F = (0.25 \times 3000) + 1500$$
$$F = 2250 \text{ N}$$ ... Eq. (ii)

Equating Eqs. (i) and (ii), we have
$$110.84 \, d^2 = 2250$$

∴
$$d = 4.51 \text{ mm}$$

The nearest value for $d = 4.51$ mm corresponds to $M4.5$.   ... **Tb. 9.8/Pg 140, DHB**

11. **The cylinder head of a reciprocating air compressor is held in place by 10 bolts. The total joint stiffness is four times the total bolt stiffness. Each bolt is tightened to an initial tension of 5 kN. The total external force acting to separate the joint is 20 kN. Find the size of the bolt so that the stress in the bolts is not to exceed 100 MPa.**

VTU – Dec. 2009/ Jan. 2010 – 08 Marks

Solution: $i = 10$, $K_g = 4K_b$, $F_i = 5000$ N, $F_a' = 20000$ N, $\sigma_t = 100$ MPa, $d = ?$

We know that
$$\sigma_t = \frac{F}{A_1}$$

$$F = \sigma_t \left(\frac{\pi d_1^2}{4}\right) = 100 \times \left(\frac{\pi d_1^2}{4}\right)$$

$$= 78.54 \, d_1^2 = 78.54 \times (0.84 \, d)^2$$

(Assuming $d_1 = 0.84 \, d$, for coarse threads)
$$F = 55.42 \, d^2$$ ... Eq. (i)

Also final load on the bolt, $F = KF_a + F_i$ **9.2(a)/ Pg 128, DHB**

But
$$K = \left(\frac{K_b}{K_b + K_g}\right) = \left(\frac{K_b}{K_b + 4K_b}\right) = \left(\frac{K_b}{4K_b}\right) = 0.2$$

Load on each bolt,
$$F_a = \frac{F_a'}{i} = \frac{20000}{10} = 2000 \text{ N}$$

∴
$$F = (0.2 \times 2000) + 5000$$
$$F = 5400 \text{ N}$$ ... Eq. (ii)

Equating Eqs. (i) and (ii), we have
$$55.42 \, d^2 = 5400$$

∴
$$d = 9.87 \text{ mm}$$

The nearest value for $d = 9.87$ mm corresponds to $M10$.   ... **Tb. 9.8/Pg 141, DHB**

12. **Two circular plates with $2d$ and d as outer and inner diameters are clamped together by means of a bolt as shown in Fig. 4.4. The bolt is made of plain carbon steel ($\sigma_y = 380$ MPa, $E = 207$ GPa) while the plates are made of aluminium ($E = 71$ GPa). The initial preload is 5 kN in the bolt and external force acting on the joint is 10 kN. Determine the size of the bolt if factor of safety = 2.5.**

VTU – June/ July 2015 – 08 Marks

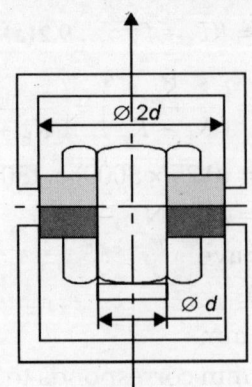

Fig. 4.4: Problem 12

Solution: $D_o = 2d$, $D_i = d$, $\sigma_y = 380$ MPa, $E_b = 207 \times 10^3$ MPa, $E_g = 71 \times 10^3$ MPa, $F_i = 5000$ N, $F_a = 10000$ N, $d = ?$, $n = 2.5$

$$\sigma_t = \frac{\sigma_{yt}}{n} = \frac{380}{2.5} = 152 \text{ MPa}$$

We know that $\qquad \sigma_t = \dfrac{F}{A_1}$

$$F = \sigma_t \left(\frac{\pi d_1^2}{4} \right) = 152 \times \left(\frac{\pi d_1^2}{4} \right)$$

$$= 119.38\, d_1^2 \qquad\qquad\qquad\qquad \text{... Eq. (i)}$$

Also final load on the bolt, $F = KF_a + F_i \qquad$ ... Eq. (ii) **9.2(a)/ Pg 128, DHB**

But $\qquad\qquad K = \dfrac{A_b E_b}{L} \Bigg/ \left(\dfrac{A_b E_b}{L} + \dfrac{A_g E_g}{t} \right)$

From **Fig. 4.4,** $\qquad L = t$

$$A_b = \left(\frac{\pi d^2}{4} \right) = 0.7854\, d_1^2$$

But $\qquad\qquad A_g = \left[\dfrac{\pi(D_o^2 - D_i^2)}{4} \right] = \left[\dfrac{\pi((2d)^2 - d^2)}{4} \right] = 2.356\, d_1^2$

$$K = \frac{0.7854\, d^2 \times (207 \times 10^3)}{[0.7854\, d^2 \times (207 \times 10^3)] + [2.356\, d^2 \times (71 \times 10^3)]}$$

$$K = 0.4928$$

$\therefore$ Eq. (ii) yields... $\qquad F = (0.4928 \times 10000) + 5000$

$$F = 9928 \text{ N}$$

Equating Eqs. (i) and (ii), we have

$$119.38\, d_1^2 = 9928$$

$\therefore \qquad\qquad\qquad\qquad d_1 = 9.119 \text{ mm}$

The nearest value for $d_1 = 9.119$ mm corresponds to $d_1 = 9.852979$ mm for M12.

... Tb. 9.8/Pg 140, DHB

Thus the size of bolt is $M12 \times 1.75$.

13. **A cylinder head is fastened to the cylinder of a compressor using 6 bolts of M20 size. Bolt material is C20. The maximum fluid pressure is 3.5 MPa, cylinder diameter is 75 mm. A soft gasket is used. Assuming the initial tension required in each bolt as 40 kN, determine the factor of safety.**

VTU – Dec. 2012 – 12 Marks

Solution: $i = 6$, $d = 20$ mm, Material: C20, $p = 3.5$ MPa, $D = 75$ mm, $F_i = 40000$ N, $n = ?$, gasket: soft

We know that
$$\sigma_t = \frac{\sigma_{yt}}{n} \qquad \text{... Eq. (i)}$$

But
$$\sigma_t = \frac{F}{A_1} \qquad \text{... Eq. (ii)}$$

But final load on the bolt, $F = KF_a + F_i$ ... Eq. (iii) **9.2(a)/ Pg 128, DHB**
Total external load,

$$F_a' = p\left(\frac{\pi D^2}{4}\right) = 3.5 \times \left(\frac{\pi \times 75^2}{4}\right) = 15462.53 \text{ N}$$

Load on each bolt,

$$F_a = \frac{F_a'}{i} = \frac{15462.53}{6} = 2577.08 \text{ N}$$

For soft copper gasket, we have $K = 0.5$ **... Tb 1.8/ Pg 463, DHB**

$\therefore$ Eq. (iii) yields... $F = (0.5 \times 2577.08) + 40000 = 41288.54$ N

For $M20$ bolt, $A_1 = 245$ mm^2 **... Tb 9.8/ Pg 142, DHB**

and $\sigma_{yt} = 245$ MPa, for C20   **... Tb I.8/Pg 463, DHB**

Eq. (ii) yields... $\sigma_t = \dfrac{41288.54}{245} = 168.52$ MPa

Eq. (i) yields... $n = \dfrac{245}{168.52} = 1.45$

14. **A steam engine cylinder has an effective diameter of 350 mm and the maximum steam pressure acting on the cylinder cover is 1.25 N/mm^2. Calculate the number and size of studs required to fix the cylinder cover, assuming the permissible stress in the studs as 33 MPa.**   *VTU – June/ July 2015 – 14 Marks*

Solution: $D = 350$ mm, $p = 1.25$ MPa, $i = ?$, $d = ?$, $\sigma_t = 33$ MPa.
Upward force acting on cylinder cover

$$F = p\left(\frac{\pi D^2}{4}\right) = 1.25 \times \left(\frac{\pi \times 350^2}{4}\right) = 120264.1 \text{ N} \qquad \text{... Eq. (i)}$$

Resisting force offered by i bolts,

$$F = \sigma_t \left(\frac{\pi d_1^2}{4}\right) i \qquad \text{... Eq. (ii)}$$

Equating Eqs. (i) and (ii), we have

$$120264.1 = 33 \, i \times \left(\frac{\pi d_1^2}{4} \right)$$

$$4640.15 = i d_1^2 \qquad \text{... Eq. (iii)}$$

From Eq. (iii), the number of bolts or studs may be obtained, if the size of the bolt or stud is known and vice versa. Usually the size of the bolt is assumed.

Let us assume $\quad\quad d = 24$ mm

For $\quad\quad\quad\quad d = 24$ mm, core diameter $d_1 = 20.319392$ mm

... Tb. 9.8/ Pg 142, DHB

$\therefore$ Eq. (iii) yields...

$$4640.15 = i \times 20.319392^2$$

$$i = 11.23 \approx 12$$

Also circumferential pitch,

$$p_c = \frac{\pi D_p}{i} \qquad \text{... Eq. (iv)}$$

where $\quad\quad$ PCD, $D_p = D + 2t + 3d_h$

Assume thickness of cylinder cover as $t = 10$ mm

Diameter of hole, $\quad\quad\quad\quad d_h = d_1 + 1$ mm $= 24 + 1$ mm $= 25$ mm

$\therefore \quad\quad\quad\quad D_p = 350 + (2 \times 10) + (3 \times 25) = 445$ mm

$\therefore$ Eq. (iv) yields... $\quad p_c = \dfrac{\pi \times 445}{12} = 116.5$ mm

Check for p_c:

$$p_c)_{min} = 20\sqrt{d_h} = 20 \times \sqrt{25} = 100 \text{ mm}$$

$$p_c)_{max} = 30\sqrt{d_h} = 30 \times \sqrt{25} = 150 \text{ mm}$$

Since 100 mm < 116.5 mm < 150 mm, the size of the bolt assumed is satisfactory.

15. **The internal diameter of a steam engine is 400 mm and the maximum pressure acting on the cylinder cover is 1.8 MPa. Calculate the number of studs required to fasten the cover to the cylinder. Assume that the permissible value of stress as 1.5 times the core diameter. Assume the pitch of studs as $20\sqrt{d_1}$ on a PCD of 500 mm for a leak proof joint.**

Solution: $D = 400$ mm, $p = 1.8$ MPa, $i = ?$, $\sigma_t = 1.5d_1$, $p_c = 20\sqrt{d_1}$, $D_p = 500$ mm.

Upward force acting on cylinder cover

$$F = p\left(\frac{\pi D^2}{4} \right) = 1.8 \times \left(\frac{\pi \times 400^2}{4} \right) = 226194.67 \text{ N} \qquad \text{... Eq. (i)}$$

Resisting force offered by i bolts,

$$F = \sigma_t \left(\frac{\pi d_1^2}{4} \right) i \qquad \text{... Eq. (ii)}$$

Equating Eqs. (i) and (ii), we have

$$226194.67 = (1.5 d_1) \times i \times \left(\frac{\pi d_1^2}{4} \right)$$

$$192000 = i d_1^3$$

$$i = \frac{192000}{d_1^3} \qquad \qquad \text{... Eq. (iii)}$$

Also circumferential pitch,

$$p_c = \frac{\pi D_p}{i}$$

$$i = \frac{\pi \times 500}{20 \sqrt{d_1}} = \frac{78.54}{\sqrt{d_1}} \qquad \qquad \text{... Eq. (iv)}$$

Equating Eqs. (iii) and (iv), we have

$$\frac{192000}{d_1^3} = \frac{78.54}{\sqrt{d_1}}$$

$$d_1^{5/2} = 2444.61$$

$$d_1 = 22.66 \text{ mm}$$

The nearest value for $d_1 = 22.66$ mm corresponds to $d_1 = 22.772131$ mm for *M24*.

... Tb. 9.8/ Pg 140, DHB

Thus the size of the bolt is *M24*

$$\therefore \text{ Eq. (iii) yields...} \qquad i = \frac{192000}{22.63^3} = 16.5 \approx 17.$$

16. **The bore of a hydraulic cylinder is 350 mm and the maximum steam pressure to which the cylinder is subjected to is 1.5 MPa. Calculate the number of bolts required to fasten the cover to the cylinder. Assume the pitch of bolts as $20\sqrt{d_1}$ on a PCD of 500 mm for a leak proof joint and permissible stress in the bolts as 40 MPa.**

Solution: $D = 350$ mm, $p = 1.5$ MPa, $i = ?$, $p_c = 20\sqrt{d_1}$, $D_p = 500$ mm, $\sigma_t = 40$ MPa.

Upward force acting on cylinder cover

$$F = p \left(\frac{\pi D^2}{4} \right) = 1.5 \times \left(\frac{\pi \times 350^2}{4} \right) = 144317 \text{ N} \qquad \text{... Eq. (i)}$$

Resisting force offered by *i* bolts,

$$F = p \left(\frac{\pi D^2}{4} \right) = 40 \times i \times \left(\frac{\pi d_1^2}{4} \right) = 31.41 \, d_1^2 \, i \qquad \text{... Eq. (ii)}$$

Equating Eqs. (i) and (ii), we have

$$144317 = 31.41 d_1^2 i$$

$$i = \frac{4593.75}{d_1^2} \qquad \qquad \text{... Eq. (iii)}$$

Also circumferential pitch,

$$p_c = \frac{\pi D_p}{i}$$

$$i = \frac{\pi \times 500}{20\sqrt{d_1}} = \frac{78.54}{\sqrt{d_1}} \qquad \dots \text{Eq. (iv)}$$

Equating Eqs. (iii) and (iv), we have

$$\frac{4593.75}{d_1^2} = \frac{78.54}{\sqrt{d_1}}$$

$$d_1^{3/2} = 58.49$$

$$d_1 = 15.07 \text{ mm}$$

The nearest value for $d_1 = 15.07$ mm corresponds to $d_1 = 15.546261$ mm for $M18$
... Tb. 9.8/ Pg 140, DHB

Thus the size of the bolt is $M18 \times 2$.

$$\therefore \text{ Eq. (iii) yields} \qquad i = \frac{4593.75}{\sqrt{15.07^2}} = 20.23 \approx 21$$

4.8 EFFECT OF FATIGUE OR DYNAMIC LOADING

The importance of preload is even greater for fatigue loaded joints than for those that are statically loaded. In most cases the type of fatigue loading encountered in the analysis of bolted joints is one in which the externally applied load fluctuates between some minimum and maximum value of F.

We know that $\qquad F = KF_a + F_i \qquad \dots$ from (Eq. 4.27)

Let the bolt be subjected to a varying load from F_{max} to F_{min}. Thus the total load on the bolt is

$$F_{max} = KF_{a})_{max} + F_i \qquad \dots \text{(Eq. 4.30)}$$

$$F_{min} = KF_{a})_{min} + F_i \qquad \dots \text{(Eq. 4.31)}$$

* Mean or average load,

$$F_m = \frac{F_{max} + F_{min}}{2}$$

* Alternating or variable load,

$$F_a = \frac{F_{max} - F_{min}}{2} \qquad \dots \textbf{2.17(a)/ Pg 24, DHB}$$

* Mean stress in the bolt,

$$\sigma_m = \frac{F_m}{A_1} = \frac{F_{max} + F_{min}}{2A_1}$$

* Alternating stress in the bolt,

$$\sigma_a = \frac{F_a}{A_1} = \frac{F_{max} - F_{min}}{2A_1}$$

According to Soderberg, the bolt size may be determined by the equation

$$\left(\frac{1}{n}\right) = \frac{K_{tf} \cdot \sigma_a}{ABC\,\sigma_{en}} + \frac{\sigma_m}{\sigma_{yp}} \qquad \dots \text{(Eq. 4.32)} \; \mathbf{2.21(c)/\,Pg\,25,\,DHB}$$

where A, B and C are correction factors for load, size and surface respectively.

(Refer Unit 3)

K_{tf} = fatigue stress concentration factor for normal stress

$K_{tf} = 1 + q(K_t - 1)$ **... 2.5/ Pg 21, DHB**

K_t = theoretical stress concentration factor for normal stress

A_1 = stress area of the bolt $= \dfrac{\pi d_1^2}{4}$

Note: The value of K_{tf}:
For rolled threads, K_{tf} = **2.2 to 3.0**
For machined threads, K_{tf} = **2.8 to 3.8**

17. **A steam engine of effective diameter 300 mm is subjected to a steam pressure of 1.5 MPa. The cylinder head is connected by 8 bolts having yield point 330 MPa and endurance limit at 240 MPa. The bolts are tightened with an initial preload of 1.5 times the steam load. A soft copper gasket is used to make the joint leak-proof. Assuming a factor of safety 2, find the size of bolt required. The stiffness factor for copper gasket may be taken as 0.5 and the stress concentration factor is 2.8.**

Solution: $D = 300$ mm, $p = 1.5$ MPa, $i = 8$, $\sigma_{yp} = 330$ MPa, $\sigma_{en} = 240$ MPa, $F_i = 1.5 F_a$, $n = 2$, $d = ?$, $K = 0.5$, $K_{tf} = 2.8$.

Method 1:
According to Soderberg,

$$\left(\frac{1}{n}\right) = \frac{K_{tf} \cdot \sigma_a}{ABC\,\sigma_{en}} + \frac{\sigma_m}{\sigma_{yp}} \qquad \dots \text{Eq. (i)} \; \mathbf{2.21(c)/\,Pg\,25,\,DHB}$$

- We know that $F = KF_a + F_i$ **... Eq. (ii) 9.2(a)/ Pg 128, DHB**

Steam load on cylinder,

$$F_a' = p\left(\frac{\pi D^2}{4}\right) = 1.5 \times \left(\frac{\pi \times 300^2}{4}\right) = 106028.75 \text{ N}$$

Load on each bolt,

$$F_a = \frac{F_a'}{i} = \frac{106028.75}{8} = 13253.60 \text{ N}$$

Preload $F_i = 1.5 F_a = 1.5 \times 13253.60 = 19880.40 \text{ N}$

$\therefore$ $F_a)_{max} = 13253.60 \text{ N and } F_a)_{min} = 0 \text{ N}$

$\therefore$ Eq. (ii) yields...

Maximum load on bolt,

$$F_{max} = KF_a)_{max} + F_i$$
$$= (0.5 \times 13253.60) + 19880.40$$
$$F_{max} = 26507.2 \text{ N}$$

Minimum load on bolt,

$$F_{min} = KF_a)_{min} + F_i$$
$$= (0.5 \times 0) + 19880.40$$
$$F_{min} = 19880.40 \text{ N}$$

- Mean stress $\quad \sigma_m = \dfrac{\sigma_{max} + \sigma_{min}}{2} = \dfrac{F_m}{A_1}$ ... **2.16(a)/ Pg 23, DHB**

But $\quad F_m = \dfrac{F_{max} + F_{min}}{2}$ and $F_a = \dfrac{F_{max} - F_{min}}{2}$ ... **2.17(a)/ Pg 24, DHB**

$$\sigma_m = \frac{F_{max} + F_{min}}{2A_1} = \frac{26507.2 + 19880.40}{2A_1} = \frac{23193.8}{A_1}$$

- Variable or alternating stress,

$$\sigma_a = \frac{\sigma_{max} - \sigma_{min}}{2} = \frac{F_a}{A_1}$$ ... **2.16(b)/ Pg 23, DHB**

$$\sigma_a = \frac{F_{max} - F_{min}}{2A_1} = \frac{26507.2 - 19880.40}{2A_1} = \frac{3313.4}{A_1}$$

- Fatigue stress concentration factor $K_{tf} = 2.8$ (data)
- Correction factors: Assume $A = 1, B = 1, C = 1$

$\therefore$ Eq. (i) yields... $\quad \left(\dfrac{1}{2}\right) = \dfrac{2.8}{(1 \times 1 \times 1) \times 240}\left(\dfrac{3313.4}{A_1}\right) + \dfrac{23193.8}{330 \times A_1}$

$$\left(\frac{1}{2}\right) = \frac{108.90}{A_1}$$

$$A_1 = 217.88 \text{ mm}^2$$

i.e. $\qquad \dfrac{\pi d_1^2}{4} = 217.88 \text{ mm}^2$

$\therefore \qquad d_1 = 16.66 \text{ mm}$

The nearest value for $d_1 = 16.66$ mm corresponds to $d_1 = 16.773131$ mm for $M18$.

         ... **Tb 9.8/Pg 141, DHB**

Thus the size of the bolt is $M18 \times 1$.

Method 2:
According to Soderberg,

$$\left(\frac{1}{n}\right) = \frac{K_{tf} \cdot \sigma_a}{ABC \, \sigma_{en}} + \frac{\sigma_m}{\sigma_{yp}}$$ ... Eq. (i) **2.21(c)/ Pg 25, DHB**

- We know that $\quad F = KF_a + F_i$ ... Eq. (ii) **9.2(a)/ Pg 128, DHB**
Steam load on cylinder,

$$F_a = p\left(\frac{\pi D^2}{4}\right) = 1.5 \times \left(\frac{\pi \times 300^2}{4}\right) = 106028.75 \text{ N}$$

Preload $\qquad F_i = 1.5 \, F_a = 1.5 \times 106028.75 = 159043.13 \text{ N}$

$\therefore$ Eq. (ii) yields...$F = (0.5 \times 106028.75) + 159043.13 = 212057.51 \text{ N}$

Maximum load per bolt,

$$F_{max} = \frac{F}{i} = \frac{212057.51}{8} = 26507.18 \text{ N}$$

Minimum load per bolt,

$$F_{min} = \frac{F_i}{i} = \frac{159043.13}{8} = 19880.40 \text{ N}$$

- Mean stress $\quad \sigma_m = \dfrac{\sigma_{max} + \sigma_{min}}{2} = \dfrac{F_m}{A_1} \qquad$ ... **2.16(a)/ Pg 23, DHB**

But $\quad F_m = \dfrac{F_{max} + F_{min}}{2}$ and $F_a = \dfrac{F_{max} - F_{min}}{2} \qquad$ ... **2.17(a)/ Pg 24, DHB**

$$\sigma_m = \frac{F_{max} + F_{min}}{2A_1} = \frac{26507.18 + 19880.40}{2A_1} = \frac{23193.79}{A_1}$$

- Variable or alternating stress,

$$\sigma_a = \frac{\sigma_{max} - \sigma_{min}}{2} = \frac{F_a}{A_1} \qquad \text{... } \textbf{2.16(b)/ Pg 23, DHB}$$

$$\sigma_a = \frac{F_{max} - F_{min}}{2A_1} = \frac{26507.18 - 19880.40}{2A_1} = \frac{3313.39}{A_1}$$

- Fatigue stress concentration factor $K_{tf} = 2.8$ (data)
- *Correction factors*: Assume $A = 1, B = 1, C = 1$

$\therefore$ Eq. (i) yields... $\quad \left(\dfrac{1}{2}\right) = \dfrac{2.8}{(1 \times 1 \times 1) \times 240}\left(\dfrac{3313.4}{A_1}\right) + \dfrac{23193.8}{330 \times A_1}$

$$\left(\frac{1}{2}\right) = \frac{108.90}{A_1}$$

$$A_1 = 217.88 \text{ mm}^2$$

i.e. $\quad \dfrac{\pi d_1^2}{4} = 217.88 \text{ mm}^2$

$\therefore \quad\quad\quad d_1 = 16.66 \text{ mm}$

The nearest value for $d_1 = 16.66$ mm corresponds to $d_1 = 16.773131$ mm for $M18$.
... **Tb. 9.8/ Pg 141, DHB**

Thus the size of the bolt is $M18 \times 1$.

18. **A bolted assembly is subjected to an external force which varies from 0 to 10 kN. The combined stiffness of the parts held together by the bolt is three times the stiffness of the bolt. The bolt is initially so tightened that at 50% overload condition, the parts held together by the bolt are just about to separate. The properties of bolt material are $\sigma_{ut} = 660$ MPa, $\sigma_y = 460$ MPa. The fatigue stress concentration factor is 2.4 and factor of safety is 2. Determine the size of the bolt.**

Solution: $F_a)_{min} = 0$ kN, $F_a)_{max} = 10$ kN, $K_g = 3K_b$, $F_i = 1.5 \, F_a)_{max}$, $\sigma_{ut} = 660$ MPa, $\sigma_{yp} = 460$ MPa, $K_{tf} = 2.4$, $n = 2$, $d = ?$

Case 1: Soderberg criteria
According to Soderberg,

$$\left(\frac{1}{n}\right) = \frac{K_{tf} \cdot \sigma_a}{ABC\,\sigma_{en}} + \frac{\sigma_m}{\sigma_{yp}} \qquad \text{... Eq. (i) 2.21(c)/ Pg 25, DHB}$$

- We know that $\quad F = KF_a + F_i \qquad \text{... Eq. (ii) 9.2(a)/ Pg 128, DHB}$

But $\qquad K = \left(\frac{K_b}{K_b + K_g}\right) = \left(\frac{K_b}{K_b + 3K_b}\right) = \left(\frac{K_b}{4K_b}\right) = 0.25$

Preload $\qquad F_i = 1.5\,F_a)_{max} = 1.5 \times 10000 = 15000 \text{ N}$

$\therefore$ Eq. (ii) yields...

Maximum load on bolt,

$$F_{max} = KF_a)_{max} + F_i$$
$$= (0.25 \times 10000) + 15000$$
$$F_{max} = 17500 \text{ N}$$

Minimum load on bolt,

$$F_{min} = KF_a)_{min} + F_i$$
$$= (0.5 \times 0) + 15000$$
$$F_{min} = 15000 \text{ N}$$

- Mean stress $\qquad \sigma_m = \frac{\sigma_{max} + \sigma_{min}}{2} = \frac{F_m}{A_1} \qquad \text{... 2.16(a)/ Pg 23, DHB}$

But $\qquad F_m = \frac{F_{max} + F_{min}}{2}$ and $F_a = \frac{F_{max} - F_{min}}{2}$

$$\text{... 2.17(a)/ Pg 24, DHB}$$

$$\sigma_m = \frac{F_{max} + F_{min}}{2A_1} = \frac{17500 + 15000}{2A_1} = \frac{16250}{A_1}$$

- Variable or alternating stress,

$$\sigma_a = \frac{\sigma_{max} - \sigma_{min}}{2} = \frac{F_a}{A_1} \qquad \text{... 2.16(b)/ Pg 23, DHB}$$

$$\sigma_a = \frac{F_{max} - F_{min}}{2A_1} = \frac{17500 - 15000}{2A_1} = \frac{1250}{A_1}$$

- Fatigue stress concentration factor
$$K_{tf} = 2.4 \quad \text{(data)}$$

- Correction factors:
  Load factor $A = 1$, assumed
  Size correction factor, $B = 0.85$, assumed since diameter is unknown
  Surface correction factor, $C = 0.75$, based on $\sigma_u = 660$ MPa
  $$\text{... Fig. 2.33(curve d)/ Pg 46, DHB}$$
- Endurance strength, $\sigma_{en} = 0.5\sigma_u = 0.5 \times 660 = 330$ MPa $\quad \text{... 2.13(a)/ Pg 23, DHB}$

$\therefore$ Eq. (i) yields... $\left(\dfrac{1}{2}\right) = \dfrac{2.4}{(1 \times 0.85 \times 0.75) \times 330}\left(\dfrac{1250}{A_1}\right) + \dfrac{16250}{460 \times A_1}$

$$\left(\frac{1}{2}\right) = \frac{49.58}{A_1}$$

$$A_1 = 99.16 \text{ mm}^2$$

i.e. $$\frac{\pi d_1^2}{4} = 99.16 \text{ mm}^2$$

∴ $$d_1 = 11.23 \text{ mm}$$

The nearest value for $d_1 = 11.23$ mm corresponds to $d_1 = 11.546261$ mm for $M14$.

... **Tb. 9.8/ Pg 141, DHB**

Thus the size of the bolt is $M14 \times 2$.

Case 2: Goodman criteria:

According to Goodman,

$$\left(\frac{1}{n}\right) = \frac{K_{tf} \cdot \sigma_a}{ABC\, \sigma_{en}} + \frac{\sigma_m}{\sigma_u} \qquad \qquad \text{... 2.21(a)/ Pg 25, DHB}$$

$$\left(\frac{1}{n}\right) = \frac{2.4}{(1 \times 0.85 \times 0.75) \times 330}\left(\frac{1250}{A_1}\right) + \frac{16250}{660 \times A_1}$$

$$\left(\frac{1}{n}\right) = \frac{38.88}{A_1}$$

∴ $$A_1 = 77.76 \text{ mm}^2$$

i.e. $$\frac{\pi d_1^2}{4} = 77.76 \text{ mm}^2$$

∴ $$d_1 = 9.95 \text{ mm} \qquad \qquad \text{... 9.2(a)/ Pg 128, DHB}$$

The nearest value for $d_1 = 9.95$ mm corresponds to $d_1 = 10.159696$ mm for $M12$.

... **Tb. 9.8/Pg 141, DHB**

Thus the size of the bolt is $M12 \times 1.5$.

19. **Two circular plates with $2d$ and d as outer and inner diameters are clamped together by means of a bolt subjected to a load that varies from zero to 10000 N, as shown in Fig. 4.5. The bolt is made of plain carbon steel ($\sigma_{ut} = 630$ MPa,**

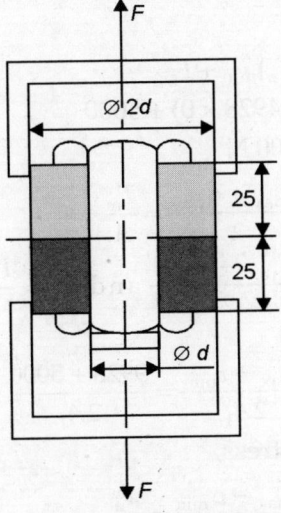

Fig. 4.5: Problem 19

σ_y = 380 MPa, E = 207 GPa) while the plates are made of aluminium (E = 71 GPa). Fatigue stress concentration factor is 2.8 and the initial preload in the bolt is 5 kN. Determine the size of the bolt if factor of safety is 3.

Solution: $D_o = 2d$, $D_i = d$, σ_{ut} = 630 MPa, σ_{yp} = 380 MPa, $E_b = 207 \times 10^3$ MPa, $E_g = 71 \times 10^3$ MPa, $K_{tf} = 2.8$, $F_i = 5$ kN, $n = 3$, $d = ?$

Case 1: Soderberg criteria

According to Soderberg,

$$\left(\frac{1}{n}\right) = \frac{K_{tf} \cdot \sigma_a}{ABC\,\sigma_{en}} + \frac{\sigma_m}{\sigma_{yp}} \qquad \text{... Eq. (i) 2.21(c)/ Pg 25, DHB}$$

- We know that $\quad F = KF_a + F_i \qquad \text{... Eq. (ii) 9.2(a)/ Pg 128, DHB}$

But $\quad K = \dfrac{A_b E_b}{L} \Big/ \left(\dfrac{A_b E_b}{L} + \dfrac{A_g E_g}{t}\right)$

From **Fig. 4.5,** $\quad L = t = 25$ mm

$$A_b = \left(\frac{\pi d^2}{4}\right) = 0.7854 d^2$$

$$A_g = \left[\frac{\pi(D_o^2 - D_i^2)}{4}\right] = \left[\frac{\pi((2d)^2 - d^2)}{4}\right] = 2.356\, d^2$$

$$K = \frac{0.7854\, d^2 \times (207 \times 10^3)}{[0.7854\, d^2 \times (207 \times 10^3)] + [2.356\, d^2 \times (71 \times 10^3)]}$$

$$K = 0.4928$$

∴ Eq. (ii) yields...

Maximum load on bolt,

$$F_{max} = KF_a)_{max} + F_i$$
$$= (0.4928 \times 10000) + 15000$$
$$F_{max} = 9928 \text{ N}$$

Minimum load on bolt,

$$F_{min} = KF_a)_{min} + F_i$$
$$= (0.4928 \times 0) + 5000$$
$$F_{min} = 5000 \text{ N}$$

- Mean stress $\quad \sigma_m = \dfrac{\sigma_{max} + \sigma_{min}}{2} = \dfrac{F_m}{A_1} \qquad \text{... 2.16(a)/ Pg 23, DHB}$

But $\quad F_m = \dfrac{F_{max} + F_{min}}{2}$ and $F_a = \dfrac{F_{max} - F_{min}}{2}$

$$\text{... 2.17(a)/ Pg 24, DHB}$$

$$\sigma_m = \frac{F_{max} + F_{min}}{2A_1} = \frac{9928 + 5000}{2A_1} = \frac{7464}{A_1}$$

- Variable or alternating stress,

$$\sigma_a = \frac{\sigma_{max} - \sigma_{min}}{2} = \frac{F_a}{A_1} \qquad \text{... 2.16(b)/ Pg 23, DHB}$$

$$\sigma_a = \frac{F_{max} - F_{min}}{2A_1} = \frac{9928 - 5000}{2A_1} = \frac{2464}{A_1}$$

- Fatigue stress concentration factor
  $$K_{tf} = 2.8 \quad \text{(data)}$$
- Correction factors:
  Load factor $A = 1$, assumed
  Size correction factor, $B = 0.85$, assumed since diameter is unknown
  Surface correction factor, $C = 0.76$, based on $\sigma_u = 630$ MPa
  ... Fig. 2.33(curve d)/ Pg 46, DHB
- Endurance strength, $\sigma_{en} = 0.5\sigma_u = 0.5 \times 630 = 315$ MPa ... **2.13(a)/ Pg 23, DHB**

$\therefore$ Eq. (i) yields... $\left(\dfrac{1}{3}\right) = \dfrac{2.8}{(1 \times 0.85 \times 0.76) \times 315}\left(\dfrac{2464}{A_1}\right) + \dfrac{7474}{380 \times A_1}$

$$\left(\frac{1}{3}\right) = \frac{53.55}{A_1}$$

$$A_1 = 160.64 \text{ mm}^2$$

i.e. $\qquad \dfrac{\pi d_1^2}{4} = 160.64 \text{ mm}^2$

$\therefore \qquad d_1 = 14.30$ mm

The nearest value for $d_1 = 11.23$ mm corresponds to $d_1 = 14.773131$ mm for $M16$.
... Tb. 9.8/ Pg 141, DHB

Thus the size of the bolt is $M16$.

Case 2: Goodman criteria:
According to Goodman,

$$\left(\frac{1}{n}\right) = \frac{K_{tf} \cdot \sigma_a}{ABC\,\sigma_{en}} + \frac{\sigma_m}{\sigma_u} \qquad \text{... 2.21(a)/ Pg 25, DHB}$$

$$\left(\frac{1}{3}\right) = \frac{2.8}{(1 \times 0.85 \times 0.76) \times 315}\left(\frac{2464}{A_1}\right) + \frac{7464}{630 \times A_1}$$

$$\left(\frac{1}{3}\right) = \frac{45.75}{A_1}$$

$\therefore \qquad A_1 = 137.26 \text{ mm}^2$

i.e. $\qquad \dfrac{\pi d_1^2}{4} = 77.76 \text{ mm}^2$

$\therefore \qquad d_1 = 13.22$ mm

The nearest value for $d_1 = 13.22$ mm corresponds to $d_1 = 13.546261$ mm for $M16$.
... Tb. 9.8/Pg 141, DHB

Thus the size of the bolt is $M16 \times 2$.

20. **A bolt connects two plates of an assembly whose combined stiffness is 4 times the stiffness of the bolt. The joint is subjected to an external load which varies from 2 kN to 6 kN. The initial tightening force on bolt is 4 kN. The bolt used is M16 coarse thread and is made of SAE 1025 annealed steel. Take $A = 1.0$, $B = 0.85$, $C = 0.9$ and $K_{ft} = 5.0$. Determine the factor of safety in design.**

VTU – Dec. 2014/ Jan. 2015 – 10 Marks

Solution: $K_g = 4K_b$, $F_a)_{min} = 2$ kN, $F_a)_{max} = 6$ kN, $F_i = 4$ kN, M16 $\Rightarrow d = 16$ mm, $A = 1.0$, $B = 0.85$, $C = 0.9$ and $K_{ft} = K_{tf} = 5.0$, $n = ?$
Material: For SAE 1025 annealed steel, $\sigma_{ut} = 462$ MPa, $\sigma_{yp} = 234$ MPa, $\sigma_{en} = 200$ MPa.

Case 1: Soderberg criteria
According to Soderberg,

$$\left(\frac{1}{n}\right) = \frac{K_{tf} \cdot \sigma_a}{ABC\,\sigma_{en}} + \frac{\sigma_m}{\sigma_{yp}} \qquad \text{... Eq. (i) } \mathbf{2.21(c)/\ Pg\ 25,\ DHB}$$

- We know that $\quad F = KF_a + F_i \qquad \text{... Eq. (ii) } \mathbf{9.2(a)/\ Pg\ 128,\ DHB}$

But $\quad K = \left(\dfrac{K_b}{K_b + K_g}\right) = \left(\dfrac{K_b}{K_b + 4K_b}\right) = \left(\dfrac{K_b}{5K_b}\right) = 0.2$

$\therefore$ Eq. (ii) yields...

Maximum load on bolt,

$$F_{max} = KF_a)_{max} + F_i$$
$$= (0.2 \times 6000) + 4000$$
$$F_{max} = 5200 \text{ N}$$

Minimum load on bolt,

$$F_{min} = KF_a)_{min} + F_i$$
$$= (0.2 \times 2000) + 4000$$
$$F_{min} = 4400 \text{ N}$$

For $d = 16$ mm and $p = 1$ mm, stress area $A_1 = 178$ mm^2

- Mean stress $\quad \sigma_m = \dfrac{\sigma_{max} + \sigma_{min}}{2} = \dfrac{F_m}{A_1} \qquad \text{... } \mathbf{2.16(a)/\ Pg\ 23,\ DHB}$

But $\quad F_m = \dfrac{F_{max} + F_{min}}{2}$ and $F_a = \dfrac{F_{max} - F_{min}}{2}$

$$\text{... } \mathbf{2.17(a)/\ Pg\ 24,\ DHB}$$

$$\sigma_m = \frac{F_{max} + F_{min}}{2A_1} = \frac{5200 + 4400}{2 \times 178} = 26.97 \text{ MPa}$$

- Variable or alternating stress,

$$\sigma_a = \frac{\sigma_{max} - \sigma_{min}}{2} = \frac{F_a}{A_1} \qquad \text{... } \mathbf{2.16(b)/\ Pg\ 23,\ DHB}$$

$$\sigma_a = \frac{F_{max} - F_{min}}{2A_1} = \frac{5200 - 4400}{2 \times 178} = 2.25 \text{ MPa}$$

- Fatigue stress concentration factor $K_{tf} = 5$ (data)
- Correction factors: $A = 1.0$, $B = 0.85$, $C = 0.9$ (data)

$\therefore$ Eq. (i) yields... $\quad \left(\dfrac{1}{n}\right) = \dfrac{5 \times 2.25}{(1 \times 0.85 \times 0.9) \times 200} + \dfrac{26.97}{234}$

$$\left(\frac{1}{n}\right) = 0.188$$

$\therefore \qquad\qquad n = 5.30 \text{ mm}$

Case 2: Goodman criteria:
According to Goodman,

$$\left(\frac{1}{n}\right) = \frac{K_{tf} \cdot \sigma_a}{ABC\,\sigma_{en}} + \frac{\sigma_m}{\sigma_u} \qquad \text{... 2.21(a)/ Pg 25, DHB}$$

$$\left(\frac{1}{n}\right) = \frac{5 \times 2.25}{(1 \times 0.85 \times 0.9) \times 200} + \frac{26.97}{462}$$

$$\left(\frac{1}{n}\right) = 0.1319$$

$$\therefore \qquad n = 7.58$$

21. **A bolt $M10 \times 1.5$ is drawn up to an initial force of 18000 N. The bolt material has a yield point value of 630 MPa and endurance limit of 410 MPa. Stress concentration factor for the threads is equal to 3. The load for bolt varies continuously from zero to 15 kN. Find the factor of safety and the value of minimum force in the part. Take $K_b = 0.785$, $K_g = 3.25$, $A = 1$, $B = 0.85$ and $C = 0.76$.**

Solution: $M10 \times 1.5 \Rightarrow d = 10$ mm, $p = 1.5$ mm, $F_i = 18000$ N, $\sigma_{yp} = 630$ MPa, $\sigma_{en} = 410$ MPa, $K_{tf} = 3$, $F_a)_{max} = 15000$ N, $F_a)_{min} = 0$ N, $n = ?$, $F_g)_{min} = ?$, $K_b = 0.785$, $K_g = 3.25$, $A = 1$, $B = 0.85$ and $C = 0.76$.

a. To find factor of safety
According to Soderberg,

$$\left(\frac{1}{n}\right) = \frac{K_{tf} \cdot \sigma_a}{ABC\,\sigma_{en}} + \frac{\sigma_m}{\sigma_{yp}} \qquad \text{... Eq. (i) 2.21(c)/ Pg 25, DHB}$$

- We know that $\qquad F = KF_a + F_i \qquad$ ... Eq. (ii) **9.2(a)/ Pg 128, DHB**

But $\qquad K = \left(\frac{K_b}{K_b + K_g}\right) = \left(\frac{0.785}{0.785 + 3.25}\right) = 0.1945$

$\therefore$ Eq. (ii) yields...

Maximum load on bolt,
$$F_{max} = KF_a)_{max} + F_i$$
$$= (0.1945 \times 15000) + 18000$$
$$F_{max} = 20917.5 \text{ N}$$

Minimum load on bolt,
$$F_{min} = KF_a)_{min} + F_i$$
$$= (0.1945 \times 0) + 18000$$
$$F_{min} = 18000 \text{ N}$$

For $d = 10$ mm and $p = 1.5$ mm, stress $A_1 = 58$ mm^2. $\qquad$ **... Tb. 9.8/ Pg 141, DHB**

- Mean stress $\qquad \sigma_m = \dfrac{\sigma_{max} + \sigma_{min}}{2} = \dfrac{F_m}{A_1} \qquad$ **... 2.16(a)/ Pg 23, DHB**

But $\qquad F_m = \dfrac{F_{max} + F_{min}}{2}$ and $F_a = \dfrac{F_{max} - F_{min}}{2}$

... 2.17(a)/ Pg 24, DHB

$$\sigma_m = \frac{F_{max} + F_{min}}{2A_1} = \frac{20917.5 + 18000}{2 \times 58} = 335.5 \text{ MPa}$$

- Variable stress,

$$\sigma_a = \frac{\sigma_{max} - \sigma_{min}}{2} = \frac{F_a}{A_1} \qquad \ldots \textbf{2.16(b)/ Pg 23, DHB}$$

$$\sigma_a = \frac{F_{max} - F_{min}}{2A_1} = \frac{20917.5 - 18000}{2 \times 58} = 26.16 \text{ MPa}$$

- Fatigue stress concentration factor $K_{tf} = 3$ (data)
- Correction factors: $A = 1$, $B = 0.85$ and $C = 0.76$ (data)

$\therefore$ Eq. (i) yields... $\left(\dfrac{1}{n}\right) = \dfrac{3 \times 25.16}{(1 \times 0.85 \times 0.76) \times 410} + \dfrac{335.5}{630}$

$$\left(\frac{1}{n}\right) = 0.818$$

$\therefore \qquad\qquad n = 1.22$

b. Minimum force on the part:

According to Goodman,

$$F_g)_{min} = KF_a - F_i = KF_a)_{max} - F_i$$

$$= F_a)_{max}\left(\frac{K_g}{K_b + K_g}\right) - F_i$$

$$= 15000 \times \left(\frac{3.25}{0.785 + 3.25}\right) - 18000$$

$\therefore \qquad\qquad F_g)_{min} = -5918.2 \text{ N}$

Negative answer indicates that no force acts on the connected parts (i.e. no separation occurs).

22. **A cylinder head is fastened to the cylinder of an air compressor using 8 numbers of bolts. Inner diameter of the cylinder is 300 mm. The pressure inside the cylinder varies from zero to a maximum pressure of 1.5 MPa. The stresses for the bolt material may be taken as $\sigma_{ut} = 500$ MPa, $\sigma_y = 300$ MPa, and $\sigma_{en} = 240$ MPa. The bolts are tightened with initial preload of 1.5 times the steam load. A copper asbestos gasket is used to make the joint leak proof. Assuming a factor of safety of 2.5, find the size of the bolt. Neglect stress concentration factor.**

VTU – Dec. 2013/ Jan. 2014 – 10 Marks

Solution: $i = 8$, $D = 300$ mm, $p_{min} = 0$ MPa, $p_{max} = 1.5$ MPa, $\sigma_u = 500$ MPa, $\sigma_{yp} = 300$ MPa, $\sigma_{en} = 240$ MPa, $F_i = 1.5 F_a)_{max}$, $n = 2.5$, $d = ?$, $K_{tf} = 1$.

Case 1: Soderberg criteria

According to Soderberg,

$$\left(\frac{1}{n}\right) = \frac{K_{tf} \cdot \sigma_a}{ABC \, \sigma_{en}} + \frac{\sigma_m}{\sigma_{yp}} \qquad \ldots \text{Eq. (i) } \textbf{2.21(c)/ Pg 25, DHB}$$

- We know that $\quad F = KF_a + F_i \qquad \ldots \text{Eq. (ii) } \textbf{9.2(a)/ Pg 128, DHB}$

For soft copper gasket, $K = 0.5$ **... Tb. 9.1/ Pg 136, DHB**

Maximum steam load on cylinder,

$$F_a)'_{max} = p_{max}\left(\frac{\pi D^2}{4}\right) = 1.5 \times \left(\frac{\pi \times 300^2}{4}\right) = 106028.75 \text{ N}$$

Minimum steam load on cylinder

$$F_a)'_{min} = p_{min}\left(\frac{\pi D^2}{4}\right) = 0 \text{ N}$$

Maximum load on each bolt,

$$F_a)_{max} = \frac{F_a)'_{max}}{i} = \frac{106028.75}{8} = 13253.60 \text{ N}$$

Minimum load on each bolt,

$$F_a)_{min} = \frac{F_a)'_{min}}{i} = 0 \text{ N}$$

Preload, $F_i = 1.5\, F_a)_{max} = 1.5 \times 13253.60 = 19880.4 \text{ N}$

$\therefore$ Eq. (ii) yields...

Maximum load on bolt,

$$F_{max} = K F_a)_{max} + F_i$$
$$= (0.5 \times 13253.60) + 19880.4$$
$$F_{max} = 26507.2 \text{ N}$$

Minimum load on bolt,

$$F_{min} = K F_a)_{min} + F_i$$
$$= (0.5 \times 0) + 19880.4$$
$$F_{min} = 19800.4 \text{ N}$$

- Mean stress $\sigma_m = \dfrac{\sigma_{max} + \sigma_{min}}{2} = \dfrac{F_m}{A_1}$ **... 2.16(a)/ Pg 23, DHB**

But $F_m = \dfrac{F_{max} + F_{min}}{2}$ and $F_a = \dfrac{F_{max} - F_{min}}{2}$

                                     ... 2.17(a)/ Pg 24, DHB

$$\sigma_m = \frac{F_{max} + F_{min}}{2A_1} = \frac{26507.2 + 19880.4}{2A_1} = \frac{23193.8}{A_1}$$

- Variable stress,

$$\sigma_a = \frac{\sigma_{max} - \sigma_{min}}{2} = \frac{F_a}{A_1}$$ **... 2.16(b)/ Pg 23, DHB**

$$\sigma_a = \frac{F_{max} - F_{min}}{2A_1} = \frac{26507.2 - 19880.4}{2A_1} = \frac{3313.4}{A_1}$$

- Fatigue stress concentration factor

$$K_{tf} = 1 \text{ (data)}$$

- Correction factors:
  Load factor $A = 1$, assumed
  Size correction factor, $B = 0.85$, assumed since diameter is unknown
  Surface correction factor, $C = 0.82$, based on $\sigma_u = 500$ MPa

  ... Fig. 2.33(curve d)/ Pg 46, DHB

$\therefore$ Eq. (i) yields...
$$\left(\frac{1}{2.5}\right) = \frac{1}{(1 \times 0.85 \times 0.82) \times 240}\left(\frac{3313.4}{A_1}\right) + \frac{23193.8}{300 \times A_1}$$

$$\left(\frac{1}{2.5}\right) = \frac{\pi d_1^2}{4}$$

$\therefore$
$$A_1 = 242.80 \text{ mm}^2$$

i.e.
$$\frac{\pi d_1^2}{4} = 242.80 \text{ mm}^2$$

$\therefore$
$$d_1 = 17.58 \text{ mm}$$

The nearest value for $d_1 = 17.58$ mm corresponds to $d_1 = 18.159696$ mm for $M20$.
Thus the size of the bolt is $M20 \times 1.5$.

Case 2: Goodman criteria:
According to Goodman,
$$\left(\frac{1}{n}\right) = \frac{K_{tf} \cdot \sigma_a}{ABC\,\sigma_{en}} + \frac{\sigma_m}{\sigma_u} \qquad \text{... 2.21(a)/ Pg 25, DHB}$$

$$\left(\frac{1}{2.5}\right) = \frac{1}{(1 \times 0.85 \times 0.82) \times 240}\left(\frac{3313.4}{A_1}\right) + \frac{23193.8}{500 \times A_1}$$

$$\left(\frac{1}{2.5}\right) = \frac{66.20}{A_1}$$

$\therefore$
$$A_1 = 165.48 \text{ mm}^2$$

i.e.
$$\frac{\pi d_1^2}{4} = 165.48 \text{ mm}^2$$

$\therefore$
$$d_1 = 14.52 \text{ mm}^2$$

The nearest value for $d_1 = 14.52$ mm corresponds to $d_1 = 14.773131$ mm for $M16$.
Thus the size of the bolt is $M16$. **... Tb 9.8/ Pg 141, DHB**

23. **A cast iron diesel engine cylinder head is held on by 8 studs with coarse threads. The maximum cylinder pressure is 5 MPa. The bore of the engine is 200 mm diameter. The initial load in the bolt is such that a cylinder pressure of 10 MPa brings the joint to opening. Assuming a factor of safety of 2 according to Soderberg's criterion, suggest a suitable size of the bolt. Take the stress concentration factor as 3.8, endurance strength in reversed axial loading as 520 MPa and the yield strength as 940 MPa. Assume $K_c = 1.45\,K_b$.**

VTU – June/ July 2008 – 10 Marks

Solution: $i = 8 = 1.5$ mm, $p_{min} = 0$ MPa, $p_{max} = 5$ MPa, $D = 200$ mm, $p_i)_{max} = 10$ MPa, $n = 2$, $d = ?$, $K_{tf} = 3.8$, $\sigma_{en} = 520$ MPa, $\sigma_{yp} = 940$ MPa, $K_c = K_g = 1.45K_b$.

According to Soderberg,

$$\left(\frac{1}{n}\right) = \frac{K_{tf} \cdot \sigma_a}{ABC\,\sigma_{en}} + \frac{\sigma_m}{\sigma_{yp}} \qquad \text{... Eq. (i) } \textbf{2.21(c)/ Pg 25, DHB}$$

- We know that $\quad F = KF_a + F_i \qquad\qquad$ ... Eq. (ii) **9.2(a)/ Pg 128, DHB**

But $\qquad K = \left(\dfrac{K_b}{K_b + K_g}\right) = \left(\dfrac{K_b}{K_b + 1.45K_b}\right) = \left(\dfrac{K_b}{2.45K_b}\right) = 0.4082$

Maximum steam load on cylinder,

$$F_a)'_{max} = p_{max}\left(\frac{\pi D^2}{4}\right) = 5 \times \left(\frac{\pi \times 200^2}{4}\right)$$

$$F_a)'_{max} = 157080 \text{ N}$$

Minimum steam load on cylinder

$$F_a)'_{min} = p_{min}\left(\frac{\pi D^2}{4}\right) = 0 \text{ N}$$

Maximum load on each bolt,

$$F_a)_{max} = \frac{F_a)'_{max}}{i} = \frac{157080}{8} = 19635 \text{ N}$$

Minimum load on each bolt,

$$F_a)_{min} = \frac{F_a)'_{min}}{i} = 0 \text{ N}$$

Preload, $\qquad F_i = p_i)_{max}\left(\dfrac{\pi D^2}{4}\right) = 10 \times \left(\dfrac{\pi \times 200^2}{4}\right) = 314160 \text{ N}$

∴ Eq. (ii) yields...

Maximum load on bolt,

$$F_{max} = KF_a)_{max} + F_i$$
$$= (0.4082 \times 19635) + 314160$$
$$F_{max} = 322175 \text{ N}$$

Minimum load on bolt,

$$F_{min} = KF_a)_{min} + F_i$$
$$= (0.4082 \times 0) + 314160$$
$$F_{min} = 314160 \text{ N}$$

- Mean stress $\quad \sigma_m = \dfrac{\sigma_{max} + \sigma_{min}}{2} = \dfrac{F_m}{A_1} \qquad$ ... **2.16(a)/ Pg 23, DHB**

But $\qquad F_m = \dfrac{F_{max} + F_{min}}{2}$ and $F_a = \dfrac{F_{max} - F_{min}}{2}$

... **2.17(a)/ Pg 24, DHB**

$$\sigma_m = \frac{F_{max} + F_{min}}{2A_1} = \frac{322175 + 314160}{2A_1} = \frac{318167.5}{A_1}$$

- Variable stress,

$$\sigma_a = \frac{\sigma_{max} - \sigma_{min}}{2} = \frac{F_a}{A_1} \qquad \text{... 2.16(b)/ Pg 23, DHB}$$

$$\sigma_a = \frac{F_{max} - F_{min}}{2A_1} = \frac{322175 - 314160}{2A_1} = \frac{4007.5}{A_1}$$

- Fatigue stress concentration factor
  $$K_{tf} = 3.8 \quad \text{(data)}$$

- Correction factors:
  Load factor $A = 1$, assumed
  Size correction factor, $B = 0.85$, assumed since diameter is unknown
  Surface correction factor, $C = 1$, assumed since σ_u is unknown

$\therefore$ Eq. (i) yields...
$$\left(\frac{1}{2}\right) = \frac{3.8}{(1 \times 0.85 \times 1) \times 520}\left(\frac{4007.5}{A_1}\right) + \frac{318167.5}{940 \times A_1}$$

$$\left(\frac{1}{2}\right) = \frac{372.93}{A_1}$$

$\therefore \qquad A_1 = 745.86 \text{ mm}^2$

i.e. $\qquad \dfrac{\pi d_1^2}{4} = 745.86 \text{ mm}^2$

$\therefore \qquad d_1 = 30.82 \text{ mm}$

The nearest value for $d_1 = 30.82$ mm corresponds to $d_1 = 31.159696$ mm for $M33$.
$$\text{... Tb. 9.8/ Pg 142, DHB}$$

Thus the size of the bolt is $M33 \times 1.5$ or $M35$.

4.9 EFFECT OF IMPACT LOADING

Impact stresses result when the bolt is subjected to suddenly applied or impact loads.
   Impact energy or resilience,

$$U = \frac{F\delta}{2} \qquad \text{... Eq. (4.33) 2.27(a)/ Pg 28, DHB}$$

where F = load caused by impact
   δ = deformation caused by impact.

24. **A $M10$ steel bolt of 125 mm long is subjected to an impact load. The kinetic energy absorbed by the bolt is 2.5 J. Determine:**
    a. Stress in the shank of the bolt if there is no threaded position between the nut and the bolt.
    b. Stress in the shank if the area of the shank is reduced to that of the root area of the thread or the entire length of bolt is threaded.

VTU – Dec. 2014/Jan. 2015 – 10Marks, Dec. 2013/Jan. 2014 – 10Marks,
June/July 2013 – 12 Marks

Solution: $M10 \Rightarrow d = 10$ mm, $L = 125$ mm, $U = 2.5$ N·m $= 2.5 \times 10^3$ N·mm, $\sigma' = ?$
We know that impact stress,

$$\sigma' = \frac{F}{A_1} \qquad \text{... Eq. (i)}$$

- For $d = 10$ mm, stress area $A_1 = 58$ mm^2 ... **Tb. 9.8/ Pg 141, DHB**
- But impact energy

$$U = \frac{F\delta}{2} \quad\quad\quad\quad\quad ... \text{2.27(a)/ Pg 28, DHB}$$

$$U = \frac{F^2 L}{2AE} \quad\quad\quad\quad ... \text{Eq. (ii) using } \textbf{1.2(b)/ Pg 3, DHB}$$

a. Stress based on shank area:

Here $A = \dfrac{\pi d^2}{4} = \dfrac{\pi \times 10^2}{4} = 78.54$ mm^2

$\therefore$ Eq. (ii) yields...

$$2.5 \times 10^3 = \frac{F^2 \times 125}{2 \times 78.54 \times 210 \times 10^3} \quad\quad (\text{Assume } E = 210 \text{ GPa})$$

$$F = 25685.30 \text{ N}$$

$\therefore$ Eq. (i) yields... $\sigma' = \dfrac{25685.30}{58} = 442.85$ MPa

b. Stress based on core area:

Here $A = A_1 = 58$ mm

$\therefore$ Eq. (ii) yields...

$$2.5 \times 10^3 = \frac{F^2 \times 125}{2 \times 58 \times 210 \times 10^3}$$

$$F = 22072.61 \text{ N}$$

$\therefore$ Eq. (i) yields... $\sigma' = \dfrac{22072.61}{58} = 380.56$ MPa

25. **A M20 × 2 steel bolt of 100 mm is subjected to impact load. The energy absorbed by the bolt is 2 N·m.**
    a. Determine the stress in the shank of the bolt if there is no thread portion between the nut and bolt head.
    b. Determine the stress in the shank, if the entire length of the bolt is threaded.
    Assume modulus of elasticity for steel as 206 GPa.

VTU – June/July 2013 – 08 Marks, May/June 2010 – 08 Marks,
Dec. 07/Jan. 2008 – 10 Marks

Solution: $M20 \times 2 \Rightarrow d = 20$ mm, $p = 2$ mm, $L = 100$ N·m $= 2 \times 10^3$ N·mm, $\sigma' = ?$, $E = 206 \times 10^3$ MPa.

We know that impact stress,

$$\sigma' = \frac{F}{A_1} \quad\quad\quad\quad\quad\quad\quad ... \text{Eq. (i)}$$

- For $d = 20$ mm and $p = 2$ mm, stress area $A_1 = 258$ mm^2... **Tb. 9.8/ Pg 141, DHB**
- But impact energy

$$U = \frac{F\delta}{2} \quad\quad\quad\quad\quad ... \text{2.27(a)/ Pg 28, DHB}$$

$$U = \frac{F^2 L}{2AE} \qquad \text{... Eq. (ii) using } \mathbf{1.2(b)/ Pg\ 3, DHB}$$

a. Stress based on shank area:

Here
$$A = \frac{\pi d^2}{4} = \frac{\pi \times 20^2}{4} = 314.16 \text{ mm}^2$$

∴ Eq. (ii) yields...

$$2 \times 10^3 = \frac{F^2 \times 100}{2 \times 314.16 \times 206 \times 10^3}$$

$$F = 50879 \text{ N}$$

∴ Eq. (i) yields... $\qquad \sigma' = \dfrac{50879}{258} = 197.21 \text{ MPa}$

b. Stress based on core area:

Here $\qquad\qquad A = A_1 = 258 \text{ mm}$

∴ Eq. (ii) yields...

$$2 \times 10^3 = \frac{F^2 \times 100}{2 \times 258 \times 206 \times 10^3}$$

$$F = 46107.70 \text{ N}$$

∴ Eq. (i) yields... $\qquad \sigma' = \dfrac{46107.70}{258} = 178.71 \text{ MPa}$

4.10 ECCENTRIC LOADING OR BOLTED JOINTS IN SHEAR

In many applications, a machine member is subjected to load such that a bending moment is developed in addition to direct normal or shear loading. Such type of loading is commonly known as eccentric loading.

 • Examples include wall bracket, pillar crane, web splices in beams and girders, standard structural connections, etc.

Following are some of the cases of an eccentric load:
   a. Load parallel to the axis of the bolt
   b. Load perpendicular to the axis of the bolt
   c. Load acting in a plane containing the bolts.

4.10.1 Eccentric Load Acting Parallel to the Axis of the Bolt

Figure 4.6 represents a bracket having a rectangular base subjected a load acting parallel to the bolt axis. This load tends to rotate the bracket about the tilting edge A–A, thereby stretching the bolt by an amount depending upon its distance from the tilting edge. Further each bolt is located at a distance from the tilting edge and hence the bolts are not equally stressed. For convenience, all the bolts are made of same size.

Let F = applied load
   e = eccentricity
   N = number of bolts
   l_1 = distance between first row of bolts and the tilting edge
   F_1 = force induced in first row of bolts

Similarly l_2, F_2 are corresponding parameters.

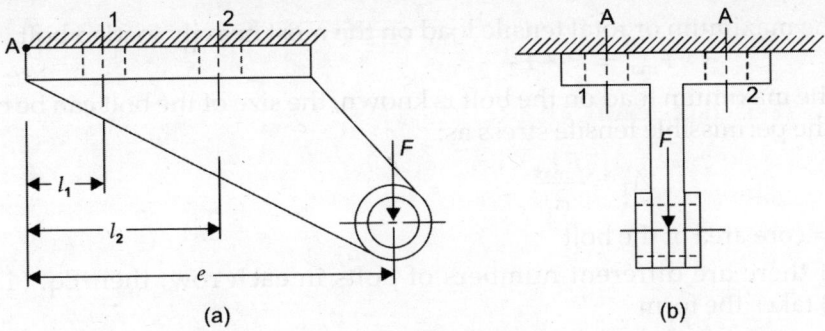

Fig. 4.6: Eccentric load parallel to bolt axis—rectangular base

Since the stresses induced in the bolts are directly proportional to the elongation which in turn is proportional to the distance of the bolts from tilting edge, we have

$$\frac{F_1}{l_1} = \frac{F_2}{l_2} \Rightarrow F_2 = \left(\frac{F_1 l_2}{l_1}\right) \qquad \text{... (Eq. 4.34)}$$

The moment (Fe) due to load F must be balanced by the sum of moments of bolt loads about the tilting edge.

$$Fe = N(F_1 l_1 + F_2 l_2)$$
$$Fe = 2(F_1 l_1 + F_2 l_2) \qquad \text{... (Eq. 4.35)}$$

(Here $N = 2$ since each row has two bolts)

i.e.
$$\frac{Fe}{2} = F_1 l_1 + \left(\frac{F_1 l_2}{l_1}\right) l_2 \qquad \text{... using (Eq. 4.34)}$$

$$= F_1 l_1 + \left(\frac{F_1 l_2^2}{l_1}\right).$$

$$= \frac{F_1}{l_1}(l_1^2 + l_2^2)$$

∴
$$F_1 = \frac{Fe l_1}{2(l_1^2 + l_2^2)} \qquad \text{... (Eq. 4.36a)}$$

Similarly,
$$F_2 = \frac{Fe l_1}{2(l_1^2 + l_2^2)} \qquad \text{... (Eq. 4.36b)}$$

Repeated in general, the most heavily loaded bolts are those which are situated at the greatest distance from the tilting edge, i.e. bolts located at l_2.

i.e.
$$F_{max} = F_2 = \frac{Fe l_2}{2(l_1^2 + l_2^2)} \qquad \text{... (Eq. 4.37)}$$

Further when the load is parallel to the axis of the bolt, each bolt will be subjected to tensile loading only.

i.e.
$$F' = \frac{F}{N} \qquad \text{... (Eq. 4.38)}$$

Thus, the maximum or total tensile load on the most heavily loaded bolt,
$$F_{max} = F' + F_2 \qquad \text{... (Eq. 4.39)}$$
When the maximum load on the bolt is known, the size of the bolt can be calculated based on the permissible tensile stress as:
$$A_1 = \frac{F_{max}}{\sigma_t} \qquad \text{... (Eq. 4.40)}$$
where A_1 = core area of the bolt

Note: If there are different numbers of bolts in each row, then Eq. (4.36a) and Eq. (4.36b) takes the form
$$F_1 = \frac{Fel_1}{N_1 l_1^2 + N_2 l_2^2} \quad \text{and} \quad F_2 = \frac{Fel_2}{N_1 l_1^2 + N_2 l_2^2} \qquad \text{... (Eq. 4.41)}$$

26. **A bracket is connected by bolts as shown in Fig. 4.7. If the permissible tensile stress for the bolt material is 60 N/mm², specify the size of the bolt. The bracket is fixed using four bolts.**

VTU – Dec. 2013/ Jan. 2014 – 14 Marks

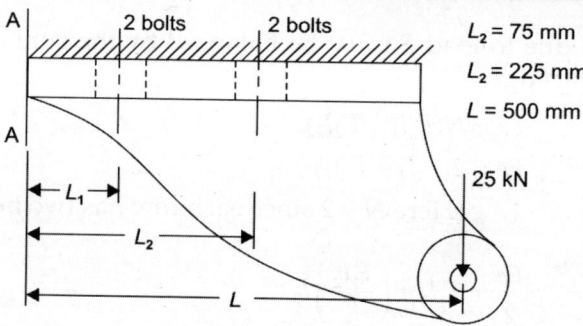

Fig. 4.7: Problem 26

Solution: $\sigma_t = 60 \text{ N/mm}^2$, $d = ?$, $N = 4$, $l_1 = 75$ mm, $l_2 = 225$ mm, $l = e = 500$ mm, $F = 25 \times 10^3$ N.

We know that
$$\sigma_t = \frac{F_{max}}{A_1} \qquad \text{... Eq. (i)}$$

But
$$F_{max} = F' + F_2 \qquad \text{... Eq. (ii)}$$

- Direct tensile load,
$$F' = \frac{F}{N} = \frac{25 \times 10^3}{4} = 6250 \text{ N}$$

- The most heavily loaded bolts are situated at the greatest distance from the tilting edge, i.e. bolts located at l_2

i.e.
$$F_2 = \frac{Fel_2}{2(l_1^2 + l_2^2)} = \frac{25 \times 10^3 \times 500 \times 225}{2(75^2 + 225^2)} = 25000 \text{ N}$$

∴ Eq. (ii) yields...
$$F_{max} = 6250 + 25000 = 31250 \text{ N}$$

Eq. (i) yields...
$$A_1 = \frac{31250}{60} = 520.84 \text{ mm}^2$$

i.e
$$\frac{\pi d_1^2}{4} = 520.84 \text{ mm}^2$$

∴
$$d_1 = 25.75 \text{ mm}$$

The nearest value for $d_1 = 25.75$ mm corresponds to $d_1 = 26.319392$ mm for $M30$
... Tb. 9.8/ Pg 142, DHB

Thus the size of the bolt is $M30 \times 3$.

4.10.2 Eccentric Load Acting Perpendicular to the Axis of the Bolt

a. Rectangular base: Figure 4.8 represents a bracket having a rectangular base subjected a load acting perpendicular to the bolt axis. This load tends to rotate the bracket in clockwise direction about the tilting edge A–A, thereby stretching the bolt by an amount depending upon its distance from the tilting edge. Further each bolt is located at a distance from the tilting edge and hence the bolts are not equally stressed. For convenience, all the bolts are made of same size.

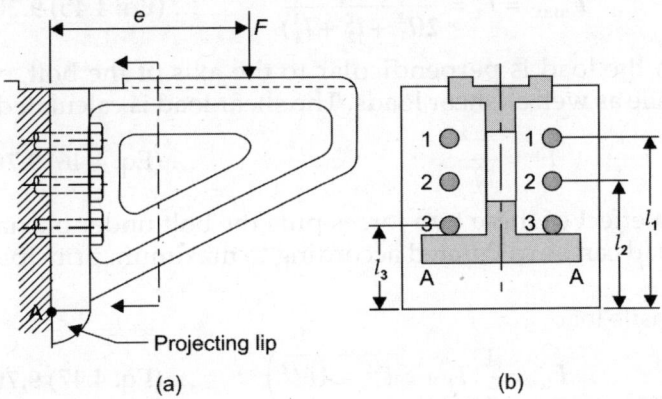

(a)   (b)

Fig. 4.8: Eccentric load perpendicular to bolt axis—rectangular base **[Fig. 9.2/Pg 130, DHB]**

Let F = applied load
  e = eccentricity
  N = number of bolts
  l_1 = distance between first row of bolts and the tilting edge
  F_1 = force induced in first row of bolts

Similarly l_2, F_2 and l_3, F_3 are corresponding parameters

Since the stresses induced in the bolts are directly proportional to the elongation which in turn is proportional to the distance of the bolts from tilting edge, we have

$$\frac{F_1}{l_1} = \frac{F_2}{l_2} = \frac{F_3}{l_3} \Rightarrow F_2 = \left(\frac{F_1 l_2}{l_1}\right), \; F_3 = \left(\frac{F_1 l_3}{l_1}\right) \qquad \text{... (Eq. 4.42)}$$

The moment (Fe) due to load F must be balanced by the sum of moments of bolt loads about the tilting edge.

$$Fe = N(F_1 l_1 + F_2 l_2 + F_3 l_3)$$
$$Fe = 2(F_1 l_1 + F_2 l_2 + F_3 l_3) \qquad \text{... (Eq. 4.43)}$$
$$\text{(Here } N = 2 \text{ since each row has two bolts)}$$

i.e. $$\frac{Fe}{2} = F_1 l_1 + \left(\frac{F_1 l_2}{l_1}\right) l_2 + \left(\frac{F_1 l_3}{l_1}\right) l_3 \qquad \text{... using (Eq. 4.42)}$$

$$= F_1 l_1 + \left(\frac{F_1 l_2^2}{l_1}\right) + \left(\frac{F_1 l_3^2}{l_1}\right)$$

$$= \frac{F_1}{l_1}(l_1^2 + l_2^2 + l_3^2)$$

$$\therefore \qquad F_1 = \frac{Fel_1}{2(l_1^2 + l_2^2 + l_3^2)} \qquad \text{... (Eq. 4.44a) Fig. 9.7(b)/Pg 130, DHB}$$

Similarly, $\qquad F_2 = \dfrac{Fel_2}{2(l_1^2 + l_2^2 + l_3^2)}$ and $F_3 = \dfrac{Fel_3}{2(l_1^2 + l_2^2 + l_3^2)}$ $\qquad$ ... (Eq. 4.44b)

In general, the most heavily loaded bolts are those which are situated at the greatest distance from the tilting edge

i.e. $\qquad F_{max} = F_1 = \dfrac{Fel_1}{2(l_1^2 + l_2^2 + l_3^2)} \qquad \text{... (Eq. 4.45) 9.7(b)/ Pg 130, DHB}$

Further when the load is perpendicular to the axis of the bolt, each bolt will be subjected to tensile as well as shear loads. The shear load is calculated as

i.e. $\qquad F' = \dfrac{F}{N} \qquad \text{... (Eq. 4.46) 9.7(a)/ Pg 130, DHB}$

The combined effect of these two forces puts the bolt under biaxial loading. Thus, the equivalent load can be calculated according to maximum principal/ normal stress theory as:

Equivalent tensile load,

$$F_{te} = \frac{1}{2}\left(F_1 + \sqrt{F_1^2 + 4F'^2} \right) \qquad \text{... (Eq. 4.47) 9.7(c)/ Pg 130, DHB}$$

Equivalent shear load,

$$F_{se} = \frac{1}{2}\sqrt{F_1^2 + 4F'^2} = \frac{1}{2}(F_1^2 + 4F'^2)^{1/2}$$

$$\text{... (Eq. 4.48) 9.7(d)/ Pg 130, DHB}$$

When the equivalent loads on the bolt are known, the size of the bolt can be calculated based on the permissible tensile stress as

$$A_1 = \frac{F_{te}}{\sigma_t} \qquad \text{... (Eq. 4.49)}$$

On the basis of shear stress,

$$A_1 = \frac{F_{se}}{\tau} \qquad \text{... (Eq. 4.50)}$$

where A_1 = core area of the bolt

> *Note:*
> - The projecting lip is provided to take care of direct shear load.
> - If there are different numbers of bolts in each row, then Eq. (4.44a) and Eq. (4.44b) takes the form

$$F_1 = \frac{Fel_1}{N_1 l_1^2 + N_2 l_2^2 + N_3 l_3^2},$$

$$F_2 = \frac{Fel_2}{N_1 l_1^2 + N_2 l_2^2 + N_3 l_3^2},$$

and
$$F_e = \frac{Fel_e}{N_1l_1^2 + N_2l_2^2 + N_3l_3^2} \qquad \text{... (Eq. 4.51)}$$

b. Circular base: Figure 4.9 represents eccentric load acting on a circular base acting perpendicular to the bolt axis.

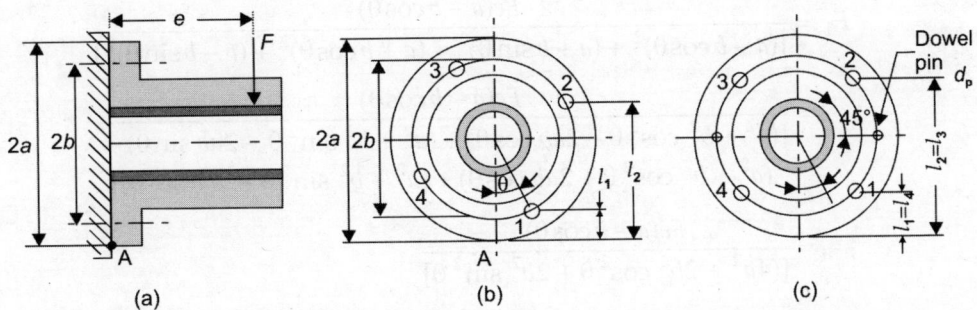

Fig. 4.9: Eccentric load acting perpendicular to axis of bolt—circular base [**Fig. 9.3/Pg 131, DHB**]

Let F = applied load
$\quad e$ = eccentricity
$\quad N$ = number of bolts
$\quad a$ = radius of flange
$\quad b$ = radius of bolt circle
$\quad l_1$ = distance between first row of bolts and the tilting edge
$\quad F_1$ = force induced in first row of bolts

Similarly l_2, F_2, l_3, F_3 and l_4, F_4 be corresponding parameters.

Since the stresses induced in the bolts are directly proportional to the elongation which in turn is proportional to the distance of the bolts from tilting edge, we have

$$\frac{F_1}{l_1} = \frac{F_2}{l_2} = \frac{F_3}{l_3} = \frac{F_4}{l_4} \Rightarrow F_2 = \left(\frac{F_1l_2}{l_1}\right), \ F_3 = \left(\frac{F_1l_3}{l_1}\right), F_4 = \left(\frac{F_1l_4}{l_1}\right)$$

$$\text{... (Eq. 4.52)}$$

The moment (Fe) due to load F must be balanced by the sum of moments of bolt loads about the tilting edge.

$$Fe = N(F_1l_1 + F_2l_2 + F_3l_3 + F_4l_4)$$
$$Fe = (F_1l_1 + F_2l_2 + F_3l_3 + F_4l_4) \qquad \text{... (Eq. 4.53)}$$
(Here $N = 1$ since each row has one bolt)

i.e.
$$Fe = F_1l_1 + \left(\frac{F_1l_2}{l_1}\right)l_2 + \left(\frac{F_1l_3}{l_1}\right)l_3 + \left(\frac{F_1l_4}{l_1}\right)l_4 \qquad \text{... using (Eq. 4.42)}$$

$$= F_1l_1 + \left(\frac{F_1l_2^2}{l_1}\right) + \left(\frac{F_1l_3^2}{l_1}\right) + \left(\frac{F_1l_4^2}{l_1}\right)$$

$$= \frac{F_1}{l_1}(l_1^2 + l_2^2 + l_3^2 + l_4^2)$$

$$\therefore \qquad F_1 = \frac{Fel_1}{(l_1^2 + l_2^2 + l_3^2 + l_4^2)} \qquad \text{... (Eq. 4.54) Fig. 9.8(b)/Pg 131, DHB}$$

From the geometry of **Fig. 4.8(b)**, we have distances

$$l_1 = a - b \cos\theta \qquad l_2 = a + b \sin\theta$$
$$l_3 = a + b \cos\theta \qquad l_4 = a - b \sin\theta \qquad \ldots \text{(Eq. 4.55)}$$

Substituting (Eq. 4.55) in (Eq. 4.54), we have

$$F_1 = \frac{Fe(a - b\cos\theta)}{[(a - b\cos\theta)^2 + (a + b\sin\theta)^2 + (a + b\cos\theta)^2 + (a - b\sin\theta)^2]}$$

$$= \frac{Fe(a - b\cos\theta)}{[(a^2 + b^2\cos^2\theta - 2ab\cos\theta) + (a^2 + b^2\sin^2\theta + 2ab\sin\theta) + (a^2 + b^2\cos^2\theta + 2ab\cos\theta) + (a^2 + b^2\sin^2\theta - 2ab\sin\theta)]}$$

$$= \frac{Fe(a - b\cos\theta)}{[(4a^2 + 2b^2\cos^2\theta + 2b^2\sin^2\theta]}$$

$$\therefore \qquad F_1 = \frac{Fe(a - b\cos\theta)}{4a^2 + 2b^2} = \frac{Fel_1}{4a^2 + 2b^2} \qquad (\because \sin^2\theta + \cos^2\theta = 1)$$

$$\ldots \text{(Eq. 4.56a) } \textbf{9.8(b)/Pg 131, DHB}$$

Similarly, $\quad F_2 = \dfrac{Fel_2}{4a^2 + 2b^2}, F_3 = \dfrac{Fel_3}{4a^2 + 2b^2}$ and $F_4 = \dfrac{Fel_4}{4a^2 + 2b^2} \qquad \ldots \text{(Eq. 4.56b)}$

Thus for N bolts (Eq. 4.56a) yields...

$$F_1 = \frac{Fe(a - b\cos\theta)}{4a^2 + 2b^2}$$

$$= \frac{Fe(a - b\cos\theta)}{2(2a^2 + b^2)}$$

$$= \frac{2Fe(a - b\cos\theta)}{4(2a^2 + b^2)} \quad \text{(Multiply and divide by 2)} \qquad \ldots \text{(Eq. 4.56c)}$$

Here 4 refers to the number of bolts.
Thus for N bolts, we have

i.e. $\qquad F_{1-n} = \dfrac{2Fe(a - b\cos\theta)}{(2a^2 + b^2)N} \qquad \ldots \text{(Eq. 4.56d) } \textbf{9.8(c)/ Pg 131, DHB}$

The load will be maximum if $\cos\theta = -1$ or $\theta = 180°$ in (Eq. 4.55a) or (Eq. 4.55d). (Eq. 4.56a) yields...

$$F_{\max} = \frac{Fe(a + b)}{4a^2 + 2b^2} = \frac{Fe(a + b)}{2(2a^2 + b^2)}$$

$$= \frac{2Fe(a + b)}{4(2a^2 + b^2)} \quad \text{(Multiply and divide by 2)} \qquad \ldots \text{(Eq. 4.57)}$$

Thus for N bolts, we have

$$F_{\max} = \frac{2Fe(a + b)}{(2a^2 + b^2)N} \qquad \ldots \text{(Eq. 4.58) } \textbf{9.8(d)/Pg 131, DHB}$$

Equation (4.58) is used if the direction of the load F changes with relation to the bolts (*as in the case of pillar crane*).

But when the direction of load is fixed, then the maximum load on the bolts can be reduced by locating the bolts in such a way that two of them are *equally stressed* as shown in **Fig. 4.9(c)**, by using dowel pins.

Then maximum load is given as

$$F_{max} = 2Fe\left[\frac{a + b\cos(180/N)^\circ}{(2a^2 + b^2)N}\right] \quad \text{... (Eq. 4.59)} \text{ 9.8(e)/Pg 131, DHB}$$

The bolts are relieved of shear stress by using two dowel pins as shown in **Fig. 4.9(c)**. Hence, bolts are designed to carry tensile load only.

When the maximum load on the bolt is known, the size of the bolt can be calculated based on the permissible tensile stress as

$$A_1 = \frac{F_{max}}{\sigma_t} \quad \text{... (Eq. 4.60)}$$

where A_1 = core area of the bolt

27. **A bracket is fixed to the wall by means of four bolts and loaded as shown in Fig. 4.10. Calculate the size of the bolts if the load is 10 kN and allowable shear stress in the bolt material is 40 MPa.**

VTU – Dec. 2012 – 10 Marks

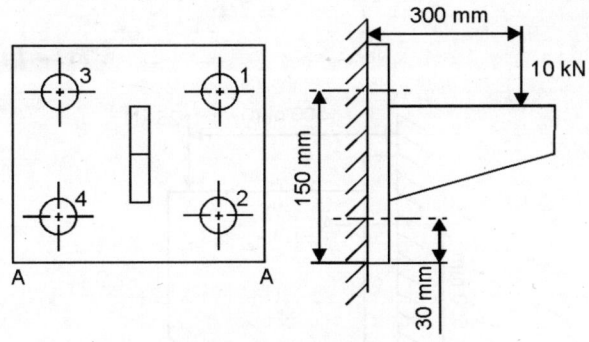

Fig. 4.10: Problem 27

Solution: $N = 4$, $d = ?$, $\tau = 40$ MPa, $l_1 = l_3 = 150$ mm, $l_2 = l_4 = 30$ mm, $F = 10 \times 10^3$ N, $e = 300$ mm.

We know that
$$\tau = \frac{F_{se}}{A_1} \quad \text{... Eq. (i)}$$

But equivalent shear load,
$$F_{se} = \frac{1}{2}\sqrt{F_1^2 + 4F'^2} \quad \text{... Eq. (ii)} \text{ 9.7(d)/ Pg 130, DHB}$$

- Direct shear load,
$$F' = \frac{F}{N} = \frac{10 \times 10^3}{4} = 2500 \text{ N} \quad \text{... 9.7(a)/ Pg 130, DHB}$$

- Maximum secondary tensile force,
$$F_1 = \frac{Fel_1}{2(l_1^2 + l_2^2)} \quad \text{... 9.7(b)/ Pg 130, DHB}$$

$$= \frac{(10 \times 10^3) \times 300 \times 150}{2(150^2 + 30^2)}$$

$$F_1 = 9615.38 \text{ N}$$

∴ Eq. (ii) yields... $\quad F_{se} = \frac{1}{2}\sqrt{9615.38^2 + (4 \times 2500^2)} = 5418.85 \text{ N}$

∴ Eq. (i) yields... $\quad A_1 = \frac{5418.85}{40} = 135.47 \text{ mm}^2$

i.e. $\quad\quad\quad \frac{\pi d_1^2}{4} = 135.47 \text{ mm}^2$

∴ $\quad\quad\quad\quad\quad d_1 = 13.13 \text{ mm}$

The nearest value for $d_1 = 13.13$ mm corresponds to $d_1 = 13.546261$ mm for $M16$

... Tb. 9.8/ Pg 141, DHB

Thus the size of the bolt is $M16 \times 2$.

28. **A wall bracket is attached to a wall by means of 4 identical bolts, two at A and two at B, as shown in Fig. 4.11. Assuming that the bracket is held against the wall and prevented from tipping about C, by all four bolts, and using an allowable stress in the bolts as 35 MPa, determine the size of the bolts on the basis of maximum principal stress theory, selecting ISO, metric threads of not more than 1.5 mm pitch.**

VTU – June 2012 – 14 Marks

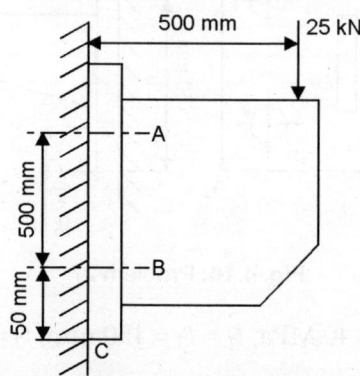

Fig. 4.11: Problem 28

Solution: $N = 4$, $d = ?$, $\tau = 35$ MPa, pitch $p \ngtr 1.5$ mm, $l_1 = l_3 = 550$ mm, $l_2 = l_4 = 50$ mm, $F = 25 \times 10^3$ N, $e = 500$ mm.

We know that $\quad\quad \tau = \frac{F_{se}}{A_1}$ $\quad\quad\quad\quad\quad\quad$ ... Eq. (i)

But equivalent shear load,

$$F_{se} = \frac{1}{2}\sqrt{F_1^2 + 4F'^2}$$ $\quad\quad$ ... Eq. (ii) **9.7(d)/ Pg 130, DHB**

• Direct shear load,

$$F' = \frac{F}{N} = \frac{25 \times 10^3}{4} = 6250 \text{ N}$$ $\quad\quad$ ... **9.7(a)/ Pg 130, DHB**

• Maximum secondary tensile force,

$$F_1 = \frac{Fel_1}{2(l_1^2 + l_2^2)} \qquad \text{... 9.7(b)/ Pg 130, DHB}$$

$$= \frac{(25 \times 10^3) \times 500 \times 550}{2(550^2 + 50^2)}$$

$$F_1 = 11270.50 \text{ N}$$

∴ Eq. (ii) yields... $F_{se} = \frac{1}{2}\sqrt{11270.50^2 + (4 \times 6250^2)} = 8415.37 \text{ N}$

∴ Eq. (i) yields... $A_1 = \frac{8415.37}{35} = 240.44 \text{ mm}^2$

i.e. $\frac{\pi d_1^2}{4} = 240.44 \text{ mm}^2$

∴ $d_1 = 17.50 \text{ mm}$

The nearest value for $d_1 = 17.50$ mm corresponds to $d_1 = 18.159696$ mm for *M20*.
... Tb. 9.8/ Pg 141, DHB

Thus the size of the bolt is *M20 × 2*.

29. **A bracket is fixed to a wall by means of four bolts and loaded as shown in Fig. 4.12. Calculate the size of the bolts if the load is 25 kN and the yield stress is 380 MPa. The factor of safety is taken as 2.5. Use maximum shear stress theory.**

VTU – June/ July 2009 – 10 Marks; Dec. 08/ Jan. 2009 – 10 Marks

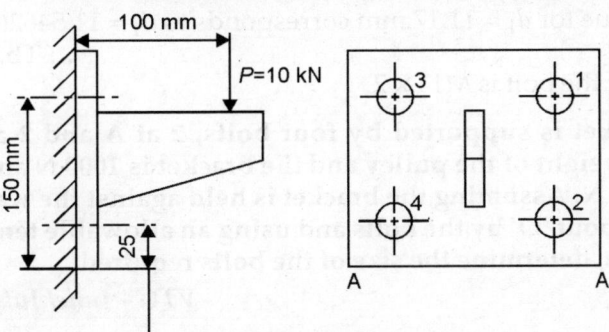

Fig. 4.12: Problem 29

Solution: $N = 4$, $d = ?$, $F = 25 \times 10^3$ N, $\sigma_y = 380$ MPa, $n = 2.5$, $l_1 = l_3 = 150$ mm, $l_2 = l_4 = 25$ mm, $e = 100$ mm.

We know that $\sigma_t = \frac{\sigma_y}{n} = \frac{380}{2.5} = 152 \text{ MPa}$

Also $\tau = \frac{\sigma_t}{2} = \frac{152}{2} = 76 \text{ MPa}$

We know that $\tau = \frac{F_{se}}{A_1}$ $\qquad$ ... Eq. (i)

But equivalent shear load,

$$F_{se} = \frac{1}{2}\sqrt{F_1^2 + 4F'^2} \qquad \text{... Eq. (ii) 9.7(d)/ Pg 130, DHB}$$

• Direct shear load,

$$F' = \frac{F}{N} = \frac{25 \times 10^3}{4} = 6250 \text{ N} \qquad \text{... 9.7(a)/ Pg 130, DHB}$$

• Maximum secondary tensile force,

$$F_1 = \frac{Fel_1}{2(l_1^2 + l_2^2)} \qquad \text{... 9.7(b)/ Pg 130, DHB}$$

$$= \frac{(25 \times 10^3) \times 100 \times 150}{2(150^2 + 25^2)}$$

$$F_1 = 8108.11 \text{ N}$$

∴ Eq. (ii) yields... $F_{se} = \frac{1}{2}\sqrt{8108.11^2 + (4 \times 6250^2)} = 7450 \text{ N}$

∴ Eq. (i) yields... $A_1 = \frac{7450}{76} = 98.02 \text{ mm}^2$

i.e. $\frac{\pi d_1^2}{4} = 98.02 \text{ mm}^2$

∴ $d_1 = 11.17 \text{ mm}$

The nearest value for $d_1 = 11.17$ mm corresponds to $d_1 = 11.546261$ mm for $M14$.
... Tb. 9.8/ Pg 141, DHB

Thus the size of the bolt is $M14 \times 2$.

30. **A pulley bracket is supported by four bolts, 2 at A and 2 at B as shown in Fig. 4.13. The weight of the pulley and the bracket is 1000 N and the load on the pulley is 20000 N. Assuming the bracket is held against the wall and prevented from tipping about 'O' by the bolts and using an allowable tensile stress for the bolts of 40 MPa, determine the size of the bolts required.**

VTU – June/ July 2008 – 10 Marks

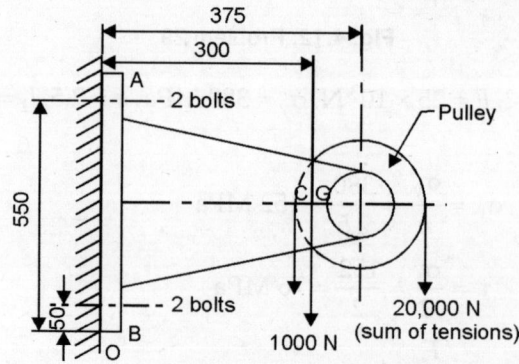

Fig. 4.13: Problem 30

Solution: $N = 4$, $W = 1000$ N, $T_1 + T_2 = 20000$ N, $\sigma_t = 40$ MPa, $d = ?$, $l_1 = l_3 = 550$ mm, $l_2 = l_4 = 50$ mm, $e_1 = 375$ mm, $e_2 = 300$ mm.

We know that $\qquad \sigma_t = \dfrac{F_{te}}{A_1}$ $\qquad \qquad$ ... Eq. (i)

But equivalent tensile load,

$$F_{te} = \frac{1}{2}\left(F_1 + \sqrt{F_1^2 + 4F'^2}\right) \qquad \text{... Eq. (ii) } \mathbf{9.7(c)/ Pg\ 130, DHB}$$

Here $\qquad F = T_1 + T_2 + W = 20000 + 1000 = 21000$ N

- Direct shear load,

$$F' = \frac{F}{N} = \frac{21000}{4} = 5250 \text{ N} \qquad \text{... } \mathbf{9.7(a)/ Pg\ 130, DHB}$$

- Maximum secondary tensile force,

$$F_1 = \frac{F e l_1}{2(l_1^2 + l_2^2)} \qquad \text{... } \mathbf{9.7(b)/ Pg\ 130, DHB}$$

$$= \frac{[(T_1 + T_2)e_1 + We_2]l_1}{2(l_1^2 + l_2^2)}$$

$$F_1 = \frac{[(20000 \times 375) + (1000 \times 300)] \times 550}{2(550^2 + 50^2)}$$

$$= 7032.78 \text{ N}$$

$\therefore$ Eq. (ii) yields... $F_{te} = \dfrac{1}{2}\left[7032.78 + \sqrt{7032.78^2 + (4 \times 5250^2)}\right] = 9835.21$ N

$\therefore$ Eq. (i) yields... $A_1 = \dfrac{9835.21}{40} = 245.88 \text{ mm}^2$

i.e. $\qquad \dfrac{\pi d_1^2}{4} = 245.88 \text{ mm}^2$

$\therefore \qquad d_1 = 17.69$ mm

The nearest value for $d_1 = 17.69$ mm corresponds to $d_1 = 18.159696$ mm for $M20$.
$\qquad \qquad \qquad \qquad \qquad \qquad \qquad$ ... **Tb. 9.8/ Pg 141, DHB**
Thus the size of the bolt is $M20 \times 1.5$.

31. **Determine the size of the bolts for the loaded bracket as shown in Fig. 4.14 if the allowable tensile stress in the bolt material is limited to 80 MPa.**
$\qquad \qquad \qquad$ *VTU – June/ July 2013 – 12 Marks; May/ June 2010 – 12 Marks*

Solution: $d = ?$, $\sigma_t = 80$ MPa, $N = 4$, $F = 20000$ N, $\theta = 30°$, $l_1 = l_3 = 200$ mm, $l_2 = l_4 = 50$ mm.

Force component:

Horizontal component,

$$F_H = F \cos \theta = 20000 \times \cos(30) = 17320.51 \text{ N}$$

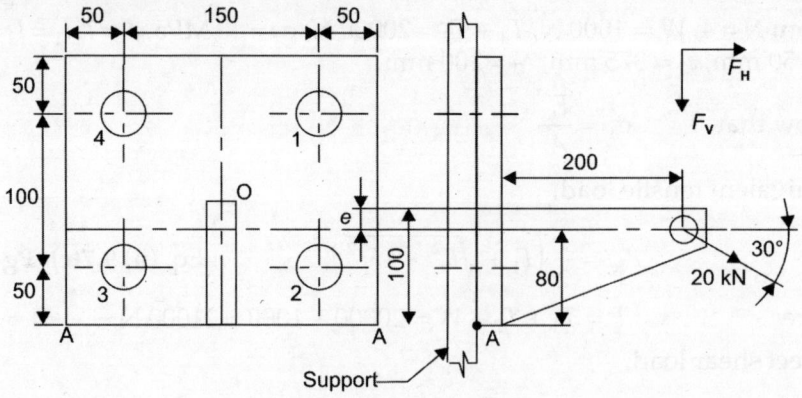

Fig. 4.14: Problem 31

Vertical component,

$$F_V = F \sin \theta = 20000 \times \sin(30) = 10000 \text{ N}$$

Loads:

Horizontal component acts parallel to the axis of the bolt:

Direct tensile load $\quad F_t' = \dfrac{F_H}{N} = \dfrac{17320.51}{4} = 4330.13 \text{ N}$

Vertical component acts perpendicular to the axis of the bolt:

Direct shear load $\quad F' = \dfrac{F_V}{N} = \dfrac{10000}{4} = 2500 \text{ N}$

Eccentric distance:

From **Fig. 4.14**, eccentric distances are:

$$e_H = 200 \text{ mm}$$

$$e_V = 100 - 80 = 20 \text{ mm} \quad \text{(CG of bolts is 100 mm and distance of load is 80 mm from A–A respectively)}$$

Moments:

Turning moment due to F_H about CG

$$M_H = F_H \cdot e_V = 17320.51 \times 20 = 346.41 \times 10^3 \text{ N·mm (CCW)}$$

Turning moment due to F_V about CG

$$M_V = F_V \cdot e_H = 10000 \times 200 = 2 \times 10^6 \text{ N·mm (CW)}$$

Net turning moment

$$M = M_V - M_H = 2 \times 10^6 - 346.41 \times 10^3 = 1.65 \times 10^6 \text{ N·mm}$$

We know that $\quad \sigma_t = \dfrac{F_{te}}{A_1}$ $\qquad\qquad$ … Eq. (i)

But equivalent tensile load,

$$F_{te} = \frac{1}{2}\left(F_1 + \sqrt{F_1^2 + 4F'^2} \right) \qquad\qquad \text{… 9.7(c)/ Pg 130, DHB}$$

i.e. $$F_{te} = \frac{1}{2}\left(F_t + \sqrt{F_t^2 + 4F'^2}\right) \qquad \text{... Eq. (i)}$$

Here $$F_t = F_1 + F_t' \qquad \text{... Eq. (iii)}$$

- Maximum secondary tensile force,

$$F_1 = \frac{Fel_1}{2(l_1^2 + l_2^2)} \qquad \text{... 9.7(b)/ Pg 130, DHB}$$

$$= \frac{Ml_1}{2(l_1^2 + l_2^2)}$$

$$= \frac{(1.65 \times 10^6) \times 150}{2(150^2 + 50^2)}$$

$$F_1 = 4950 \text{ N}$$

∴ Eq. (iii) yields... $F_t = 4950 + 4330.13 = 9280.13$ N

∴ Eq. (ii) yields... $F_{te} = \frac{1}{2}\left[9280.13 + \sqrt{9280.13^2 + (4 \times 2500^2)}\right] = 9910.76$ N

∴ Eq. (i) yields... $A_1 = \frac{9910.76}{80} = 123.88 \text{ mm}^2$

i.e. $\frac{\pi d_1^2}{4} = 123.88 \text{ mm}^2$

∴ $d_1 = 12.56 \text{ mm}$

The nearest value for $d_1 = 12.56$ mm corresponds to $d_1 = 12.773131$ mm for $M14$.

... Tb. 9.8/ Pg 141, DHB

Thus the size of the bolt is $M14$.

32. **An offset bracket is fixed to a vertical steel column by means of four bolts as shown in Fig. 4.15. Determine the diameter of the bolts. Take $\sigma_t = 100$ MPa.**

VTU – June/ July 2015 – 12 Marks

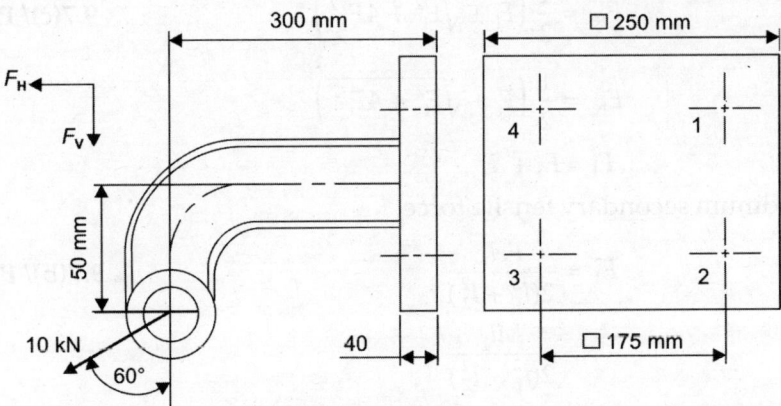

Fig. 4.15: Problem 32

Solution: $N = 4$, $d = ?$, $\sigma_t = 100$ MPa, $\theta = 60°$, $l_2 = l_3 = \left(\frac{250 - 175}{2}\right) = 37.5$ mm,

$l_1 = l_4 = 37.5 + 175 = 212.5$ mm, $F = 10000$ N.

Force component:

Horizontal component,
$$F_H = F \sin\theta = 10000 \times \sin(60) = 8660.25 \text{ N}$$

Vertical component,
$$F_V = F \sin\theta = 10000 \times \cos(60) = 5000 \text{ N}$$

Loads:

Horizontal component acts parallel to the axis of the bolt:

Direct tensile load $\quad F_t' = \dfrac{F_H}{N} = \dfrac{8660.25}{4} = 2165.06 \text{ N}$

Vertical component acts perpendicular to the axis of the bolt:

Direct shear load $\quad F' = \dfrac{F_V}{N} = \dfrac{5000}{4} = 1250 \text{ N}$

Eccentric distance:

From **Fig. 4.14**, eccentric distances are:
$$e_H = 300 \text{ mm}$$
$$e_V = 50 \text{ mm}$$

Moments:

Turning moment due to F_H about CG
$$M_H = F_H \cdot e_V = 8660.25 \times 50 = 433.01 \times 10^3 \text{ N·mm (CW)}$$

Turning moment due to F_V about CG
$$M_V = F_V \cdot e_H = 5000 \times 300 = 1.5 \times 10^6 \text{ N·mm (CCW)}$$

Net turning moment
$$M = M_V - M_H = 1.5 \times 10^6 - 433.01 \times 10^3 = 1.07 \times 10^6 \text{ N·mm}$$

We know that $\qquad \sigma_t = \dfrac{F_{te}}{A_1}$ $\qquad\qquad$ ... Eq. (i)

But equivalent tensile load,

$$F_{te} = \frac{1}{2}\left(F_1 + \sqrt{F_1^2 + 4F'^2} \right) \qquad \text{... 9.7(c)/ Pg 130, DHB}$$

i.e. $\qquad\qquad F_{te} = \dfrac{1}{2}\left(F_t + \sqrt{F_t^2 + 4F'^2} \right)$ $\qquad$ ... Eq. (ii)

Here $\qquad\qquad F_t = F_1 + F_t'$ $\qquad\qquad\qquad$ ... Eq. (iii)

- Maximum secondary tensile force,

$$F_1 = \frac{Fel_1}{2(l_1^2 + l_2^2)} \qquad\qquad \text{... 9.7(b)/ Pg 130, DHB}$$

$$= \frac{Ml_1}{2(l_1^2 + l_2^2)}$$

$$= \frac{(1.07 \times 10^6) \times 212.5}{2(212.5^2 + 37.5^2)}$$

$$F_1 = 2434.74 \text{ N}$$

$\therefore$ Eq. (iii) yields... $\quad F_t = 2434.74 + 2165.06 = 4599.8 \text{ N}$

$\therefore$ Eq. (ii) yields... $F_{te} = \dfrac{1}{2}\left[4599.8 + \sqrt{4599.8^2 + (4 \times 1250^2)}\right] = 4917.54$ N

$\therefore$ Eq. (i) yields... $A_1 = \dfrac{4917.54}{100} = 49.18$ mm^2

i.e. $\dfrac{\pi d_1^2}{4} = 49.18$ mm^2

$\therefore$ $d_1 = 7.91$ mm

The nearest value for $d_1 = 7.91$ mm corresponds to $d_1 = 8.519696$ mm for $M10$.

... Tb. 9.8/ Pg 141, DHB

Thus the size of the bolt is $M10 \times 1.5$.

33. **Suggest suitable size of bolts, if the bracket shown in Fig. 4.16 is subjected to a load of 20 kN at 60° from the vertical. The allowable tensile stress in the bolts is 120 MPa. The bracket is fixed using 4 bolts.**

VTU – Dec. 2010 – 14 Marks

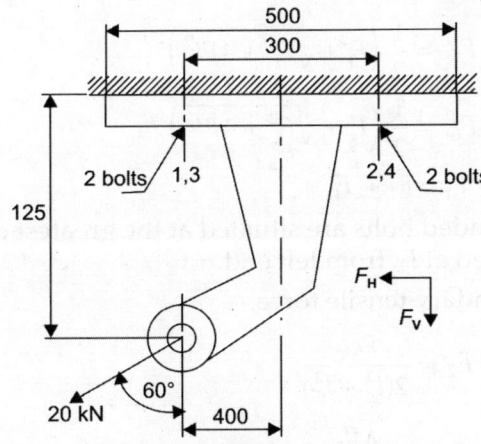

Fig. 4.16: Problem 33

Solution: $d = ?$, $F = 20000$ N, $\theta = 60°$, $\sigma_t = 120$ MPa, $l_1 = l_3 = \left(\dfrac{500 - 300}{2}\right) = 100$ mm, $N = 4$, $l_2 = l_4 = 100 + 300 = 400$ mm.

Force component:

Horizontal component,
$$F_H = F \sin\theta = 20000 \times \sin(60) = 17320.51 \text{ N}$$

Vertical component,
$$F_V = F \cos\theta = 20000 \times \cos(60) = 10000 \text{ N}$$

Loads:

Horizontal component acts perpendicular to the axis of the bolt:

Direct shear load $F' = \dfrac{F_H}{N} = \dfrac{17320.51}{4} = 4330.13$ N

Vertical component acts parallel to the axis of the bolt:

Direct tensile load $F_t' = \dfrac{F_V}{N} = \dfrac{10000}{4} = 2500$ N

Eccentric distance:

From **Fig. 4.16**, eccentric distances are:

$$e_H = 400 \text{ mm}$$
$$e_V = 125 \text{ mm}$$

Moments:

Turning moment due to F_H about CG

$$M_H = F_H \cdot e_V = 17320.51 \times 125 = 2.17 \times 10^6 \text{ N·mm (CW)}$$

Turning moment due to F_V about CG

$$M_V = F_V \cdot e_H = 10000 \times 400 = 4 \times 10^6 \text{ N·mm (CCW)}$$

Net turning moment

$$M = M_V - M_H = 4 \times 10^6 - 2.17 \times 10^6 = 1.83 \times 10^6 \text{ N·mm}$$

We know that

$$\sigma_t = \frac{F_{te}}{A_1} \qquad \qquad \text{... Eq. (i)}$$

But equivalent tensile load,

$$F_{te} = \frac{1}{2}\left(F_1 + \sqrt{F_1^2 + 4F'^2}\right) \qquad \qquad \text{... 9.7(c)/ Pg 130, DHB}$$

i.e.

$$F_{te} = \frac{1}{2}\left(F_t + \sqrt{F_t^2 + 4F'^2}\right) \qquad \qquad \text{... Eq. (ii)}$$

Here

$$F_t = F_1 + F_t' \qquad \qquad \text{... Eq. (iii)}$$

The most heavily loaded bolts are situated at the greatest distance from the tilting edge, i.e. bolts located at l_2, from left end.

- Maximum secondary tensile force,

$$F_2 = \frac{Fel_2}{2(l_1^2 + l_2^2)} \qquad \qquad \text{... 9.7(b)/ Pg 130, DHB}$$

$$= \frac{Ml_2}{2(l_1^2 + l_2^2)}$$

$$= \frac{(1.83 \times 10^6) \times 400}{2(100^2 + 400^2)}$$

$$F_2 = 2152.94 \text{ N}$$

∴ Eq. (iii) yields... $F_t = 2152.94 + 2500 = 4652.94 \text{ N}$

∴ Eq. (ii) yields... $F_{te} = \frac{1}{2}\left[4652.94 + \sqrt{4652.94^2 + (4 \times 4330.13^2)}\right] = 7242 \text{ N}$

∴ Eq. (i) yields... $A_1 = \dfrac{7242}{120} = 60.35 \text{ mm}^2$

i.e.

$$\frac{\pi d_1^2}{4} = 60.35 \text{ mm}^2$$

∴

$$d_1 = 8.76 \text{ mm}$$

The nearest value for $d_1 = 8.76$ mm corresponds to $d_1 = 8.773131$ mm for M10.

... Tb. 9.8/ Pg 141, DHB

Thus the size of the bolt is M10.

34. **For the eccentrically loaded bracket with M20 bolts shown in Fig. 4.17, calculate the maximum load that can be applied if the allowable tensile stress in the bolt is limited to 90 MPa.**

VTU – July/ Aug. 2004 – 10 Marks

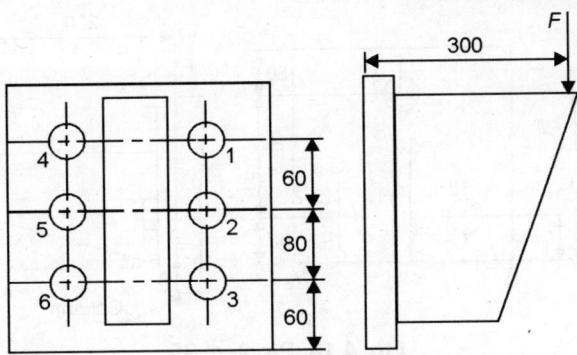

Fig. 4.17: Problem 34

Solution: $M20 \Rightarrow d = 20$ mm, $N = 6$, $F = ?$, $\sigma_t = 90$ MPa, $l_1 = l_4 = 200$ mm, $l_2 = l_5 = 140$ mm, $l_3 = l_6 = 60$ mm, $e = 300$ mm.

We know that $\qquad \sigma_t = \dfrac{F_{te}}{A_1}$

For *M20* bolt, $\qquad A_1 = 245$ mm^2 $\qquad\qquad$ **... 9.8/ Pg 142, DHB**

$$245 = \frac{F_{te}}{90}$$

$$F_{te} = 22050 \text{ N} \qquad\qquad\qquad \text{... Eq. (i)}$$

But equivalent tensile load,

$$F_{te} = \frac{1}{2}\left(F_1 + \sqrt{F_1^2 + 4F'^2}\right) \qquad \text{... Eq. (ii) 9.7(c)/ Pg 130, DHB}$$

• Direct shear load,

$$F' = \frac{F}{N} = \frac{F}{6} = 0.1667 \, F \qquad\qquad \text{... 9.7(a)/ Pg 130, DHB}$$

• Maximum secondary tensile force,

$$F_1 = \frac{Fel_1}{2(l_1^2 + l_2^2 + l_3^2)} \qquad\qquad \text{... 9.7(b)/ Pg 130, DHB}$$

$$= \frac{F \times 300 \times 200}{2(200^2 + 140^2 + 60^2)}$$

$$= 0.4747 \, F$$

$\therefore$ Eq. (ii) yields... $\quad F_{te} = \dfrac{1}{2}\left[0.4747\,F + \sqrt{(0.4747\,F)^2 + [4 \times (0.1667\,F)^2}\,\right] = 0.5274\,F$

$$\text{... Eq. (iii)}$$

Equating Eqs. (i) and (iii), we have,

$$22050 = 0.5274 \, F$$

$$F = 41808.87 \text{ N}$$

35. **A bracket as shown in Fig. 4.18 is fixed to a vertical steel column by means of three standard M16 × 2 bolts. Determine the safe load F, if the allowable tensile stress in the bolt material is 80 MPa.**

VTU – Dec. 2009/Jan. 2010 – 10 Marks

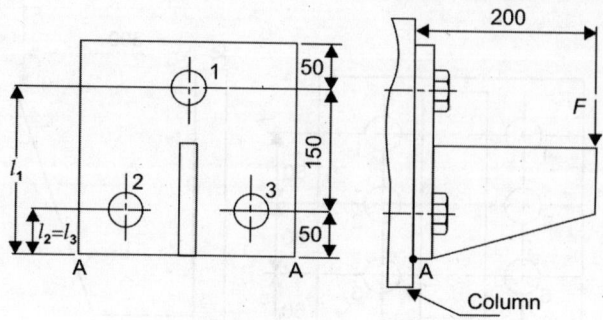

Fig. 4.18: Problem 35

Solution: $M16 \times 2 \Rightarrow d = 16$ mm, pitch $p = 2$ mm, $N = 3$, $F = ?$, $\sigma_t = 80$ MPa, $l_1 = 200$ mm, $l_2 = l_3 = 50$ mm, $e = 200$ mm.

We know that $\qquad \sigma_t = \dfrac{F_{te}}{A_1}$

For $M16 \times 2$ bolt, $\quad A_1 = 157$ mm^2 $\qquad$ **... Tb. 9.8/ Pg 142, DHB**

$$157 = \frac{F_{te}}{80}$$

$$F_{te} = 12560 \text{ N} \qquad \qquad \text{... Eq. (i)}$$

But equivalent tensile load,

$$F_{te} = \frac{1}{2}\left(F_1 + \sqrt{F_1^2 + 4F'^2}\right) \qquad \text{... Eq. (ii) 9.7(c)/ Pg 130, DHB}$$

• Direct shear load,

$$F' = \frac{F}{N} = \frac{F}{3} = 0.3334\,F \qquad \text{... 9.7(a)/ Pg 130, DHB}$$

• Maximum secondary tensile force,

$$F_1 = \frac{Fel_1}{l_1^2 + 2l_2^2} \qquad \text{... 9.7(b)/ Pg 130, DHB}$$

$$= \frac{F \times 200 \times 200}{200^2 + (2 \times 50^2)}$$

$$F_1 = 0.8889\,F$$

$\therefore$ Eq. (ii) yields... $\quad F_{te} = \dfrac{1}{2}\left[0.8889\,F + \sqrt{(0.8889\,F)^2 + [4 \times (0.3334\,F)^2]}\right] = 1\,F$

$$\text{... Eq. (iii)}$$

Equating Eqs. (i) and (iii), we have,

$$12560 = 1\,F$$

$$F = 12560 \text{ N}$$

36. **The pillar crane shown in Fig. 4.19 is fastened by eight bolts spaced equally on a bolt circle of diameter 1.6 m. The diameter of the pillar base is 1.8 m. Determine the size of bolts when the crane carries a load of 60 kN at a distance of 4.5 m from the centre of the base. The allowable stress for the bolt material is 60 MPa.**

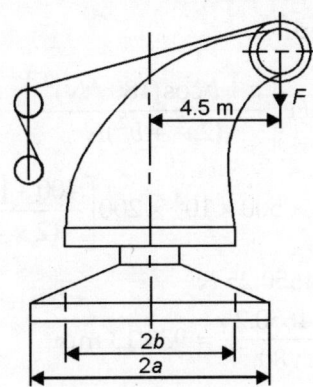

Fig. 4.19: Problem 36

Solution: $N = 8$, $2b = 1600$ mm $\Rightarrow b = 800$ mm, $2a = 1800$ mm $\Rightarrow a = 900$ mm, $F = 60 \times 10^3$ N, $L = 4500$ mm, $\sigma_t = 80$ MPa, $d = ?$

We know that $\qquad \sigma_t = \dfrac{F_{max}}{A_1}$ $\qquad\qquad\qquad$ ... Eq. (i)

For N bolts, equally spaced,

$$F_{max} = \frac{2Fe(a + b)}{(2a^2 + b^2)N} \qquad\qquad \text{... 9.8(d)/ Pg 131, DHB}$$

Here $\qquad\qquad e = L - a = 4500 - 900 = 3600$ mm

$$F_{max} = \frac{2 \times 60 \times 10^3 \times 3600(900 + 800)}{(2 \times 900^2 + 800^2) \times 8}$$

$$= 40619.47 \text{ N}$$

$\therefore$ Eq. (i) yields... $\quad A_1 = \dfrac{40619.47}{60} = 677 \text{ mm}^2$

i.e. $\qquad\qquad \dfrac{\pi d_1^2}{4} = 677 \text{ mm}^2$

$\therefore \qquad\qquad\qquad d_1 = 29.35 \text{ mm}$

The nearest value for $d_1 = 29.35$ mm corresponds to $d_1 = 30.546261$ for $M33$.

... Tb. 9.8/ Pg 141, DHB

Thus the size of the bolt is $M33 \times 2$.

37. **A flanged bearing, is fastened to a frame by means of four bolts spaced equally on 600 mm bolt circle. The diameter of bearing flange is 800 mm and a load of 500 kN acts at a distance of 200 mm from the frame. Determine the size of the bolts, taking safe tensile stress as 80 MPa for the material of the bolts. Two dowel pins are used to take up the shear load.**

Solution: $N = 4$, $2b = 600$ mm $\Rightarrow b = 300$ mm, $2a = 800$ mm $\Rightarrow a = 400$ mm, $F = 500 \times 10^3$ N, $e = 200$ mm, $\sigma_t = 80$ MPa, $d = ?$

We know that $\qquad \sigma_t = \dfrac{F_{max}}{A_1} \qquad\qquad\qquad$ ... Eq. (i)

For N bolts, equally stressed,

$$F_{max} = 2Fe \left[\frac{a + b\cos(180/N)^0}{(2a^2 + b^2)N} \right] \qquad \textbf{... Tb. 9.8(e)/ Pg 131, DHB}$$

$$= 2 \times 500 \times 10^3 \times 200 \left[\frac{400 + [300 \times \cos(180/4)]}{(2 \times 400^2 + 300^2) \times 4} \right]$$

$$F_{max} = 74650.25 \text{ N}$$

$\therefore$ Eq. (i) yields... $\quad A_1 = \dfrac{74650.25}{80} = 933.13 \text{ mm}^2$

i.e. $\qquad\qquad \dfrac{\pi d_1^2}{4} = 933.13 \text{ mm}^2$

$\therefore \qquad\qquad\qquad d_1 = 34.47 \text{ mm}$

The nearest value for $d_1 = 34.47$ mm corresponds to $d_1 = 35.319392$ for $M39$.

$\qquad\qquad\qquad\qquad\qquad\qquad\qquad\qquad$ **... Tb. 9.8/ Pg 141, DHB**

Thus the size of the bolt is $M39 \times 3$.

4.10.3 Load Acting in a Plane Containing the Bolts

Let $\qquad\qquad\qquad\qquad F$ = applied load

$\qquad\qquad\qquad\qquad\qquad e$ = eccentricity

$\qquad\qquad\qquad\qquad N$ = number of bolts

c_1, c_2, c_3 and c_4 = radial distance of respective bolts from center of gravity (CG) of the bolt group

$\qquad\qquad\qquad\qquad F'$ = direct shear force induced in each bolt

F_1'', F_2'', F_3'' and F_4'' = secondary shear force in bolts 1, 2, 3 and 4 respectively

$\theta_1, \theta_2, \theta_3$ and θ_4 = angle between F' and F_1'', F' and F_2'', F' and F_3'', and F' and F_4'' respectively

F_{R1}, F_{R2}, F_{R3} and F_4 = resultant load or force in respective bolts

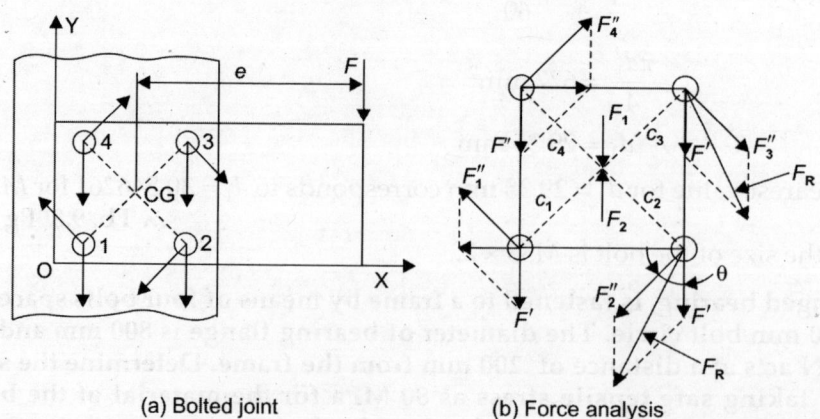

(a) Bolted joint $\qquad\qquad\qquad\qquad$ (b) Force analysis

Fig. 4.20: Eccentric loading on rectangular plates (in plate loading) **[Fig. 9.4/Pg 132, DHB]**

For force analysis of the above system, the following procedure is adopted:

1. To find of CG of the bolt group:

    Let x_1, x_2, x_3 and x_4 be the distances of respective bolts from Y axis

    y_1, y_2, y_3 and y_4 be the distances of respective bolts from X axis

$$\bar{x} = \frac{\Sigma x}{N} = \frac{x_1 + x_2 + x_3 + ... + x_N}{N}$$

and
$$\bar{y} = \frac{\Sigma y}{N} = \frac{y_1 + y_2 + y_3 + ... + y_N}{N} \qquad ...(Eq.\ 4.61)$$

2. To find radial distances:

$$c_n = \sqrt{x_n'^2 + y_n'^2} \qquad ...(Eq.\ 4.62)$$

    where $\qquad n = 1, 2, 3$ and 4 for respective bolts

    x_n' and y_n' = refers to the distances of respective bolts from CG in X and Y directions.

3. We introduce two forces F_1 and F_2 at the CG of the rivet system, which are equal and opposite to F as shown in **Fig. 4.20(b)**. Here we have two types of forces:

    a. Direct shear force due to external load F.

    b. Moment $M = Fe$ which tries to rotate the joint about CG.

    • The effect of $F_1 = F$ is to produce direct shear load on each bolt of equal magnitude.

    • Direct shear force, $F' = \dfrac{F}{N}$, acting parallel to the load F

    $$...(Eq.\ 4.63)\ \textbf{9.9(a)/ Pg 132, DHB}$$

    • The effect of $F_2 = F$ is to produce a turning moment of magnitude $F \cdot e$ which tends to rotate the joint about CG of the system in a clockwise direction. Due to the turning moment, secondary shear load on each rivet is produced. The secondary shear load is calculated as

$$F_1'' = \frac{Fec_1}{(c_1^2 + c_2^2 + c_3^2 + ...)}$$

$$F_2'' = \frac{Fec_2}{(c_1^2 + c_2^2 + c_3^2 + ...)} \text{ and so on...}$$

    i.e. in general secondary shear force on any bolt,

$$F_n'' = \frac{Fec_n}{\Sigma c^2} \qquad ...(Eq.\ 4.64)\ \textbf{9.9(d)/ Pg 132, DHB}$$

    and the maximum secondary shear force is,

$$F_{max}'' = \frac{Fec_{max}}{\Sigma c^2} \qquad ...(Eq.\ 4.65)\ \textbf{9.9(e)/ Pg 132, DHB}$$

4. The resultant shear force (F_R) on respective bolts is found as:

$$F_R = \sqrt{F'^2 + F''^2 + 2F'F'' \cos\theta}$$

$$...(Eq.\ 4.66)\ \textbf{9.9(g)/ Pg 132, DHB}$$

    where θ = smallest angle between the primary or direct shear load and secondary shear load.

$$\cos\theta_n = \frac{x_n'}{c_n}$$

When the secondary shear load on each rivet is equal, then the heavily loaded rivet will be one in which the included angle between the direct shear load and secondary shear load is minimum. The maximum loaded rivet becomes the critical one for determining the strength of the riveted joint. [*i.e. the most heavily loaded bolts are those which are situated at the greatest distance from the tilting edge, i.e. bolts located at c_3 and/or c_2*].

5. When the maximum load on the bolt is known, the size of the bolt can be calculated based on the permissible shear stress as:

$$A_1 = \frac{F_R}{\tau} \qquad \qquad \text{... (Eq. 4.67)}$$

where A_1 = core area of the bolt

Note: The topic discussed here is also applicable for riveted joints in shear.

38. **A bracket is bolted as shown in Fig. 4.21(a). All the bolts are identical and have yield strength of 400 MPa. Determine the size of the bolts, assuming a factor of safety of 3.**

VTU – Dec. 06/ Jan. 2007 – 10 Marks; Dec. 2011 – 14 Marks

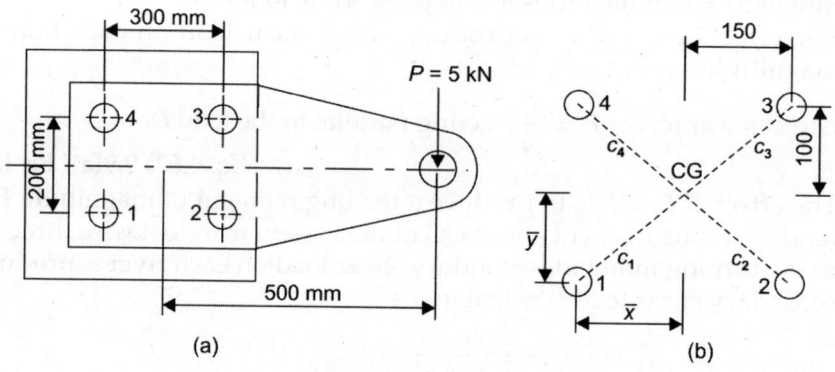

(a) (b)

Fig. 4.21: Problem 38

Solution: $\sigma_y = 400$ MPa, $n = 3$, $d = ?$, Number of bolts, $N = 4$, $F = 5000$ N, $e = 500$ mm.

We know that
$$\sigma_t = \frac{\sigma_y}{n} = \frac{400}{3} = 133.34 \text{ MPa}$$

Also
$$\tau = \frac{\sigma_t}{2} = \frac{133.34}{2} = 66.67 \text{ MPa}$$

We know that
$$\tau = \frac{F_R}{A_1} \qquad \qquad \text{... Eq. (i)}$$

a. *To find CG of the bolt group*: From **Fig. 4.21(a)**, taking bolt '1' as the reference, we have

Distance	Bolt Nos.			
(mm)	1	2	3	4
x_n	0	300	300	0
y_n	0	0	200	200

$$\bar{x} = \frac{\Sigma x}{N} = \frac{x_1 + x_2 + x_3 + \dots + x_N}{N} = \frac{0 + 300 + 300 + 0}{4} = 150 \text{ mm}$$

$$\bar{y} = \frac{\Sigma y}{N} = \frac{y_1 + y_2 + y_3 + \dots + y_N}{N} = \frac{0 + 0 + 200 + 200}{4} = 100 \text{ mm}$$

b. *To find radial distances* (c_n): From CG of the bolt [Fig. 4.21(b)], we have

Distance (mm)	Bolt Nos.			
	1	2	3	4
x'_n	150	150	150	150
x'_y	100	100	100	100
$c_n = \sqrt{x'^2_n + y'^2_n}$	180.28	180.28	180.28	180.28
$\cos\theta_n = x'_n/c_n$	0.83	0.83	0.83	0.83

c. *Shear loads*:

i. Direct or primary shear loads:

$$F' = \frac{F}{N} = \frac{5000}{4} = 1250 \text{ N} \qquad \textbf{... 9.9(a)/ Pg 132, DHB}$$

ii. Secondary shear load: The most heavily loaded bolts are those which are situated at the greatest distance from the tilting edge, i.e. bolts located at c_3

$$F''_n = \frac{Fec_n}{\Sigma c^2} \qquad \textbf{... 9.9(d)/ Pg 132, DHB}$$

i.e. $$F''_3 = \frac{Fec_3}{(c_1^2 + c_2^2 + c_3^2 + c_4^2)} = \frac{5000 \times 500 \times 180.28}{(180.28^2 + 180.28^2 + 180.28^2 + 180.28^2)}$$

$$F''_3 = 3466.83 \text{ N} = F''$$

d. *Resultant shear load*:

$$F_R = \sqrt{F'^2 + F''^2 + 2F'F'' \cos\theta} \qquad \textbf{... 9.9(g)/ Pg 132, DHB}$$

$$= \sqrt{1250^2 + 3466.83^2 + (2 \times 1250 \times 3466.83 \times 0.83)} \quad \text{(Here } \cos\theta_3 = 0.83\text{)}$$

$$= 4558 \text{ N}$$

e. *Diameter of the bolts*:

Eq. (i) yields... $$A_1 = \frac{4558}{66.67} = 68.37 \text{ mm}^2$$

i.e. $$\frac{\pi d_1^2}{4} = 68.37 \text{ mm}^2$$

$$d_1 = 9.33 \text{ mm}$$

The nearest value for $d_1 = 9.33$ mm corresponds to $d_1 = 9.852979$ for $M12$.

$$\textbf{... 9.9/Pg 141, DHB}$$

Thus the size of the bolt is $M12 \times 1.75$.

39. **Determine the size of the bolt for the loaded bracket as shown in Fig. 4.22(a). All the bolts are identical. The bolts are made from plain carbon steel 30C8 and factor of safety is 2.5. Take $\sigma_y = 400$ N/mm².**

VTU – Dec. 2014/Jan. 2015 – 10 Marks; Dec. 2015/Jan. 2016 – 10 Marks; June/July 2014 – 12 Marks

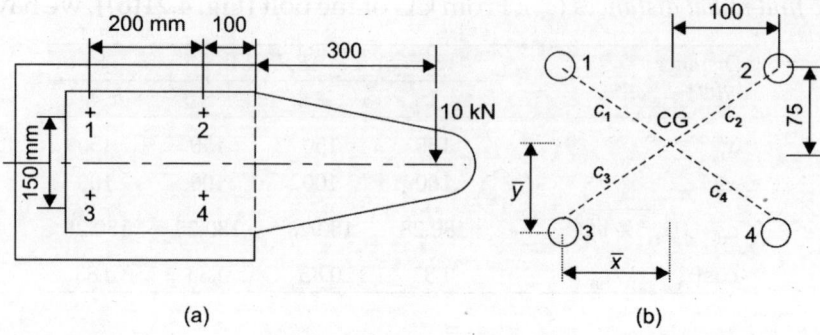

Fig. 4.22: Problem 39

Solution: $\sigma_y = 400$ MPa, $n = 2.5$, $d = ?$, Number of bolts, $N = 4$, $F = 10000$ N, $e = 300 + 100 + (200/2) = 500$ mm.

We know that $\qquad \sigma_t = \dfrac{\sigma_y}{n} = \dfrac{400}{2.5} = 160$ MPa

Also $\qquad\qquad \tau = \dfrac{\sigma_t}{2} = \dfrac{160}{2} = 80$ MPa

We know that $\qquad \tau = \dfrac{F_R}{A_1}$ $\qquad\qquad\qquad\qquad$ ... Eq. (i)

a. *To find CG of the bolt group:* From **Fig. 4.22(a)**, taking bolt '3' as the reference, we have

Distance (mm)	Bolt Nos.			
	1	2	3	4
x_n	0	200	0	200
y_n	150	150	0	0

$$\bar{x} = \frac{\Sigma x}{N} = \frac{x_1 + x_2 + x_3 + \dots + x_N}{N} = \frac{0 + 200 + 0 + 200}{4} = 100 \text{ mm}$$

$$\bar{y} = \frac{\Sigma y}{N} = \frac{y_1 + y_2 + y_3 + \dots + y_N}{N} = \frac{150 + 150 + 0 + 0}{4} = 75 \text{ mm}$$

b. *To find radial distances (c_n):* From CG of the bolt [**Fig. 4.22(b)**], we have

Distance (mm)	Bolt Nos.			
	1	2	3	4
x'_n	100	100	100	100
x'_y	75	75	75	75
$c_n = \sqrt{x'^2_n + y'^2_n}$	125	125	125	125
$\cos\theta_n = x'_n/c_n$	0.8	0.8	0.8	0.8

c. *Shear loads*:

i. Direct or primary shear loads:

$$F' = \frac{F}{N} = \frac{10000}{4} = 2500 \text{ N} \qquad \text{... 9.9(a)/ Pg 132, DHB}$$

ii. Secondary shear load: The most heavily loaded bolts are those which are situated at the greatest distance from the tilting edge, i.e. bolts located at c_3

$$F_n'' = \frac{Fec_n}{\Sigma c^2} \qquad \text{... 9.9(d)/ Pg 132, DHB}$$

i.e. $$F_2'' = \frac{Fec_2}{(c_1^2 + c_2^2 + c_3^2 + c_4^2)} = \frac{10000 \times 500 \times 125}{(125^2 + 125^2 + 125^2 + 125^2)}$$

$$F_2'' = 10000 \text{ N} - F''$$

d. *Resultant shear load*:

$$F_R = \sqrt{F'^2 + F''^2 + 2F'F'' \cos\theta} \qquad \text{... 9.9(g)/ Pg 132, DHB}$$

$$= \sqrt{2500^2 + 10000^2 + (2 \times 2500 \times 10000 \times 0.8)} \quad (\text{Here } \cos\theta_2 = 0.55)$$

$$= 12093.38 \text{ N}$$

e. *Diameter of the bolts*:

Eq. (i) yields... $A_1 = \dfrac{12093.38}{80} = 151.17 \text{ mm}^2$

i.e. $$\frac{\pi d_1^2}{4} = 151.17 \text{ mm}^2$$

* $$d_1 = 13.87 \text{ mm}$$

The nearest value for $d_1 = 13.87$ mm corresponds to $d_1 = 14.159696$ for $M16$.

... **9.9/Pg 141, DHB**

Thus the size of the bolt is $M12 \times 1.5$.

Note: Design of fasteners and/or rivets share the common procedure, except that rivets and bolts are used in respective chapters/units. For more problems students are advised to refer to Unit 6 (Riveted & Welded joints).

VTU QUESTION PAPERS

July/Aug. 2004 (AU46)

1. For the eccentrically loaded bracket with M20 bolts shown in **Fig. U4.1**, calculate the maximum load that can be applied if the allowable tensile stress in the bolt is limited to 90 MPa. **(10 Marks)**

Jan/ Feb. 2005 (AU46)

2. **Figure U4.2** shows a 15 mm × 200 mm rectangular steel bar cantilevered to a 250 mm steel channel using four bolts. Based on the external load of 16 kN, find:
   i. The resultant load on each bolt
   ii. The maximum bolt shear stress
   iii. The maximum bearing stress. **(10 Marks)**

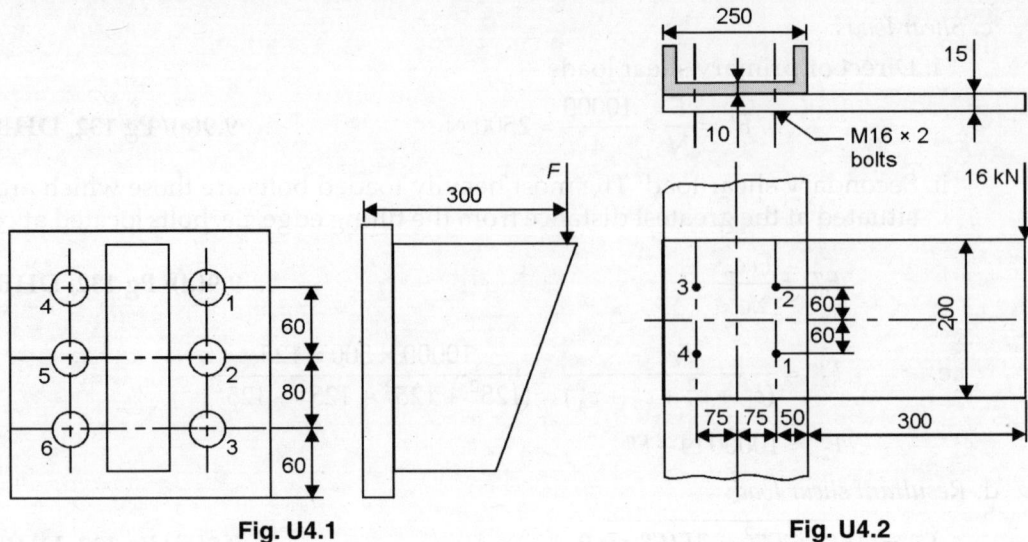

| **Fig. U4.1** | **Fig. U4.2** |

July/Aug. 2005 (AU46)

3. A cover plate is bolted on to the flanged end of a pressure vessel through 6 bolts. The inner diameter of the pressure vessel is 200 mm and is subjected to an internal pressure of 10 MPa. Selecting carbon steel C40 as the material for the bolts, determine the size of the bolts also considering the initial tension for the following cases:
   i. Metal to metal joint
   ii. A gasket joint. **(10 Marks)**

Jan/Feb. 2006 (AU46)

4. Explain the effect of initial tension of bolts. **(04 Marks)**

Dec. 06/Jan. 2007 (AU46)

5. A bracket is bolted as shown in **Fig. U4.3**. All the bolts are identical and have yield strength of 400 MPa. Determine the size of the bolts, assuming a factor of safety of 3. **(10 Marks)**

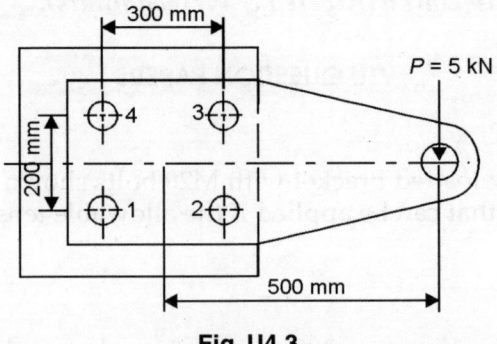

Fig. U4.3

July 2007 (AU46)

6. The cylinder head of a steam engine is subjected to a steam pressure of $0.7 \, \text{N/mm}^2$. It is held in position by means of 12 bolts. A soft copper gasket is used to make the

joint leak proof. The effective diameter of the cylinder is 300 mm. Find the size of the bolt so that the stresses in the bolt is not to exceed 100 N/mm². **(10 Marks)**

Dec. 07/Jan. 2008 (AU46)

7. A $M20 \times 2$ steel bolt, 100 mm long is subjected to impact load. The energy absorbed by the bolt is 2 N·m.
   i. Determine the stress in the shank of bolt if there is no threaded portion between the nut and bolt head.
   ii. Determine the stress in the shank if the entire length of the bolt is threaded.

   (10 Marks)

June/ July 2008 (AU46)

8. a. A cast iron diesel engine cylinder head is held on by 8 studs with coarse threads. The maximum cylinder pressure is 5 MPa. The bore of the engine is 200 mm diameter. The initial load in the bolt is such that a cylinder pressure of 10 MPa brings the joint to opening. Assuming a factor of safety of 2 according to Soderberg's criterion, suggest a suitable size of the bolt. Take the stress concentration factor as 3.8, endurance strength in reversed axial loading as 520 MPa and the yield strength as 940 MPa. Assume $K_c = 1.45\, K_b$. **(10 Marks)**
   b. A pulley bracket is supported by four bolts, 2 at A and 2 at B as shown in **Fig. U4.4**. The weight of the pulley and the bracket is 1000 N and the load on the pulley is 20000 N. Assuming the bracket is held against the wall and prevented from tipping about 'O' by the bolts and using an allowable tensile stress for the bolts of 40 MPa, determine the size of the bolts required. **(10 Marks)**

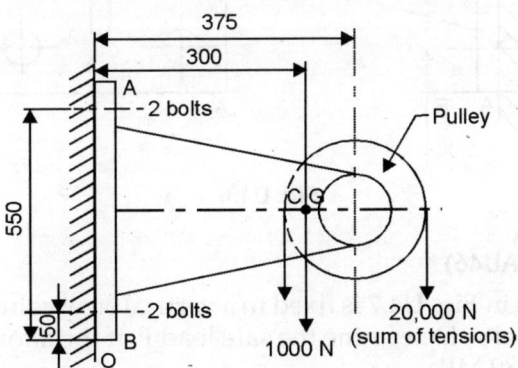

Fig. U4.4

Dec. 08/ Jan. 2009 (ME5T2)

9. A bracket is fixed to a wall by means of four bolts and loaded as shown in **Fig. U4.5**. Calculate the size of the bolts if the load is 25 kN and the yield stress is 380 N/mm². The factor of safety is taken as 2.5. Use maximum shear stress theory.

   (10 Marks)

Dec. 08/ Jan. 2009 (06ME-AU52)

10. a. Explain the stresses induced in a screw fastening subjected to static, dynamic and impact loading. **(12 Marks)**
    b. A bolt subjected to initial loading of 5 kN and final tensile load of 9 kN. Determine the size of the bolt, if the allowable stress is 80 MPa and $K = 0.05$.

    (08 Marks)

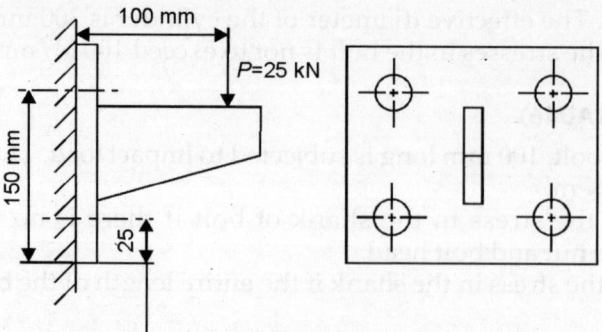

Fig. U4.5

June/July 2009 (06ME52)

11. A bracket is fixed to a wall by means of four bolts and loaded as shown in **Fig. U4.6**. Calculate the size of the bolts if the load is 25 kN and the yield stress is 380 N/mm². The factor of safety is taken as 2.5. Use maximum shear stress theory. **(10 Marks)**

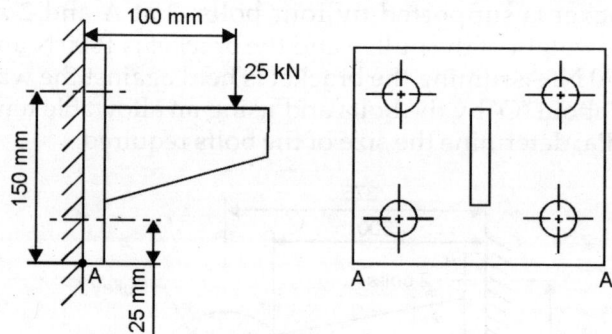

Fig. U4.6

Dec. 2009/ Jan. 2010 (AU46)

12. A bracket as shown in **Fig. U4.7** is fixed to a vertical steel column by means of three standard M16 × 2 bolts. Determine the safe load F, if the allowable tensile stress in the bolt material is 80 MPa. **(10 Marks)**

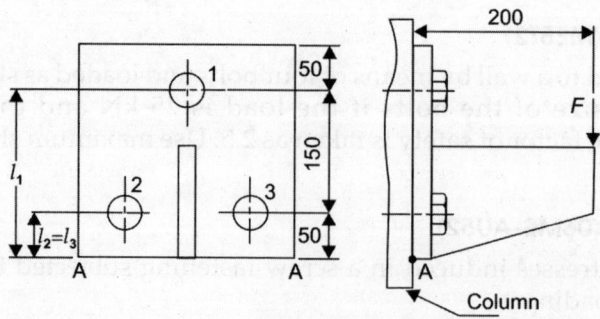

Fig. U4.7

Dec. 2009/Jan. 2010 (06ME52)

13. a. The cylinder head of a reciprocating air compressor is held in place by 10 bolts. The total joint stiffness is four times the total bolt stiffness. Each bolt is tightened to an initial tension of 5 kN. The total external force acting to separate the joint is 20 kN. Find the size of the bolt so that the stress in the bolts is not to exceed 100 MPa. **(08 Marks)**

   b. A radial drilling machine with circular base is mounted to a base plate by means of three steel bolts equally spaced on a bolt circle diameter of 0.3 m. The diameter of circular base is 0.4 m. The spindle is positioned at a radial distance of 0.335 m from the center of the column. During drilling operation, the spindle is subjected to a force of 4.5 kN. Determine the size of the bolts, if the allowable stress in the bolt material is limited to 100 MPa. **(12 Marks)**

May/June 2010 (06ME52)

14. a. An M20 × 2 steel bolt, 100 mm long is subjected to an impact load. The energy absorbed by the bolt is 2 N·m. Take $E = 206$ GPa.
   i. Determine the stress in the shank of the bolt if there is no thread portion between the nut and the bolt.
   ii. Determine the stress in the shank if the entire length of the bolt is threaded. **(08 Marks)**

   b. Determine the size of the bolt for the loaded bracket shown in **Fig. U4.8,** if the allowable tensile stress in the bolt material is limited to 80 MPa. **(12 Marks)**

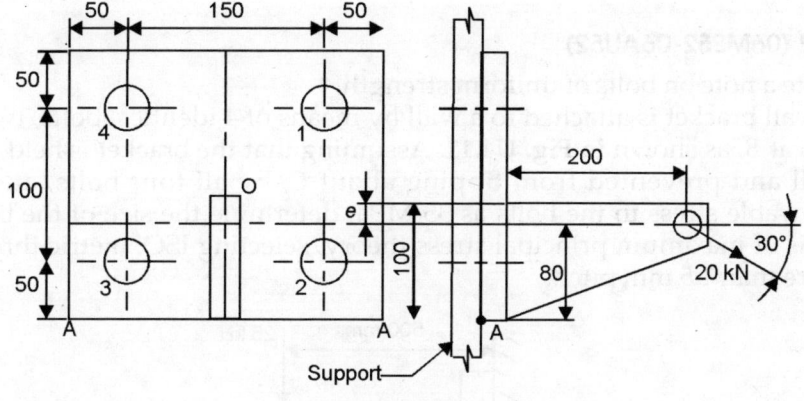

Fig. U4.8

Dec. 2010 (06ME52)

15. a. Explain the various types of stresses in threaded fasteners. **(08 Marks)**
   b. Suggest suitable size of bolts, if the bracket shown in **Fig. U4.9** is subjected to a load of 20 kN at 60° from the vertical. The allowable tensile stress in the bolts is 120 MPa. The bracket is fixed using 4 bolts. **(14 Marks)**

June/July 2011 (06ME52)

16. The cylinder head of a steam engine is subjected to a steam pressure of 0.7 N/mm². It is held in position by means of 12 bolts. A soft copper gasket is used to make the joint leak-proof. The effective diameter of the cylinder is 300 mm. Find the size of the bolts so that the stress in the bolts in not to exceed 100 N/mm². **(10 Marks)**

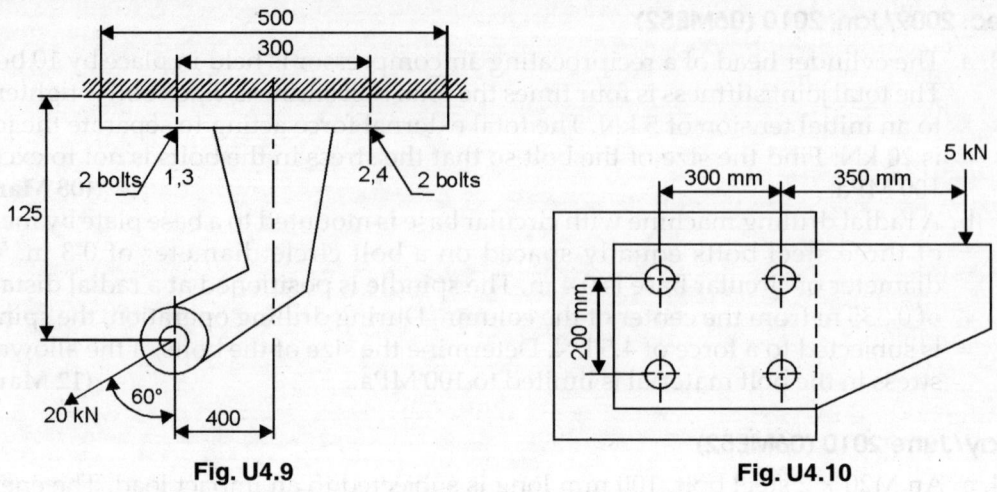

Fig. U4.9   **Fig. U4.10**

Dec. 2011 (06ME52)

17. a. A bolt carries a tensile load of 8 kN and tightening load is 3 kN. It is made of steel having allowable tensile stress of 120 MPa. Find its size. A soft copper gasket is used. **(06 Marks)**

   b. A bracket is bolted as shown in **Fig.U4.10**. All the bolts are identical and have an yield strength of 400 MPa. Determine the size of the bolts assuming a factor of safety as 3. **(14 Marks)**

June 2012 (06ME52-06AU52)

18. a. Write a note on bolts of uniform strength. **(06 Marks)**

   b. A wall bracket is attached to a wall by means of 4 identical bolts, two at A and two at B, as shown in **Fig. U4.11**. Assuming that the bracket is held against the wall and prevented from tipping about C, by all four bolts, and using an allowable stress in the bolts as 35 MPa, determine the size of the bolts on the basis of maximum principal stress theory, selecting ISO, metric threads of not more than 1.5 mm pitch. **(14 Marks)**

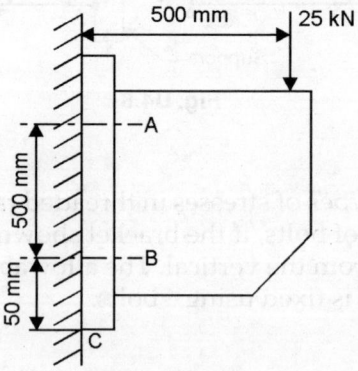

Fig. U4.11

Dec. 2012 (10ME52)

19. a. Obtain the expression for total load on a bolt in a bolted joint with gasket. **(08 Marks)**

b. A cylinder head is fastened to the cylinder of a compressor using 6 bolts of M20 size. Bolt material is C20. The maximum fluid pressure is 3.5 MPa, cylinder diameter is 75 mm. A soft gasket is used. Assuming the initial tension required in each bolt is 40 kN, determine the factor of safety. **(12 Marks)**

Dec. 2012 (06ME52)

20. a. A cover plate is bolted on to the flanged end of a pressure vessel through 6 bolts. The inner diameter of the pressure vessel is 200 mm and is subjected to an internal pressure of 10 MPa. Selecting carbon steel C40 with σ_y = 328.6 MPa as the material for the bolts determine the size of the bolts, considering initial tension for the following cases:
   i. Metal to metal joints
   ii. A copper gasket **(10 Marks)**

b. A bracket is fixed to the wall by means of four bolts and loaded as shown in **Fig. U4.12.** Calculate the size of the bolts if the load is 10 kN and allowable shear stress in the bolt material is 40 MPa. **(10 Marks)**

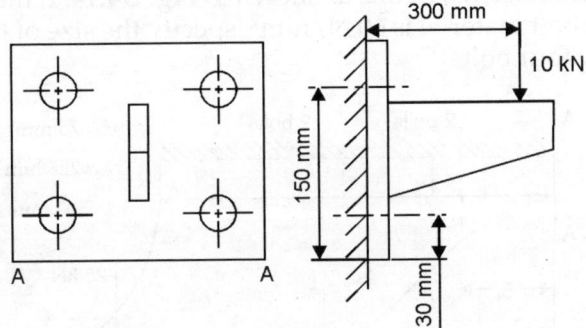

Fig. U4.12

June/July 2013 (06ME52)

21. a. Explain the steps involved in the design procedure of eccentrically loaded joints with circular base, when the load is perpendicular to the bolt axis. **(10 Marks)**

b. A M10 bolt of 125 mm long is subjected to an impact load. The kinetic energy absorbed by the bolt is 2.5 Joules. Determine:
   i. Stress in the shank of the bolt if there is no thread portion between the nut and the bolt head.
   ii. Stress in the shank, if area of shank is reduced to that of root area of the thread or the entire length of the bolt is threaded. **(12 Marks)**

June/July 2013 (10ME52)

22. a. An M20 × 2 steel bolt of 100 mm is subjected to impact load. The energy absorbed by the bolt is 2 N·m.
   i. Determine the stress in the shank of the bolt if there is no thread portion between the nut and bolt head.
   ii. Determine the stress in the shank, if the entire length of the bolt is threaded. Assume modulus of elasticity for steel as 206 GPa. **(08 Marks)**

b. Determine the size of the bolts for the loaded bracket as shown in **Fig. U4.13** if the allowable tensile stress in the bolt material is limited to 80 MPa. **(12 Marks)**

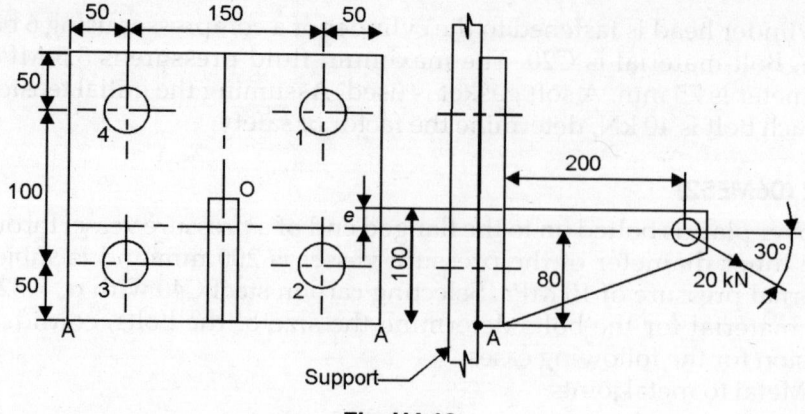

Fig. U4.13

23. a. Explain the various types of stresses in threaded fasteners. **(06 Marks)**
    b. A bracket is connected by bolts as shown in **Fig. U4.14**. If the permissible tensile stress for the bolt material is 60 N/mm², specify the size of the bolt. The bracket is fixed using four bolts. **(14 Marks)**

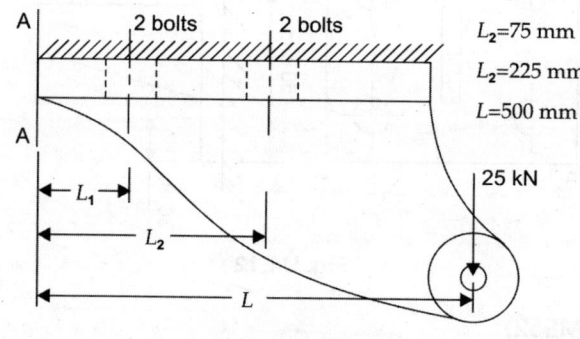

Fig. U4.14

24. a. A cylinder head is fastened to the cylinder of an air compressor using 8 numbers of bolts. Inner diameter of the cylinder is 300 mm. The pressure inside the cylinder varies from zero to a maximum pressure of 1.5 N/mm². The stresses for the bolt material may be taken as σ_{ut} = 500 N/mm², σ_y = 300 N/mm², and σ_{en} = 240 N/mm². The bolts are tightened with initial preload of 1.5 times the steam load. A copper asbestos gasket is used to make the joint leak proof. Assuming a factor of safety of 2.5, find the size of the bolt. Neglect stress concentration factor. **(10 Marks)**
    b. A M10 bolt of 125 mm long is subjected to an impact load. The kinetic energy absorbed by the bolt is 2.5 Joules. Determine:
       i. Stress in the shank of the bolt if there is no thread portion between the nut and the bolt head.
       ii. Stress in the shank, if area of shank is reduced to that of root area of the thread or the entire length of the bolt is threaded. **(10 Marks)**

June/July 2014 (06ME52)

25. a. A cover plate is bolted on to the flanged end of a pressure vessel by means of 6 bolts. The inside diameter of the pressure vessel is 180 mm and is subjected to an internal pressure of 12 MPa. Selecting a factor of safety as 2 and carbon steel C30 ($\sigma_y = 300$ MPa) as the material for bolts, determine the size of the bolts considering the initial tension for the following cases:

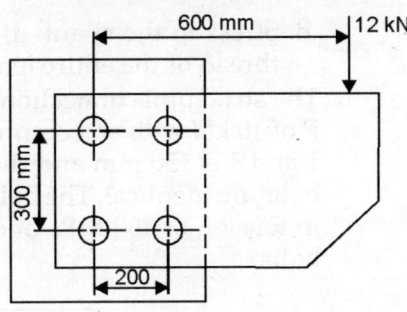

Fig. U4.15

   i. Metal to metal contact
   ii. A copper gasket is used. **(10 Marks)**

   b. A bracket is bolted as shown in **Fig. U4.15**. All the bolts are made of same size and are made of steel having allowable shear stress as 72 MPa. Determine the size of the bolts to be used. **(12 Marks)**

June/July 2014 (10ME52)

26. a. Explain the stresses induced in a screw fastening subjected to static, dynamic and impact loading. **(12 Marks)**

   b. A bolt is subjected to initial loading of 5 kN and final tensile load of 9 kN. Determine the size of the bolt, if allowable stress is 80 MPa and $K = 0.05$. **(08 Marks)**

Dec. 2014/Jan. 2015 (06ME52)

27. a. A bolt connects two plates of an assembly whose combined stiffness is 4 times the stiffness of the bolt. The joint is subjected to an external load which varies from 2 kN to 6 kN. The initial tightening force on bolt is 4 kN. The bolt used is M16 coarse thread and is made of SAE 1025 annealed steel. Take $A = 1.0$, $B = 0.85$, $C = 0.9$ and $K_{ft} = 5.0$. Determine the factor of safety in design. **(10 Marks)**

   b. Determine the size of the bolt for the loaded bracket as shown in **Fig. U4.16**. All the bolts are identical. The bolts are made from plain carbon steel 30C8 and factor of safety is 2.5. Take $\sigma_y = 400 \text{ N/mm}^2$. **(10 Marks)**

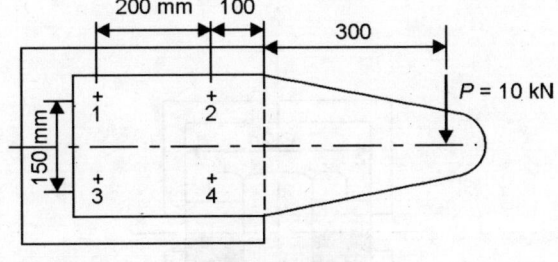

Fig. U4.16

Dec. 2014/Jan. 2015 (10ME52)

28. a. A M10 steel bolt of 125 mm long is subjected to an impact load. The kinetic energy absorbed by the bolt is 2.5 J. Determine:
   i. Stress in the shank of the bolt if there is no threaded position between the nut and the bolt.

ii. Stress in the shank, if area of shank is reduced to that of root area of the thread or the entire length of the bolt is threaded. **(10 Marks)**

b. The structural connection shown in **Fig. U4.17** is subjected to an eccentric load P of 10 kN with an eccentricity of 500 mm. The center distance between bolts at 1 and 3 is 150 mm and the center distance between 1 and 2 is 200 mm. All the bolts are identical. The bolts are made of plain carbon steel having yield strength in tension of 400 MPa and the factor of safety is 2.5. Determine the size of the bolts. **(10 Marks)**

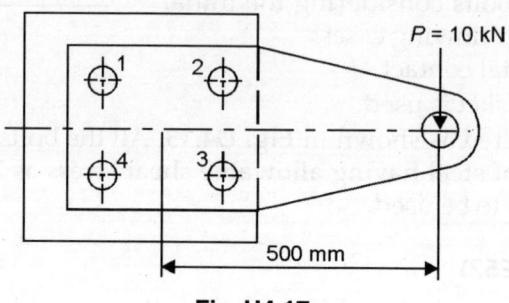

Fig. U4.17

June/July 2015 (06ME52)

29. a. Explain the effect of initial tension of bolts. **(06 Marks)**

b. A steam engine cylinder has an effective diameter of 350 mm and the maximum steam pressure acting on the cylinder cover is 1.25 N/mm². Calculate the number and size of studs required to fix the cylinder cover, assuming the permissible stress in the studs as 33 MPa. **(14 Marks)**

June/July 2015 (10ME52)

30. a. Two circular plates with $2d$ and d as outer and inner diameters are clamped together by means of a bolt as shown in **Fig. U4.18**. The bolt is made of plain carbon steel ($\sigma_y = 380$ MPa, $E = 207$ GPa) while the plates are made of aluminium ($E = 71$ GPa). The initial pre-load is 5 kN in the bolt and external force acting on the joint is 10 kN. Determine the size of the bolt if factor of safety = 2. Take $\sigma_t = 152$ N/mm². **(08 Marks)**

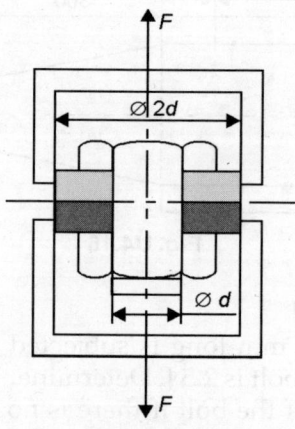

Fig. U4.18

b. An offset bracket is fixed to a vertical steel column by means of four bolts as shown in **Fig. U4.19**. Determine the diameter of the bolts. Take $\sigma_t = 100$ MPa.

(12 Marks)

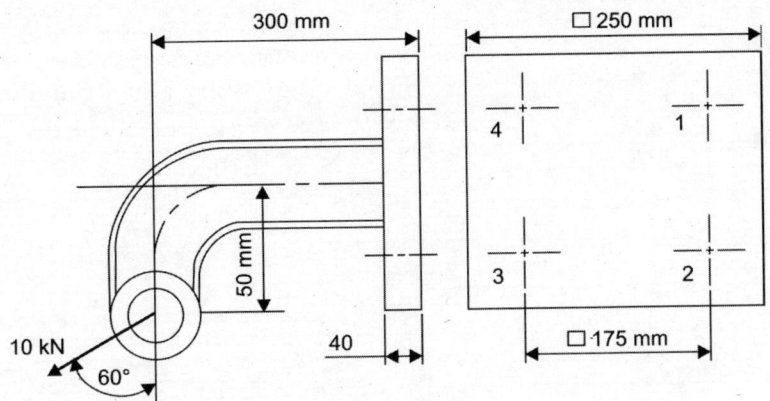

Fig. U4.19

Dec. 2015/ Jan. 2016 (10ME52)

31. a. A flat circular plate is used to close the flanged end of a pressure vessel of internal diameter 300 mm. The vessel carries a fluid pressure of 0.7 N/mm². A soft copper gasket is used to make the joint leak proof. Twelve blots are used to fasten the cover plate on the pressure vessel. Find the size of the bolt, so that the stress in the bolt is not to exceed 100 N/mm². **(10 Marks)**

b. The structural joint shown in **Fig. U4.20** is eccentric load P of 10 kN with an eccentricity of 500 mm from the centre of gravity of bolts arrangement. Distance between the bolts is 200 mm and 150 mm perpendicular and parallel to the direction of the load action. Bolts are identical and made of plain carbon steel having yield strength of 40 N/mm². Determine the size of the bolts taking factor of safety as 2.5. **(10 Marks)**

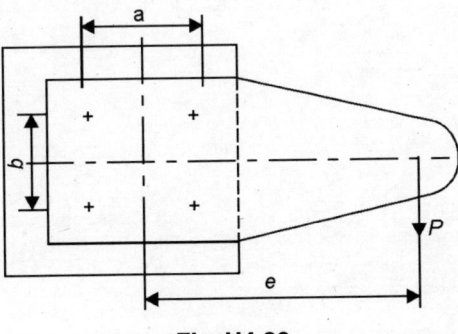

Fig. U4.20

b. An offset bracket is fixed and is acted on by a crank pin by means of four forces as shown in Fig. Q4.19. Determine the diameter. Take σ_b, Take $\sigma_t = 100$ MPa.
(14 Marks)

Fig. Q4.19

4 a. A flat circular plate is used to close the flange end of a pressure vessel of internal diameter 350 mm. It is tested to pressure 5 fluid pressure of 2.2 N/mm². A set of copper gaskets used to make the joint is tightened up. Predict the stress in the bolts and the pressure vessel. If the plate is fixed to the flange, the stress in the bolts not exceed 10.33 N/mm².
(10 Marks)

b. The bracket shown in Fig. Q4.20 is loaded. C = 0.1C₁ and C₂ = 10 kN, predict the eccentricity of loading. If the range of gravity of bolt arrangement, distance between the bolts is 200 mm and 80 mm respectively. The plate and parallel to the direction of the load section. Bolts are M 16 gross area of plate section having yield strength of 90 N/mm². Calculate the ratio of the bolts taking factor of safety as 2.5.
(10 Marks)

Fig. Q4.20

Part B

5. Design of Shafts

6. Cotter and Knuckle Joints, Keys and Couplings

7. Riveted and Welded Joints

8. Power Screws

5

Design of Shafts

5.1 INTRODUCTION

The term shaft usually refers to a relatively long member of circular cross-section that rotates and transmits power. Various members such as gears, bearings, pulleys, sprockets, cams, flywheels, cranks, etc. are mounted on the shaft for power transmission. These members are secured to the shaft by means of pins, keys, splines, snap rings and other devices.

However, a shaft can have a noncircular cross-section and need not be rotating, such as axles and spindles.

- **Axle** is a nonrotating member used for supporting rotating wheels, pulleys, etc. and do not transmit any torque.
- **Spindle** is simply defined as a short shaft. Examples: Lathe spindles, drill press spindle, etc.

5.2 TYPES OF SHAFTS

Shafts are divided into two main groups.

- **Transmission shafts:** Shafts used to transmit power between the source and the machines absorbing power are called transmission shafts. These shafts carry machine parts or members such as pulleys, gears etc., and therefore are subjected to bending in addition to twisting.
  Examples: Counter shafts, line shafts, overhead shafts and all factory shafts.
- **Machine shafts:** These shafts form an integral part of the machine itself.
  Examples: Crankshaft

5.3 SOME DEFINITIONS

- **Line shaft:** It refers to a shaft which transmits power to several machines by means of belts.
- **Counter shaft:** A shaft that connects a prime mover to a line shaft of a machine is referred to as counter shaft.
- **Flexible shaft:** A flexible shaft transmits motion between two points (say motor and machine), where the rotational axes are at an angle with respect to one another.

5.4 MATERIALS USED FOR SHAFTS

The material used for ordinary shafts is mild steel. When high strength is required, alloy steel such as nickel, nickel-chromium or chromium-vanadium steel is used.

Shafts are generally formed by hot rolling and finished to size by cold drawing or turning and grinding. Cold rolling produces a stronger shaft than hot rolling but has high residual stresses which cause distortion of the shaft when it is subjected to machining operations like slotting and milling.

Thus, most of the shafts after being hot rolled are turned and ground and are commonly referred to as T shafting and G shafting.

Note:
- *Properties of shaft materials* ... **Table 3.3/ Pg 56, DHB**
- *Standard sizes of shaft* ... **Table 3.5(a)/ Pg 57, DHB**

5.5 MAXIMUM PERMISSIBLE WORKING OR DESIGN STRESS

The following stresses are induced in the shafts:
- Shear stresses due to torque.
- Bending stresses (tensile or compressive) due to the elements mounted on the shaft (such as gears, pulleys, etc.)
- Stresses due to combined torsional and bending loads.
  - *Working stresses for shaft* ... **Table 3.5(b)/ Pg 57, DHB**

5.6 DESIGN OF SHAFT

Shafts may be subjected to axial, bending and torsional loads along with a combination of the above depending upon the type of configuration of the mechanical system mounted on it. While designing a shaft, its diameter is determined such that the shaft will be able to carry the loads imposed on it. In addition to satisfying strength requirements, shafts must be designed so that deflections are within acceptable limits.

Shafts are designed in the following two ways:
1. Based on strength:
   a. Shaft subjected to torque (T) only
   b. Shaft subjected to bending moment (BM) only
   c. Shafts subjected to combined T and BM
   d. Shafts subjected to combined axial load (F), T and BM.
2. Based on rigidity:
   a. Torsional rigidity
   b. Lateral rigidity.

5.7 SHAFT DESIGN BASED ON STRENGTH

5.7.1 Shafts Subjected to Torque (*T*) Only

When the shaft is subjected to a twisting moment, then the diameter of the shaft may be obtained from the torsional equation and is given as follows:

a. **For hollow shaft:** Outside diameter of shaft is found as

$$d_o = \left[\frac{16T}{\pi\tau_d}\left(\frac{1}{1-K^4}\right)\right]^{1/3} \quad \text{... (Eq. 5.1) } \textbf{3.4(a)/ Pg 50, DHB}$$

b. **For solid shaft:** Diameter of solid shaft is found by substituting $K = 0$ and $d_o = d$, in (Eq. 5.1)

i.e.
$$d = \left[\frac{16T}{\pi\tau_d}\right]^{1/3} \quad \text{... (Eq. 5.2)}$$

where d = diameter of solid shaft (mm)
   d_o = outer diameter of hollow shaft (mm)
   d_i = inner diameter of hollow shaft (mm)

$$K = \frac{d_i}{d_o} = \text{ratio of inner diameter to outer diameter of hollow shaft}$$

T = torque transmitted (N·mm)

τ_d = design shear stress (MPa)   **... Tb. 3.5(b)/ Pg 57, DHB**

$$= \frac{\tau_e B}{R K_s}$$

R = reliability factor   **... Tb. 2.7/ Pg 33, DHB**

B = size factor   **... 2.9(b)/ Pg 22, DHB**

τ_e = shear stress at elastic limit (MPa)

K_s = theoretical stress concentration factor for shear stress

5.7.2 Shafts Subjected to Bending Moment (BM) Only

When the shaft is subjected to a pure bending moment, then the maximum stress (tensile or compressive) may be obtained from by the bending equation and is given below.

a. **For hollow shaft:** Outside diameter of shaft is found as

$$d_o = \left[\frac{32M}{\pi \sigma_d} \left(\frac{1}{1 - K^4} \right) \right]^{1/3} \quad \text{... (Eq. 5.3) 3.4(b)/ Pg 50, DHB}$$

b. **For solid shaft:** Diameter of solid shaft is found by substituting $K = 0$ and $d_o = d$, in (Eq. 5.3)

i.e. $$d = \left[\frac{32M}{\pi \sigma_d} \right]^{1/3} \quad \text{... (Eq. 5.4)}$$

where σ_d = design stress (MPa)   **... Tb. 3.5(b)/ Pg 57, DHB**

$$= \frac{\sigma_e B}{R K_t}$$

σ_e = stress at elastic limit (MPa)

K_t = theoretical stress concentration factor for normal stress (tensile or bending).

5.7.3 Shafts Subjected to Combined T and BM

When the shaft is subjected to combined twisting moment and bending moment, the design is based on either the maximum normal stress theory or the maximum shear stress theory.

a. **For hollow shaft:**

   i. According to maximum normal stress theory, outside diameter of shaft is found as:

$$d_o = \left[\frac{16}{\pi \sigma_{max}} \left(M + \sqrt{M^2 + T^2} \right) \left(\frac{1}{1 - K^4} \right) \right]^{1/3}$$

$$\text{... (Eq. 5.5) 3.5(a)/ Pg 50, DHB}$$

   ii. According to maximum shear stress theory, outside diameter of shaft is found as:

$$d_o = \left[\frac{16}{\pi \tau_{max}} \left(\sqrt{M^2 + T^2} \right) \left(\frac{1}{1 - K^4} \right) \right]^{1/3}$$

$$\text{... (Eq. 5.6) 3.5(b)/ Pg 50, DHB}$$

b. **For solid shaft:** Diameter of solid shaft is found by substituting $K = 0$ and $d_o = d$, in (Eq. 5.5) and (Eq. 5.6).

    i. According to maximum normal stress theory, diameter of shaft is found as:

$$d = \left[\frac{16}{\pi\sigma_{max}} \left(M + \sqrt{M^2 + T^2} \right) \right]^{1/3} \qquad \text{... (Eq. 5.7)}$$

    ii. According to maximum shear stress theory, diameter of shaft is found as:

$$d = \left[\frac{16}{\pi\tau_{max}} \left(\sqrt{M^2 + T^2} \right) \right]^{1/3} \qquad \text{... (Eq. 5.8)}$$

where σ_{max} = maximum normal stress (MPa)

        τ_{max} = maximum shear stress (MPa)

Note:

- $$\sigma_{max} = \sigma_1 = \frac{\sigma_e \text{ or } \sigma_y}{n}$$

- $$\tau_{max} = \frac{\tau_e \text{ or } \tau_y}{n} = \frac{\sigma_e \text{ or } \sigma_y}{2n}$$

where σ_e or σ_y = yield strength of the material

          n = factor of safety

          $\tau_e = \dfrac{\sigma_e}{2}$, since the shear stress at yield point in a simple tension test is equal to one-half the yield stress in tension

- The term $\left(M + \sqrt{M^2 + T^2} \right)$ is called the equivalent bending moment.

- The term $\left(\sqrt{M^2 + T^2} \right)$ is called the equivalent twisting moment.

5.8 SHAFT DESIGN BASED ON RIGIDITY

Here the shaft acts like a beam which deflects transversely and at the same time is a torsion bar that deflects torsionally.

5.8.1 Torsional Rigidity (Shafts as Torsion Bars)

A shaft is said to be torsionally rigid, if it does not twist too much under the action of external torque.

Examples: Cam shaft, machine tool spindles, etc.

The angle of twist or angular deformation may be obtained from the torsional equation and is given as follows:

a. **For solid shaft:** $\theta = \dfrac{584TL}{Gd^4}$ (deg)   ... (Eq. 5.9) **3.2/ Pg 50, DHB**

b. **For hollow shaft:** $\theta = \dfrac{584TL}{G(d_o^4 - d_i^4)}$ (deg)   ... (Eq. 5.10) **3.2/ Pg 50, DHB**

where θ = angle of twist (deg)

                   T = torsional moment (N·mm)

                   L = length of the shaft (mm)

- The standard and widely used relation is that the deflection should not exceed 1° in a length equal to twenty times the diameter of the shaft.
- The permissible amount of twist for machine tool spindles, e.g. cam shaft should not exceed 0.25° per meter length.
- For line shafts 2.5° to 3° per meter length may be used as the limiting value.

5.8.2 Lateral Rigidity (Shafts as Beams)

A shaft is said to be laterally rigid, if it does not deflect too much under the action of external forces and bending moment.

The lateral rigidity is important for maintaining proper bearing clearances and for correct gear teeth alignment. If the shaft is of uniform cross-section, then the lateral deflection of a shaft may be obtained by using the deflection formulae as in 'Strength of Materials'. But when the shaft is of variable cross-section, then the lateral deflection may be determined either by the graphical method or from the fundamental equation for the elastic curve of a beam as

$$\frac{M}{EI} = \frac{d^2y}{dx^2} \qquad \qquad \dots \text{(Eq. 5.11)}$$

5.9 ASME CODE FOR SHAFT DESIGN

Till now it was assumed that the loads are steady. But in actual practice, it is observed that the loads are never steady and are always accompanied by certain amount of shock, fatigue and impact effects.

In order to take care of these effects, ASME (American Society of Mechanical Engineers) has introduced the following factors in design:

C_m = combined shock and fatigue factor applied to bending moment.

C_t = combined shock and fatigue factor applied to torsional moment.

Introducing these factors into Eqs. (5.5) to (5.8), we have:

a. **For hollow shaft:**

i. According to maximum normal stress theory, outside diameter of shaft is found as:

$$d_o = \left[\frac{16}{\pi\sigma_{max}} \left(C_m M + \sqrt{(C_m M)^2 + (C_t T)^2} \right) \left(\frac{1}{1 - K^4} \right) \right]^{1/3}$$

$$\dots \text{(Eq. 5.12) } \textbf{3.6(a)/ Pg 51, DHB}$$

ii. According to maximum shear stress theory, outside diameter of shaft is found as:

$$d_o = \left[\frac{16}{\pi\tau_{max}} \left(\sqrt{(C_m M)^2 + (C_t T)^2} \right) \left(\frac{1}{1 - K^4} \right) \right]^{1/3}$$

$$\dots \text{(Eq. 5.13) } \textbf{3.6(b)/ Pg 51, DHB}$$

b. **For solid shaft:** Diameter of solid shaft is found by substituting $K = 0$ and $d_o = d$, in Eqs (5.12) and (5.13):

i. According to maximum normal stress theory, diameter of shaft is found as:

$$d = \left[\frac{16}{\pi\sigma_{max}} \left(C_m M + \sqrt{(C_m M)^2 + (C_t T)^2} \right) \right]^{1/3} \qquad \dots \text{(Eq. 5.14)}$$

ii. According to maximum shear stress theory, diameter of shaft is found as:

$$d_o = \left[\frac{16}{\pi \tau_{max}} \left(\sqrt{(C_m M)^2 + (C_t T)^2} \right) \right]^{1/3} \qquad \text{... (Eq. 5.15)}$$

Note:

- **The values of C_m and C_t for various types of loads are obtained from**
  ... **Tb. 3.1/ Pg 56, DHB**

- **Working stresses for shaft** ... **Tb. 3.5(b)/ Pg 57, DHB**
  - ☛ ASME code suggests that the allowable design stresses (τ_{max} and σ_{max}) to be considered for steel shafting.
  - ☛ ASME code for *commercial steel shafting*:
    i. *Without keyway*:
    $$\sigma_{max} = 110 \text{ MPa}$$
    and $$\tau_{max} = 55 \text{ MPa}$$

    ii. *With keyway*: The above values are to be reduced by 25% in the presence of keyways,

    i.e. $$\sigma_{max} = (1 - 0.25) \times 110 = 82.5 \approx 83 \text{ MPa}$$
    and $$\tau_{max} = (1 - 0.25) \times 55 = 41.5 \approx 41 \text{ MPa}$$

  - ☛ ASME code for *steel purchased under definite specifications*
    i. *Without keyway*: For bending, the stress should be 30% of the yield strength but not over 18% of the ultimate strength in tension for shafts without keyways.

    i.e. $$\left. \begin{array}{l} \sigma_{max} = 0.6\, \sigma_{yt} \\ \sigma_{max} = 0.36\, \sigma_{ut} \end{array} \right\} \text{ Take the least value among the two.}$$

    $$\left. \begin{array}{l} \tau_{max} = 0.3\, \sigma_{yt} \\ \tau_{max} = 0.18\, \sigma_{ut} \end{array} \right\} \text{ Take the least value among the two.}$$

    ii. *With keyway*: For torsion and combined state, the stress should be 30% of the yield strength but not over 18% of the ultimate strength in tension for shafts without keyways.

    These values are to be reduced by 25% in the presence of keyways.

    i.e. $$\left. \begin{array}{l} \sigma_{max-1} = (1 - 0.25)\, 0.6\, \sigma_{yt} \\ \sigma_{max-1} = (1 - 0.25)\, 0.36\, \sigma_{ut} \end{array} \right\} \text{ Take the least value among the two.}$$

    $$\left. \begin{array}{l} \tau_{max-1} = (1 - 0.25)\, 0.3\, \sigma_{yt} \\ \tau_{max-1} = (1 - 0.25)\, 0.18\, \sigma_{ut} \end{array} \right\} \text{ Take the least value among the two.}$$

Example: A shaft made of 40C8 has $\sigma_{ut} = 630$ MPa and $\sigma_{yt} = 324$ MPa

Without keyway:

- $$\sigma_{max} = 0.6\, \sigma_{yt} = 0.6 \times 324 = 194.4 \text{ MPa}$$
  and $$\sigma_{max} = 0.36\, \sigma_{ut} = 0.36 \times 630 = 226.8 \text{ MPa}$$

  Take the least value among the two, we have,
  $$\sigma_{max} = 194.4 \text{ MPa}$$

- $$\tau_{max} = 0.3\, \sigma_{yt} = 0.3 \times 324 = 97.2 \text{ MPa}$$
  and $$\tau_{max} = 0.18\, \sigma_{ut} = 0.18 \times 630 = 113.4 \text{ MPa}$$

  Take the least value among the two, we have,
  $$\tau_{max} = 97.2 \text{ MPa}$$

  or $$\tau_{max} = \frac{\sigma_{max}}{2} = \frac{194.2}{2} = 97.2 \text{ MPa}$$

With keyway:

- $$\sigma_{max-1} = (1 - 0.25)\,\sigma_{max} = 0.75\,\sigma_{max} = 0.75 \times 194.4 = 145.8 \text{ MPa}$$
- $$\tau_{max-1} = (1 - 0.25)\,\tau_{max} = 0.75\,\tau_{max} = 0.75 \times 97.2 \text{ MPa} = 72.9 \text{ MPa}$$

or $$\tau_{max-1} = \frac{\sigma_{max-1}}{2} = \frac{145.8}{2} = 72.9 \text{ MPa}$$

5.10 SHAFTS SUBJECTED TO COMBINED AXIAL LOAD, TOGETHER WITH TORSIONAL AND BENDING MOMENTS (F, T AND BM)

When the shaft is subjected to an axial load (F) in addition to torsion and bending loads as in propeller shafts of ships and shafts for driving worm gears, then the stress due to axial load must be added to the bending stress.

If the shafts are quite long, they behave as a column and tend to buckle. To take care of this a factor called *column factor* is introduced and the relations for axial stress is given as

$$\sigma = \frac{4\alpha F}{\pi d_o^2 (1 - K^2)}, \text{ for hollow shaft} \qquad \dots \text{(Eq. 5.16)}$$

Substituting $K = 0$ and $d_o = d$, in (Eq. 5.16) we have

$$\sigma = \frac{4\alpha F}{\pi d^2}, \text{ for solid shaft} \qquad \dots \text{(Eq. 5.17)}$$

a. **For hollow shaft:**

   i. According to maximum normal stress theory, outside diameter of shaft is found as:

$$d_o = \left[\frac{16}{\pi \sigma_{max}} \left[\left(C_m M + \frac{\alpha F d_o (1 + K^2)}{8} \right) \right. \right.$$
$$\left. \left. + \sqrt{\left(C_m M + \frac{\alpha F d_o (1 + K^2)}{8} \right)^2 + (C_t T)^2} \right] \left(\frac{1}{1 - K^4} \right) \right]^{1/3}$$

... (Eq. 5.18) **3.8(a)/ Pg 51, DHB**

   ii. According to maximum shear stress theory, outside diameter of shaft is found as:

$$d_o = \left[\frac{16}{\pi \tau_{max}} \left\{ \sqrt{\left(C_m M + \frac{\alpha F d_o (1 + K^2)}{8} \right)^2 + (C_t T)^2} \right\} \left(\frac{1}{1 - K^4} \right) \right]^{1/3}$$

... (Eq. 5.19) **3.8(b)/ Pg 51, DHB**

where α = column factor, depends upon slenderness ratio (L/k)

$$= \frac{1}{1 - 0.0044(L/k)}, \text{ for } L/k < 115 \qquad \dots \textbf{Tb. 3.2/ Pg 56, DHB}$$

$$= \frac{\sigma_{yp}}{n\pi^2 E}(L/k)^2, \text{ for } L/k > 115 \text{ (Euler's formula)}$$

L = length of shaft between bearings (mm)

$k = \sqrt{I/A}$ = radius of gyration of the shaft (mm)

I = moment of inertia

A = area of cross-section

σ_{yp} = yield stress in compression (MPa)

E = modulus of elasticity (MPa)

n = constant for the type of column support

= 1.0, for free or hinged ends

= 1.60, for both ends pinned, guided and partly restrained

= 2.25, for both ends fixed.

Note: Assume the type of loading if not given from ... **Tb. 3.1/ Pg 56, DHB**

b. **For solid shaft:** Diameter of solid shaft is found by substituting $K = 0$ and $d_o = d$, in Eqs. (5.18) and (5.19) respectively.

5.11 SHAFT SUBJECTED TO FLUCTUATING LOADS

a. For hollow shaft:

i. According to maximum normal stress theory, outside diameter of shaft is found as:

$$d_o = \left[\frac{16}{\pi\sigma_{max}} \left[\left(M_m + \frac{K_t\sigma_{yp}}{\sigma_{en}} M_a \right) \right. \right.$$

$$\left. \left. + \sqrt{\left(M_m + \frac{K_t\sigma_{yp}}{\sigma_{en}} M_a \right)^2 + \left(T_m + \frac{K_s\sigma_{yp}}{\sigma_{en}} T_a \right)^2} \right] \left(\frac{1}{1-K^4} \right) \right]^{1/3}$$

... (Eq. 5.20) **3.7(a)/ Pg 51, DHB**

ii. According to maximum shear stress theory, outside diameter of shaft is found as:

$$d_o = \left[\frac{16}{\pi\tau_{max}} \left[\sqrt{\left(M_m + \frac{K_t\sigma_{yp}}{\sigma_{en}} M_a \right)^2 + \left(T_m + \frac{K_s\sigma_{yp}}{\sigma_{en}} T_a \right)^2} \right] \left(\frac{1}{1-K^4} \right) \right]^{1/3}$$

... (Eq. 5.21) **3.7(b)/ Pg 51, DHB**

iii. According to Hencky von Mises theory, outside diameter of shaft is found as:

$$d_o = \left[\frac{16}{\pi\sigma_{max}} \left[\sqrt{4M_m^2 + 3T_m^2} + \left(\frac{K_t\sigma_{yp}}{\sigma_{en}} \sqrt{4M_a^2 + 3T_a^2} \right) \right] \left(\frac{1}{1-K^4} \right) \right]^{1/3}$$

... (Eq. 5.22) **3.7(c)/ Pg 51, DHB**

where

Mean or average moment

$$M_m = \frac{M_{max} + M_{min}}{2}$$

Variable or alternating moment,

$$M_a = \frac{M_{max} - M_{min}}{2}$$

Mean or average torque,

$$T_m = \frac{T_{max} + T_{min}}{2}$$

Variable or alternating torque,

$$T_a = \frac{T_{max} - T_{min}}{2}$$

M_{max} = maximum bending moment
M_{min} = minimum bending moment
T_{max} = maximum torsional moment
T_{min} = minimum torsional moment

b. **For solid shaft:** Diameter of solid shaft is found by substituting $K = 0$ and $d_o = d$, in Eqs. (5.20) to (5.22) respectively.

5.12 POWER EQUATION

The torque transmitted by a shaft is found from the power equation as

$$T = \frac{9.55 \times 10^6 (P)}{n} \text{(N·mm)} \quad \text{... (Eq. 5.23) } \textbf{3.3(a)/ Pg 50, DHB}$$

5.13 EVALUATION OF TRANSMISSION FORCES

5.13.1 Forces Due to Belt Drive

Figure 5.1 represents forces acting on the shaft due to belt drive.

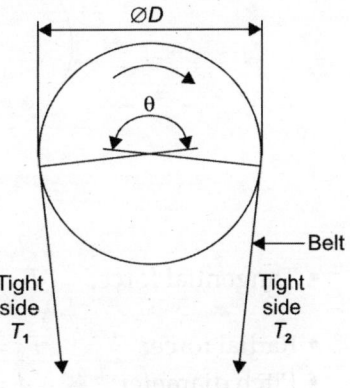

Let, T_1 = tension on tight side of the belt
T_2 = tension on slack side of the belt
θ = angle of contact or lap angle
D = diameter of pulley

Ratio of tensions: $\dfrac{T_1}{T_2} = e^{\mu\theta}$, for a flat belt

... **14.3(a)/ Pg 290, DHB**

$$\frac{T_1}{T_2} = e^{\mu_1\theta}, \text{ for a V-belt}$$

... **14.12/ Pg 294, DHB**

Fig. 5.1: Belt drive

where μ = coefficient of friction between the pulley and the belt

$\mu_1 = \dfrac{\mu}{\sin(\alpha/2)}$ is the apparent coefficient of friction.

α = groove angle of the pulley

• Effective or net pull, $F_t = (T_1 - T_2)$ ... **14.4/ Pg 291, DHB**
• Torque, $T = (T_1 - T_2)R$
• Total force or tension in the direction of belt drive
$$= (T_1 + T_2)$$

5.13.2 Forces Due to Gear Drive

Figures 5.2 and 5.3 represent forces acting on the shaft due to gears drive in horizontal and vertical positions respectively.

Let F_t = tangential or peripheral force (mm)
F_r = radial force (N)
d = diameter of pinion or gear (mm)
α = pressure angle (deg)

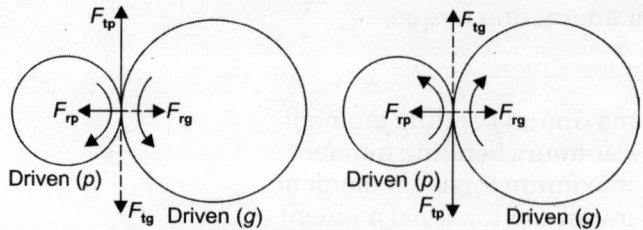

Fig. 5.2: Gears in horizontal position

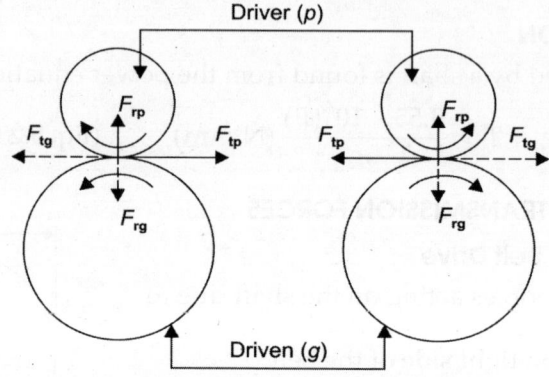

Fig. 5.3: Gears in vertical position

- Tangential force: $F_t = \dfrac{2M_t}{d}$ ... **12.8(a)/ Pg 206, DHB**

- Radial force: $F_r = F_t \tan \alpha$ ... **12.8(b)/ Pg 206, DHB**

- Pitch diameter: $d = mz$ ... **12.1(e)/ Pg 203, DHB**

  where m = module (mm)

       z = number of teeth

       M_t = torque transmitted (N·mm)

1. **A mild steel shaft has to transmit 75 kW at 200 rpm. The allowable stress in the shaft material is limited to 40 MPa and the angle of twist is not to exceed 1° in a length of 20 diameters. Calculate the suitable diameter of the shaft.**

Solution: $P = 75$ kW, $n = 200$ rpm, $\tau = 40$ MPa, $\theta = 1°$, $L = 20d$, $d = ?$

We know that $T = \dfrac{9.55 \times 10^6 (P)}{n} = \dfrac{9.55 \times 10^6 \times (75)}{200} = 3.58 \times 10^6$ N·mm

                     ... **3.3(a)/Pg 50, DHB**

Shaft diameter:

  a. Based on strength:

$$\tau = \frac{16T}{\pi d^3} \qquad \text{... 3.1/ Pg 50, DHB}$$

$$40 = \frac{16 \times 3.58 \times 10^6}{\pi d^3}$$

$$d = 76.96 \text{ mm} \qquad \text{... Eq. (a)}$$

b. Based on rigidity:

$$\theta = \frac{584TL}{Gd^4}$$ ... 3.2/ Pg 50, DHB

$$G = 78.5 \times 10^3 \, \text{MPa}$$ ... Tb 1.1/Pg 11, DHB

$$1 = \frac{584 \times 3.58 \times 10^6 \times (20d)}{(78.5 \times 10^3) d^4}$$

$$d = 81.06 \, \text{mm}$$ ... Eq. (b)

Based on Eqs. (a) and (b), select maximum diameter for design, i.e.

$$d = 81.06$$

∴ Standard size of shaft,

$$d = 90 \, \text{mm}$$ ... Tb. 3.5(a)/Pg 57, DHB

2. **A hollow shaft of diameter ratio 3/8 is required to transmit 500 kW at 110 rpm, the maximum torque being 20% greater than the mean. The shear stress is not to exceed 60 MPa and angle of twist in a length of 3 m is not to exceed 1.4°. Calculate the shaft diameter if G = 84 GPa.**

Solution: $K = 3/8$, $P = 500$ kW, $n = 110$ rpm, $T_{\text{max}} = 1.2T$, $\tau = 60$ MPa, $L = 3000$ mm, $\theta = 1.4°$, $G = 84 \times 10^3$ MPa, $d = ?$

We know that $T_{\text{max}} = 1.2T$ ... Eq. (i)

But $$T = \frac{9.55 \times 10^6 (P)}{n} = \frac{9.55 \times 10^6 \times (500)}{110} = 43.41 \times 10^6 \, \text{N·mm}$$

... 3.3(a)/Pg 50, DHB

∴ Eq. (i) yields... $T_{\text{max}} = 1.2 \times (43.41 \times 10^6) = 52.10 \times 10^6 \, \text{N·mm}$.

Shaft diameter:

a. Based on strength:

$$\tau = \frac{16T_{\text{max}}}{\pi d_o^3} \left[\frac{1}{1 - K^4} \right]$$ ... 3.1/ Pg 50, DHB

$$60 = \frac{16 \times 52.1 \times 10^6}{\pi d_o^3} \left[\frac{1}{1 - (3/8)^4} \right]$$

$$d_o = 165.24 \, \text{mm}$$ ... Eq. (a)

b. Based on rigidity:

$$\theta = \frac{584 T_{\text{max}} L}{G(d_o^4 - d_i^4)} = = \frac{584 T_{\text{max}} L}{G d_o^4 (1 - K^4)}$$ ... 3.2/ Pg 50, DHB

$$1.4 = \frac{584 \times (52.1 \times 10^6) \times 3000}{84 \times 10^3 \times d_o^4 \left[(1 - \left(\frac{3}{8} \right)^4 \right]}$$

$$d_o = 167.75 \, \text{mm}$$ ... Eq. (b)

Based on Eqs. (a) and (b), select maximum diameter for design, i.e.

$$d_o = 167.75 \, \text{mm}$$

∴ Standard size of shaft,

$$d_o = 180 \, \text{mm}$$ ... Tb. 3.5(a)/Pg 57, DHB

and $$d_i = (3/8) \times 180 = 67.5 \, \text{mm}.$$

3. **A hollow shaft transmits 200 kW at 150 rpm. The total angle of twist in a length of 5 m is 3°. Find the inner and outer diameters of the shaft, if the shear stress is limited to 60 MPa. Take $G = 80$ GPa.**

Solution: $P = 200$ kW, $n = 150$ rpm, $\theta = 3°$, $L = 5000$ mm, $G = 80 \times 10^3$ MPa, $\tau = 60$ MPa, $d_o, d_i = ?$

We know that
$$T = \frac{9.55 \times 10^6 (P)}{n} = \frac{9.55 \times 10^6 \times (200)}{150} = 12.73 \times 10^6 \text{ N·mm}$$

... 3.3(a)/Pg 50, DHB

Shaft diameter:

a. Based on strength:

$$\tau = \frac{16T}{\pi d_o^3}\left[\frac{1}{1-K^4}\right]$$

... 3.1/ Pg 50, DHB

$$60 = \frac{16 \times 12.73 \times 10^6}{\pi d_o^3}\left[\frac{1}{1-K^4}\right]$$

$$\therefore \quad d_o^3(1-K^4) = 1.08 \times 10^6$$

... Eq. (a)

b. Based on rigidity:

$$\theta = \frac{584TL}{G(d_o^4 - d_i^4)} = = \frac{584TL}{Gd_o^4(1-K^4)}$$

... 3.2/ Pg 50, DHB

$$3 = \frac{584 \times 12.73 \times 10^6 \times 5000}{(80 \times 10^3)d_o^4(1-K^4)}$$

$$d_o^3(1-K^4) = \frac{1.55 \times 10^8}{d_o}$$

... Eq. (b)

Equating Eqs. (a) and (b), we have

$$1.08 \times 10^6 = \frac{1.55 \times 10^8}{d_o}$$

$$d_o = 143.52 \text{ mm}$$

$\therefore$ Standard size of shaft,

$$d_o = 160 \text{ mm}$$

... Tb. 3.5(a)/Pg 57, DHB

Eq. (a) yields ...

$$160^3 \times (1 - K_4) = 1.08 \times 10^6$$

$$1 - K^4 = 0.2637$$

$$\therefore \quad K = 0.9263$$

Also
$$K = \frac{d_i}{d_o}$$

$$0.9263 = \frac{d_i}{160}$$

$$\therefore \quad d_i = 148.21 \text{ mm}$$

4. **Compare the weight, strength and stiffness of a hollow shaft with that of a solid shaft having same material and length.**

Solution: $L = L_S = L_H$.

Let d = diameter of solid shaft

d_o = outer diameter of hollow shaft

d_i = inner diameter of hollow shaft

$K = \dfrac{d_i}{d_o}$ = ratio of inner diameter to outer diameter of hollow shaft

L = length of the shaft

τ_d = shear stress of shaft material

ρ = density of shaft material

W_H, W_S = weight of hollow shaft and solid shaft respectively

T_H, T_S = torque transmitted by hollow shaft and solid shaft respectively

S_H, S_S = stiffness of hollow shaft and solid shaft respectively.

a. **Comparison of weight:** We know that

$$\text{Weight} = \text{density} \times \text{volume} = \text{density} \times (\text{area} \times \text{length})$$
$$W = \rho A L$$

Thus for a solid shaft,

$$W_S = \rho A_s L = \rho L \frac{\pi d^2}{4} \qquad \dots \text{Eq. (i)}$$

and for a hollow shaft,

$$W_H = \rho A_H L = \rho L \frac{\pi(d_o^2 - d_i^2)}{4} \qquad \dots \text{Eq. (ii)}$$

Dividing Eq. (ii) by Eq. (i) yields

$$\frac{W_H}{W_S} = \frac{\rho L[\pi(d_o^2 - d_i^2)/4]}{\rho L(\pi d^2/4)} = \frac{d_o^2 - d_i^2}{d^2}$$

$$\therefore \quad \frac{W_H}{W_S} = \frac{d_o^2(1 - K^2)}{d^2} \qquad \dots \text{Eq. (iii)}$$

b. **Comparison of strength:** For a hollow shaft,

$$d_o = \left[\frac{16T_H}{\pi \tau_d} \left(\frac{1}{1 - K^4} \right) \right]^{1/3} \qquad \dots \textbf{3.4(a)/ Pg 50, DHB}$$

$$T_H = \left(\frac{\pi}{16} \right) d_o^3 \tau_d (1 - K^4) \qquad \dots \text{Eq. (iv)}$$

For a solid shaft substituting $K = 0$ and $d_o = d$, in Eq. (iv), we have

$$T_s = \left(\frac{\pi}{16} \right) d^3 \tau_d \qquad \dots \text{Eq. (v)}$$

Dividing Eq. (iv) by Eq. (v) yields

$$\frac{T_H}{T_s} = \frac{(\pi/16)d_o^3 \tau_d (1 - K^4)}{(\pi/16) d^3 \tau_d}$$

$$\therefore \quad \frac{T_H}{T_s} = \frac{d_o^3(1 - K^4)}{d^3} \qquad \dots \text{Eq. (vi)}$$

Since the material is same, equating Eqs. (i) and (ii), we have

$$\rho L[\pi(d_o^2 - d_i^2)/4] = \rho L(\pi d^2/4)$$

$$d_o^2(1 - K^2) = d^2$$

$$d_o\sqrt{(1 - K^2)} = d \qquad \qquad \text{... Eq. (iii-a)}$$

Substituting Eq. (iii-a) in Eq. (vi), we have

$$\frac{T_H}{T_S} = \frac{d_o^3(1 - K^4)}{\left[d_o\sqrt{(1 - K^2)}\right]^3} = \frac{(1 - K^4)}{\left[\sqrt{(1 - K^2)}\right]^3} = \frac{(1 + K^2)(1 - K^2)}{(1 - K^2)\sqrt{(1 - K^2)}}$$

$$\therefore \qquad \frac{T_H}{T_S} = \frac{(1 + K^2)}{\sqrt{(1 - K^2)}} \qquad \qquad \text{... Eq. (vi-a)}$$

c. **Comparison of stiffness:** Stiffness is defined as

$$S = \frac{T}{\theta} \qquad \qquad \text{... Eq. (vii)}$$

We know that $\quad \dfrac{T}{J} = \dfrac{G\theta}{L} = \dfrac{\tau}{r}$ **... 1.3(b)/ Pg 3, DHB**

$$S = \frac{T}{\theta} = \frac{GJ}{L}$$

For a solid shaft, $J = \left[\dfrac{\pi d^4}{32}\right]$ and for a hollow shaft $J = \left[\dfrac{\pi(d_o^4 - d_i^4)}{32}\right]$

... Tb. 1.3(b)/ Pg 14, DHB

For a hollow shaft,

$$S_H = \frac{G}{L}\left[\frac{\pi(d_o^4 - d_i^4)}{32}\right] = \frac{G}{L}\left[\frac{\pi d_o^4(1 - K^4)}{32}\right] \qquad \text{... Eq. (viii)}$$

For a solid shaft substituting $K = 0$ and $d_o = d$ in Eq. (viii), we have

$$S_S = \frac{G}{L}\left[\frac{\pi d^4}{32}\right] \qquad \qquad \text{... Eq. (ix)}$$

Dividing Eq. (viii) by Eq. (ix) yields

$$\frac{S_H}{S_S} = \frac{(G/L) \times [\pi d_o^4(1 - K^4)/32]}{(G/L) \times (\pi d^4/32)}$$

$$\therefore \qquad \frac{S_H}{S_S} = \frac{d_o^4(1 - K^4)}{d^4} \qquad \qquad \text{... Eq. (x)}$$

Substituting Eq. (iii-a) in Eq. (vi), we have

$$\frac{S_H}{S_S} = \frac{d_o^4(1 - K^4)}{\left[d_o\sqrt{(1 - K^2)}\right]^4} = \frac{(1 - K^4)}{\left[\sqrt{(1 - K^2)}\right]^4} = \frac{(1 + K^2)(1 - K^2)}{(1 - K^2)^2}$$

$$\therefore \qquad \frac{S_H}{S_S} = \frac{(1 + K^2)}{(1 - K^2)} \qquad \qquad \text{... Eq. (x-a)}$$

5. **Compare the strength and stiffness of a hollow shaft of same outside diameter as that of a solid shaft.**

VTU – June/ July 2008 – 06 Marks

Solution: $d_o = d$.

Proceeding on similar lines as in problem 4, we have:

a. **Comparison of strength:**

$$\frac{T_H}{T_S} = \frac{d_o^3(1 - K^4)}{d^3} \qquad \text{... using Eq. (vi)}$$

Since $d_o = d$, we have

$$\frac{T_H}{T_S} = \frac{d_o^3(1 - K^4)}{d^3} = (1 - K^4) \qquad \text{... Eq. (vi-a)}$$

b. **Comparison of stiffness:**

$$\frac{S_H}{S_S} = \frac{d_o^4(1 - K^4)}{d^4} \qquad \text{... using Eq. (x)}$$

Since $d_o = d$, we have

$$\frac{S_H}{S_S} = \frac{d_o^4(1 - K^4)}{d^4} = (1 - K^4) \qquad \text{... Eq. (x-a)}$$

6. **Prove that a hollow shaft is stronger and stiffer than a solid shaft of same length, weight and material.**

VTU – June/ July – 13 Marks

Solution: Refer to *Problem 4*.

7. **Compare the weight, strength and stiffness of a hollow shaft with that of a solid shaft having same material and length. The external diameter of hollow shaft is same as that of solid shaft, while the internal diameter of hollow shaft is half the external diameter of hollow shaft.**

Solution: $d_o = d$, $d_i = d_o/2 = K = \dfrac{d_i}{d_o} = 0.5$, $L = L_S = L_H$.

Let, L = length of the shaft

d = diameter of solid shaft

d_o = outer diameter of hollow shaft

d_i = inner diameter of hollow shaft

$K = \dfrac{d_i}{d_o}$ = ratio of inner diameter to outer diameter of hollow shaft

τ_d = shear stress of shaft material

ρ = density of shaft material

W_H, W_S = weight of hollow shaft and solid shaft respectively

T_H, T_S = torque transmitted by hollow shaft and solid shaft respectively

S_H, S_S = stiffness of hollow shaft and solid shaft respectively

a. **Comparison of weight:** We know that

$$\text{Weight} = \text{density} \times \text{volume} = \text{density} \times (\text{area} \times \text{length})$$
$$W = \rho A L$$

Thus for a solid shaft,

$$W_S = \rho A_S L = \rho L \frac{\pi d^2}{4} \qquad \text{... Eq. (i)}$$

and for a hollow shaft,

$$W_H = \rho A_H L = \rho L \frac{\pi(d_o^2 - d_i^2)}{44} \qquad \text{... Eq. (ii)}$$

Dividing Eq. (ii) by Eq. (i) yields

$$\frac{W_H}{W_S} = \frac{\rho L[\pi(d_o^2 - d_i^2)/4]}{\rho L(\pi d^2/4)} = \frac{d_o^2 - d_i^2}{d^2}$$

$$\therefore \quad \frac{W_H}{W_S} = \frac{d_o^2(1 - K^2)}{d^2} \qquad \text{... Eq. (iii)}$$

Since $\quad d_o = d$

we have $\quad \dfrac{W_H}{W_S} = (1 - K^2) = (1 - 0.5^2)$

$$\therefore \quad \frac{W_H}{W_S} = 0.75 \qquad \text{... Eq. (iv)}$$

b. **Comparison of strength:** For a hollow shaft,

$$d_o = \left[\frac{16 T_H}{\pi \tau_d} \left(\frac{1}{1 - K^4} \right) \right]^{1/3} \qquad \text{... 3.4(a)/ Pg 50, DHB}$$

$$T_H = \left(\frac{\pi}{16} \right) d_o^3 \tau_d (1 - K^4) \qquad \text{... Eq. (v)}$$

For a solid shaft substituting $K = 0$ and $d_o = d$, in Eq. (v), we have

$$T_S = \left(\frac{\pi}{16} \right) d^3 \tau_d \qquad \text{... Eq. (vi)}$$

Dividing Eq. (v) by Eq. (vi) yields

$$\frac{T_H}{T_S} = \frac{(\pi/16) d_o^3 \tau_d (1 - K^4)}{(\pi/16) d^3 \tau_d}$$

$$\therefore \quad \frac{T_H}{T_S} = \frac{d_o^3(1 - K^4)}{d^3} \qquad \text{... Eq. (vii)}$$

Since $d_o = d$, we have

$$\frac{T_H}{T_S} = (1 - K^4) = (1 - 0.5^4)$$

$$\therefore \quad \frac{T_H}{T_S} = 0.9375 \qquad \text{... Eq. (viii)}$$

c. **Comparison of stiffness:** Stiffness is defined as

$$S = \frac{T}{\theta} \qquad \qquad \text{... Eq. (ix)}$$

We know that $\dfrac{T}{J} = \dfrac{G\theta}{L} = \dfrac{\tau}{r}$ **... 1.3(b)/ Pg 3, DHB**

$$S = \frac{T}{\theta} = \frac{GJ}{L}$$

For a solid shaft, $J = \left[\dfrac{\pi d^4}{32}\right]$ and for a hollow shaft $J = \left[\dfrac{\pi(d_o^4 - d_i^4)}{32}\right]$

... Tb. 1.3(b)/ Pg 14, DHB

For a hollow shaft,

$$S_H = \frac{G}{L}\left[\frac{\pi(d_o^4 - d_i^4)}{32}\right] = \frac{G}{L}\left[\frac{\pi d_o^4(1 - K^4)}{32}\right] \qquad \text{... Eq. (x)}$$

For a solid shaft,

$$S_S = \frac{G}{L}\left[\frac{\pi d^4}{32}\right] \qquad \qquad \text{... Eq. (xi)}$$

Dividing Eq. (x) by Eq. (xi) yields

$$\frac{S_H}{S_S} = \frac{(G/L) \times [\pi d_o^4(1 - K^4)/32]}{(G/L) \times (\pi d^4/32)}$$

$$\therefore \qquad \frac{S_H}{S_S} = \frac{d_o^4(1 - K^4)}{d^4} \qquad \qquad \text{... Eq. (xii)}$$

Since $d_o = d$, we have

$$\frac{S_H}{S_S} = (1 - K^4) = (1 - 0.5^4)$$

$$\therefore \qquad \frac{S_H}{S_S} = 0.9375 \qquad \qquad \text{... Eq. (xiii)}$$

8. **Compare the strength of a hollow shaft with that of a solid shaft for the same diameter and material. The diameter ratio of hollow shaft is 0.75.**

    VTU – Dec. 08/ Jan. 2009 – 06 Marks

Solution: $K = 0.75 = \dfrac{d_i}{d_o}$, $d_o = d$,

Let d = diameter of solid shaft

       d_o = outer diameter of hollow shaft

       d_i = inner diameter of hollow shaft

       $K = \dfrac{d_i}{d_o}$ = ratio of inner diameter to outer diameter of hollow shaft

From case (b) of *Problem 7*, we have

$$\therefore \qquad \frac{T_H}{T_S} = \frac{d_o^3(1 - K^4)}{d^3} \qquad \qquad \text{... using Eq. (vii)}$$

Since $d_o = d$, we have

$$\frac{T_H}{T_S} = (1 - K^4) = (1 - 0.75^4) = 0.6836$$

9. **A solid shaft and a hollow shaft are made of same material and have equal strength in torsion. The outside diameter of hollow shaft is 25% larger than the solid shaft. What will be the ratio weight of hollow shaft to solid shaft?**

Solution: $d_o = 1.25d$.

Let d = diameter of solid shaft
d_o = outer diameter of hollow shaft
d_i = inner diameter of hollow shaft

$K = \dfrac{d_i}{d_o}$ = ratio of inner diameter to outer diameter of hollow shaft

τ_d = shear stress of shaft material

For a hollow shaft,

$$d_o = \left[\frac{16T_H}{\pi\tau_d}\left(\frac{1}{1-K^4}\right)\right]^{1/3} \qquad \text{... 3.4(a)/ Pg 50, DHB}$$

$$T_H = \left(\frac{\pi}{16}\right)d_o^3\tau_d(1 - K^4) \qquad \text{... Eq. (i)}$$

For a solid shaft substituting $K = 0$ and $d_o = d$, in Eq. (i), we have

$$T_s = \left(\frac{\pi}{16}\right)d^3\tau_d \qquad \text{... Eq. (ii)}$$

Since the material is same, equating Eqs. (i) and (ii), we have

$$\left(\frac{\pi}{16}\right)d_o^3\tau_d(1 - K^4) = \left(\frac{\pi}{16}\right)d^3\tau_d$$

$$d_o^3(1 - K^4) = d^3$$

$$(1.25d)^3(1 - K^4) = d^3$$

$$(1 - K^4) = 0.512$$

$$\therefore \qquad K = 0.8358$$

From **Problem 8**, we have

$$\frac{W_H}{W_S} = \frac{d_o^2(1 - K^2)}{d^2} = \frac{(1.25d)^2(1 - 0.8358^2)}{d^2} = 0.4709$$

$$\text{... using Eq. (iii)}$$

10. **Determine the diameter of a solid circular shaft to transmit a power of 50 kW at a rated speed of 1000 rpm selecting a suitable material and choosing an appropriate value for factor of safety. Replace this solid shaft by a hollow circular shaft assuming the value of 0.6 for the ratio of diameters selecting the same material and the same factor of safety. As the consequences of this replacement, determine:**

    a. Percentage of reduction in weight assuming same length for the shafts.

    b. The ratio of torsional stiffness of the hollow shaft to that of the solid shaft.

VTU – July/ Aug. 2005 – 08 Marks

Solution: $d = ?$, $P = 50$ kW, $n = 1000$ rpm, $K = 0.6$, d_o, $d_i = ?$

a. Percentage saving in weight = ? b. $\dfrac{T_H}{T_S} = ?$

Material: Assume hot rolled or forged steel, having

$$\sigma_{ut} = 451 \text{ MPa and } \sigma_{yt} = 245 \text{ MPa} \qquad \text{... Tb. 3.3/ Pg 56, DHB}$$

According to ASME,

$$\tau_{max} = 0.3\sigma_{yt} = 0.3 \times 245 = 73.5 \text{ MPa}$$

and $\qquad\qquad \tau_{max} = 0.18\sigma_{ut} = 0.18 \times 451 = 81.18 \text{ MPa}$

Take the least value among the two, we have,

$$\tau_{max} = 73.5 \text{ MPa}$$

We know that $\qquad T = \dfrac{9.55 \times 10^6 (P)}{n} = \dfrac{9.55 \times 10^6 \times (50)}{1000} = 477.5 \times 10^3 \text{ N·mm}$

$$\text{... 3.3(a)/ Pg 50, DHB}$$

Shaft diameter:

• For a solid shaft, $\tau = \dfrac{16T}{\pi d^3}$ $\qquad\qquad$ ... **3.1/ Pg 50, DHB**

$$73.5 = \dfrac{16 \times 477.5 \times 10^3}{\pi d^3}$$

$$d = 32.10 \text{ mm}$$

∴ Standard size of shaft, $d = 36$ mm $\qquad$ ... **Tb. 3.5(a)/ Pg 57, DHB**

• For a hollow shaft,

$$\tau = \dfrac{16T}{d_o^3}\left[\dfrac{1}{1 - K^4}\right] \qquad\qquad \text{... 3.1/ Pg 50, DHB}$$

$$73.5 = \dfrac{16 \times 477.5 \times 10^3}{\pi d_o^3}\left[\dfrac{1}{1 - 0.6^4}\right]$$

$$d = 33.62 \text{ mm}$$

∴ Standard size of shaft, $d_o = 36$ mm $\qquad$ ... **Tb. 3.5(a)/ Pg 57, DHB**

and $\qquad\qquad d_i = 0.6 \times 36 = 21.6$

a. Percentage saving in weight $= \left(1 - \dfrac{W_H}{W_S}\right) \times 100$

Since the material is same, cancelling the common terms, we have

$$= \left(1 - \dfrac{A_H}{A_S}\right) \times 100$$

$$= \left[1 - \dfrac{d_o^2(1 - K^2)}{d^2}\right] \times 100$$

$$= \left[1 - \dfrac{36^2(1 - 0.6^2)}{36^2}\right] \times 100$$

∴ Percentage saving in weight = 36%.

b. The ratio of torsional stiffness of the hollow shaft to that of the solid shaft

We know that $\dfrac{T_H}{T_s} = \dfrac{d_o^3(1 - K^4)}{d^3}$

... using Eq. (vi), Problem 4 or Eq. (vii) Problem 7

$= \dfrac{36^3(1 - 0.6^4)}{36^3}$

∴ $\dfrac{T_H}{T_s} = 0.8704$

11. **A solid shaft of diameter d is used in power transmission. Due to modification of existing transmission system, it is required to replace the solid shaft by a hollow shaft of the same material and equally strong in torsion. Further, the weight of the hollow shaft per meter length should be half of solid shaft. Determine the outer diameter of hollow shaft in terms of d.**

VTU – Dec. 2012 – 10 Marks

Solution: $T_H = T_S$, $W_H = W_S/2$.

Let, d = diameter of solid shaft

      d_o = outer diameter of hollow shaft

      d_i = inner diameter of hollow shaft

      $K = \dfrac{d_i}{d_o}$ = ratio of inner diameter to outer diameter of hollow shaft

      L = length of shaft

      τ_d = shear stress of shaft material

      ρ = density of shaft material

      T_H, T_S = torque transmitted by hollow shaft and solid shaft respectively

      W_H, W_S = weight of hollow shaft and solid shaft respectively

For a hollow shaft, $d_o = \dfrac{16T_H}{\pi\tau_d}\left[\dfrac{1}{1 - K^4}\right]^{1/3}$ ... **3.4(a)/ Pg 50, DHB**

$$T_H = \left(\dfrac{\pi}{16}\right) d_o^3 \tau_d (1 - K^4) \qquad \text{... Eq. (i)}$$

For a solid shaft substituting $K = 0$ and $d_o = d$, in Eq. (i), we have

$$T_S = \left(\dfrac{\pi}{16}\right) d^3 \tau_d \qquad \text{... Eq. (ii)}$$

Since the material is equally strong in torsion, equating Eq. (ii) and Eq. (i) yields

$$T_H = T_S$$

$$\left(\dfrac{\pi}{16}\right) d_o^3 \tau_d (1 - K^4) = \left(\dfrac{\pi}{16}\right) d^3 \tau_d$$

$$d_o^3 (1 - K^4) = d^3$$

$$d_o^3 \left(1 - \dfrac{d_i^4}{d_o^4}\right) = d^3$$

$$\left(d_o^3 - \frac{d_i^4}{d_o}\right) = d^3$$

$$\frac{d_o^4 - d_i^4}{d_o} = d^3$$

$\therefore \qquad\qquad\qquad d_i^4 = d_o^4 - d^3 d_o$ ... Eq. (iii)

Also $\qquad\qquad\qquad W_H = W_S/2$

$$\rho A_H L = \rho A_S L/2$$

$$A_H = A_S/2$$

$$\frac{\pi(d_o^2 - d_i^2)}{4} = \frac{1}{2}\left(\frac{\pi d^2}{4}\right)$$

$$(d_o^2 - d_i^2) = \frac{d^2}{2}$$

$$(d_o^2 - d_i^2) = 0.5d^2$$

$$d_i^2 = d_o^2 - 0.5d^2$$

Squaring both sides, we have

$\therefore \qquad\qquad\qquad d_i^4 = (d_o^2 - 0.5d^2)^2$ ... Eq. (iv)

Equating Eqs. (iii) and (iv), we have

$$d_o^4 - d^3 d_o = (d_o^2 - 0.5d^2)^2$$

$$= d_o^4 + 0.25d^4 - d_o^2 d^2$$

i.e. $(d^2)d_o^2 - (d^3)d_o - 0.25d^4 = 0$ ... Eq. (v)

This is a quadratic equation, having $a = d^2$, $b = -d^3$ and $c = -0.25d^4$

$$d_o = \frac{-(-d^3) \pm \sqrt{d^6 - [4d^2(-0.25d^4)]}}{2d^2}$$

$$= \frac{d^3 \pm \sqrt{d^6 + d^6}}{2d^2} = \frac{d^3 \pm \sqrt{2d^6}}{2d^2}$$

$$= \frac{d^2(d \pm \sqrt{2d^2})}{2d^2} = \frac{(d \pm \sqrt{2}d)}{2}$$

Thus the roots are $\quad d_o = \dfrac{(d + \sqrt{2}d)}{2}$ and $d_o = \dfrac{(d - \sqrt{2}d)}{2}$

12. **A 250 mm diameter solid shaft is used to drive the propeller of a marine vessel. It is necessary to replace the weight of the shaft by 70%. What would be the dimensions of the hollow shaft made of same material as that of solid shaft?**

VTU – Dec. 2011 – 10 Marks

Solution: $d = 250$ mm, $W_H/W_s = 0.7$, $\Rightarrow W_H = 0.7W_S$.

Let, $\qquad d =$ diameter of solid shaft

$\qquad\qquad d_o =$ outer diameter of hollow shaft

d_i = inner diameter of hollow shaft

$K = \dfrac{d_i}{d_o}$ = ratio of inner diameter to outer diameter of hollow shaft

L = length of shaft

τ_d = shear stress of shaft material

ρ = density of shaft material

T_H, T_S = torque transmitted by hollow shaft and solid shaft respectively

W_H, W_S = weight of hollow shaft and solid shaft respectively

For a hollow shaft, $\quad d_o = \dfrac{16T_H}{\pi\tau_d}\left[\dfrac{1}{1-K^4}\right]^{1/3}$ ... **3.4(a)/ Pg 50, DHB**

$$T_H = \left(\frac{\pi}{16}\right)d_o^3\tau_d(1-K^4) \qquad\qquad \text{... Eq. (i)}$$

For a solid shaft substituting $K = 0$ and $d_o = d$, in Eq. (i), we have

$$T_S = \left(\frac{\pi}{16}\right)d^3\tau_d \qquad\qquad\qquad \text{... Eq. (ii)}$$

Since the material is same, equating Eq. (ii) and Eq. (i) yields

$$T_H = T_S$$

$$\left(\frac{\pi}{16}\right)d_o^3\tau_d(1-K^4) = \left(\frac{\pi}{16}\right)d^3\tau_d$$

$$d_o^3(1-K^4) = d^3$$

$$d_o^3\left(1 - \frac{d_i^4}{d_o^4}\right) = d^3$$

$$\left(d_o^3 - \frac{d_i^4}{d_o^4}\right) = d^3$$

$$\frac{d_o^4 - d_i^4}{d_o} = d^3$$

$\therefore \qquad\qquad\qquad d_i^4 = d_o^4 - d^3 d_o$ ... Eq. (iii)

Also $\qquad\qquad\qquad W_H = 0.7\, W_s$

$$\rho A_H L = 0.7\rho A_s L$$

$$A_H = 0.7 A_s$$

$$\frac{\pi(d_o^2 - d_i^2)}{4} = 0.7\left(\frac{\pi d^2}{4}\right)$$

$$(d_o^2 - d_i^2) = 0.7d^2$$

$$d_i^2 = d_o^2 - 0.7d^2$$

Squaring both sides, we have

$\therefore \qquad\qquad\qquad d_i^4 = (d_o^2 - 0.7d^2)^2$ ... Eq. (iv)

Equating Eqs. (iii) and (iv), we have

$$d_o^4 - d^3 d_o = (d_o^2 - 0.7d^2)^2$$
$$= d_o^4 + 0.49d^4 - 1.4d_o^2 d^2$$

i.e.
$$(1.4d^2)d_o^2 - (d^3)d_o - 0.49d^4 = 0$$
$$(1.4 \times 250^2)d_o^2 - d_o \times 250^3 - 0.49 \times 250^4 = 0$$
$$87500d_o^2 - 15.625 \times 10^6 d_o - 1.914 \times 10^9 = 0$$

This is a quadratic equation, having

$$a = 875000, b = -15.625 \times 10^6 \text{ and } c = -1.914 \times 10^{19}$$

Thus the roots are $d_o = 262 \text{ mm}, -83.48 \text{ mm}$

∴ Standard size of shaft,

$$d_o = 280 \text{ mm} \qquad \text{... Tb. 3.5(a)/ Pg 57, DHB}$$

Eq. (iii) yields... $d_i^4 = 280^4 - (250^3 \times 280)$

∴ $d_i = 205.16 \text{ mm}$

Note: *The above problem may also be of the form: "It is necessary to replace a solid shaft of 250 mm diameter by a hollow shaft. Both the shafts are made of same material. What would be the dimensions of the hollow shaft if 30% material has to be saved?"*

Solution: Since 30% material is to be saved, we have
$$W_H = (1 - 0.3) W_S \Rightarrow W_H = 0.7W_S$$

13. **A shaft of a motor is supported at two points which are 800 mm apart. The armature of the motor can be considered as a uniformly distributed load of 15 N/mm, centrally spread over a length of 500 mm, selecting a suitable material and choosing appropriate value for the factor of safety, determine the diameter of the motor shaft. The motor develops 15 kW at 1500 rpm.**

VTU – July 2006 – 12 Marks

Solution: $w = 15 \text{ N/mm}$, total length $L = 800 \text{ mm}$, udl length $l = 500 \text{ mm}$, $d = ?$, $P = 15 \text{ kW}$, $n = 1500 \text{ rpm}$.

Based on given data, the problem is represented as a line diagram as shown in **Fig. 5.4**.

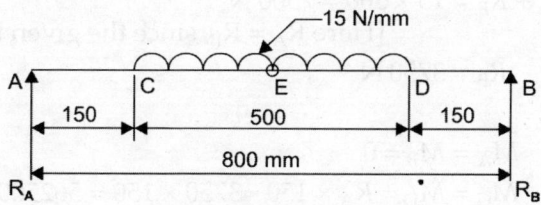

Fig. 5.4: Problem 13

Material: Assume 40C8 having $\sigma_{ut} = 630 \text{ MPa}$ and $\sigma_{yt} = 324 \text{ MPa}$ and factor of safety $n' = 1.5$ and no keyway

$$\sigma_u = \frac{\sigma_{ut}}{n'} = \frac{630}{1.5} = 420 \text{ MPa}$$

$$\sigma_y = \frac{\sigma_{yt}}{n'} = \frac{324}{1.5} = 216 \text{ MPa}$$

$\rightarrow$ $\qquad\qquad \sigma_{max} = 0.36\sigma_u = 0.36 \times 420 = 151.2 \text{ MPa}$

and $\qquad\qquad \sigma_{max} = 0.6\sigma_y = 0.6 \times 216 = 129.6 \text{ MPa}$

Take the least value among the two, we have,

$\qquad\qquad \sigma_{max} = 129.6 \text{ MPa}$

$\rightarrow$ $\qquad\qquad \tau_{max} = 0.18\sigma_u = 0.18 \times 420 = 75.6 \text{ MPa}$

and $\qquad\qquad \tau_{max} = 0.3\sigma_y = 0.3 \times 216 = 64.8 \text{ MPa}$

Take the least value among the two, we have,

$\qquad\qquad \tau_{max} = 64.8 \text{ MPa}$

or $\qquad\qquad \tau_{max} = \dfrac{\sigma_{max}}{2} = \dfrac{129.6}{2} = 64.8 \text{ MPa}$

a. **According to maximum normal stress theory:**

$$d_o = \left[\frac{16}{\pi \sigma_{max}} \left\{ C_m M + \sqrt{(C_m M)^2 + (C_t T)^2} \right\} \left(\frac{1}{1 - K^4} \right) \right]^{1/3}$$

... **3.6(a)/ Pg 51, DHB**

For a solid shaft, it is found by substituting $K = 0$ and $d_o = d$, we have

$$d = \left[\frac{16}{\pi \sigma_{max}} \left\{ C_m M + \sqrt{(C_m M)^2 + (C_t T)^2} \right\} \right]^{1/3}$$ ... Eq. (i)

- **Torque:** We know that

$$T = \frac{9.55 \times 10^6 (P)}{n} = \frac{9.55 \times 10^6 \times (15)}{1500} = 95.5 \times 10^3 \text{ N·mm}$$

... **3.3(a)/ Pg 50, DHB**

- **Maximum bending moment:** From **Fig. 5.4,** taking moments about 'A' and equating to zero, we have

$$R_B \times 800 = 15 \times 500 \times \left(\frac{500}{2} + 150 \right)$$

$\therefore \qquad\qquad R_B = 3750 \text{ N}$

Also $\quad R_A + R_B = 15 \times 500 = 7500 \text{ N}$

$\qquad\qquad$ [Here $R_A = R_B$, since the given Fig. 5.4 is symmetric]

$\therefore \qquad\qquad R_B = 3750 \text{ N}$

Moments:

$\qquad\qquad M_A = M_B = 0$

$\qquad\qquad M_C = M_D = R_A \times 150 = 3750 \times 150 = 562500 \text{ N·m}$

$$M_E = (R_A \times 400) - \left[15 \times 250 \left(\frac{250}{2} \right) \right]$$

$$= (3750 \times 400) - \left[15 \times 250 \left(\frac{250}{2} \right) \right] = 1.03 \times 10^6 \text{ N·mm}$$

Thus maximum bending moment on the shaft is

$\qquad\qquad M = M_E = 1.03 \times 10^6 \text{ N·mm}$

- Assuming steady loads, we have

$$C_m = 1.5 \text{ and } C_t = 1 \qquad \text{... Tb. 3.1/ Pg 56, DHB}$$

∴ Eq. (i) yields...

$$d = \left[\frac{16}{\pi \times 129.6} \left\{ (1.5 \times 1.03 \times 10^6) \right. \right.$$
$$\left. \left. + \sqrt{(1.5 \times 1.03 \times 10^6)^2 + (1 \times 95.5 \times 10^3)^2} \right\} \right]^{1/3}$$

∴ $\qquad d = 49.54 \text{ mm} \qquad \text{... Eq. (ii)}$

b. According to maximum shear stress theory:

$$d_o = \left[\frac{16}{\pi \tau_{max}} \left(\sqrt{(C_m M)^2 + (C_t T)^2} \right) \left(\frac{1}{1 - K^4} \right) \right]^{1/3}$$

For a solid shaft is found by substituting $K = 0$ and $d_o = d$, we have

$$d = \left[\frac{16}{\pi \tau_{max}} \left(\sqrt{(C_m M)^2 + (C_t T)^2} \right) \right]^{1/3} \quad \text{... Tb. 3.6(b)/ Pg 51, DHB}$$

$$= \left[\frac{16}{\pi \times 64.8} \sqrt{(1.5 \times 1.03 \times 10^6)^2 + (1 \times 95.5 \times 10^3)^2} \right]^{1/3}$$

∴ $\qquad d = 49.55 \text{ mm} \qquad \text{... Eq. (iii)}$

Based on Eqs. (ii) and (iii), select maximum diameter for design, i.e.

$$d = 49.55 \text{ mm}$$

∴ Standard size of shaft,

$$d = 50 \text{ mm} \qquad \text{... Tb. 3.5(a)/Pg 57, DHB}$$

14. **Design the shaft of the armature of a motor, if the magnetic pull on the shaft is equivalent to an uniformly distributed load of 10 N per mm length over the middle one-third of the 600 mm length of the shaft between bearings. The motor transmits a power of 15 kW at 1200 rpm. The allowable shear stress is 50 MPa. Take $C_m = 1.5$ and $C_t = 1.25$.**

VTU – July/ Aug. 2004 – 10 Marks

Solution: $w = 10 \text{ N/mm}$, total length $L = 600 \text{ mm}$, udl length $l = 200 \text{ mm}$, $d = ?$, $P = 15 \text{ kW}$, $n = 1200 \text{ rpm}$, $\tau_{max} = 50 \text{ MPa}$, $C_m = 1.5$, $C_t = 1.25$.

Based on given data, the problem is represented as a line diagram as shown in **Fig. 5.5.**

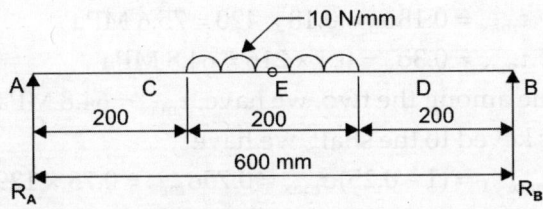

Fig. 5.5: Problem 14

According to maximum shear stress theory:

$$d = \left[\frac{16}{\pi\tau_{max}}\left(\sqrt{(C_m M)^2 + (C_t T)^2}\right)\right]^{1/3} \qquad \text{... 3.6(b)/Pg 51, DHB}$$

But
$$T = \frac{9.55 \times 10^6 (P)}{n} = \frac{9.55 \times 10^6 \times (15)}{1200} = 119.38 \times 10^3 \text{ N} \cdot \text{mm}$$

$$\text{... 3.3(a)/Pg 50, DHB}$$

Maximum bending moment on the shaft is
$$M = M_E = 250 \times 10^3 \text{ N·mm}$$

$\therefore$
$$d = 34.51 \text{ mm}$$

$\therefore$ Standard size of shaft, $d = 36$ mm   **... Tb. 3.5(a)/Pg 57, DHB**

15. **Repeat Problem 13, if a pulley is keyed to the shaft at distance of 300 mm to the right support. The pulley has tensions on tight side as 3000 N and on the slack side as 1500 N.**

Solution: $w = 15$ N/mm, total length $L = 800$ mm, udl length $l = 500$ mm, $d = ?$, $P = 15$ kW, $n = 1500$ rpm, $T_1 = 3000$ N, $T_2 = 1500$ N.

Based on given data, the problem is represented as a line diagram as shown in **Fig. 5.6.**

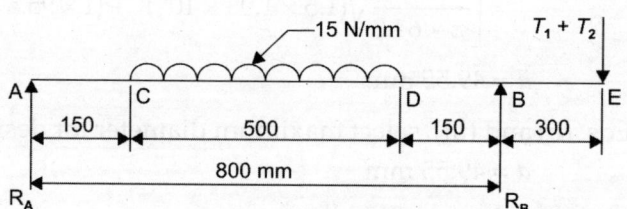

Fig. 5.6: Problem 15

Material: Assume 40C8 having $\sigma_{ut} = 630$ MPa and $\sigma_{yt} = 324$ MPa and factor of safety $n' = 1.5$.

$$\sigma_u = \frac{\sigma_{ut}}{n'} = \frac{630}{1.5} = 420 \text{ MPa}$$

$$\sigma_y = \frac{\sigma_{yt}}{n'} = \frac{324}{1.5} = 216 \text{ MPa}$$

$\rightarrow$
$$\sigma_{max} = 0.36\sigma_u = 0.36 \times 420 = 151.2 \text{ MPa}$$

and
$$\sigma_{max} = 0.6\sigma_y = 0.6 \times 216 = 129.6 \text{ MPa}$$

Take the least value among the two, we have,
$$\sigma_{max} = 129.6 \text{ MPa}$$

$\rightarrow$
$$\tau_{max} = 0.18\sigma_u = 0.18 \times 420 = 75.6 \text{ MPa}$$

and
$$\tau_{max} = 0.3\sigma_y = 0.3 \times 216 = 64.8 \text{ MPa}$$

Take the least value among the two, we have, $\tau_{max} = 64.8$ MPa

Since the pulley is keyed to the shaft, we have

$\rightarrow$
$$\sigma_{max-1} = (1 - 0.25)\sigma_{max} = 0.75\sigma_{max} = 0.75 \times 129.6 = 97.2 \text{ MPa}$$

$\rightarrow$
$$\tau_{max-1} = (1 - 0.25)\tau_{max} = 0.75\tau_{max} = 0.75 \times 64.8 = 48.6 \text{ MPa}$$

a. According to maximum normal stress theory:

$$d = \left[\frac{16}{\pi\sigma_{max-1}} \left\{ C_m M + \sqrt{(C_m M)^2 + (C_t T)^2} \right\} \right]^{1/3}$$

... Eq. (i) **3.6(a)/Pg 51, DHB**

- Torque: We know that

$$T = \frac{9.55 \times 10^6 (P)}{n} = \frac{9.55 \times 10^6 \times (15)}{1500} = 95.5 \times 10^3 \text{ N·mm}$$

... **3.3(a)/ Pg 50, DHB**

- Maximum bending moment: From **Fig. 5.6,** taking moments about 'A' and equating to zero, we have

$$R_B \times 800 = \left[15 \times 500 \times \left(\frac{500}{2} + 150 \right) \right] + (4500 \times 1100)$$

$$\because T_1 + T_2 = 4500 \text{ N}$$

$$\therefore \qquad R_B = 9937.50 \text{ N}$$

Also $\quad R_A + R_B = (15 \times 500) + 4500$

$$\therefore \qquad R_A = 2062.50 \text{ N}$$

Moments:

$$M_A = M_E = 0$$
$$M_C = 2062.5 \times 150 = 0.31 \times 10^6 \text{ N·mm}$$
$$M_D = 9937.50 \times 150 = 1.49 \times 10^6 \text{ N·mm}$$
$$M_B = -4500 \times 300 = -1.35 \times 10^6 \text{ N·mm}$$

Thus maximum bending moment on the shaft is

$$M = M_B = 1.49 \times 10^6 \text{ N·mm}$$

- Assuming steady loads, we have

$$C_m = 1.5 \text{ and } C_t = 1 \qquad\qquad \text{... Tb. 3.1/ Pg 56, DHB}$$

$\therefore$ Eq. (i) yields...

$$d = \left[\frac{16}{\pi \times 97.2} \left\{ (1.5 \times 1.49 \times 10^6) \right. \right.$$

$$\left. \left. + \sqrt{(1.5 \times 1.49 \times 10^6)^2 + (1 \times 95.5 \times 10^3)^2} \right\} \right]^{1/3}$$

$$\therefore \qquad d = 61.65 \text{ mm} \qquad\qquad \text{... Eq. (ii)}$$

b. According to maximum shear stress theory:

$$d_o = \left[\frac{16}{\pi\tau_{max-1}} \left(\sqrt{(C_m M)^2 + (C_t T)^2} \right) \right]^{1/3}$$

... **Tb. 3.6(b)/ Pg 51, DHB**

$$= \left[\frac{16}{\pi \times 48.6} \sqrt{(1.5 \times 1.49 \times 10^6)^2 + (1 \times 95.5 \times 10^3)^2} \right]^{1/3}$$

$$\therefore \qquad d = 61.66 \text{ mm} \qquad\qquad \text{... Eq. (iii)}$$

Based on Eqs. (ii) and (iii), select maximum diameter for design, i.e.

$$d = 66.66 \text{ mm}$$

∴ Standard size of shaft,
$$d = 63 \text{ mm} \qquad \text{... Tb. 3.5(a)/Pg 57, DHB}$$

16. **A shaft is driven by means of a motor, placed vertically, below it as shown in Fig. 5.7. The diameter of the pulley is 1.5 m and has belt tensions 5.4 kN and 1.8 kN on tight and slack sides of the belt respectively. Find the diameter of the shaft, assuming a maximum allowable shear stress of 42 MPa.**

VTU – Dec. 2010 – 10 Marks

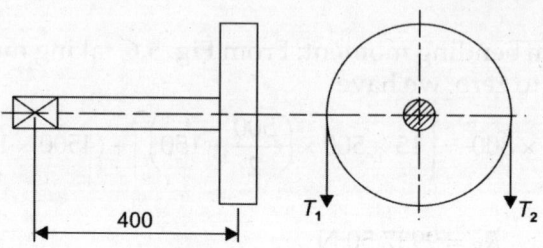

Fig. 5.7: Problem 16

Solution: $D = 1500$ mm, $T_1 = 5400$ N, $T_2 = 1800$ N, $d = ?$, $\tau = \tau_{max} = 42$ MPa, beam length $L = 400$ mm.

According to maximum shear stress theory, for a solid shaft

$$d = \left[\frac{16}{\pi \tau_{max}} \left(\sqrt{(C_m M)^2 + (C_t T)^2} \right) \right]^{1/3}$$

...Eq. (i) **3.6(b)/Pg 51, DHB**

- Torque: We know that
$$T = (T_1 - T_2)R = (5400 - 1800) \times 750 = 2.7 \times 10^6 \text{ N·mm}$$

- Bending moment:
$$M = (T_1 + T_2)L = (5400 + 1800) \times 400 = 2.88 \times 10^6 \text{ N·mm}$$

- Assuming steady loads, we have
$$C_m = 1.5 \text{ and } C_t = 1 \qquad \text{...Tb. 3.1/Pg 56, DHB}$$

∴ Eq. (i) yields...
$$d = \left[\frac{16}{\pi \times 42} \sqrt{(1.5 \times 2.88 \times 10^6)^2 + (1 \times 2.7 \times 10^6)^2} \right]^{1/3}$$

∴
$$d = 85.17 \text{ mm}$$

∴ Standard size of shaft, $d = 90$ mm. **...Tb. 3.5(a)/Pg 57, DHB**

17. **Design a shaft to transmit power from an electric motor to a lathe head stock through a pulley by means of a belt drive. The pulley weighs 200 N and is located at 300 mm from the center of bearing. The diameter of the pulley is 200 mm and the maximum power transmitted is 1 kW at 120 rpm. The angle of lap of the belt is 180⁰ and coefficient of friction between the belt and the pulley is 0.3. The shock and fatigue factors for bending and twisting are 1.5 and 2.0. The allowable shear stress in the shaft may be taken as 35 MPa.**

VTU – Dec. 2012 – 10 Marks

Solution: $W = 200$ N, $L = 300$ mm, $D = 200$ mm, $P = 1$ kW, $n = 120$ rpm, lap angle $\theta = 180° = 3.142$ rad, $\mu = 0.3$, $C_m = 1.5$, $C_t = 2$, $\tau = \tau_{max} = 35$ MPa.

Based on the data in the problem, the layout is shown in **Fig. 5.8**.

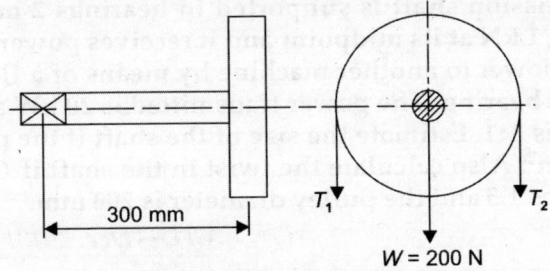

300 mm

$W = 200$ N

Fig. 5.8: Problem 17

According to maximum shear stress theory, for a solid shaft

$$d = \left[\frac{16}{\pi \tau_{max}} \left(\sqrt{(C_m M)^2 + (C_t T)^2} \right) \right]^{1/3}$$

...Eq. (i) **3.6(a)/Pg 51, DHB**

- Torque: We know that

$$T = \frac{9.55 \times 10^6 (P)}{n} = \frac{9.55 \times 10^6 \times (1)}{120} = 79.58 \times 10^3 \text{ N·mm}$$

... **3.3(a)/Pg 50, DHB**

- Maximum bending moment:

Here $M = (T_1 + T_2 + W)L$ ...Eq. (ii)

But $T = (T_1 - T_2)R$

$79.58 \times 10^3 = (T_1 - T_2) \times 100$

$(T_1 - T_2) = 795.8$ N   ...Eq. (iii)

Also $\dfrac{T_1}{T_2} = e^{\mu\theta} = e^{0.3 \times 3.142}$ ...**14.3(a)/Pg 290, DHB**

$T_1 = 2.57 T_2$ ...Eq. (iv)

∴ Eq. (iii) yields...

$(2.57 T_2 - T_2) = 795.8$

$1.57 T_2 = 795.8$

∴ $T_2 = 506.88$ N

∴ Eq. (iv) yields...

$T_1 = 2.57 \times 506.88 = 1302.68$ N

∴ Eq. (ii) yields...

$M = (1302.68 + 506.88 + 200) \times 300 = 602.87 \times 10^3$ N·mm

∴ Eq. (i) yields... $d = \left[\dfrac{16}{\pi \times 35} \sqrt{(1.5 \times 602.87 \times 10^3)^2 + (2 \times 79.58 \times 10^3)^2} \right]^{1/3}$

∴ $d = 51.12$ mm

∴ Standard size of shaft,

$d = 56$ mm   ...**Tb. 3.5(a)/Pg 57, DHB**

18. **A power transmission shaft is supported in bearings 2 m apart and carries a pulley weighing 1 kN at its midpoint and it receives power by a belt drive. The shaft transmits power to another machine by means of a flexible coupling just outside the right bearing. The power transmitted is 20 kW at 120 rpm. The ratio of belt tensions is 3:1. Estimate the size of the shaft if the permissible stress in shear is 54 N/mm². Also calculate the twist in the shaft if $G = 0.8 \times 10^5$ N/mm². Take C_m and C_t as 1.5 and the pulley diameter is 200 mm.**

VTU – Dec. 2013/ Jan. 2014 – 20 Marks

Solution: $W = 1000$ N, $L = 2000$ mm, $D = 200$ mm, $P = 20$ kW, $n = 120$ rpm, $T_1 = 3T_2$, $G = 0.8 \times 10^5$ N/mm², $\tau = \tau_{max} = 54$ MPa, $C_m = C_t = 1.5$, $d = ?$, $\theta = ?$

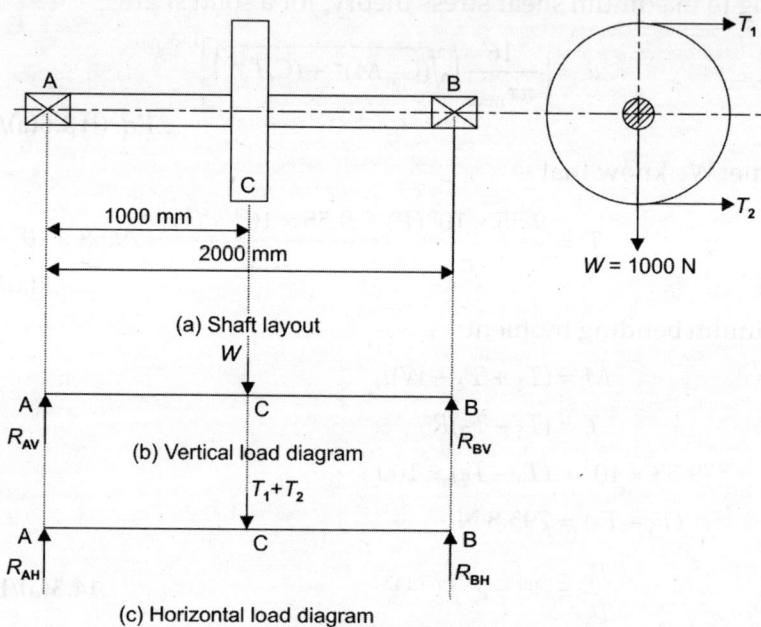

Fig. 5.9: Problem 18

a. **To find shaft diameter:** According to maximum shear stress theory, for a solid shaft

$$d = \left[\frac{16}{\pi \tau_{max}} \left(\sqrt{(C_m M)^2 + (C_t T)^2} \right) \right]^{1/3}$$

...Eq. (i) **3.6(a)/Pg 51, DHB**

- Torque: We know that

$$T = \frac{9.55 \times 10^6 (P)}{n} = \frac{9.55 \times 10^6 \times (20)}{120} = 1.59 \times 10^6 \text{ N·mm}$$

...**3.3(a)/Pg 50, DHB**

But torque on pulley,

$$T = (T_1 - T_2)R$$

$$1.59 \times 10^6 = (T_1 - T_2) \times \left(\frac{200}{2} \right)$$

$$\therefore \quad T_1 - T_2 = 15900 \text{ N}$$

Also $\quad\quad T_1 = 3T_2$ ... (data)

i.e. $\quad 3T_2 - T_2 = 15900$

$\therefore \quad\quad\quad T_2 = 7950$ N

and $\quad\quad T_1 = 3 \times 7950 = 23850$ N

- Maximum bending moment:

  a. Vertical loading: **Figure 5.9(b)** represents the vertical load diagram.
  - Taking moments about bearing 'A', and equating to zero, we have

$$R_{BV} \times 2000 = W \times 1000$$
$$= 1000 \times 1000$$

$\therefore \quad\quad\quad R_{BV} = 500$ N

Also $\quad R_{AV} + R_{BV} = W$

$$R_{AV} + 500 = 1000$$

$\therefore \quad\quad\quad R_{AV} = 500$ N

  - Moments:

$$M_{AV} = M_{BV} = 0$$
$$M_{CV} = R_{AV} \times 1000 = 500 \times 1000 = 500 \times 10^3 \text{ N·mm}$$

  b. Taking moments about bearing 'A', and equating to zero, we have

$$R_{BH} \times 2000 = (T_1 + T_2) \times 1000$$
$$= (23850 + 7950) \times 1000$$

$\therefore \quad\quad\quad R_{BV} = 15900$ N

Also $\quad R_{AH} + R_{BH} = (T_1 + T_2)$

$$R_{AH} + 15900 = (23850 + 7950)$$

$\therefore \quad\quad\quad R_{AV} = 15900$ N

  - Moments:

$$M_{AH} = M_{BH} = 0$$
$$M_{CH} = R_{AH} \times 1000 = 15900 \times 1000 = 15.9 \times 10^6 \text{ N·mm}$$

Resultant moment at C,

$$M_C = \sqrt{M_{CV}^2 + M_{CH}^2} = \sqrt{(500 \times 10^3)^2 + (15.9 \times 10^6)^2}$$
$$= 15.91 \times 10^6 \text{ N·mm}$$

$\therefore$ Eq. (i) yields...

$$d = \left[\frac{16}{\pi \times 54} \sqrt{(1.5 \times 15.91 \times 10^6)^2 + (1.5 \times 1.59 \times 10^6)^2} \right]^{1/3}$$

$\therefore \quad\quad\quad d = 131.12$ mm

$\therefore$ Standard size of shaft, $d = 140$ mm $\quad\quad$ **...Tb. 3.5(a)/Pg 57, DHB**

b. **To find θ:** We know that

$$\theta = \frac{584 TL}{GD^4} = \frac{584 \times (1.59 \times 10^6) \times 1000}{(0.8 \times 10^5) \times 140^4} = 0.0302 \text{ deg}$$

...Eq. (i) 3.6(a)/Pg 51, DHB

19. **A shaft is supported by two bearings placed 1 m apart. A 600 mm diameter pulley is mounted at a distance of 300 mm to the right of left hand bearing and this drives a pulley directly below it with the help of a belt having maximum tension of 2.25 kN. Another pulley 400 mm diameter is placed 200 mm to the left of right hand bearing and is driven with the help of electric motor and belt, which is placed horizontally to the right. The angle of contact for both the pulleys is 180° and μ = 0.24. Determine the suitable diameter for a solid shaft allowing working stress of 63 MPa in tension and 42 MPa in shear for the material of the shaft. Assume that the torque on one pulley is equal to that on the other pulley.**

VTU – June/ July 2015 – 20 Marks; (Similar) Dec. 2014/ Jan. 2015 – 20 Marks; (Similar) Jan/ Feb. 2006 – 20 Marks; (Similar) June/ July 2008 – 14 Marks

Solution: The layout of the shaft as per given data is shown in **Fig. 5.10 (a).**

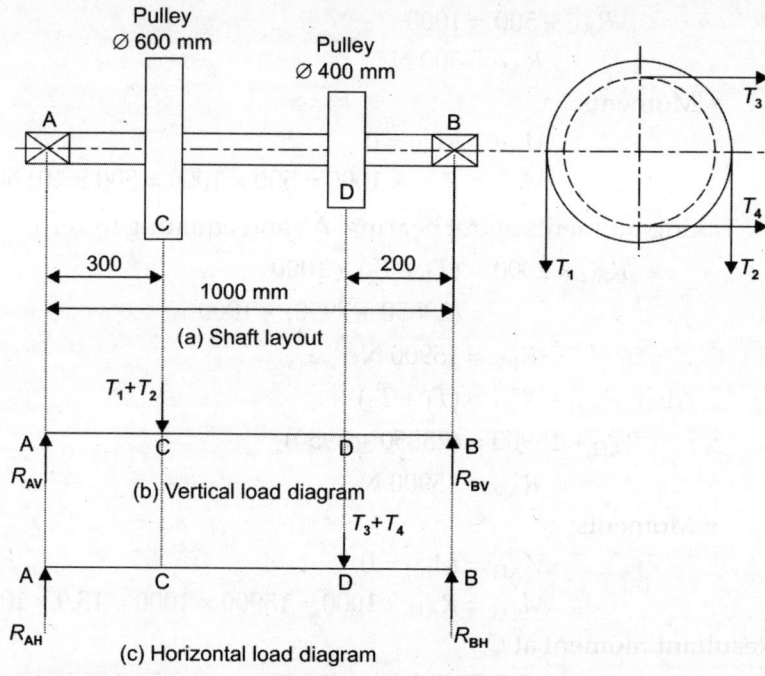

Fig. 5.10: Problem 19

Left pulley: Diameter D_C = 600 mm, maximum tension T_1 = 2250 N

... drive is vertical

Right pulley: Diameter D_D = 400 mm   ... drive is horizontal

Angle of contact $\theta_C = \theta_D$ = 180° = 3.142 rad, $\sigma = \sigma_{max}$ = 63 MPa, $\tau = \tau_{max}$ = 42 MPa, μ = 024, torque pulley is equal $T_L = T_R$, d = ?

Analysis of left pulley: We know that

$$\frac{T_1}{T_2} = e^{\mu\theta} \qquad\qquad ... \textbf{14.3(a)/ Pg 290, DHB}$$

$$= e^{0.24 \times 3.142} = 2.125$$

$$\frac{2250}{T_2} = 2.125$$

$$\therefore \qquad T_2 = 1058.60 \text{ N}$$

Torque on left pulley,

$$T_C = (T_1 - T_2)R_C = (2250 - 1058.60) \times (600/2) = 357420 \text{ N·mm}$$

Analysis of right pulley: Given torque on both pulleys are equal

$$T_C = T_D = 357420 \text{ N·mm}$$

Torque on right pulley,

$$T_D = (T_3 - T_4)R_D \qquad \text{... Eq. (i)}$$

Also

$$\frac{T_3}{T_4} = e^{\mu\theta} = 2.125$$

$$T_3 = 2.125 T_4 \qquad \text{...Eq. (ii)}$$

∴ Eq. (i) yields...

$$357420 = (2.125 - 1)T_4 \times (400/2)$$

$$T_4 = 1588.53 \text{ N}$$

∴ Eq. (ii) yields... $\quad T_3 = 2.125 \times 1588.53 = 3375.63 \text{ N}$

To find maximum bending moment:

a. Vertical loading: **Figure 5.10(b)** represents the vertical load diagram.

- Taking moments about bearing 'A', and equating to zero, we have

$$R_{BV} \times 1000 = (T_1 + T_2) \times 300$$

$$= (2250 + 1058.60) \times 300$$

$$\therefore \qquad R_{BV} = 992.58 \text{ N}$$

Also, $R_{AV} + R_{BV} = (T_1 + T_2)$

$$R_{AV} + 992.58 = (2250 + 1058.60)$$

$$\therefore \qquad R_{AV} = 2316.02 \text{ N}$$

- Moments:

$$M_{AV} = M_{BV} = 0$$

$$M_{CV} = R_{AV} \times 300 = 2316.02 \times 300 = 694806 \text{ N·mm}$$

$$M_{DV} = R_{BV} \times 200 = 992.58 \times 200 = 198516 \text{ N·mm}$$

b. Horizontal loading: **Figure 5.10(c)** represents the horizontal load diagram.

- Taking moments about bearing 'A', and equating to zero, we have

$$R_{BH} \times 1000 = (T_3 + T_4) \times 800$$

$$= (3375.63 + 1588.53) \times 800$$

$$\therefore \qquad R_{BH} = 3971.33 \text{ N}$$

Also, $R_{AH} + R_{BH} = (T_3 + T_4)$

$$R_{AH} + 3971.33 = (3375.63 + 1588.53)$$

$$\therefore \qquad R_{AH} = 992.83 \text{ N}$$

- Moments:

$$M_{AH} = M_{BH} = 0$$

$$M_{CH} = R_{AH} \times 300 = 992.38 \times 300 = 297849 \text{ N·mm}$$

$$M_{DH} = R_{BH} \times 200 = 3971.33 \times 200 = 794266 \text{ N·mm}$$

Resultant moment at C,

$$M_C = \sqrt{M_{CV}^2 + M_{CH}^2} = \sqrt{694806^2 + 297849^2}$$

$$= 755955.55 \text{ N·mm}$$

Resultant moment at D,

$$M_D = \sqrt{M_{DV}^2 + M_{DH}^2} = \sqrt{198516^2 + 794266^2}$$

$$= 818698.41 \text{ N·mm}$$

Thus maximum bending moment occurs at 'D', i.e.

$$M_D = M = 818698.41 \text{ N·mm}$$

a. **According to maximum normal stress theory:** For a solid shaft

$$d = \left[\frac{16}{\pi \sigma_{max}} \left\{ C_m M + \sqrt{(C_m M)^2 + (C_t T)^2} \right\} \right]^{1/3}$$

...3.6(a)/Pg 51, DHB

Assuming steady loads, we have

$$C_m = 1.5 \text{ and } C_t = 1 \qquad \text{...Tb. 3.1/Pg 56, DHB}$$

$$= \left[\frac{16}{\pi \times 63} \left\{ (1.5 \times 818698.41) \right.\right.$$

$$\left.\left. + \sqrt{(1.5 \times 818698.41)^2 + (1 \times 357420)^2} \right\} \right]^{1/3}$$

$$\therefore \qquad d = 58.74 \text{ mm} \qquad \text{... Eq. (a)}$$

b. **According to maximum shear stress theory:**

For a solid shaft $\quad d = \left[\frac{16}{\pi \tau_{max}} \sqrt{(C_m M)^2 + (C_t T)^2} \right]^{1/3} \quad$ ... 3.6(b)/Pg 51, DHB

$$= \left[\frac{16}{\pi \times 42} \sqrt{(1.5 \times 818698.41)^2 + (1 \times 357420)^2} \right]^{1/3}$$

$$\therefore \qquad d = 53.73 \text{ mm} \qquad \text{... Eq. (b)}$$

Based on Eqs (a) and (b), select maximum diameter for design, i.e.

$$d = 58.74 \text{ mm}$$

$\therefore$ Standard size of shaft,

$$d = 63 \text{ mm} \qquad \text{... Tb. 3.5(a)/Pg 57, DHB}$$

20. **A shaft is supported in bearings 600 mm apart. It carries a pulley of diameter 500 mm at 250 mm to the right of left bearing and another pulley of diameter 380 mm at 130 mm to the right of right bearing. The belt drive in the left pulley is vertically downward while that on the right pulley is horizontal. The permissible shear stress is not to exceed 42 MPa. The maximum tension in the smaller pulley is not to exceed 5500 N, coefficient of friction is 0.3 and angle of contact is 180°. Find the diameter of the shaft.**

VTU – June/ July 2015 – 20 Marks

Solution: The layout of the shaft as per given data is shown in **Fig. 5.11(a)**.
Left pulley: Diameter $D_C = 500$ mm, maximum tension   ... drive in vertical
Right pulley: Diameter $D_D = 380$ mm, $T_3 = 5500$ N   ...drive is horizontal
Angle of contact $\theta_C = \theta_D = 180° = 3.142$ rad, $\mu = 0.3$, $\tau = \tau_{max} = 42$ MPa, $d = ?$

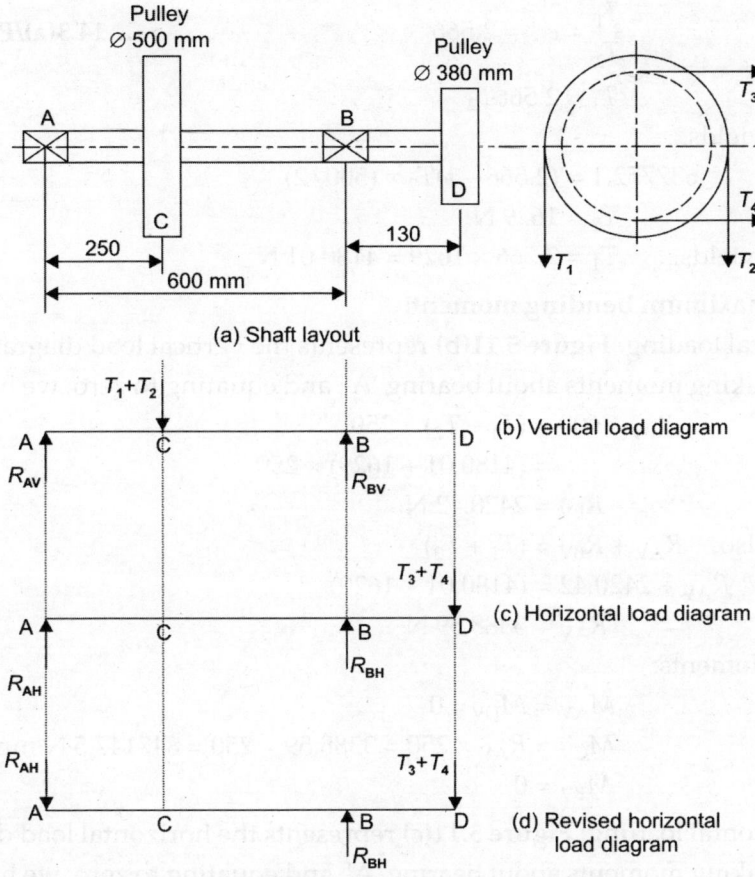

(a) Shaft layout

(b) Vertical load diagram

(c) Horizontal load diagram

(d) Revised horizontal load diagram

Fig. 5.11: Problem 20

Analysis of right pulley: We know that

$$\frac{T_3}{T_4} = e^{\mu\theta} \qquad\qquad \text{...14.3(a)/Pg 290, DHB}$$

$$\frac{T_3}{T_4} = e^{0.3 \times 3.142} = 2.566$$

$$\frac{5500}{T_4} = 2.566$$

$$\therefore \qquad\qquad T_4 = 2143.41 \text{ N}$$

Torque on right pulley,

$$T_R = (T_3 - T_4)R_D = (5500 - 2143.41) \times (380/2)$$
$$= 637752.1 \text{ N·mm}$$

Analysis of left pulley: Assuming torque on both pulleys are equal

$$T_C = T_D = 637752.1 \text{ N·mm}$$

Torque on left pulley,

$$T_C = (T_1 - T_2)R_C \qquad \text{...Eq. (i)}$$

Also

$$\frac{T_1}{T_2} = e^{\mu\theta} = 2.566 \qquad \textbf{...14.3(a)/Pg 290, DHB}$$

$$T_1 = 2.566T_2 \qquad \text{...Eq. (ii)}$$

∴ Eq. (i) yields...

$$637752.1 = (2.566 - 1)T_2 \times (500/2)$$
$$T_2 = 1629 \text{ N}$$

∴ Eq. (ii) yields... $T_1 = 2.566 \times 1629 = 4180.01 \text{ N}$

To find maximum bending moment:

a. Vertical loading: **Figure 5.11(b)** represents the vertical load diagram.

- Taking moments about bearing 'A', and equating to zero, we have

$$R_{BV} \times 600 = (T_1 + T_2) \times 250$$
$$= (4180.01 + 1629) \times 250$$
$$\therefore \qquad R_{BV} = 2420.42 \text{ N}$$

Also, $R_{AV} + R_{BV} = (T_1 + T_2)$

$$R_{AV} + 2420.42 = (4180.01 + 1629)$$
$$\therefore \qquad R_{AV} = 3388.59 \text{ N}$$

- Moments:

$$M_{AV} = M_{DV} = 0$$
$$M_{CV} = R_{AV} \times 250 = 3388.59 \times 250 = 847147.5 \text{ N·mm}$$
$$M_{BV} = 0$$

b. Horizontal loading: **Figure 5.11(c)** represents the horizontal load diagram.

- Taking moments about bearing 'A', and equating to zero, we have

$$R_{BH} \times 600 = (T_3 + T_4) \times 730$$
$$= (5500 + 2143.41) \times 730$$
$$\therefore \qquad R_{BH} = 9299.48 \text{ N}$$

Also $R_{AH} + R_{BH} = (T_3 + T_4)$

$$R_{AH} + 9299.48 = (5500 + 2143.41)$$
$$\therefore \qquad R_{AH} = -1656.07 \text{ N}$$

Since the reaction is negative, R_{AH} acts in opposite direction as shown in **Fig. 5.11(d)**.

- Moments:

$$M_{AH} = M_{DH} = 0$$
$$M_{CH} = R_{AH} \times 250 = -1656.07 \times 250 = -414017.5 \text{ N·mm}$$
$$M_{BH} = -(T_3 + T_4) \times 130 = -(5500 + 2143.41) \times 130$$
$$= 993643.3 \text{ N·mm}$$

Resultant moment at C,

$$M_C = \sqrt{M_{CV}^2 + M_{CH}^2} = \sqrt{847147.5^2 + (-414017.5)^2}$$

$$= 942904.76 \text{ N·mm}$$

Resultant moment at B,

$$M_D = \sqrt{M_{BV}^2 + M_{BH}^2} = \sqrt{0^2 + (-993643.3)^2}$$

$$= 993643.3 \text{ N·mm}$$

According to maximum normal stress theory: For a solid shaft

$$d = \left[\frac{16}{\pi \tau_{max}} \sqrt{(C_m M)^2 + (C_t T)^2}\right]^{1/3} \qquad \text{...3.6(b)/Pg 51, DHB}$$

Assuming steady loads, we have

$$C_m = 1.5 \text{ and } C_t = 1 \qquad \text{...Tb. 3.1/Pg 56, DHB}$$

$$= \left[\frac{16}{\pi \times 42} \sqrt{(1.5 \times 993643.3)^2 + (1 \times 637752.1)^2}\right]^{1/3}$$

$\therefore \qquad d = 58.14 \text{ mm}$

$\therefore$ Standard size of shaft, $d = 63$ mm. $\qquad \text{...Tb. 3.5(a)/Pg 57, DHB}$

21. **A steel shaft (C45) transmitting 15 kW at 210 rpm is supported between two bearings 750 mm apart. On this two spur gears are mounted. The gear having 80 teeth of module 6 mm is located 100 mm to the left of right bearing and receives power from a driving gear such that the tangential force acts vertical. The pinion having 24 teeth and module 6 mm is located 150 mm to the right of left bearing and delivers power to a gear mounted behind it. Taking combined shock and fatigue factors 1.75 in bending and 1.25 in torsion, determine the shaft diameter.** *VTU – Dec. 08/ Jan. 2009 – 14 Marks*

Solution: The layout of the shaft as per given data is shown in **Fig. 5.12(a)**.

$P = 15$ kW, $n = 210$ rpm, $C_m = 1.75$, $C_t = 1.25$, $d = ?$, Material: Steel C45.

Left gear: Number of teeth $z_C = 80$, module $m = 6 \Rightarrow D_C = mz_C = 6 \times 80 = 480$ mm.

Right gear: Number of teeth $z_D = 24$, module $m = 6 \Rightarrow D_D = mz_D = 6 \times 24 = 144$ mm.

Material: For C45 steel, $\sigma_u = (618 \text{ to } 696) = 650$ MPa, $\sigma_{yt} = 353$ MPa.

$\qquad \text{...Tb. I.8/Pg 464, DHB}$

Without keyway:

$\rightarrow \qquad \sigma_{max} = 0.6\sigma_{yt} = 0.6 \times 353 = 211.8$ MPa

and $\qquad \sigma_{max} = 0.36\sigma_{ut} = 0.36 \times 650 = 234$ MPa.

Take the least value among the two, we have, $\sigma_{max} = 211.8$ MPa

$\rightarrow \qquad \tau_{max} = 0.3\sigma_{yt} = 0.3 \times 353 = 105.9$ MPa

and $\qquad \tau_{max} = 0.18\sigma_{ut} = 0.18 \times 650 = 117$ MPa

Take the least value among the two, we have,

$$\tau_{max} = 105.9 \text{ MPa}$$

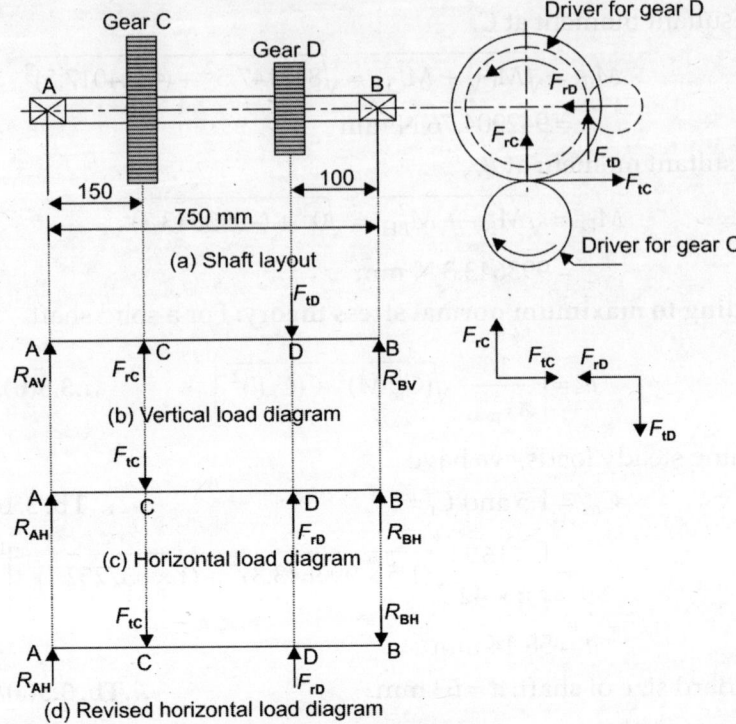

Gear C

Gear D

A ⊠ ⊠ B

150 ↔ ↔ 100

↔ 750 mm ↔

(a) Shaft layout

Driver for gear D

F_{rD}

F_{rC}

F_{tD}

F_{tC}

Driver for gear C

A ▲ C ▲ D ▲ B
R_{AV} F_{rC} R_{BV}

(b) Vertical load diagram

F_{tD}

F_{rC}

F_{tC} F_{rD}

F_{tD}

A ▲ C ▲ D ▲ B
F_{tC}

(c) Horizontal load diagram

A ▲ C ▲ D ▲ B
R_{AH} F_{rD} R_{BH}

F_{tC} R_{BH}

A ▲ C ▲ D ▲ B
R_{AH} F_{rD}

(d) Revised horizontal load diagram

Fig. 5.12: Problem 21

With keyway:

→ $\sigma_{max-1} = (1 - 0.25)\sigma_{max} = 0.75\sigma_{max} = 0.75 \times 211.8 = 158.85$ MPa

→ $\tau_{max-1} = (1 - 0.25)\tau_{max} = 0.75\tau_{max} = 0.75 \times 105.9 = 79.43$ MPa

Torque: We know that

$$T = \frac{9.55 \times 10^6 (P)}{n} = \frac{9.55 \times 10^6 \times (15)}{210} \quad \text{...3.3(a)/Pg 50, DHB}$$

$$= 6.82 \times 10^5 \text{ N·mm} = M_t$$

Analysis of gears:

- Left gear C: We know that tangential force,

$$F_{tC} = \frac{2M_t}{D_C} = \frac{2 \times 6.82 \times 10^5}{480} = 2842.26 \text{ N} \quad \text{...12.8(a)/Pg 206, DHB}$$

Radial force, $F_{rC} = F_{tC} \tan\alpha$ **...12.8(b)/Pg 206, DHB**

Assume pressure angle, $\alpha = 20°$

$$F_{rC} = 2842.26 \times \tan 20° = 1034.50 \text{ N}$$

- Right gear D: We know that tangential force,

$$F_{tD} = \frac{2M_t}{D_D} = \frac{2 \times 6.82 \times 10^5}{144} = 9474.21 \text{ N} \quad \text{...12.8(a)/Pg 206, DHB}$$

Radial force, $F_{rD} = F_{tD} \tan\alpha = 9474.21 \times \tan 20° = 3448.33 \text{ N}$

                                                  ...12.8(b)/Pg 206, DHB

To find maximum bending moment:

a. Vertical loading: **Figure 5.12(b)** represents the vertical load diagram.

- Taking moments about bearing 'A', and equating to zero, we have

$$R_{BV}(AB) = F_{tD}(AD) - F_{rC}(AC)$$
$$R_{BV} \times 750 = (9474.21 \times 650) - (1034.50 \times 150)$$
$$\therefore \qquad R_{BV} = 8004.08 \text{ N}$$

Also $R_{AV} + R_{BV} = F_{tD} - F_{rC}$
$$R_{AV} + 8004.08 = 9474.21 - 1034.50$$
$$\therefore \qquad R_{AV} = 435.63 \text{ N}$$

- Moments:

$$M_{AV} = M_{BV} = 0$$
$$M_{CV} = R_{AV} \times 150 = 435.63 \times 150 = 65344.5 \text{ N·mm}$$
$$M_{DV} = R_{BV} \times 100 = 8004.08 \times 100 = 800408 \text{ N·mm}$$

b. Horizontal loading: **Figure 5.12(c)** represents the horizontal load diagram.

- Taking moments about bearing 'A', and equating to zero, we have

$$R_{BH}(AB) + F_{rD}(AD) = F_{tC}(AC)$$
$$R_{BH} \times 750 + (3448.33 \times 650) = (2842.26 \times 150)$$
$$\therefore \qquad R_{BH} = -2420.10 \text{ N}$$

Since the reaction is negative, R_{BH} acts in opposite direction as shown in **Fig. 5.12(d)**.

Thus $\qquad R_{BH} = 2420.10 \text{ N}$

Also from **Fig. 5.12(d)**, we have

$$R_{AH} + F_{rD} = F_{tC} + R_{BH}$$
$$R_{AH} + 3448.33 = (2842.26 + 2420.10)$$
$$\therefore \qquad R_{AH} = 1814.03 \text{ N}$$

- Moments:

$$M_{AH} = M_{BH} = 0$$
$$M_{CH} = R_{AH} \times 150 = 1814.03 \times 150 = 272104.5 \text{ N·mm}$$
$$M_{DH} = -R_{BH} \times 100 = -2420.10 \times 100 = -242010 \text{ N·mm}$$

Resultant moment at C,

$$M_C = \sqrt{M_{CV}^2 + M_{CH}^2} = \sqrt{65344.5^2 + 272104.5^2}$$
$$= 279840.60 \text{ N·mm}$$

Resultant moment at D,

$$M_D = \sqrt{M_{DV}^2 + M_{DH}^2} = \sqrt{800408^2 + (-242010)^2}$$
$$= 836194.84 \text{ N·mm}$$

This maximum bending moment occurs at D, i.e. $M_D = M = 836194.84$ N·mm

According to maximum normal stress theory: For a solid shaft

$$d = \left[\frac{16}{\pi \sigma_{max-1}} \left\{ C_m M + \sqrt{(C_m M)^2 + (C_t T)^2} \right\} \right]^{1/3}$$

...3.6(a)/Pg 51, DHB

$$= \left[\frac{16}{\pi \times 158.85} \left\{ (1.75 \times 836194.84) + \sqrt{(1.75 \times 836194.84)^2 + \left(1.25 \times 6.82 \times 10^5\right)^2} \right\} \right]^{1/3}$$

$$\therefore \qquad d = 46.60 \text{ mm} \qquad \qquad \qquad \text{...Eq. (i)}$$

According to maximum shear stress theory: For a solid shaft

$$d = \left[\frac{16}{\pi \tau_{max-1}} \sqrt{(C_m M)^2 + (C_t T)^2} \right]^{1/3} \qquad \text{...3.6(b)/Pg 51, DHB}$$

$$= \left[\frac{16}{\pi \times 79.43} \sqrt{(1.75 \times 836194.84)^2 + \left(1.25 \times 6.82 \times 10^5\right)^2} \right]^{1/3}$$

$$\therefore \qquad d = 47.71 \text{ mm} \qquad \qquad \qquad \text{...Eq. (ii)}$$

Based on Eqs. (i) and (ii), select maximum diameter for design, i.e.

$$d = 47.71 \text{ mm}$$

$\therefore$ Standard size of shaft, $d = 50$ mm.   **...Tb. 3.5(a)/Pg 57, DHB**

22. **A horizontal steel shaft, supported on bearings A at the left end and B at the right end, carries two gears C and D, located at distances 250 mm and 400 mm respectively from the center lines of left and right end bearings. The pitch diameter of gear C is 600 mm and that of gear D is 200 mm. The pressure angle is 20°. The distance between the center lines of the bearings is 2400 mm. The shaft transmits 20 kW power at 120 rpm. The power is delivered to the shaft at gear C and is taken out at gear D in such a manner that the tooth pressures F_{tC} and F_{tD} of gears C and D act vertically downwards. Find the diameter of the shaft, if the working stresses are 100 MPa in tension and 56 MPa in shear. The gears C and D weigh 950 N and 350 N respectively. Take $C_m = 1.5$ and $C_T = 1.2$.**

VTU – June/ July 2014 – 20 Marks; Dec. 2010 – 20 Marks

Solution: The layout of the shaft as per given data is shown in **Fig. 5.13(a)**.
$P = 20$ kW, $n = 120$ rpm, $C_m = 1.5$, $C_t = 1.2$, $\alpha = 20°$, $d = ?$, $\sigma = \sigma_{max} = 100$ MPa, $\tau = \sigma_{max} = 56$ MPa.
Left gear: $D_C = 600$ mm, $W_C = 950$ N.
Right gear: $D_D = 200$ mm, $W_D = 350$ N.
Torque: We know that

$$T = \frac{9.55 \times 10^6 (P)}{n} = \frac{9.55 \times 10^6 \times (20)}{120} \qquad \text{...3.3(a)/Pg 50, DHB}$$

$$= 1.59 \times 10^6 \text{ N·mm} = M_t$$

Analysis of gears:

• Left gear C: We know that tangential force,

$$F_{tC} = \frac{2M_t}{D_C} = \frac{2 \times 1.59 \times 10^6}{600} = 5300 \text{ N} \qquad \text{...12.8(a)/Pg 206, DHB}$$

Radial force, $F_{rC} = F_{tC} \tan \alpha = 5300 \times \tan 20 = 1929.04$ N

                                      ...12.8(b)/Pg 206, DHB

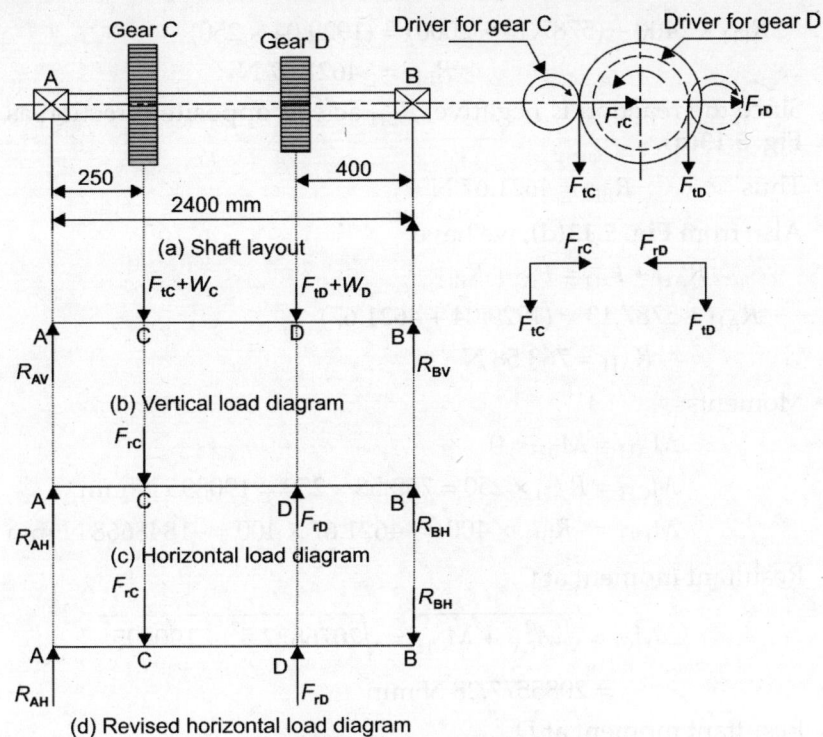

Fig. 5.13: Problem 22

- Right gear D: We know that tangential force,

$$F_{tD} = \frac{2M_t}{D_D} = \frac{2 \times 1.59 \times 10^6}{200} = 15900 \text{ N}$$

Radial force, $F_{rD} = F_{tD} \tan \alpha = 15900 \times \tan 20 = 5787.13$ N

To find maximum bending moment:

a. Vertical loading: **Figure 5.13(b)** represents the vertical load diagram.

- Taking moments about bearing 'A', and equating to zero, we have

$$R_{BV}(AB) = [F_{tC} + W_C](AC) + [F_{tD} + W_D](AD)$$

$$R_{BV} \times 2400 = [(5300 + 950) \times 250] + [(15900 + 350) \times 2000]$$

∴ $R_{BV} = 14192.71$ N

Also $R_{AV} + R_{BV} = (F_{tC} + W_C) + (F_{tD} + W_D)$

$$R_{AV} + 14192.71 = (5300 + 950) + (15900 + 350)$$

∴ $R_{AV} = 8307.29$ N

- Moments:

$$M_{AV} = M_{BV} = 0$$

$$M_{CV} = R_{AV} \times 250 = 8307.29 \times 250 = 2076822.5 \text{ N·mm}$$

$$M_{DV} = R_{BV} \times 400 = 14192.71 \times 400 = 5677084 \text{ N·mm}$$

b. Horizontal loading: **Figure 5.13(c)** represents the horizontal load diagram.

- Taking moments about bearing 'A', and equating to zero, we have

$$R_{BH}(AB) + F_{rD}(AD) = F_{rC}(AC)$$

$$R_{BH} \times 2400 + (5787.13 \times 2000) = (1929.04 \times 250)$$

$$\therefore \qquad R_{BH} = -4621.67 \text{ N}$$

Since the reaction is negative, R_{BH} acts in opposite direction as shown in **Fig. 5.13(d)**.

Thus $\qquad R_{BH} = 4621.67 \text{ N}$

Also from **Fig. 5.13(d)**, we have

$$R_{AH} + F_{rD} = F_{rC} + R_{BH}$$

$$R_{AH} + 5787.13 = (1929.04 + 4621.67)$$

$$\therefore \qquad R_{AH} = 763.58 \text{ N}$$

- Moments:

$$M_{AH} = M_{BH} = 0$$

$$M_{CH} = R_{AH} \times 250 = 763.58 \times 250 = 190895 \text{ N·mm}$$

$$M_{DH} = -R_{BH} \times 400 = -4621.67 \times 400 = -1848668 \text{ N·mm}$$

Resultant moment at C,

$$M_C = \sqrt{M_{CV}^2 + M_{CH}^2} = \sqrt{2076822.5^2 + 190895^2}$$

$$= 2085577.28 \text{ N·mm}$$

Resultant moment at D,

$$M_D = \sqrt{M_{DV}^2 + M_{DH}^2} = \sqrt{5677084^2 + (-1848668)^2}$$

$$= 5970498.82 \text{ N·mm}$$

Thus maximum bending moment occurs at 'D', i.e.

$$M_D = M = 5970498.82 \text{ N·mm}$$

a. **According to maximum normal stress theory:** For a solid shaft

$$d = \left[\frac{16}{\pi\sigma_{max}} \left\{ C_m M + \sqrt{(C_m M)^2 + (C_t T)^2} \right\} \right]^{1/3}$$

...3.6(a)/Pg 51, DHB

$$= \left[\frac{16}{\pi \times 100} \left\{ (1.5 \times 5970498.82) \right. \right.$$

...3.6(a)/Pg 51, DHB

$$\left. \left. + \sqrt{(1.5 \times 5970498.82)^2 + \left(1.2 \times 1.59 \times 10^6\right)^2} \right\} \right]^{1/3}$$

$$\therefore \qquad d = 97.34 \text{ mm} \qquad\qquad \text{...Eq. (i)}$$

b. **According to maximum shear stress theory:** For a solid shaft

$$d = \left[\frac{16}{\pi\tau_{max}} \sqrt{(C_m M)^2 + (C_t T)^2} \right]^{1/3}$$

...3.6(b)/Pg 51, DHB

$$= \left[\frac{16}{\pi \times 56} \sqrt{(1.5 \times 5970498.82)^2 + \left(1.2 \times 1.59 \times 10^6\right)^2} \right]^{1/3}$$

$$\therefore \qquad d = 94.08 \text{ mm} \qquad\qquad \text{...Eq. (ii)}$$

Based on Eqs. (i) and (ii), select maximum diameter for design, i.e.

$$d = 97.34 \text{ mm}$$

∴ Standard size of shaft, $d = 100$ mm. **...Tb. 3.5(a)/Pg 57, DHB**

23. **A pulley A and a gear B are mounted on bearings C and D on a shaft as shown in Fig. 5.14(a). The shaft transmits 15 kW at 500 rpm. The tangential force acts vertically upwards. The pulley delivers the power through a belt to another pulley. The ratio of tensions in the belt is 2. The gear and the pulley weigh 800 N and 2400 N respectively. The permissible shear stress for the material of the shaft is 60 MPa. Determine its diameter. Assume $C_m = 2$, $C_t = 1.5$. (use $F_r = F_t \tan 20°$).**

VTU – June/ July 2013 – 20 Marks

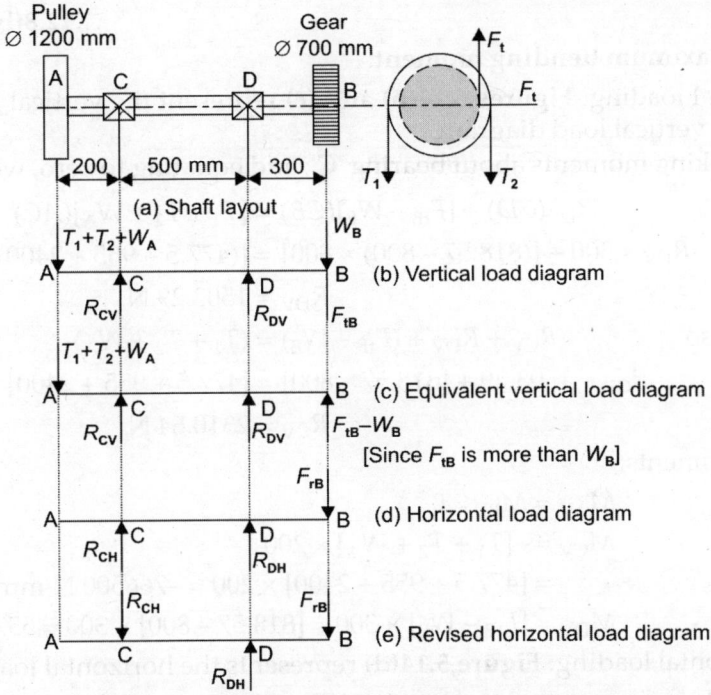

Fig. 5.14: Problem 23

Solution: $P = 15$ kW, $n = 500$ rpm, $\dfrac{T_1}{T_2} = 2$, $\tau = \tau_{max} = 60$ MPa, $C_m = 2$ and $C_t = 1.5$, $\alpha = 20°$, $d = ?$

Pulley: $D_A = 600$ mm, weight of pulley $W_A = 2400$ N.

Gear: $D_B = 700$ mm, weight of gear $W_B = 800$ N.

Torque: We know that

$$T = \frac{9.55 \times 10^6 (P)}{n} = \frac{9.55 \times 10^6 \times (15)}{500} \quad \text{...3.3(a)/Pg 50, DHB}$$

$$= 286500 \text{ N·mm} = M_t$$

Analysis of pulley: Assuming torque on pulley and gear are equal

$$T_A = T_B = 286500 \text{ N·mm}$$

Torque on pulley $\quad T_A = (T_1 - T_2)R_A$

But $\qquad\qquad \dfrac{T_1}{T_2} = 2$ $\qquad\qquad\qquad\qquad\qquad\qquad$ ... (data)

$$286500 = (2T_2 - T_2) \times (1200/2)$$

$\therefore \qquad\qquad\qquad T_2 = 477.5 \text{ N}$

and $\qquad\qquad\qquad T_1 = 955 \text{ N}$

Analysis of gears: We know that tangential force

$$F_{tB} = \frac{2M_t}{D_B} = \frac{2 \times 286500}{700} = 818.57 \text{ N} \qquad \textbf{...12.8(a)/Pg 206, DHB}$$

Radial force, $\qquad F_{rB} = F_{tB} \tan \alpha = 818.57 \times \tan 20° = 297.94 \text{ N}$

$\qquad\qquad\qquad\qquad\qquad\qquad\qquad\qquad\qquad$ **...12.8(b)/Pg 206, DHB**

To find maximum bending moment:

a. Vertical loading: **Figures 5.14(b) and (c)** represent the vertical load and equivalent vertical load diagram.

- Taking moments about bearing 'C', and equating to zero, we have

$$R_{DV}(CD) + [F_{tB} - W_B](CB) = [T_1 + T_2 + W_A](AC)$$

$$R_{DV} \times 500 + [(818.57 - 800) \times 800] = [(477.5 + 955 + 2400) \times 200]$$

$\therefore \qquad\qquad\qquad\qquad R_{DV} = 1503.29 \text{ N}$

$\quad$ Also $\qquad R_{CV} + R_{DV} + (F_{tB} - W_B) = (T_1 + T_2 + W_A)$

$$R_{CV} + 1503.29 + [818.57 - 800] = [477.5 + 955 + 2400]$$

$\therefore \qquad\qquad\qquad\qquad R_{CV} = 2310.64 \text{ N}$

- Moments:

$$M_{AV} = M_{BV} = 0$$
$$M_{CV} = -[T_1 + T_2 + W_A] \times 200$$
$$= [477.5 + 955 + 2400] \times 200 = -766500 \text{ N·mm}$$
$$M_{DV} = [F_{tB} - W_B] \times 300 = [818.57 - 800] \times 300 = 5571 \text{ N·mm}$$

b. Horizontal loading: **Figure 5.14(d)** represents the horizontal load diagram.

- Taking moments about bearing 'C', and equating to zero, we have

$$R_{DH}(CD) = F_{rB}(CB)$$
$$R_{DH} \times 500 = (297.94 \times 800)$$

$\therefore \qquad\qquad\qquad R_{DH} = 476.70 \text{ N}$

$\quad$ Also $R_{CH} + R_{DH} = F_{rB}$

$$R_{CH} + 476.70 = 297.94$$

$\therefore \qquad\qquad\qquad R_{CH} = -178.76 \text{ N}$

Since the reaction is negative, R_{CH} acts in opposite direction as shown in **Fig. 5.14(e)**.

- Moments:

$$M_{AH} = M_{CH} = M_{BH} = 0$$
$$M_{DH} = -F_{rB} \times 300 = -297.94 \times 300 = -89382 \text{ N·mm}$$

Resultant moment at C,

$$M_C = \sqrt{M_{CV}^2 + M_{CH}^2} = \sqrt{(-766500^2) + 0} = 766500 \text{ N·mm}$$

Resultant moment at D,

$$M_D = \sqrt{M_{DV}^2 + M_{DH}^2} = \sqrt{5571^2 + (-89382)^2} = 89555.45 \text{ N.mm}$$

Thus maximum bending moment occurs at 'D', i.e.

$$M_C = M = 89555.45 \text{ N·mm}$$

According to maximum shear stress theory: For a solid shaft

$$d = \left[\frac{16}{\pi \tau_{max}} \sqrt{(C_m M)^2 + (C_t T)^2} \right]^{1/3} \qquad \text{...3.6(b)/Pg 51, DHB}$$

$$= \left[\frac{16}{\pi \times 60} \sqrt{(2 \times 766500)^2 + (1.5 \times 286500)^2} \right]^{1/3}$$

$\therefore \qquad d = 51.32 \text{ mm}$

$\therefore$ Standard size of shaft, $d = 56$ mm.   **...Tb. 3.5(a)/Pg 57, DHB**

24. **A uniform circular carbon steel shaft made of SAE 1025 annealed is mounted on two bearings 850 mm apart as shown in Fig. 5.15(a). The shaft carries a gear 'A' at 200 mm to the right of the left bearing and a pulley 'B' at 250 mm to the left of right bearing. The gear is subjected to horizontal pressure of 3500 N and a vertical upward pressure of 9600 N. The pulley is driven by a belt with a tension on tight side to be 6000 N and on the slack side to be 2000 N. The shock and fatigue factors for bending and torsion are $K_m = 2$ and $K_t = 1.5$ respectively and weight of the pulley to be 1500 N. Design the diameter of the shaft for yield strength taking factor of safety as 3. Draw neatly the sketch with loading and bending moment diagrams.**

VTU – Dec. 2015/ Jan. 2016 – 20 Marks; (Similar) Dec. 2013/ Jan. 2014 – 20 Marks

Solution: Material: Carbon steel SAE 1025 annealed, FoS = 3, $C_m = K_m = 2$, $C_t = K_t = 1.5$, $d = ?$

Gear: $F_{AH} = 3500$ N, $F_{AV} = 9600$ N.

Pulley: $T_1 = 6000$ N, $T_2 = 2000$ N, weight of pulley $W_B = 1500$ N. Assume $D_B = 600$ mm.

Material: For SAE 1025 annealed steel, $\sigma_{ut} = 462$ MPa, $\sigma_{yt} = 234$ MPa.

Since design is based on yield strength (as per data), we have

$$\sigma_{max} = \frac{\sigma_{yt}}{FoS} = \frac{234}{3} = 78 \text{ MPa}$$

$$\tau_{max} = \frac{\sigma_{max}}{2} = \frac{78}{2} = 39 \text{ MPa}$$

Assuming that the keyway effect is included in the above values, we have

$$\sigma_{max-1} = \sigma_{max} = 78 \text{ MPa}$$

$$\tau_{max-1} = \tau_{max} = 39 \text{ MPa}$$

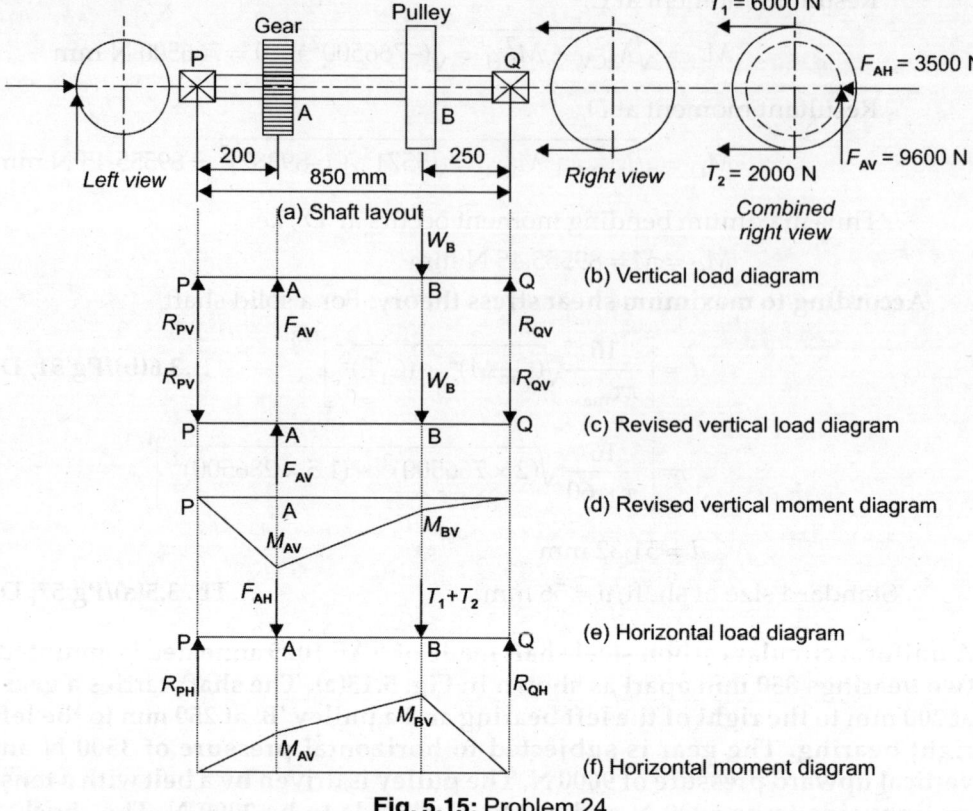

Fig. 5.15: Problem 24

Torque: Torque on pulley,
$$T_B = (T_1 - T_2)R_B = (6000 - 2000) \times (600/2) = 12 \times 10^5 \text{ N·mm.}$$

To find maximum bending moment:

a. Vertical loading: **Figure 5.15(b)** represents the vertical load diagram.

- Taking moments about bearing 'P', and equating to zero, we have
$$R_{QV}(PQ) + F_{AV}(PA) = W_B(PB)$$
$$R_{QV} \times 850 + 9600 \times 200 = 1500 \times 600$$
$$\therefore \qquad R_{QV} = -1200 \text{ N}$$

- Since the reaction is negative, R_{QV} acts in opposite direction as shown in **Fig. 5.15(c)**.

  Also $\qquad R_{PV} + F_{AV} = R_{QV} + W_B$ \hfill ...using Fig. 5.15(b)
  $$R_{PV} + 9600 = 1200 + 1500$$
  $$\therefore \qquad R_{PV} = -6900 \text{ N}$$

Since the reaction is negative, R_{PV} acts in opposite direction as shown in **Fig. 5.15(c)**.

- Moments:
$$M_{PV} = M_{QV} = 0$$
$$M_{AV} = -R_{PV} \times 200 = -6900 \times 200 = -1380000 \text{ N·mm}$$
$$M_{BV} = -R_{QV} \times 250 = -1200 \times 250 = -300000 \text{ N·mm}$$

Figure 5.15(d) represents the vertical moment diagram.

b. Horizontal loading: **Figure 5.15(e)** represents the horizontal load diagram.

- Taking moments about bearing 'P', and equating to zero, we have

$$R_{QH}(PQ) = [T_1 + T_2](PB) + F_{AH}(PA)$$

$$R_{QH} \times 850 = [(6000 + 2000) \times 600] + (3500 \times 200)$$

$$\therefore \quad R_{QH} = 6470.59 \text{ N}$$

Also $R_{PH} + R_{QH} = [T_1 + T_2] + F_{AH}$

$$R_{PH} + 6470.59 = (6000 + 2000) + 3500$$

$$\therefore \quad R_{PH} = 502.21 \text{ N}$$

- Moments:

$$M_{PH} = M_{QH} = 0$$

$$M_{AH} = R_{PH} \times 200 = 5029.21 \times 200 = 1005882 \text{ N·mm}$$

$$M_{BH} = R_{QH} \times 250 = 6470.59 \times 250 = 1617647.5 \text{ N·mm}$$

Resultant moment at A,

$$M_A = \sqrt{M_{AV}^2 + M_{AH}^2} = \sqrt{(-1380000^2) + (1005882)}$$

$$= 1707688.09 \text{ N·mm}$$

Resultant moment at B,

$$M_B = \sqrt{M_{BV}^2 + M_{BH}^2} = \sqrt{(-300000)^2 + 1617647.5^2}$$

$$= 1645230.51 \text{ N·mm}$$

Thus maximum bending moment occurs at 'A', i.e.

$$M_A = M = 1707688.09 \text{ N·mm}$$

Figure 5.15(f) represents the vertical moment diagram.

a. **According to maximum normal stress theory:** For a solid shaft

$$d = \left[\frac{16}{\pi \sigma_{max-1}} \left\{ C_m M + \sqrt{(C_m M)^2 + (C_t T)^2} \right\} \right]^{1/3}$$

...3.6(a)/Pg 51, DHB

$$= \left[\frac{16}{\pi \times 78} \left\{ (2 \times 1707688.09) \right. \right.$$

$$\left. \left. + \sqrt{(2 \times 1707688.09)^2 + \left(1.5 \times 12 \times 10^5\right)^2} \right\} \right]^{1/3}$$

$$\therefore \quad d = 78.03 \text{ mm} \qquad \qquad \text{...Eq. (i)}$$

b. **According to maximum shear stress theory:** For a solid shaft

$$d = \left[\frac{16}{\pi \tau_{max-1}} \sqrt{(C_m M)^2 + (C_t T)^2} \right]^{1/3} \qquad \text{...3.6(b)/Pg 51, DHB}$$

$$= \left[\frac{16}{\pi \times 39} \sqrt{(2 \times 1707688.09)^2 + \left(1.5 \times 12 \times 10^5\right)^2} \right]^{1/3}$$

$$\therefore \quad d = 79.59 \text{ mm} \qquad \qquad \text{...Eq. (ii)}$$

Based on Eqs. (i) and (ii), select maximum diameter for design, i.e.

$$d = 79.59 \text{ mm}$$

$\therefore$ Standard size of shaft, $d = 80$ mm. ...Tb. 3.5(a)/Pg 57, DHB

25. A horizontal piece of commercial shafting is supported by two bearings 1.5 m apart. A keyed gear, 20° involute and 175 mm in diameter, is located 400 mm to the left of right bearing and is driven by a gear directly behind it. A 600 mm diameter pulley is keyed to the shaft 600 mm to the right of left bearing and drives a pulley with a horizontal belt directly behind it. The tension ratio of the belt is 3:1, with slack side on top. The drive transmits 45 kW at 330 rpm. Take $C_m = C_t = 1.5$. Calculate the necessary shaft diameter and angular deflection in degrees. Use allowable shear stress of 40 MPa and $G = 80$ GPa.

VTU – Dec. 2014/ Jan. 2015 – 20 Marks; Dec. 2011 – 20 Marks; Dec. 07/ Jan. 2008 – 20 Marks

Solution: The layout of the shaft as per given data is shown in **Fig. 5.16(a)**.

$\alpha = 20°$, $\dfrac{T_1}{T_2} = 3$, $P = 45$ kW, $n = 330$ rpm, $C_m = C_t = 1.5$, $d = ?$, $\tau = \tau_{max} = 40$ MPa,

$G = 80 \times 10^3$ MPa.

Pulley: $D_C = 600$ mm.

Gear: $D_D = 175$ mm.

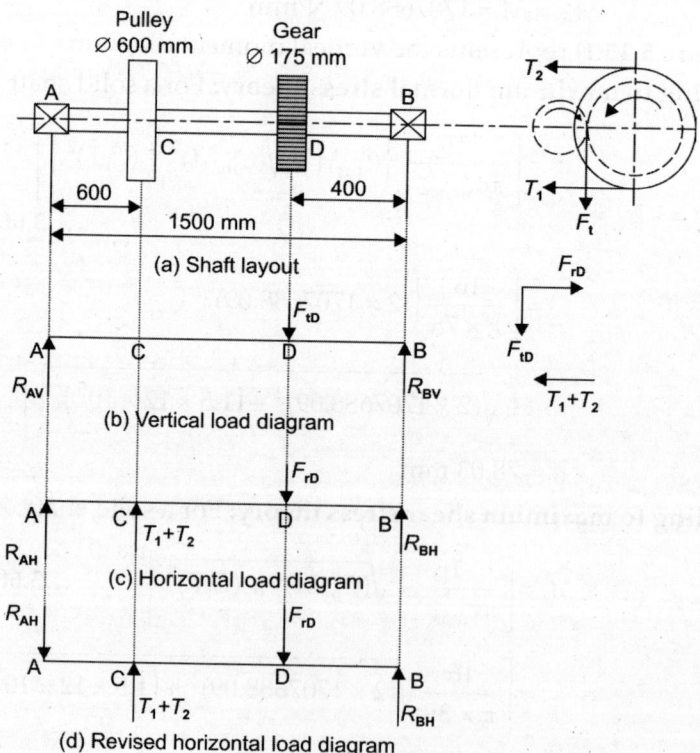

Fig. 5.16: Problem 25

Torque: We know that

$$T = \frac{9.55 \times 10^6 (P)}{n} = \frac{9.55 \times 10^6 \times (45)}{330} \qquad ...3.3(a)/Pg\ 50,\ DHB$$

$$= 1302272.73\ \text{N·mm} = M_t$$

Analysis of pulley: Assuming torque on pulley and gear is equal

$$T_C = T_D = 1302272.73\ \text{N·mm}$$

Torque on pulley $\quad T_C = (T_1 - T_2)R_C$

But $\qquad\qquad \dfrac{T_1}{T_2} = 3 \qquad\qquad\qquad\qquad\qquad\qquad\qquad$ ... (data)

$$1302272.73 = (3T_2 - T_2) \times (600/2)$$

$\therefore \qquad\qquad\qquad T_2 = 2170.45\ \text{N}$

and $\qquad\qquad\qquad T_1 = 6511.35\ \text{N}$

Analysis of gears: We know that tangential force

$$F_{tD} = \frac{2M_t}{D_B} = \frac{2 \times 1302272.73}{175} = 14883.12\ \text{N}$$

$$...12.8(a)/Pg\ 206,\ DHB$$

Radial force, $\quad F_{rD} = F_{tB} \tan \alpha = 14883.12 \times \tan 20° = 5417.01\ \text{N}$

$$...12.8(b)/Pg\ 206,\ DHB$$

To find maximum bending moment:

a. Vertical loading: **Figure 5.16(b)** represents the vertical load diagram.

- Taking moments about bearing 'A', and equating to zero, we have

$$R_{BV}(AB) = F_{tD}(AD)$$

$$R_{BV} \times 1500 = 14883.12 \times 1100$$

$\therefore \qquad\qquad R_{BV} = 10914.29\ \text{N}$

Also $\qquad\qquad R_{AV} + R_{BV} = F_{tD}$

$$R_{AV} + 10914.29 = 14883.2$$

$\therefore \qquad\qquad R_{AV} = 3968.83\ \text{N}$

- Moments:

$$M_{AV} = M_{BV} = 0$$

$$M_{CV} = R_{AV} \times 600 = 3968.83 \times 600 = 2381298\ \text{N·mm}$$

$$M_{DV} = R_{BV} \times 400 = 10914.29 \times 400 = 4365716\ \text{N·mm}$$

b. Horizontal loading: **Figure 5.16(c)** represents the horizontal load diagram.

- Taking moments about bearing 'A', and equating to zero, we have

$$R_{BH}(AB) + [T_1 + T_2](AC) = F_{rD}(AD)$$

$$R_{BH} \times 1500 + [(6511.35 + 2170.45) \times 600] = (5417.01 \times 1100)$$

$\therefore \qquad\qquad\qquad\qquad R_{BH} = 499.75\ \text{N}$

Also $\qquad\qquad R_{AH} + R_{BH} + [T_1 + T_2] = F_{rD}$

$$R_{AH} + 499.75 + (6511.35 + 2170.45) = 5417.01$$

$\therefore \qquad\qquad\qquad\qquad R_{AH} = -3764.54\ \text{N}$

Since the reaction is negative, R_{AH} acts in opposite direction as shown in **Fig. 5.16(d)**.

- **Moments:**

$$M_{AH} = M_{BH} = 0$$

$$M_{CH} = R_{AH} \times 600 = -3764.54 \times 600 = -2258724 \text{ N·mm}$$

$$M_{DH} = R_{BH} \times 400 = 499.75 \times 400 = 199900 \text{ N·mm}$$

Resultant moment at C,

$$M_A = \sqrt{M_{CV}^2 + M_{CH}^2} = \sqrt{2381298^2 + (-2258724)^2}$$

$$= 3282135.63 \text{ N·mm}$$

Resultant moment at D,

$$M_B = \sqrt{M_{DV}^2 + M_{DH}^2} = \sqrt{4365716^2 + (199900)^2}$$

$$= 4370290.17 \text{ N·mm}$$

Thus maximum bending moment occurs at 'D', i.e.

$$M_D = M = 4370290.17 \text{ N·mm}$$

According to maximum shear stress theory: For a solid shaft

$$d = \left[\frac{16}{\pi \tau_{max}} \sqrt{(C_m M)^2 + (C_t T)^2} \right]^{1/3} \qquad \textbf{...3.6(b)/Pg 51, DHB}$$

$$= \left[\frac{16}{\pi \times 40} \sqrt{(1.5 \times 4370290.17)^2 + (1.5 \times 1302272.73)^2} \right]^{1/3}$$

$$\therefore \qquad d = 95.49 \text{ mm}$$

∴ Standard size of shaft, $d = 56$ mm.   **...Tb. 3.5(a)/Pg 57, DHB**

To find θ: We know that

$$\theta = \frac{584TL}{GD^4} = \frac{584 \times (1302272.73) \times 500}{(80 \times 10^3) \times 100^4} = 0.0475 \text{ deg}$$

     ...3.2/Pg 57, DHB

26. **A power transmission shaft 1500 mm long is supported at two points A and B. While A is at the left extreme end of the shaft, B is at a distance of 400 mm from the right extreme end of the shaft. The shaft receives a power of 50 kW at a rated speed of 500 rpm through a belt drive located at the right extreme end of the shaft. The belt pulley has a diameter of 400 mm and weighs 1 kN. The belts moving on the pulley is directed away from the observer below the horizontal and inclined at 45° to it. The ratio of belt tensions is 3. This power is given out through a gear drive located at a distance of 500 mm from the right support B. The gear mounted on the shaft has a pitch diameter of 200 mm and weighs 400 N. The other gear, which meshes with this gear is placed exactly in front. The gear teeth have a pressure angle of 20°. Selecting a suitable material and choosing an appropriate value of factor of safety, determine the diameter of the solid circular shaft required for power transmission.**

     VTU – Dec. 2012 – 17 Marks; July 2006 – 20 Marks;
     (similar) Dec. 2011 – 20 Marks; (similar) May/ June 2010 – 20 Marks

Solution: The layout of the shaft as per given data is shown in **Fig. 5.17 (a).**

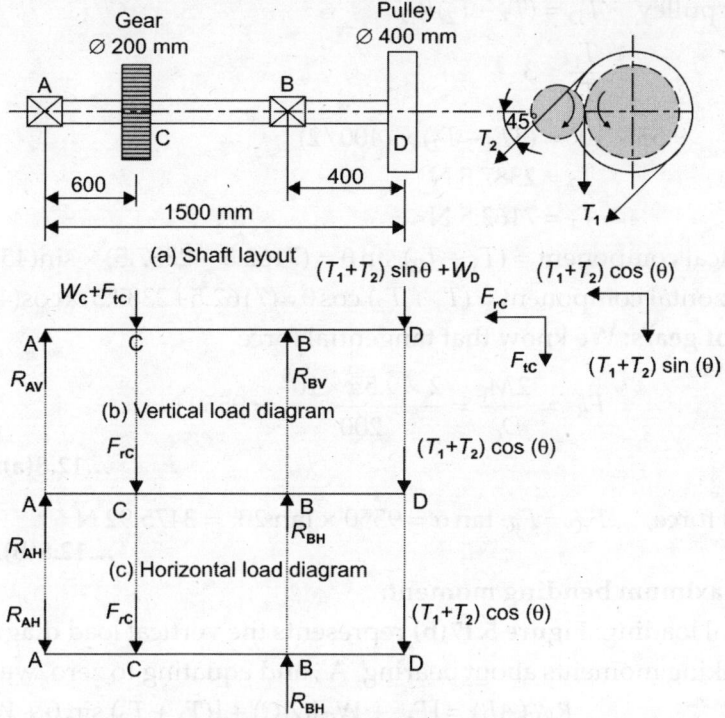

(a) Shaft layout

(b) Vertical load diagram

(c) Horizontal load diagram

(d) Revised horizontal load diagram

Fig. 5.17: Problem 26

$P = 50$ kW, $n = 500$ rpm, $\alpha = 20°$, $\dfrac{T_1}{T_2} = 3$, $d = ?$

Gear: $D_C = 200$ mm, $W_C = 400$ N.

Pulley: $D_D = 400$ mm, $W_D = 1000$ N, angle of contact $\theta = 45°$.

Material: Assume C45 steel having $\sigma_{yt} = 353$ MPa and FoS = 2.5.

...Tb. 1.8/Pg 464, DHB

$$\sigma_{max} = \frac{\sigma_{yt}}{FoS} = \frac{353}{2.5} = 141.2 \text{ MPa}$$

$$\tau_{max} = \frac{\sigma_{max}}{2} = \frac{141.2}{2} = 70.6 \text{ MPa}$$

Assuming that the keyway effect is included in the above values, we have

$$\sigma_{max-1} = \sigma_{max} = 141.2 \text{ MPa}$$
$$\tau_{max-1} = \tau_{max} = 70.6 \text{ MPa}$$

Torque: We know that

$$T = \frac{9.55 \times 10^6 (P)}{n} = \frac{9.55 \times 10^6 \times (50)}{500} \quad \text{...3.3(a)/Pg 50, DHB}$$

$$= 9.55 \times 10^5 \text{ N·mm} = M_t$$

Analysis of pulley: Assuming torque on pulley and gear is equal

$$T_C = T_D = 9.55 \times 10^5 \text{ N·mm}$$

Torque on pulley $T_D = (T_1 - T_2)R_D$

But $\dfrac{T_1}{T_2} = 3$ ... (data)

$$9.55 \times 10^5 = (3T_2 - T_2) \times (400/2)$$

$\therefore$ $T_2 = 2387.5 \text{ N}$

and $T_1 = 7162.5 \text{ N}$

Thus vertical component $= (T_1 + T_2) \sin\theta = (7162.5 + 2387.5) \times \sin(45) = 6752.87 \text{ N}$

horizontal component $= (T_1 + T_2) \cos\theta = (7162.5 + 2387.5) \times \cos(45) = 6752.87 \text{ N}$

Analysis of gears: We know that tangential force

$$F_{tC} = \frac{2M_t}{D_C} = \frac{2 \times 9.55 \times 10^5}{200} = 9550 \text{ N}$$

...12.8(a)/Pg 206, DHB

Radial force, $F_{rC} = F_{tC} \tan\alpha = 9550 \times \tan 20° = 3475.92 \text{ N}$

...12.8(b)/Pg 206, DHB

To find maximum bending moment:

a. Vertical loading: **Figure 5.17(b)** represents the vertical load diagram.

• Taking moments about bearing 'A', and equating to zero, we have

$$R_{BV}(AB) = [F_{tC} + W_C](AC) + [(T_1 + T_2)\sin\theta + W_D](AD)$$

$$R_{BV} \times 1100 = [(9550 + 400) \times 600] + [(6752.87 + 1000) \times 1500]$$

$\therefore$ $R_{BV} = 15999.73 \text{ N}$

Also $R_{AV} + R_{BV} = [F_{tC} + W_C] + [(T_1 + T_2)\sin\theta + W_D]$

$$R_{AV} + 15999.37 = (9550 + 400) + (6752.87 + 1000)$$

$\therefore$ $R_{AV} = 1703.50 \text{ N}$

• Moments:

$$M_{AV} = M_{DV} = 0$$

$$M_{CV} = R_{AV} \times 600 = 1703.50 \times 600 = 1022100 \text{ N·mm}$$

$$M_{BV} = -[(T_1 + T_2)\sin\theta + W_D] \times 400$$

$$= -(6752.87 + 1000) \times 400 = -3101148 \text{ N·mm}$$

b. Horizontal loading: **Fig. 5.17(c)** represents the horizontal load diagram.

• Taking moments about bearing 'A', and equating to zero, we have

$$R_{BH}(AB) = F_{rC}(AC) + [T_1 + T_2]\cos\theta(AD)$$

$$R_{BH} \times 1100 = (3475.92 \times 600) + (6752.87 \times 1500)$$

$\therefore$ $R_{BH} = 11104.42 \text{ N}$

Also, $R_{AH} + R_{BH} = F_{rC} + [(T_1 + T_2)\cos\theta]$

$$R_{AH} + 11104.42 = 3475.92 + 6752.87$$

$\therefore$ $R_{AH} = -875.63 \text{ N}$

Since the reaction is negative, R_{AH} acts in opposite direction as shown in **Fig. 5.17(d)**.

• Moments:

$$M_{AH} = M_{DH} = 0$$

$$M_{CH} = R_{AH} \times 600 = -875.63 \times 600 = -525378 \text{ N·mm}$$

$$M_{BH} = -[(T_1 + T_2) \cos \theta] \times 400 = -6752.87 \times 400 = -2701148 \text{ N·mm}$$

Resultant moment at C,

$$M_C = \sqrt{M_{CV}^2 + M_{CH}^2} = \sqrt{1022100^2 + (-525378)^2}$$

$$= 1149221.67 \text{ N·mm}$$

Resultant moment at B,

$$M_B = \sqrt{M_{BV}^2 + M_{BH}^2} = \sqrt{(-3101148)^2 + (-2701148)^2}$$

$$= 4112580.63 \text{ N·mm}$$

Thus maximum bending moment occurs at 'B', i.e.

$$M_B = M = 4112580.63 \text{ N·mm}$$

a. **According to maximum normal stress theory:** For a solid shaft

$$d = \left[\frac{16}{\pi\sigma_{max-1}} \left\{ C_m M + \sqrt{(C_m M)^2 + (C_t T)^2} \right\} \right]^{1/3}$$

...3.6(a)/Pg 51, DHB

Assuming minor shocks, we have $C_m = 1.75$ and $C_t = 1.25$

...Tb. 3.1/Pg 56, DHB

$$= \left[\frac{16}{\pi \times 141.2} \left\{ (1.75 \times 4112580.63) \right. \right.$$

$$\left. \left. + \sqrt{(1.75 \times 4112580.63)^2 + \left(1.25 \times 9.55 \times 10^5\right)^2} \right\} \right]^{1/3}$$

$$\therefore \qquad d = 80.55 \text{ mm} \qquad\qquad\qquad\qquad \text{...Eq. (i)}$$

b. **According to maximum shear stress theory:** For a solid shaft

$$d = \left[\frac{16}{\pi \cdot \tau_{max-1}} \sqrt{(C_m M)^2 + (C_t T)^2} \right]^{1/3} \qquad \text{...3.6(b)/Pg 51, DHB}$$

$$= \left[\frac{16}{\pi \times 70.6} \sqrt{(1.75 \times 4112580.63)^2 + \left(1.25 \times 9.55 \times 10^5\right)^2} \right]^{1/3}$$

$$\therefore \qquad d = 80.74 \text{ mm} \qquad\qquad\qquad\qquad \text{...Eq. (ii)}$$

Based on Eqs. (i) and (ii), select maximum diameter for design, i.e.

$$d = 80.74 \text{ mm}$$

$\therefore$ Standard size of shaft, $d = 90$ mm.   ...Tb. 3.5(a)/Pg 57, DHB

27. **A steel shaft 950 mm long supported between bearings 750 mm apart, has a cast iron pulley 600 mm diameter, weighing 800 N overhanging to the right of bearing by 200 mm as shown in Fig. 5.18(a). The pulley receives 25 kW at 1000 rpm from a belt drive; the belt is inclined at 60° to the horizontal (inclined upwards). The power from the shaft is transmitted through a 14½° spur pinion of diameter 200 mm to a spur gear mounted directly above the pinion. The pinion is keyed to the shaft at a distance of 150 mm to the right of left bearing.**

Taking the ratio of belt tension as 3:1, ultimate stress and yield stress for the material of the shaft as 500 MPa and 310 MPa respectively. Determine the diameter of the shaft. Use $K_b = 2$ and $K_t = 1.5$.

VTU – Dec. 06/Jan. 2007 – 20 Marks; (similar) June/July 2009 – 20 Marks;
(similar) June/July 2009 – 20 Marks;
(similar) July/ Aug. 2004 – 20 Marks; Jan/ Feb. 2005 – 20 Marks

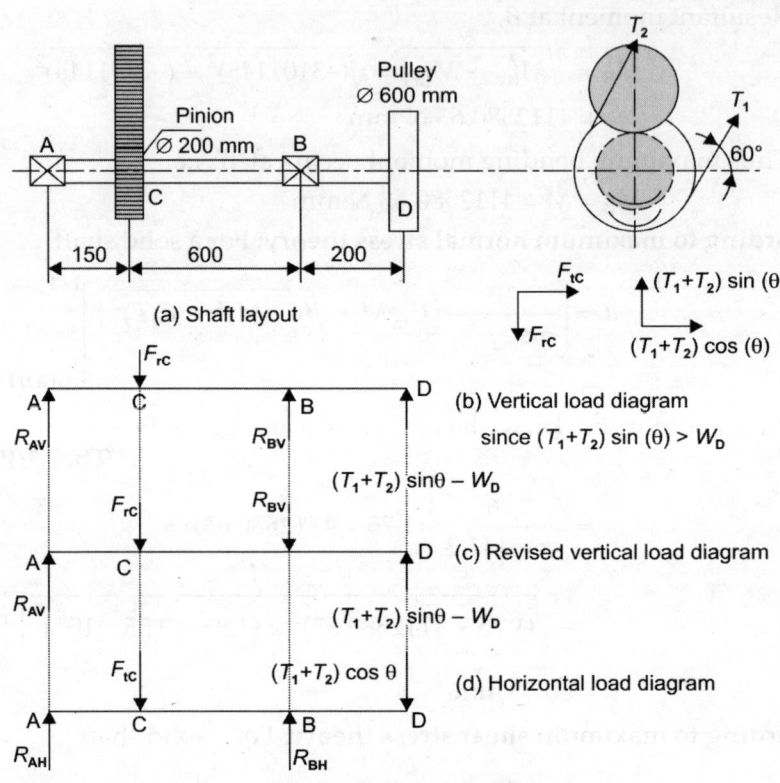

(a) Shaft layout

(b) Vertical load diagram

since $(T_1+T_2)\sin(\theta) > W_D$

(c) Revised vertical load diagram

(d) Horizontal load diagram

Fig. 5.18: Problem 27

Solution: $P = 25$ kW, $n = 1000$ rpm, $\alpha = 14.5°$, $\dfrac{T_1}{T_2} = 3$, $d = ?$, $\sigma_{ut} = 500$ MPa, $\sigma_{yt} = 310$ MPa, $K_b = C_m = 2$, $K_t = C_t = 15$.

Gear: $D_C = 200$ mm.

Pulley: $D_D = 400$ mm, $W_D = 800$ N, angle of contact $\theta = 60°$.

Design stresses:

Without keyway:

$\rightarrow \qquad \sigma_{max} = 0.6\sigma_{yt} = 0.6 \times 310 = 186$ MPa

and $\qquad \sigma_{max} = 0.36\sigma_{ut} = 0.36 \times 500 = 180$ MPa.

Take the least value among the two, we have, $\sigma_{max} = 180$ MPa

$\rightarrow \qquad \tau_{max} = 0.3\sigma_{yt} = 0.3 \times 310 = 93$ MPa

and $\qquad \tau_{max} = 0.18\sigma_{ut} = 0.18 \times 500 = 90$ MPa

Take the least value among the two, we have,

$\qquad \tau_{max} = 90$ MPa

With keyway:

$\rightarrow$ $\qquad\qquad \sigma_{max-1} = (1 - 0.25)\sigma_{max} = 0.75\sigma_{max} = 0.75 \times 180 = 135 \, \text{MPa}$

$\rightarrow$ $\qquad\qquad \tau_{max-1} = (1 - 0.25)\tau_{max} = 0.75\tau_{max} = 0.75 \times 90 = 67.5 \, \text{MPa}$

Torque: We know that

$$T = \frac{9.55 \times 10^6 (P)}{n} = \frac{9.55 \times 10^6 \times (25)}{1000} \qquad \text{...3.3(a)/Pg 50, DHB}$$

$$= 238750 \, \text{N·mm} = M_t$$

Analysis of pulley: Assuming torque on pulley and gear is equal

$$T_C = T_D = 238750 \, \text{N·mm}$$

Torque on pulley $\qquad T_D = (T_1 - T_2)R_D$

But $\qquad\qquad\qquad \dfrac{T_1}{T_2} = 3 \qquad\qquad\qquad\qquad\qquad\qquad\qquad\qquad \text{... (data)}$

$$238750 = (3T_2 - T_2) \times (600/2)$$

$\therefore \qquad\qquad\qquad T_2 = 397.92 \, \text{N}$

and $\qquad\qquad\qquad T_1 = 1193.76 \, \text{N}$

Thus,

Vertical component $= (T_1 + T_2) \sin \theta = (1193.76 + 397.92) \times \sin(60) = 1378.44 \, \text{N}$

Horizontal component $= (T_1 + T_2) \cos \theta = (1193.76 + 397.92) \times \cos(60) = 795.84 \, \text{N}$

Analysis of gears: We know that tangential force

$$F_{tC} = \frac{2M_t}{D_C} = \frac{2 \times 238750}{200} = 2387.50 \, \text{N} \qquad \text{...12.8(a)/Pg 206, DHB}$$

Radial force, $\quad F_{rC} = F_{tC} \tan \alpha = 2387.50 \times \tan(14.5) = 617.45 \, \text{N}$

$$\text{...12.8(b)/Pg 206, DHB}$$

To find maximum bending moment:

a. Vertical loading: **Figure 5.18(b)** represents the vertical load diagram.

• Taking moments about bearing 'A', and equating to zero, we have

$$R_{BV}(AB) + [(T_1 + T_2) \sin \theta - W_D](AD) = F_{rC}(AD)$$

$$R_{BV} \times 750 + [(1378.44 - 800) \times 950] = (617.45 \times 150)$$

$\therefore \qquad\qquad\qquad\qquad R_{BV} = -609.20 \, \text{N}$

Since the reaction is negative, R_{BV} acts in opposite direction as shown in **Fig. 5.18(c).**

Also $\qquad R_{AV} + [(T_1 + T_2) \sin \theta - W_D] = F_{rC} + R_{BV}$

$$R_{AV} + (1378.44 - 800) = 617.45 + 609.20$$

$\therefore \qquad\qquad\qquad\qquad R_{AV} = 648.21 \, \text{N}$

- Moments:
$$M_{AV} = M_{DV} = 0$$
$$M_{CV} = R_{AV} \times 150 = 648.21 \times 150 = 97231.50 \text{ N·mm}$$
$$M_{BV} = -[(T_1 + T_2)\sin\theta - W_D] \times 200$$
$$= -(1378.44 - 800) \times 200 = -115688 \text{ N·mm}$$

b. Horizontal loading: **Figure 5.18(d)** represents the horizontal load diagram.

- Taking moments about bearing 'A', and equating to zero, we have
$$R_{BH}(AB) = F_{tC}(AC) + [T_1 + T_2]\cos\theta(AD)$$
$$R_{BH} \times 750 = (2387.50 \times 150) + (795.84 \times 950)$$
$$\therefore \qquad R_{BH} = 1485.56 \text{ N}$$
Also $\qquad R_{AH} + R_{BH} = F_{tC} + [(T_1 + T_2)\cos\theta]$
$$R_{AH} + 1485.56 = 2387.50 + 795.84$$
$$\therefore \qquad R_{AH} = 1697.78 \text{ N}$$

- Moments:
$$M_{AH} = M_{DH} = 0$$
$$M_{CH} = R_{AH} \times 150 = 1697.78 \times 150 = 254667 \text{ N·mm}$$
$$M_{BH} = -[(T_1 + T_2)\cos\theta] \times 200 = -795.84 \times 200$$
$$= -159168 \text{ N·mm}$$

Resultant moment at C,
$$M_C = \sqrt{M_{CV}^2 + M_{CH}^2} = \sqrt{97231.50^2 + 254667^2}$$
$$= 272597.22 \text{ N·mm}$$

Resultant moment at B,
$$M_B = \sqrt{M_{BV}^2 + M_{BH}^2} = \sqrt{(-115688)^2 + (-159168)^2}$$
$$= 196769.32 \text{ N·mm}$$

Thus maximum bending moment occurs at 'C', i.e. $M = M_C = 272597.22$ N·mm.

a. **According to maximum normal stress theory:** For a solid shaft
$$d = \left[\frac{16}{\pi\sigma_{max-1}} \left\{ C_m M + \sqrt{(C_m M)^2 + (C_t T)^2} \right\} \right]^{1/3}$$

...3.6(a)/Pg 51, DHB

$$= \left[\frac{16}{\pi \times 135} \left\{ (2 \times 272597.22) \right. \right.$$
$$\left. \left. + \sqrt{(2 \times 272597.22)^2 + (1.5 \times 238750)^2} \right\} \right]^{1/3}$$
$$\therefore \qquad d = 35.61 \text{ mm} \qquad\qquad \text{...Eq. (i)}$$

b. **According to maximum shear stress theory:** For a solid shaft
$$d = \left[\frac{16}{\pi\tau_{max-1}} \sqrt{(C_m M)^2 + (C_t T)^2} \right]^{1/3} \qquad \textbf{...3.6(b)/Pg 51, DHB}$$

$$= \left[\frac{16}{\pi \times 67.5} \sqrt{(2 \times 272597.22)^2 + (1.5 \times 238750)^2} \right]^{1/3}$$

$$\therefore \qquad d = 36.65 \text{ mm} \qquad\qquad\qquad \text{...Eq. (ii)}$$

Based on Eqs. (i) and (ii), select maximum diameter for design, i.e.

$$d = 36.65 \text{ mm}$$

$$\therefore \text{ Standard size of shaft, } d = 40 \text{ mm.} \qquad\qquad \text{...Tb. 3.5(a)/Pg 57, DHB}$$

28. **A transmission shaft running at 500 rev/min is supported on bearings 800 mm apart. 20 kW power is supplied to the shaft through a 450 mm diameter pulley which is located 400 mm to the right of right bearing and receives power from a motor placed directly below the shaft. The shaft further transmits this power to spur gear of 300 mm pitch circle diameter, which is located 400 mm to the right of left bearing. The gear has 20° involute teeth and ratio of belt tensions is 3:1. The gear drives another gear which is placed directly above the shaft. The gear and the pulley are keyed to the shaft. Selecting the material as steel having σ_{ut} = 700 MPa and σ_{yt} = 460 MPa as per ASME code, determine the diameter of the shaft. Assume shock factors for bending and torsion as 1.5.**

VTU – June 2012 – 20 Marks; Dec. 2010 – 20 Marks

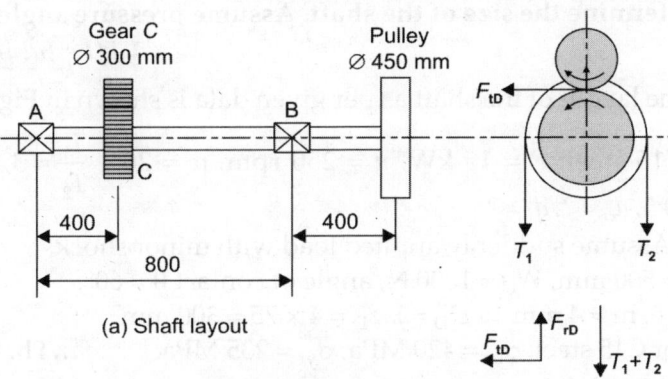

Fig. 5.19: Problem 28

Solution: Procedure similar to Problem 25.

29. **A mild shaft transmits 15 kW at 600 rpm. It is supported on two bearings 1.2 m apart. The shaft receives power through a 420 mm diameter pulley mounted at 200 mm to the right of left bearing. The power is given out through a gear of 200 mm diameter located at 250 mm to the left of right bearing. The belt drive is downward at an angle of 60° to the horizontal with tension ratio of 2.7. The gear drives with a downward tangential force. Find suitable diameter of the shaft taking allowable normal and shear stresses as 90 MPa and 54 MPa respectively. The combined shock and fatigue factors in bending and torsion are 1.75 and 1.25 respectively.**

VTU – June/ July 2014 – 20 Marks

Solution: Procedure similar to Problem 26.

30. **A hollow C15 steel shaft transmits 15 kW at 250 rpm. It is supported on two bearings 750 mm apart. A 500 mm diameter pulley whose weight is 1000 N is**

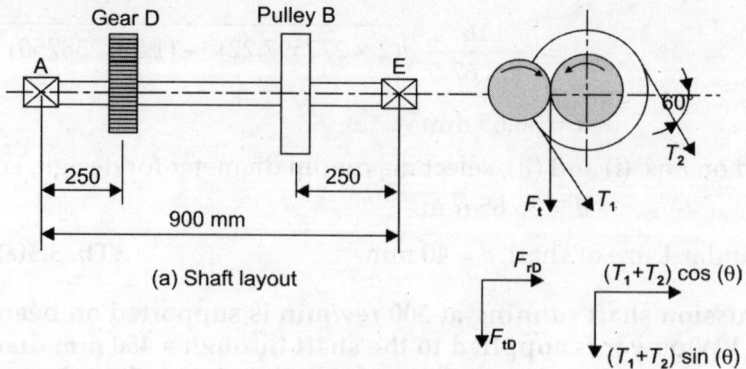

(a) Shaft layout

Fig. 5.20: Problem 29

keyed to the shaft at a distance of **100 mm to the left of left hand bearing**. A pinion having 75 teeth and 4 mm module is mounted at 150 mm to the left of right hand bearing. The pulley is driven by a belt downward at an angle of 60° to the horizontal and towards the observer. The pinion drives a gear placed directly over it. Ratio of belt tension is 3, diameter ratio is 0.5. Use ASME code, assume suddenly applied load with minor shock. Consider keyway effect. Assume the shaft rotates in clockwise direction when viewed from the right bearing. Determine the size of the shaft. Assume pressure angle = 20°.

VTU – July 2007 – 20 Marks

Solution: The layout of the shaft as per given data is shown in **Fig. 5.21(a)**.

Material: C15 steel, P = 15 kW, n = 250 rpm, α = 20°, $\dfrac{T_1}{T_2}$ = 3, diameter ratio $K = d_i/d_o = 0.5$, d_o = ?, d_i = ?

Condition: Assume suddenly applied load with minor shock.

Pulley: D_C = 500 mm, W_C = 1000 N, angle of contact θ = 60°.

Gear: Z_D = 75, m = 4 mm $\Rightarrow D_D = mz_D = 4 \times 75 = 300$ mm.

Material: For C15 steel, σ_{ut} = 420 MPa, σ_{yt} = 235 MPa. **...Tb. I.8/Pg 463, DHB**

Without keyway:

→ $\qquad \sigma_{max} = 0.6\sigma_{yt} = 0.6 \times 235 = 141$ MPa

and $\qquad \sigma_{max} = 0.36\sigma_{ut} = 0.36 \times 420 = 151.2$ MPa.

Take the least value among the two, we have, σ_{max} = 141 MPa

→ $\qquad \tau_{max} = 0.3\sigma_{yt} = 0.3 \times 235 = 70.5$ MPa

and $\qquad \tau_{max} = 0.18\sigma_{ut} = 0.18 \times 420 = 75.6$ MPa

Take the least value among the two, we have,

$\qquad \tau_{max}$ = 70.5 MPa

With keyway:

→ $\qquad \sigma_{max-1} = (1 - 0.25)\sigma_{max} = 0.75\sigma_{max} = 0.75 \times 141 = 105.75$ MPa

→ $\qquad \tau_{max-1} = (1 - 0.25)\tau_{max} = 0.75\tau_{max} = 0.75 \times 70.5 = 52.88$ MPa

Torque: We know that

$$T = \frac{9.55 \times 10^6 (P)}{n} = \frac{9.55 \times 10^6 \times (15)}{250} \qquad \text{...3.3(a)/Pg 50, DHB}$$

$$= 573000 \text{ N·mm} = M_t$$

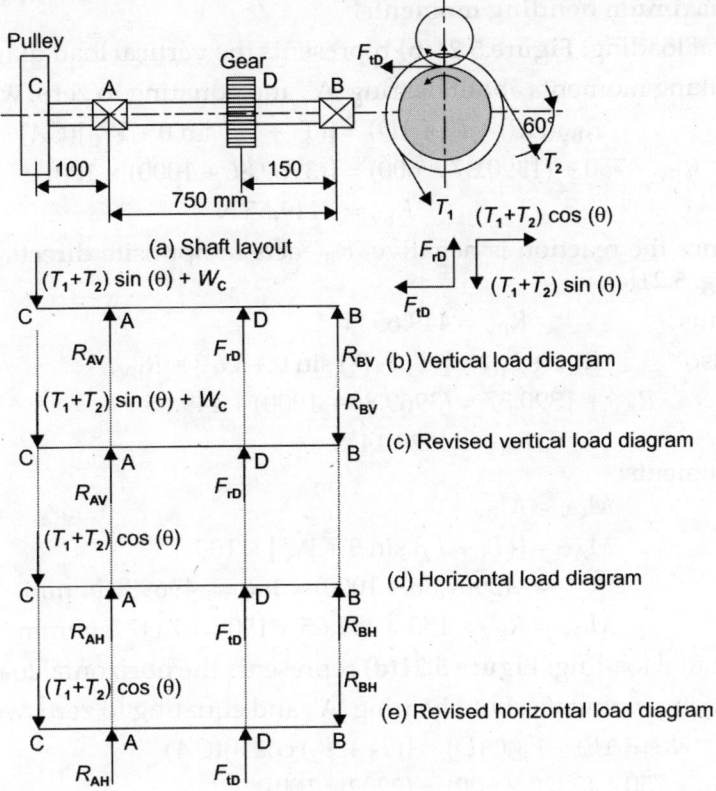

Fig. 5.21: Problem 30

Analysis of pulley: Assuming torque on pulley and gear is equal

$$T_C = T_D = 573000 \text{ N·mm}$$

Torque on pulley $T_C = (T_1 - T_2)R_C$

But $\dfrac{T_1}{T_2} = 3$ ... (data)

$$573000 = (3T_2 - T_2) \times (500/2)$$

∴ $T_2 = 1146 \text{ N}$

and $T_1 = 3438 \text{ N}$

Thus,

Vertical component $= (T_1 + T_2) \sin\theta = (3438 + 1146) \times \sin(60) = 3969.86 \text{ N}$

Horizontal component $= (T_1 + T_2) \cos\theta = (3428 + 1146) \times \cos(60) = 2292 \text{ N}$

Analysis of gear: We know that tangential force

$$F_{tD} = \frac{2M_t}{D_D} = \frac{2 \times 573000}{300} = 3820 \text{ N} \qquad \textbf{...12.8(a)/Pg 206, DHB}$$

Radial force, $F_{rD} = F_{tD} \tan\alpha = 3820 \times \tan(20°) = 1390.37 \text{ N}$

...12.8(b)/Pg 206, DHB

To find maximum bending moment:

a. Vertical loading: **Figure 5.21(b)** represents the vertical load diagram.

- Taking moments about bearing 'A', and equating to zero, we have

$$R_{BV}(AB) + F_{rD}(AD) = [(T_1 + T_2)\sin\theta + W_C](CA)$$

$$R_{BV} \times 750 + (1390.37 \times 600) = [(3969.86 + 1000) \times 100]$$

$$\therefore \qquad R_{BV} = -449.65\ N$$

Since the reaction is negative, R_{BV} acts in opposite direction as shown in **Fig. 5.21(c).**

Thus $\qquad R_{BV} = 449.65\ N$

Also $\qquad R_{AV} + F_{rD} = [(T_1 + T_2)\sin\theta + W_C] + R_{BV}$

$$R_{AV} + 1390.37 = (3969.86 + 1000) + 449.65$$

$$\therefore \qquad R_{AV} = 4029.14\ N$$

- Moments:

$$M_{CV} = M_{BV} = 0$$

$$M_{AV} = [(T_1 + T_2)\sin\theta + W_C] \times 100$$

$$= -(3969.86 + 1000) \times 100 = -496986\ N{\cdot}mm$$

$$M_{DV} = R_{BV} \times 150 = 449.65 \times 150 = 67447.5\ N{\cdot}mm$$

b. Horizontal loading: **Figure 5.21(d)** represents the horizontal load diagram.

- Taking moments about bearing 'A', and equating to zero, we have

$$R_{BH}(AB) + F_{tD}(AD) = [(T_1 + T_2)\cos\theta](CA)$$

$$R_{BH} \times 750 + (3820 \times 600) = (2292 \times 100)$$

$$\therefore \qquad R_{BH} = -2750.4\ N$$

Since the reaction is negative, R_{BH} acts in opposite direction as shown in **Fig. 5.21(e).**

Thus $\qquad R_{BH} = 2750.4\ N$

Also $\qquad R_{AH} + F_{tD} = [(T_1 + T_2)\cos\theta] + R_{BH}$

$$R_{AH} + 3820 = 2292 + 2750.04$$

$$\therefore \qquad R_{AH} = 1222.4\ N$$

- Moments:

$$M_{CH} = M_{BH} = 0$$

$$M_{AH} = -[(T_1 + T_2)\cos\theta] \times 100 = -2292 \times 100 = -229200\ N{\cdot}mm$$

$$M_{DH} = R_{BH} \times 150 = 2750.4 \times 150 = 412560\ N{\cdot}mm$$

Resultant moment at A,

$$M_A = \sqrt{M_{AV}^2 + M_{AH}^2} = \sqrt{(-496986)^2 + (-229200)^2}$$

$$= 547291.26\ N{\cdot}mm$$

Resultant moment at D,

$$M_B = \sqrt{M_{DV}^2 + M_{DH}^2} = \sqrt{67447.5^2 + 412560^2}$$

$$= 418041.82\ N{\cdot}mm$$

Thus maximum bending moment occurs at 'A', i.e.

$$M_A = M = 547291.26\ N{\cdot}mm$$

a. **According to maximum normal stress theory:** For a hollow shaft

$$d_o = \left[\frac{16}{\pi\sigma_{max-1}}\left\{C_m M + \sqrt{(C_m M)^2 + (C_t T)^2}\right\}\right]^{1/3}$$

...3.6(a)/Pg 51, DHB

For suddenly applied load with minor shock, we have $C_m = 1.75$ and $C_t = 1.25$.

...Tb. 3.1/Pg 56, DHB

$$= \left[\frac{16}{\pi \times 105.75}\left\{(1.75 \times 547291.26)\right.\right.$$

$$\left.\left. + \sqrt{(1.75 \times 547291.26)^2 + (1.25 \times 573000)^2}\right\}\left(\frac{1}{1-0.5^4}\right)\right]^{1/3}$$

$\therefore \qquad d_o = 48.04$ mm $\qquad\qquad$ ...Eq. (i)

b. **According to maximum shear stress theory:** For a solid shaft

$$d = \left[\frac{16}{\pi\tau_{max-1}}\left\{\sqrt{(C_m M)^2 + (C_t T)^2}\right\}\left(\frac{1}{1-K^4}\right)\right]^{1/3}$$

...3.6(b)/Pg 51, DHB

$$= \left[\frac{16}{\pi \times 52.88}\left\{\sqrt{(1.75 \times 547291.26)^2 + (1.25 \times 573000)^2}\right\}\left(\frac{1}{1-0.5^4}\right)\right]^{1/3}$$

$\therefore\ d_o = 49.71$ mm $\qquad\qquad$ ...Eq. (ii)

Based on Eqs. (i) and (ii), select maximum diameter for design, i.e.

$$d = 49.71 \text{ mm}$$

$\therefore$ Standard size of shaft, $d = 50$ mm. $\qquad$ ...Tb. 3.5(a)/Pg 57, DHB

31. **A hoisting drum of 0.5 m in diameter is keyed to a shaft which is supported in two bearings and driven through a 12:1 reduction ratio by an electric motor. Determine the power of the driving motor, if the maximum load of 8 kN is hoisted at a speed of 50 m/min and the efficiency of the drive is 80%. Also determine the torque on the drum shaft and the speed of the motor in rpm. Determine also the diameter of the shaft made of machinery steel, the working stresses of which are 115 MPa in tension and 50 MPa in shear. The drive gear whose diameter is 450 mm is mounted at the end of the shaft such that it overhangs the nearest bearing by 150 mm. The combined shock and fatigue factors for bending and torsion may be taken as 2 and 1.5 respectively.**

VTU – June/July 2011 – 20 Marks; Jan./Feb. 2006 – 20 Marks;
June/July 2008 – 12 Marks; (similar) June/July 2009 – 08 Marks

Solution: Drum diameter $D = 500$ mm, gear ratio $i = 12:1$, motor power $P_m = ?$, $W = 8000$ N, $V = 50$ m/min $= 0.834$ m/s, $\eta = 80\% = 0.8$, torque on drum $T_d = ?$, speed of motor $n_m = ?$

$d = ?$, $\sigma = 115$ MPa, $\tau = 50$ MPa, diameter of gear $d_g = 450$ mm, overhang $L = 150$ mm, $C_m = 2$, $C_t = 1.5$.

Assume $\alpha = 20°$.

Power: Power at drum,

$$P_d = WV = 8000 \times 0.834 = 6.67 \times 10^3 \text{ W} = 6.67 \text{ kW}$$

Power at motor, $\quad P_m = \dfrac{P_d}{\eta} = \dfrac{6.67}{0.8} = 8.34 \text{ kW}$

Speed: Speed of drum,

$$V = \dfrac{\pi D n_d}{60}$$

$$0.834 = \dfrac{\pi \times 0.5 n_d}{60}$$

$$n_d = 31.86 \text{ rpm}$$

Speed of motor, $\quad n_m = i n_d = 12 \times 31.86 = 382.32 \text{ rpm}$

Torque: Torque transmitted by gears to drum,

$$T_d = \dfrac{9.55 \times 10^6 (P_m)}{n_d} = \dfrac{9.55 \times 10^6 \times (8.34)}{31.86} \quad \text{...3.3(a)/Pg 50, DHB}$$

$$= 2.5 \times 10^6 \text{ N·mm} = M_t$$

Analysis of gear: We know that tangential force

$$F_t = \dfrac{2M_t}{d_g} = \dfrac{2 \times (2.5 \times 10^6)}{450} = 11111.11 \text{ N}$$

$$\text{...12.8(a)/Pg 206, DHB}$$

Radial force, $\quad F_r = F_t \tan \alpha = 11111.11 \times \tan(20°) = 4044.11 \text{ N}$

$$\text{...12.8(b)/Pg 206, DHB}$$

Moment: Horizontal moment,

$$M_H = F_t L = 11111.11 \times 150 = 1.67 \times 10^6 \text{ N·mm}$$

Vertical moment,

$$M_V = F_r L = 4044.11 \times 150 = 606616.5 \text{ N·mm}$$

Resultant moment,

$$M = \sqrt{M_H^2 + M_V^2} = \sqrt{(1.67 \times 10^6)^2 + (606616.5)^2}$$

$$= 1.78 \times 10^6 \text{ N·mm}$$

a. According to maximum normal stress theory: For a hollow shaft

$$d_o = \left[\dfrac{16}{\pi \sigma_{max}} \left\{ C_m M + \sqrt{(C_m M)^2 + (C_t T)^2} \right\} \right]^{1/3}$$

$$\text{...3.6(a)/Pg 51, DHB}$$

$$= \left[\dfrac{16}{\pi \times 115} \left\{ (2 \times 1.78 \times 10^6) \right. \right.$$

$$\left. \left. + \sqrt{(2 \times 1.78 \times 10^6)^2 + \left(1.5 \times 2.5 \times 10^6 \right)^2} \right\} \right]^{1/3}$$

$$\therefore \qquad d = 72.85 \text{ mm} \qquad \qquad \text{...Eq. (i)}$$

b. According to maximum shear stress theory: For a solid shaft

$$d = \left[\dfrac{16}{\pi \tau_{max}} \left\{ \sqrt{(C_m M)^2 + (C_t T)^2} \right\} \right]^{1/3} \quad \text{...3.6(b)/Pg 51, DHB}$$

$$= \left[\frac{16}{\pi \times 50} \sqrt{(1 \times 1.78 \times 10^6)^2 + (1.5 \times 2.5 \times 10^6)^2} \right]^{1/3}$$

∴ $d = 80.75$ mm ...Eq. (ii)

Based on Eqs. (i) and (ii), select maximum diameter for design, i.e.

$d = 80.75$ mm

∴ Standard size of shaft, $d \approx 80$ mm. **...Tb. 3.5(a)/Pg 57, DHB**

32. **A solid steel shaft of length 1.8 m between bearings rotates at 250 rpm in clockwise direction as seen from right side. A 20° involute spur gear D of 300 mm diameter is located at 150 mm to the left of right hand bearing. Two pulleys B and C are located at distances of 450 mm and 1200 mm respectively to the right of left hand bearing. Pulley B is 600 mm and pulley C is of 750 mm in diameter. The ratio of belt tensions for both pulleys B and C is 2. A power of 29.5 kW is supplied to the gear D by another gear directly below it. At pulley B, a power of 18.5 kW is taken off by means of a belt drive inclined at 60° to the horizontal below the shaft and behind it. The allowable shear stress for shaft material is 40 MPa. The combined shock and fatigue factors for torsion and bending are 1.5 and 2 respectively. Calculate the size of the shaft.**

VTU – Dec. 2009/ Jan. 2010 – 20 Marks

Solution: The layout of the shaft as per given data is shown in **Fig. 5.22(a)**.

$n = 250$ rpm, $\tau = \tau_{max} = 40$ MPa, $C_m = 2$, $C_t = 1.5$, $d = ?$

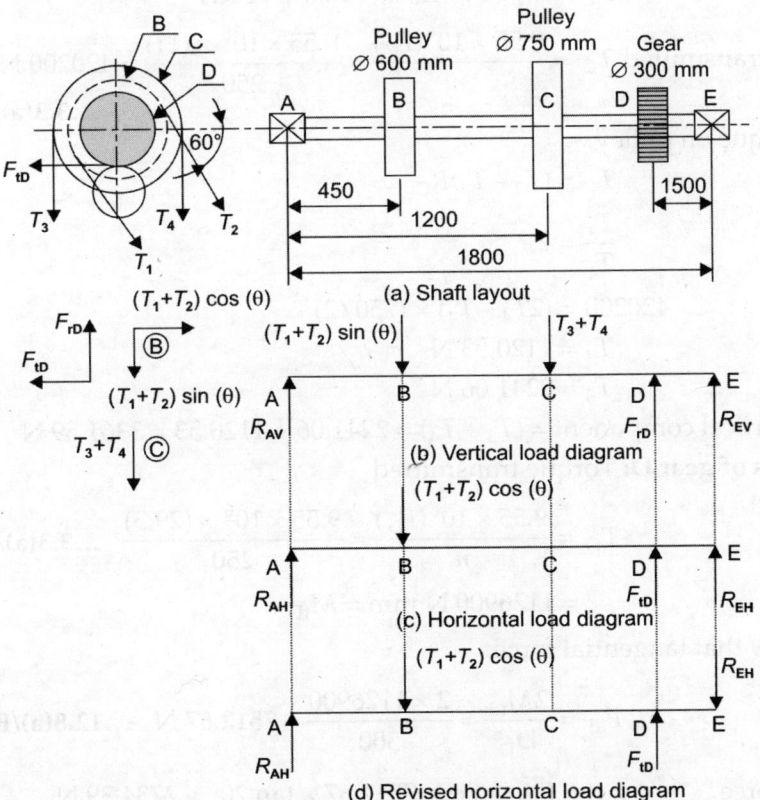

Fig. 5.22: Problem 32

Pulley B: $D_B = 600$ mm, $P_B = 18.5$ kW, $\dfrac{T_1}{T_2} = 2 = \dfrac{T_3}{T_4}$, angle of contact $\theta = 60°$.

Pulley C: $D_C = 750$ mm.

Gear D: $\alpha = 20°$, $D_D = 300$ mm, $P_D = 29.5$ kW.

Analysis of pulley B: Torque transmitted

$$T_B = \frac{9.55 \times 10^6 (P_B)}{n} = \frac{9.55 \times 10^6 \times (18.5)}{250} = 706700 \text{ N} \cdot \text{mm}$$

...3.3(a)/Pg 50, DHB

Also torque on pulley,

$$T_B = (T_1 - T_2) R_B$$

But

$$\frac{T_1}{T_2} = 2 \qquad \text{... (data)}$$

$$706700 = (2T_2 - T_2) \times (600/2)$$

$\therefore$ $\qquad T_2 = 2355.67$ N

and $\qquad T_1 = 4711.34$ N

Thus,

Vertical component $= (T_1 + T_2) \sin\theta = (4711.34 + 2355.67) \times \sin(60°) = 6120.21$ N

Horizontal component $= (T_1 + T_2) \cos\theta = (4711.34 + 2355.67) \times \cos(60°) = 3533.51$ N

Analysis of pulley C: Power available at C,

$$P_C = P_D - P_B = 29.5 - 18.5 = 11 \text{ kW}$$

Torque transmitted $T_C = \dfrac{9.55 \times 10^6 (P_C)}{n} = \dfrac{9.55 \times 10^6 \times (11)}{250} = 420200 \text{ N} \cdot \text{mm}$

...3.3(a)/Pg 50, DHB

Also torque on pulley,

$$T_C = (T_3 - T_4) R_C$$

But $\qquad \dfrac{T_3}{T_4} = 2 \qquad$ ... (data)

$$420200 = (2T_4 - T_4) \times (750/2)$$

$\therefore$ $\qquad T_4 = 1120.53$ N

and $\qquad T_3 = 2241.06$ N

Thus vertical component $= (T_3 + T_4) = 2241.06 + 1120.53 = 3361.59$ N

Analysis of gear D: Torque transmitted

$$T_D = \frac{9.55 \times 10^6 (P_D)}{n} = \frac{9.55 \times 10^6 \times (29.5)}{250} \qquad \text{...3.3(a)/Pg 50, DHB}$$

$$= 1126900 \text{ N·mm} = M_{tD}$$

We know that tangential force,

$$F_{td} = \frac{2M_{td}}{D_D} = \frac{2 \times 1126900}{300} = 7512.67 \text{ N} \quad \text{...12.8(a)/Pg 206, DHB}$$

Radial force, $\qquad F_{rD} = F_{tD} \tan\alpha = 7512.67 \times \tan 20° = 2734.39$ N

...12.8(b)/Pg 206, DHB

To find maximum bending moment:

a. Vertical loading: **Figure 5.22(b)** represents the vertical load diagram.

- Taking moments about bearing 'A', and equating to zero, we have

$$R_{EV}(AE) + F_{rD}(AD) = [(T_1 + T_2)\sin\theta](AB) = (T_3 + T_4)(AC)$$

$$(R_{EV} \times 1800) + (2734.39 \times 1650) = (6120.21 \times 450) + (3361.59 \times 1200)$$

$$\therefore \qquad R_{EV} = 1264.59 \text{ N}$$

Also
$$R_{AV} + F_{rD} + R_{EV} = [(T_1 + T_2)\sin\theta] + (T_3 + T_4)$$

$$R_{AV} + 2734.39 + 1264.59 = 6120.21 + 3361.59$$

$$\therefore \qquad R_{AV} = 5482.82.21 \text{ N}$$

- Moments:

$$M_{AV} = M_{EV} = 0$$

$$M_{BV} = R_{AV}(AB) = 5482.82 \times 450 = 2467269 \text{ N·mm}$$

$$M_{CV} = R_{AV}(AC) - [(T_1 + T_2)\sin\theta](BC)$$

$$= (5482.82 \times 1200) - (6120.21 \times 750) = 1989226.5 \text{ N·mm}$$

$$M_{DV} = R_{EV}(DE) = 1264.59 \times 150 = 189688.5 \text{ N·mm}$$

b. Horizontal loading: **Figure 5.22(c)** represents the horizontal load diagram.

- Taking moments about bearing 'A', and equating to zero, we have

$$R_{EH}(AE) + F_{tD}(AD) = [(T_1 + T_2)\cos\theta](AB)$$

$$(R_{EH} \times 1800) + (7512.67 \times 1650) = (3533.51 \times 450)$$

$$\therefore \qquad R_{EH} = -6003.29 \text{ N}$$

Since the reaction is negative, R_{EH} acts in opposite direction as shown in **Fig. 5.22(d)**.

Thus
$$R_{EH} = 6003.29 \text{ N}$$

Also
$$R_{AH} + F_{tD} = [(T_1 + T_2)\cos\theta] + R_{EH}$$

$$R_{AH} + 7512.67 = 3533.51 + 6003.29$$

$$\therefore \qquad R_{AH} = 2024.13 \text{ N}$$

Moments:

$$M_{AH} = M_{EH} = 0$$

$$M_{BH} = R_{AH}(AB) = 2024.13 \times 450 = 910858.5 \text{ N·mm}$$

$$M_{CH} = R_{AH}(AC) - [(T_1 + T_2)\cos\theta](BC)$$

$$= (2024.13 \times 1200) - (3533.51 \times 750) = -221176.5 \text{ N·mm}$$

$$M_{DH} = -R_{EH}(DE) = -(6003.29 \times 150) = -900493.5 \text{ N·mm}$$

Resultant moment at B,

$$M_B = \sqrt{M_{BV}^2 + M_{BH}^2} = \sqrt{2467269^2 + 910858.5^2}$$

$$= 2630034.23 \text{ N·mm}$$

Resultant moment at C,

$$M_C = \sqrt{M_{CV}^2 + M_{CH}^2} = \sqrt{1989226.5^2 + (-221176.5)^2}$$

$$= 2001484.73 \text{ N·mm}$$

Resultant moment at D,

$$M_D = \sqrt{M_{DV}^2 + M_{DH}^2} = \sqrt{189688.5^2 + (-900493.5)^2}$$

$$= 920255.57 \text{ N·mm}$$

Thus maximum bending moment occurs at 'B', i.e.

$$M_B = M = 2630034.13 \text{ N·mm}$$

and maximum twisting moment occurs at 'D',

$$T_D = T = 1126900 \text{ N·mm}$$

a. **According to maximum shear stress theory:** For a solid shaft

$$d = \left[\frac{16}{\pi \tau_{max}} \left\{ \sqrt{(C_m M)^2 + (C_t T)^2} \right\} \right]^{1/3} \qquad \text{...3.6(b)/Pg 51, DHB}$$

$$= \left[\frac{16}{\pi \times 40} \sqrt{(2 \times 2630034.13)^2 + (1.5 \times 1126900)^2} \right]^{1/3}$$

$$\therefore \qquad d = 88.93 \text{ mm}$$

∴ Standard size of shaft, $d \approx 90$ mm.   **...Tb. 3.5(a)/Pg 57, DHB**

33. **A power transmission shaft 1800 mm long, is supported at two points A and B. Whereas A is at a distance of 300 mm from the left extreme end of the shaft, B is at right extreme end. A power of 50 kW is received at 500 rpm, through a gear drive located at the left extreme end of the shaft. The gear mounted on the shaft here, has a pitch diameter of 300 mm and weighs 700 N. The driver gear is located exactly behind. 30 kW of this power is given out through a belt drive located at a distance of 600 mm from the left support. The pulley mounted on the shaft has as diameter of 400 mm and weighs 1000 N. The belt is directed towards the observer below the horizontal and inclined at 45° to it. The ratio of belt tensions is 3. The remaining power is given out through a gear drive located at a distance of 400 mm from the right support. The driver gear has a pitch diameter of 200 mm and weighs 500 N. The driven gear is located exactly above. Selecting C40 steel (σ_y = 328 MPa and assuming a factor of safety of 3, determine the diameter of a solid shaft for the purpose. Take k_b = 1.75, k_t = 1.5 and pressure angle α = 20° for both the gears.**

VTU – May/ June 2010 – 20 Marks

Solution: The layout of the shaft as per given data is shown in **Fig. 5.23(a).**

n = 500 rpm, σ_y = 328.6 MPa, FoS = 3, d = ?, α = 20°, τ = τ_{max} = 40 MPa, $C_m = k_b = 1.75$, $C_t = k_t = 1.5$.

Gear C: P_C = 50 kW, D_C = 300 mm, W_C = 700 N.

Pulley D: P_D = 30 kW, D_D = 400 mm, W_D = 1000 N, angle of contact θ = 45°, $\dfrac{T_1}{T_2}$ = 3.

Gear E: D_E = 200 mm., W_E = 500 N

Design stresses:

$$\sigma_{max} = \frac{\sigma_{yt}}{FoS} = \frac{328.6}{3} = 109.53 \text{ MPa}$$

$$\tau_{max} = \frac{\sigma_{max}}{2} = \frac{109.53}{2} = 54.77 \text{ MPa}$$

Assuming that the keyway effect is included in the above values, we have

$$\sigma_{max-1} = \sigma_{max} = 109.53 \text{ MPa}$$

$$\tau_{max-1} = \tau_{max} = 54.77 \text{ MPa}$$

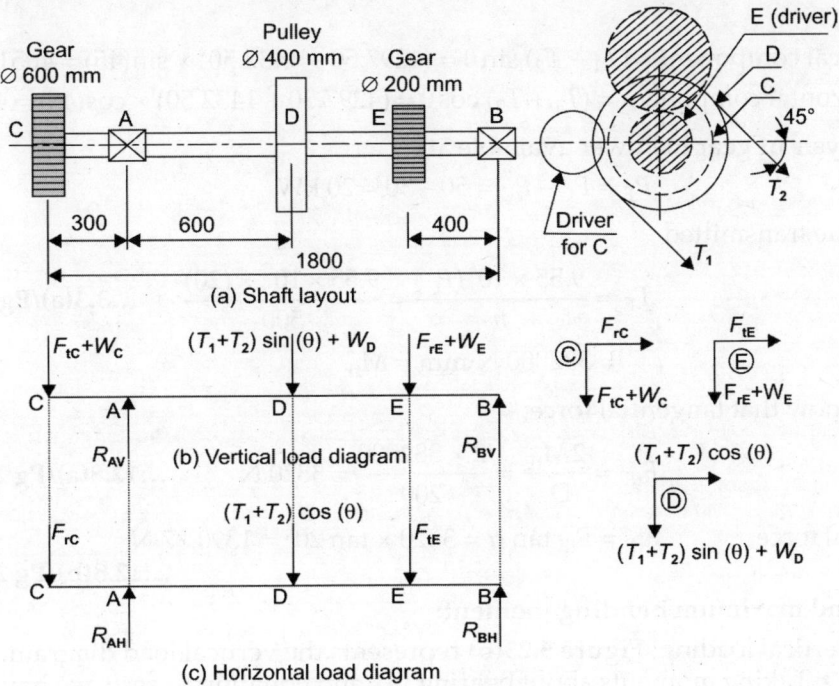

(a) Shaft layout

(b) Vertical load diagram

(c) Horizontal load diagram

Fig. 5.23: Problem 33

Analysis of gear C: Torque transmitted

$$T_D = \frac{9.55 \times 10^6 (P_D)}{n} = \frac{9.55 \times 10^6 \times (50)}{500} \qquad \text{...3.3(a)/Pg 50, DHB}$$

$$= 955000 \text{ N·mm} = M_{tC}$$

We know that tangential force,

$$F_{tC} = \frac{2M_{tC}}{D_C} = \frac{2 \times 955000}{300} = 6366.67 \text{ N} \qquad \text{...12.8(a)/Pg 206, DHB}$$

Radial force, $\qquad F_{rC} = F_{tC} \tan \alpha = 6366.67 \times \tan 20 = 2317.28 \text{ N}$

$$\text{...12.8(b)/Pg 206, DHB}$$

Analysis of pulley D: Torque transmitted

$$T_D = \frac{9.55 \times 10^6 (P_D)}{n} = \frac{9.55 \times 10^6 \times (30)}{500} \qquad \text{...3.3(a)/Pg 50, DHB}$$

$$= 573000 \text{ N·mm} = M_{tD}$$

Also torque on pulley,

$$T_D = (T_1 - T_2)R_D$$

But $\qquad\qquad \dfrac{T_1}{T_2} = 3 \qquad\qquad\qquad\qquad\qquad\qquad \text{... (data)}$

$$573000 = (3T_2 - T_2) \times (400/2)$$

$\therefore \qquad\qquad\qquad T_2 = 1432.50 \text{ N}$

and $\qquad\qquad\qquad T_1 = 4297.50 \text{ N}$

Thus,

Vertical component $= (T_1 + T_2) \sin \theta = (4297.50 + 1432.50) \times \sin(45) = 4051.72$ N

Horizontal component $= (T_1 + T_2) \cos \theta = (4297.50 + 1432.50) \times \cos(45) = 4051.72$ N

Analysis of gear E: Power available at C,

$$P_E = P_C - P_D = 50 - 30 = 20 \text{ kW}$$

Torque transmitted

$$T_E = \frac{9.55 \times 10^6 (P_C)}{n} = \frac{9.55 \times 10^6 \times (20)}{500} \qquad \textbf{...3.3(a)/Pg 50, DHB}$$

$$= 382000 \text{ N·mm} = M_{tE}$$

We know that tangential force,

$$F_{tE} = \frac{2M_{tE}}{D_E} = \frac{2 \times 382000}{200} = 3820 \text{ N} \qquad \textbf{...12.8(a)/Pg 206, DHB}$$

Radial force, $F_{rE} = F_{tE} \tan \alpha = 3820 \times \tan 20° = 1390.37$ N

$$\textbf{...12.8(b)/Pg 206, DHB}$$

To find maximum bending moment:

a. **Vertical loading: Figure 5.23(b)** represents the vertical load diagram.
- Taking moments about bearing 'A', and equating to zero, we have

$$R_{BV}(AB) + (F_{tC} + W_C)(CA) = [(T_1 + T_2) \sin \theta + W_D] (AD)$$
$$+ (F_{rE} + W_E)(AE)$$

$$(R_{BV} \times 1500) + (6366.67 + 700) \times 300 = (4051.72 + 1000) \times 600$$
$$+ (1390.37 + 500) \times 1100$$

$$\therefore \qquad R_{BV} = 1993.63 \text{ N}$$

Also $R_{AV} + R_{BV} = (F_{tC} + W_C) + [(T_1 + T_2) \sin \theta + W_D](AD)$
$$+ (F_{rE} + W_E)(AE)$$

$$R_{AV} + 1993.63 = (6366.67 + 700) + (4051.72 + 1000)$$
$$+ (1390.37 + 500)$$

$$\therefore \qquad R_{AV} = 12015.13 \text{ N}$$

- Moments:

$$M_{CV} = M_{BV} = 0$$

$$M_{AV} = -(F_{tC} + W_C)(CA) = (6366.67 + 700) \times 300 = -2120001 \text{ N·mm}$$

$$M_{DV} = -(F_{tC} + W_C)(CD) + R_{AV}(AD)$$

$$= -[(6366.67 + 700) \times 900] + (12015.13 \times 600) = 849075 \text{ N·mm}$$

$$M_{EV} = R_{EV}(BE) = 1993.63 \times 400 = 797452 \text{ N·mm}$$

b. **Horizontal loading: Figure 5.23(c)** represents the horizontal load diagram.
- Taking moments about bearing 'A', and equating to zero, we have

$$R_{BH}(AB) = [(T_1 + T_2) \cos \theta](AD)$$
$$+ F_{tE}(AE) + F_{rC}(CA)$$

$$(R_{BH} \times 1500) + (4051.72 \times 600) + (3820 \times 1100) = (2317.28 \times 300)$$

$$\therefore \qquad R_{BH} = 3958.57 \text{ N}$$

Also
$$R_{AH} + R_{BH} = [(T_1 + T_2)\cos\theta] + F_{tE} + F_{rC}$$
$$R_{AH} + 3958.57 = 4051.72 + 3820 + 2317.28$$
$$\therefore \qquad R_{AH} = 6230.43 \text{ N}$$

- **Moments:**

$$M_{CH} = M_{BH} = 0$$
$$M_{AH} = -F_{rC}(CA) = -(2317.28 \times 300) = -695184 \text{ N·mm}$$
$$M_{DH} = -F_{rC}(CD) + R_{AH}(AD) = -(2317.28 \times 900) + (6230.43 \times 600)$$
$$= 1652706 \text{ N·mm}$$
$$M_{EH} = R_{BH}(BE) = (3958.57 \times 400) = 1583428 \text{ N·mm}$$

Resultant moment at A,

$$M_A = \sqrt{M_{AV}^2 + M_{AH}^2} = \sqrt{(-2120001)^2 + (-695184)^2}$$
$$= 2231072.62 \text{ N·mm}$$

Resultant moment at D,

$$M_D = \sqrt{M_{DV}^2 + M_{DH}^2} = \sqrt{849075^2 + 1652706^2}$$
$$= 1858054.22 \text{ N·mm}$$

Resultant moment at E,

$$M_E = \sqrt{M_{EV}^2 + M_{EH}^2} = \sqrt{797452^2 + (1583428)^2}$$
$$= 1772900 \text{ N·mm}$$

Thus maximum bending moment occurs at 'A', i.e.

$$M_A = M = 2231072.62 \text{ N·mm}$$

and maximum twisting moment occurs at 'C',

$$T_C = T = 955000 \text{ N·mm}$$

a. **According to maximum normal stress theory:** For a solid shaft

$$d = \left[\frac{16}{\pi \tau_{max-1}} \left\{ C_m M + \sqrt{(C_m M)^2 + (C_t T)^2} \right\} \right]^{1/3}$$

...3.6(a)/Pg 51, DHB

$$= \left[\frac{16}{\pi \times 109.53} \left\{ (1.75 \times 2231072.62) \right. \right.$$
$$\left. \left. + \sqrt{(1.75 \times 2231072.62)^2 + (1.5 \times 955000)^2} \right\} \right]^{1/3}$$

$$\therefore \qquad d = 72.11 \text{ mm} \qquad \qquad \text{...Eq. (i)}$$

b. **According to maximum shear stress theory:** For a solid shaft

$$d = \left[\frac{16}{\pi \tau_{max-1}} \left\{ \sqrt{(C_m M)^2 + (C_t T)^2} \right\} \right]^{1/3} \quad \text{...3.6(b)/Pg 51, DHB}$$

$$= \left[\frac{16}{\pi \times 54.77} \sqrt{(1.75 \times 2231072.62)^2 + (1.5 \times 955000)^2} \right]^{1/3}$$

$$\therefore \qquad d = 72.86 \text{ mm} \qquad \qquad \text{...Eq. (ii)}$$

Based on Eqs. (i) and (ii), select maximum diameter for design, i.e.

$$d = 72.86 \text{ mm}$$

∴ Standard size of shaft, $d \approx 80$ mm. **...Tb. 3.5(a)/Pg 57, DHB**

34. **A hollow propeller shaft of 0.6 m outside diameter and 0.3 m inside diameter is used to drive a propeller of a marine vessel. The shaft is mounted in bearings 5 m apart and it transmits 6 MW power at 100 rpm. The maximum propeller thrust is 600 kN and shaft weighs 60 kN. Determine:**

   a. Maximum shear stress developed in the shaft and

   b. Angle of twist of the shaft between the bearings.

   Assume the modulus of rigidity as 84 GPa.

VTU – June/ July 2013 – 12 Marks

Solution: $d_o = 600$ mm, $d_i = 300$ mm, $K = d_i/d_o = 300/600 = 0.5$, $L = 5000$ mm, $P = 6000$ kW, $n = 100$ rpm, $F = 600 \times 10^3$ N, $W = 60 \times 10^3$ N, $\tau_{max} = ?$, $\theta = ?$

a. To find τ_{max}: According to maximum shear stress theory, outside diameter of shaft is found as:

$$d_o = \left[\frac{16}{\pi \tau_{max}} \left\{ \sqrt{\left(C_m M + \frac{\alpha F d_o (1 + K^2)}{8} \right) + (C_t T)^2} \right\} \frac{1}{1 - K^4} \right]^{1/3}$$

... Eq. (i) 3.6(a)/Pg 51, DHB

$$T = \frac{9.55 \times 10^6 (P)}{n} = \frac{9.55 \times 10^6 \times (6000)}{100} = 573 \times 10^6 \text{ N·mm}$$

... 3.3(a)/Pg 50, DHB

$$M = \frac{WL}{8}, \text{ for a simply supported beam with udl over entire span}$$

... Tb. 1.4, Fig. 6/Pg 16, DHB

$$M = \frac{60 \times 10^3 \times 5000}{8} = 37.5 \times 10^6 \text{ N·mm}$$

$$k = \sqrt{\frac{1}{k}} = \frac{\sqrt{(d_o^2 + d_i^2)}}{4} = \frac{\sqrt{600^2 + 300^2}}{4} = 167.71 \text{ mm}$$

...Tb. 1.3(a), Fig. h/Pg 13, DHB

$$\frac{L}{k} = \frac{5000}{167.71} = 29.81 < 115$$

$$\alpha = \frac{1}{1 - 0.0044(L/k)} \quad \text{for } L/k < 115$$

$$= \frac{1}{1 - (0.0044 \times 29.81)}$$

$$\alpha = 1.15$$

Assume $C_m = 1.5$ and $C_t = 1.0$ **...Tb. 3.1/Pg 56, DHB**

$$\text{Now,} \left[C_m M + \frac{\alpha F d_o (1 + K^2)}{8} \right] = \left[(1.5 \times 37.5 \times 10^6) \right.$$

$$\left. + \frac{1.15 \times 600 \times 10^3 \times 600(1 + 0.5)^2}{8} \right] = 121 \times 10^6$$

∴ Eq. (i) yields...

$$(600)^3 = \left[\frac{16}{\pi\tau_{max}} \left\{ \sqrt{(121 \times 10^6)^2 + (1 \times 573 \times 10^6)^2} \right\} \left(\frac{1}{1 - 0.5^4} \right) \right]$$

$$\tau_{max} = 14.72 \text{ MPa}$$

b. To find θ: We know that

$$\theta = \frac{584TL}{G(d_o^4 - d_i^4)} = \frac{584 \times (573 \times 10^6) \times 5000}{(84 \times 10^3) \times (600^4 - 300^4)} = 0.164 \text{ deg}$$

... 3.2/Pg 50, DHB

VTU QUESTION PAPERS

Mar. 2001 (ME5T2)

1. a. What is meant by cold-rolling shafting and hot rolled T and G shafting?
   (04 Marks)

   b. A horizontal piece of commercial shafting is supported by two bearings 1.5 m apart. A keyed gear, 20° involute and 175 mm in diameter, is located 400 mm to the left of right bearing and is driven by a gear directly behind it. A 600 mm diameter pulley is keyed to the shaft 600 mm to the right of left bearing and drives a pulley with a horizontal belt directly behind it. The tension ratio of the belt is 3:1, with a slack on top side. The drive transmits 45 kW at 330 rpm. Take $K_s = 1.5$. Calculate the necessary shaft diameter and angular deflection in degrees. Use allowable shear stress of 40 MPa and $G = 80$ GPa. **(16 Marks)**

July/Aug. 2004 (AU46)

2. A steel shaft 900 mm long between bearings receives a power of 18 kW at 900 rpm through a 20° involute spur gear of 200 mm diameter located 250 mm to the right of left hand bearing by a gear directly below the shaft. This power is transmitted by a 400 mm diameter pulley to another pulley, which is behind the shaft and above it. The belt drive axis is inclined at 60° to the horizontal. The pulley is located at a distance of 250 mm to the left of right hand bearing. The angle of lap of the belt is 1800° and the coefficient of friction is 0.3. The shaft rotates in clockwise direction as seen from the left side bearing. Design the shaft diameter if the allowable shear stress for the shaft material is 60 MPa. **(20 Marks)**

3. Design the shaft of the armature of a motor, if the magnetic pull on the shaft is equivalent to an uniformly distributed load of 10 N per mm length over the middle one-third of the 600 mm length of the shaft between bearings. The motor transmits a power of 15 kW at 1200 rpm. The allowable shear stress is 50 MPa. Take $C_m = 1.5$ and $C_t = 1.25$. **(10 Marks)**

Jan/Feb. 2005 (AU46)

4. Machine shaft turning at 600 rev/min is supported on bearings 750 mm and 15 kN is supplied to the shaft through a 450 mm pulley located 250 mm to the right of right bearing. The power is transmitted from a shaft through a 200 mm spur gear located 250 mm to the right of left bearing. The drive is at an angle of 60° above the horizontal. The pulley weighs 800 N and provides some flywheel effects. The ratio of belt tensions is 3:1. The gear has a 20° tooth form and mates with another gear located directly above the shaft. If the shaft material selected has an ultimate

strength of 500 MN/m² and yield point of 310 MN/m², determine the necessary diameter. Use $K_b = 1.5$ and $K_t = 1.0$. **(20 Marks)**

July/Aug. 2005 (AU46)

5. A power transmission shaft 1500 mm long is supported at two points A and B, while A is at a distance of 500 mm from the left extreme end of the shaft, B is at the right extreme end of the shaft. The shaft receives a power of 40 kW through a gear drive located at the left extreme end of the shaft at a rated speed of 500 rpm. The gear mounted on the shaft to be designed here has a pitch diameter of 200 mm and weighs 500 N. The gear meshing with this gear is placed behind such that the line of centers is directed away from the observer below the horizontal and inclined at 30° to it. The gear tooth is having a pressure angle of 20°. This power is given out through a belt drive located at a distance of 400 mm from the right support. The belt pulley has a pitch diameter of 350 mm and weighs 800 N. The belt moving on the pulley is directed towards observer below the horizontal and inclined at 45° to it. The ratio of belt tensions may be taken as 3. Selecting carbon steel C40 as a material for the shaft and choosing a value of 2.5 for the factor of safety, determine the diameters of the hollow shaft assuming its inner diameter to be 0.6 times the outer diameter. **(20 Marks)**

6. Determine the diameter of a solid circular shaft to transmit a power of 50 kW at a rated speed of 1000 rpm selecting a suitable material and choosing an appropriate value for factor of safety. Replace this solid shaft by a hollow circular shaft assuming the value of 0.6 for the ratio of diameters selecting the same material and the same factor of safety. As the consequences of this replacement, determine:
   a. Percentage of reduction in weight assuming same length for the shafts.
   b. The ratio of torsional stiffness of the hollow shaft to that of the solid shaft. **(08 Marks)**

Jan/Feb. 2006 (AU46)

7. A shaft is supported by two bearings placed 1.2 m apart. A 600 mm diameter pulley is mounted at a distance of 300 mm to the right of left hand bearing and this drives a pulley directly below it with the help of a belt having a maximum tension of 2 kN. Another pulley 400 mm diameter is placed 200 mm to the left of right hand bearing and is driven with the help of electric motor and belt, which is placed horizontally to the right. The angle of contact for both the pulleys is 180° and $\mu = 0.25$. Determine the suitable diameter for a solid shaft, allowing working stress of 63 MPa in tension and 42 MPa in shear for the material of the shaft. Assume that the torque on one pulley is equal to that on the other pulley. **(20 Marks)**

8. A hoisting drum of 0.5 m diameter is keyed to a shaft which is supported in two bearings and driven through a 12:1 reduction ratio by an electric motor. Determine the power of the driving motor, if the maximum load of 8 kN is hoisted at a speed of 50 m/min and the efficiency of the drive is 80%. Also determine the torque on the drum shaft and the speed of the motor in rpm. Determine also the diameter of the shaft made of machinery steel, the working stresses of which are 115 MPa in tension and 50 MPa in shear. The drive gear whose diameter is 450 mm is mounted at the end of the shaft such that it overhangs the nearest bearing by 150 mm. The combined shock and fatigue factors for bending and torsion may be taken as 2 and 1.5 respectively. **(20 Marks)**

July 2006 (AU46)

9. A power transmission shaft 1500 mm long is supported at two points A and B. While A is at the left extreme end of the shaft, B is at a distance of 400 from the right extreme end of the shaft. The shaft receives a power of 50 kW at a rated speed of 500 rpm through a belt drive located at the right extreme end of the shaft. The belt pulley has a diameter of 400 mm and weighs 1 kN. The belts moving on the pulley is directed away from the observer below the horizontal and inclined at 45° to it. The ratio of belt tensions is 3. This power is given out through a gear drive located at a distance of 500 mm from the right support B. The gear mounted on the shaft has a pitch diameter of 200 mm and weighs 400 N. The other gear, which meshes with this gear is placed exactly in front. The gear teeth have a pressure angle of 20°. Selecting a suitable material and choosing an appropriate value of factor of safety, determine the diameter of the solid circular shaft required for power transmission. **(20 Marks)**

10. A shaft of a motor is supported at two points which are 800 mm apart. The armature of the motor can be considered as a uniformly distributed load of 15 N/mm, centrally spread over a length of 500 mm. Selecting a suitable material and choosing appropriate value for the factor of safety, determine the diameter of the motor shaft. The motor develops 15 kW at 1500 rpm. **(12 Marks)**

Dec. 06/Jan. 2007 (AU46)

11. A steel shaft 950 mm long supported between bearings 750 mm apart, has a cast iron pulley 600 mm diameter, weighing 800 N overhanging to the right of bearing by 200 mm as shown in **Fig. U5.1**. The pulley receives 25 kW at 1000 rpm from a belt drive; the belt is inclined at 60° to the horizontal (inclined upwards). The power from the shaft is transmitted through a 14½° spur pinion of diameter 200 mm to a spur gear mounted directly above the pinion. The pinion is keyed to the shaft at a distance of 150 mm to the right of left bearing. Taking the ratio of belt tension as 3:1, ultimate stress and yield stress for the material of the shaft as 500 MPa and 310 MPa respectively. Determine the diameter of the shaft. Use $K_b = 2$ and $K_t = 1.5$. **(20 Marks)**

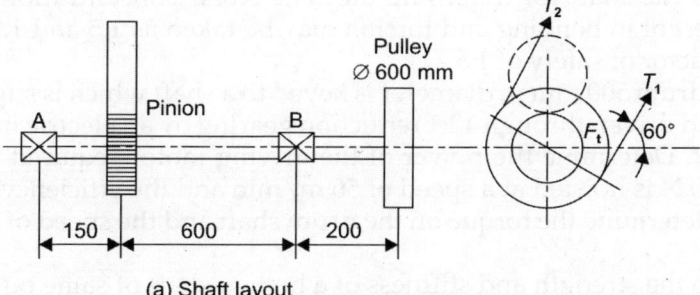

(a) Shaft layout

Fig. U5.1

July 2007 (AU46)

12. A pulley is keyed to a shaft midway between two antifriction bearings. The bending moment at the pulley varies from –170 N·m to 510 N·m as the torsional moment in the shaft varies from 55 N·m to 165 N·m. The frequency of the variation of the loads is same as the shaft speed. The shaft is made of cold drawn steel having an ultimate strength of 538 MPa and yield strength of 400 MPa. Determine the

required diameter for an indefinite life. The stress concentration factor for the keyway in bending and torsion may be taken as 1.6 and 1.3 respectively. Use design factor of 1.5. **(12 Marks)**

13. A hollow C15 steel shaft transmits 15 kW at 250 rpm. It is supported on two bearings 750 mm apart. A 500 diameter pulley whose weight is 1000 N is keyed to the shaft at a distance of 100 mm to the left of left hand bearing. A pinion having 75 teeth and 4 mm module is mounted at 150 mm to the left of right hand bearing. The pulley is driven by a belt downward at an angle of 60° to the horizontal and towards the observer. The pinion drives a gear placed directly over it. Ratio of belt tension is 3, diameter ratio is 2. Use ASME code, assume suddenly applied load with minor shock. Consider keyway effect. Assume the shaft rotates in clockwise direction when viewed from the right bearing. Determine the size of the shaft. Assume pressure angle = 20°. **(20 Marks)**

Dec. 07/Jan. 2008 (AU46)

14. A horizontal piece of commercial shafting is supported by two bearings 1.5 m apart. A keyed gear, 20° involute and 175 mm in diameter, is located 400 mm to the left of right bearing and is driven by a gear directly behind it. A 600 mm diameter pulley is keyed to the shaft 600 mm to the right of left bearing and drives a pulley with a horizontal belt directly behind it. The tension ratio of the belt is 3:1, with a slack on top side. The drive transmits 45 kW at 330 rpm. Take $K_s = K_t = 1.5$. Calculate the necessary shaft diameter and angular deflection in degrees. Use allowable shear stress of 40 MPa and $G = 80$ GPa. **(20 Marks)**

June/July 2008 (AU46)

15. A pulley is mounted on a shaft midway between two bearings. The bending moment at the pulley varies from 200 N·m to 600 N·m and the torsional moment varies from 60 N·m to 180 N·m. The frequency of variation of loads is the same as that of the shaft speed. The shaft is made of cold drawn steel having an ultimate strength of 550 MPa and yield strength of 400 MPa. Determine the required diameter of the shaft for indefinite life. The stress concentration factor for the keyway present in bending and torsion may be taken as 1.5 and 1.2 respectively. Assume a factor of safety of 1.5. **(12 Marks)**

16. A hoisting drum 500 mm in diameter is keyed to a shaft which is supported in two bearings and driven through 12:1 reduction gearing by an electric motor as shown in **Fig. U5.2**. Determine the power of the driving motor required if a maximum load of 8000 N is hoisted at a speed of 50 m/min and the efficiency of the drive is 80%. Also determine the torque on the drum shaft and the speed of the motor. **(12 Marks)**

17. a. Compare the strength and stiffness of a hollow shaft of same outside diameter as that of a solid shaft. **(06 Marks)**
    b. A shaft 900 mm between the bearings supports a 600 mm diameter pulley 300 mm to the right of left hand bearing. The belt drives the pulley directly below it. Another pulley 450 mm in diameter is located 200 mm to the left of right hand bearing and the belt is driven from a pulley horizontally to the right. The angle of lap on both the pulleys is 180° and the tension ratio is 2.2. The maximum tension in the belt on 600 mm diameter pulley is 2250 N. Determine the suitable diameter for the solid shaft assuming allowable stresses in bending and torsion as 63 MPa and 42 MPa respectively. **(14 Marks)**

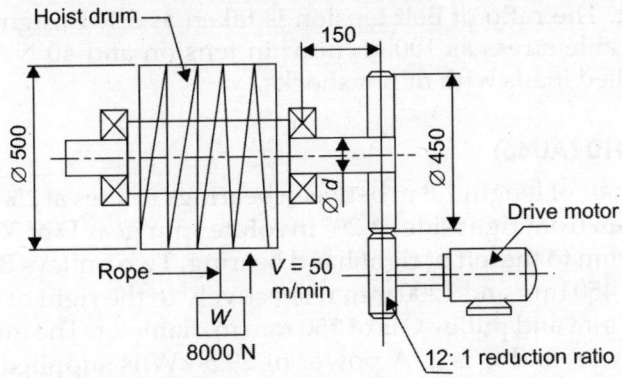

Fig. U5.2

Dec. 08/Jan. 2009 (06ME/AU52)

18. a. Compare the strength of a hollow shaft with that of a solid shaft for the same diameter and material. The diameter ratio of hollow shaft is 0.75.   **(06 Marks)**
    b. A steel shaft (C45) transmitting 15 kW at 210 rpm is supported between two bearings 1000 mm apart. On this two spur gears are mounted. The gear having 80 teeth of module 6 mm is located 100 mm to the left of right bearing and receives power from a driving gear such that the tangential force acts vertical. The pinion having 24 teeth and module 6 mm is located 200 mm to the right of left bearing and delivers power to a gear mounted behind it. Taking combined shock and fatigue factors 1.75 in bending and 1.25 in torsion, determine the shaft diameter.   **(14 Marks)**

June/July 2009 (AU46)

19. A shaft supported between bearings 400 mm apart gets its drive through a gear drive. A gear is mounted 200 mm to the right of the left hand bearing and is driven by a pinion just above it. The gear has a module of 10 mm, number of teeth is equal to 40 and pressure angle $\varphi = 20°$. The power received is 20 kW at 500 rpm. Overhanging to the right hand bearing by 200 mm there is a pulley of diameter 200 mm; the belt drive is inclined at an angle of 30^0 with the vertical and is away from the shaft. The ratio of belt tension is taken as 3. Design a shaft assuming the allowable stress as 100 N/mm² in tension and compression and 40 N/mm² in shear.   **(20 Marks)**

20. A hoisting drum of 500 mm diameter is keyed on to a shaft and is for lifting a load of 20 kN at a velocity of 31.4 m/minute. The shaft is supported on two bearings and carries a gear of 400 mm diameter, overhanging the nearest bearing by 200 mm (200 mm to the right of right bearing). The gear ratio is 12:1. Determine the power and rpm of the motor required assuming a driving efficiency of 90%.   **(08 Marks)**

June/July 2009 (06ME52)

21. A shaft supported between bearings 400 mm apart gets its drive through a gear drive. A gear is mounted 200 mm to the right of left hand bearing and is driven by a pinion just above it. The gear has a module of 10 mm, number of teeth is equal to 40 and pressure angle is $\varphi = 20°$, the power received is 20 kW at 500 rpm. Overhanging to the right hand bearing by 200 mm, there is a pulley of diameter 200 mm. The belt drive is inclined at an angle of 30° with the vertical and is away

from the shaft. The ratio of belt tension is taken as 3:1. Design a shaft assuming that the allowable stress as 100 N/mm^2 in tension and 40 N/mm^2 in shear for suddenly applied loads with minor shocks. **(20 Marks)**

Dec. 2009/Jan. 2010 (AU46)

22. A solid steel shaft of length 1.8 m between bearings rotates at 250 rpm in clockwise direction as seen from right side. A 20° involute spur gear D of 300 mm diameter is located at 150 mm to the left of right hand bearing. Two pulleys B and C are located at distances of 450 mm and 1200 mm respectively to the right of left hand bearing. Pulley B is 600 mm and pulley C is of 750 mm in diameter. The ratio of belt tensions for both pulleys B and C is 2. A power of 29.5 kW is supplied to the gear D by another gear directly below it. At pulley B a power of 18.5 kW is taken off by means off a belt drive inclined at 60° to the horizontal below the shaft and behind it. The allowable shear stress for shaft material is 40 MPa. The combined shock and fatigue factors for tension and bending are 1.5 and 2 respectively. Calculate the size of the shaft. **(20 Marks)**

Dec. 2009/Jan. 2010 (06ME52)

23. A shaft is supported between two bearings located 0.6 m apart. Gear 'A' of pitch circle diameter 0.1 m is keyed to the shaft 0.1 m to the right of the left bearing. Gear 'B' of 0.15 m diameter is keyed to the shaft 0.3 m to the right of left bearing. Another gear 'C' of pitch circle diameter 0.08 m is keyed to the shaft 0.1 m to the left of right bearing. Gear 'B' receives 10 kW power at 500 rpm from a mating gear mounted directly below it. Gear 'A' delivers 6 kW power to another gear mounted directly in front of it, such that the tangential force acts vertically upwards. Gear 'C' delivers the remaining power to its mating gear mounted directly behind it such that the tangential force acts vertically downwards. All gears are of 20° full depth involute form. The shaft is made of steel which has an ultimate strength of 510 MPa and a yield strength of 330 MPa. Determine the required diameter if the shaft under steady load condition using ASME code. **(20 Marks)**

May/June 2010 (06ME52)

24. A power transmission shaft 1800 mm long, is supported at two points A and B. Whereas A is at a distance of 300 mm from the left extreme end of the shaft, B is at right extreme end. A power of 50 kW is received at 500 rpm, through a gear drive located at the left extreme end of the shaft. The gear mounted on the shaft here, has a pitch diameter of 300 mm and weighs 700 N. The driver gear is located exactly behind. 30 kW of this power is given out through a belt drive located at a distance of 600 mm from the left support. The pulley mounted on the shaft has a diameter of 400 mm and weighs 1000 N. The belt is directed towards the observer below the horizontal and inclined at 45° to it. The ratio of belt tensions is 3. The remaining power is given out through a gear drive located at a distance of 400 mm from the right support. The driver gear has a pitch diameter of 200 mm and weighs 500 N. The driven gear is located exactly above. Selecting C40 steel (σ_y = 328.6 MPa) and assuming a factor of safety of 3, determine the diameter of a solid shaft for the purpose. Take k_o = 1.75, k_t =1.5 and pressure angle φ = 20° for both the gears. **(20 Marks)**

Dec. 2010 (AU46)

25. A shaft is driven by means of a motor, placed vertically below it, as shown in **Fig. U5.3**. The diameter of the pulley is 1.5 m and has belt tensions 5.4 kN and 1.8 kN on tight and slack sides of the belt respectively. Find the diameter of the shaft, assuming a maximum allowable shear stress of 42 MPa. **(10 Marks)**

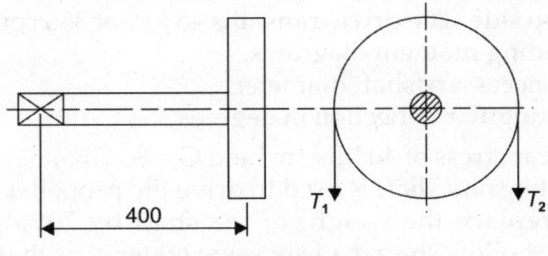

Fig. U5.3

26. A transmission shaft is carrying a spur gear and a pulley. This shaft is mounted on two bearings placed at a distance of 800 mm. Gear is mounted on the shaft in between these bearings at center and pulley overhang to the right side bearing to a distance of 400 mm. The diameters of the pulley and the gear are 450 mm and 300 mm respectively. Pulley receives the power from the motor, placed below it, while the gear delivers 20 kW at 500 rpm to another gear just placed above it. The shaft is made of commercial cold rolled steel with allowable shear stress of 122.5 MPa. Determine the shaft diameter if the shaft is subjected to gradually applied loads. **(20 Marks)**

Dec. 2010 (06ME52)

27. A horizontal steel shaft, supported on bearings $A$$A$ at the left end and B at the right end, carries two gears C and D, located at distances 250 mm and 400 mm respectively from the center lines of left and right end bearings. The pitch diameter of gear C is 600 mm and that of gear D is 200 mm. The pressure angle is 20°. The distance between the center lines of the bearings is 2400 mm. The shaft transmits 20 kW power at 120 rpm. The power is delivered to the shaft at gear C and is taken out at gear D in such a manner that the tooth pressures F_{+C} and F_{+D} of gears C and D act vertically downwards. Find the diameter of the shaft, if the working stresses are 100 MPa in tension and 56 MPa in shear. The gears C and D weigh 950 N and 350 N respectively. Take $C_m = 1.5$ and $C_x = 1.2$. **(20 Marks)**

June/July 2011 (06ME52)

28. A hoisting drum of 0.5 m is diameter is keyed to a shaft which is supported in two bearings and driven through a 12:1 reduction ratio by an electric motor. Determine the power of the driving motor, if the maximum load of 8 kN is hoisted at a speed of 50 m/min and the efficiency of the drive is 80%. Also determine the torque on the drum shaft and the speed of the motor in rpm. Determine also the diameter of the shaft made of machinery steel, the working stresses of which are 115 MPa in tension and 50 MPa in shear. The drive gear whose diameter is 450 mm is mounted at the end of the shaft such that it overhangs the nearest bearing by 150 mm. The combined shock and fatigue factors for bending and torsion may be taken as 2 and 1.5 respectively. **(20 Marks)**

Dec. 2011 (AU46)

29. A horizontal piece of commercial shafting is supported by two bearings 1.5 m apart. A keyed gear, 20° involute and 175 mm in diameter, is located 400 mm to the left of right bearing and is driven by a gear directly behind it. A 600 mm diameter pulley is keyed to the shaft 600 mm to the right of left bearing and drives a pulley with a horizontal belt directly behind it. The tension ratio of the belt is 3:1, with a slack on top side. The drive transmits 45 kW at 330 rpm. Take $K_b = K_t = 1.5$.
    i. Draw the bending moment diagrams.
    ii. Calculate the necessary shaft diameter.
    iii. Calculate the angular deflection in degrees.

    Use allowable shear stress of 40 MN/m² and G = 80 GPa. **(20 Marks)**

30. A 250 mm diameter solid shaft is used to drive the propeller of a marine vessel. It is necessary to replace the weight of the shaft by 70%. What would be the dimensions of the hollow shaft made of same material as that of solid shaft?
    (10 Marks)

Dec. 2011 (06ME52)

31. A horizontal piece of commercial shafting is supported by two bearings 1.5 m apart. A keyed gear 20° involute and 175 mm diameter, is located 400 mm to the left of the right bearing and is driven by a gear directly behind it. A 600 mm diameter pulley is keyed to the shaft 600 mm to the right of the left bearing and drives a another pulley by means of a belt drive inclined at 45° to the horizontal below the shaft and in front of it. The tension ratio of the belt is 3:1. The drive transmits 45 kW at 330 rpm CW when viewed from right side. The allowable shear stress for shaft material is 40 MPa. The combined shock and fatigue factors for torsion and bending are 1.5 and 2.0 respectively. Draw the moment diagrams and calculate the necessary shaft diameter. **(20 Marks)**

June 2012 (06ME52/06AU52)

32. A transmission shaft running at 500 rev/min is supported on bearings 800 mm apart. 20 kW power is supplied to the shaft through a 450 mm diameter pulley which is located 400 mm to the right of right bearing and receives power from a motor placed directly below the shaft. The shaft further transmits this power to spur gear of 300 mm pitch circle diameter, which is located 400 mm to the right of left bearing. The gear has 20° involute teeth and ratio of belt tensions is 3:1. The gear drives another gear which is placed directly above the shaft. The gear and the pulley are keyed to the shaft. Selecting the material as steel having $\sigma_{ut} = 700$ MPa and $\sigma_{yt} = 460$ MPa as per ASME code, determine the diameter of the shaft. Assume shock factors for bending and torsion as 1.5. **(20 Marks)**

Dec. 2012 (10ME52)

33. a. Briefly explain the advantages of hollow shaft over solid shafts. **(03 Marks)**
    b. A power transmission shaft 1300 mm long is supported in bearings at its extreme ends A and B. A power of 30 kW is received at 500 rpm through a gear drive located at 400 mm to the right of the extreme end of the shaft. The gear mounted in the shaft has a pitch diameter of 300 mm and weighs 800 N. this gear receives power from a gear located exactly behind. The power is delivered through a belt drive located 500 mm to the left of right bearing. The pulley mounted on the shaft has a diameter of 400 mm and weighs 1 kN. The belt is

directed towards the observer below the horizontal and inclined at 45°. Ratio of belt tensions is 3. Material of the shaft is C40 steel. Assuming a factor of safety of 2.5 and loading to be with minor shocks, determine the diameter of solid shaft. **(17 Marks)**

Dec. 2012 (06ME52)

34. a. Design a shaft to transmit power from an electric motor to a lathe head stock through a pulley by means of a belt drive. The pulley weighs 200 N and is located at 300 mm from the center of bearing. The diameter of the pulley is 200 mm and the maximum power transmitted is 1 kW at 120 rpm. The angle of lap of the belt is 180° and coefficient of friction between the belt and the pulley is 0.3. The shock and fatigue factors for bending and twisting are 1.5 and 2.0. The allowable shear stress in the shaft may be taken as 35 MPa.   **(10 Marks)**

   b. A solid shaft of diameter d is used in power transmission. Due to modification of existing transmission system, it is required to replace the solid shaft by a hollow shaft of the same material and equally strong in torsion. Further, the weight of the hollow shaft per meter length should be half of solid shaft. Determine the outer diameter of hollow shaft in terms of d.   **(10 Marks)**

June/July 2013 (06ME52)

35. A pulley A and a gear B are mounted on bearings C and D on a shaft as shown in **Fig. U5.4**. The shaft transmits 15 kW at 500 rpm. The tangential force acts vertically upwards. The pulley delivers the power through a belt to another pulley. The ratio of tensions in the belt is 2. The gear and the pulley weigh 800 N and 2400 N respectively. The permissible shear stress for the material of the shaft is 60 MPa. Determine its diameter. Assume $C_m = 2$, $C_t = 1.5$. (use $F_r = F_t \tan 20°$).   **(20 Marks)**

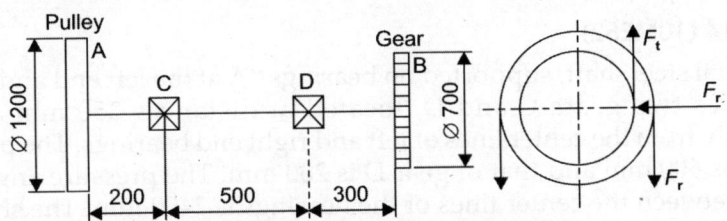

Fig. U5.4: (All dimensions in mm)

June/July 2013 (10ME52)

36. a. Prove that a hollow shaft is stronger and stiffer than a solid shaft of same length, weigh and material.   **(08 Marks)**

   b. A hollow propeller shaft of 0.6 m outside diameter and 0.3 m inside diameter is used to drive a propeller of a marine vessel. The shaft is mounted in bearings 5 m apart and it transmits 6 MW power qt 100 rpm. The maximum propeller thrust is 600 kN and shaft weighs 60 kN. Determine:
       i. Maximum shear stress developed in the shaft and
       ii. Angle of twist of the shaft between the bearings.
   Assume the modulus of rigidity as 84 GPa.   **(12 Marks)**

Dec. 2013/Jan. 2014 (06ME52)

37. A power transmission shaft is supported in bearings 2 m apart and carries a pullet weighing 1 kN at its midpoint and it receives power by a belt drive. The shaft

transmits power to another machinery by means of a flexible coupling just outside the right bearing. The power transmitted is 20 kW at 120 rpm. The ratio of belt tensions is 3:1. Estimate the size of the shaft if the permissible stress in shear is 54 N/mm². Also calculate the twist in the shaft if $G = 0.8 \times 10^5$ N/mm². Take C_m and C_t as 1.5 and the pulley diameter is 200 mm. **(20 Marks)**

Dec. 2013/Jan. 2014 (10ME52)

38. A commercial shaft 1 meter long supported between bearings has a pulley of 600 mm diameter weighing 1 kN, driven by a horizontal belt drive keyed to a shaft at a distance of 400 mm to the left of the right bearing and receives 25 kW at 1000 rpm. Power from the shaft is transmitted from the 20° spur pinion of a pitch circle diameter 200 mm which is mounted at 200 mm to the right of the left bearing to a gear such that tangential force on the gear acts upwards. Take the ratio of the belt tensions as 3. Determine the size of the shaft based on maximum shear stress theory. Assume $C_m = 1.75$ and $C_t = 1.25$. **(20 Marks)**

June/July 2014 (06ME52)

39. A mild shaft transmits 15 kW at 600 rpm. It is supported on two bearings 1.2 m apart. The shaft receives power through a 420 mm diameter pulley mounted at 200 mm to the right of left bearing. The power is given out through a gear of 200 mm diameter located at 250 mm to the left of right bearing. The belt drive is downward at an angle of 60° to the horizontal with tension ratio of 2.7. The gear drives with a downward tangential force. Find suitable diameter of the shaft taking allowable normal and shear stresses as 90 MPa and 54 MPa respectively. The combined shock and fatigue factors in bending and torsion are 1.75 and 1.25 respectively. **(20 Marks)**

June/July 2014 (10ME52)

40. A horizontal steel shaft, supported on bearings "A at the left end and B at the right end, carries two gears C and D, located at distances 250 mm and 400 mm respectively from the center lines of left and right end bearings. The pitch diameter of gear C is 600 mm and that of gear D is 200 mm. The pressure angle is 20°. The distance between the center lines of the bearings is 2400 mm. The shaft transmits 20 kW power at 120 rpm. The power is delivered to the shaft at gear C and is taken out at gear D in such a manner that the tooth pressures F_{+C} and F_{+D} of gears C and D act vertically downwards. Find the diameter of the shaft, if the working stresses are 100 MPa in tension and 56 MPa in shear. The gears C and D weigh 950 N and 350 N respectively. Take $C_m = 1.5$ and $C_t = 1.2$. **(20 Marks)**

Dec. 2014/Jan. 2015 (06ME52)

41. A shaft is supported by two bearings placed 1.2 m apart. A 600 mm diameter pulley is mounted at a distance of 300 mm to the right of left hand bearing and this drives a pulley directly below it with the help of a belt having maximum tension of 2 kN. Another pulley 400 mm diameter is placed 200 mm to the left of right hand bearing and is driven with the help of electric motor and belt, which is placed horizontally to the right. The angle of contact for both the pulleys is 180° and μ = 0.25. Determine the suitable diameter for a solid shaft allowing working stress of 63 MPa in tension and 42 MPa in shear for the material of the shaft. Assume that the torque on one pulley is equal to that on the other pulley. **(20 Marks)**

Dec. 2014/Jan. 2015 (10ME52)

42. A horizontal piece of commercial shafting is supported by two bearings 1.5 m apart. A keyed gear, 20° involute and 175 mm in diameter, is located 400 mm to the left of right bearing and is driven by a gear directly behind it. A 600 mm diameter pulley is keyed to the shaft 600 mm to the right of left bearing and drives a pulley with a horizontal belt directly behind it. The tension ratio of the belt is 3:1, with slack side on top. The drive transmits 45 kW at 330 rpm. Take $C_m = C_t = 1.5$. Calculate the necessary shaft diameter and angular deflection in degrees. Use allowable shear stress of 40 MPa and $G = 80$ GPa. **(20 Marks)**

June/July 2015 (06ME52)

43. A shaft is supported by two bearings placed 1 m apart. A 600 mm diameter pulley is mounted at a distance of 300 mm to the right of left hand bearing and this drives a pulley directly below it with the help of a belt having maximum tension of 2.25 kN. Another pulley 400 mm diameter is placed 200 mm to the left of right hand bearing and is driven with the help of electric motor and belt, which is placed horizontally to the right. The angle of contact for both the pulleys is 180° and $\mu = 0.24$. Determine the suitable diameter for a solid shaft allowing working stress of 63 MPa in tension and 42 MPa in shear for the material of the shaft. Assume that the torque on one pulley is equal to that on the other pulley. **(20 Marks)**

June/July 2015 (10ME52)

44. A shaft is supported in bearings 600 mm apart. It carries a pulley of diameter 500 mm at 250 mm to the right of left bearing and another pulley of diameter 380 mm at 130 mm to the right of right bearing. The belt drive in the left pulley is vertically downward while that on the right pulley is horizontal. The permissible shear stress is not to exceed 42 MPa. The maximum tension in the smaller pulley is not to exceed 5500 N, coefficient of friction is 0.3 and angle of contact is 180°. Find the diameter of the shaft. **(20 Marks)**

Dec. 2015/Jan 2016 (10ME52)

45. A uniform circular carbon steel shaft made of SAE 1025 annealed is mounted on two bearings 850 mm apart as shown in **Fig. U5.5**. The shaft carries a gear 'A' at 200 mm to the right of the left bearing and a pulley 'B' at 250 mm to the left of right bearing. The gear is subjected to horizontal pressure of 3500 N and a vertical upward pressure of 9600 N. The pulley is driven by a belt with a tension on tight side to be 6000 N and on the slack side to be 2000 N. The shock and fatigue factors for bending and torsion are $K_m = 2$ and $K_t = 1.5$ respectively and weight of the pulley to be 1500 N. Design the diameter of the shaft for yield strength taking factor of safety as 3. Draw neatly the sketch with loading and bending moment diagrams. **(20 Marks)**

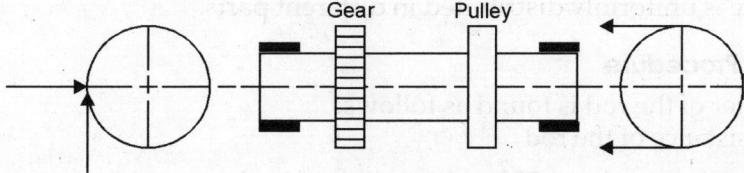

Fig. U5.5

Cotter and Knuckle Joints, Keys and Couplings

6.1 COTTER JOINT

A cotter joint is a temporary fastening used to connect two coaxial rods which are subjected to axial tensile or compressive forces. A cotter is a flat wedge shaped piece of rectangular cross-section and its width is tapered (either on one side or both sides) from one end to another. The taper is usually 1 in 24. The cotter is usually made of mild steel.

Applications: It is widely used to connect the piston rod and crosshead of a reciprocating steam engine, as a joint between the piston rod and the tailor pump rod, foundation bolt, strap end of connecting rod, etc.

Advantages of Cotter Joint

- Simple to design and manufacture.
- Can be easily assembled and dismantled with ease.
- Very high tightening force due to wedge action, which prevents loosening of parts in service.

6.2 TYPES OF COTTER JOINT

Following are the commonly used cotter joints:
1. Socket and spigot cotter joint
2. Sleeve and cotter joint
3. Gib and cotter joint.

6.3 SOCKET AND SPIGOT COTTER JOINT

Cotter joint has mainly three components as shown in **Fig. 6.1**.
1. Spigot
2. Socket
3. Cotter.

Assumptions for stress analysis of cotter joint
- The rods are subjected to axial tensile force.
- The effect of stress concentration due to holes is neglected.
- The force is uniformly distributed in different parts.

6.3.1 Design Procedure

The diameter of the rod is found as follows.
Tearing resistance of the rod

$$P = \frac{\pi d^2}{4} \sigma_t$$

... 4.16(a)/ Pg 65, DHB

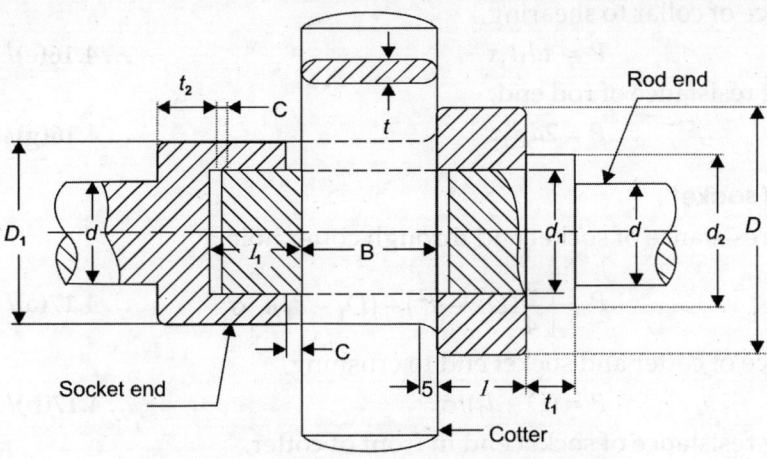

Fig. 6.1: Cotter joint **[Fig. 4.4/Pg. 66, DHB]**

The above equation gives the value of d, and is rounded off to a whole number. Based on d, the proportions of the joint are found as follows.

Parameters	**... Fig. 4.4/ Pg 66, DHB**

- Diameter of solid rod d
- Diameter of rod end $d_1 = 1.25d$
- Thickness of cotter $t = 0.25d_1$
- Width of cotter $B = b = 5t$
- Diameter of socket $D = 2d_1$
- Diameter of socket across cotter hole $D_1 = 2d$
- Diameter of collar $d_2 = 1.5d$
- Length $l_1 = 0.75d$ and $l = 1.25d$
- Thickness of collar $t_1 = 0.5d$
- Thickness of socket end $t_2 = 0.5d$
- Length of cotter (assumed) $L = 4d$
- Clearance $C = 3$ mm

Empirical relations: The following relations are used to check the stresses against the specified values.

I. Design of rod

1. The resistance of cotter and rod end to crushing,

$$P = d_1 t \sigma_c \qquad\qquad \text{... 4.16(b)/ Pg 65, DHB}$$

2. The tearing resistance of rod end through cotter hole,

$$P = \left(\frac{\pi d_1^2}{4} - d_1 t\right)\sigma_t \qquad\qquad \text{... 4.16(c)/ Pg 65, DHB}$$

3. The resistance of collar in compression,

$$P = \frac{\pi}{4}(d_2^2 - d_1^2)\sigma_c \qquad\qquad \text{... 4.16(d)/ Pg 65, DHB}$$

4. Resistance of collar to shearing,
$$P = \pi d_1 t_1 \tau$$
$$\qquad \text{... 4.16(e)/ Pg 65, DHB}$$

5. Shearing resistance of rod end,
$$P = 2d_1 l_1 \tau'$$
$$\qquad \text{... 4.16(g)/ Pg 65, DHB}$$

II. Design of socket

6. Tearing resistance of socket end through cotter hole,

$$P = \left[\frac{\pi}{4}(D_1^2 - d_1^2) - (D_1 - d_1)t\right]\sigma_t$$
$$\qquad \text{... 4.17(a)/ Pg 67, DHB}$$

7. Resistance of cotter and socket end to crushing,
$$P = (D - d_1)t\sigma_c$$
$$\qquad \text{... 4.17(b)/ Pg 67, DHB}$$

8. Shearing resistance of socket end in front of cotter,
$$P = 2(D - d_1)l\tau'$$
$$\qquad \text{... 4.17(c)/ Pg 67, DHB}$$

9. Shearing resistance of solid rod from socket end,
$$P = \pi dt_2 \tau'$$
$$\qquad \text{... 4.17(e)/ Pg 67, DHB}$$

III. Design of cotter

10. Shearing resistance of cotter,
$$P = 2bt\tau$$
$$\qquad \text{... 4.18(a)/ Pg 67, DHB}$$

Note: The design of cotter joints can be done in two methods:
- In the first method, the parameters are found using standard relations and the stresses are checked using empirical relations.
- In the second case, the empirical relations are used to find the parameters and then checked against the standard proportions.

1. **Design a cotter joint to carry an axial force of 12 kN. Use the following stresses: Allowable stress in tension and bending = 40 MPa, allowable stress in crushing = 80 MPa, allowable stress shear = 32 MPa. Sketch two views of the joint showing major dimensions.**

VTU – June/ July 2013 – 15 Marks; June/ July 2015 – 10 Marks

Solution: $P = 12 \times 10^3$ N, $\sigma_t = 40$ MPa, $\sigma_c = 80$ MPa, $\tau = \tau' = 32$ MPa
Tearing resistance of the rod,

$$P = \frac{\pi d^2}{4}\sigma_t$$
$$\qquad \text{... 4.16(a)/ Pg 65, DHB}$$

$$12 \times 10^3 = \frac{\pi d^2}{4} \times 40$$

$$d = 19.54 \text{ mm} \approx 20 \text{ mm}$$

Parameters   **... Fig. 4.4/ Pg 66, DHB**

- Diameter of solid rod $d = 20$ mm
- Diameter of rod end $d_1 = 1.25d = 1.25 \times 20 = 25$ mm ≈ 26 mm
- Thickness of cotter $t = 0.25d_1 = 0.25 \times 26 = 6.5$ mm ≈ 8 mm
- Width of cotter $B = b = 5t = 5 \times 8 = 40$ mm

- Diameter of socket $\qquad D = 2d_1 = 2 \times 26 = 52$ mm
- Diameter of socket across cotter hole $\quad D_1 = 2d = 2 \times 20 = 40$ mm
- Diameter of collar $\qquad d_2 = 1.5d = 1.5 \times 20 = 30$ mm
- Length $\qquad l_1 = 0.75d = 0.75 \times 20 = 15$ mm; and
  $\qquad l = 1.25d = 1.25 \times 20 = 25$ mm
- Thickness of collar $\qquad t_1 = 0.5d = 0.5 \times 20 = 10$ mm
- Thickness of socket end $\qquad t_2 = 0.5d = 0.5 \times 20 = 10$ mm
- Length of cotter (assumed) $\qquad L = 4d = 4 \times 20 = 80$ mm
- Clearance $\qquad C = 3$ mm

I. Design of rod

1. The resistance of cotter and rod end to crushing,

$$P = d_1 t \sigma_c \qquad \qquad \textbf{... 4.16(b)/ Pg 65, DHB}$$
$$12 \times 10^3 = 26 \times 8 \times \sigma_c$$
$$\sigma_c = 57.70 \text{ MPa} < 80 \text{ MPa}$$

2. The tearing resistance of rod end through cotter hole,

$$P = \left(\frac{\pi d_1^2}{4} - d_1 t \right) \sigma_t \qquad \qquad \textbf{... 4.16(c)/ Pg 65, DHB}$$

$$12 \times 10^3 = \left(\frac{\pi \times 26^2}{4} - 26 \times 8 \right) \sigma_t$$

$$\sigma_t = 37.16 \text{ MPa} < 40 \text{ MPa}$$

3. The resistance of collar in compression,

$$P = \frac{\pi}{4} (d_2^2 - d_1^2) \sigma_c \qquad \qquad \textbf{... 4.16(d)/ Pg 65, DHB}$$

$$12 \times 10^3 = \frac{\pi}{4} (30^2 - 26^2) \sigma_c$$

$$\sigma_c = 68.21 \text{ MPa} < 80 \text{ MPa}$$

4. Resistance of collar to shearing,

$$P = \pi d_1 t_1 \tau \qquad \qquad \textbf{... 4.16(e)/ Pg 65, DHB}$$
$$12 \times 10^3 = \pi \times 26 \times 10 \times \tau$$
$$\tau = 14.70 \text{ MPa} < 32 \text{ MPa}$$

5. Shearing resistance of rod end,

$$P = 2d_1 l_1 \tau' \qquad \qquad \textbf{... 4.16(g)/ Pg 65, DHB}$$
$$12 \times 10^3 = 2 \times 26 \times 15 \times \tau'$$
$$\tau' = 15.38 \text{ MPa} < 32 \text{ MPa}$$

II. Design of socket

6. Tearing resistance of socket end through cotter hole,

$$P = \left[\frac{\pi}{4} (D_1^2 - d_1^2) - (D_1 - d_1)t \right] \sigma_t \qquad \qquad \textbf{... 4.17(a)/ Pg 67, DHB}$$

$$12 \times 10^3 = \left[\frac{\pi}{4}(40^2 - 26^2) - (40 - 26) \times 8\right]\sigma_t$$

$$\sigma_t = 19.55 \text{ MPa} < 40 \text{ MPa}$$

7. Resistance of cotter and socket end to crushing,

$$P = (D - d_1)t\sigma_c \qquad \text{... 4.17(b)/ Pg 67, DHB}$$

$$12 \times 10^3 = (52 - 26) \times 8 \times \sigma_c$$

$$\sigma_c = 57.70 \text{ MPa} < 80 \text{ MPa}$$

8. Shearing resistance of socket end in front of cotter,

$$P = 2(D - d_1)l\tau' \qquad \text{... 4.17(c)/ Pg 67, DHB}$$

$$12 \times 10^3 = 2 \times (52 - 26) \times 25 \times \tau'$$

$$\tau' = 9.23 \text{ MPa} < 32 \text{ MPa}$$

9. Shearing resistance of solid rod from socket end,

$$P = \pi d t_2 \tau' \qquad \text{... 4.17(e)/ Pg 67, DHB}$$

$$12 \times 10^3 = \pi \times 20 \times 10 \times \tau'$$

$$\tau' = 19.10 \text{ MPa} < 32 \text{ MPa}$$

III. Design of cotter

10. Shearing resistance of cotter,

$$P = 2bt\tau \qquad \text{... 4.18(a)/ Pg 67, DHB}$$

$$12 \times 10^3 = 2 \times 40 \times 8 \times \tau$$

$$\tau = 18.75 \text{ MPa} < 32 \text{ MPa}$$

Since the calculated stresses are less than the allowable stresses, design of cotter joint is safe.

2. **Design a socket and spigot type cotter joint to sustain an axial load of 100 kN. The material selected for the joint has the following design stresses: $\sigma_t = 100$ MPa, $\sigma_c = 150$ MPa and $\tau = 60$ MPa.**

VTU – Dec. 2012 – 10 Marks; Dec. 2013/ Jan. 2014 – 10 Marks; June/ July – 10 Marks

Solution: $P = 100 \times 10^3$ N, $\sigma_t = 100$ MPa, $\sigma_c = 150$ MPa, $\tau = \tau' = 60$ MPa

Tearing resistance of the rod,

$$P = \frac{\pi d^2}{4}\sigma_t \qquad \text{... 4.16(a)/ Pg 65, DHB}$$

$$100 \times 10^3 = \frac{\pi d^2}{4} \times 100$$

$$d = 35.68 \text{ mm} \approx 40 \text{ mm} \text{ (multiples of 5)}$$

Parameters   ... Fig. 4.4/ Pg 66, DHB

- Diameter of solid rod $d = 40$ mm
- Diameter of rod end $d_1 = 1.25d = 1.25 \times 40 = 50$ mm
- Thickness of cotter $t = 0.25d_1 = 0.25 \times 50 = 12.5$ mm ≈ 14 mm
- Width of cotter $B = b = 5t = 5 \times 14 = 70$ mm

- Diameter of socket $\qquad$ $D = 2d_1 = 2 \times 50 = 100$ mm
- Diameter of socket across cotter hole $\quad D_1 = 2d = 2 \times 40 = 80$ mm
- Diameter of collar $\qquad$ $d_2 = 1.5d = 1.5 \times 40 = 60$ mm
- Length $\qquad$ $l_1 = 0.75d = 0.75 \times 40 = 30$ mm; and
  $\qquad\qquad\qquad\qquad\qquad\qquad l = 1.25d = 1.25 \times 40 = 50$ mm
- Thickness of collar $\qquad$ $t_1 = 0.5d = 0.5 \times 40 = 20$ mm
- Thickness of socket end $\qquad$ $t_2 = 0.5d = 0.5 \times 40 = 20$ mm
- Length of cotter (assumed) $\qquad$ $L = 4d = 4 \times 40 = 160$ mm
- Clearance $\qquad$ $C = 3$ mm

I. Design of rod

1. The resistance of cotter and rod end to crushing,

$$P = d_1 t \sigma_c \qquad\qquad \text{... 4.16(b)/ Pg 65, DHB}$$

$$100 \times 10^3 = 50 \times 14 \times \sigma_c$$

$$\sigma_c = 142.86 \text{ MPa} < 150 \text{ MPa}$$

2. The tearing resistance of rod end through cotter hole,

$$P = \left(\frac{\pi d_1^2}{4} - d_1 t \right) \sigma_t \qquad\qquad \text{... 4.16(c)/ Pg 65, DHB}$$

$$100 \times 10^3 = \left(\frac{\pi \times 50^2}{4} - 50 \times 14 \right) \sigma_t$$

$$\sigma_t = 79.15 \text{ MPa} < 100 \text{ MPa}$$

3. The resistance of collar in compression,

$$P = \frac{\pi}{4} (d_2^2 - d_1^2) \sigma_c \qquad\qquad \text{... 4.16(d)/ Pg 65, DHB}$$

$$100 \times 10^3 = \frac{\pi}{4} (60^2 - 50^2) \sigma_c$$

$$\sigma_c = 115.75 \text{ MPa} < 150 \text{ MPa}$$

4. Resistance of collar to shearing,

$$P = \pi d_1 t_1 \tau \qquad\qquad \text{... 4.16(e)/ Pg 65, DHB}$$

$$100 \times 10^3 = \pi \times 50 \times 20 \times \tau$$

$$\tau = 31.83 \text{ MPa} < 60 \text{ MPa}$$

5. Shearing resistance of rod end,

$$P = 2 d_1 l_1 \tau' \qquad\qquad \text{... 4.16(g)/ Pg 65, DHB}$$

$$100 \times 10^3 = 2 \times 50 \times 30 \times \tau'$$

$$\tau' = 33.33 \text{ MPa} < 60 \text{ MPa}$$

II. Design of socket

6. Tearing resistance of socket end through cotter hole,

$$P = \left[\frac{\pi}{4} (D_1^2 - d_1^2) - (D_1 - d_1)t \right] \sigma_t \qquad\qquad \text{... 4.17(a)/ Pg 67, DHB}$$

$$100 \times 10^3 = \left[\frac{\pi}{4} (80^2 - 50^2) - (80 - 50) \times 14 \right] \sigma_t$$

$$\sigma_t = 37.84 \text{ MPa} < 100 \text{ MPa}$$

7. Resistance of cotter and socket end to crushing,

$$P = (D - d_1)t\sigma_c \qquad \qquad \text{... 4.17(b)/ Pg 67, DHB}$$

$$100 \times 10^3 = (100 - 50) \times 14 \times \sigma_c$$

$$\sigma_c = 142.86 \text{ MPa} < 150 \text{ MPa}$$

8. Shearing resistance of socket end in front of cotter,

$$P = 2(D - d_1)l\tau' \qquad \qquad \text{... 4.17(c)/ Pg 67, DHB}$$

$$100 \times 10^3 = 2 \times (100 - 50) \times 50 \times \tau'$$

$$\tau' = 20 \text{ MPa} < 60 \text{ MPa}$$

9. Shearing resistance of solid rod from socket end,

$$P = \pi d t_2 \tau' \qquad \qquad \text{... 4.17(e)/ Pg 67, DHB}$$

$$100 \times 10^3 = \pi \times 40 \times 20 \times \tau'$$

$$\tau' = 38.78 \text{ MPa} < 60 \text{ MPa}$$

III. Design of cotter

10. Shearing resistance of cotter,

$$P = 2bt\tau \qquad \qquad \text{... 4.18(a)/ Pg 67, DHB}$$

$$100 \times 10^3 = 2 \times 70 \times 14 \times \tau$$

$$\tau = 51.02 \text{ MPa} < 60 \text{ MPa}$$

Since the calculated stresses are less than the allowable stresses, design of cotter joint is safe.

3. **Design a socket and spigot type cotter joint to connect two rods subjected to a steady axial pull of 100 kN. The material used for the spigot end and the cotter is (40 steel $C_{40}C_8$) having tensile yield strength of 328.6 MPa. Take factor of safety as 4 for tension, 6 for shear and 3 for crushing based on tensile yield strength.**

VTU – Dec. 07/ Jan. 2008 – 12 Marks; June/ July 2009 – 10 Marks; (Similar) July 2006 – 10 Marks.

Solution: $P = 100 \times 10^3$ N, Material: $C_{40}C_8$ having $\sigma_{yt} = 328.6$ MPa, $n = 4$ for tension, 3 for crushing and 6 for shear.

Allowable stresses: $\sigma_t = \dfrac{\sigma_{yt}}{n} = \dfrac{328.6}{4} = 82.15$ MPa

$$\sigma_c = \frac{\sigma_{yt}}{n} = \frac{328.6}{3} = 109.53 \text{ MPa}$$

$$\tau = \tau' = \frac{\sigma_{yt}}{n} = \frac{328.6}{6} = 54.77 \text{ MPa or } \tau = \tau' = 0.5\sigma_c$$

Tearing resistance of the rod

$$P = \frac{\pi d^2}{4} \sigma_t \qquad \qquad \text{... 4.16(a)/ Pg 65, DHB}$$

$$100 \times 10^3 = \frac{\pi d^2}{4} \times 82.15$$

$$d = 39.36 \text{ mm} \approx 45 \text{ mm}$$

Parameters ... **Fig. 4.4/ Pg 66, DHB**

- Diameter of solid rod $\qquad d = 45 \text{ mm}$
- Diameter of rod end $\qquad d_1 = 1.25d = 1.25 \times 45 = 56.25 \text{ mm} \;\square\; 60 \text{ mm}$
- Thickness of cotter $\qquad t = 0.25d_1 = 0.25 \times 60 = 15 \text{ mm} \approx 16 \text{ mm}$
- Width of cotter $\qquad B = b = 5t = 5 \times 16 = 80 \text{ mm}$
- Diameter of socket $\qquad D = 2d_1 = 2 \times 60 = 120 \text{ mm}$
- Diameter of socket across cotter hole $\;D_1 = 2d = 2 \times 45 = 90 \text{ mm}$
- Diameter of collar $\qquad d_2 = 1.5d = 1.5 \times 45 = 67.5 \text{ mm} \approx 70 \text{ mm}$
- Length $\qquad l_1 = 0.75d = 0.75 \times 45 = 33.75 \text{ mm} \approx 35 \text{ mm};$
  and $l = 1.25d = 1.25 \times 45 = 56.25 \text{ mm} \approx 58 \text{ mm}$
- Thickness of collar $\qquad t_1 = 0.5d = 0.5 \times 45 = 22.5 \text{ mm} \approx 23 \text{ mm}$
- Thickness of socket end $\qquad t_2 = 0.5d = 0.5 \times 45 = 22.5 \text{ mm} \approx 23 \text{ mm}$
- Length of cotter (assumed) $\qquad L = 4d = 4 \times 45 = 180 \text{ mm}$
- Clearance $\qquad C = 3 \text{ mm}$

I. Design of rod

1. The resistance of cotter and rod end to crushing,

$$P = d_1 t \sigma_c \qquad \text{... 4.16(b)/ Pg 65, DHB}$$

$$100 \times 10^3 = 60 \times 16 \times \sigma_c$$

$$\sigma_c = 104.17 \text{ MPa} < 109.53 \text{ MPa}$$

2. The tearing resistance of rod end through cotter hole,

$$P = \left(\frac{\pi d_1^2}{4} - d_1 t \right) \sigma_t \qquad \text{... 4.16(c)/ Pg 65, DHB}$$

$$100 \times 10^3 = \left(\frac{\pi \times 60^2}{4} - 60 \times 16 \right) \sigma_t$$

$$\sigma_t = 53.55 \text{ MPa} < 82.15 \text{ MPa}$$

3. The resistance of collar in compression,

$$P = \frac{\pi}{4}(d_2^2 - d_1^2) \sigma_c \qquad \text{... 4.16(d)/ Pg 65, DHB}$$

$$100 \times 10^3 = \frac{\pi}{4}(70^2 - 60^2) \sigma_c$$

$$\sigma_c = 97.94 \text{ MPa} < 109.53 \text{ MPa}$$

4. Resistance of collar to shearing,

$$P = \pi d_1 t_1 \tau \qquad \text{... 4.16(e)/ Pg 65, DHB}$$

$$100 \times 10^3 = \pi \times 60 \times 23 \times \tau$$

$$\tau = 23.07 \text{ MPa} < 54.77 \text{ MPa}$$

5. Shearing resistance of rod end,
$$P = 2d_1l_1\tau'$$ ... **4.16(g)/ Pg 65, DHB**
$$100 \times 10^3 = 2 \times 60 \times 35 \times \tau'$$
$$\tau' = 23.81 \text{ MPa} < 54.77 \text{ MPa}$$

II. Design of socket

6. Tearing resistance of socket end through cotter hole,
$$P = \left[\frac{\pi}{4}(D_1^2 - d_1^2) - (D_1 - d_1)t\right]\sigma_t$$ ... **4.17(a)/ Pg 67, DHB**

$$100 \times 10^3 = \left[\frac{\pi}{4}(90^2 - 60^2) - (90 - 60) \times 16\right]\sigma_t$$

$$\sigma_t = 32.74 \text{ MPa} < 82.15 \text{ MPa}$$

7. Resistance of cotter and socket end to crushing,
$$P = (D - d_1)t\sigma_c$$ ... **4.17(b)/ Pg 67, DHB**
$$100 \times 10^3 = (120 - 60) \times 16 \times \sigma_c$$
$$\sigma_c = 104.17 \text{ MPa} < 109.53 \text{ MPa}$$

8. Shearing resistance of socket end in front of cotter,
$$P = 2(D - d_1)l\tau'$$ ... **4.17(c)/ Pg 67, DHB**
$$100 \times 10^3 = 2 \times (120 - 60) \times 58 \times \tau'$$
$$\tau' = 14.37 \text{ MPa} < 54.77 \text{ MPa}$$

9. Shearing resistance of solid rod from socket end,
$$P = \pi dt_2\tau'$$ ... **4.17(e)/ Pg 67, DHB**
$$100 \times 10^3 = \pi \times 45 \times 23 \times \tau'$$
$$\tau' = 30.75 \text{ MPa} < 54.77 \text{ MPa}$$

III. Design of cotter

10. Shearing resistance of cotter,
$$P = 2bt\tau$$ ... **4.18(a)/ Pg 67, DHB**
$$100 \times 10^3 = 2 \times 80 \times 16 \times \tau$$
$$\tau = 39.06 \text{ MPa} < 54.77 \text{ MPa}$$

Since the calculated stresses are less than the allowable stresses, design of cotter joint is safe.

4. **A cotter joint is to be designed to connect two rods to carry a load of 120 kN. If the socket and the cotter are made of SAE 1045 steel, design the cotter joint.**

VTU – Dec. 2010 – 10 Marks

Solution: $P = 120 \times 10^3$ N, Material: SAE 1045; $\sigma_{yt} = \sigma_{yc} = 310$ MPa, $\tau_y = 180$ MPa

... **Tb. I.18/ Pg 473, DHB**

Assume $n = 4$ for tension, 3 for crushing and 4 for shear.

Allowable stresses: $\sigma_t = \dfrac{\sigma_{yt}}{n} = \dfrac{310}{4} = 77.5$ MPa

$$\sigma_c = \frac{\sigma_{yt}}{n} = \frac{310}{3} = 103.34 \text{ MPa}$$

$$\tau = \tau' = \frac{\sigma_{yt}}{n} = \frac{180}{4} = 45 \text{ MPa}$$

Tearing resistance of the rod

$$P = \frac{\pi d^2}{4} \sigma_t \qquad \text{... 4.16(a)/ Pg 65, DHB}$$

$$120 \times 10^3 = \frac{\pi d^2}{4} \times 77.5$$

$$d = 44.40 \text{ mm} \approx 50 \text{ mm}$$

Parameters
... Fig. 4.4/ Pg 66, DHB

- Diameter of solid rod $\qquad d = 50$ mm
- Diameter of rod end $\qquad d_1 = 1.25d = 1.25 \times 50 = 62.5$ mm ≈ 65 mm
- Thickness of cotter $\qquad t = 0.25d_1 = 0.25 \times 65 = 16.25$ mm ≈ 18 mm
- Width of cotter $\qquad B = b = 5t = 5 \times 18 = 90$ mm
- Diameter of socket $\qquad D = 2d_1 = 2 \times 65 = 130$ mm
- Diameter of socket across cotter hole $D_1 = 2d = 2 \times 50 = 100$ mm
- Diameter of collar $\qquad d_2 = 1.5d = 1.5 \times 50 = 75$ mm
- Length $\qquad l_1 = 0.75d = 0.75 \times 50 = 37.5$ mm ≈ 38 mm;
  $\qquad$ and $l = 1.25d = 1.25 \times 50 = 62.5$ mm ≈ 65 mm
- Thickness of collar $\qquad t_1 = 0.5d = 0.5 \times 50 = 25$ mm
- Thickness of socket end $\qquad t_2 = 0.5d = 0.5 \times 50 = 25$ mm
- Length of cotter (assumed) $\qquad L = 4d = 4 \times 50 = 200$ mm
- Clearance $\qquad C = 3$ mm

I. Design of rod

1. The resistance of cotter and rod end to crushing,

$$P = d_1 t \sigma_c \qquad \text{... 4.16(b)/ Pg 65, DHB}$$
$$120 \times 10^3 = 65 \times 18 \times \sigma_c$$
$$\sigma_c = 102.56 \text{ MPa} < 103.34 \text{ MPa}$$

2. The tearing resistance of rod end through cotter hole,

$$P = \left(\frac{\pi d_1^2}{4} - d_1 t \right) \sigma_t \qquad \text{... 4.16(c)/ Pg 65, DHB}$$

$$120 \times 10^3 = \left(\frac{\pi \times 65^2}{4} - 65 \times 18 \right) \sigma_t$$

$$\sigma_t = 55.86 \text{ MPa} < 77.5 \text{ MPa}$$

3. The resistance of collar in compression,

$$P = \frac{\pi}{4} (d_2^2 - d_1^2) \sigma_c \qquad \text{... 4.16(d)/ Pg 65, DHB}$$

$$120 \times 10^3 = \frac{\pi}{4}(75^2 - 65^2)\sigma_c$$

$$\sigma_c = 109.13 \text{ MPa} > 103.34 \text{ MPa}.$$

Hence collar fails in compression.

4. Resistance of collar to shearing,

$$P = \pi d_1 t_1 \tau \qquad \qquad \text{... 4.16(e)/ Pg 65, DHB}$$

$$120 \times 10^3 = \pi \times 65 \times 25 \times \tau$$

$$\tau = 23.51 \text{ MPa} < 45 \text{ MPa}$$

5. Shearing resistance of rod end,

$$P = 2d_1 l_1 \tau' \qquad \qquad \text{... 4.16(g)/ Pg 65, DHB}$$

$$120 \times 10^3 = 2 \times 65 \times 38 \times \tau'$$

$$\tau' = 24.30 \text{ MPa} < 45 \text{ MPa}$$

II. Design of socket

6. Tearing resistance of socket end through cotter hole,

$$P = \left[\frac{\pi}{4}(D_1^2 - d_1^2) - (D_1 - d_1)t\right]\sigma_t \qquad \text{... 4.17(a)/ Pg 67, DHB}$$

$$120 \times 10^3 = \left[\frac{\pi}{4}(100^2 - 65^2) - (100 - 60) \times 18\right]\sigma_t$$

$$\sigma_t = 30.72 \text{ MPa} < 77.5 \text{ MPa}$$

7. Resistance of cotter and socket end to crushing,

$$P = (D - d_1)t\sigma_c \qquad \qquad \text{... 4.17(b)/ Pg 67, DHB}$$

$$120 \times 10^3 = (130 - 65) \times 18 \times \sigma_c$$

$$\sigma_c = 102.56 \text{ MPa} < 103.34 \text{ MPa}$$

8. Shearing resistance of socket end in front of cotter,

$$P = 2(D - d_1)l\tau' \qquad \qquad \text{... 4.17(c)/ Pg 67, DHB}$$

$$120 \times 10^3 = 2 \times (130 - 65) \times 65 \times \tau'$$

$$\tau' = 14.20 \text{ MPa} < 45 \text{ MPa}$$

9. Shearing resistance of solid rod from socket end,

$$P = \pi d t_2 \tau' \qquad \qquad \text{... 4.17(e)/ Pg 67, DHB}$$

$$120 \times 10^3 = \pi \times 50 \times 25 \times \tau'$$

$$\tau' = 30.56 \text{ MPa} < 45 \text{ MPa}$$

III. Design of cotter

10. Shearing resistance of cotter,

$$P = 2bt\tau \qquad \qquad \text{... 4.18(a)/ Pg 67, DHB}$$

$$120 \times 10^3 = 2 \times 90 \times 18 \times \tau$$

$$\tau = 37.04 \text{ MPa} < 45 \text{ MPa}$$

Since the calculated stresses are less than the allowable stresses, design of cotter joint is safe.

6.4 KNUCKLE JOINT

A knuckle joint is used to connect two rods which are under the action of tensile loads. This joint permits angular misalignment of the rods and may take compressive load if it is guided.

Applications: Cycle chain links, tie rod joint for roof truss, valve and eccentric rod, pump rod joint, tension link in bridge structure, lever and rod connections of various types.

Advantages

- Simple to design and manufacture
- The joint can withstand large tensile loads.
- Can be easily assembled and dismantled with ease.

6.4.1 Design Procedure

A typical knuckle joint has the following parts as shown in **Fig. 6.2.**
- Fork end
- Eye end
- Knuckle pin
- Collar
- Taper pin

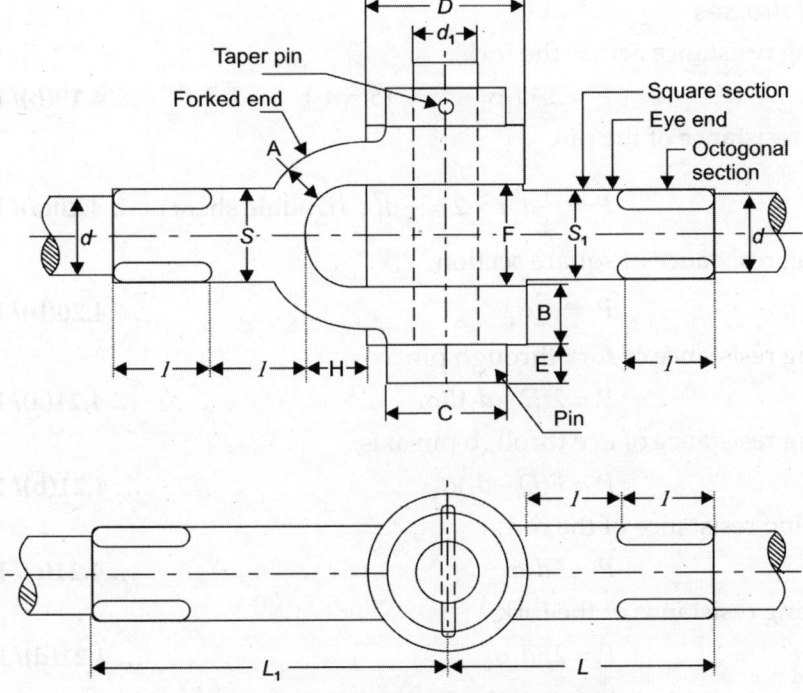

Fig. 6.2: Knuckle joint **[Fig. 4.5/Pg 68, DHB]**

The diameter of the rod is found as follows:
Tearing resistance of the rod,

$$P = \frac{\pi d^2}{4} \sigma_t$$

... **4.19(a)/ Pg 67, DHB**

The above equation gives the value of d, and is rounded off to a whole number. Based on d, the proportions of the joint are found as follows.

Parameters   ... Fig. 4.5/ Pg 68, DHB

- Diameter of solid rod d
- Side of square $S = S_1 = 1.2d$
- Thickness of eye $F = 1.5d$
- Diameter of knuckle pin $\delta = d = d_1$
- Diameter of knuckle pin collar $C = 1.5d$

- Thickness of pin head $E = \dfrac{d}{2}$

- Thickness of fork $B = 0.75d$
- Diameter of eye $D = 2d$
- Others $H = 0.80d$
                                          $A = 0.6d$
                                          $l = 2d$
                                          $L = 4d$
                                          $L_1 = 4.8d$

Check for stresses

1. Tearing resistance across the fork,

$$P = 2Ad_2\sigma_t \qquad (S = d_2) \qquad \text{... 4.19(b)/ Pg 67, DHB}$$

2. Shear resistance of the pin,

$$P = \frac{\pi}{4}d_1^2\tau \times 2 = \frac{\pi}{2}d_1^2\tau \ \text{(Double shear)} \quad \text{... 4.20(a)/ Pg 67, DHB}$$

3. Tearing resistance of square section,

$$P = d_2^2\sigma_t \qquad\qquad \text{... 4.20(b)/ Pg 67, DHB}$$

4. Tearing resistance of fork through pin axis,

$$P = 2(D - d_1)B\sigma_t \qquad \text{... 4.21(a)/ Pg 67, DHB}$$

5. Tearing resistance of eye through pin axis,

$$P = F(D - d_1)\sigma_t \qquad \text{... 4.21(b)/ Pg 67, DHB}$$

6. Crushing resistance of the rod,

$$P = Fd_1\sigma_c \qquad\qquad \text{... 4.21(c)/ Pg 67, DHB}$$

7. Crushing resistance of the fork,

$$P = 2Bd_1\sigma_c \qquad\qquad \text{... 4.21(d)/ Pg 67, DHB}$$

5. **Design a knuckle joint to transmit 150 kN. The design stress may be taken as 75 MPa in tension, 60 MPa in shear and 150 MPa in crushing.**

VTU – June/July 2015 – 12 Marks; Dec. 2014/Jan. 2015 – 08 Marks;
June/ July 2011 – 10 Marks; July 2007 – 10 Marks;
(similar) Dec. 2009/ Jan. 2010 – 10 Marks

Solution: $P = 150 \times 10^3$ N, $\sigma_t = 75$ MPa, $\sigma_c = 150$ MPa, $\tau = 60$ MPa

Tearing resistance of the rod,

$$P = \frac{\pi d^2}{4} \sigma_t \qquad \qquad \text{... 4.19(a)/ Pg 67, DHB}$$

$$150 \times 10^3 = \frac{\pi d^2}{4} \times 75$$

$$d = 50.46 \text{ mm} \approx 55 \text{ mm} \text{ (multiple of 5)}$$

Parameters
... Fig. 4.5/ Pg 68, DHB

- Diameter of solid rod $d = 55$ mm
- Side of square $S = S_1 = 1.2d = 1.2 \times 55 = 66$ mm
- Thickness of eye $F = 1.5d = 1.5 \times 55 = 82.5 \text{ mm} \approx 85$ mm
- Diameter of knuckle pin $\delta = d = d_1 = 55$ mm
- Diameter of knuckle pin collar $C = 1.5d = 1.5 \times 55 = 82.5 \text{ mm} \approx 28$ mm
- Thickness of pin head $E = \frac{d}{2} = \frac{55}{2} = 27.5 \text{ mm} \Box 28$ mm
- Thickness of fork $B = 0.75d = 0.75 \times 55 = 41.35 \text{ mm} \approx 42$ mm
- Diameter of eye $D = 2d = 2 \times 55 = 110$ mm
- Others $H = 0.80d = 0.8 \times 55 = 44$ mm
                                 $A = 0.6d = 0.6 \times 55 = 33$ mm
                                 $l = 2d = 2 \times 55 = 110$ mm
                                 $L = 4d = 4 \times 55 = 220$ mm
                                 $L_1 = 4.8d = 4.8 \times 55 = 264$ mm

Check for stresses

1. Tearing resistance across the fork,

$$P = 2Ad_2\sigma_t \qquad \qquad \text{... 4.19(b)/ Pg 67, DHB}$$

$$150 \times 10^3 = 2 \times 33 \times 66 \times \sigma_t \qquad [d_2 = S = 66 \text{ mm}]$$

$$\sigma_t = 34.44 \text{ MPa} < 75 \text{ MPa}$$

2. Shear resistance of the pin,

$$P = \frac{\pi}{2} d_1^2 \tau \qquad \qquad \text{... 4.20(a)/ Pg 67, DHB}$$

$$150 \times 10^3 = \left(\frac{\pi}{2}\right) \times 55^2 \times \tau$$

$$\tau = 31.57 \text{ MPa} < 60 \text{ MPa}$$

3. Tearing resistance of square section,

$$P = d_2^2 \sigma_t \qquad \qquad \text{... 4.20(b)/ Pg 67, DHB}$$

$$150 \times 10^3 = 66^2 \times \sigma_t \qquad [d_2 = S = 66 \text{ mm}]$$

$$\sigma_t = 34.44 \text{ MPa} < 75 \text{ MPa}$$

4. Tearing resistance of fork through pin axis,

$$P = 2(D - d_1)B\sigma_t \qquad \qquad \text{... 4.21(a)/ Pg 67, DHB}$$

$$150 \times 10^3 = 2 \times (110 - 55) \times 42 \times \sigma_t$$

$$\sigma_t = 32.47 \text{ MPa} < 75 \text{ MPa}$$

5. Tearing resistance of eye through pin axis,

$$P = F(D - d_1)\sigma_t \qquad \text{... 4.21(b)/ Pg 67, DHB}$$

$$150 \times 10^3 = 85 \times (110 - 55) \times \sigma_t$$

$$\sigma_t = 32.09 \text{ MPa} < 75 \text{ MPa}$$

6. Crushing resistance of the rod,

$$P = Fd_1\sigma_c \qquad \text{... 4.21(c)/ Pg 67, DHB}$$

$$150 \times 10^3 = 85 \times 55 \times \sigma_c$$

$$\sigma_c = 32.09 \text{ MPa} < 150 \text{ MPa}$$

7. Crushing resistance of the fork,

$$P = 2Bd_1\sigma_c \qquad \text{... 4.21(d)/ Pg 67, DHB}$$

$$150 \times 10^3 = 2 \times 42 \times 55 \times \sigma_c$$

$$\sigma_c = 32.47 \text{ MPa} < 150 \text{ MPa}$$

Since the calculated stresses are less than the allowable stresses, design of knuckle joint is safe.

6. **Design a knuckle joint for a tie rod of circular cross-section to sustain a maximum tensile load of 70 kN. The ultimate tensile strength of the rod against tension is 420 MPa. The ultimate tensile and shearing stresses for the pin material are 500 MPa and 360 MPa respectively. Take a factor of safety of 6.**

VTU – Dec. 2010 – 14 Marks; Jan/ Feb. 2006 – 10 Marks

Solution: $P = 70 \times 10^3$ N, $\sigma_{ut} = 420$ MPa; Pin: $\sigma_{ut} = 500$ MPa, $\tau_u = 360$ MPa, $n = 6$.

Allowable stresses: $\sigma_t = \dfrac{\sigma_{ut}}{n} = \dfrac{420}{6} = 70$ MPa

$$\tau = \frac{\tau_u}{n} = \frac{360}{6} = 60 \text{ MPa}$$

Tearing resistance of the rod

$$P = \frac{\pi d^2}{4}\sigma_t \qquad \text{... 4.19(a)/ Pg 67, DHB}$$

$$70 \times 10^3 = \frac{\pi d^2}{4} \times 70$$

$$d = 35.68 \text{ mm} \approx 40 \text{ mm} \text{ [multiples of 5]}$$

Parameters

... **Fig. 4.5/ Pg 68, DHB**

- Diameter of solid rod $d = 40$ mm
- Side of square $S = S_1 = 1.2d = 1.2 \times 50 = 48$ mm
- Thickness of eye $F = 1.5d = 1.5 \times 40 = 60$ mm
- Diameter of knuckle pin $\delta = d = d_1 = 40$ mm
- Diameter of knuckle pin collar $C = 1.5d = 1.5 \times 40 = 60$ mm

- Thickness of pin head $E = \dfrac{d}{2} = \dfrac{40}{2} = 20$ mm

- Thickness of fork $B = 0.75d = 0.75 \times 40 = 30$ mm
- Diameter of eye $D = 2d = 2 \times 40 = 80$ mm

- Others
$$H = 0.80d = 0.8 \times 40 = 32 \text{ mm}$$
$$A = 0.6d = 0.6 \times 40 = 24 \text{ mm}$$
$$l = 2d = 2 \times 40 = 80 \text{ mm}$$
$$L = 4d = 4 \times 40 = 160 \text{ mm}$$
$$L_1 = 4.8d = 4.8 \times 40 = 192 \text{ mm}$$

Check for stresses

1. Tearing resistance across the fork,

$$P = 2Ad_2\sigma_t \qquad \qquad \text{... 4.19(b)/ Pg 67, DHB}$$
$$70 \times 10^3 = 2 \times 24 \times 48 \times \sigma_t \qquad [d_2 = S = 48 \text{ mm}]$$
$$\sigma_t = 30.38 \text{ MPa} < 70 \text{ MPa}$$

2. Shear resistance of the pin,

$$P = \frac{\pi}{4}d_1^2\tau \qquad \qquad \text{... 4.20(a)/ Pg 67, DHB}$$

$$70 \times 10^3 = \left(\frac{\pi}{2}\right) \times 40^2 \times \tau$$

$$\tau = 27.85 \text{ MPa} < 60 \text{ MPa}$$

3. Tearing resistance of square section,

$$P = d_2^2\sigma_t \qquad \qquad \text{... 4.20(b)/ Pg 67, DHB}$$
$$70 \times 10^3 = 48^2 \times \sigma_t \qquad [d_2 = S = 48 \text{ mm}]$$
$$\sigma_t = 30.38 \text{ MPa} < 70 \text{ MPa}$$

4. Tearing resistance of fork through pin axis,

$$P = 2(D - d_1)B\sigma_t \qquad \qquad \text{... 4.21(a)/ Pg 67, DHB}$$
$$70 \times 10^3 = 2 \times (80 - 40) \times 30 \times \sigma_t$$
$$\sigma_t = 29.17 \text{ MPa} < 70 \text{ MPa}$$

5. Tearing resistance of eye through pin axis,

$$P = F(D - d_1)\sigma_t \qquad \qquad \text{... 4.21(b)/ Pg 67, DHB}$$
$$70 \times 10^3 = 60 \times (80 - 40) \times \sigma_t$$
$$\sigma_t = 29.17 \text{ MPa} < 70 \text{ MPa}$$

Since the calculated stresses are less than the allowable stresses, design of knuckle joint is safe.

6.5 KEYS

A key is defined as a machine element inserted axially between the shaft and the part (hub) mounted on it to prevent relative motion between the two. The portion of the mounted member (coupling, gears, pulleys, sprockets, flywheel, etc.) in contact with the shaft is called the hub.

According to ASME, key is defined as *"a demountable machinery part which, when assembled into keyseats, provides a positive means for transmitting torque between the shaft and the hub"*.

- Keys are wedge shaped pieces made of cold rolled steel and are always inserted parallel to the axis of the shaft.

- Keys are placed in keyways or key seats provided on the exterior surface of the shaft and the interior surface of the hub.
- A key transmits torque or power by rotation and hence is subjected to shearing and crushing stresses.
- The taper provided is usually 1 in 100.

Note: The most commonly used material for keys include 45C8 and 50C8 in order to withstand shear and compressive stresses resulting from torque transmission. Further according to Indian standards, strength not less than 60 MPa shall be used as the material of the key.

6.6 TYPES OF KEYS

A wide variety of keys are available based on design requirements. The type of key for a particular application depends upon several factors such as torque or power to be transmitted, type of loading, type of fit, stability of connection and cost.

Keys are classified under two broad categories:
1. Light and medium duty keys
2. Heavy duty keys.

6.6.1 Light and Medium Duty Keys

These include square key, rectangular key, taper key, Gib-head key, woodruff key, flat key and saddle key.

Square key [Figs 6.3(a) and (b)]: This is the most commonly used key for power transmission having equal keyway depths in shaft and the hub. This is used for light duty applications and is most common in industrial machinery.

Width of key, $\quad b = \dfrac{d}{4}$ **... 4.1/ Pg 61, DHB**

Thickness or height of the key

$$h = \dfrac{d}{4}$$

i.e. for a square key, $\quad b = h = \dfrac{d}{4}$

where $\quad\quad\quad\quad\quad d$ = diameter of the shaft

Rectangular key [Figs 6.3(c) and (d)]: This is a modification of a square key and is used where stability of the connection is desired.

Width of key, $\quad b = \dfrac{d}{4}$ **... 4.1/ Pg 61, DHB**

Thickness or height of the key

$$h = \dfrac{d}{6}$$ **... 4.2(b)/ Pg 61, DHB**

The square and rectangular keys may be parallel or tapered. In tapered keys, the width is kept uniform while the height is tapered by 1:100.

Gib-head key [Fig. 6.3(e)]: This key is similar to square or rectangular key but has a head projecting from the large end of the key. The extended head provides the means of extracting the key from the same end at which it was installed. The taper of the Gib-head is 1:100.

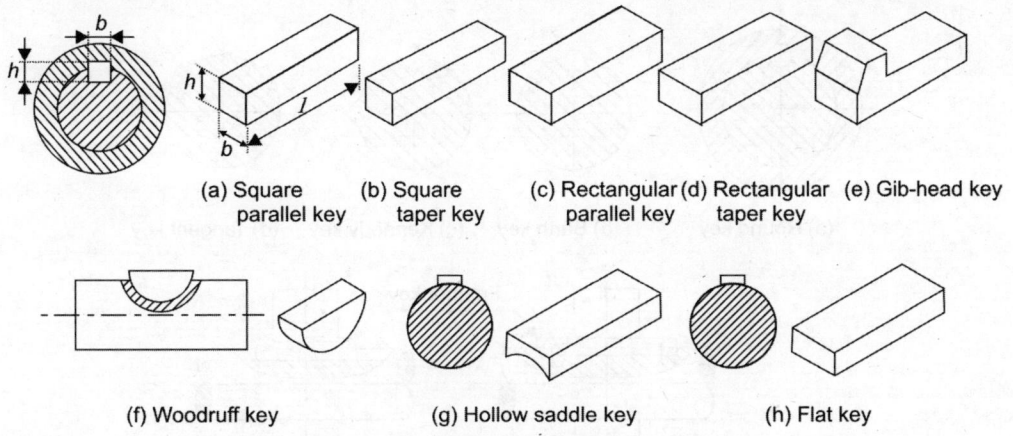

Fig. 6.3: Light and medium duty keys

Woodruff key [Fig. 6.3(f)]: Where light loading and relatively easy assembly and disassembly are desired, the Woodruff key should be considered. The circular groove in the shaft holds the key in position while the mating part is slide over the key. This is extensively used in automotive and machine tool industries.

Saddle key [Fig. 6.3(g)]: When the bottom surface of a flat key is given a concave shape to match the shaft radius, then the resulting key is called the Saddle key. This is also known as *friction key*. It is usually tapered because the torque transmission capacity depends upon the friction between the shaft and the hub.

Flat key [Fig. 6.3(h)]: This is used for light loads. Here the key slot is cut only in the hub and a set screw is used to hold the key in the shaft.

6.6.2 Heavy Duty Keys

These include round key, Barth key, Kennedy key, tangent key and feather key.

Round key [Fig. 6.4(a)]: It is essentially a tapered pin used for heavy duty service. It is also known as *pin key* or *Nordberg key*. The usual taper provided is 1:200.

Barth key [Fig. 6.4(b)]: It is a rectangular key with the two ends beveled off at 45°. Under the load, the key remains in compression rather than in shear.

Kennedy key [Fig. 6.4(c)]: It consists of two keys driven at 90° or 120° apart and fitted diagonally. It is used for heavy duty power transmission in either direction.

Tangent key [Fig. 6.4(d)]: The tangent keys are fitted in pair at right angles. Each key is to withstand torsion in one direction only. These are used in large heavy duty shafts.

Feather key [Fig. 6.4(e)]: This is used where it is necessary to slide a keyed gear or pulley along the shaft. The key is made as tight fit in the shaft and the hub and a sliding fit in the other. When making a tight fit in the shaft, it is screwed to the shaft and for a tight fit in the hub, gib heads are provided on both sides of the key as shown in **Fig. 6.4(e).**

Note:
- *Dimensions of parallel keys and keyways*   **... Table 4.1/ Pg 69, DHB**
- *Taper keys and keyways*   **... Table 4.2/ Pg 70, DHB**
- *Standard values of diameter and length for light duty taper pins*
      ... Table 4.3(a)/ Pg 71, DHB

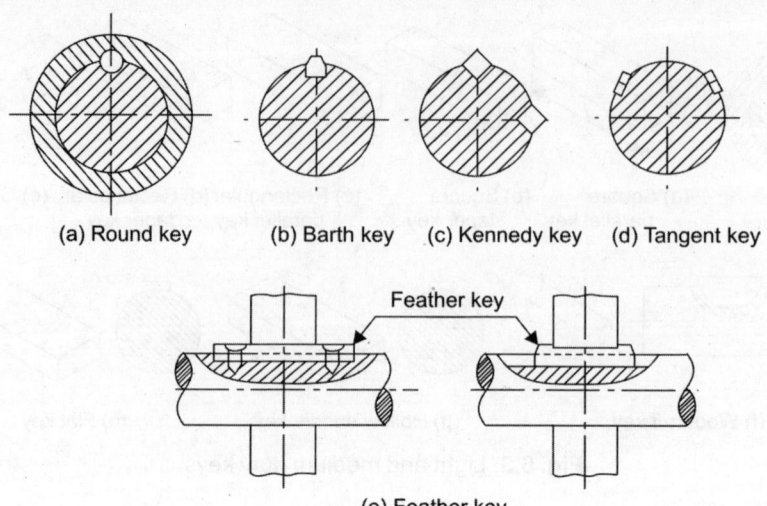

(a) Round key   (b) Barth key   (c) Kennedy key   (d) Tangent key

(e) Feather key

Fig. 6.4: Heavy duty keys

- *Standard values of diameter and length for heavy duty taper pins*
  ... Table 4.3(b)/ Pg 71, DHB
- *Standard dimensions for straight sided splines*   **... Table 4.4/ Pg 72, DHB**
- *Standard dimensions for involute splines*   **... Table 4.5/ Pg 73, DHB**
- *Standard dimensions for Gib-head keys*   **... Table 4.6/ Pg 74, DHB**

6.7 DESIGN OF SUNK KEY

When a key is inserted into a keyway which is partly in the shaft and partly in the hub, then the key is said to be a sunk key.

Let T = torque transmitted by the shaft

     F = tangential force acting on the circumference of the shaft

     R = reaction of the hub on the key

     d = diameter of the shaft

     b = width of the key

     h = height or thickness of the key

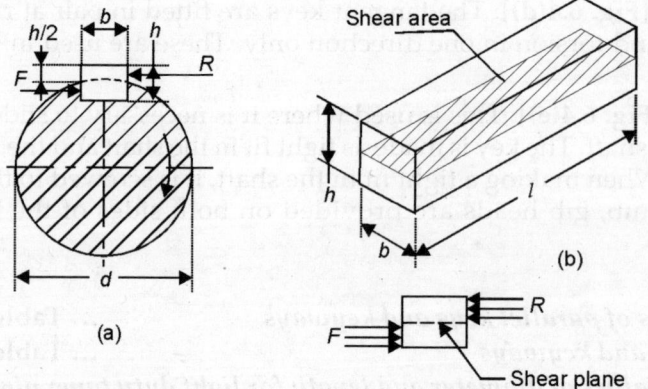

Fig. 6.5: Forces acting on a rectangular key **[Fig. 4.1(a)/Pg 62, DHB]**

l = length of the key

τ_1 = shear stress for key material

σ_{b1} = bearing or crushing or compressive stress for key material.

Keys are designed to fail when an applied torque exceeds a critical value. Failure may be due to shear or compressive bearing stresses induced in the key due to torque transmitted.

Torque transmitted by the shaft,

$$T = F\left(\frac{d}{2}\right)$$

$$F = \frac{2T}{d} \qquad \qquad \dots \text{(Eq. 6.1)}$$

a. **Failure due to shear:** The tangential force acting at shaft radius may cause shear in the key. The shear area is represented in **Fig. 6.5(b)** which is equal to lb.

Shear stress $\qquad \tau_1 = \dfrac{F}{A_s} = \dfrac{F}{lb} = \dfrac{2T}{lbd} \qquad \qquad \dots \text{using (Eq. 6.1)}$

$\therefore \qquad \qquad T = \dfrac{1}{2}\tau_1 lbd \qquad \qquad \dots \text{(Eq. 6.2) } \textbf{4.5(a)/ Pg 62, DHB}$

b. **Failure due to compressive or bearing stress:** The failure in bearing is related to the compressive stress on the side of the key, the side of the shaft keyseat, or the side of the hub keyseat. The area in compression is the same for either of these zones, $lh/2$. Thus, the failure occurs on the surface with the lowest compressive yield strength.

Compressive stress,

$$\sigma_{b1} = \frac{F}{A} = \frac{F}{(lh/2)} = \frac{4T}{lhd}$$

$\therefore \qquad \qquad T = \dfrac{1}{4}\sigma_{b1} lhd \qquad \qquad \dots \text{(Eq. 6.3) } \textbf{4.4(b)/ Pg 62, DHB}$

Note:

- To avoid failure, $\sigma_{b1} < \sigma_d$ and $\tau_1 < \tau_d$
- Shear stress in the shaft

$$\tau_s = \frac{16T}{\pi d^3} \qquad \qquad \dots \text{(Eq. 6.4) } \textbf{3.1/ Pg 50, DHB}$$

6.8 EFFECT OF KEYWAYS FOR SUNK KEY

Due to the keyway cut in the shaft, the load carrying capacity of the shaft is reduced. Keyways result in stress concentrations, thereby reducing the torsional strength of the shaft. HF Moore has shown the weakening effect of a keyway on the strength of the shaft less than 60 mm in diameter.

The torsional strength at the elastic limit of the shaft with a keyway to the strength of the shaft without a keyway was as follows.

Shaft strength factor,

$$K_e = 1.0 - \frac{0.2b}{d} - \frac{1.1h}{d} \qquad \qquad \dots \text{(Eq. 6.5) } \textbf{3.10/ Pg 52, DH}$$

where b and h are width and half-depth of keyway in mm

- *Shaft strength factor is defined as the ratio of strength of shaft with keyway to the shaft without keyway.*

  It is usually assumed that the strength of the keyed shaft is 75% of the solid shaft. In case the keyway is too long and the key is of sliding type, then the angle of twist is in the ratio K_e given as follows.

  Reduction factor angle of twist,

$$K_e = 1.0 + \frac{0.4b}{d} - \frac{0.7h}{d} \qquad \text{... (Eq. 6.6) } \textbf{3.11/ Pg 52, DHB}$$

- *Reduction factor is defined as the ratio of angular twist of the shaft with keyway to the shaft without keyway.*

  Note: Strength of the shaft with keyway

$$T = \frac{\pi d^3}{16}\tau_s K_e \qquad \text{... (Eq. 6.7)}$$

7. **Find the length of a square key of size *d*/4 such that the shaft and the key are made up of same material.**

   VTU – June/ July 2013 – 06 Marks

Solution: $l = ?$, key: square, width $b = d/4$.

Let d = diameter of the shaft

      b = width of the key

      h = height or thickness of the key

      l = length of the key

      τ_1 = shear stress for key material

      τ_s = shear stress for shaft material

For key, shear stress

$$T = \frac{1}{2}\tau_1 lbd \qquad\qquad \text{... 4.5(a)/ Pg 62, DHB}$$

$$\therefore \qquad \tau_1 = \frac{2T}{lbd}$$

For shaft, $\qquad \tau_s = \frac{16T}{\pi d^3} \qquad\qquad \text{... 3.1/ Pg 50, DHB}$

Since the shaft and the key are made up of same material, we have

$$\tau_1 = \tau_s$$

$$\frac{16T}{\pi d^3} = \frac{2T}{lbd}$$

$$\frac{8}{\pi d^2} = \frac{1}{lb}$$

$$\frac{8}{\pi d^2} = \frac{1}{l(d/4)} \qquad (\because b = d/4, \text{ data})$$

$$\frac{2}{\pi d} = \frac{1}{l}$$

$$l = 1.57d$$

Note: In general the length of the key should at least be equal to the shaft diameter for satisfactory proportions.

8. **Find the length of a square key of size** $d/4$ **such that the shaft and the key have equal strength in shear. The strength of the shaft is reduced by 25% due to keyway.**

Solution: l = ?, key: square, width $b = d/4$, shear stress for shaft = $(1 - 0.25)\tau_s = 0.75\tau_s$.

Let d = diameter of the shaft

$\quad b$ = width of the key

$\quad h$ = height or thickness of the key

$\quad l$ = length of the key

$\quad \tau_1$ = shear stress for key material

$\quad \tau_s$ = shear stress for shaft material

For key, shear stress

$$T = \frac{1}{2}\tau_1 lbd \qquad \qquad \text{... Eq. (i) } \textbf{4.5(a)/ Pg 62, DHB}$$

For shaft $\qquad \qquad \tau_s = \dfrac{16T}{\pi d^3} \qquad \qquad \text{... } \textbf{3.1/ Pg 50, DHB}$

$\therefore \qquad \qquad 0.75\tau_s = \dfrac{16T}{\pi d^3}$

$$T = \frac{0.75\pi d^3 \tau_s}{16} \qquad \qquad \text{... Eq. (ii)}$$

Since the shaft and the key have equal strength in shear, equating Eqs. (i) and (ii), we have

$$\frac{1}{2}\tau_1 lbd = \frac{0.75\pi d^3 \tau_s}{16}$$

$$lb = 0.2945d^2$$

$$l(d/4) = 0.2945d^2$$

$$l = 1.178d$$

9. **Prove that a square key is equally strong in shear and compression.**

VTU – July 2006 – 05 Marks; Dec. 2011– 04 Marks

Solution: We know that shear stress of key is

$$T = \frac{1}{2}\tau_1 lbd \qquad \qquad \text{... Eq. (i) } \textbf{4.5(a)/ Pg 62, DHB}$$

Compressive stress, $\quad T = \dfrac{1}{4}\sigma_{b1} lbd \qquad \qquad \text{... Eq. (ii) } \textbf{4.4(b)/ Pg 62, DHB}$

Since the key is equally strong in shear and compression, equating the above equations, we have

$$\frac{1}{2}\tau_1 lbd = \frac{1}{4}\sigma_{b1} lhd$$

$$\tau_1 b = \frac{1}{2}\sigma_{b1} h$$

But for a square key, $b = h$

$\therefore \qquad \qquad \sigma_{b1} = 2\tau_1 \qquad \qquad \text{... Eq. (iii)}$

This means crushing strength is twice that of shear strength or the shear stress is half of crushing strength.

Substituting Eq. (iv) into Eq. (iii) yields

$$\tau_1 b = \frac{1}{2} 2\tau_1 h$$

$$b = h$$

Thus, square key is equally strong in shear and compression.

10. **It is required to design a square key for fixing a gear on a shaft, of diameter 25 mm, 15 kW of power at 720 rpm is to be transmitted from the shaft to the gear. The key is made of steel 50C4 ($\sigma_{yt} = 460$ N/mm^2) and the factor of safety is 3. The yield strength in compression can be assumed to be equal to the yield strength in tension. Determine the dimensions of the key.**

VTU – Dec. 08/ Jan. 2009 – 10 Marks; (Similar) Dec. 2010 – 06 Marks

Solution: $d = 25$ mm, $P = 15$ kW, $n = 720$ rpm, $\sigma_{yt} = 460$ MPa, FoS = 3, $\sigma_{yt} = \sigma_{yc}$, key dimensions = ?

Allowable stresses: $\sigma_t = \sigma_{b1} = \dfrac{\sigma_{yt}}{\text{FoS}} = \dfrac{460}{3} = 153.33$ MPa

$$\tau_1 = 0.5\sigma_t = 0.5 \times 153.33 = 76.67 \text{ MPa}$$

a. **Based on shear stress:**

We know that $T = \dfrac{1}{2}\tau_1 lbd$ ... Eq. (i) **4.5(a)/ Pg 62, DHB**

But $T = \dfrac{9.55 \times 10^6 (P)}{n} = \dfrac{(9.55 \times 10^6) \times 15}{720} = 198.96 \times 10^3$ N·mm

... **3.3(a)/ Pg 50, DHB**

Also for shaft diameter, $d = 25$ mm, we have $b = h = 8$ mm (square key)

... **Tb. 4.1/ Pg 69, DHB**

∴ Eq. (i) yields...

$$198.96 \times 10^3 = \frac{1}{2} \times 76.67 \times l \times 8 \times 25$$

$$l = 25.59 \text{ mm}$$ ... Eq. (A)

b. **Based on compressive stress:**

We know that $T = \dfrac{1}{4}\sigma_{b1} lhd$ ... **4.4(b)/ Pg 62, DHB**

$$198.96 \times 10^3 = \frac{1}{4} \times 153.33 \times l \times 8 \times 25$$

$$l = 25.95 \text{ mm}$$ ... Eq. (B)

Based on Eqs. (A) and (B), select maximum length

$$l = 25.95 \text{ mm} \approx 26 \text{ mm}$$

Thus the key dimensions are $8 \times 8 \times 26$.

Note: Here Eqs. (A) and (B) yield the same result, since $\sigma_{b1} = 2\tau_1$.

11. **A square key 12 mm × 12 mm is used to transmit a power of 100 kW at 560 rpm. The key is made up of SAE 1045 annealed steel. Using the ASME code procedure, determine the length of the key required.**

VTU – Dec. 2010 – 05 Marks

Solution: $b = h = 12$ mm, $P = 100$ kW, $n = 560$ rpm, Material: SAE 1045 annealed steel, $l = ?$

For SAE 1045 annealed steel that $\sigma_{yt} = 310$ MPa and $\tau_y = 180$ MPa.

... **Tb. I.18/ Pg 473, DHB**

Allowable stresses: Assume a FoS = 2.

$$\sigma_t = \sigma_{b1} = \frac{\sigma_{yt}}{\text{FoS}} = \frac{310}{2} = 155 \text{ MPa}$$

$$\tau_1 = \frac{\tau_y}{\text{FoS}} = \frac{180}{2} = 90 \text{ MPa}$$

a. **Based on shear stress:**

We know that $\quad T = \frac{1}{2}\tau_1 lbd \quad\quad$ ... Eq. (i) **4.5(a)/ Pg 62, DHB**

But $\quad T = \frac{9.55 \times 10^6 (P)}{n} = \frac{(9.55 \times 10^6) \times 100}{560} = 1.71 \times 10^6$ N·mm

... **3.3(a)/ Pg 50, DHB**

Also for a square key,

$$b = h = \frac{d}{4} \quad\quad \text{... 4.1/ Pg 69, DHB}$$

$$d = 4b = 12 \times 4 = 48 \text{ mm}$$

∴ Eq. (i) yields...

$$1.71 \times 10^6 = \frac{1}{2} \times 90 \times l \times 12 \times 48$$

$$l = 65.97 \text{ mm} \quad\quad\quad\quad \text{... Eq. (A)}$$

b. **Based on compressive stress:**

We know that $\quad T = \frac{1}{4}\sigma_{b1} lhd \quad\quad$ **4.4(b)/ Pg 62, DHB**

$$1.71 \times 10^3 = \frac{1}{4} \times 155 \times l \times 12 \times 48$$

$$l = 76.61 \text{ mm} \quad\quad\quad\quad \text{... Eq. (B)}$$

Based on Eqs. (A) and (B), select maximum length

$$l = 76.61 \text{ mm} \approx 78 \text{ mm}$$

12. **A rectangular sunk key used on a 50 mm diameter shaft and of 14 mm width and 9 mm thickness is required to transmit 40 kW at 300 rpm. Determine the length of the key if the allowable shear stresses are 56 MPa and allowable crushing stresses are 168 MPa.**

VTU – June/ July 2013 – 14 Marks

Solution: $d = 50$ mm, $b = 14$ mm, $h = 9$ mm, $P = 40$ kW, $n = 300$ rpm, $l = ?$, $\tau_1 = 56$ MPa, $\sigma_{b1} = 168$ MPa.

a. **Based on shear stress:**

We know that $T = \dfrac{1}{2}\tau_1 lbd$ ... Eq. (i) **4.5(a)/ Pg 62, DHB**

But $T = \dfrac{9.55 \times 10^6 (P)}{n} = \dfrac{(9.55 \times 10^6) \times 40}{300} = 1.27 \times 10^6$ N·mm

... **3.3(a)/ Pg 50, DHB**

∴ Eq. (i) yields...

$$1.27 \times 10^6 = \dfrac{1}{2} \times 56 \times l \times 14 \times 50$$

$$l = 64.80 \text{ mm} \qquad\qquad\qquad ... \text{Eq. (A)}$$

b. **Based on compressive stress:**

We know that $T = \dfrac{1}{4}\sigma_{b1} lhd$ ... **4.4(b)/ Pg 62, DHB**

$$1.27 \times 10^6 = \dfrac{1}{4} \times 168 \times l \times 9 \times 50$$

$$l = 67.19 \text{ mm} \qquad\qquad\qquad ... \text{Eq. (B)}$$

Based on Eqs. (A) and (B), select maximum length

$$l = 67.19 \text{ mm} \approx 68 \text{ mm}$$

13. **The standard cross-section of a flat key, which is fitted on a 50 mm diameter shaft is 16 mm × 10 mm. The key is transmitting 475 N·m torque from the shaft to the hub. The key is made of commercial steel for which yield strength in both tension and compression may be taken as 230 MPa. Determine the minimum length of the key required if factor of safety is 3.**

VTU – June 2012 – 06 Marks

Solution: $d = 50$ mm, $b = 16$ mm, $T = 475 \times 10^3$ N·mm, $\sigma_{yt} = \sigma_{yc} = 230$ MPa, FoS = 3, $h = 10$ mm, $l = ?$

Allowable stresses: $\sigma_t = \sigma_{b1} = \dfrac{\sigma_{yt}}{\text{FoS}} = \dfrac{230}{3} = 76.67$ MPa

$$\tau_1 = 0.5\sigma_t = 0.5 \times 76.67 = 38.34 \text{ MPa}$$

a. **Based on shear stress:**

We know that $T = \dfrac{1}{2}\tau_1 lbd$ ... Eq. (i) **4.5(a)/ Pg 62, DHB**

$$475 \times 10^3 = \dfrac{1}{2} \times 38.34 \times l \times 16 \times 50$$

$$l = 30.97 \text{ mm} \qquad\qquad\qquad ... \text{Eq. (A)}$$

b. **Based on compressive stress:**

We know that $T = \dfrac{1}{4}\sigma_{b1} lhd$ ... **4.4(b)/ Pg 62, DHB**

$$475 \times 10^3 = \dfrac{1}{4} \times 76.67 \times l \times 10 \times 50$$

$$l = 49.56 \text{ mm} \qquad\qquad\qquad ... \text{Eq. (B)}$$

Based on Eqs. (A) and (B), select maximum length

$$l = 49.56 \text{ mm} \approx 50 \text{ mm}$$

Thus the key dimensions are $16 \times 10 \times 50$.

14. **A rectangular sunk key 14 mm wide × 10 mm thick × 75 mm long is required to transmit 1200 N·m torque from a 50 mm diameter solid shaft. Determine whether the length is sufficient or not if the permissible shear stress and crushing stress are limited to 56 MPa and 168 MPa respectively.**

VTU – Dec. 2012 – 06 Marks

Solution: $b = 14$ mm, $h = 10$ mm, $l = 75$ mm, $T = 1200 \times 10^3$ N·mm, $d = 50$ mm, $\tau_1 = 56$ MPa, $\sigma_{b1} = 168$ MPa.

a. **Based on shear stress:**

We know that $\quad T = \dfrac{1}{2}\tau_1 lbd$ $\qquad$ ... Eq. (i) **4.5(a)/ Pg 62, DHB**

$$1200 \times 10^3 = \frac{1}{2} \times 56 \times l \times 14 \times 50$$

$$l = 61.22 \text{ mm} < 75 \text{ mm}$$

b. **Based on compressive stress:**

We know that $\quad T = \dfrac{1}{4}\sigma_{b1} lhd$ $\qquad$ ... **4.4(b)/ Pg 62, DHB**

$$1200 \times 10^3 = \frac{1}{4} \times 168 \times l \times 10 \times 50$$

$$l = 57.14 \text{ mm} < 75 \text{ mm}$$

Thus the given key length is sufficient.

15. **A square key is used to key a gear and a shaft of diameter 35 mm. The hub length of the gear is 60 mm. Both the key and shaft are made of same material having allowable shear stress of 55 MPa. What are the dimensions of the key according to maximum stress theory, if 395 N·m of torque is to be transmitted?**

VTU – Dec. 2015/ Jan. 2016 – 05 Marks

Solution: $d = 35$ mm, $l = 60$ mm, $\tau_1 = 55$ MPa, $T = 395 \times 10^3$ N·mm, $b = h = ?$

We know that $\quad T = \dfrac{1}{2}\tau_1 lbd$ $\qquad$ ... Eq. (i) **4.5(a)/ Pg 62, DHB**

$$395 \times 10^3 = \frac{1}{2} \times 55 \times 60 \times b \times 35$$

$$b = 6.84 \text{ mm}$$

Since the given key is square cross-section, therefore the minimum size of the key is $b = h = 6.84$ mm.

From **Tb 4.1/Pg 69, DHB** for $d = 35$ mm, $b = 10$ mm, $h = 8$ mm.

Thus adopt a square key of size $b = h = 10$ mm. Hence the dimensions of the key are 10 mm × 10 mm × 60 mm.

16. A 45 mm diameter shaft is made of steel with yield strength of 400 MPa. A parallel key of size 14 mm wide and 9 mm thick made of steel with yield strength of 340 MPa. Find the required length of the key, if the shaft is loaded to transmit the maximum permissible torque. Design based on maximum shear stress theory and FoS = 2.

VTU – June/ July 2009 – 06 Marks

Solution: d = 45 mm, yield strength for shaft material σ_{yt} = 400 MPa, b = 14 mm, h = 9 mm, yield strength for key material σ_{yt} = 340 MPa, l = ?, FoS = 2.

Allowable stresses:

For shaft, $\sigma_t = \dfrac{\sigma_{yt}}{\text{FoS}} = \dfrac{400}{2} = 200$ MPa

and $\tau_s = 0.5\sigma_t = 0.5 \times 200 = 100$ MPa

For key, $\sigma_{t1} = \sigma_{b1} = \dfrac{\sigma_{yt}}{\text{FoS}} = \dfrac{340}{2} = 170$ MPa

and $\tau_1 = 0.5\sigma_{t1} = 0.5 \times 170 = 85$ MPa

a. **Based on shear stress:**

We know that $T = \dfrac{1}{2}\tau_1 lbd$ ... Eq. (i) **4.5(a)/ Pg 62, DHB**

But $\tau_s = \dfrac{16T}{\pi d^3}$ ... **3.1/ Pg 50, DHB**

$100 = \dfrac{16T}{\pi \times 45^3}$

$T = 1.78 \times 10^6$ N·mm

∴ Eq. (i) yields...

$1.78 \times 10^6 = \dfrac{1}{2} \times 85 \times l \times 14 \times 45$

$l = 66.48$ mm ... Eq. (A)

b. **Based on compressive stress:**

We know that $T = \dfrac{1}{4}\sigma_{b1} lhd$ ... **4.4(b)/ Pg 62, DHB**

$1.78 \times 10^6 = \dfrac{1}{4} \times 170 \times l \times 9 \times 45$

$l = 103.41$ mm ... Eq. (B)

Based on Eqs. (A) and (B), select maximum length

$l = 103.41$ mm $\approx$ 104 mm

17. A belt pulley is fastened to a 50 mm shaft running at 400 rpm, by means of a key 14 mm wide by 150 mm long. The permissible stresses in the key are 60 MPa and 100 MPa in shear and compression respectively. Determine:
   a. The power transmitted
   b. Depth of key

Solution: $d = 50$ mm, $n = 400$ rpm, $b = 14$ mm, $l = 150$ mm, $\tau_1 = 60$ MPa, $\sigma_{b1} = 100$ MPa, a. $P = ?$, b. $h = ?$.

a. **To find power:**

We know that $\qquad T = \dfrac{9.55 \times 10^6 (P)}{n}$ $\qquad$ ... Eq. (i) **3.3(a)/ Pg 50, DHB**

But $\qquad\qquad T = \dfrac{1}{2} \tau_1 lbd$ $\qquad\qquad\qquad$ ... **4.5(a)/ Pg 62, DHB**

$\qquad\qquad\qquad = \dfrac{1}{2} \times 60 \times 150 \times 14 \times 50$

$\qquad\qquad T = 3.15 \times 10^6$ N·mm

$\therefore$ Eq. (i) yields...

$\qquad\qquad 3.15 \times 10^6 = \dfrac{(9.55 \times 10^6) \times P}{400}$

$\qquad\qquad\qquad P = 131.94$ kW

b. **To find h:**

We know that $\qquad T = \dfrac{1}{4} \sigma_{b1} lhd$ $\qquad\qquad$ ... **4.4(b)/ Pg 62, DHB**

$\qquad\qquad 3.15 \times 10^6 = \dfrac{1}{4} \times 100 \times 150 \times h \times 50$

$\qquad\qquad\qquad h = 16.8$ mm

18. **A 900 mm diameter pulley is keyed to a 60 mm diameter shaft and is driven by a 14 mm × 14 mm × 150 mm key. The key material has an ultimate strength of 350 MPa in compression and 294 MPa in shear. If there is 2500 N difference between the total pull on the tight side and slack sides of the belt, determine:**
    a. The shear stress induced in the key
    b. Factor of safety for the key.

Solution: Diameter of pulley $D = 900$ mm, $d = 60$ mm, $b = h = 14$ mm, $l = 150$ mm, $\sigma_{uc} = 350$ MPa, $\tau_u = 294$ MPa, $(T_1 - T_2) = 2500$ N, a. $\tau_1 = ?$, b. FoS $= ?$.

a. **To find shear stress:**

We know that $\qquad T = \dfrac{1}{2} \tau_1 lbd$ $\qquad\qquad$ ... Eq. (i) **4.5(a)/ Pg 62, DHB**

But $\qquad\qquad T = (T_1 - T_2)(D/2) = 2500 \times (900/2) = 1.125 \times 10^6$ N·mm

$\therefore$ Eq. (i) yields...

$\qquad\qquad 1.125 \times 10^6 = \dfrac{1}{2} \times \tau_1 \times 150 \times 14 \times 60$

$\qquad\qquad\qquad \tau_1 = 17.86$ MPa

b. **Factor of safety:**

i. Based on shear stress:

$$\text{FoS} = \frac{\tau_u}{\tau_1} = \frac{294}{17.86} = 16.46$$

ii. Based on crushing stress:

$$FoS = \frac{\sigma_u}{\sigma_{b1}} \qquad \qquad \text{... Eq. (ii)}$$

but
$$T = \frac{1}{4}\sigma_{b1}lhd \qquad \qquad \text{... 4.4b/Pg 62, DHB}$$

$$1.125 \times 10^6 = \frac{1}{4} \times \sigma_{b1} \times 150 \times 14 \times 60$$

$$\sigma_{b1} = 35.71 \text{ MPa}$$

∴ Eq. (ii) yields...

$$FoS = \frac{350}{35.71} = 9.80$$

19. **A 15 kW 960 rpm motor has a mild steel shaft of 40 mm diameter and the extension being 75 mm. The permissible shear and crushing stresses for the mild steel key are 56 MPa and 112 MPa. Design the keyway in the motor shaft extension. Check the shear strength of the key against the normal strength of the shaft.**

VTU – Aug. 1995

Solution: P = 15 kW, n = 960 rpm, d = 40 mm, τ_1 = 56 MPa, σ_{b1} = 112 MPa, l = 75 mm. Design.

a. **To find torque:**

We know that $\quad T = \dfrac{9.55 \times 10^6(P)}{n} = \dfrac{(9.55 \times 10^6) \times 15}{960} = 149.22 \times 10^3 \text{ N·mm}$

... 3.3(a)/ Pg 50, DHB

b. **Key dimensions:**

For d = 40 mm, b = 12 mm, h = 8 mm $\qquad \qquad$ **... Tb 4.1/ Pg 69, DHB**

Since $\sigma_{b1} = 2\tau_1$, hence the key has to be a square key.

For a square key, $b = h = \dfrac{d}{4} = \dfrac{40}{4} = 10$ mm < 12 mm $\qquad$ **... 4.1/ Pg 61, DHB**

Thus the dimensions of the key are 10 mm × 10 mm × 75 mm.

c. **Shaft strength factor:**

$$K_e = 1.0 - \frac{0.2b}{d} - \frac{1.1h}{d} \qquad \qquad \text{... 3.10/ Pg 52, DHB}$$

where b and h are width and half-depth of keyway in mm.

$$= 1.0 - \frac{0.2b}{d} - \frac{1.1h}{2d} \qquad \qquad \text{(here } h = h/2\text{)}$$

$$= 1.0 - \frac{0.2 \times 10}{40} - \frac{1.1 \times 10}{2 \times 40}$$

$$K_e = 0.8125$$

$$\frac{\text{Shear strength of key}}{\text{Shear strength of shaft with keyway}} = \frac{\tau_1 lbd/2}{(\pi d^3 \tau_s/16)K_e}$$

$$= \frac{lbd/2}{(\pi d^3/16)K_e} \quad \text{(assume } \tau_1 = \tau_s\text{)}$$

$$= \frac{75 \times 10 \times 40/2}{(\pi \times 40^3/16) \times 0.8125}$$

$$= 1.47$$

20. **A 20 kW, 1500 rpm motor has a steel shaft, the extension of the shaft is 75 mm and the diameter is 45 mm. The motor pull out torsional moment is 3.5 times the average full load torsional moment of the motor and shock factor is 2.54. Assuming $\tau_1 = 55$ MPa and $\sigma_{b1} = 110$ MPa, find the size of the key. Check the shear strength of the key against the normal shear strength of the shaft.**

Solution: $P = 20$ kW, $n = 1500$ rpm, $d = 45$ mm, $T_{max} = 3.5T$, $l = 75$ mm, $\tau_1 = 55$ MPa, $\sigma_{b1} = 110$ MPa, Design.

   a. **To find torque:**

$$T_{max} = 3.5T \qquad \qquad \text{... Eq. (i)}$$

But
$$T = \frac{9.55 \times 10^6(P)}{n} = \frac{(9.55 \times 10^6) \times 20}{1500} = 127.34 \times 10^3 \text{ N·mm}$$

$$\text{... 3.3(a)/ Pg 50, DHB}$$

   $\therefore$ Eq. (i) yields...
$$T_{max} = 3.5 \times (127.34 \times 10^3) = 445.70 \times 10^3 \text{ N·mm}$$

   b. **Key dimensions:**

   For $d = 45$ mm, $b = 14$ mm, $h = 9$ mm $\qquad$ **... Tb 4.1/ Pg 69, DHB**

   Since $\sigma_{b1} = 2\tau_1$, hence the key has to be a square key.

   For a square key, $b = h = \dfrac{d}{4} = \dfrac{45}{4} = 11.25$ mm ≈ 12 mm < 14 mm

$$\text{... 4.1/ Pg 61, DHB}$$

   Thus the dimensions of the key are 12 mm × 12 mm × 75 mm.

   c. **Shaft strength factor:**

$$K_e = 1.0 - \frac{0.2b}{d} - \frac{1.1h}{d} \qquad \qquad \text{... 3.10/ Pg 52, DHB}$$

   where b and h are width and half-depth of keyway in mm.

$$= 1.0 - \frac{0.2b}{d} - \frac{1.1h}{2d} \qquad \text{(here } h = h/2)$$

$$= 1.0 - \frac{0.2 \times 12}{45} - \frac{1.1 \times 12}{2 \times 45}$$

$$K_e = 0.8$$

$$\frac{\text{Shear strength of key}}{\text{Shear strength of shaft with keyway}} = \frac{\tau_1 lbd/2}{(\pi d^3 \tau_s/16)K_e}$$

$$= \frac{lbd/2}{(\pi d^3/16)K_e} \quad \text{(assume } \tau_1 = \tau_s)$$

$$= \frac{75 \times 12 \times 45/2}{(\pi \times 45^3/16) \times 0.8}$$

$$= 1.41$$

6.9 DESIGN OF A TAPER KEY

In tapered keys, the torque is transmitted by the frictional force between the shaft and the key and hub and the key. The relationship between the circumferential force (F_t) and the pressure force (F) between the shaft and the hub is given as:

$$F_t = \mu_1 F \qquad \text{... (Eq. 6.8) } \textbf{4.6/ Pg 62, DHB}$$

where μ_1 is the coefficient of friction between the shaft and the hub and may be taken as 0.25.

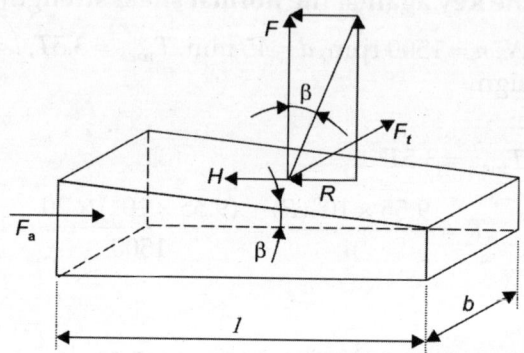

Fig. 6.6: Forces acting on a taper key [**Fig. 4.2/Pg 63, DHB**]

The pressure force between the shaft and the hub is given as

$$F = plb \qquad \text{... (Eq. 6.9) } \textbf{4.7/ Pg 62, DHB}$$

where p = pressure or compressive stress in the key.

The relationship between the torque (T) and the circumferential force is given as

$$T = \frac{1}{2}F_t d = \frac{1}{2}\mu_1 plbd \qquad \text{... (Eq. 6.10) } \textbf{4.8/ Pg 63, DHB}$$

Thus the necessary length of the key is

$$l = \frac{2T}{\mu_1 pbd} \qquad \text{... (Eq. 6.11) } \textbf{4.9/ Pg 63, DHB}$$

The axial effort (F_a) necessary to drive the key home is

$$F_a = H + R = 2F\mu_2 + F \tan \beta \qquad \text{... (Eq. 6.12) } \textbf{4.10/ Pg 63, DHB}$$

where μ_2 is the coefficient of friction between the key and the shaft and may be taken as 0.10, for greased key

and, $\qquad \tan \beta = 0.0104.$

21. **Design a taper key for a shaft of diameter 60 mm transmitting 40 kW at 250 rpm. The allowable compressive stress may be taken as 120 MPa.**

Solution: $d = 60$ mm, $P = 40$ kW, $n = 250$ rpm, compressive stress or pressure $\sigma_c = p = 120$ MPa.

a. **To find torque:**

We know that $\qquad T = \dfrac{9.55 \times 10^6 (P)}{n} = \dfrac{(9.55 \times 10^6) \times 40}{250} = 1.528 \times 10^6$ N·mm

... **3.3(a)/ Pg 50, DHB**

b. **Key dimensions:**

For $d = 60$ mm, $b = 18$ mm, $h = 11$ mm   **... Tb 4.2/ Pg 70, DHB**

For a rectangular key,

$$b = \frac{d}{4} = \frac{60}{4} = 15 \text{ mm} < 18 \text{ mm} \qquad \text{... 4.2(a)/ Pg 61, DHB}$$

$$h = \frac{d}{4} = \frac{60}{6} = 10 \text{ mm} < 11 \text{ mm} \qquad \text{... 4.2(b)/ Pg 61, DHB}$$

Based on compressive stress

$$l = \frac{2T}{\mu_1 pbd} \qquad \text{... 4.9/ Pg 63, DHB}$$

$\mu_1 = 0.25$, $\mu_2 = 0.10$, $\tan \beta = 0.0104$

$$= \frac{2 \times 1.528 \times 10^6}{0.25 \times 120 \times 15 \times 60}$$

$$l = 113.20 \text{ mm} \approx 115 \text{ mm}$$

Thus the dimensions of the key are 15 mm × 10 mm × 115 mm.

c. **Axial force:**

The axial effort (F_a) necessary to drive the key home is

$$F_a = 2F\mu_2 + F \tan \beta \qquad \text{...Eq. (i) } \textbf{4.10/ Pg 53, DHB}$$

But $F = blp$ **...4.7/ Pg 62, DHB**

$$= 15 \times 115 \times 120$$

$$F = 207 \text{ kN}$$

∴ Eq. (i) yields...

$$F_a = (2 \times 207 \times 10^3 \times 0.10) + (207 \times 10^3 \times 0.0104)$$

$$F_a = 43.55 \text{ kN}$$

22. **Design a taper key to transmit 15 kW at 750 rpm. For key material assume $\tau_1 = 75$ MPa, $\sigma_{b1} = 140$ MPa.**

Solution: $P = 15$ kW, $n = 750$ rpm, $\tau_1 = 75$ MPa, $\sigma_{b1} = 140$ MPa.

a. **To find diameter:**

We know that $\tau_s = \dfrac{16T}{\pi d^3}$ **... Eq. (i) 3.1/ Pg 50, DHB**

But $T = \dfrac{9.55 \times 10^6 (P)}{n} = \dfrac{(9.55 \times 10^6) \times 15}{750} = 191 \times 10^3 \text{ N} \cdot \text{mm}$

     ... 3.3(a)/ Pg 50, DHB

∴ Eq. (i) yields...

$$75 = \frac{16 \times 191 \times 10^3}{\pi d^3} \qquad (\text{assume } \tau_s = \tau_1)$$

$$d = 23.5 \text{ mm}$$

Hence adopt a diameter of $d = 25$ mm in the range (22 to 30 mm)

     ... Tb. 4.2/ Pg 70, DHB

b. **Key dimensions:**

For $d = 25$ mm, $b = 8$ mm, $h = 7$ mm$\grave{}$ **... Tb 4.2/ Pg 70, DHB**

- For a rectangular key,

$$b = \frac{d}{4} = \frac{25}{4} = 6.25 \text{ mm} \approx 8 \text{ mm} \qquad \text{... 4.2(a)/ Pg 61, DHB}$$

$$h = \frac{d}{4} = \frac{25}{6} = 4.17 \text{ mm} \approx 6 \text{ mm} < 7 \text{ mm}$$

$$\text{... 4.2(b)/ Pg 61, DHB}$$

- We know that

$$T = \frac{1}{2}\tau_1 lbd \qquad \text{... 4.5(a)/ Pg 62, DHB}$$

$$191 \times 10^3 = \frac{1}{2} \times 75 \times l \times 8 \times 25$$

$$l = 25.46 \text{ mm} \qquad \text{... Eq. (A)}$$

- We know that

$$T = \frac{1}{4}\sigma_{b1} lhd \qquad \text{... 4.5(b)/ Pg 62, DHB}$$

$$191 \times 10^3 = \frac{1}{4} \times 140 \times l \times 6 \times 25$$

$$l = 36.38 \text{ mm} \qquad \text{... Eq. (B)}$$

Based on Eqs. (A) and (B), select maximum length $l = 36.38$ mm ≈ 38 mm.

Thus the dimensions of the key are 8 mm × 6 mm × 38 mm.

c. **Axial force:**

The axial effort (F_a) necessary to drive the key home is

$$F_a = 2F\mu_2 + F \tan \beta \qquad \text{...Eq. (ii) } \textbf{4.10/ Pg 53, DHB}$$

But $\qquad F_t = \mu_1 F \qquad \text{... Eq. (iii) } \textbf{4.6/ Pg 62, DHB}$

Here $\qquad \mu_1 = 0.25, \mu_2 = 0.10, \tan \beta = 0.0104$

Also $\qquad T = \frac{1}{2}F_t d \qquad \text{...4.8/ Pg 63, DHB}$

$$191 \times 10^3 = \frac{1}{2} \times F_t \times 25$$

$$F_t = 12580 \text{ N}$$

$\therefore$ Eq. (iii) yields...

$$12580 = 0.25F$$

$$F = 61120 \text{ N}$$

$\therefore$ Eq. (ii) yields...

$$F_a = (2 \times 61120 \times 0.10) + (61120 \times 0.0104)$$

$$F_a = 12.86 \text{ kN.}$$

6.10 SPLINES

A spline can be described as a series of axial keys machined into a shaft, with corresponding grooves machined into the bore of the mating part (gear, sheave, sprocket, etc.). Splined shafts are most generally used in three types of applications.

- For coupling shafts when relatively heavy torques are to be transmitted without slippage
- For transmitting power to slidably-mounted or permanently-fixed gears, pulleys, and other rotating members
- For attaching parts that may require removal for indexing or change in angular position.

There are two forms of splines.
1. Straight side splines
2. Involute tooth splines.

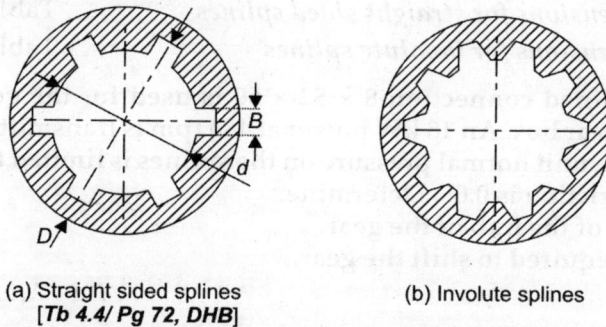

(a) Straight sided splines
[*Tb 4.4/ Pg 72, DHB*]

(b) Involute splines

Fig. 6.7: Types of splines—splined shaft and hub profile.

Straight side splines have square cross-section and may be regarded as an arrangement of multiple keys. Involute splines have geometry similar to gears, except that the pressure angle is 30° and the depth of the tooth is generally one-half that of an involute gear tooth. Other standard pressure angles are 37.5° and 45°. Involute splines are stronger than parallel sided splines because stress concentrations are lower and better surface quality can be achieved in manufacturing.

According to BIS the number of splines on the shaft has been standardized as 4, 6, 10, or 16. The fit between mating splines is characterized as sliding, close, or press. When there is relative axial motion (sliding) in a splined connection, the side pressure on the splines should be limited to about 7 MPa.

Applications: Machine tools, automatic equipment, to connect the transmission output shaft to the drive shaft in automobiles, where the suspension movement causes axial motion between the components.

According to BIS, splines are specified by 4 characteristics as: $NK \times d \times D$

$$\dots \text{(Eq. 6.13)}$$

where N = number of splines
K = type of fit (sliding, close or press)
d = minor diameter of splined shaft
D = major diameter of splined shaft

The torque transmission capacity of a splined shaft depends upon the bearing capacity of the spline. Based on bearing capacity, for a *parallel side or straight sided or square side spline*, torque transmitted between the sides of the splines is given as

$$T = \frac{1}{2} p_b L h N (D - h) \qquad \dots \text{(Eq. 6.14)} \text{ \textbf{4.14/Pg 64, DHB}}$$

where D = major diameter of splined shaft (mm)

N = number of splines

L = engaged length of spline (mm)

h = height of spline = $\dfrac{(D-d)}{2}$ (mm)

= h_1 for press fit or permanent fit

= $1.5h_1$ for close fit (hub to slide when not under load)

= $2h_1$ for close fit (hub to slide when under load)

p_b = allowable bearing pressure (MPa)

= 7 MPa, for sliding fit

= 14 MPa, for close fit

= 21MPa, for press fit

Note:

- *Standard dimensions for straight sided splines* ... **Table 4.4/ Pg 72, DHB**
- *Standard dimensions for involute splines* ... **Table 4.5/ Pg 73, DHB**

23. **A standard splined connection 8 × 52 × 60 is used for the gear and the shaft assembly of a gear box. An 18 kW power at 440 rpm is transmitted by the splined connection. The unit normal pressure on the splines is limited to 6.5 N/mm². The coefficient of friction is 0.05. Determine:**
    a. The length of the hub of the gear
    b. The force required to shift the gear.

VTU – Mar. 2001 – 10 Marks

Solution: 8 × 52 × 60 ⇒ N = 8, d = 52 mm, D = 60 mm, P = 18 kW, n = 440 rpm, p_b = 6.5 N/mm², μ_1 = 0.05, L = ?, F_t = ?

a. **To find length:**

We know that $T = \dfrac{1}{2} p_b LhN(D-h)$ ... Eq. (i) **4.14/ Pg 64, DHB**

But $T = \dfrac{9.55 \times 10^6 (P)}{n} = \dfrac{(9.55 \times 10^6) \times 18}{440} = 390.68 \times 10^3$ N·mm

... **3.3(a)/ Pg 50, DHB**

Also $h = \dfrac{(D-d)}{2} = \left(\dfrac{60-52}{2}\right) = 4$ mm

∴ Eq. (i) yields...

$$390.68 \times 10^3 = \dfrac{1}{2}[6.5 \times L \times 4 \times 8 \times (60-4)]$$

$$L = 67.08 \text{ mm} \approx 68 \text{ mm}$$

b. **To find force required to shift the gear:**

We know that $F_t = \mu_1 F$ ... Eq. (ii) **4.6/ Pg 62, DHB**

But $T = F\left(\dfrac{D+d}{4}\right)$

$$390.68 \times 10^3 = F\left(\dfrac{60+52}{4}\right)$$

$$F = 13.95 \times 10^3 \text{ N}$$

$\therefore$ Eq. (iii) yields...
$$F_t = (13.95 \times 10^3) \times 0.05 = 697.64 \text{ N}$$

24. **A standard splined connection 8 × 36 × 40 is used for a gear and shaft assembly, rotating at 700 rpm. The length of the gear hub is 50 mm and the normal pressure on the splines is limited to 6.5 N/mm². Calculate the power that can be transmitted from the gear to the shaft.**

VTU – Dec. 2011 – 06 Marks

Solution: $8 \times 36 \times 40 \Rightarrow N = 8$, $d = 36$ mm, $D = 40$ mm, $n = 700$ rpm, $L = 50$ mm, $p_b = 6.5 \text{ N/mm}^2$, $p = ?$

We know that $\quad T = \dfrac{9.55 \times 10^6 (P)}{n}$ $\qquad$ ... Eq. (i) **3.3(a)/ Pg 50, DHB**

But $\qquad T = \dfrac{1}{2} p_b L h N (D - h)$ $\qquad$ ... Eq. (ii) **4.14/ Pg 64, DHB**

Also $\qquad h = \dfrac{(D-d)}{2} = \left(\dfrac{40-36}{2}\right) = 2$ mm

$\therefore$ Eq. (ii) yields...

$$T = \frac{1}{2}[6.5 \times 50 \times 2 \times 8 \times (40 - 2)] = 98.8 \times 10^3 \text{ N·mm}$$

$\therefore$ Eq. (i) yields...

$$98.8 \times 10^3 = \frac{9.55 \times 10^6 (P)}{700}$$

$$P = 7.24 \text{ kW}$$

25. **A splined connection in an automobile transmission consists of 10 splines cut in a 58 mm diameter shaft. The height of each spline is 5.5 mm and the keyways in the hub are 45 mm long. Determine the power that may be transmitted at 2500 rev/min if the allowable normal pressure on the splines is limited to 4.8 MPa.**

VTU – June/ July 2011 – 10 Marks

Solution: $N = 10$, $D = 58$ mm, $h = 5.5$ mm, $L = 45$ mm, $P = ?$, $n = 2500$ rpm, $p_b = 4.8$ MPa.

We know that $\quad T = \dfrac{9.55 \times 10^6 (P)}{n}$ $\qquad$ ... Eq. (i) **3.3(a)/ Pg 50, DHB**

But $\qquad T = \dfrac{1}{2} p_b L h N (D - h)$ $\qquad$ ... Eq. (ii) **4.14/ Pg 64, DHB**

Also $\qquad h = \dfrac{(D-d)}{2}$

$$d = D - 2h = 58 - (2 \times 5.5) = 47 \text{ mm}$$

$\therefore$ Eq. (ii) yields...

$$T = \frac{1}{2}[4.8 \times 45 \times 10 \times 5.5 \times (58 - 5.5)] = 311.85 \times 10^3 \text{ N} \cdot \text{mm}$$

$\therefore$ Eq. (i) yields...

$$311.85 \times 10^3 = \frac{9.55 \times 10^6 (P)}{2500}$$

$$P = 81.64 \text{ kW}$$

26. **Design a spline shaft required to transmit 25 kW at 1200 rpm. The shaft is made of C40 steel. Assume $N = 6$, $L = 1.5D$, FoS = 4 and $B = h = 0.1D$.**

Solution: $P = 25$ kW, $n = 1200$ rpm, $N = 6$, $L = 1.5D$, FoS = 4 and $B = h = 0.1D$, Material: C40.

For C40 steel, $\qquad \sigma_y = 324$ MPa $\qquad\qquad$ **... Tb 1.8/ Pg 464, DHB**

Hence $\qquad\qquad \sigma_t = \dfrac{\sigma_{yt}}{\text{FoS}} = \dfrac{324}{4} = 81$ MPa

and $\qquad\qquad \tau_1 = 0.5\sigma_t = 0.5 \times 81 = 40.5$ MPa

a. **To find torque:**

We know that $\qquad T = \dfrac{9.55 \times 10^6 (P)}{n} = \dfrac{9.55 \times 10^6 \times (25)}{1200} = 198.96 \times 10^3$ N·mm

$\qquad\qquad\qquad\qquad\qquad\qquad\qquad\qquad$ **... 4.14/ Pg 64, DHB**

b. **To find major diameter:**

We know that $\qquad T = \dfrac{1}{2} p_b L h N (D - h)$ $\qquad$ **... Eq. (i) 4.14/ Pg 64, DHB**

Given $\qquad\qquad N = 6$

$\qquad\qquad\qquad L = 1.5D$

$\qquad\qquad\qquad B = h = 0.1D$

Assume $\qquad\qquad p_b = 7$ MPa, for sliding fit $\qquad\qquad$ **... 4.14/ Pg 64, DHB**

∴ Eq. (i) yields...

$$198.96 \times 10^3 = \dfrac{1}{2}[7 \times 1.5D \times 0.1D \times 6 \times (D - 0.1D)]$$

$$198.96 \times 10^3 = 2.835D^3$$

$$D = 41.25 \text{ mm}$$

Thus the standard diameter is

$$D = 45 \text{ mm} \qquad\qquad\qquad \textbf{... Tb. 3.5(a)/ Pg 57, DHB}$$

Thus the dimensions are

$$D = 45 \text{ mm}$$

$$B = h = 0.1 \times 45 = 4.5 \text{ mm} \approx 5 \text{ mm}$$

$$L = 1.5 \times 45 = 67.5 \text{ mm} \approx 68 \text{ mm}$$

$$d = D - 2h = 45 - (2 \times 5) = 35 \text{ mm}$$

Key dimensions are $N \times d \times D = 6$ mm $\times 35$ mm $\times 45$ mm

c. **Check for stresses:**

i. Shear stress in the shaft:

We know that

$$\tau_s = \dfrac{16T}{\pi d^3} \qquad\qquad\qquad\qquad \textbf{... 3.1/ Pg 50, DHB}$$

$$= \dfrac{16 \times 198.96 \times 10^3}{\pi \times 35^3}$$

$$\tau_s = 23.64 \text{ MPa} < 40.5 \text{ MPa}$$

ii. Shear stress in the key:

We know that

$$T = \frac{1}{2}\tau_1 lbd \qquad\qquad \text{... 4.5(a)/ Pg 62, DHB}$$

$$T = \left[\frac{1}{2}\tau_1 LBd\right] N$$

$$198.96 \times 10^3 = \frac{1}{2}[\tau_1 \times 68 \times 5 \times 35 \times 6]$$

$$\tau_1 = 5.57 \text{ MPa} < 40.5 \text{ MPa}$$

6.11 COUPLINGS

The term coupling refers to a device used to connect two shafts together at their ends for the purpose of transmitting power. Coupling may be rigid or they may provide flexibility and compensate for misalignment. They may also reduce shock loading and vibration.

In general, there are two types of couplings:
1. Rigid couplings
   a. Sleeve or muff or box coupling.
   b. Clamp or split-muff or compression or ribbed coupling.
   c. Flange coupling:
      i. Protected type
      ii. Unprotected type
      iii. Marine or solid flange type
2. Flexible couplings
   a. Based on kinematic flexibility:
      i. Universal or Hooke's coupling
      ii. Oldham coupling
   b. Based on incorporated flexibility:
      i. Bushed-pin coupling
      ii. Leather pad type, etc.

Rigid couplings should be used only when the alignment of the two shafts can be maintained very accurately. Further shafts are often subjected to radial, angular, and axial misalignment, thereby leading to failure by fatigue. In these situations, flexible couplings must be used. Rigid couplings have no backlash, making them useful for precision machines and servo mechanisms. Rigid couplings have essentially no energy loss, which can be a significant advantage compared to flexible couplings.

Flexible couplings are used to connect two shafts having both lateral and angular misalignment. The three basic functions of a flexible coupling are:
- To transmit power
- To accommodate misalignment
- To compensate for end movement.

6.12 FLANGE COUPLING

This is basically a rigid coupling used to transmit heavy torque. It consists of two cast iron flanges, keyed to the shaft ends and connected together by bolts (4 or 6). Power is transmitted from the driving shaft to one of the flanges by a key and then to the other flange by means of bolts and then finally to the driven shaft by means of a key. To

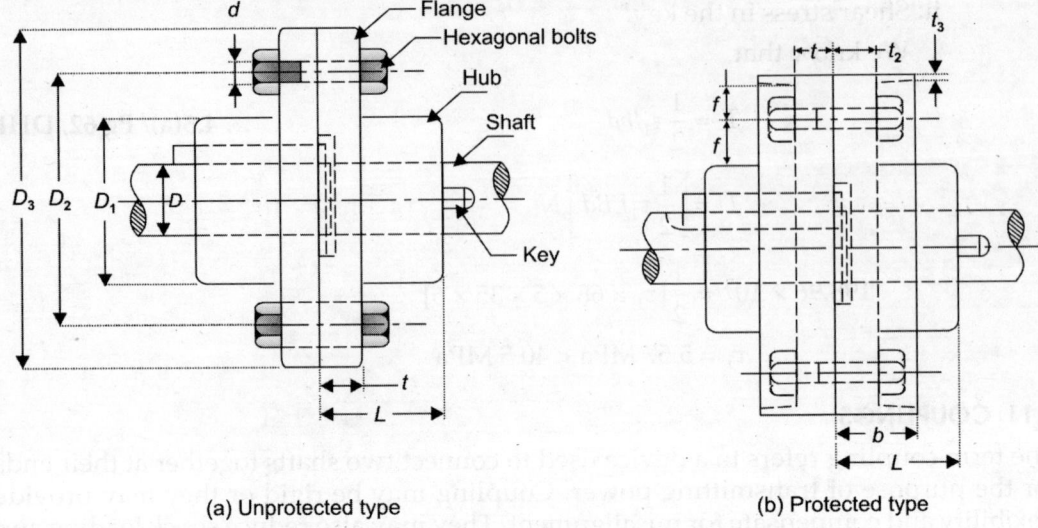

Fig. 6.8: Flange coupling **[Fig. 13.1(a & b)/Pg 251/DHB]**

ensure proper alignment, the end of one shaft may enter into the recess provided in the flange attached to the other shaft. The flanges are generally made from cast iron by casting or steel by a forging process. Protected type of couplings **[Fig. 6.8(b)]** is often used to provide safety to the operator. These flanges project beyond the heads of the bolts and nuts.

Applications: Marine propeller shafts, vertical hydroturbines, etc.

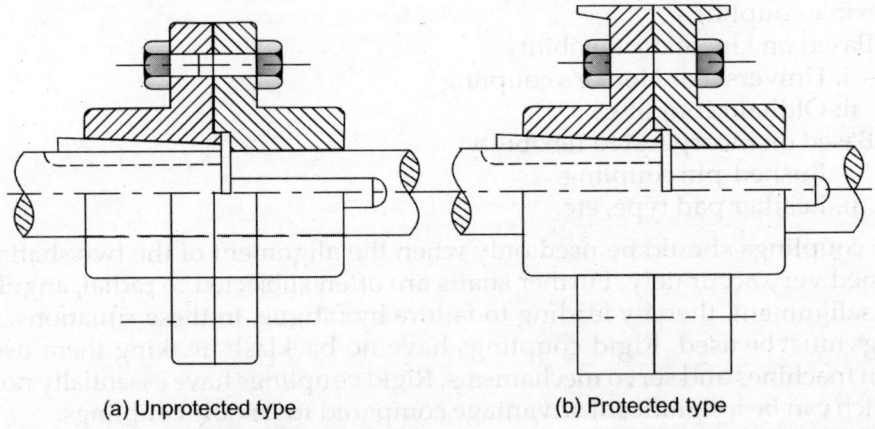

Fig. 6.9: Flange coupling—top half in section

6.12.1 Design Procedure for Flange Coupling

The flange coupling shown in **Fig. 6.8** consists of the following components:

- Shaft
- Hub
- Key
- Bolts
- Flange.

Parameters:

Let
D = diameter of the shaft
D_1 = diameter of the hub
D_2 = bolt circle diameter or pitch circle diameter of bolts
D_3 = diameter of the flange
d = diameter of the bolt
L = length of the hub
i = number of bolts
T = torque transmitted
τ_s = shear stress in shaft material
τ_1, τ_b, τ_c = shear stress in key, bolt and flange respectively
σ_b, σ_{b1} = crushing stress for bolt and key materials respectively.

I. Design of shaft

1. The torque transmitted is found as

$$T = \frac{9.55 \times 10^6 (P)}{n} \qquad \dots \text{3.3(a)/ Pg 50, DHB}$$

2. The shaft diameter is found using

$$\tau_s = \frac{16T}{\pi D^3} \qquad \dots \text{3.1/ Pg 50, DHB}$$

Standardize the shaft diameter using...   ... Tb. 3.5(a)/Pg 57, DHB

II. Design of hub

3. Hub diameter $D_1 = 1.5D + 25$ mm   ... 13.1(d)/ Pg 252, DHB
4. Hub length $L = 1.2D + 20$ mm   ... 13.1(g)/ Pg 252, DHB

III. Design of key

5. If crushing strength of the key is twice the shear strength in the key ($\sigma_{b1} = 2\tau_1$), then use square key.
6. Based on diameter of the shaft obtained in step (2), choose proper values of b and h for the type of key from ...Tb. 4.1/ Pg 69 and/or Tb.4.2/ Pg 70, DHB
7. The length of key in each part is kept equal to length of hub, i.e. $l = L$.
8. Check for stresses:
   a. Shear stress in the key is found using,

$$T = \frac{1}{2} \tau_1 lbD \qquad \dots \text{4.5(a)/Pg 62, DHB}$$

   b. Crushing stress in the key is found using

$$T = \frac{1}{4} \sigma_{b1} lhD \qquad \dots \text{4.4(b)/Pg 62, DHB}$$

For safe design, the calculated stresses should be less than the allowable stresses.

IV. Design of bolts

9. The number of bolts* is found as

$$i = \frac{3D}{80} + 2 \qquad \text{... 13.1(a)/ Pg 251, DHB}$$

10. The diameter of the bolts is found as

$$d = \frac{0.423D}{\sqrt{i}} + 7.5 \text{ mm} \qquad \text{... 13.1(c)/ Pg 251, DHB}$$

Standardize the bolt diameter using...   **... Tb. 9.8/Pg 140, DHB**

11. PCD of bolts is found as

$$D_2 = D_1 + 3.2d \qquad \text{... 13.1(e)/ Pg 252, DHB}$$

12. Check for stresses:

a. Shear stress in the bolt is found using

$$T = \frac{\tau_b \pi i d^2 D_2}{8} \qquad \text{... 13.2(c)/ Pg 252, DHB}$$

b. Crushing stress in the bolt and flange is found using

$$T = \frac{\sigma_b i t d D_2}{2} \qquad \text{... 13.2(d)/ Pg 252, DHB}$$

where i = number of effective bolts, taken as:

= i, if bolts are used in *reamed and ground holes*, for **[Eq. 13.2(c)]**,

= $\dfrac{i}{2}$, if bolts are used in *clearance holes*, for **[Eq. 13.2(d)]**

- In case of **reamed holes**, torque transmission is by shear resistance of bolts and not by torsional shear stress **[Eq. 13.2(c)]**. Here the bolts are finger tight and there is no clearance between the holes and the nominal diameter of the bolts.
- While in case of **clearance holes** the bolts are tightened with a preload and the torque is transmitted by friction between the two flanges **[Eq. 13.2(d)]**.
  In this case, the frictional torque is calculated as

$$T = \mu F R$$

where F = axial force caused due to bolt loading (N)

     μ = coefficient of friction between the flanges

$$R = \frac{1}{3}\left(\frac{D_o^3 - D_i^3}{D_o^2 - D_i^2}\right), \text{ friction radius assuming uniform pressure distribu-}$$

tion (mm)

D_o = outer diameter of contact/flange

D_i = inner (recess) diameter of contact/flange

Until unless specified, the bolts are fitted in reamed and ground holes.
For safe design, the calculated stresses should be less than the allowable stresses.

V. Design of flange

Flange is made of cast iron

13. Outside diameter of the flange is found as

$$D_3 = D_1 + 6d \qquad \text{... 13.1(f)/ Pg 252, DHB}$$

---

*Should be rounded to the next higher even number.

14. Thickness of the flange is found as
$$t = 0.35D + 9 \text{ mm} \qquad \text{... 13.1(h)/ Pg 252, DHB}$$

15. Check for stresses:

    Shear stress in the flange is found using,
$$T = \frac{\tau_c \pi D_1^2 t}{2} \qquad \text{... 13.2(e)/ Pg 252, DHB}$$

For safe design, the calculated stresses should be less than the allowable stresses.

VI. Other parameters

Values of b, c, f, t_1, t_2, t_3 and a are obtained using empirical relations from...
$$\text{... Fig. 13.1(a \& b)/ Pg 251, DHB}$$

Note:
- The shaft is made of plain carbon steel C30, C40 or C45 while the flange is made of gray cast iron FG 200.
- The most commonly used material used for keys include 45C8 and 50C8 in order to withstand shear and compressive stresses resulting from torque transmission. Further according to Indian standards, strength not less than 60 MPa shall be used as the material of the key.
- Until unless specified, the shaft and key are assumed to be made of same material.

27. **Design a CI flange coupling to transmit 18 kW at 1440 rpm. The allowable stresses for shafts, keys and bolts are 75 MPa in shear and 150 MPa in crushing. The allowable shear stress for CI flange is 5 MPa.**

VTU – June/ July 2014 – 10 Marks; Dec. 07/ Jan. 2008 – 10 Marks; (similar) July/ Aug. 2004 – 10 Marks

Solution: $P = 18$ kW, $n = 1440$ rpm, $\tau_s = \tau_1 = \tau_b = 75$ MPa, $\sigma_b = \sigma_{b1} = \sigma_b = 150$ MPa, $\tau_c = 5$ MPa.

I. Design of shaft:

1. We know that
$$T = \frac{9.55 \times 10^6 (P)}{n} = \frac{9.55 \times 10^6 \times (18)}{1440} = 119.38 \times 10^3 \text{ N·mm}$$
$$\text{... 3.3(a)/ Pg 50, DHB}$$

2. Shaft diameter,
$$\tau_s = \frac{16T}{\pi D^3} \qquad \text{... 3.1/ Pg 50, DHB}$$
$$75 = \frac{16 \times 119.38 \times 10^3}{\pi D^3}$$
$$D = 20.08 \text{ mm}$$

∴ Standard size of shaft,
$$D = 22 \text{ mm} \qquad \text{... Tb. 3.5(a)/ Pg 57, DHB}$$

II. Design of hub:

3. Hub diameter
$$D_1 = 1.5D + 25 \text{ mm} = (1.5 \times 22) + 25 = 58 \text{ mm}$$
$$\text{... 13.1(d)/ Pg 252, DHB}$$

4. Hub length $L = 1.2D + 20$ mm $= (1.2 \times 22) + 20 = 46.4$ mm ≈ 48 mm

... **13.1(g)/ Pg 252, DHB**

III. Design of key:

5. Since $\sigma_{b1} = 2\tau_1$, use square key.

6. For $D = 22$ mm, $b = h = 6$ mm.   ... **Tb. 4.1/ Pg 69, DHB**

7. The length of key in each part is kept equal to length of hub, i.e. $l = L = 48$ mm.

8. *Check for stresses*:

   a. Shear stress in the key:

$$T = \frac{1}{2}\tau_1 lbD \qquad \qquad \text{... } \textbf{4.5(a)/ Pg 62, DHB}$$

$$119.38 \times 10^3 = \frac{1}{2}[\tau_1 \times 48 \times 6 \times 22]$$

$$\tau_1 = 37.68 \text{ MPa} < 75 \text{ MPa, hence safe.}$$

   b. *Crushing stress in the key*:

$$T = \frac{1}{4}\sigma_{b1} lhD \qquad \qquad \text{... } \textbf{4.4(b)/ Pg 62, DHB}$$

$$119.38 \times 10^3 = \frac{1}{4}[\sigma_{b1} \times 48 \times 6 \times 22]$$

$$\sigma_{b1} = 75.37 \text{ MPa} < 150 \text{ MPa, hence safe.}$$

IV. Design of bolts:

9. Number of bolts:

$$i = \frac{3D}{80} + 2 = \frac{3 \times 22}{80} + 2 \qquad \text{... } \textbf{13.1(a)/ Pg 251, DHB}$$

$$= 2.825 \approx 4 \text{ (next higher even number)}$$

10. Diameter of the bolts:

$$d = \frac{0.423D}{\sqrt{i}} + 7.5 \text{ mm} = \frac{0.423 \times 22}{\sqrt{4}} + 7.5 \text{ mm} = 12.15 \text{ mm}$$

... **13.1(c)/ Pg 251, DHB**

$\therefore$ Standard size of bolt, $d = 14$ mm   ... **Tb. 9.8/ Pg 141, DHB**

11. PCD of bolts:

$$D_2 = D_1 + 3.2d = 58 + (3.2 \times 14) = 102.8 \text{ mm} \approx 105 \text{ mm}$$

... **13.1(e)/ Pg 252, DHB**

12. *Check for stresses*:

   Shear stress in the bolt:

$$T = \frac{\tau_b \pi i d^2 D_2}{8} \qquad \qquad \text{... } \textbf{13.2(c)/ Pg 252, DHB}$$

$$119.38 \times 10^3 = \frac{\tau_b \times \pi \times 4 \times 14^2 \times 105}{8}$$

$$\tau_b = 3.69 \text{ MPa} < 75 \text{ MPa, hence safe.}$$

V. **Design of flange:** Flange is made of cast iron.

13. Outside diameter of the flange:

$$D_3 = D_1 + 6d = 58 + (6 \times 14) = 142 \text{ mm} \quad \dots \textbf{13.1(f)/ Pg 252, DHB}$$

14. Thickness of the flange:

$$t = 0.35D + 9 \text{ mm} = (0.35 \times 22) + 9 = 16.7 \text{ mm} \approx 17 \text{ mm}$$
$$\dots \textbf{13.1(h)/ Pg 252, DHB}$$

15. *Check for stresses*:

a. Shear stress in the flange:

$$T = \frac{\tau_c \pi D_1^2 t}{2} \quad \dots \textbf{13.2(e)/ Pg 252, DHB}$$

$$119.38 \times 10^3 = \frac{\tau_c \times \pi \times 58^2 \times 17}{2}$$

$$\tau_c = 1.33 \text{ MPa} < 5 \text{ MPa, hence safe.}$$

b. *Crushing stress in the bolt and flange*:

$$T = \frac{\sigma_b itdD_2}{2} \quad \dots \textbf{13.2(d)/ Pg 252, DHB}$$

$$119.38 \times 10^3 = \frac{\sigma_b \times 4 \times 17 \times 14 \times 105}{2}$$

$$\sigma_b = 2.39 \text{ MPa} < 150 \text{ MPa, hence safe.}$$

VI. **Other parameters:** $\qquad\qquad\qquad$ ... **13.1(a & b)/Pg 251, DHB**

$$b = 0.5D + 25 \text{ mm} = (0.5 \times 22) + 25 = 36 \text{ mm}$$
$$c = 0.1D + 2.5 \text{ mm} = (0.1 \times 22) + 2.5 = 4.7 \text{ mm}$$
$$f = 1.5d = 1.5 \times 14 = 21 \text{ mm}$$
$$t_1 = 0.25D + 6.35 \text{ mm} = (0.25 \times 22) + 6.35 = 11.85 \text{ mm}$$
$$t_2 = 0.30D + 7.50 \text{ mm} = (0.30 \times 22) + 7.50 = 14.1 \text{ mm}$$
$$t_3 = 0.10D + 5.00 \text{ mm} = (0.10 \times 22) + 5.00 = 7.2 \text{ mm}$$
$$a = 0.20D + 5.00 \text{ mm} = (0.20 \times 22) + 5 = 9.4 \text{ mm}$$

Problems on Torque

28. **Design a protected type CI flange coupling for a steel shaft transmitting 30 kW at 200 rpm. The allowable shear stress in the shaft and key material is 40 MPa. The maximum torque transmitted is to be 20% greater than the full torque. The allowable shear stress in the bolts is 60 MPa and the allowable shear stress in the CI flange is 40 MPa. Sketch the coupling indicating salient dimensions.**

VTU – Dec. 06/ Jan. 2007 – 20 Marks; May/ June 2010 – 06 Marks

Solution: $P = 30$ kW, $n = 200$ rpm, $\tau_s = \tau_1 = 40$ MPa, $T_{max} = 1.2T$, $\tau_b = 60$ MPa, $\tau_c = 40$ MPa.

Assume $\qquad\qquad \sigma_{b_1} = 2\tau_1 = 2 \times 40 = 80$ MPa and
$$\sigma_b = 2\tau_b = 2 \times 60 = 120 \text{ MPa}$$

I. **Design of shaft:**

1. Given $\qquad T_{max} = 1.2T \qquad\qquad\qquad\qquad\qquad\qquad\qquad$ ... Eq. (i)

But $\qquad\qquad T = \frac{9.55 \times 10^6 (P)}{n} = \frac{9.55 \times 10^6 \times (30)}{200} = 1.43 \times 10^6 \text{ N} \cdot \text{mm}$

$$\dots \textbf{3.3(a)/ Pg 50, DHB}$$

∴ Eq. (i) yields...
$$T_{max} = 1.2 \times (1.43 \times 10^6) = 1.72 \times 10^6 \text{ N·mm}$$

2. Shaft diameter,

$$\tau_s = \frac{16T_{max}}{\pi D^3} \qquad \text{... 3.1/ Pg 50, DHB}$$

$$40 = \frac{16 \times 1.72 \times 10^6}{\pi D^3}$$

$$D = 60.28 \text{ mm}$$

∴ Standard size of shaft,
$$D = 63 \text{ mm} \qquad \text{... Tb. 3.5(a)/ Pg 57, DHB}$$

II. Design of hub:

3. Hub diameter
$$D_1 = 1.5D + 25 \text{ mm} = (1.5 \times 63) + 25 = 119.5 \text{ mm} \approx 120 \text{ mm}$$
$$\text{... 13.1(d)/ Pg 252, DHB}$$

4. Hub length $L = 1.2D + 20 \text{ mm} = (1.2 \times 63) + 20 = 95.6 \text{ mm} \approx 96 \text{ mm}$
$$\text{... 13.1(g)/ Pg 252, DHB}$$

III. Design of key:

5. Since $\sigma_{b1} = 2\tau_1$, use square key.
6. For $D = 63$ mm, $b = h = 18$ mm.   ... **Tb. 4.1/ Pg 69, DHB**
7. The length of key in each part is kept equal to length of hub, i.e. $l = L = 96$ mm.
8. *Check for stresses:*

   a. Shear stress in the key:

$$T_{max} = \frac{1}{2}\tau_1 lbD \qquad \text{... 4.5(a)/ Pg 62, DHB}$$

$$1.72 \times 10^3 = \frac{1}{2}[\tau_1 \times 96 \times 18 \times 63]$$

$$\tau_1 = 31.60 \text{ MPa} < 40 \text{ MPa, hence safe.}$$

   b. *Crushing stress in the key*:

$$T_{max} = \frac{1}{4}\sigma_{b1} lhD \qquad \text{... 4.4(b)/ Pg 62, DHB}$$

$$1.72 \times 10^3 = \frac{1}{4}[\sigma_{b1} \times 96 \times 18 \times 63]$$

$$\sigma_{b1} = 63.20 \text{ MPa} < 80 \text{ MPa, hence safe.}$$

IV. Design of bolts:

9. Number of bolts:

$$i = \frac{3D}{80} + 2 = \frac{3 \times 63}{80} + 2 \qquad \text{... 13.1(a)/ Pg 251, DHB}$$

$$= 4.36 \approx 6 \text{ (next higher even number)}$$

10. Diameter of the bolts:

$$d = \frac{0.423D}{\sqrt{i}} + 7.5 \text{ mm} = \frac{0.423 \times 63}{\sqrt{6}} + 7.5 \text{ mm} = 18.38 \text{ mm}$$
$$\text{... 13.1(c)/ Pg 251, DHB}$$

∴ Standard size of bolt, $d = 20$ mm   ... **Tb. 9.8/ Pg 141, DHB**

11. PCD of bolts:
$$D_2 = D_1 + 3.2d = 120 + (3.2 \times 20) = 184 \text{ mm}$$
$$\text{... } \mathbf{13.1(e)/ Pg~252, DHB}$$

12. *Check for stresses*:
   Shear stress in the bolt:

$$T_{max} = \frac{\tau_b \pi i d^2 D_2}{8} \qquad \text{... } \mathbf{13.2(c)/ Pg~252, DHB}$$

$$1.72 \times 10^6 = \frac{\tau_b \times \pi \times 6 \times 20^2 \times 184}{8}$$

$$\tau_b = 9.91 \text{ MPa} < 60 \text{ MPa, hence safe.}$$

V. **Design of flange:**

13. Outside diameter of the flange:
$$D_3 = D_1 + 6d = 120 + (6 \times 20) = 240 \text{ mm...} \mathbf{13.1(f)/ Pg~252, DHB}$$

14. Thickness of the flange:
$$t = 0.35D + 9 \text{ mm} = (0.35 \times 63) + 9 = 31.05 \text{ mm} \approx 32 \text{ mm}$$
$$\text{... } \mathbf{13.1(h)/ Pg~252, DHB}$$

15. *Check for stresses*:
   a. Shear stress in the flange:

$$T_{max} = \frac{\tau_c \pi D_1^2 t}{2} \qquad \text{... } \mathbf{13.2(e)/ Pg~252, DHB}$$

$$1.72 \times 10^6 = \frac{\tau_c \times \pi \times 120^2 \times 32}{2}$$

$$\tau_c = 2.38 \text{ MPa} < 40 \text{ MPa, hence safe.}$$

   b. Crushing stress in the bolt and flange:

$$T_{max} = \frac{\sigma_b i t d D_2}{2} \qquad \text{... } \mathbf{13.2(d)/ Pg~252, DHB}$$

$$1.72 \times 10^6 = \frac{\sigma_b \times 6 \times 32 \times 20 \times 184}{2}$$

$$\sigma_b = 4.87 \text{ MPa} < 120 \text{ MPa, hence safe.}$$

VI. **Other parameters:** $\qquad\qquad\qquad$ ... **13.1(a & b)/Pg 251, DHB**

$$b = 0.5D + 25 \text{ mm} = (0.5 \times 63) + 25 = 56.5 \text{ mm}$$
$$c = 0.1D + 2.5 \text{ mm} = (0.1 \times 63) + 2.5 = 8.87 \text{ mm}$$
$$f = 1.5d = 1.5 \times 20 = 30 \text{ mm}$$
$$t_1 = 0.25D + 6.35 \text{ mm} = (0.25 \times 63) + 6.35 = 22.1 \text{ mm}$$
$$t_2 = 0.30D + 7.50 \text{ mm} = (0.30 \times 63) + 7.50 = 26.4 \text{ mm}$$
$$t_3 = 0.10D + 5.00 \text{ mm} = (0.10 \times 22) + 5.00 = 11.3 \text{ mm}$$
$$a = 0.20D + 5.00 \text{ mm} = (0.20 \times 63) + 5 = 17.6 \text{ mm}$$

29. **Design a protective CI flange coupling for a steel shaft transmitting 15 kW at 200 rpm and having an allowable shear stress of 40 MPa. The working stress in the bolt should not exceed 30 MPa. Assume that the same material is used for shaft and key and the existing stress is twice its value in shear stress. The maximum torque is 25% greater than the full load torque. The shear stress for CI is 14 MPa.**

VTU – June/ July 2015 – 10 Marks

Solution: $P = 15$ kW, $n = 200$ rpm, $\tau_s = \tau_1 = 40$ MPa, $\tau_b = 30$ MPa, $\sigma_{b1} = 2\tau_1 = 80$ MPa, $T_{max} = 1.25T$, $\tau_c = 14$ MPa.

I. Design of shaft:

1. Given $\qquad T_{max} = 1.25T$ $\qquad\qquad\qquad\qquad\qquad$ ... Eq. (i)

$\quad$ But $\qquad T = \dfrac{9.55 \times 10^6 (P)}{n} = \dfrac{9.55 \times 10^6 \times (15)}{200} = 716.25 \times 10^3$ N·mm

$\qquad\qquad\qquad\qquad\qquad\qquad\qquad\qquad\qquad\qquad$ ... **3.3(a)/ Pg 50, DHB**

$\quad \therefore$ Eq. (i) yields...

$\qquad\qquad T_{max} = 1.25 \times (716.25 \times 10^6) = 895.31 \times 10^3$ N·mm

2. Shaft diameter,

$$\tau_s = \frac{16 T_{max}}{\pi D^3} \qquad\qquad\qquad\qquad \text{... } \textbf{3.1/ Pg 50, DHB}$$

$$40 = \frac{16 \times 895.31 \times 10^3}{\pi D^3}$$

$$D = 48.48 \text{ mm}$$

$\quad \therefore$ Standard size of shaft,

$$D = 50 \text{ mm} \qquad\qquad\qquad\qquad \text{... } \textbf{Tb. 3.5(a)/ Pg 57, DHB}$$

II. Design of hub:

3. Hub diameter

$$D_1 = 1.5D + 25 \text{ mm} = (1.5 \times 50) + 25 = 100 \text{ mm}$$

$\qquad\qquad\qquad\qquad\qquad\qquad\qquad\qquad$ ... **13.1(d)/ Pg 252, DHB**

4. Hub length $\quad L = 1.2D + 20$ mm $= (1.2 \times 50) + 20 = 80$ mm

$\qquad\qquad\qquad\qquad\qquad\qquad\qquad\qquad$ ... **13.1(g)/ Pg 252, DHB**

III. Design of key:

5. Since $\sigma_{b1} = 2\tau_1$, use square key.

6. For $D = 50$ mm, $b = h = 14$ mm. $\qquad\qquad$ ... **Tb. 4.1/ Pg 69, DHB**

7. The length of key in each part is kept equal to length of hub, i.e. $l = L = 80$ mm.

8. *Check for stresses*:

$\quad$ a. Shear stress in the key:

$$T_{max} = \frac{1}{2} \tau_1 lbD \qquad\qquad\qquad\qquad \text{... } \textbf{4.5(a)/ Pg 62, DHB}$$

$$895.31 \times 10^3 = \frac{1}{2} [\tau_1 \times 80 \times 14 \times 50]$$

$$\tau_1 = 31.97 \text{ MPa} < 40 \text{ MPa, hence safe.}$$

$\quad$ b. Crushing stress in the key:

$$T_{max} = \frac{1}{4} \sigma_{b1} lhD \qquad\qquad\qquad\qquad \text{... } \textbf{4.4(b)/ Pg 62, DHB}$$

$$895.31 \times 10^3 = \frac{1}{4} [\sigma_{b1} \times 80 \times 14 \times 50]$$

$$\sigma_{b1} = 63.95 \text{ MPa} < 80 \text{ MPa, hence safe.}$$

IV. **Design of bolts:**

9. Number of bolts:

$$i = \frac{3D}{80} + 2 = \frac{3 \times 50}{80} + 2 \qquad \text{... 13.1(a)/ Pg 251, DHB}$$

$$= 3.875 \approx 4 \text{ (next higher even number)}$$

10. Diameter of the bolts:

$$d = \frac{0.423D}{\sqrt{i}} + 7.5 \text{ mm} = \frac{0.423 \times 50}{\sqrt{4}} + 7.5 \text{ mm} = 18.08 \text{ mm}$$

$$\text{... 13.1(c)/ Pg 251, DHB}$$

$\therefore$ Standard size of bolt, $d = 20$ mm ... **Tb. 9.8/ Pg 141, DHB**

11. PCD of bolts:

$$D_2 = D_1 + 3.2d = 100 + (3.2 \times 20) = 164 \text{ mm}$$

$$\text{... 13.1(e)/ Pg 252, DHB}$$

12. *Check for stresses*:

Shear stress in the bolt:

$$T_{max} = \frac{\tau_b \pi i d^2 D_2}{8} \qquad \text{... 13.2(c)/ Pg 252, DHB}$$

$$895.31 \times 10^6 = \frac{\tau_b \times \pi \times 4 \times 20^2 \times 164}{8}$$

$$\tau_b = 8.69 \text{ MPa} < 30 \text{ MPa, hence safe.}$$

V. **Design of flange:**

13. Outside diameter of the flange:

$$D_3 = D_1 + 6d = 100 + (6 \times 20) = 120 \text{ mm... } \textbf{13.1(f)/ Pg 252, DHB}$$

14. Thickness of the flange:

$$t = 0.35D + 9 \text{ mm} = (0.35 \times 50) + 9 = 26.5 \text{ mm} \approx 27 \text{ mm}$$

$$\text{... 13.1(h)/ Pg 252, DHB}$$

15. *Check for stresses*:

Shear stress in the flange:

$$T_{max} = \frac{\tau_c \pi D_1^2 t}{2} \qquad \text{... 13.2(e)/ Pg 252, DHB}$$

$$895.31 \times 10^3 = \frac{\tau_c \times \pi \times 100^2 \times 27}{2}$$

$$\tau_c = 2.11 \text{ MPa} < 14 \text{ MPa, hence safe.}$$

VI. **Other parameters:** ... **13.1(a & b)/Pg 251, DHB**

$$b = 0.5D + 25 \text{ mm} = (0.5 \times 50) + 25 = 50 \text{ mm}$$

$$c = 0.1D + 2.5 \text{ mm} = (0.1 \times 50) + 2.5 = 7.5 \text{ mm}$$

$$f = 1.5d = 1.5 \times 20 = 30 \text{ mm}$$

$$t_1 = 0.25D + 6.35 \text{ mm} = (0.25 \times 50) + 6.35 = 18.85 \text{ mm}$$

$$t_2 = 0.30D + 7.50 \text{ mm} = (0.30 \times 50) + 7.50 = 22.5 \text{ mm}$$

$$t_3 = 0.10D + 5.00 \text{ mm} = (0.10 \times 50) + 5.00 = 10 \text{ mm}$$

$$a = 0.20D + 5.00 \text{ mm} = (0.20 \times 50) + 5 = 15 \text{ mm}$$

30. **It is required to design a rigid type flange coupling to connect two shafts. The input shaft transmits 37.5 kW at 180 rev/min to the output shaft through the coupling. The starting torque is 50% higher than the rated torque. Select material for flanges as cast iron FG200 (σ_{ut} = 200 MPa) with a factor of safety 6, material for shafts as carbon steel with σ_{yt} = 380 MPa, with a factor of safety 2.5, material for key and bolts may be taken as steel with σ_{yt} = 400 MPa (in tension) and σ_{yC} = 600 MPa (in compression) respectively and a factor of safety 2.5. Design the coupling and give the major dimensions.**

VTU – June 2012 – 14 Marks

Solution: P = 37.5 kW, n = 180 rpm, T_{max} = 1.50T.
Material:

Flange:	FG 200:	σ_{ut} = 200 MPa, FoS = 6
Shaft:	Carbon steel:	σ_{yt} = 380 MPa, FoS = 2.5
Keys and bolts:	Steel:	σ_{yt} = 400 MPa, σ_{yc} = 600 MPa, FoS = 2.5

Allowable stresses:

Flange:
$$\tau_c = \frac{0.5\,\sigma_{ut}}{\text{FoS}} = \frac{0.5 \times 200}{6} = 16.67 \text{ MPa}$$

Shaft:
$$\tau_s = \frac{0.5\,\sigma_{yt}}{\text{FoS}} = \frac{0.5 \times 380}{2.5} = 76 \text{ MPa}$$

Keys and bolts:
$$\tau_1 = \tau_b = \frac{0.5\,\sigma_{yt}}{\text{FoS}} = \frac{0.5 \times 400}{2.5} = 80 \text{ MPa}$$

$$\sigma_{b1} = \frac{\sigma_{yc}}{\text{FoS}} = \frac{600}{2.5} = 240 \text{ MPa}$$

I. **Design of shaft:**
1. Given $T_{max} = 1.5T$ ... Eq. (i)

But
$$T = \frac{9.55 \times 10^6 (P)}{n} = \frac{9.55 \times 10^6 \times (37.5)}{180} = 1.98 \times 10^6 \text{ N·mm}$$
... **3.3(a)/ Pg 50, DHB**

Eq. (i) yields...
$$T_{max} = 1.5 \times (1.98 \times 10^6) = 2.98 \times 10^3 \text{ N·mm}$$

2. Shaft diameter,
$$\tau_s = \frac{16 T_{max}}{\pi D^3}$$
... **3.1/ Pg 50, DHB**

$$76 = \frac{16 \times 2.98 \times 10^6}{\pi D^3}$$

$$D = 58.47 \text{ mm}$$

∴ Standard size of shaft,
$$D = 63 \text{ mm}$$
... **Tb. 3.5(a)/ Pg 57, DHB**

II. **Design of hub:**
3. Hub diameter
$$D_1 = 1.5D + 25 \text{ mm} = (1.5 \times 63) + 25 = 119.5 \text{ mm} \approx 120 \text{ mm}$$
... **13.1(d)/ Pg 252, DHB**

4. Hub length $L = 1.2D + 20 \text{ mm} = (1.2 \times 63) + 20 = 95.6 \text{ mm} \approx 96 \text{ mm}$
... **13.1(g)/ Pg 252, DHB**

III. Design of key:

5. Since $\sigma_{b1} \neq 2\tau_1$, use square key.
6. For $D = 63$ mm, $b = 18$ mm and $h = 11$ mm.   ... **Tb. 4.1/ Pg 69, DHB**
7. The length of key in each part is kept equal to length of hub, i.e. $l = L = 96$ mm.
8. *Check for stresses*:

a. Shear stress in the key:

$$T_{max} = \frac{1}{2}\tau_1 lbD \qquad\qquad ... \textbf{4.5(a)/ Pg 62, DHB}$$

$$2.98 \times 10^6 = \frac{1}{2}[\tau_1 \times 96 \times 18 \times 63]$$

$$\tau_1 = 54.75 \text{ MPa} < 80 \text{ MPa, hence safe.}$$

b. Crushing stress in the key:

$$T_{max} = \frac{1}{4}\sigma_{b1} lhD \qquad\qquad ... \textbf{4.4(b)/ Pg 62, DHB}$$

$$2.98 \times 10^6 = \frac{1}{4}[\sigma_{b1} \times 96 \times 11 \times 63]$$

$$\sigma_{b1} = 179.17 \text{ MPa} < 240 \text{ MPa, hence safe.}$$

IV. Design of bolts:

9. Number of bolts:

$$i = \frac{3D}{80} + 2 = \frac{3 \times 63}{80} + 2 \qquad\qquad ... \textbf{13.1(a)/ Pg 251, DHB}$$

$$= 4.36 \approx 6 \text{ (next higher even number)}$$

10. Diameter of the bolts:

$$d = \frac{0.423D}{\sqrt{i}} + 7.5 \text{ mm} = \frac{0.423 \times 63}{\sqrt{6}} + 7.5 \text{ mm} = 18.38 \text{ mm}$$

$$... \textbf{13.1(c)/ Pg 251, DHB}$$

∴ Standard size of bolt, $d = 20$ mm   ... **Tb. 9.8/ Pg 141, DHB**

11. PCD of bolts:

$$D_2 = D_1 + 3.2d = 120 + (3.2 \times 20) = 184 \text{ mm}$$

$$... \textbf{13.1(e)/ Pg 252, DHB}$$

12. *Check for stresses*:

Shear stress in the bolt:

$$T_{max} = \frac{\tau_b \pi i d^2 D_2}{8} \qquad\qquad ... \textbf{13.2(c)/ Pg 252, DHB}$$

$$2.98 \times 10^6 = \frac{\tau_b \times \pi \times 6 \times 20^2 \times 184}{8}$$

$$\tau_b = 17.18 \text{ MPa} < 80 \text{ MPa, hence safe.}$$

V. Design of flange: Flange is made of cast iron

13. Outside diameter of the flange:

$$D_3 = D_1 + 6d = 120 + (6 \times 20) = 240 \text{ mm} ... \textbf{13.1(f)/ Pg 252, DHB}$$

14. Thickness of the flange:
$$t = 0.35D + 9 \text{ mm} = (0.35 \times 63) + 9 = 31.05 \text{ mm} \approx 32 \text{ mm}$$
$$\text{... 13.1(h)/ Pg 252, DHB}$$

15. *Check for stresses:*

a. Shear stress in the flange:

$$T_{max} = \frac{\tau_c \pi D_1^2 t}{2} \qquad \text{... 13.2(e)/ Pg 252, DHB}$$

$$2.98 \times 10^6 = \frac{\tau_c \times \pi \times 120^2 \times 32}{2}$$

$$\tau_c = 4.11 \text{ MPa} < 16.67 \text{ MPa, hence safe.}$$

b. Crushing stress in the bolt and flange:

$$T_{max} = \frac{\sigma_b itdD_2}{2} \qquad \text{... 13.2(d)/ Pg 252, DHB}$$

$$2.98 \times 10^6 = \frac{\sigma_b \times 6 \times 32 \times 20 \times 184}{2}$$

$$\sigma_b = 8.43 \text{ MPa} < 240 \text{ MPa, hence safe.}$$

VI. **Other parameters:**   **... 13.1(a & b)/Pg 251, DHB**

$$b = 0.5D + 25 \text{ mm} = (0.5 \times 63) + 25 = 56.5 \text{ mm}$$
$$c = 0.1D + 2.5 \text{ mm} = (0.1 \times 63) + 2.5 = 8.87 \text{ mm}$$
$$f = 1.5d = 1.5 \times 20 = 30 \text{ mm}$$
$$t_1 = 0.25D + 6.35 \text{ mm} = (0.25 \times 63) + 6.35 = 22.1 \text{ mm}$$
$$t_2 = 0.30D + 7.50 \text{ mm} = (0.30 \times 63) + 7.50 = 26.4 \text{ mm}$$
$$t_3 = 0.10D + 5.00 \text{ mm} = (0.10 \times 63) + 5.00 = 11.3 \text{ mm}$$
$$a = 0.20D + 5.00 \text{ mm} = (0.20 \times 63) + 5 = 17.6 \text{ mm}.$$

Problems on Material Specification

31. **Design a flange coupling to connect the shafts of a motor and centrifugal pump for the following specifications:**
Total head = 20 m, pump output = 3000 liters/min, pump speed = 600 rpm, pump efficiency = 70%. Select C40 steel for shaft and C35 steel for bolts with factor of safety = 2. Use allowable shear stress in the cast iron flange = 15 N/mm².

VTU – Dec. 2014/ Jan. 2015 – 12 Marks; Mar. 2001 – 10 Marks;
(Similar) June/ July 2014 – 10 Marks; (similar)June/ July 2013 – 14 Marks

Solution: H = 20 m, Q = 3000 liters/min = 3 m³/min = $\frac{3}{60}$ = 0.05 m³/sec, n = 600 rpm, η = 70% = 0.7, FoS = 2, τ_c = 15 N/mm².

Material:

Shaft:	C40 steel:	σ_{yt} = 324 MPa
Bolts:	C35 steel:	σ_{yt} = 304 MPa

Allowable stresses:

Shaft: $$\sigma_t = \frac{\sigma_{yt}}{\text{FoS}} = \frac{324}{2} = 162 \text{ MPa}$$

$$\tau_s = 0.5\sigma_t = 0.5 \times 162 = 81 \text{ MPa}$$

Bolts: $$\sigma_b = \frac{\sigma_{yt}}{FoS} = \frac{304}{2} = 152 \text{ MPa}$$

$$\tau_b = 0.5\sigma_t = 0.5 \times 152 = 76 \text{ MPa}$$

I. Design of shaft:

1. We know that

$$T = \frac{9.55 \times 10^6 (P)}{n} \qquad \text{... Eq. (i)}$$

But $$P = \frac{\omega QH}{\eta} = \frac{9.81 \times 0.05 \times 20}{0.7} = 14.01 \text{ kW}$$

∴ Eq. (i) yields...

$$T = \frac{9.55 \times 10^6 \times (14.01)}{600} = 223 \times 10^3 \text{ N·mm}$$

... 3.3(a)/ Pg 50, DHB

2. Shaft diameter,

$$\tau_s = \frac{16T}{\pi D^3} \qquad \text{... 3.1/ Pg 50, DHB}$$

$$81 = \frac{16 \times 223 \times 10^3}{\pi D^3}$$

$$D = 24.11 \text{ mm}$$

∴ Standard size of shaft,

$$D = 25 \text{ mm} \qquad \text{... Tb. 3.5(a)/ Pg 57, DHB}$$

II. Design of hub:

3. Hub diameter
$$D_1 = 1.5D + 25 \text{ mm} = (1.5 \times 25) + 25 = 62.5 \text{ mm} \approx 65 \text{ mm}$$
... 13.1(d)/ Pg 252, DHB

4. Hub length $L = 1.2D + 20 \text{ mm} = (1.2 \times 25) + 20 = 50 \text{ mm}$
... 13.1(g)/ Pg 252, DHB

III. Design of key:

5. Since $\sigma_{b1} = 2\tau_1$, use square key.

6. For $D = 25$ mm, $b = 8$ mm and $h = 8$ mm.   ... Tb. 4.1/ Pg 69, DHB

7. The length of key in each part is kept equal to length of hub, i.e. $l = L = 50$ mm.

8. *Check for stresses:*

   a. Shear stress in the key:

$$T = \frac{1}{2}\tau_1 lbD \qquad \text{... 4.5(a)/ Pg 62, DHB}$$

$$223 \times 10^3 = \frac{1}{2}[\tau_1 \times 50 \times 8 \times 25]$$

$$\tau_1 = 44.6 \text{ MPa} < 81 \text{ MPa, hence safe.}$$

b. Crushing stress in the key:

$$T = \frac{1}{4}\sigma_{b1}lhD \qquad \text{... 4.4(b)/ Pg 62, DHB}$$

$$223 \times 10^3 = \frac{1}{4}[\sigma_{b1} \times 50 \times 8 \times 25]$$

$$\sigma_{b1} = 89.17 \text{ MPa} < 162 \text{ MPa, hence safe.}$$

IV. **Design of bolts:**

9. Number of bolts:

$$i = \frac{3D}{80} + 2 = \frac{3 \times 25}{80} + 2 \qquad \text{... 13.1(a)/ Pg 251, DHB}$$

$$= 2.94 \approx 4 \text{ (next higher even number)}$$

10. Diameter of the bolts:

$$d = \frac{0.423D}{\sqrt{i}} + 7.5 \text{ mm} = \frac{0.423 \times 25}{\sqrt{4}} + 7.5 \text{ mm} = 12.78 \text{ mm}$$
$$\text{... 13.1(c)/ Pg 251, DHB}$$

$$\therefore \text{ Standard size of bolt, } d = 16 \text{ mm} \qquad \text{... Tb. 9.8/ Pg 141, DHB}$$

11. PCD of bolts:

$$D_2 = D_1 + 3.2d = 65 + (3.2 \times 16) = 116.2 \text{ mm} \approx 118 \text{ mm}$$
$$\text{... 13.1(e)/ Pg 252, DHB}$$

12. *Check for stresses*:

Shear stress in the bolt:

$$T = \frac{\tau_b \pi i d^2 D_2}{8} \qquad \text{... 13.2(c)/ Pg 252, DHB}$$

$$223 \times 10^6 = \frac{\tau_b \times \pi \times 6 \times 16^2 \times 118}{8}$$

$$\tau_b = 4.70 \text{ MPa} < 76 \text{ MPa, hence safe.}$$

V. **Design of flange:** Flange is made of cast iron.

13. Outside diameter of the flange:

$$D_3 = D_1 + 6d = 65 + (6 \times 16) = 161 \text{ mm} \quad \text{... 13.1(f)/ Pg 252, DHB}$$

14. Thickness of the flange:

$$t = 0.35D + 9 \text{ mm} = (0.35 \times 25) + 9 = 17.75 \text{ mm} \approx 18 \text{ mm}$$
$$\text{... 13.1(h)/ Pg 252, DHB}$$

15. *Check for stresses*:

a. Shear stress in the flange:

$$T = \frac{\tau_c \pi D_1^2 t}{2} \qquad \text{... 13.2(e)/ Pg 252, DHB}$$

$$223 \times 10^3 = \frac{\tau_c \times \pi \times 65^2 \times 18}{2}$$

$$\tau_c = 1.87 \text{ MPa} < 15 \text{ MPa, hence safe.}$$

b. Crushing stress in the bolt and flange:

$$T = \frac{\sigma_b itdD_2}{2} \qquad \text{... 13.2(d)/ Pg 252, DHB}$$

$$223 \times 10^3 = \frac{\sigma_b \times 4 \times 18 \times 16 \times 118}{2}$$

$$\sigma_b = 3.28 \text{ MPa} < 152 \text{ MPa, hence safe.}$$

VI. Other parameters: ... 13.1(a and b)/Pg 251, DHB

$$b = 0.5D + 25 \text{ mm} = (0.5 \times 25) + 25 = 37.5 \text{ mm}$$
$$c = 0.1D + 2.5 \text{ mm} = (0.1 \times 25) + 2.5 = 5 \text{ mm}$$
$$f = 1.5d = 1.5 \times 16 = 24 \text{ mm}$$
$$t_1 = 0.25D + 6.35 \text{ mm} = (0.25 \times 25) + 6.35 = 12.6 \text{ mm}$$
$$t_2 = 0.30D + 7.50 \text{ mm} = (0.30 \times 25) + 7.50 = 15 \text{ mm}$$
$$t_3 = 0.10D + 5.00 \text{ mm} = (0.10 \times 25) + 5.00 = 7.5 \text{ mm}$$
$$a = 0.20D + 5.00 \text{ mm} = (0.20 \times 25) + 5 = 10 \text{ mm}.$$

32. A mild steel shaft has to transmit 40 kW power at 600 rpm. The maximum torque to be transmitted is 30% greater than the average torque. Design a rigid flange coupling for this application.

VTU – Dec. 2012 – 10 Marks

Solution: $P = 40$ kW, $n = 600$ rpm, $T_{max} = 1.3T$.

Repeat the steps which are similar to Problem 30, assuming that shaft and key are made of same material C40 steel, bolts of C35 steel and flange of CI having a shear stress as 14 MPa.

Problems Based on Known Diameter

33. A cast iron protective type flange coupling is used to connect two shafts of 80 mm diameter. The shaft runs at 250 rpm and transmits a torque of 4300 N·m. The permissible shear stress for shaft and bolt materials is 50 MPa and permissible shear stress for the flange is 8 MPa. Design the bolts, hub and flange for the coupling.

VTU – Dec. 2011 – 14 Marks

Solution: $D = 80$ mm, $n = 250$ rpm, $T = 4300$ N·m $= 4.3 \times 10^6$ N·mm, $\tau_s = \tau_b = 50$ MPa, $\tau_c = 8$ MPa.

I. Design of hub:

1. Hub diameter

$$D_1 = 1.5D + 25 \text{ mm} = (1.5 \times 80) + 25 = 145 \text{ mm}$$
     ... 13.1(d)/ Pg 252, DHB

2. Hub length $L = 1.2D + 20 \text{ mm} = (1.2 \times 80) + 20 = 116 \text{ mm}$
     ... 13.1(g)/ Pg 252, DHB

II. Design of bolts:

3. Number of bolts:

$$i = \frac{3D}{80} + 2 = \frac{3 \times 80}{80} + 2 \qquad \text{... 13.1(a)/ Pg 251, DHB}$$

$$= 5 \approx 6 \text{ (next higher even number)}$$

4. Diameter of the bolts:

$$d = \frac{0.423D}{\sqrt{i}} + 7.5 \text{ mm} = \frac{0.423 \times 80}{\sqrt{6}} + 7.5 \text{ mm} = 21.32 \text{ mm}$$

... **13.1(c)/ Pg 251, DHB**

∴ Standard size of bolt, $d = 24$ mm   ... **Tb. 9.8/ Pg 141, DHB**

5. PCD of bolts:

$$D_2 = D_1 + 3.2d = 145 + (3.2 \times 24) = 221.8 \text{ mm} \approx 222 \text{ mm}$$

... **13.1(e)/ Pg 252, DHB**

6. *Check for stresses*:

Shear stress in the bolt:

$$T = \frac{\tau_b \pi i d^2 D_2}{8}$$ ... **13.2(c)/ Pg 252, DHB**

$$4.33 \times 10^6 = \frac{\tau_b \times \pi \times 6 \times 24^2 \times 222}{8}$$

$$\tau_b = 14.37 \text{ MPa} < 50 \text{ MPa, hence safe.}$$

III. **Design of flange:**

7. Outside diameter of the flange:

$$D_3 = D_1 + 6d = 145 + (6 \times 24) = 289 \text{ mm} \approx 290 \text{ mm}$$

... **13.1(f)/ Pg 252, DHB**

8. Thickness of the flange:

$$t = 0.35D + 9 \text{ mm} = (0.35 \times 80) + 9 = 37 \text{ mm}$$

... **13.1(h)/ Pg 252, DHB**

9. *Check for stresses*:

Shear stress in the flange:

$$T = \frac{\tau_c \pi D_1^2 t}{2}$$ ... **13.2(e)/ Pg 252, DHB**

$$4.33 \times 10^6 = \frac{\tau_c \times \pi \times 145^2 \times 37}{2}$$

$$\tau_c = 3.54 \text{ MPa} < 8 \text{ MPa, hence safe.}$$

34. **Design a cast iron flange coupling to connect two shafts of 45 mm diameter to transmit 20 kW power at 400 rpm. The permissible shear strength for the shaft, bolt and key is 50 MPa and the permissible compressive stress is 120 MPa. The permissible shear strength for cast iron is 15 MPa. Assume maximum torque transmitted to be 30% greater than the normal torque. Design the coupling assuming the bolts are fitted in reamed holes.**

VTU – Dec. 2014/ Jan. 2015 – 12 Marks; Dec. 2009/ Jan. 2010 – 20 Marks

Solution: $D = 45$ mm, $P = 20$ kW, $n = 400$ rpm, $\tau_s = \tau_b = \tau_1 = 50$ MPa, $\sigma_s = \sigma_b = \sigma_1 = 1200$ MPa, $\tau_c = 15$ MPa, $T_{max} = 1.3T$.

I. **Design of shaft:**

1. Given $T_{max} = 1.3T$ ... Eq. (i)

But $T = \dfrac{9.55 \times 10^6 (P)}{n} = \dfrac{9.55 \times 10^6 \times (20)}{400} = 477.5 \times 10^3$ N·mm

... **3.3(a)/ Pg 50, DHB**

∴ Eq. (i) yields...

$T_{max} = 1.3 \times (477.5 \times 10^6) = 620.75 \times 10^3$ N·mm

... **3.3(a)/ Pg 50, DHB**

2. Shaft diameter,

$D = 45$ mm (data)

II. **Design of hub:**

3. Hub diameter

$D_1 = 1.5D + 25$ mm $= (1.5 \times 45) + 25 = 92.5$ mm ≈ 95 mm

... **13.1(d)/ Pg 252, DHB**

4. Hub length $L = 1.2D + 20$ mm $= (1.2 \times 45) + 20 = 74$ mm

... **13.1(g)/ Pg 252, DHB**

III. **Design of key:**

5. Since $\sigma_{b1} \neq 2\tau_1$, use rectangular key.

6. For $D = 25$ mm, $b = 14$ mm and $h = 9$ mm. ... **Tb. 4.1/ Pg 69, DHB**

7. The length of key in each part is kept equal to length of hub, i.e. $l = L = 74$ mm.

8. *Check for stresses*:

a. Shear stress in the key:

$$T_{max} = \frac{1}{2}\tau_1 lbD \qquad \text{... 4.5(a)/ Pg 62, DHB}$$

$$620.75 \times 10^3 = \frac{1}{2}[\tau_1 \times 74 \times 14 \times 45]$$

$\tau_1 = 26.63$ MPa < 50 MPa, hence safe.

b. Crushing stress in the key:

$$T_{max} = \frac{1}{4}\sigma_{b1} lhD \qquad \text{... 4.4(b)/ Pg 62, DHB}$$

$$620.75 \times 10^3 = \frac{1}{4}[\sigma_{b1} \times 74 \times 9 \times 45]$$

$\sigma_{b1} = 82.85$ MPa < 120 MPa, hence safe.

IV. **Design of bolts:**

9. Number of bolts:

$$i = \frac{3D}{80} + 2 = \frac{3 \times 45}{80} + 2 \qquad \text{... 13.1(a)/ Pg 251, DHB}$$

$= 3.69 \approx 4$ (next higher even number)

10. Diameter of the bolts:

$$d = \frac{0.423D}{\sqrt{i}} + 7.5 \text{ mm} = \frac{0.423 \times 45}{\sqrt{4}} + 7.5 \text{ mm} = 17.02 \text{ mm}$$

... **13.1(c)/ Pg 251, DHB**

∴ Standard size of bolt, $d = 20$ mm   ... **Tb. 9.8/ Pg 141, DHB**

11. PCD of bolts:

$$D_2 = D_1 + 3.2d = 95 + (3.2 \times 20) = 159 \text{ mm}$$

... **13.1(e)/ Pg 252, DHB**

12. *Check for stresses*:

Shear stress in the bolt:

$$T_{max} = \frac{\tau_b \pi i d^2 D_2}{8}$$

... **13.2(c)/ Pg 252, DHB**

$$620.75 \times 10^3 = \frac{\tau_b \times \pi \times 6 \times 20^2 \times 159}{8}$$

$$\tau_b = 6.21 \text{ MPa} < 50 \text{ MPa, hence safe.}$$

V. **Design of flange:**

13. Outside diameter of the flange:

$$D_3 = D_1 + 6d = 95 + (6 \times 20) = 215 \text{ mm}$$

... **13.1(f)/ Pg 252, DHB**

14. Thickness of the flange:

$$t = 0.35D + 9 \text{ mm} = (0.35 \times 45) + 9 = 24.75 \text{ mm} \approx 25 \text{ mm}$$

... **13.1(h)/ Pg 252, DHB**

15. *Check for stresses*:

a. Shear stress in the flange:

$$T_{max} = \frac{\tau_c \pi D_1^2 t}{2}$$

... **13.2(e)/ Pg 252, DHB**

$$620.75 \times 10^3 = \frac{\tau_c \times \pi \times 95^2 \times 25}{2}$$

$$\tau_c = 1.75 \text{ MPa} < 50 \text{ MPa, hence safe.}$$

b. Crushing stress in the bolt and flange:

$$T = \frac{\sigma_b itdD_2}{2}$$

... **13.2(d)/ Pg 252, DHB**

$$620.75 \times 10^3 = \frac{\sigma_b \times 4 \times 25 \times 20 \times 159}{2}$$

$$\sigma_b = 3.90 \text{ MPa} < 120 \text{ MPa, hence safe.}$$

VI. **Other parameters:**   ... **13.1(a & b)/Pg 251, DHB**

$$b = 0.5D + 25 \text{ mm} = (0.5 \times 45) + 25 = 47.5 \text{ mm}$$
$$c = 0.1D + 2.5 \text{ mm} = (0.1 \times 45) + 2.5 = 7 \text{ mm}$$
$$f = 1.5d = 1.5 \times 20 = 30 \text{ mm}$$
$$t_1 = 0.25D + 6.35 \text{ mm} = (0.25 \times 45) + 6.35 = 17.6 \text{ mm}$$
$$t_2 = 0.30D + 7.50 \text{ mm} = (0.30 \times 45) + 7.50 = 21 \text{ mm}$$
$$t_3 = 0.10D + 5.00 \text{ mm} = (0.10 \times 45) + 5.00 = 9.5 \text{ mm}$$
$$a = 0.20D + 5.00 \text{ mm} = (0.20 \times 45) + 5 = 14 \text{ mm}$$

35. In a rigid flange coupling designed to transmit 50 kW at 200 rpm, a tapered key of dimensions 18 × 11 × 100 is used to key the shafts of 60 mm diameter to flange. Five bolts are used on a bolt circle of 170 mm diameter. Taking the materials of bolts same as that of shaft, determine:
    a. The shear stress induced in the shaft and the key.
    b. The size of bolts required.

VTU – June/ July 2009 – 12 Marks

Solution: $P = 50$ kW, $n = 200$ rpm, taper key: $18 \times 11 \times 100$ mm $\Rightarrow b = 14$ mm, $h = 11$ mm, $l = 100$ mm, $D = 60$ mm, $i = 5$, PCD of bolts, $D_2 = 170$ mm, a. $\tau_s = ?$, $\tau_1 = ?$ b. $d = ?$, if $\tau_s = \tau_b$.

a. **To find shear stresses:**

    i. *Shear stress in the shaft*:
    We know that

$$\tau_s = \frac{16T}{\pi D^3} \qquad \text{...Eq. (i) } \textbf{3.1/ Pg 50, DHB}$$

But

$$T = \frac{9.55 \times 10^6 (P)}{n} = \frac{9.55 \times 10^6 \times (50)}{200} = 2.39 \times 10^6 \text{ N·mm}$$

$$\text{... } \textbf{3.3(a)/ Pg 50, DHB}$$

$\therefore$ Eq. (i) yields...

$$\tau_s = \frac{16 \times 2.39 \times 10^6}{\pi \times 60^3} = 56.35 \text{ MPa}$$

    ii. Shear stress in the key:
    We know that

$$T = \frac{1}{2}\tau_1 lbD \qquad \text{... } \textbf{4.5(a)/ Pg 62, DHB}$$

$$2.39 \times 10^6 = \frac{1}{2}[\tau_1 \times (100 \times 14 \times 60)]$$

$$\tau_1 = 56.90 \text{ MPa}$$

b. **Size of bolt:**
    Shear stress in the bolt,

$$T = \frac{\tau_b \pi i d^2 D_2}{8} \qquad \text{... } \textbf{13.2(c)/ Pg 252, DHB}$$

$$2.39 \times 10^6 = \frac{56.35 \times \pi \times 5 \times d^2 \times 170}{8} \quad (\because \tau_s = \tau_b) \text{ data}$$

$$d = 11.27 \text{ mm}$$

$\therefore$ Standard size of bolt,

$$d = 14 \text{ mm} \qquad \text{... Tb. 9.8/Pg 141, DHB}$$

36. **A rigid coupling has four bolts on a pitch circle of 125 mm diameter and transmitting 20 kW power at 720 rpm. The bolts are made of carbon steel (C45) and has a factor of safety of 3. Determine the diameter of the bolt.**

VTU – Dec. 08/ Jan. 2009 – 06 Marks

Solution: $i = 4$, PCD of bolts, $D_2 = 125$ mm, $P = 20$ kW, $n = 720$ rpm, bolt material: C45, FoS = 3, $d = ?$

Material: Bolts: C45 steel: $\sigma_{yt} = 353$ MPa   **... Tb. I.8/ Pg 464, DHB**
Allowable stresses: Bolts:

$$\sigma_b = \frac{\sigma_{yt}}{\text{FoS}} = \frac{353}{3} = 117.67 \text{ MPa}$$

$$\tau_b = 0.5\sigma_t = 0.5 \times 117.67 = 58.84 \text{ MPa}$$

Shear stress in the bolt,

$$T = \frac{\tau_b \pi i d^2 D_2}{8} \qquad \text{... Eq. (i) } \textbf{13.2(c)/ Pg 252, DHB}$$

But $$T = \frac{9.55 \times 10^6 (P)}{n} = \frac{9.55 \times 10^6 \times (20)}{720} = 265.27 \times 10^3 \text{ N·mm}$$

... 3.3(a)/ Pg 50, DHB

∴ Eq. (i) yields...

$$265.27 \times 10^3 = \frac{58.84 \times \pi \times 4 \times d^2 \times 125}{8}$$

$$d = 4.80 \text{ mm}$$

∴ Standard size of bolt,

$$d = 6 \text{ mm} \qquad\qquad\qquad \text{... Tb. 9.8/ Pg 141, DHB}$$

37. **The following specifications refer to rigid coupling: Outer diameter of flange = 160 mm, diameter of recess = 95 mm, number of bolts = 6, preload of each bolt = 10 kN, coefficient of friction = 0.15, speed = 100 rpm. The bolts are fitted in large clearance holes. Calculate the power transmitting capacity of the coupling.**

Solution: $D_o = 160$ mm, $D_i = 95$ mm, $i = 6$, $F = 10 \times 10^3$ N, $\mu = 0.15$, $n = 100$ rpm, $P = ?$

We know that $$T = \frac{9.55 \times 10^6 (P)}{n} \qquad \text{... Eq. (i) } \textbf{3.3(a)/ Pg 50, DHB}$$

But $$T = \mu F R \qquad\qquad \text{... Eq. (ii) } \textbf{13.2(b)/ Pg 252, DHB}$$

where $$R = \frac{1}{3}\left(\frac{D_o^3 - D_i^3}{D_o^2 - D_i^2}\right) = \frac{1}{3}\left(\frac{160^3 - 95^3}{160^2 - 95^2}\right) = 65.13 \text{ mm}$$

∴ Eq. (ii) yields... $T = 0.15 \times 10 \times 10^3 \times 65.13$

$$T = 97695 \text{ N·mm}$$

Thus the torque transmitted by i bolts $= 97695 \times 6 = 586170$ N·mm.

∴ Eq. (i) yields...

$$586170 = \frac{9.55 \times 10^6 (P)}{100} \Rightarrow P = 6.14 \text{ kW}$$

Shaft Design Based

38. **A mild steel shaft has to transmit 75 kW at 200 rev/min. The allowable stress in the shaft material is limited to 40 MPa and the angle of twist is not to exceed 1° in a length of 20 diameters. Calculate the suitable diameter of the shaft. Design**

a cast iron flange coupling for this shaft. Assume the allowable stress in the material of the bolts to be 30 MPa and the bolts are fitted in reamed holes. Assume the allowable shear stress in the cast iron flange equal to 15 MPa.

VTU – June/ July 2008 – 12 Marks; Dec. 2013/ Jan. 2014 – 10 Marks;
(Similar) Jan/ Feb. 2005 – 20 Marks

Solution: $P = 75$ kW, $n = 200$ rpm, $\tau_s = 40$ MPa, $\theta = 1°$, $L = 20D$, $D = ?$, $\tau_b = 30$ MPa, $\tau_c = 15$ MPa.

Assume that the shaft and key are made of same material; and a square key

i.e. $\qquad \tau_s = \tau_1 = 40$ MPa

$\qquad \tau_{b1} = 2\tau_1 = 2 \times 40 = 80$ MPa

and $\qquad \sigma_b = 2\tau_b = 2 \times 30 = 60$ MPa

I. Design of shaft:

1. We know that

$$T = \frac{9.55 \times 10^6 (P)}{n} = \frac{9.55 \times 10^6 \times (75)}{200} = 3.58 \times 10^6 \text{ N·mm}$$

$\qquad\qquad\qquad\qquad\qquad\qquad\qquad$ ... **3.3(a)/ Pg 50, DHB**

2. Shaft diameter,

 a. Based on strength:

$$\tau_s = \frac{16T}{\pi D^3} \qquad\qquad\qquad\qquad \text{... 3.1/ Pg 50, DHB}$$

$$40 = \frac{16 \times 3.58 \times 10^6}{\pi D^3}$$

$$D = 76.96 \text{ mm} \qquad\qquad\qquad\qquad\qquad\qquad \text{... Eq. (a)}$$

 b. Based on rigidity:

$$\theta = \frac{584TL}{GD^4} \qquad\qquad\qquad\qquad\qquad \text{... 3.1/ Pg 50, DHB}$$

$$G = 78.5 \times 10^3 \text{ MPa, for steel} \qquad\qquad \text{... Tb. 1.1/ Pg 11, DHB}$$

$$1 = \frac{584 \times 3.58 \times 10^6 \times (20D)}{(78.5 \times 10^3)D^4}$$

$$D = 81.06 \text{ mm} \qquad\qquad\qquad\qquad\qquad\qquad \text{... Eq. (b)}$$

Based on Eqs. (a) and (b), select maximum diameter for design, i.e.

$$D = 81.06 \text{ mm}$$

∴ Standard size of shaft,

$$D = 90 \text{ mm} \qquad\qquad\qquad\qquad \text{... Tb. 3.5(a)/ Pg 57, DHB}$$

II. Design of hub:

3. Hub diameter

$$D_1 = 1.5D + 25 \text{ mm} = (1.5 \times 90) + 25 = 160 \text{ mm}$$

$\qquad\qquad\qquad\qquad\qquad\qquad\qquad$ ... **13.1(d)/ Pg 252, DHB**

4. Hub length $\quad L = 1.2D + 20 \text{ mm} = (1.2 \times 90) + 20 = 128 \text{ mm}$

$\qquad\qquad\qquad\qquad\qquad\qquad\qquad$ ... **13.1(g)/ Pg 252, DHB**

III. **Design of key:**

   5. Since $\sigma_{b1} = 2\tau_1$, use square key.

   6. For $D = 90$ mm, $b = h = 25$ mm.   ... **Tb. 4.1/ Pg 69, DHB**

   7. The length of key in each part is kept equal to length of hub, i.e. $l = L = 128$ mm.

   8. *Check for stresses:*

   a. Shear stress in the key:

$$T = \frac{1}{2}\tau_1 lbD \qquad\qquad ... \textbf{4.5(a)/ Pg 62, DHB}$$

$$3.58 \times 10^6 = \frac{1}{2}[\tau_1 \times 128 \times 25 \times 90]$$

$$\tau_1 = 24.86 \text{ MPa} < 40 \text{ MPa, hence safe.}$$

   b. Crushing stress in the key:

$$T = \frac{1}{4}\sigma_{b1} lhD \qquad\qquad ... \textbf{4.4(b)/ Pg 62, DHB}$$

$$3.58 \times 10^6 = \frac{1}{4}[\sigma_{b1} \times 128 \times 25 \times 90]$$

$$\sigma_{b1} = 49.72 \text{ MPa} < 80 \text{ MPa, hence safe.}$$

IV. **Design of bolts:**

   9. Number of bolts:

$$i = \frac{3D}{80} + 2 = \frac{3 \times 90}{80} + 2 \qquad\qquad ... \textbf{13.1(a)/ Pg 251, DHB}$$

$$= 5.375 \approx 6 \text{ (next higher even number)}$$

   10. Diameter of the bolts:

$$d = \frac{0.423D}{\sqrt{i}} + 7.5 \text{ mm} = \frac{0.423 \times 90}{\sqrt{6}} + 7.5 \text{ mm} = 23.04 \text{ mm}$$

  ... **13.1(c)/ Pg 251, DHB**

$$\therefore \text{ Standard size of bolt, } d = 27 \text{ mm} \qquad ... \textbf{Tb. 9.8/ Pg 141, DHB}$$

   11. PCD of bolts:

$$D_2 = D_1 + 3.2d = 160 + (3.2 \times 27) = 246.4 \text{ mm} \approx 250 \text{ mm}$$

  ... **13.1(e)/ Pg 252, DHB**

   12. *Check for stresses:*

   Shear stress in the bolt:

$$T = \frac{\tau_b \pi i d^2 D_2}{8} \qquad\qquad ... \textbf{13.2(c)/ Pg 252, DHB}$$

$$3.58 \times 10^6 = \frac{\tau_b \times \pi \times 6 \times 27^2 \times 250}{8}$$

$$\tau_b = 8.34 \text{ MPa} < 30 \text{ MPa, hence safe.}$$

V. **Design of flange:**

   13. Outside diameter of the flange:

$$D_3 = D_1 + 6d = 160 + (6 \times 27) = 322 \text{ mm} ... \textbf{13.1(f)/ Pg 252, DHB}$$

14. Thickness of the flange:
$$t = 0.35D + 9 \text{ mm} = (0.35 \times 90) + 9 = 40.5 \text{ mm} \approx 42 \text{ mm}$$
$$\text{... } \textbf{13.1(h)/ Pg 252, DHB}$$

15. *Check for stresses*:
    a. Shear stress in the flange:

$$T = \frac{\tau_c \pi D_1^2 t}{2} \qquad \text{... } \textbf{13.2(e)/ Pg 252, DHB}$$

$$3.58 \times 10^6 = \frac{\tau_c \times \pi \times 160^2 \times 42}{2}$$

$$\tau_c = 2.12 \text{ MPa} < 15 \text{ MPa, hence safe.}$$

   b. Crushing stress in the bolt and flange:

$$T = \frac{\sigma_b i t d D_2}{2} \qquad \text{... } \textbf{13.2(e)/ Pg 252, DHB}$$

$$3.58 \times 10^6 = \frac{\sigma_b \times 6 \times 42 \times 27 \times 250}{2}$$

$$\sigma_b = 4.21 \text{ MPa} < 60 \text{ MPa, hence safe.}$$

VI. **Other parameters:** $\qquad\qquad\qquad$ **... 13.1(a & b)/Pg 251, DHB**

$$b = 0.5D + 25 \text{ mm} = (0.5 \times 90) + 25 = 70 \text{ mm}$$
$$c = 0.1D + 2.5 \text{ mm} = (0.1 \times 90) + 2.5 = 11.5 \text{ mm}$$
$$f = 1.5d = 1.5 \times 27 = 40.5 \text{ mm}$$
$$t_1 = 0.25D + 6.35 \text{ mm} = (0.25 \times 90) + 6.35 = 28.5 \text{ mm}$$
$$t_2 = 0.30D + 7.50 \text{ mm} = (0.30 \times 90) + 7.50 = 34.5 \text{ mm}$$
$$t_3 = 0.10D + 5.00 \text{ mm} = (0.10 \times 90) + 5.00 = 14 \text{ mm}$$
$$a = 0.20D + 5.00 \text{ mm} = (0.20 \times 90) + 5 = 23 \text{ mm}$$

6.13 FLEXIBLE COUPLING: BUSH–PIN TYPE

The most common coupling is the bush-pin type used when the driving and driven members are mounted on a monoblock. Here motion from one-half of the flange to the other half is transmitted by pins or bolts. This coupling can take up parallel misalignment of shafts up to 0.25 mm per 100 mm outside diameter of the coupling and an angular misalignment of 1.5°.

The coupling has two dissimilar halves with a clearance of 3 to 5 mm, as shown in **Fig. 6.10**. The construction of flexible coupling is similar to flange coupling except that the bolts are replaced by pins and bush. These pins are rigidly fastened by nuts to one of the flanges while their diameters are enlarged and covered with flexible materials like leather or rubber bush. The rubber bush is provided with brass lining at the inner surface to avoid excessive wear of the rubber component. The rubber bushing absorbs shocks and vibration during operation. Power is transmitted from the input shaft to the input flange through key and from the flange to the pin through the bush. The pin then transmits the power to the output flange by shear resistance. Finally power is transmitted from output flange to the output shaft through the key.

Applications: Mostly used to couple electric motors and machines such as a prime mover connected to generator, compressor connected to electric motor, electric motor connected to centrifugal blower, etc.

6.13.1 Design Procedure for Flexible Coupling: Bush and Pin Type

The bush-pin type flexible coupling shown in **Fig. 6.10** consists of the following components:

- Shaft
- Hub
- Key
- Pins or bolts
- Bush
- Flange.

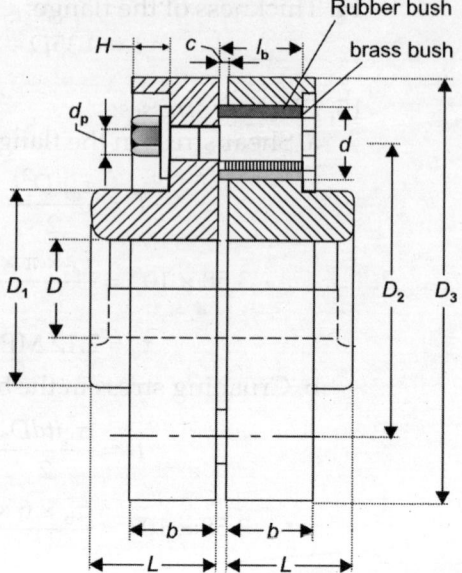

Fig. 6.10: Flexible coupling—Bush-pin type **[Fig. 13.6 (a & b)/Pg 255, DHB]**

Parameters

Let D = diameter of the shaft

D_1 = diameter of the hub

D_2 = bolt circle diameter or pitch circle diameter of bolts

D_3 = diameter of the flange

d_p = diameter of the pin

L = length of the hub

i = number of bolts

T = torque transmitted

l_b = length of the bush

c = clearance between the hubs

τ_s = shear stress in shaft material

τ_1, τ_b, τ_c = shear stress in key, bolt and flange respectively

σ_b, σ_{b1} = crushing stress for bolt and key materials respectively.

I. Design of shaft

1. The torque transmitted is found as

$$T = \frac{9.55 \times 10^6 (P)}{n} \qquad \text{... 3.3(a)/ Pg 50, DHB}$$

2. The shaft diameter is found using

$$\tau_s = \frac{16T}{\pi D^3} \qquad \text{... 3.1/ Pg 50, DHB}$$

Standardize the shaft diameter using... **... Tb. 3.5(a)/Pg 57, DHB**

II. Design of hub

3. Hub diameter $D_1 = 1.5D + 25$ mm **... 13.1(d)/ Pg 252, DHB**
4. Hub length $L = 1.2D + 20$ mm **... 13.1(g)/ Pg 252, DHB**

III. Design of key

5. If crushing strength of the key is twice the shear strength in the key ($\sigma_{b1} = 2\tau_1$) then use square key.
6. Based on diameter of the shaft obtained in step (2), choose proper value of b and h for the type of key from... **...Tb. 4.1/ Pg 69 and/or Tb.4.2/ Pg 70, DHB**

7. The length of key in each part is kept equal to length of hub, i.e. $l = L$.

8. Check for stresses:

   a. Shear stress in the key is found using,

$$T = \frac{1}{2}\tau_1 lbD$$

... 4.5(a)/Pg 62, DHB

   b. Crushing stress in the key is found using

$$T = \frac{1}{4}\sigma_{b1} lhD$$

... 4.4(b)/Pg 62, DHB

   For safe design, the calculated stresses should be less than the allowable stresses.

IV. Design of Pin

9. The number of pins* is found as

$$i = \frac{3D}{80} + 2$$

... 13.1(a)/ Pg 251, DHB

   The minimum number of pins is taken as 6.

10. The diameter of the pin is found as

$$d_p = \frac{0.423D}{\sqrt{i}} + 7.5 \text{ mm}$$

... 13.1(c)/ Pg 251, DHB

   Standardize the pin diameter using... **... Tb. 9.8/Pg 140, DHB**

11. PCD of pins is found as

$$D_2 = D_1 + 3.2d_p$$

... 13.1(e)/ Pg 252, DHB

V. Design of Bush

12. Assume

   Thickness of brass bush (t_b) = 4 mm (effective both sides)

   Thickness of rubber bush (t_r) = 12 mm (effective both sides)

   Allowance for enlarged diameter (*allw*) = 4 mm (effective both sides)

13. Outside diameter of bush

$$d' = d_p + t_b + t_r + allw$$

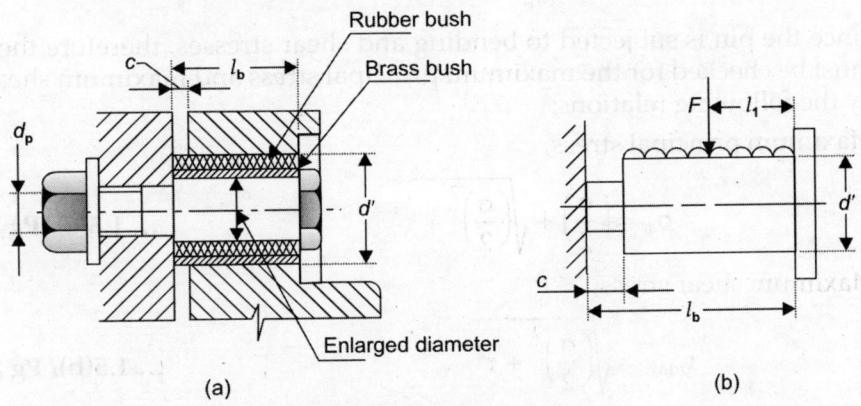

(a)   (b)

Fig. 6.11: Details of pin and bush

*Should be rounded to the next higher even number.

14. Length of the bush is found as

$$p_b = \frac{F}{l_b \cdot d'}$$ ... Eq. (A)/**Pg 351, DHB**

Also torque transmitted by i pins is

$$T = \left(\frac{FD_2}{2}\right) i$$ ... Eq. (B)

From Eqs. (A) and (B), values of l_b and F are obtained.

15. Check for stresses:
    a. Shear stress in the bolt is found using

$$T = \frac{\tau_p \pi i d_p^2 D_2}{8}$$ ... **13.5(b)/ Pg 254, DHB**

    b. Bending stress in the pin is found using

$$\sigma_{bp} = \frac{M}{Z}$$ ... Eq. (C)

Since the pin and the rubber bush are not rigidly held in the right hand flange, therefore the tangential force (F) at the enlarged portion will introduce a bending stress in the pin. Assuming the force (F) to be uniformly distributed on the rubber bush as shown in **Fig. 6.11(b)**, the maximum bending moment on the pin is

$$M = Fl_1 = \frac{F(l_b + c)}{2}$$

where $$l_1 = \frac{1}{2}(l_b - c) + c = \frac{(l_b + c)}{2}; \quad c = \text{clearance (3 to 5 mm)}$$

and $$Z = \frac{\pi d_p^3}{32}$$ $$\left[\text{According to } \mathbf{DHB}, \frac{l}{2} = \frac{(l_b + c)}{2}\right]$$

∴ Eq. (C) yields...

$$\sigma_{bp} = \frac{16F(l_b + c)}{\pi d_p^3}$$ ... **13.5(e)/ Pg 254, DHB**

Since the pin is subjected to bending and shear stresses, therefore the design must be checked for the maximum principal stress and maximum shear stress by the following relations:

c. Maximum principal stress,

$$\sigma_1 = \left(\frac{\sigma}{2}\right) + \sqrt{\left(\frac{\sigma}{2}\right)^2 + \tau^2}$$ ... **1.5(a)/ Pg 3, DHB**

d. Maximum shear stress,

$$\tau_{max} = \sqrt{\left(\frac{\sigma}{2}\right)^2 + \tau^2}$$ ... **1.5(b)/ Pg 3, DHB**

For safe design, the calculated stresses should be less than the allowable stresses.

VI. Design of Flange

16. Outside diameter of the flange is found as

$$D_3 = D_1 + 6d_p \qquad \qquad \text{... 13.1(f)/ Pg 252, DHB}$$

17. Thickness of the flange is found at

$$t = 0.35D + 9 \text{ mm} \qquad \qquad \text{... 13.1(h)/ Pg 252, DHB}$$

18. Check for stresses:

Since stress in the flange is found using,

$$T = \frac{\tau_c \pi D_1^2 t}{2} \qquad \qquad \text{... 13.2(e)/ Pg 252, DHB}$$

For safe design, the calculated stresses should be less than the allowable stresses.

Note:
- The shaft is made of plain carbon steel C30, C40 or C45 while the flange is made of gray cast iron FG 200.
- The most commonly used material used for keys include 45C8 and 50C8 in order to withstand shear and compressive stresses resulting from torque transmission. Further according to Indian standards, strength not less than 60 MPa shall be used as the material of the key.
- Until unless specified, the shaft and key are assumed to be made of same material.

39. **Design a bushed-pin type flexible coupling to connect a pump shaft to a motor shaft transmitting 32 kW at 960 rpm. The overall torque is 20% more than mean torque. The material properties are as follows:**
   i. **The allowable shear and crushing stress for shaft and key material is 40 MPa and 80 MPa respectively.**
   ii. **The allowable shear stress for cast iron is 15 MPa.**
   iii. **The allowable bearing pressure for rubber bush is 0.8 N/mm².**
   iv. **The material of the pin is same as that of shaft and key.**

   VTU – June/ July 2009 – 14 Marks; (Similar)Dec. 2009/ Jan. 2010 – 10 Marks

Solution: $P = 32$ kW, $n = 960$ rpm, $T_{max} = 1.2T$, $\tau_s = \tau_1 = \tau_p = 40$ MPa, $\sigma_b = \sigma_{b1} = \sigma_{bp} = 80$ MPa, $\tau_c = 15$ MPa, $p_b = 0.8$ N/mm².

I. **Design of shaft:**

1. Given $\qquad T_{max} = 1.2T \qquad \qquad \text{... Eq. (i)}$

   But $\qquad T = \dfrac{9.55 \times 10^6 (P)}{n} = \dfrac{9.55 \times 10^6 \times (32)}{960} = 318.34 \times 10^3$ N·mm

   $\qquad \qquad \qquad \qquad \qquad \qquad \qquad \qquad \text{... 3.3(a)/ Pg 50, DHB}$

   $\therefore$ Eq. (i) yields...

   $$T_{max} = 1.2 \times (318.34 \times 10^6) = 382 \times 10^3 \text{ N·mm}$$

2. Shaft diameter,

   $$\tau_s = \frac{16T}{\pi D^3} \qquad \qquad \text{... 3.1/ Pg 50, DHB}$$

   $$40 = \frac{16 \times 382 \times 10^3}{\pi D^3}$$

   $$D = 36.50 \text{ mm}$$

   $\therefore$ Standard size of shaft,

   $$\dot{D} = 40 \qquad \qquad \text{... Tb. 3.5(a)/ Pg 57, DHB}$$

II. **Design of hub:**

3. Hub diameter

$$D_1 = 1.5D + 25 \text{ mm} = (1.5 \times 40) + 25 = 85 \text{ mm}$$

... **13.1(d)/ Pg 252, DHB**

4. Hub length $L = 1.2D + 20 \text{ mm} = (1.2 \times 40) + 20 = 68 \text{ mm}$

... **13.1(g)/ Pg 252, DHB**

III. **Design of key:**

5. Since $\sigma_{b1} = 2\tau_1$, use square key.

6. For $D = 40$ mm, $b = h = 12$ mm.   ... **Tb. 4.1/ Pg 69, DHB**

7. The length of key in each part is kept equal to length of hub, i.e. $l = L = 68$ mm.

8. *Check for stresses*:

   a. Shear stress in the key:

$$T_{\max} = \frac{1}{2}\tau_1 lbD$$

... **4.5(a)/ Pg 62, DHB**

$$382.75 \times 10^3 = \frac{1}{2}[\tau_1 \times 68 \times 12 \times 40]$$

$$\tau_1 = 23.41 \text{ MPa} < 54 \text{ MPa, hence safe.}$$

   b. Crushing stress in the key:

$$T_{\max} = \frac{1}{4}\sigma_{b1} lhD$$

... **4.4(b)/ Pg 62, DHB**

$$382 \times 10^3 = \frac{1}{4}[\sigma_{b1} \times 68 \times 12 \times 40]$$

$$\sigma_{b1} = 46.81 \text{ MPa} < 80 \text{ MPa, hence safe.}$$

IV. **Design of pins:**

9. Number of pins:

$$i = \frac{3D}{80} + 2 = \frac{3 \times 40}{80} + 2$$

... **13.1(a)/ Pg 251, DHB**

$$= 3.5 \approx 4 \text{ (next higher even number)}$$

But the minimum number of pins for a flexible coupling is 6, hence i = 6.

10. Diameter of the pin:

$$d_p = \frac{0.423D}{\sqrt{i}} + 7.5 \text{ mm} = \frac{0.423 \times 40}{\sqrt{6}} + 7.5 \text{ mm} = 14.41 \text{ mm}$$

... **13.1(c)/ Pg 251, DHB**

$\therefore$ Standard size of pin, $d_p = 16$ mm   ... **Tb. 9.8/ Pg 141, DHB**

11. PCD of pins:

$$D_2 = D_1 + 3.2d_p = 85 + (3.2 \times 16) = 136.2 \text{ mm} \approx 140 \text{ mm}$$

... **13.1(e)/ Pg 252, DHB**

V. **Design of Bush:**

12. Assume:

Thickness of brass bush (t_b) = 4 mm	(effective both sides)
Thickness of rubber bush (t_r) = 12 mm	(effective both sides)
Allowance for enlarged diameter (*allw*) = 4 mm	(effective both sides)

13. Outside diameter of bush

$$d' = d_p + t_b + t_r + allw$$

$$d' = 16 + 4 + 12 + 4 = 36 \text{ mm}$$

14. Length of the bush is found as

$$p_b = \frac{F}{l_b \cdot d'}$$

$$0.8 = \frac{F}{l_b \times 36}$$

$$F = 28.8\, l_b \qquad\qquad\qquad\qquad \text{... Eq. (a)}$$

Also torque transmitted by i pins is

$$T_{max} = \left(\frac{FD_2}{2}\right)i \qquad\qquad \text{OR} \qquad T_{max} = \frac{p_b i l_b d' D_2}{2}$$

$$382 \times 10^3 = \left(\frac{28.8 l_b \times 140}{2}\right) \times 6 \qquad 382 \times 10^3 = \left(\frac{0.8 \times 6 \times l_b \times 36 \times 140}{2}\right)$$

$$l_b = 31.58 \text{ mm} \approx 32 \text{ mm} \qquad\qquad l_b = 31.58 \text{ mm} \approx 32 \text{ mm}$$

∴ Eq. (a) yields...

$$F = 28.8 \times 32 = 921.6 \text{ N}$$

15. *Check for stresses*:

a. Shear stress in the pin:

$$T_{max} = \frac{\tau_p \pi i d_p^2 D_2}{8} \qquad\qquad\qquad \text{... 13.5(b)/ Pg 254, DHB}$$

$$382 \times 10^3 = \left(\frac{\tau_p \times \pi \times 6 \times 16^2 \times 140}{8}\right)$$

$$\tau_p = 4.52 \text{ MPa} < 40 \text{ MPa}.$$

b. Bending stress in the pin:

$$\sigma_{bp} = \frac{16F(l_b + c)}{\pi d_p^3} \qquad\qquad\qquad \text{... 13.5(e)/ Pg 254, DHB}$$

$$= \frac{16 \times 921.6 \times (32 + 5)}{\pi \times 16^3} \qquad \text{(Assume } c = 5 \text{ mm)}$$

$$\sigma_{bp} = 42.40 \text{ MPa} < 80 \text{ MPa}.$$

Since the pin is subjected to bending and shear stresses, therefore the design must be checked for the maximum principal stress and maximum shear stress.

c. Maximum principal stress,

$$\sigma_1 = \left(\frac{\sigma}{2}\right) + \sqrt{\left(\frac{\sigma}{2}\right)^2 + \tau^2} \qquad\qquad\qquad \text{... 1.5(a)/ Pg 3, DHB}$$

Here $\sigma = \sigma_{bp} = 42.40$ MPa and $\tau = \tau_p = 4.52$ MPa.

$$\sigma_1 = \left(\frac{42.40}{2}\right) + \sqrt{\left(\frac{42.40}{2}\right)^2 + 4.52^2}$$

$\therefore \qquad \sigma_1 = 42.88$ MPa < 80 MPa.

d. Maximum shear stress,

$$\tau_{max} = \sqrt{\left(\frac{\sigma}{2}\right)^2 + \tau^2} \qquad \qquad \text{... 1.5(b)/ Pg 3, DHB}$$

$$= \sqrt{\left(\frac{42.40}{2}\right)^2 + 4.52^2}$$

$\therefore \qquad \tau_{max} = 21.68$ MPa < 40 MPa.

VI. **Design of flange:**

16. Outside diameter of the flange:
$$D_3 = D_1 + 6d_p = 85 + (6 \times 16) = 181 \text{ mm} \approx 182 \text{ mm}$$
$$\text{... 13.1(f)/ Pg 252, DHB}$$

17. Thickness of the flange:
$$t = 0.35D + 9 \text{ mm} = (0.35 \times 40) + 9 = 23 \text{ mm}$$
$$\text{... 13.1(h)/ Pg 252, DHB}$$

18. *Check for stresses*:

a. Shear stress in the flange:

$$T_{max} = \frac{\tau_c \pi D_1^2 t}{2} \qquad \qquad \text{... 13.2(e)/ Pg 252, DHB}$$

$$382 \times 10^3 = \frac{\tau_c \times \pi \times 85^2 \times 23}{2}$$

$$\tau_c = 1.46 \text{ MPa} < 15 \text{ MPa, hence safe.}$$

40. **Design a flexible flanged coupling to transmit a power of 25 kW at a rated speed of 500 rpm.**

VTU – July/ Aug. 2005 – 12 Marks; (Similar) July 2006 – 12 Marks; (Similar) Dec. 08/ Jan. 2009 – 14 Marks; (Similar) Dec. 2010 (AU46) – 14 Marks

Solution: $P = 25$ kW, $n = 500$ rpm.

Material:

Assumption:	Shaft, key and pins:	C40 steel	$\sigma_{yt} = 324$ MPa, FoS = 2
	Flange:	FG 200	$\sigma_{yt} = 200$ MPa, FoS = 6
	Bearing pressure:	$p_b = 0.5$ MPa	

Allowable stresses:

Shaft, key and pins: $\sigma_t = \dfrac{\sigma_{yt}}{\text{FoS}} = \dfrac{324}{2} = 162$ MPa

$$\tau_s = 0.5\sigma_t = 0.5 \times 162 = 81 \text{ MPa}$$

Flange: $\sigma_t = \dfrac{\sigma_{yt}}{\text{FoS}} = \dfrac{200}{6} = 33.34$ MPa

$$\tau_c = 0.5\sigma_t = 0.5 \times 33.34 = 16.67 \text{ MPa}$$

i.e.
$$\tau_s = \tau_1 = \tau_p = 81 \text{ MPa}, \sigma_t = \sigma_{b1} = \sigma_{bp} = 162 \text{ MPa}$$

$$\tau_c = 16.67 \text{ MPa}.$$

I. Design of shaft:

1. We know that

$$T = \frac{9.55 \times 10^6 (P)}{n} = \frac{9.55 \times 10^6 \times (25)}{500} = 477.5 \times 10^3 \text{ N·mm}$$

... 3.3(a)/ Pg 50, DHB

2. Shaft diameter,

$$\tau_s = \frac{16T}{\pi D^3}$$

... 3.1/ Pg 50, DHB

$$81 = \frac{16 \times 477.5 \times 10^3}{\pi D^3}$$

$$D = 31.08 \text{ mm}$$

∴ Standard size of shaft,

$$D = 32 \text{ mm}$$

... Tb. 3.5(a)/ Pg 57, DHB

II. Design of hub:

3. Hub diameter

$$D_1 = 1.5D + 25 \text{ mm} = (1.5 \times 32) + 25 = 73 \text{ mm}$$

... 13.1(d)/ Pg 252, DHB

4. Hub length $\quad L = 1.2D + 20 \text{ mm} = (1.2 \times 32) + 20 = 58.4 \text{ mm} \approx 60 \text{ mm}$

... 13.1(g)/ Pg 252, DHB

III. Design of key:

5. Since $\sigma_{b1} = 2\tau_1$, use square key.

6. For $D = 32$ mm, $b = h = 10$ mm.   **... Tb. 4.1/ Pg 69, DHB**

7. The length of key in each part is kept equal to length of hub, i.e. $l = L = 60$ mm.

8. *Check for stresses*:

   a. Shear stress in the key:

$$T = \frac{1}{2}\tau_1 lbD$$

... 4.5(a)/ Pg 62, DHB

$$477.5 \times 10^3 = \frac{1}{2}[\tau_1 \times 60 \times 10 \times 32]$$

$$\tau_1 = 49.74 \text{ MPa} < 81 \text{ MPa, hence safe.}$$

   b. Crushing stress in the key:

$$T = \frac{1}{4}\sigma_{b1} lhD$$

... 4.4(b)/ Pg 62, DHB

$$477.5 \times 10^3 = \frac{1}{4}[\sigma_{b1} \times 60 \times 10 \times 32]$$

$$\sigma_{b1} = 99.48 \text{ MPa} < 162 \text{ MPa, hence safe.}$$

IV. **Design of pins:**

9. Number of pins:

$$i = \frac{3D}{80} + 2 = \frac{3 \times 32}{80} + 2 \qquad \text{... 13.1(a)/ Pg 251, DHB}$$

$$= 3.2 \approx 4 \text{ (next higher even number)}$$

But the minimum number of pins for a flexible coupling is 6, hence i = 6.

10. Diameter of the pin:

$$d_{\mathrm{p}} = \frac{0.423D}{\sqrt{i}} + 7.5 \text{ mm} = \frac{0.423 \times 32}{\sqrt{6}} + 7.5 \text{ mm} = 13.03 \text{ mm}$$

$$\text{... 13.1(c)/ Pg 251, DHB}$$

∴ Standard size of pin, $d_{\mathrm{p}} = 16$ mm   **... Tb. 9.8/ Pg 141, DHB**

11. PCD of pins:

$$D_2 = D_1 + 3.2d_{\mathrm{p}} = 73 + (3.2 \times 16) = 124.2 \text{ mm} \approx 125 \text{ mm}$$

$$\text{... 13.1(e)/ Pg 252, DHB}$$

V. **Design of Bush:**

12. Assume:

Thickness of brass bush (t_{b}) = 4 mm   (effective both sides)
Thickness of rubber bush (t_{r}) = 12 mm   (effective both sides)
Allowance for enlarged diameter (*allw*) = 4 mm   (effective both sides)

13. Outside diameter of bush
$$d' = d_{\mathrm{p}} + t_{\mathrm{b}} + t_{\mathrm{r}} + allw$$
$$d' = 16 + 4 + 12 + 4 = 36 \text{ mm}$$

14. Length of the bush is found as

$$p_{\mathrm{b}} = \frac{F}{l_{\mathrm{b}} \cdot d'}$$

$$0.5 = \frac{F}{l_{\mathrm{b}} \times 36}$$

$$F = 18 \, l_{\mathrm{b}} \qquad \text{... Eq. (a)}$$

Also torque transmitted by *i* pins is

$$T_{\max} = \left(\frac{FD_2}{2}\right) i \qquad \text{OR} \qquad T_{\max} = \frac{p_{\mathrm{b}} i l_{\mathrm{b}} d' D_2}{2}$$

$$477.5 \times 10^3 = \left(\frac{18 l_{\mathrm{b}} \times 125}{2}\right) \times 6 \qquad 477.5 \times 10^3 = \left(\frac{0.5 \times 6 \times l_{\mathrm{b}} \times 36 \times 125}{2}\right)$$

$$l_{\mathrm{b}} = 70.74 \text{ mm} \approx 72 \text{ mm} \qquad l_{\mathrm{b}} = 70.74 \text{ mm} \approx 72 \text{ mm}$$

∴ Eq. (a) yields...
$$F = 18 \times 72 = 1296 \text{ N}$$

15. *Check for stresses:*

a. Shear stress in the pin:

$$T = \frac{\tau_{\mathrm{p}} \pi i d_{\mathrm{p}}^2 D_2}{8} \qquad \text{... 13.5(b)/ Pg 254, DHB}$$

$$477.5 \times 10^3 = \left(\frac{\tau_p \times \pi \times 6 \times 16^2 \times 125}{8} \right)$$

$$\tau_p = 6.33 \text{ MPa} < 81 \text{ MPa}.$$

b. Bending stress in the pin:

$$\sigma_{bp} = \frac{16F(l_b + c)}{\pi d_p^3} \qquad \qquad \text{... 13.5(e)/ Pg 254, DHB}$$

$$= \frac{16 \times 1296 \times (72 + 5)}{\pi \times 16^3} \qquad \text{(Assume } c = 5 \text{ mm)}$$

$$\sigma_{bp} = 124.08 \text{ MPa} < 162 \text{ MPa}.$$

Since the pin is subjected to bending and shear stresses, therefore the design must be checked for the maximum principal stress and maximum shear stress.

c. Maximum principal stress,

$$\sigma_1 = \left(\frac{\sigma}{2} \right) + \sqrt{\left(\frac{\sigma}{2} \right)^2 + \tau^2} \qquad \qquad \text{... 1.5(a)/ Pg 3, DHB}$$

Here $\sigma = \sigma_{bp} = 124.08$ MPa and $\tau = \tau_p = 6.33$ MPa.

$$\sigma_1 = \left(\frac{124.08}{2} \right) + \sqrt{\left(\frac{124.08}{2} \right)^2 + 6.33^2}$$

$$\therefore \qquad \sigma_1 = 124.40 \text{ MPa} < 162 \text{ MPa}.$$

d. Maximum shear stress,

$$\tau_{max} = \sqrt{\left(\frac{\sigma}{2} \right)^2 + \tau^2} \qquad \qquad \text{... 1.5(b)/ Pg 3, DHB}$$

$$= \sqrt{\left(\frac{124.08}{2} \right)^2 + 6.33^2}$$

$$\therefore \qquad \tau_{max} = 62.36 \text{ MPa} < 81 \text{ MPa}.$$

VI. **Design of flange:** Flange is made of cast iron.

16. Outside diameter of the flange:

$$D_3 = D_1 + 6d_p = 73 + (6 \times 16) = 169 \text{ mm} \approx 170 \text{ mm}$$
$$\text{... 13.1(f)/ Pg 252, DHB}$$

17. Thickness of the flange:

$$t = 0.35D + 9 \text{ mm} = (0.35 \times 32) + 9 = 20.2 \text{ mm} \approx 21 \text{ mm}$$
$$\text{... 13.1(h)/ Pg 252, DHB}$$

18. *Check for stresses:*

a. Shear stress in the flange:

$$T_{max} = \frac{\tau_c \pi D_1^2 t}{2} \qquad \qquad \text{... 13.2(e)/ Pg 252, DHB}$$

$$477.5 \times 10^3 = \frac{\tau_c \times \pi \times 73^2 \times 21}{2}$$

$$\tau_c = 2.72 \text{ MPa} < 15 \text{ MPa, hence safe.}$$

Typical Problem: Diameter Range

41. **Design a flexible bushed pin type coupling suitable for transmitting 40 kW of power at 1000 rpm. The overall torque is 20% greater than the mean torque. The material properties are as follows:**

   i. **The allowable shear and crushing stress for shaft and key material is 40 N/mm² and 120 N/mm² respectively.**
   ii. **The allowable shear stress for cast iron is 10 N/mm².**
   iii. **The allowable bearing pressure for rubber bush is 0.45 N/mm².**
   iv. **The material for the pin is same as that of shaft and key having allowable stress in bending of 152 N/mm². Motor shaft diameter is 50 mm and pump shaft diameter is 45 mm.**

VTU – Dec. 2013/ Jan. 2014 – 10 Marks

Solution: $P = 40$ kW, $n = 1000$ rpm, $T_{max} = 1.2\ T$, $\tau_s = \tau_1 = \tau_p = 40$ N/mm², $\sigma_b = \sigma_{b1} = 120$ N/mm², $\tau_c = 10$ N/mm², $p_b = 0.45$ N/mm², $\sigma_{bp} = 152$ N/mm², motor shaft diameter (driver) $D_{max} = 50$ mm, pump shaft diameter (driven) $D_{min} = 45$ mm.

I. **Design of shaft:** Since the diameter range is given, the maximum rating of the coupling at 100 rpm has to be found out, based on which the dimensions of the coupling are taken from **Tb. 13.3/Pg 282, DHB.**

1. Load rating at 100 rpm,

$$P = \frac{(\text{kW}) \times \text{service factor} \times 100}{\text{rpm of application}} \qquad \text{... 13.5(a)/ Pg 254, DHB}$$

Based on driven machine, service factor = 1.5   ... **Tb 13.3/ Pg 282, DHB**

$$P = \frac{40 \times 1.5 \times 100}{1000}$$

$$P = 6 \text{ kW}$$

From **Tb. 13.2(c)/Pg 281, DHB** for $P \geq 6$ kW, the type of coupling is FB 8 having a load rating of 7.36 kW, the dimensions are as follows:

$$D_{max} = 60 \text{ mm}$$

and $D_{min} = 42$ mm   Given value of D falls in this range

i.e. 42 mm < 50 mm < 60 mm

$$D_3 = 180 \text{ mm}, D_1 = 102 \text{ mm}, L = 70 \text{ mm}, b = 38 \text{ mm}, c = 3 \text{ mm}$$

2. Torque transmitted:

Given $T_{max} = 1.2\ T$ ... Eq. (i)

$$T = \frac{9.55 \times 10^6 (P)}{n} = \frac{9.55 \times 10^6 \times (40)}{1000} = 382 \times 10^3 \text{ N·mm}$$

... **3.3(a)/ Pg 50, DHB**

∴ Eq. (i) yields...

$$T_{max} = 1.2 \times (382 \times 10^6) = 458.4 \times 10^3 \text{ N·mm}$$

II. **Design of key:**

3. Since $\sigma_{b1} \neq 2\tau_1$, use rectangular key.
4. For $D = 50$ mm, $b = 14$ mm, $h = 9$ mm. ... **Tb. 4.1/ Pg 69, DHB**
5. The length of key in each part is kept equal to length of hub, i.e. $l = L = 70$ mm.

6. *Check for stresses*:
   a. Shear stress in the key:

$$T_{max} = \frac{1}{2}\tau_1 lbD \qquad\qquad \text{... 4.5(a)/ Pg 62, DHB}$$

$$458.4 \times 10^3 = \frac{1}{2}[\tau_1 \times 70 \times 14 \times 50]$$

$$\tau_1 = 18.71 \text{ MPa} < 40 \text{ MPa, hence safe.}$$

   b. Crushing stress in the key:

$$T_{max} = \frac{1}{4}\sigma_{b1} lhD \qquad\qquad \text{... 4.4(b)/ Pg 62, DHB}$$

$$458.4 \times 10^3 = \frac{1}{4}[\sigma_{b1} \times 70 \times 9 \times 50]$$

$$\sigma_{b1} = 58.21 \text{ MPa} < 120 \text{ MPa, hence safe.}$$

III. Design of pins:

7. Number of pins:

$$i = \frac{3D}{80} + 2 = \frac{3 \times 50}{80} + 2 \qquad\qquad \text{... 13.1(a)/ Pg 251, DHB}$$

$$= 3.88 \approx 4 \text{ (next higher even number)}$$

But the minimum number of pins for a flexible coupling is 6, hence i = 6.

8. Diameter of the pin:

$$d_P = \frac{0.423D}{\sqrt{i}} + 7.5 \text{ mm} = \frac{0.423 \times 50}{\sqrt{6}} + 7.5 \text{ mm} = 16.13 \text{ mm}$$

$$\text{... 13.1(c)/ Pg 251, DHB}$$

∴ Standard size of pin, d_P = 16 mm   ... Tb. 9.8/ Pg 141, DHB

9. PCD of pins:

$$D_2 = D_1 + 3.2d_P = 102 + (3.2 \times 18) = 159.6 \text{ mm} \approx 160 \text{ mm}$$

$$\text{... 13.1(e)/ Pg 252, DHB}$$

IV. Design of Bush:

10. Assume:
    Thickness of brass bush (t_b) = 4 mm   (effective both sides)
    Thickness of rubber bush (t_r) = 12 mm   (effective both sides)
    Allowance for enlarged diameter (*allw*) = 4 mm   (effective both sides)

11. Outside diameter of bush

$$d' = d_P + t_b + t_r + allw$$

$$d' = 18 + 4 + 12 + 4 = 38 \text{ mm}$$

12. Length of the bush is found as

$$p_b = \frac{F}{l_b \cdot d'}$$

$$0.45 = \frac{F}{l_b \times 38}$$

$$F = 17.1 \, l_b \qquad\qquad \text{... Eq. (a)}$$

Also torque transmitted by i pins is

$$T_{max} = \left(\frac{FD_2}{2}\right)i \qquad\qquad\qquad \text{OR} \qquad T_{max} = \frac{p_b i l_b d' D_2}{2}$$

$$458.4 \times 10^3 = \left(\frac{17.1 l_b \times 160}{2}\right) \times 6 \qquad 458.4 \times 10^3 = \left(\frac{0.45 \times 6 \times l_b \times 38 \times 160}{2}\right)$$

$$l_b = 55.85 \text{ mm} \approx 56 \text{ mm} \qquad\qquad l_b = 55.85 \text{ mm} \approx 56 \text{ mm}$$

∴ Eq. (a) yields...

$$F = 17.1 \times 56 = 957.6 \text{ N}$$

13. *Check for stresses*:

a. Shear stress in the pin:

$$T_{max} = \frac{\tau_p \pi i d_p^2 D_2}{8} \qquad\qquad\qquad \text{... 13.5(b)/ Pg 254, DHB}$$

$$458.4 \times 10^3 = \left(\frac{\tau_p \times \pi \times 6 \times 18^2 \times 160}{8}\right)$$

$$\tau_p = 3.75 \text{ MPa} < 40 \text{ MPa.}$$

b. Bending stress in the pin:

$$\sigma_{bp} = \frac{16F(l_b + c)}{\pi d_p^3} \qquad\qquad\qquad \text{... 13.5(e)/ Pg 254, DHB}$$

$$= \frac{16 \times 957.6 \times (56 + 3)}{\pi \times 18^3} \qquad \text{(data } c = 3 \text{ mm)}$$

$$\sigma_{bp} = 49.34 \text{ MPa} < 152 \text{ MPa.}$$

Since the pin is subjected to bending and shear stresses, therefore the design must be checked for the maximum principal stress and maximum shear stress.

c. Maximum principal stress,

$$\sigma_1 = \left(\frac{\sigma}{2}\right) + \sqrt{\left(\frac{\sigma}{2}\right)^2 + \tau^2} \qquad\qquad \text{... 1.5(a)/ Pg 3, DHB}$$

Here $\qquad \sigma = \sigma_{bp} = 49.34$ MPa and $\tau = \tau_p = 3.75$ MPa.

$$\sigma_1 = \left(\frac{49.34}{2}\right) + \sqrt{\left(\frac{49.34}{2}\right)^2 + 3.75^2}$$

∴ $\qquad\qquad \sigma_1 = 49.62 \text{ MPa} < 152 \text{ MPa.}$

d. Maximum shear stress,

$$\tau_{max} = \sqrt{\left(\frac{\sigma}{2}\right)^2 + \tau^2} \qquad\qquad\qquad \text{... 1.5(b)/ Pg 3, DHB}$$

$$= \sqrt{\left(\frac{49.34}{2}\right)^2 + 3.75^2}$$

∴ $\qquad\qquad \tau_{max} = 24.95 \text{ MPa} < 40 \text{ MPa.}$

V. **Design of flange:** Flange is made of cast iron.

14. Outside diameter of the flange:

$$D_3 = D_1 + 6d_p = 102 + (6 \times 18) = 210 \text{ mm}$$

... **13.1(f)/ Pg 252, DHB**

15. Thickness of the flange:

$$t = 0.35D + 9 \text{ mm} = (0.35 \times 50) + 9 \text{ mm} = 26.5 \text{ mm} \approx 27 \text{ mm}$$

... **13.1(h)/ Pg 252, DHB**

16. *Check for stresses*:

a. Shear stress in the flange:

$$T_{max} = \frac{\tau_c \pi D_1^2 t}{2}$$

... **13.2(e)/ Pg 252, DHB**

$$458.4 \times 10^3 = \frac{\tau_c \times \pi \times 102^2 \times 27}{2}$$

$$\tau_c = 1.04 \text{ MPa} < 10 \text{ MPa, hence safe.}$$

6.14 OLDHAM'S COUPLING

Oldham couplings are a three piece design comprising two hubs or flanges and a center piece or member, as shown in **Fig. 6.12**. It is used to connect two parallel shafts whose axes are at a small distance apart. Two flanges, each having a rectangular slot, are keyed, one on each shaft. The two flanges are positioned such that, the slot in one is at right angle to the slot in the other. A circular disc with two rectangular projections (tongues) on either side and at right angle to each other, is placed between the two flanges. During motion, the central disc slides in the slots of the flanges. Power transmission takes place between the shafts, because of the positive connection between the flanges and the central disc.

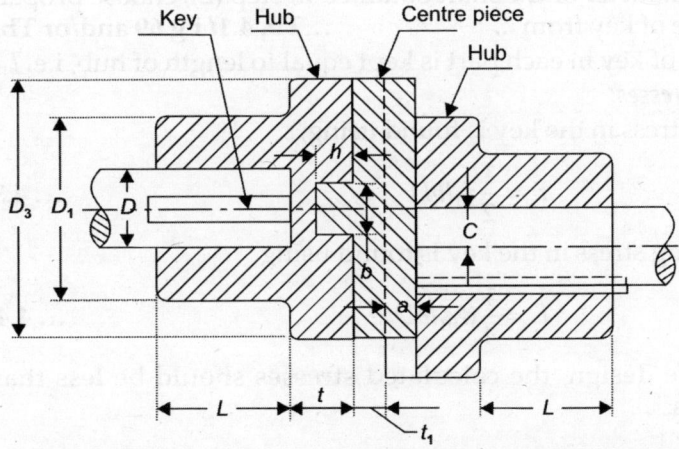

Fig. 6.12: Oldham's flexible coupling **[Fig. 13.7(a)/Pg 256, DHB]**

The coupling is usually made of cast iron or steel. The maximum speed is limited to 1500 rpm to prevent undue vibrations. The allowable pressure between the faces of the grooves is not to exceed 8.5 MPa

6.14.1 Design Procedure Oldham's Coupling

I. Design of shaft

1. The torque transmitted is found as

$$T = \frac{9.55 \times 10^6 (P)}{n}$$ ... 3.3(a)/ Pg 50, DHB

2. The shaft diameter is found using

$$\tau_s = \frac{16T}{\pi D^3}$$ ... 3.1/ Pg 50, DHB

Standardize the shaft diameter using... ... Tb. 3.5(a)/Pg 57, DHB

II. Dimensions/Parameters ... 13.6(d)/ Pg 255 & 256, DHB

3. Hub diameter $D_1 = 1.8D + 20$ mm
4. Hub length $L = 0.75D + 12.5$ mm

Eccentricity or distance between shaft centers $C = 0.003D$

Flange diameter $D_3 = 3D + C$

Width of tongues $b = 0.45D$

$$t = 0.6D + 0.25C$$

$$a = t_1 = h = 0.25D + 0.1C$$

Check for bearing pressure $T = \frac{phD_3^2}{6}$ ... 13.6(c)/ Pg 255, DHB

Value of $p \leq 8.5$ MPa, allowable pressure between the faces of the groove.

III. Design of Key

5. If crushing strength of the key is twice the shear strength in the key ($\sigma_{b1} = 2\tau_1$), then use square key.
6. Based on diameter of the shaft obtained in step (2), choose proper value of b and h for the type of key from ... ...Tb. 4.1/ Pg 69 and/or Tb.4.2/ Pg 70, DHB
7. The length of key in each part is kept equal to length of hub, i.e. $l = L$.
8. *Check for stresses*:
   a. Shear stress in the key is found using,

$$T = \frac{1}{2}\tau_1 lbD$$ ... 4.5(a)/ Pg 62, DHB

   b. Crushing stress in the key is found using

$$T = \frac{1}{4}\sigma_{b1} lbD$$ ... 4.4(b)/ Pg 62, DHB

For safe design, the calculated stresses should be less than the allowable stresses.

VTU QUESTION PAPERS

Mar. 2001 (ME5T2)

1. a. A standard splined connection $8 \times 52 \times 60$ is used for the gear and the shaft assembly of a gear box. An 18 kW power at 440 rpm is transmitted by the spline

connection. The unit normal pressure on the splines is limited to 6.5 N/mm^2. The coefficient of friction is 0.05. Determine:

   i. The length of the hub of the gear

   ii. The force required to shift the gear. **(10 Marks)**

  b. Design a flange coupling to connect the shafts of a motor and centrifugal pump for the following specifications:

Pump output = 3000 liters per minute, total head = 20 m, pump speed = 600 rpm, pump efficiency = 70%.

Select C40 steel for shaft and C35 steel for bolts, with factor of safety 2. Use allowable shear stress in cast iron flanges equal to 15 N/mm^2. **(10 Marks)**

July/Aug. 2004 (AU46)

2. Design a cast iron rigid flange coupling to transmit a power of 15 kW at 1200 rpm. The allowable shear and normal stresses for the shaft and bolts are 60 MPa and 100 MPa respectively. The allowable shear and normal stresses for the flange are 38 MPa and 32 MPa respectively. Do not design the key but suggest the type. **(10 Marks)**

3. Design a knuckle joint to transmit a load of 40 kN. The allowable tensile stress is 100 MPa and the allowable shear and compressive stresses are 55 MPa and 100 MPa respectively. **(10 Marks)**

Jan/Feb. 2005 (AU46)

4. Design a flange coupling for connecting the motor and centrifugal pump shafts. The details of the duty required from the coupling are:

Power to be transmitted = 18 kW, speed = 1000 rev/min, allowable stress in the shaft is limited to 50 N/mm^2 and the angle of twist is not to exceed 0.75 degrees in a length of 20 diameters. The allowable shear stress in the coupling bolts is 30 N/mm^2. Assume the torsional moment to be transmitted is 20% more than the mean torsional moment. **(20 Marks)**

July/Aug. 2005 (AU46)

5. Design a flexible flanged coupling to transmit a power of 45 kW at a rated speed of 500 rpm. **(12 Marks)**

6. Design a cotter joint to sustain an axial load of 100 kN. Allowable stresses for the material of the joints are as follows:

Allowable stress in tension = 80 MPa

Allowable stress in compression = 120 MPa

Allowable stress in shear = 60 MPa

Allowable bearing pressure = 40 MPa. **(10 Marks)**

Jan/Feb. 2006 (AU46)

7. Explain with neat sketches the following types of keys used in power transmission:

   i. Woodruff key

   ii. Gib-head key **(06 Marks)**

8. Design a knuckle joint for a tie rod of a circular section to sustain a maximum pull of 60 kN. The ultimate strength of the material of the rod against tearing is 420 MPa. The ultimate tensile and shearing strength of the pin material are 510 MPa and 396 MPa respectively. Determine the tie rod section and pin section. Take factor of safety = 6. **(10 Marks)**

July 2006 (AU46)

9. Design a flexible flanged coupling to transmit a power of 50 kW at a rated speed of 500 rpm. **(12 Marks)**

10. Prove that a square key is equally strong in shear and compression. **(05 Marks)**

11. Design a cotter joint to join two round rods capable of sustaining an axial load of 100 kN. **(10 Marks)**

Dec. 06/Jan. 2007 (AU46)

12. Design a protected type CI flange coupling for a steel shaft transmitting 30 kW at 200 rpm. The allowable shear stress in the shaft and key material is 40 MPa. The maximum torque transmitted is to be 20% greater than the full torque. The allowable shear stress in the bolts is 60 MPa and the allowable shear stress in the CI flange is 40 MPa. Sketch the coupling indicating salient dimensions. **(20 Marks)**

13. Design and sketch the assembly of a knuckle joint to connect two mild steel rods, subjected to an axial pull of 100 kN. The material selected for the joint has the following design stresses: σ_t = 100 MPa, σ_c =130 MPa, τ =60 MPa. **(12 Marks)**

July 2007 (AU46)

14. A flexible flanged coupling has to transmit a power of 45 kW at a rated speed of 500 rpm. Select C40 steel for the shaft and the pin. Assume factor of safety as 2.5. Determine the maximum normal stress, maximum shear stress induced in the pin, torque capacity based on shearing of bolts. **(04 Marks)**

15. Design a knuckle joint to transmit 150 kN. The design stresses may be taken as 75 N/mm² in tension, 60 N/mm² in shear and 150 N/mm² in compression. **(10 Marks)**

Dec. 07/Jan. 2008 (AU46)

16. Design a rigid flange coupling to transmit 18 kW at 1440 rpm. The allowable shear stress in the cast iron flange is 4 MPa. The shaft and the key are made of annealed steel material of allowable shear stress 93.384 N/mm². **(10 Marks)**

17. Design a socket and spigot type cotter joint to connect two rods subjected to a steady axial pull of 100 kN. The material used for the spigot end and the cotter is (40 steel $C_{40}C_8$) having tensile yield strength of 328.6 MPa. Take factor of safety as 4 for tension, 6 for shear and 3 for crushing based on tensile yield strength. **(12 Marks)**

June/July 2008 (AU46)

18. a. Enumerate the requirements of a good coupling. Distinguish between a rigid coupling and a flexible coupling. **(05 Marks)**

   b. A mild steel shaft has to transmit 75 kW at 200 rev/min. The allowable stress in the shaft material is limited to 40 MPa and the angle of twist is not to exceed 1° in a length of 20 diameters. Calculate the suitable diameter of the shaft. Design a cast iron flange coupling for this shaft. Assume the allowable stress in the material of the bolts to be 30 MPa and the bolts are fitted in reamed holes. Assume the allowable shear stress in the cast iron flange equal to 15 MPa. **(12 Marks)**

Dec. 08/Jan. 2009 (ME5T2)

19. It is required to design a square key for fixing a gear on a shaft of diameter 25 mm. 15 kW of power at 720 rpm is to be transmitted from the shaft to the gear. The key is made of steel 50C4 (σ_{yt} = 460 N/mm^2) and the factor of safety is 3. The yield strength in compression can be assumed to be equal to the yield strength in tension. Determine the dimensions of the key. **(10 Marks)**

Dec. 08/ Jan. 2009 (06ME-AU52)

20. a. A rigid coupling has four bolts on a pitch circle of 125 mm diameter and transmitting 20 kW power at 720 rpm. The bolts are made of carbon steel (C45) and has a factor of safety of 3. Determine the diameter of the bolt. **(06 Marks)**

   b. Design a bush pin type flexible coupling to transmit 25 kW at 500 rpm. Select suitable materials for shaft, key and bolts. **(14 Marks)**

June/July 2009 (AU46)

21. In a rigid flange coupling designed to transmit 50 kW at 200 rpm, a tapered key of dimensions 18 × 11 × 100 is used to key the shafts of 60 mm diameter to flange.
   Five bolts are used on a bolt circle of 170 mm diameter. Taking the materials of bolts same as that of shaft, determine:

   i. The shear stress induced in the shaft and the key.

   ii. The size of bolts required. **(12 Marks)**

22. Design a socket and spigot type cotter joint to connect two rods subjected to a steady axial pull of 100 kN. The material used for the spigot end, socket end and the cotter is C$_{40}$ steel. Take factor of safety as 4 for tension, 6 for shear and 3 for crushing based on tensile yield strength. **(10 Marks)**

June/July 2009 (06ME52)

23. a. A 45 mm diameter shaft is made of steel with yield strength of 40 MPa. A parallel key of size 14 mm wide and 9 mm thick made of steel with yield strength of 340 MPa. Find the required length of the key, if the shaft is loaded to transmit the maximum permissible torque. Design based on maximum shear stress theory and FoS = 2. **(06 Marks)**

   b. Design a bushed-pin type flexible coupling to connect a pump shaft to a motor shaft transmitting 32 kW at 960 rpm. The overall torque is 20 percent more than mean torque. The material properties are as follows:

   i. The allowable shear and crushing stress for shaft and key material is 40 MPa and 80 MPa respectively.

   ii. The allowable shear stress for cast iron is 15 MPa.

   iii. The allowable bearing pressure for rubber bush is 0.8 N/mm^2.

   iv. The material of the pin is same as that of shaft and key. **(14 Marks)**

Dec. 2009/Jan. 2010 (AU46)

24. Design a cast iron flange coupling to connect two shafts of 45 mm diameter to transmit 20 kW power at 400 rpm. The permissible shear strength for the shaft, bolt and key is 50 MPa and the permissible compressive stress is 120 MPa. The permissible shear strength for cast iron is 15 MPa. Assume maximum torque transmitted to be 30% greater than the normal torque. **(20 Marks)**

25. Design a socket and a spigot type of cotter joint to sustain an axial load of 40 kN. The material used for spigot and cotter has the following properties: σ_t = 200 MPa, σ_c = 420 MPa, τ = 160 MPa. Assume a factor of safety of 4. **(14 Marks)**

Dec. 2009/ Jan. 2010 (06ME52)

26. a. Design a knuckle joint to connect two mild steel rods to sustain an axial pull of 150 kN. The pin and the rods are made of same material. Assume the working stresses in the material as 80 MPa in tension, 40 MPa in shear and 120 MPa in crushing. **(10 Marks)**

   b. Design a bushed pin type flexible coupling to connect a motor shaft to a pump shaft transmitting 20 kW power at 1440 rpm. The allowable shear and crushing stress for steel shafts, keys and pins are 40 MPa and 80 MPa respectively. The allowable shear stress for cast iron flange is 10 MPa and the allowable bearing pressure for rubber bush is 0.5 MPa. **(10 Marks)**

May/June 2010 (06ME52)

27. a. Design a protective type cast iron flange coupling for a steel shaft transmitting 30 kW at 200 rpm. The allowable shear stress in the shaft and key material is 40 MPa. The maximum torque transmitted is 20% greater than the full load torque. The allowable shear stress in the bolt is 60 MPa and allowable shear stress in the flange is 40 MPa. **(06 Marks)**

   b. Design a sleeve type cotter joint, to connect two tie rods, subjected to an axial pull of 60 kN. The allowable stresses of C30 material used for the rods and cotters are $\sigma_t = 65 \, \text{N/mm}^2$, $\sigma_c = 75 \, \text{N/mm}^2$, $\tau = 35 \, \text{N/mm}^2$; cast steel used for the sleeve has the following allowable stresses $\sigma_t = 70 \, \text{N/mm}^2$, $\sigma_c = 110 \, \text{N/mm}^2$, $\tau = 45 \, \text{N/mm}^2$. **(14 Marks)**

Dec. 2010 (AU46)

28. a. A flexible coupling is used to transmit 15 kW power at 100 rpm. Choose the appropriate material for the shaft and the flanges. Also design other components and calculate the stress induced in each component of the flange. **(04 Marks)**

   b. A square key 12 mm × 12 mm is used to transmit a power of 100 kW at 560 rpm. The key is made up of SAE 1045 annealed steel. Using the ASME code procedure, determine the length of the key required. **(06 Marks)**

29. A cotter joint is to be designed to connect two rods to carry a load of 120 kN. If the socket and the cotter are made of SAE 1045 steel, design the cotter joint. **(10 Marks)**

Dec. 2010 (06ME52)

30. a. Design a square key for fixing a gear on a shaft of 25 mm diameter. 15 kW power at 720 rpm is transmitted from the shaft to the gear. The allowable compressive stress in the material is 150 MPa and allowable shear stress is 88 MPa. **(06 Marks)**

   b. Design a knuckle joint for a tie rod of circular cross-section to sustain a maximum tensile load of 70 kN. The ultimate tensile strength of the rod against tension is 420 N/mm². The ultimate tensile and shearing stresses for the pin material are 500 N/mm² and 360 N/mm² respectively. Take a factor of safety of 6. **(14 Marks)**

June/July 2011 (06ME52)

31. a. Design a knuckle joint to transmit 150 kW. The design stresses may be taken as 75 N/mm² in tension, 60 N/mm² in shear and 150 N/mm² in compression. **(10 Marks)**

b. A splined connection in an automobile transmission consists of 10 splines cut in a 58 mm diameter shaft. The height of each spline is 5.5 mm and the keyways in the hub are 45 mm long. Determine the power that may be transmitted at 2500 rev/min if the allowable normal pressure on the splines is limited to 4.8 MPa. **(10 Marks)**

Dec. 2011 (AU46)

32. a. Prove that a square key is equally strong in shear and in compression.
(04 Marks)

   b. A standard splined connection 8 × 36 × 40 is used for a gear and shaft assembly, rotating at 700 rpm. The length of the gear hub is 50 mm and the normal pressure on the splines is limited to 6.5 N/mm². Calculate the power that can be transmitted from the gear to the shaft. **(06 Marks)**

33. Two rod ends of a machine are joined by means of a cotter joint by employing a sleeve and two cotters for the joint. Design the joint for an axial load of 150 kN, which alternatively changer from tensile to compressive. The allowable stresses for the material use for sleeve and cotter are 80 MPa in tension, 60 MPa in shear and 160 MPa in crushing. **(10 Marks)**

Dec. 2011 (06ME52)

34. a. Design and sketch the assembly of a cotter joint to connect two rods, subjected to an axial pull of 600 kN. The material selected for the joint has the following permissible stresses: 300 MPa in tension, 220 MPa in shear and 450 MPa in crushing. **(12 Marks)**

   b. A cast iron protective type flange coupling is used to connect two shafts of 80 mm diameter. The shaft runs at 250 rpm and transmits a torque of 4300 N·m. The permissible shear stress for shaft and bolt materials is 50 MPa and permissible shear stress for the flange is 8 MPa. Design the bolts, hub and flange for the coupling. **(14 Marks)**

June 2012 (06ME52-06AU52)

35. a. The standard cross-section of a flat key, which is fitted on a 50 mm diameter shaft is 16 × 10 mm. The key is transmitting 475 N·m torque from the shaft to the hub. The key is made of commercial steel for which yield strength in both tension and compression may be taken as 230 N/mm². Determine the minimum length of the key required if factor of safety is 3. **(06 Marks)**

   b. It is required to design a rigid type flange coupling to connect two shafts. The input shaft transmits 37.5 kW at 180 rev/min to the output shaft through the coupling. The starting torque is 50% higher than the rated torque. Select material for flanges as cast iron FG200 (σ_{ut} = 200 MPa) with a factor of safety 6, material for shafts as carbon steel with σ_{yt} = 380 MPa, with a factor of safety 2.5, material for key and bolts may be taken as steel with σ_{yt} = 400 MPa (in tension) and σ_{yc} = 600 MPa (in compression) respectively and a factor of safety 2.5. Design the coupling and give the major dimensions. **(14 Marks)**

Dec. 2012 (10ME52)

36. a. A mild steel shaft has to transmit 40 kW power at 600 rpm. The maximum torque to be transmitted is 30% greater than the average torque. Design a rigid flange coupling for this application. **(10 Marks)**

b. Design a knuckle joint to connect two mild steel rods. The joint has to transmit a tensile load of 80 kN. Material for the rods has the following allowable stresses: $\sigma_t = 120$ MPa, $\sigma_{cr} = 120$ MPa, $\tau = 40$ MPa. **(10 Marks)**

Dec. 2012 (06ME52)

37. a. Design a socket and spigot type cotter joint to sustain a axial load of 100 kN. The material selected for the joint has the following design stresses: $\sigma_t = 100$ MPa, $\sigma_c = 150$ M/mm^2 and $\tau = 60$ MPa. **(10 Marks)**

b. A rectangular sink key 14 mm wide × 10 mm thick × 75 mm long is required to transmit 1200 N·m torque from a 50 mm diameter solid shaft. Determine whether the length is sufficient or not if the permissible shear stress and crushing stress are limited to 56 MPa and 168 MPa respectively. **(06 Marks)**

c. What is coupling? What are the requirements of a good coupling? **(04 Marks)**

June/July 2013 (06ME52)

38. a. Design a cotter joint to carry an axial force of 12 kN. Use the following stresses:
Allowable stress in tension and bending = 40 MPa
Allowable stress in crushing = 80 MPa
Allowable stress shear = 32 MPa
Sketch two views of the joint showing major dimensions. **(15 Marks)**

b. A rectangular sunk key used on a 50 mm diameter shaft and of 14 mm width and 9 mm thickness is required to transmit 40 kW at 300 rpm. Determine the length of the key if the allowable shear stresses are 56 MPa and allowable crushing stresses are 168 MPa. **(14 Marks)**

June/July 2013 (10ME52)

39. a. If the shaft and the key are made of same material, determine the length of the key required in terms of shaft diameter, taking key width $b = d/4$ and key thickness $h = 3d/16$. Assume keyway factor of safety as 0.75. **(06 Marks)**

b. Design a rigid flange coupling to transmit 18 kW at 1440 rpm. The allowable shear stress in the cast iron flange is 4 MPa. The shaft and keys are made of AISI 1040 annealed steel with ultimate strength and yield stress values as 518.8 MPa and 353.4 MPa, respectively. Use ASME code to design the shaft and the key. **(14 Marks)**

Dec. 2013/Jan. 2014 (06ME52)

40. a. Design a knuckle joint suitable for connecting two rods subjected to axial force of 12 kN. The permissible stresses are 40 N/mm^2 in tension, 80 N/mm^2 in compression and 32 N/mm^2 in shear. Give a neat dimensioned sketch. **(10 Marks)**

b. Design a flexible bushed pin type coupling suitable for transmitting 40 kW of power at 1000 rpm. The overall torque is 20 percent greater than the mean torque. The material properties are as follows:
   i. The allowable shear and crushing stress for shaft and key material is 40 N/mm^2 and 120 N/mm^2 respectively.
   ii. The allowable shear stress for cast iron is 10 N/mm^2.
   iii. The allowable bearing pressure for rubber bush is 0.45 N/mm^2.
   iv. The material for the pin is same as that of shaft and key having allowable stress in bending of 152 N/mm^2.
Motor shaft diameter is 50 mm and pump shaft diameter is 45 mm. **(10 Marks)**

Dec. 2013/ Jan. 2014 (10ME52)

41. a. Design a socket and a spigot type cotter joint to sustain an axial load of 100 kN. The material selected for the joint has the following design stresses: $\sigma_c = 100 \text{ N/mm}^2$, $\sigma_c = 150 \text{ N/mm}^2$ and $\tau = 60 \text{ N/mm}^2$. **(10 Marks)**

   b. Design a cast iron flanged coupling for a steel shaft transmitting 100 kW at 250 rpm. Take the allowable shear stress for the shaft as 40 N/mm². The angle of twist is not to exceed 1° in a length of 20 diameters. Allowable shear stress for the bolts is 13 N/mm². The allowable shear stress in the flange is 14 N/mm². For the key, shear stress is 40 N/mm² and compressive stress is 80 N/mm². **(10 Marks)**

June/July 2014 (06ME52)

42. a. Design a cotter joint to connect two round rods and support an axial load of 120 kN. The allowable stresses are: 90 MPa in tension, 60 MPa in shear and 150 MPa in crushing. **(10 Marks)**

   b. Design a CI flange coupling to transmit 18 kW at 1440 rpm. The allowable stresses for shafts, keys and bolts are 75 MPa in shear and 150 MPa in crushing. The allowable shear stress for CI flange is 5 MPa. **(10 Marks)**

June/July 2014 (10ME52)

43. a. Design a cotter joint to sustain an axial load of 100 kN. The allowable stresses are 80 MPa in tension, 120 MPa in compression and 60 MPa in shear. The allowable bearing pressure is 40 MPa. **(10 Marks)**

   b. Design a flanged coupling to connect the shafts of motor and pump transmitting 15 kW power at 600 rpm. Select C40 steel for shaft and C35 steel for bolts, with factor of safety = 2. Use allowable shear stress for cast iron flanges = 15 N/mm²; $\sigma_{allow} = 162 \text{ N/mm}^2$; and $\tau_{allow} = 81 \text{ N/mm}^2$ for bolts $\sigma = 152 \text{ N/mm}^2$ and $\tau = 76 \text{ N/mm}^2$. **(10 Marks)**

Dec. 2014/Jan. 2015 (06ME52)

44. a. Design a knuckle joint to transmit 150 kN. The design stress may be taken as 75 MPa in tension, 60 MPa in shear and 150 MPa in crushing. **(08 Marks)**

   b. Design a flange coupling to connect the shafts of a motor and centrifugal pump for the following specifications:
   Total head = 20 m, pump output = 3000 liters/min, pump speed = 600 rpm, pump efficiency = 70%.
   Select C40 steel for shaft and C35 steel for bolts with factor of safety = 2. Use allowable shear stress in the cast iron flange = 15 N/mm². **(12 Marks)**

Dec. 2014/Jan. 2015 (10ME52)

45. a. Design a cast iron flange coupling to connect two shafts of 45 mm diameter to transmit 20 kW power at 400 rpm. The permissible shear strength for the shaft, bolt and key is 50 MPa and the permissible compressive stress is 120 MPa. The permissible shear strength for cast iron is 15 MPa. Assume starting torque is 30 percent higher than the nominal torque. Design the coupling assuming the bolts are fitted in reamed hole. **(12 Marks)**

   b. Design the assembly of a knuckle joint to connect two mild steel rods subjected to an axial pull of 100 kN. The allowable stress for the pin and the rods are 100 MPa, 130 MPa and 60 MPa in tension, crushing and shear respectively. The bending of the pin is prevented by selection of proper fit. **(08 Marks)**

June/July 2015 (06ME52)

46. a. Enumerate the requirements of a good coupling. Distinguish between a rigid coupling and a flexible bearing. **(08 Marks)**

    b. Design a knuckle joint to transmit 150 kN. The design stress may be taken as 75 MPa in tension, 60 MPa in shear and 150 MPa in crushing. **(12 Marks)**

June/July 2015 (10ME52)

47. a. Design a cotter joint to resist a load of 12 kN which acts along the axis of the rod having the following permissible stresses.
    $\sigma_c = 80 \text{ N/mm}^2$, $\sigma_t = 40 \text{ N/mm}^2$, $\tau = 32 \text{ N/mm}^2$. **(10 Marks)**

    b. Design a protective CI flange coupling for a steel shaft transmitting 15 kW at 200 rpm and having an allowable shear stress of 40 MPa. The working stress in the bolt should not exceed 30 MPa. Assume that the same material is used for shaft and key and the existing stress is twice its value in shear stress. The maximum torque is 25% greater than the full load torque. The shear stress for CI is 14 MPa. **(10 Marks)**

Dec. 2015/Jan. 2016 (10ME52)

48. a. Design a cotter joint for an axial load of 50 kN which alternately changes from tensile to compressive, assuming allowable stresses in the components under and compression as 52.5 N/mm², bearing stress as 63 N/mm² and shearing stress as 35 N/mm². Sketch the joint and show the dimensions. **(15 Marks)**

    b. A square key is used to key a gear and a shaft of diameter 35 mm. The hub length of the gear is 60 mm. Both the key and shaft are made of same material having allowable shear stress of 55 MPa. What are the dimensions of the key according to maximum stress theory, if 395 N·m of torque is to be transmitted? **(05 Marks)**

7

Riveted and Welded Joints

RIVETED JOINTS

7.1 INTRODUCTION

A rivet is a cylindrical body having a head at one end and a shank at the other end as shown in **Fig. 7.1**. The purpose of the rivet is to join together two plates permanently. The plates to be joined by rivets are drilled with holes. The rivet is then inserted in the holes and held firmly by a backup bar while the protruding end (shank) is given adequate mechanical force

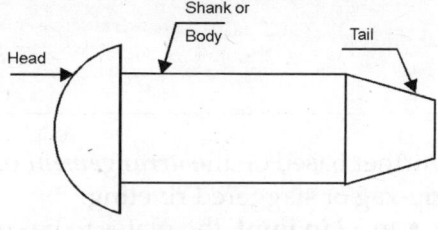

Fig. 7.1: A rivet

to form a second head (known as point) on the tail on the rivet as shown in **Fig. 7.2**. The mechanical force may be hydraulic, pneumatic or steam power.

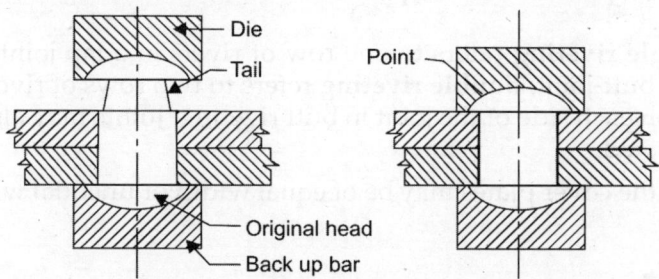

Fig. 7.2: Typical head forming of rivet

Further rivets may be hot driven or cold driven. *Cold driving* (cold riveting) is done at ambient temperature and does not require heating the shank portion of the rivet. *Hot driving* (hot riveting) is done by heating the shank to red hot condition, followed by hammering.

Applications: Pressure vessels, boilers, roof truss, bridges, ship hull, cranes, structural works, aircraft structures, etc.

7.2 TYPES OF FASTENING

These are classified into two groups:
   a. Permanent joints: Permanent joints are those which cannot be disassembled without causing damage to the connected parts.
   Examples: Welding, riveting, brazing, adhesives, etc.

b. Temporary joints: Temporary joints are those which can be disassembled without causing damage to the connected parts.
Examples: Keys, cotter and knuckle joints, couplings, screws, bolts and nuts.

7.3 TYPES OF RIVETED JOINTS

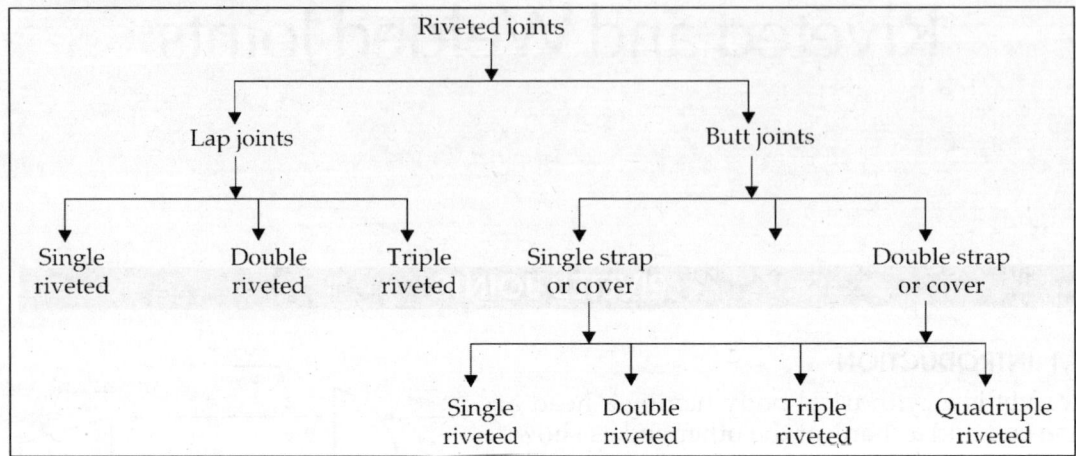

Further based on the *arrangement* of the rivets they are classified as chain riveting and zig-zag or staggered riveting.

- In a **lap joint**, the plates to be connected overlap each other and are held together by one or more rows of rivets. Lap joints may also be made with inside or outside cover plates.
- In the **butt-joint**, the plates to be connected are in the same plane and are joined by means of a cover plate or butt strap, which is riveted to both plates by one or more rows of rivets.
- The term **single riveting** refers to one row of rivets in a lap joint or one row on each side of a butt-joint; **double riveting** refers to two rows of rivets in a lap-joint or two rows on each side of the joint in butt riveting. Joints may also be triple and quadruple riveted.

For butt joints, the cover plates may be of equal width or unequal width.

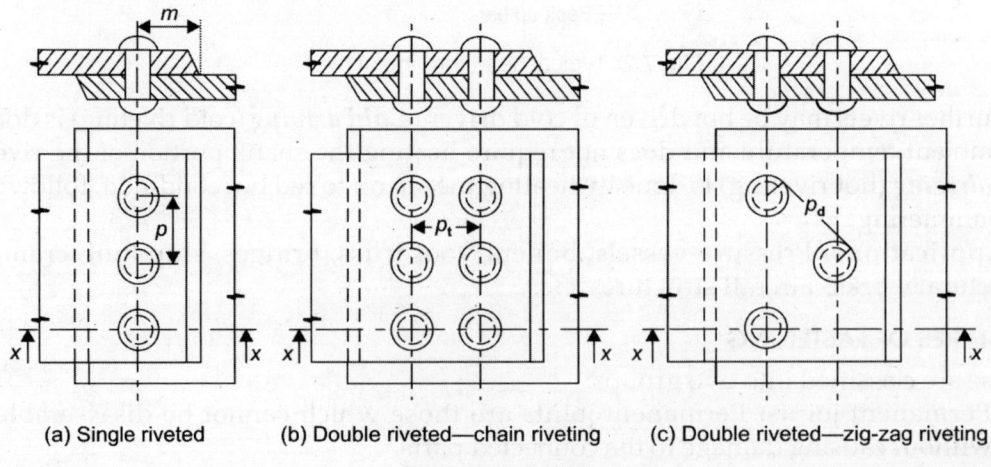

(a) Single riveted   (b) Double riveted—chain riveting   (c) Double riveted—zig-zag riveting

Fig. 7.3: Lap joint

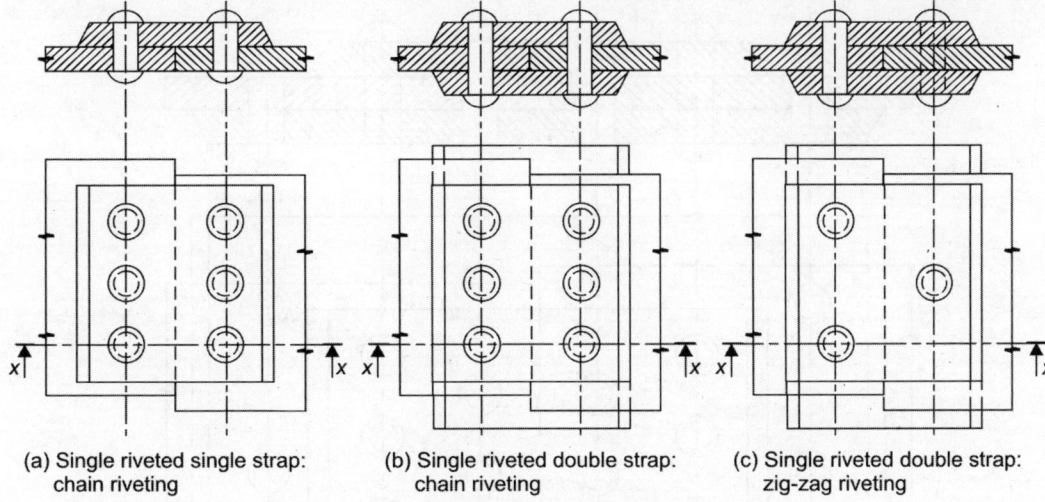

(a) Single riveted single strap:
chain riveting

(b) Single riveted double strap:
chain riveting

(c) Single riveted double strap:
zig-zag riveting

Fig. 7.4: Butt joint—single rivet

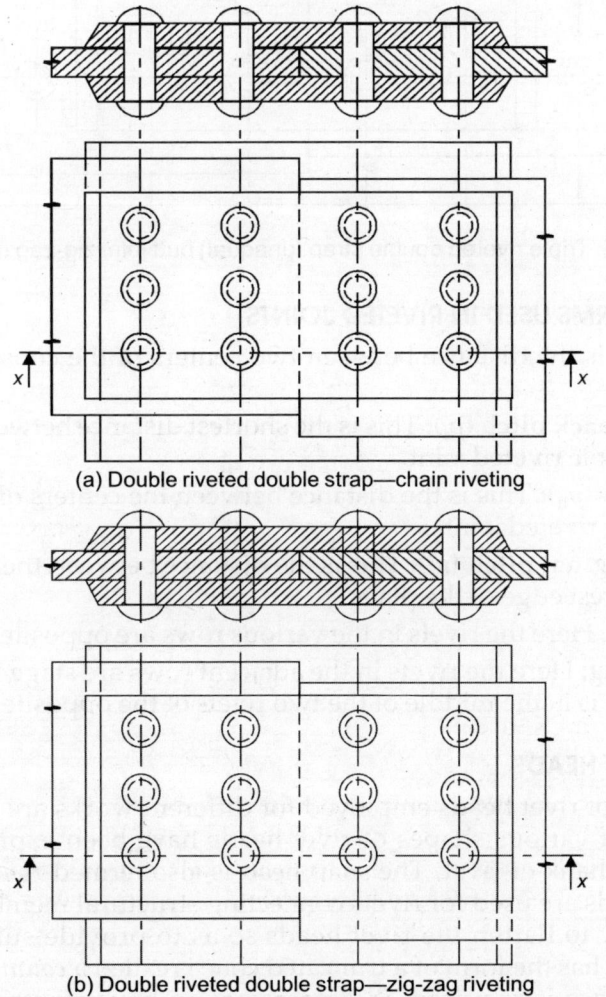

(a) Double riveted double strap—chain riveting

(b) Double riveted double strap—zig-zag riveting

Fig. 7.5: Butt joint—double rivet

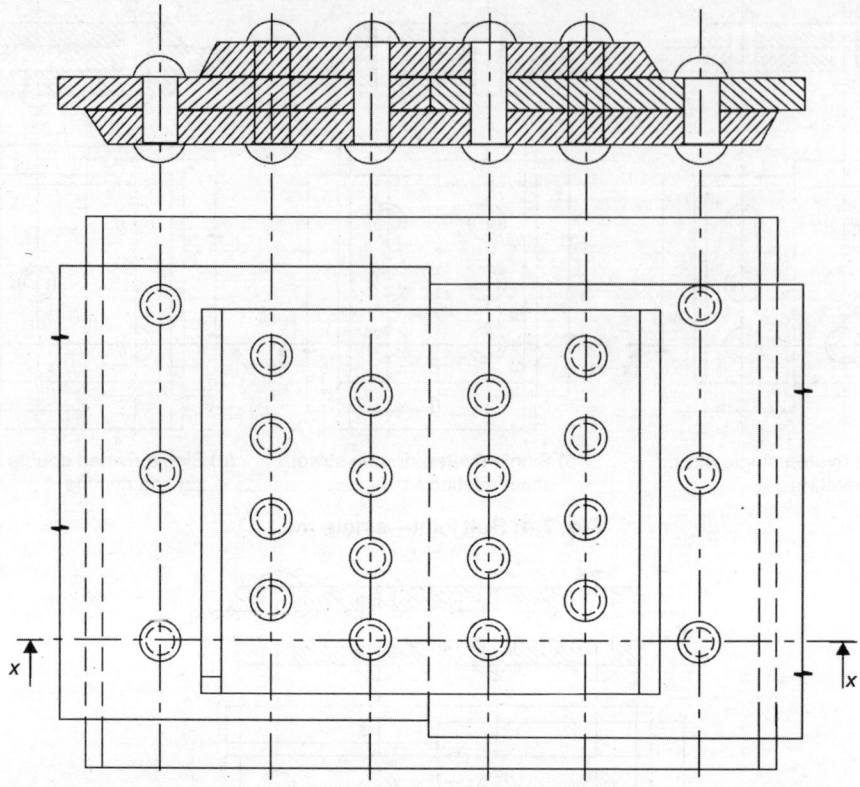

Fig. 7.6: Triple riveted double strap (unequal) butt joint zig-zag riveting

7.4 IMPORTANT TERMS USED IN RIVETED JOINTS

- **Pitch (p):** This is the distance between two centers of the consecutive rivets in a single row.
- **Transverse or back pitch (p_t):** This is the shortest distance between two successive rows in a multiple riveted joint.
- **Diagonal pitch (p_d):** This is the distance between the centers of rivets in adjacent rows of zig-zag riveted joint.
- **Margin or marginal pitch (m):** This is the distance between the centre of the rivet hole to the nearest edge of the plate.
- **Chain riveting:** Here the rivets in the various rows are opposite to each other.
- **Zig-zag riveting:** Here the rivets in the adjacent rows are staggered in such a way that every rivet is in the middle of the two rivets of the opposite row.

7.5 TYPES OF RIVET HEADS

The various types of rivet heads employed for different works are shown in **Fig. 7.7**. The proportions of various shapes of rivet heads have been expressed in terms of diameter d of the shank of rivet. The snap head is also termed *round head and button head*. The snap heads are used for rivets connecting structural members. Sometimes it becomes necessary to flatten the rivet heads so as to provide sufficient clearance. A rivet head which has the form of a truncated cone is called a *countersunk head*. When a smooth flat surface is required, it is necessary to have rivets countersunk and chipped.

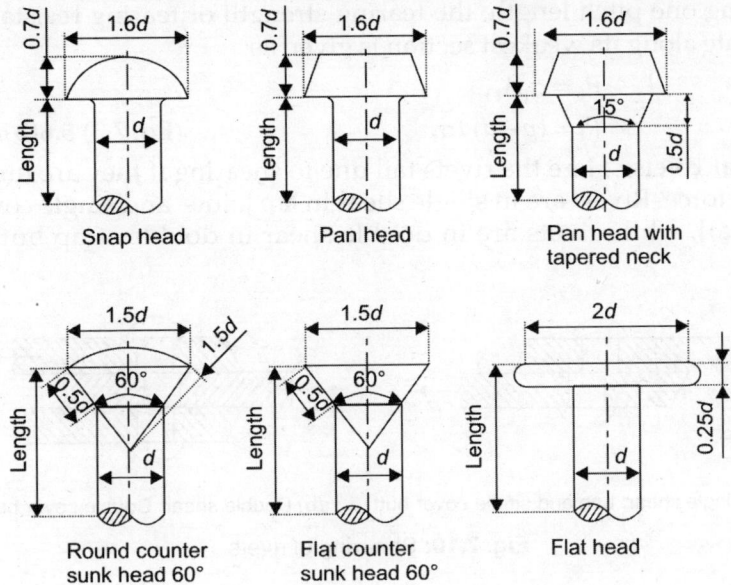

Fig. 7.7: Various forms of rivet heads

7.6 MATERIALS FOR RIVETS

The materials used for rivets should be strong and ductile. The most commonly used material for rivets is mild steel, low carbon steel, aluminum and brass. For structural and machine-member purposes rivets are usually made of wrought iron or soft steel, but for aircraft and other applications where light weight or resistance to corrosion is important. Copper, aluminum alloy, monel, inconel, etc. may be used as rivet material.

7.7 FAILURES OF RIVETED JOINTS

A riveted joint may fail in the following ways:

- Tearing of a plate at an edge
- Tearing of plates across a row of rivets
- Shearing of rivets
- Bearing or crushing of rivets/plates.

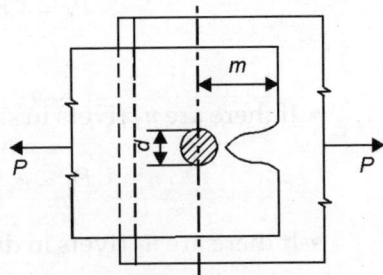

Fig. 7.8: Tearing of plate at an edge

1. **Tearing of a plate at an edge:** This type of failure occurs due to insufficient margin (i.e. distance from the centre of the rivet to the edge of the plate), as shown in **Fig. 7.8.** The failure can be avoided by keeping margin value as
   $m = 1.5d$, where d is the diameter of rivet
   ... (Eq. 7.1) **5.16/ Pg 83, DHB**

2. **Tearing of plates across a row of rivets:** The strength of the plate is reduced due to the presence of rivet hole and the plate or cover plates may tear off across a row or line of rivets, as shown in **Fig. 7.9.** This is due to large value of tensile stress acting on the row of weaker holes.

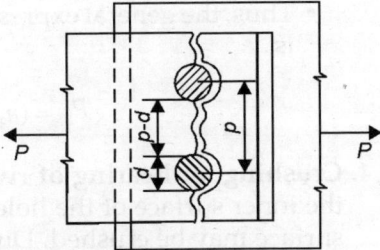

Fig. 7.9: Tearing of plate across a row of rivets

Considering one pitch length, the tearing strength or tearing resistance of a unit strip of plate along its weakest section is given as:

$$P_t = \sigma_t A_t \qquad \ldots \text{(Eq. 7.2)}$$
$$P_t = (p - d)\, t\sigma_t \qquad \ldots \text{(Eq. 7.3)} \;\textbf{5.6(b)/ Pg 80, DHB}$$

3. **Shearing of rivets:** Here the rivets fail due to shearing if they are unable to resist the tensile force. Rivets are in single shear in lap joints and single cover butt joint **[Fig. 7.10(a)]**, while rivets are in double shear in double strap butt joints **[Fig. 7.10(b)]**.

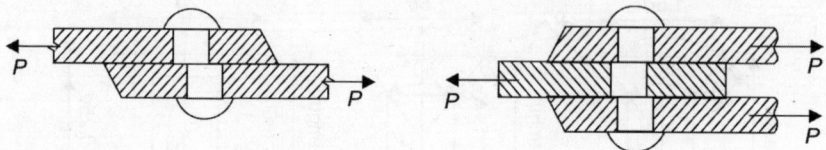

(a) Single shear: Lap and single cover butt   (b) Double shear: Double cover butt

Fig. 7.10: Shearing of rivets

Shearing resistance per pitch length,

$$P_s = \tau A_s \qquad \ldots \text{(Eq. 7.4)}$$

$$P_s = \left(\frac{\pi d^2}{4}\right)\tau, \text{ for single shear} \qquad \ldots \text{(Eq. 7.5)}$$

$$P_s = 2\left(\frac{\pi d^2}{4}\right)\tau, \text{ for double shear} \qquad \ldots \text{(Eq. 7.6)}$$

$$P_s = 1.875\left(\frac{\pi d^2}{4}\right)\tau, \text{ for double shear according to Indian Boiler}$$
$$\text{Regulations (IBR)}$$
$$\ldots \text{(Eq. 7.7)} \;\textbf{5.6(c)/ Pg 80, DHB}$$

- If there are n_1 rivets in single shear, then

$$P_s = n_1\left(\frac{\pi d^2}{4}\right)\tau, \text{ for single shear} \qquad \ldots \text{(Eq. 7.8)}$$

- If there are n_2 rivets in double shear, then

$$P_s = n_2\left[1.875\left(\frac{\pi d^2}{4}\right)\tau\right], \text{ according to IBR} \qquad \ldots \text{(Eq. 7.9)}$$

- Thus, the general expression for shearing resistance of all the rivets in unit strip is

$$P_s = (n_1 + 1.875 n_2)\left(\frac{\pi d^2}{4}\right)\tau \qquad \ldots \text{(Eq. 7.10)} \;\textbf{5.6(d)/ Pg 80, DHB}$$

4. **Crushing or bearing of rivets or plates:** Due to rivet being compressed against the inner surface of the hole, there is a possibility that either the rivet or the hole surface may be crushed. Due to this, the rivet hole becomes of an oval shape and hence the joint becomes loose as shown in **Fig. 7.11**. The area, which resists this action, is the projected area of hole or rivet on diametral plane and is given as $A_c = dt$.

The crushing resistance of the rivet per pitch length,

$$P_c = \sigma_c A_c = \sigma_c dt \quad \text{... (Eq. 7.11)}$$

- If there are n number of rivets in a pitch length, then

$$P_c = ndt\sigma_c \quad \text{... (Eq. 7.12)}$$

- Thus, the general expression for crushing resistance of all the rivets,

$$P_c = (n_1 t_i + n_2 t) d\sigma_c \quad \text{... (Eq. 7.13) 5.6(e)/ Pg 80, DHB}$$

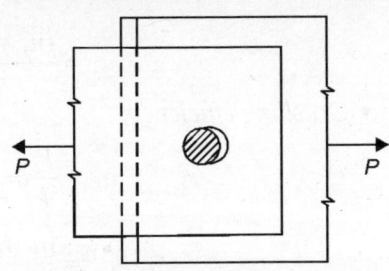

Fig. 7.11: Crushing of a rivets

where t_i = thickness of the inner cover plate
t = thickness of main plate
n_1 = number of rivets in single shear
n_2 = number of rivets in double shear
σ_c = compressive stress

Note: Number of rivets under crushing is equal to the number of rivets under shear.

7.8 STRENGTH OF A RIVETED JOINT

It is defined as the maximum force which a riveted joint can withstand without failure, i.e. the least value of P_t, P_s and P_c, from Eqs. (7.3), (7.10) and (7.13).

7.9 EFFICIENCY OF A RIVETED JOINT

The efficiency of a riveted joint is defined as the ratio of the strength of riveted joint to the strength of the solid or unriveted plate.

Efficiency, $\eta = \dfrac{\text{strength of riveted joint}}{\text{strength of solid plate}}$ ... (Eq. 7.14)

where   strength of riveted joint is the least value of P_t, P_s and P_c, from Eqs. (7.3), (7.10) and (7.13)
and   strength of solid plate $P = pt\sigma_t$ ... (Eq. 7.15) **5.6(a)/ Pg 80, DHB**

i.e. $\eta = \dfrac{\text{least value of } P_t, P_s \text{ and } P_c}{P}$ or least of η_t, η_s and η_c

... (Eq. 7.16)

- *Tearing or plate efficiency:*

$$\eta_t = \frac{P_t}{P} = \frac{(p-d)t\sigma_t}{pt\sigma_t} \quad \text{... using Eqs. [(5.6(b) and 5.6(a)/DHB]}$$

$$= \frac{p-d}{p} \quad \text{... (Eq. 7.17) 5.9(e)/Pg 81, DHB}$$

- *Shearing or rivet efficiency:*

$$\eta_s = \frac{P_s}{P} = \frac{(n_1 + 1.875 n_2)\left(\dfrac{\pi d^2}{4}\right)\tau}{pt\sigma_t}$$

... using Eqs. [(5.6(d) and 5.6(a)/DHB]

$$= \frac{(n_1 + 1.875n_2)\pi d^2 \tau}{4pt\sigma_t} \qquad \text{... (Eq. 7.18) } \mathbf{5.9(f)/Pg\ 81,\ DHB}$$

- *Crushing efficiency*:

$$\eta_c = \frac{P_c}{P} = \frac{(n_1 t_i + n_2 t)d\sigma_c}{pt\sigma_t} \quad \text{... using } \mathbf{Eqs\ [(5.6(e)\ and\ 5.6(a)/DHB]}$$

$$= \frac{[n_1(t_i/t) + n_2(t/t)]d\sigma_c}{p\sigma_t} = \frac{[n_1(t_i/t) + n_2]d\sigma_c}{p\sigma_t} \qquad \text{... (Eq. 7.19a)}$$

Note:
- For lap joints, put $(t_i/t) = 1 \Rightarrow t_i = t$ and $n_2 = 0$. Here $n_1 = n$.   ... [+]**Pg 81, DHB**
- For butt joint with equal cover plates, put $n_1 = 0$.   ... [+]**Pg 81, DHB**
- **Table 5.1/ Pg 84, DHB**, *gives the values of efficiency for commercial boiler joints.*

1. **A double riveted lap joint is made between 16 mm thick plates. The rivet diameter and pitch are 20 mm and 80 mm respectively. If the permissible stresses are 80 MPa in tension, 60 MPa in shear and 120 MPa in crushing, find the minimum force per pitch which will rupture the joint.**

Solution: Type: Lap joint – double riveted $\Rightarrow$ number of rivets $n = 2$, plate thickness $t = 16$ mm, rivet diameter $d = 20$ mm, pitch $p = 80$ mm, $\sigma_t = 80$ MPa, $\tau = 60$ MPa, $\sigma_c = 120$ MPa, $P_{min} = ?$

Tearing resistance, $\quad P_t = (p - d)t\sigma_t \qquad \qquad$ ... **5.6(b)/ Pg 80, DHB**

$$= (80 - 20) \times 16 \times 80$$

$$P_t = 76800 \text{ N} \qquad \qquad \qquad \text{... Eq. (i)}$$

Shearing resistance, $P_s = (n_1 + 1.875n_2)\left(\dfrac{\pi d^2}{4}\right)\tau \qquad$ ... **5.6(d)/Pg 80, DHB**

For a lap joint, $\qquad n_2 = 0, t_i = t \qquad \qquad$ ... **5.10(b)/ Pg 81 or [+] Pg 81, DHB**

$\therefore \qquad \qquad \qquad n_1 = n = 2$

$$P_s = (2 + 1.875 \times 0)\left(\frac{\pi \times 20^2}{4}\right) \times 60$$

$$P_s = 37699.11 \text{ N} \qquad \qquad \qquad \text{... Eq. (ii)}$$

Crushing resistance,

$$P_c = (n_1 t_i + n_t t)d\sigma_c \qquad \qquad \text{... } \mathbf{5.6(e)/\ Pg\ 80,\ DHB}$$

$$= (2 \times 16 + 0) \times 20 \times 120$$

$$P_c = 76800 \text{ N} \qquad \qquad \qquad \text{... Eq. (iii)}$$

Thus the minimum force per pitch is the minimum of Eqs. (i), (ii) and (iii)

i.e. $\qquad \qquad P_{min} = P_c = 37699.11 \text{ N}$

2. **A double riveted double cover butt joint with plates 20 mm thick is made with 25 mm diameter rivets at 100 mm pitch. The permissible stresses are $\sigma_t = 120$ MPa, $\tau = 100$ MPa and $\tau_c = 150$ MPa. Find the efficiency of the joint, taking the strength of the rivet in double shear as twice that of single shear.**

VTU – June/ July 2015 – 10 Marks; (similar) Jan./Feb. 2006 – 10 Marks

Solution: Type: Butt joint – double riveted double cover $\Rightarrow$ number of rivets $n = 2$, plate thickness $t = 20$ mm, rivet diameter $d = 25$ mm, pitch $p = 100$ mm, $\sigma_t = 120$ MPa, $\tau = 100$ MPa, $\sigma_c = 150$ MPa, $\eta = ?$

Method 1:

Tearing or plate efficiency:

$$\eta_t = \frac{P_t}{P} = \frac{p - d}{p} \qquad \qquad \text{... 5.9(e)/Pg 81, DHB}$$

$$= \frac{100 - 25}{100} = 0.75$$

$$\eta_t = 75\% \qquad \qquad \text{... Eq. (i)}$$

Shearing or rivet efficiency:

$$\eta_s = \frac{P_s}{P} = \frac{(n_1 + 1.875 \, n_2)\pi d^2 \tau}{4pt\sigma_t}$$

$$\text{... 5.9(f)/Pg 81, DHB or 5.7/ Pg 80, DHB}$$

For equal cover butt joint,

$$n_1 = 0 \qquad \qquad \text{... 5.10(b)/ Pg 81, DHB}$$

$$\therefore \qquad n_2 = n = 2$$

$$\eta_s = \frac{(0 + 1.875 \times 2)\,\pi \times 25^2 \times 100}{4 \times 100 \times 20 \times 120} = 0.7669$$

$$\eta_s = 76.69\% \qquad \qquad \text{... Eq. (ii)}$$

Crushing efficiency:

$$\eta_c = \frac{P_c}{P} = \frac{(n_1 t_i + n_2 t)d\sigma_c}{pt\sigma_t}$$

$$= \frac{(0 + 2 \times 20) \times 25 \times 150}{100 \times 20 \times 120} = 0.6250$$

$$\eta_c = 62.50\% \qquad \qquad \text{... Eq. (iii)}$$

Thus the efficiency is the least of Eqs. (i), (ii) and (iii), i.e.

$$\eta = \eta_c = 62.50\%.$$

Method 2: We know that

$$\eta = \frac{\text{least value of } P_t, P_s \text{ and } P_c}{P} \qquad \qquad \text{... Eq. (iv)}$$

Tearing resistance,

$$P_t = (p - d)t\sigma_t \qquad \qquad \text{... 5.6(b)/ Pg 80, DHB}$$

$$= (100 - 25) \times 20 \times 120 = 180000 \text{ N}$$

Shearing resistance,

$$P_s = (n_1 + 1.875 \, n_2)\left(\frac{\pi d^2}{4}\right)\tau \qquad \qquad \text{... 5.6(d)/ Pg 80, DHB}$$

$$P_s = (0 + 1.875 \times 2)\left(\frac{\pi \times 25^2}{4}\right) \times 100 = 184077.70 \text{ N}$$

Crushing resistance,

$$P_c = (n_1 t_i + n_2 t)d\sigma_c \qquad \qquad \text{... 5.6(e)/ Pg 80, DHB}$$

$$P_c = (0 + 2 \times 20) \times 25 \times 150 = 150000 \text{ N}$$

Strength of solid plate,

$$P = pt\sigma_t \qquad \text{... 5.6(a)/ Pg 80, DHB}$$
$$P = 100 \times 20 \times 120 = 240000 \text{ N}$$

Eq. (iv) yields... $\eta = \dfrac{150000}{240000} = 0.6250 = 62.50\%$

7.10 DESIGN OF BOILER JOINTS

A cylindrical pressure vessel has two dimensions—the length and the diameter. The cylindrical sections are obtained by bending the sheets and joining the edges by a riveted joint. These sections are then joined together by another riveted joint along circumference.

Thus, there are two types of joints: Longitudinal and circumferential.
- A **longitudinal joint** is used to join the ends of the plate to get the required diameter of a boiler. For this purpose, a triple riveted butt joint with two cover plates is used.
- A **circumferential joint** is used to get the required length of the boiler. For this purpose, a lap joint with one ring overlapping the other alternately is used.

7.10.1 Assumptions in Designing Boiler Joints
- Load is assumed to be uniformly distributed among all the rivets.
- Stress in plate is assumed to be uniform.
- Shear stress is assumed to be uniformly distributed over the gross area of rivets.
- Bearing stress is assumed to be uniform between the contact surfaces of plate and rivet.
- Bending stress in rivet is neglected.
- Rivet hole is assumed to be completely filled by the rivet.
- Friction between plates is neglected.

7.11 DESIGN PROCEDURE FOR LONGITUDINAL BUTT JOINT

According to Indian Boiler Regulations (IBR), the following procedure should be adopted for the design of longitudinal butt joint for a boiler.

1. **Type of joint:** Select the type of joint from **Table 5.2/ Pg 84, DHB,** based on the diameter of the shell, if not given.
2. **Thickness of boiler shell:** The thickness of the boiler shell is determined, by using thin cylinder formula as

$$t = \frac{p_i D}{2\sigma_t \eta} \qquad \text{... (Eq. 7.20) 5.1/ Pg 79, DHB}$$

where p_i = internal steam pressure
D = internal diameter of the boiler shell
σ_t = permissible stress of the shell material
η = efficiency of the longitudinal joint.

The efficiency of the joint may be obtained from
... Table 5.4(b)/ Pg 85 or Table 5.1/ Pg 84, DHB
- Value of thickness to be standardized using **... Table 5.3(c)/ Pg 85, DHB**
3. **Diameter of rivet hole and rivet:**
   a. If the thickness is more than 8 mm ($t > 8$ mm), the diameter of the rivet hole is obtained from Unwin's formula as:

$$d = 6.325\sqrt{t} \qquad \text{... (Eq. 7.21) 5.11(d)/ Pg 81, DHB}$$

b. If $t < 8$ mm, then the diameter of the rivet hole is obtained by equating the shearing resistance of the rivets to crushing resistance as:

$$P_s = P_c$$

$$(n_1 + 1.875\,n_2)\left(\frac{\pi d^2}{4}\right)\tau = (n_1 t_i + n_2 t)d\sigma_c \quad \text{... using Eqs. [(5.6(d) and 5.6(e)/DHB]}$$

i.e. $$d = \frac{4(n_1 t_i + n_2 t)\sigma_c}{\pi(n_1 + 1.875\,n_2)\tau} \quad \text{...(Eq. 7.22) 5.10(a)/ Pg 81, DHB}$$

- The diameter of rivet hole (d) must be rounded off to the nearest standard value with the help of the following table and the corresponding diameter of rivet (d_1) is noted.

Standard rivet hole and rivet diameters												
Dia. of rivet hole (d)	13	15	17	19	21	23	25	28.5	31.5	34.5	37.5	41	44
Dia. of rivet (d_1)	12	14	16	18	20	22	24	27	30	33	36	39	42

From the above table, we observe that

$$d = d_1 + 1 \text{ mm}, \quad \text{for } 12 \text{ mm} \le d \le 24 \text{ mm}$$
$$d = d_1 + 1.5 \text{ mm}, \quad \text{for } 27 \text{ mm} \le d \le 36 \text{ mm}$$
$$d = d_1 + 2 \text{ mm}, \quad \text{for } 39 \text{ mm} \le d \le 48 \text{ mm}$$

- The nominal diameter of rivets may also be obtained from **Table 5.3(b)/ Pg 84, DHB**

Note: Use diameter of rivet hole for all calculations.

4. **Pitch of the rivets:**

   a. The pitch of the rivets is obtained by equating the shearing resistance of the rivets to the tearing resistance of the plate as:

   $$P_s = P_t$$

   $$(n_1 + 1.875\,n_2)\left(\frac{\pi d^2}{4}\right)\tau = (p - d)t\sigma_t \quad \text{... using Eqs.[(5.6(d) and 5.6(b)/DHB]}$$

   i.e. optimum pitch

   $$p = \frac{(n_1 + 1.875\,n_2)\pi d^2 \tau}{4t\sigma_t} + d$$

   $$\text{... (Eq. 7.23) 5.12(a)/ Pg 81, DHB}$$

   - For a butt joint with equal cover plates, put $n_1 = 0$.

   b. According to IBR, the maximum pitch for a longitudinal joint is

   $$p_{max} = k_1 t + 41 \text{ mm} \quad \text{... (Eq. 7.24) 5.12(b)/Pg 81, DHB}$$

   Value of k_1 **... Table 5.4(a)/Pg 85, DHB**

   Adopt lower value of p from the above Eqs. (7.23) and (7.24) for further calculations.

5. **Transverse pitch (distance between the rows of rivets):** According to IBR:

   a. The transverse pitch for equal number of rivets in a row is:

   i. Chain riveting: $p_t \ge 2d$ **... 5.14(a)/Pg 82, DHB**

   ii. Zig-zag or staggered riveting: $p_t \ge 0.33p + 0.67d$ **... 5.14(b)/Pg 82, DHB**

b. For joints in which the longer pitch (outer row) is double the shorter one (inner row) and the inner rows are chain riveted:
   i. Transverse pitch between outer row and inner row:
$$p \geq 2d$$
  or$\qquad\qquad p_t \geq 0.33p + 0.67d$ **... 5.14(c)/ Pg 82, DHB**
   ii. Transverse pitch between successive inner rows:
$$p_t \geq 2d$$ **... 5.14(d)/ Pg 82, DHB**

c. For joints in which the longer pitch (outer row) is double the shorter one (inner row) and the inner rows are zig-zag riveted:
   i. Transverse pitch between outer row and inner row:
$$p_t \geq 0.2p + 1.15d$$ **... 5.15(a)/ Pg 82, DHB**
   ii. Transverse pitch between successive inner rows:
$$p_t \geq 0.165p + 0.67d$$ **... 5.15(b)/ Pg 83, DHB**

Note: p is the pitch of the rivets in the outer row.

6. **Thickness of cover plate or butt strap:** According to IBR
  a. The thickness in no case shall be less than 10 mm.
  b. For single butt strap with ordinary riveting:
$$t_i = 1.125t$$ **... 5.4(a)/ Pg 79, DHB**
  c. For single butt strap having alternate rivets in outer rows omitted:
$$t_i = 1.125t \left(\frac{p-d}{p-2d} \right)$$ **... 5.4(b)/ Pg 80, DHB**
  d. For double butt strap of equal width having ordinary riveting:
$$t_i = t_o = 0.625t$$ **... 5.4(c)/ Pg 80, DHB**
  e. For double straps of equal width having every alternate rivet in outer rows omitted:
$$t_i = t_o = 0.625t \left(\frac{p-d}{p-2d} \right)$$ **... 5.4(d)/ Pg 80, DHB**
  f. For double butt strap of unequal width:
   i. $t_o = 0.625t$, for ordinary riveting.   **... 5.4(e)/ Pg 80, DHB**
   ii. $t_i = 0.75t$, for alternate rivets in outer rows omitted: **... 5.4(f)/ Pg 80, DHB**

7. **Margin:** Margin is calculated as $m = 1.5d$ **... 5.16/ Pg 83, DHB**

8. **Efficiency:**
$$\eta = \frac{\text{least value of } P_t, \, P_s \text{ and } P_c}{P} \text{ or least of } \eta_t, \, \eta_s \text{ and } \eta_c$$
[... as discussed in Section 7.9]

Note: The above procedure can also be used for ordinary riveted joint.

7.12 DESIGN PROCEDURE FOR CIRCUMFERENTIAL LAP JOINT

The circumferential joint is always a lap joint made with one ring overlapping the other alternately.

1. **Thickness of boiler shell:**   *... as discussed in longitudinal butt joint*
2. **Diameter of rivet hole:**   *... as discussed in longitudinal butt joint*

3. **Number of rivets:** As the circumferential joint is a lap riveted joint, therefore the rivets will be in single shear.

$$n = \frac{\text{steam load}}{\text{shear strength of one rivet}} = \frac{(\pi D^2/4)p_i}{(\pi d^2/4)\tau} \qquad \text{... (Eq. 7.25)}$$

where D = inner diameter of boiler shell, d = diameter of rivet hole

4. **Pitch:**
   a. The pitch is calculated as

   $$p = \frac{(n_1 + 1.875 n_2)\pi d^2 \tau}{4t\sigma_t} + d$$

   ... using (Eq. 7.23) **5.12(a)/ Pg 81, DHB**

   For a lap joint, $n_2 = 0$

   b. According to IBR, the maximum pitch for a longitudinal joint is

   $$p_{max} = k_1 t + 41 \text{ mm} \qquad \text{... using (Eq. 7.24)} \textbf{ 5.12(b)/ Pg 81, DHB}$$

   Value of k_1 **... Table 5.4(a)/ Pg 85, DHB**

   Adopt lower value of p from the above Eqs. (7.23) and (7.24) for further calculations.

5. **Number of rivets per row:** For a circumferential joint, the number of rivets arranged in a row can be computed as

   $$n' = \frac{\pi(D + t)}{p} \qquad \text{... (Eq. 7.26)}$$

6. **Number of rows (Z):** The circumferential joint is always a double riveted butt joint, hence $Z = 2$.   ... (Eq. 7.27)

7. **Transverse pitch (distance between the rows of rivets):** For zig-zag or staggered riveting,

   $$p_t \geq 0.33p + 0.67d \qquad \text{... } \textbf{5.14(b)/ Pg 82, DHB}$$

8. **Overlap:** The overlap of the plate is fixed as

   $$\text{overlap} = (Z - 1)p_t + 2m \text{ or using type of joint} \qquad \text{... (Eq. 7.28)}$$

9. **Efficiency:** $\eta = \dfrac{\text{least value of } P_t, P_s \text{ and } P_c}{P}$

   or least of η_c, η_s and η_c *... as discussed in Section 7.9*

   Note:
   - **Table 5.1/ Pg 84, DHB,** *gives the values of efficiency for commercial boiler joints.*
   - **Table 5.2/ Pg 84, DHB,** *gives the recommended type of joints, based on diameter of boiler shell.*
   - **Table 5.3(b)/ Pg 84, DHB,** *gives the nominal diameter of the rivets.*
   - **Table 5.3(c)/ Pg 85, DHB,** *gives the thickness of plates for various applications.*
   - **Table 5.4(b)/ Pg 85, DHB,** *gives the recommended values of rivet hole diameter, pitch and efficiency.*
   - *Pressure vessels are designed based on a factor of safety of 5, as given under note section of* **Tb. 5.6/ Pg 86, DHB.**

Problems on Lap Joint

3. **Design a double riveted lap joint with zig-zag riveting for 13 mm thick plates. The working stresses to be used are $\sigma_t = 80$ MPa, $\tau = 60$ MPa and $\sigma_c = 120$ MPa. State how the joint will fail and find the efficiency of the joint.**

   VTU – June/ July 2011 – 10 Marks

Solution: $t = 13$ mm, $\sigma_t = 80$ MPa, $\tau = 60$ MPa, $\sigma_c = 120$ MPa, $\eta = ?$

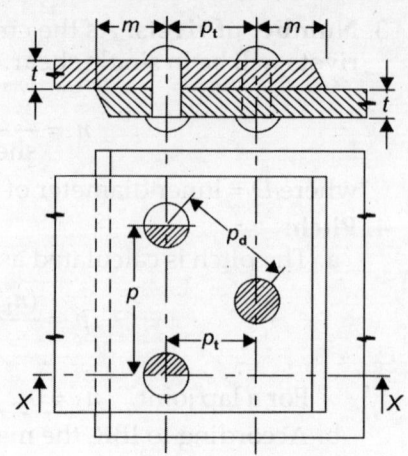

Fig. 7.12: Problem 3

1. **Type of joint:** Lap joint – Double riveted double cover $\Rightarrow n = 2$.

   Here Number of rivets in single shear,
   $n_1 = n = 2$
   Number of rivets in double shear,
   $n_2 = 0$
   Thickness of inner plate,
   $t_i = t = 13$ mm   ... *Pg 81/ DHB

2. **Thickness of plate:**

   $$t = 13 \text{ mm (data)}$$

3. **Diameter of rivet hole:** From Unwin's formula, for $t > 8$ mm, we have

   $$d = 6.325\sqrt{t} \qquad \text{... 5.11(d)/ Pg 81, DHB}$$

   $$= 6.325\sqrt{13}$$

   $$d = 22.81 \text{ mm}$$

   Thus the standard diameter of rivet hole,

   $$d = 23 \text{ mm}$$

   and the diameter of rivet,

   $$d = d_1 + 1 \text{ mm}, \quad \text{for } 12 \text{ mm} \le d \le 24 \text{ mm}$$
   $$d_1 = 23 - 1 = 22 \text{ mm}$$

4. **Pitch of the rivets:**

   a. Optimum pitch:

   $$p = \frac{(n_1 + 1.875n_2)\pi d^2 \tau}{4t\sigma_t} + d \qquad \text{... 5.12(a)/ Pg 81, DHB}$$

   $$p = \frac{2\pi \times 23^2 \times 60}{4 \times 13 \times 80} + 23 \qquad \text{...}n_2 = 0, \text{ from step 1}$$

   $$p = 70.94 \text{ mm} \qquad \text{... Eq. (i)}$$

   b. Maximum pitch:

   $$p_{max} = k_1 t + 41 \text{ mm} \qquad \text{... 5.12(b)/ Pg 81, DHB}$$
   $$k_1 = 2.62, \text{ for a lap joint with two rivets per pitch}$$
   $$\text{... Tb. 5.4(a)/ Pg 85, DHB}$$
   $$p_{max} = (2.62 \times 13) + 41 = 75.06 \qquad \text{... Eq. (ii)}$$

   Thus, the standard pitch is the lower value from Eqs. (i) and (ii)
   i.e. $p = 70.94 \text{ mm} \approx 71 \text{ mm}$

5. **Transverse pitch (distance between the rows of rivets):**

   For zig-zag or staggered riveting,
   $$p_t \ge 0.33p + 0.67d \qquad \text{... 5.14(b)/ Pg 82, DHB}$$
   $$\ge (0.33 \times 71) + (0.67 \times 23)$$
   $$p_t = 38.84 \text{ mm} \approx 40 \text{ mm}$$

6. **Margin:** Margin is calculated as
$$m = 1.5d = 1.5 \times 23 = 34.5 \text{ mm} \qquad \text{... 5.16/Pg 83, DHB}$$

7. **Efficiency:** We know that
$$\eta = \frac{\text{least value of } P_t, P_s \text{ and } P_c}{P} \text{ or least of } \eta_t, \eta_s \text{ and } \eta_c$$

- Tearing or plate efficiency:
$$\eta_t = \frac{P_t}{P} = \frac{p - d}{p} = \frac{71 - 23}{71} = 0.6761 = 67.61\%$$
$$\text{... Eq. (iii) } \textbf{5.9(e)/Pg 81, DHB}$$

- Shearing or rivet efficiency:
$$\eta_s = \frac{P_s}{P} = \frac{(n_1 + 1.875 n_2)\pi d^2 \tau}{4pt\sigma_t} = \frac{(2 + 0)\pi \times 23^2 \times 60}{4 \times 71 \times 13 \times 80} = 0.6572$$
$$\text{... } \textbf{5.9(f)/Pg 81, DHB}$$
$$\eta_s = 67.52\% \qquad\qquad \text{... Eq. (iv)}$$

- Crushing efficiency:
$$\eta_c = \frac{P_c}{P} = \frac{(n_1 t_i + n_2 t)d\sigma_c}{pt\sigma_t}$$
$$= \frac{(2 \times 13 + 0) \times 23 \times 120}{71 \times 13 \times 80} = 0.9718 = 97.18\% \qquad \text{... Eq. (v)}$$

Thus, the efficiency is the least of Eqs. (iii), (iv) and (v), i.e. $\eta = \eta_s = 67.52\%$. The joint will fail by shear.

4. **Design a double riveted lap joint with chain riveting for mild steel plates of 20 mm thick taking the allowable value of stress in shear, tension and compression to 60 MPa, 90 MPa and 120 MPa respectively.**

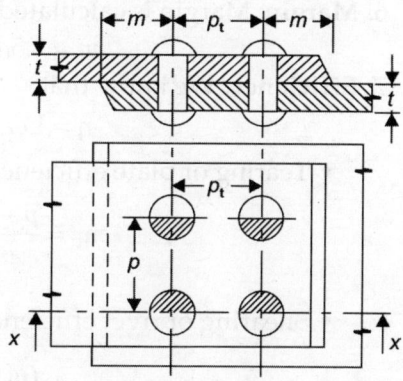

Fig. 7.13: Problem 4

VTU – Dec. 08/ Jan. 2009 – 12 Marks; June/July 2014 – 10 Marks

Solution: $t = 20$ mm, $\sigma_t = 90$ MPa, $\tau = 60$ MPa, $\sigma_c = 120$ MPa, $\eta = ?$

1. **Type of joint:** Lap joint – Double riveted double-chain rivetting cover $\Rightarrow n = 2$.
   Here Number of rivets in single shear, $n_1 = n = 2$
   Number of rivets in double shear, $n_2 = 0$
   Thickness of inner plate, $t_i = t = 20$ mm ... *Pg 81/ DHB

2. **Thickness of plate:**
$$t = 20 \text{ mm (data)}$$

3. **Diameter of rivet hole:** From Unwin's formula, for $t > 8$ mm, we have
$$d = 6.325\sqrt{t} \qquad \text{... 5.11(d)/ Pg 81, DHB}$$
$$= 6.325\sqrt{20}$$
$$d = 28.28 \text{ mm}$$

Thus, the standard diameter of rivet hole,
$$d = 28.5 \text{ mm}$$

and the diameter of rivet,
$$d = d_1 + 1.5 \text{ mm}, \quad \text{for } 27 \text{ mm} \leq d \leq 36 \text{ mm}$$
$$d_1 = 28.5 - 1.5 = 27 \text{ mm}$$

4. **Pitch of the rivets:**

a. Optimum pitch:

$$p = \frac{(n_1 + 1.875 n_2)\pi d^2 \tau}{4 t \sigma_t} + d \qquad \text{... 5.12(a)/ Pg 81, DHB}$$

$$p = \frac{2\pi \times 28.5^2 \times 60}{4 \times 20 \times 90} + 28.5 \qquad \text{...} n_2 = 0, \text{ from step 1}$$

$$p = 71.03 \text{ mm} \qquad \qquad \text{... Eq. (i)}$$

b. Maximum pitch:

$$p_{\max} = k_1 t + 41 \text{ mm} \qquad \text{... 5.12(b)/ Pg 81, DHB}$$

$$k_1 = 2.62, \text{ for a lap joint with two rivets per pitch}$$
$$\text{... Tb. 5.4(a)/ Pg 85, DHB}$$

$$p_{\max} = (2.62 \times 20) + 41 = 93.40 \text{ mm} \qquad \text{... Eq. (ii)}$$

Thus, the standard pitch is the lower value from Eqs. (i) and (ii)

i.e. $\qquad\qquad p = 71.03 \text{ mm} \approx 71 \text{ mm}$

5. **Transverse pitch (distance between the rows of rivets):**

For chain riveting, $\quad p_t \geq 2d = 2 \times 28.5 = 57 \text{ mm} \qquad \text{... 5.14(a)/ Pg 82, DHB}$

6. **Margin:** Margin is calculated as
$$m = 1.5d = 1.5 \times 28.5 = 42.75 \text{ mm} \qquad \text{... 5.16/Pg 83, DHB}$$

7. **Efficiency:** We know that
$$\eta = \text{Least of } \eta_t, \eta_s \text{ and } \eta_c$$

- Tearing or plate efficiency:

$$\eta_t = \frac{p - d}{p} = \frac{71 - 28.5}{71} = 0.5986 = 59.86\%$$
$$\text{... Eq. (iii) 5.9(e)/Pg 81, DHB}$$

- Shearing or rivet efficiency:

$$\eta_s = \frac{(n_1 + 1.875 n_2)\pi d^2 \tau}{4 p t \sigma_t} = \frac{(2 + 0)\pi \times 28.5^2 \times 60}{4 \times 71 \times 20 \times 90} = 0.5990$$
$$\text{... 5.9(f)/Pg 81, DHB}$$

$$\eta_s = 59.90\% \qquad\qquad \text{... Eq. (iv)}$$

- Crushing efficiency:

$$\eta_c = \frac{P_c}{P} = \frac{(n_1 t_i + n_2 t)d\sigma_c}{p t \sigma_t}$$

$$= \frac{(2 \times 20 + 0) \times 28.5 \times 120}{71 \times 20 \times 90} = 1.0704 = 107.04\% \qquad \text{... Eq. (v)}$$

Thus the efficiency is the least of Eqs. (iii), (iv) and (v), i.e. $\eta = \eta_s = 69.86\%$.

Problems on Butt Joint

5. **Two plates 10 mm thick each are to be joined by means of a single riveted double strap butt joint. Determine the rivet diameter, pitch, strap thickness and efficiency of the joint. Take σ_t = 80 MPa, τ = 60 MPa**

VTU – June/ July 2015 – 10 Marks

Solution: t = 10 mm, d = ?, p = ?, $t_i = t_o$ = ?, η = ?, σ_t = 80 MPa, τ = 60 MPa.

Type of joint: Butt joint – Single riveted double strap/cover $\Rightarrow n = 1$. Assume equal cover.

Here   Number of rivets in single shear, $n_1 = 0$

Number of rivets in double shear, $n_2 = n = 1$

Thickness of main plate, t = 10 mm   … *Pg 81/ DHB

1. **Diameter of rivet hole:** From Unwin's formula, for $t > 8$ mm, we have

$$d = 6.325\sqrt{t} \qquad \text{… 5.11(d)/ Pg 81, DHB}$$

$$= 6.325\sqrt{10}$$

$$= 20 \text{ mm}$$

Thus the standard diameter of rivet hole,

$$d = 21 \text{ mm}$$

and the diameter of rivet,

$$d = d_1 + 1 \text{ mm}, \quad \text{for } 12 \text{ mm} \le d \le 24 \text{ mm}$$

$$d_1 = 21 - 1 = 20 \text{ mm}$$

2. **Pitch of the rivets:**

a. Optimum pitch:

$$p = \frac{(n_1 + 1.875n_2)\pi d^2 \tau}{4t\sigma_t} + d \qquad \text{… 5.12(a)/ Pg 81, DHB}$$

$$p = \frac{(1.875 \times 1) \times \pi \times 21^2 \times 60}{4 \times 10 \times 80} + 21 \qquad …n_1 = 0, \text{ from step 1}$$

$$p = 69.71 \text{ mm} \qquad \text{… Eq. (i)}$$

b. Maximum pitch:

$$p_{max} = k_1 t + 41 \text{ mm} \qquad \text{… 5.12(b)/ Pg 81, DHB}$$

$$k_1 = 1.75, \text{ for a double strap butt joint having one rivet per}$$
$$\text{pitch} \qquad \text{… Tb. 5.4(a)/ Pg 85, DHB}$$

$$p_{max} = (1.75 \times 10) + 41 = 58.5 \text{ mm} \qquad \text{… Eq. (ii)}$$

Thus the standard pitch is the lower value from Eqs. (i) and (ii)

i.e. $\qquad p = 58.5 \text{ mm} \approx 60 \text{ mm}$

3. **Strap thickness:**

For double butt strap of equal width having ordinary riveting

$$t_i = t_o = 0.625t = 0.625 \times 10 \qquad \text{… 5.4(c)/ Pg 80, DHB}$$

$$t_i = t_o = 6.25 \text{ mm}$$

4. **Efficiency:** We know that

$$\eta = \text{Least of } \eta_t \text{ and } \eta_s$$

- Tearing or plate efficiency:

$$\eta_t = \frac{P_t}{P} = \frac{p-d}{p} = \frac{60-21}{60} = 0.65 = 65\%$$

... Eq. (iii) **5.9(e)/Pg 81, DHB**

- Crushing efficiency:

$$\eta_s = \frac{P_s}{P} = \frac{(n_1 + 1.875n_2)\pi d^2 \tau}{4pt\sigma_t}$$ ... **5.9(f)/Pg 81, DHB**

$$= \frac{(0 + 1.875 \times 1)\pi \times 21^2 \times 60}{4 \times 60 \times 10 \times 80} = 0.8118$$

$$\eta_s = 81.18\%$$ ... Eq. (iv)

Thus the efficiency is the least of Eqs. (iii) and (iv), i.e. $\eta = \eta_t = 65\%$.

6. **Design a double riveted butt joint with equal widths of cover plates to join two plates of thickness 10 mm. The allowable stress for the material of the rivets and for the plates are as follows: For plate material in tension, $\sigma_t = 80$ MPa; for rivet material in compression, $\sigma_c = 120$ MPa; for rivet material in shear, $\tau = 60$ MPa.**

VTU – July/ Aug. 2005 – 10 Marks; July 2006 – 10 Marks

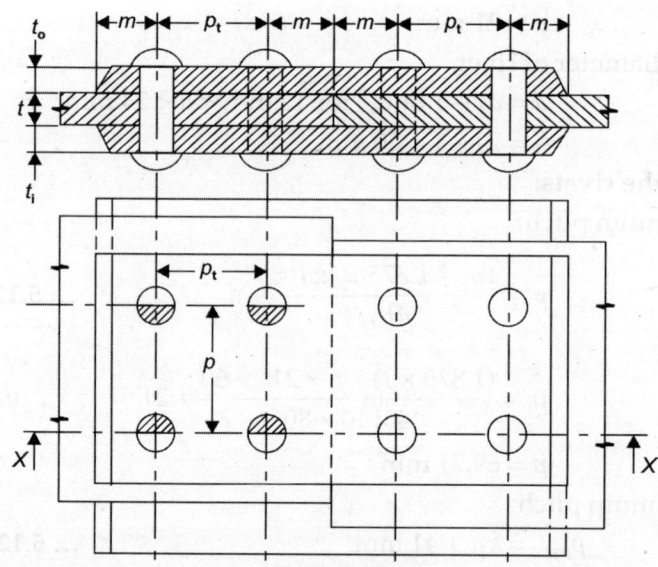

Fig. 7.14: Problem 6

Solution: $t = 10$ mm, $\sigma_t = 80$ MPa, $\sigma_c = 120$ MPa, $\tau = 60$ MPa.

1. **Type of joint:** Butt joint – Double riveted double strap - equal cover $\Rightarrow n = 2$.
   Assume chain riveting.
   Here   Number of rivets in single shear, $n_1 = 0$
      Number of rivets in double shear, $n_2 = n = 2$ ... *Pg 81/ DHB

2. **Thickness of plate:**
   $$t = 10 \text{ mm (data)}$$

3. **Diameter of rivet hole:** From Unwin's formula, for $t > 8$ mm, we have

   $$d = 6.325\sqrt{t}$$ ... **5.11(d)/ Pg 81, DHB**

   $$= 6.325\sqrt{10} = 20 \text{ mm}$$

Thus the standard diameter of rivet hole,
$$d = 21 \text{ mm}$$
and the diameter of rivet,
$$d = d_1 + 1 \text{ mm}, \quad \text{for } 12 \text{ mm} \le d \le 24 \text{ mm}$$
$$d_1 = 21 - 1 = 20 \text{ mm}$$

4. **Pitch of the rivets:**

    a. Optimum pitch:
    $$p = \frac{(n_1 + 1.875n_2)\pi d^2 \tau}{4t\sigma_t} + d \qquad \text{... 5.12(a)/ Pg 81, DHB}$$

    $$p = \frac{(1.875 \times 2) \times \pi \times 21^2 \times 60}{4 \times 10 \times 80} + 21 \qquad ...n_1 = 0, \text{ from step 1}$$

    $$p = 118.41 \text{ mm} \qquad \text{... Eq. (i)}$$

    b. Maximum pitch:
    $$p_{max} = k_1 t + 41 \text{ mm} \qquad \text{... 5.12(b)/ Pg 81, DHB}$$
    $$k_1 = 3.5, \quad \text{for a double strap butt joint having two rivets per}$$
    $$\text{pitch} \qquad \text{... Tb. 5.4(a)/ Pg 85, DHB}$$
    $$p_{max} = (3.5 \times 10) + 41 = 76 \text{ mm} \qquad \text{... Eq. (ii)}$$

    Thus the standard pitch is the lower value from Eqs. (i) and (ii),

    i.e. $\qquad\qquad p = 76 \text{ mm}$

5. **Transverse pitch (distance between the rows of rivets):**

    For chain riveting, $\quad p_t \ge 2d = 2 \times 21 = 42 \text{ mm} \qquad \text{... 5.14(a)/ Pg 82, DHB}$

6. **Strap thickness:**

    For double butt strap of equal width having ordinary riveting
    $$t_i = t_o = 0.625t = 0.625 \times 10 \qquad \text{... 5.4(c)/ Pg 80, DHB}$$
    $$t_i = t_o = 6.25 \text{ mm}$$

7. **Margin:** Margin is calculated as
    $$m = 1.5d = 1.5 \times 21 = 31.5 \text{ mm} \qquad \text{... 5.16/ Pg 83, DHB}$$

8. **Efficiency:** We know that
    $$\eta = \text{Least of } \eta_t, \eta_s \text{ and } \eta_c$$

    • Tearing or plate efficiency:
    $$\eta_t = \frac{p - d}{p} = \frac{76 - 21}{76} = 0.7264 = 72.64\%$$
    $$\text{... Eq. (iii) 5.9(e)/Pg 81, DHB}$$

    • Shearing or rivet efficiency:
    $$\eta_s = \frac{(n_1 + 1.875n_2)\pi d^2 \tau}{4pt\sigma_t} \qquad \text{... 5.9(f)/Pg 81, DHB}$$

    $$= \frac{(0 + 1.875 \times 2)\pi \times 21^2 \times 60}{4 \times 76 \times 10 \times 80} = 1.282$$

    $$\eta_s = 128.2\% \qquad \text{... Eq. (iv)}$$

- Crushing efficiency:

$$\eta_c = \frac{P_c}{P} = \frac{(n_1 t_i + n_2 t)d\sigma_c}{pt\sigma_t}$$

$$= \frac{(0 + 2 \times 10) \times 21 \times 120}{76 \times 10 \times 80} = 0.8290$$

$$\eta_s = 82.90\% \qquad \qquad \text{... Eq. (iv)}$$

Thus the efficiency is the least of Eqs. (iii), (iv) and (v), i.e. $\eta = \eta_t = 72.64\%$.

7. **Design a double riveted zig-zag butt joint with equal cover plates to connect two plates 20 mm thick. Calculate the efficiency of the joint. The joint should be leak proof. Take $\sigma_t = 100$ MPa, $\tau = 60$ MPa and $\sigma_c = 120$ MPa.**

VTU – Dec. 08/ Jan. 2009 – 10 Marks; Dec. 07/ Jan. 2008 – 10 Marks

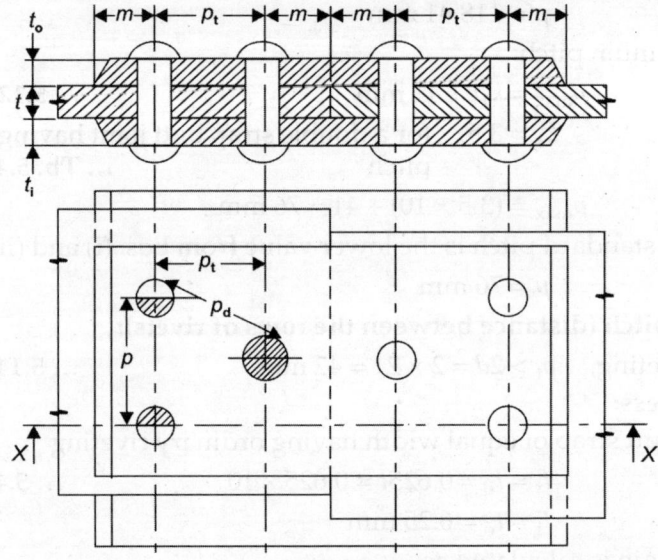

Fig. 7.15: Problem 7

Solution: $t = 20$ mm, $\sigma_t = 100$ MPa, $\sigma_c = 120$ MPa, $\tau = 60$ MPa.

1. **Type of joint:** Butt joint – Double riveted double strap—equal cover with zig-zag riveting $\Rightarrow n = 2$.

   Here, number of rivets in single shear, $n_1 = 0$

   number of rivets in double shear, $n_2 = n = 2$ ... *Pg 81/ DHB

2. **Thickness of plate:**

   $$t = 20 \text{ mm (data)}$$

3. **Diameter of rivet hole:** From Unwin's formula, for $t > 8$ mm, we have

   $$d = 6.325\sqrt{t} \qquad \qquad \text{... 5.11(d)/ Pg 81, DHB}$$

   $$= 6.325\sqrt{20} = 28.28 \text{ mm}$$

   Thus the standard diameter of rivet hole,

   $$d = 28.5 \text{ mm}$$

and the diameter of rivet,

$$d = d_1 + 1.5 \text{ mm}, \quad \text{for } 12 \text{ mm} \le d \le 36 \text{ mm}$$

$$d_1 = 28.5 - 1.5 = 27 \text{ mm}$$

4. Pitch of the rivets:

a. Optimum pitch:

$$p = \frac{(n_1 + 1.875 n_2)\pi d^2 \tau}{4 t \sigma_t} + d \qquad \text{... 5.12(a)/ Pg 81, DHB}$$

$$p = \frac{(1.875 \times 2) \times \pi \times 28.5^2 \times 60}{4 \times 20 \times 100} + 28.5 \qquad ...n_1 = 0, \text{ from step 1}$$

$$p = 100.27 \text{ mm} \qquad \text{... Eq. (i)}$$

b. Maximum pitch:

$$p_{max} = k_1 t + 41 \text{ mm} \qquad \text{... 5.12(b)/ Pg 81, DHB}$$

$$k_1 = 3.5, \quad \text{for a double strap butt joint having two rivets per pitch} \qquad \text{... Tb. 5.4(a)/ Pg 85, DHB}$$

$$p_{max} = (3.5 \times 20) + 41 = 111 \text{ mm} \qquad \text{... Eq. (ii)}$$

Thus the standard pitch is the lower value from Eqs. (i) and (ii),

i.e. $$p = 100.27 \text{ mm} \approx 102 \text{ mm}$$

For leak proof joint,

$$p \le 6d \qquad \text{... 5.12(d)/ Pg 82, DHB}$$

i.e. $$\frac{p}{d} < 6 \Rightarrow \frac{102}{28.5} < 6$$

$3.57 < 6$, hence the joint is leak proof.

5. Transverse pitch (distance between the rows of rivets): For zig-zag or staggered riveting,

$$p_t \ge 0.33 p + 0.67 d \qquad \text{... 5.14(b)/ Pg 82, DHB}$$

$$\ge (0.33 \times 102) + (0.67 \times 28.5)$$

$$p_t = 52.76 \text{ mm} \approx 53 \text{ mm}$$

6. Strap thickness:

For double butt strap of equal width having ordinary riveting,

$$t_i = t_o = 0.625 t = 0.625 \times 20 \qquad \text{... 5.4(c)/ Pg 80, DHB}$$

$$t_i = t_o = 12.5 \text{ mm}$$

7. Margin: We know that

$$m = 1.5 d = 1.5 \times 28.5 = 42.75 \text{ mm} \qquad \text{... 5.16/ Pg 83, DHB}$$

8. Efficiency: We know that

$$\eta = \text{Least of } \eta_t, \eta_s \text{ and } \eta_c$$

- Tearing or plate efficiency:

$$\eta_t = \frac{p - d}{p} = \frac{102 - 28.5}{102} = 0.7206 = 72.06\%$$

$$\text{... Eq. (iii) 5.9(e)/Pg 81, DHB}$$

- Shearing or rivet efficiency:

$$\eta_s = \frac{(n_1 + 1.875 n_2)\pi d^2 \tau}{4 p t \sigma_t} \qquad \text{... 5.9(f)/Pg 81, DHB}$$

$$= \frac{(0 + 1.875 \times 2)\pi \times 28.5^2 \times 120}{4 \times 102 \times 20 \times 100} = 0.7036$$

$$\eta_s = 70.36\% \qquad \text{... Eq. (iv)}$$

- Crushing efficiency:

$$\eta_c = \frac{P_c}{P} = \frac{(n_1 t_i + n_2 t)d\sigma_c}{p t \sigma_t}$$

$$= \frac{(0 + 2 \times 20) \times 28.5 \times 120}{102 \times 20 \times 100} = 0.6705$$

$$= 67.05\% \qquad \text{... Eq. (iv)}$$

Thus the efficiency is the least of Eqs. (iii), (iv) and (v), i.e. $\eta = \eta_c = 67.05\%$.

8. **Design a triple riveted butt joint with equal cover plates and staggered riveting to connect two plates 20 mm thick. The allowable tensile stress for the plate is 100 MPa and allowable shear and compressive stresses for the rivet material are 55 MPa and 110 MPa respectively. Sketch the designed joint showing main dimensions and calculate the joint efficiency.**

VTU – July/ Aug. 2004 – 10 Marks

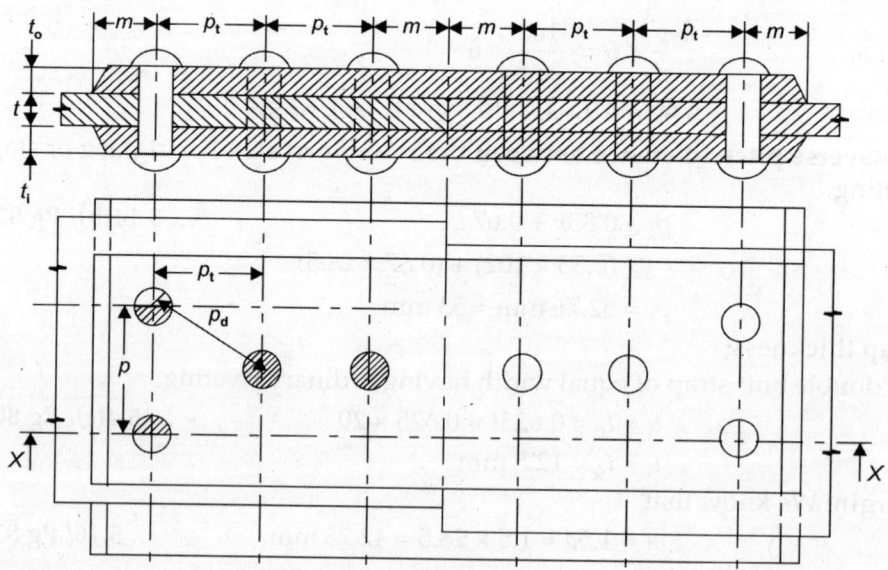

Fig. 7.16: Problem 8

Solution: $t = 20$ mm, $\sigma_t = 100$ MPa, $\sigma_c = 110$ MPa, $\tau = 55$ MPa.

1. **Type of joint:** Butt joint – Triple riveted double strap—equal cover, zig-zag riveting $\Rightarrow n = 3$.

Here Number of rivets in single shear, $n_1 = 0$

Number of rivets in double shear, $n_2 = n = 3$ ... *Pg 81/ DHB

2. **Thickness of plate:**
$$t = 20 \text{ mm (data)}$$

3. **Diameter of rivet hole:** From Unwin's formula, for $t > 8$ mm, we have
$$d = 6.325\sqrt{t} \hspace{2cm} \text{... 5.11(d)/ Pg 81, DHB}$$

$$= 6.325\sqrt{20} = 28.28 \text{ mm}$$

Thus the standard diameter of rivet hole,
$$d = 28.5 \text{ mm}$$

and the diameter of rivet,
$$d = d_1 + 1.5 \text{ mm}, \quad \text{for } 27 \text{ mm} \le d \le 36 \text{ mm}$$
$$d_1 = 28.5 - 1.5 = 27 \text{ mm}$$

4. **Pitch of the rivets:**

a. Optimum pitch:
$$p = \frac{(n_1 + 1.875 n_2)\pi d^2 \tau}{4 t \sigma_t} + d \hspace{1cm} \text{... 5.12(a)/ Pg 81, DHB}$$

$$p = \frac{(1.875 \times 3) \times \pi \times 28.5^2 \times 55}{4 \times 20 \times 100} + 28.5 \hspace{0.3cm} ...n_1 = 0, \text{ from step 1}$$

$$p = 127.18 \text{ mm} \hspace{3cm} \text{... Eq. (i)}$$

b. Maximum pitch:
$$p_{\max} = k_1 t + 41 \text{ mm} \hspace{2cm} \text{... 5.12(b)/ Pg 81, DHB}$$
$$k_1 = 4.63, \text{ for a double strap butt joint having three rivets per}$$
$$\text{pitch} \hspace{2cm} \text{... Tb. 5.4(a)/ Pg 85, DHB}$$
$$p_{\max} = (4.63 \times 20) + 41 = 133.6 \text{ mm} \hspace{1cm} \text{... Eq. (ii)}$$

Thus the standard pitch is the lower value from Eqs. (i) and (ii),

i.e. $\hspace{2cm} p = 127.18 \text{ mm} \approx 128 \text{ mm}$

5. **Transverse pitch (distance between the rows of rivets):** For zig-zag or staggered riveting,
$$p_t \ge 0.33 p + 0.67 d \hspace{2cm} \text{... 5.14(b)/ Pg 82, DHB}$$
$$\ge (0.33 \times 128) + (0.67 \times 28.5)$$
$$p_t = 61.34 \text{ mm} \approx 62 \text{ mm}$$

6. **Strap thickness:**

For double butt strap of equal width having ordinary riveting
$$t_i = t_o = 0.625 t = 0.625 \times 20 \hspace{1.5cm} \text{... 5.4(c)/ Pg 80, DHB}$$
$$t_i = t_o = 12.5 \text{ mm}$$

7. **Margin:** We know that
$$m = 1.5 d = 1.5 \times 28.5 = 42.75 \text{ mm} \hspace{1cm} \text{... 5.16/ Pg 83, DHB}$$

8. **Efficiency:** We know that
$$\eta = \text{Least of } \eta_t, \eta_s \text{ and } \eta_c$$

• Tearing or plate efficiency:

$$\eta_t = \frac{p - d}{p} = \frac{128 - 28.5}{128} = 0.7773 = 77.73\%$$
$$\text{... Eq. (iii) 5.9(e)/Pg 81, DHB}$$

• Shearing or rivet efficiency:

$$\eta_s = \frac{(n_1 + 1.875 n_2)\pi d^2 \tau}{4pt\sigma_t} \qquad \ldots \text{5.9(f)/Pg 81, DHB}$$

$$= \frac{(0 + 1.875 \times 3)\pi \times 28.5^2 \times 55}{4 \times 128 \times 20 \times 100} = 0.7709$$

$$\eta_s = 77.90\% \qquad \ldots \text{Eq. (iv)}$$

• Crushing efficiency:

$$\eta_c = \frac{P_c}{P} = \frac{(n_1 t_i + n_2 t)d\sigma_c}{pt\sigma_t} \qquad \ldots \text{5.9(f)/Pg 81, DHB}$$

$$= \frac{(0 + 3 \times 20) \times 28.5 \times 110}{128 \times 20 \times 100} = 0.7348$$

$$= 73.48\% \qquad \ldots \text{Eq. (v)}$$

Thus the efficiency is the least of Eqs. (iii), (iv) and (v), i.e. $\eta = \eta_t = 73.48\%$.

Note: If unequal cover plates are used, then $n_1 = 1$ and $n_2 = 2$.

9. **Design a triple riveted butt joint to join two plates of thickness 10 mm. The pitch of the rivets in the extreme rows, which are in single shear is twice the pitch of rivets in the inner rows which are in double shear. The design stresses of the materials of the main plate and the rivets are as follows:**

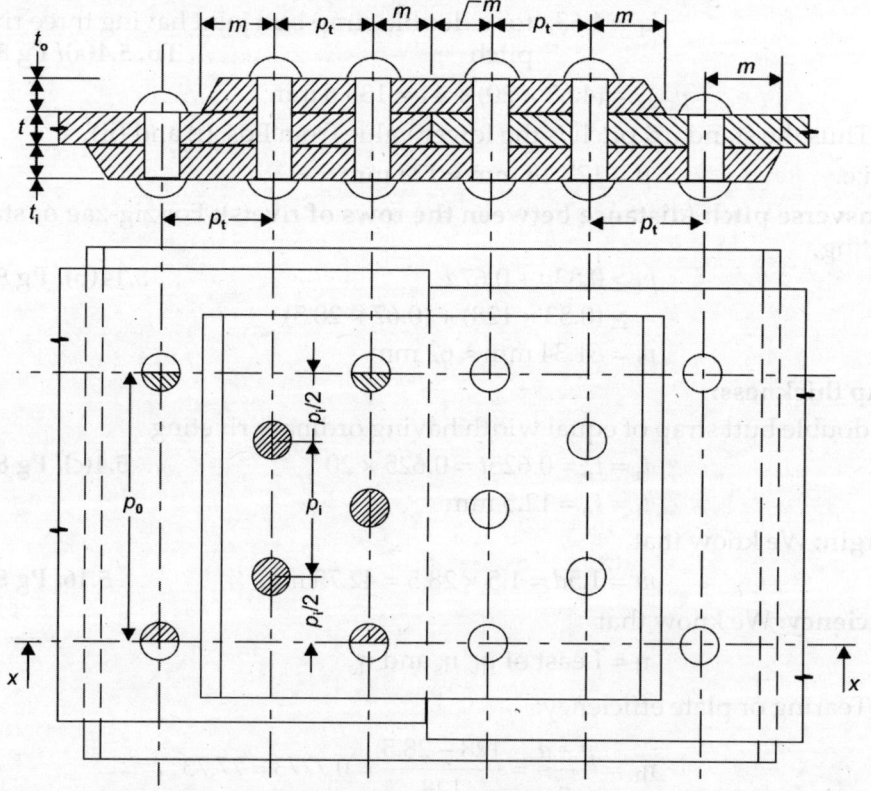

Fig. 7.17: Problem 9

For plate material in tension, σ_t = 120 MPa, for rivet material in compression, σ_c = 160 MPa and for rivet material in shear, τ = 80 MPa.

VTU – Dec. 2014/ Jan. 2015 – 12 Marks

Solution: t = 10 mm, p_o = $2p_i$, σ_t = 120 MPa, σ_c = 160 MPa, τ = 80 MPa.

1. **Type of joint:** Butt joint – Triple riveted double strap. Assume unequal cover with zig-zag riveting.
   - Let us arrange the joint in such a manner that the alternate rivets in outer rows are omitted. The rivets in the outer row will be in single shear, while those in the inner row will be in double shear, as shown in **Fig. 7.17**. In one length (per pitch), there are 4 rivets which are in double shear while 1 is in single shear.

     Here, number of rivets in single shear, n_1 = 1

     number of rivets in double shear, n_2 = 4

2. **Thickness of plate:**
$$t = 10 \text{ mm (data)}$$

3. **Diameter of rivet hole:** From Unwin's formula, for t > 8 mm, we have
$$d = 6.325\sqrt{t} \qquad \text{... 5.11(d)/ Pg 81, DHB}$$
$$= 6.325\sqrt{10} = 20 \text{ mm}$$

Thus the standard diameter of rivet hole,
$$d = 21 \text{ mm}$$

and the diameter of rivet,
$$d = d_1 + 1 \text{ mm, for } 12 \text{ mm} \leq d \leq 24 \text{ mm}$$
$$d_1 = 21 - 1 = 20 \text{ mm}$$

4. **Pitch of the rivets:**
   a. Optimum pitch:
$$p = \frac{(n_1 + 1.875n_2)\pi d^2 \tau}{4t\sigma_t} + d \qquad \text{... 5.12(a)/ Pg 81, DHB}$$

$$p = \frac{(1 + 1.875 \times 4) \times \pi \times 21^2 \times 80}{4 \times 10 \times 120} + 21 \quad ...n_1 = 1, \text{ from step 1}$$

$$p = 217.27 \text{ mm} \qquad \text{... Eq. (i)}$$

   b. Maximum pitch:
$$p_{max} = k_1 t + 41 \text{ mm} \qquad \text{... 5.12(b)/ Pg 81, DHB}$$
$$k_1 = 6, \quad \text{for a double cover butt joint having five rivets per pitch} \qquad \text{... Tb. 5.4(a)/ Pg 85, DHB}$$
$$p_{max} = (6 \times 10) + 41 = 101 \text{ mm} \qquad \text{... Eq. (ii)}$$

Thus the standard pitch is the lower value from Eqs. (i) and (ii),

i.e. outer pitch p_o = 101 mm

Since $p_o = 2p_i$, inner pitch, $p_i = \dfrac{p_o}{2} = \dfrac{101}{2} = 50.5$

5. **Transverse pitch (distance between the rows of rivets):** For zig-zag or staggered riveting,

- The transverse pitch between the outer and inner row,

$$p_t \geq 0.2p + 1.15d \qquad \qquad \text{... 5.15(a)/ Pg 82, DHB}$$
$$\geq (0.2 \times 101) + (1.15 \times 21)$$
$$p_t = 47.38 \text{ mm} \approx 44 \text{ mm}$$

- The transverse pitch between the successive inner row,

$$p_t \geq 0.165p + 0.67d \qquad \qquad \text{... 5.15(b)/ Pg 83, DHB}$$
$$\geq (0.165 \times 101) + (0.67 \times 21)$$
$$p_t = 30.74 \text{ mm} \approx 31 \text{ mm}$$

6. **Strap thickness:**
- Thickness of outer cover plate,

$$t_o = 0.625t = 0.625 \times 10 = 6.25 \text{ mm} \qquad \text{... 5.4(e)/ Pg 80, DHB}$$

- Thickness of inner cover plate,

$$t_i = 0.75t = 0.75 \times 10 = 7.5 \text{ mm} \qquad \text{... 5.4(f)/ Pg 80, DHB}$$

7. **Margin:** Margin is calculated as

$$m = 1.5d = 1.5 \times 21 = 31.5 \text{ mm} \qquad \text{... 5.16/ Pg 83, DHB}$$

8. **Efficiency:** We know that

$$\eta = \text{Least of } \eta_t, \eta_s \text{ and } \eta_c$$

- Tearing or plate efficiency:

$$\eta_t = \frac{p - d}{p} = \frac{101 - 21}{101} = 0.7921 = 79.21\%$$

... Eq. (iii) **5.9(e)/Pg 81, DHB**

- Shearing or rivet efficiency:

$$\eta_s = \frac{(n_1 + 1.875n_2)\pi d^2 \tau}{4pt\sigma_t} \qquad \qquad \text{... 5.9(f)/Pg 81, DHB}$$

$$= \frac{[1 + (1.875 \times 4)]\pi \times 21^2 \times 80}{4 \times 101 \times 10 \times 120} = 1.9433$$

$$\eta_s = 194.32\% \qquad \qquad \text{... Eq. (iv)}$$

- Crushing efficiency:

$$\eta_c = \frac{P_c}{P} = \frac{(n_1 t_i + n_2 t)d\sigma_c}{pt\sigma_t}$$

$$= \frac{[(1 + 7.5) + (4 \times 10)] \times 21 \times 160}{101 \times 10 \times 120} = 1.3168$$

$$= 131.68\% \qquad \qquad \text{... Eq. (v)}$$

- Failure due to tearing of plate at inner row and shearing of rivets in outer row:

$$\eta_{ts} = \frac{(p - 2d)t\sigma_t + k\tau(\pi d^2/4)}{pt\sigma_t} \qquad \text{... 5.8(b)/Pg 80, DHB}$$

Here $\qquad k = 1$ for rivets in single shear

$$n_{ts} = \frac{[(101 - 2 \times 21) \times 10 \times 120] + [1 \times 80 \times (\pi \times 21^2/4)]}{101 \times 10 \times 120}$$

$$= 0.8128 = 81.28\% \qquad\qquad \text{... Eq. (vi)}$$

- Failure of plate due to combined action of tearing of plate at inner row and crushing of rivets in outer row:

$$\eta_{tc} = \frac{(p - 2d)t\sigma_t + dt\sigma_c}{pt\sigma_t} \qquad\qquad \text{... 5.9(b)/Pg 81, DHB}$$

$$= \frac{[(101 - 2 \times 21) \times 10 \times 120] + [21 \times 10 \times 160]}{101 \times 10 \times 120}$$

$$= 0.8614 = 86.14\% \qquad\qquad \text{... Eq. (vii)}$$

- Failure of plate due to combined action of shearing of rivets in outer row and crushing of rivets in inner row:

$$\eta_{sc} = \frac{\tau(\pi d^2/4) + ndt\sigma_c}{pt\sigma_t} \quad \text{here } n = n_2 \qquad \text{... 5.9(d)/Pg 80, DHB}$$

$$= \frac{[80 \times (\pi \times 21^2/4)] + [4 \times 21 \times 10 \times 160]}{101 \times 10 \times 120}$$

$$\eta_{sc} = 1.338 = 133.84\% \qquad\qquad \text{... Eq. (viii)}$$

Thus the efficiency is the least of Eqs. (iii) to (viii), i.e. $\eta = \eta_t = 79.21\%$.

Note: Equations (vi) to (viii) have to be calculated for a triple riveted zig-zag butt joint having unequal cover plates.

Problems on Boiler Connections

10. **Design a double riveted butt joint, with single cover plate, for the longitudinal seam for a boiler shell of diameter 1000 mm and pressure 1.5 MPa. Allowable tensile stress for the plate is 100 MPa and allowable shear and crushing stresses for rivets are 70 and 150 MPa respectively.**

VTU – Dec. 2010 – 15 Marks

Solution: $D = 1000$ mm, $p_i = 1.5$ MPa, $\sigma_t = 100$ MPa, $\tau = 70$ MPa, $\sigma_c = 150$ MPa.

1. **Type of joint:** Butt joint – Double riveted single strap—equal cover. Assume chain riveting

Here, number of rivets in single shear, $n_1 = 0$

number of rivets in double shear, $n_2 = 2$ $\qquad$ ... *Pg 81/ DHB

2. **Thickness of plate:** We know that

$$t = \frac{p_i D}{2\sigma_t \eta} \qquad\qquad \text{... 5.1/Pg 79, DHB}$$

Assume efficiency of the joint $\eta = 75\%$, since η is not available for single strap butt joint in **Tb 5.4(b)/Pg 85, or Tb 5.1/Pg 84, DHB.**

$$t = \frac{1.5 \times 1000}{2 \times 100 \times 0.75} = 10 \text{ mm}$$

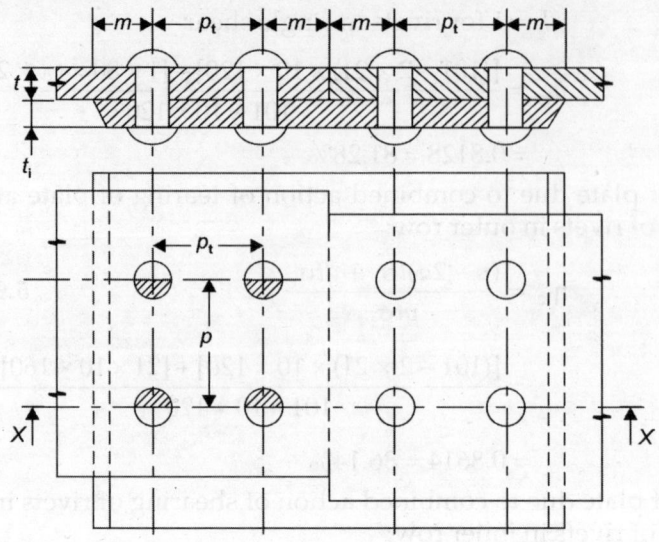

Fig. 7.18: Problem 10

Standard thickness,

$$t = 10 \text{ mm} \qquad \text{... Tb 5.3(c)/Pg 85/ DHB}$$

3. **Diameter of rivet hole:** From Unwin's formula, for $t > 8$ mm, we have

$$d = 6.325\sqrt{t}$$

$$= 6.325\sqrt{10} = 20 \text{ mm} \qquad \text{... 5.11(d)/ Pg 81, DHB}$$

Thus the standard diameter of rivet hole,

$$d = 21 \text{ mm}$$

and the diameter of rivet,

$$d = d_1 + 1 \text{ mm}, \quad \text{for } 12 \text{ mm} \le d \le 24 \text{ mm}$$

$$d_1 = 21 - 1 = 20 \text{ mm}$$

4. **Pitch of the rivets:**

a. Optimum pitch:

$$p = \frac{(n_1 + 1.875 n_2)\pi d^2 \tau}{4 t \sigma_t} + d \qquad \text{... 5.12(a)/ Pg 81, DHB}$$

$$p = \frac{(0 + 1.875 \times 2) \times \pi \times 21^2 \times 70}{4 \times 10 \times 100} + 21 \quad ...n_1 = 0, \text{ from step 1}$$

$$p = 111.92 \text{ mm} \qquad \text{... Eq. (i)}$$

b. Maximum pitch:

$$p_{\max} = k_1 t + 41 \text{ mm} \qquad \text{... 5.12(b)/ Pg 81, DHB}$$

$$k_1 = 3.06, \text{ for a single strap butt joint having two rivets per}$$
$$\text{pitch} \qquad \text{... Tb. 5.4(a)/ Pg 85, DHB}$$

$$p_{\max} = (3.06 \times 10) + 41 = 71.6 \text{ mm} \qquad \text{... Eq. (ii)}$$

Thus the standard pitch is the lower value from Eqs. (i) and (ii),

i.e. $\qquad p = 71.6 \text{ mm} \approx 72 \text{ mm}$

5. **Transverse pitch (distance between the rows of rivets):** For chain riveting,
$$p_t \geq 2d = 2 \times 21 = 42 \text{ mm} \qquad \text{... 5.14(a)/ Pg 82, DHB}$$

6. **Strap thickness:**
For single butt strap with ordinary riveting
$$t_i = 1.125t = 1.125 \times 10 = 11.25 \text{ mm} \qquad \text{... 5.4(a)/ Pg 79, DHB}$$

7. **Margin:** Margin is calculated as
$$m = 1.5d = 1.5 \times 21 = 31.5 \text{ mm} \qquad \text{... 5.16/ Pg 83, DHB}$$

8. **Efficiency:** We know that
$$\eta = \text{Least of } \eta_t, \eta_s \text{ and } \eta_c$$

- Tearing or plate efficiency:
$$\eta_t = \frac{p-d}{p} = \frac{72-21}{72} = 0.7083 = 70.83\%$$
$$\text{... Eq. (iii) } \textbf{5.9(e)/Pg 81, DHB}$$

- Shearing or rivet efficiency:
$$\eta_s = \frac{(n_1 + 1.875n_2)\pi d^2 \tau}{4pt\sigma_t} \qquad \text{... 5.9(f)/Pg 81, DHB}$$
$$= \frac{[0 + (1.875 \times 2)]\pi \times 21^2 \times 70}{4 \times 72 \times 10 \times 100} = 1.2627$$
$$\eta_s = 126.27\% \qquad \text{... Eq. (iv)}$$

- Crushing efficiency:
$$\eta_c = \frac{P_c}{P} = \frac{(n_1 t_i + n_2 t)d\sigma_c}{pt\sigma_t}$$
$$= \frac{[0 + (2 \times 10)] \times 21 \times 150}{72 \times 10 \times 100} = 0.875$$
$$= 87.5\% \qquad \text{... Eq. (v)}$$

Thus the efficiency is the least of Eqs. (iii), (iv) and (v), i.e. $\eta = \eta_t = 70.83\%$.

11. **Design a double riveted butt joint with two cover plates for the longitudinal seam of a boiler shell 1.5 m in diameter subjected to a steam pressure of 0.95 N/mm². Assume an efficiency of 75%, allowable tensile stress in the plate of 90 MPa, allowable compressive stress of 140 MPa and an allowable shear stress in the rivets as 56 MPa.**

VTU – Dec. 2009/ Jan. 2010 – 10 Marks; Dec. 2013/ Jan. 2014 – 10 Marks; Dec. 2013/ Jan. 2014 – 12 Marks; Dec. 2014/ Jan. 2015 – 10 Marks.
[Similar: June/ July 2008 – 10 Marks; June 2012 – 10 Marks; June/ July 2014 – 10 Marks; Dec. 08/ Jan. 2009 – 12 Marks]

Solution: $D = 1500$ mm, $p_i = 0.95$ MPa, $\eta = 75\% = 0.75$, $\sigma_t = 90$ MPa, $\sigma_c = 140$ MPa, $\tau = 56$ MPa

1. **Type of joint:** Butt joint – Double riveted double strap - equal cover. Assume chain riveting
Here   Number of rivets in single shear, $n_1 = 0$
Number of rivets in double shear, $n_2 = 2$ ... **Pg 81, DHB**

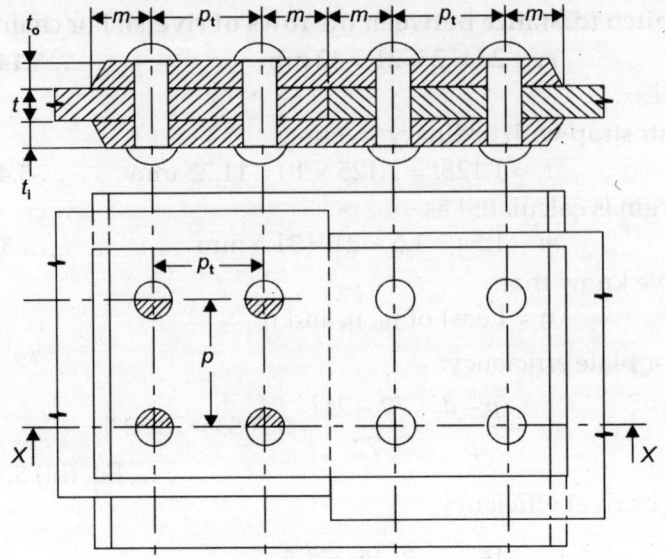

Fig. 7.19: Problem 11

2. **Thickness of plate:** We know that

$$t = \frac{p_i D}{2\sigma_t \eta} \qquad \text{... 5.1/Pg 79, DHB}$$

$$t = \frac{0.95 \times 1500}{2 \times 90 \times 0.75} = 10.56 \text{ mm}$$

Standard thickness,

$$t = 12 \text{ mm} \qquad \text{... Tb 5.3(c)/Pg 85, DHB}$$

3. **Diameter of rivet hole:** From Unwin's formula, for $t > 8$ mm, we have

$$d = 6.325\sqrt{t}$$

$$= 6.325\sqrt{12} = 21.91 \text{ mm} \qquad \text{... 5.11(d)/ Pg 81, DHB}$$

Thus the standard diameter of rivet hole,

$$d = 23 \text{ mm}$$

and the diameter of rivet,

$$d = d_1 + 1 \text{ mm}, \quad \text{for } 12 \text{ mm} \leq d \leq 24 \text{ mm}$$

$$d_1 = 23 - 1 = 22 \text{ mm}$$

4. **Pitch of the rivets:**

a. Optimum pitch:

$$p = \frac{(n_1 + 1.875 n_2)\pi d^2 \tau}{4t\sigma_t} + d \qquad \text{... 5.12(a)/ Pg 81, DHB}$$

$$p = \frac{(0 + 1.875 \times 2) \times \pi \times 23^2 \times 56}{4 \times 12 \times 90} + 23 \quad \text{...} n_1 = 0, \text{ from step 1}$$

$$p = 103.79 \text{ mm} \qquad \text{... Eq. (i)}$$

b. **Maximum pitch:**

$$p_{max} = k_1 t + 41 \text{ mm} \qquad \text{... 5.12(b)/ Pg 81, DHB}$$

$$k_1 = 3.5, \quad \text{for a double strap butt joint having two rivets per pitch} \qquad \text{... Tb. 5.4(a)/ Pg 85, DHB}$$

$$p_{max} = (3.5 \times 12) + 41 = 83 \text{ mm} \qquad \text{... Eq. (ii)}$$

Thus the standard pitch is the lower value from Eqs. (i) and (ii),

i.e. $\qquad p = 83 \text{ mm}$

5. **Transverse pitch (distance between the rows of rivets):** For chain riveting,

$$p_t \geq 2d = 2 \times 23 = 46 \text{ mm} \qquad \text{... 5.14(a)/ Pg 82, DHB}$$

6. **Strap thickness:**

For double butt strap of equal width having ordinary riveting

$$t_i = t_o = 0.625t = 0.625 \times 12 = 7.5 \text{ mm} \qquad \text{... 5.4(c)/ Pg 80, DHB}$$

7. **Margin:** Margin is calculated as

$$m = 1.5d = 1.5 \times 23 = 34.5 \text{ mm} \qquad \text{... 5.16/ Pg 83, DHB}$$

8. **Efficiency:** We know that

$$\eta = \text{Least of } \eta_t, \eta_s \text{ and } \eta_c$$

- Tearing or plate efficiency:

$$\eta_t = \frac{p - d}{p} = \frac{83 - 23}{83} = 0.7229 = 72.29\%$$

$$\text{... Eq. (iii) 5.9(e)/Pg 81, DHB}$$

- Shearing or rivet efficiency:

$$\eta_s = \frac{(n_1 + 1.875n_2)\pi d^2 \tau}{4pt\sigma_t} \qquad \text{... 5.9(f)/Pg 81, DHB}$$

$$= \frac{[0 + (1.875 \times 2)]\pi \times 23^2 \times 56}{4 \times 83 \times 10 \times 90} = 0.9773$$

$$\eta_s = 97.73\% \qquad \text{... Eq. (iv)}$$

- Crushing efficiency:

$$\eta_c = \frac{P_c}{P} = \frac{(n_1 t_i + n_2 t)d\sigma_c}{pt\sigma_t}$$

$$= \frac{[0 + (2 \times 12)] \times 23 \times 140}{83 \times 12 \times 90} = 0.8621$$

$$= 86.21\% \qquad \text{... Eq. (v)}$$

Thus the efficiency is the least of Eqs. (iii), (iv) and (v), i.e. $\eta = \eta_t = 72.29\%$.

12. **Design a longitudinal double riveted double strap butt joint with unequal straps for a pressure vessel. The internal diameter of the pressure vessel is 1 m and is subjected to an internal pressure of 2.2 MPa. The pitch of the rivet in the outer row is to be double the pitch in inner row. The allowable tensile stress in the plate is 124 N/mm². The allowable shear and crushing of the rivets are 93 N/mm² and 165 N/mm² respectively. The resistance of the rivets in double shear is to be taken as 1.875 times that of single shear.**

VTU – Dec. 2009/ Jan. 2010 – 10 Marks

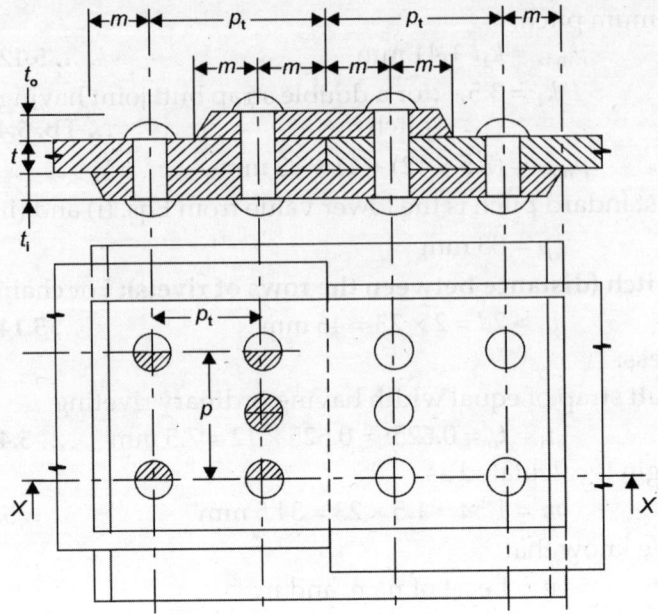

Fig. 7.20: Problem 12

Solution: $D = 1$ m $= 1000$ mm, $p_i = 2.2$ MPa, $p_o = 2p_i$, $\sigma_t = 124$ MPa, $\sigma_c = 165$ MPa, $\tau = 93$ MPa

1. **Type of joint:** Butt joint – Double riveted double strap—unequal cover. Assume chain riveting.

   • Let us arrange the joint in such a manner that the alternate rivets in outer rows are omitted. The rivets in the outer row will be in single shear, while those in the inner row will be in double shear, as shown in **Fig. 7.20.**
   In one length (per pitch), there are 2 rivets which are in double shear while 1 is in single shear.
   Here, number of rivets in single shear, $n_1 = 1$
   number of rivets in double shear, $n_2 = 2$

2. **Thickness of boiler shell:** We know that

$$t = \frac{p_i D}{2\sigma_t \eta} \qquad \qquad \text{... 5.1/Pg 79, DHB}$$

Efficiency of the joint $\eta = 75\%$, for double riveted double strap butt joint.
$$\text{... Tb 5.4(b)/Pg 85, DHB}$$

$$t = \frac{2.2 \times 1000}{2 \times 124 \times 0.75} = 11.82 \text{ mm}$$

Standard thickness,

$$t = 12 \text{ mm} \qquad \qquad \text{... Tb 5.3(c)/Pg 85, DHB}$$

3. **Diameter of rivet hole:** From Unwin's formula, for $t > 8$ mm, we have

$$d = 6.325\sqrt{t}$$

$$= 6.325\sqrt{12} = 21.91 \text{ mm} \qquad \qquad \text{... 5.11(d)/ Pg 81, DHB}$$

Thus the standard diameter of rivet hole,
$$d = 23 \text{ mm}$$
and the diameter of rivet,
$$d = d_1 + 1 \text{ mm}, \quad \text{for } 12 \text{ mm} \le d \le 24 \text{ mm}$$
$$d_1 = 23 - 1 = 22 \text{ mm}$$

4. **Pitch of the rivets:**

   a. Optimum pitch:
   $$p = \frac{(n_1 + 1.875 n_2) \pi d^2 \tau}{4 t \sigma_t} + d \qquad \text{... 5.12(a)/ Pg 81, DHB}$$

   $$p = \frac{(1 + 1.875 \times 2) \times \pi \times 23^2 \times 93}{4 \times 12 \times 124} + 23 \quad \text{...} n_1 = 1, \text{ from step 1}$$

   $$p = 146.34 \text{ mm} \qquad \qquad \text{... Eq. (i)}$$

   b. Maximum pitch:
   $$p_{max} = k_1 t + 41 \text{ mm} \qquad \text{... 5.12(b)/ Pg 81, DHB}$$
   $$k_1 = 4.63, \quad \text{for a double strap butt joint having three rivets per}$$
   $$\text{pitch} \qquad \qquad \text{... Tb. 5.4(a)/ Pg 85, DHB}$$
   $$p_{max} = (4.63 \times 12) + 41 = 95.56 \text{ mm} \qquad \text{... Eq. (ii)}$$

   Thus the standard pitch is the lower value from Eqs. (i) and (ii),

   i.e. outer pitch $\quad p_o = 95.56 \text{ mm} \approx 98 \text{ mm and } p_i = p_o/2 = 98/2 = 49 \text{ mm}.$

5. **Transverse pitch (distance between the rows of rivets):** For joints in which the longer pitch (outer row) is double the shorter one (inner row) and the inner row is chain riveted:

   - Transverse pitch between outer row and inner row:
   $$p_t \ge 2d = 2 \times 23 = 46 \text{ mm} \qquad \text{... 5.14(c)/ Pg 82, DHB}$$
   - Transverse pitch between successive inner rows:
   $$p_t \ge 2d = 2 \times 23 = 46 \text{ mm} \qquad \text{... 5.14(d)/ Pg 82, DHB}$$

6. **Strap thickness:**
   - Thickness of outer cover plate
   $$t_o = 0.625t = 0.625 \times 12 = 7.5 \text{ mm} \qquad \text{... 5.4(e)/ Pg 80, DHB}$$
   - Thickness of inner cover plate
   $$t_i = 0.75t = 0.75 \times 12 = 9 \text{ mm} \qquad \text{... 5.4(f)/ Pg 80, DHB}$$

7. **Margin:** Margin is calculated as
   $$m = 1.5d = 1.5 \times 23 = 34.5 \text{ mm} \qquad \text{... 5.16/ Pg 83, DHB}$$

8. **Efficiency:** We know that
   $$\eta = \text{Least of } \eta_t, \eta_s \text{ and } \eta_c$$

   - Tearing or plate efficiency:
   $$\eta_t = \frac{p - d}{p} = \frac{98 - 23}{98} = 0.7653 = 76.53\%$$
   $$\text{... Eq. (iii) 5.9(e)/Pg 81, DHB}$$

- Shearing or rivet efficiency:

$$\eta_s = \frac{(n_1 + 1.875n_2)\pi d^2 \tau}{4pt\sigma_t} \qquad \text{... 5.9(f)/Pg 81, DHB}$$

$$= \frac{[(1 + 1.875 \times 2)]\pi \times 23^2 \times 93}{4 \times 98 \times 12 \times 124} = 1.2586$$

$$\eta_s = 125.86\% \qquad \text{... Eq. (iv)}$$

- Crushing efficiency:

$$\eta_c = \frac{P_c}{P} = \frac{(n_1 t_i + n_2 t)d\sigma_c}{pt\sigma_t}$$

$$= \frac{[(1 \times 9) + (2 \times 12)] \times 23 \times 165}{98 \times 12 \times 124} = 0.8588$$

$$= 85.88\% \qquad \text{... Eq. (v)}$$

- Failure due to tearing of plate at inner row and shearing of rivets in outer row:

$$\eta_{ts} = \frac{(p - 2d)t\sigma_t + k\tau(\pi d^2/4)}{pt\sigma_t} \qquad \text{... 5.8(b)/Pg 80, DHB}$$

Here $\qquad k = 1$ for rivets in single shear

$$n_{ts} = \frac{[(98 - 2 \times 23) \times 12 \times 124] + [1 \times 93 \times (\pi \times 23^2/4)]}{98 \times 12 \times 124}$$

$$= 0.7956 = 79.56\% \qquad \text{... Eq. (vi)}$$

- Failure of plate due to combined action of tearing of plate at inner row and crushing of rivets in outer row:

$$\eta_{tc} = \frac{(p - 2d)t\sigma_t + dt\sigma_c}{pt\sigma_t} \qquad \text{... 5.9(b)/Pg 81, DHB}$$

$$= \frac{[(98 - 2 \times 23) \times 12 \times 124] + [23 \times 12 \times 165]}{98 \times 12 \times 124}$$

$$= 0.8429 = 84.29\% \qquad \text{... Eq. (vii)}$$

- Failure of plate due to combined action of shearing of rivets in outer row and crushing of rivets in inner rows:

$$\eta_{sc} = \frac{\tau(\pi d^2/4) + ndt\sigma_c}{pt\sigma_t} \quad \text{here } n = n_2 \qquad \text{... 5.9(d)/Pg 80, DHB}$$

$$= \frac{[93 \times (\pi \times 23^2/4)] + [2 \times 23 \times 12 \times 165]}{98 \times 12 \times 124}$$

$$\eta_{sc} = 0.8896 = 88.96\% \qquad \text{... Eq. (viii)}$$

Thus the efficiency is the least of Eqs. (iii) to (viii), i.e. $\eta = \eta_t = 76.53\%$.

13. **Design a triple riveted butt joint with double straps of equal width longitudinal butt joint for a boiler shell of 1.5 m diameter. The maximum steam pressure in the boiler is limited to 2.4 MPa. The rivet pitch is to be same in all rows and chain**

riveting is to be used. The allowable stresses in tension, shear and crushing are 124 MPa, 93 MPa and 165 MPa respectively. Assume that the rivets in double shear are 1.875 times stronger than in single shear. Take the corrosion allowance in thickness of plate as 1 mm. Sketch the joint with all the dimensions.

VTU – Dec. 06/ Jan. 2007 – 10 Marks

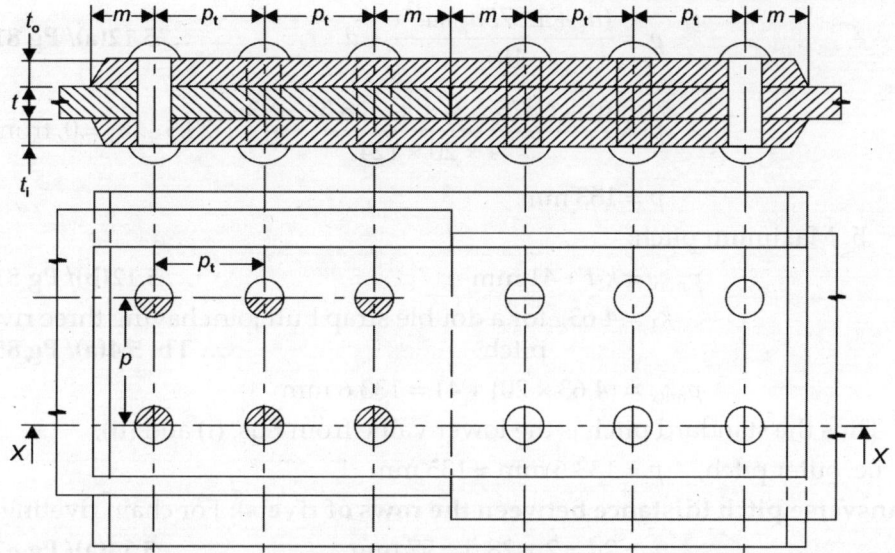

Fig. 7.21: Problem 13

Solution: $D = 1.5$ m $= 1500$ mm, $p_i = 2.4$ MPa, $\sigma_t = 124$ MPa. Corrosion allowance (CA) = 1 mm, $\sigma_c = 165$ MPa, $\tau = 93$ MPa

1. **Type of joint:** Butt joint – Triple riveted double strap—equal cover with chain riveting

   Here, number of rivets in single shear, $n_1 = 0$

   number of rivets in double shear, $n_2 = 3$ ... *Pg 81, DHB

2. **Thickness of boiler shell:** We know that

$$t = \frac{p_i D}{2\sigma_t \eta} + CA$$

Efficiency of the joint $\eta = 85\%$, for triple riveted double strap butt joints.

... **Tb 5.4(b)/Pg 85, DHB**

$$t = \frac{2.4 \times 1500}{2 \times 124 \times 0.85} + 1 = 18.07 \text{ mm}$$

Standard thickness,

$t = 20$ mm   ... **Tb 5.3(c)/Pg 85, DHB**

3. **Diameter of rivet hole:** From Unwin's formula, for $t > 8$ mm, we have

$$d = 6.325\sqrt{t}$$

$$= 6.325\sqrt{20} = 28.28 \text{ mm}$$ ... **5.11(d)/ Pg 81, DHB**

Thus the standard diameter of rivet hole,

$d = 28.5$ mm

and the diameter of rivet,

$$d = d_1 + 1.5 \text{ mm}, \quad \text{for } 27 \text{ mm} \le d \le 36 \text{ mm}$$
$$d_1 = 28.5 - 1.5 = 27 \text{ mm}$$

4. **Pitch of the rivets:**

   a. Optimum pitch:

   $$p = \frac{(n_1 + 1.875n_2)\pi d^2 \tau}{4t\sigma_t} + d \qquad \text{... 5.12(a)/ Pg 81, DHB}$$

   $$p = \frac{(0 + 1.875 \times 3) \times \pi \times 28.5^2 \times 93}{4 \times 20 \times 124} + 28.5 \quad \text{...} n_1 = 0, \text{ from step 1}$$

   $$p = 163 \text{ mm} \qquad \text{... Eq. (i)}$$

   b. Maximum pitch:

   $$p_{max} = k_1 t + 41 \text{ mm} \qquad \text{... 5.12(b)/ Pg 81, DHB}$$

   $$k_1 = 4.63, \quad \text{for a double strap butt joint having three rivets per pitch} \qquad \text{... Tb. 5.4(a)/ Pg 85, DHB}$$

   $$p_{max} = (4.63 \times 20) + 41 = 133.6 \text{ mm} \qquad \text{... Eq. (ii)}$$

   Thus the standard pitch is the lower value from Eqs. (i) and (ii),

   i.e. outer pitch, $p = 133.6 \text{ mm} \approx 135 \text{ mm}$

5. **Transverse pitch (distance between the rows of rivets):** For chain riveting,

   $$p_t \ge 2d = 2 \times 28.5 = 57 \text{ mm} \qquad \text{... 5.14(a)/ Pg 82, DHB}$$

6. **Strap thickness:**

   For double butt strap of equal width having ordinary riveting

   $$t_i = t_o = 0.625t = 0.625 \times 20 = 12.5 \text{ mm} \qquad \text{... 5.4(c)/ Pg 80, DHB}$$

7. **Margin:** Margin is calculated as

   $$m = 1.5d = 28.5 \times 42.75 \text{ mm} \approx 43 \text{ mm} \qquad \text{... 5.16/ Pg 83, DHB}$$

8. **Efficiency:** We know that

   $$\eta = \text{Least of } \eta_t, \eta_s \text{ and } \eta_c$$

   - Tearing or plate efficiency:

   $$\eta_t = \frac{p - d}{p} = \frac{135 - 28.5}{135} = 0.7888 = 78.88\%$$

   $$\text{... Eq. (iii) 5.9(e)/Pg 81, DHB}$$

   - Shearing or rivet efficiency:

   $$\eta_s = \frac{(n_1 + 1.875n_2)\pi d^2 \tau}{4pt\sigma_t} \qquad \text{... 5.9(f)/Pg 81, DHB}$$

   $$= \frac{[0 + (1.875 \times 3)]\pi \times 28.5^2 \times 93}{4 \times 135 \times 20 \times 124} = 0.9967$$

   $$\eta_s = 99.67\% \qquad \text{... Eq. (iv)}$$

   - Crushing efficiency:

   $$\eta_c = \frac{P_c}{P} = \frac{(n_1 t_i + n_2 t)d\sigma_c}{pt\sigma_t}$$

$$= \frac{[0 + (3 \times 20)] \times 28.5 \times 165}{135 \times 20 \times 124} = 0.8428$$

$$= 84.28\% \qquad \qquad \ldots \text{Eq. (v)}$$

Thus the efficiency is the least of Eqs. (iii), (iv) and (v), i.e. $\eta = \eta_t = 78.88\%$.

14. **Design a triple riveted longitudinal double strap butt joint with unequal straps for a boiler. The inside diameter of the congest course of the drum is 1.3 m. The joint is to be designed for a steam pressure of 2.4 MPa. The working stresses to be used are σ_t = 77 MPa, τ = 62 MPa and σ_c = 120 MPa Assume the efficiency of the joint as 81%. The longer pitch in the outer row is twice the pitch in the inner row and the inner rows are zig-zag.**

VTU – Dec. 2011 – 12 Marks; July 2007 – 10 Marks

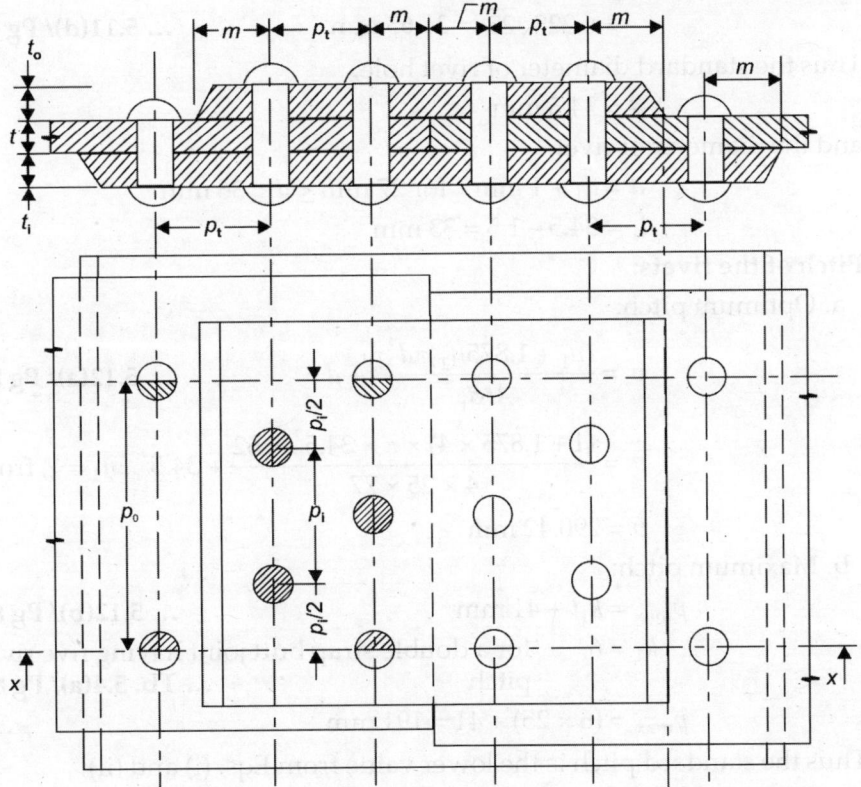

Fig. 7.22: Problem 14

Solution: D = 1.3 m = 1300 mm, p_i = 2.4 MPa, σ_t = 77 MPa, σ_c = 120 MPa, τ = 62 MPa, η = 81%, $p_o = 2p_i$.

1. **Type of joint:** Butt joint – Triple riveted double strap—unequal cover with zig-zag riveting.

   - Let us arrange the joint in such a manner that the alternate rivets in outer rows are omitted. The rivets in the outer row will be in single shear, while those in the inner row will be in double shear, as shown in **Fig. 7.22**.
   In one length (per pitch), there are 4 rivets which are in double shear while 1 is in single shear.

Hence number of rivets in single shear, $n_1 = 1$ and number of rivets in double shear, $n_2 = 4$.

2. **Thickness of boiler shell:** We know that

$$t = \frac{p_i D}{2\sigma_t \eta} \qquad \text{... 5.1/Pg 79, DHB}$$

$$t = \frac{2.4 \times 1300}{2 \times 77 \times 0.81} = 25.01 \text{ mm}$$

Standard thickness,

$$t = 25 \text{ mm} \qquad \text{... Tb 5.3(c)/Pg 85, DHB}$$

3. **Diameter of rivet hole:** From Unwin's formula, for $t > 8$ mm, we have

$$d = 6.325\sqrt{t}$$

$$= 6.325\sqrt{25} = 31.63 \text{ mm} \qquad \text{... 5.11(d)/ Pg 81, DHB}$$

Thus the standard diameter of rivet hole,

$$d = 34.5 \text{ mm}$$

and the diameter of rivet,

$$d = d_1 + 1 \text{ mm}, \quad \text{for } 27 \text{ mm} \le d \le 36 \text{ mm}$$

$$d_1 = 34.5 - 1.5 = 33 \text{ mm}$$

4. **Pitch of the rivets:**

   a. Optimum pitch:

$$p = \frac{(n_1 + 1.875 n_2)\pi d^2 \tau}{4t\sigma_t} + d \qquad \text{... 5.12(a)/ Pg 81, DHB}$$

$$p = \frac{(1 + 1.875 \times 4) \times \pi \times 34.5^2 \times 62}{4 \times 25 \times 77} + 34.5 \ ...n_1 = 1, \text{ from step 1}$$

$$p = 290.42 \text{ mm} \qquad \text{... Eq. (i)}$$

   b. Maximum pitch:

$$p_{max} = k_1 t + 41 \text{ mm} \qquad \text{... 5.12(b)/ Pg 81, DHB}$$

$$k_1 = 6, \quad \text{for a double strap butt joint having five rivets per pitch} \qquad \text{... Tb. 5.4(a)/ Pg 85, DHB}$$

$$p_{max} = (6 \times 25) + 41 = 191 \text{ mm} \qquad \text{... Eq. (ii)}$$

Thus the standard pitch is the lower value from Eqs. (i) and (ii),

i.e. outer pitch $\quad p_o = 191$ mm

Since $\qquad p_o = 2p_i$

inner pitch, $\qquad p_i = \dfrac{p_o}{2} = \dfrac{191}{2} = 95.5$ mm

5. **Transverse pitch (distance between the rows of rivets):** For zig-zag or staggered riveting:

   • Transverse pitch between outer row and inner row:

$$p_t \ge 0.2p + 1.15d \qquad \text{... 5.15(a)/ Pg 82, DHB}$$

$$\ge (0.2 \times 191) + (1.15 \times 34.5)$$

$$p_t \ge 77.88 \text{ mm} \approx 78 \text{ mm}$$

- Transverse pitch between successive inner rows:

$$p_t \geq 0.165p + 0.67d \qquad \text{... 5.15(b)/ Pg 83, DHB}$$
$$\geq (0.165 \times 191) + (0.67 \times 34.5)$$
$$p_t \geq 54.63 \text{ mm} \approx 55 \text{ mm}$$

6. **Strap thickness:**

- Thickness of outer cover plate

$$t_o = 0.625t = 0.625 \times 25 = 15.63 \text{ mm} \approx 16 \text{ mm}$$
$$\text{... 5.4(e)/ Pg 80, DHB}$$

- Thickness of inner cover plate

$$t_i = 0.75t = 0.75 \times 25 = 18.75 \text{ mm} \approx 19 \text{ mm}$$
$$\text{... 5.4(f)/ Pg 80, DHB}$$

7. **Margin:** Margin is calculated as

$$m = 1.5d = 1.5 \times 34.5 = 51.75 \text{ mm} \approx 52 \text{ mm}$$
$$\text{... 5.16/ Pg 83, DHB}$$

8. **Efficiency:** We know that

$$\eta = \text{Least of } \eta_t, \eta_s \text{ and } \eta_c$$

- Tearing or plate efficiency:

$$\eta_t = \frac{p-d}{p} = \frac{191 - 34.5}{191} = 0.8194 = 81.94\%$$
$$\text{... Eq. (iii) 5.9(e)/Pg 81, DHB}$$

- Shearing or rivet efficiency:

$$\eta_s = \frac{(n_1 + 1.875n_2)\pi d^2 \tau}{4pt\sigma_t} \qquad \text{... 5.9(f)/Pg 81, DHB}$$
$$= \frac{[(1 + 1.875 \times 4)]\pi \times 34.5^2 \times 62}{4 \times 191 \times 25 \times 77} = 1.340$$
$$\eta_s = 134\% \qquad \text{... Eq. (iv)}$$

- Crushing efficiency:

$$\eta_c = \frac{P_c}{P} = \frac{(n_1 t_i + n_2 t)d\sigma_c}{pt\sigma_t}$$
$$= \frac{[(1 + 19) + (4 \times 25)] \times 34.5 \times 120}{191 \times 25 \times 77} = 1.340$$
$$= 134\% \qquad \text{... Eq. (v)}$$

- Failure due to tearing of plate at inner row and shearing of rivets in outer row:

$$\eta_{ts} = \frac{(p - 2d)t\sigma_t + k\tau(\pi d^2/4)}{pt\sigma_t} \qquad \text{... 5.8(b)/Pg 80, DHB}$$

Here $k = 1$ for rivets in single shear

$$n_{ts} = \frac{[(191 - 2 \times 34.5) \times 25 \times 77] + [1 \times 62 \times (\pi \times 34.5^2/4)]}{191 \times 25 \times 77}$$
$$= 0.7964 = 79.64\% \qquad \text{... Eq. (vi)}$$

- Failure of plate due to combined action of tearing of plate at inner row and crushing of rivets in outer row:

$$\eta_{tc} = \frac{(p - 2d)t\sigma_t + dt\sigma_c}{pt\sigma_t}$$

$$= \frac{[(191 - 2 \times 34.5) \times 25 \times 77] + [34.5 \times 25 \times 120]}{191 \times 25 \times 77}$$

$$= 0.9202 = 92.02\% \qquad \qquad \dots \text{Eq. (vii)}$$

- Failure of plate due to combined action of shearing of rivets in outer row and crushing of rivets in inner rows:

$$\eta_{sc} = \frac{\tau(\pi d^2/4) + ndt\sigma_c}{pt\sigma_t} \quad \text{here } n = n_2 \qquad \dots \textbf{5.9(d)/Pg 80, DHB}$$

$$= \frac{[62 \times (\pi \times 34.5^2/4)] + [4 \times 34.5 \times 25 \times 120]}{191 \times 25 \times 77}$$

$$\eta_{sc} = 1.284 = 128.4\% \qquad \qquad \dots \text{Eq. (viii)}$$

Thus the efficiency is the least of Eqs. (iii) to (viii), i.e. $\eta = \eta_{ts} = 79.64\%$.

15. Design a longitudinal seam joint of a steam drum whose inner diameter is 1680 mm and the pressure of steam is 2.1 MPa by gauge. The longitudinal joint is triple riveted butt joint with an efficiency of 85%. The pitch of outer rows of rivet is to be double of that in the inner rows and the widths of the cover plates are unequal. The ultimate tensile, crushing and shear stresses are 470 MPa, 780 MPa and 390 MPa respectively. Adopt a factor of safety of 5. The rivet in double shear is to be not greater than 87.5% over that in single shear.

VTU – Dec. 2011 – 10 Marks

Solution: $D = 1680$ mm, $p_i = 2.1$ MPa, $\eta = 85\%$, $p_o = 2p_i$, $\sigma_{ut} = 470$ MPa, $\sigma_{uc} = 780$ MPa, $\tau_u = 390$ MPa, FoS = 2.

Allowable stress: $\sigma_t = \dfrac{\sigma_{ut}}{\text{FoS}} = \dfrac{470}{5} = 94$ MPa

$$\sigma_c = \frac{\sigma_{uc}}{\text{FoS}} = \frac{780}{5} = 156 \text{ MPa}$$

$$\tau = \frac{\tau_u}{\text{FoS}} = \frac{390}{5} = 78 \text{ MPa}$$

The rest part of the problem is similar to Problem 14.

16. Determine the main dimensions for longitudinal and circumferential joints of a boiler whose inner diameter is 1.7 m and pressure of steam is 2.05 MPa. The ultimate stresses are $\sigma_{uc} = 780$ MPa, $\sigma_{ut} = 470$ MPa and $\tau_u = 390$ MPa. Assume a factor of safety of 5. The rivet in double shear will have an effective resisting area not greater than 87.5% over that in single shear.

VTU – Jan/ Feb. 2005 – 20 Marks

Solution: $D = 1.7$ m $= 1700$ mm, $p_i = 2.05$ MPa, $\sigma_{uc} = 780$ MPa, $\sigma_{ut} = 470$ MPa, $\tau_u = 390$ MPa, FoS = 5.

Allowable stress: $\sigma_t = \dfrac{\sigma_{ut}}{\text{FoS}} = \dfrac{470}{5} = 94$ MPa

$$\sigma_c = \frac{\sigma_{uc}}{FoS} = \frac{780}{5} = 156 \text{ MPa}$$

$$\tau = \frac{\tau_u}{FoS} = \frac{390}{5} = 78 \text{ MPa}$$

Case A: Longitudinal joint:

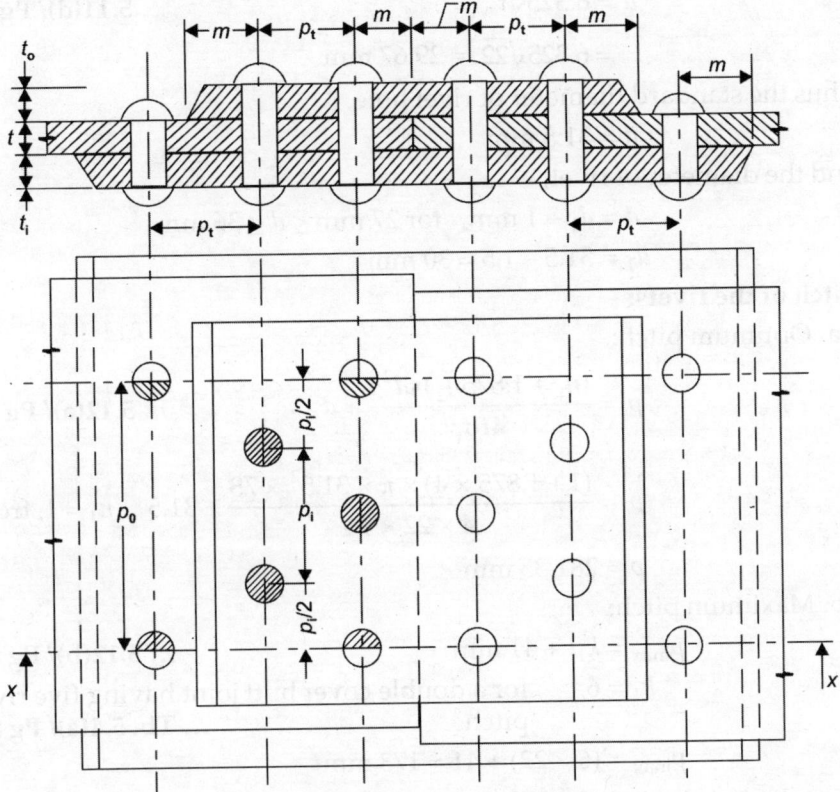

Fig. 7.23: Problem 16

1. **Type of joint:** Butt joint – Triple riveted double strap—unequal cover with zig-zag riveting.
   - For given diameter, the joint will be a triple riveted double strap butt joint.
     ... **Tb 5.2/Pg 84, DHB**
   - Since η is not given, we have η = 85%.   ... **Tb 5.4(b)/Pg 85, DHB**
   - Let us arrange the joint in such a manner that the alternate rivets in outer rows will be in single shear, while those in the inner row will be in double shear, as shown in **Fig. 7.23.**
     In one length (per pitch), there are 4 rivets which are in double shear while 1 is in single shear.
     Hence number of rivets in single shear, $n_1 = 1$ and number or rivets in double shear, $n_2 = 4$.

2. **Thickness of boiler shell:** We know that

$$t = \frac{p_i D}{2\sigma_t \eta} \qquad \qquad \text{... 5.1/Pg 79, DHB}$$

$$t = \frac{2.05 \times 1700}{2 \times 94 \times 0.85} = 21.81 \text{ mm}$$

Standard thickness,

$$t = 22 \text{ mm} \qquad \qquad \text{... Tb 5.3(c)/Pg 85, DHB}$$

3. **Diameter of rivet hole:** From Unwin's formula, for $t > 8$ mm, we have

$$d = 6.325\sqrt{t} \qquad \qquad \text{... 5.11(d)/ Pg 81, DHB}$$

$$= 6.325\sqrt{22} = 29.67 \text{ mm}$$

Thus the standard diameter of rivet hole,

$$d = 31.5 \text{ mm}$$

and the diameter of rivet,

$$d = d_1 + 1 \text{ mm}, \quad \text{for } 27 \text{ mm} \le d \le 36 \text{ mm}$$

$$d_1 = 31.5 - 1.5 = 30 \text{ mm}$$

4. **Pitch of the rivets:**

    a. Optimum pitch:

$$p = \frac{(n_1 + 1.875 n_2)\pi d^2 \tau}{4 t \sigma_t} + d \qquad \qquad \text{... 5.12(a)/ Pg 81, DHB}$$

$$p = \frac{(1 + 1.875 \times 4) \times \pi \times 31.5^2 \times 78}{4 \times 22 \times 94} + 31.5 \text{ ...} n_1 = 1, \text{from step 1}$$

$$p = 281.35 \text{ mm} \qquad \qquad \text{... Eq. (i)}$$

    b. Maximum pitch:

$$p_{\max} = k_1 t + 41 \text{ mm} \qquad \qquad \text{... 5.12(b)/ Pg 81, DHB}$$

$$k_1 = 6, \qquad \text{for a double cover butt joint having five rivets per}$$
$$\text{pitch} \qquad \qquad \text{... Tb. 5.4(a)/ Pg 85, DHB}$$

$$p_{\max} = (6 \times 22) + 41 = 173 \text{ mm} \qquad \qquad \text{... Eq. (ii)}$$

Thus the standard pitch is the lower value from Eqs. (i) and (ii),

i.e. outer pitch $p_o = 173$ mm say ≈ 174 mm

Since $p_o = 2p_i$

inner pitch, $p_i = \dfrac{p_o}{2} = \dfrac{174}{2} = 87$ mm

5. **Transverse pitch (distance between the rows of rivets):** For zig-zag or staggered riveting:

    • Transverse pitch between outer row and inner row:

$$p_t \ge 0.2p + 1.15d \qquad \qquad \text{... 5.15(a)/ Pg 82, DHB}$$

$$\ge (0.2 \times 174) + (1.15 \times 31.5)$$

$$p_t \ge 71.03 \text{ mm} \approx 72 \text{ mm}$$

    • Transverse pitch between successive inner rows:

$$p_t \ge 0.165p + 0.67d \qquad \qquad \text{... 5.14(a)/ Pg 82, DHB}$$

$$\ge (0.165 \times 174) + (0.67 \times 31.5)$$

$$p_t \ge 49.82 \text{ mm} \approx 50 \text{ mm}$$

6. Strap thickness:

- Thickness of outer cover plate

$$t_o = 0.625t = 0.625 \times 22 \qquad \text{... 5.4(e)/ Pg 80, DHB}$$
$$= 13.75 \text{ mm} \approx 14 \text{ mm}$$

- Thickness of inner cover plate

$$t_i = 0.75t = 0.75 \times 22 = 16.5 \text{ mm} \approx 17 \text{ mm}$$
$$\text{... 5.4(f)/ Pg 80, DHB}$$

7. Margin: Margin is calculated as

$$m = 1.5d = 1.5 \times 31.5 = 47.25 \text{ mm} \approx 48 \text{ mm}$$
$$\text{... 5.16/ Pg 83, DHB}$$

8. Efficiency: We know that

$$\eta = \text{Least of } \eta_t, \eta_s \text{ and } \eta_c$$

- Tearing or plate efficiency:

$$\eta_t = \frac{p-d}{p} = \frac{174 - 31.5}{174} = 0.8190 = 81.90\%$$
$$\text{... Eq. (iii) 5.9(e)/Pg 81, DHB}$$

- Shearing or rivet efficiency:

$$\eta_s = \frac{(n_1 + 1.875n_2)\pi d^2 \tau}{4pt\sigma_t} \qquad \text{... 5.9(f)/Pg 81, DHB}$$

$$= \frac{[(1 + 1.875 \times 4)]\pi \times 31.5^2 \times 78}{4 \times 174 \times 22 \times 94} = 1.436$$

$$\eta_s = 143.60\% \qquad \text{... Eq. (iv)}$$

- Crushing efficiency:

$$\eta_c = \frac{P_c}{P} = \frac{(n_1 t_i + n_2 t)d\sigma_c}{pt\sigma_t}$$

$$= \frac{[(1 \times 17) + (4 \times 22)] \times 31.5 \times 156}{174 \times 22 \times 94} = 1.433$$

$$= 143.3\% \qquad \text{... Eq. (v)}$$

- Failure due to tearing of plate at inner row and shearing of rivets in outer row:

$$\eta_{ts} = \frac{(p - 2d)t\sigma_t + k\tau(\pi d^2/4)}{\pi t\sigma_t} \qquad \text{... 5.8(b)/Pg 80, DHB}$$

Here $\quad k = 1$ for rivets in single shear

$$n_{ts} = \frac{[(174 - 2 \times 31.5) \times 22 \times 94] + [1 \times 78 \times (\pi \times 31.5^2/4)]}{174 \times 22 \times 94}$$

$$= 0.8069 \doteq 80.69\% \qquad \text{... Eq. (vi)}$$

- Failure of plate due to combined action of tearing of plate at inner row and crushing of rivets in outer row:

$$\eta_{tc} = \frac{(p - 2d)t\sigma_t + dt\sigma_c}{pt\sigma_t} \qquad \ldots 5.9(b)/Pg\ 81,\ DHB$$

$$= \frac{[(174 - 2 \times 31.5) \times 22 \times 94] + [31.5 \times 22 \times 156]}{174 \times 22 \times 94}$$

$$= 0.9384 = 93.84\% \qquad \ldots Eq.\ (vii)$$

- Failure of plate due to combined action of shearing or rivets in outer row and crushing of rivets in inner rows:

$$\eta_{sc} = \frac{\tau(\pi d^2/4) + ndt\sigma_c}{pt\sigma_t} \quad \text{here } n = n_2 \qquad \ldots 5.9(d)/Pg\ 81,\ DHB$$

$$= \frac{[78 \times (\pi \times 31.5^2/4)] + [4 \times 31.5 \times 22 \times 156]}{174 \times 22 \times 94}$$

$$\eta_{sc} = 1.371 = 137.1\% \qquad \ldots Eq.\ (viii)$$

Thus the efficiency is the least of Eqs. (iii) to (viii), i.e. $\eta = \eta_{ts} = 80.69\%$.

Case B: Circumferential joint: The circumferential joint is always a lap joint made with one ring overlapping the other alternatively.

1. **Type of joint:** Double riveted lap joint with zig-zag riveting. $\Rightarrow n = 2$ **(Refer to Fig. 7.12)**

   Hence Number of rivets in single shear, $n_1 = n = 2$
   Number of rivets in double shear, $n_2 = 0$
   Thickness of inner plate, $t_i = t = 22$ mm   ... *Pg 81, DHB

   Since η is not given, we have $\eta = 70\%$.   ... Tb. 5.4(b)/Pg 84, DHB

2. **Dimensions of longitudinal joint:** From longitudinal joint, we have
   Thickness of boiler shell $t = 22$ mm
   Diameter of rivet hole $d = 31.5$ mm
   Diameter of rivet hole $d_1 = 30$ mm
   Margin $m = 48$ mm

3. **Number of rivets:** As the circumferential joint is a lap riveted joint, therefore the rivets will be in single shear.

$$n = \frac{\text{steam load}}{\text{shear strength of one rivet}}$$

$$= \frac{(\pi D^2/4)p_i}{(\pi d^2/4)\tau} = \frac{(\pi \times 1700^2/4) \times 2.05}{(\pi \times 31.5^2/4) \times 78} = 76.54 \approx 78 \text{ rivets}$$

4. **Pitch:**

   a. Optimum pitch:

$$p = \frac{(n_1 + 1.875n_2)\pi d^2 \tau}{4t\sigma_t} + d \qquad \ldots 5.12(a)/\ Pg\ 81,\ DHB$$

$$= \frac{(2 + 0) \times \pi \times 31.5^2 \times 78}{4 \times 22 \times 94} + 31.5 \qquad \text{(from step 1)}$$

$$p = 90.29 \text{ mm} \qquad \ldots Eq.\ (a)$$

b. Maximum pitch:

$$p_{max} = k_1 t + 41 \text{ mm} \qquad \qquad \text{... 5.12(b)/ Pg 81, DHB}$$

$$k_1 = 2.62, \text{ for a lap joint with two rivets per pitch}$$
$$\text{... Tb. 5.4(a)/ Pg 85, DHB}$$

$$p_{max} = (2.62 \times 22) + 41 = 98.64 \text{ mm} \qquad \qquad \text{... Eq. (b)}$$

Thus the standard pitch is the lower value from Eqs. (i) and (ii),

i.e. $$p = 90.29 \text{ mm} \approx 92 \text{ mm}$$

5. **Number of rivets per row:** For a circumferential joint, the number of rivets arranged in a row can be computed as

$$n' = \frac{\pi(D + t)}{p} = \frac{\pi(1700 + 22)}{92} = 58.8 \approx 60 \text{ rivets}$$

Thus the total number of rivets in two rows = $2 \times 60 = 120$

6. **Number of rows:** The circumferential is always a double riveted butt joint, hence
$$Z = 2$$

7. **Transverse pitch (distance between the rows of rivets):** For zig-zag or staggered riveting:

- Transverse pitch between outer row and inner row:

$$p_t \geq 0.33p + 0.67d \qquad \qquad \text{... 5.14(b)/ Pg 82, DHB}$$
$$\geq (0.33 \times 92) + (0.67 \times 31.5)$$
$$p_t \geq 51.47 \text{ mm} \approx 52 \text{ mm}$$

8. **Overlap:** The overlap of the plate is fixed as
$$O = (Z - 1)p_t + 2m \text{ or using type of joint}$$
$$O = [(2 - 1) \times 52] + (2 \times 48)$$
$$O = 148 \text{ mm}$$

9. **Efficiency:** We know that
$$\eta = \text{Least of } \eta_t, \eta_s \text{ and } \eta_c$$

- Tearing or plate efficiency:

$$\eta_t = \frac{p - d}{p} = \frac{92 - 31.5}{92} = 0.6576 = 65.76\%$$
$$\text{... Eq. (c) 5.9(e)/Pg 81, DHB}$$

- Shearing of rivet efficiency:

$$\eta_s = \frac{(n_1 + 1.875n_2)\pi d^2 \tau}{4pt\sigma_t} \qquad \qquad \text{... 5.9(f)/Pg 81, DHB}$$

$$= \frac{(2 + 0) \pi \times 31.5^2 \times 78}{4 \times 92 \times 22 \times 94} = 0.6390$$

$$\eta_s = 63.90\% \qquad \qquad \text{... Eq. (d)}$$

- Crushing efficiency:

$$\eta_c = \frac{P_c}{P} = \frac{(n_1 t_i + n_2 t)d\sigma_c}{pt\sigma_t}$$

$$= \frac{(2 \times 22 + 0) \times 31.5 \times 156}{92 \times 22 \times 94} = 1.1364$$

$$= 113.64\% \qquad \qquad \text{... Eq. (e)}$$

Thus the efficiency is the least of Eqs. (c), (d) and (e), i.e. $\eta = \eta_s = 63.90\%$.

7.13 STRUCTURAL JOINTS OR TIES (DIAMOND OR LOZENGE JOINT)

Diamond or lozenge joints are used for connecting bridges, girders, tie bars, etc. The joints are usually of double cover butt type with rivets so arranged that there is only one rivet in the outermost row and their number increases as we proceed towards inner row, as shown in **Fig. 7.24**, for equal cover butt joints. This arrangement of rivets gives uniform strength to the structure.

Let,
$\qquad b$ = width of plate
$\qquad t$ = thickness of plate
$\qquad d$ = diameter of rivet hole
$\qquad F$ = force applied on the joint

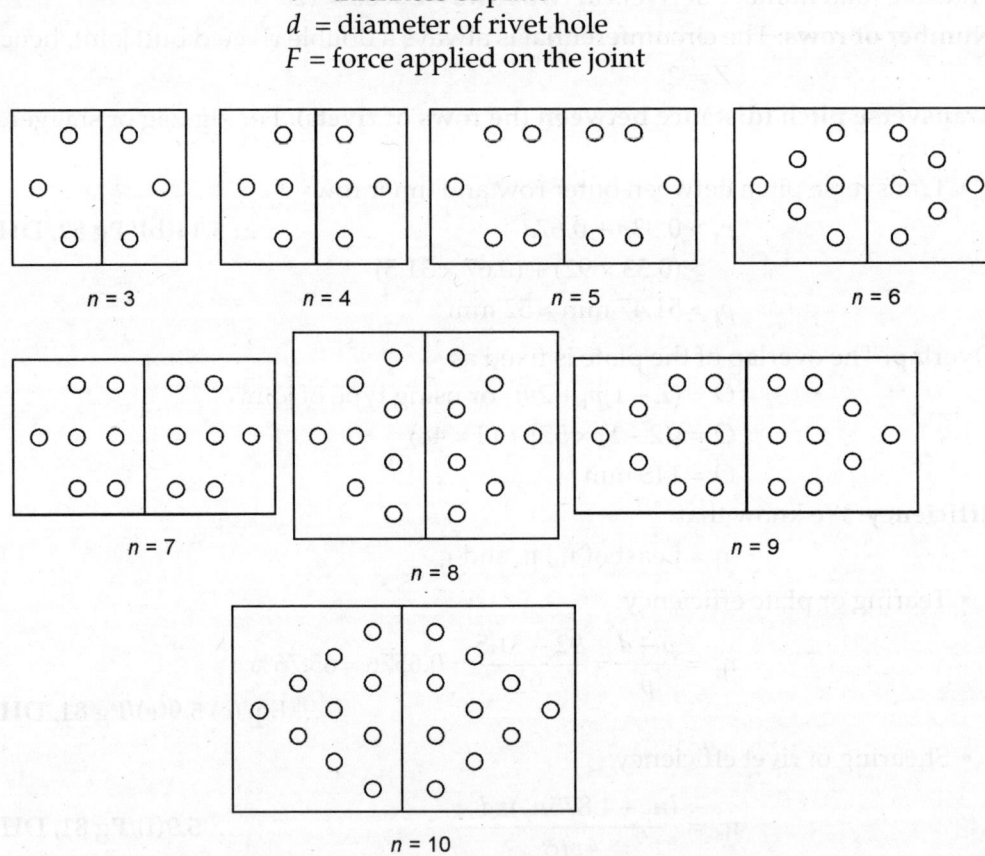

Fig. 7.24: Various arrangements of diamond joints

1. **Diameter of rivet hole and rivet:** The diameter of the rivet hole is obtained from Unwin's formula as:

$$d = 6.325\sqrt{t} \qquad \qquad \text{... (Eq. 7.29)} \textbf{ 5.11(d)/ Pg 81, DHB}$$

   • The diameter of rivet hole (d) must be rounded off to the nearest standard value with the help of the following table and the corresponding diameter of rivet (d_1) is noted.

Standard rivet hole and rivet diameters												
Dia. of rivet hole (d)	13	15	17	19	21	23	25	28.5	31.5	34.5	37.5	41	44
Dia. of rivet (d_1)	12	14	16	18	20	22	24	27	30	33	36	39	42

From table we observe that,

$$d = d_1 = 1 \text{ mm} \qquad \text{for } 12 \text{ mm} \le d \le 24 \text{ mm}$$
$$d = d_1 + 1.5 \text{ mm} \qquad \text{for } 27 \text{ mm} \le d \le 36 \text{ mm}$$
$$d = d_1 + 2 \text{ mm} \qquad \text{for } 39 \text{ mm} \le d \le 48 \text{ mm}$$

- The nominal diameter of rivets may also be obtained from **Table 5.3(b)/ Pg 84, DHB**

Note: Use diameter of rivet hole for all calculations.

2. **Number of rivets:** The number of rivets is calculated as

$$n = \frac{P_t}{\text{least value of } P_s \text{ and } P_c} \qquad \dots \text{(Eq. 7.30)}$$

- Tearing resistance of plate is given as,

$$P_t = (b - d)t\sigma_t \qquad \dots \text{(Eq. 7.31) } \textbf{5.6(b)/ Pg 80, DHB}$$
$$\textbf{[replace } p \textbf{ with } b \textbf{ in 5.6(b)/ Pg 80, DHB]}$$

- Shearing resistance of one rivet,

$$P_s = 1.875 \left(\frac{\pi d^2}{4} \right) \tau \qquad \dots \text{(Eq. 7.32) } \textbf{5.6(c)/ Pg 80, DHB}$$

- Crushing resistance of one rivet,

$$P_c = dt\sigma_c \qquad \dots \text{(Eq. 7.33)}$$

3. **Thickness of cover plate:** According to IBR,

for double butt strap of equal width having ordinary riveting:

$$t_i = t_o = 0.625t \qquad \dots \textbf{5.4(c)/ Pg 80, DHB}$$

4. **Arrangement of rivets: Figure 7.25** represents a typical structural joint.

5. **Margin:** Margin is calculated as

$$m = 1.5d \qquad \dots \textbf{5.16/ Pg 83, DHB}$$

6. **Pitch:** Pitch is calculated based on the number of rivets in the innermost section (i.e. section 3-3).

Width, $\qquad b = 2m + n'p = 2m + 2p \text{ (in this case, } n' = 2) \qquad \dots \text{(Eq. 7.34)}$

where n' = number of pitches in the innermost section, obtained based on arrangement in step 4.

7. **Transverse pitch (distance between the rows of rivets):** For chain riveting:

$$p_t \ge 2d \qquad \dots \textbf{5.14(a)/ Pg 82, DHB}$$

8. **Efficiency:**

   a. Tearing resistance: [With respect to **Fig. 7.25**]

   - Along section 1-1:

$$P_{t1} = (b - d)\tau\sigma_t \qquad \dots \text{(Eq. 7.35)}$$

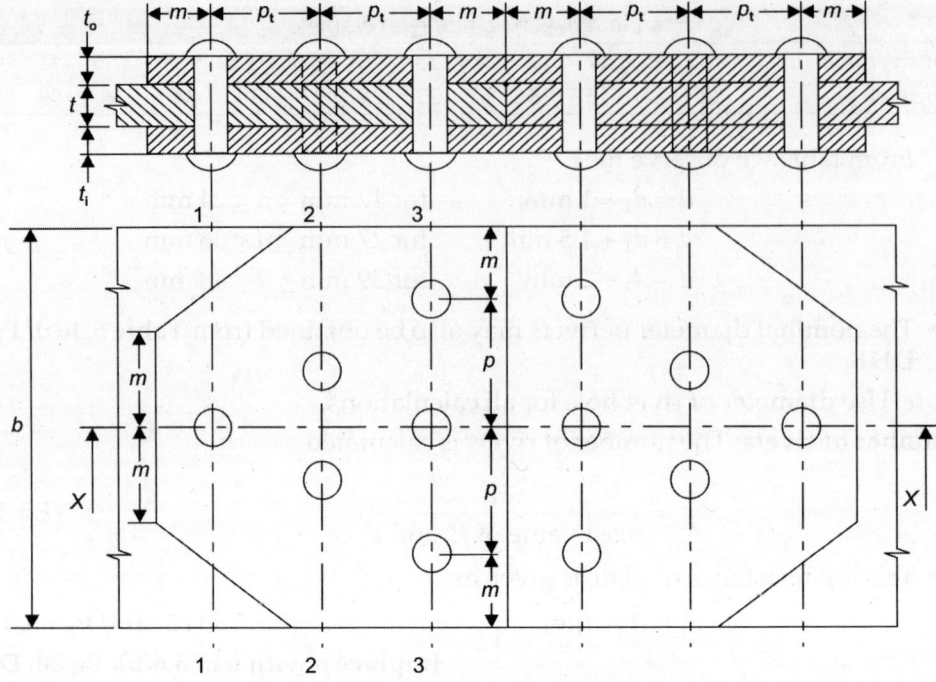

Fig. 7.25: A typical structural joint

- Along section 2-2:

$$P_{t2} = (b - 2d)t\sigma_t + \text{strength of one rivet in front of section 2-2}$$

$$P_{t2} = (b - 2d)t\sigma_t + \left[1.875\left(\frac{\pi d^2}{4}\right)\tau\right] = (b - 2d)t\sigma_t + P_s$$

... (Eq. 7.36)

- Along section 3-3:

$$P_{t3} = (b - 3d)t\sigma_t + \text{strength of three rivets in front of section 3-3}$$

$$P_{t3} = (b - 3d)t\sigma_t + 3 \times \left[1.875\left(\frac{\pi d^2}{4}\right)\tau\right] = (b - 3d)t\sigma_t + 3P_s$$

... (Eq. 7.37)

and so on.　　(depending on number of rivets)

b. Shearing resistance of all rivets:

$$P_s' = \text{number of rivets} \times P_s = n \cdot P_s \qquad \text{... (Eq. 7.38)}$$

c. Crushing resistance of all rivets:

$$P_c' = \text{number of rivets} \times P_c = n \cdot P_c \qquad \text{... (Eq. 7.39)}$$

d. Strength of solid plate:

$$P = bt\sigma_t \qquad \text{... (Eq. 7.40)} \textbf{ 5.6(a)/ Pg 80, DHB}$$

$$\therefore \qquad \eta = \frac{\text{strength of riveted joint}}{\text{strength of solid plate}}$$

$$= \frac{\text{least value of Eqs. (7.35) to (7.39)}}{\text{Eq. (7.40)}} \qquad \text{... (Eq. 7.41)}$$

17. **Two lengths of a mild steel tie rod having width 200 mm and thickness 12.5 mm are to be connected by means of a butt joint with double cover plate. Design the joint if the permissible stresses are 105 N/mm² in tension, 70 N/mm² in shear and 180 N/mm² in crushing. Assume to double shear strength 1.75 times in single shear.**

VTU – June/ July 2009 – 10 Marks

Solution: $b = 200$ mm, $t = 12.5$ mm, $\sigma_t = 105$ N/mm², $\tau = 70$ N/mm², $\sigma_c = 180$ N/mm².

1. **Diameter of rivet hole and rivet:** From Unwin's formula, for $t > 8$ mm, we have

$$d = 6.325\sqrt{t}$$

$$= 6.325\sqrt{12.5} = 22.36 \text{ mm} \qquad \text{... 5.11(d)/ Pg 81, DHB}$$

Thus the standard diameter of rivet hole,

$$d = 23 \text{ mm}$$

and the diameter of rivet,

$$d = d_1 + 1 \text{ mm}, \quad \text{for } 12 \text{ mm} \le d \le 24 \text{ mm}$$

$$d_1 = 23 - 1 = 22 \text{ mm}$$

2. **Number of rivets:** The number of rivets is calculated as

$$n = \frac{P_t}{\text{least value of } P_s \text{ and } P_c} \qquad \text{... Eq. (a)}$$

- Tearing resistance of plate,

$$P_t = (b - d)t\sigma_t \qquad \text{... 5.6(b)/Pg 80, DHB}$$

$$= (200 - 23) \times 12.5 \times 105$$

$$P_t = 232312.5 \text{ N} \qquad \text{... Eq. (b)}$$

- Shearing resistance of one rivet,

$$P_s = 1.875\left(\frac{\pi d^2}{4}\right)\tau \qquad \text{... 5.6(c)/Pg 80, DHB}$$

$$= 1.75\left(\frac{\pi d^2}{4}\right)\tau = 1.75\left(\frac{\pi \times 23^2}{4}\right) \times 70 \qquad \text{... (As per data)}$$

$$P_s = 50895.75 \text{ N} \qquad \text{... Eq. (c)}$$

- Crushing resistance of one rivet,

$$P_c = dt\sigma_c = 23 \times 12.5 \times 180 = 51750 \text{ N} \qquad \text{... Eq. (d)}$$

Thus the least value of Eqs. (c) and (d) is

$$P_s = 50895.76 \text{ N}$$

Eq. (a) yields...

$$n = \frac{232312.5}{50895.76} = 4.56 \approx 5$$

3. **Thickness of cover plate:** According to IBR,

for double butt strap of equal width having ordinary riveting:

$$t_i = t_o = 0.625t = 0.625 \times 12.5 \qquad \text{... 5.4(c)/Pg 80, DHB}$$

$$t_i = t_o = 7.81 \text{ mm} \approx 8 \text{ mm}$$

4. **Arrangement of rivets:** Type of joint: Double riveted equal cover butt joint, as shown in **Fig. 7.26**.

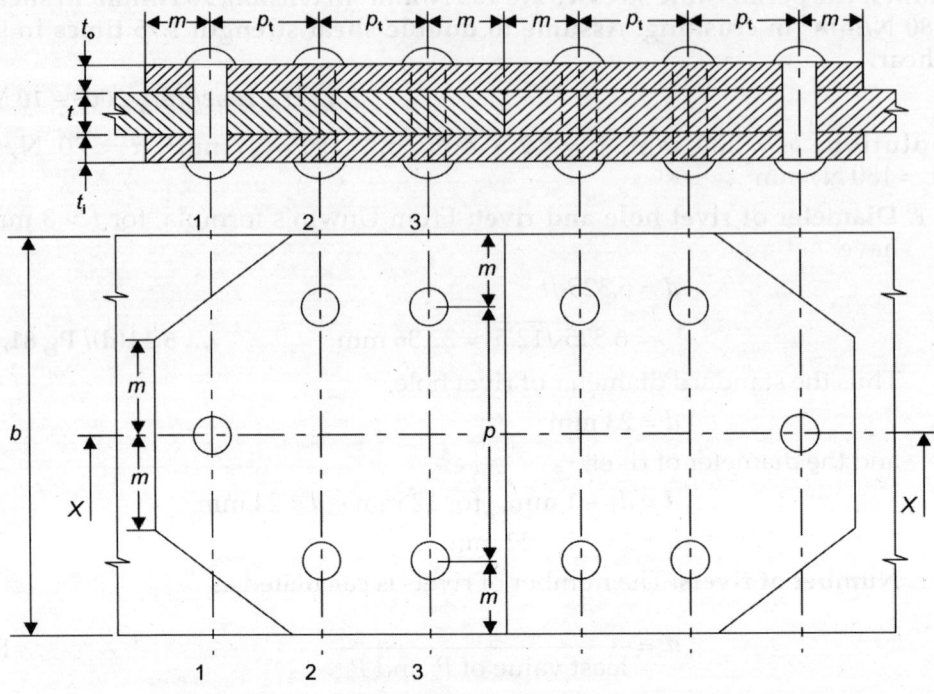

Fig. 7.26: Problem 17

5. **Margin:** Margin is calculated as

$$m = 1.5d = 1.5 \times 23 = 34.5 \text{ mm} \approx 35 \text{ mm} \qquad \text{... 5.16/Pg 83, DHB}$$

6. **Pitch of the rivets:** Pitch is calculated based on the number of rivets in the innermost section (i.e. section 3-3).

From **Fig. 7.26**, we have width

$$b = 2m + n'p$$

where n' = number of pitches in the innermost section

$$b = 2m + 1p$$
$$200 = (2 \times 35) + 1p$$
$$p = 130 \text{ mm}$$

7. **Transverse pitch (distance between the rows of rivets):**

For chain riveting,

$$p_t \geq 2d = 2 \times 23 = 46 \text{ mm} \qquad \text{... 5.14(a)/ Pg 82, DHB}$$

8. **Efficiency:**

   a. Tearing resistance:

     • Along section 1-1:

$$P_{t1} = (b - d)t\sigma_t = (200 - 23) \times 12.5 \times 105 = 232312.5 \text{ N} \qquad \text{... Eq. (i)}$$

     • Along section 2-2:

$$P_{t2} = (b - 2d)t\sigma_t + \text{Strength of one rivet in front of section 2-2}$$

$$= (b - 2d)t\sigma_t + 1.75\left(\frac{\pi d^2}{4}\right)\tau = (b - 2d)t\sigma_t + P_s$$

$$\dots (1.75, \text{ as per data})$$

$$= [(200 - 2 \times 23) \times 12.5 \times 105] + 50895.76$$

$$P_{t2} = 253020.76 \text{ N} \qquad\qquad\qquad \dots \text{Eq. (ii)}$$

- Along section 3-3:

$$P_{t3} = (b - 2d)t\sigma_t + \text{Strength of three rivets in front of section 3-3}$$

$$= (b - 2d)t\sigma_t + 3 \times \left[1.75\left(\frac{\pi d^2}{4}\right)\tau\right] = (b - 2d)t\sigma_t + 3P_s$$

$$= [(200 - 2 \times 23) \times 12.5 \times 105] + (50895.76 \times 3)$$

$$P_{t3} = 354812.30 \text{ N} \qquad\qquad\qquad \dots \text{Eq. (iii)}$$

b. Shearing resistance of all rivets:

$$P_s' = n \times P_s = 5 \times 50895.76 = 254478.82 \text{ N} \qquad \dots \text{Eq. (iv)}$$

c. Crushing resistance of all rivets:

$$P_c' = n \times P_c = 5 \times 51750 = 258750 \text{ N} \qquad\qquad \dots \text{Eq. (v)}$$

Thus the least value of Eqs. (i) to (v) is

$$P_{t1} = 232312.5 \text{ N}$$

d. Strength of solid plate:

$$P = bt\sigma_t = 200 \times 12.5 \times 105 = 262500 \text{ N}$$

$$\dots \text{Eq. (vi)} \ \textbf{5.6(a)/Pg 80, DHB}$$

$$\therefore \qquad \eta = \frac{\text{least value}}{\text{strength of solid plate}} = \frac{232312.5}{262500} = 0.885 = 88.5\%$$

18. **A tie bar in a bridge consists of plate 350 mm wide and 20 mm thick. It is connected by a plate of same thickness by a cover butt joint. Design an economical structural joint, if permissible stresses are 90 N/mm² in tension, 60 N/mm² in shear and 150 N/mm² in compression.**

VTU – June/ July 2009 – 10 Marks

Solution: $b = 350$ mm, $t = 20$ mm, $\sigma_t = 90$ N/mm², $\tau = 60$ N/mm², $\sigma_c = 150$ N/mm².

1. **Diameter of rivet hole and rivet:** From Unwin's formula, for $t > 8$ mm, we have

$$d = 6.325\sqrt{t}$$

$$= 6.325\sqrt{20} = 28.28 \text{ mm} \qquad \dots \textbf{5.11(d)/ Pg 81, DHB}$$

Thus the standard diameter of rivet hole,

$$d = 28.5 \text{ mm}$$

and the diameter of rivet,

$$d = d_1 + 1 \text{ mm}, \ \text{ for } 27 \text{ mm} \le d \le 36 \text{ mm}$$

$$d_1 = 28.5 - 1.5 = 27 \text{ mm}$$

2. **Number of rivets:** The number of rivets is calculated as

$$n = \frac{P_t}{\text{least value of } P_s \text{ and } P_c} \qquad\qquad \dots \text{Eq. (a)}$$

- Tearing resistance of plate,

$$P_t = (b - d)t\sigma_t \qquad \text{... 5.6(b)/Pg 80, DHB}$$
$$= (350 - 28.5) \times 20 \times 90$$
$$P_t = 578700 \text{ N} \qquad \text{... Eq. (b)}$$

- Shearing resistance of one rivet,

$$P_s = 1.875 \left(\frac{\pi d^2}{4} \right) \tau \qquad \text{... 5.6(c)/Pg 80, DHB}$$

$$= 1.875 \left(\frac{\pi \times 28.5^2}{4} \right) \times 60 = 71768.21 \text{ N} \qquad \text{... Eq. (c)}$$

- Crushing resistance of one rivet,

$$P_c = dt\sigma_c = 28.5 \times 20 \times 150 = 85500 \text{ N} \qquad \text{... Eq. (d)}$$

Thus the least value of Eqs. (c) and (d) is

$$P_s = 71768.21 \text{ N}$$

Eq. (a) yields...

$$n = \frac{578700}{71768.21} = 8.06 \approx 9$$

3. **Thickness of cover plate:** According to IBR,
   for double butt strap of equal width having ordinary riveting:

$$t_i = t_o = 0.625t = 0.625 \times 20 \qquad \text{... 5.4(c)/Pg 80, DHB}$$
$$t_i = t_o = 12.5 \text{ mm} \approx 14 \text{ mm}$$

4. **Arrangement of rivets:** Type of joint: Double riveted equal cover butt joint, as shown in **Fig. 7.27**.

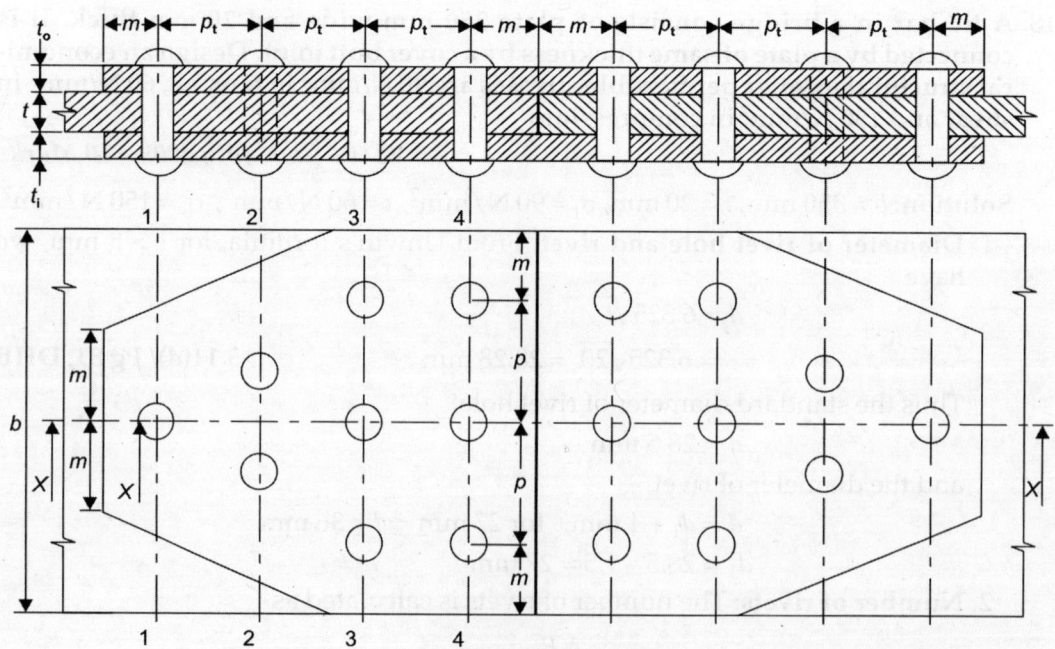

Fig. 7.27: Problem 18

5. **Margin:** Margin is calculated as
$$m = 1.5d = 1.5 \times 28.5 = 42.75 \text{ mm} \approx 45 \text{ mm}$$
... 5.16/Pg 83, DHB

6. **Pitch of the rivets:** Pitch is calculated based on the number of rivets in the innermost section (i.e. section 4-4).

    From **Fig. 7.27**, we have width
    $$b = 2m + n'p$$
    where n' = number of pitches in the innermost section
    $$b = 2m + 2p$$
    $$350 = (2 \times 45) + 2p$$
    $$p = 130 \text{ mm}$$

7. **Transverse pitch (distance between the rows of rivets):**

    For chain riveting,
    $$p_t \geq 2d = 2 \times 28.5 = 57 \text{ mm} \approx 60 \text{ mm} \qquad \text{... 5.14(a)/ Pg 82, DHB}$$

8. **Efficiency:**

    a. Tearing resistance:
    - Along section 1-1:
    $$P_{t1} = (b - d)t\sigma_t = (350 - 28.5) \times 20 \times 90 = 578700 \text{ N} \qquad \text{... Eq. (i)}$$

    - Along section 2-2:
    $$P_{t2} = (b - 2d)t\sigma_t + \text{Strength of one rivet in front of section 2-2}$$
    $$= (b - 2d)t\sigma_t + P_s$$
    $$= [(350 - 2 \times 28.5) \times 20 \times 90] + 71768.21$$
    $$P_{t2} = 599168.21 \text{ N} \qquad \text{... Eq. (ii)}$$

    - Along section 3-3:
    $$P_{t3} = (b - 3d)t\sigma_t + \text{Strength of three rivets in front of section 3-3}$$
    $$= (b - 3d)t\sigma_t + 3P_s$$
    $$= [(350 - 3 \times 28.5) \times 20 \times 90] + (3 \times 71768.21)$$
    $$P_{t3} = 691404.63 \text{ N} \qquad \text{... Eq. (iii)}$$

    - Along section 4-4:
    $$P_{t4} = (b - 3d)t\sigma_t + \text{Strength of six rivets in front of section 4-4}$$
    $$= (b - 3d)t\sigma_t + 6P_s$$
    $$= [(350 - 3 \times 28.5) \times 20 \times 90] + (6 \times 71768.21)$$
    $$P_{t4} = 906709.26 \text{ N} \qquad \text{... Eq. (iv)}$$

    b. Shearing resistance of all rivets:
    $$P_s' = n \times P_s = 9 \times 71768.21 = 645913.90 \text{ N} \qquad \text{... Eq. (v)}$$

    c. Crushing resistance of all rivets:
    $$P_c' = n \times P_c = 9 \times 85500 = 769500 \text{ N} \qquad \text{... Eq. (vi)}$$

    Thus the least value of Eqs. (i) to (v) is
    $$P_{t1} = 578700 \text{ N}$$

    d. Strength of solid plate:
    $$P = bt\sigma_t = 350 \times 20 \times 90 = 630000 \text{ N}$$
    ... Eq. (vii) 5.6(a)/Pg 80, DHB

    $$\therefore \qquad \eta = \frac{\text{least value}}{\text{strength of solid plate}} = \frac{578700}{630000} = 0.9186 = 91.86\%$$

19. **Two lengths of a flat tie bar, 15 mm thick, is connected by a butt joint with equal cover plates on either side. If 400 kN is acting on the tie bar, design the joint, such that the section of the bar is not reduced by more than one rivet hole. Working stresses for the material of the bar are 85 MPa in tension, 60 MPa in shear and 110 MPa in crushing.**

VTU – May/ June 2010 – 10 Marks; Mar. 2001 – 10 Marks

Solution: $t = 15$ mm, $F = P_t = 400$ kN, $\sigma_t = 85$ MPa, $\tau = 60$ MPa, $\sigma_c = 110$ MPa.

1. **Diameter of rivet hole and rivet:** From Unwin's formula, for $t > 8$ mm, we have

$$d = 6.325\sqrt{t} \qquad \text{... 5.11(d)/Pg 81, DHB}$$

$$= 6.325\sqrt{15} = 24.50 \text{ mm}$$

Thus the standard diameter of rivet hole,

$$d = 25 \text{ mm}$$

and the diameter of rivet,

$$d = d_1 + 1 \text{ mm}, \quad \text{for } 12 \text{ mm} \le d \le 24 \text{ mm}$$

$$d_1 = 25 - 1 = 24 \text{ mm}$$

2. **Width of plate:** We know that, tearing resistance of plate

$$P_t = (b - d)t\sigma_t \qquad \text{... 5.6(b)/Pg 80, DHB}$$

$$400 \times 10^3 = (b - 25) \times 15 \times 85$$

$$b = 338.73 \text{ mm} \approx 340 \text{ mm}$$

3. **Number of rivets:** We know that, tearing resistance of plate

$$n = \frac{P_t}{\text{least value of } P_s \text{ and } P_c} \qquad \text{... Eq. (a)}$$

- Shearing resistance of one rivet,

$$P_s = 1.875\left(\frac{\pi d^2}{4}\right)\tau \qquad \text{... 5.6(c)/Pg 80, DHB}$$

$$= 1.875\left(\frac{\pi \times 25^2}{4}\right) \times 60 = 55223.31 \text{ N} \qquad \text{... Eq. (b)}$$

- Crushing resistance of one rivet,

$$P_c = dt\sigma_c = 25 \times 15 \times 110 = 41250 \text{ N} \qquad \text{... Eq. (c)}$$

Thus the least value of Eqs. (b) and (c) is

$$P_c = 41250 \text{ N}$$

Eq. (a) yields...

$$n = \frac{400 \times 10^3}{41250} = 9.690 \approx 10$$

4. **Thickness of cover plate:** According to IBR,

for double butt strap of equal width having ordinary riveting:

$$t_i = t_o = 0.625t = 0.625 \times 15 \qquad \text{... 5.4(c)/Pg 80, DHB}$$

$$t_i = t_o = 9.38 \text{ mm} \approx 10 \text{ mm}$$

5. **Arrangement of rivets:** Type of joint: Double riveted equal cover butt joint, as shown in **Fig. 7.28**.

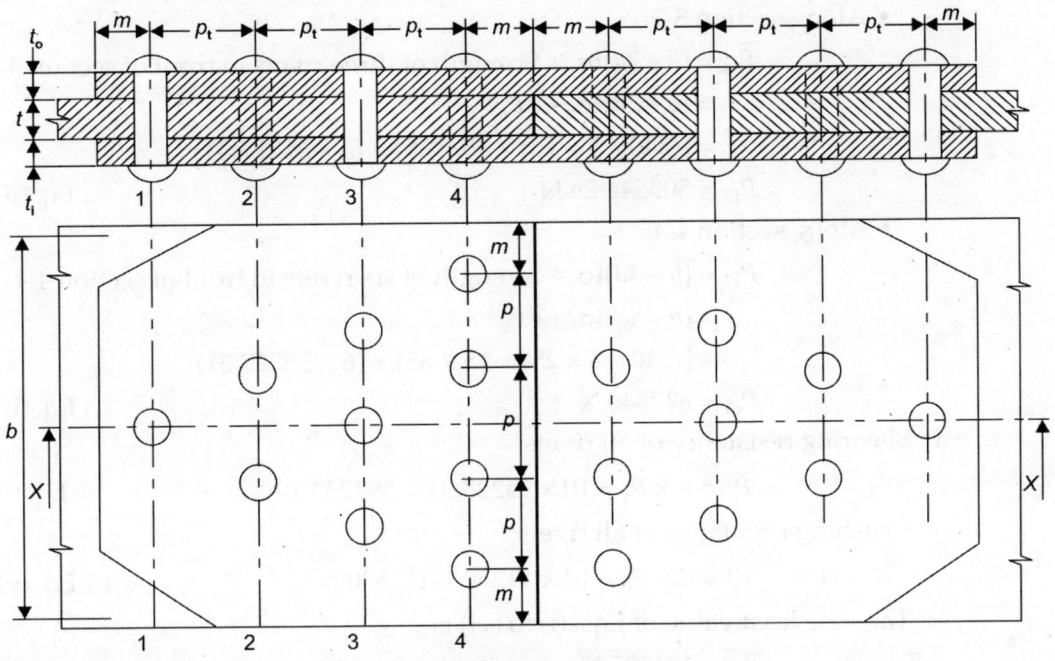

Fig. 7.28: Problem 19

6. **Margin:** Margin is calculated as
$$m = 1.5d = 1.5 \times 25 = 37.5 \text{ mm} \approx 38 \text{ mm}$$
... 5.16/Pg 83, DHB

7. **Pitch of the rivets:** Pitch is calculated based on the number of rivets in the innermost section (i.e. section 4-4).

From **Fig. 7.28**, we have width
$$b = 2m + n'p$$
where n' = number of pitches in the innermost section
$$b = 2m + 3p$$
$$340 = (2 \times 38) + 3p$$
$$p = 88 \text{ mm}$$

8. **Transverse pitch (distance between the rows of rivets):**
For chain riveting,
$$p_t \geq 2d = 2 \times 25 = 50 \text{ mm}$$
... 5.14(a)/ Pg 82, DHB

9. **Efficiency:**
   a. Tearing resistance:
   • Along section 1-1:
   $$P_{t1} = (b - d)t\sigma_t = (340 - 25) \times 15 \times 85 = 401625 \text{ N}$$
   ... Eq. (i)
   • Along section 2-2:
   $$P_{t2} = (b - 2d)t\sigma_t + \text{Strength of one rivet in front of section 2-2}$$
   $$= (b - 2d)t\sigma_t + P_s$$

$$= [(340 - 2 \times 25) \times 15 \times 85] + 55223.31$$

$$P_{t2} = 424973.31 \text{ N} \qquad \qquad \text{... Eq. (ii)}$$

- Along section 3-3:

$$P_{t3} = (b - 3d)t\sigma_t + \text{Strength of three rivets in front of section 3-3}$$

$$= (b - 3d)t\sigma_t + 3P_s$$

$$= [(340 - 3 \times 25) \times 15 \times 85] + (3 \times 55223.31)$$

$$P_{t3} = 503544.26 \text{ N} \qquad \qquad \text{... Eq. (iii)}$$

- Along section 4-4:

$$P_{t3} = (b - 4d)t\sigma_t + \text{Strength of six rivets in front of section 4-4}$$

$$= (b - 4d)t\sigma_t + 6P_s$$

$$= [(340 - 4 \times 25) \times 15 \times 85] + (6 \times 55223.31)$$

$$P_{t3} = 637340 \text{ N} \qquad \qquad \text{... Eq. (iv)}$$

b. Shearing resistance of all rivets:

$$P_s' = n \times P_s = 10 \times 55223.31 = 552233.1 \text{ N} \qquad \qquad \text{... Eq. (v)}$$

c. Crushing resistance of all rivets:

$$P_c' = n \times P_c = 10 \times 41250 = 412500 \text{ N} \qquad \qquad \text{... Eq. (vi)}$$

Thus the least value of Eqs. (i) to (vi) is

$$P_{t1} = 401625 \text{ N}$$

d. Strength of solid plate:

$$P = bt\sigma_t = 340 \times 15 \times 85 = 433500 \text{ N}$$

$$\text{... Eq. (vii)} \textbf{ 5.6(a)/Pg 80, DHB}$$

i.e. $$\eta = \frac{\text{least value}}{\text{strength of solid plate}} = \frac{401625}{433500} = 0.9265 = 92.65\%$$

20. **Design a diamond lap joint for a mild steel flat tie bar 200 mm × 10 mm using 21 mm diameter rivets. Number of rivets in the joint is 8. Allowable stresses are: σ_t = 120 MPa, τ = 80 MPa, σ_{cr} = 210 MPa. Assume hole diameter to be equal to the rivet diameter.** *VTU – Dec. 2012 – 10 Marks*

Solution: b = 200 mm, t = 10 mm, $d = d_1$ = 21 mm, n = 8, σ_t = 120 MPa, τ = 80 MPa, σ_c = 210 MPa.

1. **Diameter of rivet hole and rivet:**

$$d = d_1 = 21 \text{ mm (data)}$$

2. **Number of rivets:** Check for n: (n = 8, as per data)

$$n = \frac{P_t}{\text{least value of } P_s \text{ and } P_c} \qquad \qquad \text{... Eq. (a)}$$

- Shearing resistance of plate,

$$P_t = (b - d)t\sigma_t \qquad \qquad \textbf{... 5.6(b)/Pg 80, DHB}$$

$$= (200 - 21) \times 10 \times 120$$

$$P_t = 214800 \text{ N} \qquad \qquad \text{... Eq. (b)}$$

- Shearing resistance of plate,

$$P_s = \left(\frac{\pi d^2}{4} \right) \tau \qquad \qquad \text{... 5.6(c)/Pg 80, DHB}$$

$$= \left(\frac{\pi \times 21^2}{4} \right) \times 80 = 27708.85 \text{ N} \qquad \text{... Eq. (c)}$$

- Crushing resistance of one rivet,

$$P_c = dt\sigma_c = 21 \times 10 \times 210 = 44100 \text{ N} \qquad \text{... Eq. (d)}$$

Thus the least value of Eqs. (c) and (d) is $P_s = 27708.5$ N

Eq. (a) yields...

$$n = \frac{214800}{27708.5} = 7.75 \approx 8$$

3. **Arrangement of rivets:** Type of joint: Lap joint, as shown in **Fig. 7.29**.

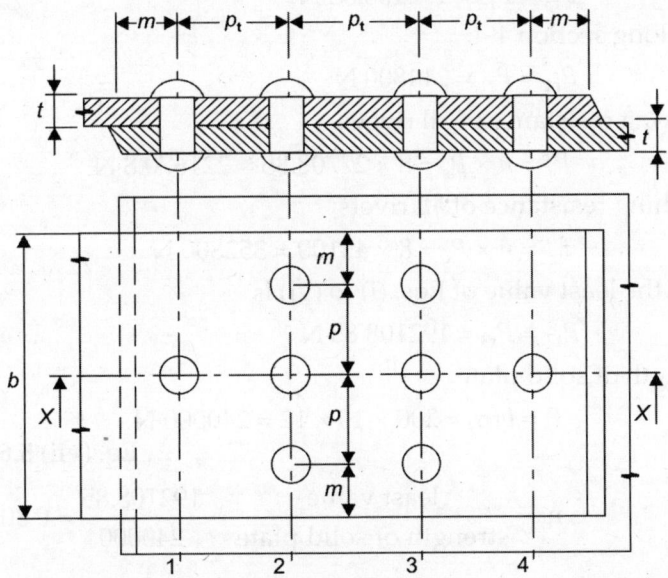

Fig. 7.29: Problem 20

4. **Margin:** Margin is calculated as

$$m = 1.5d = 1.5 \times 21 = 31.5 \text{ mm} \approx 35 \text{ mm}$$

... 5.16/Pg 83, DHB

5. **Pitch of the rivets:** Pitch is calculated based on the number of rivets in the innermost section (i.e. section 2-2 or 3-3).

From **Fig. 7.29**, we have width

$$b = 2m + n'p$$

where n' = number of pitches in the innermost section

$$b = 2m + 2p$$

$$200 = (2 \times 35) + 2p$$

$$p = 65 \text{ mm}$$

6. **Transverse pitch (distance between the rows of rivets):**
   For chain riveting,
   $$p_t \geq 2d = 2 \times 21 = 42 \text{ mm} \qquad \textbf{... 5.14(a)/ Pg 82, DHB}$$

7. **Efficiency:**

   a. Tearing resistance:
   - Along section 1-1:
     $$P_{t1} = (b - d)t\sigma_t = (200 - 21) \times 10 \times 120 = 214800 \text{ N} \qquad \text{... Eq. (i)}$$
   - Along section 2-2:
     $$P_{t2} = (b - 3d)t\sigma_t + \text{Strength of one rivet in front of section 2-2}$$
     $$= (b - 3d)t\sigma_t + P_s$$
     $$= [(200 - 3 \times 21) \times 10 \times 120] + 27708.85$$
     $$P_{t2} = 192108.85 \text{ N} \qquad \text{... Eq. (ii)}$$
   - Along section 3-3:
     $$P_{t3} = P_{t2} = 192108.85 \text{ N} \qquad \text{... Eq. (iii)}$$
   - Along section 4-4:
     $$P_{t4} = P_{t1} = 214800 \text{ N} \qquad \text{... Eq. (iv)}$$

   b. Shearing resistance of all rivets:
   $$P_s' = n \times P_s = 8 \times 27708.85 = 221670.8 \text{ N} \qquad \text{... Eq. (v)}$$

   c. Crushing resistance of all rivets:
   $$P_c' = n \times P_c = 8 \times 44100 = 352800 \text{ N} \qquad \text{... Eq. (vi)}$$

   Thus the least value of Eqs. (i) to (vi) is
   $$P_{t2} = P_{t3} = 192108.85 \text{ N}$$

   d. Strength of solid plate:
   $$P = bt\sigma_t = 200 \times 10 \times 12 = 240000 \text{ N}$$
   $$\text{... Eq. (vii)} \textbf{ 5.6(a)/Pg 80, DHB}$$

   i.e. $$\eta = \frac{\text{least value}}{\text{strength of solid plate}} = \frac{192108.85}{240000} = 0.8005 = 80.05\%$$

7.14 ECCENTRIC LOADED RIVETED JOINTS

When the line of action of the load does not pass through the centroid of the rivet system then the joint is said to be an eccentric loaded riveted joint. This eccentric load can be replaced by an equal load passing through the centre of gravity (CG) of the rivet group and a couple acting about the CG of the rivet group and whose moment is equal to the product of the load and the perpendicular distance between the CG of the rivet group and the original line of action of load. The load acting through the CG of the rivet group produces a primary or direct shear force and/or stress and the couple produces a secondary shear force and/or stress in the rivets. The primary shear has the same magnitude in all directions while the secondary shear depends upon the location of rivets from CG of the rivet group. Thus, the resultant force varies from one rivet to another.

The rivet groups may be classified as:
   a. Horizontal group
   b. Vertical group
   c. Compound group.

7.14.1 Load Acting in a Plane Containing the Rivets—Compound Group

The analysis is similar to that discussed for bolted joints in shear *(Refer to Section 4.10.3).*

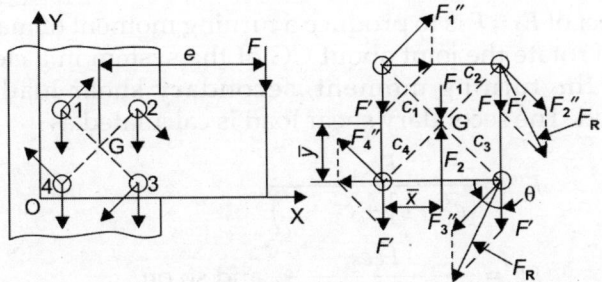

Fig. 7.30: Riveted joint with eccentric load [**Fig. 5.1/Pg 83, DHB**]

Let $\qquad$ F = applied load

e = eccentricity

n = number of rivets

c_1, c_2, c_3 and c_4 = radial distance of respective rivets from center of gravity (CG) of the rivet group

F' = direct shear force induced in each rivet

F_1'', F_2'', F_3'' and F_4'' = secondary shear force in rivets 1, 2 3 and 4 respectively

$\theta_1, \theta_2, \theta_3$ and θ_4 = angle between F' and F_1'', F' and F_2'', F' and F_3'', and F' and F_4'', respectively

F_{R1}, F_{R2}, F_{R3} and F_{R4} = resultant load or force in respective rivets.

For the force analysis of the above system, the following procedure is adopted:

1. To find CG (G) of the rivet group:

Let $\quad x_1, x_2, x_3$ and x_4 be the distances of respective rivets from Y-axis

$\quad y_1, y_2, y_3$ and y_4 be the distances of respective rivets from X-axis

$$\bar{x} = \frac{\Sigma x}{n} = \frac{x_1 + x_2 + x_3 + ... + x_n}{n}$$

and $\qquad \bar{y} = \frac{\Sigma y}{n} = \frac{y_1 + y_2 + y_3 + ... + y_n}{n}$ $\qquad$ ... (Eq. 7.42)

2. To find radial distances:

$$c_n = \sqrt{x_n'^2 + y_n'^2}$$ $\qquad$ ... (Eq. 7.43)

where n = 1, 2, 3 and 4 for respective rivets

x_n' and y_n' refer to the distances of respective rivets from CG in X and Y directions.

3. We introduce two forces F_1 and F_2 at the CG of the rivet system, which are equal and opposite to F as shown in **Fig. 4.20(b)**. Here we have two types of forces:

a. Direct shear force due to external load F.

b. Momemt $M = Fe$ which tries to rotate the joint about CG.

- The effect of $F_1 = F$ is to produce direct shear load on each rivet of equal magnitude.

Direct shear force,

$$F' = \frac{F}{n}, \text{ acting parallel to the load } F$$

... (Eq. 7.44) **5.18/ Pg 83, DHB**

- The effect of $F_2 = F$ is to produce a turning moment of magnitude $F \cdot e$ which tends to rotate the joint about CG of the system in a clockwise direction. Due to the turning moment, secondary shear load on each rivet is produced. The secondary shear load is calculated as

$$F_1'' = \frac{F e c_1}{\left(c_1^2 + c_2^2 + c_3^2 + ...\right)},$$

$$F_2'' = \frac{F e c_2}{\left(c_1^2 + c_2^2 + c_3^2 + ...\right)} \text{ and so on...}$$

i.e. in general secondary shear force on any rivet,

$$F_n'' = \frac{F e c_n}{\Sigma c^2}$$

... (Eq. 7.45) **5.20/ Pg 83, DHB**

and the maximum secondary shear force is ,

$$F_{max}'' = \frac{F e c_{max}}{\Sigma c^2}$$

... (Eq. 7.46)

4. The resultant shear force (F_R) on respective rivets is found as:

$$F_R = \sqrt{F'^2 + F''^2 + 2F'F'' \cos\theta} \quad ... \text{(Eq. 7.47)} \textbf{ 5.21/ Pg 83, DHB}$$

where θ = smallest angle between the primary or direct shear load and secondary shear load.

$$\cos\theta_n = \frac{x_n'}{c_n}$$

When the secondary shear load on each rivet is equal, then the heavily loaded rivet will be one in which the included angle between the direct shear load and secondary shear load is minimum. The maximum loaded rivet becomes the critical one for determining the strength of the riveted joint [*i.e. the most heavily loaded rivets are those which are situated at the greatest distance from the tilting edge, i.e. rivets located at c_3 and/or c_2*].

5. When the maximum load on the rivet is known, the size of the rivet can be calculated based on the permissible shear stress as:

$$A_1 = \frac{F_R}{\tau}$$

... (Eq. 7.48)

where A_1 = core area of the rivet

Note: The topic discussed here is applicable also for bolted joints in shear. Refer to Eqs. [9.9(a) to 9.9(g)/ Pg 132, DHB].

21. **Determine the size of rivets required for the bracket shown in Fig. 7.31(a). Take the permissible shear stress for the rivet material as 100 MPa.**

Solution: $d_1 = ?, \tau = 100$ MPa, $F = 100 \times 10^3$ N, number of bolts $n = 6, e = 200$ mm.

We know that $\qquad \tau = \frac{F_R}{A}$ ... Eq. (i)

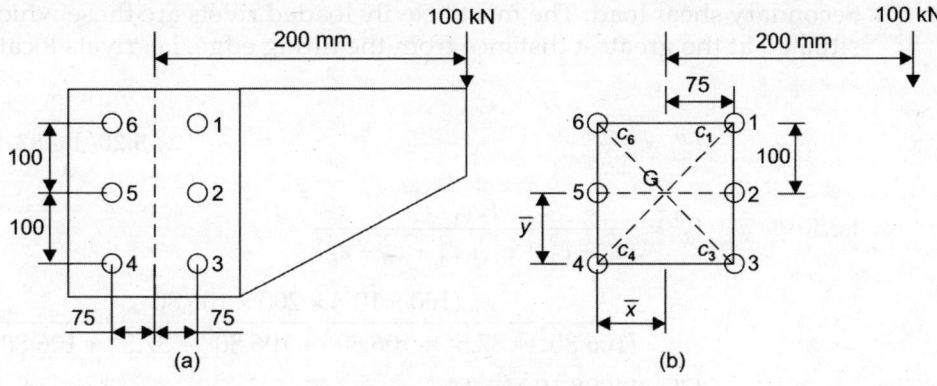

Fig. 7.31: Problem 21

Method-1

a. To find CG of the rivet group: From **Fig. 7.31(a)**, taking rivet '4' as the reference, we have

Distance (mm)	Rivet Nos.					
	1	2	3	4	5	6
x_n	75	75	75	0	0	0
y_n	200	100	0	0	100	200

$$\bar{x} = \frac{\Sigma x}{n} = \frac{x_1 + x_2 + x_3 + \dots + x_n}{n}$$

$$\therefore \quad \bar{x} = \frac{75 + 75 + 75 + 0 + 0 + 0}{6} = 37.5 \text{ mm}$$

$$\bar{y} = \frac{\Sigma y}{n} = \frac{y_1 + y_2 + y_3 + \dots + y_n}{n}$$

$$\therefore \quad \bar{y} = \frac{200 + 100 + 0 + 0 + 100 + 200}{6} = 100 \text{ mm}$$

b. To find radial distances (c_n): From CG of the rivet **[Fig. 7.31(b)]**, we have

Distance from CG (mm)	Rivet Nos.					
	1	2	3	4	5	6
$x'_n = (\bar{x} \sim x_n)$	37.5	37.5	37.5	37.5	37.5	37.5
$y'_n = (\bar{y} \sim y_n)$	100	0	100	100	0	100
$c_n = \sqrt{x'^2_n + y'^2_n}$	106.80	37.5	106.80	106.80	37.5	106.80
$\cos\theta_n = x'_n / c_n$	0.35	1	0.35	0.35	1	0.35

c. Shear loads:

i. Direct or primary shear load:

$$F' = \frac{F}{n} = \frac{100 \times 10^3}{6} = 16666.67 \text{ N} \qquad \text{... 5.18/ Pg 83, DHB}$$

ii. Secondary shear load: The most heavily loaded rivets are those which are situated at the greatest distance from the tilting edge, i.e. rivets located at c_1

$$F_n'' = \frac{Fec_n}{\Sigma c^2} \qquad \textbf{... 5.20/ Pg 83, DHB}$$

i.e. $$F_1'' = \frac{Fec_1}{(c_1^2 + c_2^2 + c_3^2 + c_4^2 + c_5^2 + c_6^2)}$$

$$= \frac{(100 \times 10^3) \times 200 \times 106.80}{(106.80^2 + 37.5^2 + 106.80^2 + 106.80^2 + 37.5^2 + 106.80^2)}$$

$$F_1'' = 44098.10 \text{ N} = F''$$

d. Resultant shear load:

$$F_R = \sqrt{F'^2 + F''^2 + 2F'F'' \cos\theta} \qquad \textbf{... 5.21/ Pg 83, DHB}$$

$$= \sqrt{16666.67^2 + 44098.10^2 + (2 \times 16666.67 \times 44098.10 \times 0.35)}$$

$$\text{(Here } \cos\theta_1 = 0.35)$$

$$F_R = 52315.37 \text{ N}$$

e. Diameter of the rivet hole:

Eq. (i) yields...

$$A = \frac{52315.37}{100} = 523.15 \text{ mm}^2$$

i.e. $$\frac{\pi d^2}{4} = 523.15 \text{ mm}^2$$

$\therefore$ $$d = 25.81 \text{ mm}$$

Thus the standard diameter of rivet hole,

$$d = 28.5 \text{ mm}$$

and the diameter of rivet,

$$d = d_1 + 1.5 \text{ mm}, \quad \text{for } 27 \text{ mm} \leq d \leq 36 \text{ mm}$$

$$d_1 = 28.5 - 1.5 = 27 \text{ mm}$$

Method-2

a. To find CG of the rivet group: From **Fig. 7.31(a)**, taking rivet '4' as the reference, we have

Distance (mm)	Rivet Nos.					
	1	2	3	4	5	6
x_n	75	75	75	0	0	0
y_n	200	100	0	0	100	200

$$\bar{x} = \frac{\Sigma x}{n} = \frac{x_1 + x_2 + x_3 + ... + x_n}{n}$$

$\therefore$ $$\bar{x} = \frac{75 + 75 + 75 + 0 + 0 + 0}{6} = 37.5 \text{ mm}$$

$$\overline{y} = \frac{\Sigma y}{n} = \frac{y_1 + y_2 + y_3 + \dots + y_n}{n}$$

$$\therefore \quad \overline{y} = \frac{200 + 100 + 0 + 0 + 100 + 200}{6} = 100 \text{ mm}$$

b. To find radial distances (c_n): From CG of the rivet **[Fig. 7.31(b)]**, we have

Distance from CG (mm)	Rivet Nos.					
	1	2	3	4	5	6
$x'_n = (\overline{x} \sim x_n)$	37.5	37.5	37.5	37.5	37.5	37.5
$y'_n = (\overline{y} \sim y_n)$	100	0	100	100	0	100
$c_n = \sqrt{x'^2_n + y'^2_n}$	106.80	37.5	106.80	106.80	37.5	106.80
$\cos\theta_n = x'_n / c_n$	0.35	1	0.35	0.35	1	0.35

c. Shear loads:
  i. Direct or primary shear load:

$$F' = \frac{F}{n} = \frac{100 \times 10^3}{6} = 16666.67 \text{ N} \qquad \textbf{... 5.18/ Pg 83, DHB}$$

  ii. Secondary shear load:

$$F''_n = \frac{Fec_n}{\Sigma c^2} \qquad \textbf{... 5.20/ Pg 83, DHB}$$

i.e. $\quad F''_1 = \dfrac{Fec_2}{(c_1^2 + c_2^2 + c_3^2 + c_4^2 + c_5^2 + c_6^2)}$

$$= \frac{(100 \times 10^3) \times 200 \times 106.80}{(106.80^2 + 37.5^2 + 106.80^2 + 106.80^2 + 37.5^2 + 106.80^2)}$$

$$F''_1 = 44098.10 \text{ N} \qquad \qquad \text{... Eq. (a)}$$

$$F''_2 = F''_1\left(\frac{c_2}{c_1}\right) = 44098.10 \times \left(\frac{37.5}{106.80}\right) = 15483.88 \text{ N} \quad \text{... Eq. (b)}$$

$$F''_3 = F''_1\left(\frac{c_3}{c_1}\right) = 44098.10 \times \left(\frac{106.80}{106.80}\right) = 44098.10 \text{ N} \quad \text{... Eq. (c)}$$

$$F''_4 = F''_1\left(\frac{c_3}{c_1}\right) = 44098.10 \times \left(\frac{106.80}{106.80}\right) = 44098.10 \text{ N} \quad \text{... Eq. (d)}$$

$$F''_5 = F''_1\left(\frac{c_5}{c_1}\right) = 44098.10 \times \left(\frac{37.5}{106.80}\right) = 15483.88 \text{ N} \quad \text{... Eq. (e)}$$

$$F''_6 = F''_1\left(\frac{c_6}{c_1}\right) = 44098.10 \times \left(\frac{106.80}{106.80}\right) = 44098.10 \text{ N} \quad \text{... Eq. (f)}$$

Thus F'' is the maximum of Eqs. (a) to (f), i.e.

$$F'' = 44098.10 \text{ N} = F''_1 = F''_3 = F''_4 = F''_6$$

d. Resultant shear load:

$$F_R = \sqrt{F'^2 + F''^2 + 2F'F'' \cos\theta} \qquad \text{... 5.21/ Pg 83, DHB}$$

$$= \sqrt{16666.67^2 + 44098.10^2 + 2 \times 16666.67 \times 44098.10 \times 0.35}$$

$$\text{(Here } \cos\theta_1 = 0.35)$$

$$F_R = 52315.37 \text{ N}$$

e. Diameter of the rivet hole:

Eq. (i) yields...

$$A = \frac{52315.37}{100} = 523.15 \text{ mm}^2$$

i.e.

$$\frac{\pi d^2}{4} = 523.15 \text{ mm}^2$$

∴

$$d = 25.81 \text{ mm}$$

Thus the standard diameter of rivet hole,

$$d = 28.5 \text{ mm}$$

and the diameter of rivet,

$$d = d_1 + 1.5 \text{ mm}, \quad \text{for } 27 \text{ mm} \le d \le 36 \text{ mm}$$

$$d_1 = 28.5 - 1.5 = 27 \text{ mm}$$

22. **Determine the size of rivets, for the 20 mm thick flat plate, riveted to a column as shown in Fig. 7.32(a). The allowable stresses in the rivets are 56 MPa in shear and 100 MPa in crushing.**

VTU – Dec. 2010 – 10 Marks

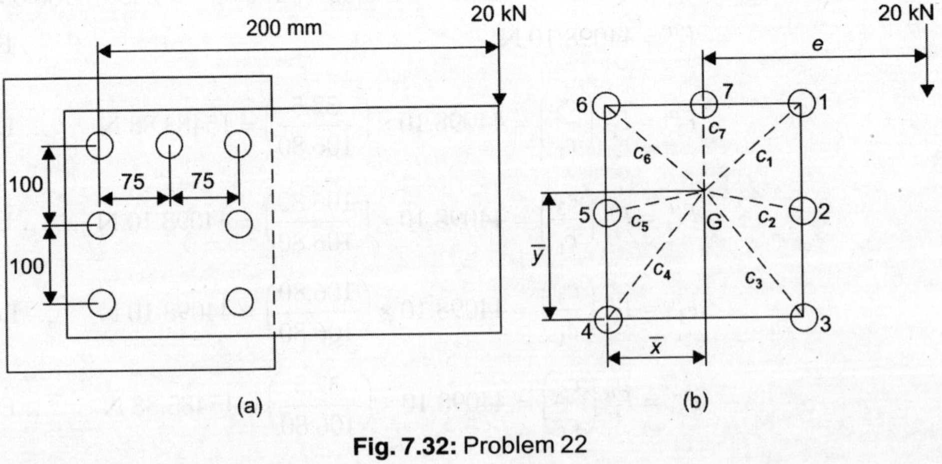

Fig. 7.32: Problem 22

Solution: $d_1 = ?$, $t = 20$ MPa, $\tau = 56$ MPa, $\sigma_c = 100$ MPa, $F = 20 \times 10^3$ N, number of bolts $n = 7$, $e = 200 - 75 = 125$ mm.

We know that $\qquad \tau = \dfrac{F_R}{A} \qquad$ ... Eq. (i)

Method-1

a. To find CG of the rivet group: From **Fig. 7.32(a)**, taking rivet '4' as the reference, we have

Distance (mm)	Rivet Nos.						
	1	2	3	4	5	6	7
x_n	150	150	150	0	0	0	75
y_n	200	100	0	0	100	200	200

$$\overline{x} = \frac{\Sigma x}{n} = \frac{x_1 + x_2 + x_3 + \dots + x_n}{n}$$

$\therefore \qquad \overline{x} = \frac{150 + 150 + 150 + 0 + 0 + 0 + 75}{7} = 75 \text{ mm}$

$$\overline{y} = \frac{\Sigma y}{n} = \frac{y_1 + y_2 + y_3 + \dots + y_n}{n}$$

$\therefore \qquad \overline{y} = \frac{200 + 100 + 0 + 0 + 100 + 200 + 200}{7} = 114.29 \text{ mm}$

b. To find radial distances (c_n): From CG of the rivet **[Fig. 7.32(b)]**, we have

Distance from CG (mm)	Rivet Nos.						
	1	2	3	4	5	6	7
$x'_n = (\overline{x} \sim x_n)$	75	75	75	75	75	75	0
$y'_n = (\overline{y} \sim y_n)$	85.71	14.29	114.29	114.29	14.29	85.71	85.71
$c_n = \sqrt{x'^2_n + y'^2_n}$	113.89	76.35	136.70	136.70	76.35	113.89	85.71
$\cos\theta_n = x'_n/c_n$	0.66	0.98	0.55	0.55	0.98	0.66	0

c. Shear loads:

  i. Direct or primary shear load:

$$F' = \frac{F}{n} = \frac{20 \times 10^3}{7} = 2857.14 \text{ N} \qquad \dots \textbf{5.18/ Pg 83, DHB}$$

  ii. Secondary shear load: The most heavily loaded rivets are those which are situated at the greatest distance from the tilting edge, i.e. rivets located at c_1 and c_3.

  Based on observation, it is found that, c_3 will be heavily loaded since it has two rivets in that particular row compared to topmost row.

$$F''_n = \frac{Fec_n}{\Sigma c^2} \qquad \dots \textbf{5.20/ Pg 83, DHB}$$

  i.e. $\quad F''_3 = \dfrac{Fec_3}{(c_1^2 + c_2^2 + c_3^2 + c_4^2 + c_5^2 + c_6^2 + c_7^2)}$

$$= \frac{(20 \times 10^3) \times 125 \times 136.7}{(113.89^2 + 76.35^2 + 136.7^2 + 136.7^2 + 76.35^2 + 113.89^2 + 85.71^2)}$$

$$F''_3 = 4151.34 \text{ N} = F''$$

d. Resultant shear load:

$$F_R = \sqrt{F'^2 + F''^2 + 2F'F''\cos\theta} \qquad \textbf{... 5.21/ Pg 83, DHB}$$

$$= \sqrt{2587.14^2 + 4151.34^2 + (2 \times 2587.14 \times 4151.24 \times 0.55)}$$

$$\text{(Here } \cos\theta_3 = 0.35)$$

$$F_R = 6200.32 \text{ N}$$

e. Diameter of the rivet hole:

Eq. (i) yields...

$$A = \frac{6200.32}{56} = 110.71 \text{ mm}^2$$

i.e.

$$\frac{\pi d^2}{4} = 110.71 \text{ mm}^2$$

$$\therefore \qquad d = 11.87 \text{ mm}$$

Thus the standard diameter of rivet hole,

$$d = 13 \text{ mm}$$

and the diameter of rivet,

$$d = d_1 + 1 \text{ mm}, \quad \text{for } 12 \text{ mm} \le d \le 24 \text{ mm}$$

$$d_1 = 13 - 1 = 12 \text{ mm}$$

Method-2

a. To find CG of the rivet group: From **Fig. 7.32(a)**, taking rivet '4' as the reference, we have

Distance (mm)	Rivet Nos.						
	1	2	3	4	5	6	7
x_n	150	150	150	0	0	0	75
y_n	200	100	0	0	100	200	200

$$\bar{x} = \frac{\Sigma x}{n} = \frac{x_1 + x_2 + x_3 + ... + x_n}{n}$$

$$\therefore \qquad \bar{x} = \frac{150 + 150 + 150 + 0 + 0 + 0 + 75}{7} = 75 \text{ mm}$$

$$\bar{y} = \frac{\Sigma y}{n} = \frac{y_1 + y_2 + y_3 + ... + y_n}{n}$$

$$\therefore \qquad \bar{y} = \frac{200 + 100 + 0 + 0 + 100 + 200 + 200}{7} = 114.29 \text{ mm}$$

b. To find radial distances (c_n): From CG of the rivet **[Fig. 7.32(b)]**, we have

Distance from CG (mm)	Rivet Nos.						
	1	2	3	4	5	6	7
$x'_n = (\bar{x} \sim x_n)$	75	75	75	75	75	75	0
$y'_n = (\bar{y} \sim y_n)$	85.71	14.29	114.29	114.29	14.29	85.71	85.71
$c_n = \sqrt{x'^2_n + y'^2_n}$	113.89	76.35	136.70	136.70	76.35	113.89	85.71
$\cos\theta_n = x'_n/c_n$	0.66	0.98	0.55	0.55	0.98	0.66	0

c. Shear loads:
  i. Direct or primary shear load:

$$F' = \frac{F}{n} = \frac{20 \times 10^3}{7} = 2857.14 \text{ N} \qquad \text{... 5.18/ Pg 83, DHB}$$

  ii. Secondary shear load:

$$F_n'' = \frac{Fec_n}{\Sigma c^2} \qquad \text{... 5.20/ Pg 83, DHB}$$

i.e. $\quad F_1'' = \dfrac{Fec_1}{\left(c_1^2 + c_2^2 + c_3^2 + c_4^2 + c_5^2 + c_6^2 + c_7^2 \right)}$

$$= \frac{(20 \times 10^3) \times 125 \times 113.89}{(113.89^2 + 76.35^2 + 136.7^2 + 136.7^2 + 76.35^2 + 113.80^2 + 85.71^2)}$$

$F_1'' = 3458.83 \text{ N} \qquad\qquad\qquad\qquad\qquad\qquad\qquad\qquad \text{... Eq. (a)}$

$$F_2'' = F_1'' \left(\frac{c_2}{c_1} \right) = 3458.83 \times \left(\frac{76.35}{113.89} \right) = 2318.61 \text{ N} \qquad \text{... Eq. (b)}$$

$$F_3'' = F_1'' \left(\frac{c_3}{c_1} \right) = 3458.83 \times \left(\frac{136.7}{113.89} \right) = 4151.34 \text{ N} \qquad \text{... Eq. (c)}$$

$$F_4'' = F_1'' \left(\frac{c_3}{c_1} \right) = 3458.83 \times \left(\frac{136.7}{113.89} \right) = 4151.34 \text{ N} \qquad \text{... Eq. (d)}$$

$$F_5'' = F_1'' \left(\frac{c_5}{c_1} \right) = 3458.83 \times \left(\frac{136.7}{113.89} \right) = 2318.61 \text{ N} \qquad \text{... Eq. (e)}$$

$$F_6'' = F_1'' \left(\frac{c_6}{c_1} \right) = 3458.83 \times \left(\frac{113.89}{113.89} \right) = 3458.83 \text{ N} \qquad \text{... Eq. (f)}$$

$$F_7'' = F_1'' \left(\frac{c_7}{c_1} \right) = 3458.83 \times \left(\frac{85.71}{113.89} \right) = 2603.04 \text{ N} \qquad \text{... Eq. (g)}$$

Thus F'' is the maximum of Eqs. (a) to (g), i.e.

$$F'' = 4151.34 = F_3'' = F_4''$$

d. Resultant shear load:

$$F_R = \sqrt{F'^2 + F''^2 + 2F'F'' \cos\theta} \qquad \text{... 5.21/ Pg 83, DHB}$$

$$= \sqrt{2587.14^2 + 4151.34^2 + (2 \times 2587.14 \times 4151.34 \times 0.55)}$$

$$\text{... (Here } \cos\theta_3 = 0.35)$$

$$F_R = 6200.32 \text{ N}$$

e. Diameter of the rivet hole:
  Eq. (i) yields...

$$A = \frac{6200.32}{56} = 110.71 \text{ mm}^2$$

i.e. $\qquad\qquad \dfrac{\pi d^2}{4} = 110.71 \text{ mm}^2$

$\therefore \qquad\qquad\qquad d = 11.87 \text{ mm}$

Thus the standard diameter of rivet hole,

$$d = 13 \text{ mm}$$

and the diameter of rivet,

$$d = d_1 + 1 \text{ mm}, \quad \text{for } 12 \text{ mm} \le d \le 24 \text{ mm}$$

$$d_1 = 13 - 1 = 12 \text{ mm}$$

23. **Determine the size of rivets required for the bracket shown in Fig. 7.33(a). Take the permissible shear stress for the rivet material as 100 MPa.**

VTU – July 2007 – 10 Marks

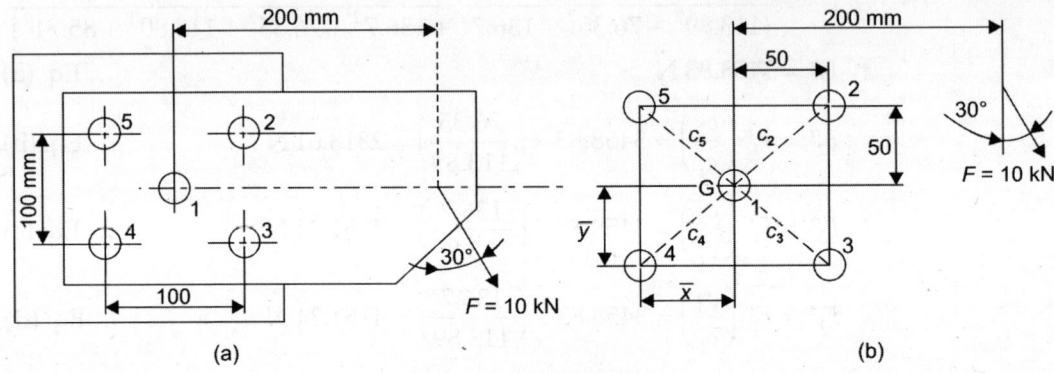

Fig. 7.33: Problem 23

Solution: $d_1 = ?$, $\tau = 100$ MPa, $F = 10 \times 10^3$ N, number of bolts $n = 5$, $e = 200$ mm, $\alpha = 30°$.

We know that $\qquad \tau = \dfrac{F_R}{A}$ $\qquad\qquad$ ... Eq. (i)

a. To find CG of the rivet group: From **Fig. 7.33(a)**, taking rivet '4' as the reference, we have

Distance (mm)	Rivet Nos.				
	1	2	3	4	5
x_n	50	100	100	0	0
y_n	50	100	0	0	100

$$\overline{x} = \frac{\Sigma x}{n} = \frac{x_1 + x_2 + x_3 + \dots + x_n}{n}$$

$$\therefore \quad \overline{x} = \frac{50 + 100 + 100 + 0 + 0}{5} = 50 \text{ mm}$$

$$\overline{y} = \frac{\Sigma y}{n} = \frac{y_1 + y_2 + y_3 + \dots + y_n}{n}$$

$$\therefore \quad \overline{y} = \frac{50 + 100 + 0 + 0 + 100}{5} = 50 \text{ mm}$$

b. To find radial distances (c_n): From CG of the rivet **[Fig. 7.33(b)]**, we have

Distance from CG (mm)	Rivet Nos.				
	1	2	3	4	5
$x_n' = (\bar{x} \sim x_n)$	0	50	50	50	50
$y_n' = (\bar{y} \sim y_n)$	0	50	50	50	50
$c_n = \sqrt{x_n'^2 + y_n'^2}$	0	70.71	70.71	70.71	70.71
$\cos\theta_n = x_n'/c_n$	0	0.71	0.71	0.71	0.71
θ_n (deg)	90	45	45	45	45

c. Shear loads:
   i. Direct or primary shear load:

$$F' = \frac{F}{n} = \frac{10 \times 10^3}{5} = 2000 \text{ N} \qquad \textbf{... 5.18/ Pg 83, DHB}$$

   ii. Secondary shear load: The most heavily loaded rivets are those which are situated at the greatest distance from the tilting edge, i.e. rivets located at c_2 and/or c_3.

$$F_n'' = \frac{Fec_n}{\Sigma c^2} \qquad \textbf{... 5.20/ Pg 83, DHB}$$

i.e.
$$F_2'' = \frac{Fec_2}{(c_1^2 + c_2^2 + c_3^2 + c_4^2 + c_5^2)}$$

$$= \frac{(10 \times 10^3) \times 200 \times 70.71}{0 + (4 \times 70.71^2)}$$

$$F_2'' = 7071.14 \text{ N} = F''$$

d. Resultant shear load:

$$F_R = \sqrt{F'^2 + F''^2 + 2F'F''\cos\theta} \qquad \textbf{... 5.21/ Pg 83, DHB}$$

Since load is applied at an angle, we have $\cos\theta = (\cos 45° - \cos 30°) = \cos 15°$

$$= \sqrt{2000^2 + 7071.14^2 + (2 \times 2000 \times 7071.14 \times \cos 15°)}$$

$$F_R = 9017.86 \text{ N}$$

e. Diameter of the rivet hole:
   Eq. (i) yields...

$$A = \frac{9017.86}{100} = 90.178 \text{ mm}^2$$

i.e.
$$\frac{\pi d^2}{4} = 90.178 \text{ mm}^2$$

$\therefore \qquad d = 10.71 \text{ mm}$

Thus the standard diameter of rivet hole,

$$d = 13 \text{ mm}$$

and the diameter of rivet,

$$d = d_1 + 1 \text{ mm}, \quad \text{for } 12 \text{ mm} \leq d \leq 24 \text{ mm}$$
$$d_1 = 13 - 1 = 12 \text{ mm}$$

24. **For the riveted joint shown in Fig. 7.34(a), determine the size of the rivet taking permissible shear stress in rivets as 60 MPa.**

VTU – Dec. 06/ Jan 2007 – 10 Marks

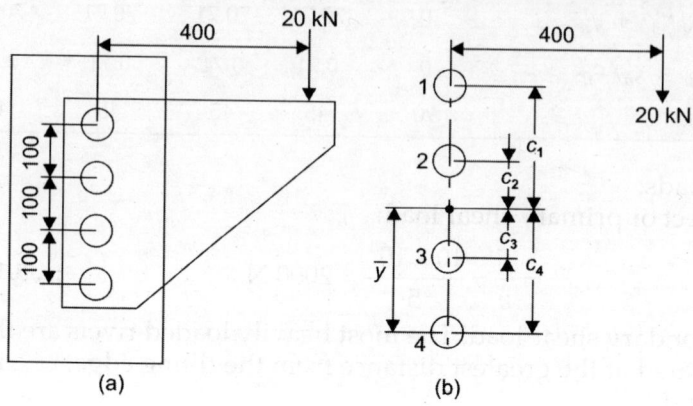

Fig. 7.34: Problem 24

Solution: $F = 20 \times 10^3$ N, $e = 400$ mm, $\tau = 60$ MPa, $d_1 = ?$

We know that $\qquad \tau = \dfrac{F_R}{A}$ $\qquad\qquad$ ... Eq. (i)

a. To find CG of the rivet group: From **Fig. 7.34(a)**, taking rivet '4' as the reference, we have

Distance (mm)	Rivet Nos.			
	1	2	3	4
x_n	0	0	0	0
y_n	300	200	100	0

$$\bar{x} = \frac{\Sigma x}{n} = 0$$

and

$$\bar{y} = \frac{\Sigma y}{n} = \frac{y_1 + y_2 + y_3 + \dots + y_n}{n}$$

$\therefore \qquad\qquad \bar{y} = \dfrac{300 + 200 + 100 + 0}{4} = 150 \text{ mm}$

b. To find radial distances (c_n): From CG of the rivet [**Fig. 7.34(b)**], we have

Distance from CG (mm)	Rivet Nos.			
	1	2	3	4
$x_n' = (\bar{x} \sim x_n)$	0	0	0	0
$y_n' = (\bar{y} \sim y_n)$	150	50	50	150
$c_n = \sqrt{x_n'^2 + y_n'^2}$	150	50	50	150
$\cos\theta_n = x_n'/c_n$	0	0	0	0

c. Shear loads:

  i. Direct or primary shear load:

$$F' = \frac{F}{n} = \frac{20 \times 10^3}{5} = 5000 \text{ N} \qquad \text{... 5.18/ Pg 83, DHB}$$

  ii. Secondary shear load: The most heavily loaded rivets are those which are situated at the greatest distance from the tilting edge, i.e. rivets located at c_1.

$$F_n'' = \frac{Fec_n}{\Sigma c^2} \qquad \text{... 5.20/ Pg 83, DHB}$$

i.e.

$$F_1'' = \frac{Fec_1}{(c_1^2 + c_2^2 + c_3^2 + c_4^2)}$$

$$= \frac{(20 \times 10^3) \times 400 \times 150}{(150^2 + 50^2 + 50^2 + 150^2)}$$

$$F_1'' = 24000 \text{ N} = F''$$

d. Resultant shear load:

$$F_R = \sqrt{F'^2 + F''^2 + 2F'F'' \cos\theta} \qquad \text{... 5.21/ Pg 83, DHB}$$

$$= \sqrt{5000^2 + 24000^2 + (2 \times 5000 \times 24000 \times 0)}$$

(Here $\cos\theta_1 = 0$)

$$F_R = 24515.30 \text{ N}$$

e. Diameter of the rivet hole:

  Eq. (i) yields...

$$A = \frac{24515.30}{60} = 405.58 \text{ mm}^2$$

i.e.

$$\frac{\pi d^2}{4} = 405.58 \text{ mm}^2$$

$\therefore \qquad d = 22.81 \text{ mm}$

Thus the standard diameter of rivet hole,

$$d = 23 \text{ mm}$$

and the diameter of rivet,

$$d = d_1 + 1 \text{ mm}, \quad \text{for } 12 \text{ mm} \le d \le 24 \text{ mm}$$

$$d_1 = 23 - 1 = 22 \text{ mm}$$

25. **A bracket is supported by means of four rivets of same size as shown in Fig. 7.35(a). Determine the diameter of the rivet if the maximum shear stress in the rivet is 90 N/mm².**

VTU – June/ July 2013 – 10 Marks

Solution: $F = 10 \times 10^3 \text{ N}$, $e = 200 + 60 = 260 \text{ mm}$, $\tau = 90 \text{ MPa}$, $d_1 = ?$

We know that $\qquad \tau = \frac{F_R}{A}$ $\qquad$ ... Eq. (i)

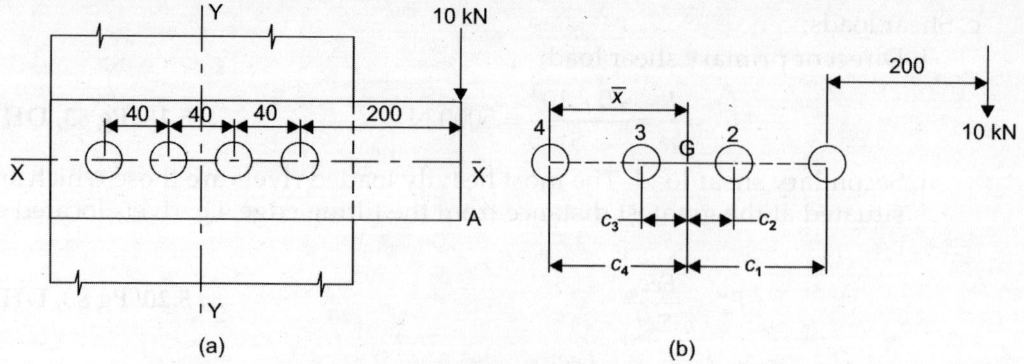

Fig. 7.35: Problem 25

a. To find CG of the rivet group: From **Fig. 7.35(a)**, taking rivet '4' as the reference, we have

Distance (mm)	Rivet Nos.			
	1	2	3	4
x_n	120	80	40	0
y_n	0	0	0	0

$$\bar{x} = \frac{\Sigma x}{n} = \frac{x_1 + x_2 + x_3 + \dots x_n}{n}$$

$$\therefore \qquad \bar{x} = \frac{120 + 80 + 40 + 0}{4} = 60 \text{ mm}$$

and $\qquad \bar{y} = \frac{\Sigma y}{n} = 0$

b. To find radial distances (c_n): From CG of the rivet **[Fig. 7.35(b)]**, we have

Distance from CG (mm)	Rivet Nos.			
	1	2	3	4
$x'_n = (\bar{x} \sim x_n)$	60	20	20	60
$y'_n = (\bar{y} \sim y_n)$	0	0	0	0
$c_n = \sqrt{x'^2_n + y'^2_n}$	60	20	20	60
$\cos\theta_n = x'_n / c_n$	1	1	1	1

c. Shear loads:
   i. Direct or primary shear load:

$$F' = \frac{F}{n} = \frac{10 \times 10^3}{4} = 2500 \text{ N} \qquad \text{... 5.18/ Pg 83, DHB}$$

   ii. Secondary shear load: The most heavily loaded rivets are those which are situated at the greatest distance from the tilting edge, i.e. rivets located at c_1.

$$F''_n = \frac{Fec_n}{\Sigma c^2} \qquad \text{... 5.20/ Pg 83, DHB}$$

i.e.
$$F_1'' = \frac{Fec_1}{(c_1^2 + c_2^2 + c_3^2 + c_4^2)}$$

$$= \frac{(10 \times 10^3) \times 260 \times 60}{(60^2 + 20^2 + 20^2 + 60^2)}$$

$$F_1'' = 19500 \text{ N} = F''$$

d. Resultant shear load:

$$F_R = \sqrt{F'^2 + F''^2 + 2F'F''\cos\theta} \qquad \text{... 5.21/ Pg 83, DHB}$$

$$= \sqrt{2500^2 + 19500^2 + (2 \times 2500 \times 19500 \times 1)}$$

(Here $\cos\theta_1 = 1$)

$$F_R = 22000 \text{ N}$$

e. Diameter of the rivet hole:

Eq. (i) yields...

$$A = \frac{22000}{90} = 244.44 \text{ mm}^2$$

i.e.
$$\frac{\pi d^2}{4} = 244.44 \text{ mm}^2$$

$$\therefore \qquad d = 17.64 \text{ mm}$$

Thus the standard diameter of rivet hole,

$$d = 19$$

and the diameter of rivet,

$$d = d_1 + 1 \text{ mm}, \quad \text{for } 12 \text{ mm} \le d \le 24 \text{ mm}$$

$$d_1 = 19 - 1 = 18 \text{ mm}$$

26. **Find the diameter of the rivet shown in Fig. 7.36(a). The maximum shearing stress on the most heavily loaded rivet is 56 N/mm².**

VTU – Dec. 07/ Jan. 2008 – 08 Marks

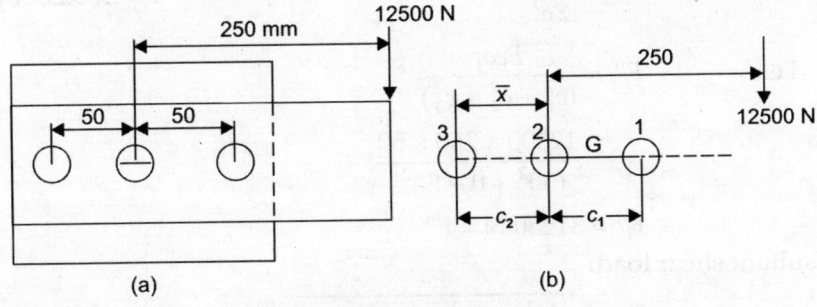

Fig. 7.36: Problem 26

Solution: $F = 12500$ N, $e = 250$ mm, $\tau = 56$ MPa, $d_1 = ?$

We know that
$$\tau = \frac{F_R}{A} \qquad \text{... Eq. (i)}$$

a. To find CG of the rivet group: From **Fig. 7.36(a)**, taking rivet '3' as the reference, we have

Distance (mm)	Rivet Nos.		
	1	2	3
x_n	100	50	0
y_n	0	0	0

$$\bar{x} = \frac{\Sigma x}{n} = \frac{x_1 + x_2 + x_3 + ... x_n}{n}$$

$$\therefore \quad \bar{x} = \frac{100 + 50 + 0}{3} = 50 \text{ mm}$$

and $$\bar{y} = \frac{\Sigma y}{n} = 0$$

b. To find radial distances (c_n): From CG of the rivet [**Fig. 7.36(b)**], we have

Distance from CG (mm)	Rivet Nos.		
	1	2	3
$x'_n = (\bar{x} \sim x_n)$	50	0	50
$y'_n = (\bar{y} \sim y_n)$	0	0	0
$c_n = \sqrt{x'^2_n + y'^2_n}$	50	0	50
$\cos\theta_n = x'_n/c_n$	1	0	1

c. Shear loads:
   i. Direct or primary shear load:

$$F' = \frac{F}{n} = \frac{12500}{3} = 4166.67 \text{ N} \qquad \text{... 5.18/ Pg 83, DHB}$$

   ii. Secondary shear load: The most heavily loaded rivets are those which are situated at the greatest distance from the tilting edge, i.e. rivets located at c_1.

$$F''_n = \frac{Fec_n}{\Sigma c^2} \qquad \text{... 5.20/ Pg 83, DHB}$$

   i.e. $$F''_1 = \frac{Fec_1}{(c_1^2 + c_2^2 + c_3^2)}$$

$$= \frac{12500 \times 250 \times 50}{(50^2 + 0 + 50^2)}$$

$$F''_1 = 31250 \text{ N} = F''$$

d. Resultant shear load:

$$F_R = \sqrt{F'^2 + F''^2 + 2F'F'' \cos\theta} \qquad \text{... 5.21/ Pg 83, DHB}$$

$$= \sqrt{4166.67^2 + 31250^2 + (2 \times 4166.67 \times 31250 \times 1)}$$

$$\text{(Here } \cos\theta_1 = 1)$$

$$F_R = 35416.67 \text{ N}$$

e. Diameter of the rivet hole:

Eq. (i) yields…

$$A = \frac{35416.67}{56} = 632.44 \text{ mm}^2$$

i.e.

$$\frac{\pi d^2}{4} = 632.44 \text{ mm}^2$$

$$\therefore \qquad d = 28.37 \text{ mm}$$

Thus the standard diameter of rivet hole,

$$d = 28.5 \text{ mm}$$

and the diameter of rivet,

$$d = d_1 + 1 \text{ mm}, \quad \text{for } 27 \text{ mm} \leq d \leq 36 \text{ mm}$$

$$d_1 = 28.5 - 1.5 = 27 \text{ mm}$$

27. **Find the value of rivet diameter for the joint shown in Fig. 7.37(a) based on a working shear stress of 100 MPa.**

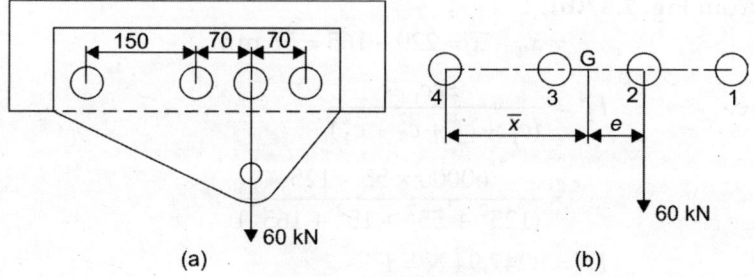

(a) (b)

Fig. 7.37: Problem 27

Solution: $F = 60000 \text{ N}, \tau = 100 \text{ MPa}, n = 4, d_1 = ?$

We know that $\qquad \tau = \dfrac{F_R}{A} \qquad\qquad$ … Eq. (i)

a. To find CG of the rivet group: From **Fig. 7.37(a)**, taking rivet '4' as the reference, we have

Distance (mm)	Rivet Nos.			
	1	2	3	4
x_n	290	220	150	0
y_n	0	0	0	0

$$\bar{x} = \frac{\Sigma x}{n} = \frac{x_1 + x_2 + x_3 + \dots x_n}{n}$$

$$\therefore \qquad \bar{x} = \frac{290 + 220 + 150 + 0}{4} = 165 \text{ mm}$$

and $\qquad \bar{y} = \dfrac{\Sigma y}{n} = 0$

b. To find radial distances (c_n): From CG of the rivet **[Fig. 7.37(b)]**, we have

Distance from CG (mm)	Rivet Nos.			
	1	2	3	4
$x'_n = (\bar{x} \sim x_n)$	125	55	15	165
$y'_n = (\bar{y} \sim y_n)$	0	0	0	0
$c_n = \sqrt{x'^2_n + y'^2_n}$	125	55	15	165
$\cos\theta_n = x'_n / c_n$	1	1	1	1

i. Direct or primary shear load:

$$F' = \frac{F}{n} = \frac{60000}{4} = 15000 \text{ N} \qquad \textbf{... 5.18/ Pg 83, DHB}$$

ii. Secondary shear load: Based on observations, it is found that rivet at c_1 is heavily loaded.

$$F''_n = \frac{Fec_n}{\Sigma c^2} \qquad \textbf{... 5.20/ Pg 83, DHB}$$

From **Fig. 7.37(b)**,

$$e = x_2 \sim \bar{x} = 220 - 165 = 55 \text{ mm}$$

i.e.

$$F''_1 = \frac{Fec_1}{(c_1^2 + c_2^2 + c_3^2 + c_4^2)}$$

$$= \frac{60000 \times 55 \times 125}{(125^2 + 55^2 + 15^2 + 165^2)}$$

$$F''_1 = 8947.94 \text{ N} = F''$$

c. Resultant shear load:

$$F_R = \sqrt{F'^2 + F''^2 + 2F'F'' \cos\theta} \qquad \textbf{... 5.21/ Pg 83, DHB}$$

$$= \sqrt{15000^2 + 8947.94^2 + (2 \times 15000 \times 8947.94 \times 1)}$$

(Here $\cos\theta_1 = 1$)

$$F_R = 23947.94 \text{ N}$$

d. Diameter of the rivet hole:

Eq. (i) yields...

$$A = \frac{23947.94}{100} = 239.48 \text{ mm}^2$$

i.e.

$$\frac{\pi d^2}{4} = 239.48 \text{ mm}^2$$

$\therefore \qquad d = 17.46 \text{ mm}$

Thus the standard diameter of rivet hole,

$$d = 19 \text{ mm}$$

and the diameter of rivet,

$$d = d_1 + 1 \text{ mm}, \quad \text{for } 12 \text{ mm} \le d \le 24 \text{ mm}$$

$$d_1 = 19 - 1 = 18 \text{ mm}$$

28. **Figure 7.38(a) shows an arrangement of rivets subjected to eccentric load. If all the rivets have a common diameter of 16 mm, find the distance 'a' if the maximum shear stress in the rivet is limited to 95 MPa.**

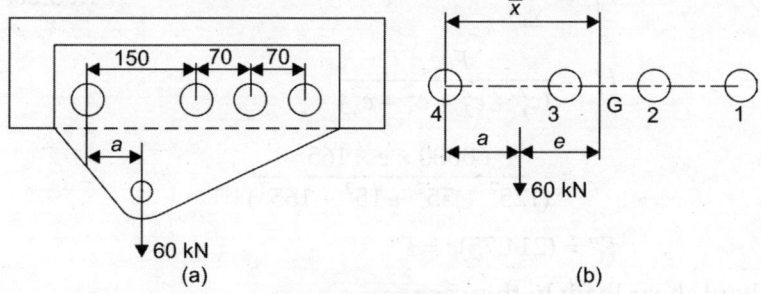

Fig. 7.38: Problem 28

Solution: $F = 60000$ N, $d = 16$ mm, $\tau = 95$ MPa, $n = 4$, $a = ?$

We know that
$$\tau = \frac{F_R}{A}$$

∴
$$F_R = 95 \times \left(\frac{\pi \times 16^2}{4}\right) = 19100.88 \text{ N} \qquad \text{... Eq. (i)}$$

a. To find CG of the rivet group: From **Fig. 7.38(a)**, taking rivet '4' as the reference, we have

Distance (mm)	Rivet Nos.			
	1	2	3	4
x_n	290	220	150	0
y_n	0	0	0	0

$$\bar{x} = \frac{\Sigma x}{n} = \frac{x_1 + x_2 + x_3 + \dots x_n}{n}$$

∴
$$\bar{x} = \frac{290 + 220 + 150 + 0}{4} = 165 \text{ mm}$$

and
$$\bar{y} = \frac{\Sigma y}{n} = 0$$

b. To find radial distances (c_n): From CG of the rivet [**Fig. 7.38(b)**], we have

Distance from CG (mm)	Rivet Nos.			
	1	2	3	4
$x'_n = (\bar{x} \sim x_n)$	125	55	15	165
$y'_n = (\bar{y} \sim y_n)$	0	0	0	0
$c_n = \sqrt{x'^2_n + y'^2_n}$	125	55	15	165
$\cos\theta_n = x'_n/c_n$	1	1	1	1

i. Direct or primary shear load:

$$F' = \frac{F}{n} = \frac{60000}{4} = 15000 \text{ N} \qquad \text{... 5.18/ Pg 83, DHB}$$

ii. Secondary shear load: Based on observations, it is found that rivet at c_4 is heavily loaded.

$$F_n'' = \frac{Fec_n}{\Sigma c^2}$$

... 5.20/ Pg 83, DHB

i.e.

$$F_1'' = \frac{Fec_4}{(c_1^2 + c_2^2 + c_3^2 + c_4^2)}$$

$$= \frac{60000 \times e \times 165}{(125^2 + 55^2 + 15^2 + 165^2)}$$

$$F_1'' = (214.75)e = F''$$

c. Resultant shear load: In this case

$$F_R = F' + F''$$

$$F_R = 15000 + (214.75)e$$

... Eq. (ii)

Equating Eqs. (i) and (ii), we have

$$19100.88 = 15000 + (214.75)e$$

$$e = 19.10 \text{ mm}$$

But from **Fig. 7.37(b)**, $a = \bar{x} - e = 165 - 19.10 = 145.9$ mm

7.14.2 Load Acting Perpendicular to the Axis of the Rivet

The concepts and problems dealt in this section are similar to those dealt in Unit 4 (**Threaded fasteners, Sec. 4.10.2**), except that N is replaced with n, as given below.

Equivalent tensile load,

$$F_{te} = \frac{1}{2}\left(F_1 + \sqrt{F_1^2 + 4F'^2}\right)$$

... 9.7(c)/Pg 130, DHB

Equivalent shear load,

$$F_{se} = \frac{1}{2}\sqrt{F_1^2 + 4F'^2} = \frac{1}{2}(F_1^2 + 4F'^2)^{1/2}$$

... 9.7(d)/Pg 130, DHB

In general, the most heavily loaded rivets are those which are situated at the greatest distance from the tilting edge, i.e. bolts located at l_n

i.e.

$$F_n = F_1 = \frac{Fel_n}{l_1^2 + l_2^2 + l_3^2 + ...} = \frac{Fel_n}{\Sigma l^2}$$

... 9.7(b)/Pg 130, DHB

where suffix 'n' refers to the rivet number.

and

$$F' = \frac{F}{n}$$

... 9.7(a)/Pg 130, DHB

When the equivalent loads on the rivet are known, the size of the rivet can be calculated based on the permissible tensile stress as:

$$A = \frac{F_{te}}{\sigma_t}$$

... (Eq. 4.49)

On the basis of shear stress,

$$A = \frac{F_{se}}{\tau} \qquad \qquad \dots \text{(Eq. 4.50)}$$

where

$$A = \frac{\pi d^2}{4} \text{ and } d = \text{diameter of rivet hole}$$

29. **Figure 7.39(a) shows a bracket fixed on a steel column by means of four rivets. Find the diameter of rivet required to take up a load of 20 kN. Assume permissible tensile and shear stress in the rivet material to be 77 MPa and 56 MPa respectively.**

VTU – Dec. 2011 – 10 Marks

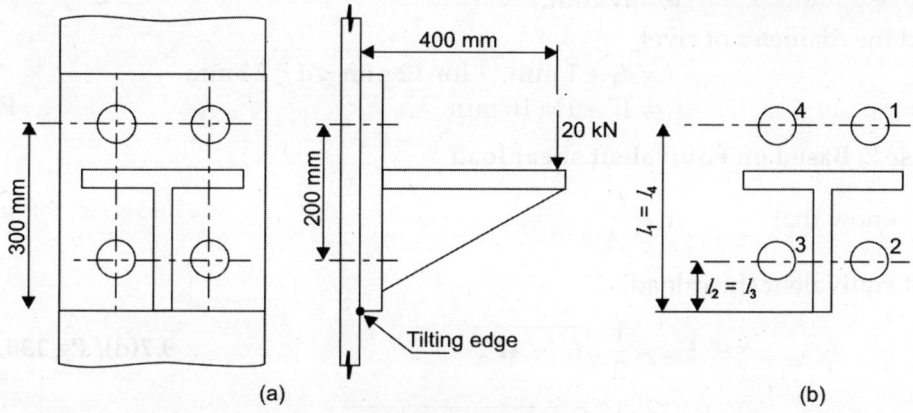

(a)   (b)

Fig. 7.39: Problem 29

Solution: $n = 4$, $d = ?$, $F = 20 \times 10^3$ N, $\sigma_t = 77$ MPa, $\tau = 56$ MPa.
From **Fig. 7.39(b)**, $l_1 = l_4 = 300$ mm, $l_2 = l_3 = 100$ mm, $e = 400$ mm.

Case 1: Based on equivalent tensile load:

We know that $\quad \sigma_t = \dfrac{F_{te}}{A_1} \qquad \qquad \dots \text{Eq. (i)}$

But equivalent tensile load,

$$F_{te} = \frac{1}{2}\left(F_1 + \sqrt{F_1^2 + 4F'^2}\right) \qquad \dots \text{Eq. (ii) 9.7(c)/ Pg 130, DHB}$$

- Direct shear load,

$$F' = \frac{F}{n} = \frac{20 \times 10^3}{4} = 5000 \qquad \dots \text{9.7(a)/ Pg 130, DHB}$$

- Maximum secondary tensile force,

$$F_1 = \frac{Fel_n}{\Sigma l^2} \qquad \qquad \dots \text{9.7(b)/ Pg 130, DHB}$$

$$= \frac{Fel_1}{2\left(l_1^2 + l_2^2\right)}$$

$$F_1 = \frac{(20 \times 10^3) \times 400 \times 300}{2(300^2 + 100^2)} = 12000 \text{ N}$$

∴ Eq. (ii) yields...

$$F_{te} = \frac{1}{2}\left[12000 + \sqrt{12000^2 + (4 \times 5000^2)}\right] = 13810.25 \text{ N}$$

∴ Eq. (i) yields...

$$A_1 = \frac{13810.25}{77} = 179.35 \text{ mm}^2$$

i.e.

$$\frac{\pi d^2}{4} = 179.35 \text{ mm}^2$$

∴

$$d = 15.11 \text{ mm}$$

Thus the standard diameter of rivet hole,

$$d = 17 \text{ mm}$$

and the diameter of rivet,

$$d = d_1 + 1 \text{ mm}, \quad \text{for } 12 \text{ mm} \leq d \leq 24 \text{ mm}$$
$$d_1 = 17 - 1 = 16 \text{ mm} \qquad \qquad \text{... Eq. (iii)}$$

Case 2: Based on equivalent shear load

We know that $\qquad \tau = \dfrac{F_{se}}{A_1} \qquad \qquad$ ... Eq. (iv)

But equivalent shear load,

$$F_{se} = \frac{1}{2}\sqrt{F_1^2 + 4F'^2} \qquad \qquad \text{... 9.7(d)/ Pg 130, DHB}$$

or

$$F_{se} = \frac{1}{2}\sqrt{12000^2 + (4 \times 5000^2)} = 7810.25 \text{ N}$$

∴ Eq. (iv) yields $\qquad A_1 = \dfrac{7810.25}{56} = 139.47 \text{ mm}^2$

i.e.

$$\frac{\pi d^2}{4} = 139.47 \text{ mm}^2$$

∴

$$d = 13.32 \text{ mm}$$

Thus the standard diameter of rivet hole,

$$d = 15 \text{ mm}$$

and the diameter of rivet,

$$d = d_1 + 1 \text{ mm} \quad \text{for } 12 \text{ mm} \leq d \leq 24 \text{ mm}$$
$$d_1 = 15 - 1 = 14 \text{ mm} \qquad \qquad \text{... Eq. (v)}$$

Based on Eqs. (iii) and (v), select maximum diameter. Hence $d = 16$ mm.

30. **Determine the safe value of P for a joint loaded as shown in Fig. 7.40, limiting the maximum normal stress induced to 80 MPa and maximum shear stress induced to 60 MPa.**

VTU – July/ Aug. 2005 – 10 Marks

Solution: $n = 6$, $P = ?$, $\sigma_t = 80$ MPa, $\tau = 60$ MPa.
From **Fig. 7.40**, $d_1 = d_6 = 25$ mm, $d_2 = d_5 = 20$ mm, $d_3 = d_4 = 15$ mm, $l_1 = l_6 = 900$ mm, $l_2 = l_5 = 500$ mm, $l_3 = l_4 = 200$ mm, $e = 1000$ mm.

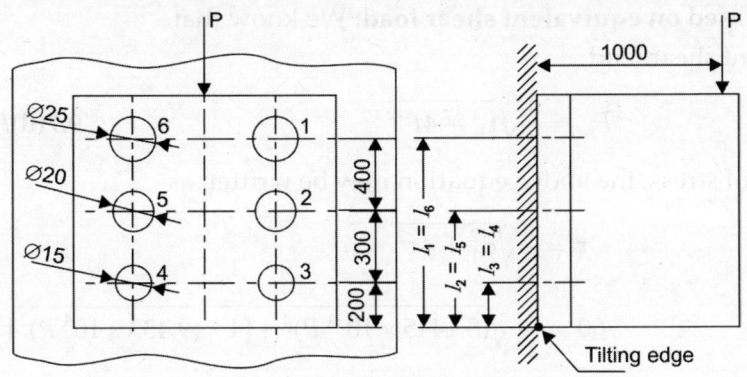

Fig. 7.40: Problem 30

Case 1: Based on equivalent tensile load: We know that
Equivalent tensile load,

$$F_{te} = \frac{1}{2}\left(F_1 + \sqrt{F_1^2 + 4F'^2}\right) \qquad \ldots 9.7(c)/\ Pg\ 130,\ DHB$$

In terms of stress, the above equation may be written as

$$\sigma_t = \frac{1}{2}\left(\sigma_1 + \sqrt{\sigma_1^2 + 4\tau^2}\right) \qquad \ldots Eq.\ (i)$$

In this problem the safe load the system can carry depends upon the least diameter of the rivet. Hence we have d_3.

- Direct shear load,

$$F' = \frac{F}{n} = \frac{P}{6} = 0.1667\,P \qquad \ldots 9.7(a)/\ Pg\ 130,\ DHB$$

and shear stress,

$$\tau = \frac{F'}{A} = \frac{0.1667\,P}{\pi \times 15^2/4} = (9.433 \times 10^{-4})P$$

- Maximum secondary tensile force,

$$F_1 = \frac{Fel_n}{\Sigma l^2} \qquad \ldots 9.7(b)/\ Pg\ 130,\ DHB$$

i.e.

$$F_3 = \frac{Pel_3}{2\left(l_1^2 + l_2^2 + l_3^2\right)} = \frac{P \times 1000 \times 200}{2(900^2 + 500^2 + 200^2)} = (90.91 \times 10^{-3})P$$

and tensile stress,

$$\sigma_3 = \frac{F_3}{A} = \frac{(90.91 \times 10^{-3})P}{\pi \times 15^2/4} = \left(5.1445 \times 10^{-4}\right)P$$

∴ Eq. (i) yields...

$$80 = \frac{1}{2}\left[(5.1445 \times 10^{-4})\,P + \sqrt{(5.1445 \times 10^{-4}\,P)^2 + [4 \times (9.433 \times 10^{-4}\,P)^2]}\right]$$

$$= 1.235 \times 10^{-3}\,P$$

∴ $\qquad P = 64777.33\ N \qquad \ldots Eq.\ (ii)$

Case 2: Based on equivalent shear load: We know that

Equivalent shear load,

$$F_{se} = \frac{1}{2}\sqrt{F_1^2 + 4F'^2} \qquad \text{... 9.7(d)/Pg 130, DHB}$$

In terms of stress, the above equation may be written as

$$\tau = \frac{1}{2}\sqrt{\sigma_1^2 + 4\tau^2}$$

$$60 = \frac{1}{2}\left[\sqrt{(5.1445 \times 10^{-4}\,P)^2 + [4 \times (9.433 \times 10^4\,P)^2]}\right]$$

$$60 = 9.777 \times 10^{-4}\,P$$

∴ $\qquad\qquad P = 61368.52\,\text{N} \qquad\qquad \text{... Eq. (iii)}$

Based on Eqs. (ii) and (iii), select the minimum load as the safe load for the joint.

i.e. $\qquad\qquad P = 61368.52\,\text{N}$

31. **Determine the maximum stresses induced in the worst stressed rivet in a riveted joint as shown in Fig. 7.41.**

VTU – July 2006 – 10 Marks

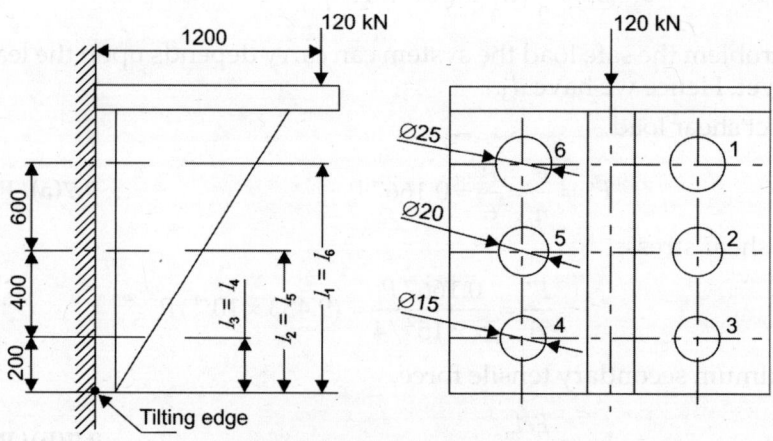

Fig. 7.41: Problem 31

Solution: $n = 6$, $F = 120 \times 10^3\,\text{N}$, $\sigma_t = ?$, $\tau = ?$.

From **Fig. 7.41**, $d_1 = d_6 = 25$ mm, $d_2 = d_5 = 20$ mm, $d_3 = d_4 = 15$ mm, $l_1 = l_6 = 1200$ mm, $l_2 = l_5 = 600$ mm, $l_3 = l_4 = 200$ mm, $e = 1200$ mm.

Case 1: Based on equivalent tensile load: We know that

Equivalent tensile load,

$$F_{te} = \frac{1}{2}\left(F_1 + \sqrt{F_1^2 + 4F'^2}\right) \qquad \text{... 9.7(c)/ Pg 130, DHB}$$

In terms of stress, the above equation may be written as

$$\sigma_t = \frac{1}{2}\left(\sigma_1 + \sqrt{\sigma_1^2 + 4\tau^2}\right) \qquad\qquad \text{... Eq. (i)}$$

In this problem the worst stress rivet having the least diameter, i.e. d_3.

- Direct shear load,

$$F' = \frac{F}{n} = \frac{120 \times 10^3}{6} = 20000 \text{ N} \qquad \text{... 9.7(a)/ Pg 130, DHB}$$

and shear stress,

$$\tau = \frac{F'}{A} = \frac{20000}{\pi \times 15^2/4} = 113.18 \text{ MPa}$$

- Maximum secondary tensile force,

$$F_1 = \frac{Fel_n}{\Sigma l^2} \qquad \text{... 9.7(b)/ Pg 130, DHB}$$

i.e.

$$F_3 = \frac{Fel_3}{2\left(l_1^2 + l_2^2 + l_3^2\right)} = \frac{120 \times 10^3 \times 1200 \times 200}{2(1200^2 + 600^2 + 200^2)} = 7826.08 \text{ N}$$

and tensile stress,

$$\sigma_3 = \frac{F_3}{A} = \frac{7826.08}{\pi \times 15^2/4} = 44.29 \text{ MPa}$$

∴ Eq. (i) yields...

$$\sigma_t = \frac{1}{2}\left[44.29 + \sqrt{44.29^2 + (4 \times 113.18^2)}\right] = 137.47 \text{ MPa}$$

Case 2: Based on equivalent shear load: We know that
Equivalent shear load,

$$F_{se} = \frac{1}{2}\sqrt{F_1^2 + 4F'^2} \qquad \text{... 9.7(d)/Pg 130, DHB}$$

In terms of stress, the above equation may be written as

$$\tau = \frac{1}{2}\sqrt{\sigma_1^2 + 4\tau^2}$$

$$60 = \frac{1}{2}\left[\sqrt{44.29^2 + (4 \times 113.18^2)}\right] = 115.33 \text{ MPa}$$

Note: *For more problems, repeat problems under Sec. 4.10.2 in Unit 4 by replacing the term bolt with rivets.*

WELDED JOINTS

7.15 INTRODUCTION

A welded joint is a permanent joint which is obtained by the fusion of the edges of two parts to be joined together. Welding is the process of joining two similar or dissimilar metals by the application of heat and/ or application of pressure and addition of filler material. The most commonly employed method of heat generation for fusion of parts is the electric arc method due to greater speed of welding.

Advantages

- Welded structures are comparatively lighter than corresponding riveted structures.
- Welded joints are economical to riveted joint.
- The welded joints provide high efficiency.
- Welded joint has greater strength compared to that of riveted joint.
- A welded structure has better finish and appearance than the corresponding riveted structure.
- Alterations and additions to the existing structure are easy.
- Difficult shapes can be more easily welded.
- It is possible to weld any part of a structure, but riveting always requires enough clearance.
- In welded connections, the tension members are not weakened as in the case of riveted joints.
- Less noisy.

Disadvantages

- Welding requires skilled labor and supervision.
- Due to uneven heating and cooling of the members during the welding, the members may distort resulting in additional stresses.
- Since there is no provision for expansion and contraction in welded connection, there is possibility of cracks.
- Inspection of welding work is more difficult and costlier than the riveting work.

7.16 TYPES OF WELDED JOINTS

In general welded joints are of two types:

1. **Lap or fillet weld:** A joint obtained by overlapping two members and then welding their edges together is referred to as a lap or fillet joint. A fillet weld has an approximate triangular cross-section joining two surfaces at right angles to each other as in Tee and corner joints. Fillet welds are usually cheaper than butt welds. The most common types of lap joints are shown in **Fig. 7.42. [Fig. 6.2/ Pg 90, DHB]**
   a. Single transverse fillet weld
   b. Double transverse fillet weld
   c. Double parallel fillet weld

Parallel weld: Welds parallel to the direction of applied load are called parallel or longitudinal welds.

Transverse weld: Welds perpendicular to the direction of applied load are called transverse or normal welds.

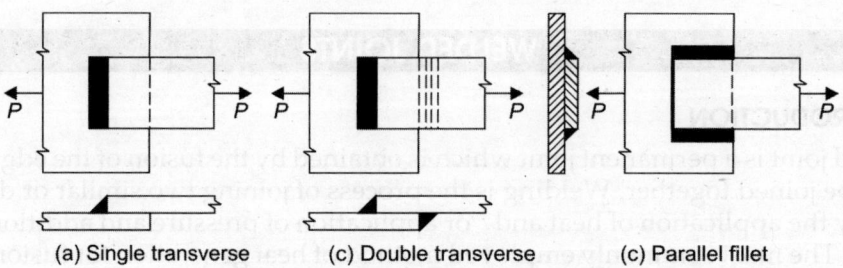

(a) Single transverse   (c) Double transverse   (c) Parallel fillet

Fig. 7.42: Types of lap of fillet joints

2. **Butt or V welds:** A joint obtained by butting (touching) the edges of two members which are in the same plane and then welding them together is referred to as a butt joint. Butt weld is also termed groove weld. These are used to join structural members carrying direct compression or tension.

The most common types of butt joints are shown in **Fig. 7.43**.

   a. Square butt joint
   b. Single V-butt joint
   c. Single U-butt joint
   d. Double V-butt joint
   e. Double U-butt joint.

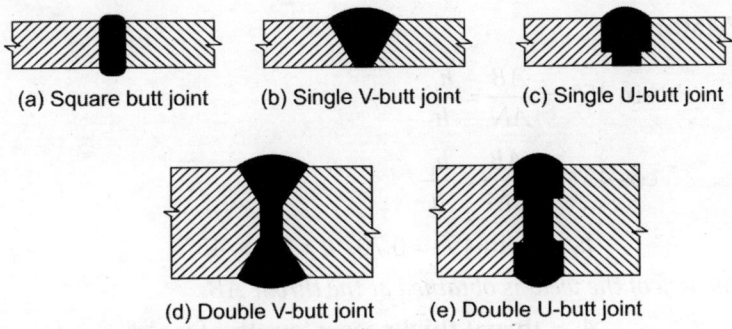

(a) Square butt joint   (b) Single V-butt joint   (c) Single U-butt joint

(d) Double V-butt joint   (e) Double U-butt joint

Fig. 7.43: Types of butt joints

Other forms of welded joints include Tee joint, corner joint and edge joint as shown in **Fig. 7.44**.

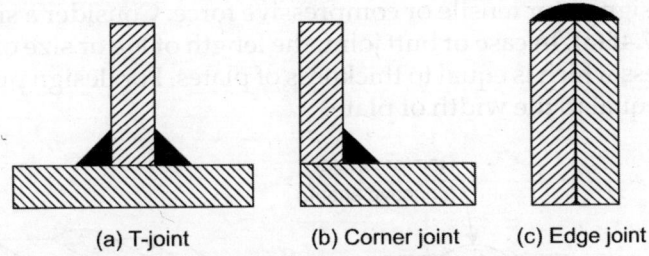

(a) T-joint   (b) Corner joint   (c) Edge joint

Fig. 7.44: Other joints

7.17 DETAILS OF FILLET WELD

Consider a fillet weld as shown in **Fig. 7.45**.

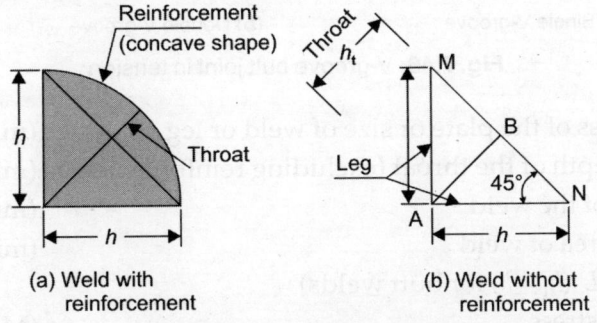

(a) Weld with reinforcement   (b) Weld without reinforcement

Fig. 7.45: Details of fillet weld

Let h = thickness of the plate or size of weld or leg (mm)

h_t = weld depth of the throat   (mm)

L = length of the weld   (mm)

In most applications, fillet or lap welds are employed since fillet welds are stronger than butt welds. Although it is desirable to make fillet weld slightly concave [**Fig. 7.45(a)**], yet a reinforced weld obtained from welding is ground to obtain a right angled triangular section (AMN) with two sides equal to the thickness (h) of plates that are joined. For the purpose of calculations, the concave shape above the triangle is neglected, as shown in **Fig. 7.45(b)**. The minimum area of the weld is obtained at the throat AB.

From **Fig. 7.45(b)**,

$$\sin 45° = \frac{AB}{AN} = \frac{h_t}{h}$$

or

$$\cos 45° = \frac{AB}{AM} = \frac{h_t}{h}$$

∴ $h_t = h \sin 45° = 0.707\,h = h \cos 45°$ ... (Eq. 7.49)

The minimum area of the weld is obtained at the throat AB.

i.e. A_t = throat thickness × length of weld

= $AB × L$

∴ $A_t = h_t \cdot L = 0.707\,hL$ ... (Eq. 7.50)

7.18 STRENGTH OF BUTT WELD

Butt joints are designed for tensile or compressive force. Consider a single V-butt joint as shown in **Fig. 7.46(a)**. In case of butt joint, the length of leg or size of weld is equal to the throat thickness which is equal to thickness of plates. For design purpose the length of weld is taken equal to the width of plate.

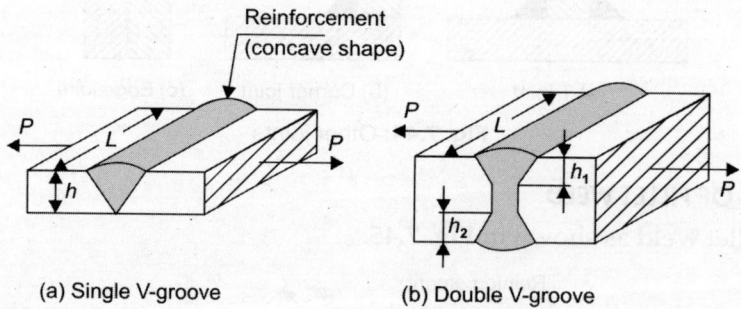

(a) Single V-groove   (b) Double V-groove

Fig. 7.46: V-groove butt joint in tension

Let h = thickness of the plate or size of weld or leg   (mm)

h_t = weld depth of the throat (excluding reinforcement) (mm)

L = length of the weld   (mm)

A_t = throat area of weld   (mm²)

= $h_t \cdot L = h \cdot L$ ($h_t = h$, for butt welds)

σ = normal stress   (MPa)

We know that

$$\text{Normal stress} = \frac{\text{Load}}{\text{Area}}$$

- For a single V-groove butt joint subjected to tensile and/or compressive load [**Fig. 7.46(a)**],

$$\sigma = \frac{P}{A_t} = \frac{P}{h_t \cdot L} = \frac{P}{h \cdot L} \qquad \text{... (Eq. 7.51) \textbf{6.1(a)/ Pg 89, DHB}}$$

- For a double V-groove butt joint subjected to tensile and/or compressive load [**Fig. 7.46(b)**],

$$\sigma = \frac{P}{A_t} = \frac{P}{(h_1 + h_2)L} \qquad \text{... (Eq. 7.52) \textbf{Tb. 6.1/ Pg 92, DHB}}$$

where h_1 = throat thickness at top,

h_2 = throat thickness at bottom

Note:
- *According to experiments carried out at Lincoln Electric Co, a properly made butt joint has equal strength than the plate and hence there is no need for calculating the stresses in the weld.*
- *In calculating the value of throat, reinforcement is neglected. The reinforcement may be desirable in order to compensate for flaws, but the amount of reinforcement varies along the length of the weld and produces stress concentration at end points.*

7.19 STRENGTH OF FILLET WELD

7.19.1 Transverse or Normal Fillet Welds

Welds perpendicular to the direction of applied load are called transverse or normal welds. These joints are designed for tensile strength.

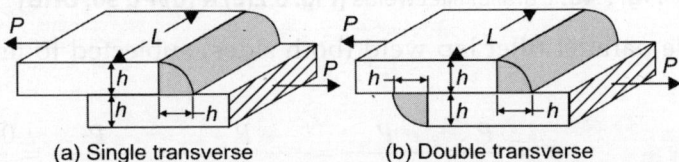

(a) Single transverse   (b) Double transverse

Fig. 7.47: Transverse fillet welds [**Fig. 6.2(a) & (b)/Pg 90, DHB**]

Let h = thickness of the plate or size of weld or leg   (mm)
h_t = weld depth of the throat (excluding reinforcement) (mm)
L = length of each weld   (mm)
$A_t = h_t \cdot L$ = throat area of weld   (mm²)
σ = normal stress   (MPa)
We know that

$$\text{Normal stress} = \frac{\text{Load}}{\text{Area}}$$

- For a single transverse fillet lap weld subjected to tensile load [**Fig. 7.47(a)**],

$$\sigma = \frac{P}{A_t} = \frac{P}{h_t \cdot L} = \frac{P}{0.707\,hL} = \frac{1.414\,P}{hL}$$

$$\text{... (Eq. 7.53) \textbf{6.2(a)/ Pg 90, DHB}}$$

The area resisting the load is always assumed to be the throat area, because weld failures are more often occurs across the throat.

Hence $\qquad A_t = h_t \cdot L = 0.707\,hL$ $\qquad$ ... using (Eq. 7.50)

- For a double transverse fillet lap weld subjected to tensile load **[Fig. 7.47(b)]**,

$$\sigma = \frac{P}{2A_t} = \frac{P}{2(h_t \cdot L)} = \frac{P}{2(0.707\,hL)} = \frac{P}{1.414\,hL} = \frac{0.707\,P}{hL}$$
$$\text{... (Eq. 7.54) } \mathbf{6.2(b)/ \ Pg\ 90,\ DHB}$$

7.19.2 Parallel or Longitudinal Fillet Welds

Welds parallel to the direction of applied load are called parallel or longitudinal welds. These joints are designed for shear strength since the mode of failure is shear.

- For a double parallel fillet lap weld (one side) subjected to tensile load **[Fig. 7.48(a)]**,

$$\sigma = \frac{P}{2A_t} = \frac{P}{2(h_t \cdot L)} = \frac{P}{2(0.707\,hL)} = \frac{P}{1.414\,hL} = \frac{0.707\,P}{hL}$$
$$\text{... (Eq. 7.55) } \mathbf{6.2(c)/ \ Pg\ 90,\ DHB}$$

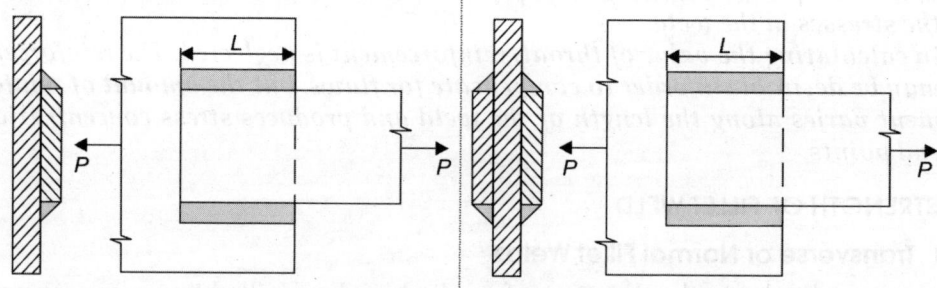

(a) Double parallel fillet (one side of plate) $\qquad$ (b) Double parallel fillet (both sides of plate)

Fig. 7.48: Parallel fillet welds **[Fig. 6.2(c) & (d)/Pg 90, DHB]**

- For a double parallel fillet lap weld (both sides) subjected to tensile load **[Fig. 7.48(b)]**,

$$\sigma = \frac{P}{4A_t} = \frac{P}{4(h_t \cdot L)} = \frac{P}{4(0.707\,hL)} = \frac{P}{2.828\,hL} = \frac{0.354\,P}{hL}$$
$$\text{... (Eq. 7.56) } \mathbf{Tb.\ 6.2(d)/ \ Pg\ 90,\ DHB}$$

Since the parallel fillet welds are subjected to shear stress, on similar lines we have:

- For a double parallel fillet lap weld (one side of plate) subjected to tensile load, the allowable shear stress is given as:

$$\tau = \frac{P}{2A_t} = \frac{P}{2(h_t \cdot L)} = \frac{P}{2(0.707\,hL)} = \frac{P}{1.414\,hL} = \frac{0.707\,P}{hL}$$
$$\text{... (Eq. 7.57)}$$

- For a double parallel fillet lap weld (both sides of plate) subjected to tensile load, the allowable shear stress is given as:

$$\tau = \frac{P}{4A_t} = \frac{P}{4(h_t \cdot L)} = \frac{P}{4(0.707\,hL)} = \frac{P}{2.828\,hL} = \frac{0.354\,P}{hL}$$
$$\text{... (Eq. 7.58)}$$

Note: *According to experiments carried out, transverse fillet welds are somewhat stronger than parallel fillet welds. However the common practice is to treat both of these fillet welds as being of equal strength.*

7.19.3 Combined Parallel and Transverse Fillet Welds

Figure 7.49 indicates a welded joint having both transverse and parallel fillet welds subjected to tensile load. Here the total strength of the joint is given as

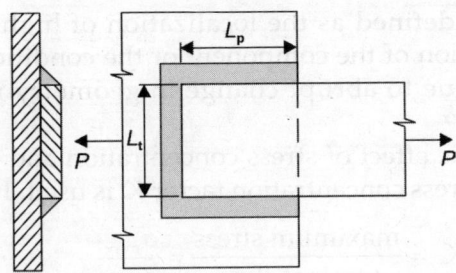

Fig. 7.49: Combined transverse and parallel fillet welds

Total strength of the joint,

$$P = P_t + P_p \qquad \qquad \text{... (Eq. 7.59)}$$

where P_t = strength of transverse weld $= \dfrac{hL_t\sigma}{1.414}$

$$\text{... using (Eq. 7.53) } \textbf{6.2(a)/ Pg 90, DHB}$$

P_p = strength of parallel fillet weld $= \dfrac{hL_p\tau}{0.707}$

$$\text{... using (Eq. 7.57) } \textbf{6.2(d)/ Pg 90, DHB}$$

P = total strength of the joint = σwh
w = width of plate
L_t = length of transverse weld
L_p = length of each parallel weld.

Thus $\qquad \qquad P = \dfrac{hL_t\sigma}{1.414} + \dfrac{hL_p\tau}{0.707}$

or $\qquad \qquad P = 0.707\,hL_t\sigma + 1.414\,hL_p\tau \qquad \text{... (Eq. 7.60)}$

Note:

• *In determining the length of weld required, normally 10 to 15 mm is added to the length of each weld to take care of starting and stopping of weld run or bead.*
• *Stresses in welds subjected to different loadings* ... **Table 6.1/Pg 92, DHB**
• *Design stresses for welds made with mild steel electrodes.*
  ... **Table 6.4/Pg 94, DHB**
• *Strength of shield arc steel welds subjected to repeated loads.*
  ... **Table 6.5/Pg 95, DHB**

AWS = American Welding Society

- *Plate thickness and minimum size of fillet welds.* ... **Table 6.6(a)/Pg 95, DHB**
- *Allowable loads on mild steel fillet welds.* ... **Table 6.6(b)/Pg 95, DHB**
- *Allowable loads on mild steel butt welds.* ... **Table 6.6(c)/Pg 95, DHB**
- *Properties for typical fillet welds, treating weld as a line.*

  ... **Table 6.7/Pg 96, DHB**

7.20 STRESS CONCENTRATION FACTORS

Stress concentration is defined as the localization of high stresses due to abrupt changes in the cross-section of the component or the condition where high localized stresses are produced due to abrupt change in geometry is called stress concentration.

In order to consider the effect of stress concentration and determine the localized stresses, a factor called stress concentration factor K_t is used. It is given as

$$K_t = \frac{\text{maximum stress}}{\text{nominal stress}} = \frac{\sigma_{max}}{\sigma} \qquad \text{... (Eq. 7.61)}$$

where K_t = theoretical elastic stress concentration factor for normal stress (tension or bending)

σ_{max} = maximum stress at the notch

σ = nominal stress

- For direct stress, $\sigma_{max} = \sigma K_t = \left(\dfrac{F}{A}\right) K_t$

  ... (Eq. 7.62) **2.1(a)/Pg 20, DHB [Fig. 2.1(a)/Pg 20, DHB]**

- For bending, $\sigma_{max} = \sigma_b K_t = \left(\dfrac{M}{Z}\right) K_t$

  ... (Eq. 7.63) **2.1(b)/Pg 20, DHB [Fig. 2.1(b)/Pg 20, DHB]**

- For torsion, $\tau_{max} = \tau K_s = \left(\dfrac{Tr}{J}\right) K_s = \left(\dfrac{T}{Z_p}\right) K_s$

  ... (Eq. 7.64) **2.1(c)/Pg 20, DHB [Fig. 2.1(c)/Pg 20, DHB]**

  K_s = theoretical elastic stress concentration factor for shear

Note:

- *For static load conditions, stress concentration factor is taken as unity.*
- *Stress concentration factors for various welds.* ... **Table 6.3/ Pg 94, DHB**

32. **Show that the plane of maximum shear force occurs at 45° for a parallel load on a fillet weld of equal legs.**

Consider a Tee joint having two parallel fillet (load parallel to weld length) welds of equal legs and subjected to tensile load along the weld length as shown in **Fig. 7.50(a)**. The detailed or enlarged portion of the weld ABC is shown in **Fig. 7.50(b)**.

Let h = thickness of the plate or size of weld or leg

h_t = weld depth of the throat

L = length of the each weld

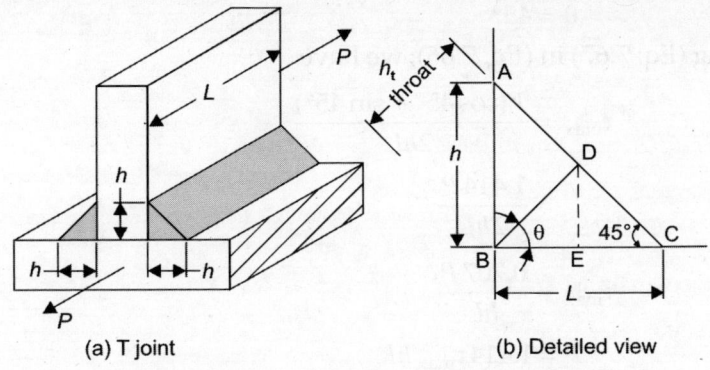

(a) T joint   (b) Detailed view

Fig. 7.50: Tee joint with parallel fillet welds

θ = angle of plane of maximum shear stress

From triangle ABC, we have

$$AB = BC = h$$

$$BC = BE + EC$$

$$= BE + ED \ (\because EC = DE, \text{ as } \angle ECD = 45°)$$

$$= BD \cos\theta + BD \sin\theta$$

$$= BD(\cos\theta + \sin\theta)$$

$$h = h_t(\cos\theta + \sin\theta)$$

$\therefore$
$$h_t = \frac{h}{(\cos\theta + \sin\theta)} \qquad \dots \text{(Eq. 7.65)}$$

For a double parallel fillet weld subjected to tensile load, the shear stress is given as:

$$\tau = \frac{P}{2A_t} = \frac{P}{2(h_t L)} \qquad \dots \text{using (Eq. 7.57)}$$

$$= \frac{P}{2L[h/(\cos\theta + \sin\theta)]}$$

$\therefore$
$$\tau = \frac{P(\cos\theta + \sin\theta)}{2hL} \qquad \dots \text{(Eq. 7.66)}$$

For maximum shear stress, differentiate (Eq. 7.66) with respect to θ and equate to zero.

i.e.
$$\frac{\partial \tau}{\partial \theta} = 0$$

$$\frac{\partial}{\partial \theta}\left[\frac{P(\cos\theta + \sin\theta)}{2hL}\right] = 0$$

$$\left[\frac{P(-\sin\theta + \cos\theta)}{2hL}\right] = 0$$

$$-\sin\theta + \cos\theta = 0$$

$$\sin\theta = \cos\theta$$

i.e.
$$\tan\theta = 1$$

$$\therefore \qquad \theta = 45° \qquad \qquad \text{... (Eq. 7.67)}$$

Substituting (Eq. 7.67) in (Eq. 7.66), we have

$$\tau_{max} = \frac{P(\cos 45° + \sin 45°)}{2hL}$$

$$= \frac{1.414\,P}{2\,hL}$$

$$\therefore \qquad \tau_{max} = \frac{0.707\,P}{hL} \qquad \qquad \text{... (Eq. 7.68a)}$$

or $\qquad\qquad\qquad P = 1.414\tau_{max}\,hL \qquad\qquad\qquad\qquad$ ... (Eq. 7.68b)

Note: (Eq. 7.68a) is same as Eq. (7.57).

33. **Show that the plane of maximum shear force occurs at 67½° for a transverse load on a fillet weld of equal legs or prove that the ratio of strength of parallel to transverse fillet welds is 1.17 or prove that the ratio of strength of transverse to parallel fillet welds is 0.85.**

VTU – Jan/ Feb. 2005 – 06 Marks

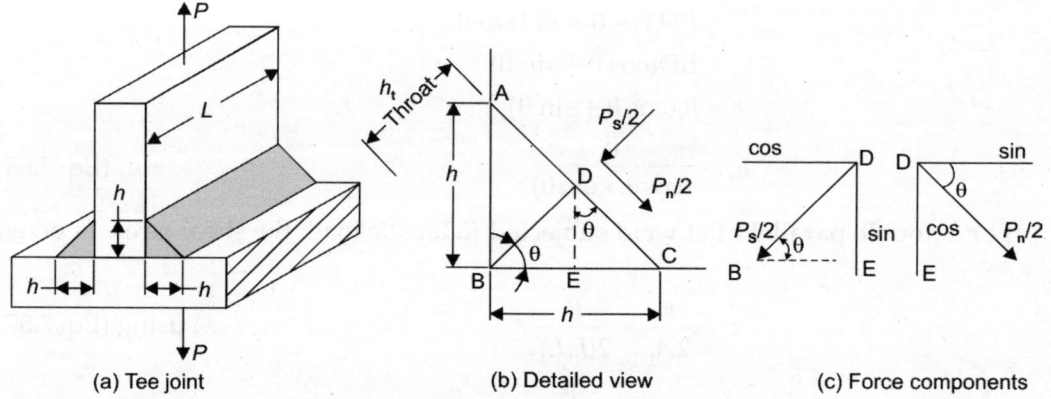

Fig. 7.51: Tee joint with transverse fillet welds

Consider a Tee joint having two transverse fillets (load perpendicular to weld length) welds of equal legs and subjected to tensile load as shown in **Fig. 7.51(a)**. The detailed or enlarged portion of the weld ABC is shown in **Fig. 7.51(b)**. The forces acting on the welds along with components are shown in **Fig. 7.51(c)**.

Let h = thickness of the plate or size of weld or leg

$\quad h_t$ = weld depth of the throat

$\quad L$ = length of the each weld

$\quad \theta$ = angle of plane of maximum shear stress

$\quad P_s$ = shear force

$\quad P_n$ = normal force

From triangle ABC, we have

$$AB = BC = h$$
$$BC = BE + EC$$
$$= BE + ED \;(\because EC = DE, \text{ as } \angle ECD = 45°)$$

$$= BD \cos \theta + BD \sin \theta$$

$$BC = BD(\cos \theta + \sin \theta)$$

$$h = h_t(\cos \theta + \sin \theta)$$

$$\therefore \qquad h_t = \frac{h}{(\cos \theta + \sin \theta)} \qquad \qquad \dots \text{(Eq. 7.69)}$$

Assuming that the two welds share the load equally, therefore summing up the vertical components, from **Fig. 7.51(c)**, we have

$$P = 2\left[\frac{P_s}{2} \sin \theta + \frac{P_n}{2} \cos \theta\right] \qquad \text{(Here 2 refers to both welds)}$$

$$P = P_s \sin \theta + P_n \cos \theta \qquad \qquad \dots \text{(Eq. 7.70)}$$

Assuming that the resultant of $\dfrac{P_s}{2}$ and $\dfrac{P_n}{2}$ is vertical, their horizontal components must be equal and opposite,

i.e. $\qquad \dfrac{P_s}{2} \cos \theta = \dfrac{P_n}{2} \sin \theta$

$$P_n = \frac{P_s \cos \theta}{\sin \theta} \qquad \qquad \dots \text{(Eq. 7.71)}$$

Substituting (Eq. 7.71) in (Eq. 7.70), we have

$$P = P_s \sin \theta + \left(\frac{P_s \cos \theta}{\sin \theta}\right) \cos \theta$$

$$P = P_s \sin \theta + \left(\frac{P_s \cos^2 \theta}{\sin \theta}\right)$$

$$P \sin \theta = P_s \sin^2 \theta + P_s \cos^2 \theta = P_s(\sin^2 \theta + \cos^2 \theta)$$

$$P \sin \theta = P_s \qquad \qquad \dots \text{(Eq. 7.72)}$$

For a double parallel fillet weld subjected to tensile load, the shear stress is given as:

$$\tau = \frac{P_s}{2A_t} = \frac{P_s}{2(h_t \cdot L)}$$

$$= \frac{P \sin \theta}{2L[h/(\cos \theta + \sin \theta)]}$$

$$\therefore \qquad \tau = \frac{P \sin \theta(\cos \theta + \sin \theta)}{2hL} \qquad \qquad \dots \text{(Eq. 7.73)}$$

For maximum shear stress, differentiate (Eq. 7.66) with respect to θ and equate to zero,

i.e. $$\frac{\partial \tau}{\partial \theta} = 0$$

$$\frac{\partial}{\partial \theta}\left[\frac{P \sin \theta(\cos \theta + \sin \theta)}{2hL}\right] = 0$$

$$\frac{\partial}{\partial\theta}\left[\sin\theta\left(\cos\theta+\sin\theta\right)\right]=0$$

$$\left[\sin\theta\left(-\sin\theta+\cos\theta\right)\right]+\left[\left(\cos\theta+\sin\theta\right)\cos\theta\right)\right]=0$$

$$\left[-\sin^2\theta+\sin\theta\cos\theta\right]+\left[\cos^2\theta+\sin\theta\cos\theta\right)\right]=0$$

$$\left(\cos^2\theta-\sin^2\theta\right)+2\sin\theta\cos\theta=0$$

but, $\qquad\qquad\qquad\qquad \cos^2\theta-\sin^2\theta=\cos2\theta$ and $2\sin\theta\cos\theta=\sin2\theta$

Thus $\qquad\qquad\qquad\qquad\qquad \cos2\theta+\sin2\theta=0$

$$\cos2\theta=-\sin2\theta$$

i.e. $\qquad\qquad\qquad\qquad\qquad\qquad \tan2\theta=-1$

$$2\theta=135°$$

$\therefore$ $\qquad\qquad\qquad\qquad\qquad\qquad\qquad \theta=67.5°$ $\qquad\qquad$ ... (Eq. 7.74)

Substituting (Eq. 7.74) in (Eq. 7.73), we have

$$\tau_{max}=\frac{P\sin67.5°(\cos67.5°+\sin67.5°)}{2hL}$$

$\therefore$ $\qquad\qquad \tau_{max}=\frac{1.21P}{2hL}=\frac{0.605P}{hL}$ $\qquad\qquad$ ... (Eq. 7.75a)

or $\qquad\qquad P=1.652\tau_{max}hL$ $\qquad\qquad$ ... (Eq. 7.75b)

From Eqs. (7.68b) and (7.75b), we have

$$\frac{P_{trans}}{P_{fillet}}=\frac{1.414\,\tau_{max}\,hL}{1.652\,\tau_{max}\,hL}=0.855\approx0.86$$ $\qquad$ ... (Eq. 7.76a)

or $\qquad\qquad \frac{P_{fillet}}{P_{trans}}=\frac{1.652\,\tau_{max}\,hL}{1.414\,\tau_{max}\,hL}=1.168\approx1.17$ $\qquad$ ... (Eq. 7.76b)

34. **A plate 60 mm wide and 10 mm thick is welded to another plate by two transverse fillet welds as shown in Fig. 7.52. Determine the safe load that the joint can carry, if the allowable stress for the weld material is 80 MPa.**

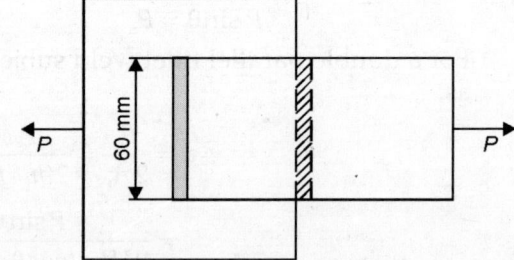

Fig. 7.52: Problem 34

Solution: Width of plate, $w=60$ mm, $h=10$ mm, $\sigma=80$ MPa, $P=?$

For a double transverse fillet lap weld subjected to tensile load

$$\sigma=\frac{P}{2A_t}=\frac{0.707\,P}{hL}$$ $\qquad\qquad$ ... 6.2(b)/ Pg 90, DHB

$$80=\frac{0.707\,P}{10\times60}$$

$\therefore$ $\qquad\qquad P=67892.50$ N

On the other hand, for a single transverse fillet lap weld subjected to tensile load

$$\sigma = \frac{P}{A_t} = \frac{1.414\,P}{hL} \qquad \text{... 6.2(a)/ Pg 90, DHB}$$

$$80 = \frac{1.414\,P}{10 \times 60}$$

$$\therefore \qquad P = 33946.25 \text{ N}$$

35. **Two plates 100 mm wide by 10 mm thick are joined together by double transverse fillet welds as shown in Fig. 7.53. Find the length of the weld required, if the strength of weld is equal to the strength of the plates. Take the allowable stress as 90 MPa.**

    Solution: $w = 100$ mm, $h = 10$ mm, $\sigma = 90$ MPa, $L = ?$

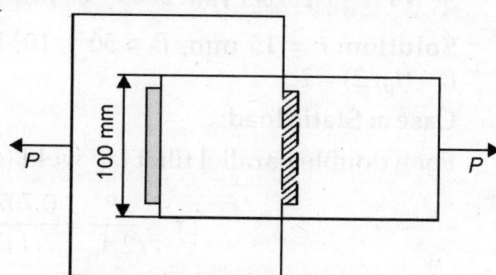

Fig. 7.53: Problem 35

For a double transverse fillet lap weld subjected to tensile load

$$\sigma = \frac{P}{2A_t} = \frac{0.707\,P}{hL} \qquad \text{... Eq. (i) } \textbf{6.2(b)/ Pg 90, DHB}$$

But strength of plate,

$$P = \sigma \cdot A = \sigma(wh) = 90 \times 100 \times 10 = 90 \times 10^3 \text{ N}$$

$\therefore$ Eq. (i) yields...

$$90 = \frac{0.707 \times (90 \times 10^3)}{10 \times L}$$

$$\therefore \qquad L = 70.7 \text{ mm}$$

Adding 10 mm for starting and stopping of weld run (bead), we have length of each weld,

$$L = 70.7 + 10 = 80.7 \text{ mm}$$

$$\therefore \qquad L \approx 81 \text{ mm}$$

36. **A plate 60 mm wide and 10 mm thick is welded to another plate by two parallel fillet welds as shown in Fig. 7.54. Determine the safe load that the joint can carry, if the allowable stress in shear for the weld material is 75 MPa.**

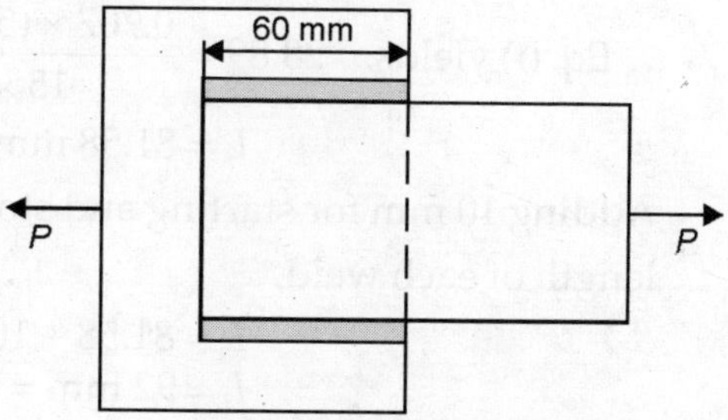

    Solution: $w = 60$ mm, $h = 10$ mm, $\tau = 75$ MPa, $L = 60$ mm, $P = ?$

Fig. 7.54: Problem 36

For a double parallel fillet lap weld (one side) subjected to shear stress, we have

$$\tau = \frac{P}{2A_t} = \frac{0.707\,P}{hL} \qquad \text{... 6.2(c)/ Pg 90, DHB}$$

$$75 = \frac{0.707 \times P}{10 \times 60}$$

$$\therefore \qquad P = 63649.22 \text{ N}$$

37. **A mild steel plate of 15 mm thickness is welded to another plate by two parallel welds to carry a load of 50 kN as shown in Fig. 7.55. Determine the length of the weld required: a) load is static   b) load is dynamic.**

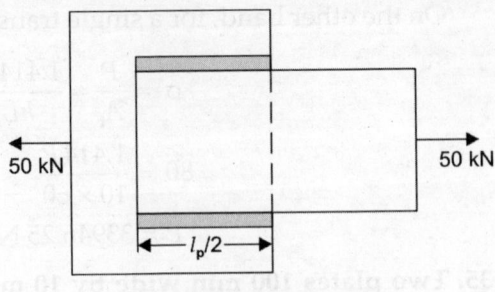

VTU – Dec. 08/ Jan. 2009 – 08 Marks

Fig. 7.55: Problem 37

Solution: $h = 15$ mm, $P = 50 \times 10^3$ N, $L = (l_p/2) = ?$

Case a: Static load:

For a double parallel fillet lap weld (one side) subjected to shear stress, we have

$$\tau = \frac{P}{2A_t} = \frac{0.707\,P}{hL} \qquad \text{... Eq. (i) 6.2(c)/ Pg 90, DHB}$$

Assume shear stress $\tau = 78$ MPa **... Tb. 6.4/ Pg 94, DHB**

$$78 = \frac{0.707 \times (50 \times 10^3)}{15 \times L}$$

$$\therefore \qquad L = 30.21 \text{ mm}$$

Adding 10 mm for starting and stopping of weld run (bead), we have length of each weld,

$$L = 30.21 + 10 = 40.21 \text{ mm}$$

$$\therefore \qquad L \approx 41 \text{ mm} = l_p/2$$

Case b: Dynamic load:

For torsion, $\tau_{max} = \tau K_s$ **... 2.1(c)/ Pg 20, DHB**

i.e. $\tau = \tau' K_s$

Here $K_s = 2.7$ **... Tb. 6.3/ Pg 94, DHB**

$$78 = \tau' \times 2.7$$

$$\therefore \qquad \tau' = 28.89 \text{ MPa}$$

$\therefore$ Eq. (i) yields... $28.89 = \dfrac{0.707 \times (50 \times 10^3)}{15 \times L}$

$$\therefore \qquad L = 81.58 \text{ mm}$$

Adding 10 mm for starting and stopping of weld run (bead), we have length of each weld,

$$L = 81.58 + 10 = 91.58 \text{ mm}$$

$$\therefore \qquad L \approx 92 \text{ mm} = l_p/2$$

38. **For the joint shown in Fig. 7.56, determine the length of the weld, assuming a shear stress of 75 MPa.**

Solution: $w = 80$ mm, $h = 10$ mm, $\tau = 75$ MPa, $P = 400 \times 10^3$ N, $L = ?$

Case a: [Fig. 7.56(a)]

For a double parallel fillet lap weld (one side) subjected to shear stress, we have

$$\tau = \frac{P}{2A_t} = \frac{0.707\,P}{hL} \qquad \text{... 6.2(c)/ Pg 90, DHB}$$

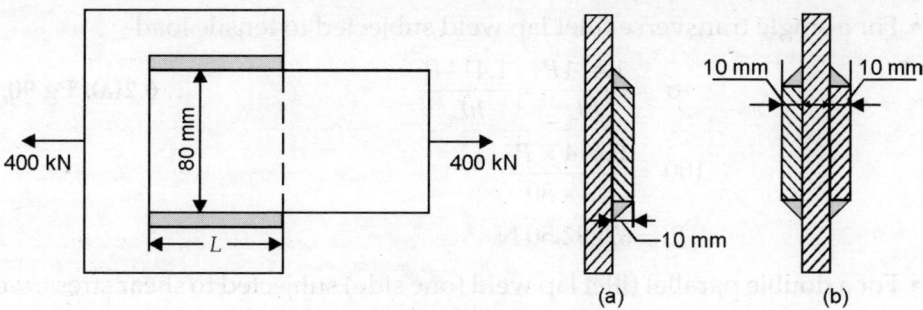

$$75 = \frac{0.707 \times (400 \times 10^3)}{10 \times L}$$

∴ $L = 377.06$ mm

Adding 10 mm for starting and stopping of weld run (bead), we have length of each weld,

$$L = 377.06 + 10 = 387.06 \text{ mm}$$

∴ $L \approx 390$ mm

Case b: [Fig. 7.56(b)]

For a double parallel fillet lap weld (both sides) subjected to shear stress, we have

$$\tau = \frac{P}{4A_t} = \frac{0.354 P}{hL} \qquad \text{... 6.2(d)/ Pg 90, DHB}$$

$$75 = \frac{0.354 \times (400 \times 10^3)}{10 \times L}$$

∴ $L = 188.80$ mm

Adding 10 mm for starting and stopping of weld run (bead), we have length of each weld,

$$L = 188.80 + 10 = 198.80 \text{ mm}$$

∴ $L \approx 200$ mm

39. A 80 mm wide, 12 mm thick plate carrying an axial load of 96 kN is welded to a support as shown in Fig. 7.57. The following tensile and shear stress in the weld are 100 MPa and 70 MPa respectively. Find the length of each parallel fillet weld.

VTU – June/ July 2014 – 10 Marks

Solution: $w = L_t = 80$ mm, $h = 12$ mm, $P = 96 \times 10^3$ N, $\sigma = 100$ MPa, $\tau = 70$ MPa, $L_p = ?$

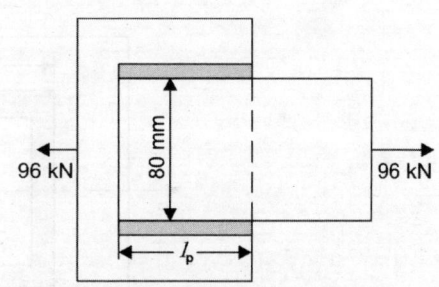

Fig. 7.57: Problem 39

For combined loading, we have

$$P = P_t + P_p \qquad \text{... Eq. (i)}$$

- For a single transverse fillet lap weld subjected to tensile load

$$\sigma = \frac{1.414\,P}{hL} = \frac{1.414\,P_t}{hL_t} \qquad \text{... 6.2(a)/ Pg 90, DHB}$$

$$100 = \frac{0.414 \times P_t}{12 \times 80}$$

$$\therefore \qquad P_t = 67892.50 \text{ N}$$

- For a double parallel fillet lap weld (one side) subjected to shear stress, we have

$$\tau = \frac{0.707\,P}{hL} = \frac{0.707\,P_p}{hL_p} \qquad \text{... 6.2(c)/ Pg 90, DHB}$$

$$70 = \frac{0.707 \times P_p}{12 \times L_p}$$

$$\therefore \qquad P_p = 1188.12\,L_p$$

$\therefore$ Eq. (i) yields...

$$96 \times 10^3 = 67892.50 + 1188.12\,L_p$$

$$\therefore \qquad L_p = 23.65 \text{ mm}$$

Adding 10 mm for starting and stopping of weld run (bead), we have

Length of each parallel weld,

$$L_p = 23.65 + 10 = 33.65 \text{ mm}$$

$$\therefore \qquad L_p \approx 35 \text{ mm}$$

40. **A 80 mm wide and 12 mm thick plate subjected to axial tensile load is welded to a vertical support by a single transverse fillet weld and a double parallel fillet weld as shown in Fig. 7.58. The maximum tensile and shear stresses in the weld are 100 MPa and 70 MPa respectively. Find the length of each parallel weld, if the joint is subjected to:**
   i. Static loading
   ii. Fatigue loading

VTU – Dec. 06/Jan. 2007 – 10 Marks

Solution: $w = L_t = 80$ mm, $h = 12$ mm, $\sigma = 100$ MPa, $\tau = 70$ MPa, $L_p = (l_p/2) = ?$

For combined loading, we have

$$P = P_t + P_p \qquad \text{... Eq. (i)}$$

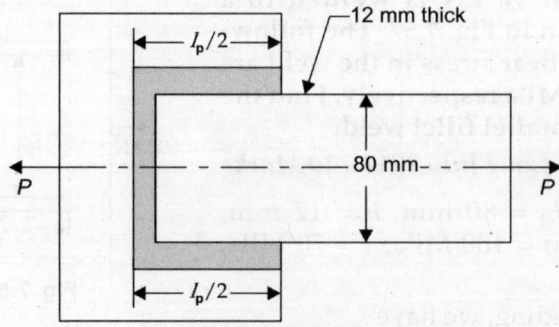

Fig. 7.58: Problem 40

- Strength of plate,
$$P = \sigma wh = 100 \times 80 \times 12 = 96000 \text{ N}$$

Case a: Static load

- For a single transverse fillet lap weld subjected to tensile load

$$\sigma = \frac{1.414P}{hL} = \frac{1.414P_t}{hL_t} \qquad \text{... Eq. (ii) 6.2(a)/ Pg 90, DHB}$$

$$100 = \frac{1.414 \times P_t}{12 \times 80}$$

$$\therefore \qquad P_t = 67892.50 \text{ N}$$

- For a double parallel fillet lap weld (one side) subjected to shear stress, we have

$$\tau = \frac{0.707P}{hL} = \frac{0.707P_p}{hL_p} \qquad \text{... 6.2(c)/ Pg 90, DHB}$$

$$70 = \frac{0.707 \times P_p}{12 \times L_p}$$

$$\therefore \qquad P_p = 1188.12 \, L_p$$

$\therefore$ Eq. (i) yields...

$$96 \times 10^3 = 67892.50 + 1188.12 \, L_p$$

$$\therefore \qquad L_p = 23.65 \text{ mm}$$

Adding 10 mm for starting and stopping of weld run (bead), we have length of each parallel weld,

$$L_p = 23.65 + 10 = 33.65 \text{ mm}$$

$$\therefore \qquad L_p \approx 35 \text{ mm} = (l_p/2)$$

Case b: Fatigue or dynamic load

- For torsion $\quad \tau_{max} = \tau K_s$ ... 2.1(c)/ Pg 20, DHB
  i.e. $\quad\quad\quad\quad \tau = \tau' K_s$
  Here $\quad\quad\quad\quad K_s = 2.7$, for torsion
  and $\quad\quad\quad\quad K_t = 1.5$, for axial load   ... Tb. 6.3/ Pg 24, DHB
  $\quad\quad\quad\quad\quad\quad 70 = \tau' \times 2.7$
  $\therefore \quad\quad\quad\quad\quad \sigma' = 25.93 \text{ MPa}$

- For direct stress
  $$\sigma_{max} = \sigma K_t \qquad \text{... 2.1(a)/ Pg 20, DHB}$$
  i.e. $\quad\quad\quad\quad \sigma = \sigma' K_t$
  $$100 = \sigma' \times 1.5$$
  $\therefore \quad\quad\quad\quad\quad \sigma' = 66.67 \text{ MPa}$

$\therefore$ Eq. (ii) yields...

$$\sigma' = \frac{1.414P_t}{hL_t}$$

$$66.67 = \frac{1.414P_t}{12 \times 80}$$

$$P_t = 45264 \text{ N}$$

Eq. (iii) yields... $\tau' = \dfrac{0.707\,P_p}{hL_p}$

$$25.93 = \dfrac{0.707 \times P_p}{12 \times L_p}$$

$\therefore$ $P_p = (440.11)\,L_p$

$\therefore$ Eq. (i) yields...

$$96 \times 10^3 = 45264 + (440.11)\,L_p$$

$\therefore$ $L_p = 115.28$ mm

Adding 10 mm for starting and stopping of weld run (bead), we have

length of each parallel weld,

$$L_p = 115.28 + 10 = 125.28 \text{ mm}$$

$\therefore$ $L_p \approx 126 \text{ mm} = (l_p/2)$

Note: For the joint shown in **Fig. 7.59**, since the maximum size of the weld should not exceed the plate thickness, we have:

- **Width of plate** $w = (80 - h) = 80 - 12 = 68$ mm
- **Strength of plate,** $P = \sigma wh = 100 \times 68 \times 12 = 81600$ N
  - For static loading,

    $$L_p \approx 31 \text{ mm} = (l_p/2)$$

  - For dynamic loading,

    $$L_p \approx 110 \text{ mm} = (l_p/2)$$

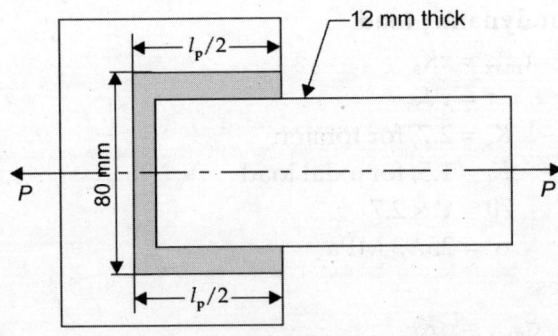

Fig. 7.59

7.21 UNSYMMETRICAL WELDS SUBJECTED TO AXIAL LOADS

Figure 7.60 represents an angle section welded to a plate by means of two unequal parallel fillet welds. If a tensile force P is applied so as to pass through the centre of gravity of the section, then the length of the fillet nearer to CG (L_1) will take greater proportion of the force P than the length of fillet weld which is away from CG. The lengths L_1 and L_2 are to be so proportioned that the forces carried by two fillet welds exert no moment about centre of gravity axis. The two fillets are at distances of e_1 and e_2 respectively from CG.

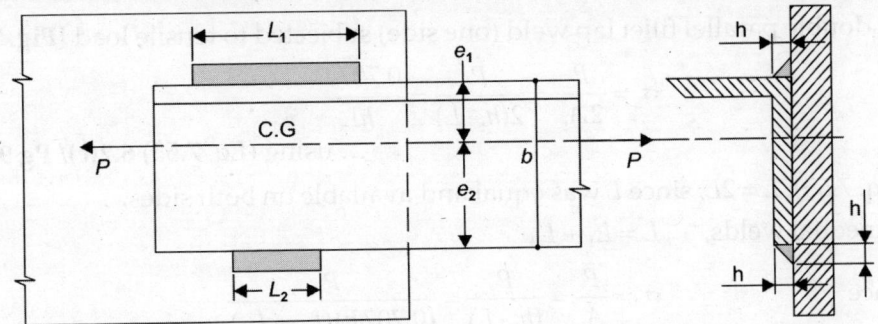

Fig. 7.60: Unsymmetrical welded joint in tension **[Fig. 6.2(e)/Pg 90, DHB]**

Let

P = tensile load (N)

b = distance between the welds (mm)

L_1 = length of weld at top (mm)

L_2 = length of weld at bottom (mm)

$L = L_1 + L_2$ = total length of weld (mm)

e_1 = distance of top weld from CG (mm)

e_2 = distance of bottom weld from CG (mm)

σ = average normal stress (MPa)

τ = allowable shear stress (MPa)

If 's' is the resistance offered by the weld per unit length, then

• Moment of the top weld about CG = $L_1 \cdot s \cdot e_1$
• Moment of the bottom weld about CG = $L_2 \cdot s \cdot e_2$

Since the sum of the moments of the weld about the gravity axis must be zero, we have

$$L_1 \cdot s \cdot e_1 - L_2 \cdot s \cdot e_2 = 0$$

$$L_1 \cdot e_1 = L_2 \cdot e_2 \qquad \qquad \text{... Eq. (a)}$$

$$L_1 = \frac{L_2 \cdot e_2}{e_1} \quad \text{or} \quad L_2 = \frac{L_1 \cdot e_1}{e_2} \qquad \text{... Eq. (b)}$$

Also

$$L = L_1 + L_2 \qquad \qquad \text{... Eq. (c)}$$

$$= L_1 + \frac{L_1 \cdot e_1}{e_2}$$

$$= \frac{L_1 \cdot e_2 + L_1 \cdot e_1}{e_2} = \frac{L_1(e_1 + e_2)}{e_2}$$

$$\therefore \qquad L_1 = \frac{L e_2}{(e_1 + e_2)} = \frac{L e_2}{b} \qquad \text{... Eq. (7.77) 6.2(f)/Pg 90, DHB}$$

On similar lines $\qquad L_2 = \frac{L e_1}{(e_1 + e_2)} = \frac{L e_1}{b} \qquad \text{... Eq. (7.78) 6.2(g)/Pg 90, DHB}$

Equations (7.77) and (7.78) are used to find the length of respective welds.

For a double parallel fillet lap weld (one side) subjected to tensile load [**Fig. 7.48(a)**],

$$\sigma = \frac{P}{2A_t} = \frac{P}{2(h_t \cdot L)} = \frac{0.707\,P}{hL}$$

... using (Eq. 7.55) **6.2(c)/ Pg 90, DHB**

In (Eq. 7.55), $L = 2L$, since L was equal and available on both sides.

For unequal welds, $L = L_1 + L_2$

and hence $\sigma = \dfrac{P}{A_t} = \dfrac{P}{(h_t \cdot L)} = \dfrac{P}{(0.707\,h)(L_1 + L_2)}$

$\therefore$ $\sigma = \dfrac{1.414\,P}{h(L_1 + L_2)} = \dfrac{1.414\,P}{hL}$ ... (Eq. 7.79) **6.2(e)/Pg 90, DHB**

Since the parallel fillet welds are subjected to shear stress, on similar lines we have

$$\tau = \frac{1.414\,P}{h(L_1 + L_2)} = \frac{1.414\,P}{hL}$$ **(Replace σ with τ in Eq. 7.79)**

... (Eq. 7.80) **6.2(e)/Pg 90, DHB**

Note: Strength of weld per mm length (i.e. $L = 1$ mm) is obtained from (Eq. 7.80) as

$$P = \frac{\tau h}{1.414} = 0.707\,\tau h$$ ... (Eq. 7.81)

41. An 125 × 100 × 10 mm unequal leg angle section is to be welded to a steel plate by fillet welds along the edges of the 125 mm leg as shown in Fig. 7.61. The angle is subjected to a tensile load of 100 kN passing through the center of gravity of the angle. Determine the weld lengths if the size of the weld is 8 mm and allowable shear stress in the weld is 102 MPa. All dimensions are in mm.

VTU – Dec. 2015/ Jan. 2016 – 06 Marks

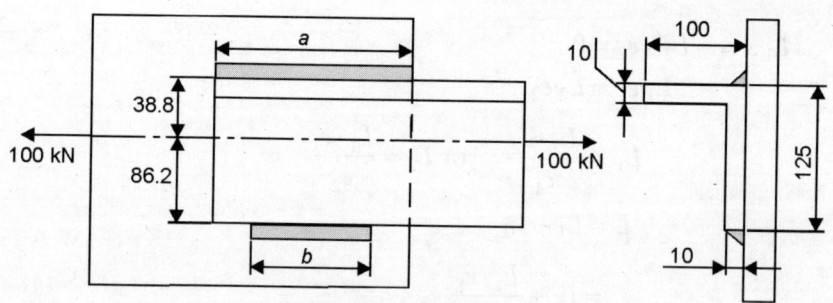

Fig. 7.61: Problem 41

Solution: $P = 100 \times 10^3$ N, weld size, $h = 8$ mm, $\tau = 102$ MPa, $L_1, L_2 = ?$
From **Fig. 7.61**, we have:

$e_1 = 38.8$ mm, $e_2 = 86.2$ mm, $b = (e_1 + e_2) = 125$ mm.

Method 1:

Length of top weld $L_1 = \dfrac{1.414\,Pe_2}{\tau h b} = \dfrac{1.414 \times (100 \times 10^3) \times 86.2}{102 \times 8 \times 125} = 119.50$ mm

... **6.2(f)/ Pg 90, DHB**

Length of short weld

$$L_2 = \frac{1.414 P e_1}{\tau h b} = \frac{1.414 \times (100 \times 10^3) \times 38.8}{102 \times 8 \times 125} = 53.78 \text{ mm}$$

... **6.2(g)/ Pg 90, DHB**

Adding 10 mm for starting and stopping of weld run (bead), we have

$$L_1 = 119.50 + 10 = 129.50 \approx 130 \text{ mm}$$

$$L_2 = 53.78 + 10 = 63.78 \approx 64 \text{ mm}$$

Method 2:

We know that, $\qquad \tau = \dfrac{1.414 P}{h(L_1 + L_2)} = \dfrac{1.414 P}{hL}$

(Replace σ with τ in **Eq. 6.2(e)/ Pg 90, DHB)** ... Eq. (i)

From Eq. (i), strength of weld per mm length ($L = 1$ mm) is obtained as

$$P = \frac{\tau h}{1.414} = \frac{102 \times 8}{1.414} = 577.08 \text{ N}$$

Hence total length of weld required,

$$L = \frac{\text{total load}}{\text{load per unit length}}$$

$$= \frac{100 \times 10^3}{577.08}$$

∴ $\qquad L = (L_1 + L_2) = 173.28 \text{ mm}$

Length of top weld,

$$L_1 = \frac{L e_2}{(e_1 + e_2)} = \frac{173.28 \times 86.2}{125} = 119.50 \text{ mm}$$

... **6.2(f)/ Pg 90, DHB**

Length of short weld,

$$L_2 = \frac{L e_1}{(e_1 + e_2)} = \frac{173.28 \times 38.8}{125} = 53.78 \text{ mm}$$

... **6.2(g)/ Pg 90, DHB**

or $\qquad L_2 = L - L_1 = 173.28 - 119.50 = 53.78 \text{ mm}$

Adding 10 mm for starting and stopping of weld run (bead), we have

$$L_1 = 119.50 + 10 = 129.50 \approx 130 \text{ mm}$$

$$L_2 = 53.78 + 10 = 63.78 \approx 64 \text{ mm}$$

42. **A tie beam of a roof truss consists of an angle 90 × 90 × 8 mm and is subjected to a load of 125 kN. The tie is connected to a gusset plate by welding. Design the joint if the size of the weld is 6 mm. Take maximum allowable shear stress in the weld as 102.5 MPa. The distance between the neutral axis and edges of the angle section are 28.7 mm and 61.3 mm.**

Solution: $P = 125 \times 10^3$ N, weld size, $h = 6$ mm, $\tau = 102.5$ MPa, $L_1, L_2 = ?$

Based on given data, the dimensions are shown in **Fig. 7.62.**

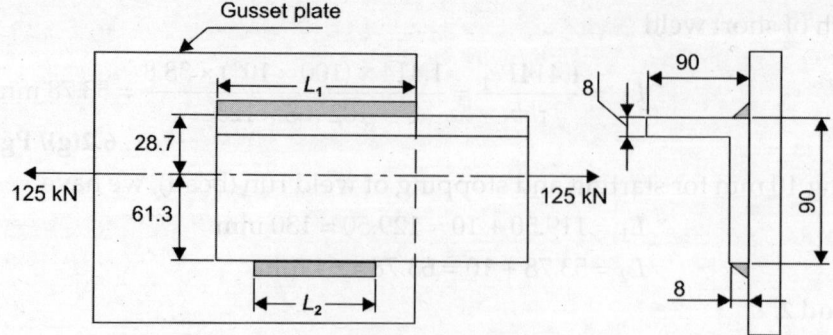

Fig. 7.62: Problem 42

From **Fig. 7.62**, we have:

$$e_1 = 28.7 \text{ mm}, e_2 = 61.3 \text{ mm}, b = (e_1 + e_2) = 90 \text{ mm}.$$

Method 1:

Length of top weld $L_1 = \dfrac{1.414 P e_1}{\tau h b} = \dfrac{1.414 \times (125 \times 10^3) \times 61.3}{102.5 \times 6 \times 90} = 195.75 \text{ mm}$

... **6.2(f)/ Pg 90, DHB**

Length of short weld

$$L_2 = \frac{1.414 P e_1}{\tau h b} = \frac{1.414 \times (125 \times 10^3) \times 28.7}{102.5 \times 6 \times 90} = 91.65 \text{ mm}$$

... **6.2(g)/ Pg 90, DHB**

Adding 10 mm for starting and stopping of weld run (bead), we have

$$L_1 = 195.70 + 10 = 205.75 \approx 206 \text{ mm}$$
$$L_2 = 91.65 + 10 = 101.65 \approx 102 \text{ mm}$$

43. **An 150 × 75 × 10 mm angle is to be welded to a steel plate by fillet welds along the longer leg of the angle. If the angle is subjected to a static load of 100 kN, find the length of weld at the top and bottom. The allowable shear stress for static loading may be taken as 120 MPa.**

Solution: $P = 100 \times 10^3 \text{ N}, h = 10 \text{ mm}, \tau = 120 \text{ MPa}, L_1, L_2 = ?$

Based on given data, the dimensions are shown in **Fig. 7.63**.

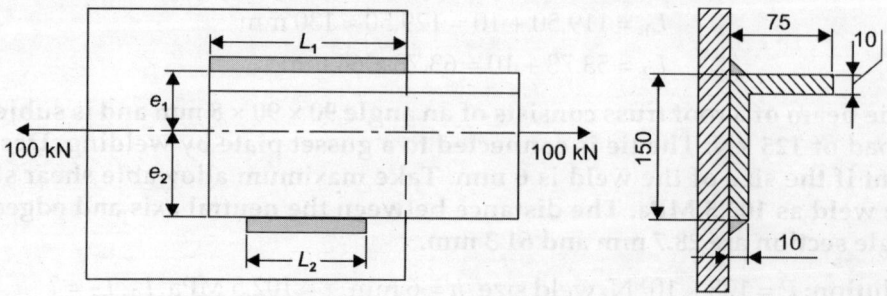

Fig. 7.63: Problem 43

From **Fig. 7.63**, we have:
$$b = (e_1 + e_2) = 150 \text{ mm.}$$

a. To find L:

We know that,
$$\tau = \frac{1.414\,P}{h(L_1 + L_2)} = \frac{1.414\,P}{hL}$$

(Replace σ with τ in **Eq. 6.2(e)/Pg 90, DHB**)

$$120 = \frac{1.414 \times (100 \times 10^3)}{10 \times L}$$

∴ $$L = 117.83 \approx 120 \text{ mm}$$

b. To find e_1, e_2:

Distance of CG from top edge (short leg),

$$e_1 = \bar{y} = \frac{\Sigma ay}{\Sigma a}$$

$$= \frac{[(150 \times 10) \times (150/2)] + [(75 - 10) \times 10 \times (10/2)]}{(150 \times 10) + (75 - 10) \times 10}$$

∴ $$e_1 = 53.84 \text{ mm}$$

Distance of CG from bottom edge (long leg),
$$e_2 = (b - e_1) = 150 - 53.84 = 96.16 \text{ mm}$$

c. To find L_1, L_2:

Length of top weld $\quad L_1 = \dfrac{Le_2}{(e_1 + e_2)} = \dfrac{120 \times 96.16}{150} = 76.93 \text{ mm}$

... **6.2(f)/ Pg 90, DHB**

Length of short weld

$$L_2 = \frac{Le_1}{(e_1 + e_2)} = \frac{120 \times 53.84}{150} = 43.07 \text{ mm}$$

... **6.2(g)/ Pg 90, DHB**

or $\qquad L_2 = L - L_1 = 120 - 76.93 = 43.07 \text{ mm}$

Adding 10 mm for starting and stopping of weld run (bead), we have
$$L_1 = 76.93 + 10 = 86.93 \approx 87 \text{ mm}$$
$$L_2 = 43.07 + 10 = 53.07 \approx 54 \text{ mm}$$

44. **Two 100 × 75 × 10 mm angles are welded to a gusset plate as shown in Fig. 7.64. The tie member is subjected to a load of 400 kN. Design the welded joint if shear stress is limited to 100 MPa.**

Solution: Total load for two angles $2P = 400 \times 10^3$ N, $h = 10$ mm, $\tau = 100$ MPa, L_1, $L_2 = ?$

Hence load acting on single angle,
$$P = 200 \times 10^3 \text{ N}$$

From **Fig. 7.64**, we have:
$$e_1 = 31.9 \text{ mm}, \; e_2 = 68.1 \text{ mm}, \; b = (e_1 + e_2) = 100 \text{ mm.}$$

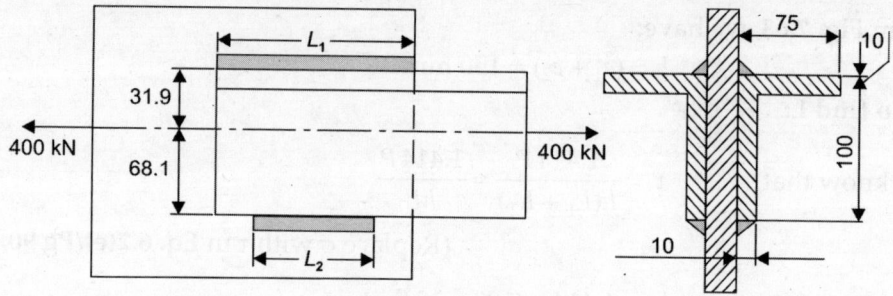

Fig. 7.64: Problem 44

Method 1:

Length of top weld $L_1 = \dfrac{1.414 Pe_2}{\tau h b} = \dfrac{1.414 \times (200 \times 10^3) \times 68.1}{100 \times 10 \times 100} = 192.58$ mm

... **6.2(f)/ Pg 90, DHB**

Length of short weld

$$L_2 = \dfrac{1.414 Pe_1}{\tau h b} = \dfrac{1.414 \times (200 \times 10^3) \times 31.9}{100 \times 10 \times 100} = 90.21 \text{ mm}$$

... **6.2(g)/ Pg 90, DHB**

Adding 10 mm for starting and stopping of weld run (bead), we have

$$L_1 = 192.58 + 10 = 202.58 \approx 203 \text{ mm}$$
$$L_2 = 90.21 + 10 = 100.21 \approx 101 \text{ mm}$$

Thus for both angles, effective length,

$$L_{1e} = 2 \times 203 = 406 \text{ mm}$$
$$L_{2e} = 2 \times 101 = 202 \text{ mm}$$

Method 2: *[This method is applicable, if e_1 and e_2 are unknown]*
a. To find L:

We know that, $\tau = \dfrac{1.414 P}{h(L_1 + L_2)} = \dfrac{1.414 P}{hL}$

(Replace σ with τ in **Eq. 6.2(e)/Pg 90, DHB**)

$$100 = \dfrac{1.414 \times (200 \times 10^3)}{10 \times L}$$

∴ $L = (L_1 + L_2) = 282.8$ mm (This value is only for single angle)
b. To find e_1, e_2:

Distance of CG from top edge (short leg),

$$e_1 = \bar{y} = \dfrac{\Sigma a y}{\Sigma a}$$

$$= \dfrac{[(100 \times 10) \times (100/2)] + [(75 - 10) \times 10 \times (10/2)]}{(100 \times 10) + [(75 - 10) \times 10]}$$

∴ $e_1 = 32.27$ mm

Distance of CG from bottom edge (long leg),
$$e_2 = (b - e_1) = 100 - 32.27 = 67.73 \text{ mm}$$

c. To find L_1, L_2:

Length of top weld $L_1 = \dfrac{Le_2}{(e_1 + e_2)} = \dfrac{282.8 \times 67.73}{100} = 191.54 \text{ mm}$

... **6.2(f)/ Pg 90, DHB**

Length of short weld

$$L_2 = \dfrac{Le_1}{(e_1 + e_2)} = \dfrac{282.8 \times 32.27}{100} = 91.26 \text{ mm}$$

... **6.2(g)/ Pg 90, DHB**

Adding 10 mm for starting and stopping of weld run (bead), we have
$$L_1 = 191.54 + 10 = 201.54 \approx 202 \text{ mm}$$
$$L_2 = 91.26 + 10 = 101.26 \approx 102 \text{ mm}$$

Thus for both angles, effective length,
$$L_{1e} = 2 \times 202 = 404 \text{ mm}$$
and $$L_{2e} = 2 \times 102 = 204 \text{ mm}$$

45. **Two angles 200 × 150 × 10 mm plates are welded to a gusset plate by means of parallel welds along the longer leg of the angle. Determine the length of the welds required if the angles carry a load of 250 kN and the allowable shear stress is limited to 90 MPa.**

Solution: Load for two angles $2P = 250 \times 10^3$ N, $h = 10$ mm, $\tau = 90$ MPa, L_1, $L_2 = ?$

Hence load acting on single angle,
$$P = 125 \times 10^3 \text{ N}$$

Based on given data, the dimensions are shown in **Fig. 7.65**.

From **Fig. 7.65**, we have
$$b = (e_1 + e_2) = 100 \text{ mm}.$$

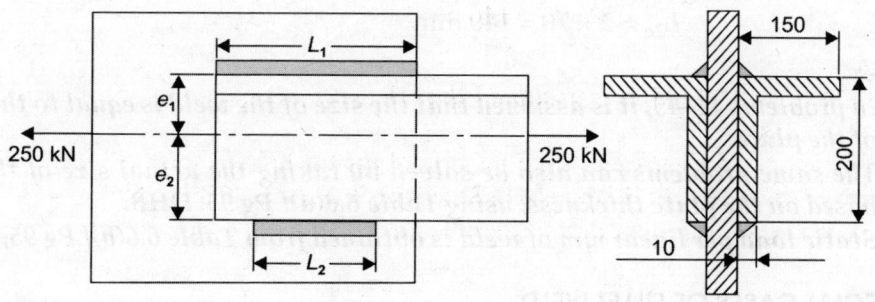

Fig. 7.65: Problem 45

a. To find L:

We know that, $\tau = \dfrac{1.414P}{h(L_1 + L_2)} = \dfrac{1.414P}{hL}$

(Replace σ with τ in **Eq. 6.2(e)/Pg 90, DHB**)

$$90 = \frac{1.414 \times (125 \times 10^3)}{10 \times L}$$

$$\therefore \qquad L = 196.38 \approx 197 \text{ mm}$$

b. To find e_1, e_2:

Distance of CG from top edge (short leg),

$$e_1 = \bar{y} = \frac{\Sigma ay}{\Sigma a}$$

$$= \frac{[(200 \times 10) \times (200/2)] + [(150 - 10) \times 10 \times (10/2)]}{(200 \times 10) + [(150 - 10) \times 10]}$$

$$\therefore \qquad e_1 = 60.88 \text{ mm}$$

Distance of CG from bottom edge (long leg),

$$e_2 = (b - e_1) = 200 - 60.88 = 139.12 \text{ mm}$$

c. To find L_1, L_2:

Length of top weld $\quad L_1 = \dfrac{Le_2}{(e_1 + e_2)} = \dfrac{197 \times 139.12}{200} = 137.03 \text{ mm}$

$$\text{... 6.2(f)/ Pg 90, DHB}$$

Length of short weld

$$L_2 = \frac{Le_1}{(e_1 + e_2)} = \frac{197 \times 60.88}{200} = 59.97 \text{ mm}$$

$$\text{... 6.2(g)/ Pg 90, DHB}$$

or $\qquad L_2 = L - L_1 = 197 - 137.03 = 59.97 \text{ mm}$

Adding 10 mm for starting and stopping of weld run (bead), we have

$$L_1 = 137.03 + 10 = 147.03 \approx 148 \text{ mm}$$

$$L_2 = 59.97 + 10 = 69.97 \approx 70 \text{ mm}$$

Thus for both angles, effective length,

$$L_{1e} = 2 \times 148 = 296 \text{ mm}$$

and $\qquad L_{2e} = 2 \times 70 = 140 \text{ mm}$

Note:

- *In problems 41–45, it is assumed that the size of the weld is equal to thickness of the plate.*
- *The same problems can also be solved by taking the actual size of the weld based on the plate thickness, using Table 6.6(a)/ Pg 95, DHB.*
- *Static load per linear mm of weld is obtained from Table 6.6(b)/ Pg 95, DHB*

7.22 SPECIAL CASES OF FILLET WELD

7.22.1 Tee Joint: Parallel Fillet Weld Subjected to Bending Moment

A Tee joint with parallel fillet welds subjected to bending moment (M) is shown in **Fig. 7.66**.

The bending stress is given as

$$\sigma_b = \sigma = \frac{M}{Z} \qquad\qquad \text{... 1.1(b)/ Pg 2, DHB}$$

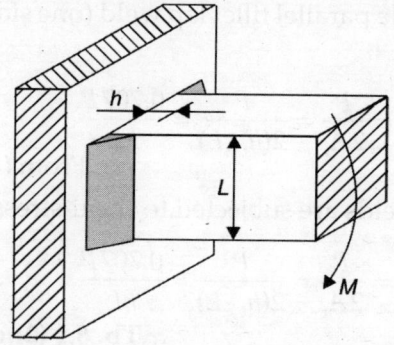

Fig. 7.66: Tee joint: Parallel fillet weld subjected to bending moment

Assuming that the failure of weld occurs at the throat (minimum resisting area), we have

$$Z = \frac{h_t L^2}{6}$$

where

$$h_t = h \sin 45° = 0.707\,h = h \cos 45° \qquad \text{... From (Eq. 7.49)}$$

$$\therefore \qquad \sigma_b = \frac{M}{2(0.70\,h)L^2/6}$$

[Here 2 refers to double parallel fillet lap weld (one side)]

$$= \frac{6M}{1.414\,hL^2}$$

$$\therefore \qquad \sigma_b = \sigma = \frac{4.24M}{hL^2} \qquad \text{... (Eq. 7.82)}$$

... Tb. 6.1 (1st row, 3rd col.)/Pg 93, DHB

7.22.2 Tee Joint: Parallel Fillet Weld Subjected to Eccentric Load

A Tee joint with parallel fillet welds subjected to eccentric load (P) acting at eccentricity (e) is shown in **Fig. 7.67**. Due to this eccentric load, two types of stresses namely the shear stress and the bending stress is produced. The strength of the joint for combined action of bending moment and shear force is calculated as follows.

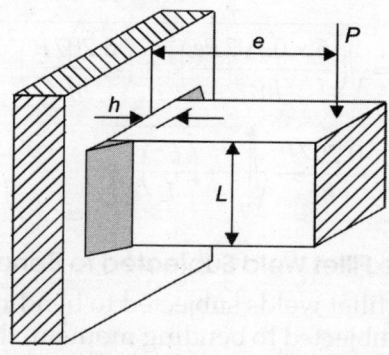

Fig. 7.67: Tee joint: Parallel fillet weld subjected to eccentric load

We know that for a double parallel fillet lap weld (one side) subjected to tensile load [**Fig. 7.48(a)**],

$$\sigma = \frac{P}{2A_t} = \frac{P}{2(h_t \cdot L)} = \frac{0.707P}{hL}$$

$$\text{... From (Eq. 7.55) 6.2(c)/Pg 90, DHB}$$

Since the parallel fillet welds are subjected to shear stress, we have

$$\tau = \frac{P}{2A_t} = \frac{P}{2(h_t \cdot L)} = \frac{0.707P}{hL} \qquad \text{... From (Eq. 7.57)}$$

$$\text{...Tb. 6.1 (2nd row, 1st col.)/Pg 93, DHB}$$

The bending stress is given as

$$\sigma_b = \sigma = \frac{M}{Z} \qquad \text{... 1.1(b)/ Pg 2, DHB}$$

$$\sigma_b = \sigma = \frac{Pe}{Z} \qquad (\because M = Pe)$$

Assuming that the failure of weld occurs at the throat (minimum resisting area), we have

$$Z = \frac{h_t L^2}{6}$$

where $\qquad h_t = h \sin 45° = 0.707\, h = h \cos 45°$ $\qquad$ ... From (Eq. 7.49)

$\therefore \qquad\qquad\qquad \sigma_b = \dfrac{Pe}{2(0.70h)L^2/6}$

[Here 2 refers to double parallel fillet lap weld (one side)]

$$= \frac{6Pe}{1.414\,hL^2} = \frac{6 \times 0.707\,Pe}{hL^2}$$

$\therefore \qquad\qquad\qquad \sigma_b = \sigma = \dfrac{4.24Pe}{hL^2}$ $\qquad\qquad$ ... (Eq. 7.83)

$$\text{... Tb. 6.1 (2nd row, 1st col.)/ Pg 93, DHB}$$

The resultant stress is calculated as

$$\sigma_{max} = \sqrt{\sigma^2 + \tau^2} \qquad \text{... 1.7(g)/ Pg 4, DHB}$$

$$= \sqrt{\left(\frac{6 \times 0.707\,Pe}{hL^2}\right)^2 + \left(\frac{0.707P}{hL}\right)^2}$$

$\therefore \qquad\qquad \sigma_{max} = \dfrac{0.707P}{hL}\sqrt{\left[1 + \left(\dfrac{6e}{L}\right)^2\right]}$ $\qquad\qquad$ ... (Eq. 7.84)

7.22.3 Tee Joint: Transverse Fillet Weld Subjected to Bending Moment

A Tee joint with transverse fillet welds subjected to bending moment (M) is shown in **Fig. 7.68**. When the joint is subjected to bending moment, the magnitude of tensile and compressive force in the weld is given by $\sigma L h_t$.

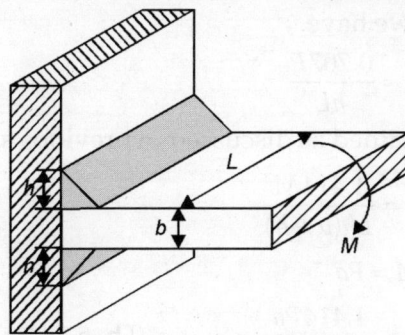

Fig. 7.68: Tee joint: Transverse fillet weld subjected to bending moment

Equating the bending moment to the moment of internal resistance, we have

$$M = \sigma L h_t(b + h)$$

$$\sigma = \frac{M}{L h_t(b + h)} \qquad \text{... (Eq. 7.85)}$$

where

$$h_t = h \sin 45° = 0.707\,h = h \cos 45° \qquad \text{... From (Eq. 7.49)}$$

$$\sigma = \frac{M}{L(0.707\,h)\,(b + h)}$$

$$\therefore \quad \sigma = \frac{1.414M}{Lh(b + h)} \qquad \text{... (Eq. 7.86)}$$

... Tb. 6.1 (4th row, 3rd col.)/Pg 92, DHB

7.22.4 Tee Joint: Transverse Fillet Weld Subjected to Eccentric Load

A Tee joint with transverse fillet welds subjected to eccentric load (P) acting at eccentricity (a) is shown in **Fig. 7.69.** Due to this eccentric load, two types of stresses namely the normal stress and the bending stress are produced. The strength of the joint for combined action of bending moment and shear load is calculated as follows.

We know that for a double transverse fillet lap weld subjected to tensile load **[Fig. 7.47(b)]**,

$$\sigma = \frac{P}{2A_t} = \frac{P}{2(h_t \cdot L)} = \frac{0.707P}{hL}$$

... From (Eq. 7.54) 6.2(b)/Pg 90, DHB

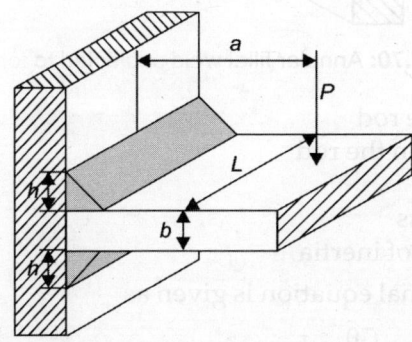

Fig. 7.69: Tee joint: Transverse fillet weld subjected to eccentric load

In terms of shear stress, we have

$$\tau = \frac{0.707P}{hL}$$

The bending stress is obtained as discussed in previous article as,

$$\sigma = \frac{1.414M}{Lh(b+h)} \qquad \text{... From (Eq. 7.86)}$$

According to **Fig. 7.69**, $M = Pa$

$$\sigma = \frac{1.414Pa}{Lh(b+h)} \qquad \text{... Tb. 6.1 (1st row, 1st col.)/ Pg 93, DHB}$$

The resultant stress is calculated as

$$\sigma_{max} = \sqrt{\sigma^2 + \tau^2} \qquad \text{... 1.7(g)/ Pg 4, DHB}$$

$$= \sqrt{\left(\frac{1.414Pa}{Lh(b+h)}\right)^2 + \left(\frac{0.707P}{hL}\right)^2}$$

$$= \frac{P}{hL(b+h)}\sqrt{(1.414a)^2 + [0.707(b+h)]^2}$$

$$\therefore \qquad \sigma_{max} = \frac{P}{hL(b+h)}\sqrt{2a^2 + \frac{(b+h)^2}{2}}$$

$$\text{... (Eq. 7.87) Tb. 6.1 (1st row, 1st col.)/ Pg 93, DHB}$$

7.22.5 Annular or Circular Fillet Weld Subjected to Torsion

Consider a circular rod welded to a plate using fillet weld as shown in **Fig. 7.70**.

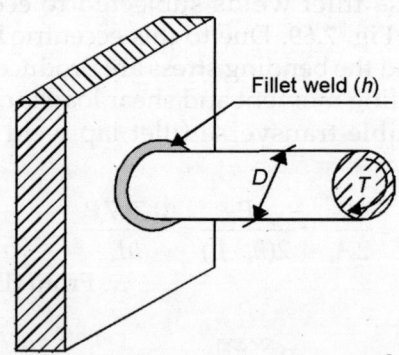

Fig. 7.70: Annular fillet weld subjected to torsion

Let D = diameter of the rod
    T = torque acting on the rod
    h = size of the leg
    h_t = throat thickness
    J = polar moment of inertia   ... **Tb. 6.7/ Pg 96, DHB**

We know that the torsional equation is given as

$$\frac{T}{J} = \frac{G\theta}{L} = \frac{\tau}{r} \qquad \text{... 1.3(b)/ Pg 3, DHB}$$

Based on strength or shear stress, we have

$$\frac{T}{J} = \frac{\tau}{R} \quad \text{(Replace '}r\text{' with '}R\text{')}$$

$$\tau = \frac{TR}{J}$$

Here $\qquad R = D/2$

$$J = \frac{\pi m^3 h_t}{4} \qquad \text{... Tb. 6.7(last row, last col.)/ Pg 97, DHB}$$

Comparing the above parameters with respect to **Fig. 7.70**, we have $m = D$

$\therefore \qquad\qquad J = \dfrac{\pi D^3 h_t}{4}$

Thus $\qquad\qquad \tau = \dfrac{T(D/2)}{\pi D^3 h_t/4} = \dfrac{2T}{\pi D^2 h_t}$

But $\qquad\qquad h_t = h \sin 45° = 0.707\,h = h \cos 45° \qquad\qquad$ ... From (Eq. 7.49)

$\therefore \qquad\qquad \tau = \dfrac{2T}{\pi D^2 (0.707\,h)}$

$\therefore \qquad\qquad \tau = \dfrac{2.83T}{\pi h D^2} \qquad\qquad\qquad\qquad$ ... (Eq. 7.88)

$\qquad\qquad\qquad\qquad\qquad\qquad$ ... **Tb. 6.1 (3rd row, 2nd col.)/ Pg 93, DHB**

7.22.6 Annular or Circular Fillet Weld Subjected to Bending Moment

Consider a circular rod welded to a plate using fillet weld as shown in Fig. 7.71.

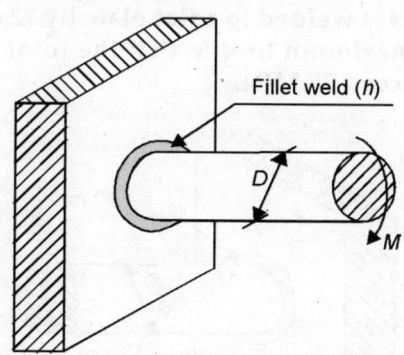

Fig. 7.71: Annular fillet weld subjected to bending moment

Let $\quad D$ = diameter of the rod

$\qquad M$ = bending moment acting on the rod

$\qquad h$ = size of the leg

$\qquad h_t$ = throat thickness

$\qquad Z$ = section modulus $\qquad\qquad\qquad\qquad\qquad$ ... **Tb. 6.7/ Pg 96, DHB**

We know that the torsional equation is given as [**Fig. 1.1(b)/Pg 2, DHB**]

$$\frac{M}{I} = \frac{E}{R} = \frac{\sigma}{c} \qquad \text{... 1.3(a)/ Pg 3, DHB}$$

$$\sigma = \sigma_b = \frac{Mc}{I} = \frac{M}{Z} \qquad \text{... 1.1(b)/ Pg 2, DHB}$$

Here
$$Z = \frac{\pi m^2 h_t}{4} \qquad \text{... Tb. 6.7(last row, 2nd col.)/ Pg 96, DHB}$$

Comparing the above parameters with respect to **Fig.7.71**, we have $m = D$

$$\therefore \quad Z = \frac{\pi D^2 h_t}{4}$$

Thus
$$\sigma = \sigma_b = \frac{M}{\pi D^2 h_t / 4} = \frac{4M}{\pi D^2 h_t}$$

But
$$h_t = h\sin 45° = 0.707\, h = h\cos 45° \qquad \text{... From (Eq. 7.49)}$$

$$\therefore \quad \sigma = \sigma_b = \frac{4M}{\pi D^2 (0.707\, h)}$$

$$\therefore \quad \sigma = \sigma_b = \frac{5.66M}{\pi h D^2} \qquad \text{... (Eq. 7.89)}$$

$$\text{... Tb. 6.1 (3rd row, 1st col.)/ Pg 93, DHB}$$

46. **Prove that normal stress in case of annular fillet weld subjected to bending is given by** $\sigma_b = \dfrac{5.66\, M_b}{\pi h D^2}$.

VTU – Dec. 2009/ Jan. 2010 – 06 Marks

Solution: Refer to Section 7.22.6.

47. **A 60 mm diameter shaft is welded to a flat plate by 12 mm fillet welds as shown in Fig. 7.72. Find the maximum torque that the joint can sustain, if maximum shear stress is not to exceed 75 MPa.**

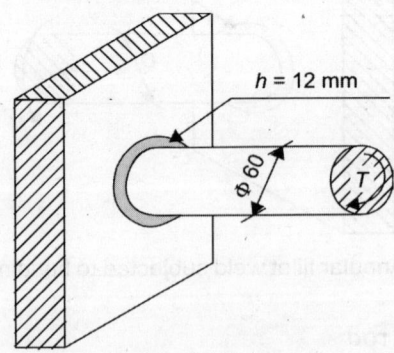

Fig. 7.72: Problem 47

Solution: $D = 60$ mm, $h = 12$ mm, $T = ?$, $\tau = 75$ MPa.

Here
$$\tau = \frac{2.83T}{\pi h D^2} \qquad \text{... Tb. 6.1 (3rd row, 2nd col.)/Pg 93, DHB}$$

$$75 = \frac{2.83T}{\pi \times 12 \times 60^2}$$

$$\therefore \qquad T = 3.6 \times 10^6 \, \text{N·mm}$$

48. **A circular steel rod of 50 mm diameter and 200 mm long is welded perpendicularly to a steel plate to form a cantilever to be loaded with a moment of 1 kN·m as shown in Fig. 7.73. Determine the size of the weld, assuming allowable stress as 100 MPa in the welds.**

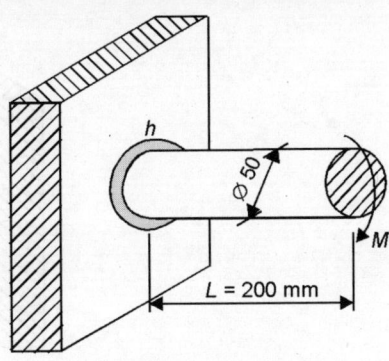

Fig. 7.73: Problem 48

Solution: $D = 50$ mm, $L = 200$ mm, $\sigma = 75$ MPa, $M = 1 \times 10^6$ N·mm, $h = ?$

Here $\qquad \sigma = \sigma_b = \dfrac{5.66M}{\pi h D^2}$ ... **Tb. 6.1 (3rd row, 1st col.)/ Pg 93, DHB**

$$100 = \frac{5.66 \times (1 \times 10^6)}{\pi \times h \times 50^2}$$

$$\therefore \qquad h = 7.21 \, \text{mm}$$

49. **A 600 mm long plate is welded to another plate at right angles to each by 10 mm fillet welds as shown in Fig. 7.74. Find the bending moment that the joint can sustain, if allowable stress is not to exceed 100 MPa.**

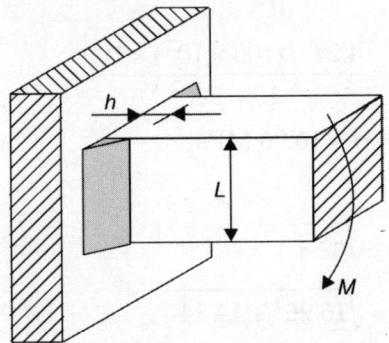

Fig. 7.74: Problem 49

Solution: $L = 600$ mm, $h = 10$ mm, $M = ?$, $\sigma = 120$ MPa.

Here $\qquad \sigma_b = \sigma = \dfrac{4.24M}{hL^2}$ ... **Tb. 6.1 (1st row, 3rd col.)/ Pg 93, DHB**

$$100 = \frac{4.24M}{10 \times 600^2}$$

$$\therefore \qquad M = 84.91 \times 10^6 \, \text{N·mm}$$

50. **A Tee joint with parallel fillet welds subjected to eccentric load is shown in Fig. 7.75. Find the bending stress, shear stress and the resultant stresses using the following data:** $P = 100$ kN, $e = 100$ mm, $h = 10$ mm, $L = 500$ mm.

Solution: $P = 100$ kN, $e = 100$ mm, $h = 10$ mm, $L = 500$ mm, $\sigma = ?$, $\tau = ?$, $\sigma_{max} = ?$

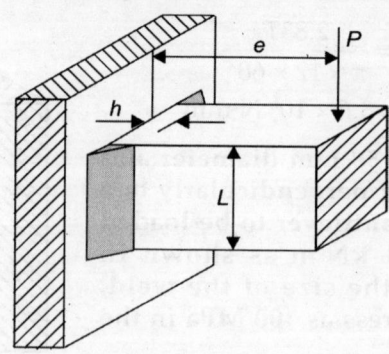

Fig. 7.75: Problem 50

a. Shear stress:

We know that $\qquad \tau = \dfrac{0.707P}{hL} \qquad$ ... **Tb. 6.1 (2nd row, 1st col.)/ Pg 93, DHB**

$$= \dfrac{0.707 \times 100 \times 10^3}{10 \times 500}$$

$\therefore \qquad \tau = 14.14$ MPa

b. Bending stress:

We know that $\qquad \sigma_b = \sigma = \dfrac{4.24Pe}{hL^2} \qquad$ ... **Tb. 6.1 (2nd row, 1st col.)/ Pg 93, DHB**

$$= \dfrac{4.24 \times (100 \times 10^3) \times 100}{10 \times 500^2}$$

$\therefore \qquad \sigma_b = \sigma = 16.96$ MPa

c. Resultant stress:

We know that $\qquad \sigma_{max} = \sqrt{\sigma^2 + \tau^2} \qquad$ ... **1.7(g)/ Pg 4, DHB**

$$= \sqrt{16.96^2 + 14.14^2}$$

$\therefore \qquad \sigma_{max} = 22.08$ MPa

or $\qquad \sigma_{max} = \dfrac{0.707P}{hL}\sqrt{\left[1 + \left(\dfrac{6e}{L}\right)^2\right]}$

$$= \dfrac{0.707 \times (100 \times 10^3)}{10 \times 500}\sqrt{\left[1 + \left(\dfrac{6 \times 100}{500}\right)^2\right]}$$

$\therefore \qquad \sigma_{max} = 22.08$ MPa

51. **A Tee joint with transverse fillet welds subjected to eccentric load is shown in Fig. 7.76. Find the bending stress, shear stress and the resultant stresses using the following data: $P = 100$ kN, $a = 100$ mm, $h = 10$ mm, $b = 25$ mm, $L = 500$ mm.**

Solution: $P = 100$ kN, $a = 100$ mm, $h = 10$ mm, $b = 25$ mm, $L = 500$ mm, $\sigma = ?$, $\tau = ?$, $\sigma_{max} = ?$

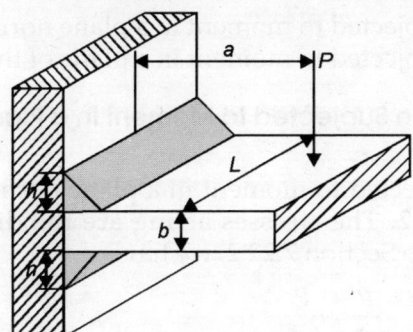

Fig. 7.76: Problem 51

a. Shear stress:

We know that $\qquad \tau = \dfrac{0.707P}{hL}$ ... **Tb. 6.1 (1st row, 1st col.)/ Pg 93, DHB**

$$= \dfrac{0.707 \times 100 \times 10^3}{10 \times 500}$$

$\therefore \qquad\qquad\qquad \tau = 14.14\ \text{MPa}$

b. Bending stress:

We know that $\qquad \sigma_b = \sigma = \dfrac{1.414Pa}{Lh(b+h)}$ ... **Tb. 6.1 (1st row, 1st col.)/ Pg 93, DHB**

$$= \dfrac{1.414 \times (100 \times 10^3) \times 100}{10 \times 500 \times (25 + 10)}$$

$\therefore \qquad\qquad\qquad \sigma_b = \sigma = 80.8\ \text{MPa}$

c. Resultant stress:

We know that $\qquad \sigma_{max} = \sqrt{\sigma^2 + \tau^2}$ ... **1.7(g)/ Pg 4, DHB**

$$= \sqrt{80.8^2 + 14.14^2}$$

$\therefore \qquad\qquad\qquad \sigma_{max} = 82.03\ \text{MPa}$

or $\qquad\qquad \sigma_{max} = \dfrac{P}{hL(b+h)}\sqrt{2a^2 + \dfrac{(b+h)^2}{2}}$ ... (Eq. 7.87)

                               ... **Tb. 6.1 (1st row, 1st col.)/ Pg 93, DHB**

$$= \dfrac{100 \times 10^3}{10 \times 500 \times (25 + 10)}\sqrt{(2 \times 100^2) + \dfrac{(25 + 10)^2}{2}}$$

$\therefore \qquad\qquad\qquad \sigma_{max} = 82.04\ \text{MPa}$

7.23 ECCENTRIC LOAD ON WELDED CONNECTIONS

In eccentric joint, two types of stresses are produced, namely direct shear stress and the other either bending or torsion shear stress. There are two types of eccentric welded connections:

1. Welded connection subjected to moment in a plane normal to the plane of weld.
2. Welded connection subjected to moment in a plane of the weld.

7.23.1 Welded Connection Subjected to Moment in a Plane Normal to the Plane of Weld

A welded connection subjected to moment in a plane normal to the plane of weld is explained in Section 7.22.2. The stresses acting are the direct shear stress and the bending stress. Referring to Section 7.22.2, we have

shear stress, $\qquad \tau = \dfrac{P}{A} = \dfrac{P}{h_t L}$ $\qquad$ ... **6.1 (b)/ Pg 89, DHB**

where $\qquad\qquad L$ = total length of weld

and $\qquad\qquad h_t = 0.707\,h$

Bending stress, $\qquad \sigma_b = \sigma = \dfrac{M}{Z} = \dfrac{Pe}{Z}$ $\qquad$ ... **Tb. 6.1 (c)/ Pg 89, DHB**

where $\qquad\qquad Z$ = section modulus obtained from **Tb 6.7/ Pg 96, DHB** based on weld.

For biaxial loading:

According to maximum normal stress theory,

$$\sigma_{max} = \left(\frac{\sigma}{2}\right) + \sqrt{\left(\frac{\sigma}{2}\right)^2 + \tau^2} \qquad \text{... (Eq. 7.90) } \textbf{1.5(a)/ Pg 3, DHB}$$

According to maximum shear stress theory,

$$\tau_{max} = \sqrt{\left(\frac{\sigma}{2}\right)^2 + \tau^2} \qquad \text{... (Eq. 7.91) } \textbf{1.5(b)/ Pg 3, DHB}$$

52. **Determine the maximum normal stress and the maximum shear stress in the weld shown in Fig. 7.77.**

VTU – June/ July 2013 – 10 Marks

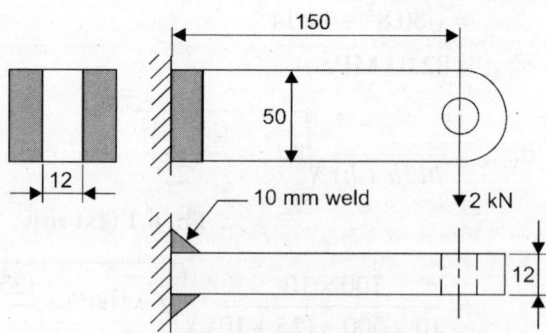

Fig. 7.77: Problem 52

Solution: $P = 2000$ N, $e = 150$ mm, $w = L = 50$ mm, $h = 12$ mm, $\sigma_{max} = ?$, $\tau_{max} = ?$

Bending stress $\qquad \sigma = \dfrac{M}{Z} = \dfrac{Pe}{Z} = \dfrac{4.24Pe}{hL^2} = \dfrac{4.24 \times 2000 \times 150}{12 \times 50^2} = 42.4$ MPa

$\qquad\qquad$ ... **Tb. 6.1 (2nd row, 1st col.)/Pg 93, DHB**

Shear stress, $\quad \tau = \dfrac{0.707P}{hL} = \dfrac{0.707 \times 2000}{12 \times 50} = 2.36 \text{ MPa}$

$$\quad\quad\quad\quad\quad\quad\quad\quad\quad\quad\quad\quad \textbf{... Tb. 6.1 (2nd row, 1st col.)/Pg 93, DHB}$$

According to maximum normal stress theory,

$$\sigma_{max} = \left(\frac{\sigma}{2}\right) + \sqrt{\left(\frac{\sigma}{2}\right)^2 + \tau^2} \quad\quad\quad \textbf{... 1.5(a)/ Pg 3, DHB}$$

$$= \left(\frac{42.4}{2}\right) + \sqrt{\left(\frac{42.4}{2}\right)^2 + 2.36^2}$$

$\therefore \quad\quad\quad\quad \sigma_{max} = 42.53 \text{ MPa}$

According to maximum shear stress theory,

$$\tau_{max} = \sqrt{\left(\frac{\sigma}{2}\right)^2 + \tau^2} \quad\quad\quad\quad \textbf{... 1.5(b)/ Pg 3, DHB}$$

$$= \sqrt{\left(\frac{42.4}{2}\right)^2 + 2.36^2}$$

$\therefore \quad\quad\quad\quad \tau_{max} = 21.33 \text{ MPa}$

53. A welded joint as shown in Fig. 7.78 is subjected to an eccentric load of 2.5 kN. Find the size of the weld, if the maximum shear stress in the weld is 25 MPa.

$$\textit{VTU – Jan. /Feb. 2006 – 14 Marks}$$

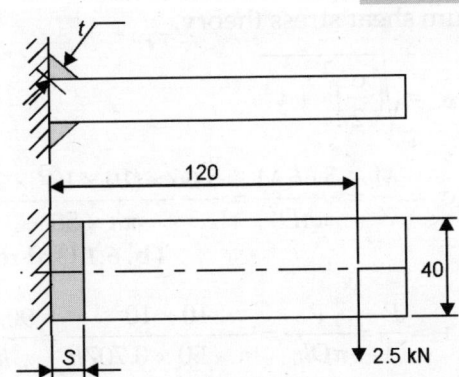

Fig. 7.78: Problem 53

Solution: $P = 2500 \text{ N}, e = 120 \text{ mm}, w = L = 40 \text{ mm}, h = ?, \tau_{max} = ?$

According to maximum shear stress theory,

$$\tau_{max} = \sqrt{\left(\frac{\sigma}{2}\right)^2 + \tau^2} \quad\quad\quad\quad \textbf{... Eq. (i) 1.5(b)/ Pg 3, DHB}$$

Bending stress $\quad \sigma = \dfrac{4.24Pe}{hL^2} = \dfrac{4.24 \times 2500 \times 120}{h \times 40^2} = \dfrac{795}{h}$

$$\quad\quad\quad\quad\quad\quad\quad\quad\quad\quad\quad \textbf{... Tb. 6.1 (2nd row, 1st col.)/Pg 93, DHB}$$

Shear stress, $\quad \tau = \dfrac{0.707P}{hL} = \dfrac{0.707 \times 2500}{h \times 40} = \dfrac{44.19}{h}$

$$\quad\quad\quad\quad\quad\quad\quad\quad\quad\quad\quad \textbf{... Tb. 6.1 (2nd row, 1st col.)/Pg 93, DHB}$$

∴ Eq. (i) yields... $25 = \sqrt{\left(\dfrac{795}{2h}\right)^2 + \left(\dfrac{44.19}{h}\right)^2}$

$$25^2 = \dfrac{160 \times 10^3}{h^2}$$

∴ $h = 16$ mm

54. A circular shaft 50 mm in diameter is welded to a support by means of a fillet weld and loaded as shown in Fig. 7.79. Determine the size of the weld if the permissible shear stress in the weld is limited to 100 MPa.

VTU – June 2012 – 10 Marks

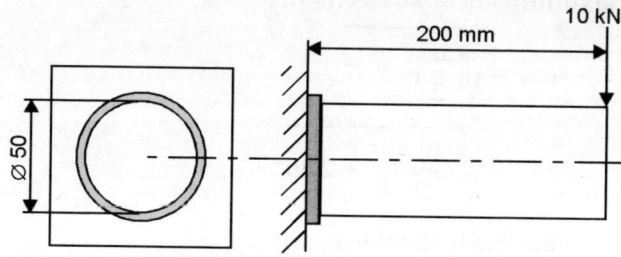

Fig. 7.79: Problem 54

Solution: $P = 10 \times 10^3$ N, $e = 200$ mm, $D = 50$ mm, $h = ?$, $\tau_{max} = 100$ MPa.

According to maximum shear stress theory,

$$\tau_{max} = \sqrt{\left(\dfrac{\sigma}{2}\right)^2 + \tau^2} \qquad \text{... Eq. (i) } \mathbf{1.5(b)/\ Pg\ 3,\ DHB}$$

Bending stress $\sigma = \dfrac{M}{Z} = \dfrac{5.66\,M}{\pi h D^2} = \dfrac{5.66 \times (10 \times 10^3 \times 200)}{\pi h \times 50^2} = \dfrac{1441.31}{h}$

... **Tb. 6.1 (3rd row, 1st col.)/Pg 93, DHB**

Shear stress, $\tau = \dfrac{P}{A} = \dfrac{P}{\pi D h_t} = \dfrac{10 \times 10^3}{\pi \times 50 \times 0.707h} = \dfrac{90.05}{h}$

∴ Eq. (i) yields... $100 = \sqrt{\left(\dfrac{1441.31}{2h}\right)^2 + \left(\dfrac{90.05}{h}\right)^2}$

$$100^2 = \dfrac{527.45 \times 10^3}{h^2}$$

∴ $h = 7.26$ mm ≈ 8 mm

55. A shaft of rectangular cross-section is welded to a support by means of fillet welds as shown in Fig. 7.80. Determine the size of the welds, if permissible shear stress in the weld is limited to 75 MPa.

VTU – Dec. 2014/ Jan. 2015 – 10 Marks; June/July 2008 – 10 Marks

Solution: $P = 25 \times 10^3$ N, $e = 500$ mm, $n = 100$ mm, $m = 150$ mm, $h = ?$, $\tau_{max} = 75$ MPa.

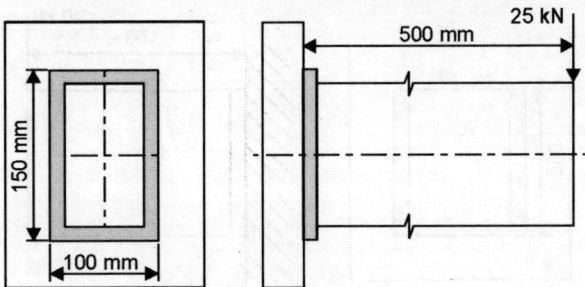

Fig. 7.80: Problem 55

According to maximum shear stress theory,

$$\tau_{max} = \sqrt{\left(\frac{\sigma}{2}\right)^2 + \tau^2} \qquad \text{... Eq. (i) } \textbf{1.5(b)/ Pg 3, DHB}$$

Bending stress $\qquad \sigma = \dfrac{M}{Z} \qquad$ ... Eq. (ii)

Here $\qquad M = P \cdot e = (25 \times 10^3) \times 500 = 12.5 \times 10^6 \text{ N·mm}$

$$Z = h_t\left(nm + \frac{m^2}{3}\right) \quad \textbf{... Tb. 6.7 (2nd row, 2nd col.)/Pg 97, DHB}$$

$$= 0.707\,h\left[(100 \times 150) + \frac{150^2}{3}\right]$$

$$Z = (15907.5)\,h$$

$\therefore$ Eq. (ii) yields... $\qquad \sigma = \dfrac{12.5 \times 10^6}{(15907.5)h} = \dfrac{785.80}{h}$

Shear stress, $\qquad \tau = \dfrac{P}{A} = \dfrac{P}{Lh_t}$

Here total length of weld,

$$L = (2n + 2m) \text{ and } h_t = 0.707\,h$$

$\therefore \qquad A = Lh_t = (2n + 2m)h_t$

$$= [(2 \times 100) + (2 \times 150)] \times 0.707\,h = (353.5)\,h$$

$$\tau = \frac{25 \times 10^3}{(353.5)h} = \frac{70.72}{h}$$

$\therefore$ Eq. (i) yields... $\qquad 75 = \sqrt{\left(\dfrac{785.80}{2h}\right)^2 + \left(\dfrac{70.72}{h}\right)^2}$

$$75^2 = \frac{159.37 \times 10^3}{h^2}$$

$\therefore \qquad h = 5.32 \text{ mm} \approx 6 \text{ mm}$

56. **A bracket is welded to a vertical plate as shown in Fig. 7.81. Determine the size of the welds, if permissible shear stress in the weld is limited to 60 MPa.**

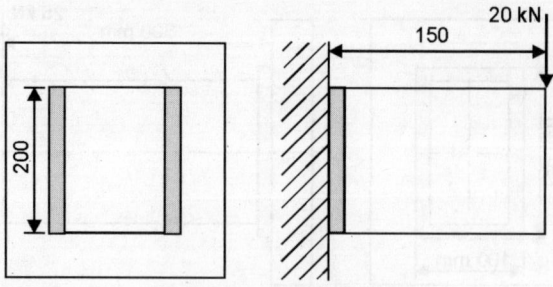

Fig. 7.81: Problem 56

Solution: $P = 20 \times 10^3$ N, $e = 150$ mm, $m = 200$ mm, $h = ?$, $\tau_{max} = 60$ MPa.

According to maximum shear stress theory,

$$\tau_{max} = \sqrt{\left(\frac{\sigma}{2}\right)^2 + \tau^2} \qquad \text{... Eq. (i) } \textbf{1.5(b)/ Pg 3, DHB}$$

Bending stress $\quad \sigma = \dfrac{M}{Z} \qquad\qquad\qquad\qquad$ ... Eq. (ii)

Here $\qquad\qquad M = P{\cdot}e = (20 \times 10^3) \times 150 = 3 \times 10^6$ N·mm

$$Z = \frac{h_t m^2}{3} \qquad \text{... } \textbf{Tb. 6.7 (4th row, 2nd col.)/Pg 96, DHB}$$

$$= \frac{0.707h \times 200^2}{3}$$

$$Z = (9426.67)\, h$$

∴ Eq. (ii) yields... $\quad \sigma = \dfrac{3 \times 10^6}{(9426.67)h} = \dfrac{318.25}{h}$

Shear stress, $\qquad \tau = \dfrac{P}{A} = \dfrac{P}{L h_t}$

Here total length of weld,

$$L = 2m,\ h_t = 0.707\,h$$

∴ $\qquad\qquad A = L h_t = (2m)h_t$

$$= (2 \times 200) \times 0.707\,h = (282.8)\,h$$

$$\tau = \frac{20 \times 10^3}{(282.8)h} = \frac{70.72}{h}$$

∴ Eq. (i) yields... $\quad 60 = \sqrt{\left(\dfrac{318.25}{2h}\right)^2 + \left(\dfrac{70.72}{h}\right)^2}$

$$60^2 = \frac{30.32 \times 10^3}{h^2}$$

∴ $\qquad\qquad h = 2.90$ mm ≈ 3 mm

57. **A bracket is welded to a vertical plate as shown in Fig. 7.82. Determine the size of the welds, if permissible shear stress in the weld is limited to 90 MPa.**

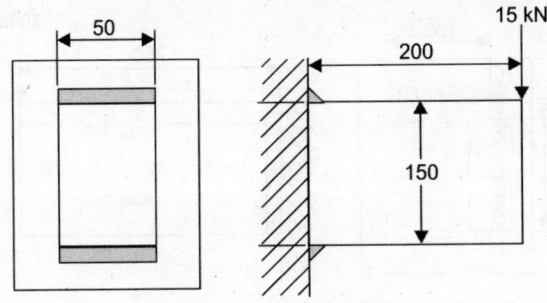

Fig. 7.82: Problem 57

Solution: $P = 15 \times 10^3$ N, $e = 200$ mm, $n = 50$ mm, $m = 150$ mm, $h = ?$, $\tau_{max} = 90$ MPa.
According to maximum shear stress theory,

$$\tau_{max} = \sqrt{\left(\frac{\sigma}{2}\right)^2 + \tau^2} \qquad \text{... Eq. (i) \textbf{1.5(b)/ Pg 3, DHB}}$$

Bending stress $\qquad \sigma = \dfrac{M}{Z} \qquad\qquad\qquad\qquad\qquad\qquad$ ... Eq. (ii)

Here $\qquad\qquad M = P \cdot e = (15 \times 10^3) \times 200 = 3 \times 10^6$ N·mm

$\qquad\qquad\qquad Z = h_t nm \qquad$ ... **Tb. 6.7 (3rd row, 2nd col.)/Pg 96, DHB**

$\qquad\qquad\qquad\quad = 0.707\, h \times 50 \times 150$

$\qquad\qquad\qquad\quad = (5302.5)\, h$

$\therefore$ Eq. (ii) yields... $\qquad \sigma = \dfrac{3 \times 10^6}{(5302.5)h} = \dfrac{565.77}{h}$

Shear stress, $\qquad\qquad \tau = \dfrac{P}{A} = \dfrac{P}{Lh_t}$

Here total length of weld,

$\qquad\qquad\qquad L = 2n, h_t = 0.707\, h$

$\therefore \qquad\qquad\qquad A = Lh_t = (2n)h_t$

$\qquad\qquad\qquad\quad = (2 \times 50) \times 0.707\, h = (70.7)\, h$

$\qquad\qquad\qquad \tau = \dfrac{15 \times 10^3}{(70.7)h} = \dfrac{212.16}{h}$

$\therefore$ Eq. (i) yields... $\qquad 90 = \sqrt{\left(\dfrac{565.77}{2h}\right)^2 + \left(\dfrac{212.16}{h}\right)^2}$

$\qquad\qquad\qquad 90^2 = \dfrac{125.04 \times 10^3}{h^2}$

$\therefore \qquad\qquad\qquad h = 3.93$ mm ≈ 4 mm

58. **Determine the size of the weld for the bracket shown in Fig. 7.83. The allowable shear stress may be taken as 80 MPa.**

    Solution: $P = 20 \times 10^3$ N, $e = 750$ mm, $n = 100$ mm, $m = 200$ mm, $h = ?$, $\tau_{max} = 80$ MPa.

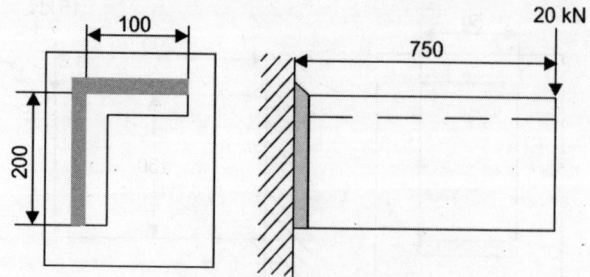

Fig. 7.83: Problem 58

According to maximum shear stress theory,

$$\tau_{max} = \sqrt{\left(\frac{\sigma}{2}\right)^2 + \tau^2} \qquad \text{... Eq. (i) } \textbf{1.5(b)/ Pg 3, DHB}$$

Bending stress $\qquad \sigma = \dfrac{M}{Z_{min}} \qquad\qquad\qquad\qquad\qquad$ ... Eq. (ii)

Here $\qquad\qquad M = P \cdot e = (20 \times 10^3) \times 750 = 15 \times 10^6 \text{ N·mm}$

From **Tb. 6.7 (5th row, 2nd col.)/Pg 96, DHB** , we have

$$Z_{top} = h_t \left(\frac{4nm + m^2}{6}\right)$$

$$= 0.707 h \left(\frac{4 \times 100 \times 200 + 200^2}{6}\right) = (14140)h$$

$$Z_{bottom} = h_t \left[\frac{m^2(4nm + m)}{6(2n + m)}\right]$$

$$= 0.707 h \left[\frac{200^2(4 \times 100 \times 200 + 200)}{6(2 \times 100 + 200)}\right] = (945023.3)h$$

Thus $\qquad\qquad Z_{min} = (14140)\,h$

$\therefore$ Eq. (ii) yields... $\qquad \sigma = \dfrac{15 \times 10^6}{(14140)h} = \dfrac{1060.82}{h}$

Shear stress, $\qquad \tau = \dfrac{P}{A} = \dfrac{P}{Lh_t}$

Here total length of weld,

$$L = (m + n),\ h_t = 0.707\,h$$

$\therefore \qquad\qquad A = Lh_t = (m + n)h_t$

$$= (200 + 100) \times 0.707\,h = (212.1)\,h$$

$$\tau = \frac{20 \times 10^3}{(212.1)h} = \frac{94.29}{h}$$

$\therefore$ Eq. (i) yields... $\qquad 80 = \sqrt{\left(\dfrac{1060.82}{2h}\right)^2 + \left(\dfrac{94.29}{h}\right)^2}$

$$80^2 = \frac{290.234 \times 10^3}{h^2}$$

$$\therefore \qquad h = 6.73 \text{ mm} \approx 7 \text{ mm}$$

59. Determine the size of the weld for the bracket shown in Fig. 7.84. The allowable shear stress may be taken as 80 MPa.

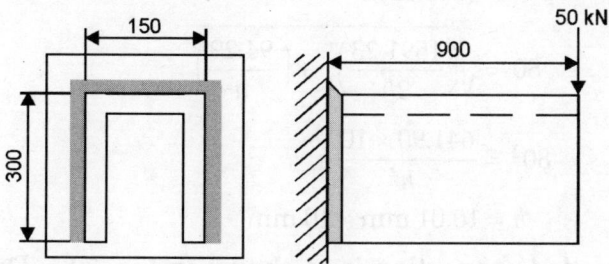

Fig. 7.84: Problem 59

Solution: $P = 50 \times 10^3$ N, $e = 900$ mm, $n = 150$ mm, $m = 300$ mm, $h = ?$, $\tau_{max} = 80$ MPa.

According to maximum shear stress theory,

$$\tau_{max} = \sqrt{\left(\frac{\sigma}{2}\right)^2 + \tau^2} \qquad \text{... Eq. (i) } \mathbf{1.5(b)/ \ Pg \ 3, \ DHB}$$

Bending stress $\qquad \sigma = \dfrac{M}{Z_{min}} \qquad\qquad\qquad\qquad$ ... Eq. (ii)

Here $\qquad M = P \cdot e = (50 \times 10^3) \times 900 = 45 \times 10^6$ N·mm

From **Tb. 6.7 (1st row, 2nd col.)/Pg 97, DHB**, we have

$$Z_{top} = h_t \left(\frac{2nm + m^3}{3}\right)$$

$$= 0.707 \, h \left(\frac{(2 \times 150 \times 300) + 300^3}{3}\right) = (6384210) h$$

$$Z_{bottom} = h_t \left[\frac{m^2 (2n + m)}{3(n + m)}\right]$$

$$= 0.707 \, h \left[\frac{300^2 (2 \times 150 + 300)}{3(150 + 300)}\right] = (28280) h$$

Thus $\qquad Z_{min} = (28280) \, h$

$\therefore$ Eq. (ii) yields... $\qquad \sigma = \dfrac{45 \times 10^6}{(28280) h} = \dfrac{1591.23}{h}$

Shear stress, $\qquad \tau = \dfrac{P}{A} = \dfrac{P}{L h_t}$

Here total length of weld,

$$L = (2m + n), h_t = 0.707 h$$

$$\therefore \qquad A = Lh_t = (2m + n)h_t$$

$$= (2 \times 300 + 150) \times 0.707 h = (530.25) h$$

$$\tau = \frac{50 \times 10^3}{(530.25)h} = \frac{94.29}{h}$$

∴ Eq. (i) yields... $\quad 80 = \sqrt{\left(\frac{1591.23}{2h}\right)^2 + \left(\frac{94.29}{h}\right)^2}$

$$80^2 = \frac{641.90 \times 10^3}{h^2}$$

$$\therefore \qquad h = 10.01 \text{ mm} \approx 10 \text{ mm}$$

60. **An eccentric loaded connection is as shown in Fig. 7.85. Determine the size of the weld, if maximum shear stress induced in the weld is not to exceed 75 N/mm².**

VTU – June/ July 2009 – 10 Marks

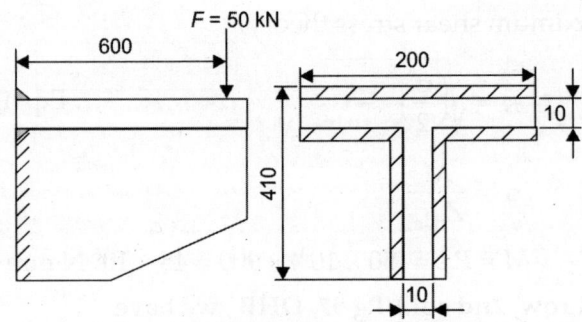

Fig. 7.85: Problem 60

Solution: $P = 50 \times 10^3$ N, $e = 600$ mm, $n = 200$ mm, $m = 410$ mm, $h = ?$, $\tau_{max} = 75$ N/mm².

According to maximum shear stress theory,

$$\tau_{max} = \sqrt{\left(\frac{\sigma}{2}\right)^2 + \tau^2} \qquad \text{... Eq. (i)} \textbf{ 1.5(b)/ Pg 3, DHB}$$

Bending stress $\qquad \sigma = \dfrac{M}{Z_{min}}$ $\qquad\qquad$ ... Eq. (ii)

Here $\qquad M = P \cdot e = (50 \times 10^3) \times 600 = 30 \times 10^6$ N·mm

From **Tb. 6.7 (4th row, 2nd col.)/Pg 97, DHB** , we have

$$Z_{top} = h_t \left(\frac{4nm + m^2}{3}\right)$$

$$= 0.707h\left(\frac{(4 \times 200 \times 410) + 410^2}{3}\right) = (116914.23)h$$

$$Z_{bottom} = h_t \left[\frac{(4nm^2 + m^3)}{(6n + 3m)} \right]$$

$$= 0.707 \, h \left[\frac{(4 \times 200 \times 410^2) + 410^3}{(6 \times 200 + 3 \times 410)} \right] = (59178.81) h$$

Thus $Z_{min} = (59178.81) \, h$

∴ Eq. (ii) yields... $\sigma = \dfrac{30 \times 10^6}{(59178.81) h} = \dfrac{506.94}{h}$

Shear stress, $\tau = \dfrac{P}{A} = \dfrac{P}{L h_t}$

Here total length of weld,

$$L = n + (n - 10) + 2(m - 10)$$

$$= 200 + 190 + [2 \times (410 - 10)]$$

$$L = 1190 \text{ mm}$$

and $h_t = 0.707 \, h$

∴ $A = L h_t = 1190 \times 0.707 \, h = (841.33) \, h$

$$\tau = \frac{50 \times 10^3}{(841.33) h} = \frac{59.43}{h}$$

∴ Eq. (i) yields... $75 = \sqrt{\left(\dfrac{506.94}{2h} \right)^2 + \left(\dfrac{59.43}{h} \right)^2}$

$$75^2 = \frac{67.78 \times 10^3}{h^2}$$

∴ $h = 3.48 \text{ mm} \approx 4 \text{ mm}$

61. **An eccentric loaded connection is as shown in Fig. 7.86. Determine the size of the weld, if maximum shear stress induced in the weld is not to exceed 60 MPa.**

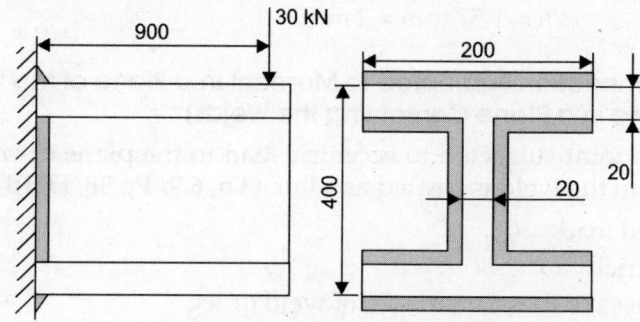

Fig. 7.86: Problem 61

Solution: $P = 30 \times 10^3$ N, $e = 900$ mm, $n = 200$ mm, $m = 400$ mm, $h = ?$, $\tau_{max} = 60$ MPa.

According to maximum shear stress theory,

$$\tau_{max} = \sqrt{\left(\frac{\sigma}{2}\right)^2 + \tau^2} \qquad \text{... Eq. (i) } \textbf{1.5(b)/ Pg 3, DHB}$$

Bending stress $\qquad \sigma = \dfrac{M}{Z} \qquad\qquad\qquad\qquad\qquad$ ... Eq. (ii)

Here $\qquad\qquad M = P{\cdot}e = (30 \times 10^3) \times 900 = 27 \times 10^6 \text{ N·mm}$

From **Tb. 6.7 (6th row, 2nd col.)/Pg 97, DHB** , we have

$$Z = h_t \left(2nm + \frac{m^2}{3} \right)$$

$$= 0.707\, h \left((2 \times 200 \times 400) + \frac{400^2}{3} \right) = (150826.67)h$$

$$\therefore \qquad\qquad \sigma = \frac{27 \times 10^6}{(158026.67)h} = \frac{179.01}{h}$$

Shear stress, $\qquad\qquad \tau = \dfrac{P}{A} = \dfrac{P}{Lh_t}$

Here total length of weld,

$$L = 2[n + (n - t_w)] + 2(m - 2t_f) \quad [t_w = \text{web}, t_f = \text{flange}]$$

$$= 2[200 + (200 - 20)] + 2(400 - 2 \times 20)$$

$$L = 1480 \text{ mm}$$

$$\therefore \qquad A = Lh_t = 1480 \times 0.707\, h = (1046.36)\, h$$

$$\tau = \frac{30 \times 10^3}{(1046.36)h} = \frac{28.67}{h}$$

$\therefore$ Eq. (i) yields... $\qquad 60 = \sqrt{\left(\dfrac{179.01}{2h}\right)^2 + \left(\dfrac{28.67}{h}\right)^2}$

$$60^2 = \frac{8.83 \times 10^3}{h^2}$$

$$\therefore \qquad\qquad h = 1.57 \text{ mm} \approx 2 \text{ mm}$$

7.23.2 Welded Connection Subjected to Moment in a Plane of the Weld (Load Acting in a Plane Containing the Welds)

Consider a welded joint subjected to eccentric load in the plane of weld as shown in **Fig. 7.87(a)**, wherein the weld is treated as a line **(Tb. 6.7/ Pg 96, DHB)**.

Let $\quad P$ = applied load

$\quad e$ = eccentricity

$\quad h$ = thickness of the plate or size of weld or leg

$\quad h_t$ = weld depth of the throat = $h \cos 45° = 0.707\, h$

$\quad n$ = horizontal length of weld

$\quad m$ = vertical length of weld

$\quad G$ = center of gravity (CG) of weld

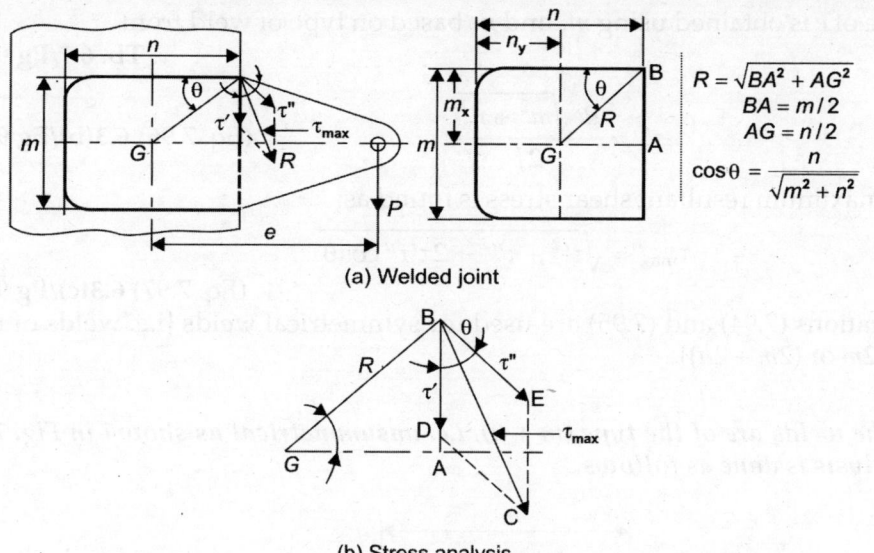

(a) Welded joint

(b) Stress analysis

Fig. 7.87: Eccentrically loaded welded joint **[Fig. 6.3/Pg 91, DHB]**

m_x = distance of CG from top
n_y = distance of CG from left
J = polar moment of inertia   **... Tb. 6.7/ Pg 96, DHB**
τ' = direct or primary shear stress
τ'' = secondary shear stress
τ_{max} = maximum resultant shear stress
θ = angle between primary and secondary shear stresses

The stresses acting are the direct shear stress and the torsional shear stress. The analysis is similar to that as discussed under riveted joints subjected to shear.

• Direct or primary shear stress,

$$\tau' = \frac{P}{A_t} = \frac{P}{h_t L} = \frac{P}{(h\cos 45°)L} \quad \text{... (Eq. 7.92) 6.3(a)/Pg 91, DHB}$$

• Secondary shear stress,

$$\tau'' = \frac{TR}{J} = \frac{(P \cdot e)R}{J} \quad \text{... (Eq. 7.93)}$$

From **Fig. 7.87(b)**, we have

$$R = BG = \sqrt{BA^2 + AG^2}$$

But $BA = (m/2)$ and $AG = (n/2)$, from **Fig. 7.87(a)**

Hence $$R = \sqrt{\left(\frac{m}{2}\right)^2 + \left(\frac{n}{2}\right)^2} = \frac{\sqrt{m^2 + n^2}}{2} \quad \text{... (Eq. 7.94)}$$

$$\cos\theta = \frac{AG}{BG} = \frac{n/2}{R} = \frac{n/2}{\sqrt{(m^2+n^2)}/2} = \frac{n}{\sqrt{m^2+n^2}}$$

... (Eq. 7.95) 6.3(d)/ Pg 91, DHB

Value of e is obtained using m_x and n_y based on type of weld from

... **Tb. 6.7/Pg 96, DHB**

Thus $\qquad \tau'' = \dfrac{Pe\sqrt{m^2 + n^2}}{2J}$ ... **(Eq. 7.96) 6.3(b)/Pg 91, DHB**

The maximum resultant shear stress is found as:

$$\tau_{max} = \sqrt{\tau'^2 + \tau''^2 + 2\tau'\tau'' \cos\theta}$$

... **(Eq. 7.97) 6.3(c)/Pg 91, DHB**

- Equations (7.94) and (7.95) are used for symmetrical welds [i.e. welds of the type $2n$, $2m$ or $(2m + 2n)$].

Note:
- *If the welds are of the type $(m + n)$, i.e. unsymmetrical as shown in Fig. 7.88, the analysis is done as follows.*

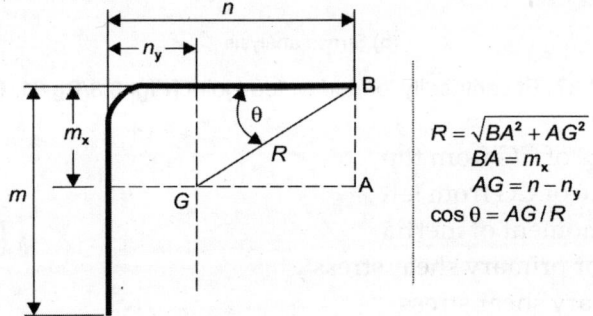

Fig. 7.88: To find R

We know that $\qquad \tau'' = \dfrac{TR}{J} = \dfrac{(P \cdot e)R}{J}$ ... Using (Eq. 7.93)

Here $\qquad R = \sqrt{BA^2 + AG^2}$ ... (Eq. 7.98)

where $\qquad BA = m_x$ and $AG = n - n_y$,

and $\qquad \cos\theta = \dfrac{AG}{BG} = \dfrac{AG}{R}$ ... (Eq. 7.99)

- *Equations (7.98) and (7.99) are used for unsymmetrical welds [i.e. welds of the type n, m, $(m + n)$, $(2m + n)$, $(2n + m)$]*

* In solving problems, the dimensions are shown by treating the welds as a line, irrespective of thickness of the weld.

62. **A bracket carrying a load of 15 kN is to be welded as shown in Fig. 7.89(a). Find the size of the weld required if the allowable shear stress is not to exceed 80 MPa.**

VTU – June/July 2015 – 10 Marks, Dec. 13/Jan. 2014 – 08 Marks,
June/July 2011– 10 Marks, July 2007 – 10 Marks

Solution: $P = 15 \times 10^3$ N, $n = 50$ mm, $m = 80$ mm, $\tau_{max} = 80$ MPa, $h = ?$

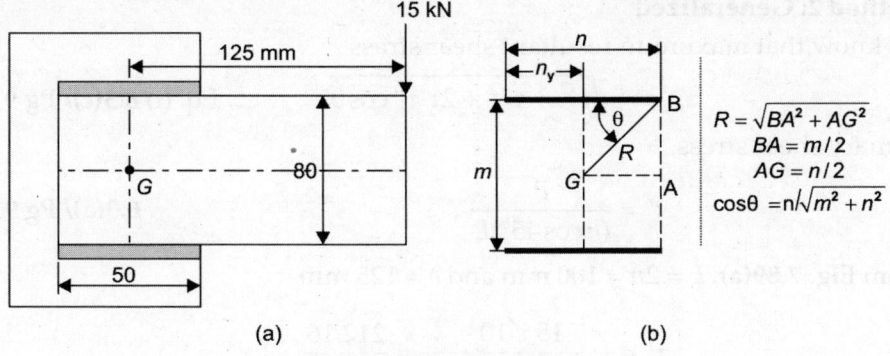

Fig. 7.89: Problem 62

Method 1: As per formulae

Here the welds are of the type $2n$ (symmetric) as shown in **Fig. 7.89(b)**.

We know that maximum resultant shear stress

$$\tau_{max} = \sqrt{\tau'^2 + \tau''^2 + 2\tau'\tau'' \cos\theta} \qquad \dots \text{Eq. (i) } \textbf{6.3(c)/ Pg 91, DHB}$$

Primary shear stress,

$$\tau' = \frac{P}{(h\cos 45°)L} \qquad \dots \textbf{6.3(a)/ Pg 91, DHB}$$

From **Fig. 7.89(a)**, $L = 2n = 100$ mm and $e = 125$ mm

$$\therefore \qquad \tau' = \frac{15 \times 10^3}{(h\cos 45°) \times 100} = \frac{212.16}{h}$$

Secondary shear stress,

$$\tau'' = \frac{Pe\sqrt{m^2 + n^2}}{2J} \qquad \dots \textbf{6.3(b)/Pg 91, DHB}$$

Here

$$J = \frac{h_t n(3m^2 + n^2)}{6} \qquad \dots \textbf{Tb. 6.7 (3rd row, 3rd col.)/Pg 96, DHB}$$

$$= \frac{(0.707 h) \times 50(3 \times 80^2 + 50^2)}{6}$$

$$J = (127.85 \times 10^3) h$$

$$\therefore \qquad \tau'' = \frac{(15 \times 10^3) \times 125 \times \sqrt{80^2 + 50^2}}{2 \times (127.85 \times 10^3)h} = \frac{691.78}{h}$$

Also

$$\cos\theta = \frac{AG}{BG} = \frac{n}{\sqrt{m^2 + n^2}} = \frac{50}{\sqrt{80^2 + 50^2}} = 0.530$$

$\therefore$ Eq. (i) yields...

$$80 = \sqrt{\left(\frac{212.16}{h}\right)^2 + \left(\frac{691.78}{h}\right)^2 + 2\left(\frac{212.16}{h}\right)\left(\frac{691.78}{h}\right) \times 0.530}$$

$$80^2 = \frac{67.15 \times 10^3}{h^2}$$

$$\therefore \qquad h = 10.30 \text{ mm} \approx 11 \text{ mm}$$

Method 2: Generalized

We know that maximum resultant shear stress

$$\tau_{max} = \sqrt{\tau'^2 + \tau''^2 + 2\tau'\tau''\cos\theta} \qquad \text{... Eq. (i) 6.3(c)/ Pg 91, DHB}$$

Primary shear stress,

$$\tau' = \frac{P}{(h\cos 45°)L} \qquad \text{... 6.3(a)/ Pg 91, DHB}$$

From **Fig. 7.89(a)**, $L = 2n = 100$ mm and $e = 125$ mm

$$\therefore \qquad \tau' = \frac{15 \times 10^3}{(h\cos 45°) \times 100} = \frac{212.16}{h}$$

Secondary shear stress,

$$\tau'' = \frac{TR}{J} = \frac{(P \cdot e)R}{J} \qquad \text{... Eq. (ii)}$$

- $$m_x = AB = \frac{m}{2} = \frac{80}{2} = 40 \text{ mm}$$

- $$n_y = AG = \frac{n}{2} = \frac{50}{2} = 25 \text{ mm}$$

- $$R = \sqrt{BA^2 + AG^2} = \sqrt{40^2 + 25^2} = 47.17 \text{ mm}$$

- $$\cos\theta = \frac{AG}{R} = \frac{25}{47.17} = 0.530$$

- Also $$J = \frac{h_t n(3m^2 + n^2)}{6} \qquad \text{... Tb. 6.7 (3rd row, 3rd col.)/Pg 96, DHB}$$

$$= \frac{(0.707 h) \times 50(3 \times 80^2 + 50^2)}{6}$$

$$J = (127.85 \times 10^3)h$$

$$\therefore \text{Eq. (ii) yields...} \quad \tau'' = \frac{15 \times 10^3 \times 125 \times 47.17}{(127.85 \times 10^3)h} = \frac{691.78}{h}$$

$$\therefore \text{Eq. (i) yields...} \quad 80 = \sqrt{\left(\frac{212.16}{h}\right)^2 + \left(\frac{691.78}{h}\right)^2 + 2\left(\frac{212.16}{h}\right)\left(\frac{691.78}{h}\right) \times 0.530}$$

$$80^2 = \frac{67.15 \times 10^3}{h^2}$$

$$\therefore \qquad h = 10.30 \text{ mm} \approx 11 \text{ mm}$$

Note: *Method 2 is preferred in most cases.*

63. **A bracket shown in Fig. 7.90 carries a load of 10 kN. Find the size of the weld if the allowable shear stress is not to exceed 80 MPa.**

VTU – Dec. 2011 – 08 Marks

Solution: $P = 10 \times 10^3$ N, $n = 60$ mm, $m = 100$ mm, $\tau_{max} = 80$ MPa, $h = ?$

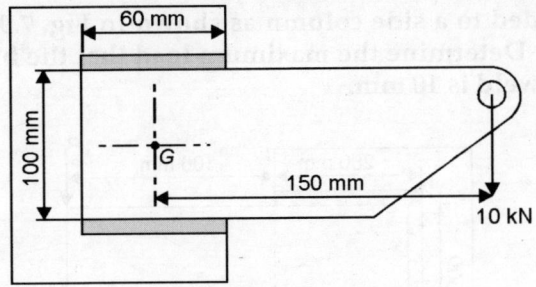

Fig. 7.90: Problem 63

Method 1: As per formulae

Here the welds are of the type 2n (symmetric) as shown in **Fig. 7.90**.

We know that maximum resultant shear stress

$$\tau_{max} = \sqrt{\tau'^2 + \tau''^2 + 2\tau'\tau''\cos\theta} \qquad \text{... Eq. (i) } \textbf{6.3(c)/ Pg 91, DHB}$$

Primary shear stress,

$$\tau' = \frac{P}{(h\cos 45°)L} \qquad \text{... } \textbf{6.3(a)/ Pg 91, DHB}$$

From **Fig. 7.90**, $L = 2n = 120$ mm and $e = 150$ mm

$$\therefore \qquad \tau' = \frac{10 \times 10^3}{(h\cos 45°) \times 120} = \frac{117.87}{h}$$

Secondary shear stress,

$$\tau'' = \frac{Pe\sqrt{m^2 + n^2}}{2J} \qquad \text{... } \textbf{6.3(b)/Pg 91, DHB}$$

Here

$$J = \frac{h_t n(3m^2 + n^2)}{6} \qquad \text{... Tb. 6.7 (3rd row, 3rd col.)/Pg 96, DHB}$$

$$= \frac{(0.707\,h) \times 60(3 \times 100^2 + 60^2)}{6}$$

$$J = (237.55 \times 10^3)h$$

$$\therefore \qquad \tau'' = \frac{(10 \times 10^3) \times 150 \times \sqrt{100^2 + 60^2}}{2 \times (237.55 \times 10^3)h} = \frac{368.19}{h}$$

Also

$$\cos\theta = \frac{AG}{BG} = \frac{n}{\sqrt{m^2 + n^2}} = \frac{60}{\sqrt{100^2 + 60^2}} = 0.515$$

$\therefore$ Eq. (i) yields...

$$80 = \sqrt{\left(\frac{117.87}{h}\right)^2 + \left(\frac{368.19}{h}\right)^2 + 2\left(\frac{117.87}{h}\right)\left(\frac{368.19}{h}\right) \times 0.515}$$

$$80^2 = \frac{194.16 \times 10^3}{h^2}$$

$$\therefore \qquad h = 5.51 \text{ mm} \approx 6 \text{ mm}$$

64. A bracket is welded to a side column as shown in Fig. 7.91 with a permissible stress of 80 MPa. Determine the maximum load that the bracket can withstand if the size of the weld is 10 mm.

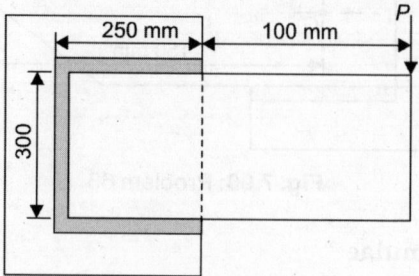

Fig. 7.91: Problem 64

Solution: $\tau_{max} = 80$ MPa, $P = ?$, $n = 250$ mm, $m = 300$ mm, $h = 10$ mm.

Method 1: As per formulae

Here the welds are of the type $2n$ (symmetric) as shown in **Fig. 7.91**.

We know that maximum resultant shear stress

$$\tau_{max} = \sqrt{\tau'^2 + \tau''^2 + 2\tau'\tau''\cos\theta} \qquad \text{... Eq. (i) } \textbf{6.3(c)/ Pg 91, DHB}$$

Primary shear stress,

$$\tau' = \frac{P}{(h\cos 45°)L} \qquad \text{... 6.3(a)/ Pg 91, DHB}$$

From **Fig. 7.91**, $L = 2n = 500$ mm and $e = 100 + (250/2) = 225$ mm

$$\therefore \qquad \tau' = \frac{P}{(10\cos 45°) \times 500} = 2.83 \times 10^{-4} P$$

Secondary shear stress,

$$\tau'' = \frac{Pe\sqrt{m^2 + n^2}}{2J} \qquad \text{... 6.3(b)/Pg 91, DHB}$$

Here $\qquad J = \dfrac{h_t n(3m^2 + n^2)}{6} \qquad$ **... Tb. 6.7 (3rd row, 3rd col.)/Pg 96, DHB**

$$= \frac{(0.707 \times 10) \times 250(3 \times 300^2 + 250^2)}{6}$$

$$J = 97.95 \times 10^6 \text{ mm}^4$$

$$\therefore \qquad \tau'' = \frac{P \times 225 \times \sqrt{300^2 + 250^2}}{2 \times (97.95 \times 10^6)} = 4.49 \times 10^{-4} P$$

Also $\qquad \cos\theta = \dfrac{AG}{BG} = \dfrac{n}{\sqrt{m^2 + n^2}} = \dfrac{250}{\sqrt{300^2 + 250^2}} = 0.640$

$\therefore$ Eq. (i) yields...

$$80 = \sqrt{(2.83 \times 10^{-4}P)^2 + (4.49 \times 10^{-4}P)^2 + [2(2.83 \times 10^{-4}P)(4.49 \times 10^{-4}P) \times 0.640]}$$

$$80^2 = 4.44 \times 10^{-7}P^2$$

$\therefore \quad P = 120 \text{ kN}$

65. **A 16 mm thick plate is welded to a vertical support by two fillet welds as shown in Fig. 7.92(a). Determine the size of the weld, if the permissible shear stress for the weld material is 75 MPa.**

VTU – May/ June 2010 – 10 Marks; Dec. 07/ Jan. 2008 – 10 Marks

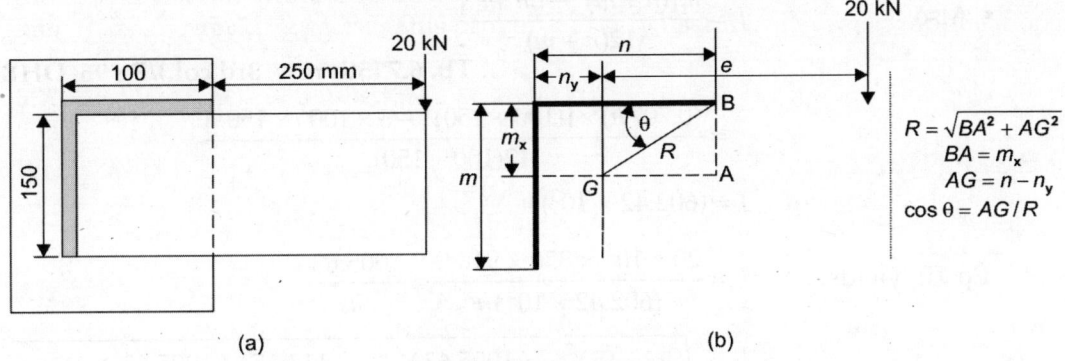

(a)   (b)

Fig. 7.92: Problem 65

Solution: $P = 20$ kN, $n = 100$ mm, $m = 150$ mm, $h = ?$, $\tau_{max} = 75$ MPa.

Method 2: Generalized

Here the welds are of type $m + n$ (unsymmetrical) as shown in **Fig. 7.92**.

We know that maximum resultant shear stress

$$\tau_{max} = \sqrt{\tau'^2 + \tau''^2 + 2\tau'\tau'' \cos\theta} \qquad \text{... Eq. (i) } \textbf{6.3(c)/ Pg 91, DHB}$$

Primary shear stress,

$$\tau' = \frac{P}{(h\cos 45°)L} \qquad \text{... } \textbf{6.3(a)/ Pg 91, DHB}$$

From **Fig. 7.92(a)**, $\quad L = m + n = 150 + 100 = 250$ mm.

$$\therefore \qquad \tau' = \frac{20 \times 10^3}{(h\cos 45°) \times 250} = \frac{113.15}{h}$$

Secondary shear stress,

$$\tau'' = \frac{TR}{J} = \frac{(P \cdot e)R}{J} \qquad \text{... Eq. (ii)}$$

$$\bullet \qquad m_x = \frac{m^2}{2(n+m)} = \frac{150^2}{2(100+150)} = 45 \text{ mm}$$

$$\bullet \qquad n_y = \frac{n^2}{2(n+m)} = \frac{100^2}{2(100+150)} = 20 \text{ mm}$$

... **Tb. 6.7 (5th row, 1st col.)/Pg 96, DHB**

From **Fig. 7.92(a)**, $e = (250 + 100) - n_y = 350 - 20 = 330$ mm

- $$R = \sqrt{BA^2 + AG^2}$$
  $$BA = m_x = 45 \text{ mm}$$
  $$AG = n - n_y = 100 - 20 = 80 \text{ mm}$$
  $$R = \sqrt{45^2 + 80^2} = 91.79 \text{ mm}$$

- $$\cos\theta = \frac{AG}{R} = \frac{80}{91.79} = 0.872$$

- Also $$J = \frac{h_t[(n+m)^4 - 6n^2 m^2]}{12(n+m)}$$

  ... **Tb. 6.7 (5th row, 3rd col.)/Pg 96, DHB**

  $$= \frac{(0.707\,h) \times [(100+150)^4 - 6 \times 100^2 \times 150^2]}{12(100+150)}$$

  $$J = (602.42 \times 10^3)\,h$$

∴ Eq. (ii) yields... $$\tau'' = \frac{20 \times 10^3 \times 330 \times 91.79}{(602.42 \times 10^3)h} = \frac{1005.63}{h}$$

∴ Eq. (i) yields... $$75 = \sqrt{\left(\frac{113.15}{h}\right)^2 + \left(\frac{1005.63}{h}\right)^2 + 2\left(\frac{113.15}{h}\right)\left(\frac{1005.63}{h}\right) \times 0.872}$$

$$75^2 = \frac{1.22 \times 10^6}{h^2}$$

∴ $$h = 14.74 \text{ mm} \approx 15 \text{ mm}$$

66. **A steel bracket is welded to the structure and loaded by a vertical load of 35 kN at a distance of 480 mm from the support as shown in Fig. 7.93(a). Calculate the size of the weld required at the three sides as shown, if the allowable shear stress in the weld is 90 MPa.**

VTU – Dec. 2011 – 10 Marks, Dec. 2009/Jan. 2010 – 10 Marks,
(similar) Jan/Feb. 2005 – 14 Marks

Solution: $P = 35$ kN, $n = 120$ mm, $m = 240$ mm, $h = ?$, $\tau_{max} = 90$ MPa.

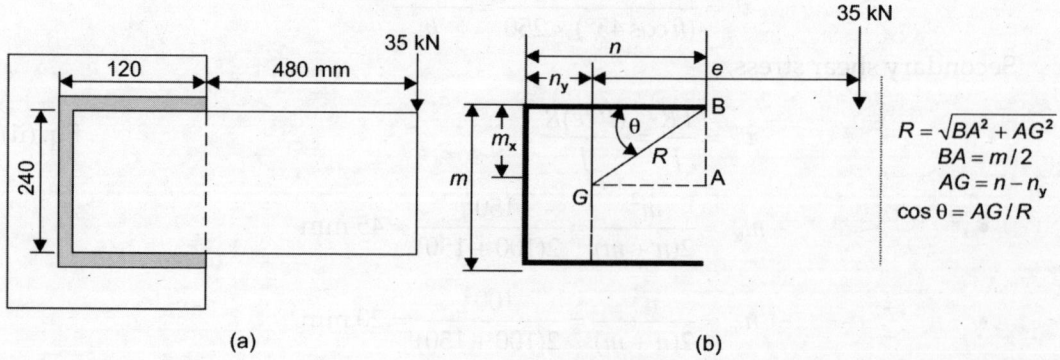

(a)   (b)

Fig. 7.93: Problem 66

Method 2: Generalized

Here the welds are of the type $(m + 2n)$ [unsymmetrical] as shown in **Fig. 7.93**.

We know that maximum resultant shear stress

$$\tau_{max} = \sqrt{\tau'^2 + \tau''^2 + 2\tau'\tau'' \cos\theta} \quad \text{... Eq. (i) } \textbf{6.3(c)/ Pg 91, DHB}$$

Primary shear stress,

$$\tau' = \frac{P}{(h\cos 45°)L} \quad \text{... 6.3(a)/ Pg 91, DHB}$$

From **Fig. 7.93(a)**, $L = (m + 2n) = [240 + (2 \times 120)] = 480$ mm.

$$\therefore \qquad \tau' = \frac{35 \times 10^3}{(h\cos 45°) \times 480} = \frac{103.14}{h}$$

Secondary shear stress,

$$\tau'' = \frac{TR}{J} = \frac{(P \cdot e)R}{J} \qquad \text{... Eq. (ii)}$$

- $$m_x = \frac{m}{2} = \frac{240}{2} = 120 \text{ mm}$$

- $$n_y = \frac{n^2}{2n + m} = \frac{120^2}{[(2 \times 120) + 240]} = 30 \text{ mm}$$
  $$\text{... Tb. 6.7 (6th row, 1st col.)/Pg 96, DHB}$$

From **Fig. 7.93(a)**, $e = (480 + 120) - n_y = 600 - 30 = 570$ mm

- $$R = \sqrt{BA^2 + AG^2}$$

  $$BA = m_x = 120 \text{ mm}$$

  $$AG = n - n_y = 120 - 30 = 90 \text{ mm}$$

  $$R = \sqrt{120^2 + 90^2} = 150 \text{ mm}$$

- $$\cos\theta = \frac{AG}{R} = \frac{90}{150} = 0.6$$

- Also $$J = h_t\left[\frac{(2n + m)^3}{12} - \frac{n^2(n + m)^2}{(2n + m)}\right]$$
  $$\text{... Tb. 6.7 (6th row, 3rd col.)/Pg 96, DHB}$$

  $$= (0.707h) \times \left[\frac{(2 \times 120 + 240)^3}{12} - \frac{120^2 \times (120 + 240)^2}{(2 \times 120 + 240)}\right]$$

  $$J = (3.77 \times 10^6)h$$

$\therefore$ Eq. (ii) yields... $$\tau'' = \frac{35 \times 10^3 \times 570 \times 150}{(3.77 \times 10^6)h} = \frac{794.42}{h}$$

$\therefore$ Eq. (i) yields... $$90 = \sqrt{\left(\frac{103.14}{h}\right)^2 + \left(\frac{794.42}{h}\right)^2 + 2\left(\frac{103.14}{h}\right)\left(\frac{794.42}{h}\right) \times 0.6}$$

$$90^2 = \frac{784.64 \times 10^3}{h^2}$$

$$\therefore \qquad h = 9.56 \text{ mm} \approx 10 \text{ mm}$$

Note: *Students are hereby advised to solve more problems based on Problem 66, since numerous question papers have the same pattern.*

67. **An eccentrically loaded bracket is welded to a support as shown in Fig. 7.94. The permissible shear stress for the weld material is 80 MPa. Determine the size of the weld.**

VTU – June/ July 2015 – 10 Marks

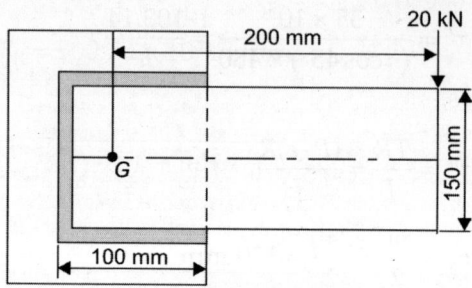

Fig. 7.94: Problem 67

Solution: $P = 20$ kN, $n = 100$ mm, $m = 150$ mm, $h = ?$, $\tau_{max} = 80$ MPa.

Here the welds are of the type $(m + 2n)$ [unsymmetrical] as shown in **Fig. 7.94**.

We know that maximum resultant shear stress

$$\tau_{max} = \sqrt{\tau'^2 + \tau''^2 + 2\tau'\tau'' \cos\theta} \qquad \text{... Eq. (i) 6.3(c)/ Pg 91, DHB}$$

Primary shear stress,

$$\tau' = \frac{P}{(h\cos 45°)L} \qquad \text{... 6.3(a)/ Pg 91, DHB}$$

From **Fig. 7.94,** $\qquad L = (m + 2n) = [150 + (2 \times 100)] = 350$ mm.

$$\therefore \qquad \tau' = \frac{20 \times 10^3}{(h\cos 45°) \times 350} = \frac{80.82}{h}$$

Secondary shear stress,

$$\tau'' = \frac{TR}{J} = \frac{(P \cdot e)R}{J} \qquad \text{... Eq. (ii)}$$

- $$m_x = \frac{m}{2} = \frac{150}{2} = 75 \text{ mm}$$

- $$n_y = \frac{n^2}{2n + m} = \frac{100^2}{(2 \times 100) + 150} = 28.57 \text{ mm}$$

$$\text{... Tb. 6.7 (6th row, 1st col.)/Pg 96, DHB}$$

From **Fig. 7.94,** $e = 200$ mm

- $$R = \sqrt{BA^2 + AG^2}$$

$$BA = m_x = 75 \text{ mm}$$

$$AG = n - n_y = 100 - 28.57 = 71.43 \text{ mm}$$

$$R = \sqrt{75^2 + 71.43^2} = 103.57 \text{ mm}$$

- $$\cos \theta = \frac{AG}{R} = \frac{71.43}{103.57} = 0.689$$

- Also $$J = h_t \left[\frac{(2n + m)^3}{12} - \frac{n^2(n + m)^2}{(2n + m)} \right]$$

$$\text{... Tb. 6.7 (6th row, 3rd col.)/Pg 96, DHB}$$

$$= (0.707\, h) \times \left[\frac{(2 \times 100 + 150)^3}{12} - \frac{100^2 \times (100 + 150)^2}{(2 \times 100 + 150)} \right]$$

$$J = (1.26 \times 10^6)\, h$$

$\therefore$ Eq. (ii) yields... $$\tau'' = \frac{20 \times 10^3 \times 200 \times 103.57}{(1.26 \times 10^6)h} = \frac{327.87}{h}$$

$\therefore$ Eq. (i) yields... $$80 = \sqrt{\left(\frac{80.82}{h}\right)^2 + \left(\frac{327.87}{h}\right)^2 + 2\left(\frac{80.82}{h}\right)\left(\frac{327.87}{h}\right) \times 0.689}$$

$$80^2 = \frac{150.54 \times 10^3}{h^2}$$

$\therefore$ $$h = 4.85 \text{ mm} \approx 5 \text{ mm}$$

68. **Determine the size of the weld required for a flat plate, welded to a steel column and loaded as shown in Fig. 7.95. The allowable shear stress in the weld is limited to 80 MPa at the throat section.**

VTU – Dec. 2010 – 10 Marks

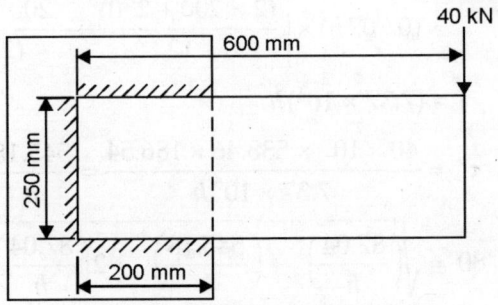

Fig. 7.95: Problem 68

Solution: $P = 40$ kN, $n = 200$ mm, $m = 250$ mm, $h = ?$, $\tau_{max} = 80$ MPa.

Here the welds are of the type $(m + 2n)$ [unsymmetrical] as shown in **Fig. 7.95**.

We know that maximum resultant shear stress

$$\tau_{max} = \sqrt{\tau'^2 + \tau''^2 + 2\tau'\tau'' \cos\theta} \qquad \text{... Eq. (i) 6.3(c)/ Pg 91, DHB}$$

Primary shear stress,

$$\tau' = \frac{P}{(h\cos 45°)L} \qquad \text{... 6.3(a)/ Pg 91, DHB}$$

From **Fig. 7.95,** $L = (m + 2n) = [250 + (2 \times 200)] = 650$ mm.

$\therefore \qquad \tau' = \dfrac{40 \times 10^3}{(h\cos 45°) \times 650} = \dfrac{87.04}{h}$

Secondary shear stress,

$$\tau'' = \dfrac{TR}{J} = \dfrac{(P \cdot e)R}{J} \qquad\qquad \text{... Eq. (ii)}$$

- $m_x = \dfrac{m}{2} = \dfrac{250}{2} = 125$ mm

- $n_y = \dfrac{n^2}{2n + m} = \dfrac{200^2}{(2 \times 200 + 250)} = 61.54$ mm

  ... **Tb. 6.7 (6th row, 1st col.)/Pg 96, DHB**

From **Fig. 7.95,** $e = (600 - n_y) = 600 - 61.54 = 538.46$ mm

- $R = \sqrt{BA^2 + AG^2}$

  $BA = m_x = 125$ mm

  $AG = n - n_y = 200 - 61.54 = 138.46$ mm

  $R = \sqrt{125^2 + 138.46^2} = 186.54$ mm

- $\cos\theta = \dfrac{AG}{R} = \dfrac{138.46}{186.54} = 0.742$

- Also $J = h_t\left[\dfrac{(2n + m)^3}{12} - \dfrac{n^2(n + m)^2}{(2n + m)}\right]$

  ... **Tb. 6.7 (6th row, 3rd col.)/Pg 96, DHB**

  $= (0.707\,h) \times \left[\dfrac{(2 \times 200 + 250)^3}{12} - \dfrac{200^2 \times (200 + 250)^2}{(2 \times 200 + 250)}\right]$

  $J = (7.37 \times 10^6)\,h$

$\therefore$ Eq. (ii) yields... $\tau'' = \dfrac{40 \times 10^3 \times 538.46 \times 186.54}{7.37 \times 10^6\,h} = \dfrac{545.18}{h}$

$\therefore$ Eq. (i) yields... $80 = \sqrt{\left(\dfrac{87.04}{h}\right)^2 + \left(\dfrac{545.18}{h}\right)^2 + 2\left(\dfrac{87.04}{h}\right)\left(\dfrac{545.18}{h}\right) \times 0.742}$

$80^2 = \dfrac{357.22 \times 10^3}{h^2}$

$\therefore \qquad h = 7.66$ mm ≈ 8 mm

69. **A bracket is welded to a side column as shown in Fig. 7.96 with a permissible stress of 80 MPa. Determine the maximum load that the bracket can withstand if the size of the weld is 10 mm.**

VTU – Dec. 2013/ Jan. 2014 – 10 Marks

Solution: $\tau_{max} = 80$ MPa, $h = 10$ mm, $n = 250$ mm, $m = 300$ mm, $P = ?$

Here the welds are of the type $(m + 2n)$ [unsymmetrical] as shown in **Fig. 7.96.**

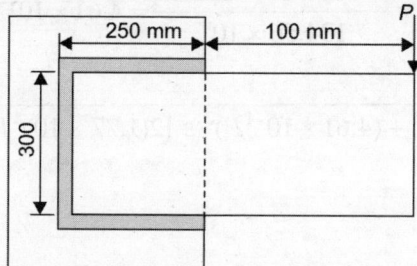

Fig. 7.96: Problem 69

We know that maximum resultant shear stress

$$\tau_{max} = \sqrt{\tau'^2 + \tau''^2 + 2\tau'\tau''\cos\theta} \qquad \text{... Eq. (i) 6.3(c)/ Pg 91, DHB}$$

Primary shear stress,

$$\tau' = \frac{P}{(h\cos 45°)L} \qquad \text{... 6.3(a)/ Pg 91, DHB}$$

From **Fig. 7.96**, $\quad L = (m + 2n) = [300 + (2 \times 250)] = 800$ mm.

$$\therefore \qquad \tau' = \frac{P}{(10 \times h\cos 45°) \times 800} = 1.77 \times 10^{-4}\, P$$

Secondary shear stress,

$$\tau'' = \frac{TR}{J} = \frac{(P \cdot e)R}{J} \qquad \text{... Eq. (ii)}$$

- $m_x = \dfrac{m}{2} = \dfrac{300}{2} = 150$ mm

- $n_y = \dfrac{n^2}{2n + m} = \dfrac{250^2}{(2 \times 250 + 300)} = 78.13$ mm

  $\text{... Tb. 6.7 (6th row, 1st col.)/Pg 96, DHB}$

From **Fig. 7.96**, $\quad e = (250 + 100 - n_y) = 350 - 78.13 = 271.87$ mm

- $R = \sqrt{BA^2 + AG^2}$

  $BA = m_x = 150$ mm

  $AG = n - n_y = 250 - 78.13 = 171.87$ mm

  $R = \sqrt{150^2 + 171.87^2} = 228.12$ mm

- $\cos\theta = \dfrac{AG}{R} = \dfrac{171.87}{228.12} = 0.753$

- Also $\quad J = h_t\left[\dfrac{(2n + m)^3}{12} - \dfrac{n^2(n + m)^2}{(2n + m)}\right]$

  $\text{... Tb. 6.7 (6th row, 3rd col.)/Pg 96, DHB}$

  $= (0.707 \times 10) \times \left[\dfrac{(2 \times 250 + 300)^3}{12} - \dfrac{250^2 \times (250 + 300)^2}{(2 \times 250 + 300)}\right]$

  $J = 134.56 \times 10^6$ mm^4

∴ Eq. (ii) yields...　　$\tau'' = \dfrac{P \times 271.87 \times 228.12}{134.56 \times 10^6} = 4.61 \times 10^{-4}\,P$

∴ Eq. (i) yields...

$$80 = \sqrt{(1.77 \times 10^{-4}P)^2 + (4.61 \times 10^{-4}P)^2 + [2(1.77 \times 10^{-4}P)(4.61 \times 10^{-4}P) \times 0.753]}$$

$$80^2 = 3.66 \times 10^{-7}\,P^2$$

∴　　$P = 132.10$ kN

VTU QUESTION PAPERS

Mar. 2001 (ME5T2)

1. Two lengths of a flat tie bar 15 mm thick are connected by a butt joint with equal cover plates. If a load of 400 kN is acting on the tie bar, design the joint such that the section of the bar is not reduced by more than one rivet hole. Working stresses for the material of the bar are 85 MPa in tension, 60 MPa in shear and 110 MPa in crushing. **(10 Marks)**

July/Aug. 2004 (AU46)

2. Design a triple riveted butt joint with equal cover plates and staggered riveting to connect two plates 20 mm thick. The allowable tensile stress for the plate is 100 MPa and allowable shear and compressive stresses for the rivet material are 55 MPa and 110 MPa respectively. Sketch the designed joint showing main dimensions and calculate the joint efficiency. **(10 Marks)**

3. a. Design a lozenge joint to connect two plates 20 mm thick and 350 mm wide. The allowable tensile stress for the plate is 90 MPa and the allowable shear and compressive stresses for the rivet material are 55 MPa and 110 MPa respectively. Sketch the designed joint showing main dimensions and calculate the joint efficiency. **(10 Marks)**

   b. Calculate the maximum force F that can be applied to the eccentrically loaded welded joint as shown in **Fig. U7.1**. The fillet welds have an allowable shear stress of 80 MPa. **(10 Marks)**

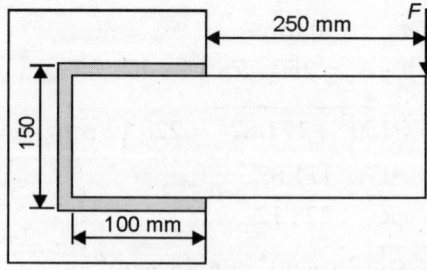

Fig. U7.1

Jan./Feb. 2005 (AU46)

4. Determine the main dimensions for longitudinal and circumferential joints of a boiler whose inner diameter is 1.7 m and pressure of steam is 2.05 N/mm². The ultimate stresses are $\sigma_c = 780$ N/mm², $\sigma_t = 470$ N/mm² and $\tau = 390$ N/mm².

Assume a factor of safety of 5. The rivet in double shear will have an effective resisting area not greater than 87.5% over that in single shear. **(20 Marks)**

5. a. Determine the size of fillet weld required for the flat plate loaded as shown in **Fig. U7.2**. Allowable stress = 94 MN/m^2 **(14 Marks)**

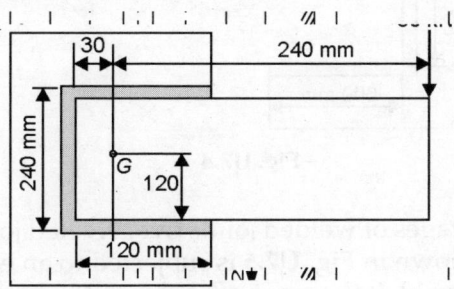

Fig. U7.2

b. Show that the plane of maximum shear force occurs at 67.5° for a transverse load on a fillet weld of equal legs. **(06 Marks)**

July/Aug. 2005 (AU46)

6. Design a double riveted butt joint with equal widths of cover plates to join two plates of thickness 10 mm. The allowable stress for the material of the rivets and for the plates are as follows:

For plate material in tension, σ_t = 80 MPa
For rivet material in compression, σ_u = 120 MPa
For rivet material in shear, τ = 60 MPa **(10 Marks)**

7. a. Determine the safe value of P for a joint loaded as shown in **Fig. U7.3**, limiting the maximum normal stress induced to 80 MPa and maximum shear stress induced to 60 MPa. **(10 Marks)**

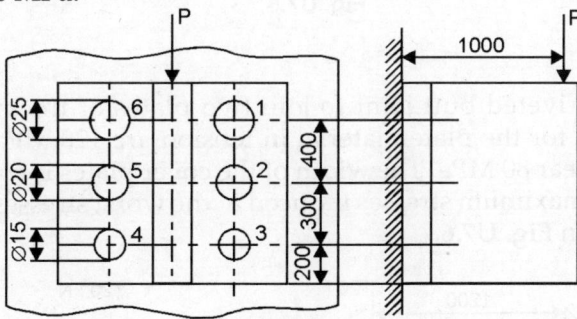

Fig. U7.3

b. Determine the size of the weld for the welded joint as shown in **Fig. U7.4**. **(10 Marks)**

Jan./Feb. 2006 (AU46)

8. A double riveted double cover butt joint in plates 20 mm thick is made with 25 mm diameter rivets of 110 mm pitch. The permissible stresses are: σ_t = 120 MPa, τ = 100 MPa and σ_c = 150 MPa. Find the efficiency of the joint, taking the strength of the rivet in double shear as twice than that of single shear. **(10 Marks)**

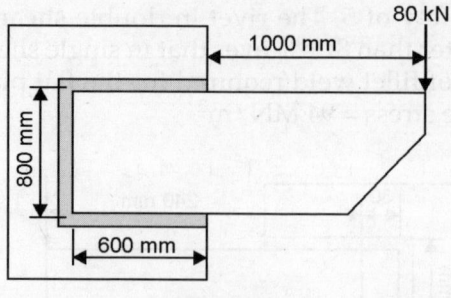

Fig. U7.4

9. a. What are the advantages of welded joints over riveted joints?   **(06 Marks)**
   b. A welded joint as shown in **Fig. U7.5** is subjected to an eccentric load of 2.5 kN. Find the size of the weld, if the maximum shear stress in the weld is 25 MPa.

   (14 Marks)

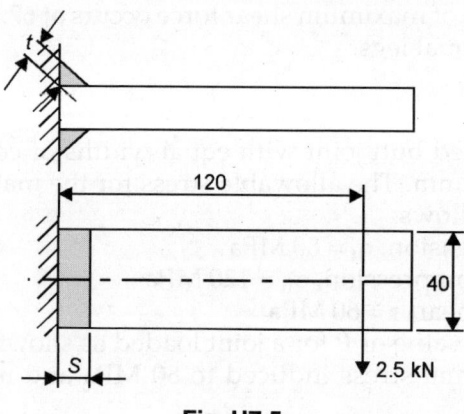

Fig. U7.5

July 2006 (AU46)

10. Design a double riveted butt joint to join two plates of thickness 10 mm. The allowable stresses for the plate material in tension are 120 MPa, in compression 160 MPa and in shear 80 MPa. The width of the cover plates is equal.   **(10 Marks)**
11. a. Determine the maximum stresses induced in the worst stresses rivet in a riveted joint as shown in **Fig. U7.6**.   **(10 Marks)**

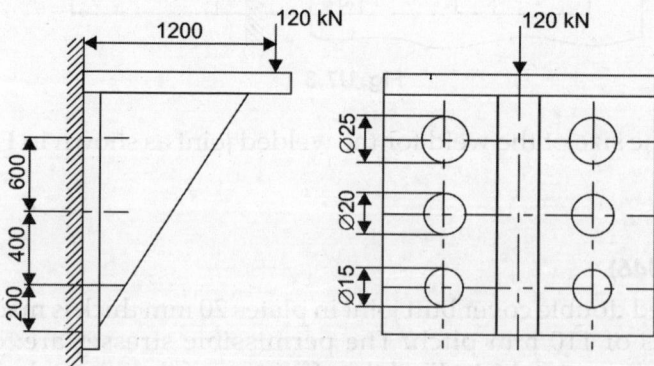

Fig. U7.6

b. Determine the weld size for a welded joint as shown in **Fig. U7.7.**   (**10 Marks**)

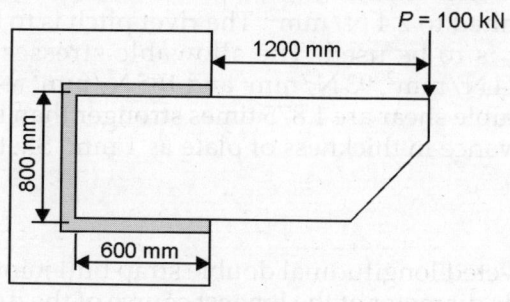

Fig. U7.7

Dec. 2006/ Jan. 2007 (AU46)

12. For the riveted joint shown in **Fig. U7.8**, determine the size of the rivet taking permissible shear stress in rivets as 60 MPa.   (**10 Marks**)

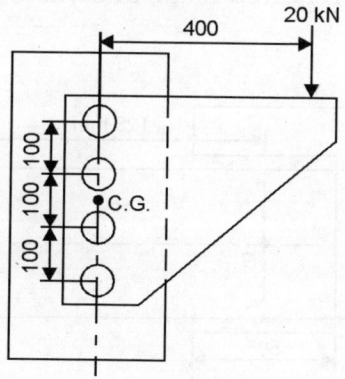

Fig. U7.8

13. a. A 80 mm wide and 12 mm thick plate subjected to axial tensile load is welded to a vertical support by a single transverse fillet weld and a double parallel fillet weld as shown in **Fig. U7.9**. The maximum tensile and shear stresses in the weld are 100 MPa and 70 MPa respectively. Find the length of each parallel weld, if the joint is subjected to:
    i. Static loading
    ii. Fatigue loading
    (**10 Marks**)

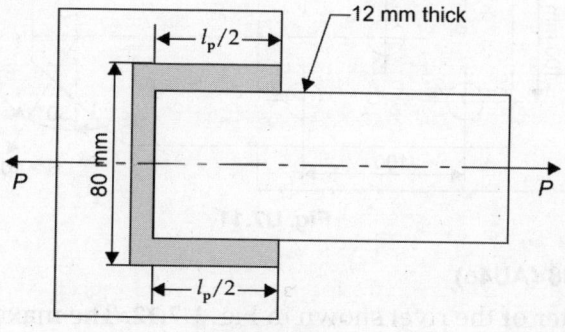

Fig. U7.9

b. Design a triple riveted butt joint with double straps of equal width longitudinal butt joint for a boiler shell of 1.5 m diameter. The maximum steam pressure in the boiler is limited to 2.4 N/mm². The rivet pitch is to be same in all rows and chain riveting is to be used. The allowable stresses in tension, shear and crushing are 124 N/mm², 93 N/mm² and 165 N/mm² respectively. Assume that the rivets in double shear are 1.875 times stronger than in single shear. Take the corrosion allowance in thickness of plate as 1 mm. Sketch the joint with all the dimensions. **(10 Marks)**

July 2007 (AU46)

14. Design a triple riveted longitudinal double strap butt joint with unequal strap for a boiler. The inside diameter of the longest course of the drum is 1.3 m. The joint is to be designed for a steam pressure of 2.4 N/mm². The working stresses to be used are $\sigma_t = 77$ N/mm² for plate material in tension, $\tau = 62$ N/mm² for rivet material in shear, $\sigma_c = 120$ N/mm² for rivet material in compression. Assume joint efficiency as 81%. **(10 Marks)**

15. a. A bracket carrying a load of 15 kN is to be welded as shown in **Fig. U7.10**. Find the size of the weld required if the allowable shear stress is not to exceed 80 N/mm². **(10 Marks)**

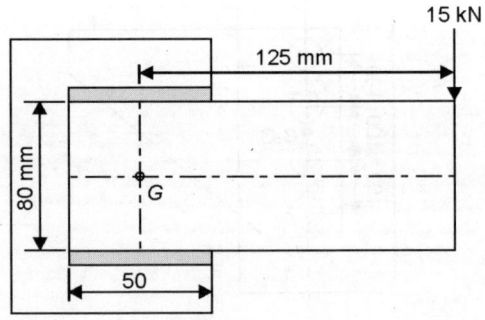

Fig. U7.10

b. Determine the size of rivets required for the bracket shown in Fig. **U7.11**. Take the permissible shear stress for the rivet material as 100 MPa.

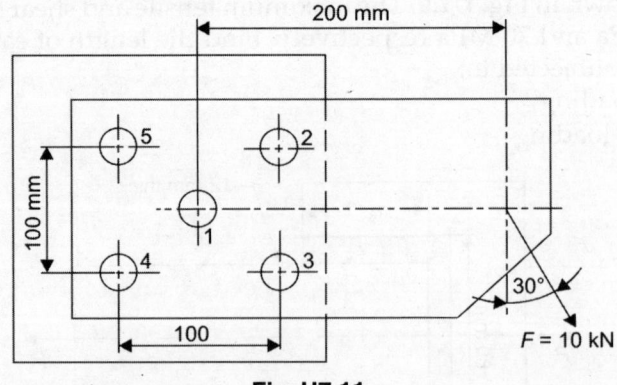

Fig. U7.11

Dec. 2007/Jan. 2008 (AU46)

16. Find the diameter of the rivet shown in Fig. **U7.12**. The maximum shearing stress on the most heavily loaded rivet is 56 N/mm². **(08 Marks)**

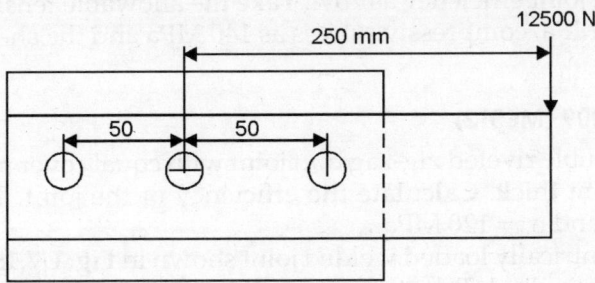

Fig. U7.12

17. a. Design a double riveted butt joint to connect two plates 20 mm thick. The joint is zig-zag riveted and has equal width cover plates. The allowable tensile stress for the plate is 100 MPa. The allowable shear and crushing stresses for rivet material are 60 MPa and 120 MPa respectively. Calculate the efficiency of the joint. The joint should be leak proof. **(10 Marks)**

   b. A 16 mm thick plate is welded to a vertical support by two fillet welds as shown in **Fig. U7.13**. Determine the size of the weld if the permissible shear stress for the weld material is 75 N/mm². **(10 Marks)**

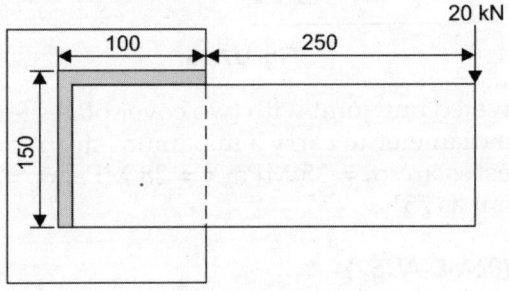

Fig. U7.13

June/July 2008 (AU46)

18. a. A shaft of rectangular cross-section is welded to a support by means of fillet welds as shown in **Fig. U7.14**. Determine the size of the weld if the permissible shear stress in the weld material is limited to 75 MPa. (10 Marks)

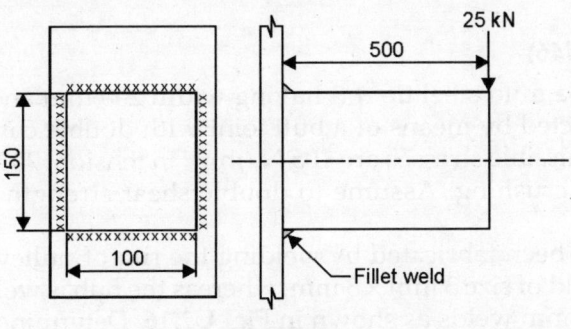

Fig. U7.14

   b. Design a longitudinal double riveted butt joint with two cover plates for a boiler shell of 1500 mm in diameter subjected to an internal pressure of 0.915 MPa.

Assume the joint efficiency as 75%. Take the allowable tensile stress in the plate equal to 84 MPa, compressive stress as 140 MPa and the shear stress in the rivet as 56 MPa. **(10 Marks)**

Dec. 2008/Jan. 2009 (ME5T2)

19. a. Design a double riveted zig-zag butt joint with equal cover plates to connect two plates 20 mm thick. Calculate the efficiency of the joint. Take $\sigma_\theta = 100$ MPa, $\tau = 60$ MPa and $\sigma_c = 120$ MPa. **(10 Marks)**

b. For the eccentrically loaded welded joint shown in **Fig. U7.15**, determine the size of the weld required. Take the permissible stress for the weld as 75 MPa. **(10 Marks)**

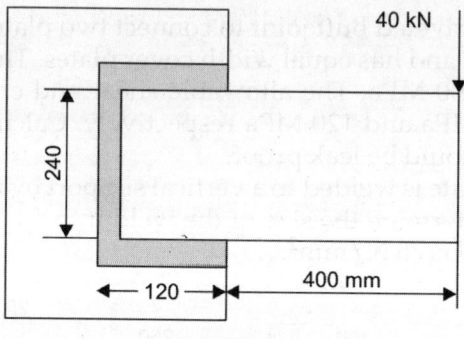

Fig. U7.15

20. Design a double riveted butt joint with two cover plates for longitudinal seam of a boiler shell, 0.75 m diameter to carry a maximum steam pressure of 1.05 N/mm². The allowable stresses are $\sigma_t = 35$ MPa, $\tau = 28$ MPa, $\sigma_c = 52.5$ MPa. Assume the efficiency of the joint as 75%. **(12 Marks)**

Dec. 2008/Jan. 2009 (06ME-AU52)

21. a. Design a double riveted lap joint with chain riveting for mild steel plates of 20 mm thick taking the allowable value of stress in shear, tension and compression to 60, 90 and 120 MPa respectively. **(12 Marks)**

b. A mild steel plate of 15 mm thickness is welded to another plate by two parallel welds to carry a load of 50 kN. Determine the size of the weld required, if:
    i. Load is static
    ii. Load is dynamic **(08 Marks)**

June/July 2009 (AU46)

22. Two lengths of a mild steel tie rod having width 200 mm and thickness 12.5 mm are to be connected by means of a butt joint with double cover plate. Design the joint if the permissible stresses are 105 N/mm² in tension, 70 N/mm² in shear and 180 N/mm² in crushing. Assume to double shear strength 1.75 times in single shear. **(10 Marks)**

23. a. A pulley has been fabricated by welding the rim of pulley to the annular web plate by a weld of size 3 mm × 3 mm, whereas the hub is welded to the web plate by 5 mm × 5 mm welds as shown in Fig. **U7.16**. Determine the safe power that can be transmitted by this pulley and welded pulley considering only the welded joint strength. Assume allowable stress for welds 80 N/mm². **(10 Marks)**

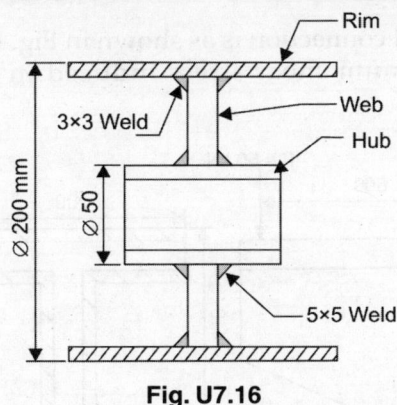

Fig. U7.16

b. Figure **U7.17** shows connections of eccentrically loaded welded joints. The allowable shear stress in the fillet weld using MS bar electrodes can be taken as 80 N/mm². Find the thickness of the plate. **(10 Marks)**

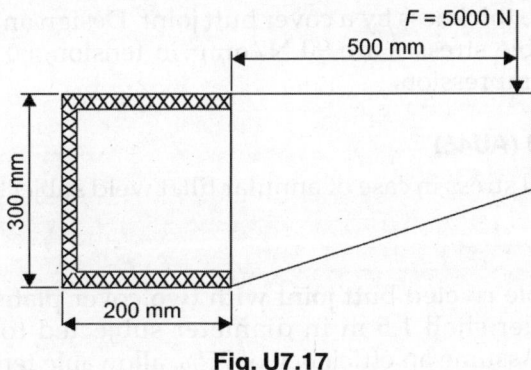

F = 5000 N

500 mm

300 mm

200 mm

Fig. U7.17

June/July 2009 (06ME52)

24. a. A pulley has been fabricated by welding the rim of a pulley to the annular web plate by a weld of size 3 mm × 3 mm, whereas hub is welded to the web plate by 5 mm × 5 mm weld. Determine safe power that can be transmitted by this pulley and welded considering only welded joint. [Refer **Fig. U7.18**]

(10 Marks)

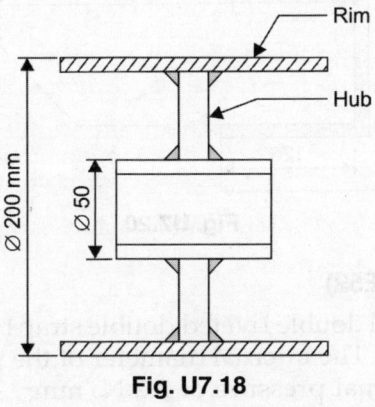

Fig. U7.18

b. An eccentric loaded connection is as shown in Fig. **U7.19**. Determine the size of the weld, if maximum shear stress induced in the weld is not to exceed 75 N/mm². **(10 Marks)**

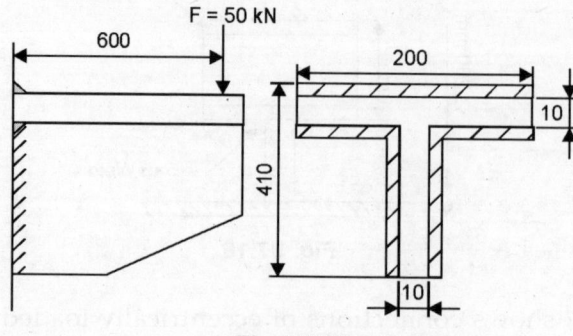

Fig. U7.19

25. A tie bar in a bridge consists of plate 350 mm wide and 20 mm thick. It is connected by a plate of same thickness by a cover butt joint. Design an economical structural joint, if permissible stresses are 90 N/mm² in tension, 60 N/mm² in shear and 150 N/mm² in compression. **(10 Marks)**

Dec. 2009/ Jan. 2010 (AU46)

26. Prove that normal stress in case of annular fillet weld subjected to bending is given by: $\sigma_b = \dfrac{5.66 M_b}{\pi h D^2}$. **(06 Marks)**

27. a. Design a double riveted butt joint with two cover plates for the longitudinal seam of a boiler shell 1.5 m in diameter subjected to a steam pressure of 0.95 N/mm². Assume an efficiency of 75%, allowable tensile stress in the plate as 90 N/mm², allowable compressive stress of 140 N/mm² and an allowable shear stress in the rivets as 56 N/mm². **(10 Marks)**

b. A steel plate is welded by fillet welds to a structure and is loaded as shown in **Fig. U7.20**. Calculate the size of the weld if the load is 35 kN and allowable shear stress for the weld material is 90 MPa. **(10 Marks)**

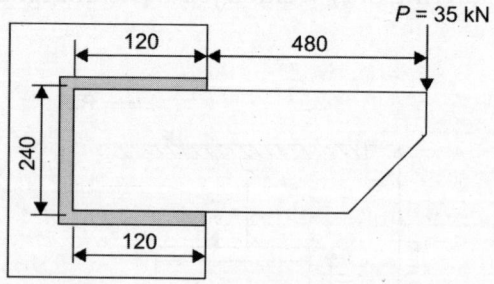

Fig. U7.20

Dec. 2009/ Jan. 2010 (06ME52)

28. a. Design a longitudinal double riveted double strap butt joint with unequal straps for a pressure vessel. The internal diameter of the pressure vessel is 1 m and is subjected to an internal pressure of 2.2 N/mm². The pitch of the rivet in the

outer row is to be double the pitch in inner row. The allowable tensile stress in the plate is 124 N/mm². The allowable shear and crushing of the rivets are 93 N/mm² and 165 N/mm² respectively. The resistance of the rivets in double shear is to be taken as 1.875 times that of single shear. **(10 Marks)**

b. One end of a rectangular bar of 120 mm × 70 mm cross-section is welded to a vertical support by four fillet welds along its circumference. A steady transverse load of 10 kN is applied at the free end of the bar of length 160 mm and is parallel to 120 mm side. Determine the size of the weld, if the allowable stress in the material is limited to 115 MPa. **(10 Marks)**

May/June 2010 (06ME52)

29. a. The length of a flat tie bar, 15 mm thick, is connected by a butt joint with equal cover plates on either side. If 400 kN is acting on the tie bar, design the joint, such that the section of the bar is not reduced by more than one rivet hole. Working stresses for the material of the bar are 85 MPa in tension, 60 MPa in shear and 110 MPa in crushing. **(10 Marks)**

b. A 16 mm thick plate is welded to a vertical support by two fillet welds as shown in **Fig. U7.21**. Determine the size of the weld, if the permissible shear stress for the weld material is 75 MPa. **(10 Marks)**

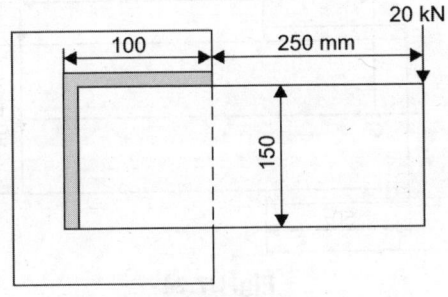

Fig. U7.21

Dec. 2010 (AU46)

30. a. Design a double riveted butt joint, with single cover plate, for the longitudinal seam for a boiler shell of diameter 1000 mm and pressure 1.5 MPa. Allowable tensile stress for the plate is 100 MPa and allowable shear and crushing stresses for rivets are 70 MPa and 150 MPa respectively. **(15 Marks)**

b. What are the advantages and disadvantages of welded joints over riveted joints? **(05 Marks)**

Dec. 2010 (06ME52)

31. a. Determine the size of the weld required for a flat plate, welded to a steel column and loaded as shown in **Fig. U7.22**. The allowable shear stress in the weld is limited to 80 MPa at the throat section. **(10 Marks)**

b. Determine the size of rivets, for the 20 mm thick flat plate, riveted to a column as shown in **Fig. U7.23**. The allowable stresses in the rivets are 56 MPa in shear and 100 MPa in crushing. **(10 Marks)**

June/July 2011 (06ME52)

32. a. Design a double riveted lap joint with zigzag riveting for 13 mm thick plates. The working stresses to be used are σ_t = 80 MPa, τ = 60 MPa and σ_c = 120 MPa.

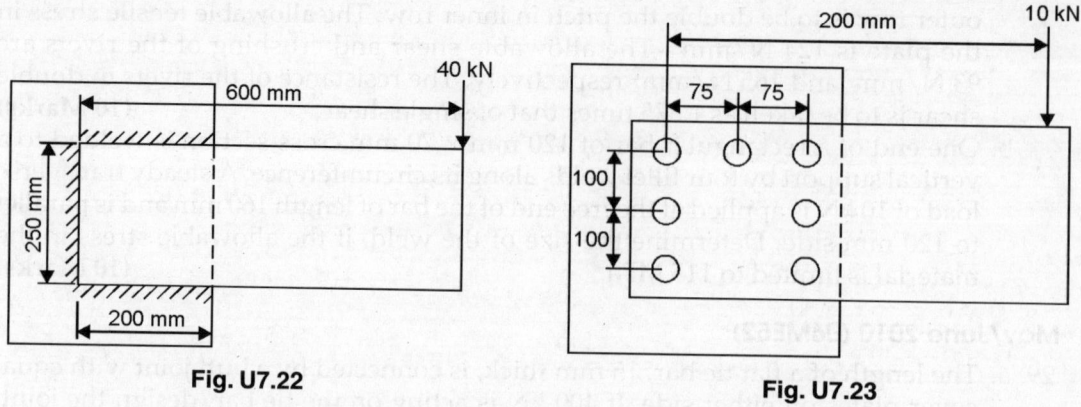

Fig. U7.22   **Fig. U7.23**

State how the joint will fail and find the efficiency of the joint.   **(10 Marks)**

b. A bracket carrying a load of 15 kN is to be welded as shown in **Fig. U7.24**. Find the size of the weld required if the allowable shear stress is not to exceed 80 MPa.
   (10 Marks)

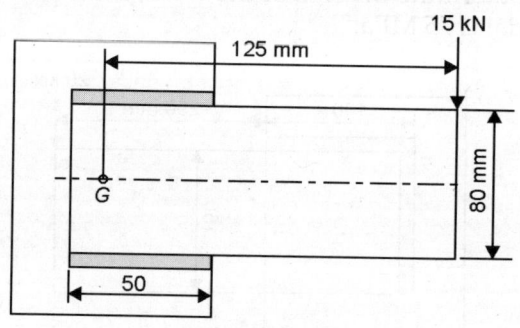

Fig. U7.24

Dec. 2011 (AU46)

33. Design a longitudinal seam joint of a steam drum whose inner diameter is 1680 mm and the pressure of steam is 2.1 MPa by gauge. The longitudinal joint is triple riveted butt joint with an efficiency of 85%. The pitch of outer rows of rivet is to be double of that in the inner rows and the width of the cover plates are unequal. The ultimate tensile, crushing and shear stresses are 470 MPa, 780 MPa and 390 MPa respectively. Adopt a factor of safety of 5. The rivet in double shear is to be not greater than 87.5% over that in single shear.   **(10 Marks)**

34. a. A steel bracket is welded to the structure and loaded by a vertical load of 35 kN at a distance of 480 mm from the support as shown in **Fig. U7.25**. Calculate the size of the weld required at the three sides as shown, if the allowable shear stress in the weld is 90 MN/m². **(10 Marks)**

   b. **Figure U7.26** shows a bracket fixed on a steel column by means of four rivets. Find the diameter of rivet required to take up a load of 20 kN. Assume permissible tensile and shear stress in the rivet material to be 77 MPa and 56 MPa respectively.   **(10 Marks)**

Dec. 2011 (06ME52)

35. a. Design a triple riveted longitudinal double strap butt joint with unequal straps for a boiler. The inside diameter of the congest course of the drum is 1.3 m. The

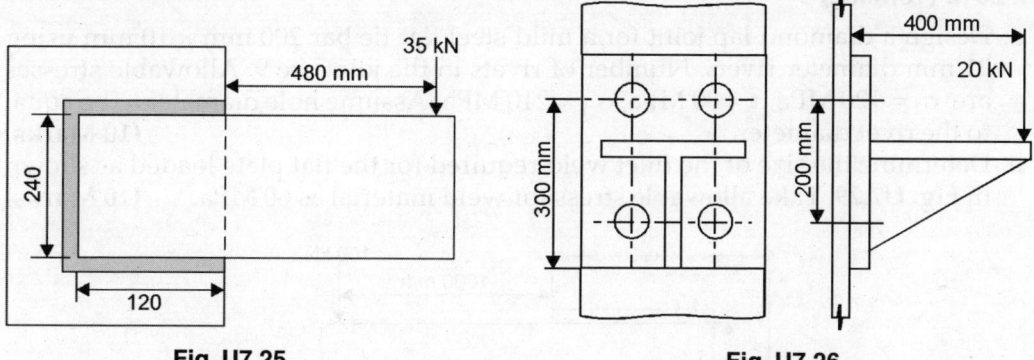

Fig. U7.25   **Fig. U7.26**

joint is to be designed for a steam pressure of 2.4 MPa. The working stresses to be used are σ_t = 77 MPa, τ = 62 MPa and σ_c = 120 MPa. Assume the efficiency of the joint as 81%. The longer pitch in the outer row is twice the pitch in the inner row and the inner rows are zigzag.   **(12 Marks)**

b. A bracket shown in **Fig. U7.27** carries a load of 10 kN. Find the size of the weld if the allowable shear stress is not to exceed 80 MPa.   **(08 Marks)**

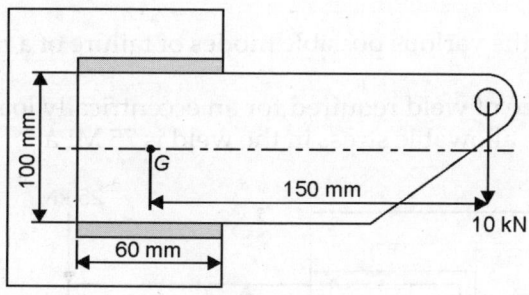

Fig. U7.27

June 2012 (06ME52-06AU52)

36. a. Design a double riveted butt joint with two cover plates for the longitudinal seam of a boiler shell 1.5 m in diameter subjected to a steam pressure or 0.9 MPa. Assume joint efficiency as 75%. Allowable stress in tension for the plate is 83 MPa in compression 138 MPa and shear stress in rivets may be assumed as 55 MPa. Assume chain riveted joint.   **(10 Marks)**

b. A circular shaft 50 mm in diameter is welded to a support by means of a fillet weld and loaded as shown in Fig. **U7.28**. Determine the size of the weld if the permissible shear stress in the weld is limited to 100 MPa.   **(10 Marks)**

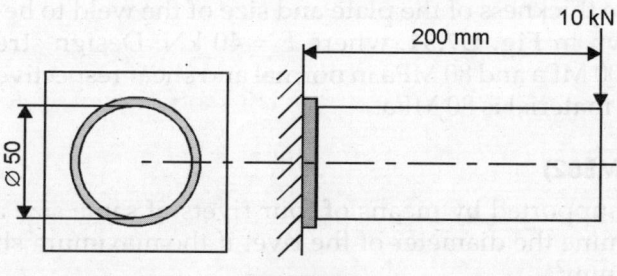

Fig. U7.28

Dec. 2012 (10ME52)

37. a. Design a diamond lap joint for a mild steel flat tie bar 200 mm × 10 mm using 21 mm diameter rivets. Number of rivets in the joint are 9. Allowable stresses are: $\sigma_1 = 120$ MPa, $\tau = 80$ MPa, $\sigma_{cr} = 210$ MPa. Assume hole diameter to be equal to the rivet diameter. **(10 Marks)**

b. Determine the size of the fillet weld required for the flat plate loaded as shown in **Fig. U7.29**. Take allowable stress for weld material as 60 MPa. **(10 Marks)**

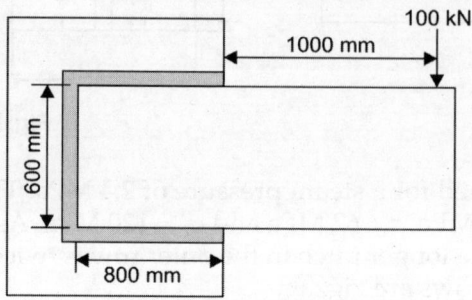

Fig. U7.29

Dec. 2012 (06ME52)

38. a. Explain in detail the various possible modes of failure of a riveted joint. **(10 Marks)**

b. Determine the size of weld required for an eccentrically loaded weld as shown in **Fig. U7.30**. The allowable stress in the weld is 75 MPa. **(10 Marks)**

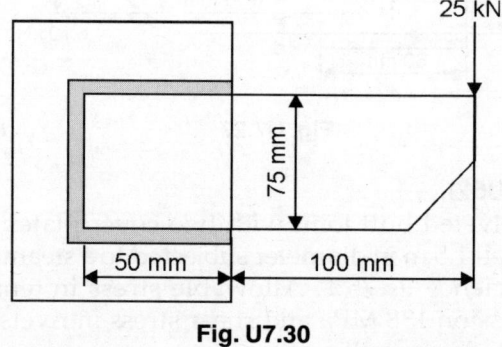

Fig. U7.30

June/July 2013 (06ME52)

39. a. Explain the possible failures of riveted joints by means of simple sketches. **(08 Marks)**

b. Determine the thickness of the plate and size of the weld to be specified for the bracket shown in **Fig. U7.31**, where $F = 40$ kN. Design stress for the plate materials is 100 MPa and 80 MPa in normal and shear respectively. Design stress for the throat material is 80 MPa. **(12 Marks)**

June/July 2013 (10ME52)

40. a. A bracket is supported by means of four rivets of same size as shown in **Fig. U7.32**. Determine the diameter of the rivet if the maximum shear stress in the rivet is 90 N/mm². **(10 Marks)**

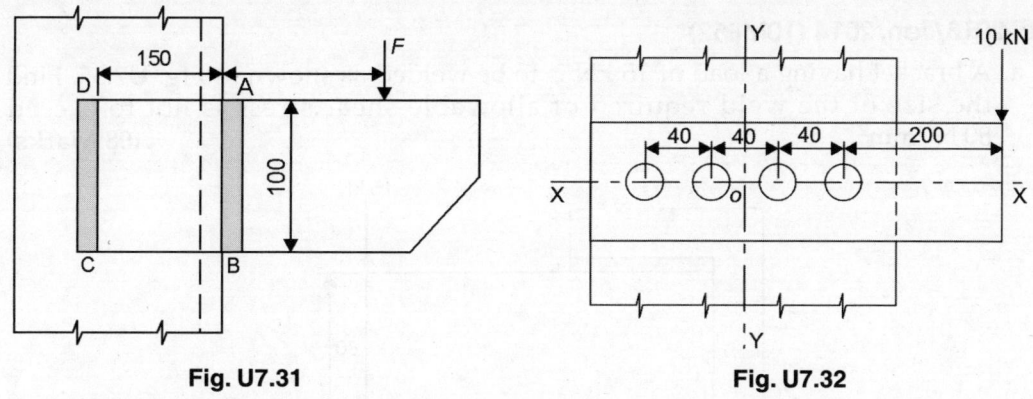

Fig. U7.31   Fig. U7.32

b. Determine the maximum normal stress and the maximum shear stress in the weld shown in **Fig. U7.33**.   **(10 Marks)**

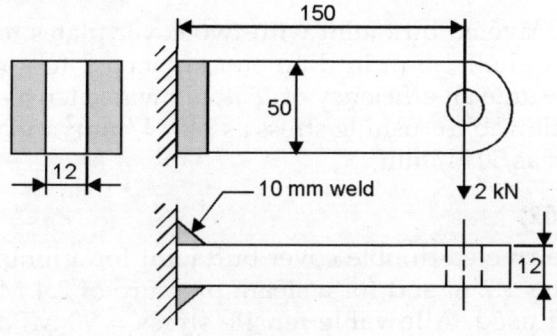

Fig. U7.33

Dec. 2013/Jan. 2014 (06ME52)

41. a. Design a double riveted butt joint with two cover plates for longitudinal seam of a boiler shell 1.5 m in diameter and subjected to steam pressure of 0.95 N/mm². Assume joint efficiency as 75%, allowable tensile stress is 90 N/mm², compressive stress is 140 N/mm² and shear stress is 56 N/mm².
    (10 Marks)

   b. A bracket is welded to a side column as shown in **Fig. U7.34** with a permissible stress of 80 N/mm². Determine the maximum load that the bracket can withstand if the size of the weld is 10 mm.   **(10 Marks)**

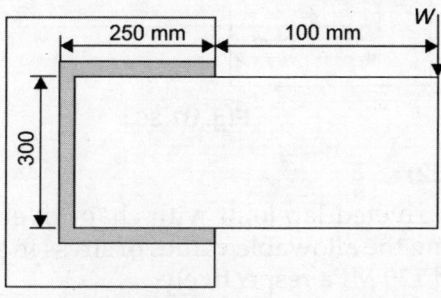

Fig. U7.34

Dec. 2013/Jan. 2014 (10ME52)

42. a. A bracket having a load of 15 kN is to be welded as shown in **Fig. U7.35**. Find the size of the weld required of allowable shear stress is not to exceed 80 N/mm². **(08 Marks)**

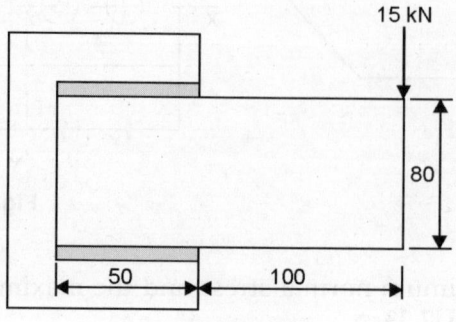

Fig. U7.35

b. Design a double riveted butt joint with two cover plates for the longitudinal seam of a boiler shell 1.5 m in diameter subjected to a steam pressure of 0.95 N/mm². Assume an efficiency of 75%, allowable tensile stress in the plate as 90 N/mm², allowable crushing stress as 140 N/mm² and an allowable shear stress in the rivet as 50 N/mm². **(12 Marks)**

June/July 2014 (06ME52)

43. a. Design a double riveted double cover butt joint for a longitudinal seam of a boiler of diameter 1.2 m and for a steam pressure of 2.4 MPa. The following stresses may be used. Allowable tensile stress = 90 MPa, allowable shear stress = 60 MPa and allowable crushing stress = 150 MPa. Assume a joint efficiency of 80%. **(10 Marks)**

b. A 80 mm wide, 12 mm thick plate carrying an axial load of 96 kN is welded to a support as shown in **Fig. U7.36**. The following tensile and shear stress in the weld are 100 MPa and 70 MPa respectively. Find the length of each parallel fillet weld.

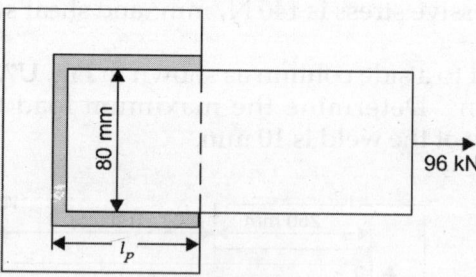

Fig. U7.36

June/July 2014 (10ME52)

44. a. Design a double riveted lap joint with chain riveting for mild steel plates of 20 mm thick taking the allowable values of stress in shear, tension and compression to 60, 90 and 120 MPa respectively. **(10 Marks)**

b. Determine the size of the weld for a welded joint loaded shown in **Fig. U7.37**, if permissible shear stress for the weld material is 75 MPa. **(10 Marks)**

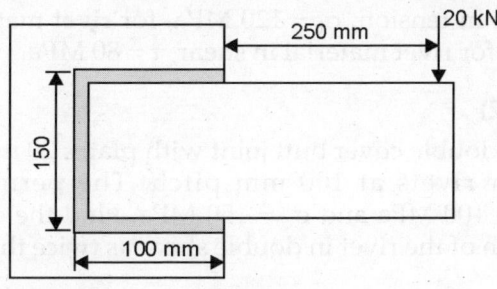

Fig. U7.37

Dec. 2014/Jan. 2015 (06ME52)

45. a. Design a double riveted butt joint with two plates for the longitudinal seam of a boiler shell 1.5 m in diameter subjected to a steam pressure of 0.95 N/mm². Assume an efficiency of 75%, allowable tensile stress in the plate of 90 N/mm², allowable compressive stress of 140 N/mm² and an allowable shear stress of 56 N/mm² in the rivets. **(10 Marks)**

   b. A shaft of rectangular cross-section is welded to a support by means of fillet welds as shown in **Fig. U7.38**. Determine the size of the welds, if permissible shear stress in the weld is limited to 75 N/mm². **(10 Marks)**

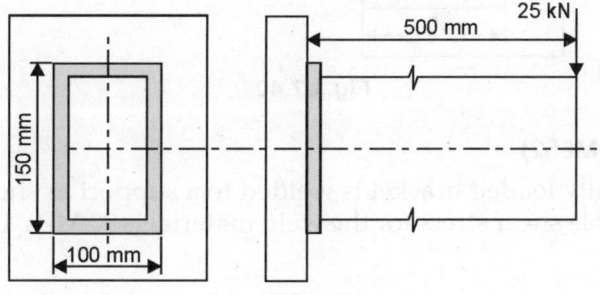

Fig. U7.38

Dec. 2014/ Jan. 2015 (10ME52)

46. a. Determine the size of the weld required for an eccentrically loaded weld as shown in **Fig. U7.39**. Assume steady load and fillet weld. **(08 Marks)**

   b. Design a triple riveted butt joint to join two plates of thickness 10 mm. The pitch of the rivets in the extreme rows which are in single shear is twice the pitch of rivets in the inner rows which are in double shear. The design stresses of the materials of the main plate and the rivets are as follows:

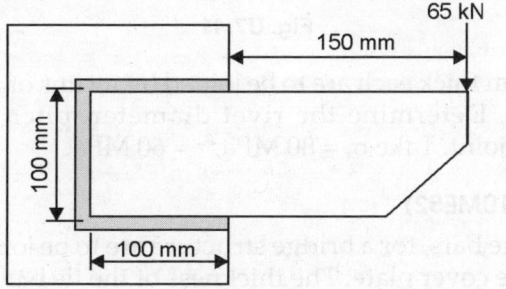

Fig. U7.39

For plate material in tension, σ_t = 120 MPa, for rivet material in compression, σ_c = 160 MPa and for rivet material in shear, τ = 80 MPa. (12 Marks)

June/July 2015 (06ME52)

47. a. A double riveted double cover butt joint with plates 20 mm thick is made with 25 mm diameter rivets at 100 mm pitch. The permissible stresses are σ_t = 120 MPa, τ = 100 MPa and σ_c = 150 MPa. Find the efficiency of the joint, taking the strength of the rivet in double shear as twice that of single shear. **(10 Marks)**

    b. A bracket carrying a load of 15 kN is to be welded as shown in **Fig. U7.40**. Find the size of the weld required if the allowable shear stress is not to exceed 80 MPa. **(10 Marks)**

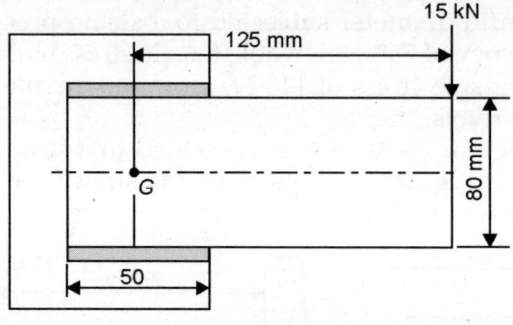

Fig. U7.40

June/ July 2015 (10ME52)

48. a. An eccentrically loaded bracket is welded to a support as shown in **Fig. U7.41**. The permissible shear stress for the weld material is 80 MPa. Determine the size of the weld. **(10 Marks)**

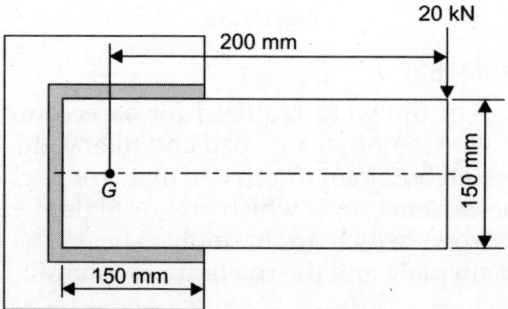

Fig. U7.41

    b. Two plates 10 mm thick each are to be joined by means of a single riveted double strap butt joint. Determine the rivet diameter, pitch, strap thickness and efficiency of the joint. Take σ_t = 80 MPa, τ = 60 MPa. **(10 Marks)**

Dec. 2015/ Jan 2016 (10ME52)

49. a. Two mild steel tie bars, for a bridge structure are to be joined by means of a butt joint with double cover plate. The thickness of the tie bar is 15 mm and carries a tensile load of 300 kN. Design an economical joint completely taking the

allowable stresses as $\sigma_t = 80$ MPa, $\sigma_c = 160$ MPa and $\tau = 64$ MPa. Draw neatly a proportional top and front views of the arrangements of the rivets with dimensions. (14 Marks)

b. An 125 × 100 × 10 mm unequal leg angle section is to be welded to a steel plate by fillet welds along the edges of the 125 mm leg as shown in **Fig. U7.42**. The angle is subjected to a tensile load of 100 kN passing through the center of gravity of the angle. Determine the weld lengths if the size of the weld is 8 mm and allowable shear stress in the weld is 102 MPa. All dimensions are in mm.

(06 Marks)

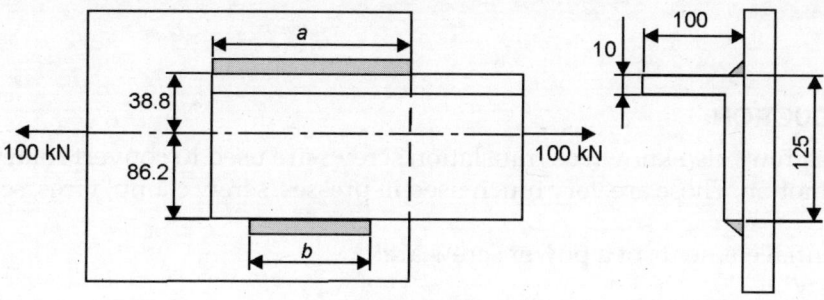

Fig. U7.42

8

Power Screws

8.1 INTRODUCTION

The power screws also known as translation screws are used to convert rotary motion into linear motion. These are very much used in presses, screw clamp, vices, screw jack, etc.

The essential elements of a power screw are:
- A screw
- A nut threaded to engage the screw.

In most of the power screws, the nut has axial motion against the resisting axial force while the screw rotates in its bearings; while in some cases, the screw rotates and moves axially against the resisting force while the nut is stationary and in others, the nut rotates while the screw moves axially with no rotation.

Applications include lead screw and presses for high efficiency; screw jacks, clamps and vices for low efficiency.

8.2 TYPES OF SCREW THREAD

The most commonly used screw thread forms are: (a) square threads, (b) acme threads and (c) buttress threads, as shown in **Figs 8.1 (a), (b) and (c)** respectively.

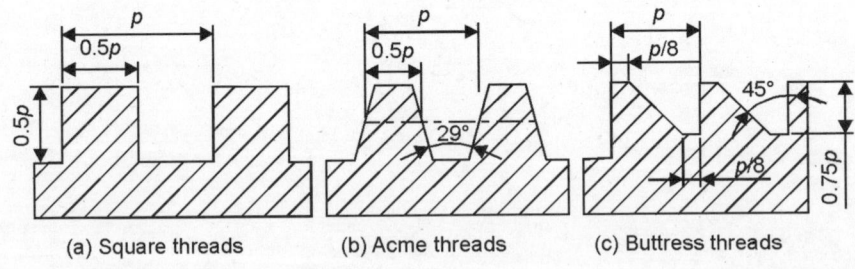

(a) Square threads   (b) Acme threads   (c) Buttress threads

Fig. 8.1: Forms of threads

a. Square Threads
- These are widely used because of high efficiency of power transmission in either direction.
- Eliminates the radial component of force (bursting pressure) between the screw and nut.
- Expensive and difficult to cut using taps and dies, but can be cut on a lathe using single point tool.

- It cannot be easily compensated for wear.
- Found in feed mechanisms of machine tools, valves, spindles, screw jack, etc.

Note:
- **Figure 9.10/ Pg 148, DHB**, *indicates basic profile of square thread.*
- **Table 9.9/ Pg 146, DHB**, *gives basic dimensions of square threads – Fine series.*
- **Table 9.10/ Pg 149, DHB**, *gives basic dimensions of square threads – Nominal series.*
- **Table 9.11/ Pg 151, DHB**, *gives basic dimensions of square threads – Coarse series.*

b. Acme Threads

- It is a modified version of square thread and is much stronger than square thread.
- Included angle is 29°.
- Efficiency is slightly less than square threads due to slope.
- It induces bursting pressure on the nut, but increases its area in shear.
- Wear can be compensated by providing an adjustable split nut, as in the lead screw of a lathe.
- Used in screw cutting lathes, brass valves and bench vices.

c. Buttress threads

- Used to transmit power in single direction.
- It has high efficiency and easy to cut.
- It has the advantages of both square and V-threads.
- It is stronger than other forms due to greater thickness at the base of the thread.
- Found in bench vice spindles.

Power screws can have either single or multistart threads. Multistart threads are employed when a large lead with fine threads or high efficiency is desired, e.g. high speed actuators.

8.3 TERMINOLOGY OF POWER SCREWS

- **Pitch:** It is defined as the distance between two consecutive threads, denoted by 'p'.
- **Helix/ Lead angle (α):** It is defined as the angle made by the helix of the thread with a plane perpendicular to axis of the screw. It is also called the lead angle.
  If one complete turn of a screw thread is unwound from the body of the screw and developed, it will form an inclined plane as shown in **Fig. 8.2(b)**. The relationship between the helix angle, mean diameter of the screw and the lead is expressed as:

$$\tan \alpha = \frac{l}{\pi d_2} \qquad \text{... (Eq. 8.1) } \textbf{9.10(b)/ Pg 133, DHB}$$

- **Lead (l):** It is defined as the distance which a screw thread advances axially in one rotation of the nut.
  In general, lead = number of starts × pitch
  i.e. $\qquad\qquad l = n \cdot p \qquad\qquad$ ... (Eq. 8.2) **9.10(b)/ Pg 133, DHB**
  where $n = 1$, for single start threads
  $\qquad n = 2$, for double start threads
  $\qquad n = 3$, for triple start threads and so on.
- **Nominal or major or outer diameter (d):** It is the largest diameter of a screw thread.

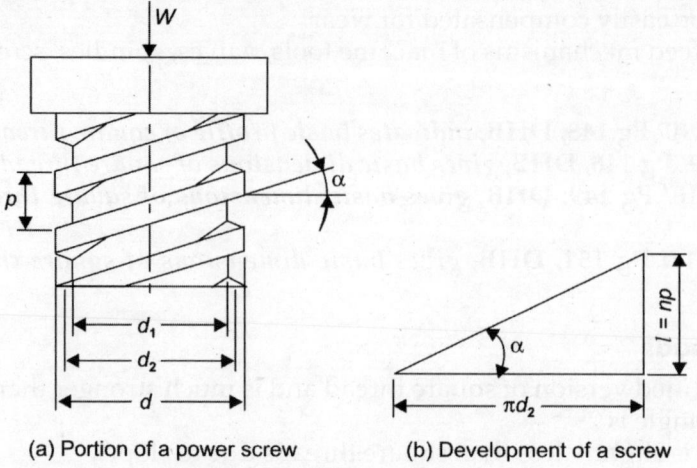

(a) Portion of a power screw   (b) Development of a screw

Fig. 8.2: Terminology of power screw

- **Root or core or minor or inner diameter (d_1):** It is the smallest diameter of an external or internal screw thread.
- **Mean or pitch diameter (d_2):** It is defined as the theoretical diameter between the major and minor diameters.

$$d_2 = [d - (p/2)] = [(d_1 + d_1)/2] \qquad \qquad \text{... (Eq. 8.2a)}$$

- **Frictional force (fF_N):** It is defined as the opposing force, which acts in the opposite direction of the movement of the load (W). This is due to the relative motion between two parts.
- **Coefficient of friction (f):** It is defined as the ratio of the limiting friction (F) to the normal reaction (F_N) between the two bodies.

Mathematically, $\qquad f = \dfrac{F}{F_N}$ $\qquad \qquad \qquad$ ... (Eq. 8.3)

also $\qquad \qquad \quad f = \tan \phi$ $\qquad$ ... (Eq. 8.4) **9.10(c)/ Pg 133, DHB**

where $\qquad \qquad \quad \phi$ = friction angle

Values of coefficient of friction f are available in... $\qquad$ ... **Tb. 9.3/ Pg136, DHB**

The coefficient of friction depends upon the material of screw and nut, their surface finish, type of lubricant used, unit bearing pressure and the rubbing speed.

8.4 MECHANICS OF POWER SCREW: FORCE AND TORQUE ANALYSIS

8.4.1 Torque Required to Raise the Load

Consider a single square threaded power screw subjected to compressive load W, as shown in **Fig. 8.3(a)**. Here the screw is assumed to be an inclined plane with inclination α, as shown in **Fig. 8.3(a)**. When the load is being raised, the forces and their components acting at a point on the inclined plane are shown in **Fig. 8.3(b)**. The system is in equilibrium under the action of these forces.

Let $\quad W$ = axial compressive load

$\qquad d$ = major diameter of the screw

$\qquad d_2$ = mean or pitch diameter of screw

$\qquad d_1$ = minor diameter of screw

$\qquad \alpha$ = helix angle

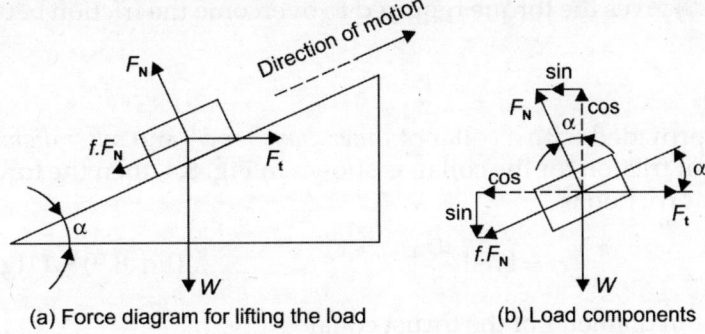

(a) Force diagram for lifting the load   (b) Load components

Fig. 8.3: Torque required to raise or lift the load

l = lead of screw
p = pitch
f = coefficient of friction between screw and nut = $\tan\phi$
ϕ = friction angle
F_t = tangential force acting at mean radius of the screw

Resolving the forces along the horizontal, we have

$$F_t = fF_N \cos\alpha + F_N \sin\alpha \qquad \ldots \text{(Eq. 8.5)}$$

Resolving the forces along the vertical, we have

$$W + fF_N \sin\alpha = F_N \cos\alpha$$

$$\therefore \qquad W = F_N \cos\alpha - fF_N \sin\alpha \qquad \ldots \text{(Eq. 8.6)}$$

Dividing (Eq. 8.5) by (Eq. 8.6) yields

$$\frac{F_t}{W} = \frac{fF_N \cos\alpha + F_N \sin\alpha}{F_N \cos\alpha - fF_N \sin\alpha}$$

$$= \frac{F_N(f\cos\alpha + \sin\alpha)}{F_N(\cos\alpha - f\sin\alpha)} = \frac{(f\cos\alpha + \sin\alpha)}{(\cos\alpha - f\sin\alpha)}$$

Dividing the RHS of above equation with $\cos\alpha$, yields

$$\frac{F_t}{W} = \frac{f + \tan\alpha}{1 - f\tan\alpha}$$

$$\therefore \qquad F_t = W\left(\frac{f + \tan\alpha}{1 - f\tan\alpha}\right) \qquad \ldots \text{(Eq. 8.7)} \text{ \textbf{9.11(a)/ Pg 134, DHB}}$$

But coefficient of friction,

$$f = \tan\phi$$

(Eq. 8.7) yields... $\qquad F_t = W\left(\dfrac{\tan\phi + \tan\alpha}{1 - \tan\phi\tan\alpha}\right) = W\tan(\phi + \alpha)$

$$\ldots \text{(Eq. 8.7a)} \text{ \textbf{9.11(a)/ Pg 134, DHB}}$$

The torque required to raise the load,

$$T = F_t\left(\frac{d_2}{2}\right) = \left(\frac{Wd_2}{2}\right)\tan(\phi + \alpha)$$

$$\ldots \text{(Eq. 8.8)} \text{ \textbf{9.11(b)/ Pg 134, DHB}}$$

Equation (8.8) gives the torque required to overcome the friction between the screw and the nut.

Collar Friction

If the screw is provided with a collar of *inner diameter d″* and *outer diameter d′* and if is the coefficient of friction for the collar as shown in **Fig. 8.4**, then the torque required to overcome collar friction is

$$T_C = Wf_c\left(\frac{d_c}{2}\right)$$
... (Eq. 8.9) **9.11(g)/ Pg 134, DHB**

where d_c = mean diameter of the thrust collar

$$= \left(\frac{d' + d''}{2}\right), \text{for uniform wear condition}$$

$$= \frac{2}{3}\left(\frac{d'^3 - d''^3}{d'^2 - d''^2}\right), \text{for uniform pressure condition}$$

f_c = coefficient of friction for the collar   ... **Tb. 9.6/ Pg 137, DHB**
d' = *outer diameter* of the collar
d'' = *inner diameter* of the collar

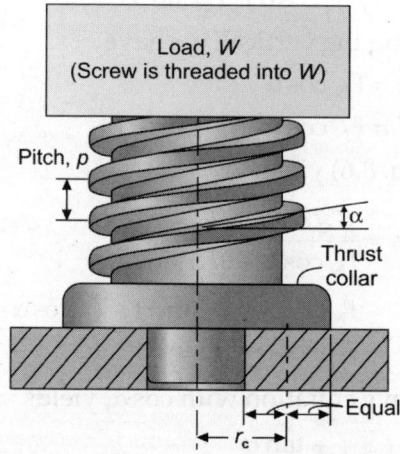

Fig. 8.4: Power screw with collar **[Pg 126, DHB]**

When the axial load is taken up by a thrust collar the load does not rotate with the screw.

Thus, the total torque required for square threads in raising the load is obtained by adding Eqs. (8.8) and (8.9)

$$T = \left[\left(\frac{Wd_2}{2}\right)\tan(\phi + \alpha)\right] + Wf_c\left(\frac{d_c}{2}\right)$$

i.e. $$T = \frac{W}{2}[d_2\tan(\phi + \alpha) + f_c d_c]$$

$$T = \frac{W}{2}\left[d_2\left(\frac{f + \tan\alpha}{1 - f\tan\alpha}\right) + f_c d_c\right] = T_R$$

... (Eq. 8.10) **9.12(a)/ Pg 135, DHB**

Note: Uniform pressure theory is applicable when the collar surface is new, while uniform wear theory is used after the collar surface is subjected to initial wear. *Hence in general, uniform wear theory is used for collar friction.*

8.4.2 Torque Required to Lower the Load

When the load is being lowered, the forces and their components acting at a point on the inclined plane are shown in **Fig. 8.5(b)**. The system is in equilibrium under the action of these forces. Proceeding on similar lines as discussed in **Sec. 8.4.1**.

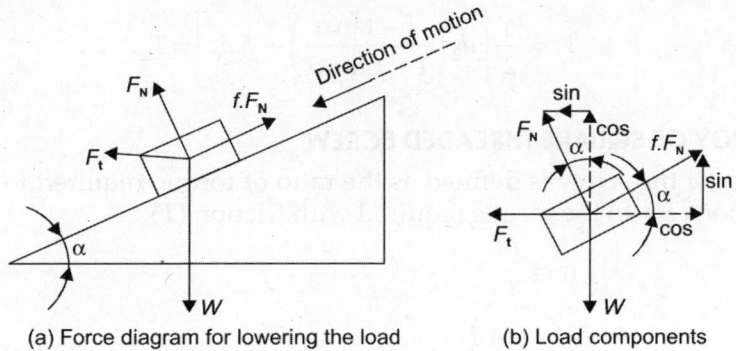

(a) Force diagram for lowering the load   (b) Load components

Fig. 8.5: Torque required to lower the load

Resolving the forces along the horizontal, we have

$$F_t + F_N \sin\alpha = fF_N \cos\alpha$$

$\therefore \qquad F_t = fF_N \cos\alpha - F_N \sin\alpha \qquad \qquad \text{... (Eq. 8.11)}$

Resolving the forces along the vertical, we have

$$W = F_N \cos\alpha + fF_N \sin\alpha \qquad \qquad \text{... (Eq. 8.12)}$$

Dividing (Eq. 8.11) by (Eq. 8.12) yields

$$\frac{F_t}{W} = \frac{fF_N \cos\alpha - F_N \sin\alpha}{F_N \cos\alpha + fF_N \sin\alpha}$$

$$= \frac{F_N(f\cos\alpha - \sin\alpha)}{F_N(\cos\alpha + f\sin\alpha)} = \frac{(f\cos\alpha - \sin\alpha)}{(\cos\alpha + f\sin\alpha)}$$

Dividing the RHS of above equation with $\cos\alpha$, yields

$$\frac{F_t}{W} = \frac{f - \tan\alpha}{1 + f\tan\alpha}$$

$\therefore \qquad F_t = W\left(\dfrac{f - \tan\alpha}{1 + f\tan\alpha}\right) \qquad \text{... (Eq. 8.13)}$ **9.11(d)/ Pg 134, DHB**

But coefficient of friction,

$$f = \tan\phi$$

(Eq. 8.13) yields... $\qquad F_t = W\left(\dfrac{\tan\phi - \tan\alpha}{1 + \tan\phi\tan\alpha}\right) = W\tan(\phi - \alpha)$

... (Eq. 8.13a) **9.11(d)/ Pg 134, DHB**

The torque required to raise the load,

$$T = F_t \left(\frac{d_2}{2} \right) = \left(\frac{Wd_2}{2} \right) \tan(\phi - \alpha)$$

... (Eq. 8.14) **9.11(e)/ Pg 134, DHB**

On similar lines to (Eq. 8.10), the total torque required for square thread in lowering the load is given by:

$$T = \frac{W}{2} \left[d_2 \tan(\phi - \alpha) + f_c d_c \right]$$

$$T = \frac{W}{2} \left[d_2 \left(\frac{f - \tan\alpha}{1 + f \tan\alpha} \right) + f_c d_c \right] = T_L \qquad \text{... (Eq. 8.15)}$$

8.5 EFFICIENCY OF SQUARE THREADED SCREW

The efficiency of the screw is defined as the ratio of torque required to raise the load without friction (T') to the torque required with friction (T).

i.e.
$$\eta = \frac{T'}{T}$$

Here
$$T = \left(\frac{Wd_2}{2} \right) \tan(\phi + \alpha) \qquad \text{... 9.11(a)/ Pg 134, DHB}$$

In the absence of friction,

$$T' = \left(\frac{Wd_2}{2} \right) \tan\alpha \qquad \text{... (Eq. 8.16) 9.11(c)/ Pg 134, DHB}$$

$$\therefore \quad \eta = \frac{\left[\left(\frac{Wd_2}{2} \right) \tan\alpha \right]}{\left[\left(\frac{Wd_2}{2} \right) \tan(\phi + \alpha) \right]} = \frac{\tan\alpha}{\tan(\phi + \alpha)}$$

... (Eq. 8.17) **9.11(f)/ Pg 134, DHB**

If the collar friction is considered, then

$$\eta = \frac{\left[\left(\frac{Wd_2}{2} \right) \tan\alpha \right]}{\dfrac{W}{2} \left[d_2 \left(\dfrac{f + \tan\alpha}{1 - f \tan\alpha} \right) + f_c d_c \right]}$$

$$\therefore \quad \eta = \frac{d_2 \tan\alpha}{\left[d_2 \left(\dfrac{f + \tan\alpha}{1 - f \tan\alpha} \right) + f_c d_c \right]} = \frac{1}{\pi [d_2 \tan(\phi + \alpha) + f_c d_c]}$$

... (Eq. 8.18) **9.12(b)/ Pg 135, DHB**

8.6 SELF LOCKING AND OVERHAULING IN POWER SCREWS

We know that the torque required to raise the load,

$$T = \left(\frac{Wd_2}{2} \right) \tan(\phi + \alpha) \qquad \text{... 9.11(b)/ Pg 134, DHB}$$

where α = helix angle and ϕ = friction angle

If $\phi < \alpha$ in the above expression, then torque required to lower the load will be **negative**, indicating that the load will start moving downward without the application of any torque. Such a condition is known as **overhauling of screws or back driving of screw**. This condition is not useful in screw jack applications but can be found in Yankee-screw driver.

The overhauling condition for square threads is given as

$$\tan\alpha \geq \frac{fd_2 + f_c d_c}{d_2 - f\,f_c d_c} \qquad \text{... 9.12(c)/ Pg 135, DHB}$$

On the other hand, if $\phi \geq \alpha$, the torque required to lower the load will be **positive**, indicating that an effort is to be applied in order to lower the load. Such a screw is known as **self-locking screw**. This property is very useful in screw jack applications.

8.7 EFFICIENCY OF SELF LOCKING SCREW

We know that
$$\eta = \frac{\tan\alpha}{\tan(\phi + \alpha)} \qquad \text{... 9.11(f)/ Pg 134, DHB}$$

For self locking, $\quad \phi \geq \alpha$ or $\alpha \leq \phi$

$\therefore \qquad \eta \leq \dfrac{\tan\phi}{\tan(\phi + \phi)}$

$\qquad\qquad \leq \dfrac{\tan\phi}{\tan 2\phi}$

$\qquad\qquad \leq \dfrac{\tan\phi(1 - \tan^2\phi)}{2\tan\phi} \qquad \because \tan 2\phi = \dfrac{2\tan\phi}{(1 - \tan^2\phi)}$

$\therefore \qquad \eta \leq \dfrac{1}{2} - \dfrac{\tan^2\phi}{2} \qquad\qquad\qquad \text{... (Eq. 8.19)}$

Thus, the efficiency of self-locking screw is $\leq 50\%$. On the other hand, if the efficiency is more than 50%, then the screw is said to be *overhauling*.

8.8 V-THREADS OR ANGULAR THREADS

For a V-thread, the included angle is as shown in **Fig. 8.6.**

where 2β = angle of V-thread

$\qquad$ = 29° for acme thread

$\qquad$ = 30° for ISO metric trapezoidal thread.

$\qquad \beta$ = semi angle of V-thread

From **Fig. 8.6,** we have

$$\cos\beta = \frac{W}{F_N}$$

i.e. $\qquad F_N = \dfrac{W}{\cos\beta}$

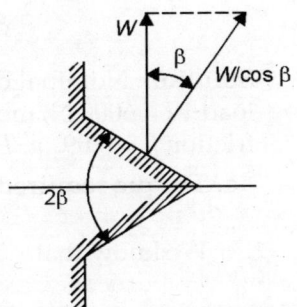

Fig. 8.6: Forces on V-thread **[Fig. 9.5(b)/Pg 133, DHB]**

But frictional force = $\quad fF_N = \dfrac{fW}{\cos\beta} = fW\sec\beta \qquad\qquad \text{... (Eq. 8.20)}$

The effect of thread angle is to increase the frictional force by a term $\sec\beta$. To account for this effect, the coefficient of friction f is taken as $f\sec\beta$ instead of f as derived for square threads.

On similar lines as derived for square threads, we have:

Tangential force of V-threads acting at mean radius of the screw,

$$F_{t1} = W\left(\frac{\tan\alpha + f\sec\beta}{1 - f\tan\alpha\sec\beta}\right) \quad \ldots \text{(Eq. 8.21)} \textbf{ 9.10(f)/ Pg 134, DHB}$$

Total torque required for V-threads,

$$T = \frac{W}{2}\left[d_2\left(\frac{\tan\alpha + f\sec\beta}{1 - f\tan\alpha\sec\beta}\right) + f_c d_c\right]$$

$$\ldots \text{(Eq. 8.22)} \textbf{ 9.10(h)/ Pg 134, DHB}$$

Efficiency,
$$\eta = \frac{d_2\tan\alpha}{\left[d_2\left(\dfrac{\tan\alpha + f\sec\beta}{1 - f\tan\alpha\sec\beta}\right) + f_c d_c\right]} \quad \ldots \text{(Eq. 8.23)}$$

Note: *From Tb. 9.8/Pg 140, DHB*

	External thread	Internal thread
Major or nominal or outside diameter [Column 3]	d	D
Mean or pitch diameter [Column 4]	d_2	D_2
Root or core or minor diameter	d_1 [column 5]	D_1 [column 6]

1. **A square threaded power screw has a nominal diameter of 30 mm and a pitch of 6 mm with double threads. The load on the screw is 6 kN and the mean diameter of the thread collar is 40 mm. The coefficient of friction for the screw is 0.1 and the collar is 0.09. Determine:**

   a. **Torque required to raise the screw against the load**

   b. **Torque required to lower the screw with the load**

   c. **Overall efficiency**

   d. **Is the screw self-locking?**

   VTU – Dec. 07/ Jan. 2008 – 10 Marks; Dec. 2012 – 15 Marks

Solution: Nominal diameter $d = 30$ mm, pitch $p = 6$ mm, number of threads $n = 2$, load $W = 6000$ N, mean diameter of collar $d_c = 40$ mm, screw friction $f = 0.1$, collar friction $f_c = 0.09$. a. $T_R = ?$, b. $T_L = ?$, c. $\eta = ?$ d. self locking?

a. **Torque required to raise the load:**

We know that $\quad T_R = \dfrac{W}{2}\left[d_2\left(\dfrac{f + \tan\alpha}{1 - f\tan\alpha}\right) + f_c d_c\right]$

$$\ldots \text{Eq. (i)} \textbf{ 9.12(a)/ Pg 135, DHB}$$

Mean or pitch diameter,

$$d_2 = d - \left(\frac{p}{2}\right) = 30 - \left(\frac{6}{2}\right) = 27 \text{ mm}$$

Lead angle $\quad \tan\alpha = \dfrac{l}{\pi d_2} = \dfrac{np}{\pi d_2} = \dfrac{2 \times 6}{\pi \times 27} = 0.1415 \quad \ldots \textbf{9.10(b)/ Pg 133, DHB}$

∴ Eq. (i) yields…

$$T_R = \frac{6000}{2}\left[27 \times \left(\frac{0.1 + 0.1415}{1 - 0.1 \times 0.1415}\right) + (0.09 \times 40)\right]$$

$$T_R = 30642.27 \text{ N·mm}$$

b. **Torque required to lower the load:**

We know that $T_L = \dfrac{W}{2}\left[d_2\left(\dfrac{f - \tan\alpha}{1 + f\tan\alpha}\right) + f_c d_c\right]$

$$= \frac{6000}{2}\left[27 \times \left(\frac{0.1 - 0.1415}{1 + 0.1 \times 0.1415}\right) + (0.09 \times 40)\right]$$

$$T_L = 7485.40 \text{ N·mm}$$

c. **Efficiency:**

We know that $\quad \eta = \dfrac{d_2 \tan\alpha}{\left[d_2\left(\dfrac{f + \tan\alpha}{1 - f\tan\alpha}\right) + f_c d_c\right]}$ … **9.12(b)/ Pg 135, DHB**

$$= \frac{27 \times 0.1415}{\left[27\left(\dfrac{0.1 + 0.1415}{1 - 0.1 \times 0.1415}\right) + (0.09 \times 40)\right]}$$

$$\eta = 37.40\%$$

d. **Self locking:** Since efficiency of screw is < 50%, the given screw is self locking.

2. **A single start square threaded power screw is used to raise a load of 120 kN. The screw has a mean diameter of 24 mm and four threads per 24 mm length. The mean collar diameter is 40 mm. The coefficient of friction is estimated as 0.1 for both thread and the collar.**
   a. **Determine the major diameter of the screw.**
   b. **Estimate the screw torque required to raise the load.**
   c. **Estimate the overall efficiency.**
   d. **If collar friction is eliminated, what minimum value of thread coefficient is needed to prevent the screw from overhauling?**

   VTU – June/ July 2014 – 15 Marks; Dec. 2009/ Jan. 2010 – 10 Marks

Solution: Number of starts $n = 1$, $W = 120 \times 10^3$ N, mean diameter $d_2 = 24$ mm, number of threads $n_1 = 4$, thread length $l_n = 24$ mm, $d_c = 40$ mm, $f = f_c = 0.1$. a. $d = ?$, b. $T_R = ?$, c. $\eta = ?$, d. $f = ?$ for overhauling

a. **Major diameter:**

We know that $\qquad d_2 = d - \left(\dfrac{p}{2}\right)$

But length of nut $\quad l_n = n_1 p$ … **9.13(b)/ Pg 135, DHB**

$$24 = 4p$$

$$p = 6 \text{ mm}$$

i.e. $\qquad 24 = d - \dfrac{6}{2}$

$$d = 27 \text{ mm}$$

b. **Torque required to lower the load:**

We know that $T_R = \dfrac{W}{2}\left[d_2\left(\dfrac{f + \tan\alpha}{1 - f\tan\alpha}\right) + f_c d_c\right]$

...Eq. (i) **9.12(a)/ Pg 135, DHB**

But lead angle,

$$\tan\alpha = \frac{l}{\pi d_2} = \frac{np}{\pi d_2} = \frac{1 \times 6}{\pi \times 24} = 0.0796 \qquad \text{... 9.10(b)/ Pg 133, DHB}$$

$\therefore$ Eq. (i) yields... $T_R = \dfrac{120 \times 10^3}{2}\left[24 \times \left(\dfrac{0.1 + 0.0796}{1 - 0.1 \times 0.0796}\right) + (0.1 \times 40)\right]$

$$T_R = 500.70 \times 10^3 \text{ N·mm}$$

c. **Efficiency:**

We know that $\eta = \dfrac{d_2 \tan\alpha}{\left[d_2\left(\dfrac{f + \tan\alpha}{1 - f\tan\alpha}\right) + f_c d_c\right]}$ ... **9.12(b)/ Pg 135, DHB**

$$= \frac{24 \times 0.0796}{\left[24\left(\dfrac{0.1 + 0.0796}{1 - 0.1 \times 0.0796}\right) + (0.1 \times 40)\right]}$$

$$\eta = 22.90\%$$

d. **Minimum value of f:**

We know that the condition for overhauling is

$$\phi < \alpha$$

i.e. $\tan\phi < \tan\alpha$

or $\tan\alpha > \tan\phi$

Thus, minimum value of f to prevent overhauling of the screw is

$$f = 0.0796$$

3. **A single threaded power screw of 25 mm diameter has a pitch of 5 mm. A vertical load on the screw reaches a maximum load of 500 N. The coefficient of friction is 0.05 for collar and 0.08 for the screw. The frictional diameter of the collar is 30 mm. Find the torque required to raise and lower the load. Also find the efficiency of the power screw.**

VTU – June/ July 2009 – 10 Marks

Solution: $n = 1$, $d = 25$ mm, $p = 5$ mm, $W = 500$ N, $f = 0.08$, $f_c = 0.05$, $d_c = 30$ mm.
a. $T_R = ?$, b. $\eta = ?$

a. **Torque required to raise the load:**

We know that $T_R = \dfrac{W}{2}\left[d_2\left(\dfrac{f + \tan\alpha}{1 - f\tan\alpha}\right) + f_c d_c\right]$

... Eq. (i) **9.12(a)/ Pg 135, DHB**

Mean or pitch diameter,

$$d_2 = d - \left(\frac{p}{2}\right) = 25 - \left(\frac{5}{2}\right) = 22.5 \text{ mm}$$

Lead angle $\quad \tan\alpha = \dfrac{l}{\pi d_2} = \dfrac{np}{\pi d_2} = \dfrac{1 \times 5}{\pi \times 22.5} = 0.0707 \quad \ldots$ **9.10(b)/ Pg 133, DHB**

$\therefore$ Eq. (i) yields...

$$T_R = \frac{500}{2}\left[22.5 \times \left(\frac{0.08 + 0.0707}{1 - 0.08 \times 0.0707}\right) + (0.05 \times 30)\right]$$

$$T_R = 1227.51 \text{ N·mm}$$

b. **Efficiency:**

We know that $\quad \eta = \dfrac{d_2 \tan\alpha}{\left[d_2\left(\dfrac{f + \tan\alpha}{1 - f\tan\alpha}\right) + f_c d_c\right]} \quad \ldots$ **9.12(b)/ Pg 135, DHB**

$$= \frac{22.5 \times 0.0707}{\left[22.5\left(\dfrac{0.08 + 0.0707}{1 - 0.08 \times 0.0707}\right) + (0.05 \times 30)\right]}$$

$$\eta = 32.40\%$$

4. **The double threaded screw of a screw jack has the following specifications:**
   Load to be raised: 90 kN   OD of square thread: 75 mm
   Mean collar diameter: 125 mm   Pitch: 16 mm
   Coefficient of friction for thread: 0.1   Coefficient of friction for collar: 0.12

   Determine the torque required to operate the screw jack and the efficiency of the screw.

   VTU – July/Aug. 2004 – 10 Marks

Solution: $n = 2$, $W = 90 \times 10^3$ N, $d = 75$ mm, $d_c = 125$ mm, $p = 16$ mm, $f = 0.1$, $f_c = 0.12$. a. $T_R = ?$, b. $\eta = ?$

a. **Torque required to raise the load:**

We know that $\quad T_R = \dfrac{W}{2}\left[d_2\left(\dfrac{f + \tan\alpha}{1 - f\tan\alpha}\right) + f_c d_c\right]$

$\ldots$ Eq. (i) **9.12(a)/ Pg 135, DHB**

Mean or pitch diameter,

$$d_2 = d - \left(\frac{p}{2}\right) = 75 - \left(\frac{16}{2}\right) = 67 \text{ mm}$$

Lead angle $\quad \tan\alpha = \dfrac{l}{\pi d_2} = \dfrac{np}{\pi d_2} = \dfrac{2 \times 16}{\pi \times 67} = 0.1520 \quad \ldots$ **9.10(b)/ Pg 133, DHB**

$\therefore$ Eq. (i) yields...

$$T_R = \frac{90 \times 10^3}{2}\left[67 \times \left(\frac{0.1 + 0.1520}{1 - 0.1 \times 0.1520}\right) + (0.12 \times 125)\right]$$

$$T_R = 1.45 \times 10^6 \text{ N·mm}$$

b. **Efficiency:**

We know that $\quad \eta = \dfrac{d_2 \tan\alpha}{\left[d_2\left(\dfrac{f + \tan\alpha}{1 - f\tan\alpha}\right) + f_c d_c\right]} \quad \ldots$ **9.12(b)/ Pg 135, DHB**

$$= \frac{67 \times 0.1520}{\left[67 \left(\frac{0.1 + 0.1520}{1 - 0.1 \times 0.1520} \right) + (0.12 \times 125) \right]}$$

$$\eta = 31.68\%$$

5. **A vertical two start square threaded screw of 100 mm mean diameter and 20 mm pitch supports a vertical load of 18 kN. The axial thrust on the screw is taken by a collar bearing of 250 mm outside diameter and 100 mm inside diameter. Find the force required at the end of the lever which is 400 mm long in order to lift and lower the load. The coefficient of friction for the vertical screw and nut is 0.15 and that for collar bearing is 0.20.**

VTU – June/ July 2015 – 14 Marks

Solution: $n = 2$, $d_2 = 100$ mm, $p = 20$ mm, $W = 18 \times 10^3$ N, $d' = 250$ mm, $d'' = 100$ mm, $f = 0.15$, $f_c = 0.20$, length of lever $L = 400$ mm. a. $F_R = ?$, b. $F_L = ?$

a. **Force required to raise the load:** Since the torque is equal to bending moment, torque required to raise the load = effort × length of handle

i.e. $\qquad\qquad T_R = F_R L$ $\qquad\qquad\qquad\qquad\qquad\qquad$ ... Eq. (i)

but $\qquad\qquad T_R = \frac{W}{2} \left[d_2 \left(\frac{f + \tan \alpha}{1 - f \tan \alpha} \right) + f_c d_c \right]$

$\qquad\qquad\qquad\qquad\qquad\qquad\qquad$ ... Eq. (ii) **9.12(a)/ Pg 135, DHB**

Lead angle $\quad \tan \alpha = \frac{l}{\pi d_2} = \frac{np}{\pi d_2} = \frac{2 \times 20}{\pi \times 100} = 0.1273$ $\quad$ ... **9.10(b)/ Pg 133, DHB**

Mean diameter of collar,

$$d_c = \left(\frac{d' + d''}{2} \right), \text{ assuming uniform wear condition}$$

$$d_c = \left(\frac{250 + 100}{2} \right) = 175 \text{ mm}$$

Eq. (ii) yields...

$$T_R = \frac{18 \times 10^3}{2} \left[100 \times \left(\frac{0.15 + 0.1273}{1 - 0.15 \times 0.1273} \right) + (0.2 \times 175) \right]$$

$$T_R = 569.43 \times 10^3 \text{ N·mm}$$

Eq. (i) yields...

$$569.43 \times 10^3 = F_R \times 400 \Rightarrow F_R = 1423.57 \text{ N}$$

b. **Force required to lower the load:**

Here $\qquad\qquad T_L = F_L L$ $\qquad\qquad\qquad\qquad\qquad\qquad$ ... Eq. (iii)

But $\qquad\qquad T_L = \frac{W}{2} \left[d_2 \left(\frac{f - \tan \alpha}{1 + f \tan \alpha} \right) + f_c d_c \right]$

$$= \frac{18 \times 10^3}{2} \left[100 \times \left(\frac{0.15 - 0.1273}{1 + 0.15 \times 0.1273} \right) + (0.2 \times 175) \right]$$

$$T_L = 335.05 \times 10^3 \text{ N·mm}$$

Eq. (iii) yields...

$$335.05 \times 10^3 = F_L \times 400$$

$$F_L = 837.62 \text{ N}$$

6. **The cutter of a broaching machine is pulled by a square threaded screw 55 mm outer diameter having 10 mm pitch. The operating nut takes an axial load of 400 N on a flat surface 60 mm inner diameter and 90 mm outer diameter. If f at threads and collar is 0.15, find:**
   a. **The torque on the screw**
   b. **The power required for the motor at a cutting speed of 6 m/min**
   c. **Efficiency of the screw.**

VTU – June/ July 2011 – 12 Marks; Dec. 2013/ Jan. 2014 – 15 Marks; Jan/ Feb. 2006 – 10 Marks

Solution: $d = 55$ mm, $p = 10$ mm, $W = 400$ N, $d' = 90$ mm, $d'' = 60$ mm, $f = 0.15 = f_c$. a. $F_R = ?$, b. $P = ?$, if cutting speed $= 6$ m/min, c. $\eta = ?$

a. **Torque required**

We know that $\quad T_R = \dfrac{W}{2}\left[d_2 \left(\dfrac{f + \tan\alpha}{1 - f\tan\alpha} \right) + f_c d_c \right]$

$$\text{... Eq. (i) } \textbf{9.12(a)/ Pg 135, DHB}$$

Mean or pitch diameter,

$$d_2 = d - \left(\frac{p}{2} \right) = 55 - \left(\frac{10}{2} \right) = 50 \text{ mm}$$

Lead angle $\quad \tan\alpha = \dfrac{l}{\pi d_2} = \dfrac{np}{\pi d_2} = \dfrac{1 \times 10}{\pi \times 50} = 0.0637 \quad \text{... } \textbf{9.10(b)/ Pg 133, DHB}$

Mean diameter of collar,

$$d_c = \left(\frac{d' + d''}{2} \right), \text{ assuming uniform wear condition}$$

$$d_c = \left(\frac{90 + 60}{2} \right) = 75 \text{ mm}$$

Eq. (i) yields...

$$T_R = \frac{400}{2}\left[50 \times \left(\frac{0.15 + 0.0637}{1 - 0.15 \times 0.0637} \right) + (0.15 \times 75) \right]$$

$$T_R = 4407.62 \text{ N·mm}$$

b. **Power:**

We know that $\quad T_R = \dfrac{9.55 \times 10^6 (P)}{n'} \quad \text{... } \textbf{3.3(a)/Pg 50, DHB}$

But $\quad n' = \dfrac{\text{cutting speed}}{\text{lead}} = \dfrac{6000 \text{ mm/min}}{1 \times 10 \text{ mm}} = 600 \text{ rpm}$

$$4407.62 = \frac{9.55 \times 10^6 (P)}{600}$$

$$P = 0.277 \text{ kW.}$$

c. **Efficiency:**

We know that $\quad \eta = \dfrac{d_2 \tan\alpha}{\left[d_2 \left(\dfrac{f + \tan\alpha}{1 - f \tan\alpha} \right) + f_c d_c \right]}$ ... **9.12(b)/ Pg 135, DHB**

$$= \frac{50 \times 0.0637}{\left[50 \left(\dfrac{0.15 + 0.0637}{1 - 0.15 \times 0.0637} \right) + (0.15 \times 75) \right]}$$

$$\eta = 14.45\%$$

7. **An electric motor driven power screw moves a nut in a horizontal plane against a force of 75 kN at 300 mm/min. The screw has a single thread of 6 mm pitch on a major diameter of 40 mm. The friction coefficient at screw threads is 0.1. Estimate the power of the motor.**

VTU – June/ July 2015 – 10 Marks

Solution: $W = 75 \times 10^3$ N, cutting speed $= 300$ mm/min, $n = 1$, $p = 6$ mm, $d = 40$ mm, $f = 0.1$, $P = ?$

We know that $\quad T_R = \dfrac{9.55 \times 10^6 (P)}{n'}$ ... Eq. (i) **3.3(a)/Pg 50, DHB**

But $\quad n' = \dfrac{\text{cutting speed}}{\text{lead}} = \dfrac{300 \text{ mm/min}}{1 \times 6 \text{ mm}} = 50$ rpm

Also $\quad T_R = \dfrac{W d_2}{2} \left(\dfrac{f + \tan\alpha}{1 - f \tan\alpha} \right)$ ... Eq. (ii) **9.11(b)/Pg 134, DHB**

Mean or pitch diameter,

$$d_2 = d - \left(\frac{p}{2} \right) = 40 - \left(\frac{6}{2} \right) = 37 \text{ mm}$$

Lead angle $\quad \tan\alpha = \dfrac{l}{\pi d_2} = \dfrac{np}{\pi d_2} = \dfrac{1 \times 6}{\pi \times 37} = 0.0516$ ... **9.10(b)/ Pg 133, DHB**

Eq. (ii) yields...

$$T_R = \frac{(75 \times 10^3) \times 37}{2} \left(\frac{0.1 + 0.0516}{1 - 0.1 \times 0.0516} \right)$$

$$T_R = 211.44 \times 10^3 \text{ N·mm}$$

Eq. (i) yields...

$$211.44 \times 10^3 = \frac{9.55 \times 10^6 (P)}{50}$$

$$P = 1.107 \text{ kW.}$$

8. **The square thread of a screw jack with a specification of 80 × 16, with a double start is to raise a load of 100 kN. The mean collar diameter is 130 mm. The coefficient of friction for the threads and the collar are 0.1 and 0.12 respectively. Determine:**
   a. **The torque required to raise the load**
   b. **The efficiency of the screw**
   c. **Whether self-locking exists?**

VTU – July 2006 – 15 Marks

Solution: Specification: $80 \times 16 \Rightarrow d = 80$ mm, $p = 16$ mm, $n = 2$, $W = 100 \times 10^3$ N, $d_c = 130$ mm, $f = 0.1$, $f_c = 0.12$. a. $T_R = ?$, b. $\eta = ?$, c. self-locking?

a. Torque required to raise the load

We know that $T_R = \dfrac{W}{2}\left[d_2\left(\dfrac{f + \tan\alpha}{1 - f\tan\alpha}\right) + f_c d_c \right]$

... Eq. (i) **9.12(a)/ Pg 135, DHB**

Mean or pitch diameter,

$$d_2 = d - \left(\frac{p}{2}\right) = 80 - \left(\frac{16}{2}\right) = 72 \text{ mm}$$

Lead angle $\tan\alpha = \dfrac{l}{\pi d_2} = \dfrac{np}{\pi d_2} = \dfrac{2 \times 16}{\pi \times 72} = 0.1415$ ... **9.10(b)/ Pg 133, DHB**

∴ Eq. (i) yields...

$$T_R = \frac{100 \times 10^3}{2}\left[72 \times \left(\frac{0.1 + 0.1415}{1 - 0.1 \times 0.1415}\right) + (0.12 \times 130) \right]$$

$$T_R = 1.66 \times 10^6 \text{ N·mm}$$

b. Efficiency:

We know that $\eta = \dfrac{d_2 \tan\alpha}{\left[d_2\left(\dfrac{f + \tan\alpha}{1 - f\tan\alpha}\right) + f_c d_c \right]}$ ... **9.12(b)/ Pg 135, DHB**

$$= \frac{72 \times 0.1415}{\left[72\left(\dfrac{0.1 + 0.1415}{1 - 0.1 \times 0.1415}\right) + (0.12 \times 130) \right]}$$

$$\eta = 30.65\%$$

c. **Self-locking:** Since η of screw is $< 50\%$, the given screw is self-locking.

9. **A power screw for a jack has square threads of proportion 50 × 42 × 8. The coefficient of friction at the threads is 0.1 while that at the collar is 0.12. Determine the weight that can be lifted by this jack through a human effort of 400 N through a hand lever of span 400 mm.**

VTU – July/ Aug. 2005 – 16 Marks

Solution: Specification: $50 \times 42 \times 8 \Rightarrow d = 80$ mm, $d_1 = 42$ mm, $p = 8$ mm, $f = 0.1$, $f_c = 0.12$, $W = ?$, $L = 400$ mm, $F = 400$ N.

We know that $T_R = FL = 400 \times 400 = 160000$ N·mm   ... Eq. (i)

Also $T_R = \dfrac{W}{2}\left[d_2\left(\dfrac{f + \tan\alpha}{1 - f\tan\alpha}\right) + f_c d_c \right]$

... Eq. (ii) **9.12(a)/ Pg 135, DHB**

Mean or pitch diameter,

$$d_2 = d - \left(\frac{p}{2}\right) = 50 - \left(\frac{8}{2}\right) = 46 \text{ mm}$$

Lead angle $\tan\alpha = \dfrac{p}{\pi d_2} = \dfrac{8}{\pi \times 46} = 0.0554$ ... **9.10(b)/ Pg 133, DHB**

Assume, outside diameter of collar,

$$d' = 1.75d = 1.75 \times 50 = 87.5 \text{ mm}$$

Assume, inside diameter of collar

$$d'' = 0.25d' = 0.25 \times 87.5 = 21.88 \text{ mm} \approx 22 \text{ mm}$$

Mean diameter of collar,

$$d_c = \left(\frac{d' + d''}{2}\right), \text{ assuming uniform wear condition}$$

$$d_c = \left(\frac{87.5 + 22}{2}\right) = 54.75 \text{ mm}$$

Eq. (ii) yields…

$$T_R = \frac{W}{2}\left[46 \times \left(\frac{0.1 + 0.0554}{1 - 0.1 \times 0.0554}\right) + (0.12 \times 54.75)\right]$$

$$T_R = 6.87W$$

From Eqs. (i) and (ii), we have

$$6.87W = 160000$$

$$W = 23.28 \text{ kN}$$

10. **A single threaded power screw has a major diameter restriction of 36 mm. Design the screw, if the frictional coefficient for thread and collar are 0.13 and 0.1 respectively. Estimate the power input to rotate the screw at 1 rpm, if the load to be lifted is 5 kN.**

VTU – Dec. 06/ Jan. 2007 – 10 Marks

Solution: $n = 1, d = 36 \text{ mm}, f = 0.13, f_c = 0.1, P = ?, n' = 1 \text{ rpm}, W = 5000 \text{ N}.$

We know that $\qquad T_R = \dfrac{9.55 \times 10^6 (P)}{n'} \qquad$ … Eq. (i) **3.3(a)/Pg 50, DHB**

but $\qquad T_R = \dfrac{W}{2}\left[d_2\left(\dfrac{f + \tan\alpha}{1 - f\tan\alpha}\right) + f_c d_c\right]$

… Eq. (ii) **9.12(a)/ Pg 135, DHB**

For $\qquad d = 36 \text{ mm}$, from **Tb. 9.10/Pg 149, DHB**, we have

Minor diameter of thread

$$d_1 = 30 \text{ mm and pitch } p = 6 \text{ mm}$$

Mean or pitch diameter,

$$d_2 = d - \left(\frac{p}{2}\right) = 36 - \left(\frac{6}{2}\right) = 33 \text{ mm}$$

Lead angle $\qquad \tan\alpha = \dfrac{p}{\pi d_2} = \dfrac{6}{\pi \times 33} = 0.0579 \qquad$ … **9.10(b)/ Pg 133, DHB**

Assume, outside diameter of collar,

$$d' = 1.75d = 1.75 \times 36 = 63 \text{ mm}$$

Assume, inside diameter of collar

$$d'' = 0.25d' = 0.25 \times 63 = 15.75 \text{ mm} \approx 16 \text{ mm}$$

Mean diameter of collar,

$$d_c = \left(\frac{d' + d''}{2}\right), \text{ assuming uniform wear condition}$$

$$d_c = \left(\frac{63 + 16}{2}\right) = 39.5 \text{ mm}$$

Eq. (ii) yields…

$$T_R = \frac{5000}{2}\left[33 \times \left(\frac{0.13 + 0.0579}{1 - 0.13 \times 0.0579}\right) + (0.1 \times 39.5)\right]$$

$$T_R = 25.47 \times 10^3 \text{ N·mm}$$

Eq. (i) yields…

$$25.47 \times 10^3 = \frac{9.55 \times 10^6 (P)}{1}$$

$$P = 0.002667 \text{ kW} = 2.6672 \text{ W}$$

11. **In a large gate valve used to a high pressure water line, the gate weighs 6000 N and friction force due to water pressure, resisting opening is 2000 N. The valve stem is nonrotating and is raised by a rotating wheel with internal threads acting as a rotating nut on the valve stem. The outside diameter of the valve stem screw is 38 mm. The wheel presses against a supporting collar of 40 mm inside diameter and 75 mm outside diameter. The valve stem is fitted with square threads (single start) having an 8.5 mm pitch. Assuming the coefficient of friction for the collar as 0.25 and for the threads as 0.1, determine:**
    a. **The torque that must be applied to the wheel to raise the valve gate.**
    b. **The torque that must be applied to the wheel to lower the valve gate.**
    c. **The efficiency of the screw and collar mechanism.**

VTU – Jan/ Feb. 2005 – 10 Marks

Solution: $W = 6000$ N, $F = 2000$ N, $d = 38$ mm, $d'' = 40$ mm, $d' = 75$ mm, $n = 1$, $p = 8.5$ mm, $f = 0.1$, $f_c = 0.25$. a. $T_R = ?$, b. $T_L = ?$, c. $\eta = ?$

a. **Torque required to raise the load:**

We know that $\quad T_R = \dfrac{W_R}{2}\left[d_2\left(\dfrac{f + \tan\alpha}{1 - f\tan\alpha}\right) + f_c d_c\right]$

$\qquad\qquad\qquad\qquad\qquad$ … Eq. (i) **9.12(a)/ Pg 135, DHB**

Here $\qquad\qquad W_R = W + F = 6000 + 2000 = 8000$ N

Mean or pitch diameter,

$$d_2 = d - \left(\frac{p}{2}\right) = 38 - \left(\frac{8.5}{2}\right) = 33.75 \text{ mm}$$

Lead angle $\quad \tan\alpha = \dfrac{l}{\pi d_2} = \dfrac{np}{\pi d_2} = \dfrac{1 \times 8.5}{\pi \times 33.75} = 0.0802 \quad$ … **9.10(b)/ Pg 133, DHB**

Mean diameter of collar,

$$d_c = \left(\frac{d' + d''}{2}\right), \text{ assuming uniform wear condition}$$

$$d_c = \left(\frac{75 + 40}{2}\right) = 57.5 \text{ mm}$$

Eq. (i) yields…

$$T_R = \frac{8000}{2}\left[33.75 \times \left(\frac{0.1 + 0.0802}{1 - 0.1 \times 0.0802}\right) + (0.25 \times 57.5)\right]$$

$$T_R = 82.02 \times 10^3 \text{ N·mm}$$

b. Force required to lower the load:

We know that $T_L = \dfrac{W_L}{2}\left[d_2\left(\dfrac{f - \tan\alpha}{1 + f\tan\alpha}\right) + f_c d_c\right]$

Here $W_L = W - F = 6000 - 2000 = 4000 \text{ N}$

$$= \frac{4000}{2}\left[33.75 \times \left(\frac{0.1 - 0.0802}{1 + 0.1 \times 0.0802}\right) + (0.25 \times 57.5)\right]$$

$$T_L = 30.08 \times 10^3 \text{ N·mm}$$

c. Efficiency:

We know that $\eta = \dfrac{d_2\tan\alpha}{\left[d_2\left(\dfrac{f + \tan\alpha}{1 - f\tan\alpha}\right) + f_c d_c\right]}$ … **9.12(b)/ Pg 135, DHB**

$$= \frac{33.75 \times 0.0802}{\left[33.75\left(\frac{0.1 + 0.0802}{1 - 0.1 \times 0.0802}\right) + (0.25 \times 57.5)\right]}$$

$$\eta = 13.20\%$$

12. **A double threaded power screw with trapezoidal ISO thread is used to raise a load of 300 kN. The nominal diameter is 100 mm and the pitch is 12 mm. The coefficient of friction is 0.15. Neglecting the collar friction, calculate:**
    a. Torque required to raise the load.
    b. Torque required to lower the load.
    c. Efficiency of the screw.

VTU – Dec. 2010 – 10 Marks

Solution: $n = 2$, trapezoidal thread $\beta = 15°$, $W = 300 \times 10^3$ N, $d = 100$ mm, pitch $p = 12$ mm, $f = 0.15$, $f_c = 0$. a. $T_R = ?$, b. $T_L = ?$, c. $\eta = ?$

a. Torque required to raise the load:

We know that $T_R = \dfrac{W}{2}\left[d_2\left(\dfrac{f\sec\beta + \tan\alpha}{1 - f\sec\beta\tan\alpha}\right) + f_c d_c\right]$

… Eq. (i) **9.10(h)/ Pg 134, DHB**

Mean or pitch diameter,

$$d_2 = d - \left(\frac{p}{2}\right) = 100 - \left(\frac{12}{2}\right) = 94 \text{ mm}$$

Lead angle $\tan\alpha = \dfrac{l}{\pi d_2} = \dfrac{np}{\pi d_2} = \dfrac{2 \times 12}{\pi \times 94} = 0.0813$ … **9.10(b)/ Pg 133, DHB**

$$\sec\beta = \frac{1}{\cos\beta} = \frac{1}{\cos(15)} = 1.0353$$

Eq. (i) yields...

$$T_R = \frac{300 \times 10^3}{2} \left[94 \times \left(\frac{0.15 \times 1.0353 + 0.0813}{1 - 0.15 \times 1.0353 \times 0.0813} \right) + 0 \right]$$

$$T_R = 3.38 \times 10^6 \, \text{N·mm}$$

b. **Torque required to lower the load:**

We know that $T_L = \dfrac{W}{2} \left[d_2 \left(\dfrac{f \sec\beta - \tan\alpha}{1 + f \sec\beta \tan\alpha} \right) + f_c d_c \right]$

$$= \frac{300 \times 10^3}{2} \left[94 \times \left(\frac{0.15 \times 1.0353 - 0.0813}{1 + 0.1 \times 1.0353 \times 0.0813} \right) + 0 \right]$$

$$T_L = 1.03 \times 10^6 \, \text{N·mm}$$

c. **Efficiency:**

We know that $\quad \eta = \dfrac{d_2 \tan\alpha}{\left[d_2 \left(\dfrac{f \sec\beta + \tan\alpha}{1 - f \sec\beta \tan\alpha} \right) + f_c d_c \right]}$ ... 9.10(j)/ Pg 134, DHB

[θ for triangular thread; β for trapezoidal and acme threads]

$$= \frac{94 \times 0.0813}{\left[94 \left(\dfrac{0.15 \times 1.0353 + 0.0813}{1 - 0.15 \times 1.0353 \times 0.0813} \right) + 0 \right]}$$

$$\eta = 33.93\%$$

13. **The lead screw of a machine has single start trapezoidal threads of 30 mm outside diameter and 6 mm pitch. It drives the tool carriage against an axial load of 1500 N. The thrust collar has a mean diameter of 40 mm. The carriage is moved at a speed of 0.72m/min. The coefficient of friction for both screw and collar is 0.14. Find the power required to drive the screw and the efficiency.**

VTU – June/ July 2014 – 10 Marks

Solution: $n = 1$, trapezoidal thread $\beta = 15°$, $d = 30$ mm, pitch $p = 6$ mm, $W = 1500$ N, $d_c = 40$ mm, $n' = 0.72$ m/min, $f = f_c = 0.14$. a. $P = ?$, b. $\eta = ?$

a. **Power:**

We know that $\quad T_R = \dfrac{9.55 \times 10^6 (P)}{n'}$ ... Eq. (i) 3.3(a)/ Pg 50, DHB

$$n' = \frac{\text{cutting speed}}{\text{lead}} = \frac{0.72 \times 1000 \, \text{mm/min}}{1 \times 6 \, \text{mm}} = 120 \, \text{rpm}$$

But $\quad T_R = \dfrac{W}{2} \left[d_2 \left(\dfrac{f \sec\beta + \tan\alpha}{1 - f \sec\beta \tan\alpha} \right) + f_c d_c \right]$

... Eq. (ii) 9.10(h)/ Pg 134, DHB

Mean or pitch diameter,

$$d_2 = d - \left(\frac{p}{2} \right) = 30 - \left(\frac{6}{2} \right) = 27 \, \text{mm}$$

Lead angle $\quad \tan\alpha = \dfrac{l}{\pi d_2} = \dfrac{np}{\pi d_2} = \dfrac{1 \times 6}{\pi \times 27} = 0.0707 \qquad$ ... **9.10(b)/ Pg 133, DHB**

$$\sec\beta = \dfrac{1}{\cos\beta} = \dfrac{1}{\cos(15)} = 1.0353$$

Eq. (ii) yields...

$$T_R = \dfrac{1500}{2}\left[27 \times \left(\dfrac{0.14 \times 1.0353 + 0.0707}{1 - 0.14 \times 1.0353 \times 0.0707}\right) + (0.14 \times 40)\right]$$

$$T_R = 8.61 \times 10^3 \, \text{N·mm}$$

Eq. (i) yields...

$$8.61 \times 10^3 = \dfrac{9.55 \times 10^6 (P)}{120}$$

$$P = 0.1082 \, \text{kW}$$

b. **Efficiency:**

We know that $\quad \eta = \dfrac{d_2 \tan\alpha}{\left[d_2\left(\dfrac{f\sec\beta + \tan\alpha}{1 - f\sec\beta\tan\alpha}\right) + f_c d_c\right]} \qquad$ ... **9.10(j)/ Pg 134, DHB**

[θ for triangular thread; β for trapezoidal and acme threads]

$$= \dfrac{27 \times 0.0707}{\left[27\left(\dfrac{0.14 \times 1.0353 + 0.0707}{1 - 0.14 \times 1.0353 \times 0.0707}\right) + (0.14 \times 40)\right]}$$

$$\eta = 16.63\%$$

14. **The lead screw of a lathe has single start ISO metric trapezoidal threads of 52 mm nominal diameter and 8 mm pitch. The screw is required to exert an axial force of 2 kN in order to drive the tool carriage during turning operation. The thrust is carried on a collar of 100 mm outer diameter and 60 mm inner diameter. The values of coefficient of friction at the screw threads and collar are 0.15 and 0.12 respectively. The lead screw rotates at 30 rev/min. Calculate:**
    a. **The power required to drive the screw.**
    b. **The efficiency of the screw.**

VTU – June 2012 – 14 Marks

Solution: $n = 1$, trapezoidal thread $\beta = 15°$, $d = 52$ mm, pitch $p = 8$ mm, $W = 2000$ N, $d' = 100$ mm, $d'' = 60$ mm, $f = 0.15$, $f_c = 0.12$, $n' = 30$ rpm. a. $P = ?$, b. $\eta = ?$

a. **Power:**

We know that $\quad T_R = \dfrac{9.55 \times 10^6 (P)}{n'} \qquad$ ... Eq. (i) **3.3(a)/ Pg 50, DHB**

But $\quad T_R = \dfrac{W}{2}\left[d_2\left(\dfrac{f\sec\beta + \tan\alpha}{1 - f\sec\beta\tan\alpha}\right) + f_c d_c\right]$

... Eq. (ii) **9.10(h)/ Pg 134, DHB**

Mean or pitch diameter,

$$d_2 = d - \left(\dfrac{p}{2}\right) = 52 - \left(\dfrac{8}{2}\right) = 48 \, \text{mm}$$

Lead angle $\quad \tan\alpha = \dfrac{l}{\pi d_2} = \dfrac{np}{\pi d_2} = \dfrac{1 \times 8}{\pi \times 48} = 0.0531 \qquad$ ... **9.10(b)/ Pg 133, DHB**

$$\sec\beta = \dfrac{1}{\cos\beta} = \dfrac{1}{\cos(15)} = 1.0353$$

Mean diameter of collar,

$$d_c = \left(\dfrac{d' + d''}{2}\right), \text{ assuming uniform wear condition}$$

$$d_c = \left(\dfrac{100 + 60}{2}\right) = 80 \text{ mm}$$

Eq. (ii) yields...

$$T_R = \dfrac{2000}{2}\left[48 \times \left(\dfrac{0.15 \times 1.0353 + 0.0531}{1 - 0.15 \times 1.0353 \times 0.0531}\right) + (0.12 \times 80)\right]$$

$$T_R = 19.69 \times 10^3 \text{ N·mm}$$

Eq. (i) yields...

$$19.69 \times 10^3 = \dfrac{9.55 \times 10^6 (P)}{30}$$

$$P = 0.0618 \text{ kW}$$

b. **Efficiency:**

We know that $\quad \eta = \dfrac{d_2 \tan\alpha}{\left[d_2\left(\dfrac{f\sec\beta + \tan\alpha}{1 - f\sec\beta\tan\alpha}\right) + f_c d_c\right]} \qquad$ ... **9.10(j)/ Pg 134, DHB**

[θ for triangular thread; β for trapezoidal and acme threads]

$$= \dfrac{48 \times 0.0531}{\left[48\left(\dfrac{0.15 \times 1.0353 + 0.0531}{1 - 0.15 \times 1.0353 \times 0.0531}\right) + (0.12 \times 80)\right]}$$

$$\eta = 12.95\%$$

15. **Following data apply to machinists clamp. Outside diameter of the screw = 14 mm, root diameter = 9.5 mm, pitch = 4 mm (single thread), collar friction radius = 6 mm, collar friction coefficient = 0.15, screw friction coefficient = 0.15, thread angle = 30°. Assume that the machinist can comfortably exert a maximum force of 120 N on the handle whose radius is 130 mm. Calculate the maximum clamping force that can be developed between the jaws of the clamp and the efficiency of the clamp.**

VTU – July 2007 – 10 Marks

Solution: $d = 14$ mm, $d_1 = 9.5$ mm, pitch $p = 4$ mm, $n = 1$, $r_c = 6$ mm, $f_c = 0.15$, $f = 0.15$, thread angle $2\beta = 30°$, $\beta = 15°$, $F = 120$ N, $R = 130$ mm. a. $W = ?$, b. $\eta = ?$

a. **To find W:**

We know that $\quad T_R = FR = 120 \times 130 = 15600$ N·mm $\qquad$ ... Eq. (i)

But $\qquad T_R = \dfrac{W}{2}\left[d_2\left(\dfrac{f\sec\beta + \tan\alpha}{1 - f\sec\beta\tan\alpha}\right) + f_c d_c\right]$

... Eq. (ii) **9.10(h)/ Pg 134, DHB**

Mean or pitch diameter,

$$d_2 = \left(\frac{d + d_1}{2}\right) = \left(\frac{14 + 9.5}{2}\right) = 11.75 \text{ mm}$$

Lead angle $\quad \tan\alpha = \dfrac{l}{\pi d_2} = \dfrac{np}{\pi d_2} = \dfrac{1 \times 4}{\pi \times 11.75} = 0.1084 \quad \dots$ **9.10(b)/ Pg 133, DHB**

$$\sec\beta = \frac{1}{\cos\beta} = \frac{1}{\cos(15)} = 1.0353$$

Mean diameter of collar,

$$d_c = 2r_c = 2 \times 6 = 12 \text{ mm}$$

Eq. (ii) yields...

$$T_R = \frac{W}{2}\left[11.75 \times \left(\frac{0.15 \times 1.0353 + 0.1084}{1 - 0.15 \times 1.0353 \times 0.1084}\right) + (0.15 \times 12)\right]$$

$$T_R = 2.476 \, W \qquad\qquad\qquad\qquad\qquad\qquad\qquad \dots \text{Eq. (iii)}$$

From Eqs. (i) and (iii), we have

$$2.476W = 15600$$

$$W = 6300 \text{ N}$$

b. **Efficiency:**

We know that $\quad \eta = \dfrac{d_2 \tan\alpha}{\left[d_2\left(\dfrac{f\sec\beta + \tan\alpha}{1 - f\sec\beta\tan\alpha}\right) + f_c d_c\right]} \quad \dots$ **9.10(j)/ Pg 134, DHB**

[θ for triangular thread; β for trapezoidal and acme threads]

$$= \frac{11.75 \times 0.1084}{\left[11.75\left(\dfrac{0.15 \times 1.0353 + 0.1084}{1 - 0.15 \times 1.0353 \times 0.1084}\right) + (0.15 \times 12)\right]}$$

$$\eta = 25.72\%$$

16. **In a hand vice, the screw has double start acme threads of 25 mm nominal diameter and 4 mm pitch. If the length of the lever is 300 mm, the maximum force that can be applied at the end of the lever is 250 N. Determine the force with which the job is held between the jaws of the vice. Take coefficient of friction at the threads as 0.14, angle of thread = 20 – 29°. Neglect collar friction.**

VTU – Dec. 2009/ Jan. 2010 – 10 Marks

Solution: $n = 2$, $d = 25$ mm, $p = 4$ mm, $L = 300$ mm, $F = 250$ N, $f = 0.14$, acme thread $\beta = 14.5°$, $W = ?$

We know that $\quad T_R = FR = 250 \times 300 = 75000 \text{ N·mm} \qquad \dots \text{Eq. (i)}$

But $\quad T_R = \dfrac{W}{2}\left[d_2\left(\dfrac{f\sec\beta + \tan\alpha}{1 - f\sec\beta\tan\alpha}\right) + f_c d_c\right]$

$\qquad\qquad\qquad\qquad\qquad\qquad\qquad\qquad \dots \text{Eq. (ii)}$ **9.10(h)/ Pg 134, DHB**

Mean or pitch diameter,

$$d_2 = d - \left(\frac{p}{2}\right) = 25 - \left(\frac{4}{2}\right) = 23 \text{ mm}$$

Lead angle $\quad \tan\alpha = \dfrac{l}{\pi d_2} = \dfrac{np}{\pi d_2} = \dfrac{2 \times 4}{\pi \times 23} = 0.1107 \quad$ ... **9.10(b)/ Pg 133, DHB**

$$\sec\beta = \frac{1}{\cos\beta} = \frac{1}{\cos(14.5)} = 1.0329$$

Eq. (ii) yields... $\quad T_R = \dfrac{W}{2}\left[23 \times \left(\dfrac{0.14 \times 1.0329 + 0.1107}{1 - 0.14 \times 1.0329 \times 0.1107} \right) + 0 \right]$

$$T_R = 2.984 \, W \qquad\qquad\qquad\qquad\qquad ... \text{Eq. (iii)}$$

From Eqs. (i) and (iii), we have

$$2.984W = 75000$$
$$W = 25134.04 \text{ N}$$

17. **A machine slide weighing 4000 N is elevated by two start acme thread 50 mm diameter, 8 mm pitch at the rate of 0.8 m/min. If the coefficient of friction is 0.14, calculate the power of the motor to drive the slide. The end of the screw is carried on a thrust collar 40 mm inside, 60 mm outside diameter. The coefficient of friction at the collar is 0.12. Assume uniform wear.**

VTU – Dec. 2011 – 10 Marks

Solution: $W = 4000$ N, $n = 2$, acme thread $\beta = 14.5°$, $d = 50$ mm, $p = 8$ mm, $v = 0.8$ m/min, $f = 0.14$, $P = ?$, $d' = 60$ mm, $d'' = 40$ mm, $f_c = 0.12$.

We know that $\quad T_R = \dfrac{9.55 \times 10^6 (P)}{n'} \qquad$ ... Eq. (i) **3.3(a)/ Pg 50, DHB**

$$n' = \frac{\text{cutting speed}}{\text{lead}} = \frac{0.8 \times 1000 \text{ mm/min}}{2 \times 8 \text{ mm}} = 50 \text{ rpm}$$

But $\quad T_R = \dfrac{W}{2}\left[d_2 \left(\dfrac{f \sec\beta + \tan\alpha}{1 - f \sec\beta \tan\alpha} \right) + f_c d_c \right]$

... Eq. (ii) **9.10(h)/ Pg 134, DHB**

Mean or pitch diameter,

$$d_2 = d - \left(\frac{p}{2}\right) = 50 - \left(\frac{8}{2}\right) = 46 \text{ mm}$$

Lead angle $\quad \tan\alpha = \dfrac{l}{\pi d_2} = \dfrac{np}{\pi d_2} = \dfrac{2 \times 8}{\pi \times 46} = 0.1107 \quad$ ... **9.10(b)/ Pg 133, DHB**

$$\sec\beta = \frac{1}{\cos\beta} = \frac{1}{\cos(14.5)} = 1.0329$$

Mean diameter of collar

$$d_c = \left(\frac{d' + d''}{2}\right) \text{ for uniform wear condition}$$

$\therefore \qquad\qquad d_c = \left(\dfrac{60 + 40}{2}\right) = 50 \text{ mm}$

Eq. (ii) yields...

$$T_R = \frac{4000}{2}\left[46 \times \left(\frac{0.14 \times 1.0329 + 0.1107}{1 - 0.14 \times 1.0329 \times 0.1107}\right) + (0.12 \times 50)\right]$$

$$T_R = 35.87 \times 10^3 \text{ N·mm}$$

Eq. (i) yields...

$$35.87 \times 10^3 = \frac{9.55 \times 10^6 (P)}{50}$$

$$P = 0.1878 \text{ kW}$$

18. **The mean diameter of the square threaded screw having pitch of 10 mm is 50 mm. A load of 20 kN is lifted through a distance of 170 mm. Find the work done in lifting the load and the efficiency of the screw, when:**
   a. **The load rotates with the screw.**
   b. **The load rests on the loose head which does not rotate with the screw. The external and internal diameters of the bearing surface of the loose head are 100 mm and 60 mm respectively. The coefficient of friction for the screw and the bearing surface may be taken as 0.08.**

VTU – Feb. 2015 – 10 Marks

Solution: $d_2 = 50$ mm, $p = 10$ mm, $W = 20 \times 10^3$ N, lift $L = 170$ mm, $d' = 100$ mm, $d'' = 60$ mm, $f = f_c = 0.08$.
   a. Load rotates with the screw, $f_c = 0$. i. $W = ?$, ii. $\eta = ?$
   b. The load rests on the loose head which does not rotate with the screw, $f_c = 0.08$. i. $W = ?$, ii. $\eta = 2$.
   a. **Load rotates with the screw, $f_c = 0$**
   i. **Work done:**

We know that $\quad T_R = \dfrac{9.55 \times 10^6 (P)}{n'}$ ... Eq. (i) **3.3(a)/ Pg 50, DHB**

$$n' = \frac{\text{lift}}{\text{lead}} = \frac{170}{10} = 17 \text{ rpm}$$

But $\quad\quad T_R = \dfrac{W}{2}\left[d_2\left(\dfrac{f + \tan\alpha}{1 - f\tan\alpha}\right) + f_c d_c\right]$

            ... Eq. (ii) **9.12(a)/ Pg 135, DHB**

Lead angle $\quad \tan\alpha = \dfrac{l}{\pi d_2} = \dfrac{np}{\pi d_2} = \dfrac{1 \times 10}{\pi \times 50} = 0.0637$ ... **9.10(b)/ Pg 133, DHB**

Mean diameter of collar,

$$d_c = \left(\frac{d' + d''}{2}\right), \text{ assuming uniform wear condition}$$

$$d_c = \left(\frac{100 + 60}{2}\right) = 80 \text{ mm}$$

Eq. (ii) yields...

$$T_R = \frac{20 \times 10^3}{2}\left[50 \times \left(\frac{0.08 + 0.0637}{1 - 0.08 \times 0.0637}\right) + 0\right]$$

$$T_R = 72.22 \times 10^3 \text{ N·mm}$$

Eq. (i) yields...

$$72.22 \times 10^3 = \frac{9.55 \times 10^6 (P)}{17}$$

$$P = 0.1286 \text{ kW}$$

And work done $W = 60P = 60 \times 0.1286 = 7.71 \text{ kN·m}$

or
$$W = 2\pi n T_R = 2\pi \times 17 \times 72.22 \times 10^3$$
$$= 7.71 \times 10^6 \text{ N·mm} = 7.71 \text{ kN·m}$$

ii. Efficiency:

We know that
$$\eta = \frac{d_2 \tan \alpha}{\left[d_2 \left(\dfrac{f + \tan \alpha}{1 - f \tan \alpha} \right) + f_c d_c \right]} \qquad \text{... 9.12(b)/ Pg 135, DHB}$$

$$= \frac{50 \times 0.0637}{\left[50 \times \left(\dfrac{0.08 + 0.0637}{1 - 0.08 \times 0.0637} \right) + 0 \right]}$$

$$\eta = 44.10\%$$

b. Load does not rotate with the screw, $f_c = 0.08$

i. Work done:

∴ Eq. (ii) yields...

$$T_R = \frac{20 \times 10^3}{2} \left[50 \times \left(\frac{0.08 + 0.0637}{1 - 0.08 \times 0.0637} \right) + (0.08 \times 35) \right]$$

$$T_R = 100.22 \times 10^3 \text{ N·mm}$$

Eq. (i) yields...

$$100.22 \times 10^3 = \frac{9.55 \times 10^6 (P)}{17}$$

$$P = 0.1784 \text{ kW}$$

and work done $W = 60P = 60 \times 0.1784 = 10.70 \text{ kN·m}$

or
$$W = 2\pi n T_R = 2\pi \times 17 \times 100.22 \times 10^3$$
$$= 10.70 \times 10^6 \text{ N·mm} = 10.70 \text{ kN·m}$$

ii. Efficiency:

We know that
$$\eta = \frac{d_2 \tan \alpha}{\left[d_2 \left(\dfrac{f + \tan \alpha}{1 - f \tan \alpha} \right) + f_c d_c \right]} \qquad \text{... 9.12(b)/ Pg 135, DHB}$$

$$= \frac{50 \times 0.0637}{\left[50 \times \left(\dfrac{0.08 + 0.0637}{1 - 0.08 \times 0.0637} \right) + (0.08 \times 35) \right]}$$

$$\eta = 31.78\%$$

8.9 STRESSES IN POWER SCREWS

Following types of stresses are induced in the screw.

8.9.1 Direct Stress (Tensile or Compressive)

Power screws are subjected to direct tensile and compressive stresses, obtained by dividing the axial load by the minimum cross-sectional area of the screw,

i.e.
$$\sigma_c = \frac{W}{A_1} = \sigma_t \qquad \text{... (Eq. 8.24) } \textbf{1.1(a)/ Pg 2, DHB}$$

where W = axial load

A_1 = core or minor or root area of the screw

$$= \frac{\pi d_1^2}{4}, \text{ for external threads}$$

$$= \frac{\pi D_1^2}{4}, \text{ for internal threads}$$

8.9.2 Torsional Shear Stress

This is due to twisting moment induced in the screw.

$$\tau = \frac{16T}{\pi d_1^3} \qquad \text{... (Eq. 8.25) } \textbf{1.1(d)/ Pg 2, DHB}$$

where
$$T_R = T = \frac{W}{2}\left[d_2\left(\frac{f + \tan\alpha}{1 - f\tan\alpha}\right) + f_c d_c \right] \quad \text{... } \textbf{9.12(a)/ Pg 135, DHB}$$

The resultant stress due to combined action of direct and shear stresses may be found as follows:

According to maximum normal stress theory,

$$\sigma_{max} = \left(\frac{\sigma_c}{2}\right) + \sqrt{\left(\frac{\sigma_c}{2}\right)^2 + \tau^2} \qquad \text{... (Eq. 8.26) } \textbf{1.5(a)/ Pg 3, DHB}$$

According to maximum shear stress theory,

$$\tau_{max} = \sqrt{\left(\frac{\sigma_c}{2}\right)^2 + \tau^2} \qquad \text{... (Eq. 8.27) } \textbf{1.5(b)/ Pg 3, DHB}$$

8.9.3 Direct Shear Stress

The screw thread is considered to be loaded as a cantilevered beam. The load is assumed to be uniformly distributed over the mean radius of the screw. Hence, both the threads on the screw and the threads on the nut experience a transverse shear stress at their roots.

Shear stress in the screw,

$$\tau_{screw} = \frac{W}{A_s)_{screw}} = \frac{W}{n\pi d_1 t} \qquad \text{... (Eq. 8.28)}$$

Shear stress in the nut,

$$\tau_{nut} = \frac{W}{(A_s)_{nut}} = \frac{W}{n\pi dt} \qquad \text{... (Eq. 8.29)}$$

where n = number of threads in contact

d_1 = minor/core/root diameter of external thread

d = major/outer/nominal diameter of external thread

t = thickness or width of thread = $p/2$

p = pitch

8.9.4 Bearing Pressure

The direct compression or bearing stress p_b is the pressure between the surface of the screw thread and the contacting surface of the nut. The area used for the stress calculation is the *projected* area for each thread given as $\pi(d^2 - D_1^2)/4$.

Assuming that the load is uniformly distributed over the threads in contact, the bearing pressure on the threads is given by

$$p_b = \frac{4W}{n\pi(d^2 - d_1^2)} \qquad \text{... (Eq. 8.30) 9.13(a)/ Pg 135, DHB}$$

Values of bearing pressure are available in $\qquad$ **... Tb. 9.5/ Pg 137, DHB**

19. **A power screw has 6 mm pitch and 40 mm diameter. The screw is subjected to an axial load of 6 kN. The nut length is 12 mm. Determine:**
    a. The bearing pressure between the threads.
    b. Shear stress in the threads due to axial load.
    c. Compressive stress in the screw.

VTU – June/ July 2014 – 10 Marks

Solution: $p = 6$ mm, $d = 40$ mm, $W = 6000$ N, $l_n = 12$ mm, a. $p_b = ?$, b. τ_{screw}, $\tau_{nut} = ?$, c. $\sigma_c = ?$

a. **Bearing pressure:**

We know that $\quad p_b = \dfrac{4W}{n\pi(d^2 - d_1^2)} \qquad$ **... 9.13(a)/ Pg 135, DHB**

Mean or pitch diameter

$$d_2 = d - \left(\frac{p}{2}\right) = 40 - \left(\frac{6}{2}\right) = 37 \text{ mm}$$

Minor diameter,

$$d_1 = d - p = 40 - 6 = 34 \text{ mm}$$

Also $\qquad l_n = np \qquad$ **... 9.13(b)/ Pg 135, DHB**

$$12 = 6n$$

$$n = 2 \text{ threads}$$

$$\therefore \qquad p_b = \frac{4 \times 6000}{2\pi \times (40^2 - 34^2)} = 8.60 \text{ MPa}$$

b. **Shear stresses in the threads:**

Shear stress in the screw,

$$\tau_{screw} = \frac{W}{A_s)_{screw}} = \frac{W}{n\pi d_1 t}$$

Thickness of nut, $t = p/2 = 6/2 = 3$ mm

$$\tau_{screw} = \frac{6000}{2\pi \times 34 \times 3} = 9.36 \text{ MPa}$$

Shear stress in the nut,

$$\tau_{nut} = \frac{W}{A_s)_{nut}} = \frac{W}{n\pi dt} = \frac{6000}{2\pi \times 40 \times 3} = 7.96 \text{ MPa}$$

c. **Compressive stress in the screw:**

We know that $\quad \sigma_c = \dfrac{W}{A_1} = \dfrac{4W}{\pi d_1^2} = \dfrac{4 \times 6000}{\pi \times 34^2} = 6.61 \text{ MPa}$ $\qquad$ ... **1.1(a)/ Pg 2, DHB**

20. **A triple threaded power screw is used in a screw jack, has a nominal diameter of 50 mm and a pitch if 8 mm. The threads are square shape and the length of the nut is 48 mm. The screw jack is used to lift a load of 7.5 kN. The coefficient of friction at the threads is 0.12 and the collar friction is negligible. Calculate:**
    a. **The principal shear stresses in the screw rod.**
    b. **The transverse shear stresses in the screw and the nuts.**
    c. **The unit bearing pressure for threads.**
    d. **State whether the screw is self-locking.**

VTU – Mar. 2001 – 16 Marks; June/ July 2009 – 10 Marks

Solution: $n = 3$, $d = 50$ mm, $p = 8$ mm, $l_n = 48$ mm, $W = 7500$ N, $f = 0.12$, $f_c = 0$.
a. $\tau_{max} = ?$, b. τ_{screw} , $\tau_{nut} = ?$ c. $p_b = ?$ d. self-locking = ?

a. **To find shear stresses in the screw:**

We know that $\tau_{max} = \sqrt{\left(\dfrac{\sigma_c}{2}\right)^2 + \tau^2}$ $\qquad$ ... Eq. (i) **1.5(b)/ Pg 3, DHB**

But $\qquad \sigma_c = \dfrac{W}{A_1} = \dfrac{4W}{\pi d_1^2}$ $\qquad$ ... **1.1(a)/ Pg 2, DHB**

Mean or pitch diameter,

$$d_2 = d - \left(\frac{p}{2}\right) = 50 - \left(\frac{8}{2}\right) = 46 \text{ mm}$$

Minor diameter, $d_1 = d - p = 50 - 8 = 42$ mm

Lead angle $\quad \tan\alpha = \dfrac{l}{\pi d_2} = \dfrac{np}{\pi d_2} = \dfrac{3 \times 8}{\pi \times 46} = 0.1661$ $\qquad$ ... **9.10(b)/ Pg 133, DHB**

$\therefore \qquad\qquad \sigma_c = \dfrac{4 \times 7500}{\pi \times 42^2} = 5.41 \text{ MPa}$

Also $\qquad\qquad \tau = \dfrac{16 T_R}{\pi d_1^3}$ $\qquad$ ... **1.1(d)/ Pg 2, DHB**

$$T_R = \frac{W}{2}\left[d_2\left(\frac{f + \tan\alpha}{1 - f\tan\alpha}\right) + f_c d_c\right] \quad \text{... 9.12(a)/ Pg 135, DHB}$$

$$= \frac{7500}{2}\left[46 \times \left(\frac{0.12 + 0.1661}{1 - 0.12 \times 0.1661}\right) + 0\right]$$

$$T_R = 50.36 \times 10^3 \, \text{N·mm}$$

$$\therefore \qquad \tau = \frac{16 \times 50.36 \times 10^3}{\pi \times 42^3} = 3.46 \, \text{MPa}$$

Eq. (i) yields...

$$\tau_{max} = \sqrt{\left(\frac{5.41}{2}\right)^2 + 3.46^2} = 4.39 \, \text{MPa}$$

b. **The transverse shear stresses in the screw and the nuts:**

Shear stress in the screw,

$$\tau_{screw} = \frac{W}{A_s)_{screw}} = \frac{W}{n_1 \pi d_1 t}$$

Thickness of nut, $t = p/2 = 8/2 = 4 \, \text{mm}$

Also $\qquad l_n = n_1 p \qquad\qquad\qquad\qquad$ ... 9.13(b)/ Pg 135, DHB

$$48 = 8n_1$$

$$n_1 = 6 \, \text{threads}$$

$$\therefore \qquad \tau_{screw} = \frac{7500}{6\pi \times 42 \times 4} = 2.37 \, \text{MPa}$$

Shear stress in the nut,

$$\tau_{nut} = \frac{W}{A_s)_{nut}} = \frac{W}{n_1 \pi d t} = \frac{7500}{6\pi \times 50 \times 4} = 1.99 \, \text{MPa}$$

c. **Bearing pressure:**

We know that $\qquad p_b = \dfrac{4W}{n_1 \pi (d^2 - d_1^2)} \qquad\qquad$ ... 9.13(a)/ Pg 135, DHB

$$= \frac{4 \times 7500}{6\pi \times (50^2 - 42^2)}$$

$$p_b = 2.16 \, \text{MPa}$$

d. **Self-locking:**

We know that $\qquad \eta = \dfrac{d_2 \tan\alpha}{\left[d_2\left(\dfrac{f + \tan\alpha}{1 - f\tan\alpha}\right) + f_c d_c\right]} \qquad$ ... 9.12(b)/ Pg 135, DHB

$$= \frac{46 \times 0.1661}{\left[46\left(\dfrac{0.12 + 0.1661}{1 - 0.12 \times 1.1661}\right) + 0\right]}$$

$$\eta = 56.90\%$$

Since $\eta > 60\%$, the screw is not self-locking.

21. **A power screw having double start square threads of 25 mm nominal diameter and 5 mm pitch is acted upon by an axial load of 10 kN. The outer and inner diameters of screw collar are 50 mm and 20 mm respectively. The coefficient of thread friction and collar friction may be assumed as 0.2 and 0.15 respectively. The screw rotates at 12 rpm. Assuming uniform wear conditions at the collar and allowable bearing pressure of 5.8 MPa, find:**
    a. **The power required to rotate the screw.**
    b. **The stresses in the screw.**
    c. **Number of threads of nut in engagement with screw.**
    d. **The height of the nut.**

VTU – June/ July 2013 – 15 Marks

Solution: $n = 2$, $d = 25$ mm, $p = 5$ mm, $W = 10 \times 10^3$ N, $d' = 50$ mm, $d'' = 20$ mm, $f = 0.2$, $f_c = 0.15$, $n' = 12$ rpm, $p_b = 5.8$ MPa. a. $P = ?$, b. $\tau_{max} = ?$, c. $n_1 = ?$, d. $l_n = ?$

a. **Power:**

We know that $\quad T_R = \dfrac{9.55 \times 10^6 (P)}{n'}$ ... Eq. (i) **3.3(a)/ Pg 50, DHB**

But $\qquad T_R = \dfrac{W}{2}\left[d_2 \left(\dfrac{f + \tan\alpha}{1 - f\tan\alpha} \right) + f_c d_c \right]$

... Eq. (ii) **9.12(a)/ Pg 135, DHB**

Mean or pitch diameter,

$$d_2 = d - \left(\dfrac{p}{2}\right) = 25 - \left(\dfrac{5}{2}\right) = 22.5 \text{ mm}$$

Minor diameter,

$$d_1 = d - p = 25 - 5 = 20 \text{ mm}$$

Lead angle $\quad \tan\alpha = \dfrac{l}{\pi d_2} = \dfrac{np}{\pi d_2} = \dfrac{2 \times 5}{\pi \times 22.5} = 0.1415 \quad$ ... **9.10(b)/ Pg 133, DHB**

Mean diameter of collar,

$$d_c = \left(\dfrac{d' + d''}{2}\right), \text{ assuming uniform wear condition}$$

$$d_c = \left(\dfrac{50 + 20}{2}\right) = 35 \text{ mm}$$

Eq. (ii) yields...

$$T_R = \dfrac{10 \times 10^3}{2}\left[22.5 \times \left(\dfrac{0.2 + 0.1415}{1 - 0.2 \times 0.1415} \right) + (0.15 \times 35) \right]$$

$$T_R = 65.78 \times 10^3 \text{ N·mm}$$

Eq. (i) yields...

$$65.78 \times 10^3 = \dfrac{9.55 \times 10^6 (P)}{12}$$

$$P = 0.0827 \text{ kW}$$

b. **Stresses in screw:**

We know that $\tau_{max} = \sqrt{\left(\dfrac{\sigma_c}{2}\right)^2 + \tau^2}$ ... Eq. (iii) **1.5(b)/ Pg 3, DHB**

But
$$\sigma_c = \frac{W}{A_1} = \frac{4W}{\pi d_1^2} = \frac{4 \times 10 \times 10^3}{\pi \times 20^2} = 31.83 \text{ MPa}$$

... 1.1(a)/ Pg 2, DHB

$$\tau = \frac{16T_R}{\pi d_1^3} = \frac{16 \times 65.78 \times 10^3}{\pi \times 20^3} = 41.88 \text{ MPa}$$

... 1.1(d)/ Pg 2, DHB

Eq. (iii) yields...

$$\tau_{max} = \sqrt{\left(\frac{31.83}{2}\right)^2 + 41.88^2} = 44.80 \text{ MPa}$$

c. **Number of threads of nuts:**

We know that $p_b = \dfrac{4W}{n_1 \pi (d^2 - d_1^2)}$ ... 9.13(a)/ Pg 135, DHB

$$5.8 = \frac{4 \times 10 \times 10^3}{n_1 \pi (25^2 - 20^2)}$$

$\therefore$ $n_1 = 9.76 \approx 10$ threads

d. **The height of nut:**
Length of nut $l_n = n_1 p = 10 \times 5 = 50 \text{ mm}$ ... 9.13(b)/ Pg 135, DHB

22. **The screw of shaft straightner exerts a load of 30 kN as shown in Fig. 8.7. The screw is square threaded of outside diameter 75 mm and 6 mm pitch. Determine:**
    a. **Force required at the rim of 300 mm diameter hand wheel assuming the coefficient of friction for threads as 0.12.**
    b. **Maximum compressive stress in the screw, bearing pressure on the threads and maximum shear stress in threads.**
    c. **Efficiency of the straightner.**
    VTU – Dec. 2010 – 15 Marks

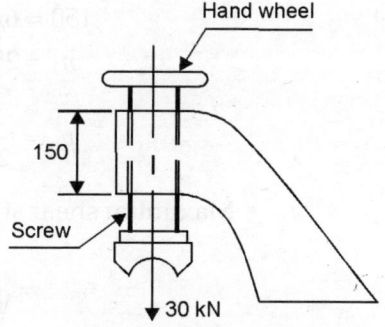

Fig. 8.7: Problem 12

Solution: $W = 30 \times 10^3$ N, $d = 75$ mm, $p = 6$ mm, $n = 2$, $D = 300$ mm, $f = 0.12$,
a. $F_R = ?$, b. $\sigma_c = ?$, $p_b = ?$, $\tau_{max} = ?$, c) $\eta = ?$

a. **Force required at the rim:**
$$T_R = F_R R \qquad \qquad \text{... Eq. (i)}$$

But
$$T_R = \frac{W}{2}\left[d_2\left(\frac{f + \tan\alpha}{1 - f\tan\alpha}\right) + f_c d_c\right]$$

... Eq. (ii) **9.12(a)/ Pg 135, DHB**

Mean or pitch diameter,
$$d_2 = d - \left(\frac{p}{2}\right) = 75 - \left(\frac{6}{2}\right) = 72 \text{ mm}$$

Minor diameter,
$$d_1 = d - p = 75 - 6 = 69 \text{ mm}$$

Lead angle $\tan\alpha = \dfrac{l}{\pi d_2} = \dfrac{np}{\pi d_2} = \dfrac{1 \times 6}{\pi \times 72} = 0.0265$ ... 9.10(b)/ Pg 133, DHB

$\therefore$ Eq. (ii) yields...

$$\therefore \qquad T_R = \frac{30 \times 10^3}{2}\left[72 \times \left(\frac{0.12 + 0.0265}{1 - 0.12 \times 0.0265}\right) + 0\right]$$

$$T_R = 158.72 \times 10^3 \text{ N·mm}$$

$\therefore$ Eq. (i) yields...

$$158.72 \times 10^3 = F_R \times (300/2)$$

$$F_R = 1058.16 \text{ N}$$

b. **To find compressive stress, bearing pressure and maximum shear stress:**
   - Shear stress in the screw,

$$\sigma_c = \frac{W}{A_1} = \frac{4W}{\pi d_1^2} = \frac{4 \times 30 \times 10^3}{\pi \times 69^2} = 8.02 \text{ MPa} \quad \dots \textbf{1.1(a)/ Pg 2, DHB}$$

   - Bearing pressure,

$$p_b = \frac{4W}{n_1 \pi (d^2 - d_1^2)} \qquad \qquad \dots \textbf{9.13(a)/ Pg 135, DHB}$$

But $\qquad l_n = n_1 p$

$$150 = 6n_1 \quad [l_n = 150 \text{ mm from } \textbf{Fig. 8.7}]$$

$$n_1 = 25 \text{ threads}$$

$$\therefore \qquad p_b = \frac{4 \times 30 \times 10^3}{25 \times \pi (75^2 - 69^2)} = 1.76 \text{ MPa}$$

   - Maximum shear stress,

$$\tau_{max} = \sqrt{\left(\frac{\sigma_c}{2}\right)^2 + \tau^2} \qquad \dots \text{Eq. (iii) } \textbf{1.5(b)/ Pg 3, DHB}$$

But $\qquad \tau = \dfrac{16T_R}{\pi d_1^3} = \dfrac{16 \times 158.72 \times 10^3}{\pi \times 69^3} = 2.46 \text{ MPa} \quad \dots \textbf{1.1(d)/ Pg 2, DHB}$

Eq. (iii) yields...

$$\tau_{max} = \sqrt{\left(\frac{8.02}{2}\right)^2 + 2.46^2} = 4.70 \text{ MPa}$$

c. **Efficiency:**

We know that $\qquad \eta = \dfrac{d_2 \tan\alpha}{\left[d_2\left(\dfrac{f + \tan\alpha}{1 - f\tan\alpha}\right) + f_c d_c\right]} \qquad \dots \textbf{9.12(b)/ Pg 135, DHB}$

$$= \frac{72 \times 0.0265}{\left[72\left(\dfrac{0.12 + 0.0265}{1 - 0.12 \times 0.0265}\right) + 0\right]}$$

$$\eta = 18.03\%$$

23. **A weight of 500 kN is raised at a speed of 6 m/min by two screw rods of double start square thread of 50 mm major diameter with a pitch of 8 mm. The two screw rods are driven through bevel gear drives by a motor. Determine:**
    a. **The torque required to raise the load.**
    b. **The speed of rotation of the screw rod.**
    c. **The maximum stresses induced on the cross-section of the screw rod.**
    d. **The efficiency of screw drive.**
    e. **The length of the nut for the purpose of supporting the load.**
    f. **Check for overhaul.**

VTU – Dec. 2014/Jan. 2015 – 16 Marks; Dec. 2013/Jan. 2014 – 15 Marks

Solution: Weight lifted by two screw rods, $2W = 500 \times 10^3$ N, Weight lifted by one screw rod, $W = 250 \times 10^3$, $v = 6$ m/min $= 6000$ mm/min, $d = 50$ mm, $p = 8$ mm. a. $T_R = ?$, b. $n' = ?$, c. τ_{max}, $\sigma_{max} = ?$, d. $\eta = ?$, e. $l_n = ?$, f. overhaul $= ?$

a. **Torque required to raise the load:**

We know that $\quad T_R = \dfrac{W}{2}\left[d_2\left(\dfrac{f + \tan\alpha}{1 - f\tan\alpha}\right) + f_c d_c\right]$

... Eq. (i) **9.12(a)/ Pg 135, DHB**

Mean or pitch diameter,

$$d_2 = d - \left(\dfrac{p}{2}\right) = 50 - \left(\dfrac{8}{2}\right) = 46 \text{ mm}$$

Minor diameter,

$$d_1 = d - p = 50 - 8 = 42 \text{ mm}$$

Lead angle $\quad \tan\alpha = \dfrac{l}{\pi d_2} = \dfrac{np}{\pi d_2} = \dfrac{2 \times 8}{\pi \times 46} = 0.1107 \quad$ ... **9.10(b)/ Pg 133, DHB**

Assume $\quad\quad f = 0.14$, for heavy machine oil

... **Tb 9.3/ Pg 136, DHB**

∴ Eq. (i) yields...

$$\therefore \quad T_R = \dfrac{250 \times 10^3}{2}\left[46 \times \left(\dfrac{0.14 + 0.1107}{1 - 0.14 \times 0.1107}\right) + 0\right]$$

$$T_R = 1.46 \times 10^6 \text{ N·mm}$$

Thus the torque required for two screw rods

$$= 2T_R = 2 \times 1.46 \times 10^6 = 2.92 \times 10^6 \text{ N·mm}$$

b. **Speed of rotation:**

$$n' = \dfrac{\text{velocity}}{\text{lead}} = \dfrac{6 \times 1000 \text{ mm/min}}{2 \times 8 \text{ mm}} = 375 \text{ rpm}$$

c. **Maximum shear stress:**

$$\tau_{max} = \sqrt{\left(\dfrac{\sigma_c}{2}\right)^2 + \tau^2} \quad\quad \text{... Eq. (ii) } \textbf{1.5(b)/ Pg 3, DHB}$$

But $\quad\quad \sigma_c = \dfrac{W}{A_1} = \dfrac{4W}{\pi d_1^2} = \dfrac{4 \times 250 \times 10^3}{\pi \times 42^2} = 180.45 \text{ MPa}$

... **1.1(a)/ Pg 2, DHB**

$$\tau = \frac{16T_R}{\pi d_1^2} = \frac{16 \times 1.46 \times 10^6}{\pi \times 42^3} = 100.36 \text{ MPa}$$

$$\text{... 1.1(d)/ Pg 2, DHB}$$

Eq. (ii) yields...

$$\tau_{max} = \sqrt{\left(\frac{180.45}{2}\right)^2 + 100.36^2} = 134.95 \text{ MPa}$$

- Maximum normal stress,

$$\sigma_{max} = \left(\frac{\sigma_c}{2}\right) + \sqrt{\left(\frac{\sigma_c}{2}\right)^2 + \tau^2} \qquad \text{... 1.5(a)/ Pg 3, DHB}$$

$$= \left(\frac{180.45}{2}\right) + \sqrt{\left(\frac{180.45}{2}\right)^2 + 100.36^2}$$

$$\sigma_{max} = 225.18 \text{ MPa}$$

d. **Efficiency:**

We know that

$$\eta = \frac{d_2 \tan\alpha}{\left[d_2\left(\dfrac{f + \tan\alpha}{1 - f\tan\alpha}\right) + f_c d_c\right]} \qquad \text{... 9.12(b)/ Pg 135, DHB}$$

$$= \frac{46 \times 0.1107}{\left[46\left(\dfrac{0.14 + 0.1107}{1 - 0.14 \times 0.1107}\right) + 0\right]}$$

$$\eta = 43.47\%$$

e. **Nut length:**

Bearing pressure,

$$p_b = \frac{4W}{n_1 \pi (d^2 - d_1^2)} \qquad \text{... 9.13(a)/ Pg 135, DHB}$$

For $v = 6 \text{ m/min}, p_b = 4.1 \text{ to } 7 \text{ MPa}$ **... Tb 9.5/ Pg 137, DHB**

Take $p_b = 5.55 \text{ MPa (average)}$

$$5.55 = \frac{4 \times 250 \times 10^3}{n_1 \times \pi(50^2 - 42^2)}$$

$$n_1 = 77.93 \text{ threads} \approx 78 \text{ threads}$$

f. **Overhaul:**

Since $\eta < 50\%$, the screw is self-locking and not overhaul.

8.10 DESIGN OF SCREW JACK

I. Design of Screw Spindle [Fig. 8.8(a)]

1. **To find core diameter:** Since the screw is under compression, the diameter of the screw is found as:

$$\sigma_c)_{screw} = \frac{W}{A_1} = \frac{4W}{\pi d_1^2} \qquad \text{...Eq. (a) 1.1(a)/ Pg 2, DHB}$$

Based on the value of d_1 obtained from Eq. (a), standardize the value of d_1 using **Tb 9.10/ Pg 149, DHB**
Based on standard value of d_1, select the values of d, D and p for normal series from ... **Tb 9.10/ Pg 149, DHB**

2. **Check for stresses:**
   a. **Maximum shear stress:**

$$\tau_{max} = \sqrt{\left(\frac{\sigma_c}{2}\right)^2 + \tau^2} \qquad \text{... Eq. (b) 1.5(b)/ Pg 3, DHB}$$

Based on standard values, find

$$\sigma_c = \frac{4W}{\pi d_1^2} \qquad \text{... 1.1(a)/ Pg 2, DHB}$$

$$\tau = \frac{16T}{\pi d_1^3} \qquad \text{... 1.1(d)/ Pg 2, DHB}$$

where $\quad T = \frac{Wd_2}{2}\left[\left(\frac{f + \tan\alpha}{1 - f\tan\alpha}\right)\right] \qquad$ ... **9.11(b)/ Pg 134, DHB**

Mean or pitch diameter,

$$d_2 = d - \left(\frac{p}{2}\right) \text{ or } \left(\frac{d + d_1}{2}\right)$$

Lead angle $\quad \tan\alpha = \dfrac{l}{\pi d_2} = \dfrac{p}{\pi d_2} \ (n = 1) \qquad$ ... **9.10(b)/ Pg 133, DHB**

Assume $\quad f = 0.14$, for heavy machine oil, if not given
... **Tb 9.3/ Pg 136, DHB**

II. Design for Nut [Fig. 8.8(b)]

The nut is generally made of phosphor bronze.

3. **Number of threads:** $n = \dfrac{4W}{p_b \pi(d^2 - d_1^2)} \qquad$ ... **9.13(a)/ Pg 135, DHB**

Based on materials for screw and nut, the value of p_b ... **Tb. 9.5/ Pg 137, DHB**

4. **Height or length of nut:**

$$l_n = np \qquad \text{... 9.13(b)/ Pg 135, DHB}$$

5. **Thickness of screw:**

$$t = \left(\frac{p}{2}\right)$$

6. **Check for stresses in screw and nut:**
   a. **Shear stress in the screw:**

$$\tau_{screw} = \frac{W}{A_s)_{screw}} = \frac{W}{n\pi d_1 t}$$

   b. **Shear stress in the nut:**

$$\tau_{nut} = \frac{W}{A_s)_{nut}} = \frac{W}{n\pi d t}$$

The calculated values of τ_{screw} and τ_{nut} should be less than permissible values, for design to be safe.

III. Design for Collar (Collar Dimensions): (D_1, D_2, t_1)

7. **Inside diameter of collar:** Based on tearing strength of nut,

$$W = \left[\frac{\pi(D_1^2 - d^2)}{4}\right]\sigma_t)_{nut}$$

8. **Outside diameter of collar:** Based on crushing strength of nut collar,

$$W = \left[\frac{\pi(D_2^2 - D_1^2)}{4}\right]\sigma_c)_{nut}$$

9. **Thickness of collar:** Based on shear strength of nut collar,

$$W = \pi D_1 t_1 \tau_{nut}$$

IV. Design of Screw Head and Handle [Fig. 8.8(c)]

10. **Diameter of screw head:**

$$D_3 = 1.75d$$

11. **Diameter of pin:** $\quad D_4 = \dfrac{D_3}{4}$

12. **Length of handle:** The handle is subjected to bending, we have

$$M = T_R = F \times L_h \qquad \qquad \text{... Eq. } (d)$$

where $\qquad \qquad F$ = effort applied

= 200 to 400 N applied by a person to rotate the handle. (300 N average)

L_h = length of handle

In general, the bending moment is taken equivalent to the torque required.

$$T_R = \frac{W}{2}\left[d_2\left(\frac{f + \tan\alpha}{1 - f\tan\alpha}\right) + f_c d_c\right]$$

$$\text{... Eq. } (e) \textbf{ 9.12(a)/ Pg 135, DHB}$$

d_c = mean diameter of the thrust collar

$$= \frac{2}{3}\left(\frac{D_3^3 - D_4^3}{D_3^2 - D_4^2}\right), \text{ for uniform pressure condition}$$

f_c = coefficient of friction for collar, based on materials for screw and nut $\qquad$ **... Tb. 9.6/ Pg 137, DHB**

or assume $\qquad \qquad f_c = f$, if not given

D_3 = diameter of screw head

D_4 = diameter of pin head

Equating Eqs. (d) and (e), we get the length of handle.

13. **Diameter of handle:** Since the handle is subjected to bending,

moment, $\qquad M = \left(\dfrac{\pi D_h^3}{32}\right)\sigma_b = T_R \qquad \qquad \text{... Eq. } (f)$

where $\qquad \qquad \sigma_b = \sigma_c$, if screw and handle are made of same material.

Solving Eq. (f) gives the diameter of handle.

14. **Height of screw head:**
$$H = 2D_h$$

15. **Check for buckling of screw rod:** Based on Johnson's parabolic formula for columns, the buckling or crippling load is given as

$$F_{cr} = A\sigma_{yp}\left[1 - \frac{\sigma_{yp}}{4n\pi^2 E}\left(\frac{L}{k}\right)^2\right] \qquad \text{... 1.16(b)/ Pg 10, DHB}$$

where $A = A_1 = \pi d_1^2/4$

σ_{yp} = yield strength of screw material, n = end condition

= 0.25, assuming one end fixed and the other end free.

... **1.16(a)/ Pg 9, DHB**

E = Young's modulus of screw material

$k = 0.25\,d_1$ = radius of gyration

L = effective length of screw

$$= \text{screw lift} + \frac{\text{length of nut}}{2}$$

For safe design, the value of
$$F_{cr} > W$$

V. Design of cup [Fig. 8.8(d)]

16. **Base diameter of cup is made equal to the diameter of screw head:**
$$D_{cb} = D_3 = 1.75d$$

17. **Top diameter of cup:**
$$D_{ct} = 2D_3$$

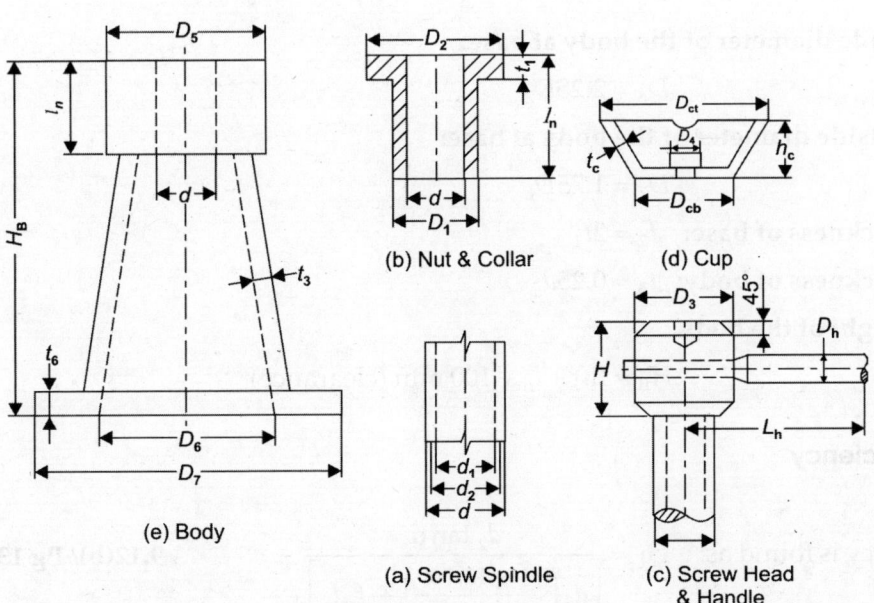

(b) Nut & Collar

(d) Cup

(e) Body

(a) Screw Spindle

(c) Screw Head & Handle

Fig. 8.8: Parts of screw jack

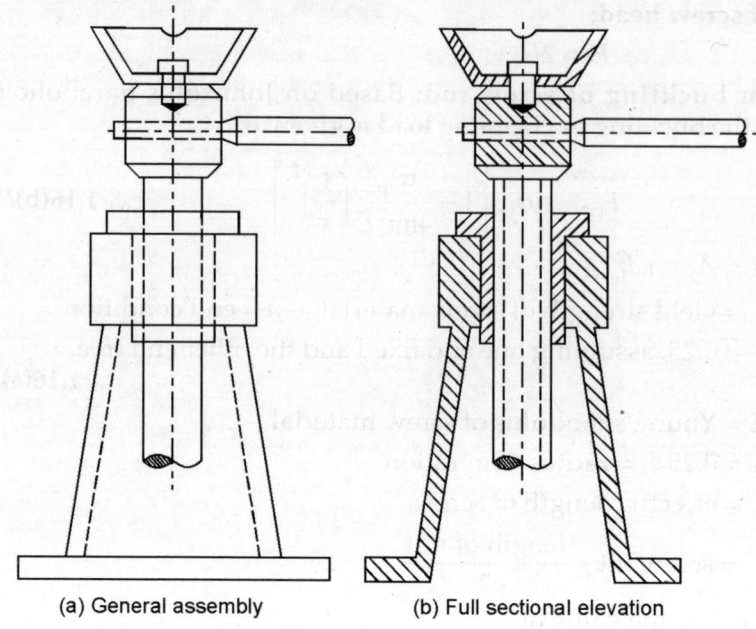

(a) General assembly   (b) Full sectional elevation

Fig. 8.9: Screw jack assembly

18. **Height of cup:** $h_c = 1.2D_2$ or 50 mm
19. **Thickness of cup:** $t_c = 10$ mm

VI. Design of Body [Fig. 8.8(e)]

20. **Diameter of the body at top:**

$$D_5 = 1.5D_2$$

21. **Inside diameter of the body at base:**

$$D_6 = 2.25D_2$$

22. **Outside diameter of the body at base:**

$$D_7 = 1.75D_6$$

23. **Thickness of base:** $t_2 = 2t_1$

24. **Thickness of body:** $t_3 = 0.25d$

25. **Height of the body:**

$$H_B = \text{lift} + l_n + 100 \text{ mm (clearance)}$$

VII. Efficiency

Efficiency is found as: $\eta = \dfrac{d_2 \tan \alpha}{\left[d_2 \left(\dfrac{f + \tan \alpha}{1 - f \tan \alpha} \right) + f_c d_c \right]}$ ... **9.12(b)/ Pg 135, DHB**

24. A screw jack is to lift a load of 80 kN through a height of 400 mm. Ultimate strengths of screw material in tension and compression are 200 N/mm² and in shear is 120 N/mm². The material for the nut is phosphor bronze for which the ultimate strength is 100 N/mm² in tension, 90 N/mm² in compression and 80 N/mm² in shear. The bearing pressure between the nut and screw is not to exceed 18 N/mm². Design the screw and the nut and check for the stresses. Take FoS = 2. Assume 25% overload for the screw rod design.

VTU – May/ June 2010 – 16 Marks; Dec. 2014/ Jan. 2015 – 16 Marks

Solution: $W' = 80000$ N, height $= 400$ mm, $\sigma_{yt})_{screw} = \sigma_{yc})_{screw} = 200$ N/mm², $\sigma_y)_{screw} = 120$ N/mm², $\sigma_{yt})_{nut} = 100$ N/mm², $\sigma_{yc})_{nut} = 90$ N/mm², $\tau_y)_{nut} = 80$ N/mm², $p_b = 18$ N/mm², FoS = 2, overload $W = 1.25$, $W' = 1.25 \times 80000 = 100000$ N.

Safe stresses:

Screw:

$$\sigma_{yt})_{screw} = \sigma_{yc})_{screw} = 200 \, N/mm^2$$

$$\Rightarrow \quad \sigma_t)_{screw} = \sigma_c)_{screw} = \frac{\sigma_{yt}}{FoS} = \frac{200}{2} = 100 \, N/mm^2 = \sigma_{max}$$

$$\tau_y)_{screw} = 120 \, N/mm^2$$

$$\Rightarrow \quad \tau_{screw} = \tau_{max} = \frac{\sigma_{yt}}{FoS} = \frac{120}{2} = 60 \, N/mm^2$$

Nut:

$$\sigma_{yt})_{nut} = 100 \, N/mm^2 \quad \Rightarrow \quad \sigma_t)_{nut} = \frac{100}{2} = 50 \, N/mm^2$$

$$\sigma_{yc})_{nut} = 90 \, N/mm^2 \quad \Rightarrow \quad \sigma_c)_{nut} = \frac{90}{2} = 45 \, N/mm^2$$

$$\tau_y)_{nut} = 80 \, N/mm^2 \quad \Rightarrow \quad \tau_{nut} = \frac{80}{2} = 40 \, N/mm^2$$

I. Design of screw spindle:

1. **To find core diameter:**

$$\sigma_c)_{screw} = \frac{W}{A_1} = \frac{4W}{\pi d_1^2} \qquad \qquad \dots 1.1(a)/ \, Pg \, 2, \, DHB$$

$$100 = \frac{4 \times 100000}{\pi d_1^2}$$

$$d_1 = 35.68 \, mm$$

Standard values for normal series are: $d_1 = 40$ mm, $d = 48$ mm, and $p = 8$ mm.

$$\dots Tb \, 9.10/ \, Pg \, 149, \, DHB$$

2. **Check for stresses:**

a. **Maximum shear stress:**

$$\tau_{max} = \sqrt{\left(\frac{\sigma_c}{2}\right)^2 + \tau^2} \qquad \qquad \dots Eq. \, (i) \, 1.5(b)/ \, Pg \, 3, \, DHB$$

Based on standard values,

$$\sigma_c = \frac{4W}{\pi d_1^2} = \frac{4 \times 100000}{\pi \times 40^2} = 79.57 \text{ MPa} \qquad \dots \textbf{1.1(a)/ Pg 2, DHB}$$

$$\tau = \frac{16T}{\pi d_1^3} \qquad \dots \text{Eq. (ii) } \textbf{1.1(d)/ Pg 2, DHB}$$

Here
$$T = \frac{Wd_2}{2}\left[\left(\frac{f + \tan\alpha}{1 - f\tan\alpha}\right)\right] \qquad \dots \text{Eq. (iii) } \textbf{9.11(b)/ Pg 134, DHB}$$

$$d_2 = d - \left(\frac{p}{2}\right) = 48 - \left(\frac{8}{2}\right) = 44 \text{ mm}$$

$$\tan\alpha = \frac{l}{\pi d_2} = \frac{p}{\pi d_2} = \frac{8}{\pi \times 44} = 0.0579 \qquad \dots \textbf{9.10(b)/ Pg 133, DHB}$$

Assume $f = 0.14$, for heavy machine oil (not given)

$$\dots \textbf{Tb. 9.3/ Pg 136, DHB}$$

Eq. (iii) yields...

$$T = \frac{100000 \times 44}{2}\left[\left(\frac{0.14 + 0.0579}{1 - 0.14 \times 0.0579}\right)\right] = 440 \times 10^3 \text{ N·mm}$$

Eq. (ii) yields...

$$\tau_{max} = \frac{16 \times 440 \times 10^3}{\pi \times 40^3} = 35.01 \text{ MPa}$$

Eq. (i) yields...

$$\tau_{max} = \sqrt{\left(\frac{79.57}{2}\right)^2 + 35.01^2} = 53 \text{ MPa} < 60 \text{ MPa, hence safe.}$$

b. **Maximum normal stress:**

$$\sigma_{max} = \left(\frac{\sigma_c}{2}\right) + \sqrt{\left(\frac{\sigma_c}{2}\right)^2 + \tau^2} \qquad \dots \textbf{1.5(a)/ Pg 3, DHB}$$

$$= \left(\frac{79.57}{2}\right) + \sqrt{\left(\frac{79.57}{2}\right)^2 + 35.01^2}$$

$$\sigma_{max} = 92.78 \text{ MPa} < 100 \text{ MPa, hence safe.}$$

II. **Design for nut:** The nut is generally made of phosphor bronze.

3. **Number of threads:**

$$n = \frac{4W}{p_b\pi(d^2 - d_1^2)} = \frac{4 \times 100000}{18\pi(48^2 - 40^2)} = 10.05 \approx 10 \text{ threads}$$

$$\dots \textbf{9.13(a)/ Pg 135, DHB}$$

4. **Height or length of nut:**

$$l_n = np = 10 \times 8 = 80 \text{ mm} \qquad \dots \textbf{9.13(b)/ Pg 135, DHB}$$

5. **Thickness of screw:**

$$t = \left(\frac{p}{2}\right) = \left(\frac{8}{2}\right) = 4 \text{ mm}$$

6. Check for stresses in screw and nut:
a. Shear stress in the screw:

$$\tau_{screw} = \frac{W}{A_s)_{screw}} = \frac{W}{n\pi d_1 t} = \frac{100000}{10\pi \times 40 \times 4}$$

$$= 19.89 \text{ MPa} < 60 \text{ MPa, hence safe.}$$

b. Shear stress in the nut:

$$\tau_{nut} = \frac{W}{A_s)_{nut}} = \frac{W}{n\pi dt} = \frac{100000}{10\pi \times 48 \times 4}$$

$$= 16.57 \text{ MPa} < 40 \text{ MPa, hence safe.}$$

III. Design for collar (collar dimensions): $[D_1, D_2, t_1]$
7. Inside diameter of collar: Based on tearing strength of nut,

$$W = \left[\frac{\pi(D_1^2 - d^2)}{4}\right]\sigma_t)_{nut}$$

$$100000 = \left[\frac{\pi(D_1^2 - 48^2)}{4}\right] \times 50$$

$$D_1 = 69.65 \text{ mm} \approx 70 \text{ mm}$$

8. Outside diameter of collar: Based on crushing strength of nut collar,

$$W = \left[\frac{\pi(D_2^2 - D_1^2)}{4}\right]\sigma_c)_{nut}$$

$$100000 = \left[\frac{\pi(D_2^2 - 70^2)}{4}\right] \times 45$$

$$D_2 = 87.91 \text{ mm} \approx 90 \text{ mm}$$

9. Thickness of collar: Based on shear strength of nut collar,

$$W = \pi D_1 t_1 \tau_{nut}$$

$$100000 = \pi \times 70 \times t_1 \times 40$$

$$t_1 = 11.37 \text{ mm} \approx 12 \text{ mm}$$

25. Design completely the screw, handle and the nut of a screw jack of capacity 40 kN. The maximum lift is limited to 0.2 m. The screw and the handle are made of C40 (40C8) steel and the nut and the cap are made of cast iron. Also find the efficiency of the screw. Check the screw for buckling load.

VTU – June/ July 2013 – 20 Marks

Solution: $W = 40 \times 10^3$ N, lift = 200 mm, Material: Screw and handle – C40 steel, Nut and cap – Cast iron.

Material properties:

Screw and handle: For C40 steel,

$$\sigma_{yt})_{screw} = \sigma_{yc})_{screw} = 324 \text{ MPa} \qquad \text{... Tb. I.8/ Pg 464, DHB}$$

Assume FoS = 3 for screws, we have

$$\sigma_t)_{screw} = \sigma_c)_{screw} = \frac{\sigma_y}{FOS} = \frac{324}{3} = 108 \text{ MPa} = \sigma_{max}$$

and $\qquad \tau_{screw} = \tau_{max} = 0.5\sigma_t = 0.5 \times 108 = 54 \text{ MPa}$

Nut and cap: For FG 200, $\sigma_{yt})_{nut} = \sigma_{yc})_{nut} = 200$ MPa   ... **Tb I.4/ Pg 461, DHB**

Assume   FoS = 5 for cast iron   ... **Tb III.a/ Pg 477, DHB**

$$\sigma_t)_{nut} = \sigma_c)_{nut} = \frac{200}{5} = 40 \text{ N/mm}^2$$

and $\tau_{nut} = 0.5\,\sigma_t = 0.5 \times 40 = 20$ MPa

I. Design of screw spindle:

1. To find core diameter:

$$\sigma_c)_{screw} = \frac{W}{A_1} = \frac{4W}{\pi d_1^2}$$ ... **1.1(a)/ Pg 2, DHB**

$$108 = \frac{4 \times 40000}{\pi d_1^2}$$

$$d_1 = 21.71 \text{ mm}$$

Standard values for normal series are: $d_1 = 30$ mm, $d = 36$ mm, and $p = 6$ mm.
                    ... **Tb 9.10/ Pg 149, DHB**

2. Check for stresses:

a. Maximum shear stress:

$$\tau_{max} = \sqrt{\left(\frac{\sigma_c}{2}\right)^2 + \tau^2}$$ ... Eq. (i) **1.5(b)/ Pg 3, DHB**

Based on standard values,

$$\sigma_c = \frac{4W}{\pi d_1^2} = \frac{4 \times 40000}{\pi \times 30^2} = 56.59 \text{ MPa}$$ ... **1.1(a)/ Pg 2, DHB**

$$\tau = \frac{16T}{\pi d_1^3}$$ ... Eq. (ii) **1.1(d)/ Pg 2, DHB**

Here $$T = \frac{Wd_2}{2}\left[\left(\frac{f + \tan\alpha}{1 - f\tan\alpha}\right)\right]$$ ... Eq. (iii) **9.11(b)/ Pg 134, DHB**

$$d_2 = d - \left(\frac{p}{2}\right) = 36 - \left(\frac{6}{2}\right) = 33 \text{ mm}$$

$$\tan\alpha = \frac{l}{\pi d_2} = \frac{p}{\pi d_2} = \frac{6}{\pi \times 33} = 0.0579$$ ... **9.10(b)/ Pg 133, DHB**

Assume $f = 0.14$, for heavy machine oil.   ... **Tb. 9.3/ Pg 136, DHB**

Eq. (iii) yields...

$$T = \frac{40 \times 10^3 \times 33}{2}\left[\left(\frac{0.14 + 0.0579}{1 - 0.14 \times 0.0579}\right)\right] = 131.68 \times 10^3 \text{ N·mm}$$

Eq. (ii) yields...

$$\tau = \frac{16 \times 131.68 \times 10^3}{\pi \times 30^3} = 24.84 \text{ MPa}$$

Eq. (i) yields...

$$\tau_{max} = \sqrt{\left(\frac{56.59}{2}\right)^2 + 24.84^2} = 37.65 \text{ MPa} < 54 \text{ MPa, hence safe.}$$

b. **Maximum normal stress:**

$$\sigma_{max} = \left(\frac{\sigma_c}{2}\right) + \sqrt{\left(\frac{\sigma_c}{2}\right)^2 + \tau^2} \qquad \text{... 1.5(a)/ Pg 3, DHB}$$

$$= \left(\frac{56.59}{2}\right) + \sqrt{\left(\frac{56.59}{2}\right)^2 + 24.84^2}$$

$$\sigma_{max} = 65.95 \text{ MPa} < 108 \text{ MPa, hence safe.}$$

II. Design for nut:

3. Number of threads:

$$n = \frac{4W}{p_b \pi (d^2 - d_1^2)} \qquad \text{... 9.13(a)/ Pg 135, DHB}$$

Bearing pressure,

$$p_b = 14 \text{ MPa, for steel and CI materials.}$$
$$\text{... Tb 9.5/ Pg 137, DHB}$$

$$n = \frac{4 \times 40000}{14\pi(36^2 - 30^2)} = 9.19 \approx 10 \text{ threads}$$

4. Height or length of nut:

$$l_n = np = 10 \times 6 = 60 \text{ mm} \qquad \text{... 9.13(b)/ Pg 135, DHB}$$

5. Thickness of screw:

$$t = \left(\frac{p}{2}\right) = \left(\frac{6}{2}\right) = 3 \text{ mm}$$

6. Check for stresses in screw and nut:

a. **Shear stress in the screw:**

$$\tau_{screw} = \frac{W}{A_s)_{screw}} = \frac{W}{n\pi d_1 t} = \frac{40000}{10\pi \times 30 \times 3}$$

$$= 14.15 \text{ MPa} < 54 \text{ MPa, hence safe.}$$

b. **Shear stress in the nut:**

$$\tau_{nut} = \frac{W}{A_s)_{nut}} = \frac{W}{n\pi d t} = \frac{40000}{10\pi \times 36 \times 3}$$

$$= 11.78 \text{ MPa} < 20 \text{ MPa, hence safe.}$$

III. Design for collar (collar dimensions): [D_1, D_2, t_1]

7. Inside diameter of collar: Based on tearing strength of nut,

$$W = \left[\frac{\pi(D_1^2 - d^2)}{4}\right]\sigma_t)_{nut}$$

$$40000 = \left[\frac{\pi(D_1^2 - 36^2)}{4}\right] \times 40$$

$$D_1 = 50.68 \text{ mm} \approx 52 \text{ mm}$$

8. **Outside diameter of collar:** Based on crushing strength of nut collar,

$$W = \left[\frac{\pi(D_2^2 - D_1^2)}{4}\right]\sigma_c)_{nut}$$

$$40000 = \left[\frac{\pi(D_2^2 - 52^2)}{4}\right] \times 40$$

$$D_2 = 63.07 \text{ mm} \approx 64 \text{ mm}$$

9. **Thickness of collar:** Based on shear strength of nut collar,

$$W = \pi D_1 t_1 \tau_{nut}$$

$$40000 = \pi \times 52 \times t_1 \times 20$$

$$t_1 = 12.24 \text{ mm} \approx 14 \text{ mm}$$

IV. **Design of screw head and handle:**

10. **Diameter of screw head:**

$$D_3 = 1.75d = 1.75 \times 36 = 63 \text{ mm} \approx 64 \text{ mm (say)}$$

11. **Diameter of pin:**

$$D_4 = \frac{D_3}{4} = \frac{64}{4} = 16 \text{ mm}$$

12. **Length of handle:** The handle is subjected to bending, we have

$$M = T_R = F \times L_h$$

where $F = 300$ N (average) effort applied by a person to rotate the handle

L_h = length of handle

$$\therefore \qquad T_R = 300L_h \qquad\qquad\qquad \dots \text{Eq. (iv)}$$

In general, the bending moment is taken equivalent to the torque required,

i.e. $$T_R = \frac{W}{2}\left[d_2\left(\frac{f + \tan\alpha}{1 - f\tan\alpha}\right) + f_c d_c\right]$$
$$\dots \text{Eq. (v)} \textbf{ 9.12(a)/Pg 135, DHB}$$

Here $f_c = 0.147$, coefficient of friction for the collar for steel and CI materials.
$$\dots \textbf{Tb. 9.6/Pg 137, DHB}$$

Mean diameter of the thrust collar

$$d_c = \frac{2}{3}\left(\frac{D_3^3 - D_4^3}{D_3^2 - D_4^2}\right), \text{ for uniform pressure condition}$$

$$= \frac{2}{3}\left(\frac{64^3 - 16^3}{64^2 - 16^2}\right)$$

$$d_c = 44.8 \text{ mm} \approx 45 \text{ mm}$$

$\therefore$ Eq. (v) yields...

$$T_R = \frac{40 \times 10^3}{2}\left[33 \times \left(\frac{0.14 + 0.0579}{1 - 0.14 \times 0.0579}\right) + (0.147 \times 45)\right]$$

$$T_R = 264 \times 10^3 \text{ N·mm}$$

and Eq. (iv) yields...

$$264 \times 10^3 = 300 \, L_h$$

$$L_h = 880 \text{ mm} \approx 900 \text{ mm}$$

13. **Diameter of handle:** Since the handle is subjected to bending,

moment, $\qquad M = \left(\dfrac{\pi d_h^3}{32}\right) \sigma_b = T_R$

Here $\sigma_b = \sigma_c = 108$ MPa, since the screw and handle are made of same material.

$$264 \times 10^3 = \left(\frac{\pi D_h^3}{32}\right) \times 108$$

$\therefore \qquad D_h = 29.20 \text{ mm} \approx 30 \text{ mm}$

14. **Height of screw head:**

$$H = 2D_h = 2 \times 30 = 60 \text{ mm}$$

15. **Check for buckling of screw rod:** Based on Johnson's parabolic formula for columns, the buckling or crippling load is given as

$$F_{cr} = A\sigma_{yp} \left[1 - \frac{\sigma_{yp}}{4n\pi^2 E} \left(\frac{L}{k}\right)^2 \right] \qquad \text{... 1.16(b)/Pg 10, DHB}$$

where $\qquad A = A_1 = \dfrac{\pi d_1^2}{4} = \dfrac{\pi \times 30^2}{4} = 706.86 \text{ mm}^2$

End condition, $n = 0.25$, assuming one end fixed and the other end free.

$$\text{... 1.16(a)/Pg 9, DHB}$$

Yield strength of screw material,

$$\sigma_{yp} = \sigma_{yc})_{screw} = 324 \text{ MPa}$$

Young's modulus of screw material,

$$E = 2.1 \times 10^5 \text{ MPa}$$

Radius of gyration,

$$k = 0.25 d_1 = 0.25 \times 30 = 7.5 \text{ mm}$$

Effective length of screw,

$$L = \text{screw lift} + \frac{\text{length of nut}}{2}$$

$$L = 200 + \frac{60}{2} = 230 \text{ mm}$$

$\therefore \qquad F_{cr} = 706.86 \times 324 \times \left[1 - \dfrac{324}{4 \times 0.25 \times \pi^2 \times (2.1 \times 10^5)} \left(\dfrac{230}{7.5}\right)^2 \right]$

$$F_{cr} = 195.35 \text{ kN} > W$$

Hence, design of screw is safe against buckling.

V. Efficiency of the screw:

We know that $\eta = \dfrac{d_2 \tan \alpha}{\left[d_2 \left(\dfrac{f + \tan \alpha}{1 - f \tan \alpha} \right) + f_c d_c \right]}$ ... **Tb. 9.12(b)/Pg 135, DHB**

$$= \dfrac{33 \times 0.0579}{\left[33 \times \left(\dfrac{0.14 + 0.0579}{1 - 0.14 \times 0.0579} \right) + (0.147 \times 45) \right]}$$

$$\eta = 14.48\%$$

26. **Design a screw jack for a capacity of 10 kN, to lift 200 mm height. Select suitable materials and factor of safety.**

VTU – Dec. 08/ Jan. 2009 – 14 Marks; (Similar) Dec. 2012 – 15 Marks

Solution: $W = 10 \times 10^3$ N, lift = 200 mm.

Material properties: Assume the materials as: Screw – C40 steel, Nut – phosphor bronze.

Screw: For C40 steel,

$\sigma_{yt})_{screw} = \sigma_{yc})_{screw} = 324$ MPa   ... **Tb. I.8/ Pg 464, DHB**

Assume FoS = 4 for screws, we have

$$\sigma_t)_{screw} = \sigma_c)_{screw} = \dfrac{\sigma_y}{FOS} = \dfrac{324}{4} = 81 \text{ MPa} = \sigma_{max}$$

and $\qquad \tau_{screw} = \tau_{max} = 0.5\,\sigma_t = 0.5 \times 81 = 40.5$ MPa

Nut: Phosphor bronze

Assume

$$\sigma_{yt})_{nut} = \sigma_{yc})_{nut} = 100 \text{ MPa}, \tau_y)_{nut} = 80 \text{ MPa and FoS} = 4$$

$$\Rightarrow \qquad \sigma_t)_{nut} = \sigma_c)_{nut} = \dfrac{100}{4} = 25 \text{ MPa}$$

$$\Rightarrow \qquad \tau_{nut} = \dfrac{80}{4} = 20 \text{ MPa}$$

I. Design of screw spindle:

1. **To find core diameter:**

$$\sigma_c)_{screw} = \dfrac{W}{A_1} = \dfrac{4W}{\pi d_1^2} \qquad \qquad \text{... 1.1(a)/ Pg 2, DHB}$$

$$81 = \dfrac{4 \times 10000}{\pi d_1^2}$$

$$d_1 = 12.54 \text{ mm}$$

Standard values for normal series are: $d_1 = 24$ mm, $d = 30$ mm, and $p = 6$ mm.

... **Tb 9.10/ Pg 149, DHB**

2. **Check for stresses:**
   a. **Maximum shear stress:**

$$\tau_{max} = \sqrt{\left(\dfrac{\sigma_c}{2} \right)^2 + \tau^2} \qquad \qquad \text{... Eq. (i) 1.5(b)/ Pg 3, DHB}$$

Based on standard values,

$$\sigma_c = \frac{4W}{\pi d_1^2} = \frac{4 \times 10000}{\pi \times 24^2} = 22.10 \text{ MPa} \qquad \textbf{... 1.1(a)/ Pg 2, DHB}$$

$$\tau = \frac{16T}{\pi d_1^3} \qquad \textbf{... Eq. (ii) 1.1(d)/ Pg 2, DHB}$$

Here $\qquad T = \frac{Wd_2}{2}\left[\left(\frac{f + \tan\alpha}{1 - f\tan\alpha}\right)\right] \qquad \textbf{... Eq. (iii) 9.11(b)/ Pg 134, DHB}$

$$d_2 = d - \left(\frac{p}{2}\right) = 30 - \left(\frac{6}{2}\right) = 27 \text{ mm}$$

$$\tan\alpha = \frac{l}{\pi d_2} = \frac{p}{\pi d_2} = \frac{6}{\pi \times 27} = 0.0707 \qquad \textbf{... 9.10(b)/ Pg 133, DHB}$$

Assume $f = 0.14$, for heavy machine oil. $\qquad \textbf{... Tb. 9.3/ Pg 136, DHB}$
Eq. (iii) yields...

$$T = \frac{10 \times 10^3 \times 27}{2}\left[\left(\frac{0.14 + 0.0707}{1 - 0.14 \times 0.0707}\right)\right] = 28.73 \times 10^3 \text{ N·mm}$$

Eq. (ii) yields...

$$\tau = \frac{16 \times 28.73 \times 10^3}{\pi \times 24^3} = 10.58 \text{ MPa}$$

Eq. (i) yields...

$$\tau_{max} = \sqrt{\left(\frac{22.10}{2}\right)^2 + 10.58^2} = 15.30 \text{ MPa} < 40.5 \text{ MPa, hence safe.}$$

b. **Maximum normal stress:**

$$\sigma_{max} = \left(\frac{\sigma_c}{2}\right) + \sqrt{\left(\frac{\sigma_c}{2}\right)^2 + \tau^2} \qquad \textbf{... 1.5(a)/ Pg 3, DHB}$$

$$= \left(\frac{22.10}{2}\right) + \sqrt{\left(\frac{22.10}{2}\right)^2 + 10.58^2}$$

$$\sigma_{max} = 26.35 \text{ MPa} < 81 \text{ MPa, hence safe.}$$

II. **Design for nut:**
3. **Number of threads:**

$$n = \frac{4W}{p_b \pi(d^2 - d_1^2)} \qquad \textbf{... 9.13(a)/ Pg 135, DHB}$$

Bearing pressure,

$$p_b = 14 \text{ MPa, for steel and CI materials.}$$

$$\textbf{... Tb 9.5/ Pg 137, DHB}$$

$$n = \frac{4 \times 10000}{14\pi(30^2 - 24^2)} = 2.81 \approx 3 \text{ threads}$$

4. **Height or length of nut:**
$$l_n = np = 3 \times 6 = 18 \text{ mm} \qquad \qquad \text{... 9.13(b)/ Pg 135, DHB}$$

5. **Thickness of screw:**
$$t = \left(\frac{p}{2}\right) = \left(\frac{6}{2}\right) = 3 \text{ mm}$$

6. **Check for stresses in screw and nut:**

   a. **Shear stress in the screw:**
   $$\tau_{screw} = \frac{W}{A_s)_{screw}} = \frac{W}{n\pi d_1 t} = \frac{10000}{3\pi \times 24 \times 3}$$
   $$= 14.74 \text{ MPa} < 40.5 \text{ MPa, hence safe.}$$

   b. **Shear stress in the nut:**
   $$\tau_{nut} = \frac{W}{A_s)_{nut}} = \frac{W}{n\pi dt} = \frac{10000}{3\pi \times 30 \times 3}$$
   $$= 11.79 \text{ MPa} < 20 \text{ MPa, hence safe.}$$

III. **Design for collar (collar dimensions): [D_1, D_2, t_1]**

7. **Inside diameter of collar:** Based on tearing strength of nut,
$$W = \left[\frac{\pi(D_1^2 - d^2)}{4}\right] \sigma_t)_{nut}$$
$$10000 = \left[\frac{\pi(D_1^2 - 30^2)}{4}\right] \times 25$$
$$D_1 = 37.54 \text{ mm} \approx 38 \text{ mm}$$

8. **Outside diameter of collar:** Based on crushing strength of nut collar,
$$W = \left[\frac{\pi(D_2^2 - D_1^2)}{4}\right] \sigma_c)_{nut}$$
$$10000 = \left[\frac{\pi(D_2^2 - 38^2)}{4}\right] \times 25$$
$$D_2 = 44.12 \text{ mm} \approx 45 \text{ mm}$$

9. **Thickness of collar:** Based on shear strength of nut collar,
$$W = \pi D_1 t_1 \tau_{nut}$$
$$10000 = \pi \times 38 \times t_1 \times 20$$
$$t_1 = 4.18 \text{ mm} \approx 5 \text{ mm}$$

IV. **Design of screw head and handle:**

10. **Diameter of screw head:**
$$D_3 = 1.75d = 1.75 \times 30 = 52.5 \text{ mm} \approx 54 \text{ mm (say)}$$

11. **Diameter of pin:**
$$D_4 = \frac{D_3}{4} = \frac{54}{4} = 13.5 \text{ mm} \approx 14 \text{ mm (say)}$$

12. **Length of handle:** The handle is subjected to bending, we have
$$M = T_R = F \times L_h$$

where $F = 300$ N (average) effort applied by a person to rotate the handle

L_h = length of handle

$\therefore$ $$T_R = 300L_h$$ ... Eq. (iv)

In general, the bending moment is taken equivalent to the torque required

i.e. $$T_R = \frac{W}{2}\left[d_2\left(\frac{f + \tan\alpha}{1 - f\tan\alpha}\right) + f_c d_c\right]$$

... Eq. (v) **9.12(a)/Pg 135, DHB**

Here $f_c = 0.081$, coefficient of friction for the collar for steel and bronze materials. ... **Tb. 9.6/Pg 137, DHB**

Mean diameter of the thrust collar

$$d_c = \frac{2}{3}\left(\frac{D_3^3 - D_4^3}{D_3^2 - D_4^2}\right),\text{ for uniform pressure condition}$$

$$= \frac{2}{3}\left(\frac{54^3 - 14^3}{54^2 - 14^2}\right)$$

$$d_c = 37.92 \text{ mm} \approx 38 \text{ mm}$$

$\therefore$ Eq. (v) yields...

$$T_R = \frac{10 \times 10^3}{2}\left[27 \times \left(\frac{0.14 + 0.0707}{1 - 0.14 \times 0.0707}\right) + (0.081 \times 38)\right]$$

$$T_R = 44.12 \times 10^3 \text{ N·mm}$$

and Eq. (iv) yields...

$$44.12 \times 10^3 = 300\, L_h$$

$$L_h = 147.06 \text{ mm} \approx 150 \text{ mm}$$

13. **Diameter of handle:** Since the handle is subjected to bending,

moment, $$M = \left(\frac{\pi d_h^3}{32}\right)\sigma_b = T_R$$

Here $\sigma_b = \sigma_c = 81$ MPa, since the screw and handle are made of same material.

$$44.12 \times 10^3 = \left(\frac{\pi D_h^3}{32}\right) \times 81$$

$\therefore$ $$D_h = 17.70 \text{ mm} \approx 18 \text{ mm}$$

14. **Height of screw head:**
$$H = 2D_h = 2 \times 18 = 36 \text{ mm}$$

15. **Check for buckling of screw rod:** Based on Johnson's parabolic formula for columns, the buckling or crippling load is given as

$$F_{cr} = A\sigma_{yp} \left[1 - \frac{\sigma_{yp}}{4n\pi^2 E} \left(\frac{L}{k} \right)^2 \right] \qquad \text{... 1.16(b)/Pg 10, DHB}$$

where

$$A = A_1 = \frac{\pi d_1^2}{4} = \frac{\pi \times 24^2}{4} = 452.39 \text{ mm}^2$$

End condition, $n = 0.25$, assuming one end fixed and the other end free.

$$\text{... 1.16(a)/Pg 9, DHB}$$

Yield strength of screw material,

$$\sigma_{yp} = \sigma_{yc})_{screw} = 324 \text{ MPa}$$

Young's modulus of screw material,

$$E = 2.1 \times 10^5 \text{ MPa}$$

Radius of gyration,

$$k = 0.25 d_1 = 0.25 \times 24 = 6 \text{ mm}$$

Effective length of screw,

$$L = \text{screw lift} + \frac{\text{length of nut}}{2}$$

$$L = 200 + \frac{18}{2} = 209 \text{ mm}$$

$$\therefore \qquad F_{cr} = 452.39 \times 324 \times \left[1 - \frac{324}{4 \times 0.25 \times \pi^2 \times (2.1 \times 10^5)} \left(\frac{209}{6} \right)^2 \right]$$

$$F_{cr} = 118.77 \text{ kN} > W$$

Hence, design of screw is safe against buckling.

V. Design of cup:

16. **Base diameter of cup is made equal to the diameter of screw head:**

$$D_{cb} = D_3 = 1.75d = 1.75 \times 30 = 52.5 \text{ mm} \approx 54 \text{ mm (say)}$$

17. **Top diameter of cup:**

$$D_{ct} = 2D_3 = 2 \times 54 = 108 \text{ mm}$$

18. **Height of cup:** $h_c = 1.2 D_2 = 1.2 \times 45 = 54 \text{ mm}$

19. **Thickness of cup:**

$$t_c = 10 \text{ mm (assumed)}$$

VI. Design of body:

20. **Diameter of body at top:**

$$D_5 = 1.5 D_2 = 1.5 \times 45 = 67.5 \text{ mm} \approx 68 \text{ mm (say)}$$

21. **Inside diameter of the body at base:**

$$D_6 = 2.25 D_2 = 2.25 \times 45 = 101.25 \text{ mm} \approx 105 \text{ mm (say)}$$

22. **Outside diameter of the body at base:**

$$D_7 = 1.75 D_6 = 1.75 \times 105 = 183.75 \text{ mm} \approx 185 \text{ mm (say)}$$

23. **Thickness of base:**
$$t_2 = 2t_1 = 2 \times 5 = 10 \text{ mm}$$

24. **Thickness of body:**
$$t_3 = 0.25d = 0.25 \times 30 = 7.5 \text{ mm}$$

25. **Height of the body:**
$$H_B = \text{lift} + l_n + 100 \text{ mm (clearance)}$$
$$= 200 + 18 + 100 \text{ mm (clearance)}$$
$$H_B = 318 \text{ mm}$$

VII. **Efficiency of the screw:**

We know that $\quad \eta = \dfrac{d_2 \tan \alpha}{\left[d_2 \left(\dfrac{f + \tan \alpha}{1 - f \tan \alpha} \right) + f_c d_c \right]}$ ... **Tb. 9.12(b)/Pg 135, DHB**

$$= \dfrac{27 \times 0.0707}{\left[27 \times \left(\dfrac{0.14 + 0.0707}{1 - 0.14 \times 0.0707} \right) + (0.081 \times 38) \right]}$$

$$\eta = 21.63\%$$

27. **A sluice gate weighing 600 kN is raised by means of two square threaded screws. The coefficient of the collar friction is 0.03 and that of thread friction is 0.14. The outer diameter of the collar is 100 mm and the inner diameter is 50 mm. The gate is raised at a rate of 0.6 m/min. The permissible stress of the screw material in tension and compression is 80 MPa and that in shear is 60 MPa. Design the screw, nut and check for the stresses induced.**

Also determine the speed of the screw and power required at the motor to raise the gate, assuming an efficiency of 75% for reduction drive. The permissible bearing pressure is 15 MPa.

VTU – Dec. 2011 – 14 Marks

Solution: Weight lifted by two screw rods, $2W = 600 \times 10^3$ N; weight lifted by one screw rod, $W = 300 \times 10^3, f = 0.14, f_c = 0.03, d' = 100$ mm, $d'' = 50$ mm, $v = 0.6$ m/min $= 600$ mm/min, $\sigma_t)_{\text{screw}} = \sigma_c)_{\text{screw}} = 80$ MPa $= \sigma_{\max}, \tau_{\text{screw}} = \tau_{\max} = 60$ MPa, $\eta = 75\%$, $p_b = 15$ MPa. a. Design of screw, b. Design of nut, c. speed $n' = ?$ d. Power, $P = ?$

I. **Design of screw spindle:**
  1. **To find core diameter:**

$$\sigma_c)_{\text{screw}} = \frac{W}{A_1} = \frac{4W}{\pi d_1^2} \qquad \text{... 1.1(a)/ Pg 2, DHB}$$

$$80 = \frac{4 \times 300 \times 10^3}{\pi d_1^2}$$

$$d_1 = 69.10 \text{ mm}$$

Standard values for normal series are: $d_1 = 78$ mm, $d = 90$ mm, and $p = 12$ mm.
... **Tb 9.10/ Pg 149, DHB**

  2. **Check for stresses:**
    a. **Maximum shear stress:**

$$\tau_{\max} = \sqrt{\left(\frac{\sigma_c}{2} \right)^2 + \tau^2} \qquad \text{... Eq. (i) 1.5(b)/ Pg 3, DHB}$$

Based on standard values,

$$\sigma_c = \frac{4W}{\pi d_1^2} = \frac{4 \times 300 \times 10^3}{\pi \times 78^2} = 62.78 \text{ MPa} \qquad \text{... } \mathbf{1.1(a)/ Pg\ 2, DHB}$$

$$\tau = \frac{16T}{\pi d_1^3} \qquad \text{... Eq. (ii) } \mathbf{1.1(d)/ Pg\ 2, DHB}$$

Here

$$T = \frac{W d_2}{2}\left[\left(\frac{f + \tan\alpha}{1 - f\tan\alpha}\right)\right] \qquad \text{... Eq. (iii) } \mathbf{9.11(b)/ Pg\ 134, DHB}$$

$$d_2 = d - \left(\frac{p}{2}\right) = 90 - \left(\frac{12}{2}\right) = 84 \text{ mm}$$

$$\tan\alpha = \frac{l}{\pi d_2} = \frac{p}{\pi d_2} = \frac{12}{\pi \times 84} = 0.0455 \qquad \text{... } \mathbf{9.10(b)/ Pg\ 133, DHB}$$

Assume $f = 0.14$, for heavy machine oil. ... **Tb. 9.3/ Pg 136, DHB**
Eq. (iii) yields...

$$T = \frac{300 \times 10^3 \times 84}{2}\left[\left(\frac{0.14 + 0.0455}{1 - 0.14 \times 0.0455}\right)\right] = 2.35 \times 10^6 \text{ N·mm}$$

Eq. (ii) yields...

$$\tau = \frac{16 \times 2.35 \times 10^6}{\pi \times 78^3} = 25.25 \text{ MPa}$$

Eq. (i) yields...

$$\tau_{max} = \sqrt{\left(\frac{62.78}{2}\right)^2 + 25.25^2} = 40.28 \text{ MPa} < 60 \text{ MPa, hence safe.}$$

b. **Maximum normal stress:**

$$\sigma_{max} = \left(\frac{\sigma_c}{2}\right) + \sqrt{\left(\frac{\sigma_c}{2}\right)^2 + \tau^2} \qquad \text{... } \mathbf{1.5(a)/ Pg\ 3, DHB}$$

$$= \left(\frac{62.78}{2}\right) + \sqrt{\left(\frac{62.78}{2}\right)^2 + 25.25^2}$$

$$\sigma_{max} = 71.68 \text{ MPa} < 80 \text{ MPa, hence safe.}$$

II. **Design for nut:**

3. **Number of threads:**

$$n = \frac{4W}{p_b \pi(d^2 - d_1^2)} = \frac{4 \times 300 \times 10^3}{15\pi(90^2 - 78^2)} = 12.63 \approx 13 \text{ threads}$$

$$\text{... } \mathbf{9.13(a)/ Pg\ 135, DHB}$$

4. **Height or length of nut:**

$$l_n = np = 13 \times 12 = 156 \text{ mm} \qquad \text{... } \mathbf{9.13(b)/ Pg\ 135, DHB}$$

5. **Thickness of screw:**

$$t = \left(\frac{p}{2}\right) = \left(\frac{12}{2}\right) = 6 \text{ mm}$$

III. **Speed:** We know that speed,

$$n' = \frac{\text{velocity}}{\text{lead}} = \frac{600}{12} = 50 \text{ rpm}$$

IV. **Power:** We know that

$$T_R = \frac{9.55 \times 10^5 (P)}{n'} \qquad \qquad \dots \textbf{3.3(a)/ Pg 50, DHB}$$

Since efficiency is given, the above equation is modified as

$$T_R = \frac{9.55 \times 10^5 (P)}{n'} \times \eta \qquad \qquad \dots \text{Eq. (iv)}$$

But $\qquad T_R = \frac{W}{2}\left[d_2\left(\frac{f + \tan\alpha}{1 - f\tan\alpha}\right) + f_c d_c \right]$

$$\dots \text{Eq. (v) } \textbf{9.12(a)/ Pg 135, DHB}$$

Mean diameter of collar,

$$d_c = \left(\frac{d' + d''}{2}\right), \text{ assuming uniform wear condition}$$

$$d_c = \left(\frac{100 + 50}{2}\right) = 75 \text{ mm}$$

∴ Eq. (v) yields...

$$T_R = \frac{300 \times 10^3}{2}\left[84 \times \left(\frac{0.14 + 0.0455}{1 - 0.14 \times 0.0455}\right) + (0.03 \times 75) \right]$$

$$T_R = 2.68 \times 10^6 \text{ N·mm}$$

Hence torque required for two screws,

$$T_R = 2 \times 2.68 \times 10^6 = 5.38 \times 10^6 \text{ N·mm}$$

∴ Eq. (iv) yields...

$$5.38 \times 10^6 = \frac{9.55 \times 10^6 (P)}{50} \times 0.75$$

$$P = 37.56 \text{ kW.}$$

28. **A vertical 2-start square threaded screw of 100 mm mean diameter and 20 mm pitch supports a vertical load of 18 kN. The nut of screw is fitted in the hub of a gear wheel having 80 teeth which meshes with a pinion of 20 teeth. The mechanical efficiency of pinion and gear wheel drive is 90%. The axial thrust on the screw is taken by the collar bearing 250 mm outside diameter and 100 mm inside diameter. Assuming uniform pressure conditions, find the diameter of pinion shaft and height of nut when friction coefficient for vertical screw and nut is 0.15 and that of collar bearing is 0.2. Take $\tau = 50$ MPa and $p_b = 1.4$ MPa.**

VTU – June/ July 2015 – 10 Marks; May/ June 2010 – 16 Marks

Solution: $n = 2$, $d_2 = 100$ mm, $p = 20$ mm, $w = 18 \times 10^3$ N, number of teeth on gear $z_g = 80$, number of teeth on pinion $z_p = 20$, $\eta = 90\%$, $d' = 250$ mm, $d'' = 100$ mm, $f = 0.15$, $f_c = 0.2$, $\tau = 50$ MPa, $p_b = 1.4$ MPa. a. Diameter of pinion, $D_p = ?$, b. $l_n = ?$

a. **Diameter of pinion:**

Shear stress, $\tau = \dfrac{16T_{net}}{\pi D_P^3}$ ... Eq. (i) **1.1(d)/ Pg 2, DHB**

But $T_{net} = \dfrac{T_P}{\eta}$ ... Eq. (ii)

Torque transmitted by pinion,

$$T_P = T_R\left(\dfrac{z_p}{z_g}\right) \qquad \text{... Eq. (iii)}$$

But $T_R = \dfrac{W}{2}\left[d_2\left(\dfrac{f + \tan\alpha}{1 - f\tan\alpha}\right) + f_c d_c\right]$

... Eq. (iv) **9.12(a)/ Pg 135, DHB**

$$\tan\alpha = \dfrac{np}{\pi d_2} = \dfrac{2 \times 20}{\pi \times 100} = 0.1273 \qquad \text{... 9.10(b)/ Pg 133, DHB}$$

$$d_c = \dfrac{2}{3}\left(\dfrac{d'^3 - d''^3}{d'^2 - d''^2}\right), \quad \text{for uniform pressure condition}$$

$$= \dfrac{2}{3}\left(\dfrac{250^3 - 100^3}{250^2 - 100^2}\right)$$

$$d_c = 185.71 \text{ mm} \approx 186 \text{ mm}$$

Eq. (iv) yields...

$$T_R = \dfrac{18 \times 10^3}{2}\left[100 \times \left(\dfrac{0.15 + 0.1273}{1 - 0.15 \times 0.1273}\right) + (0.2 \times 186)\right]$$

$$T_R = 5.89 \times 10^5 \text{ N·mm}$$

Eq. (iii) yields...

$$T_P = 5.89 \times 10^5 \times \left(\dfrac{20}{80}\right) = 1.47 \times 10^5 \text{ N·mm}$$

Eq. (ii) yields...

$$T_{net} = \dfrac{1.47 \times 10^5}{0.90} = 1.63 \times 10^5 \text{ N·mm}$$

Eq. (i) yields...

$$50 = \dfrac{16 \times 1.63 \times 10^6}{\pi D_P^3}$$

$$D_P = 25.53 \text{ mm}$$

b. Length of nut:

$$l_n = \dfrac{4Wp}{p_b \pi (d^2 - d_1^2)} \qquad \text{... 9.13(a)/ Pg 135, DHB}$$

But
$$d = d_2 + (p/2) = 100 + (20/2) = 110 \text{ mm}$$
$$d_1 = d_2 - p = 100 - 20 = 80 \text{ mm}$$
$$l_n = \frac{4 \times 18 \times 10^3 \times 20}{1.4 \times \pi(110^2 - 80^2)} = 57.44 \text{ mm} \approx 58 \text{ mm}.$$

VTU QUESTION PAPERS

Mar. 2001 (ME5T2)

1. a. Explain self-locking and overhauling in power screws. **(04 Marks)**
   b. A triple threaded power screw used in a screw jack has a nominal diameter of 50 mm and a pitch of 8 mm. The threads are square shape and the length of the nut is 48 mm. The screw jack is used to lift a load of 7.5 kN. The coefficient of friction at the threads is 0.12 and the collar friction is negligible. Calculate:
      i. The principal shear stresses in the screw rod.
      ii. The transverse shear stresses in the screw and the nuts.
      iii. The unit bearing pressure for threads.
      iv. State whether the screw is self-locking. **(16 Marks)**

July/Aug. 2004 (AU46)

2. A double threaded screw of a screw jack has the following specifications:

Load to be raised	90 kN
OD of square thread	75 mm
Pitch	16 mm
Mean collar diameter	125 mm
Coefficient of friction for thread	0.1
Coefficient of friction for collar	0.12

   Determine the torque required to operate the screw jack and the efficiency of the screw. **(10 Marks)**

Jan/Feb. 2005 (AU46)

3. In a large gate valve used in a high pressure water line, the gate weighs 6000 N and the friction force due to water pressure, resisting opening is 2000 N. The valve stem is nonrotating and is raised by a rotating wheel with internal threads acting as a rotating nut on the valve stem. The outside diameter of the valve stem screw is 38 mm. The wheel presses against a supporting collar of 40 mm inside diameter and 75 mm outside diameter. The valve stem is fitted with square threads (single start) having 8.5 mm pitch. Assuming the coefficient of friction for the collar as 0.25 and for the threads as 0.1, determine:
   i. The torque that must be applied to the wheel to raise the valve gate.
   ii. The efficiency of the screw and collar mechanism. **(10 Marks)**

July/Aug. 2005 (AU46)

4. A power screw for a jack has square threads of proportion. The coefficient of friction at the threads is 0.1 and that at the collar is 0.12. Determine the weight that can be lifted by this jack through a human effort of 400 N through a hand lever of span 400 mm. **(16 Marks)**

Jan/Feb. 2006 (AU46)

5. The cutter of a broaching machine is pulled by a square threaded screw of 50 mm external diameter and 10 mm pitch. The operating nut takes an axial load of 400 N on a flat surface of 54 mm and 84 mm internal and external diameters respectively. If the coefficient of friction is 0.15 for all contact surfaces on the nut, determine the power required to rotate the operating nut when the cutting speed is 5 m/min. Also find the efficiency of the screw. **(10 Marks)**

July 2006 (AU46)

6. The square thread of a screw jack with a specification of 80 × 16, with a double start is to raise a load of 100 kN. The mean collar diameter is 130 mm. The coefficient of friction for the threads and the collar are 0.1 and 0.12 respectively. Determine:
   i. The torque required to raise the load.
   ii. The efficiency of the screw.
   iii. Whether self-locking exists. **(15 Marks)**

Dec. 06/Jan. 2007 (AU46)

7. A single threaded power screw has a major diameter restriction of 36 mm. Design the screw, if the frictional coefficient for thread and collar are 0.13 and 0.1 respectively. Estimate the power input to rotate the screw at 1 rpm, if the load to be lifted is 5 kN. **(10 Marks)**

July 2007 (AU46)

8. Following data apply to machinists clamp. Outside diameter of the screw = 14 mm, root diameter = 9.5 mm, pitch = 4 mm (single thread), collar friction radius = 6 mm, collar friction coefficient = 0.15, screw friction coefficient = 0.15, thread angle = 30°. Assume that the machinist can comfortably exert a maximum force of 120 N on the handle whose radius is 130 mm. Calculate the maximum clamping force that can be developed between the jaws of the clamp and the efficiency of the clamp. **(10 Marks)**

Dec. 07/Jan. 2008 (AU46)

9. A square threaded power screw has a nominal diameter of 30 mm and a pitch of 6 mm with double threads. The load on the screw is 6 kN and the mean diameter of the thread collar is 40 mm. The coefficient of friction for the screw is 0.1 and the collar is 0.09. Determine:
   i. Torque required to raise the screw against the load.
   ii. Torque required to lower the screw with the load.
   iii. Overall efficiency.
   iv. Is the screw self locking? **(10 Marks)**

Dec. 08/Jan. 2009 (ME5T2)

10. a. Derive the conditions for self locking in power screws. **(06 Marks)**
    b. The lead screw of a lathe has trapezoidal threads. To drive the tool carriage, the screw has to exert an axial force of 20 kN. The thrust is carried by the collar. The length of the lead screw is 1.5 m. Coefficients of friction at the collar and the nut are 0.1 and 0.15 respectively. Determine the dimensions of the screw and the nut if the permissible bearing pressure is 4 MPa. **(14 Marks)**

Dec. 08/Jan. 2009 (06ME-AU52)

11. a. Explain self locking and overhaul of screw jack. **(06 Marks)**
    b. Design a screw jack for a capacity of 10 kN to lift 200 mm height. Select suitable materials and factor of safety. **(16 Marks)**

June/July 2009 (AU46)

12. a. A single threaded power screw of 25 mm diameter with a pitch of 5 mm. The vertical load on the screw reaches a maximum load of 500 N. The coefficient of friction is 0.05 for collar and 0.08 for the screw. The frictional diameter of the collar is 30 mm. Find the torque required to raise and lower the load. Also find the efficiency of the power screw. **(10 Marks)**
    b. Mention at least four applications of power screws. **(04 Marks)**
    c. What is self locking as applicable to power screws? Relate coefficient of friction to lead angle for the above condition. **(06 Marks)**

June/July 2009 (06ME52)

13. A triple threaded power screw used in a screw jack has a nominal diameter of 50 mm and a pitch of 8 mm. The threads are of square shape and the length of the nut is 48 mm. The screw jack is to lift a load of 7.5 kN. The coefficient of friction at the threads is 0.12 and the collar friction is negligible. Calculate:
    i. The principal shear stresses in the screw rod.
    ii. The transverse shear stress in the screw and nut.
    iii. The bearing pressure for threads.
    iv. State whether the screw is self locking. **(10 Marks)**

Dec. 2009/Jan. 2010 (AU46)

14. In a hand vice, the screw has double start acme threads of 25 mm nominal diameter and 4 mm pitch. The length of the lever is 300 mm and the maximum force that can be applied at the end of the lever is 250 N. Determine the force with which the job is held between the jaws of the vice. Take coefficient of friction at the threads as 0.14, angle of thread = 20–29°. Neglect collar friction. **(10 Marks)**

Dec. 2009/Jan. 2010 (06ME52)

15. a. Explain overhauling of screws. Derive condition for self locking of square thread with collar friction. **(05 Marks)**
    b. A single start square threaded power screw is used to raise a load of 120 kN. The screw has a mean diameter of 24 mm and four threads per 24 mm length. The mean collar diameter is 40 mm. The coefficient of friction is estimated as 0.1 for both the thread and the collar.
    i. Determine the major diameter of the screw.
    ii. Estimate the screw torque required to raise the load.
    iii. Estimate overall efficiency.
    iv. If collar friction is eliminated, what minimum value of thread coefficient is needed to prevent the screw from overhauling? **(10 Marks)**

May/June 2010 (06ME52)

16. a. Explain self locking and overhauling in power screws. **(04 Marks)**
    b. A screw jack is to lift a load of 80 kN through a height of 400 mm. Ultimate strengths of screw material in tension and compression are 200 N/mm^2 and in

shear is 120 N/mm^2. The material for the nut is phosphor bronze for which the ultimate strength is 100 N/mm^2 in tension, 90 N/mm^2 in compression and 80 N/mm^2 in shear. The bearing pressure between the nut and screw is not to exceed 18 N/mm^2. Design the screw and the nut and check for the stresses. Take FoS = 2. Assume 25% overload for the screw rod design.   **(16 Marks)**

Dec. 2010 (AU46)

17. A double threaded power screw with trapezoidal ISO thread is used to raise a load of 300 kN. The nominal diameter is 100 mm and the pitch is 12 mm. The coefficient of friction is 0.15. Neglecting the collar friction, calculate:
    i. Torque required to raise the load.
    ii. Torque required to lower the load.
    iii. Efficiency of the screw.   **(10 Marks)**

Dec. 2010 (06ME52)

18. a. Explain the terms 'overhauling' and 'self locking' with respect to power screws.
                (05 Marks)
    b. The screw of shaft straightner exerts a load of 30 kN as shown in **Fig. U8.1**. The screw is square threaded of outside diameter 75 mm and 6 mm pitch. Determine:
       i. Force required at the rim of 300 mm diameter hand wheel assuming the coefficient of friction for threads as 0.12.

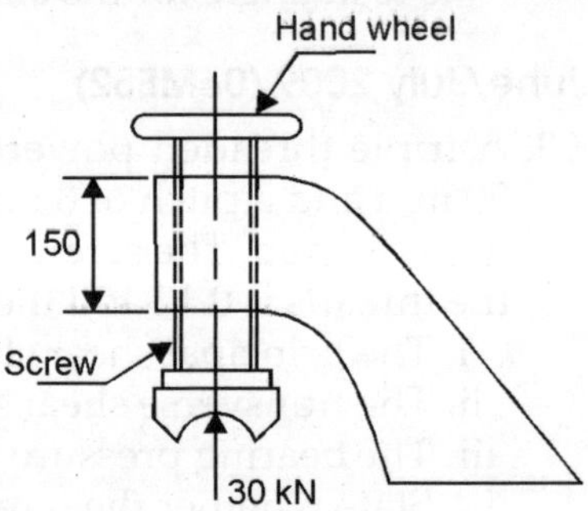

Hand wheel
150
Screw
30 kN
Fig. U8.1

       ii. Maximum compressive stress in the screw, bearing pressure on the threads and maximum shear stress in threads.
       iii. Efficiency of the straightner.   **(15 Marks)**

June/July 2011 (06ME52)

19. a. Derive the equation for maximum efficiency of a square threaded screw.
                (08 Marks)
    b. The cutter of a broaching machine is pulled by a square threaded screw of 55 mm external diameter and 10 mm pitch. The operating nut takes the axial load of 400 N on a flat surface of 60 mm and 90 mm internal and external diameters respectively. If the coefficient of friction is 0.15 for all contact surfaces, determine the power required to rotate the nut when the cutting speed is 6 m/min. Also find the efficiency of the screw.   **(12 Marks)**

Dec. 2011 (AU46)

20. A machine slide weighing 4000 N is elevated by two start acme thread of 50 mm diameter and 8 mm pitch at the rate of 0.8 m/min. If the coefficient of friction is 0.14, calculate the power of the motor to drive the slide. The end of the screw is carried on a thrust collar 40 mm inside, 60 mm outside diameter. The coefficient of friction at the collar is 0.12. Assume uniform wear.   **(10 Marks)**

Dec. 2011 (06ME52)

21. a. Explain self locking and over hauling in power screws.   **(06 Marks)**
    b. A sluice gate weighing 600 kN is raised by means of two square threaded screws. The coefficient of the collar friction is 0.3 and that of thread friction is

0.14. The outer diameter of the collar is 100 mm and the inner diameter is 50 mm. The gate is raised at a rate of 0.6 m/min. The permissible stress of the screw material in tension and compression is 80 MPa and that in shear is 60 MPa. Design the screw, nut and check for the stresses induced. Also determine the speed of the screw and power required at the motor to raise the gate, assuming an efficiency of 75% for reduction drive. The permissible bearing pressure is 15 MPa. **(14 Marks)**

June 2012 (06ME52-06AU52)

22. a. Derive an expression for the maximum efficiency of a square threaded screw and thus show that for self locking the efficiency is always less than 50%.
    (06 Marks)
   b. The lead screw of a lathe has single start ISO metric trapezoidal threads of 52 mm nominal diameter and 8 mm pitch. The screw is required to exert an axial force of 2 kN in order to drive the tool carriage during turning operation. The thrust is carried on a collar of 100 mm outer diameter and 60 mm inner diameter. The values of coefficient of friction at the screw threads and collar are 0.15 and 0.12 respectively. The lead screw rotates at 30 rev/min. Calculate:
      i. The power required to drive the screw.
      ii. The efficiency of the screw. **(14 Marks)**

Dec. 2012 (10ME52)

23. a. Obtain an expression for torque required in raising the load in case of a power screw. **(05 Marks)**
   b. Design a screw jack to lift a load of 30 kN with the following data:
      Allowable compressive stress in the material = 160 MPa
      Coefficient of friction in threads = 0.14
      Coefficient of collar friction = 0.2
      Height of lift = 150 mm. **(15 Marks)**

Dec. 2012 (06ME52)

24. a. What is self-locking of a power screw? What is the condition of self-locking? State the applications where self-locking is essential. **(05 Marks)**
   b. A square threaded power screw has a nominal diameter of 30 mm and a pitch of 6 mm with double threads. The load on the screw is 6 kN and the mean diameter of the thrust collar is 40 mm. The coefficient of friction for the screw is 0.1 and the collar is 0.09. Determine:
      i. Torque required to raise the screw against the load.
      ii. Torque required to lower the screw with the load.
      iii. Overall efficiency
      iv. Is this screw self-locking? **(15 Marks)**

June/July 2013 (06ME52)

25. a. Derive an equation for torque required to raise the load on a square thread.
    (05 Marks)
   b. A power screw having double start square threads of 25 mm nominal diameter and 5 mm pitch is acted upon by an axial load of 10 kN. The outer and inner diameters of screw collar are 50 mm and 20 mm respectively. The coefficient of thread friction and collar friction may be assumed as 0.2 and 0.15 respectively.

The screw rotates at 12 rpm. Assuming uniform wear conditions at the collar and allowable bearing pressure of 5.77 N/mm^2, find

    i. The power required to rotate the screw.

    ii. The stresses in the screw

    iii. Number of threads of nut in engagement with screw and the height of the nut.   **(15 Marks)**

June/July 2013 (10ME52)

26. Design completely the screw, handle and the nut of a screw jack of capacity 40 kN. The maximum lift is limited to 0.2 m. The screw and the handle are made of C40 (40C8) steel and the nut and the cap are made of cast iron. Also find the efficiency of the screw. Check the screw for buckling load.   **(20 Marks)**

Dec. 2013/Jan. 2014 (06ME52)

27. a. Explain self locking and overhauling in power screws.   **(05 Marks)**

    b. The cutter of a broaching machine is pulled by a square threaded screw of 55 mm outer diameter having 10 mm pitch. The operating nut takes an axial load of 400 N on a flat surface 60 mm inner diameter and 90 mm outer diameter. If μ at threads and collar is 0.15, find:

      i. The torque on the screw

      ii. The power required for the motor at a cutting speed of 6 m/min

      iii. Efficiency of the screw.   **(15 Marks)**

Dec. 2013/Jan. 2014 (10ME52)

28. a. Explain overhauling of screws. Derive the condition for self-locking of square thread with collar friction.   **(05 Marks)**

    b. A weight of 500 kN is raised at a speed of 6 m/min by two screw rods with square threads of 50×8 cut on them. The two screw rods are driven through bevel gear drives by a motor. Determine:

      i. The torque required to raise the load

      ii. The speed of rotation of the screw rod assuming the threads are double start.

      iii. The maximum stresses induced in the screw rod.

      iv. The efficiency of screw drive

      v. The length of the nut for the purpose of supporting the load.   **(15 Marks)**

June/July 2014 (06ME52)

29. a. The lead screw of a machine has single start trapezoidal threads of 30 mm outside diameter and 6 mm pitch. It drives the tool carriage against an axial load of 1500 N. The thrust collar has a mean diameter of 40 mm. The carriage is moved at a speed of 0.72 m/min. The coefficient of friction for both screw and collar is 0.14. Find the power required to drive the screw and the efficiency.   **(10 Marks)**

    b. A power screw has 6 mm pitch and 40 mm diameter. The screw is subjected to an axial load of 6 kN. The nut length is 12 mm. Determine:

      i. The bearing pressure between the threads

      ii. Shear stress in the threads due to axial load and

      iii. Compressive stress in the screw.   **(10 Marks)**

June/July 2014 (10ME52)

30. a. Explain self locking and overhauling in power screws. **(05 Marks)**
    b. A single start square threaded power screw is used to raise a load of 120 kN. The screw has a mean diameter of 24 mm and four threads per 24 mm length. The mean collar diameter is 40 mm. The coefficient of friction is estimated as 0.1 for both thread and the collar.
       i. Determine the major diameter of the screw.
       ii. Estimate the screw torque required to raise the load.
       iii. Estimate the overall efficiency.
       iv. If collar friction is eliminated, what minimum value of thread coefficient is needed to prevent the screw from overhauling? **(15 Marks)**

Dec. 2014/Jan. 2015 (06ME52)

31. a. Explain self locking and overhauling in power screws. **(04 Marks)**
    b. A weight of 500 kN is raised at a speed of 6 m/min by two screw rods of double start square thread of 50 mm major diameter with a pitch of 8 mm. The two screw rods are driven through bevel gear drives by a motor. Determine:
       i. The torque required to raise the load.
       ii. The speed of rotation of the screw rod.
       iii. The maximum stresses induced on the cross-section of the screw rod.
       iv. The efficiency of screw drive.
       v. The length of the nut for the purpose of supporting the load.
       vi. Check for overhaul. **(16 Marks)**

Dec. 2014/Jan. 2015 (10ME52)

32. a. Explain self locking and overhauling in power screws. **(04 Marks)**
    b. A screw jack is to lift a load of 80 kN through a height of 400 mm. Ultimate strengths of screw material in tension and compression are 200 N/mm^2 and in shear is 120 N/mm^2. The material for the nut is phosphor bronze for which the ultimate strength is 100 N/mm^2 in tension, 90 N/mm^2 in compression and 80 N/mm^2 in shear. The bearing pressure between the nut and screw is not to exceed 18 N/mm^2. Design the screw and the nut and check for the stresses. Take FoS = 2. Assume 25% overload for the screw rod design. **(16 Marks)**

June/July 2015 (06ME52)

33. a. Explain self locking and overhauling in power screws. **(06 Marks)**
    b. A vertical two start square threaded screw of 100 mm mean diameter and 20 mm pitch supports a vertical load of 18 kN. The axial thrust on the screw is taken by a collar bearing of 250 mm outside diameter and 100 mm inside diameter. Find the force required at the end of the lever which is 400 mm long in order to lift and lower the load. The coefficient of friction for the vertical screw and nut is 0.15 and that for collar bearing is 0.20. **(14 Marks)**

June/July 2015 (10ME52)

34. a. An electric motor driven power screw moves a nut in a horizontal plane against a force of 75 kN at 300 mm/min. The screw has a single thread of 6 mm pitch on a major diameter of 40 mm. The friction coefficient at screw threads is 0.1. Estimate the power of the motor. **(10 Marks)**

b. A vertical 2-start square threaded screw of 100 mm mean diameter and 20 mm pitch supports a vertical load of 18 kN. The nut of screw is fitted in the hub of a gear wheel having 80 teeth which meshes with a pinion of 20 teeth. The mechanical efficiency of pinion and gear wheel drive is 90%. The axial thrust on the screw is taken by the collar bearing 250 mm outside diameter and 100 mm inside diameter. Assuming uniform pressure conditions, find the diameter of pinion shaft and height of nut when friction coefficient for vertical screw and nut is 0.15 and that of collar bearing is 0.2. Take $\tau = 50$ MPa and $p_b = 1.4$ MPa.

(10 Marks)

Dec. 2015/Jan. 2016 (10ME52)

35. a. Derive the equation for torque required to lift the load on the square thread screws. **(08 Marks)**
    b. Define self locking and overhauling of power screws. **(04 Marks)**
    c. A machine slide weighing 20 kN is raised by a double start square threaded screw at the rate of 0.84 m/min. Take $\mu = 0.12$ and $\mu_c = 0.14$. The outside diameter of the screw is 44 mm and the pitch is 7 mm. The outside and inside diameters of the collar are 58 mm and 32 mm respectively. Calculate the power required to drive the slide. If the allowable shear stress in the screw is 30 MPa, is the screw strong enough to sustain the load? **(08 Marks)**

Index

A

Amplitude ratio 168
Average or mean stress 167

B

Bending stress 36
Bolts
    eccentric loads on 282
    initial tension 249, 251
    number of 442
    unstressed 250

C

Circumferential lap joint 498
Codes and standards 7
Coefficient of friction of
    screws 648
    thrust collars 650
Combined loading 201
Combined stress 35, 201
Cotter joint 402
Couplings 439
    bush and pin type 463
    flange 439
    flexible 463
    Oldham's 477
Cumulative fatigue
    damage 230

D

Design considerations 6
Designation and properties of
    materials 7
Direct stress 35
Direction of
    principal stresses 15, 16
    shear stress 16
Distortion energy theory 72

E

Eccentric loads on 58
    bolts 282
    circular base 287
    rectangular
        base 283, 285
    riveted joints 544
    welded joints 603
Effect of inertia 130
Efficiency of
    power screws 652
    riveted joints 493
Endurance limit
    modifying factors 170
Energy
    distortion 72
    impact 121
    kinetic 123
    shear strain 73
    strain 73

F

Factor
    load correction 170
    of safety 34
    reliability 171
    size correction 171
    surface correction 171
Failure
    Goodman criteria for 176
    of riveted joints 491
    Soderberg criteria for 174
    theories of 70
Fatigue
    effect of 266
    failure theories 174
    high cycle 165, 166

    low cycle 165, 166
    phenomenon or
        nature of 164
    stress concentration for 172
Flange coupling 439

G

Goodman criteria 176
Guest's theory 71

H

Helix angle 647

I

Impact stresses due to
    axial loads 121
    bending 128
    torsional loads 130
Index of sensitivity 172
Initial tension in bolts 251

J

Joints
    boiler 496
    cotter 402
    knuckle 413
    lozenge 532
    riveted 485
    welded 569

K

Keys 417
    design of 420
    effect of 421
    feather 419
    rectangular 418
    splined 435
    square 418
    tapered 432
Knuckle joint 413

L

Lead 647
Load correction factor 170
Longitudinal butt joint 496

M

Maximum normal strain
    theory 71
Maximum normal stress
    theory 70
Maximum shear stress
    theory 71

N

Normal stress theory 70
Notch sensitivity index 172

O

Oldham's coupling 477
Overhauling of screw 652

P

Poisson's ratio 12
Power screws 646
   design of 680
   efficiency of 652
   overhauling of 652
   self-locking of 652
   stresses in 672

R

Rankine's theory 70
Reliability factor 171
Riveted joints
   eccentric loads on 544
   efficiency of 493
   failure of 491

pitch of 490
rivet diameters for 497

S

Saint-Venant's theory 71
Screw
   efficiency of 652
   jack 680
   power 646
Self-locking 652
Shafts 321
   ASME code for
     design of 325
   design of 322
   effect of keyways on 421
   power transmitted by 329
   under fluctuating loads 328
Shear difference theory 71
Shear strain 12
Size factor 171
S–N diagram 169
Soderberg criteria 174
Static load 34
Strain energy theory 73
Strength of
   butt weld 572
   fillet weld 573
   key in crushing 421
   key in shear 421
   riveted joint 493
Stress
   analysis 10
   average or mean 167
   bending 36
   bi-axial 16
   combined loading 201
   concentration
     factor 90, 172, 576
   direct 35
   equivalent maximum
     shear 201
   equivalent normal 201
   equivalent shear 201

impact, axial 121
impact, bending 128
in power screws 672
in tension bolts 249
maximum shear 15
normal 14
plane 15
principal 15
range 167
ratio 167
resultant 14
shear 11, 36
tensor 17
tri-axial 17
variable 167
Stress–strain diagram 12
Surface correction factor 171

T

Theories of failure 70
   Guest theory 71
   Haigh's theory 73
   maximum shear 71
   Rankine's 70
   Saint-Venant's theory 71
   von Mises 72
Threaded fasteners 247
Tresca's theory 71

U

Unwin's formula 496

V

Variable stress 167
von Mises theory of failure 72

W

Welded joints
   eccentric loads on 603
   types of 570
   unsymmetrical 586
Wohler curves 169